OFFICIAL
FOOTBALL
YEARBOOK 2009–2010
OF THE ENGLISH AND SCOTTISH LEAGUES

Forewords by **Sir Bobby Robson** and **George Burley**

IN PARTNERSHIP WITH

DESIGN AND PRODUCTION: Richard Mulligan (Press Association Sport)
HEAD OF PRODUCTION: Chris Wiltshire
EDITORS: Phil Ascough, Peter Marshall
PRODUCTION: Danny Lambert, Robert Meaden, Chris Brady, Lynne Maxwell, Neil Morgan,
Dominic Picksley, Mark Tattersall

CONTRIBUTORS: Simon Armstrong, Duncan Bech, Mark Bowering, Alex Brooker, Roddy Brooks, Andrew Carless,
Chris Cope, Adrian Curtis, John Curtis, Ronnie Esplin, Wayne Gardiner, Jamie Gardner, Ken Gaunt, Lisa Gray,
Ross Heppenstall, Alex Lowe, Frank Malley, Carl Markham, Gavin McCafferty, Matt McGeehan, Mike McGrath,
Jon Phipps, Tom Rostance, Ben Rumsby, Andy Sims, Damian Spellman, Simon Stone, Sean Taylor, Pete Thompson,
Mark Walker, Paul Walker, Stuart Walker, Drew Williams, Simon Willis, Jim van Wijk (Press Association Sport)

Cover and inside photography © Press Association Photos

First published 2009 by
A&C Black Publishers Ltd
36 Soho Square, London W1D 3QY
www.acblack.com

Copyright © Press Association Sport 2009

ISBN 978-1-408-11333-2

All rights reserved. No part of this publication may be reproduced in any form or by any means –
graphic, electronic or mechanical, including photocopying, recording, taping or information storage
and retrieval systems – without the prior permission in writing of the publishers.

A CIP catalogue record for this book is available from the British Library.

Designed and typeset in Expert Sans by Press Association Sport, Bridgegate, Howden,
East Yorkshire, DN14 7AE
Cover and inside photography © Press Association Photos
Printed and bound by Scotprint, Haddington

This book is produced using paper that is made from wood grown in managed, sustainable forests. It
is natural, renewable and recyclable. The logging and manufacturing processes conform to the
environmental regulations of the country of origin.

PRESS
ASSOCIATION
Sport

www.pa-sport.com

CONTENTS

FOOTBALL in England went from strength to strength during another memorable season that delivered all anyone could ask for in terms of excitement and passion.

As spectators, we were treated to some thrilling contests from the top of the Barclays Premier League to the bottom of Coca-Cola League Two, and once again many of the main promotion and relegation issues were not resolved until the very end of the campaign.

For my money Manchester United were deserved Barclays Premier League champions. A year ago the goals of Ronaldo made the difference. This time around it was more of a team effort, and the proof of that came with five of their players being nominated for the PFA Players' Player of the Year award. But United were pushed all the way to the line and they will expect an even tougher challenge next season. Liverpool will be back after coming closer than anyone to upsetting their great rivals, and so will Chelsea. I expect Arsenal to strengthen, while Aston Villa now have a better idea of what it will take for them to break into that top four.

Everton can push on from their great season in the FA Cup, and Manchester City could take the Barclays Premier League by storm if they invest their money in real quality. I was delighted to see one of my old teams, Fulham, claim a place in the UEFA Europa League, especially after their escape from relegation last year.

This time the relegation battle again went down to the wire, but Stoke and Hull shocked a few of the big boys in showing that Coca-Cola Championship clubs can survive in the top flight. I was hugely disappointed to see Newcastle United relegated and I just hope they can follow the example of Birmingham, who bounced straight back, gaining promotion along with Wolves.

At the other end of the Championship it was sad to see Norwich, Southampton and Charlton relegated. All three clubs have strong Barclays Premier League traditions but their decline just shows how much the Football League has progressed. They will be inspired by the success of Leicester and Scunthorpe, but the achievement of Peterborough in winning a second successive promotion is a warning of how tough the competition will be throughout the division.

In Coca-Cola League Two, Exeter did a great job in securing a promotion place with Brentford and Wycombe just a year after returning to the Football League, and no doubt Burton and Torquay will hope to follow that example next season.

But back at the top, the real indicator of the strength of our domestic game was the presence once again of three Barclays Premier League teams in the semi-finals of the UEFA Champions League.

> **United were pushed all the way ... and they will expect an even tougher challenge next season**

Sir Bobby Robson – Former England manager

The Sir Bobby Robson Foundation raises money for the early detection and treatment of cancer. For full details please visit www.sirbobbyrobsonfoundation.org.uk

IT WAS a tremendous end to the season in the Clydesdale Bank Premier League, with Rangers and Celtic taking the title race right down to the last game of the campaign.

Rangers deservedly won the championship with an absolutely fantastic finish to the season, and all credit goes to them for their achievement.

Gordon Strachan has now left Celtic and, although I was not surprised to hear that news, I was saddened. I think everybody will look back at Gordon's spell in charge of Celtic over the last few years with admiration. He did a fantastic job there and good luck to him in the future. He is very passionate about football, he loves coaching and I'm sure he will do well wherever he goes.

Of course, at the bottom of the Clydesdale Bank Premier League it was a sad finale for my big mate Terry Butcher at Inverness as they were relegated.

You want competitive games in your domestic league and the SPL had them all the way through the season, so it has been a very interesting campaign all in all.

Next term is already looking promising as well. Scotland will have six teams in Europe for the first time and hopefully they will all do well. Last season one or two of our teams struggled in the early rounds of the European competitions, as often the foreign sides have already started their domestic campaigns by that stage and so they are fully prepared. Hopefully we can get our clubs through the first rounds of those tournaments and then they can push on from there.

As for the international scene, Scotland's challenge for a place at the World Cup finals in South Africa in 2010 is entering a really important period and by the time the qualification campaign resumes the players will have had a good break and will have been back with their clubs for pre-season training. Hopefully they will be raring to go.

It has certainly been a season to reflect upon.

You can talk about different issues in Scottish football, like international football or the leagues but, for me, the most important challenge we face is to get our youngsters to play football on a regular basis. Society has changed – kids don't play regularly at school or in parks these days, but if they are going to reach their full potential then they have to play more football.

George Burley
Scotland national team coach

" The most important challenge we face is to get our youngsters to play football on a regular basis "

CLOCKWISE FROM ABOVE: One-time 'Busby Babe' Ian Greaves, who also managed Bolton and Huddersfield; Johnny Dixon lifts the FA Cup as Aston Villa captain in 1957; Paul Birch during his time with Wolves

THE 2008/09 season saw the 20th anniversary of the Hillsborough disaster, and the occasion was marked by a service at Anfield on 15th April.

The bells of Liverpool's two cathedrals and its civic buildings rang out in memory of the 96 football fans who died at Sheffield Wednesday's stadium two decades ago. The city's public transport system also came to a standstill for two minutes at 3.06pm, the exact time that the FA Cup semi-final between Liverpool and Nottingham Forest was abandoned. Thousands of people attended the emotional memorial service at Anfield, where 96 candles were lit and a representative from the family of each victim was awarded the Freedom of Liverpool.

Liverpool's Lord Mayor, Steve Rotheram, led the tributes, saying: 'Hillsborough affected so many lives, not just on Merseyside but across the whole of the UK. I attended the match 20 years ago and the passing years do not diminish the importance and the poignancy of this occasion.'

Sheffield marked the anniversary of Britain's worst sporting disaster quietly. After consultation with the Liverpool families' organisations, a decision was taken that there would be no formal ceremony at Wednesday's ground. The Leppings Lane End – where the disaster unfolded – was opened, though, with three different memorials within a few hundred yards of the ground to provide a local focus. In Nottingham there was a two-minute silence in the city's Old Market Square, also beginning at 3.06pm.

It was a day on which fans everywhere paid their own tribute, as the victims of the tragedy were remembered.

This season also saw the passing of some of the game's true greats. Aston Villa mourned the loss of two of their post-War legends, Vic Crowe and Johnny Dixon, who died within a day of each other in January. Crowe was 76 and Dixon was 85. Crowe served the club for 17 years as a player, coach and then manager, while Dixon won a place in the hearts of the fans at Villa Park when he captained the team to victory in the 1957 FA Cup final.

A former 'Busby Babe', Ian Greaves, also died in January aged 76. He was one of the players who came through under the

CLOCKWISE FROM ABOVE: Ernie Cooksey during his Rochdale days; Steven Gerrard and Jamie Carragher lead the tributes at Anfield's Hillsborough memorial; former Celtic player and Notts County boss Jimmy Sirrel

legendary Sir Matt Busby at Manchester United before he eventually became a successful manager in his own right, winning the Division Two title with both Huddersfield (1969/70) and Bolton (1977/78).

Former Celtic player Jimmy Sirrel passed away in September and was remembered both at Parkhead and Notts County, having taken the Meadow Lane club from the old Fourth Division to the First Division as a manager between 1978 and 1982.

Blackpool and Newcastle fans, among others, were saddened by the news of Alan Suddick's death in March. He helped the Magpies to win the Division Two title in 1964/65 before being sold to Blackpool in December 1966. He went on to achieve legendary status with the Seasiders' supporters, scoring more than 60 goals in 310 appearances during a decade with the club and helping them win promotion to the top flight in 1969/70.

Ernie Cooksey was just 28 when he tragically fell victim to skin cancer in July 2008. Having first been spotted in

non-League football by Oldham, for whom he signed in the summer of 2003, Cooksey made a huge impact in his first season, featuring regularly in the first team and weighing in with some important goals. In September 2004 he was allowed to leave for Rochdale, where he spent two-and-a-half seasons before going on to play for Boston United and Grays Athletic.

Preston and Ireland stalwart Alan Kelly Snr, who played a club-record 477 league games for the Lilywhites, died in May aged 72 after a long battle with illness, while former Ipswich winger John Elsworthy died at the age of 77.

Paul Birch lost his battle with bone cancer this year, passing away aged just 46. The popular figure came through Villa's youth team and made more than 200 appearances for the club from 1980 to 1991, before he was sold to Wolves for £400,000.

Former Leicester midfielder and coach Neville Hamilton died aged 48 while Peter Aldis, who made almost 300 appearances for Villa, was 81.

October saw the death of John Sjoberg, the former Leicester defender who spent 15 years at the club, making more than 400 first-team appearances for the Foxes.

Former Tottenham winger Jimmy Neighbour – who was a member of the Spurs side that won the League Cup in 1971 – died at the age of 58. He also played for Norwich and West Ham. Just a day later, Mike Keen, a former QPR midfielder, also passed away at the age of 69, with fans remembering a 16-year career in which he made almost 700 league appearances before going on to manage Watford, Northampton and Wycombe.

John Hulme, formally of Bolton, Reading and Bury, also passed away this season.

Wolves, Manchester City and Walsall fans, meanwhile, mourned Jimmy Murray. A prolific goalscoring centre forward, he was a key member of the Wolves side that won back-to-back First Division titles in 1958 and 1959 – when he led the club's scoring charts on both occasions – and he was also a member of the team that won the FA Cup in 1960.

THE 2008/09 season was as good as I can remember in terms of the Barclays Premier League with the fight for the title and the battle for survival going all the way.

Liverpool emerged as genuine title contenders and fought Manchester United all the way. Newcastle became the biggest club ever to be relegated from the Barclays Premier League and, in my opinion, will be a sad loss.

Hull were the surprise team in the early part of the season with a string of great wins, including victory at the Emirates Stadium. However, it was Fulham who were the biggest surprise of them all in qualifying for Europe, a season after staying up on the final day of the 2007/08 campaign.

There were plenty of the usual managerial casualties, with World Cup-winning coach Luiz Felipe Scolari the biggest name of the lot to get the chop.

In Europe, the English League established itself as the strongest across the continent with three of the four semi-finalists hailing from the Barclays Premier League. Barcelona may have won the UEFA Champions League but they should never have been in the final as their win over Chelsea in the last four was, for me, the low point of the season in terms of refereeing.

Burnley not only earned promotion but were the giant-killing specialists of the season with a string of top-division scalps on their way. Former top-flight clubs Norwich, Southampton and Charlton all plunged into Coca-Cola League One, proving just how easy it is to drop down the divisions once you are on that slippery slope.

Another big club that will play in League One next season is Leeds, who failed again in the play-offs. That division saw the continuing emergence of another successful manager named Ferguson as Sir Alex's son Darren led Peterborough to promotion. The biggest story of League Two was 1988 League Cup winners Luton dropping out of the Football League after a season blighted by a huge points deduction.

In Scotland, Rangers ended Celtic's three-year domination of the Clydesdale Bank Premier League after a season in which the Old Firm didn't have it all their own way, with surprise defeats aplenty.

In fact, shock results became the norm both north and south of the border, which is why the lead continually changed in The New Football Pools Pundits League, in which my old Liverpool teammate John Barnes vied with me for the title of best predictor throughout the season.

The 2008/09 season was definitely one to remember... roll on 2009/10!

Alan Hansen – Pundit with The New Football Pools

Read Alan Hansen's weekly predictions at www.footballpools.com

Alan Hansen, pundit with The New Football Pools

What a fantastic season for British football! High drama and intensely competitive to the final day – arguably one of the most memorable in recent years!

The season also marked the re-launch of The New Football Pools, incorporating Littlewoods, Vernons and Zetters, re-establishing the iconic football pools right back at the heart of football fans and their communities. Having paid billions of pounds to millions of winners, The New Football Pools – the oldest football gaming business in the world, established in 1923 – is firmly back on the football landscape.

As an Official Licensee of the Premier League and the Football League, and an Official Partner of the Scottish Premier League and Scottish Football League, we are closer than ever to the game that we have supported over the decades.

We have a huge social responsibility too – by playing our games, customers are also contributing to the ongoing investment in grass roots football. We have contributed over £1.1billion to football and charitable causes since the 1970s, and supporting the community remains at the very heart of The New Football Pools. This season we joined forces with the Premier League to launch Premier League Health, and invested £1.63million into a scheme to assist top-flight football clubs in tackling men's health issues. A further £4.3million is to be invested across the English and Scottish Leagues in their community projects.

We look forward to the 2009/10 season, and bringing more exciting football prediction games to fans across the UK who want to get in on the action, putting their skills to the test to win big cash prizes. Join our new Mini Leagues at www.footballpools.com where your friends and colleagues can compete with and against each other in your own league, using your football knowledge to win money and the weekly bragging rights!

The New Football Pools is back and better than ever.

Ian Penrose, CEO, Sportech PLC (owner of The New Football Pools)

Howard Webb, in conversation with Manchester United's Edwin van der Sar, is among the game's most highly-rated officials

ACROSS the board, I think our referees have performed extremely well this season. There will always be the odd big decision that turns out to be wrong but, in the main, I think we can certainly prove that those occasions have been reduced dramatically, which is important.

One of the main things that has improved this season – as part of the 'Get On With The Game, Get On With The Ref, Get On With Each Other' programme – has been how we, as referees, can make better use of the captains. The captains of the Barclays Premier League clubs, in particular, have really bought into it – obviously with the guidance of their managers and the clubs themselves. Out on the field of play it has been a real bonus to the referees to have another management tool and to be able to involve the captain by getting him to calm down his team or to emphasise that if a certain way of behaviour continues, then a player may get a yellow or red card. It has

been a really good preventative tool that has been a cornerstone of the season and a big success from our point of view.

The pre-match meeting with the captain and the club officials has also been extremely beneficial, but I also think that managers have taken on board their responsibility. They are operating in a high-pressure, need-to-win environment, and the reality is that, on occasions, they have come out and said that referees have got it wrong. We don't ignore such comments – we look at them very closely and, if needs be, we will go back and talk to the individual manager concerned.

The future is good for refereeing. One of the key points of the Respect campaign – although it is still in its early days – is to work with the Football Association to get young referees to recognise that there is a career for them in the game if they want it. If they show talent and consistent levels of high performance, the system will draw them to the top. That has been proven with

younger referees who have come through. Howard Webb, for example, is still young in refereeing terms. He was out at the Confederations Cup, and in the next year he will be looking to be appointed for the World Cup. We have got young Michael Oliver in the Coca-Cola Football League who is showing great maturity. There is probably a fair bit of competition in his household with his father refereeing as well!

The development of these young men shows how far we have come. The establishment of professional referees in 2001 is, in a sense, now beginning to yield some real rewards and that has been recognised, with FIFA president Sepp Blatter recently saying that he wants to see more professional referees. For that reason, I think we are now leading the world.

Keith Hackett
General manager, Professional Game Match Officials Board

Barclays Manager of the Month
Gareth Southgate (Middlesbrough)
Barclays Player of the Month
Deco (Chelsea)
Top: Chelsea (7 points) **Bottom:** West Brom (1)
Top Scorers: Agbonlahor (Aston Villa),
Elano (Manchester C), Zaki (Wigan) 3

Coca-Cola Manager of the Month
Mick McCarthy (Wolves)
Powerade Player of the Month
Richard Chaplow (Preston)
Top: Wolves (10) **Bottom:** Derby (1)
Top Scorers: Doyle (Reading), Iwelumo (Wolves), Kightly
(Wolves), McCormack (Cardiff), Phillips (Birmingham),
Sharp (Sheff Utd), Smith (Watford), Sonko (Reading)......3

Coca-Cola Manager of the Month
Nigel Pearson (Leicester)
Powerade Player of the Month
Danny Graham (Carlisle)
Top: Leicester (10) **Bottom:** Huddersfield (2)
Top Scorers: Fryatt (Leicester), Graham (Carlisle),
Lambert (Bristol R) 5

Coca-Cola Manager of the Month
Mark Robins (Rotherham)
Powerade Player of the Month
Soloman Taiwo (Dag & Red)
Top: Dagenham (10) **Bottom:** Luton (-23)
Top Scorer: Thorne (Bradford) 5

Clydesdale Bank Manager of the Month
Jim Jefferies (Kilmarnock)
Clydesdale Bank Player of the Month
Pedro Mendes (Rangers)
Clydesdale Bank Young Player of the Month
James McArthur (Hamilton)
Top: Rangers (10) **Bottom:** Falkirk (0)
Top Scorers: Nish (Hibernian), Samaras (Celtic) 3

Irn-Bru Phenomenal Manager of the Month
First Division
Roberto Landi (Livingston)
Top: Livingston (12) **Bottom:** Morton (2)
Second Division
Brian Reid (Ayr)
Top: Ayr United (11) **Bottom:** Stranraer (4)
Third Division
Harry Cairney (Annan)
Top: Stenhousemuir (11) **Bottom:** Elgin (4)
Irn-Bru Phenomenal Player of the Month
Stephen Robertson (Airdrie)
Irn-Bru Phenomenal Young Player of the Month
Leigh Griffiths (Livingston)

WITH THE season barely under way, Rangers were already counting the cost of failing to make the UEFA Champions League group stage.

A 2–1 defeat to FBK Kaunas in Lithuania devastated the Gers' plans as they exited the competition in the second qualifying round and found themselves without even a place in the UEFA Cup to fall back on.

The Clydesdale Bank Premier League runners-up – UEFA Cup finalists during the previous season – failed to break down their visitors in a goalless first leg and had their hearts broken by a late Kaunas winner in the return fixture as their away goal advantage at 1–1 was wiped out.

Meanwhile, in the Barclays Premier League, Manchester United were held at home 1–1 to Newcastle over the first weekend of the season, while the rest of the 'Big Four' got off to winning starts, in a mixed month for the reigning champions. Having beaten Portsmouth on penalties in the Community Shield, Champions League winners United then failed to add the UEFA Super Cup to their trophy cabinet as they lost 2–1 to UEFA Cup holders Zenit St Petersburg.

Chelsea appeared a revived force under new boss Luiz Felipe Scolari, putting four past Portsmouth without reply to start their campaign, with summer signing Deco looking an inspired acquisition as he capped a fine debut with a late strike.

Hull began their first season in England's top flight with a 2–1 win over Fulham, while fellow newly-promoted sides Stoke and West Brom suffered defeats to Bolton and Arsenal respectively.

The Tigers, however, were taught a painful lesson in just their third Barclays Premier League fixture as they were beaten 5–0 by Wigan at home.

Domestic action had got under way earlier in the month both north and south of the

Sean O'Driscoll guided his newly-promoted Doncaster to an opening-day win at Derby

border, with newly-promoted Coca-Cola Championship side Doncaster producing a shock opening-day win over recently-relegated Derby at Pride Park.

Scunthorpe also suffered further misery following relegation, as fellow Coca-Cola League One promotion favourites Leeds recorded a 2–1 victory at Glanford Park.

In Coca-Cola League Two, Luton failed to make a dent in their unprecedented 30-point deduction, handed out after they were found guilty of misconduct and failing to satisfy the Football League's insolvency rules. The Hatters lost 3–1 to Port Vale on the opening day, but they made amends later in the month with two wins and a draw.

Rangers put their European woes behind them by taking 10 points from their opening four games in the SPL, including a 4–2 victory at arch-rivals Celtic, while Hamilton began life back in Scotland's top flight with impressive back-to-back wins.

The Irn-Bru Scottish Football League's newest club, Annan Athletic, kicked off their Third Division campaign with a 4–1 victory at Cowdenbeath and went unbeaten in four games until a 4–2 defeat to Albion Rovers on August 30.

The final month of the summer transfer window saw those staying put grab more headlines than those on the move. The protracted saga surrounding Cristiano Ronaldo's potential move to Real Madrid finally came to an end with Manchester United's star winger eventually ruling out a move away from Old Trafford. The much-speculated £50million-plus deal had dragged on throughout the summer, but with United unwilling to do business with the Spanish giants, Ronaldo finally broke his silence by delivering the news that United fans were so desperate to hear.

In the other main transfer story of the summer, Gareth Barry's agent claimed the midfielder would remain with Aston Villa

CLOCKWISE FROM ABOVE: Manchester United players celebrate beating Portsmouth on penalties in the Charity Shield; new Chelsea boss Luiz Felipe Scolari directs his players from the touchline; Rangers fail to overcome Lithuanian side FBK Kaunas

WHAT THEY SAID

The matter is closed now. He is a Manchester United player – it's finished. He'll be playing here next season, believe me.
– Sir Alex Ferguson gives his word that Cristiano Ronaldo will not be moving to Real Madrid after a summer of speculation

I'd like one of the big teams, someone we can make as much money from as possible because, let's face it, we're not going to win it.
– Macclesfield boss Keith Alexander spells out his side's prospects in the Carling Cup ahead of the second-round draw

I could say that I practised it every day for half an hour, but just an idiot would shoot from there!
– Bolton defender Gretar Steinsson admits his spectacular goal against Stoke was intended as a cross

It's a blow in every aspect. We just have to face it and get on with it.
– Rangers manager Walter Smith tries to come to terms with Rangers' European exit at the hands of FBK Kaunas

until January at least after Liverpool failed to match Villa manager Martin O'Neill's valuation.

Liverpool had already added to their ranks by acquiring Robbie Keane from Tottenham in a move they hoped would turn them into Barclays Premier League title contenders. The Irishman started each of Liverpool's first three league games, in which they beat Sunderland and Middlesbrough and drew with Villa.

Among those also moving clubs was striker Andrew Johnson, who completed his transfer from Everton to Fulham for an undisclosed fee, while Sunderland confirmed the signing of forwards Djibril Cisse, on a season-long loan from Marseille, and David Healy from Fulham.

Ukrainian striker Andriy Shevchenko put an end to his miserable two-year stay in the Barclays Premier League as he completed a loan return to former club AC Milan from Chelsea. Another man going back to his former club from Chelsea was winger Shaun Wright-Phillips, who rejoined Manchester City on a four-year contract for an undisclosed fee some three years after leaving Eastlands.

In the Championship, much-travelled striker Grzegorz Rasiak joined Watford from Southampton, Derby signed Arsenal youngster Nacer Barazite and defender Moritz Volz joined Ipswich from Fulham, all on loan deals.

SPL champions Celtic signed defender Glenn Loovens from Cardiff for around £2.5million and rivals Rangers landed midfielder Pedro Mendes from Portsmouth for £3million.

Barclays Manager of the Month
Phil Brown (Hull)
Barclays Player of the Month
Ashley Young (Aston Villa)
Top: Chelsea (14) **Bottom:** Tottenham (2)
Top Scorers: Adebayor (Arsenal), Defoe (Portsm'th) 3

Coca-Cola Manager of the Month
Owen Coyle (Burnley)
Powerade Player of the Month
Kevin Doyle (Reading)
Top: Wolves (22) **Bottom:** Nottm Forest (5)
Top Scorer: Doyle (Reading)..5

Coca-Cola Manager of the Month
Kenny Jackett (Millwall)
Powerade Player of the Month
Jermaine Beckford (Leeds)
Top: Leicester (19) **Bottom:** Hereford (4)
Top Scorer: Mackail-Smith (Peterborough)...................5

Coca-Cola Manager of the Month
Alan Knill (Bury)
Powerade Player of the Month
Matthew Gill (Exeter)
Top: Bury (18) **Bottom:** Luton (-19)
Top Scorers: Gill (Exeter), Yeo (Macclesfield) 4

Clydesdale Bank Manager of the Month
Gordon Strachan (Celtic)
Clydesdale Bank Player of the Month
Georgios Samaras (Celtic)
Clydesdale Bank Young Player of the Month
Scott Arfield (Falkirk)
Top: Rangers (19) **Bottom:** St Mirren (5)
Top Scorers: Samaras (Celtic)....................................4

Irn-Bru Phenomenal Manager of the Month
First Division
Jim McIntyre (Dunfermline)
Top: Livingston (18) **Bottom:** Morton (4)
Second Division
Dave Baikie (East Fife)
Top: Brechin (16) **Bottom:** Alloa (4)
Third Division
John Coughlin (Stenhousemuir)
Top: Stenhousemuir (20) **Bottom:** Elgin (4)
Irn-Bru Phenomenal Player of the Month
Paul McManus (East Fife)
Irn-Bru Phenomenal Young Player of the Month
Calum Elliot (Livingston)

SEPTEMBER began in the most dramatic fashion with the final day of the summer transfer window dominated by two £30million-plus deals and the arrival of new owners at Manchester City.

City were taken over by the Abu Dhabi United Group and promptly signed Real Madrid's Brazilian star Robinho from under the noses of Chelsea for a British record fee of £32.5million. Not only did City steal the Blues' number-one transfer target, but the Eastlands outfit emphasised their new-found status as one of the richest clubs in world football.

Across the city, Manchester United beat the midnight deadline on 1st September, paying £30.75million to Tottenham for striker Dimitar Berbatov. Fraizer Campbell went in the opposite direction on a season-long loan as part of the deal that allowed Berbatov to complete what he described as a 'dream' move to the English and European champions.

Spurs also completed the signing of Roman Pavlyuchenko from Spartak Moscow, while Espanyol winger Albert Riera joined Liverpool. Pavlyuchenko's arrival failed to have the desired impact, though, as the north London side still remained without a first Barclays Premier League win of the season at the end of the month.

In contrast, London rivals Chelsea continued to lead the way in the League despite being held at home by Spurs and United, who themselves struggled to live up to their billing as title favourites as they slipped to a 2–1 defeat against Liverpool at Anfield. Chelsea,

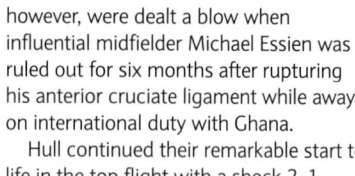

Theo Walcott scored a hat-trick for England in Croatia

however, were dealt a blow when influential midfielder Michael Essien was ruled out for six months after rupturing his anterior cruciate ligament while away on international duty with Ghana.

Hull continued their remarkable start to life in the top flight with a shock 2–1 victory at Arsenal. Phil Brown's side collected seven points from a possible nine in September.

Kevin Bond had the misfortune of becoming the first managerial casualty of the season when he was replaced by Jimmy Quinn at Bournemouth, while six other English clubs also made changes to their coaching staff.

The most notable departures came at Newcastle and West Ham as Kevin Keegan and Alan Curbishley both left amid disputes over transfer policy at their respective clubs. The end of Keegan's second spell in the hotseat at St James' Park sparked such a furore among Newcastle fans that the fallout prompted owner Mike Ashley to put the Magpies up for sale – although he later made a U-turn on that decision. The search for Keegan's successor saw Ashley turn to veteran former Wimbledon and Nottingham Forest boss Joe Kinnear, who was installed as interim manager, while Gianfranco Zola became West Ham's first ever foreign head coach.

In Coca-Cola League One, struggling Cheltenham replaced Keith Downing with one-time Leicester boss Martin Allen following five successive defeats in all competitions, while Kit Symons took charge at Colchester as caretaker manager after Geraint Williams' reign came to an end following a 3–0 defeat to MK Dons.

While Bond left the Cherries, fellow Coca-Cola League Two sides Grimsby and Port Vale also parted company with Alan Buckley and Lee Sinnott respectively.

In the Coca-Cola Championship, Owen Coyle picked up the manager of the month award after leading Burnley to four wins and a draw and also into the fourth round of the Carling Cup following a 1–0 win over Fulham. Brighton also caused an upset in the Carling Cup when they beat Manchester City on penalties in their rearranged second-round clash at the Withdean, while Watford beat West Ham. However, the Hornets'

CLOCKWISE FROM ABOVE: Robinho scores on his Manchester City debut; Dimitar Berbatov becomes Manchester United's record signing; Kevin Keegan left Newcastle United in controversial circumstances

WHAT THEY SAID

It's my opinion that a manager must have the right to manage and clubs should not impose upon any manager any player that he does not want.
– Kevin Keegan quits as Newcastle boss just eight months after his emotional return to St James' Park

My lads were well up for it and we needed to do something big after losing to Walsall's nine men on Saturday.
– Brighton boss Micky Adams after his side put Manchester City out of the Carling Cup

I've never seen anything like it. It's like a UFO landing, a mistake like that.
– Watford boss Adrian Boothroyd expresses his disbelief after seeing referee Stuart Atwell award a goal to opponents Reading when the ball had gone the wrong side of the post

I would say that I'm fairly pleased with the way we have started this season.
– Dunfermline's Jim McIntyre refuses to get too carried away after a six-game unbeaten run

month was dominated by a bizarre incident during their league game against Reading. Referee Stuart Atwell created headlines of the wrong sort when he awarded a goal to the Royals, despite the fact that the ball had gone the wrong side of the post. John Eustace's header to clear Stephen Hunt's corner bounced out of play at least three yards wide of the goal, but somehow Attwell, on his assistant referee's instruction, pointed to the centre circle as if a goal had been scored. The controversial game ended 2–2.

In Scotland, the Old Firm stamped their authority on the Clydesdale Bank Premier League with Celtic and Rangers both claiming maximum points from their three fixtures in September. Aberdeen's poor home form caused them problems as they suffered back-to-back defeats at Pittodrie against Hamilton and Dundee United before a 3–2 loss at Celtic left the Dons second from bottom of the table.

Stenhousemuir were the form side outside of the SPL, moving five points clear at the top of the Irn-Bru Third Division after

amassing nine points during the month. East Fife's Paul McManus caught the eye in the Irn-Bru Second Division, scoring five goals in two games.

On the international front, Theo Walcott scored a hat-trick as England triumphed 4–1 in Croatia after a 2–0 win in Andorra to boost their hopes of reaching the 2010 World Cup. Scotland experienced mixed fortunes as they kicked off their qualifying campaign with a 1–0 defeat in Macedonia before bouncing back with a 2–1 victory in Iceland.

Barclays Manager of the Month
Rafael Benitez (Liverpool)
Barclays Player of the Month
Frank Lampard (Chelsea)
Top: Liverpool (26) **Bottom:** Tottenham (6)
Top Scorer: Robinho (Manchester C) 4

Coca-Cola Manager of the Month
Dave Jones (Cardiff)
Powerade Player of the Month
Rob Hulse (Derby)
Top: Wolves (31) **Bottom:** Doncaster (8)
Top Scorers: Ebanks-Blake (Wolves), Hulse (Derby),
Lita (Norwich), McCormack (Cardiff) 4

Coca-Cola Manager of the Month
Paul Trollope (Bristol R)
Powerade Player of the Month
Rickie Lambert (Bristol R)
Top: Scunthorpe (29) **Bottom:** Crewe (9)
Top Scorer: Lambert (Bristol R) 7

Coca-Cola Manager of the Month
Peter Jackson (Lincoln)
Powerade Player of the Month
Jamie Ward (Chesterfield)
Top: Wycombe (27) **Bottom:** Luton (-14)
Top Scorer: Ward (Chesterfield) 7

Clydesdale Bank Manager of the Month
Gus MacPherson (St Mirren)
Clydesdale Bank Player of the Month
Scott Brown (Celtic)
Clydesdale Bank Young Player of the Month
Steven Fletcher (Hibernian)
Top: Celtic (25) **Bottom:** Hamilton (9)
Top Scorers: Brown (Celtic), Boyd (Rangers), Bryson
(Kilmarnock), Fletcher (Hibernian), Loovens (Celtic),
Lovell (Falkirk), Miller (Aberdeen), Porter (Motherwell),
Riordan (Hibernian)...2

Irn-Bru Phenomenal Manager of the Month
First Division
Derek McInnes (St Johnstone)
Top: Queen of the South (21) **Bottom:** Morton (10)
Second Division
Michael O'Neill (Brechin)
Top: Brechin (25) **Bottom:** Arbroath (6)
Third Division
Jim Chapman (Dumbarton)
Top: Stenhousemuir (21) **Bottom:** Elgin (8)
Irn-Bru Phenomenal Player of the Month
Steven Milne (St Johnstone)
Irn-Bru Phenomenal Young Player of the Month
Dominic Shimmin (Morton)

CHELSEA'S incredible unbeaten home record in the Barclays Premier League came to an end as Liverpool showcased their title credentials in west London. Having gone 86 league games without defeat at Stamford Bridge – a run that began in February 2004 – Xabi Alonso's deflected goal gave the Reds a 1–0 victory at the end of the month and ensured Rafael Benitez's side led the way heading into November.

Steven Gerrard, in particular, produced another outstanding performance against Chelsea. He had started October by notching his 100th goal for the Reds during the 3–1 win over PSV Eindhoven at Anfield in the UEFA Champions League. Also on target against the Dutch champions was Robbie Keane, who, in the process, scored his first goal since his summer move to Merseyside.

While Liverpool were setting the pace at the top of the table, Keane's former club Tottenham struggled at the opposite end. A 2–1 defeat at Stoke ensured Spurs made their worst-ever start to a season and, to compound their misery, Gareth Bale and Michael Dawson were both sent off at the Britannia Stadium. Juande Ramos was sacked less than a week later, just eight months after helping the club to win the Carling Cup, and Harry Redknapp left his post at Portsmouth to take charge at White Hart Lane.

Fresh from his FA Cup success at Pompey five months earlier, Redknapp wasted little time in reviving Tottenham's fortunes. He masterminded the club's first league win of the campaign, a 2–0 victory over Bolton, a matter of hours after arriving. Then came an incredible 4–4 draw against arch-rivals Arsenal. Trailing 4–2 with only a few minutes remaining, Spurs struck late through Jermaine Jenas and Aaron Lennon to spark wild scenes among the travelling Tottenham

Shrewsbury striker Grant Holt scored five goals against Wycombe

supporters who had opted not to leave early at the Emirates Stadium.

Former Gunners captain Tony Adams was subsequently unveiled as Redknapp's replacement at Portsmouth for his first managerial role since his short spell at Wycombe Wanderers.

Another Barclays Premier League manager in the headlines was David Moyes, who signed a new five-year deal at Everton after protracted negotiations. Moyes has worked wonders at Goodison Park since making the move from Preston in 2002, but not even he could prevent the Toffees from crashing out of the UEFA Cup to Standard Liège. Motherwell were also ousted by French side Nancy, while Tottenham, Aston Villa, Manchester City and Portsmouth all progressed to the group stage.

Ramos was not the only managerial casualty in October as QPR sacked Iain Dowie after 15 games in charge with the club lying ninth in the Coca-Cola Championship and into the last 16 of the Carling Cup. Gareth Ainsworth took temporary charge at Loftus Road, while former Scotland international Paul Lambert replaced Geraint Williams at Colchester and Mike Newell made his return to the dugout at Coca-Cola League Two side Grimsby. Newell – who was previously in charge of Luton and Hartlepool – succeeded Alan Buckley with the Mariners without a victory and two points above the relegation places.

There were plenty of eye-catching results in the Johnstone's Paint Trophy as Rotherham upset the odds to beat Yorkshire rivals Leeds 4–2, while Shrewsbury thrashed Wycombe 7–0 thanks to five goals from Grant Holt.

Like Holt, Wayne Rooney also enjoyed a purple patch in front of goal in October, scoring seven times in as many games for Manchester United and England. Rooney also scored successive braces on international duty in England's 5–1 and 3–1 wins over Kazakhstan and Belarus to ensure Fabio Capello's men made decent progress towards qualifying for World Cup 2010. He also found the net in

CLOCKWISE FROM ABOVE: Geovanni scores Hull's winner against Tottenham; Xabi Alonso's goal for Liverpool ends Chelsea's unbeaten home run; Scotland forward Chris Iwelumo can't believe it as he misses from close range against Norway

WHAT THEY SAID

I must thank God for this success. Credit also goes to chairman Dave Whelan and manager Steve Bruce.
– Wigan striker Amr Zaki reflects on his success

There's people dancing in the dressing room so we don't have to do a warm-down any more.
– Manager Phil Brown after Hull's 1–0 victory over West Ham propelled them to third in the Premier League

We did a seven-a-side game where the punishment for missing the target was to take off an item of clothing.
– Motherwell boss Mark McGhee reveals the cold-weather preparation behind his side's victory at Inverness

I don't think the fans will expect me to score five every game – one a week will do!
– Shrewsbury's Grant Holt following his five goals against Wycombe

I feel like Superman, I could fly home.
– Tottenham midfielder David Bentley after scoring in the 4–4 draw with Arsenal

United's convincing 3–0 Champions League victory over Celtic at Old Trafford and the Barclays Premier League games against Blackburn and West Brom.

After a prolific start to the season with Wolves, Chris Iwelumo had a Scotland debut to forget as he squandered a gilt-edged chance from close range during the goalless stalemate against Norway at Hampden Park. Iwelumo's miss aside, it was a game best remembered for the furore generated when boss George Burley opted to leave striker Kris Boyd on the bench.

Boyd in turn announced he would not play for Scotland again while Burley was the national team's manager.

John Toshack's Wales beat Liechtenstein 2–0 at the Millennium Stadium – where West Ham striker Craig Bellamy missed a penalty – before losing 1–0 against Germany, while Nigel Worthington's Northern Ireland went down to two late goals from Slovenia. The Republic of Ireland, under veteran Italian coach Giovanni Trapattoni, beat Cyprus 1–0 at Croke Park, with Liverpool striker Keane –

forgetting about any frustrations at club level – scoring the winner.

In the Scottish domestic game, Rangers edged into the semi-finals of the Co-operative Insurance Cup with a 2–0 home win over Hamilton. Old Firm rivals Celtic joined them in the last four with a comfortable 3–1 victory against Kilmarnock at Rugby Park.

Airdrie and Ross County beat Partick Thistle and Morton 1–0 and 4–1 respectively to reach the final of the ALBA Challenge Cup.

Barclays Manager of the Month
Gary Megson (Bolton)
Barclays Player of the Month
Nicolas Anelka (Chelsea)
Top: Chelsea (33) **Bottom:** West Brom (11)
Top Scorer: Anelka (Chelsea).........................7

Coca-Cola Manager of the Month
Mick McCarthy (Wolves)
Powerade Player of the Month
Chris Iwelumo (Wolves)
Top: Wolves (47) **Bottom:** Doncaster (15)
Top Scorers: Beattie (Sheff Utd), Doyle (Reading),
Iwelumo (Wolves) 6

Coca-Cola Manager of the Month
Roberto Di Matteo (MK Dons)
Powerade Player of the Month
Dean Lewington (MK Dons)
Top: Leicester (38) **Bottom:** Crewe (9)
Top Scorer: Cox (Swindon).........................5

Coca-Cola Manager of the Month
Peter Taylor (Wycombe)
Powerade Player of the Month
Grant Holt (Shrewsbury)
Top: Wycombe (37) **Bottom:** Luton (-11)
Top Scorers: Forte (Notts Co), Holt (Shrewsbury) 4

Clydesdale Bank Manager of the Month
Gordon Strachan (Celtic)
Clydesdale Bank Player of the Month
Bruno Aguiar (Hearts)
Clydesdale Bank Young Player of the Month
Sone Aluko (Aberdeen)
Top: Celtic (43) **Bottom:** St Mirren (12)
Top Scorer: Boyd (Rangers).........................6

Irn-Bru Phenomenal Manager of the Month
First Division
Jocky Scott (Dundee)
Top: St Johnstone (28) **Bottom:** Airdrie (14)
Second Division
Brian Reid (Ayr)
Top: Raith (32) **Bottom:** Stranraer (10)
Third Division
Jim McInally (East Stirling)
Top: Stenhousemuir (29) **Bottom:** Elgin (8)
Irn-Bru Phenomenal Player of the Month
Bryan Prunty (Ayr)
Irn-Bru Phenomenal Young Player of the Month
Kyle Benedictis (Dundee)

THE FIRST major piece of silverware of the season in English and Scottish football was decided by a thrilling penalty shoot-out as Marc Smyth held his nerve to help Airdrie United win the ALBA Challenge Cup.

Smyth converted the decisive spot-kick as the Diamonds beat Ross County 3–2 on penalties on 16th November after the sides were deadlocked at 2–2 following extra-time. Earlier, David Nixon's own goal had opened the scoring and Stephen McKenna levelled for Airdrie before Andy Dowie turned the ball into his own net and Sean Higgins powered home a headed equaliser to set up a tense finish.

Airdrie were not the only team enjoying success from the penalty spot in November as Burnley's Carling Cup campaign went from strength to strength. Having already accounted for Fulham in September, Owen Coyle's side raised more eyebrows when they beat the then-Barclays Premier League leaders Chelsea 5–4 on penalties after drawing 1–1 in their fourth-round tie at Stamford Bridge. Goalkeeper Brian Jensen was the hero, saving brilliantly from Wayne Bridge and John Obi Mikel.

Chelsea had started the month with a 5–0 demolition of Sunderland, with Nicolas Anelka scoring a hat-trick and Frank Lampard netting his 100th Barclays Premier League goal, while Tottenham's revival continued with vital wins over Liverpool and Manchester City.

Wayne Rooney was another player celebrating a century milestone, his 100th goal in club football giving Manchester United all three points and local bragging rights following a 1–0 win at rivals Manchester City.

Stoke showed their battling qualities with a 2–1 success against Arsenal at the Britannia Stadium, but they were left licking their wounds a fortnight later following a 5–0 humbling at Old Trafford. The Gunners, meanwhile, made amends for their sluggish showing in Staffordshire by beating United 2–1 thanks to two goals from Samir Nasri, and they then triumphed by the same scoreline at Chelsea. Arsenal came from behind at Stamford Bridge, with Robin van Persie scoring twice. However, those superb results against their traditional rivals at the top of the table were recorded either side of a home defeat to the rising stars of Aston Villa, whose 2–0 win at the Emirates came thanks to Gael Clichy's own goal and a Gabriel Agbonlahor strike.

While England's sides progressed in the UEFA Champions League, the magic of the FA Cup was evident as the first and second rounds of the world's oldest cup competition produced plenty of shocks. Non-League Blyth Spartans and Curzon Ashton ousted Shrewsbury and Exeter respectively in round one, while Leeds were the fall guys in the next round, losing 1–0 to Blue Square Premier side Histon.

Eastwood Town also enjoyed their day as they beat Coca-Cola League Two leaders Wycombe 2–0 at Coronation Park, while Luton knocked out Walsall and Rotherham overcame Leicester in the Johnstone's Paint Trophy.

More managers came and went, with Adrian Boothroyd and Alan Pardew the most high profile to lose their jobs after leaving Watford and Charlton.

Wolves went through November unbeaten in the Coca-Cola Championship and MK Dons enhanced their hopes of promotion with four wins in as many Coca-Cola League One outings. Wycombe found some consolation from their FA Cup exit as they stretched their unbeaten run in League Two to 17 games by the end of the month. Jocky Scott's return to management for a third spell at Dundee in the Irn-Bru First Division coincided with an upturn in fortunes for the

Mick McCarthy's Wolves were unbeaten in November

CLOCKWISE FROM ABOVE: Samir Nasri scores his second in Arsenal's victory over Manchester United; Airdrie United players take a lap of honour after winning the ALBA Challenge Cup; Burnley's Brian Jensen is mobbed after a penalty shoot-out win over Chelsea in the Carling Cup

WHAT THEY SAID

If he wants to come over and see a game here we would be very pleased to have him, but I think he might be a bit busy.
— West Ham boss Gianfranco Zola does not expect to see the club's most famous newly-discovered fan, Barack Obama, at Upton Park any time soon

It's a magnificent day for us and if there's a hard way for us to do it, we'll try it.
— Airdrie United boss Kenny Black hails his players after their ALBA Challenge Cup final penalty shoot-out victory against Ross County

To come to Chelsea and knock them out of the Cup is a great moment. This will give the town a big lift.
— Burnley boss Owen Coyle after the Carling Cup victory at Stamford Bridge

We had our pants pulled down and our backsides slapped at Old Trafford, but we've come back and the attitude was first class.
— Stoke manager Tony Pulis after his side bounced back from a 5–0 defeat against Manchester United to beat West Brom 1–0

Dees, who then forged a four-game unbeaten run.

Free-scoring Ayr United continued to catch the eye in the Irn-Bru Second Division – hitting the net 13 times in four games – while East Stirling's promotion challenge gathered pace after three wins from four in the Irn-Bru Third Division.

Scottish football also mourned the death of former Gretna owner Brooks Mileson after a long illness. It was with the help of Mileson's extensive financial backing that Gretna achieved successive promotions in three seasons before they completed their ascent into the Clydesdale Bank Premier League in 2007.

Celtic's early exit from the UEFA Champions League – confirmed after a 2–1 defeat against Aalborg in Denmark – was offset by their fine form in the SPL as Gordon Strachan's men won six successive league games. Rangers were also in ominous form, clinically seeing off Inverness and Kilmarnock 5–0 and 4–0 respectively.

Goals from Ronaldinho and Filippo Inzaghi denied Portsmouth what would have been a famous win as they were held 2–2 by AC Milan in the UEFA Cup at Fratton Park, while Tottenham and Manchester City beat NEC and Schalke respectively.

Both England and Scotland were in international friendly action, although they endured mixed fortunes. While John Terry's late winner handed England a 2–1 victory over Germany, Maxi Rodriguez's goal gave Argentina a narrow success over Scotland at Hampden Park in Diego Maradona's first game in charge of the South Americans.

Barclays Manager of the Month
Martin O'Neill (Aston Villa)
Barclays Player of the Month
Ashley Young (Aston Villa)
Top: Liverpool (45) **Bottom:** West Brom (18)
Top Scorer: Gerrard (Liverpool) 5

Coca-Cola Manager of the Month
Steve Coppell (Reading)
Powerade Player of the Month
Stephen Hunt (Reading)
Top: Wolves (58) **Bottom:** Charlton (19)
Top Scorers: Maynard (Bristol C), Morrison (Coventry), Scotland (Swansea) 4

Coca-Cola Manager of the Month
Nigel Pearson (Leicester)
Powerade Player of the Month
Matty Fryatt (Leicester)
Top: Leicester (51) **Bottom:** Crewe (16)
Top Scorers: Fryatt (Leicester), Hughes (Oldham), Mclean (Peterborough) 4

Coca-Cola Manager of the Month
John Still (Dag & Red)
Powerade Player of the Month
Marcus Bean (Brentford)
Top: Wycombe (46) **Bottom:** Luton (-1)
Top Scorers: Benson (Dag & Red), Gritton (Macclesfield), Lowe (Chester), Patulea (Lincoln) 4

Clydesdale Bank Manager of the Month
Gus MacPherson (St Mirren)
Clydesdale Bank Player of the Month
Lee Miller (Aberdeen)
Clydesdale Bank Young Player of the Month
James McCarthy (Hamilton)
Top: Celtic (50) **Bottom:** Hamilton (17)
Top Scorer: Boyd (Rangers).........5

Irn-Bru Phenomenal Manager of the Month
First Division
John Brown (Clyde)
Top: St Johnstone (36) **Bottom:** Airdrie (18)
Second Division
David Baikie (East Fife)
Top: Raith (38) **Bottom:** Stranraer (11)
Third Division
Jimmy Crease (Berwick)
Top: Stenhousemuir (33) **Bottom:** Elgin (8)
Irn-Bru Phenomenal Player of the Month
Alan Main (St Johnstone)
Irn-Bru Phenomenal Young Player of the Month
Chris McMenamin (Berwick)

THE FIFA Club World Cup in Japan provided the stage for Manchester United to put the seal on a memorable 2008 as they added another title to their glittering trophy cabinet. Not content with winning the Barclays Premier League and UEFA Champions League in the previous season, United were officially crowned as the best club side on the planet as they beat Ecuador's Liga de Quito 1–0 in the Tokyo final.

Wayne Rooney grabbed the only goal of the game after Nemanja Vidic had been sent off, and there was a further accolade for United to celebrate in December as Cristiano Ronaldo received the coveted Ballon d'Or award to become European footballer of the year ahead of Lionel Messi and Fernando Torres. That prize was further recognition of Ronaldo's outstanding form for both club and country – and the Portugal star proved integral once more as United kept the pressure on their Barclays Premier League title rivals, Liverpool and Chelsea.

It was Liverpool who finished the year at the top of the league table thanks to a brilliant 5–1 win at Newcastle and a creditable draw at Arsenal, although those results were tempered somewhat by disappointing home stalemates against West Ham and Hull.

Their Merseyside rivals, Everton, were also beginning to find their form after an indifferent start to the season. David Moyes' Toffees won at both Middlesbrough and Manchester City in a productive month.

Arsenal's indifferent form continued as they became the latest top-flight side to crash out of the Carling Cup to battling Burnley. Two goals from midfielder Kevin McDonald saw the Clarets claim a place in the semi-finals along with fellow Coca-Cola Championship side Derby, Manchester United and Tottenham.

The Rams were also triumphant against Barclays Premier League

Scotland international Lee Miller was in hot form for Aberdeen during December

opposition, beating Stoke 1–0 at the Britannia Stadium, while Spurs came from behind to win 2–1 at Watford.

Harry Redknapp's side also reached the last 32 of the UEFA Cup along with Aston Villa and Manchester City, but Portsmouth failed to progress past the group stage of the competition.

Chelsea left it until the final group game to book their place in the last 16 of the Champions League – Didier Drogba climbing off the bench to score his first European goal of the campaign in the 2–1 win over CFR Cluj at Stamford Bridge.

The FA Cup produced yet more shocks as several lower-league sides once again hit the headlines in their second-round replays. Fresh from ousting Shrewsbury in round one, Blyth Spartans claimed a second Coca-Cola League Two scalp thanks to Ged Dalton's late effort in the 1–0 win over 10-man Bournemouth, while Kettering Town came from a goal down to beat Notts County 2–1.

After two postponements and a 2–2 draw, Droylsden appeared set to finally progress into the third round as Sean Newton's brace helped seal a 2–1 replay win over Chesterfield. However, the Blue Square North side's celebrations were cut short when it emerged that Newton had been ineligible to face the Spireites due to suspension and Droylsden, despite lodging an appeal, were subsequently expelled from the competition.

Celtic ended the calendar year seven points clear at the top of the Clydesdale Bank Premier League after Scott McDonald's goal saw them emerge as 1–0 winners from an insipid Old Firm derby against Rangers, who began the month with a 7–1 thrashing of Hamilton.

St Mirren gave their survival hopes a timely boost by claiming maximum points in December, while Lee Miller's three goals in as many games helped Aberdeen beat Falkirk, Inverness and Hearts.

Veteran St Johnstone goalkeeper Alan Main rolled back the years with a string of impressive displays, conceding just one goal in four appearances, while East Fife edged into the play-off places in the Irn-Bru Second Division.

CLOCKWISE FROM ABOVE: MK Dons boss Roberto Di Matteo guided his side to four wins from five; Gary McAllister was sacked by Leeds; Tim Cahill scores in another impressive Everton win, this time at Manchester City; Manchester United captain Rio Ferdinand lifts the Club World Cup trophy

WHAT THEY SAID

I could sit here and say I haven't had the chance, but I've brought in lots of players. I have absolutely no excuses.
– Roy Keane shortly before resigning as Sunderland boss

I was rushing to get a 'for sale' sign on him for the TV, but I couldn't find a pen.
– Crystal Palace manager Neil Warnock on Shefki Kuqi, whom he was looking to sell, after the striker scored in a win over Southampton

If that happens I will go to the nearest bridge and throw myself off!
– Dave Pace, chairman of Droylsden, reacts to the news that his side could be thrown out of the FA Cup for fielding an ineligible player. They were cast out of the competition although, thankfully, Pace was not true to his word

We're the worst team in the League and I'm the worst manager.
– Motherwell boss Mark McGhee takes no prisoners following his side's 2–0 derby defeat at Hamilton

Berwick Rangers claimed four wins from four in the Irn-Bru Third Division, including a 3–2 success over leaders Stenhousemuir and a stunning 10-man victory by the same scoreline against Montrose.

The scramble for promotion from the Championship intensified as Reading emerged from the hectic festive period with an impressive return of five wins – including a 3–1 triumph at fellow high-flyers Birmingham – and two draws.

Leicester led the way in Coca-Cola League One heading into 2009 following an unbeaten month for Nigel Pearson's side, while Dagenham were the stand-out performers in League Two, winning three games out of four.

Elsewhere, not even the season of goodwill could prevent the managerial merry-go-round from spinning and claiming another set of victims.

Roy Keane resigned from Sunderland after 27 months in charge at the Stadium of Light and his former Old Trafford teammate Paul Ince was sacked by Blackburn having presided over just three wins from 17 Barclays Premier League games. Former Bolton and Newcastle manager Sam Allardyce returned to the game to succeed Ince at Ewood Park, while coach Ricky Sbragia took the reins from Keane.

In the Football League, Nottingham Forest, Derby and Leeds parted company with Colin Calderwood, Paul Jewell and Gary McAllister respectively. Simon Grayson left his post at Blackpool to fill the vacant position at Elland Road and return to the club at which he started his playing career in the 1980s.

Barclays Manager of the Month
Sir Alex Ferguson (Manchester Utd)
Barclays Player of the Month
Nemanja Vidic (Manchester Utd)
Top: Manchester Utd (53) **Bottom:** West Brom (22)
Top Scorers: Berbatov (Man Utd), Cole (West Ham),
Davies (Bolton), Ronaldo (Man Utd) 3

Coca-Cola Manager of the Month
Roberto Martinez (Swansea)
Powerade Player of the Month
Joe Ledley (Cardiff)
Top: Wolves (62) **Bottom:** Charlton (22)
Top Scorer: Saganowski (Southampton),
Scotland (Swansea) 4

Coca-Cola Manager of the Month
Paul Lambert (Colchester)
Powerade Player of the Month
Matt Oakley (Leicester)
Top: Leicester (64) **Bottom:** Cheltenham (21)
Top Scorer: Wilbraham (MK Dons) 6

Coca-Cola Manager of the Month
Alan Knill (Bury)
Powerade Player of the Month
Dany N'Guessan (Lincoln)
Top: Wycombe (53) **Bottom:** Luton (2)
Top Scorers: N'Guessan (Lincoln),
Rhodes (Brentford) 4

Clydesdale Bank Manager of the Month
Billy Reid (Hamilton)
Clydesdale Bank Player of the Month
Tomas Cerny (Hamilton)
Clydesdale Bank Young Player of the Month
James McCarthy (Hamilton)
Top: Celtic (54) **Bottom:** Inverness (11)
Top Scorers: Boyd (Rangers), Mensing (Hamilton) 4

Irn-Bru Phenomenal Manager of the Month
First Division
Ian McCall (Partick)
Top: St Johnstone (38) **Bottom:** Airdrie (23)
Second Division
Allan Moore (Stirling)
Top: Raith (46) **Bottom:** Stranraer (12)
Third Division
Danny Lennon (Cowdenbeath)
Top: Cowdenbeath (44) **Bottom:** Elgin (9)
Irn-Bru Phenomenal Player of the Month
Willie McLaren (Clyde)
Irn-Bru Phenomenal Young Player of the Month
Robert Barr (Albion)

PLAYERS moving clubs – and one in particular who stayed put – dominated the headlines in January as the mid-season transfer window opened for business.

Meanwhile, on the pitch, the domestic cup competitions came to the fore as the big guns were once again tested by lower-division opposition.

Manchester City made full use of the window to bolster their squad and, having agreed a deal with Chelsea for defender Wayne Bridge, they also brought in West Ham's Craig Bellamy and Nigel de Jong from German side Hamburg before the end of the month. However, City did not have things all their own way as a bid for Blackburn Rovers striker Roque Santa Cruz came to nothing and an astonishing £100million deal to bring AC Milan star Kaka to Eastlands fell through.

At one stage it appeared as though the Brazilian playmaker could be on his way to the Barclays Premier League when Milan agreed to open discussions over a deal. The player himself soon made it clear that he had no desire to quit the San Siro, though, leaving City to rue what might have been. 'If you want my personal opinion they [AC Milan] bottled it,' said Manchester City's executive chairman Garry Cook.

City were not the only side spending money and Tottenham attempted to ease their relegation fears by re-signing Jermain Defoe and Pascal Chimbonda. The striker and defender were joined at the club by Wilson Palacios, bought for around £14million from Wigan, and goalkeeper Carlo Cudicini, who arrived from Chelsea on a free transfer.

Elsewhere in the Barclays Premier League, Aston Villa completed the signing of Wigan's Emile Heskey for £3.5million,

Robbie Keane returned to Tottenham from Liverpool – and was installed as captain

paving the way for Colombian striker Hugo Rodallega to join the Latics, while Hull demonstrated their ambition with the signing of Jimmy Bullard for £5million from Fulham.

The biggest moves outside of the top flight saw QPR make a flurry of signings, capturing Gary Borrowdale, Heidar Helguson, Wayne Routledge, Liam Miller and Lee Cook, while Leicester borrowed Tom Cleverley from Manchester United and Scunthorpe secured talented Arsenal youngster Henri Lansbury on loan. In Coca-Cola League Two, Anthony Elding joined Lincoln from Crewe and Brentford loaned Ipswich striker Jordan Rhodes.

Scottish giants Celtic captured Cardiff's Willo Flood, who had been on loan at Dundee United, while Rangers offloaded Chris Burke and Jean-Claude Darcheville.

January also saw the return of a familiar surname at Derby as Nigel Clough followed in the footsteps of his father, Brian, to become the club's new manager.

In the Barclays Premier League, Manchester United finished the month five points clear at the top of the table thanks to a Cristiano Ronaldo penalty in a 1–0 win over Everton. That goal capped a wonderful month for Ronaldo, who was named FIFA World Player of the Year at a ceremony in Zurich.

Inverness Caledonian Thistle sacked manager Craig Brewster in the Clydesdale Bank Premier League, with Scotland assistant manager Terry Butcher taking over and combining the role with his duties for the national team.

Meanwhile, Aberdeen began the new year with impressive home results against the Old Firm teams. Two goals in three minutes from Zander Diamond secured a 4–2 win over Celtic and the Dons followed that up by holding Rangers to a 0–0 draw.

Stirling Albion's fine run of four wins in four games – including an 8–2 victory over Stranraer – saw them steal the headlines in the Irn–Bru Second Division, while their Irn-Bru Third Division counterparts Cowdenbeath took 13 points from a possible 15.

In the Co-operative Insurance Cup semi-final, Celtic and Dundee United endured a marathon penalty shoot-

CLOCKWISE FROM ABOVE: Nathan Tyson grabs Nottingham Forest's opening goal in their FA Cup demolition of Manchester City; Swansea enjoy their victory at struggling Portsmouth; new manager Terry Butcher gives orders to his Inverness Caledonian Thistle team

WHAT THEY SAID

We made an offer and it was turned down. We offered Stoke-on-Trent.
– Stoke boss Tony Pulis jokes that, like Manchester City, his attempts to sign Brazilian playmaker Kaka were unsuccessful

I said we would go out of the Cup if we weren't up for it. I was proved right.
– Portsmouth boss Tony Adams after his side lost to Swansea in the FA Cup

When we mess up, we do it big style.
– Wolves boss Mick McCarthy's verdict on his side's 3–1 home defeat by Preston

I think a few of the lads will be getting a haircut and getting the fake tan on!
– Ayr United manager Brian Reid on his side's Scottish Cup game against Kilmarnock being televised

My missus could have scored it.
– Tottenham boss Harry Redknapp makes Darren Bent feel even worse about the late miss that cost Spurs a win against Portsmouth

out, which the Glasgow team eventually won 11–10. The other semi-final saw Rangers make lighter work of Falkirk, beating them 3–0.

In the Carling Cup, Coca-Cola Championship side Burnley's amazing run finally came to an end – but not before they had threatened another remarkable upset in the semi-final against Tottenham. The Clarets – 4–1 down from the first leg – stormed into a 3–0 lead after 90 minutes at Turf Moor and looked well placed to progress to the Wembley showpiece.

However, extra-time goals from Roman Pavlyuchenko and Defoe spared Tottenham's blushes as they edged through to the final 6–4 on aggregate.

In the other semi-final, Kris Commons scored the only goal as Derby beat Manchester United 1–0 in the first leg at Pride Park, only for United to restore order in the return leg as they won 4–2 for a 4–3 aggregate victory.

There was also drama in the FA Cup as Barclays Premier League side Stoke lost 2–0 at Hartlepool and non-League Torquay beat

Blackpool 1–0. Arguably the story of the third round, however, was Championship strugglers Nottingham Forest knocking out big-spending Manchester City with a stunning 3–0 win at Eastlands.

West Brom, Chelsea, Portsmouth and Hull were all taken to a replay by lower-league opposition before moving through to the fourth round. However, holders Pompey were soon out of the tournament they had won just eight months earlier as in-form Swansea beat Tony Adams' faltering side 2–0 at Fratton Park.

Barclays Manager of the Month
David Moyes (Everton)
Barclays Player of the Month
Phil Jagielka (Everton)
Top: Manchester Utd (62) **Bottom:** West Brom (22)
Top Scorer: Torres (Liverpool) 3

Coca-Cola Manager of the Month
Chris Coleman (Coventry)
Powerade Player of the Month
Jason Scotland (Swansea)
Top: Wolves (64) **Bottom:** Charlton (27)
Top Scorers: Adebola (Bristol C), Ebanks-Blake (Wolves) ..4

Coca-Cola Manager of the Month
Gudjon Thordarson (Crewe)
Powerade Player of the Month
Aaron McLean (Peterborough)
Top: Leicester (74) **Bottom:** Cheltenham (21)
Top Scorer: McLean (Peterborough) 5

Coca-Cola Manager of the Month
Sammy McIlroy (Morecambe)
Powerade Player of the Month
Charlie MacDonald (Brentford)
Top: Brentford (62) **Bottom:** Luton (9)
Top Scorer: MacDonald (Brentford) 5

Clydesdale Bank Manager of the Month
Mark McGhee (Motherwell)
Clydesdale Bank Player of the Month
Andy Dorman (St Mirren)
Clydesdale Bank Young Player of the Month
Lee Wallace (Hearts)
Top: Rangers (60) **Bottom:** Inverness (22)
Top Scorers: Dorman (St Mirren), Nakamura (Celtic)....3

Irn-Bru Phenomenal Manager of the Month
First Division
Jocky Scott (Dundee)
Top: St Johnstone (44) **Bottom:** Airdrie (27)
Second Division
Allan Maitland (Alloa)
Top: Raith (48) **Bottom:** Stranraer (12)
Third Division
Jim McInally (East Stirling)
Top: Cowdenbeath (48) **Bottom:** Elgin (15)
Irn-Bru Phenomenal Player of the Month
Gary Harkins (Partick)
Irn-Bru Phenomenal Young Player of the Month
Fraser McLaren (Berwick)

WIDESPREAD wintery weather across Britain caused havoc at the start of February as the big freeze hit the football fixture programme hard.

Plummeting temperatures and the worst snowfall in some regions for 18 years inevitably took its toll, with a total of 25 games in the FA Cup, Football League and Blue Square Premier postponed on the first midweek match night of the month alone.

Several key matches in Scotland also fell victim to the weather, the most notable of which was Inverurie Locos' Homecoming Scottish Cup fourth-round clash against Motherwell. It had been postponed four times at the back end of January, although when the tie at Inverurie's Harlaw Park was finally able to go ahead, at the fifth time of asking, John Sutton's brace and a goal from David Clarkson sealed a comfortable 3–0 victory for Mark McGhee's men.

Prolonged snow showers also led to the delayed closure of the winter transfer window, which was put back further due to the adverse conditions. When the paperwork was eventually completed, it was deals involving Robbie Keane, Andrei Arshavin and Shay Given that dominated the headlines. Just over six months after leaving White Hart Lane to join Liverpool, Keane returned to Tottenham, while Russian star Arshavin joined Arsenal from Zenit St Petersburg and goalkeeper Given ended his 11-year association with Newcastle by moving to Manchester City.

On the pitch, Liverpool endured a mixed month as attempts to get their faltering title challenge in the Barclays Premier League back on track were hampered by a 1–1 draw with Manchester City and a 2–0 defeat at struggling Middlesbrough.

Dan Gosling's dramatic extra-

Leicester's Matty Fryatt helped the Foxes stay at the top of League One

time winner for Merseyside rivals Everton also sent the Reds crashing out of the FA Cup in the fourth round, but Rafael Benitez's side did gain plenty of plaudits for their 1–0 win against Real Madrid at the Bernabeu in the first leg of their last-16 clash in the UEFA Champions League.

Arsenal and Chelsea both made home advantage count in their European ties – running out 1–0 victors against Roma and Juventus respectively – while Manchester United and Inter Milan played out a goalless draw at the San Siro.

Away from European competition, Chelsea's bid to keep the pressure on United and Liverpool at the top of the Barclays Premier League hit problems as a string of disappointing results – including a defeat at Anfield – culminated in the end of Luiz Felipe Scolari's tenure at Stamford Bridge after just seven months in charge.

The Brazilian departed on the same day that Tony Adams' reign at Portsmouth, which had lasted just 15 weeks, was also cut short. Russia coach Guus Hiddink took charge of the Blues until the end of the season, while Paul Hart was installed as the new man in charge at Fratton Park.

Blackburn striker Roque Santa Cruz ended Manchester United's run of 1,334 minutes without conceding a goal – a new Barclays Premier League record – but still ended up on the losing side at Old Trafford as goals from Wayne Rooney and Cristiano Ronaldo ensured the Red Devils continued to lead the way in the Barclays Premier League, while West Brom's top-flight survival hopes faded after three successive defeats.

The Baggies were also knocked out of the FA Cup by Burnley to compound matters further for boss Tony Mowbray, with Steven Thompson's second-half brace proving the difference during the 3–1 defeat at Turf Moor.

Elsewhere in the oldest knockout competition in the world, Coventry became the only team outside the top flight to book their place in the quarter-finals with a 1–0 win over a Blackburn side

CLOCKWISE FROM ABOVE: Luton win the Johnstone's Paint Trophy southern final; Robin van Persie fires Arsenal ahead against Roma; Guus Hiddink leads Chelsea to a 1–0 Champions League win over Juventus; Gabriel Agbonlahor scores in Aston Villa's sixth consecutive away win

WHAT THEY SAID

I did everything I had to do and did everything possible to play, but sometimes the manager just doesn't fancy you, simple as that.
– Robbie Keane reveals why his Liverpool career lasted barely six months

After kamikaze pilot, I would guess football manager has about the same sort of job security.
– Bolton boss Gary Megson on the manager's lifespan, following Chelsea's sacking of Luiz Felipe Scolari

His lifestyle, the way he looks after himself, his desire to always want to win is a credit to him and also an inspiration to any young kid who wants to become a footballer.
– Sir Alex Ferguson pays tribute to Ryan Giggs after he signs a new deal at Manchester United

I thought Swansea was in England, because they play there. But obviously I found out it's in Wales, which was quite shocking.
– Jason Scotland reveals the thorough research which preceded his move to the Swans two years ago

seemingly more concerned with their relegation battle. Leon Best grabbed the only goal of the game in their fifth-round replay at the Ricoh Arena.

Upsets were also few and far between in the Scottish Cup, with Falkirk's 1–0 win at Clydesdale Bank Premier League rivals Hearts proving the most unlikely result of the fifth round.

In the UEFA Cup, Manchester City were the only English representatives to make the final 16 thanks to Craig Bellamy's brace in the 4–3 aggregate victory over FC Copenhagen, while Tottenham and Aston Villa paid the price for fielding weakened teams against Shakhtar Donetsk and CSKA Moscow respectively.

Meanwhile, there was cup success for Luton and Grimsby, who won the southern and northern finals of the Johnstone's Paint Trophy to secure a Wembley place.

The SPL title race intensified as Gordon Strachan's Celtic were held to successive draws by Inverness, Rangers and Motherwell before Shunsuke Nakamura's hat-trick helped set up a 7–0 thrashing of St Mirren. As for the Gers, they finished the month at the top of the table on goal difference following their 3–1 success over Kilmarnock, despite going behind, and a 1–0 win at Hamilton, which was sealed courtesy of captain Barry Ferguson's first goal of the campaign.

Dundee emerged as potential promotion contenders with seven points from their three games in the Irn-Bru First Division, while Alloa boosted their survival prospects in the Irn-Bru Second Division with their first two away wins of the season.

Barclays Manager of the Month
Rafael Benitez (Liverpool)
Barclays Player of the Month
Steven Gerrard (Liverpool)
Top: Manchester Utd (65) **Bottom:** West Brom (24)
Top Scorer: Gerrard (Liverpool) 4

Coca-Cola Manager of the Month
Kevin Blackwell (Sheff Utd)
Powerade Player of the Month
Robbie Blake (Burnley)
Top: Wolves (77) **Bottom:** Charlton (29)
Top Scorers: Cotterill (Sheff Utd), Ebanks-Blake (Wolves),
Gallagher (Plymouth), Kuqi (Palace), Long (Reading),
Parkin (Preston), Porter (Derby) 3

Coca-Cola Manager of the Month
Darren Ferguson (Peterborough)
Powerade Player of the Month
Simon Cox (Swindon)
Top: Leicester (82) **Bottom:** Cheltenham (31)
Top Scorer: Cox (Swindon)..................................8

Coca-Cola Manager of the Month
Lee Richardson (Chesterfield)
Powerade Player of the Month
Reuben Reid (Rotherham)
Top: Brentford (71) **Bottom:** Luton (22)
Top Scorer: Reid (Rotherham) 8

Clydesdale Bank PREMIER LEAGUE

Clydesdale Bank Manager of the Month
Mixu Paatelainen (Hibernian)
Clydesdale Bank Player of the Month
Scott McDonald (Celtic)
Clydesdale Bank Young Player of the Month
Steven Fletcher (Hibernian)
Top: Celtic (64) **Bottom:** Falkirk (27)
Top Scorers: McDonald (Celtic), Sandaza (Dundee U) ..3

Irn-Bru Phenomenal Manager of the Month
First Division
Paul Hegarty (Livingston)
Top: St Johnstone (51) **Bottom:** Clyde (31)
Second Division
Brian Reid (Ayr)
Top: Ayr (61) **Bottom:** Stranraer (31)
Third Division
Dick Campbell (Forfar)
Top: Cowdenbeath (56) **Bottom:** Elgin (19)
Irn-Bru Phenomenal Player of the Month
Kevin Rutkiewicz (St Johnstone)
Irn-Bru Phenomenal Young Player of the Month
Leigh Griffiths (Livingston)

MARCH was a tale of two halves for Manchester United as it began with yet another piece of silverware heading back to Old Trafford, but ended in frustration as the Barclays Premier League title race was blown wide open by Liverpool.

Ben Foster was the hero for United in the Carling Cup final. Sir Alex Ferguson's side were triumphant for the second time in seven months at Wembley following their Community Shield victory back in August as they held their nerve again in another penalty shoot-out. Foster saved Jamie O'Hara's spot-kick and David Bentley blazed his effort wide as holders Tottenham lost the shoot-out 4–1.

Despite his penalty exploits, Foster returned to his usual role as understudy to first-choice goalkeeper Edwin van der Sar three days later at Newcastle as the Dutchman saw his record-breaking run without conceding a goal in the Barclays Premier League come to an end. It was Magpies striker Peter Lovenkrands who eventually found a way past Van der Sar, but the Red Devils showed resolve to come from behind and claim a valuable 2–1 win at St James' Park thanks to goals from England ace Wayne Rooney and Bulgarian Dimitar Berbatov.

Another historic feat was achieved later in the month when David Beckham came on as a second-half substitute in England's 4–0 friendly thrashing of Slovakia to earn his 109th cap and surpass the late Bobby Moore's record for an outfield player.

At Hampden Park, Celtic claimed the bragging rights by edging out Rangers 2–0 to win the Co-operative Insurance Cup final. The Bhoys' Darren O'Dea and Aiden

Charlie MacDonald's goals helped Brentford's promotion push from League Two

McGeady scored decisive goals in extra-time after a tense 90 minutes had produced no goals.

The game finally exploded into life two minutes into the first period of extra-time, O'Dea breaking the deadlock against the holders when he rose well to head home a Shunsuke Nakamura free-kick. Gers defender Kirk Broadfoot was then sent off in the third minute of added time after he had denied McGeady a clear goalscoring opportunity, and the Republic of Ireland international made no mistake from the resulting penalty.

Fresh from thrashing Real Madrid 5–0 on aggregate in the last 16 of the UEFA Champions League, Liverpool sent shockwaves through the Barclays Premier League and pushed themselves firmly back into the reckoning for the title with a 4–1 away victory at leaders Manchester United. Rafael Benitez, who later in the month signed a new long-term deal with the club, saw his side battle back from a goal down after Cristiano Ronaldo had opened the scoring from the penalty spot.

Fernando Torres and Steven Gerrard turned the match on its head before the break, with Fabio Aurelio and Andrea Dossena easing Liverpool well clear late on, while United finished the game with 10 men following Nemanja Vidic's dismissal.

Things went from bad to worse for Sir Alex Ferguson's men a week later as they went down 2–0 at Fulham, and Liverpool cut their lead at the top of the table to just one point as a Gerrard hat-trick helped inspire a 5–0 demolition of Aston Villa.

At the other end of the table, it was a bad month for the three north-east sides as they all faced up to the possibility of being involved in one of the tightest relegation run-ins in years.

Newcastle's problems continued as a return of one point from a possible 12 saw them drop into the bottom three, while local rivals Sunderland and Middlesbrough fared no better.

There was a major shock in the Homecoming Scottish Cup as Irn-Bru First Division side Dunfermline booked their place in the semi-finals with a penalty shoot-out win over Aberdeen, which saw Paul Gallacher save

CLOCKWISE FROM ABOVE: Aiden McGeady scores for Celtic in the Co-operative Insurance Cup final; Sir Alex Ferguson holds aloft the Carling Cup trophy; Fernando Torres scores in Liverpool's 4–1 defeat of Manchester United; Sheffield United boss Kevin Blackwell saw his side unbeaten throughout March

WHAT THEY SAID

We probably know the inside leg measurements of Rafa's [Liverpool boss Rafael Benitez] trousers.
– Chelsea secretary David Barnard commenting on a fifth Liverpool match-up in as many seasons following the UEFA Champions League quarter-final draw

If you had said before the game we would get three points, I would have said you'd had too much gin.
– Inverness manager Terry Butcher after his team's shock win against Rangers

We've got three away games where we cover 1,200 miles in just a few days. If we win all of them, I'll show my backside on Sheffield Town Hall steps.
– Crystal Palace boss Neil Warnock played down his side's chances of maximum points from trips to Burnley, Swansea and Barnsley

The players are being treated like amateurs.
– Darlington boss Dave Penney shares his frustration after the club's administrators refused to sanction an overnight stay ahead of their match at Barnet

from Scott Severin and Richard Foster. David Gormley's second-half strike helped Ayr United emerge 1–0 victors over Irn-Bru Second Division promotion rivals Raith at Stark's Park and Brian Reid's men followed that up with wins over East Fife and Stranraer.

In the Coca-Cola Championship, Kevin Blackwell's Sheffield United reduced the gap on leaders Wolves and Birmingham with an impressive string of results. The Blades went through March unbeaten and recorded four wins from six, including a 2–1

success over Birmingham and a 3–0 triumph at fellow high-flyers Cardiff.

Leicester and Peterborough continued to lead the way in Coca-Cola League One, while at the bottom Cheltenham manager Martin Allen informed his entire squad that they were up for sale in a bid to prevent the club from going into administration. Allen's side responded by embarking upon a five-game unbeaten run, which kept their hopes of avoiding the drop alive.

In Coca-Cola League Two, Brentford remained top of the table during the

month, picking up a vital win at Grimsby but losing at home to Chesterfield.

The line-up for the FA Cup semi-finals had a familiar feel about it as Manchester United brushed aside Fulham 4–0, Chelsea beat Coventry 2–0 and Everton and Arsenal beat Middlesbrough and Hull respectively. United, Arsenal and Chelsea also progressed along with Liverpool into the last eight of the Champions League, while Manchester City needed penalties to beat Danish side Aalborg and reach the quarter-finals of the UEFA Cup.

Barclays Manager of the Month
Sir Alex Ferguson (Manchester Utd)
Barclays Player of the Month
Andrey Arshavin (Arsenal)
Top: Manchester Utd (77) **Bottom:** West Brom (28)
Top Scorer: Arshavin (Arsenal) 5

Coca-Cola Manager of the Month
Alan Irvine (Preston)
Powerade Player of the Month
Kyle Naughton (Sheff Utd)
Top: Wolves (87) **Bottom:** Charlton (36)
Top Scorer: McCormack (Cardiff) 5

Coca-Cola Manager of the Month
Roberto Di Matteo (MK Dons)
Powerade Player of the Month
Lloyd Owusu (Brighton)
Top: Leicester (93) **Bottom:** Hereford (34)
Top Scorer: Owusu (Brighton).....................................6

Coca-Cola Manager of the Month
Andy Scott (Brentford)
Powerade Player of the Month
Sam Saunders (Dag & Red)
Top: Brentford (82) **Bottom:** Luton (26)
Top Scorer: Clarke (Brentford)...................................6

Clydesdale Bank Manager of the Month
Walter Smith (Rangers)
Clydesdale Bank Player of the Month
Andy Dorman (St Mirren)
Clydesdale Bank Young Player of the Month
Calum Elliot (Hearts)
Top: Celtic (74) **Bottom:** Falkirk (28)
Top Scorers: Dorman (St Mirren), Vennegoor of
Hesselink (Celtic), Boyd (Rangers) 4

Irn-Bru Phenomenal Manager of the Month
First Division
Gordon Chisholm (Queen of the South)
Top: St Johnstone (59) **Bottom:** Clyde (35)
Second Division
John McGlynn (Raith)
Top: Raith (72) **Bottom:** Stranraer (16)
Third Division
Jim Chapman (Dumbarton)
Top: Dumbarton (61) **Bottom:** Elgin (23)
Irn-Bru Phenomenal Player of the Month
Stephen Dobbie (Queen of the South)
Irn-Bru Phenomenal Young Player of the Month
Kevin Moon (St Johnstone)

A MONTH of high drama on and off the pitch began with Allan McGregor and Barry Ferguson being exiled from the Scotland national team after breaking curfew. Due to a late-night drinking session in the aftermath of defeat to Holland and apparent obscene gestures made to television cameras while on the bench during Scotland's World Cup 2010 qualifier against Iceland a few days later, the Rangers pair were told that they would never again be selected.

Although George Burley's side beat Iceland 2–1, it was the actions of McGregor and Ferguson, who were also given two-week unpaid bans by their club, which hit the headlines.

Other international action saw England maintain their 100 per cent record in Group Six with a 2–1 win over Ukraine, while Northern Ireland remained top of Group Three thanks to a 1–0 success over Slovenia, and Wales lost 2–0 to Germany. An 88th-minute goal from Tottenham's Robbie Keane saw the Republic of Ireland draw 1–1 in Italy to stay just two points behind the World Cup holders in second place in Group Eight.

Newcastle turned to the club's all-time record goalscorer, Alan Shearer, to revive their fortunes due to Joe Kinnear's ill-health as the former England international took charge of the final eight games of the Barclays Premier League season, despite initial speculation that the story was in fact an elaborate April Fool's Day hoax.

Shearer's tenure at St James' Park began in disappointing fashion with a 2–0 defeat at the hands of a Chelsea side who later in the month drew 4–4 with Liverpool in what was dubbed the 'match of the millennium' by one Italian newspaper.

The UEFA

Alan Shearer was installed as Newcastle's interim boss

Champions League quarter-final second leg at Stamford Bridge was expected to be something of a formality after the Blues emerged 3–1 victors at Anfield in the first encounter. But first-half goals from Fabio Aurelio and Xabi Alonso catapulted the visitors back into the tie before Guus Hiddink's side produced a sensational comeback of their own – scoring three times in the second half to lead 6–3 on aggregate at one stage. Yet the incredible contest took another twist when Liverpool scored twice in as many minutes to leave them just one goal away from a sensational victory. However, Frank Lampard's second goal of the match in the 89th minute secured a 4–4 draw on the night and a date with Barcelona in the last four.

Elsewhere, Manchester United and Arsenal beat Porto and Villarreal respectively to move into the semi-finals of the Champions League, although England's last remaining representative in the UEFA Cup, Manchester City, exited at the quarter-final stage 4–3 on aggregate to SV Hamburg.

In the Clydesdale Bank Premier League, Rangers enjoyed a perfect month by claiming four victories out of four games while Celtic dropped two points against Hearts to let their fierce rivals back into the title race. Gordon Strachan's side failed to build on Jan Vennegoor of Hesselink's early strike at Tynecastle as Bruno Aguiar's spectacular free-kick earned Hearts a 1–1 draw.

There was more delight for Rangers in the Homecoming Scottish Cup, as they eased past St Mirren 3–0 to set up a final showdown against Falkirk, who beat Dunfermline 2–0.

St Johnstone continued their march towards the Irn-Bru First Division title despite being held 1–1 by closest rivals Partick at the beginning of the month. The Saints went ahead after 65 minutes through Steven Milne, but Partick equalised with just three minutes remaining when Gary Harkins fired home from a tight angle.

Clyde's relegation fears worsened after a 7–1 hammering at Queen of

CLOCKWISE FROM ABOVE: Leicester players celebrate securing promotion back to the Championship; Andrey Arshavin silences Anfield with four goals for Arsenal; Leighton Baines scores in Everton's penalty shoot-out win against Manchester United in the FA Cup semi-finals; Charlton's Matt Holland looks dejected after his side's relegation to League One

WHAT THEY SAID

What do we want now? Do we want to be playing in front of 10,000 or 12,000 people next season in grounds not as good as ours, or do we want to be playing here and going to Old Trafford and Anfield?
– Alan Shearer lays out the reality to his Newcastle squad after returning to the club in a managerial capacity

There is a lot of ice in that dressing room – it's like the dining room on the Titanic in there.
– Celtic boss Gordon Strachan on his side's bruising draw at Hearts

If you said to me when we returned for pre-season training that with three games to go we'd be in with a chance of automatic promotion, I'd have broken your legs and your arms.
– Sheffield United boss Kevin Blackwell appears surprised by his team's form

If I wasn't up for challenges I'd be walking my dogs today – I think my dogs need a break.
– Roy Keane returns to football management with Championship side Ipswich

the South. Stephen Dobbie helped himself to a magnificent four goals for the hosts to leave John Brown's side rooted to the bottom.

Promotion and relegation issues were decided in England as Wolves sealed their place in the Barclays Premier League thanks to a 1–0 victory over QPR and Mick McCarthy's side went on to be crowned champions a week later at Barnsley.

Two teams also leaving the Coca-Cola Championship, but at the opposite end of the table, were Charlton and Southampton.

The Addicks were first to fall after a 2–2 home draw with Blackpool, while the Saints' fate was sealed in the same month that the club's parent company went into administration.

Peterborough and Leicester clinched promotion from Coca-Cola League One, while Luton's 89-year stay in the Football League came to an end just a week after Mick Harford's men had beaten Scunthorpe 3–2 in the Johnstone's Paint Trophy final.

In the FA Cup, meanwhile, Everton edged past Manchester United in a penalty shoot-out to book a final place against Chelsea, who came from behind to see off London rivals Arsenal 2–1 at Wembley.

While Sir Alex Ferguson's hopes of an incredible 'quintuple' were dashed by their FA Cup exit, his side moved closer to a third successive Barclays Premier League title thanks to four wins in April. They were also aided by Liverpool dropping two points at home to Arsenal, the Reds drawing 4–4 just days after their classic European tie against Chelsea, with Andrey Arshavin scoring all four goals for the Gunners.

Winners Manchester United
Champions League qualifiers
Manchester United, Liverpool, Chelsea, Arsenal
Europa League qualifiers Everton, Aston Villa, Fulham
Relegated Newcastle, Middlesbrough, West Brom

Winners Wolves
Promoted Birmingham, Burnley
Play-offs Sheffield United, Reading, Burnley, Preston
Relegated Norwich, Southampton, Charlton

Winners Leicester
Promoted Peterborough, Scunthorpe
Play-offs MK Dons, Leeds, Millwall, Scunthorpe
Relegated Northampton, Crewe, Cheltenham, Hereford

Winners Brentford
Promoted Exeter, Wycombe, Gillingham
Play-offs Bury, Gillingham, Rochdale, Shrewsbury
Relegated Chester, Luton

Winners Rangers
Champions League qualifiers Celtic
Europa League qualifiers Hearts, Aberdeen, Falkirk, Motherwell
Relegated Inverness

FIRST DIVISION
Winners St Johnstone
Relegated Clyde, Airdrie (play-off)
SECOND DIVISION
Winners Raith
Promoted Ayr (play-off)
Play-offs Brechin, Peterhead
Relegated Stranraer, Queen's Park (play-off)
THIRD DIVISION
Winners Dumbarton
Promoted Stenhousemuir (play-off)
Play-offs Cowdenbeath, East Stirling

MANCHESTER UNITED'S hopes of securing a historic quadruple of major trophies were extinguished in Rome as Barcelona produced a footballing master-class to confirm their status as European champions.

The two continental heavyweights clashed on 27th May in one of the most eagerly-anticipated UEFA Champions League finals in the competition's history.

United had booked their place in the final with a 4–1 aggregate win over Arsenal, while Barca disposed of another English side in the last four, overcoming Chelsea on away goals courtesy of Andres Iniesta's injury-time strike in the second leg during a night of drama at Stamford Bridge that saw referee Tom Ovrebo controversially rejecting several penalty appeals by Chelsea.

All the signs pointed to a classic final, but Barcelona outclassed their opponents and goals from Samuel Eto'o and Lionel Messi gave them a deserved 2–0 win to complete a memorable season following their La Liga and Copa del Rey triumphs.

Despite that defeat, Sir Alex Ferguson can look back fondly on May after United clinched their third consecutive Barclays Premier League title with a goalless draw against Arsenal on the penultimate weekend of the season. That meant Liverpool could only finish second, although a new contract for star striker Fernando Torres at the end of the month will give the Reds' faithful much optimism heading into 2009/10.

It was also crunch time in the Clydesdale Bank Premier League title race as Rangers headed into the final weekend of the season knowing victory at Dundee United would end Celtic's three-year domination. Walter Smith's men duly obliged with

Rangers assistant boss Ally McCoist holds aloft the SPL trophy

goals from Kyle Lafferty, Pedro Mendes and Kris Boyd handing them a comprehensive 3–0 win.

For United, the defeat meant they were pipped to the final European berth by Aberdeen who, despite qualifying for the Europa League after a 2–1 win over Hibernian, were left managerless as Jimmy Calderwood departed.

Falkirk and Motherwell also qualified for the Europa League.

At the bottom of the SPL, Inverness were relegated to the Irn-Bru First Division after a 1–0 home defeat to Falkirk on the final day. The Bairns' joy was short-lived, though, as a Nacho Novo goal ended their hopes of lifting the Homecoming Scottish Cup with Rangers edging a close final 1–0.

St Johnstone secured the First Division title and ended their seven-year absence from Scotland's top flight after a 3–1 victory over Morton. Meanwhile, Clyde and Airdrie United were relegated from the second tier with Raith Rovers and Ayr United going the opposite way.

Queens Park were relegated from the Irn-Bru Second Division after a play-off defeat to Stenhousemuir, who went on to secure promotion thanks to a play-off final victory over Cowdenbeath.

In England, Louis Saha scored the fastest FA Cup final goal – clocked at 25 seconds – to give Everton the perfect start at a sun-soaked Wembley. The Toffees failed to hang on, though, as Didier Drogba equalised before Frank Lampard scored the winner with 18 minutes left to give Chelsea the trophy in Guus Hiddink's last game in charge.

Back in the Barclays Premier League, the race for survival went down to the final day, with Newcastle, Middlesbrough, Hull and Sunderland battling to avoid relegation. It proved an unhappy end for north-east sides Newcastle and Middlesbrough as defeats at Aston Villa and West Ham

CLOCKWISE FROM ABOVE: The spotlight falls on Alan Shearer after Newcastle are relegated; Cristiano Ronaldo looks solemn after losing the Champions League final; Chelsea lift the FA Cup; Burnley's Wade Elliot picks up the play-off final trophy

WHAT THEY SAID

The great challenge now is to try to win it next year because that would be something special. It would give us a special place in the club's history.
– Sir Alex Ferguson turns his attention to Manchester United beating Liverpool's 18 English titles

It will be a Charlton Heston job, like the film 'El Cid', when they patched him up to go into battle.
– Kilmarnock boss Jim Jefferies on his bid to get striker Kevin Kyle fit for the Clydesdale Bank Premier League relegation battle against Inverness

We won't change. We are what we are. A proper football club. There are not many billionaires floating around on a night out in Burnley.
– Chairman Barry Kilby insists Burnley will keep it real in the Barclays Premier League

To score in a Champions League final against Manchester United and win the league title is just unbelievable.
– Barcelona star Lionel Messi

respectively consigned them to Coca-Cola Championship football next season. Despite a 1–0 home defeat to a weakened Manchester United side, Hull lived to fight another day and, although Sunderland survived, manager Ricky Sbragia decided to relinquish his post.

Birmingham became one of the three teams to replace Newcastle, Boro and West Brom – relegated after a 2–0 defeat to Liverpool – after Alex McLeish's side secured second spot in the Championship with a last-day victory at Reading. The

defeat consigned the Royals to the play-offs and they were left disappointed after a 3–0 aggregate defeat to Burnley in the semi-finals spelt the end for manager Steve Coppell. The Clarets went on to beat Sheffield United 1–0 in the final at Wembley.

Norwich were relegated from the Championship after a 4–2 defeat at Charlton in their final match, while Scunthorpe beat Millwall 3–2 in the Coca-Cola League One play-off final.

At the bottom, Northampton were relegated from League One after a last-day

defeat at Leeds. The Coca-Cola League Two season ended in dramatic style as Wycombe and Exeter secured automatic promotion, while Gillingham beat Shrewsbury 1–0 in the play-off final.

There were off-field dramas during a hectic last month of the season, including billionaire businessman Dr Sulaiman Al Fahim's proposed takeover at Portsmouth.

Gordon Strachan resigned from his post as Celtic manager and his Hibs counterpart Mixu Paatelainen also stepped down, while Carlo Ancelotti took over at Chelsea.

IT'S BEEN a great 2008/09 Premier 10 season as the official pools game of the Barclays Premier League has proven to be a massive success with an estimated jackpot of £20,000 on offer every week.

It's simple to play, all you have to do is predict a home win, away win or draw for the 10 fixtures to have a chance of winning big money. It only costs £1 to play so is well worth a punt, especially as Premier 10 also pays out for nine correct predictions. This year's winners showed that it pays to play with your head rather than your heart as one lucky Spurs fan backed Hull to win at White Hart Lane among his selections and scooped £100,000 as a result!

Newcastle proved themselves to be the draw specialists of the division followed closely by Arsène Wenger's young guns and ever-improving Everton. Manchester was the place to be for home victories as both United and City led the way, whereas Liverpool and Chelsea both proved they were the teams to back on the road. To help with players' choices, throughout the 2008/09 season, expert pundits Alan Hansen, John Barnes and Tony Cascarino provided advice, views and predictions on footballpools.com.

The 2008/09 season also saw us introduce our exciting Premier 10 Mini Leagues which have proven to be a big hit with our players. Not only can you win bragging rights over your mates but you can also win cash by out-predicting them. Whoever wins the Mini League each week nets both the kudos and the mini-pot.

There will be plenty of new developments for the 2009/10 season on footballpools.com so make sure you and your friends come to join the banter and you too could be a big winner!

Dawn Primarolo (Minister of State for Public Health), Richard Scudamore (chief executive of the Premier League), Ian Penrose (chief executive of Sportech), George Cohen (World Cup winner) launch the Premier League Health programme, above. Sunderland's Stadium of Light was built with the help of the Football Trust, which was backed by The New Football Pools, below

A LONG HISTORY OF GIVING MONEY TO GOOD CAUSES

Supporting the community is at the very heart of The New Football Pools having contributed over £1.1billion to arts, sporting and good causes since 1923.

From 1975 to 2000, Littlewoods, Vernons and Zetters provided virtually the only source of external funding for British football, through the Football Grounds Improvement Trust. Then, via the Football Trust, which was established in 1979, it channelled funds to assist clubs in implementing the recommendations contained in Lord Justice Taylor's report on the Hillsborough disaster.

Altogether almost £530million was given to British football by the pools companies, providing an essential lifeline when the game's wealth was a fraction of what it enjoys today. It enabled clubs to rebuild, modernise and make their

mini LEAGUES

It's better together

The New Football Pools

www.footballpools.com

THE NEW FOOTBALL POOLS PLAYER OF THE SEASON

This season, The New Football Pools panel of football experts and pundits has analysed team and individual player performances across all 92 English League clubs to produce its definitive 2008/09 'Player of the Season' in The Official Football Yearbook. From Arsenal to Yeovil, the panel looked at criteria such as clean sheets, goals scored, assists, number of games played and man of the match performances, to cherry pick those players who made the biggest impact during the exhilarating 2008/09 campaign. We'd like to congratulate every winner of this terrific accolade, including those pictured below. Read on to see whether your favourite player matches the verdict of our panel....

Steven Gerrard (Liverpool)

Marcus Tudgay (Sheffield Wednesday)

Fabian Delph (Leeds)

Sam Wood (Brentford)

grounds safer and helped the game to tackle its social problems, helping transform its appeal to television companies, sponsors and partners.

The legacy of the Trust can be seen in the scores of new and rebuilt stadiums in all parts of the UK – from Huddersfield, Sunderland, Reading and Bolton to Chester, Derby, Stoke and Northampton – none of which would have been built in the 1980s and 1990s without Football Trust assistance.

PREMIER LEAGUE HEALTH

Continuing our support of good causes, this season The New Football Pools joined forces with the Premier League in a new partnership to tackle men's health problems. Premier League Health is a unique £1.63million scheme funded by The New Football Pools to improve men's health in deprived area across the country by working with 16 Barclays Premier League Clubs throughout the UK.

MAKE EVERY PLAYER COUNT

A further £2.6million of funding by The New Football Pools will help launch the Football League's Make Every Player Count campaign, which helps up to 40 Football League clubs across the country to engage in disability football.

BARCLAYS PREMIER LEAGUE STATISTICS 2008/09

Player of the season
Nemanja Vidic (Manchester Utd)

Manager of the season
Sir Alex Ferguson (Manchester Utd)

The player with the most...

Shots on target	
Cristiano Ronaldo (Manchester Utd)	115
Shots off target	
Steven Gerrard (Liverpool)	61
Shots without scoring	
Stewart Downing (Middlesbrough)	70
Shots per goal	
David Bentley (Tottenham)	62
Assists	
Dimitar Berbatov (Man Utd/Tottenham)	
Steven Gerrard (Liverpool)	
Frank Lampard (Chelsea)	
Robin van Persie (Arsenal)	
Cesc Fabregas (Arsenal)	10
Offsides	
Marlon King (Middlesbrough)	66
Fouls	
Kevin Davies (Bolton)	115
Fouls without a card	
Emile Heskey (Aston Villa/Wigan)	26
Free-kicks won	
Kevin Davies (Bolton)	92
Penalties scored	
Danny Murphy (Fulham)	5
Goals scored direct from free-kicks	
Mikel Arteta (Everton)	
Cristiano Ronaldo (Manchester Utd)	
Chris Brunt (West Brom)	
Matthew Taylor (Bolton)	3
Saves made	
Mark Schwarzer (Fulham)......................	233
Defensive clearances	
Michael Turner (Hull)	102
Defensive blocks	
Gary Cahill (Bolton)	37

The team with the most...

Shots on target	Manchester Utd	376
Shots off target	Liverpool	302
Shots per Goal	Middlesbrough	15.3
Corners	Liverpool	271
Fouls	Hull	536
Woodwork strikes	Liverpool	19
Offsides	Hull	137
Penalties conceded	Newcastle	9
Yellow cards	Blackburn	77
Red cards	Newcastle	8

TOTALS 2008/09

Goals	
Total	942
Home	532
Away	410
Cards	
Yellow	1198
Average per game	3.15
Reds	63
Average per game	0.17
Attendances	
Total	13,527,815

SIR ALEX FERGUSON won his 11th Premier League title, Ryan Giggs became the PFA Footballer of the Year and Manchester United drew level with Liverpool's record of 18 league championships.

Domestic football seasons do not get much better than that. Which is why, every morning when he rises at six o'clock and heads for United's Carrington training ground, Ferguson should thank his wife Cathy for talking him out of retiring seven years ago. Actually, football fans everywhere should be grateful because United claimed another league title by staying true to the club's finest traditions of attacking, exciting football.

Cristiano Ronaldo produced moments of genius, Michael Carrick and Darren Fletcher provided unsung solidity, goalkeeper Edwin van der Sar racked up a European record of 14 consecutive clean sheets, Nemanja Vidic and Rio Ferdinand enhanced their reputation as Britain's meanest central defenders and Wayne Rooney was simply superb. They were so consistently brilliant that, even though Liverpool recorded a 4–1 league victory at Old Trafford on the day Vidic put in a shocking performance, United's title challenge was never seriously in doubt.

True, Liverpool came closer than they have for 19 years to winning the title they once dominated – and Fernando Torres and Steven Gerrard in tandem were at times unplayable – but, whenever they threatened, United always fashioned the required response.

Elsewhere, Arsene Wenger's Arsenal were disappointing. They played pretty football but lacked a dominating force in central defence and a midfield enforcer to support captain and playmaker Cesc Fabregas. They produced the odd head-turning result, such as beating Manchester United at home and Chelsea at Stamford Bridge, but they struggled for consistency, being defeated at home 2–1 by Hull and away at Stoke.

Such erratic form consigned them to fourth place, behind a Chelsea side who will always wonder what might have been if they had acquired the managerial services of Guus Hiddink at the start of the season, rather than after Luis Felipe Scolari had wrought uncertainty and tactical confusion at Stamford Bridge.

Yet while the 'big four' as usual vied for the top spots, it was a season which for

> ❝ **United claimed another league title by staying true to the club's traditions of exciting football** ❞

long periods was the tightest, most unpredictable for years.

Aston Villa, with the pacy Ashley Young and Gabriel Agbonlahor, threatened to break into the top four before fading late in the season. Everton defied a spate of injuries which claimed all the club's strikers to prove what organisation can achieve under manager David Moyes.

Roy Hodgson was many people's idea of the manager of the year for his rejuvenation of Fulham, gaining a Europa League spot, while Harry Redknapp worked his magic after taking over a Tottenham side that were rock bottom. Gianfranco Zola also proved a splendid choice in his debut season with a West Ham side which made light of the club's financial worries.

It was a campaign which saw Roy Keane walk out on Sunderland, with six Barclays Premier League clubs changing managers mid-term and one, Newcastle, sporting four managers in the course of 10 months. In the end even Alan Shearer, a Geordie legend and the last of that quartet, could not deliver salvation and Newcastle slid into the Coca-Cola Championship in the tamest of fashions.

Middlesbrough joined them, manager Gareth Southgate unable to coax his side to score enough goals. West Brom were the other side relegated, ending another brief stay in the top flight.

Hull breathed a sigh of relief big enough to alert the shipping forecast after a dramatic season which saw them shock the top division with a fantastic start, beating Arsenal and Tottenham, before imploding in the final months. In the end they were saved by a single point which saw manager Phil Brown 'celebrating' a final defeat by Manchester United with a raucous rendition of 'This is the best trip I've ever been on' in the centre circle at the KC Stadium. Somehow it summed up perfectly the rollercoaster nature of Barclays Premier League football.

Manchester United's jubilant players hold the Barclays Premier League trophy having beaten Liverpool to the title in a thrilling season. United finally claimed the trophy thanks to a 0–0 draw against Arsenal in front of their own fans at Old Trafford

FINAL BARCLAYS PREMIER LEAGUE TABLE

Pos		P	HOME					AWAY					GD	Pts	PU
			W	D	L	F	A	W	D	L	F	A			
1	Manchester Utd	38	16	2	1	43	13	12	4	3	25	11	44	**90**	33
2	Liverpool	38	12	7	0	41	13	13	4	2	36	14	50	**86**	23
3	Chelsea	38	11	6	2	33	12	14	2	3	35	12	44	**83**	29
4	Arsenal	38	11	5	3	31	16	9	7	3	37	21	31	**72**	28
5	Everton	38	8	6	5	31	20	9	6	4	24	17	18	**63**	25
6	Aston Villa	38	7	9	3	27	21	10	2	7	27	27	6	**62**	21
7	Fulham	38	11	3	5	28	16	3	8	8	11	18	5	**53**	26
8	Tottenham	38	10	5	4	21	10	4	4	11	24	35	0	**51**	29
9	West Ham	38	9	2	8	23	22	5	7	7	19	23	-3	**51**	30
10	Manchester City	38	13	0	6	40	18	2	5	12	18	32	8	**50**	34
11	Wigan	38	8	5	6	17	18	4	4	11	17	27	-11	**45**	29
12	Stoke	38	10	5	4	22	15	2	4	13	16	40	-17	**45**	29
13	Bolton	38	7	5	7	21	21	4	3	12	20	32	-12	**41**	24
14	Portsmouth	38	8	3	8	26	29	2	8	9	12	28	-19	**41**	29
15	Blackburn	38	6	7	6	22	23	4	4	11	18	37	-20	**41**	28
16	Sunderland	38	6	3	10	21	25	3	6	10	13	29	-20	**36**	30
17	Hull	38	3	5	11	18	36	5	6	8	21	28	-25	**35**	29
18	Newcastle	38	5	7	7	24	29	2	6	11	16	30	-19	**34**	29
19	Middlesbrough	38	5	9	5	17	20	2	2	15	11	37	-29	**32**	28
20	West Brom	38	7	3	9	26	33	1	5	13	10	34	-31	**32**	30

PU – Players Used

Hull's Nick Barmby celebrates after the Tigers avoided relegation on the last day of the season

THE OFFICIAL UK FOOTBALL POOL OF THE PREMIER LEAGUE

PREMIER LEAGUE
OFFICIAL LICENSEE

The New Football Pools
www.footballpools.com

SEASON REVIEW

BARCLAYS PREMIER LEAGUE RESULTS GRID

Away teams read across the grid ▶

Home teams read from top to bottom ▼

	ARSENAL	ASTON VILLA	BLACKBURN	BOLTON	CHELSEA	EVERTON	FULHAM	HULL	LIVERPOOL	MAN CITY	MAN UTD	MIDDLESBRO	NEWCASTLE	PORTSMOUTH	STOKE	SUNDERLAND	TOTTENHAM	WEST BROM	WEST HAM	WIGAN
ARSENAL	–	0-2	4-0	1-0	1-4	3-1	0-0	1-2	1-1	2-0	2-1	2-0	3-0	1-0	4-1	0-0	4-4	1-0	0-0	1-0
ASTON VILLA	2-2	–	3-2	4-2	0-1	3-3	0-0	1-0	0-0	4-2	0-0	1-2	1-0	0-0	2-2	2-1	1-2	2-1	1-1	0-0
BLACKBURN	0-4	0-2	–	2-2	0-2	0-0	1-0	1-1	1-3	2-2	0-2	1-1	3-0	2-0	3-0	1-2	2-1	0-0	1-1	2-0
BOLTON	1-3	1-1	0-0	–	0-2	0-1	1-3	1-1	0-2	2-0	0-1	4-1	1-0	2-1	3-1	0-0	3-2	0-0	2-1	0-1
CHELSEA	1-2	2-0	2-0	4-3	–	0-0	3-1	0-0	0-1	1-0	1-1	2-0	0-0	4-0	2-1	5-0	1-1	2-0	1-1	2-1
EVERTON	1-1	2-3	2-3	3-0	0-0	–	1-0	2-0	0-2	1-2	1-1	1-1	2-2	0-3	3-1	3-0	0-0	2-0	3-1	4-0
FULHAM	1-0	3-1	1-2	2-1	2-2	0-2	–	0-1	0-1	1-1	2-0	3-0	2-1	3-1	1-0	0-0	2-1	2-0	1-2	2-0
HULL	1-3	0-1	1-2	0-1	0-3	2-2	2-1	–	1-3	2-2	0-1	2-1	1-1	0-0	1-2	1-4	1-2	2-2	1-0	0-5
LIVERPOOL	4-4	5-0	4-0	3-0	2-0	1-1	0-0	2-2	–	1-1	2-1	2-1	3-0	1-0	0-0	2-0	3-1	3-0	0-0	3-2
MAN CITY	3-0	2-0	3-1	1-0	1-3	0-1	1-3	5-1	2-3	–	0-1	1-0	2-1	6-0	3-0	1-0	1-2	4-2	3-0	1-0
MAN UTD	0-0	3-2	2-1	2-0	3-0	1-0	3-0	4-3	1-4	2-0	–	1-0	1-1	2-0	5-0	1-0	5-2	4-0	2-0	1-0
MIDDLESBRO	1-1	1-1	0-0	1-3	0-5	0-1	0-1	3-1	2-0	2-0	0-2	–	0-0	1-1	2-1	1-1	2-1	0-1	1-1	0-0
NEWCASTLE	1-3	2-0	1-2	1-0	0-0	0-0	1-1	1-2	1-5	2-2	1-2	3-1	–	0-0	2-2	1-1	2-1	2-1	2-2	2-2
PORTSMOUTH	0-3	0-1	3-2	1-0	0-1	2-1	1-1	2-2	2-3	2-0	0-1	2-1	0-3	–	2-1	3-1	2-0	2-2	1-4	1-2
STOKE	2-1	3-2	1-0	2-0	0-2	2-3	0-0	1-1	0-0	1-0	0-1	1-0	1-1	2-2	–	1-0	2-1	1-0	0-1	2-0
SUNDERLAND	1-1	1-2	0-0	1-4	2-3	0-2	1-1	1-0	0-1	0-3	1-2	2-0	2-1	1-2	2-0	–	1-1	4-0	0-1	1-2
TOTTENHAM	0-0	1-2	1-0	2-0	1-0	0-1	0-0	0-1	2-1	2-1	0-0	4-0	1-0	1-1	3-1	1-2	–	1-0	1-0	0-0
WEST BROM	1-3	1-2	2-2	1-1	0-3	1-2	1-0	0-3	0-2	2-1	0-5	3-0	2-3	1-1	0-2	3-0	2-0	–	3-2	3-1
WEST HAM	0-2	0-1	4-1	1-3	0-1	1-3	3-1	2-0	0-3	1-0	0-1	2-1	3-1	0-0	2-1	2-0	0-2	0-0	–	2-1
WIGAN	1-4	0-4	3-0	0-0	0-1	1-0	0-0	1-0	1-1	2-1	1-2	0-1	2-1	1-0	0-0	1-1	1-0	2-1	0-1	–

NICOLAS ANELKA (CHELSEA)

BARCLAYS
RACE FOR THE GOLDEN BOOT

Player	(Team)	Goals
Nicolas Anelka	(Chelsea)	19
Cristiano Ronaldo	(Man Utd)	18
Steven Gerrard	(Liverpool)	16
Fernando Torres	(Liverpool)	14
Robinho	(Man City)	14
Dirk Kuyt	(Liverpool)	12
Wayne Rooney	(Man Utd)	12
Darren Bent	(Tottenham)	12
Gabriel Agbonlahor	(Aston Villa)	12
Frank Lampard	(Chelsea)	12

ON THE CLOCK
BARCLAYS PREMIER LEAGUE

FROM THE START OF A MATCH

Quickest goal
Steve Sidwell 0:31
(Aston Villa v Everton)

Quickest card
■ Stephen Warnock 0:53
(Blackburn v Hull)

Last-gasp goal
Andy Dawson 94:56
(Hull v Stoke)

BY A SUBSTITUTE

Quickest goal
Matt Derbyshire..............................0:40
(Blackburn v Portsmouth)

Quickest card
■ Elano 0:52
(Manchester City v Stoke)

Substitute being substituted
Amr Zaki 10:56
(Wigan v West Brom)

EDWIN VAN DER SAR (MAN UTD)

BARCLAYS
RACE FOR THE GOLDEN GLOVE

Player	(Team)	Clean Sheets
Edwin Van der Sar	(Man Utd)	21
Jose Reina	(Liverpool)	20
Petr Cech	(Chelsea)	19
Tim Howard	(Everton)	17
Mark Schwarzer	(Fulham)	15
Manuel Almunia	(Arsenal)	14
Brad Friedel	(Aston Villa)	13
Heurelho Gomes	(Tottenham)	12
Thomas Sorensen	(Stoke)	12
Chris Kirkland	(Wigan)	11
Robert Green	(West Ham)	10

DISCIPLINARY RECORDS

INCLUDES ALL DOMESTIC COMPETITIONS

	Fouls	Y	R
Arsenal			
Robin van Persie	50	6	1
Alexandre Song	44	7	0
Cesc Fabregas	33	7	0
Gael Clichy	23	7	0
Emmanuel Adebayor	30	4	1
Aston Villa			
Gareth Barry	56	9	0
Ashley Young	37	7	1
Stiliyan Petrov	42	7	0
James Milner	39	6	0
Luke Young	23	6	0
Blackburn			
Stephen Warnock	42	8	0
Andre Ooijer	40	8	0
Ryan Nelsen	28	8	0
Aaron Mokoena	22	7	0
Benedict McCarthy	24	5	1
Bolton			
Gavin McCann	63	9	1
Gretar Steinsson	38	8	0
Fabrice Muamba	43	5	0
Andrew O'Brien	28	5	0
Kevin Davies	115	4	0
Chelsea			
John Terry	22	7	2
Mikel	59	8	0
Michael Ballack	42	8	0
Ashley Cole	40	6	0
Jose Bosingwa	28	6	0
Everton			
Marouane Fellaini	116	13	0
Tim Cahill	85	7	1
Phil Neville	43	7	0
Steven Pienaar	29	7	0
Tony Hibbert	20	6	0
Fulham			
Danny Murphy	45	8	0
John Pantsil	42	7	0
Clint Dempsey	35	5	0

	Fouls	Y	R
Paul Konchesky	15	5	0
Brede Hangeland	35	4	0
Hull			
Ian Ashbee	50	10	0
Sam Ricketts	36	7	1
Andy Dawson	35	8	0
Dean Marney	43	6	1
Kamil Zayatte	48	7	0
Liverpool			
Alvaro Arbeloa	38	8	0
Xabi Alonso	31	7	0
Javier Mascherano	41	6	0
Leiva Lucas	42	4	1
Jamie Carragher	30	5	0
Manchester City			
Richard Dunne	42	5	2
Vincent Kompany	60	8	0
Stephen Ireland	45	6	0
Pablo Zabaleta	35	3	1
Gelson Fernandes	14	3	1
Manchester Utd			
Wayne Rooney	28	8	1
Nemanja Vidic	42	6	2
Cristiano Ronaldo	15	7	1
Paul Scholes	23	5	1
Patrice Evra	24	6	0
Middlesbrough			
Gary O'Neil	31	8	0
Emanuel Pogatetz	26	4	1
Didier Digard	24	4	1
Matthew Bates	17	4	1
Robert Huth	36	5	0
Newcastle			
Nicky Butt	55	9	1
Jonas Gutierrez	27	7	0
Sebastien Bassong	22	3	2
Steven Taylor	27	6	0
Fabricio Coloccini	30	5	0
Portsmouth			
Glen Johnson	33	11	1

	Fouls	Y	R
Sean Davis	46	6	1
Hermann Hreidarsson	28	7	0
Nadir Belhadj	30	5	1
Lassana Diarra	23	4	1
Stoke			
Ricardo Fuller	59	10	1
Andy Wilkinson	19	7	1
Liam Lawrence	18	8	0
Abdoulaye Faye	23	6	0
Richard Cresswell	22	6	0
Sunderland			
Kieran Richardson	41	11	0
Phillip Bardsley	38	11	0
Dean Whitehead	34	6	0
George McCartney	11	4	1
Steed Malbranque	37	5	0
Tottenham			
Benoit Assou-Ekotto	27	4	2
Jermaine Jenas	44	7	0
Jonathan Woodgate	29	6	0
Didier Zokora	50	5	0
Luka Modric	23	5	0
West Brom			
Paul Robinson	36	7	1
Roman Bednar	38	7	0
Jonathan Greening	36	7	0
Jonas Olsson	31	7	0
Gianni Zuiverloon	54	5	0
West Ham			
Mark Noble	31	9	1
Lucas Neill	42	8	0
Luis Boa Morte	38	8	0
Scott Parker	37	8	0
Carlton Cole	76	4	2
Wigan			
Lee Cattermole	59	11	2
Titus Bramble	30	8	0
Michael Brown	36	7	0
Antonio Valencia	40	4	1
Emmerson Boyce	18	3	1

Assists

Dimitar Berbatov (Man Utd/Spurs)	10
Cesc Fabregas (Arsenal)	10
Steven Gerrard (Liverpool)	10
Frank Lampard (Chelsea)	10
Robin van Persie (Arsenal)	10
Stephen Ireland (Manchester City)	9
Steed Malbranque (Sunderland)	9
James Milner (Aston Villa)	9
Luka Modric (Tottenham)	9
Ashley Young (Aston Villa)	9

Shots on target

Cristiano Ronaldo (Manchester Utd)	115
Frank Lampard (Chelsea)	96
Matthew Taylor (Bolton)	68
Wayne Rooney (Manchester Utd)	65
Robinho (Manchester City)	62
Nicolas Anelka (Chelsea)	60
Afonso Alves (Middlesbrough)	54
Steven Gerrard (Liverpool)	54
Djibril Cisse (Sunderland)	53
Robin van Persie (Arsenal)	50

Shots off target

Steven Gerrard (Liverpool)	61
Frank Lampard (Chelsea)	51
Cristiano Ronaldo (Manchester Utd)	51
Robin van Persie (Arsenal)	51
Djibril Cisse (Sunderland)	48
Peter Crouch (Portsmouth)	43
Wayne Rooney (Manchester Utd)	43
Geovanni (Hull)	40
Bobby Zamora (Fulham)	40
Dirk Kuyt (Liverpool)	39

Shots without scoring

Stewart Downing (Middlesbrough)	70
Dean Marney (Hull)	38
Gavin McCann (Bolton)	34
Fabrice Muamba (Bolton)	34
Tom Huddlestone (Tottenham)	33
Javier Mascherano (Liverpool)	27
Borja Valero (West Brom)	25
Paul Scharner (Wigan)	25
Jon Obi Mikel (Chelsea)	23
Nicky Butt (Newcastle)	22

Offsides

Djibril Cisse (Sunderland)	56
Emmanuel Adebayor (Arsenal)	43
Gabriel Agbonlahor (Aston Villa)	32
Andy Johnson (Fulham)	31
Wayne Rooney (Manchester Utd)	31
Nicolas Anelka (Chelsea)	30
Benni McCarthy (Blackburn)	30
Bobby Zamora (Fulham)	30
Afonso Alves (Middlesbrough)	29
Jason Roberts (Blackburn)	29

Fouls committed

Kevin Davies (Bolton)	115
Marouane Fellaini (Everton)	101
Bobby Zamora (Fulham)	77
Tim Cahill (Everton)	68
Carlton Cole (West Ham)	65
Gavin McCann (Bolton)	63
Vincent Kompany (Manchester City)	60
Lee Cattermole (Wigan)	59
Ricardo Fuller (Stoke)	59
John Carew (Aston Villa)	58

REFEREES' PERFORMANCES

Referee	Games	Yel	Red	Cd/M
Mark Clattenburg (Tyne & Wear)	1	0	0	0.00
Mark Halsey (Lancashire)	27	37	2	1.44
Lee Probert (Wiltshire)	11	27	0	2.45
Peter Walton (Northants)	27	67	3	2.59
Keith Stroud (Hampshire)	5	14	0	2.80
Alan Wiley (Staffordshire)	28	80	2	2.93
Rob Styles (Hampshire)	26	80	6	3.31
Phil Dowd (Staffordshire)	29	92	6	3.38
Chris Foy (Merseyside)	25	82	3	3.40
Mike Jones (Cheshire)	12	39	3	3.50
Howard Webb (S Yorkshire)	35	118	6	3.54
Martin Atkinson (W Yorkshire)	26	87	6	3.58
Steve Bennett (Kent)	22	79	0	3.59
Stuart Attwell (Warwickshire)	5	16	2	3.60
Andre Marriner (W Midlands)	20	68	4	3.60
Lee Mason (Lancashire)	16	58	5	3.94
Steve Tanner (Somerset)	11	41	3	4.00
Mike Riley (Yorkshire)	23	90	4	4.09
Mike Dean (Wirral)	31	123	8	4.23

MOST CARDS IN A SINGLE MATCH

Referee	Match	Date	YC	RC	Total
Stuart Attwell	Wigan v West Ham	04/03/2009	7	2	9
Steve Tanner	Manchester City v Sunderland	22/03/2009	8	1	9
Howard Webb	Manchester Utd v Chelsea	11/01/2009	8	0	8
Lee Mason	Aston Villa v Arsenal	26/12/2008	8	0	8
Mike Dean	Portsmouth v Tottenham	28/09/2008	7	1	8

SEASON REVIEW

BARCLAYS PREMIER LEAGUE GAMES SINCE...

Club	A win	A home win	An away win	A defeat	A home defeat	An away defeat	A score draw	A no-score draw	Conceding a goal	Scoring a goal	Conceeding more than 1	Scoring more than 1	Keeping a clean sheet	Failing to score	Winning consecutive games	Losing consecutive games	Gaining a point	Losing a point	Winning by more than one	Losing by more than one
Arsenal	0	0	1	2	1	**12**	5	1	0	0	2	0	1	1	3	24	0	1	0	2
Aston Villa	0	0	6	2	4	1	1	14	1	0	2	6	0	8	15	7	0	1	13	2
Blackburn	2	1	5	1	6	0	8	0	1	2	1	2	0	0	32	5	0	0	2	1
Bolton	7	3	11	0	4	0	1	2	0	1	6	6	2	0	11	5	1	0	7	9
Chelsea	0	0	0	8	11	4	18	5	0	0	0	0	1	5	0	**114**	0	**5**	1	14
Everton	0	0	0	4	2	4	6	2	1	0	4	0	0	2	0	66	0	2	0	30
Fulham	1	1	0	0	0	1	19	5	0	1	0	2	1	0	1	10	1	0	2	0
Hull	10	11	5	0	0	1	1	7	0	1	2	**14**	7	0	29	2	1	0	**29**	4
Liverpool	0	0	0	11	30	5	5	17	0	0	5	0	1	11	0	60	0	5	0	11
Manchester City	0	0	2	1	3	0	12	45	1	0	1	3	0	2	3	1	0	1	3	2
Manchester Utd	0	1	0	9	5	4	30	1	2	0	5	2	0	1	2	9	0	1	3	9
Middlesbrough	6	3	13	0	1	0	1	5	0	0	0	6	5	3	**37**	2	1	0	6	2
Newcastle	2	1	6	0	0	0	6	4	0	2	3	2	4	0	20	0	**2**	0	2	3
Portsmouth	1	0	13	0	1	0	7	4	0	1	2	1	4	0	31	2	1	0	1	2
Stoke	1	0	1	0	1	0	6	17	0	0	0	1	1	3	1	3	1	0	1	0
Sunderland	5	2	10	0	0	0	10	2	0	0	0	0	2	2	20	0	**2**	0	13	1
Tottenham	1	0	4	0	11	0	10	2	0	0	1	2	2	0	5	17	1	0	11	0
West Brom	2	1	**16**	1	0	1	6	0	0	2	1	2	0	0	31	10	0	0	2	1
West Ham	0	0	1	1	1	0	5	9	0	0	1	0	3	2	10	1	0	0	7	1
Wigan	0	0	4	1	1	0	15	4	1	0	1	9	0	1	8	1	0	1	21	1

TEAM STATISTICS

Club	Played	Shots on	Shots off	Corners	Hit woodwork	Caught offside	Offside trap	Fouls	Yellow cards	Red cards	Pens awarded	Pens con
Arsenal	38	315	239	268	17	88	**135**	420	60	3	5 (5)	5
Aston Villa	38	223	182	261	12	83	40	434	54	2	5 (4)	6
Blackburn	38	219	186	199	9	117	118	500	**77**	4	**7** (4)	6
Bolton	38	240	196	198	4	70	122	497	61	1	1 (0)	7
Chelsea	38	361	298	237	13	110	57	419	50	3	2 (2)	1
Everton	38	232	191	194	8	98	84	474	49	1	5 (4)	3
Fulham	38	232	197	192	9	88	115	416	41	1	5 (5)	2
Hull	38	212	203	188	7	**137**	95	**536**	72	3	3 (3)	3
Liverpool	38	310	**302**	**271**	**19**	99	94	425	50	0	6 (5)	2
Manchester City	38	269	220	212	9	74	120	456	50	4	**7** (6)	4
Manchester Utd	38	**376**	246	260	6	98	67	384	64	5	4 (4)	3
Middlesbrough	38	219	207	173	6	119	110	420	55	3	3 (1)	2
Newcastle	38	201	169	168	11	70	123	413	59	**8**	5 (4)	**9**
Portsmouth	38	230	210	196	15	76	119	433	61	5	4 (2)	7
Stoke	38	136	168	178	8	60	54	478	74	5	6 (5)	3
Sunderland	38	210	187	175	8	91	60	380	69	1	1 (1)	5
Tottenham	38	281	203	222	6	82	99	429	56	5	3 (3)	4
West Brom	38	255	212	232	11	95	128	434	67	1	5 (3)	4
West Ham	38	246	192	191	10	132	44	457	68	4	3 (1)	6
Wigan	38	227	255	217	6	101	95	441	61	4	5 (5)	3

Offside trap – number of times a side has caught the opposition offside. **Pens awarded** (scored in brackets). **Pens con** – number of penalties awarded to opposition. **Bold** – biggest total

Total league games played this season: **380** • Home wins: **173** (45%) • Away wins: **110** (29%)
• Draws: **97** (26%) • Average goals scored per match **2.6**

TABLES

HOME TABLE

	P	W	D	L	F	A	GD	Pts
Manchester Utd	19	16	2	1	43	13	30	50
Liverpool	19	12	7	0	41	13	28	43
Manchester City	19	13	0	6	40	18	22	39
Chelsea	19	11	6	2	33	12	21	39
Arsenal	19	11	5	3	31	16	15	38
Fulham	19	11	3	5	28	16	12	36
Tottenham	19	10	5	4	21	10	11	35
Stoke	19	10	5	4	22	15	7	35
Everton	19	8	6	5	31	20	11	30
Aston Villa	19	7	9	3	27	21	6	30
West Ham	19	9	2	8	23	22	1	29
Wigan	19	8	5	6	17	18	-1	29
Portsmouth	19	8	3	8	26	29	-3	27
Bolton	19	7	5	7	21	21	0	26
Blackburn	19	6	7	6	22	23	-1	25
Middlesbrough	19	5	9	5	17	20	-3	24
West Brom	19	7	3	9	26	33	-7	24
Newcastle	19	5	7	7	24	29	-5	22
Sunderland	19	6	3	10	21	25	-4	21
Hull	19	3	5	11	18	36	-18	14

AWAY TABLE

	P	W	D	L	F	A	GD	Pts
Chelsea	19	14	2	3	35	12	23	44
Liverpool	19	13	4	2	36	14	22	43
Manchester Utd	19	12	4	3	25	11	14	40
Arsenal	19	9	7	3	37	21	16	34
Everton	19	9	6	4	24	17	7	33
Aston Villa	19	10	2	7	27	27	0	32
West Ham	19	5	7	7	19	23	-4	22
Hull	19	5	6	8	21	28	-7	21
Fulham	19	3	8	8	11	18	-7	17
Wigan	19	4	4	11	17	27	-10	16
Tottenham	19	4	4	11	24	35	-11	16
Blackburn	19	4	4	11	18	37	-19	16
Bolton	19	4	3	12	20	32	-12	15
Sunderland	19	3	6	10	13	29	-16	15
Portsmouth	19	2	8	9	12	28	-16	14
Newcastle	19	2	6	11	16	30	-14	12
Manchester City	19	2	5	12	18	32	-14	11
Stoke	19	2	4	13	16	40	-24	10
West Brom	19	1	5	13	10	34	-24	8
Middlesbrough	19	2	2	15	11	37	-26	8

FIRST-HALF TABLE
(If points were only awarded for first-half performances)

	P	W	D	L	F	A	GD	Pts
Chelsea	38	19	14	5	32	8	24	71
Manchester Utd	38	18	15	5	31	13	18	69
Liverpool	38	15	19	4	28	12	16	64
Arsenal	38	15	16	7	27	14	13	61
Manchester City	38	14	16	8	28	16	12	58
West Ham	38	13	19	6	23	17	6	58
Fulham	38	12	21	5	19	13	6	57
Everton	38	11	21	6	20	13	7	54
Aston Villa	38	13	15	10	23	22	1	54
Tottenham	38	10	20	8	21	14	7	50
Wigan	38	12	14	12	18	17	1	50
Bolton	38	10	15	13	23	21	2	45
Middlesbrough	38	7	20	11	12	19	-7	41
Sunderland	38	7	19	12	14	21	-7	40
Blackburn	38	8	15	15	17	26	-9	39
Stoke	38	8	14	16	10	29	-19	38
Portsmouth	38	6	18	14	10	21	-11	36
Hull	38	5	16	17	15	34	-19	31
Newcastle	38	3	19	16	17	31	-14	28
West Brom	38	3	16	19	10	37	-27	25

SECOND-HALF TABLE
(If points were only awarded for second-half performances)

	P	W	D	L	F	A	GD	Pts
Liverpool	38	25	10	3	49	15	34	85
Chelsea	38	19	15	4	36	16	20	72
Manchester Utd	38	19	13	6	37	11	26	70
Everton	38	17	12	9	35	24	11	63
Arsenal	38	15	17	6	41	23	18	62
Stoke	38	13	17	8	28	26	2	56
Aston Villa	38	13	15	10	31	26	5	54
West Brom	38	14	10	14	26	30	-4	52
Manchester City	38	11	13	14	30	34	-4	46
Newcastle	38	10	16	12	23	28	-5	46
Hull	38	11	13	14	24	30	-6	46
Tottenham	38	9	17	12	24	31	-7	44
Wigan	38	9	17	12	16	28	-12	44
Portsmouth	38	10	13	15	28	36	-8	43
Fulham	38	9	15	14	20	21	-1	42
West Ham	38	9	12	17	19	28	-9	39
Blackburn	38	10	9	19	23	34	-11	39
Sunderland	38	9	10	19	20	33	-13	37
Bolton	38	7	13	18	18	32	-14	34
Middlesbrough	38	8	9	21	16	38	-22	33

SEQUENCES

Wins
Manchester Utd 11
26/12/2008–04/03/2009
Losses
Blackburn 6
09/11/2008–13/12/2008
Draws
Arsenal 5
28/01/2009–28/02/2009
Undefeated
Arsenal 21
30/11/2008–02/05/2009
Without win
Middlesbrough 14
16/11/2008–21/02/2009
Undefeated home
Liverpool 19
(All season)
Undefeated away
Chelsea 11
17/08/2008–28/12/2008
Without scoring
Middlesbrough 5
17/01/2009–21/02/2009
Without conceding
Manchester Utd 14
15/11/2008–18/02/2009
Scoring
Manchester Utd 12
17/08/2008–15/11/2008
Conceding
Hull 15
29/10/2008–31/01/2009

PENALTIES

Total awarded	85
Scored	67
Saved	13
Missed	5

WHEN THE GOALS WERE SCORED

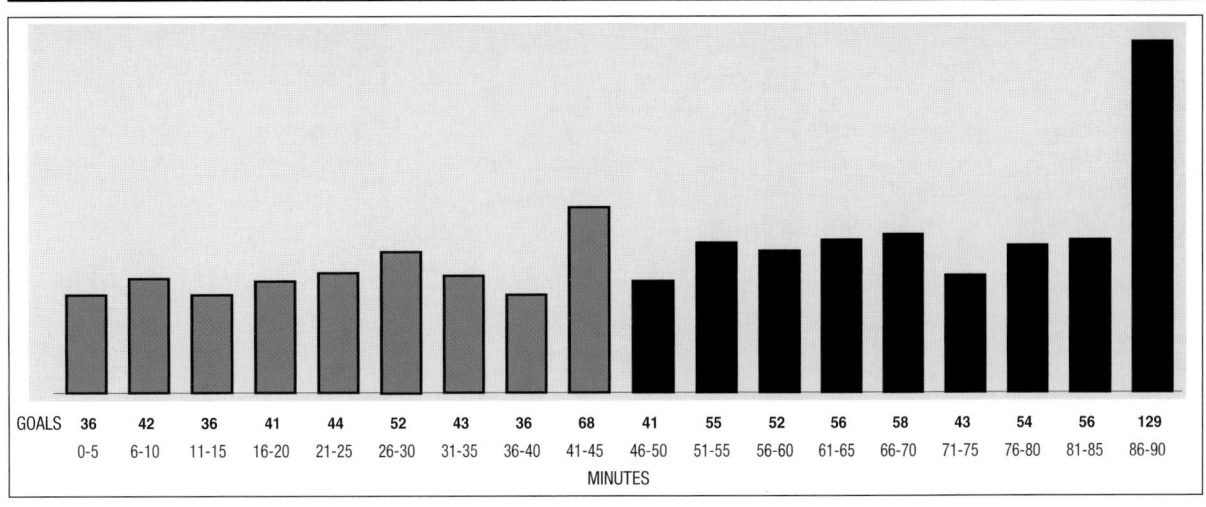

GOALS	36	42	36	41	44	52	43	36	68	41	55	52	56	58	43	54	56	129
	0-5	6-10	11-15	16-20	21-25	26-30	31-35	36-40	41-45	46-50	51-55	56-60	61-65	66-70	71-75	76-80	81-85	86-90

MINUTES

NICOLAS ANELKA'S stunning goal for Chelsea in their win at Sunderland on the final day of the season not only earned him the Golden Boot but also secured his place at the top of the Actim Index for the 2008/09 campaign.

The France international ended the year with a haul of 751 points, brought about largely by his 19 goals, although 60 shots on target and seven assists also helped.

Anelka finished the season two places clear of teammate Frank Lampard, who missed the season finale through injury and was unable to improve on his total of 653 points. Lampard's misfortune was Dirk Kuyt's gain as the hard-working Liverpool forward crept in to overtake the England playmaker and steal second place.

The 28-year-old figured in all 38 of his side's games and earned 25 points for his role in the win over Tottenham, seeing him end up two points clear of Lampard on 655 points.

Kuyt also managed to outshine his high-profile strike partner Fernando Torres, with the Spaniard ending the season in 54th, although he did only manage 24 appearances in an injury-hit season.

While Kuyt's selflessness earned many plaudits, Liverpool defender Jamie Carragher and goalkeeper Jose Reina also deserve credit for their work in helping Rafael Benitez's side to a second-place finish.

Carragher ended the campaign as the highest-scoring defender, with his 552 points seeing him finish in eighth place. The 31-year-old's consistency is highlighted by the fact his highest score was only 26. Reina finished in sixth with 573 points, making 159 saves and providing two assists.

Two players outside of the 'big four' made the Actim Index Team of the Season, with Everton's Joleon Lescott (476 points) and Aston Villa's Gareth Barry (564 points) joining the elite.

Actim player rankings for the 2008/2009 Barclays Premier League season

#	Name	Team	Index score	#	Name	Team	Index score	#	Name	Team	Index score
1	Nicolas Anelka	Chelsea	751	34	Manuel Almunia	Arsenal	423	68	Lucas Neill	West Ham	370
2	Dirk Kuyt	Liverpool	655	35	Marouane Fellaini	Everton	423	69	Patrice Evra	Man Utd	369
3	Frank Lampard	Chelsea	653	36	Wayne Rooney	Man Utd	423	70	Mikel Arteta	Everton	368
4	Dimitar Berbatov	Man Utd	586	37	Phil Neville	Everton	422	71	Andrew Johnson	Fulham	368
5	Gabriel Agbonlahor	Aston Villa	575	38	Leon Osman	Everton	416	72	Jermaine Jenas	Tottenham	364
6	Jose Reina	Liverpool	573	39	Aaron Lennon	Tottenham	411	73	Gretar Steinsson	Bolton	363
7	Gareth Barry	Aston Villa	564	40	Aaron Hughes	Fulham	410	74	Richard Dunne	Man City	362
8	Jamie Carragher	Liverpool	552	41	Brede Hangeland	Fulham	409	75	Nicklas Bendtner	Arsenal	360
9	Steven Gerrard	Liverpool	540	42	Paul Konchesky	Fulham	408	76	Steven Pienaar	Everton	358
10	Nemanja Vidic	Man Utd	540	43	Heurelho Gomes	Tottenham	408	77	Michael Carrick	Man Utd	357
11	Cristiano Ronaldo	Man Utd	517	44	Gael Clichy	Arsenal	407	78	John O'Shea	Man Utd	356
12	Petr Cech	Chelsea	513	45	Matthew Upson	West Ham	402	79	Sol Campbell	Portsmouth	356
13	John Terry	Chelsea	501	46	Abdoulaye Faye	Stoke	401	80	Curtis Davies	Aston Villa	354
14	Robbie Keane	Tottenham	482	47	Yossi Benayoun	Liverpool	401	81	Danny Collins	Sunderland	352
15	Edwin van der Sar	Man Utd	481	48	Thomas Sorensen	Stoke	400	82	Phil Jagielka	Everton	352
16	Neves Denilson	Arsenal	477	49	Samir Nasri	Arsenal	398	83	Ryan Nelsen	Blackburn	351
17	Mark Schwarzer	Fulham	477	50	Peter Crouch	Portsmouth	392	84	Titus Bramble	Wigan	350
18	Joleon Lescott	Everton	476	51	Jlloyd Samuel	Bolton	391	85	Andrew O'Brien	Bolton	348
19	Tim Howard	Everton	472	52	Bacary Sagna	Arsenal	390	86	Rio Ferdinand	Man Utd	343
20	Kevin Davies	Bolton	468	53	Leighton Baines	Everton	389	87	Florent Malouda	Chelsea	343
21	Stephen Ireland	Man City	466	54	Fernando Torres	Liverpool	389	88	Darren Fletcher	Man Utd	343
22	Ashley Cole	Chelsea	458	55	Jussi Jaaskelainen	Bolton	386	89	Darren Bent	Tottenham	343
23	Ashley Young	Aston Villa	451	56	Shay Given	Man City	382	90	Ryan Giggs	Man Utd	342
24	Robinho	Man City	450	57	Matthew Taylor	Bolton	382	91	Danny Murphy	Fulham	336
25	Brad Friedel	Aston Villa	449	58	David James	Portsmouth	381	92	Carlton Cole	West Ham	336
26	James Milner	Aston Villa	439	59	Xabi Alonso	Liverpool	381	93	Scott Carson	West Brom	335
27	Alvaro Arbeloa	Liverpool	437	60	Michael Turner	Hull	379	94	Cesc Fabregas	Arsenal	334
28	Jose Bosingwa	Chelsea	435	61	Sylvain Distin	Portsmouth	377	95	Jonathan Woodgate	Tottenham	333
29	Jon Obi Mikel	Chelsea	434	62	Ryan Shawcross	Stoke	376	96	Scott Parker	West Ham	332
30	Gary Cahill	Bolton	434	63	Emmanuel Adebayor	Arsenal	375	97	Antonio Valencia	Wigan	328
31	Tim Cahill	Everton	432	64	Luke Young	Aston Villa	373	98	Alex	Chelsea	327
32	Robert Green	West Ham	431	65	Stephen Warnock	Blackburn	372	99	John Carew	Aston Villa	325
33	Vedran Corluka	Tottenham	425	66	Herita Ilunga	West Ham	372	100	Paul Robinson	Blackburn	323
				67	John Pantsil	Fulham	371				

LEADING PLAYERS IN THE ACTIM INDEX BY POSITION

TOP 5 GOALKEEPERS

Name	Index score	Overall Index rank	Team
Jose Reina	573	6	Liverpool
Petr Cech	513	12	Chelsea
Edwin van der Sar	481	15	Manchester Utd
Mark Schwarzer	477	17	Fulham
Tim Howard	472	19	Everton

TOP 5 DEFENDERS

Name	Index score	Overall Index rank	Team
Jamie Carragher	552	8	Liverpool
Nemanja Vidic	540	10	Manchester Utd
John Terry	501	13	Chelsea
Joleon Lescott	476	18	Everton
Ashley Cole	458	22	Chelsea

TOP 5 MIDFIELDERS

Name	Index score	Overall Index rank	Team
Frank Lampard	653	3	Chelsea
Gareth Barry	564	7	Aston Villa
Steven Gerrard	540	9	Liverpool
Cristiano Ronaldo	517	11	Manchester Utd
Neves Denilson	477	16	Arsenal

TOP 5 STRIKERS

Name	Index score	Overall Index rank	Team
Nicolas Anelka	751	1	Chelsea
Dirk Kuyt	655	2	Liverpool
Dimitar Berbatov	586	4	Manchester Utd
Gabriel Agbonlahor	575	5	Aston Villa
Robbie Keane	482	14	Tottenham

BEST INDIVIDUAL MATCH SCORES

Robinho	Manchester City	82
26/10/2008: Man City 3–0 Stoke		
Andrey Arshavin	Arsenal	79
21/04/2009: Liverpool 4–4 Arsenal		
Nicolas Anelka	Chelsea	73
09/11/2008: Blackburn 0–2 Chelsea		
Emmanuel Adebayor	Arsenal	64
13/09/2008: Blackburn 0–4 Arsenal		
Gabriel Agbonlahor	Aston Villa	63
17/08/2008: Aston Villa 4–2 Man City		
Cristiano Ronaldo	Manchester Utd	62
29/10/2008: Man Utd 2–0 West Ham		
Nicolas Anelka	Chelsea	61
01/11/2008: Chelsea 5–0 Sunderland		
David Di Michele	West Ham	60
20/09/2008: West Ham 3–1 Newcastle		
Frank Lampard	Chelsea	58
04/04/2009: Newcastle 0–2 Chelsea		
Steven Gerrard	Liverpool	58
28/12/2008: Newcastle 1–5 Liverpool		
Cristiano Ronaldo	Man Utd	58
15/11/2008: Man Utd 5–0 Stoke		
Ashley Young	Aston Villa	56
07/12/2008: Everton 2–3 Aston Villa		
Wayne Rooney	Manchester Utd	56
18/10/2008: Man Utd 4–0 West Brom		
Robinho	Manchester City	55
26/12/2008: Man City 5–1 Hull		
Kenwyne Jones	Sunderland	54
13/12/2008: Sunderland 4–0 West Brom		
Gabriel Agbonlahor	Aston Villa	53
13/12/2008: Aston Villa 4–2 Bolton		

ACTIM INDEX TEAM OF THE SEASON

Joleon Lescott (476) Everton
Nemanja Vidic (540) Manchester Utd
Jose Reina (573) Liverpool
John Terry (501) Chelsea
Jamie Carragher (552) Liverpool
Gareth Barry (564) Aston Villa
Frank Lampard (653) Chelsea
Nicolas Anelka (751) Chelsea
Steven Gerrard (540) Liverpool
Dirk Kuyt (655) Liverpool
Cristiano Ronaldo (517) Manchester Utd

TOP RANK BY CLUB

	SCORE	RANK	POSITON
ARSENAL Neves Denilson	477	16	Midfielder
ASTON VILLA Gabriel Agbonlahor	575	5	Striker
BLACKBURN Stephen Warnock	372	65	Defender
BOLTON Kevin Davies	468	20	Striker
CHELSEA Nicolas Anelka	751	1	Striker
EVERTON Joleon Lescott	476	18	Defender
FULHAM Mark Schwarzer	477	17	Goalkeeper
HULL Michael Turner	379	60	Defender
LIVERPOOL Dirk Kuyt	655	2	Striker
MANCHESTER CITY Stephen Ireland	466	21	Midfielder
MANCHESTER UTD Dimitar Berbatov	586	4	Striker
MIDDLESBROUGH Marlon King	313	110	Striker
NEWCASTLE Steven Taylor	316	106	Defender
PORTSMOUTH Peter Crouch	392	50	Striker
STOKE Abdoulaye Faye	401	46	Defender
SUNDERLAND Danny Collins	352	81	Defender
TOTTENHAM Robbie Keane	482	14	Striker
WEST BROM Scott Carson	335	93	Goalkeeper
WEST HAM Robert Green	431	32	Goalkeeper
WIGAN Titus Bramble	350	84	Defender

CLUB SUMMARY

FORMED	1886
MANAGER	Arsène Wenger
GROUND	Emirates Stadium
CAPACITY	60,000
NICKNAME	The Gunners
WEBSITE	www.arsenal.com

The New Football Pools PLAYER OF THE SEASON — Robin van Persie

OVERALL

P	W	D	L	F	A	GD
61	33	16	12	113	54	59

BARCLAYS PREMIER LEAGUE

Pos	P	W	D	L	F	A	GD	Pts
4	38	20	12	6	68	37	31	72

HOME

Pos	P	W	D	L	F	A	GD	Pts
5	19	11	5	3	31	16	15	38

AWAY

Pos	P	W	D	L	F	A	GD	Pts
4	19	9	7	3	37	21	16	34

CUP PROGRESS DETAILS

Competition	Round reached	Knocked out by
FA Cup	SF	Chelsea
Champions League	SF	Man Utd
Carling Cup	QF	Burnley

BIGGEST WIN (ALL COMPS)
23/09/08 6–0 v Sheff Utd **LC3**

BIGGEST DEFEAT (ALL COMPS)
10/05/09 1–4 v Chelsea **PREM**

THE PLAYER WITH THE MOST

Shots on target
Robin van Persie 50

Shots off target
Robin van Persie 51

Shots without scoring
Bacary Sagna 13

Assists
Cesc Fabregas 10

Offsides
Emmanuel Adebayor 43

Fouls
Neves Denilson 57

Fouls without a card
Mikael Silvestre 8

Free-kicks won
Neves Denilson 76

Defensive clearances
Kolo Toure 29

actim INDEX — for the 2008/09 Barclays Premier League Season

Rank	Player	Pts
16	Neves Denilson	477
34	Manuel Almunia	423
44	Gael Clichy	407
49	Samir Nasri	398
52	Bacary Sagna	390

ATTENDANCE RECORD

High	Low	Average
60,109	59,317	60,040
v West Ham (31/01/2009)	v Wigan (06/12/2008)	

ARSÈNE WENGER was once again left to reflect on a campaign in which his young Arsenal side promised much, but too often failed to deliver.

Despite failing to build on the previous campaign and mount a serious title challenge, the Gunners did recover from early troubles when they lost five of their first 14 Barclays Premier League games, let a two-goal lead slip against arch-rivals Tottenham at home and saw defender William Gallas stripped of the captaincy after publicly questioning the desire of his teammates. An impressive 21-match unbeaten run from 30th November to 10th May saw Arsenal storm past Aston Villa and Everton to secure fourth place – and with it another crack at the Champions League, albeit via the qualifiers.

Ultimately the campaign will be remembered for the Gunners' failure to deliver when it mattered most as, within 18 days in the spring, they suffered defeat in the FA Cup semi-finals to Chelsea before seeing their Champions League dreams destroyed by holders Manchester United.

However, while some Arsenal fans are concerned about a lack of silverware in recent years, Wenger can point to some areas of relative success over the season.

A youthful team impressed as they reached the last eight of the League Cup, sweeping aside Sheffield United 6–0 and then beating Barclays Premier League outfit Wigan 3–0, before defeat to Burnley at Turf Moor in December, when they had more than enough chances to put the tie well beyond the Clarets.

The FA Cup run to the semi-finals produced some more notable performances from the fringe players, while Eduardo's double in the fourth-round win over Cardiff marked his return from the best part of a year out with a broken leg. They then overcame Hull in a quarter-final at the Emirates Stadium, although that game was overshadowed by angry scenes involving captain Cesc Fabregas and members of Hull's coaching staff which became the subject of an investigation by the Football Association.

There was, though, to be no dream finale to the campaign and, while there is no shame in losing to Chelsea, Wenger's decision to start without January signing Andrey Arshavin – who was cup-tied in Europe – was rather perplexing.

> **Wenger can point to some areas of relative success over the season**

In the Champions League, Arsenal certainly improved, and did not concede a goal at home until eventually being outclassed by United over two legs in the semi-finals.

Steve McClaren's FC Twente were comfortably dispatched in the qualifiers, while Porto, who would exact their revenge to eventually win the group, found themselves torn apart 4–0 at the Emirates on 30th September before an impressive 5–2 away victory over Fenerbahce followed. Roma awaited in the knockout stages, and after a 1–0 win in London, the Gunners eventually progressed following a nervous penalty shoot-out win at the Olympic Stadium.

Despite the promise shown in overcoming Villarreal in the last eight, there was to be no return to Rome for the final as semi-final opponents Manchester United produced a ruthless display, scoring twice in the first 11 minutes of the second leg to end the Gunners' hopes.

Arguably the most positive aspect of the campaign was the way in which Arsenal recovered from a desperate start to the campaign, which featured a 2–1 home defeat at the hands of Hull. Their brilliant run in the second half of the season included a number of impressive victories, but perhaps their most memorable game was the amazing 4–4 draw at Liverpool in April. An incredible night saw Arshavin score four times, although the Gunners were left wounded by conceding an injury-time goal that denied them a famous win.

While Arshavin impressed after his arrival, the inability of striker Emmanuel Adebayor to produce a big performance at crucial times was costly, and his future at the club is uncertain.

One man who looks certain to stay is Wenger. The manager admitted that the criticism he received during the season made him feel like he had 'killed someone', but fears he would quit to join Real Madrid have since been allayed.

CLOCKWISE FROM ABOVE: Robin van Persie scores his second goal during the league victory at Chelsea; Arsène Wenger shows off his skills; Andrey Arshavin scores one of his four goals in the 4–4 thriller at Liverpool; Manuel Almunia reflects on being beaten by Cristiano Ronaldo's brilliant free-kick in Arsenal's Champions League semi-final defeat to Manchester United

RESULTS 2008/09

August

13th ● FC Twente ....a W 0–2 **Att:** 20,000. **Ref:** A Undiano Mallenco — **Arsenal** (4-4-2): Almunia, Sagna, Djourou, Gallas¹, Clichy, Eboue, Ramsey, Denilson▮, Walcott (Randall 84), Adebayor¹, Van Persie (Bendtner 88). Subs not used: Fabianski, Vela, Wilshere, Hoyte, Gibbs.

16th ● West Brom ....h W 1–0 **Att:** 60,071. **Ref:** H Webb — **Arsenal** (4-4-2): Almunia, Sagna, Gallas, Djourou, Clichy, Walcott (Toure 72), Denilson, Nasri¹, Eboue, Adebayor, Bendtner (Van Persie 69). Subs not used: Fabianski, Vela, Ramsey, Wilshere, Randall.

23rd ● Fulham ....a L 1–0 **Att:** 25,276. **Ref:** M Atkinson — **Arsenal** (4-4-2): Almunia, Sagna, Toure (Song Billong 77), Gallas, Clichy, Walcott (Bendtner 65), Eboue, Denilson, Nasri, Adebayor, Van Persie. Subs not used: Fabianski, Ramsey, Wilshere, Djourou, Gibbs.

27th ● FC Twente ....h W 4–0 **Att:** 59,583. **Ref:** T Hauge — **Arsenal** (4-4-2): Almunia, Sagna, Gallas¹, Djourou, Clichy¹, Walcott¹, Fabregas (Song 68), Denilson, Nasri¹ (Eboue 46), Van Persie (Adebayor 65), Bendtner. Subs not used: Fabianski, Toure, Vela, Ramsey.

30th ● Newcastle ....h W 3–0 **Att:** 60,067. **Ref:** R Styles — **Arsenal** (4-4-2): Almunia, Sagna, Toure, Gallas, Clichy, Eboue (Walcott 72), Fabregas▮, Denilson¹ (Song 69), Nasri, Adebayor, Van Persie² (Vela 63). Subs not used: Fabianski, Ramsey, Djourou, Bendtner.

September

13th ● Blackburn ....a W 0–4 **Att:** 23,041. **Ref:** M Dean — **Arsenal** (4-4-2): Almunia, Sagna, Toure, Gallas, Clichy, Eboue (Ramsey 82), Fabregas, Denilson▮, Walcott (Song 64), Adebayor³, Van Persie¹ (Wilshere 84). Subs not used: Fabianski, Djourou, Bendtner, Gibbs.

17th ● Dynamo Kiev ....a D 1–1 **Att:** 20,000. **Ref:** L Medina Cantalejo — **Arsenal** (4-4-2): Almunia, Sagna▮ (Eboue 78), Toure, Gallas¹, Clichy, Walcott, Fabregas, Song (Bendtner 70), Denilson, Van Persie (Vela 83), Adebayor. Subs not used: Fabianski, Ramsey, Wilshere, Djourou.

20th ● Bolton ....a W 1–3 **Att:** 22,694. **Ref:** S Bennett — **Arsenal** (4-4-2): Almunia, Sagna, Toure, Gallas, Clichy (Djourou 46), Eboue¹ (Ramsey 85), Fabregas▮, Song▮, Denilson¹, Adebayor, Bendtner¹ (Walcott 73). Subs not used: Fabianski, Van Persie, Vela, Gibbs.

23rd ● Sheff Utd.......................h W 6–0 **Att:** 56,632. **Ref:** P Dowd — **Arsenal** (4-4-2): Fabianski, Hoyte, Djourou, Song (Lansbury 70), Gibbs, Randall, Ramsey, Merida (Coquelin 71), Wilshere¹, Bendtner² (Simpson 71), Vela³. Subs not used: Mannone, Emmanuel-Thomas, Ogogo, Frimpong.

27th ● Hull ....h L 1–2 **Att:** 60,037. **Ref:** A Wiley — **Arsenal** (4-4-2): Almunia, Sagna▮, Toure, Gallas, Clichy, Eboue (Bendtner 69), Fabregas, Denilson, Walcott (Vela 77), Adebayor, Van Persie. Subs not used: Fabianski, Ramsey, Song, Silvestre, Djourou.

30th ● FC Porto ....h W 4–0 **Att:** 59,623. **Ref:** H Fandel — **Arsenal** (4-4-2): Almunia, Sagna, Toure, Gallas, Clichy▮, Walcott (Vela 71), Fabregas, Denilson, Nasri (Eboue 64), Van Persie² (Bendtner 64), Adebayor². Subs not used: Fabianski, Ramsey, Silvestre, Djourou.

October

4th ● Sunderland ....a D 1–1 **Att:** 40,199. **Ref:** L Mason — **Arsenal** (4-4-2): Almunia, Sagna, Toure▮, Gallas, Clichy▮, Walcott (Bendtner▮ 66), Denilson (Nasri 73), Fabregas¹, Song▮ (Vela 87), Van Persie, Adebayor▮. Subs not used: Fabianski, Silvestre, Djourou, Eboue.

18th ● Everton ....h W 3–1 **Att:** 60,064. **Ref:** P Walton — **Arsenal** (4-4-2): Almunia, Song, Toure (Walcott¹ 46), Silvestre, Clichy▮, Eboue, Fabregas, Denilson, Nasri¹ (Diaby 83), Van Persie¹, Adebayor▮. Subs not used: Fabianski, Vela, Ramsey, Gibbs, Hoyte.

21st ● Fenerbahce ....a W 2–5 **Att:** 49,521. **Ref:** P Frojdfeldt — **Arsenal** (4-5-1): Almunia, Eboue, Song▮, Silvestre, Clichy, Walcott¹ (Djourou 84), Fabregas, Diaby▮ (Ramsey¹ 73), Denilson, Nasri, Adebayor¹ (Vela 86). Subs not used: Fabianski, Van Persie, Bendtner, Gibbs.

26th ● West Ham........................a W 0–2 **Att:** 34,802. **Ref:** P Dowd —**Arsenal** (4-4-2): Almunia, Eboue, Gallas, Silvestre, Clichy▮, Walcott (Adebayor¹ 67), Fabregas▮, Song▮, Nasri (Diaby 68), Bendtner, Van Persie (Sagna 90). Subs not used: Fabianski, Toure, Ramsey, Djourou.

29th ● Tottenham ....h D 4–4 **Att:** 60,043. **Ref:** M Atkinson — **Arsenal** (4-4-2): Almunia, Sagna, Silvestre¹, Gallas¹, Clichy, Walcott (Eboue 75), Fabregas, Denilson, Nasri (Song 88), Van Persie¹ (Diaby▮ 81), Adebayor¹. Subs not used: Fabianski, Toure, Vela, Bendtner.

November

1st ● Stoke ....a L 2–1 **Att:** 26,704. **Ref:** R Styles — **Arsenal** (4-4-2): Almunia, Sagna (Walcott 57), Toure, Silvestre, Clichy¹, Denilson (Van Persie 65), Fabregas▮, Song, Diaby, Adebayor▮ (Vela 72), Bendtner. Subs not used: Fabianski, Nasri, Ramsey, Djourou.

5th ● Fenerbahce ....h D 0–0 **Att:** 60,003. **Ref:** R Rosetti — **Arsenal** (4-4-2): Fabianski, Toure, Djourou▮, Silvestre (Song 83), Clichy, Ramsey (Diaby 59), Fabregas, Denilson, Nasri, Bendtner (Vela 59), Van Persie. Subs not used: Mannone, Sagna, Wilshere, Gibbs.

8th ● Man Utd ....h W 2–1 **Att:** 60,106. **Ref:** H Webb — **Arsenal** (4-4-1-1): Almunia (Fabianski 78), Sagna▮, Gallas▮, Silvestre, Clichy▮, Walcott (Song 77), Fabregas, Denilson, Nasri², Diaby (Toure 86), Bendtner. Subs not used: Vela, Ramsey, Wilshere, Djourou.

11th ● Wigan ....a W 3–0 **Att:** 59,665. **Ref:** S Tanner — **Arsenal** (4-4-2): Fabianski, Hoyte, Song Billong, Djourou, Gibbs, Wilshere (Bischoff 76), Randall, Ramsey▮, Merida, Simpson² (Lansbury 76), Vela¹ (Fonte 84). Subs not used: Mannone, Coquelin, Ogogo, Frimpong.

15th ● Aston Villa.....................h L 0–2 **Att:** 60,047. **Ref:** M Riley — **Arsenal** (4-4-1-1): Almunia, Sagna (Toure 71), Gallas, Silvestre, Clichy, Walcott, Fabregas▮, Denilson▮, Nasri, Diaby (Adebayor 61), Bendtner (Vela 68). Subs not used: Fabianski, Ramsey, Song Billong, Djourou.

22nd ● Man City ....a L 3–0 **Att:** 44,878. **Ref:** A Wiley — **Arsenal** (4-4-2): Almunia, Hoyte (Ramsey 60), Djourou, Silvestre, Clichy, Nasri, Denilson, Song▮, Diaby (Vela 69), Van Persie, Bendtner. Subs not used: Fabianski, Wilshere, Gibbs, Lansbury, Simpson.

25th ● Dynamo Kiev ....h W 1–0 **Att:** 59,374. **Ref:** A Hamer — **Arsenal** (4-4-1-1): Almunia, Djourou, Gallas, Silvestre, Clichy, Denilson, Fabregas, Song, Ramsey (Bendtner¹ 68), Vela (Wilshere 77), Van Persie. Subs not used: Fabianski, Gibbs, Hoyte, Merida, Simpson.

30th ● Chelsea ....a W 1–2 **Att:** 41,760. **Ref:** M Dean — **Arsenal** (4-4-2): Almunia, Sagna, Gallas, Djourou, Clichy, Denilson, Fabregas, Song, Nasri, Adebayor (Bendtner 83), Van Persie². Subs not used: Fabianski, Vela, Ramsey, Silvestre, Wilshere, Gibbs.

December

2nd ● Burnley ....a L 2–0 **Att:** 19,045. **Ref:** A Marriner — **Arsenal** (4-4-2): Fabianski, Hoyte, Silvestre, Ramsey, Gibbs, Rodgers (Lansbury 46), Randall (Bischoff 72), Merida▮, Wilshere (Simpson 63), Bendtner, Vela. Subs not used: Mannone, Coquelin, Steer, Frimpong.

6th ● Wigan ....h W 1–0 **Att:** 59,317. **Ref:** S Bennett — **Arsenal** (4-4-2): Almunia, Sagna, Toure, Djourou, Clichy, Denilson, Fabregas, Song Billong, Nasri (Eboue 32 (Silvestre 90)), Van Persie, Adebayor1, E Eboue (Silvestre 90). Subs not used: Fabianski, Vela, Ramsey, Wilshere, Bendtner.

10th ● FC Porto ....a L 2–0 **Att:** 37,602. **Ref:** K Vassaras — **Arsenal** (4-4-2): Almunia, Eboue▮, Gallas, Silvestre, Djourou, Ramsey (Wilshere 59), Diaby (Gibbs 59), Song (Randall 78), Denilson, Vela, Bendtner. Subs not used: Fabianski, Hoyte, Merida, Simpson.

13th ● Middlesbrough ....a D 1–1 **Att:** 27,320. **Ref:** P Walton — **Arsenal** (4-4-2): Almunia, Sagna, Gallas, Djourou, Clichy, Denilson, Fabregas, Song, Diaby▮ (Bendtner 82), Van Persie, Adebayor¹. Subs not used: Fabianski, Vela, Ramsey, Silvestre, Wilshere, Eboue.

21st ● Liverpool ....h D 1–1 **Att:** 60,094. **Ref:** H Webb — **Arsenal** (4-4-2): Almunia, Sagna▮, Djourou, Gallas, Clichy, Denilson, Fabregas (Diaby 46), Song, Nasri (Eboue 90), Adebayor▮▮, Van Persie. Subs not used: Fabianski, Vela, Ramsey, Silvestre, Wilshere.

26th ● Aston Villa.......................a D 2–2 **Att:** 42,585. **Ref:** L Mason — **Arsenal** (4-5-1): Almunia, Sagna, Eboue, Toure▮, Silvestre, Song▮ (Ramsey 43), Denilson¹, Nasri (Clichy 82), Diaby▮¹, Gallas, Van Persie. Subs not used: Fabianski, Vela, Wilshere, Bendtner.

28th ● Portsmouth ....h W 1–0 **Att:** 60,092. **Ref:** A Wiley — **Arsenal** (4-4-2): Almunia, Sagna, Gallas¹, Silvestre, Clichy, Eboue (Vela 66), Denilson, Diaby (Ramsey 75), Nasri, Adebayor, Bendtner. Subs not used: Fabianski, Toure, Van Persie, Wilshere, Gibbs.

● Barclays Premier League ● FA Cup ● Carling Cup ● UEFA Champions League ● UEFA Cup   ▮ Yellow Card ▮ Red Card

RESULTS 2008/09

January

3rd ● Plymouth .... h **W 3–1** **Att:** 59,424. **Ref:** M Jones — **Arsenal** (4-4-1-1): Fabianski, Sagna, Gallas, Djourou, Silvestre (Gibbs 30), Eboue (Vela 70), Diaby, Nasri, Ramsey, Van Persie², Bendtner (Wilshere 86). Subs not used: Almunia, Adebayor, Bischoff, Randall.

10th ● Bolton .... h **W 1–0** **Att:** 60,068. **Ref:** C Foy — **Arsenal** (4-4-2): Almunia, Sagna, Toure, Djourou▌, Clichy, Eboue (Bendtner¹ 74), Diaby (Vela 64), Denilson, Nasri, Adebayor (Ramsey▌ 88), Van Persie. Subs not used: Fabianski, Wilshere, Bischoff, Gibbs.

17th ● Hull .... a **W 1–3** **Att:** 24,924. **Ref:** A Wiley — **Arsenal** (4-4-2): Almunia, Sagna, Toure, Djourou, Clichy▌, Eboue (Bendtner¹ 69), Diaby, Denilson, Nasri¹, Adebayor¹ (Song 87), Van Persie. Subs not used: Fabianski, Vela, Ramsey, Gibbs, Merida.

25th ● Cardiff .... a **D 0–0** **Att:** 20,079. **Ref:** M Atkinson — **Arsenal** (4-4-2): Fabianski, Sagna, Toure, Djourou, Gibbs, Nasri, Ramsey (Diaby 59), Song, Eboue▌ (Adebayor 66), Van Persie, Bendtner (Wilshere 87). Subs not used: Almunia, Gallas, Vela, Denilson.

28th ● Everton .... a **D 1–1** **Att:** 37,097. **Ref:** A Marriner — **Arsenal** (4-4-2): Almunia, Sagna (Eboue 72), Djourou, Gallas, Clichy, Nasri▌, Denilson, Song (Bendtner 72), Diaby▌, Adebayor, Van Persie¹. Subs not used: Fabianski, Toure, Vela, Ramsey, Gibbs.

31st ● West Ham .... h **D 0–0** **Att:** 60,109. **Ref:** S Bennett — **Arsenal** (4-4-2): Almunia, Sagna, Toure, Gallas, Clichy, Eboue (Vela▌ 36), Diaby▌ (Song 90), Denilson, Nasri, Adebayor, Bendtner (Van Persie 68). Subs not used: Fabianski, Ramsey, Djourou, Gibbs.

February

8th ● Tottenham .... a **D 0–0** **Att:** 36,021. **Ref:** M Dean — **Arsenal** (4-4-2): Almunia, Sagna, Toure, Gallas, Clichy▌ (Gibbs 87), Eboue▌, Song, Denilson, Nasri, Adebayor (Bendtner 38), Van Persie. Subs not used: Fabianski, Eduardo, Ramsey, Djourou, Arshavin.

16th ● Cardiff .... h **W 4–0** **Att:** 57,237. **Ref:** M Halsey — **Arsenal** (4-4-2): Fabianski, Sagna, Toure, Gallas▌, Gibbs, Nasri (Ramsey 67), Denilson, Song, Vela (Bischoff 74), Eduardo² (Van Persie¹ 67), Bendtner▌. Subs not used: Almunia, Wilshere, Clichy.

21st ● Sunderland .... h **D 0–0** **Att:** 60,104. **Ref:** A Wiley — **Arsenal** (4-4-2): Almunia, Sagna, Gallas, Toure, Clichy▌ (Gibbs 85), Nasri▌, Denilson, Song (Eboue 78), Arshavin (Vela 63), Bendtner, Van Persie. Subs not used: Fabianski, Ramsey, Djourou, Merida.

24th ● Roma .... h **W 1–0** **Att:** 60,003. **Ref:** C Bo Larsen — **Arsenal** (4-4-1-1): Almunia, Sagna, Toure▌, Gallas, Clichy, Eboue (Ramsey 82), Denilson, Diaby (Song 62), Nasri▌, Van Persie¹, Bendtner (Vela 67). Subs not used: Fabianski, Djourou, Gibbs, Merida.

28th ● Fulham .... h **D 0–0** **Att:** 60,102. **Ref:** P Walton — **Arsenal** (4-4-2): Almunia, Sagna (Eboue 70), Toure, Gallas, Clichy, Arshavin, Denilson, Diaby, Nasri, Van Persie, Vela (Bendtner 63). Subs not used: Fabianski, Ramsey, Song, Djourou, Gibbs.

March

3rd ● West Brom .... a **W 1–3** **Att:** 26,244. **Ref:** S Tanner — **Arsenal** (4-4-2): Almunia, Sagna, Toure¹ (Diaby 46), Djourou, Clichy, Eboue (Ramsey 67), Song, Denilson, Nasri (Merida 83), Bendtner², Arshavin. Subs not used: Fabianski, Van Persie, Vela, Gibbs.

8th ● Burnley .... h **W 3–0** **Att:** 57,454. **Ref:** C Foy — **Arsenal** (4-4-2): Fabianski, Sagna, Djourou, Gallas, Gibbs, Eduardo¹ (Walcott 71), Song, Diaby (Ramsey 71), Vela¹ (Van Persie 60), Eboue▌, Arshavin. Subs not used: Almunia, Clichy, Bendtner, Bischoff.

11th ● Roma .... a **L 1–0** **Att:** 81,000. **Ref:** M Mejuto Gonzalez — **Arsenal** (4-2-3-1): Almunia, Sagna, Toure, Gallas, Clichy, Diaby▌, Denilson, Eboue (Walcott 74), Nasri, Bendtner (Eduardo 85), Van Persie. Subs not used: Fabianski, Djourou, Gibbs, Vela, Song.

14th ● Blackburn .... h **W 4–0** **Att:** 60,091. **Ref:** P Dowd — **Arsenal** (4-5-1): Almunia, Sagna, Toure, Djourou, Clichy, Walcott (Diaby 79), Song, Denilson, Arshavin¹, Nasri (Eboue² 83), Bendtner (Vela 79). Subs not used: Fabianski, Gallas, Van Persie, Gibbs.

17th ● Hull .... h **W 2–1** **Att:** 55,641. **Ref:** M Riley — **Arsenal** (4-3-3): Fabianski, Sagna, Gallas▌, Djourou, Gibbs, Walcott (Eboue 82), Song (Bendtner 64), Diaby, Nasri (Nasri▌ 64), Van Persie¹, Arshavin. Subs not used: Mannone, Toure, Denilson, Silvestre.

21st ● Newcastle .... a **W 1–3** **Att:** 49,972. **Ref:** M Halsey — **Arsenal** (4-4-1-1): Almunia, Sagna, Gallas▌, Toure, Clichy, Arshavin (Song Billong 74), Denilson, Diaby¹, Nasri¹, Van Persie, Bendtner¹ (Eboue 89). Subs not used: Fabianski, Eduardo, Vela, Djourou, Gibbs.

April

4th ● Man City .... h **W 2–0** **Att:** 60,097. **Ref:** H Webb — **Arsenal** (4-3-3): Almunia, Sagna, Toure▌, Gallas, Clichy, Fabregas (Ramsey 79), Song, Denilson, Walcott (Eboue 70), Adebayor² (Bendtner 70), Arshavin. Subs not used: Fabianski, Silvestre, Djourou, Gibbs.

7th ● Villarreal .... a **D 1–1** **Att:** 25,000. **Ref:** T Ovrebo — **Arsenal** (4-2-3-1): Almunia (Fabianski 28), Sagna, Toure, Gallas (Djourou 42), Clichy, Denilson, Song▌, Walcott (Eboue 78), Fabregas▌, Nasri, Adebayor¹▌. Subs not used: Vela, Silvestre, Bendtner, Gibbs.

11th ● Wigan .... a **W 1–4** **Att:** 22,954. **Ref:** A Wiley — **Arsenal** (4-4-1-1): Fabianski, Sagna, Toure, Djourou (Silvestre¹ 35), Gibbs▌, Walcott¹ (Adebayor 68), Denilson (Van Persie 63), Song▌, Arshavin¹, Fabregas, Bendtner. Subs not used: Szczesny, Nasri, Vela, Eboue.

15th ● Villarreal .... h **W 3–0** **Att:** 58,233. **Ref:** W Stark — **Arsenal** (4-4-2): Fabianski, Eboue, Toure, Gallas▌, Silvestre, Walcott¹ (Denilson 77), Song, Fabregas, Nasri, Adebayor¹ (Bendtner 83), Van Persie¹ (Diaby 77). Subs not used: Mannone, Eduardo, Vela, Ramsey.

18th ● Chelsea .... n **L 1–2** **Att:** 88,103. **Ref:** M Atkinson — **Arsenal** (4-4-1-1): Fabianski, Eboue, Toure▌, Silvestre, Gibbs, Walcott¹, Fabregas, Diaby, Denilson▌ (Nasri 86), Van Persie (Arshavin 75), Adebayor (Bendtner 83). Subs not used: Mannone, Vela, Ramsey, Song.

21st ● Liverpool .... a **D 4–4** **Att:** 44,424. **Ref:** H Webb — **Arsenal** (4-5-1): Fabianski, Sagna, Toure, Silvestre, Gibbs, Arshavin⁴, Song, Fabregas, Denilson (Walcott 65), Nasri, Bendtner (Diaby 90). Subs not used: Mannone, Eduardo, Vela, Ramsey, Eboue.

26th ● Middlesbrough .... h **W 2–0** **Att:** 60,089. **Ref:** C Foy — **Arsenal** (4-4-1-1): Almunia, Eboue, Toure, Silvestre (Djourou 46), Gibbs, Walcott (Diaby 68), Denilson, Fabregas² (Adebayor 68), Nasri, Arshavin, Bendtner. Subs not used: Fabianski, Sagna, Vela, Song Billong.

29th ● Man Utd .... a **L 1–0** **Att:** 74,733. **Ref:** C Bo Larsen — **Arsenal** (4-2-3-1): Almunia, Sagna, Toure, Silvestre, Gibbs, Song, Diaby, Walcott (Bendtner 70), Fabregas, Nasri, Adebayor (Eduardo 82). Subs not used: Fabianski, Denilson, Ramsey, Djourou, Eboue.

May

2nd ● Portsmouth .... a **W 0–3** **Att:** 20,418. **Ref:** L Mason — **Arsenal** (4-4-2): Fabianski, Sagna, Song, Djourou, Eboue, Walcott (Bischoff 64), Denilson, Ramsey (Randall 82), Arshavin▌, Bendtner² (Merida 77), Vela¹. Subs not used: Mannone, Coquelin, Emmanuel-Thomas, Frimpong.

5th ● Man Utd .... h **L 1–3** **Att:** 59,867. **Ref:** R Rosetti — **Arsenal** (4-4-1-1): Almunia, Sagna, Toure, Djourou, Gibbs (Eboue▌ 45), Walcott (Bendtner 63), Fabregas, Song, Nasri▌, Van Persie¹ (Vela 79), Adebayor▌. Subs not used: Fabianski, Silvestre, Diaby, Denilson.

10th ● Chelsea .... h **L 1–4** **Att:** 60,075. **Ref:** P Dowd — **Arsenal** (4-4-1-1): Fabianski, Sagna, Toure, Silvestre, Gibbs, Walcott (Adebayor 68), Nasri, Song (Denilson 67), Diaby (Bendtner¹ 59), Fabregas▌, Van Persie. Subs not used: Mannone, Ramsey, Djourou, Eboue.

16th ● Man Utd .... a **D 0–0** **Att:** 75,468. **Ref:** M Dean — **Arsenal** (4-5-1): Fabianski, Sagna, Toure, Song▌, Gibbs (Eboue 76), Nasri▌ (Bendtner 69), Denilson, Diaby, Fabregas▌, Arshavin▌ (Walcott 69), van Persie▌. Subs not used: Mannone, Vela, Ramsey, Silvestre.

24th ● Stoke .... h **W 4–1** **Att:** 60,082. **Ref:** M Atkinson — **Arsenal** (4-4-2): Mannone, Sagna (Eboue 57), Toure, Song, Gibbs, Diaby¹, Fabregas, Denilson▌, Arshavin (Vela 71), van Persie², Walcott (Bendtner 46). Subs not used: Szczesny, Ramsey, Silvestre, Adebayor.

● Barclays Premier League ● FA Cup ● Carling Cup ● UEFA Champions League ● UEFA Cup   ▌ Yellow Card █ Red Card

BARCLAYS PREMIER LEAGUE GOALKEEPER STATS

Player	Minutes on pitch	Appearances	Match starts	Completed matches	Sub appearances	Subbed off	SAVES BREAKDOWN: Saved with feet	Punched	Parried	Tipped over	Fumbled	Tipped round	Caught	Blocked	Clean sheets	Goals conceded	Minutes since conceding	Save %	PENALTIES: Saved	Resulting in goals	Opposition miss	Yellow cards	Red cards
Manuel Almunia	3039	32	32	31	0	1	3	17	21	5	0	3	97	0	15	26	224	85.06	2	2	0	0	0
Lukasz Fabianski	502	6	5	5	1	0	0	8	6	3	0	1	19	0	2	10	102	79.17	0	0	0	0	0
Vito Mannone	96	1	1	1	0	0	0	0	0	0	0	0	1	0	0	1	65	50.00	0	1	0	0	0

BARCLAYS PREMIER LEAGUE OUTFIELD PLAYER STATS

Player	Minutes on pitch	Appearances	Match starts	Completed matches	Substitute appearances	Subbed off	Goals scored	Minutes since scoring	Assists	Shots on target	Shots off target	Crosses	Defensive clearances	Defensive blocks	Fouls committed	Free-kicks won	Caught offside	Yellow cards	Red cards
Emmanuel Adebayor	1980	26	21	14	5	6	10	97	7	34	25	9	12	1	30	15	43	4	1
Andrey Arshavin	1052	12	12	8	0	4	6	340	7	23	8	17	1	3	14	16	3	2	0
Nicklas Bendtner	1880	31	17	9	14	8	9	93	2	35	25	9	9	1	20	17	7	1	0
Amaury Bischoff	30	1	0	0	1	0	0	-	0	0	0	1	0	0	1	0	0	0	0
Gael Clichy	2810	31	30	27	1	3	1	1814	0	4	2	31	10	8	23	34	1	7	0
Neves Denilson	3329	37	36	31	1	5	3	1741	7	19	14	18	11	1	57	76	2	3	0
Vassiriki Diaby	1549	24	16	8	8	8	3	78	2	14	9	5	8	0	31	17	0	5	0
Johan Djourou	1271	15	13	12	2	1	0	-	0	0	1	0	14	4	13	10	1	1	0
Emmanuel Eboue	1566	28	17	6	11	10	3	271	4	12	11	6	4	0	9	29	2	1	1
Cesc Fabregas	2021	22	22	19	0	3	3	286	10	30	15	44	1	0	33	31	2	7	0
William Gallas	2197	23	23	23	0	0	2	684	0	5	7	0	14	6	13	10	2	3	0
Kieran Gibbs	577	8	6	5	2	1	0	-	0	0	6	5	4	1	3	3	0	1	0
Gavin Hoyte	61	1	1	0	0	1	0	-	0	0	0	0	0	0	2	0	0	0	0
Fran Merida	27	2	0	0	2	0	0	-	0	0	1	0	0	0	0	1	0	0	0
Samir Nasri	2518	29	28	19	1	9	6	381	2	29	8	37	3	0	23	22	4	4	0
Aaron Ramsey	258	9	1	0	8	1	0	-	1	4	3	3	2	0	4	5	0	1	0
Mark Randall	12	1	0	0	1	0	0	-	0	0	0	0	0	0	0	0	0	0	0
Bacary Sagna	3113	35	34	29	1	5	0	-	1	6	7	52	16	8	21	43	1	4	0
Mikael Silvestre	1176	14	12	11	2	1	2	260	1	5	1	1	8	7	8	7	0	0	0
Alexandre Song	2211	31	23	18	8	5	1	457	1	7	10	3	12	2	44	31	1	7	0
Kolo Toure	2426	29	26	23	3	3	1	868	1	11	11	1	29	13	15	15	1	3	0
Carlos Alberto Vela	479	14	2	1	12	1	1	59	1	7	4	8	1	0	3	13	1	1	0
Theo Walcott	1319	22	16	1	6	15	2	310	2	20	20	24	0	0	6	26	6	0	0
Jack Wilshere	9	1	0	0	1	0	0	-	0	0	0	0	0	0	0	0	0	0	0
Robin van Persie	2325	28	24	19	4	4	11	55	10	50	51	41	10	1	46	40	11	5	1

SEASON TOTALS

Goals scored	68
Goals conceded	37
Clean sheets	16
Shots on target	315
Shots off target	239
Shots per goal	8.15
Pens awarded	5
Pens scored	5
Pens conceded	5
Offsides	88
Corners	268
Crosses	315
Players used	28
Fouls committed	420
Free-kicks won	470

CARDS RECEIVED

60 **3**

SEQUENCES

Wins	5
(03/03/09–11/04/09)	
Losses	2
(15/11/08–22/11/08)	
Draws	5
(28/01/09–28/02/09)	
Undefeated	21
(30/11/08–02/05/09)	
Without win	5
(28/01/09–28/02/09)	
Undefeated home	10
(06/12/08–26/04/09)	
Undefeated away	12
(30/11/08–16/05/09)	
Without scoring	4
(31/01/09–28/02/09)	
Without conceding	4
(31/01/09–28/02/09)	
Scoring	10
(30/08/08–08/11/08)	
Conceding	6
(29/10/08–30/11/08)	

League position at the end of each week

League position at the end of: August 4, September 4, October 3, November 4, December 5, January 5, February 5, March 4, April 4, May 4

SEASON INFORMATION
Highest Position: 1
Lowest Position: 14
Average goals scored per game: 1.79
Average goals conceded per game: 0.97

MATCH RECORDS

Goals scored per match

		W	D	L	Pts
Failed to score	8	0	5	3	5
Scored 1 goal	11	4	4	3	16
Scored 2 goals	6	5	1	0	16
Scored 3 goals	7	7	0	0	21
Scored 4+ goals	6	4	2	0	14

Goals conceded per match

		W	D	L	Pts
Clean sheet	16	11	5	0	38
Conceded 1 goal	14	9	4	1	31
Conceded 2 goals	4	0	1	3	1
Conceded 3 goals	1	0	0	1	0
Conceded 4+ goals	3	0	2	1	2

GOALS SCORED/CONCEDED PER FIVE-MINUTE INTERVALS

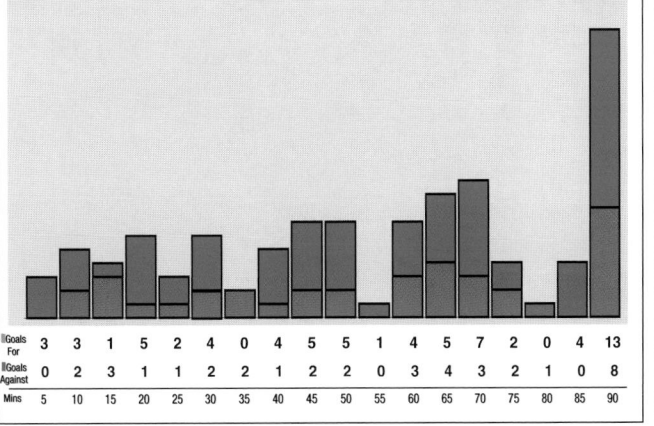

Goals For	3	3	1	5	2	4	0	4	5	5	1	4	5	7	2	0	4	13
Goals Against	0	2	3	1	1	2	2	1	2	2	0	3	4	3	2	1	0	8
Mins	5	10	15	20	25	30	35	40	45	50	55	60	65	70	75	80	85	90

QUICK-FIRE GOALS

From the start of a match
Samir Nasri (v West Brom) 3:44

By a substitute after coming on
Emmanuel Eboue (v Blackburn) 4:22

LAST-GASP GOALS

From the start of a match
Gael Clichy (v Stoke) 93:28

By a substitute after coming on
Theo Walcott (v Everton) 44:22

GOAL DETAILS

How the goals were struck

SCORED		CONCEDED
35	Right foot	17
18	Left foot	9
14	Headers	11
1	Others	0

How the goals were struck

SCORED		CONCEDED
45	Open play	19
4	Cross	6
3	Corner	4
5	Penalties	3
0	Direct from free-kick	1
7	Free-kick	1
4	Own goals	3

Distance from goal

SCORED		CONCEDED
26	6yds	12
37	18yds	19
5	18+yds	6

ASTON VILLA

CLUB SUMMARY

FORMED	1874
MANAGER	Martin O'Neill
GROUND	Villa Park
CAPACITY	42,584
NICKNAME	The Villans
WEBSITE	www.avfc.co.uk

 The New **Football Pools** PLAYER OF THE SEASON — Ashley Young

OVERALL
P	W	D	L	F	A	GD
54	24	15	15	76	67	9

BARCLAYS PREMIER LEAGUE
Pos	P	W	D	L	F	A	GD	Pts
6	38	17	11	10	54	48	6	62

HOME
Pos	P	W	D	L	F	A	GD	Pts
10	19	7	9	3	27	21	6	30

AWAY
Pos	P	W	D	L	F	A	GD	Pts
6	19	10	2	7	27	27	0	32

CUP PROGRESS DETAILS
Competition	Round reached	Knocked out by
FA Cup	R5	Everton
UEFA Cup	R-32	CSKA Moscow
Carling Cup	R3	QPR

BIGGEST WIN (ALL COMPS)
26/10/08 4–0 v Wigan **PREM**

BIGGEST DEFEAT (ALL COMPS)
22/03/09 0–5 v Liverpool **PREM**

THE PLAYER WITH THE MOST
Shots on target	
Ashley Young	44
Shots off target	
Ashley Young	36
Shots without scoring	
Craig Gardner	4
Assists	
James Milner	9
Offsides	
Gabriel Agbonlahor	32
Fouls	
John Carew	58
Fouls without a card	
Emile Heskey	26
Free-kicks won	
Ashley Young	76
Defensive clearances	
Curtis Davies	42

actim INDEX for the 2008/09 Barclays Premier League Season

Rank	Player	Pts
5	Gabriel Agbonlahor	575
7	Gareth Barry	564
23	Ashley Young	451
25	Brad Friedel	449
26	James Milner	439

ATTENDANCE RECORD
High	Low	Average
42,585	35,134	39,812
v Man Utd (22/11/2008)	v Bolton (13/12/2008)	

CLOCKWISE FROM TOP: Gareth Barry smashes home a penalty against Everton; Brad Friedel is sent off in a 5–0 defeat at Liverpool; Martin O'Neill embraces the impressive Ashley Young; Gabriel Agbonlahor scores in the 4–0 win at Wigan

ASTON VILLA secured an automatic European spot for the first time in 11 years, but there was still a sense of what might have been for Martin O'Neill's side.

Villa appeared on course to clinch a Champions League place after a 13-game unbeaten league run in mid-season. They began March holding a six-point advantage over a stuttering Arsenal side and were even challenging Chelsea at one stage for third spot in the table.

But an FA Cup fifth-round loss to Everton at Goodison Park signalled the start of a 12-match run in all competitions without a win. That was quickly followed by a rather controversial exit from the UEFA Cup when O'Neill fielded virtually a reserve side away to CSKA Moscow, angering travelling fans. O'Neill's justification for the move was that he did not have a strong enough squad to maintain a push for success on cup and league fronts. But Villa never regained momentum as his players, who had reported back in early July for Intertoto Cup duty, gradually ran out of steam. At the same time the Gunners welcomed back key players such as Cesc Fabregas, Theo Walcott and Emmanuel Adebayor from injury and comfortably reclaimed fourth spot in the table. In the end Villa claimed a Europa League spot after finishing sixth for the second year running, a point behind their main rivals outside of the Barclays Premier League's 'big four', Everton.

At their best, Villa looked to be one of the best counter-attacking teams in the top flight and at one stage chalked up a club-record seven successive away league victories. However, their inability to break down sides at home proved costly. They went four months without a victory in front of their own fans from January to early May before victories against Hull and Newcastle cemented their top-six position.

It is clear O'Neill will have to invest heavily in the transfer market this summer if Villa are to sustain the progress made during the Northern Irishman's first three years at the club. Villa sold Gareth Barry soon after the end of the season and have a massive hole to fill in the shape of skipper and central defender Martin Laursen, forced to retire because of knee problems.

O'Neill has already acknowledged maintaining a top-six position will be harder to achieve given the spending spree that the likes of Manchester City and Tottenham are likely to embark upon. O'Neill's own shopping list should include a ball-winning centre-half as Villa's defence became increasingly leaky when Laursen was absent from the back line during the second half of the campaign.

However, Villa should have the firepower to give most defences a real examination via the likes of John Carew, Emile Heskey and Gabriel Agbonlahor, as well as the ammunition supplied by Ashley Young and James Milner. Carew finished as top scorer with 15 goals despite missing the middle third of the season with a back problem. He will continue to face competition for a place from Heskey, a surprise signing in January at a time when Villa were in full flow.

O'Neill's highest hopes should be for Agbonlahor, Young, Milner and his other young talent making further progress. Winger Young's potential was recognised by his fellow professionals in being voted the PFA Young Player of the Year, with Agbonlahor finishing runner-up.

Stiliyan Petrov's rehabilitation after a difficult initial spell following his move from Celtic culminated in him being voted Player of the Year. The Bulgarian international was dropped for a spell in 2007/08 as even O'Neill's faith in the player appeared to be wavering. But Petrov has been a revelation in a holding role which has allowed others the licence to roam forward.

> ❝ **Their inability to break down sides at Villa Park proved costly** ❞

ASTON VILLA

July

19th ● Odense BK ....a D 2–2 **Att:** 12,000. **Ref:** A De Marco — **Aston Villa** (4-4-2): Taylor, Gardner, Laursen¹, Knight, Bouma, Petrov, Reo-Coker, Sidwell (Routledge 82), A Young▌, Agbonlahor, Carew▌¹. Subs not used: Parish, Harewood, Salifou, Osbourne, Maloney, Baker.

26th ● Odense BK ....h W 1–0 **Att:** 35,000. **Ref:** 266858 — **Aston Villa** (4-4-2): Taylor, Gardner, Laursen, Knight, Bouma (Barry 14), Petrov, Reo-Coker, Sidwell, Young¹, Agbonlahor, Carew. Subs not used: Parish, Harewood, Salifou, Routledge, Osbourne, Maloney.

August

14th ● FH Hafnarfjordur.................a W 1–4 **Att:** 2,200. **Ref:** R Matejek — **Aston Villa** (4-4-2): Friedel, Gardner, Davies, Laursen¹, Shorey, Reo-Coker, Petrov, Barry▌¹, Young¹, Harewood, Agbonlahor¹. Subs not used: Taylor, Delfouneso, Knight, Salifou, Routledge, Osbourne, Baker.

17th ● Man City ....h W 4–2 **Att:** 39,955. **Ref:** P Dowd — **Aston Villa** (4-4-2): Friedel, L Young, Davies, Laursen, Shorey, Reo-Coker, Petrov, Barry, A Young, Agbonlahor³, Carew¹. Subs not used: Taylor, Harewood, Knight, Salifou, Routledge, Gardner, Osbourne.

23rd ● Stoke ....a L 3–2 **Att:** 27,500. **Ref:** M Halsey — **Aston Villa** (4-4-2): Friedel, L Young, Laursen¹, Davies, Shorey (Routledge 73), Petrov, Reo-Coker, Barry, A Young, Carew¹, Agbonlahor. Subs not used: Taylor, Knight, Osbourne, Gardner, Salifou, Harewood.

28th ● FH Hafnarfjordur.................h D 1–1 **Att:** 25,415. **Ref:** B Kuipers — **Aston Villa** (4-4-2): Friedel, Gardner¹, Knight, Davies, Barry, Routledge, Reo-Coker, Osbourne, Salifou, Agbonlahor (Delfouneso¹ 62), Harewood▌. Subs not used: Taylor, Laursen, Young, Carew, Petrov, Baker.

31st ● Liverpool ....h D 0–0 **Att:** 41,647. **Ref:** M Atkinson — **Aston Villa** (4-4-2): Friedel, L Young (Milner 64), Laursen, Davies, Shorey (Gardner 79), Reo-Coker, Petrov, Barry, A Young, Carew, Agbonlahor. Subs not used: Guzan, Harewood, Salifou, Routledge.

September

15th ● Tottenham ....a W 1–2 **Att:** 36,075. **Ref:** S Bennett — **Aston Villa** (4-4-2): Friedel, L Young¹, Laursen, Davies, Shorey▌ (Gardner 88), A Young▌, Petrov, Reo-Coker¹, Barry, Agbonlahor (Harewood 84), Carew▌ (Milner 63). Subs not used: Guzan, Knight, Routledge, Cuellar.

18th ● Litex Lovech ....a W 1–3 **Att:** 7,000. **Ref:** C Zografos — **Aston Villa** (4-5-1): Friedel, Young, Cuellar, Laursen, Shorey, Gardner (Harewood 68), Barry¹ (Salifou 78), Reo-Coker¹ (Routledge 74), Petrov¹, Milner, Agbonlahor. Subs not used: Guzan, Knight, Osbourne, Delfouneso.

21st ● West Brom ....a W 1–2 **Att:** 26,011. **Ref:** M Dean — **Aston Villa** (4-4-2): Friedel, L Young▌, Davies, Laursen, Shorey (Milner 74), Reo-Coker, Petrov (Gardner 83), Barry, A Young▌, Carew▌¹ (Cuellar 89), Agbonlahor¹. Subs not used: Guzan, Harewood, Knight, Salifou.

24th ● QPR ....h L 0–1 **Att:** 21,541. **Ref:** L Mason — **Aston Villa** (4-4-2): Guzan, Gardner¹, Cuellar, Knight, Shorey, Osbourne (Routledge 67), Petrov, Barry, Young, Harewood (Agbonlahor 67), Carew. Subs not used: Friedel, Delfouneso, Davies, Salifou, Reo-Coker.

27th ● Sunderland ....h W 2–1 **Att:** 38,706. **Ref:** P Walton — **Aston Villa** (4-4-2): Friedel, L Young¹, Davies, Laursen, Shorey (Milner 70), Reo-Coker, Petrov▌, Barry, A Young, Agbonlahor, Carew▌ (Cuellar 90). Subs not used: Guzan, Harewood, Knight, Salifou, Gardner.

October

2nd ● Litex Lovech ....h D 1–1 **Att:** 27,230. **Ref:** T Chapron — **Aston Villa** (4-4-2): Friedel, L Young, Knight, Cuellar, Shorey, Routledge, Petrov, Salifou, A Young (Osbourne 85), Harewood¹, Milner. Subs not used: Guzan, Laursen, Agbonlahor, Delfouneso, Reo-Coker, Gardner.

5th ● Chelsea ....a L 2–0 **Att:** 41,593. **Ref:** C Foy — **Aston Villa** (4-4-2): Friedel, L Young (Milner 46), Davies (Cuellar▌ 46), Laursen, Shorey▌, Reo-Coker, Petrov▌, Barry, A Young, Carew (Harewood 71), Agbonlahor. Subs not used: Guzan, Knight, Salifou, Gardner.

18th ● Portsmouth ....h D 0–0 **Att:** 37,660. **Ref:** M Riley — **Aston Villa** (3-5-2): Friedel, Cuellar, Davies, Laursen (L Young 88), Milner, Reo-Coker, Petrov, Barry, A Young▌, Agbonlahor, Carew. Subs not used: Guzan, Sidwell, Harewood, Knight, Shorey, Gardner.

23rd ● Ajax.........................h W 2–1 **Att:** 36,657. **Ref:** T Einwaller — **Aston Villa** (4-3-3): Friedel, L Young, Cuellar, Laursen¹, Shorey, Reo-Coker (Gardner▌ 81), Petrov, Barry¹, Milner, Agbonlahor (Davies 90), A Young. Subs not used: Guzan, Sidwell, Harewood, Knight, Salifou.

26th ● Wigan ....a W 0–4 **Att:** 20,249. **Ref:** M Jones — **Aston Villa** (4-3-3): Friedel, L Young▌ (Davies 78), Laursen, Cuellar, Shorey, Reo-Coker▌, Petrov (Sidwell¹ 84), Barry¹ (Carew¹ 54), A Young, Agbonlahor¹, Milner. Subs not used: Guzan, Harewood, Knight, Gardner.

29th ● Blackburn ....h W 3–2 **Att:** 35,985. **Ref:** K Stroud — **Aston Villa** (4-4-2): Friedel, L Young¹, Shorey, Laursen, Cuellar, Barry¹, Milner, Petrov (Carew 46), Reo-Coker (Sidwell 83), A Young, Agbonlahor¹ (Harewood 90). Subs not used: Guzan, Davies, Knight, Gardner.

November

3rd ● Newcastle ....a L 2–0 **Att:** 44,567. **Ref:** S Bennett — **Aston Villa** (4-4-2): Friedel, L Young▌, Cuellar, Laursen, Shorey (Sidwell▌ 72), Milner, Reo-Coker (Harewood 85), Barry¹, A Young, Agbonlahor, Carew. Subs not used: Guzan, Davies, Knight, Salifou, Gardner.

6th ● Slavia Prague ....a W 0–1 **Att:** 20,322. **Ref:** C Kapitanis — **Aston Villa** (4-4-2): Guzan, Davies, Cuellar, Shorey, Knight, Sidwell▌, A Young, Salifou, Gardner▌, Agbonlahor (Barry 89), Carew¹ (Delfouneso 90). Subs not used: Friedel, L Young, Laursen, Routledge, Reo-Coker.

9th ● Middlesbrough ....h L 1–2 **Att:** 36,672. **Ref:** R Styles — **Aston Villa** (4-4-2): Friedel, Cuellar, Davies, Laursen, Shorey (Harewood 70), Reo-Coker, Sidwell¹, Barry, Milner▌, Agbonlahor, A Young▌. Subs not used: Guzan, Routledge, Salifou, Knight, Delfouneso, Gardner.

15th ● Arsenal ....a W 0–2 **Att:** 60,047. **Ref:** M Riley — **Aston Villa** (4-1-4-1): Friedel, Cuellar, Davies, Laursen, L Young, A Young, Sidwell▌, Petrov, Barry▌, Milner, Agbonlahor▌¹. Subs not used: Guzan, Harewood, Carew, Knight, Salifou, Reo-Coker, Gardner.

22nd ● Man Utd ....h D 0–0 **Att:** 42,585. **Ref:** C Foy — **Aston Villa** (4-5-1): Friedel, Reo-Coker, Davies▌, Laursen, L Young, Sidwell (Carew 81), Petrov, Barry, Milner, Agbonlahor, A Young. Subs not used: Guzan, Harewood, Knight, Salifou, Shorey, Gardner.

29th ● Fulham ....h D 0–0 **Att:** 36,625. **Ref:** M Jones — **Aston Villa** (4-3-3): Friedel, Cuellar, Laursen, Davies, L Young, Sidwell, Petrov, Barry, Milner, Agbonlahor, A Young. Subs not used: Guzan, Harewood, Delfouneso, Knight, Salifou, Shorey, Gardner.

December

4th ● MSK Zilina ....h L 1–2 **Att:** 28,797. **Ref:** E Berntsen — **Aston Villa** (4-4-2): Guzan, Reo-Coker, Knight, Cuellar, L Young, Gardner, Salifou (Barry 68), Osbourne▌ (Milner 65), A Young, Delfouneso¹ (Agbonlahor 76), Harewood. Subs not used: Friedel, Laursen, Petrov, Clarke.

7th ● Everton ....a W 2–3 **Att:** 31,922. **Ref:** M Atkinson — **Aston Villa** (4-3-3): Friedel, Cuellar, Laursen, Davies, L Young▌, Sidwell¹, Petrov, Barry, Milner, Agbonlahor. A Young. Subs not used: Guzan, Harewood, Delfouneso, Knight, Reo-Coker, Shorey, Gardner.

13th ● Bolton ....h W 4–2 **Att:** 35,134. **Ref:** L Probert — **Aston Villa** (4-3-3): Friedel, Cuellar, Laursen, Davies¹, L Young¹, Sidwell, Petrov, Barry, Milner (Reo-Coker 68), Agbonlahor² (Shorey 87), A Young (Harewood 81). Subs not used: Guzan, Delfouneso, Knight, Gardner.

17th ● Hamburg.........................a L 3–1 **Att:** 49,121. **Ref:** A Nikolayev — **Aston Villa** (4-4-2): Guzan, Young, Cuellar, Knight▌, Shorey, Gardner (Bannan 61), Sidwell▌▌, Reo-Coker, Salifou, Harewood, Delfouneso¹. Subs not used: Friedel, Davies, Petrov, Clark, Herd, Lowry.

20th ● West Ham.........................a W 0–1 **Att:** 31,353. **Ref:** M Halsey — **Aston Villa** (4-1-4-1): Friedel, Cuellar (Reo-Coker 58), Davies, Laursen, L Young, Petrov, Milner▌, Sidwell, Barry, A Young, Agbonlahor. Subs not used: Guzan, Delfouneso, Knight, Shorey, Gardner.

26th ● Arsenal ....h D 2–2 **Att:** 42,585. **Ref:** L Mason — **Aston Villa** (4-5-1): Friedel, Reo-Coker▌, Davies, Knight¹, L Young, Milner, Sidwell, Petrov▌, Barry▌¹, A Young, Agbonlahor▌. Subs not used: Guzan, Harewood, Delfouneso, Salifou, Shorey, Gardner, Osbourne.

30th ● Hull ....a W 0–1 **Att:** 24,727. **Ref:** S Bennett — **Aston Villa** (4-5-1): Friedel, Reo-Coker, Knight, Davies, L Young, Milner, Sidwell (Gardner 86), Petrov▌, Barry▌, A Young, Agbonlahor. Subs not used: Guzan, Harewood, Delfouneso, Salifou, Shorey, Osbourne.

● Barclays Premier League ● FA Cup ● Carling Cup ● UEFA Champions League ● UEFA Cup ● UEFA Intertoto Cup | ▌ Yellow Card ▌ Red Card

RESULTS 2008/09

January

4th ● Gillingham............................a W 1–2 **Att:** 10,107. **Ref:** K Stroud — **Aston Villa** (4-5-1): Friedel, Reo-Coker▮, Davies▮, Knight, Shorey, Milner², Sidwell, Petrov, Gardner, Young, Delfouneso (Harewood 72). Subs not used: Guzan, Salifou, Osbourne, Bannan, Clark, Lowry.

10th ● West Brom ....h W 2–1 **Att:** 41,757. **Ref:** S Bennett — **Aston Villa** (4-3-3): Friedel, Reo-Coker, Davies¹, Laursen▮, L Young, Sidwell (Cuellar 86), Petrov, Barry, Milner, Agbonlahor, A Young. Subs not used: Guzan, Harewood, Delfouneso, Knight, Shorey, Gardner.

17th ● Sunderland ....a W 1–2 **Att:** 40,350. **Ref:** M Dean — **Aston Villa** (4-5-1): Friedel, Reo-Coker, Davies, Cuellar, L Young¹, Milner¹, Sidwell (Gardner 73), Petrov, Barry¹, A Young▮, Agbonlahor¹. Subs not used: Guzan, Harewood, Delfouneso, Knight, Salifou, Shorey.

24th ● Doncaster ....a D 0–0 **Att:** 13,517. **Ref:** M Halsey — **Aston Villa** (4-5-1): Friedel, Davies, Cuellar, Knight, Shorey, Reo-Coker (Gardner 70), Sidwell, Petrov, Barry, Shorey, Milner, Agbonlahor. Subs not used: Harewood, Delfouneso, Salifou, Guzan, Osbourne, Clark.

27th ● Portsmouth ....a W 0–1 **Att:** 19,073. **Ref:** P Walton — **Aston Villa** (4-4-2): Friedel, Cuellar, Knight, Davies, Young, Gardner (Sidwell 65), Petrov▮, Barry, Milner▮, Agbonlahor, Heskey¹ (Shorey 83). Subs not used: Guzan, Harewood, Delfouneso, Osbourne.

31st ● Wigan ....h D 0–0 **Att:** 41,766. **Ref:** R Styles — **Aston Villa** (4-4-2): Friedel, Cuellar, Knight, Davies▮, Young, Gardner (Carew 62), Petrov, Barry, Milner, Heskey, Agbonlahor. Subs not used: Guzan, Sidwell, Delfouneso, Salifou, Shorey, Osbourne.

February

4th ● Doncaster ....h W 3–1 **Att:** 24,203. **Ref:** L Mason — **Aston Villa** (4-4-2): Guzan, L Young, Davies, Cuellar, Shorey, Gardner, Salifou, Sidwell¹▮, A Young (Osbourne 78), Delfouneso¹, Carew¹. Subs not used: Friedel, Barry, Milner, Agbonlahor, Knight, Lowry.

7th ● Blackburn ....a W 0–2 **Att:** 24,267. **Ref:** S Bennett — **Aston Villa** (4-4-2): Friedel, Cuellar (Gardner 46), Davies, Knight, L Young, Milner¹, Petrov, Barry▮, A Young, Heskey (Carew 70), Agbonlahor¹. Subs not used: Guzan, Sidwell, Delfouneso, Salifou, Shorey.

15th ● Everton ....a L 3–1 **Att:** 32,979. **Ref:** M Atkinson — **Aston Villa** (4-4-2): Friedel, Gardner, Knight, Davies, L Young, Milner¹▮, Sidwell▮ (Delfouneso 83), Petrov▮, A Young, Agbonlahor, Carew. Subs not used: Guzan, Harewood, Salifou, Shorey, Albrighton, Lowry.

18th ● CSKA Moscow ....h D 1–1 **Att:** 38,038. **Ref:** P Rasmussen — **Aston Villa** (4-4-2): Guzan, L Young▮, Davies, Knight, Shorey, Gardner, Petrov▮, Barry, A Young, Carew¹. Subs not used: Friedel, Bannan, Salifou, Lowry, Albrighton, Harewood, Delfouneso.

21st ● Chelsea ....h L 0–1 **Att:** 42,585. **Ref:** M Halsey — **Aston Villa** (4-4-2): Friedel, Cuellar▮, Davies (Carew 70), Knight, L Young, Milner, Petrov, A Young, Heskey, Agbonlahor. Subs not used: Guzan, Sidwell, Delfouneso, Salifou, Shorey, Gardner.

26th ● CSKA Moscow ....a L 2–0 **Att:** 25,650. **Ref:** F Brych — **Aston Villa** (4-5-1): Guzan, Young, Davies (Osbourne 84), Knight, Shorey, Albrighton▮, Gardner, Salifou (Harewood 46), Sidwell, Bannan▮, Delfouneso. Subs not used: Taylor, Lichaj, Clark, Lowry.

March

1st ● Stoke ....h D 2–2 **Att:** 39,641. **Ref:** H Webb — **Aston Villa** (4-4-2): Friedel, Cuellar, Knight, Davies, L Young, Milner, Petrov¹, Barry, A Young▮, Agbonlahor, Heskey (Carew¹ 76). Subs not used: Guzan, Harewood, Delfouneso, Reo-Coker, Shorey, Gardner.

4th ● Man City ....a L 2–0 **Att:** 40,137. **Ref:** C Foy — **Aston Villa** (4-4-2): Friedel, Cuellar (Gardner 88), Davies (Carew 46), Knight, L Young, Milner▮, Petrov, Barry▮, A Young, Agbonlahor, Heskey. Subs not used: Guzan, Harewood, Delfouneso, Reo-Coker, Shorey.

15th ● Tottenham............................h L 1–2 **Att:** 41,205. **Ref:** S Bennett — **Aston Villa** (4-4-2): Friedel, Reo-Coker▮, Cuellar, Knight (Carew¹ 60), L Young, Milner, Petrov, Barry, A Young, Heskey (Delfouneso 79), Heskey (Gardner 82). Subs not used: Guzan, Harewood, Davies, Shorey.

22nd ● Liverpool ....a L 5–0 **Att:** 44,131. **Ref:** M Atkinson — **Aston Villa** (4-4-2): Friedel▮, Reo-Coker (Guzan 64), Cuellar, Davies, L Young▮, Milner, Petrov, Barry¹, A Young, Heskey (Agbonlahor 58), Carew (Gardner¹ 88). Subs not used: Delfouneso, Knight, Salifou, Shorey.

April

5th ● Man Utd ....a L 3–2 **Att:** 75,409. **Ref:** M Riley — **Aston Villa** (4-4-2): Friedel, L Young, Cuellar, Davies, Shorey, Milner▮ (Reo-Coker 76), Petrov, Barry, A Young▮, Carew¹, Agbonlahor¹. Subs not used: Guzan, Delfouneso, Knight, Salifou, Gardner, Albrighton.

12th ● Everton ....h D 3–3 **Att:** 40,188. **Ref:** H Webb — **Aston Villa** (4-4-2): Friedel, L Young, Davies, Knight, Shorey, Milner¹, Petrov, Barry¹, A Young, Agbonlahor (Delfouneso 54), Carew¹. Subs not used: Guzan, Sidwell, Salifou, Reo-Coker, Gardner, Albrighton.

18th ● West Ham............................h D 1–1 **Att:** 39,534. **Ref:** R Styles — **Aston Villa** (4-4-2): Friedel, L Young, Davies, Cuellar, Shorey, Milner (Gardner 81), Petrov▮, Barry, A Young▮, Heskey¹ (Delfouneso 71), Carew. Subs not used: Guzan, Sidwell, Knight, Salifou, Reo-Coker.

25th ● Bolton ....a D 1–1 **Att:** 21,709. **Ref:** L Probert — **Aston Villa** (4-4-2): Friedel, Knight, Davies, Cuellar, Shorey, Milner, Petrov, Barry▮, Young¹, Heskey (Delfouneso 76), Carew. Subs not used: Guzan, Sidwell, Salifou, Gardner, Albrighton, Clark.

May

4th ● Hull ....h W 1–0 **Att:** 39,607. **Ref:** M Dean — **Aston Villa** (4-4-2): Friedel, L Young, Davies, Knight, Shorey, Milner, Petrov (Reo-Coker 90), Barry, A Young (Gardner 90), Carew¹ (Heskey 86), Agbonlahor. Subs not used: Guzan, Sidwell, Delfouneso, Clark.

9th ● Fulham ....a L 3–1 **Att:** 25,660. **Ref:** M Halsey — **Aston Villa** (4-4-2): Friedel, L Young¹ (Heskey 64), Knight, Davies, Shorey (Reo-Coker 64), Milner, Petrov, Barry, A Young, Carew, Agbonlahor. Subs not used: Guzan, Sidwell, Delfouneso, Gardner, Clark.

16th ● Middlesbrough ....a D 1–1 **Att:** 27,261. **Ref:** M Riley — **Aston Villa** (4-4-2): Friedel, Milner▮, Davies, Cuellar, Shorey, Young (Reo-Coker 70), Petrov, Barry▮, Agbonlahor, Carew¹, Heskey. Subs not used: Guzan, Sidwell, Delfouneso, Knight, Gardner, Clark.

24th ● Newcastle ....h W 1–0 **Att:** 42,585. **Ref:** C Foy — **Aston Villa** (4-4-2): Friedel, Gardner (Heskey 75), Davies, Cuellar, Shorey, Milner, Petrov (Reo-Coker 84), Barry, Young, Carew (Sidwell 89), Agbonlahor. Subs not used: Guzan, Delfouneso, Knight, Albrighton.

● Barclays Premier League ● FA Cup ● Carling Cup ● UEFA Champions League ● UEFA Cup ● UEFA Intertoto Cup   ▮ Yellow Card ▮ Red Card

ASTON VILLA

BARCLAYS PREMIER LEAGUE GOALKEEPER STATS

Player	Minutes on pitch	Appearances	Match starts	Completed matches	Sub appearances	Subbed off	SAVES BREAKDOWN								Clean sheets	Goals conceded	Minutes since conceding	Save %	PENALTIES			Yellow cards	Red cards
							Saved with feet	Punched	Parried	Tipped over	Fumbled	Tipped round	Caught	Blocked					Saved	Resulting in goals	Opposition miss		
Brad Friedel	3585	38	38	37	0	0	1	14	32	11	0	10	105	0	13	47	181	80.54	0	4	0	1	1
Bradley Guzan	29	1	0	0	1	0	0	0	0	0	0	0	0	0	0	1	-	0	0	2	0	0	0

BARCLAYS PREMIER LEAGUE OUTFIELD PLAYER STATS

Player	Minutes on pitch	Appearances	Match starts	Completed matches	Substitute appearances	Subbed off	Goals scored	Minutes since scoring	Assists	Shots on target	Shots off target	Crosses	Defensive clearances	Defensive blocks	Fouls committed	Free-kicks won	Caught offside	Yellow cards	Red cards
Gabriel Agbonlahor	3290	36	35	30	1	5	12	479	8	37	19	39	3	0	47	55	32	4	0
Gareth Barry	3576	38	38	37	0	1	5	604	7	23	19	70	28	5	56	45	10	9	0
John Carew	1910	27	18	11	9	7	11	127	3	26	24	12	16	0	58	24	18	2	0
Carlos Cuellar	2253	28	24	21	4	3	0	-	0	0	2	9	35	14	18	13	0	2	0
Curtis Davies	3127	35	34	31	1	3	1	1529	1	1	11	0	42	17	24	28	0	2	0
Nathan Delfouneso	94	4	0	0	4	0	0	-	0	2	0	2	0	0	1	0	0	0	0
Craig Gardner	352	14	3	0	11	3	0	-	0	2	2	6	4	0	5	4	0	1	0
Marlon Harewood	81	6	0	0	6	0	0	-	0	1	0	2	0	0	1	1	0	0	0
Emile Heskey	962	14	11	4	3	7	2	294	1	9	9	7	10	3	11	13	6	0	0
Zat Knight	1202	13	13	12	0	1	1	1109	0	2	3	0	15	12	9	7	0	0	0
Martin Laursen	1794	19	19	18	0	1	1	1615	2	5	7	2	40	14	10	32	1	1	0
James Milner	3045	36	31	28	5	3	3	602	9	34	20	107	3	7	39	31	2	6	0
Stiliyan Petrov	3344	36	36	31	0	5	1	1090	3	14	12	5	20	6	36	64	1	6	0
Nigel Reo-Coker	1903	26	19	16	7	3	1	1616	0	6	5	19	1	4	32	23	0	3	0
Wayne Routledge	22	1	0	0	1	0	0	-	0	0	0	0	0	0	0	0	0	0	0
Nicky Shorey	1664	21	19	11	2	8	0	-	1	0	1	17	6	8	3	9	0	2	0
Steve Sidwell	1066	16	11	7	5	4	3	659	0	11	9	1	16	0	24	13	1	2	0
Ashley Young	3363	36	36	32	0	3	7	249	9	44	36	148	4	4	37	76	11	7	1
Luke Young	3024	34	33	29	1	4	1	2301	0	6	3	29	18	5	23	19	0	6	0

SEASON TOTALS

Goals scored	54
Goals conceded	48
Clean sheets	13
Shots on target	223
Shots off target	182
Shots per goal	7.50
Pens awarded	5
Pens scored	4
Pens conceded	6
Offsides	83
Corners	261
Crosses	475
Players used	21
Fouls committed	434
Free-kicks won	467

CARDS RECEIVED

54 | 2

SEQUENCES

Wins	4
(30/12/08–27/01/09)	
Losses	4
(04/03/09–05/04/09)	
Draws	3
(12/04/09–25/04/09)	
Undefeated	13
(15/11/08–07/02/09)	
Without win	9
(21/02/09–25/04/09)	
Undefeated home	6
(22/11/08–31/01/09)	
Undefeated away	7
(15/11/08–07/02/09)	
Without scoring	2
(on two occasions)	
Without conceding	3
(on two occasions)	
Scoring	8
(07/12/08–27/01/09)	
Conceding	9
(21/02/09–25/04/09)	

SEASON INFORMATION

Highest Position: 1
Lowest Position: 10
Average goals scored per game: 1.42
Average goals conceded per game: 1.26

League position at the end of each week

League position at the end of: August 7, September 3, October 4, November 5, December 4, January 4, February 4, March 5, April 5, May 6

MATCH RECORDS

Goals scored per match

		W	D	L	Pts
Failed to score	10	0	5	5	5
Scored 1 goal	11	5	3	3	18
Scored 2 goals	11	7	2	2	23
Scored 3 goals	3	2	1	0	7
Scored 4+ goals	3	3	0	0	9

Goals conceded per match

		W	D	L	Pts
Clean sheet	13	8	5	0	29
Conceded 1 goal	9	5	3	1	18
Conceded 2 goals	11	4	2	5	14
Conceded 3 goals	4	0	1	3	1
Conceded 4+ goals	1	0	0	1	0

QUICK-FIRE GOALS

From the start of a match
Steve Sidwell (v Everton) 0:31

By a substitute after coming on
John Carew (v Stoke) 3:20

LAST-GASP GOALS

From the start of a match
Ashley Young (v Everton) 93:32

By a substitute after coming on
John Carew (v Tottenham) 24:34

GOAL DETAILS

How the goals were struck

SCORED		CONCEDED
28	Right foot	37
13	Left foot	5
12	Headers	6
1	Others	0

How the goals were struck

SCORED		CONCEDED
28	Open play	33
9	Cross	3
3	Corner	2
4	Penalties	6
2	Direct from free-kick	1
3	Free-kick	3
5	Own goals	0

Distance from goal

SCORED		CONCEDED
20	6yds	15
27	18yds	27
7	18+yds	6

GOALS SCORED/CONCEDED PER FIVE-MINUTE INTERVALS

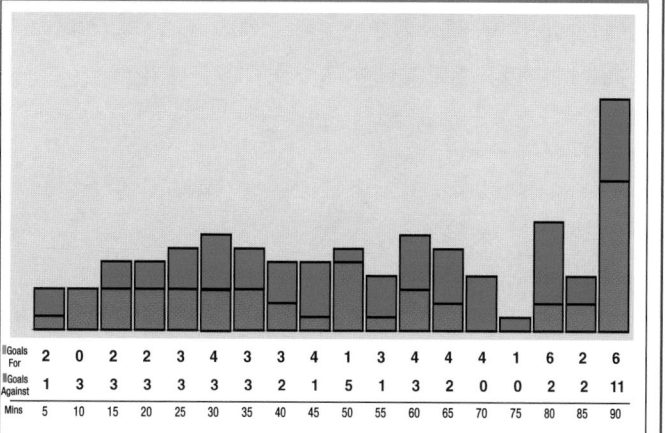

Mins	5	10	15	20	25	30	35	40	45	50	55	60	65	70	75	80	85	90
Goals For	2	0	2	2	3	4	3	4	1	3	4	4	4	1	6	2	6	
Goals Against	1	3	3	3	3	3	3	2	1	5	1	3	2	0	0	2	2	11

BLACKBURN ROVERS

CLUB SUMMARY

FORMED	1875
MANAGER	Sam Allardyce
GROUND	Ewood Park
CAPACITY	31,367
NICKNAME	Rovers
WEBSITE	www.rovers.co.uk

The New Football Pools PLAYER OF THE SEASON — Stephen Warnock

OVERALL

P	W	D	L	F	A	GD
47	15	13	19	55	71	-16

BARCLAYS PREMIER LEAGUE

Pos	P	W	D	L	F	A	GD	Pts
15	38	10	11	17	40	60	-20	41

HOME

Pos	P	W	D	L	F	A	GD	Pts
15	19	6	7	6	22	23	-1	25

AWAY

Pos	P	W	D	L	F	A	GD	Pts
12	19	4	4	11	18	37	-19	16

CUP PROGRESS DETAILS

Competition	Round reached	Knocked out by
FA Cup	R5	Coventry
Carling Cup	QF	Man Utd

BIGGEST WIN (ALL COMPS)
27/08/08 4–1 v Grimsby **LC2**

BIGGEST DEFEAT (ALL COMPS)
13/09/08 0–4 v Arsenal **PREM**

THE PLAYER WITH THE MOST

Shots on target
Morten Gamst Pedersen 36

Shots off target
Morten Gamst Pedersen 23

Shots without scoring
Carlos Villanueva 19

Assists
Morten Gamst Pedersen 8

Offsides
Benni McCarthy 30

Fouls
Christopher Samba 54

Fouls without a card
Roque Santa Cruz 15

Free-kicks won
El-Hadji Diouf 51

Defensive clearances
Christopher Samba 64

actim INDEX
for the 2008/09 Barclays Premier League Season

Rank	Player	Pts
65	Stephen Warnock	372
83	Ryan Nelsen	351
100	Paul Robinson	323
111	Andre Ooijer	311
119	Christopher Samba	304

ATTENDANCE RECORD

High	Low	Average
28,389	17,606	23,479
v West Brom (24/05/2009)	v Middlesbrough (25/10/2008)	

CLOCKWISE FROM TOP: Ryan Nelsen celebrates scoring his first ever Rovers goal in the win over Wigan; former manager Paul Ince has a bad day at the office; Benni McCarthy enjoys his extra-time winner against Sunderland in the FA Cup fourth round; Christopher Samba scores against Portsmouth

SAM ALLARDYCE'S reputation as a man who is able to get the most from under-achievers and players of limited ability was enhanced further after he steered Blackburn to Barclays Premier League safety.

Allardyce's ability to rejuvenate fading stars and produce results-driven teams was honed during an eight-year spell at Bolton. Although he could not work his magic fast enough to prevent a swift departure from Newcastle, he proved his Reebok exploits were not a flash in the pan during the second half of 2008/09.

Allardyce was installed at Ewood Park on 17th December, less than 48 hours after Paul Ince was sacked for a run of results which saw Rovers fail to win in 11 league matches. They sank to 19th in the table with just 13 points from 17 games and chairman John Williams – whose bold decision it had been to appoint Ince to his maiden top-flight job six months earlier – felt he had no option but to dispense with the former England midfielder.

Oddly, Blackburn had started the season relatively well with three victories and a draw in six matches to put them seventh in the table. However, they took just two points from October and one from November and, with confidence draining out of the squad, Ince was powerless to

turn things around. There was only one man Williams felt he could turn to in this time of crisis and that was Allardyce, who had been in the running to get the job before Ince only to pull out as he felt it was not the right time for him.

Within three days, the new manager had managed to achieve what Ince had failed to do in three months – produce a victory. The 3–0 home win over Stoke had much to do with strikers Benni McCarthy and Jason Roberts clicking instantly and sharing the goals between them. It was the signal for a turnaround in their home fortunes which, ultimately, secured their top-flight future.

Allardyce made Ewood Park a difficult place to visit once again. Prior to his arrival the team had taken just five points from eight matches, but they picked up 19 points in their subsequent 10 home games. That record could have been much better had they not thrown away points in a fashion

> **Allardyce made Ewood Park a difficult place to visit once again**

most unlike a side organised by Allardyce. Indeed six days after the Stoke win, the Ewood Park club were leading 2–0 at home to Manchester City on Boxing Day only to concede two goals in the last two minutes.

Despite that eventual result, Rovers' players were showing a new-found confidence, highlighted by their coming from 2–0 down against Bolton to get a draw with two goals in the last 24 minutes. Even defeats to Aston Villa and Manchester United and an FA Cup exit to Coca-Cola Championship side Coventry could not dampen spirits. Rovers bounced back to take seven points from their next three league matches, with wins over Hull and Fulham sandwiching a creditable goalless draw at home to Everton.

The team appeared to be heading in the right direction as they moved up to 15th on 30 points, but heavy defeats to Arsenal and Liverpool and a damaging reverse at Stoke in mid-April saw them back into the bottom three. However, two wins in their next three matches secured their safety much sooner than Allardyce could have anticipated and they were able to relax for the last fortnight of the season.

The achievement was all the greater as key strikers Roberts and Roque Santa Cruz missed the last two months of the season through injury, with Allardyce getting the best from his squad by choosing to play defender Christopher Samba in attack towards the end of the campaign.

BLACKBURN ROVERS

RESULTS 2008/09

August

16th ● Everton ....a W 2–3 **Att:** 38,675. **Ref:** A Marriner — **Blackburn** (4-4-2): Robinson, Ooijer▮, Samba, Nelsen, Warnock▮, Reid, Dunn¹ (Tugay 90), Mokoena, Pedersen (Treacy 76), Santa Cruz¹, Roberts (McCarthy 83). Subs not used: Brown, Villanueva, Simpson, Derbyshire.

23rd ● Hull ....h D 1–1 **Att:** 23,439. **Ref:** S Attwell — **Blackburn** (4-4-2): Robinson, Ooijer, Samba, Nelsen, Warnock, Reid, Mokoena (Tugay 67), Dunn (Emerton 46), Pedersen, Santa Cruz, Roberts¹ (McCarthy 81). Subs not used: Simpson, Treacy, Derbyshire, Brown.

27th ● Grimsby ....h W 4–1 **Att:** 8,379. **Ref:** M Oliver — **Blackburn** (4-4-2): Brown, Simpson, Khizanishvili, Nelsen (Judge 67), Treacy, Emerton¹ (Gallagher 70), Mokoena, Tugay, Pedersen (Marshall 76), Derbyshire², Villanueva¹. Subs not used: Robinson, Santa Cruz, Kane, Hodge.

30th ● West Ham ....a L 4–1 **Att:** 32,905. **Ref:** M Riley — **Blackburn** (4-4-2): Robinson, Ooijer▮, Samba, Nelsen▮, Warnock, Emerton▮, Reid, Grella▮ (Andrews 46), Pedersen (Treacy 66), Santa Cruz (Derbyshire 29), Roberts▮▮. Subs not used: Brown, Mokoena, Villanueva, Simpson.

September

13th ● Arsenal ....h L 0–4 **Att:** 23,041. **Ref:** M Dean — **Blackburn** (4-4-2): Robinson, Simpson (Derbyshire 73), Samba, Nelsen, Warnock▮, Emerton, Reid, Andrews, Pedersen (Treacy 69), Roberts (McCarthy 69), Santa Cruz. Subs not used: Tugay, Brown, Mokoena, Villanueva.

20th ● Fulham ....h W 1–0 **Att:** 19,398. **Ref:** L Probert — **Blackburn** (4-4-2): Robinson, Simpson, Samba, Nelsen, Warnock, Emerton, Andrews¹, Pedersen (Tugay 60), Treacy (Derbyshire¹ 75), Santa Cruz, Roberts (Villanueva 65). Subs not used: Brown, Ooijer, Mokoena, Fowler.

24th ● Everton ....h W 1–0 **Att:** 14,366. **Ref:** M Atkinson — **Blackburn** (4-4-2): Robinson (Brown 12), Simpson, Ooijer, Khizanishvili, Olsson¹, Villanueva▮ (Santa Cruz 72), Tugay, Warnock▮, Treacy (Pedersen 75), Derbyshire, Fowler. Subs not used: Samba, Nelsen, Kane, Roberts.

27th ● Newcastle ....a W 1–2 **Att:** 44,935. **Ref:** S Tanner — **Blackburn** (4-4-2): Brown, Simpson, Nelsen▮, Samba¹, Warnock▮, Emerton▮, Olsson, Tugay, Derbyshire (Ooijer 84), Santa Cruz¹ (Roberts▮ 84), Villanueva (Fowler 62). Subs not used: Bunn, Pedersen, Andrews, Treacy.

October

4th ● Man Utd ....h L 0–2 **Att:** 27,321. **Ref:** S Bennett — **Blackburn** (4-4-1-1): Brown, Ooijer, Samba▮, Nelsen, Olsson, Emerton, Tugay (Andrews 68), Warnock▮, Pedersen▮ (Treacy 58), Derbyshire, Santa Cruz (Roberts 50). Subs not used: Bunn, Mokoena, Villanueva, Fowler.

18th ● Bolton ....a D 0–0 **Att:** 24,778. **Ref:** H Webb — **Blackburn** (4-4-2): Robinson, Simpson, Samba, Ooijer, Emerton, Villanueva▮ (Derbyshire 62), Tugay▮, Warnock, Fowler (Andrews 74), Roberts (McCarthy 78). Subs not used: Brown, Grella, Khizanishvili, Treacy.

25th ● Middlesbrough ....h D 1–1 **Att:** 17,606. **Ref:** M Dean — **Blackburn** (4-4-2): Robinson, Simpson, Ooijer, Nelsen, Olsson▮ (Treacy 81), Emerton, Grella▮, Warnock, Villanueva, Santa Cruz, Derbyshire▮ (McCarthy¹ 65). Subs not used: Brown, Tugay, Khizanishvili, Andrews, Roberts.

29th ● Aston Villa ....a L 3–2 **Att:** 35,985. **Ref:** K Stroud — **Blackburn** (4-4-2): Robinson, Ooijer, Nelsen, Warnock¹ (Tugay 68), Emerton¹, Andrews, Simpson, Pedersen (Olsson 79), Villanueva, McCarthy (Derbyshire 79). Subs not used: Brown, Mokoena, Fowler, Roberts.

November

1st ● West Brom ....a D 2–2 **Att:** 24,976. **Ref:** M Jones — **Blackburn** (4-4-2): Robinson, Simpson (Tugay 46), Samba, Nelsen, Olsson (Pedersen 62), Emerton (Khizanishvili 77), Andrews¹, Grella, Warnock, McCarthy▮▮¹, Roberts. Subs not used: Brown, Villanueva, Fowler, Derbyshire.

9th ● Chelsea ....h L 0–2 **Att:** 20,670. **Ref:** C Foy — **Blackburn** (4-2-3-1): Robinson, Simpson, Khizanishvili, Nelsen, Olsson, Grella (Mokoena 45), Warnock▮, Villanueva, Andrews (Derbyshire 46), Pedersen, Roberts (Fowler 77). Subs not used: Brown, Samba, Tugay, Treacy.

12th ● Sunderland ....a W 1–2 **Att:** 18,555. **Ref:** R Styles — **Blackburn** (4-4-2): Robinson, Khizanishvili, Samba, Olsson, Tugay, Derbyshire, Mokoena▮, Treacy▮ (Warnock 67), Fowler (Villanueva 78), Haworth (Santa Cruz¹ 62). Subs not used: Brown, Ooijer, Nelsen, Judge.

15th ● Sunderland ....h L 1–2 **Att:** 21,798. **Ref:** S Tanner — **Blackburn** (4-4-2): Robinson, Ooijer, Samba¹, Khizanishvili▮, Warnock▮, Simpson, Andrews (Villanueva 62), Mokoena▮, Pedersen (Tugay 76), Santa Cruz, Roberts (Derbyshire 61). Subs not used: Brown, Fowler, Treacy, Judge.

23rd ● Tottenham ....a L 1–0 **Att:** 35,903. **Ref:** H Webb — **Blackburn** (4-4-2): Robinson, Ooijer▮, Samba, Nelsen, Olsson▮ (Derbyshire 71), Andrews▮, Mokoena, Pedersen (Treacy 81), McCarthy (Simpson 46), Santa Cruz. Subs not used: Brown, Tugay, Fowler, Roberts.

30th ● Portsmouth ....a L 3–2 **Att:** 18,111. **Ref:** M Halsey — **Blackburn** (4-4-2): Robinson, Ooijer▮, Samba, Nelsen, Warnock, Emerton, Andrews, Tugay¹, Pedersen (Villanueva 87), Santa Cruz, McCarthy (Derbyshire¹ 61). Subs not used: Brown, Mokoena, Simpson, Fowler, Roberts.

December

3rd ● Man Utd ....a L 5–3 **Att:** 53,997. **Ref:** A Wiley — **Blackburn** (4-4-2): Robinson, Olsson, Nelsen▮, Ooijer, Warnock, Treacy, Tugay (Pedersen 70), Mokoena, Emerton (McCarthy² 46), Derbyshire¹, Santa Cruz (Fowler 76). Subs not used: Brown, Villanueva, Judge, Roberts.

6th ● Liverpool ....h L 1–3 **Att:** 26,920. **Ref:** A Marriner — **Blackburn** (4-4-2): Robinson, Ooijer, Samba, Nelsen, Warnock▮, Emerton, Andrews▮, Tugay (Vogel 84), Pedersen (McCarthy 81), Santa Cruz¹, Derbyshire (Treacy 90). Subs not used: Brown, Villanueva, Simpson, Fowler.

13th ● Wigan ....a L 3–0 **Att:** 18,003. **Ref:** H Webb — **Blackburn** (4-4-2): Robinson, Ooijer, Samba, Nelsen▮, Warnock, Emerton, Tugay (Roberts 61), Andrews (Treacy 78), Pedersen (Dunn 46), Santa Cruz, Derbyshire. Subs not used: Brown, McCarthy, Villanueva, Simpson.

20th ● Stoke ....h W 3–0 **Att:** 23,004. **Ref:** P Walton — **Blackburn** (4-4-2): Robinson, Ooijer, Samba, Nelsen, Warnock, Emerton (Simpson 85), Dunn (Tugay 70), Andrews, Pedersen, McCarthy² (Derbyshire 79), Roberts¹. Subs not used: Brown, Khizanishvili, Mokoena, Judge.

26th ● Sunderland ....a D 0–0 **Att:** 44,680. **Ref:** M Atkinson — **Blackburn** (4-4-2): Robinson, Ooijer▮, Samba▮, Nelsen (Mokoena 90), Warnock, Emerton, Dunn (Tugay 62), Andrews, Pedersen, Roberts, McCarthy▮ (Derbyshire 88). Subs not used: Brown, Khizanishvili, Treacy, Olsson.

28th ● Man City ....h D 2–2 **Att:** 25,200. **Ref:** H Webb — **Blackburn** (4-4-2): Robinson, Ooijer▮, Samba, Nelsen▮, Warnock, Emerton, Tugay▮ (Mokoena 73), Andrews, Pedersen, McCarthy¹ (Derbyshire 85), Roberts¹. Subs not used: Brown, Khizanishvili, Vogel, Treacy, Olsson.

January

5th ● Blyth Spartans ....a W 0–1 **Att:** 3,445. **Ref:** A Marriner — **Blackburn** (4-4-2): Bunn, Simpson, Mokoena▮, Khizanishvili, Olsson, Vogel, Grella (Andrews 60), Treacy, Judge, Villanueva¹ (Roberts 59), Derbyshire (Hodge 83). Subs not used: Brown, Gunning, Doran, Haworth.

17th ● Newcastle ....h W 3–0 **Att:** 25,583. **Ref:** R Styles — **Blackburn** (4-4-2): Robinson, Ooijer, Samba (Dunn 45), Nelsen, Warnock, Emerton, Andrews, Tugay (Grella¹ 59), Pedersen, Roberts¹², McCarthy (Santa Cruz 70). Subs not used: Bunn, Mokoena, Treacy, Derbyshire.

24th ● Sunderland ....a D 0–0 **Att:** 22,634. **Ref:** L Probert — **Blackburn** (4-4-2): Robinson, Simpson, Samba▮, Nelsen, Warnock (Givet 73), Olsson▮ (Haworth 56), Mokoena▮, Grella, Pedersen, Santa Cruz (Villanueva 67), McCarthy. Subs not used: Bunn, Emerton, Khizanishvili, Andrews.

28th ● Bolton ....h D 2–2 **Att:** 25,205. **Ref:** M Dean — **Blackburn** (4-4-2): Robinson, Ooijer (Santa Cruz 58), Samba, Nelsen, Warnock¹, Emerton▮, Andrews, Grella▮ (Mokoena 90), Pedersen (Tugay 57), Roberts▮, McCarthy¹. Subs not used: Bunn, Villanueva, Givet, Simpson.

31st ● Middlesbrough ....a D 0–0 **Att:** 24,303. **Ref:** C Foy — **Blackburn** (4-4-2): Robinson, Ooijer▮, Nelsen▮, Samba, Warnock, Emerton (Dunn 50), Andrews (Tugay 42), Grella, Pedersen▮, McCarthy▮ (Roberts 73), Santa Cruz. Subs not used: Bunn, Villanueva, Givet, Simpson.

February

4th ● Sunderland ....h W 2–1 **Att:** 10,112. **Ref:** P Dowd — **Blackburn** (4-4-2): Robinson, Simpson▮, Khizanishvili, Nelsen (Ooijer 87), Givet, Villanueva, Mokoena▮¹, Dunn (Tugay 61), Treacy▮, Santa Cruz (McCarthy¹ 72), Roberts. Subs not used: Bunn, Pedersen, Olsson, Doran.

7th ● Aston Villa ....h L 0–2 **Att:** 24,267. **Ref:** S Bennett — **Blackburn** (4-4-2): Robinson, Ooijer, Samba, Nelsen, Warnock, Pedersen, Grella, Andrews (Tugay▮ 46), Dunn (Diouf 46), McCarthy▮, Roberts (Santa Cruz 74). Subs not used: Bunn, Khizanishvili, Villanueva, Givet.

● Barclays Premier League ● FA Cup ● Carling Cup ● UEFA Champions League ● UEFA Cup   ▮ Yellow Card ▮ Red Card

RESULTS 2008/09

14th	● Coventry ....h	D 2–2	**Att:** 15,053. **Ref:** S Tanner — **Blackburn** (4-4-2): Robinson, Simpson, Samba‖[1], Khizanishvili‖, Givet, Villanueva, Dunn (Treacy 71), Tugay (Andrews 65), Warnock, Santa Cruz[1], Roberts (McCarthy 78). Subs not used: Bunn, Nelsen, Grella, Doran.
21st	● Man Utd ....a	L 2–1	**Att:** 75,000. **Ref:** H Webb — **Blackburn** (4-1-4-1): Robinson, Ooijer, Nelsen, Givet‖, Warnock, Grella (McCarthy 79), Diouf (Treacy 83), Andrews‖, Dunn (Tugay 73), Pedersen, Santa Cruz[1]. Subs not used: Brown, Khizanishvili, Mokoena, Roberts.
24th	● Coventry ....a	L 1–0	**Att:** 22,793. **Ref:** M Riley — **Blackburn** (4-4-2): Brown‖, Simpson, Samba, Khizanishvili (Givet 81), Olsson, Villanueva (Santa Cruz 68), Mokoena, Tugay, Treacy (Warnock 68), McCarthy, Roberts. Subs not used: Robinson, Nelsen, Pedersen, Doran.

March

1st	● Hull ....a	W 1–2	**Att:** 24,612. **Ref:** M Atkinson — **Blackburn** (4-5-1): Robinson (Brown 46), Ooijer, Nelsen, Samba, Givet, Diouf‖ (Mokoena 83), Grella, Andrews[1], Warnock‖, Pedersen‖‖, Santa Cruz (Roberts 86). Subs not used: Tugay, McCarthy, Treacy, Villanueva.
4th	● Everton ....h	D 0–0	**Att:** 21,445. **Ref:** A Wiley — **Blackburn** (4-3-3): Brown, Ooijer, Samba, Nelsen, Givet‖ (Mokoena 64), Andrews, Grella (Tugay 46), Warnock, Santa Cruz, Roberts, Diouf (Treacy 88). Subs not used: Bunn, Dunn, McCarthy, Simpson.
11th	● Fulham ....a	W 1–2	**Att:** 22,259. **Ref:** R Styles — **Blackburn** (4-3-3): Robinson, Ooijer, Samba, Nelsen, Givet, Andrews (McCarthy 56), Tugay (Mokoena 82), Warnock, Diouf[1], Roberts[1], Pedersen (Dunn 86). Subs not used: Bunn, Khizanishvili, Villanueva, Simpson.
14th	● Arsenal ....a	L 4–0	**Att:** 60,091. **Ref:** P Dowd — **Blackburn** (4-5-1): Robinson, Simpson, Samba, Ooijer‖, Givet (Dunn 13), Diouf‖, Mokoena‖, Khizanishvili‖ (McCarthy 66), Warnock (Olsson 55), Pedersen, Roberts. Subs not used: Bunn, Tugay, Andrews, Treacy.
21st	● West Ham ....h	D 1–1	**Att:** 21,672. **Ref:** C Foy — **Blackburn** (4-4-2): Robinson, Ooijer (Andrews[1] 46), Samba, Nelsen‖, Givet, Diouf, Mokoena‖, Warnock, Pedersen, McCarthy, Roberts. Subs not used: Brown, Tugay, Dunn, Khizanishvili, Villanueva, Treacy.

April

4th	● Tottenham ....h	W 2–1	**Att:** 21,891. **Ref:** P Walton — **Blackburn** (4-4-2): Robinson, Andrews, Samba‖, Nelsen, Givet, Diouf, Mokoena (Tugay 63), Warnock, Pedersen (Dunn 26), Roberts (Ooijer[1] 46), McCarthy[1]. Subs not used: Brown, Villanueva, Treacy, Olsson.
11th	● Liverpool ....a	L 4–0	**Att:** 43,466. **Ref:** H Webb — **Blackburn** (4-1-4-1): Robinson, Andrews‖, Nelsen, Givet, Mokoena (Doran 46), Dunn (Villanueva 59), Tugay (Grella 66), Warnock, Treacy, Samba. Subs not used: Bunn, McCarthy, Khizanishvili, Olsson.
18th	● Stoke ....a	L 1–0	**Att:** 27,500. **Ref:** H Webb — **Blackburn** (4-5-1): Robinson, Ooijer, Samba, Nelsen, Givet, Diouf, Andrews, Mokoena (Dunn 81), Warnock‖, Pedersen, McCarthy (Villanueva 68). Subs not used: Bunn, Grella, Khizanishvili, Olsson, Doran.
26th	● Wigan ....h	W 2–0	**Att:** 25,019. **Ref:** P Walton — **Blackburn** (4-4-2): Robinson, Ooijer, Nelsen[1], Givet, Warnock, Diouf, Grella (Andrews 78), Tugay (Dunn 63), Pedersen, Samba, McCarthy[1] (Villanueva 81). Subs not used: Bunn, Khizanishvili, Olsson, Doran.

May

2nd	● Man City ....a	L 3–1	**Att:** 43,967. **Ref:** M Dean — **Blackburn** (4-4-2): Robinson, Ooijer‖, Nelsen‖, Givet, Warnock, Diouf, Grella‖, Tugay (Doran 64), Pedersen, McCarthy (Villanueva 46), Samba (Andrews[1] 64). Subs not used: Bunn, Khizanishvili, Mokoena, Olsson.
9th	● Portsmouth ....h	W 2–0	**Att:** 24,234. **Ref:** M Riley — **Blackburn** (4-4-2): Robinson, Andrews‖, Nelsen, Givet, Warnock, Diouf, Grella, Tugay, Pedersen[1], Samba, McCarthy[1] (Mokoena 83). Subs not used: Bunn, Khizanishvili, Villanueva, Treacy, Olsson, Doran.
17th	● Chelsea ....a	L 2–0	**Att:** 40,804. **Ref:** R Styles — **Blackburn** (4-4-2): Robinson, Andrews, Ooijer (Doran 44), Givet (Khizanishvili 46), Warnock, Diouf, Tugay, Grella, Pedersen (McCarthy 65), Samba, Villanueva. Subs not used: Bunn, Mokoena, Treacy, Olsson.
24th	● West Brom ....h	D 0–0	**Att:** 28,389. **Ref:** M Jones — **Blackburn** (4-4-2): Robinson, Andrews, Ooijer, Givet, Warnock, Diouf, Tugay (Olsson 85), Pedersen, Samba (Roberts‖ 59), McCarthy, Grella (Mokoena 69). Subs not used: Bunn, Khizanishvili, Villanueva, Treacy.

● Barclays Premier League ● FA Cup ● Carling Cup ● UEFA Champions League ● UEFA Cup

‖ Yellow Card ‖ Red Card

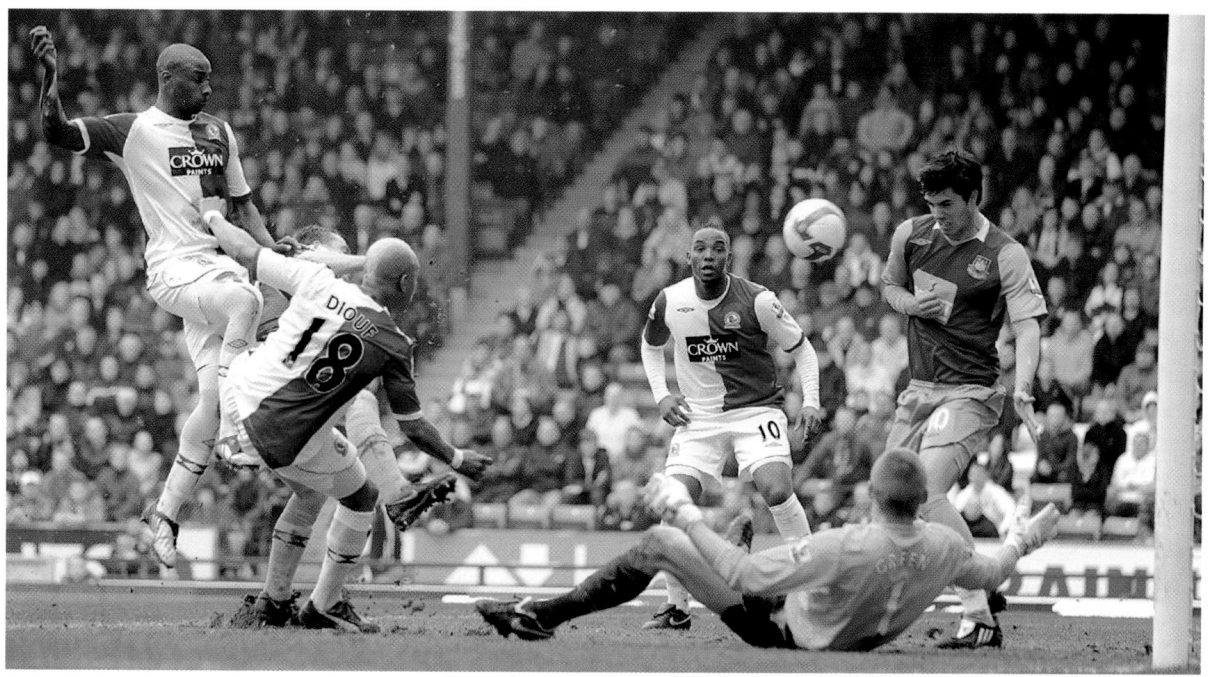

El-Hadji Diouf fires into the net in the 1–1 draw with West Ham United, but the 'goal' is ruled out for offside

BLACKBURN ROVERS

BARCLAYS PREMIER LEAGUE GOALKEEPER STATS

Player	Minutes on pitch	Appearances	Match starts	Completed matches	Sub appearances	Subbed off	SAVES BREAKDOWN Saved with feet	Punched	Parried	Tipped over	Fumbled	Tipped round	Caught	Blocked	Clean sheets	Goals conceded	Minutes since conceding	Save %	PENALTIES Saved	Resulting in goals	Opposition miss	Yellow cards	Red cards
Jason Brown	335	4	3	3	1	0	0	1	0	1	0	2	14	0	1	4	175	82.61	0	1	0	0	0
Paul Robinson	3289	35	35	34	0	1	1	24	26	6	0	5	77	1	10	56	128	72.28	0	4	1	0	0

BARCLAYS PREMIER LEAGUE OUTFIELD PLAYER STATS

Player	Minutes on pitch	Appearances	Match starts	Completed matches	Substitute appearances	Subbed off	Goals scored	Minutes since scoring	Assists	Shots on target	Shots off target	Crosses	Defensive clearances	Defensive blocks	Fouls committed	Free-kicks won	Caught offside	Yellow cards	Red cards
Keith Andrews	2524	33	27	21	6	6	4	313	0	14	10	14	13	13	43	23	0	6	0
Matt Derbyshire	752	17	5	2	12	3	2	250	1	8	4	12	2	1	5	9	10	2	0
El-Hadji Diouf	1259	14	13	10	1	3	1	883	1	7	3	42	2	1	15	27	9	3	0
Aaron Doran	130	3	0	0	3	0	0	-	0	0	0	0	0	0	2	4	1	1	0
David Dunn	800	15	7	0	8	7	1	779	0	13	4	10	2	2	9	12	1	0	0
Brett Emerton	1766	20	19	15	1	4	1	956	0	10	14	54	8	2	31	11	2	4	0
Robbie Fowler	121	3	1	0	2	1	0	-	0	0	0	0	0	0	0	1	0	0	0
Gael Givet	1173	14	14	11	0	3	0	-	0	0	0	6	7	4	6	8	0	2	0
Vincenzo Grella	1285	17	15	8	2	7	0	-	0	10	2	6	7	3	29	8	0	5	0
Tugay Kerimoglu	1642	29	15	5	14	10	1	1160	0	8	8	6	2	0	15	14	0	3	0
Zurab Khizanishvili	320	5	3	2	2	1	0	-	0	0	0	0	5	1	5	6	0	4	0
Benni McCarthy	1600	28	18	5	10	12	10	146	3	18	22	13	3	1	24	11	30	5	1
Aaron Mokoena	902	18	9	5	9	4	0	-	0	2	3	1	4	0	10	10	0	3	0
Ryan Nelsen	3288	35	35	33	0	2	1	270	1	3	7	5	61	26	27	26	0	7	0
Martin Olsson	528	9	6	3	3	2	0	-	0	0	0	3	6	4	12	3	0	2	1
Andre Ooijer	2838	32	30	28	2	2	0	480	0	6	3	19	22	18	40	15	0	8	0
Morten Gamst Pedersen	2661	33	32	16	1	15	1	228	8	36	23	83	14	1	36	42	10	3	1
Steven Reid	382	4	4	4	0	0	0	-	2	5	5	7	0	1	1	6	0	0	0
Jason Roberts	1819	26	20	10	6	9	7	254	5	30	8	10	4	1	50	39	29	4	1
Christopher Samba	3226	35	35	32	0	3	2	2225	4	15	21	3	64	16	54	36	7	4	0
Roque Santa Cruz	1571	20	17	13	3	4	4	250	2	14	21	5	7	0	15	15	14	0	0
Danny Simpson	936	12	10	8	2	2	0	-	0	1	2	15	4	0	12	9	0	2	0
Keith Treacy	347	12	2	1	10	1	0	-	0	2	1	9	3	0	6	5	1	0	0
Carlos Villanueva	693	13	6	4	7	2	0	-	1	7	12	14	2	0	12	14	1	1	0
Johann Vogel	11	1	0	0	1	0	0	-	0	0	0	0	0	0	0	0	0	0	0
Stephen Warnock	3468	37	37	35	0	2	3	1170	3	10	13	43	27	9	42	30	2	8	0

actim | BARCLAYS PREMIER LEAGUE

SEASON TOTALS

Goals scored	40
Goals conceded	60
Clean sheets	10
Shots on target	219
Shots off target	186
Shots per goal	10.12
Pens awarded	7
Pens scored	4
Pens conceded	6
Offsides	117
Corners	199
Crosses	381
Players used	28
Fouls committed	501
Free-kicks won	387

CARDS RECEIVED

77 **4**

SEQUENCES

Wins 2
(20/09/08–27/09/08)
Losses 6
(09/11/08–13/12/08)
Draws 2
(on three occasions)
Undefeated 6
(20/12/08–31/01/09)
Without win 11
(04/10/08–13/12/08)
Undefeated home 4
(20/12/08–28/01/09)
Undefeated away 2
(on three occasions)
Without scoring 2
(on three occasions)
Without conceding 2
(20/12/08–26/12/08)
Scoring 3
(on four occasions)
Conceding 9
(25/10/08–13/12/08)

League position at the end of each week

League position at the end of: August 10, September 7, October 13, November 19, December 19, January 18, February 19, March 17, April 15, May 15

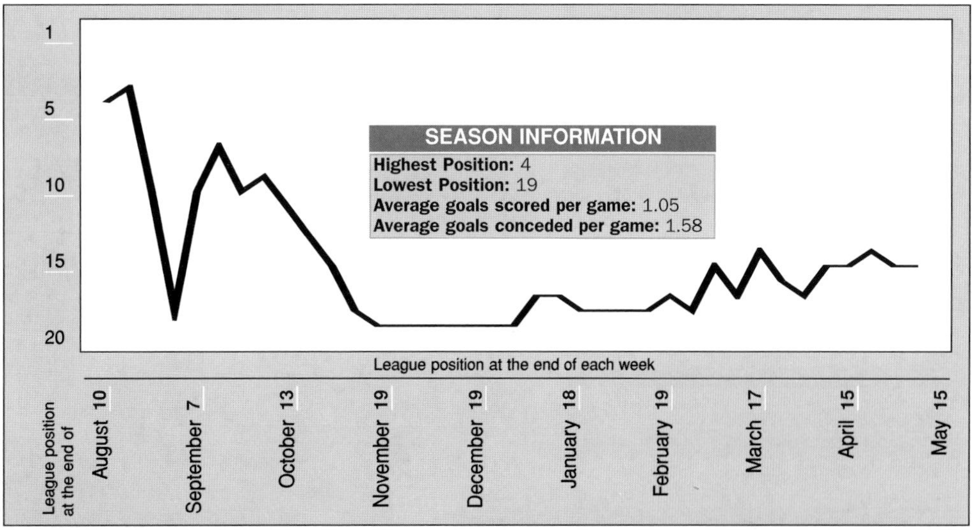

SEASON INFORMATION
Highest Position: 4
Lowest Position: 19
Average goals scored per game: 1.05
Average goals conceded per game: 1.58

MATCH RECORDS

Goals scored per match

		W	D	L	Pts
Failed to score	15	0	5	10	5
Scored 1 goal	9	1	3	5	6
Scored 2 goals	11	6	3	2	21
Scored 3 goals	3	3	0	0	9
Scored 4+ goals	0	0	0	0	0

Goals conceded per match

		W	D	L	Pts
Clean sheet	10	5	5	0	20
Conceded 1 goal	9	4	3	2	15
Conceded 2 goals	10	1	3	6	6
Conceded 3 goals	5	0	0	5	0
Conceded 4+ goals	4	0	0	4	0

GOALS SCORED/CONCEDED PER FIVE-MINUTE INTERVALS

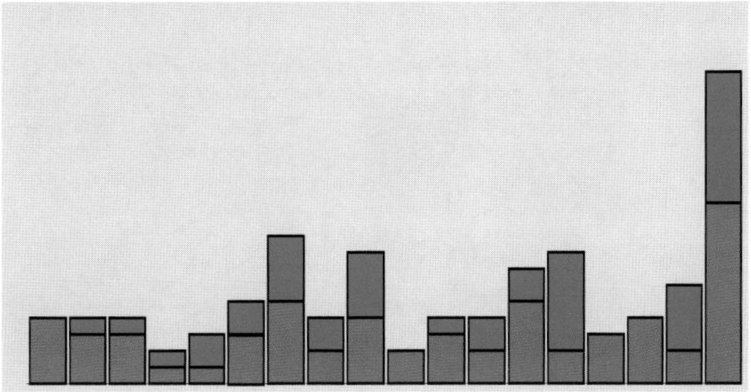

Goals For	0	1	1	1	2	2	4	2	4	0	1	2	2	6	0	0	4	8
Goals Against	4	3	3	1	1	3	5	2	4	2	3	2	5	2	3	4	2	11
Mins	5	10	15	20	25	30	35	40	45	50	55	60	65	70	75	80	85	90

QUICK-FIRE GOALS

From the start of a match
Andre Ooijer (v Arsenal) 1:14

By a substitute after coming on
Matt Derbyshire (v Portsmouth) 0:40

LAST-GASP GOALS

From the start of a match
Brett Emerton (v Aston Villa) 93:37

By a substitute after coming on
Andre Ooijer (v Tottenham) 43:35

GOAL DETAILS

How the goals were struck

SCORED		CONCEDED
21	Right foot	35
10	Left foot	14
9	Headers	9
0	Others	2

How the goals were struck

SCORED		CONCEDED
23	Open play	40
5	Cross	8
4	Corner	2
4	Penalties	5
1	Direct from free-kick	1
3	Free-kick	2
0	Own goals	2

Distance from goal

SCORED		CONCEDED
19	6yds	21
17	18yds	35
4	18+yds	4

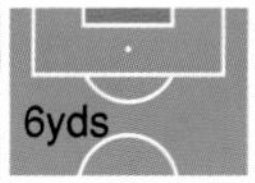

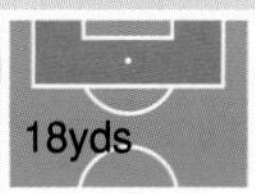

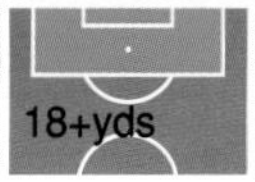

BOLTON WANDERERS

CLUB SUMMARY

FORMED	1874
MANAGER	Gary Megson
GROUND	Reebok Stadium
CAPACITY	27,879
NICKNAME	The Trotters
WEBSITE	www.bwfc.co.uk

The New **Football Pools**
PLAYER OF THE SEASON — Kevin Davies

OVERALL

P	W	D	L	F	A	GD
40	11	8	21	43	57	-14

BARCLAYS PREMIER LEAGUE

Pos	P	W	D	L	F	A	GD	Pts
13	38	11	8	19	41	53	-12	41

HOME

Pos	P	W	D	L	F	A	GD	Pts
14	19	7	5	7	21	21	0	26

AWAY

Pos	P	W	D	L	F	A	GD	Pts
13	19	4	3	12	20	32	-12	15

CUP PROGRESS DETAILS

Competition	Round reached	Knocked out by
FA Cup	R3	Sunderland
Carling Cup	R2	Northampton

BIGGEST WIN (ALL COMPS)
29/11/08 4–1 v Sunderland **PREM**

BIGGEST DEFEAT (ALL COMPS)
26/12/08 0–3 on two occasions

THE PLAYER WITH THE MOST

Shots on target
Matt Taylor..................................... 68

Shots off target
Matt Taylor..................................... 37

Shots without scoring
Gavin McCann.................................. 34

Assists
Gretar Rafn Steinsson........................ 5

Offsides
Johan Elmander 22

Fouls
Kevin Davies 115

Fouls without a card
Chris Basham 5

Free-kicks won
Kevin Davies 92

Defensive clearances
Gary Cahill 81

actim INDEX for the 2008/09 Barclays Premier League Season

Rank	Player	Pts
20	Kevin Davies	468
30	Gary Cahill	434
51	Jlloyd Samuel	391
55	Jussi Jaaskelainen	386
57	Matt Taylor	382

ATTENDANCE RECORD

High	Low	Average
26,021	19,884	22,486
v Man Utd (17/01/2009)	v Portsmouth (20/12/2008)	

CLOCKWISE FROM TOP: Kevin Davies battles for possession in Bolton's 1–0 win against Portsmouth; Ricardo Gardner celebrates scoring the only goal in a home victory over Newcastle; Gary Megson shouts his orders; Matt Taylor curls home a free-kick in the 2–1 home victory against West Ham in February

BOLTON manager Gary Megson will spend the summer trying to convince chairman Phil Gartside that new players must be signed and the cost-cutting has to stop.

Megson has been forced to work with arguably the smallest pool of players in the Barclays Premier League. Yet they managed to remain in the top flight for the second successive season under his stewardship.

Having taken over from Sammy Lee and kept Bolton in the Barclays Premier League during his first season, fans were unsure of what to expect from Megson's side in 2008/09. Predictably, many pundits tipped them to spend the campaign fighting relegation.

In truth they never really looked like going down and key players Gary Cahill, Matt Taylor and Kevin Davies all impressed enough to be mentioned as possible England call-ups. The trio enhanced their reputations, and for all those Trotters fans still doubting the manager's credentials, it should also be remembered that Cahill and Taylor were Megson's own signings.

Cahill was recruited from Aston Villa in January 2008 for a fee of £5million and is now one of the first names on the Wanderers' teamsheet. Martin O'Neill may well rue his decision to allow the England Under-21 centre-back to leave Villa Park as Megson is convinced that Cahill is destined to win full international honours.

Taylor was recruited at the same time as Cahill, the duo playing key roles in the club's successful relegation scrap of 2007/08 before blossoming further in their first full season at the Reebok Stadium. Taylor's educated left foot was a key factor in Bolton's style of play and heavy reliance on set-pieces. The former Reading and Portsmouth man grabbed a very healthy 10 goals during the campaign, and has become a real favourite with supporters.

Davies was again superb, scoring 11 league goals and proving a constant menace for opponents with his burly physique and intelligent play.

However, the jury remains firmly out on Johan Elmander after he struggled during a disappointing first season at the Reebok. Megson persuaded the Bolton hierarchy to pay Toulouse £10million for the Sweden international

last summer but, despite scoring on his debut, he could only return five goals.

Allowing skipper Kevin Nolan to join Newcastle in January looked like a gamble that could backfire spectacularly, but young midfielder Mark Davies arrived from Wolves at around the same time and showed several flashes of quality. While Davies was left frustrated by a niggling injury, he could well make a big impact in the Barclays Premier League in the 2009/10 season.

During 2008/09, long-serving goalkeeper Jaaskelainen enhanced his reputation as one of the best in the business. He was outstanding in some key games, winning particular plaudits in both the home and away games against Hull. Another success was homegrown midfielder Chris Basham who made a number of first-team appearances and looked at home in a number of positions in defence and midfield.

Looking back, Megson was pleased with his side's overall progress, although he admits that he is still struggling to win over the Reebok faithful. He said: 'There has been a lot of good things this season. We have scored more goals and let fewer in. There have been small improvements. We stayed up and made a profit. There must be a lot of other clubs having huge problems if I'm getting stick.'

However, Megson is now keen to make serious investment during the summer in all areas, apart from the goalkeeping position with Jaaskelainen only getting better with age. If funds are not forthcoming, the manager fears that Bolton might struggle to avoid the drop.

Megson said: 'Money is tight everywhere, but we have got to kick on. If we do not then we are going to have real problems next season. We have made a profit in transfer business in the last two years and the wage bill is down.

'We are pleased, but that was not my brief. If you do not keep going forward you get problems. A number of players have gone from here and because of our size not as many have been brought in. We have a chance to redress that balance and it has got to happen. We have already identified targets we would like to bring in. We want to improve.'

> **Kevin Davies was again superb, scoring 11 league goals and proving a constant menace**

RESULTS 2008/09

August

16th	● Stoke ....h	W 3–1	**Att:** 22,717. **Ref:** C Foy — **Bolton** (4-4-2): Jaaskelainen, Steinsson▮, Cahill, A O'Brien, Samuel, J O'Brien, Nolan, Muamba, Taylor, K Davies¹, Elmander¹ (McCann 76). Subs not used: Al Habsi, Hunt, Gardner, Mustapha, Shittu, Cohen.
23rd	● Newcastle ....a	L 1–0	**Att:** 47,711. **Ref:** S Bennett — **Bolton** (4-4-2): Jaaskelainen, Steinsson, Cahill, A O'Brien, Samuel, J O'Brien (Mustapha 85), Nolan, Muamba, Taylor (Gardner 65), K Davies, Elmander (McCann▮ 15). Subs not used: Al Habsi, Hunt, Dzemaili, Shittu.
26th	● Northampton ....h	L 1–2	**Att:** 7,136. **Ref:** G Laws — **Bolton** (4-3-3): Jaaskelainen, Steinsson, Cahill▮, Shittu, Samuel (Nolan¹ 64), McCann (A O'Brien 39), Muamba, J O'Brien, Mustapha (K Davies 64), Helguson, Gardner. Subs not used: Al Habsi, Hunt, Dzemaili, Fojut.
30th	● West Brom ....h	D 0–0	**Att:** 20,387. **Ref:** K Stroud — **Bolton** (4-4-1-1): Jaaskelainen, Steinsson, A O'Brien, Shittu, Samuel, J O'Brien (Riga 14), McCann▮, Muamba, Gardner, Nolan▮, K Davies. Subs not used: Al Habsi, Hunt, Helguson, Vaz Te, Dzemaili, Fojut.

September

13th	● Fulham ....a	L 2–1	**Att:** 23,656. **Ref:** S Tanner — **Bolton** (4-5-1): Jaaskelainen (Helguson 64), Shittu, A O'Brien, Samuel, Gardner, Muamba, Nolan▮, McCann (Riga 51), J O'Brien, K Davies¹. Subs not used: Al Habsi, Hunt, Vaz Te, Cohen, Fojut.
20th	● Arsenal ....h	L 1–3	**Att:** 22,694. **Ref:** S Bennett — **Bolton** (4-1-4-1): Jaaskelainen, Steinsson, Shittu, A O'Brien, Samuel, J O'Brien (McCann 61), Smolarek (Riga 56), Muamba▮ (Vaz Te 81), Nolan, Gardner, K Davies▮. Subs not used: Al Habsi, Hunt, Helguson, Cohen.
27th	● Man Utd ....a	L 2–0	**Att:** 75,484. **Ref:** R Styles — **Bolton** (4-5-1): Jaaskelainen, Steinsson, Cahill, A O'Brien, Samuel, K Davies▮, Nolan, McCann▮, Muamba, Gardner (Smolarek 73), Elmander¹ (Vaz Te 66). Subs not used: Al Habsi, Taylor, J O'Brien, Riga, Shittu.

October

5th	● West Ham.......................a	W 1–3	**Att:** 33,715. **Ref:** M Dean — **Bolton** (4-5-1): Jaaskelainen, Steinsson, A O'Brien, Cahill¹, Samuel, K Davies¹, Nolan▮, McCann, Muamba (J O'Brien 80), Gardner, Elmander (Taylor¹ 73). Subs not used: Al Habsi, Hunt, Smolarek, Riga, Shittu.
18th	● Blackburn ....h	D 0–0	**Att:** 24,778. **Ref:** H Webb — **Bolton** (4-1-4-1): Jaaskelainen (J O'Brien 77), A O'Brien, Cahill, Samuel, McCann, K Davies, Nolan, Muamba (Gardner 69), Taylor (Riga 86), Elmander. Subs not used: Al Habsi, Hunt, Smolarek, Shittu.
26th	● Tottenham ....a	L 2–0	**Att:** 35,507. **Ref:** A Marriner — **Bolton** (4-5-1): Jaaskelainen▮, Steinsson, Cahill, O'Brien, Samuel, K Davies, Nolan▮, Muamba (Gardner 85), McCann▮, Taylor, Elmander (Riga 85). Subs not used: Al Habsi, Hunt, Smolarek, Helguson, Shittu.
29th	● Everton ....h	L 0–1	**Att:** 21,692. **Ref:** P Dowd — **Bolton** (4-4-2): Jaaskelainen, Steinsson, Cahill, O'Brien, Samuel▮, Riga, Nolan, Muamba, Taylor, K Davies, Elmander. Subs not used: Al Habsi, Hunt, Smolarek, Gardner, Helguson, Shittu, Cohen.

November

2nd	● Man City ....h	W 2–0	**Att:** 21,095. **Ref:** M Riley — **Bolton** (4-5-1): Jaaskelainen▮, Steinsson, Cahill, O'Brien, Samuel, Riga (Gardner¹ 43), McCann, Nolan, Muamba, Taylor, K Davies. Subs not used: Al Habsi, Hunt, Smolarek, Helguson, Shittu, Basham.
8th	● Hull ....a	W 0–1	**Att:** 24,903. **Ref:** A Wiley — **Bolton** (4-4-2): Jaaskelainen, Steinsson, Cahill, O'Brien, Samuel, Muamba▮, Gardner▮, McCann, Taylor¹, Elmander (Smolarek 77), K Davies. Subs not used: Al Habsi, Helguson, Shittu, Basham, Sissons, Obadeyi.
15th	● Liverpool ....h	L 0–2	**Att:** 24,893. **Ref:** R Styles — **Bolton** (4-5-1): Jaaskelainen, Steinsson, Cahill, O'Brien, Samuel, Taylor (Smolarek 84), Nolan▮, Muamba (Gardner 46), McCann, Elmander, K Davies. Subs not used: Al Habsi, Helguson, Shittu, Basham, Obadeyi.
22nd	● Middlesbrough ....a	W 1–3	**Att:** 24,487. **Ref:** M Atkinson — **Bolton** (4-5-1): Jaaskelainen, Steinsson¹, Cahill▮, O'Brien, Samuel▮, Taylor¹ (Gardner 89), McCann¹, Muamba, Nolan▮, Elmander¹ (Smolarek 84), K Davies. Subs not used: Al Habsi, Riga, Shittu, Basham, Obadeyi.
29th	● Sunderland ....a	W 1–4	**Att:** 35,457. **Ref:** C Foy — **Bolton** (4-1-4-1): Jaaskelainen, Steinsson, Cahill¹, O'Brien, Samuel, Muamba, K Davies, Nolan, Taylor¹ (Gardner 46), Elmander² (Basham 89). Subs not used: Al Habsi, Smolarek, Riga, Shittu, Obadeyi.

December

6th	● Chelsea ....h	L 0–2	**Att:** 22,023. **Ref:** H Webb — **Bolton** (4-5-1): Jaaskelainen, Steinsson, Cahill, O'Brien, Samuel (Smolarek 80), K Davies▮, McCann, Nolan, Muamba (Gardner 46), Taylor, Elmander. Subs not used: Al Habsi, Riga, Shittu, Basham, Obadeyi.
13th	● Aston Villa......................a	L 4–2	**Att:** 35,134. **Ref:** L Probert — **Bolton** (4-5-1): Jaaskelainen, Steinsson, Cahill, O'Brien, Samuel, K Davies¹, McCann, Nolan, Muamba (Gardner 53), Taylor, Elmander¹ (Smolarek 74). Subs not used: Al Habsi, Riga, Shittu, Basham, Obadeyi.
20th	● Portsmouth ....h	W 2–1	**Att:** 19,884. **Ref:** M Atkinson — **Bolton** (4-5-1): Jaaskelainen, Steinsson, Cahill, O'Brien, Samuel, K Davies, Nolan, McCann, Taylor¹, Gardner¹ (Muamba 83), Elmander. Subs not used: Al Habsi, Smolarek, Riga, Shittu, Basham, Obadeyi.
26th	● Liverpool ....a	L 3–0	**Att:** 43,548. **Ref:** A Wiley — **Bolton** (4-5-1): Jaaskelainen, Steinsson▮, Cahill, O'Brien, Samuel (K Davies 46), Muamba, Nolan▮, McCann▮, Taylor (Riga 66), Gardner, Elmander (Smolarek 46). Subs not used: Al Habsi, Shittu, Basham, Obadeyi.
28th	● Wigan ....h	L 0–1	**Att:** 23,726. **Ref:** P Dowd — **Bolton** (4-4-1-1): Jaaskelainen, Steinsson, Shittu, O'Brien, Samuel (Riga 65), Taylor, Nolan▮ (Muamba 64), McCann, Gardner (Obadeyi 87), Elmander, K Davies. Subs not used: Al Habsi, Smolarek, Fogut, Basham.

January

3rd	● Sunderland ....a	L 2–1	**Att:** 20,685. **Ref:** S Bennett — **Bolton** (4-4-2): Jaaskelainen, Steinsson, Shittu▮, O'Brien, Samuel (Riga 86), Nolan▮, Muamba▮, Gardner, Taylor▮, Elmander, K Davies (Smolarek¹ 73). Subs not used: Bogdan, Basham, Obadeyi, Hunt, Fojut.
10th	● Arsenal ....a	L 1–0	**Att:** 60,068. **Ref:** C Foy — **Bolton** (4-4-2): Jaaskelainen, Basham, Shittu, O'Brien, Samuel, Taylor, Muamba, McCann▮, Gardner, Elmander (M Riga▮ 39 (Obadeyi 77)), K Davies, M Riga (Obadeyi 77). Subs not used: Bogdan, Fojut.
17th	● Man Utd ....h	L 0–1	**Att:** 26,021. **Ref:** A Marriner — **Bolton** (4-5-1): Jaaskelainen, Steinsson, Cahill, O'Brien, Samuel, K Davies, Basham, Muamba, Gardner (Puygrenier 83), Taylor, Makukula▮ (Obadeyi 64). Subs not used: Bogdan, Smolarek, Riga, Shittu, Sinclair.
28th	● Blackburn ....a	D 2–2	**Att:** 25,205. **Ref:** M Dean — **Bolton** (4-5-1): Jaaskelainen▮, Steinsson, Cahill, Puygrenier▮, Samuel, K Davies¹, Muamba, Nolan, Basham, Taylor¹, Makukula (M Davies 74). Subs not used: Al Habsi, Gardner, Riga, Shittu, O'Brien.
31st	● Tottenham ....h	W 3–2	**Att:** 21,575. **Ref:** P Dowd — **Bolton** (4-5-1): Jaaskelainen, Steinsson, Cahill, Puygrenier¹ (O'Brien 79), Samuel, Taylor, M Davies², Muamba, Gardner, K Davies, Makukula (Smolarek 61). Subs not used: Al Habsi, Riga, Shittu, Basham, Obadeyi.

February

7th	● Everton ....a	L 3–0	**Att:** 33,791. **Ref:** P Walton — **Bolton** (4-4-2): Jaaskelainen, O'Brien, Cahill, Puygrenier (Basham 60), Samuel, Steinsson, M Davies▮, Muamba (Smolarek 60), Taylor, Gardner, Makukula (Riga 83). Subs not used: Al Habsi, Shittu, Obadeyi.
21st	● West Ham ....h	W 2–1	**Att:** 21,245. **Ref:** S Tanner — **Bolton** (4-5-1): Jaaskelainen, Steinsson, Cahill, Puygrenier (O'Brien 73), Samuel, K Davies¹, M Davies, McCann, Gardner, Taylor¹, Elmander (Muamba 76). Subs not used: Al Habsi, Smolarek, Makukula, Shittu, Basham.

March

1st	● Newcastle ....h	W 1–0	**Att:** 20,763. **Ref:** A Wiley — **Bolton** (4-4-2): Jaaskelainen, Steinsson, Cahill, O'Brien, Samuel, M Davies, Muamba (Gardner¹ 46), Taylor¹, K Davies, Elmander (Smolarek▮ 78). Subs not used: Al Habsi, Puygrenier, Makukula, Shittu, Basham.
4th	● Stoke ....a	L 2–0	**Att:** 26,319. **Ref:** M Dean — **Bolton** (4-4-2): Jaaskelainen, Steinsson (Makukula 80), Cahill, O'Brien, Samuel, M Davies, Muamba (Gardner 64), McCann, Taylor, K Davies, Elmander. Subs not used: Al Habsi, Shittu, Smolarek, Puygrenier, Basham.
14th	● Fulham ....h	L 1–3	**Att:** 22,117. **Ref:** C Foy — **Bolton** (4-4-2): Jaaskelainen, Steinsson, Cahill, O'Brien, Samuel (Riga 74), Taylor, McCann, M Davies¹ (Muamba 68), Gardner, K Davies, Elmander. Subs not used: Al Habsi, Hunt, Puygrenier, Makukula, Shittu.

● Barclays Premier League ● FA Cup ● Carling Cup ● UEFA Champions League ● UEFA Cup ▮ Yellow Card ▮ Red Card

RESULTS 2008/09

21st ● West Brom ....a | D 1–1 | **Att:** 25,530. **Ref:** H Webb — **Bolton** (4-4-2): Jaaskelainen, Steinsson▌, Cahill, Puygrenier (Shittu 59), Samuel, Taylor¹, Muamba, McCann, Gardner, Elmander (Smolarek 90), Davies. Subs not used: Al Habsi, Hunt, Riga, Makukula, Cohen.

April
4th ● Middlesbrough ....h | W 4–1 | **Att:** 20,819. **Ref:** A Wiley — **Bolton** (4-4-2): Jaaskelainen, Steinsson, Cahill, Shittu▌, Samuel, Taylor¹, Muamba▌, McCann, Gardner¹, Elmander (Basham 83), K Davies¹. Subs not used: Al Habsi, Hunt, Smolarek, Puygrenier, Cohen, O'Brien.

11th ● Chelsea ....a | L 4–3 | **Att:** 41,096. **Ref:** P Walton — **Bolton** (4-3-3): Jaaskelainen, Steinsson, Cahill, Shittu (O'Brien¹ 46), Samuel, Muamba, McCann (Cohen 83), Gardner, K Davies, Elmander (Basham¹ 66), Taylor¹. Subs not used: Al Habsi, Hunt, Smolarek, Puygrenier.

18th ● Portsmouth ....a | L 1–0 | **Att:** 20,158. **Ref:** P Dowd — **Bolton** (4-3-3): Jaaskelainen, Steinsson, O'Brien, Cahill, Samuel, Basham, McCann▌, Gardner (Muamba 12), K Davies▌, Elmander, Taylor. Subs not used: Al Habsi, Hunt▌, Smolarek, Puygrenier, Makukula, Cohen.

25th ● Aston Villa...........................h | D 1–1 | **Att:** 21,709. **Ref:** L Probert — **Bolton** (4-5-1): Jaaskelainen, Steinsson, Cahill, O'Brien (Puygrenier 78), Samuel, Davies, McCann, Muamba, Cohen¹ (Basham 87), Taylor, Elmander. Subs not used: Al Habsi, Hunt, Smolarek, Riga, Makukula.

May
2nd ● Wigan ....a | D 0–0 | **Att:** 18,655. **Ref:** M Jones — **Bolton** (4-5-1): Jaaskelainen, Steinsson, Cahill, O'Brien, Samuel, K Davies, Muamba▌, McCann▌, Cohen (Riga 79), Taylor▌, Elmander. Subs not used: Al Habsi, Puygrenier, Hunt, Makukula, Smolarek, Basham.

9th ● Sunderland ....h | D 0–0 | **Att:** 24,005. **Ref:** R Styles — **Bolton** (4-5-1): Jaaskelainen, Steinsson, Cahill, O'Brien, Samuel, K Davies, Muamba, McCann, Cohen▌ (M Davies 46▌), Taylor, Elmander (Riga 67). Subs not used: Al Habsi, Smolarek, Puygrenier, Makukula, Basham.

16th ● Hull ....h | D 1–1 | **Att:** 25,085. **Ref:** P Walton — **Bolton** (4-5-1): Jaaskelainen, Steinsson¹, Cahill, Shittu, Samuel▌, K Davies, Muamba (Basham 82), McCann, M Davies, Taylor (Riga 82), Elmander (Makukula 89). Subs not used: Al Habsi, Hunt, Puygrenier, Cohen.

24th ● Man City ....a | L 1–0 | **Att:** 47,202. **Ref:** M Clattenburg — **Bolton** (4-4-2): Jaaskelainen, Steinsson, Cahill, Shittu (O'Brien 83), Samuel, M Davies, Muamba, McCann, Taylor (Basham 59), Elmander (Riga 83), K Davies. Subs not used: Al Habsi, Hunt, Puygrenier, Cohen.

● Barclays Premier League ● FA Cup ● Carling Cup ● UEFA Champions League ● UEFA Cup | ▌Yellow Card ▌Red Card

Chris Basham scores in the thrilling 4–3 defeat at Chelsea in April

BOLTON WANDERERS

BARCLAYS PREMIER LEAGUE GOALKEEPER STATS

Player	Minutes on pitch	Appearances	Match starts	Completed matches	Sub appearances	Subbed off	Saved with feet	Punched	Parried	Tipped over	Fumbled	Tipped round	Caught	Blocked	Clean sheets	Goals conceded	Minutes since conceding	Save %	Saved	Resulting in goals	Opposition miss	Yellow cards	Red cards
Jussi Jaaskelainen 3619	38	38	38	0	0	1	22	42	7	0	13	111	2	7	53	86	79.22	1	6	0	3	0

Columns under SAVES BREAKDOWN: Saved with feet, Punched, Parried, Tipped over, Fumbled, Tipped round, Caught, Blocked. Columns under PENALTIES: Saved, Resulting in goals, Opposition miss.

BARCLAYS PREMIER LEAGUE OUTFIELD PLAYER STATS

Player	Minutes on pitch	Appearances	Match starts	Completed matches	Substitute appearances	Subbed off	Goals scored	Minutes since scoring	Assists	Shots on target	Shots off target	Crosses	Defensive clearances	Defensive blocks	Fouls committed	Free-kicks won	Caught offside	Yellow cards	Red cards
Chris Basham 512	11	4	4	7	0	1	172	0	2	1	1	5	0	5	4	0	0	0
Gary Cahill 3140	33	33	33	0	0	3	725	4	13	9	7	81	37	16	31	0	1	0
Tamir Cohen 225	4	3	0	1	3	1	153	0	1	2	3	0	0	5	1	0	1	0
Kevin Davies 3573	38	37	37	1	0	12	761	3	31	18	28	11	2	115	92	19	4	0
Mark Davies 806	10	8	7	2	1	0	-	2	5	4	13	0	1	11	7	0	3	0
Johan Elmander 2441	30	30	11	0	19	5	1480	2	27	26	7	2	0	28	35	22	1	0
Ricardo Gardner 1963	29	18	13	11	5	4	116	2	21	13	17	6	4	17	43	3	1	0
Heidar Helguson 29	1	0	0	1	0	0	-	0	0	0	0	0	0	1	0	0	0	0
Ariza Makukula 306	6	4	0	2	4	0	-	1	2	5	0	2	0	7	2	4	1	0
Gavin McCann 2896	33	30	27	3	2	0	-	0	19	15	26	18	9	63	28	0	9	1
Fabrice Muamba 2979	38	33	22	5	11	0	-	0	10	24	10	11	9	43	25	2	5	0
Kevin Nolan 1868	20	20	19	0	0	0	-	2	16	17	3	21	8	36	17	5	8	0
Andrew O'Brien 2930	34	30	29	4	1	1	404	0	3	3	7	48	29	28	15	0	5	0
Joey O'Brien 384	7	5	2	2	3	0	-	2	0	1	9	9	3	4	6	0	1	0
Temitope Obadeyi 54	3	0	0	3	0	0	-	0	0	0	0	0	0	1	1	0	0	0
Sebastien Puygrenier 394	7	5	1	2	4	1	258	0	1	0	0	6	2	2	0	1	1	0
Mustapha Riga 514	17	2	0	15	2	0	-	0	8	5	19	1	1	8	7	1	1	0
Jlloyd Samuel 3506	38	38	34	0	4	0	-	2	2	3	36	36	21	31	32	0	3	0
Dan Shittu 839	10	9	7	1	2	0	-	0	2	2	1	17	7	6	4	1	1	0
Ebi Smolarek 269	12	1	0	11	1	0	-	0	1	2	0	1	0	5	3	4	1	0
Gretar Rafn Steinsson 3465	37	37	34	0	3	2	166	5	7	9	62	30	9	37	27	0	7	0
Matt Taylor 2987	34	33	25	8	10	10	546	5	68	37	67	16	4	30	33	7	3	0
Ricardo Vaz Te 38	2	0	0	2	0	0	-	0	1	0	2	0	0	0	0	1	0	0

actim

BARCLAYS PREMIER LEAGUE

SEASON TOTALS

Goals scored	41
Goals conceded	53
Clean sheets	7
Shots on target	240
Shots off target	196
Shots per goal	10.63
Pens awarded	1
Pens scored	–
Pens conceded	7
Offsides	70
Corners	198
Crosses	318
Players used	24
Fouls committed	501
Free-kicks won	424

CARDS RECEIVED

61 **1**

SEQUENCES

Wins	2
(on three occasions)	
Losses	4
(26/12/08–17/01/09)	
Draws	4
(25/04/09–16/05/09)	
Undefeated	4
(25/04/09–16/05/09)	
Without win	5
(on three occasions)	
Undefeated home	3
(on two occasions)	
Undefeated away	3
(08/11/08–29/11/08)	
Without scoring	4
(26/12/08–17/01/09)	
Without conceding	2
(on two occasions)	
Scoring	4
(14/03/09–11/04/09)	
Conceding	14
(15/11/08–21/02/09)	

SEASON INFORMATION
Highest Position: 3
Lowest Position: 18
Average goals scored per game: 1.08
Average goals conceded per game: 1.39

League position at the end of each week

League position at the end of: August 8, September 17, October 19, November 9, December 11, January 12, February 12, March 12, April 13, May 13

MATCH RECORDS
Goals scored per match

		W	D	L	Pts
Failed to score	18	0	4	14	4
Scored 1 goal	8	2	3	3	9
Scored 2 goals	5	3	1	1	10
Scored 3 goals	5	4	0	1	12
Scored 4+ goals	2	2	0	0	6

Goals conceded per match

		W	D	L	Pts
Clean sheet	7	3	4	0	13
Conceded 1 goal	17	7	3	7	24
Conceded 2 goals	8	1	1	6	4
Conceded 3 goals	4	0	0	4	0
Conceded 4+ goals	2	0	0	2	0

QUICK-FIRE GOALS
From the start of a match
Matt Taylor (v Portsmouth) 0:48
By a substitute after coming on
Ricardo Gardner (v Newcastle) 1:08

LAST-GASP GOALS
From the start of a match
Kevin Davies (v Tottenham) 86:07
By a substitute after coming on
Ricardo Gardner (v Man City) 33:55

GOAL DETAILS
How the goals were struck

SCORED		CONCEDED
19	Right foot	28
12	Left foot	13
10	Headers	12
0	Others	0

How the goals were struck

SCORED		CONCEDED
28	Open play	31
4	Cross	7
1	Corner	5
0	Penalties	6
3	Direct from free-kick	0
4	Free-kick	2
1	Own goals	2

Distance from goal

SCORED		CONCEDED
13	6yds	19
22	18yds	31
6	18+yds	3

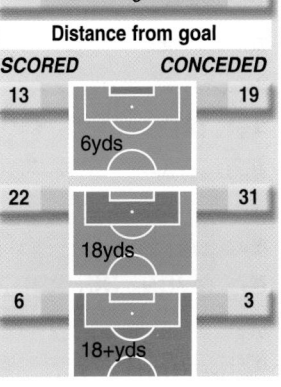

GOALS SCORED/CONCEDED PER FIVE-MINUTE INTERVALS

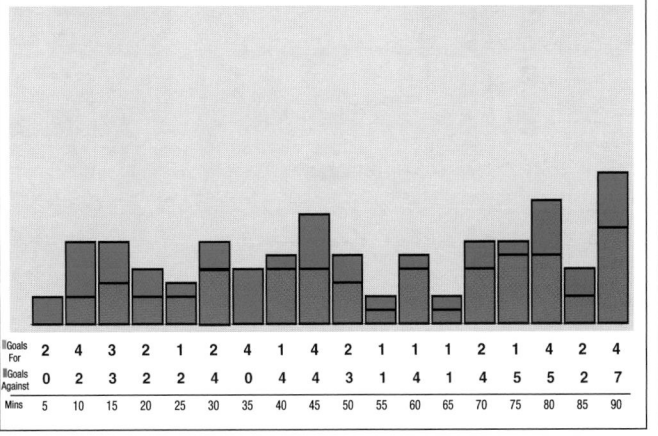

Goals For	2	4	3	2	1	2	4	1	4	2	1	1	1	2	1	4	2	4
Goals Against	0	2	3	2	2	4	0	4	4	3	1	4	1	4	5	5	2	7
Mins	5	10	15	20	25	30	35	40	45	50	55	60	65	70	75	80	85	90

OFFICIAL FOOTBALL YEARBOOK OF THE ENGLISH & SCOTTISH LEAGUES 2009–2010 **63**

CLUB SUMMARY

FORMED	1905
MANAGER	Carlo Ancelotti
GROUND	Stamford Bridge
CAPACITY	42,420
NICKNAME	The Blues
WEBSITE	www.chelseafc.com

The New Football Pools PLAYER OF THE SEASON — Frank Lampard

OVERALL

P	W	D	L	F	A	GD
59	37	16	6	110	44	66

BARCLAYS PREMIER LEAGUE

Pos	P	W	D	L	F	A	GD	Pts
3	38	25	8	5	68	24	44	83

HOME

Pos	P	W	D	L	F	A	GD	Pts
4	19	11	6	2	33	12	21	39

AWAY

Pos	P	W	D	L	F	A	GD	Pts
1	19	14	2	3	35	12	23	44

CUP PROGRESS DETAILS

Competition	Round reached	Knocked out by
FA Cup	Won	–
Champions League	SF	Barcelona
Carling Cup	R4	Burnley

BIGGEST WIN (ALL COMPS)

5–0 on two occasions

BIGGEST DEFEAT (ALL COMPS)

11/01/09 0–3 v Man Utd **PREM**

THE PLAYER WITH THE MOST

Shots on target	
Frank Lampard	96
Shots off target	
Frank Lampard	51
Shots without scoring	
Jon Obi Mikel	23
Assists	
Frank Lampard	10
Offsides	
Nicolas Anelka	30
Fouls	
Jon Obi Mikel	55
Fouls without a card	
Salomon Kalou	21
Free-kicks won	
Jon Obi Mikel	57
Defensive clearances	
John Terry	33

actim INDEX for the 2008/09 Barclays Premier League Season

Rank	Player	Pts
1	Nicolas Anelka	751
3	Frank Lampard	653
12	Petr Cech	513
13	John Terry	501
22	Ashley Cole	458

ATTENDANCE RECORD

High	Low	Average
43,417	40,280	41,588

v West Brom (26/12/2008)   v Middlesbrough (28/01/2009)

CLOCKWISE FROM TOP: Guus Hiddink parades the FA Cup trophy with his players; Frank Lampard enjoys scoring in the 5–0 win at Middlesbrough; former manager Luiz Felipe Scolari shows his frustration; Didier Drogba celebrates after Kolo Toure's own goal in the superb 4–1 victory at Arsenal in May

CHELSEA'S season began full of optimism under World Cup-winning coach Luiz Felipe Scolari. It ended in delight with a 2–1 win over Everton in the FA Cup final, but not before the Brazilian had been replaced.

Scolari, appointed last summer as a replacement for Avram Grant, was a bold choice by the Chelsea board and their decision looked to be the right one when the Blues went on a run of eight straight away victories from the start of the campaign. But it was their form at Stamford Bridge that provided the first signs of concern.

Liverpool ended their 86-match unbeaten home league record with a 1–0 success in October. Worse was to follow for Scolari as Coca-Cola Championship side Burnley booted them out of the League Cup on penalties. But when Newcastle gained a draw at the Bridge and Arsenal sent them tumbling to a second home defeat of the season, the cracks began to show.

Scolari's fate was sealed in December and January amid off-the-pitch allegations about the lack of intensity on the training ground and falling fitness levels.

In the new year, Chelsea failed to beat League One side Southend in the FA Cup third round at home and were then thumped 3–0 at Old Trafford by Manchester United. It was a result which brought Scolari's personality clash with Ivorian star Didier Drogba to a head. The striker's performance against United was lamentable and he paid the price for it by being axed from the squad for the replay against Southend, which Chelsea won 4–1.

But they lost Joe Cole for the rest of the season with knee ligament damage, adding to the absence of Michael Essien, who had been ruled out with a similar injury back in September.

A winner from Frank Lampard against Stoke then appeared to save Scolari's neck and he bought more time with victories over Ipswich in the FA Cup and Middlesbrough in the League.

But a 2–0 defeat against Liverpool at Anfield on 1st February was immediately followed by a goalless home draw with Barclays Premier League new boys Hull. Scolari was relieved of his duties by Roman Abramovich, and Guus Hiddink was appointed as an interim coach – combining his new role at Chelsea with that of coach of Russia's national side.

Hiddink proved to be a breath of fresh air. Abramovich had charged him with ensuring Chelsea finished in the top three in order to qualify automatically for next season's UEFA Champions League, and Hiddink set about working his magic.

In Europe, victory at home over Juventus was supplemented by wins over Wigan and Portsmouth in the League and Coventry in the FA Cup.

The return of Essien boosted Hiddink's armoury and the Ghanaian international repaid his faith by scoring a vital away goal in the return leg 2–2 draw against Juventus in Turin. A rare defeat at Tottenham, Hiddink's only one in the League, failed to stop Chelsea's push to catch Manchester United. In the end the gap proved too wide and a home draw with their FA Cup final opponents Everton ended their hopes.

The focus inevitably turned to Hiddink's future. A chorus of appeals from the Chelsea players for him to stay almost worked, but in the end Hiddink decided to go. He was replaced at the end of the season by Carlo Ancelotti, who left AC Milan after an eight-year stint.

Hiddink had brought Drogba back in from the cold and the striker responded with some fine goals, including the winner against Arsenal in the FA Cup semi-final. Nicolas Anelka finished the season as top scorer in the League and the only real sour note was Chelsea's controversial exit to Barcelona in the Champions League semi-final. But even then, while Drogba uttered foul-mouthed rants at the TV cameras and confronted official Tom Henning Ovrebo over his failure to award one of four penalty claims, Hiddink remained calm and dignified amid the chaos.

He managed to inspire the players to bounce back with a 4–1 victory at rivals Arsenal and finish the league season with a 3–2 win at Sunderland.

The crowning glory came at Wembley as Didier Drogba and Frank Lampard scored to seal victory after Everton had gone ahead in the first minute.

> ❝ **The crowning glory came at Wembley as Didier Drogba and Frank Lampard scored** ❞

CHELSEA

RESULTS 2008/09

August

17th ● Portsmouth ....h **W 4–0** **Att:** 41,468. **Ref:** M Dean — **Chelsea** (4-3-2-1): Cech, Bosingwa (Ferreira 83), Carvalho, Terry, A Cole¹, Ballack (Malouda 38), Lampard¹, Obi, Deco¹, J Cole (Wright-Phillips 78), Anelka. Subs not used: Hilario, Di Santo, Bridge, Alex.

24th ● Wigan ....a **W 0–1** **Att:** 18,139. **Ref:** A Wiley — **Chelsea** (4-3-3): Cech, Bosingwa, Carvalho, Terry▌, A Cole (Bridge 83), Ballack, Essien, Lampard, Deco¹, Anelka (Malouda 89), J Cole (Kalou 58). Subs not used: Hilario, Ivanovic, Alex, Belletti.

31st ● Tottenham ....h **D 1–1** **Att:** 41,790. **Ref:** H Webb — **Chelsea** (4-4-1-1): Cech, Belletti (Kalou 75), Carvalho, Terry, A Cole, Bosingwa▌, Essien, Lampard, J Cole▌ (Malouda 65), Deco▌, Anelka (Di Santo 88). Subs not used: Cudicini, Bridge, Ferreira, Alex.

September

13th ● Man City ....a **W 1–3** **Att:** 47,331. **Ref:** M Halsey — **Chelsea** (4-3-3): Cech, Bosingwa, Terry▌, Carvalho¹, A Cole, Obi, Lampard¹, Deco, J Cole (Belletti 70), Anelka¹ (Alex 79), Malouda (Drogba 70). Subs not used: Hilario, Ivanovic, Bridge, Kalou.

16th ● Bordeaux ....h **W 4–0** **Att:** 39,635. **Ref:** P Vink — **Chelsea** (4-1-4-1): Cech, Bosingwa, Carvalho, Terry, A Cole¹, Obi, J Cole (Belletti 74), Deco▌ (Ballack 61), Lampard¹, Malouda¹ (Kalou 84), Anelka¹. Subs not used: Hilario, Di Santo, Ferreira, Alex.

21st ● Man Utd ....h **D 1–1** **Att:** 41,760. **Ref:** M Riley — **Chelsea** (4-1-4-1): Cech, Bosingwa, Carvalho (Alex 12), Terry, A Cole, Obi, J Cole, Ballack (Kalou¹ 74), Lampard, Malouda (Drogba 46), Anelka. Subs not used: Cudicini, Bridge, Belletti, Ferreira.

24th ● Portsmouth ....a **W 0–4** **Att:** 15,339. **Ref:** S Bennett — **Chelsea** (4-3-3): Cech, Ivanovic, Terry, Alex, Bridge, Belletti, Ballack▌ (Ferreira 69), Lampard² (Sinclair 74), Kalou¹, Malouda¹, Drogba (Di Santo 79). Subs not used: Cudicini, Obi, Mancienne, Stoch.

27th ● Stoke ....a **W 0–2** **Att:** 27,500. **Ref:** M Atkinson — **Chelsea** (4-1-4-1): Cech, Bosingwa¹, Alex, Terry, A Cole, Obi, Kalou (Anelka¹ 46), Ballack (Ferreira 89), Lampard, Malouda▌, Drogba (Belletti 73). Subs not used: Hilario, Ivanovic, Sinclair, Bridge.

October

1st ● CFR Cluj-Napoca ....a **D 0–0** **Att:** 22,000. **Ref:** F Meyer — **Chelsea** (4-5-1): Cech, Bosingwa, Alex▌, Terry, Bridge, Mikel, Kalou (Anelka▌ 46), Ballack, Lampard, Malouda (Di Santo 74), Drogba (Belletti 58). Subs not used: Hilario, Ivanovic, Ferreira, Stoch.

5th ● Aston Villa ....h **W 2–0** **Att:** 41,593. **Ref:** C Foy — **Chelsea** (4-1-4-1): Cech, Bosingwa, Ivanovic, Terry, A Cole¹, Mikel, J Cole (Kalou 57), Ballack, Lampard, Malouda (Belletti 83), Anelka¹ (Di Santo 46). Subs not used: Hilario, Bridge, Ferreira, Mancienne.

18th ● Middlesbrough ....a **W 0–5** **Att:** 29,221. **Ref:** P Dowd — **Chelsea** (4-3-3): Cudicini, Bosingwa, Terry, Alex, Bridge (Ferreira 65), Belletti▌, Lampard¹ (Deco 73), Mikel, Kalou², Anelka (Sinclair 78), Malouda¹. Subs not used: Hilario, Ivanovic, Mancienne, Stoch.

22nd ● Roma ....h **W 1–0** **Att:** 41,002. **Ref:** K Vassaras — **Chelsea** (4-1-4-1): Cech, Bosingwa, Terry▌¹, Carvalho, Bridge, Kalou (Di Santo 77), Lampard, Mikel, Malouda▌ (Belletti 46), Deco, Anelka (Ferreira 90). Subs not used: Cudicini, Ivanovic, Alex, Stoch.

26th ● Liverpool ....h **L 0–1** **Att:** 41,705. **Ref:** H Webb — **Chelsea** (4-1-4-1): Cech, Bosingwa (Sinclair 84), Carvalho, Terry, A Cole▌, Mikel, Kalou (Di Santo 58), Deco▌, Lampard, Malouda▌ (Belletti 58), Anelka. Subs not used: Cudicini, Ivanovic, Ferreira, Alex.

29th ● Hull ....a **W 0–3** **Att:** 24,906. **Ref:** A Marriner — **Chelsea** (4-3-3): Cech, Bosingwa (Ivanovic 86), Carvalho, Terry, A Cole, Deco▌ (Kalou 78), Mikel, Lampard¹, J Cole▌ (Belletti 54), Anelka¹, Malouda¹. Subs not used: Cudicini, Di Santo, Bridge, Alex.

November

1st ● Sunderland ....h **W 5–0** **Att:** 41,693. **Ref:** M Atkinson — **Chelsea** (4-1-4-1): Cech, Bosingwa, Alex¹, Terry, A Cole (Bridge 36), Mikel, J Cole (Drogba 63), Deco, Lampard¹, Malouda, Anelka³ (Mineiro 75). Subs not used: Hilario, Ivanovic, Kalou, Belletti.

4th ● Roma ....a **L 3–1** **Att:** 38,425. **Ref:** L Medina Cantalejo — **Chelsea** (4-3-3): Cech, Bosingwa (Kalou 63), Terry¹, Alex, Bridge, Deco▌▌, Mikel, Lampard, J Cole (Belletti 46), Anelka, Malouda (Drogba 46). Subs not used: Cudicini, Ivanovic, Di Santo, Ferreira.

9th ● Blackburn ....a **W 0–2** **Att:** 20,670. **Ref:** C Foy — **Chelsea** (4-3-3): Cech, Bosingwa, Alex, Terry, Bridge, Lampard, Mikel, Deco (Ferreira 90), Kalou (Belletti 62), Anelka², Malouda▌. Subs not used: Cudicini, Ivanovic, Di Santo, Sinclair, Mineiro.

12th ● Burnley ....h **D 1–1** **Att:** 41,369. **Ref:** K Stroud — **Chelsea** (4-4-2): Cudicini, Ivanovic, Alex, Belletti (Lampard 25), Bridge, Ferreira, Deco (Mikel 46), Mineiro, Malouda, Drogba¹ (Di Santo 68), Kalou. Subs not used: Hilario, Sinclair, Terry, Woods.

15th ● West Brom ....a **W 0–3** **Att:** 26,322. **Ref:** S Bennett — **Chelsea** (4-3-3): Cudicini, Bosingwa▌, Ivanovic▌, Terry▌ (Ferreira 85), Bridge, Lampard, Mikel, Deco, Kalou (Ballack 68), Anelka² (Drogba 74), Malouda. Subs not used: Hilario, A Cole, Sinclair, Mineiro.

22nd ● Newcastle ....h **D 0–0** **Att:** 41,660. **Ref:** P Dowd — **Chelsea** (4-1-4-1): Cech, Bosingwa, Ivanovic, Terry, A Cole, Mikel, J Cole (Ballack 82), Deco, Lampard, Malouda (Kalou 72), Anelka. Subs not used: Cudicini, Sinclair, Bridge, Ferreira, Mineiro.

26th ● Bordeaux ....a **D 1–1** **Att:** 34,307. **Ref:** F De Bleeckere — **Chelsea** (4-1-4-1): Cech, Bosingwa, Ivanovic, Terry▌, A Cole▌, Mikel, J Cole▌ (Ferreira 85), Ballack, Lampard▌▌, Malouda, Anelka¹ (Drogba 63). Subs not used: Cudicini, Bridge, Kalou, Alex, Stoch.

30th ● Arsenal ....h **L 1–2** **Att:** 41,760. **Ref:** M Dean — **Chelsea** (4-1-4-1): Cech, Bosingwa, Ivanovic▌, Terry▌, A Cole, Mikel (Malouda 69), Deco (Stoch 81), Ballack, Lampard, Kalou, Anelka. Subs not used: Hilario, Bridge, Ferreira, Mineiro, Alex.

December

6th ● Bolton ....a **W 0–2** **Att:** 22,023. **Ref:** H Webb — **Chelsea** (4-1-4-1): Cech, Bosingwa (Ivanovic 89), Terry, Alex, A Cole, Mikel, Kalou (Ferreira 83), Lampard, Ballack, Deco¹, Anelka¹. Subs not used: Cudicini, Sinclair, Mineiro, Stoch, Woods.

9th ● CFR Cluj-Napoca ....h **W 2–1** **Att:** 41,060. **Ref:** P Frojdfeldt — **Chelsea** (4-5-1): Cech, A Cole, Terry, Alex, Bosingwa, Kalou¹ (Drogba¹ 64), Deco, Mikel▌ (Bridge 87), Ballack, J Cole (Belletti▌ 74), Anelka. Subs not used: Cudicini, Ivanovic, Ferreira, Stoch.

14th ● West Ham ....h **D 1–1** **Att:** 41,675. **Ref:** M Riley — **Chelsea** (4-1-4-1): Cech, Bosingwa, Alex, Terry, A Cole▌, Mikel▌ (Belletti 80), Deco, Ballack▌ (Drogba 46), Lampard, J Cole (Kalou 74), Anelka¹. Subs not used: Hilario, Ivanovic, Bridge, Ferreira.

22nd ● Everton ....a **D 0–0** **Att:** 35,655. **Ref:** P Dowd — **Chelsea** (4-3-3): Cech, Bosingwa, Alex, Terry▌, A Cole▌, Mikel, J Cole (Ivanovic 46), Ballack▌, Lampard, Deco (Bridge 87), Anelka (Drogba 46). Subs not used: Cudicini, Malouda, Kalou, Belletti.

26th ● West Brom ....h **W 2–0** **Att:** 43,417. **Ref:** R Styles — **Chelsea** (4-3-3): Cech, Bosingwa (Belletti 46), Ivanovic, Alex, A Cole, Ballack▌, Mikel, Lampard¹, J Cole (Deco 79), Drogba¹ (Malouda 66), Anelka. Subs not used: Ferreira, Kalou, Cudicini, Mineiro.

28th ● Fulham ....a **D 2–2** **Att:** 25,462. **Ref:** A Marriner — **Chelsea** (4-3-3): Cech, Bosingwa▌, Ivanovic, Alex (Carvalho 37), A Cole, Deco, Mikel, Lampard², J Cole (Kalou 72), Drogba▌ (Malouda 30). Subs not used: Cudicini, Ballack, Ferreira, Belletti.

January

3rd ● Southend ....h **D 1–1** **Att:** 41,090. **Ref:** S Attwell — **Chelsea** (4-4-2): Cudicini, Ferreira▌, Carvalho, Ivanovic, A Cole, Belletti, Lampard, Mikel▌, J Cole (Di Santo 84), Kalou¹ (Sinclair 87), Drogba. Subs not used: Hilario, Mineiro, Anelka, Mancienne, Sawyer.

● Barclays Premier League ● FA Cup ● Carling Cup ● UEFA Champions League ● UEFA Cup

▌ Yellow Card ▌ Red Card

BARCLAYS PREMIER LEAGUE

RESULTS 2008/09

11th	● Man Utd ....a	L 3–0	**Att:** 75,455. **Ref:** H Webb — **Chelsea** (4-1-4-1): Cech, Bosingwa▌ (Belletti 64), Carvalho▌, Terry▌, A Cole, Mikel▌, J Cole (Di Santo 85), Lampard▌, Ballack, Deco (Anelka 46), Drogba. Subs not used: Cudicini, Ivanovic, Ferreira, Kalou.
14th	● Southend ....a	W 1–4	**Att:** 11,314. **Ref:** C Foy — **Chelsea** (4-1-4-1): Cech, Bosingwa, Alex, Terry, A Cole, Mikel▌ (Belletti 46), J Cole (Di Santo 76), Ballack[1], Lampard[1], Kalou[1], Anelka[1]. Subs not used: Cudicini, Ivanovic, Carvalho, Mancienne, Stoch.
17th	● Stoke ....h	W 2–1	**Att:** 41,788. **Ref:** P Walton — **Chelsea** (4-3-3): Cech, Bosingwa (Belletti 78), Carvalho, Alex, A Cole, Lampard[1], Mikel (Stoch 82), Ballack, Malouda (Di Santo 60), Anelka, Kalou. Subs not used: Cudicini, Ivanovic, Mancienne, Kakuta.
24th	● Ipswich ....h	W 3–1	**Att:** 41,137. **Ref:** A Wiley — **Chelsea** (4-4-2): Cech, Bosingwa, Carvalho (Ivanovic 70), Alex, A Cole, Belletti, Ballack[2] (Deco 79), Lampard[1], Malouda (Drogba 58), Kalou, Anelka. Subs not used: Cudicini, Ferreira, Mancienne, Stoch.
28th	● Middlesbrough ....h	W 2–0	**Att:** 40,280. **Ref:** L Probert — **Chelsea** (4-1-4-1): Cech, Bosingwa, Alex, Terry, A Cole, Mikel, Kalou[2] (Deco 82), Ballack, Lampard, Malouda (Drogba 46), Anelka (Stoch 88). Subs not used: Hilario, Ivanovic, Ferreira, Mancienne.

February

1st	● Liverpool..............a	L 2–0	**Att:** 44,174. **Ref:** M Riley — **Chelsea** (4-3-3): Cech, Bosingwa, Alex, Terry▌, A Cole▌, Ballack, Mikel▌, Lampard▌▌, Kalou (Stoch 85), Anelka (Drogba 69), Malouda (Deco 69). Subs not used: Hilario, Ivanovic, Ferreira, Mancienne.
7th	● Hull ....h	D 0–0	**Att:** 41,802. **Ref:** L Mason — **Chelsea** (4-1-4-1): Hilario, Bosingwa, Alex, Terry, A Cole, Mikel▌ (Belletti 57), Quaresma (Drogba 63), Ballack (Deco 73), Lampard, Kalou, Anelka. Subs not used: Taylor, Ivanovic, Di Santo, Stoch.
14th	● Watford ....a	W 1–3	**Att:** 16,851. **Ref:** M Dean — **Chelsea** (4-3-3): Cech, Mancienne, Alex, Ivanovic, A Cole▌, Lampard, Ballack (Belletti 83), Mikel (Stoch 73), Kalou, Anelka[3], Drogba. Subs not used: Hilario, Di Santo, Quaresma, Ferreira, Deco.
21st	● Aston Villa..............a	W 0–1	**Att:** 42,585. **Ref:** M Halsey — **Chelsea** (4-1-3-2): Cech, Bosingwa▌, Alex, Terry▌, Ferreira, Mikel, Ballack▌, Lampard, Kalou (Deco 55), Anelka[1], Drogba (Belletti 90). Subs not used: Hilario, Ivanovic, Quaresma, Mancienne, Stoch.
25th	● Juventus ....h	W 1–0	**Att:** 38,079. **Ref:** O Benquerenca — **Chelsea** (4-4-2): Cech, Bosingwa, Terry, Alex, A Cole, Kalou (Malouda 72), Ballack▌ (Mancienne 81), Lampard, Mikel, Drogba[1], Anelka. Subs not used: Hilario, Ivanovic, Ferreira, Di Santo, Stoch.
28th	● Wigan ....h	W 2–1	**Att:** 40,714. **Ref:** L Probert — **Chelsea** (4-3-3): Cech, Mancienne▌ (Quaresma 81), Alex▌, Terry▌▌, A Cole, Ballack, Mikel, Lampard[1], Kalou (Belletti 75), Anelka, Drogba. Subs not used: Hilario, Ivanovic, Di Santo, Malouda, Ferreira.

March

3rd	● Portsmouth ....a	W 0–1	**Att:** 20,326. **Ref:** P Dowd — **Chelsea** (4-3-3): Cech, Bosingwa, Alex, Terry, A Cole, Mikel (Belletti 56), Ballack (Mancienne 90), Lampard, Kalou (Quaresma 60), Drogba[1], Malouda. Subs not used: Hilario, Ivanovic, Di Santo, Ferreira.
7th	● Coventry ....a	W 0–2	**Att:** 31,407. **Ref:** S Bennett — **Chelsea** (4-3-3): Cech, Bosingwa, Terry, Alex[1], A Cole, Lampard, Mikel (Essien 65), Ballack, Malouda, Drogba[1] (Di Santo 80), Kalou (Quaresma 46). Subs not used: Hilario, Carvalho, Belletti, Mancienne.
10th	● Juventus ....a	D 2–2	**Att:** 28,500. **Ref:** A Undiano Mallenco — **Chelsea** (4-1-3-2): Cech▌, Bosingwa, Terry, Alex (Carvalho 88), A Cole▌, Mikel, Ballack, Essien[1] (Belletti 66), Lampard, Drogba▌[1], Anelka▌. Subs not used: Hilario, Malouda, Deco, Kalou, Mancienne.
15th	● Man City ....h	W 1–0	**Att:** 41,810. **Ref:** M Riley — **Chelsea** (4-4-2): Cech, Bosingwa, Carvalho, Terry, A Cole, Ballack, Essien[1], Lampard, Deco (Belletti 41), Anelka, Drogba (Malouda 71). Subs not used: Hilario, Mikel, Quaresma, Kalou, Alex.
21st	● Tottenham ....a	L 1–0	**Att:** 36,034. **Ref:** M Dean — **Chelsea** (4-3-3): Cech, Bosingwa, Alex, Terry, A Cole, Essien (Malouda 76), Ballack▌, Lampard, Belletti▌ (Quaresma 61), Drogba, Anelka. Subs not used: Hilario, Ivanovic, Di Santo, Kalou, Mancienne.

April

4th	● Newcastle ....a	W 0–2	**Att:** 52,112. **Ref:** R Styles — **Chelsea** (4-3-3): Cech, Ivanovic, Alex, Terry, A Cole, Essien (Ballack 57), Mikel▌, Lampard▌, Malouda[1], Anelka (Di Santo 67), Kalou. Subs not used: Hilario, Carvalho, Belletti, Mancienne.
8th	● Liverpool ....a	W 1–3	**Att:** 42,543. **Ref:** C Bo Larsen — **Chelsea** (4-5-1): Cech, Ivanovic[2], Terry▌, Alex, A Cole, Kalou▌, Ballack, Essien, Lampard, Malouda, Drogba[1] (Anelka 79). Subs not used: Hilario, Carvalho, Belletti, Mancienne, Mikel, Deco.
11th	● Bolton ....h	W 4–3	**Att:** 41,096. **Ref:** P Walton — **Chelsea** (4-3-3): Cech, Ivanovic, Carvalho, Terry, A Cole, Ballack[1], Mikel, Lampard[1] (Deco 66), Kalou, Drogba[2] (Anelka 66), Malouda. Subs not used: Hilario, Quaresma, Alex, Belletti, Mancienne.
14th	● Liverpool ....h	D 4–4	**Att:** 38,286. **Ref:** L Medina Cantalejo — **Chelsea** (4-5-1): Cech, Ivanovic▌, Alex[1], Carvalho▌, A Cole▌, Kalou (Anelka 36), Ballack, Essien, Lampard[2], Malouda, Drogba[1] (Di Santo 90). Subs not used: Hilario, Mikel, Deco, Belletti, Mancienne.
18th	● Arsenal ....a	W 1–2	**Att:** 88,103. **Ref:** M Atkinson — **Chelsea** (4-4-2): Cech, Ivanovic▌, Alex, Terry, A Cole, Ballack▌, Lampard, Essien, Malouda[1], Anelka (Kalou 82), Drogba▌[1]. Subs not used: Hilario, Carvalho, Di Santo, Mikel, Belletti, Mancienne.
22nd	● Everton ....h	D 0–0	**Att:** 41,556. **Ref:** M Halsey — **Chelsea** (4-3-3): Cech, Ivanovic, Alex, Terry, A Cole, Ballack, Essien (Mikel 60), Lampard, Drogba, Anelka (Kalou 60), Malouda (Di Santo 77). Subs not used: Hilario, Belletti, Mancienne, Mellis.
25th	● West Ham ....a	W 0–1	**Att:** 34,749. **Ref:** M Dean — **Chelsea** (4-2-3-1): Cech, Mancienne (Ballack 83), Ivanovic, Terry, Bosingwa (A Cole 58), Mikel, Belletti, Kalou[1] (Essien 73), Lampard, Malouda, Anelka. Subs not used: Hilario, Di Santo, Drogba, Stoch.
28th	● Barcelona ....a	D 0–0	**Att:** 95,000. **Ref:** W Stark — **Chelsea** (4-2-3-1): Cech, Ivanovic, Alex▌, Terry, Bosingwa, Mikel, Ballack▌ (Anelka 90), Essien, Lampard (Belletti 71), Malouda, Drogba. Subs not used: Hilario, Di Santo, Kalou, Mancienne, Stoch.

May

2nd	● Fulham ....h	W 3–1	**Att:** 41,801. **Ref:** A Wiley — **Chelsea** (4-4-2): Cech, Bosingwa, Alex (Ivanovic 46), Terry, A Cole, Lampard, Essien (Ballack 46), Mikel, Malouda[1], Anelka[1], Drogba[1] (Di Santo 84). Subs not used: Hilario, Kalou, Belletti, Mancienne.
6th	● Barcelona ....h	D 1–1	**Att:** 37,857. **Ref:** T Ovrebo — **Chelsea** (4-3-3): Cech, Bosingwa, Alex▌, Terry, A Cole, Lampard, Essien▌[1], Ballack▌, Anelka, Drogba (Belletti 72), Malouda. Subs not used: Hilario, Ivanovic, Di Santo, Mikel, Kalou, Mancienne.
10th	● Arsenal ....a	W 1–4	**Att:** 60,075. **Ref:** P Dowd — **Chelsea** (4-3-3): Cech, Bosingwa (Ivanovic 77), Alex[1], Terry, A Cole, Essien, Mikel, Lampard, Anelka[1], Drogba, Malouda[1] (Ballack 88). Subs not used: Hilario, Di Santo, Kalou, Belletti, Mancienne.
17th	● Blackburn ....h	W 2–0	**Att:** 40,804. **Ref:** R Styles — **Chelsea** (4-3-3): Cech, Bosingwa▌, Alex, A Cole, Terry, Essien, Mikel, Lampard, Drogba, Anelka[1], Malouda[1]. Subs not used: Hilario, Ivanovic, Di Santo, Sinclair, Belletti, Mancienne, Stoch.
24th	● Sunderland ....a	W 2–3	**Att:** 42,468. **Ref:** M Halsey — **Chelsea** (4-3-3): Cech, Bosingwa, Ivanovic, Terry, A Cole▌, Essien (Kalou[1] 65), Mikel (Mancienne 78), Belletti (Ballack 27), Malouda, Drogba, Anelka. Subs not used: Hilario, Di Santo, Sinclair, Stoch.
30th	● Everton ....n	W 2–1	**Att:** 89,391. **Ref:** H Webb — **Chelsea** (4-3-3): Cech, Bosingwa, Alex, Terry, A Cole, Essien (Ballack 61), Mikel▌, Lampard▌, Anelka, Drogba[1], Malouda. Subs not used: Hilario, Ivanovic, Di Santo, Kalou, Belletti, Mancienne.

● Barclays Premier League ● FA Cup ● Carling Cup ● UEFA Champions League ● UEFA Cup ▌Yellow Card ▌Red Card

OFFICIAL FOOTBALL YEARBOOK OF THE ENGLISH & SCOTTISH LEAGUES 2009–2010 **67**

BARCLAYS PREMIER LEAGUE GOALKEEPER STATS

Player	Minutes on pitch	Appearances	Match starts	Completed matches	Sub appearances	Subbed off	SAVES BREAKDOWN								Clean sheets	Goals conceded	Minutes since conceding	Save %	PENALTIES			Yellow cards	Red cards
							Saved with feet	Punched	Parried	Tipped over	Fumbled	Tipped round	Caught	Blocked					Saved	Resulting in goals	Opposition miss		
Petr Cech	3328	35	35	0	0	0	19	34	4	0	9	99	0	19	24	4	87.30	1	0	0	0	0
Carlo Cudicini	187	2	2	0	0	0	2	0	0	0	0	6	0	2	0	70	61.54	0	0	0	0	0
Henrique Hilario	94	1	1	0	0	0	0	0	0	0	0	1	0	1	0	-	0	0	0	0	0	0

BARCLAYS PREMIER LEAGUE OUTFIELD PLAYER STATS

Player	Minutes on pitch	Appearances	Match starts	Completed matches	Substitute appearances	Subbed off	Goals scored	Minutes since scoring	Assists	Shots on target	Shots off target	Crosses	Defensive clearances	Defensive blocks	Fouls committed	Free-kicks won	Caught offside	Yellow cards	Red cards
Alex	2079	24	22	20	2	2	2	161	1	16	10	0	29	13	25	12	0	1	0
Nicolas Anelka	3052	37	33	21	4	12	19	47	7	60	36	25	5	3	20	23	30	0	0
Michael Ballack	2146	29	22	16	7	6	1	288	4	25	22	4	10	2	35	38	2	6	0
Juliano Belletti	773	20	5	2	15	3	3	340	0	5	6	1	4	1	14	13	2	2	0
Jose Bosingwa	3038	34	34	25	0	9	2	1901	3	7	18	70	18	2	28	36	5	6	0
Wayne Bridge	326	6	3	2	3	1	0	-	0	0	0	0	3	1	1	1	1	1	0
Ricardo Carvalho	1018	12	11	10	1	1	1	717	1	1	3	1	11	8	3	7	0	2	0
Ashley Cole	3105	34	33	31	1	2	2	8	2	10	14	37	16	8	36	49	3	5	0
Joe Cole	985	14	14	1	0	13	2	594	5	14	7	13	0	1	17	7	5	2	0
Deco	1621	24	17	11	7	6	3	576	2	14	10	14	2	3	26	32	1	3	0
Franco Di Santo	186	8	0	0	8	0	0	-	1	1	5	2	0	0	5	1	1	0	0
Didier Drogba	1636	24	15	9	9	6	5	315	4	24	27	13	9	4	28	32	18	1	0
Michael Essien	805	11	10	5	1	5	1	597	0	5	10	1	5	2	5	19	0	1	0
Paulo Ferreira	157	7	1	1	6	0	0	-	0	0	0	0	0	0	0	1	0	0	0
Branislav Ivanovic	1173	16	11	11	5	0	0	-	1	0	3	8	9	5	15	15	1	2	0
Salomon Kalou	1580	27	17	6	10	11	6	20	4	23	22	7	1	0	21	18	14	0	0
Frank Lampard	3429	37	37	34	0	2	12	482	10	96	51	63	21	5	31	44	9	3	1
Florent Malouda	2115	31	24	13	7	11	6	187	6	38	33	33	2	0	27	36	14	3	0
Michael Mancienne	186	4	2	0	2	2	0	-	0	1	0	0	0	0	1	0	0	1	0
Jon Obi Mikel	3022	34	33	27	1	6	0	-	2	10	13	6	12	7	55	57	2	6	0
Mineiro	17	1	0	0	1	0	0	-	0	0	0	0	0	0	0	0	0	0	0
Ricardo Quaresma	143	4	1	0	3	1	0	-	0	3	0	4	0	0	0	3	1	0	0
Scott Sinclair	23	2	0	0	2	0	0	-	0	0	0	0	0	0	1	0	0	0	0
Miroslav Stoch	42	4	0	0	4	0	0	-	0	1	0	0	0	0	1	1	0	0	0
John Terry	3236	35	35	32	0	1	1	1123	0	7	8	1	33	25	22	23	0	7	2
Shaun Wright-Phillips	14	1	0	0	1	0	0	384	1	0	0	0	0	0	0	0	1	0	0

SEASON TOTALS

Goals scored	68
Goals conceded	24
Clean sheets	22
Shots on target	361
Shots off target	298
Shots per goal	9.69
Pens awarded	2
Pens scored	2
Pens conceded	1
Offsides	110
Corners	237
Crosses	306
Players used	29
Fouls committed	419
Free-kicks won	470

CARDS RECEIVED

50 **3**

SEQUENCES

Wins	5
(25/04/09–24/05/09)	
Losses	
(–)	
Draws	2
(14/12/08–22/12/08)	
Undefeated	8
(on two occasions)	
Without win	2
(on four occasions)	
Undefeated home	11
(14/12/08–17/05/09)	
Undefeated away	10
(24/08/08–28/12/08)	
Without scoring	2
(01/02/09–07/02/09)	
Without conceding	5
(29/10/08–22/11/08)	
Scoring	8
(17/08/08–18/10/08)	
Conceding	3
(on two occasions)	

SEASON INFORMATION

Highest Position: 1
Lowest Position: 5
Average goals scored per game: 1.79
Average goals conceded per game: 0.63

League position at the end of each week

League position at the end of: August 1, September 1, October 2, November 1, December 2, January 2, February 2, March 3, April 3, May 3

MATCH RECORDS

Goals scored per match

		W	D	L	Pts
Failed to score	8	0	4	4	4
Scored 1 goal	9	5	3	1	18
Scored 2 goals	11	10	1	0	31
Scored 3 goals	5	5	0	0	15
Scored 4+ goals	5	5	0	0	15

Goals conceded per match

		W	D	L	Pts
Clean sheet	22	18	4	0	58
Conceded 1 goal	10	5	3	2	18
Conceded 2 goals	4	1	1	2	4
Conceded 3 goals	2	1	0	1	3
Conceded 4+ goals	0	0	0	0	0

QUICK-FIRE GOALS

From the start of a match
Nicolas Anelka (v Fulham) 0:51

By a substitute after coming on
Salomon Kalou (v Man Utd) 5:32

LAST-GASP GOALS

From the start of a match
Frank Lampard (v Stoke) 93:14

By a substitute after coming on
Nicolas Anelka (v Stoke) 30:48

GOAL DETAILS

How the goals were struck

SCORED		CONCEDED
37	Right foot	14
17	Left foot	5
12	Headers	5
2	Others	0

How the goals were struck

SCORED		CONCEDED
49	Open play	16
6	Cross	3
2	Corner	1
2	Penalties	0
2	Direct from free-kick	1
4	Free-kick	2
3	Own goals	1

Distance from goal

SCORED		CONCEDED
23	6yds	10
38	18yds	13
7	18+yds	1

GOALS SCORED/CONCEDED PER FIVE-MINUTE INTERVALS

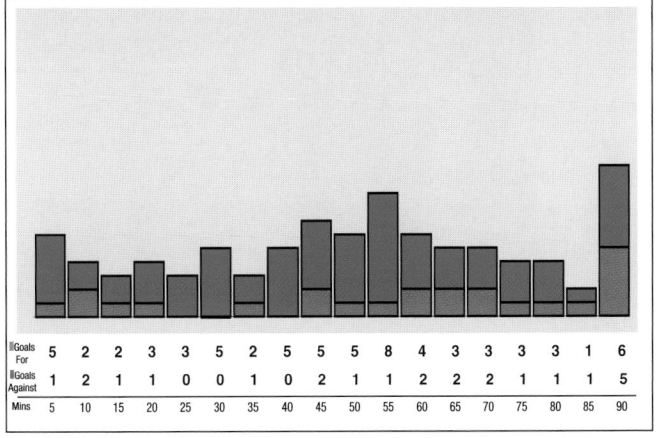

Goals For	5	2	2	3	3	5	2	5	5	5	8	4	3	3	3	3	1	6
Goals Against	1	2	1	1	0	0	1	0	2	1	1	2	2	2	1	1	1	5
Mins	5	10	15	20	25	30	35	40	45	50	55	60	65	70	75	80	85	90

EVERTON

CLUB SUMMARY

FORMED	1878
MANAGER	David Moyes
GROUND	Goodison Park
CAPACITY	40,260
NICKNAME	The Toffees
WEBSITE	www.evertonfc.co.uk

The New Football Pools PLAYER OF THE SEASON — Phil Jagielka

OVERALL

P	W	D	L	F	A	GD
48	21	15	12	67	47	20

BARCLAYS PREMIER LEAGUE

Pos	P	W	D	L	F	A	GD	Pts
5	38	17	12	9	55	37	18	63

HOME

Pos	P	W	D	L	F	A	GD	Pts
9	19	8	6	5	31	20	11	30

AWAY

Pos	P	W	D	L	F	A	GD	Pts
5	19	9	6	4	24	17	7	33

CUP PROGRESS DETAILS

Competition	Round reached	Knocked out by
FA Cup	Final	Chelsea
UEFA Cup	R2	Standard Liège
Carling Cup	R3	Blackburn

BIGGEST WIN (ALL COMPS)

05/04/09 4–0 v Wigan **PREM**

BIGGEST DEFEAT (ALL COMPS)

30/08/08 0–3 v Portsmouth **PREM**

THE PLAYER WITH THE MOST

Shots on target
Marouane Fellaini 30
Shots off target
Tim Cahill 24
Shots without scoring
Jack Rodwell 14
Assists
Steven Pienaar 8
Offsides
Tim Cahill 23
Fouls
Marouane Fellaini 101
Fouls without a card
Jo... 14
Free-kicks won
Steven Pienaar 78
Defensive clearances
Joleon Lescott 37

actim INDEX for the 2008/09 Barclays Premier League Season

Rank	Player	Pts
18	Joleon Lescott	476
19	Tim Howard	472
31	Tim Cahill	432
35	Marouane Fellaini	423
37	Phil Neville	422

ATTENDANCE RECORD

High	Low	Average
39,574	31,063	35,667
v Liverpool (27/09/2008)	v Middlesbrough (16/11/2008)	

CLOCKWISE FROM TOP: Phil Neville looks on as Chelsea lift the FA Cup; Marouane Fellaini was a key signing; Dan Gosling scores the winner against Liverpool in Everton's FA Cup fourth-round replay at Goodison Park; Everton's players celebrate beating Manchester United in their FA Cup semi-final

EVERTON'S season started with only two wins in the first 12 matches, but ended with David Moyes leading his side out at Wembley in the FA Cup final against Chelsea.

The turnaround was amazing. A small squad, in terms of numbers at least, was cruelly hit by major injuries to some of their most influential players, but still managed a top-six finish.

They even took a shock lead over Chelsea in the first minute of the FA Cup final before being overhauled late in the game to suffer an agonising 2–1 defeat.

Moyes lost all his strikers at one stage of the season and had to borrow Brazilian Jo from Manchester City and use midfielders Tim Cahill and Marouane Fellaini as emergency forwards. Moyes lost frontmen Ayegbeni Yakubu and Victor Anichebe, midfielder Mikel Arteta and even key defender Phil Jagielka by the time the sharp end of the season arrived. And the likes of Joseph Yobo, Louis Saha, James Vaughan, Leighton Baines and Tony Hibbert were all hit by lengthy lay-offs at some stage. But the adversity just produced more determination and defiance from Everton.

It would have been hard to imagine how the season would climax as winter fell at Goodison Park. Everton were out of both the League Cup and UEFA Cup by the first weekend of October, and had suffered a painful home defeat in the League at the hands of Liverpool along the way.

When they lost at Arsenal on 10th October, they were down to 16th position in the Barclays Premier League and the alarm bells were beginning to sound. But Moyes' men then embarked on a defiant run and, despite being crippled by injuries to key men, they lost just two of the next 17 matches.

Their turnaround began with a heroic home performance in a 1–1 draw with Manchester United.

Everton's transformation was proven in three unbeaten games against Liverpool in the space of 16 days just after the turn of the year. A gutsy 1–1 league draw at Anfield was followed by another 1–1 scoreline there in the FA Cup fourth round. The replay at Goodison Park then saw teenager Dan Gosling strike a late winner to send the Toffees into the quarter-finals.

The momentum, team spirit and adrenalin were in full flow by now. Cahill and record-signing Fellaini were having to play out of position up front, with no strikers fit, but they did remarkably well.

Aston Villa were crushed in the last eight of the FA Cup, bringing about the Toffees' first visit to the new Wembley.

There they took on a Manchester United side without several big names due to their UEFA Champions League commitments. And Everton took advantage, holding the champions to 0–0 after extra-time, and then winning the penalty shoot-out 4–2, with Jagielka netting the decisive spot-kick.

With final opponents Chelsea heading for the Champions League, Everton's European qualification for the third time in four seasons was confirmed a month from the end of the season – but another top-six finish was attained nonetheless.

There were heroes everywhere. Goalkeeper Tim Howard set a club clean sheets record in the Barclays Premier League while Jagielka and Baines forced their way into the England squad. Sadly, Jagielka's fine season would end in tears with a knee injury in the home game with Manchester City just six days after that semi-final triumph.

At one stage Everton lost just three of 26 games, although their season did tail off somewhat with the cup final – their first since 1995 – on the horizon. But once again Moyes had produced miracles on a shoestring, and the hope remains that he will be able to break into the top four.

> **Tim Howard set a club clean sheets record in the Barclays Premier League**

RESULTS 2008/09

August

16th ● Blackburn ....h L 2–3 **Att:** 38,675. **Ref:** A Marriner — **Everton** (4-4-1-1): Howard, Neville, Yobo▌, Lescott, Nuno Valente (Baxter 78), Arteta¹, Rodwell, Jagielka, Baines, Osman, Yakubu▌¹. Subs not used: Turner, Jutkiewicz, Gosling, Agard, Kissock, Wallace.

23rd ● West Brom ....a W 1–2 **Att:** 26,190. **Ref:** R Styles — **Everton** (4-1-4-1): Howard, Neville, Yobo, Lescott, Baines, Jagielka, Arteta, Rodwell, Osman▌¹, Baxter (Vaughan 58), Yakubu¹ (Nuno Valente 86). Subs not used: Turner, Jutkiewicz, Agard, Kissock, Wallace.

30th ● Portsmouth ....h L 0–3 **Att:** 34,418. **Ref:** M Halsey — **Everton** (4-4-2): Howard, Neville, Yobo, Lescott, Baines▌, Arteta, Rodwell, Jagielka, Osman (Baxter 71), Yakubu, Vaughan (Anichebe 58). Subs not used: Turner, Jacobsen, Nuno Valente, Kissock, Wallace.

September

14th ● Stoke ....a W 2–3 **Att:** 27,415. **Ref:** A Wiley — **Everton** (4-1-4-1): Howard, Neville, Yobo, Jagielka, Lescott, Fellaini, Anichebe¹ (Vaughan 90), Cahill¹ (Rodwell 81), Castillo, Arteta▌, Yakubu¹. Subs not used: Nash, Baines, Nuno Valente, Kissock, Baxter.

18th ● Standard Liege ....h D 2–2 **Att:** 28,312. **Ref:** G Gilewski — **Everton** (4-4-1-1): Howard, Neville, Yobo, Jagielka, Lescott, Anichebe (Vaughan 64), Castillo¹, Osman, Arteta, Cahill, Yakubu¹. Subs not used: Nash, Baines, Nuno Valente, Jutkiewicz, Baxter, Rodwell.

21st ● Hull ....a D 2–2 **Att:** 24,845. **Ref:** L Mason — **Everton** (4-4-1-1): Howard, Neville, Jagielka, Yobo, Baines (Lescott 46), Osman¹, Fellaini▌, Arteta, Castillo (Saha 46), Cahill¹, Yakubu (Vaughan 87). Subs not used: Nash, Nuno Valente, Rodwell, Baxter.

24th ● Blackburn ....a L 1–0 **Att:** 14,366. **Ref:** M Atkinson — **Everton** (4-3-3): Howard, Neville▌, Yobo, Jagielka, Lescott, Rodwell, Castillo (Cahill 46), Fellaini (Yakubu 46), Vaughan▌ (Baxter 83), Saha, Osman. Subs not used: Turner, Hibbert, Baines, Nuno Valente.

27th ● Liverpool ....h L 0–2 **Att:** 39,574. **Ref:** M Riley — **Everton** (4-4-1-1): Howard, Hibbert (Saha 63), Yobo, Jagielka, Lescott, Arteta, Neville▌, Fellaini▌, Osman, Cahill▌, Yakubu▌. Subs not used: Nash, Baines, Castillo, Vaughan, Nuno Valente, Rodwell.

October

2nd ● Standard Liege ....a L 2–1 **Att:** 27,406. **Ref:** P Sippel — **Everton** (4-4-2): Howard, Hibbert (Anichebe 63), Jagielka¹, Lescott, Baines▌, Neville (Yobo 88), Osman, Cahill, Arteta, Yakubu, Saha (Pienaar 71). Subs not used: Nash, Castillo, Nuno Valente, Rodwell.

5th ● Newcastle ....h D 2–2 **Att:** 33,805. **Ref:** H Webb — **Everton** (4-4-2): Howard, Hibbert, Jagielka, Lescott, Baines, Arteta¹, Osman, Fellaini▌¹, Pienaar (Vaughan 84), Saha (Anichebe 72), Yakubu. Subs not used: Nash, Yobo, Castillo, Nuno Valente, Rodwell.

18th ● Arsenal ....a L 3–1 **Att:** 60,064. **Ref:** P Walton — **Everton** (4-5-1): Howard, Hibbert (Vaughan 80), Jagielka, Lescott, Baines, Arteta, Osman▌¹, Rodwell, Fellaini (Saha 74), Pienaar▌, Yakubu (Neville 80). Subs not used: Nash, Nuno Valente, Gosling, Wallace.

25th ● Man Utd ....h D 1–1 **Att:** 36,069. **Ref:** A Wiley — **Everton** (4-4-2): Howard, Neville▌, Yobo, Jagielka▌, Lescott, Arteta, Fellaini▌¹, Osman, Pienaar, Saha (Vaughan 90), Yakubu (Vaughan 88). Subs not used: Nash, Baines, Castillo, Nuno Valente, Rodwell.

29th ● Bolton ....a W 0–1 **Att:** 21,692. **Ref:** P Dowd — **Everton** (4-4-2): Howard, Neville, Yobo, Jagielka, Lescott▌, Arteta (Rodwell 90), Fellaini▌¹, Osman, Pienaar, Yakubu (Cahill 63), Saha (Anichebe 83). Subs not used: Nash, Hibbert, Baines, Vaughan.

November

1st ● Fulham ....h W 1–0 **Att:** 31,278. **Ref:** L Mason — **Everton** (4-4-1-1): Howard, Neville, Yobo, Jagielka, Lescott, Arteta, Osman, Fellaini (Saha¹ 61), Pienaar (Anichebe 76), Cahill, Yakubu (Vaughan 84). Subs not used: Nash, Hibbert, Baines, Rodwell.

8th ● West Ham ....a W 1–3 **Att:** 33,961. **Ref:** M Halsey — **Everton** (4-4-2): Howard, Neville, Yobo, Jagielka, Lescott▌¹, Arteta, Cahill, Rodwell (Vaughan 65), Osman, Saha² (Hibbert 90), Anichebe (Baines 86). Subs not used: Nash, Castillo, Jutkiewicz, Gosling.

16th ● Middlesbrough ....h D 1–1 **Att:** 31,063. **Ref:** H Webb — **Everton** (4-4-2): Howard, Neville, Yobo, Jagielka, Lescott, Arteta, Fellaini, Cahill (Anichebe 85), Osman (Pienaar 72), Yakubu¹ (Vaughan 88), Saha. Subs not used: Nash, Hibbert, Baines, Castillo.

24th ● Wigan ....a L 1–0 **Att:** 18,344. **Ref:** R Styles — **Everton** (4-4-2): Howard, Neville (Baines 85), Yobo, Jagielka, Lescott, Cahill, Fellaini, Arteta, Osman, Saha (Anichebe 65), Yakubu. Subs not used: Nash, Castillo, Rodwell, Jutkiewicz, Gosling.

30th ● Tottenham ....a W 0–1 **Att:** 35,742. **Ref:** S Bennett — **Everton** (4-5-1): Howard, Neville, Yobo, Jagielka, Lescott, Arteta, Osman (Baines 88), Cahill▌, Fellaini▌, Pienaar▌¹, Yakubu (L Saha 11 (Anichebe 71)), Saha (Anichebe 71). Subs not used: Nash, Castillo, Rodwell, Gosling.

December

7th ● Aston Villa ....h L 2–3 **Att:** 31,922. **Ref:** M Atkinson — **Everton** (4-4-1-1): Howard, Neville (Van der Meyde 84), Yobo, Jagielka, Lescott▌², Osman, Fellaini▌, Arteta, Pienaar, Cahill, Anichebe (Baines 86). Subs not used: Nash, Castillo, Jutkiewicz, Gosling, Kissock.

13th ● Man City ....a W 0–1 **Att:** 41,344. **Ref:** M Halsey — **Everton** (4-5-1): Howard, Neville, Yobo, Jagielka, Lescott, Osman, Pienaar, Fellaini▌, Castillo, Arteta, Cahill¹. Subs not used: Nash, Hibbert, Baines, Van der Meyde, Rodwell, Jutkiewicz, Gosling.

22nd ● Chelsea ....h D 0–0 **Att:** 35,655. **Ref:** P Dowd — **Everton** (4-1-4-1): Howard, Hibbert, Yobo (Baines 61), Jagielka, Lescott, Neville, Osman, Arteta, Fellaini, Pienaar, Cahill. Subs not used: Nash, Van der Meyde, Rodwell, Jutkiewicz, Gosling, Kissock.

26th ● Middlesbrough ....a W 0–1 **Att:** 30,253. **Ref:** M Riley — **Everton** (4-5-1): Howard, Hibbert, Jagielka, Lescott, Baines, Arteta, Neville, Fellaini▌, Pienaar, Gosling, Cahill¹. Subs not used: Nash, Van der Meyde, Rodwell, Jutkiewicz, Anichebe, Kissock, Wallace.

28th ● Sunderland ....h W 3–0 **Att:** 39,146. **Ref:** R Styles — **Everton** (4-5-1): Howard, Hibbert, Jagielka▌, Lescott, Baines, Arteta², Osman (Gosling¹ 69), Neville, Fellaini (Anichebe 77), Pienaar, Cahill (Jutkiewicz 86). Subs not used: Nash, Van der Meyde, Rodwell, Kissock.

January

3rd ● Macclesfield ....a W 0–1 **Att:** 6,008. **Ref:** P Walton — **Everton** (4-4-2): Howard, Hibbert, Lescott, Jagielka, Baines, Osman¹, Neville, Arteta, Pienaar (Gosling 90), Anichebe, Cahill. Subs not used: Nash, Fellaini, Rodwell, Jutkiewicz, Kissock, Wallace.

10th ● Hull ....h W 2–0 **Att:** 37,527. **Ref:** M Atkinson — **Everton** (4-4-2): Howard, Hibbert, Jagielka, Lescott, Baines, Osman, Arteta¹ (Rodwell 90), Neville, Pienaar, Fellaini▌¹, Cahill▌ (Anichebe 73). Subs not used: Nash, Van der Meyde, Castillo, Jutkiewicz, Gosling.

19th ● Liverpool ....a D 1–1 **Att:** 44,382. **Ref:** H Webb — **Everton** (4-5-1): Howard, Hibbert, Lescott, Jagielka, Baines, Osman, Arteta¹, Neville, Pienaar▌, Cahill¹, Anichebe. Subs not used: Nash, Van der Meyde, Castillo, Rodwell, Jutkiewicz, Gosling, Kissock.

25th ● Liverpool ....a D 1–1 **Att:** 43,524. **Ref:** S Bennett — **Everton** (4-5-1): Howard, Hibbert, Jagielka, Lescott¹, Baines, Anichebe (Gosling 71), Castillo (Rodwell 76), Neville, Osman, Pienaar▌, Cahill▌. Subs not used: Nash, Yobo, Van der Meyde, Jacobsen, Jutkiewicz.

28th ● Arsenal ....h D 1–1 **Att:** 37,097. **Ref:** A Marriner — **Everton** (4-4-1-1): Howard, Hibbert▌, Jagielka, Lescott, Baines, Osman, Arteta▌, Neville, Pienaar, Fellaini, Cahill¹ (Anichebe 86). Subs not used: Nash, Yobo, Castillo, Rodwell, Jutkiewicz, Gosling.

31st ● Man Utd ....a L 1–0 **Att:** 75,399. **Ref:** M Halsey — **Everton** (4-4-1-1): Howard, Hibbert, Jagielka, Lescott, Baines, Osman, Arteta, Neville, Pienaar, Fellaini (Anichebe 68), Cahill. Subs not used: Nash, Yobo, Castillo, Jacobsen, Rodwell, Gosling.

February

4th ● Liverpool ....h W 1–0 **Att:** 37,918. **Ref:** A Wiley — **Everton** (4-5-1): Howard, Hibbert▌, Jagielka, Lescott, Baines, Osman, Fellaini (Gosling¹ 52), Neville▌ (Van der Meyde 106), Arteta▌, Pienaar▌ (Rodwell 60), Cahill▌. Subs not used: Nash, Yobo, Castillo, Jacobsen.

7th ● Bolton ....h W 3–0 **Att:** 33,791. **Ref:** P Walton — **Everton** (4-4-1-1): Howard, Hibbert▌, Jagielka, Lescott, Baines (Yobo 82), Gosling, Neville, Arteta¹ (Van der Meyde 85), Osman, Cahill (Rodwell 77), Jo². Subs not used: Nash, Castillo, Jacobsen, Baxter.

15th ● Aston Villa ....h W 3–1 **Att:** 32,979. **Ref:** M Atkinson — **Everton** (4-4-1-1): Howard, Hibbert▌, Jagielka, Lescott, Baines, Gosling, Neville, Arteta¹ (Castillo 90), Rodwell▌, Cahill▌, Anichebe (Yobo 88). Subs not used: Nash, Van der Meyde, Jacobsen, Baxter, Wallace.

● Barclays Premier League ● FA Cup ● Carling Cup ● UEFA Champions League ● UEFA Cup   ▌Yellow Card █ Red Card

BARCLAYS PREMIER LEAGUE

RESULTS 2008/09

| 22nd | ● Newcastle ....a | D 0–0 | **Att:** 47,683. **Ref:** L Mason — **Everton** (4-4-2): Howard, Jagielka, Yobo, Lescott, Baines, Gosling (Saha 74), Neville, Arteta (Castillo 7), Rodwell, Anichebe (Fellaini▌ 45). Subs not used: Nash, Van der Meyde, Jacobsen, Wallace. |
| 28th | ● West Brom ....h | W 2–0 | **Att:** 33,898. **Ref:** S Bennett — **Everton** (4-4-1-1): Howard, Hibbert (Osman 26), Yobo, Jagielka, Baines, Gosling, Neville, Fellaini▌ (Saha¹ 60), Pienaar, Cahill, Jo (Castillo 75). Subs not used: Nash, Lescott, Van der Meyde, Jacobsen. |

March

4th	● Blackburn ....a	D 0–0	**Att:** 21,445. **Ref:** A Wiley — **Everton** (4-4-1-1): Howard, Jagielka, Yobo, Lescott, Baines, Osman, Neville, Rodwell (Saha 71), Pienaar, Cahill, Jo (Fellaini 78). Subs not used: Nash, Van der Meyde, Castillo, Jacobsen, Gosling.
8th	● Middlesbrough ....h	W 2–1	**Att:** 37,856. **Ref:** M Halsey — **Everton** (4-4-1-1): Howard, Neville, Yobo, Jagielka, Lescott, Pienaar (Gosling 89), Rodwell (Saha¹ 46), Osman, Baines, Fellaini¹, Cahill. Subs not used: Nash, Van der Meyde, Castillo, Jacobsen, Wallace.
14th	● Stoke ....h	W 3–1	**Att:** 36,396. **Ref:** A Marriner — **Everton** (4-4-1-1): Howard, Jagielka, Yobo, Lescott¹, Baines, Osman, Neville, Cahill (Saha 46), Pienaar, Fellaini¹, Jo¹ (Rodwell 85). Subs not used: Nash, Castillo, Jacobsen, Gosling, Wallace.
21st	● Portsmouth ....a	L 2–1	**Att:** 20,388. **Ref:** P Walton — **Everton** (4-4-2): Howard, Jacobsen (Gosling 86), Jagielka, Lescott, Baines¹, Osman▌, Fellaini, Neville, Pienaar, Saha, Jo (Rodwell 90). Subs not used: Nash, Castillo, Agard, Baxter, Wallace.

April

5th	● Wigan ....h	W 4–0	**Att:** 34,427. **Ref:** P Dowd — **Everton** (4-4-1-1): Howard, Hibbert, Jagielka, Lescott, Baines, Osman¹, Neville, Cahill (Rodwell 64), Pienaar (Gosling 71), Fellaini¹ (Saha 72), Jo². Subs not used: Nash, Van der Meyde, Castillo, Jacobsen.
12th	● Aston Villa ....a	D 3–3	**Att:** 40,188. **Ref:** H Webb — **Everton** (4-4-1-1): Howard, Hibbert▌ (Jacobsen 65), Lescott, Jagielka, Baines, Osman, Neville▌, Cahill¹, Pienaar¹, Fellaini¹, Jo (Saha 81). Subs not used: Nash, Van der Meyde, Castillo, Rodwell, Gosling.
19th	● Man Utd ....a	D 0–0	**Att:** 88,141. **Ref:** M Riley — **Everton** (4-4-1-1): Howard, Hibbert, Jagielka, Lescott, Baines, Osman, Neville, Fellaini▌ (Vaughan 102), Pienaar, Cahill▌, Saha (Rodwell 70). Subs not used: Nash, Yobo, Castillo, Jacobsen, Gosling.
22nd	● Chelsea ....a	D 0–0	**Att:** 41,556. **Ref:** M Halsey — **Everton** (4-4-2): Howard, Jacobsen (Jagielka 87), Lescott, Yobo, Baines, Osman (Rodwell 89), Castillo, Neville▌, Pienaar, Jo (Saha 90), Cahill. Subs not used: Nash, Hibbert, Vaughan, Gosling.
25th	● Man City ....h	L 1–2	**Att:** 37,791. **Ref:** A Wiley — **Everton** (4-4-1-1): Howard, Hibbert, Yobo, Jagielka, Baines, Osman, Neville▌, Castillo (Gosling¹ 60), Pienaar, Fellaini (Cahill 60), Saha (Vaughan 60). Subs not used: Nash, Lescott, Rodwell, Baxter.

May

3rd	● Sunderland ....a	W 0–2	**Att:** 41,313. **Ref:** M Atkinson — **Everton** (4-4-1-1): Howard, Jacobsen (Rodwell 73), Lescott, Yobo, Baines, Gosling▌ (Castillo 86), Neville, Fellaini¹, Pienaar¹, Cahill, Jo (Saha¹ 80). Subs not used: Nash, Vaughan, Agard, Wallace.
9th	● Tottenham..........................h	D 0–0	**Att:** 36,646. **Ref:** L Mason — **Everton** (4-4-1-1): Howard, Neville, Yobo, Lescott▌, Baines, Gosling (Osman 69), Rodwell, Cahill, Pienaar¹, Fellaini, Jo (Saha 69). Subs not used: Nash, Castillo, Vaughan, Jacobsen, Wallace.
16th	● West Ham...........................h	W 3–1	**Att:** 38,501. **Ref:** P Dowd — **Everton** (4-4-1-1): Howard, Jacobsen, Yobo¹, Jagielka, Lescott, Baines▌, Osman, Neville, Cahill (Jo 80), Pienaar, Fellaini (Rodwell 69), Saha² (Vaughan 80). Subs not used: Nash, Hibbert, Castillo, Gosling.
24th	● Fulham ....a	W 0–2	**Att:** 25,497. **Ref:** M Riley — **Everton** (4-4-1-1): Howard, Hibbert, Yobo, Lescott, Baines, Neville (Gosling 76), Cahill, Rodwell, Pienaar (Vaughan 86), Osman², Saha (Castillo 79). Subs not used: Nash, Jo, Jacobsen, Lescott.
30th	● Chelsea ....n	L 2–1	**Att:** 89,391. **Ref:** H Webb — **Everton** (4-3-1-2): Howard, Hibbert▌ (Jacobsen 46), Yobo, Lescott, Baines▌, Osman (Gosling 82), Neville▌, Pienaar, Cahill, Fellaini, Saha¹ (Vaughan 77). Subs not used: Nash, Castillo, Rodwell, Baxter.

● Barclays Premier League ● FA Cup ● Carling Cup ● UEFA Champions League ● UEFA Cup   ▌Yellow Card ▌Red Card

Louis Saha fires home Everton's first goal from the penalty-spot in a 3–1 win against West Ham at Goodison Park

EVERTON

BARCLAYS PREMIER LEAGUE GOALKEEPER STATS

Player	Minutes on pitch	Appearances	Match starts	Completed matches	Sub appearances	Subbed off	SAVES BREAKDOWN								Clean sheets	Goals conceded	Minutes since conceding	Save %	PENALTIES			Yellow cards	Red cards
							Saved with feet	Punched	Parried	Tipped over	Fumbled	Tipped round	Caught	Blocked					Saved	Resulting in goals	Opposition miss		
Tim Howard	3618	38	38	38	0	0	1	17	26	4	0	12	116	0	17	37	164	82.71	0	3	0	0	0

BARCLAYS PREMIER LEAGUE OUTFIELD PLAYER STATS

Player	Minutes on pitch	Appearances	Match starts	Completed matches	Substitute appearances	Subbed off	Goals scored	Minutes since scoring	Assists	Shots on target	Shots off target	Crosses	Defensive clearances	Defensive blocks	Fouls committed	Free-kicks won	Caught offside	Yellow cards	Red cards
Victor Anichebe	637	17	5	1	12	4	1	550	1	6	5	0	0	1	12	11	2	0	0
Mikel Arteta	2366	26	26	22	0	4	5	51	6	18	12	79	8	1	32	45	0	3	0
Leighton Baines	2479	31	26	24	5	2	1	854	7	9	2	63	7	8	22	44	2	2	0
Jose Baxter	98	3	1	0	2	1	0	-	0	1	1	0	0	0	1	0	0	0	0
Tim Cahill	2541	30	28	18	2	9	8	572	5	30	24	11	20	1	68	49	23	3	1
Segundo Castillo	527	9	5	3	4	2	0	-	0	5	0	4	0	3	8	3	0	0	0
Marouane Fellaini	2521	30	28	20	2	8	8	185	3	30	17	7	12	5	101	40	17	12	0
Dan Gosling	628	11	6	3	5	3	2	178	1	7	7	3	0	0	8	7	1	1	0
Tony Hibbert	1375	17	16	12	1	4	0	-	1	0	0	15	4	2	14	18	0	4	0
Lars Jacobsen	373	5	4	1	1	3	0	-	0	0	0	0	0	0	0	1	0	0	0
Phil Jagielka	3152	34	33	33	1	0	0	-	0	2	9	4	36	24	12	40	0	2	0
Jo	959	12	11	3	1	8	5	379	2	19	8	0	0	0	8	21	19	0	0
Lukas Jutkiewicz	6	1	0	0	1	0	0	-	0	0	0	0	0	0	0	0	0	0	0
Joleon Lescott	3378	36	35	35	1	0	2	833	2	9	12	11	37	22	34	26	2	5	0
Phil Neville	3403	37	36	33	1	3	0	-	3	6		26	18	5	30	16	1	5	0
Jorge Nuno Valente	87	2	1	0	1	1	0	-	0	0	0	1	0	2	0	0	3	0	0
Leon Osman	3052	34	32	27	2	5	6	5	4	27	20	20	23	7	36	39	1	3	0
Steven Pienaar	2533	28	27	23	1	4	2	318	8	22	16	31	2	1	22	78	6	5	0
Jack Rodwell	940	19	9	7	10	2	0	-	0	6	8	0	4	3	13	4	0	0	0
Louis Saha	1212	24	10	1	14	9	6	82	1	23	17	2	9	1	12	19	7	1	0
Andy van der Meyde	18	2	0	0	2	0	0	-	0	0	0	1	0	0	2	0	0	0	0
James Vaughan	239	13	1	0	12	1	0	-	0	0	0	0	0	0	6	4	1	0	0
Ayegbeni Yakubu	1164	14	14	6	0	8	4	126	1	14	14	8	0	0	20	15	16	2	0
Joseph Yobo	2461	27	26	25	1	1	1	138	0	4	6	0	22	13	15	17	0	1	0

SEASON TOTALS

Goals scored	55
Goals conceded	37
Clean sheets	17
Shots on target	232
Shots off target	191
Shots per goal	7.69
Pens awarded	5
Pens scored	4
Pens conceded	3
Offsides	98
Corners	194
Crosses	281
Players used	25
Fouls committed	474
Free-kicks won	508

CARDS RECEIVED

49   1

SEQUENCES

Wins	3
(on two occasions)	
Losses	
(–)	
Draws	2
(on two occasions)	
Undefeated	7
(13/12/08–28/01/09)	
Without win	5
(21/09/08–25/10/08)	
Undefeated home	8
(22/12/08–05/04/09)	
Undefeated away	4
(30/11/08–19/01/09)	
Without scoring	
(–)	
Without conceding	5
(13/12/08–10/01/09)	
Scoring	7
(05/10/08–16/11/08)	
Conceding	9
(16/08/08–25/10/08)	

SEASON INFORMATION

Highest Position: 5
Lowest Position: 19
Average goals scored per game: 1.45
Average goals conceded per game: 0.97

League position at the end of each week

League position at the end of: August 17, September 14, October 12, November 7, December 6, January 6, February 6, March 6, April 6, May 5

MATCH RECORDS

Goals scored per match

		W	D	L	Pts
Failed to score	9	0	5	4	5
Scored 1 goal	12	5	4	3	19
Scored 2 goals	9	5	2	2	17
Scored 3 goals	7	6	1	0	19
Scored 4+ goals	1	1	0	0	3

Goals conceded per match

		W	D	L	Pts
Clean sheet	17	12	5	0	41
Conceded 1 goal	10	4	4	2	16
Conceded 2 goals	6	1	2	3	5
Conceded 3 goals	5	0	1	4	1
Conceded 4+ goals	0	0	0	0	0

QUICK-FIRE GOALS

From the start of a match
Leighton Baines (v Portsmouth) 3:54

By a substitute after coming on
Louis Saha (v West Brom) 9:15

LAST-GASP GOALS

From the start of a match
Dan Gosling (v Man City) 93:47

By a substitute after coming on
Dan Gosling (v Man City) 34:37

GOAL DETAILS

How the goals were struck

SCORED		CONCEDED
22	Right foot	25
17	Left foot	5
15	Headers	7
1	Others	0

How the goals were struck

SCORED		CONCEDED
31	Open play	24
5	Cross	3
4	Corner	3
4	Penalties	3
4	Direct from free-kick	1
5	Free-kick	1
2	Own goals	2

Distance from goal

SCORED		CONCEDED
25	6yds	14
23	18yds	17
7	18+yds	6

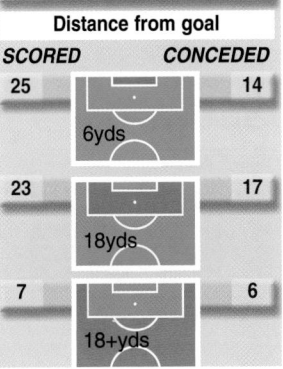

GOALS SCORED/CONCEDED PER FIVE-MINUTE INTERVALS

Goals For	1	2	0	4	2	3	1	3	4	4	5	0	6	1	2	4	3	10
Goals Against	1	1	1	1	4	0	2	1	2	3	6	1	3	5	1	0	0	5
Mins	5	10	15	20	25	30	35	40	45	50	55	60	65	70	75	80	85	90

FULHAM

CLUB SUMMARY

FORMED	1879
MANAGER	Roy Hodgson
GROUND	Craven Cottage
CAPACITY	25,350
NICKNAME	The Cottagers
WEBSITE	www.fulhamfc.co.uk

The New Football Pools PLAYER OF THE SEASON — **Brede Hangeland**

OVERALL

P	W	D	L	F	A	GD
45	18	12	15	51	46	5

BARCLAYS PREMIER LEAGUE

Pos	P	W	D	L	F	A	GD	Pts
7	38	14	11	13	39	34	5	53

HOME

Pos	P	W	D	L	F	A	GD	Pts
6	19	11	3	5	28	16	12	36

AWAY

Pos	P	W	D	L	F	A	GD	Pts
9	19	3	8	8	11	18	-7	17

CUP PROGRESS DETAILS

Competition	Round reached	Knocked out by
FA Cup	QF	Man Utd
Carling Cup	R3	Burnley

BIGGEST WIN (ALL COMPS)
20/12/08 3–0 v Middlesbrough **PREM**

BIGGEST DEFEAT (ALL COMPS)
07/03/09 0–4 v Man Utd **FAC6**

THE PLAYER WITH THE MOST

Shots on target
Andrew Johnson 40

Shots off target
Bobby Zamora 40

Shots without scoring
John Pantsil 9

Assists
Bobby Zamora 6

Offsides
Andrew Johnson 31

Fouls
Bobby Zamora 77

Fouls without a card
Diomansy Kamara 10

Free-kicks won
Bobby Zamora 42

Defensive clearances
Aaron Hughes 58

actim INDEX for the 2008/09 Barclays Premier League Season

Rank	Player	Pts
17	Mark Schwarzer	477
40	Aaron Hughes	410
41	Brede Hangeland	409
42	Paul Konchesky	408
67	John Pantsil	371

ATTENDANCE RECORD

High	Low	Average
25,661	22,259	24,344

v Liverpool (04/04/2009) v Blackburn (11/03/2009)

ONCE again Fulham defied pre-season predictions, but even the most fanatical of supporters could not have envisaged what was to come.

Annually tipped for relegation from the Barclays Premier League, the Cottagers surpassed all expectations by finishing seventh – qualifying for Europe in the process. A 2–0 defeat by Everton on the final day failed to mute the carnival scenes on the banks of the Thames as Fulham celebrated claiming a place in the 2009/10 Europa League.

Rock solid at Craven Cottage – only Manchester United, Liverpool and Manchester City won more home games – they also addressed their disastrous away form by picking up three victories on the road.

Just a year earlier they were subjected to a nerve-shredding climax to the campaign as only a second-half goal against Portsmouth prevented them from dropping into the Championship. It is a remarkable turnaround that is easily explained by the presence of one man – Roy Hodgson, a manager who was once unappreciated on these shores. The 61-year-old's impressive coaching CV, which includes stints with Inter Milan and the Switzerland and Finland national teams, was overshadowed by his sacking by Blackburn in 1998. His departure from Ewood Park always rankled, largely because he felt he had done a sound job, and it ensured he was held in higher regard in Europe than in England.

But 17 months after rescuing a club that was teetering on the brink of relegation, Hodgson has performed nothing short of miracles at Fulham. Furthermore he has managed it playing attractive, passing football and on a limited budget.

A first-rate coach on the training ground, Hodgson's technical appreciation for the game is well known and he has proved an excellent man-manager. Seeking to avoid controversy in public at all costs, Hodgson cuts a dignified figure whose fairness and honesty shames many of his rivals.

Despite Hodgson's input, luck also played its part in Fulham's highest top-flight finish – their previous best was ninth place under Chris Coleman in 2003/04. An extraordinary lack of injuries enabled Hodgson to field his first-choice XI for

---

'Hodgson has performed nothing short of miracles at Fulham'

much for the season. Hodgson enjoyed his good fortune, but also proved a shrewd operator in the transfer market with centre-back Brede Hangeland and goalkeeper Mark Schwarzer turning out to be inspired signings.

Star striker Andrew Johnson has slotted into Hodgson's system without fuss and is a key figure, even if he has not been as prolific as might have been expected.

But perhaps the canniest piece of business was the sale of Jimmy Bullard to Hull, a move that initially had fans despairing at the departure of a favourite son. Bullard's return from injury inspired Fulham's survival in 2007/08, yet Hodgson was never entirely convinced and despite public declarations that he wanted the erratic England squad midfielder to stay, he decided to let him go. Agreeing a £5million fee with Hull for a 30-year-old whose game was based on a high work rate, and who had recently returned from a career-threatening knee injury, seemed liked excellent business. And so it proved, as just 53 minutes into his Hull debut he damaged the same knee, requiring further surgery that ruled him out for the rest of the season.

With Bullard gone, Danny Murphy became the central figure in Fulham's midfield and the former Liverpool and England man emerged as one of their star performers.

The Cottagers' board will hope Hodgson maintains his fine track record in the transfer market with a crucial summer approaching. Keeping the magnificent Hangeland out of the clutches of other Barclays Premier League sides will be the greatest challenge, testing the board's resolve to keep a player signed for £2.5million yet who could now fetch four times that figure.

Despite claims to the contrary, Hodgson's transfer policy must also be shaped by Europa League commitments with Fulham's small squad sure to be put under pressure in its current state.

CLOCKWISE FROM ABOVE: Danny Murphy's penalty kick hits the back of the net in the 2–0 win over Manchester United; Brede Hangeland dispossesses Liverpool's Fernando Torres at Anfield; Erik Nevland celebrates during a 3–1 win against Portsmouth

FULHAM

RESULTS 2008/09

August

16th ● Hull ....a   L 2–1   **Att:** 24,525. **Ref:** P Walton — **Fulham** (4-5-1): Schwarzer, Pantsil, Hangeland, Hughes, Konchesky, Davies, Murphy (Andreasen 85), Ki-Hyeon¹ (Nevland 85), Bullard, Gera, Zamora (Dempsey 81). Subs not used: Zuberbuhler, Teymourian, Stoor, Kallio.

23rd ● Arsenal ....h   W 1–0   **Att:** 25,276. **Ref:** M Atkinson — **Fulham** (4-4-2): Schwarzer, Pantsil, Hughes, Hangeland¹, Kallio (Baird 74), Davies, Bullard, Murphy▌ (Teymourian▌ 81), Gera, Zamora, Ki-Hyeon (Dempsey 77). Subs not used: Stockdale, Nevland, Stoor, Milsom.

27th ● Leicester ....h   W 3–2   **Att:** 7,584. **Ref:** P Taylor — **Fulham** (4-4-2): Schwarzer, Stoor, Hangeland, Hughes, Kallio, Davies, Bullard¹, Murphy¹, Gera¹, Zamora, Ki-Hyeon (Nevland 59). Subs not used: Zuberbuhler, Pantsil, Teymourian, Dempsey, Andreasen, Baird.

September

13th ● Bolton ....h   W 2–1   **Att:** 23,656. **Ref:** S Tanner — **Fulham** (4-4-2): Schwarzer, Pantsil, Hangeland, Hughes, Konchesky, Davies, Murphy, Bullard, Gera¹, Zamora¹ (Nevland 84), Johnson (Ki-Hyeon 75). Subs not used: Zuberbuhler, Teymourian, Stoor, Dempsey, Kallio.

20th ● Blackburn ....a   L 1–0   **Att:** 19,398. **Ref:** L Probert — **Fulham** (4-4-2): Schwarzer, Pantsil, Hangeland, Hughes, Konchesky, Davies, Bullard, Murphy, Gera, Johnson, Zamora. Subs not used: Zuberbuhler, Ki-Hyeon, Nevland, Stoor, Dempsey, Andreasen, Kallio.

23rd ● Burnley ....a   L 1–0   **Att:** 7,119. **Ref:** M Jones — **Fulham** (4-4-2): Zuberbuhler, Baird, Stoor, Andreasen, Konchesky, Teymourian, Ki-Hyeon (Milsom 90), Gera (Pantsil 73), Dempsey, Kallio▌, Johnson (Nevland 72). Subs not used: Stockdale, Leijer, Brown.

27th ● West Ham ....h   L 1–2   **Att:** 23,946. **Ref:** A Marriner — **Fulham** (4-4-2): Schwarzer, Pantsil, Hughes, Hangeland▌, Konchesky▌, Gera, Murphy¹▌, Bullard, Davies, Johnson▌, Zamora. Subs not used: Zuberbuhler, Ki-Hyeon, Nevland, Dempsey, Andreasen, Kallio, Baird.

October

4th ● West Brom ....a   L 1–0   **Att:** 25,708. **Ref:** P Dowd — **Fulham** (4-4-2): Schwarzer, Pantsil (Stoor 82), Hughes, Hangeland, Konchesky, Davies, Bullard, Murphy (Andreasen¹ 87), Gera, Zamora (Ki-Hyeon 71), Dempsey. Subs not used: Zuberbuhler, Nevland, Kallio, Baird.

18th ● Sunderland ....h   D 0–0   **Att:** 25,116. **Ref:** K Stroud — **Fulham** (4-4-2): Schwarzer, Pantsil, Hughes, Hangeland, Konchesky, Davies, Murphy▌, Bullard, Gera (Dempsey 73), Zamora, Johnson. Subs not used: Zuberbuhler, Nevland, Gray, Andreasen, Kallio.

26th ● Portsmouth ....a   D 1–1   **Att:** 19,233. **Ref:** M Halsey — **Fulham** (4-4-2): Schwarzer, Pantsil (Nevland 84), Hughes, Hangeland, Konchesky, Davies, Murphy, Bullard, Gera (Dempsey¹ 71), Johnson, Zamora. Subs not used: Zuberbuhler, Ki-Hyeon, Milsom, Kallio, Baird.

29th ● Wigan ....h   W 2–0   **Att:** 22,500. **Ref:** H Webb — **Fulham** (4-4-2): Schwarzer, Pantsil, Hughes, Hangeland, Konchesky, Davies, Bullard (Baird 88), Murphy, Gera (Dempsey 72), Johnson² (Nevland 90), Zamora. Subs not used: Zuberbuhler, Gray, Stoor, Andreasen.

November

1st ● Everton ....a   L 1–0   **Att:** 31,278. **Ref:** L Mason — **Fulham** (4-4-2): Schwarzer, Pantsil, Hughes, Hangeland, Konchesky, Davies (Nevland 89), Bullard (Baird 83), Murphy, Gera (Dempsey 88), Zamora, Johnson. Subs not used: Zuberbuhler, Gray, Stoor, Andreasen.

9th ● Newcastle ....h   W 2–1   **Att:** 24,740. **Ref:** M Atkinson — **Fulham** (4-4-2): Schwarzer, Pantsil, Hughes, Hangeland, Konchesky, Davies, Bullard, Murphy¹▌ (Baird 88), Gera (Dempsey 64), Johnson¹, Zamora (Nevland 74). Subs not used: Zuberbuhler, Gray, Stoor, Andreasen.

15th ● Tottenham ....h   W 2–1   **Att:** 25,139. **Ref:** A Wiley — **Fulham** (4-4-2): Schwarzer, Pantsil, Hughes, Hangeland, Konchesky, Dempsey (Gera 87), Murphy, Bullard (Andreasen 90), Davies¹, Johnson¹, Zamora▌. Subs not used: Zuberbuhler, Nevland, Gray, Kallio, Baird.

22nd ● Liverpool ....a   D 0–0   **Att:** 43,589. **Ref:** M Halsey — **Fulham** (4-4-2): Schwarzer, Pantsil, Hangeland, Konchesky, Dempsey (Gera 84), Bullard (Baird 90), Murphy, Davies, Johnson, Zamora. Subs not used: Zuberbuhler, Nevland, Gray, Stoor, Kallio.

29th ● Aston Villa ....a   D 0–0   **Att:** 36,625. **Ref:** M Jones — **Fulham** (4-4-2): Schwarzer, Pantsil▌, Hughes, Hangeland, Konchesky, Davies, Murphy, Bullard, Dempsey▌, Johnson, Zamora (Gera 85). Subs not used: Zuberbuhler, Nevland, Gray, Etuhu, Stoor, Kallio.

December

6th ● Man City ....h   D 1–1   **Att:** 24,012. **Ref:** R Styles — **Fulham** (4-4-2): Schwarzer, Pantsil▌, Hughes, Hangeland, Konchesky, Davies, Murphy, Bullard¹▌, Dempsey, Johnson, Zamora. Subs not used: Zuberbuhler, Nevland, Gera, Etuhu, Stoor, Andreasen, Kallio.

13th ● Stoke ....a   D 0–0   **Att:** 25,287. **Ref:** S Attwell — **Fulham** (4-4-1-1): Schwarzer, Pantsil, Hangeland, Hughes, Konchesky, Davies, Bullard, Murphy, Gera▌, Dempsey, Johnson. Subs not used: Zuberbuhler, Nevland, Gray, Etuhu, Stoor, Andreasen.

20th ● Middlesbrough ....h   W 3–0   **Att:** 23,722. **Ref:** K Stroud — **Fulham** (4-4-2): Schwarzer, Pantsil, Hughes, Hangeland, Konchesky, Davies, Bullard¹ (Andreasen 85), Murphy¹ (Etuhu 79), Gera (Zamora 31), Dempsey¹, Johnson. Subs not used: Zuberbuhler, Nevland, Stoor, Kallio.

26th ● Tottenham ....a   D 0–0   **Att:** 35,866. **Ref:** P Walton — **Fulham** (4-4-2): Schwarzer, Pantsil, Baird, Hughes, Konchesky▌, Dempsey, Murphy, Bullard (Etuhu 37), Davies (Nevland 90), Johnson, Zamora. Subs not used: Zuberbuhler, Gray, Stoor, Andreasen, Kallio.

28th ● Chelsea ....h   D 2–2   **Att:** 25,462. **Ref:** A Marriner — **Fulham** (4-4-2): Schwarzer, Pantsil, Hangeland, Hughes, Davies, Etuhu (Andreasen 78), Murphy (Baird 90), Dempsey¹², Johnson, Zamora (Nevland 78). Subs not used: Zuberbuhler, Gray, Stoor, Kallio.

January

3rd ● Sheff Wed ....a   W 1–2   **Att:** 18,377. **Ref:** L Mason — **Fulham** (4-4-2): Schwarzer, Stoor, Hughes, Hangeland, Konchesky, Gray (Davies 77), Etuhu, Murphy, Dempsey, Johnson², Zamora (Nevland 69). Subs not used: Zuberbuhler, Pantsil, Andreasen, Kallio, Baird.

18th ● West Ham ....a   L 3–1   **Att:** 31,818. **Ref:** P Dowd — **Fulham** (4-4-2): Schwarzer, Pantsil▌, Hughes, Hangeland, Konchesky¹▌, Dempsey, Murphy, Etuhu (Andreasen 84), Davies▌ (Gera 74), Zamora (Nevland 72), Johnson. Subs not used: Zuberbuhler, Gray, Kallio, Baird.

24th ● Kettering ....a   W 2–4   **Att:** 5,406. **Ref:** M Riley — **Fulham** (4-4-2): Schwarzer, Stoor, Hangeland▌, Hughes, Konchesky, Davies¹, Andreasen, Etuhu (Murphy¹ 69), Gera (Zamora¹ 69), Johnson¹, Dempsey. Subs not used: Zuberbuhler, Pantsil, Nevland, Kallio, Baird.

27th ● Sunderland ....a   L 1–0   **Att:** 36,539. **Ref:** M Halsey — **Fulham** (4-4-2): Schwarzer, Pantsil, Hughes, Hangeland, Konchesky, Davies (Gera 76), Etuhu (Nevland 83), Murphy, Dempsey, Johnson, Zamora. Subs not used: Zuberbuhler, Stoor, Andreasen, Kallio, Baird.

31st ● Portsmouth ....h   W 3–1   **Att:** 23,722. **Ref:** A Wiley — **Fulham** (4-4-2): Schwarzer, Pantsil, Hughes, Hangeland, Konchesky, Dempsey (Gera 90), Etuhu, Murphy, Davies, Zamora (Nevland² 63), Johnson¹. Subs not used: Zuberbuhler, Teymourian, Gray, Stoor, Kallio.

February

7th ● Wigan ....a   D 0–0   **Att:** 16,499. **Ref:** L Probert — **Fulham** (4-4-2): Schwarzer, Pantsil▌, Hangeland, Hughes, Konchesky, Davies, Etuhu (Dacourt 45), Murphy, Dempsey▌ (Gera 90), Johnson, Zamora (Nevland 75). Subs not used: Zuberbuhler, Gray, Stoor, Baird.

14th ● Swansea ....a   D 1–1   **Att:** 16,573. **Ref:** H Webb — **Fulham** (4-5-1): Schwarzer, Stoor, Hangeland, Hughes, Nevland (Zamora 75), Gera, Murphy, Davies, Dacourt▌ (Dempsey 60), Johnson (Gray 85). Subs not used: Zuberbuhler, Pantsil, Milsom, Kallio.

18th ● Man Utd ....a   L 3–0   **Att:** 75,437. **Ref:** A Marriner — **Fulham** (4-1-4-1): Schwarzer, Pantsil▌ (Dacourt 67), Hangeland, Hughes, Kallio, Baird, Gera (Brown 86), Murphy (Milsom 80), Davies, Dempsey, Zamora. Subs not used: Zuberbuhler, Nevland, Gray, Smalling.

22nd ● West Brom ....h   W 2–0   **Att:** 22,394. **Ref:** M Atkinson — **Fulham** (4-4-2): Schwarzer, Pantsil, Hughes, Hangeland, Konchesky, Davies, Murphy (Dacourt 85), Etuhu, Dempsey, Johnson¹ (Kamara 80), Zamora¹ (Nevland 80). Subs not used: Zuberbuhler, Gray, Kallio, Baird.

24th ● Swansea ....h   W 2–1   **Att:** 12,316. **Ref:** M Halsey — **Fulham** (4-4-2): Schwarzer, Pantsil, Hughes, Hangeland, Konchesky, Davies, Dacourt (Murphy 59), Etuhu▌, Dempsey¹ (Kamara 90), Nevland (Gera 60), Zamora¹. Subs not used: Zuberbuhler, Milsom, Kallio, Baird.

● Barclays Premier League   ● FA Cup   ● Carling Cup   ● UEFA Champions League   ● UEFA Cup   ▌ Yellow Card   ▐ Red Card

BARCLAYS
PREMIER LEAGUE

RESULTS 2008/09

| 28th | ● Arsenal ....a | D 0–0 | **Att:** 60,102. **Ref:** P Walton — **Fulham** (4-4-2): Schwarzer, Baird (Stoor 46), Hangeland, Hughes, Konchesky, Davies, Murphy, Etuhu, Dempsey (Gera 88), Johnson, Zamora. Subs not used: Zuberbuhler, Nevland, Kamara, Dacourt, Kallio. |

March

4th	● Hull ....h	L 0–1	**Att:** 23,051. **Ref:** M Jones — **Fulham** (4-4-2): Schwarzer, Pantsil, Hughes, Hangeland▌, Konchesky, Davies▌, Murphy, Etuhu▌, Dempsey, Johnson, Zamora (Kamara 89). Subs not used: Zuberbuhler, Nevland, Gera, Dacourt, Stoor, Kallio.
7th	● Man Utd ....h	L 0–4	**Att:** 24,662. **Ref:** M Dean — **Fulham** (4-4-2): Schwarzer, Pantsil▌, Hangeland, Hughes, Konchesky, Davies, Etuhu, Murphy (Dacourt▌ 57), Dempsey, Zamora (Gera 67), Johnson (Kamara 60). Subs not used: Zuberbuhler, Nevland, Stoor, Kallio.
11th	● Blackburn ....h	L 1–2	**Att:** 22,259. **Ref:** R Styles — **Fulham** (4-4-2): Schwarzer, Pantsil, Hangeland, Hughes (Kallio 77), Konchesky, Davies (Nevland 90), Etuhu, Murphy▌, Gera (Kamara 80), Dempsey[1], Johnson. Subs not used: Zuberbuhler, Dacourt, Gray, Stoor.
14th	● Bolton ....a	W 1–3	**Att:** 22,117. **Ref:** C Foy — **Fulham** (4-4-2): Schwarzer, Pantsil, Hangeland, Hughes, Konchesky, Davies[1], Etuhu, Murphy, Dempsey, Johnson[1] (Nevland 90), Zamora (Kamara[1] 84). Subs not used: Zuberbuhler, Gera, Dacourt, Stoor, Smalling.
21st	● Man Utd ....h	W 2–0	**Att:** 25,652. **Ref:** P Dowd — **Fulham** (4-4-2): Schwarzer, Pantsil▌, Hughes, Hangeland, Konchesky, Dempsey▌ (Gera[1] 81), Murphy[1] (Dacourt 67), Etuhu, Davies, Johnson, Zamora (Kamara 77). Subs not used: Zuberbuhler, Nevland, Stoor, Kallio.

April

4th	● Liverpool...........................h	L 0–1	**Att:** 25,661. **Ref:** S Bennett — **Fulham** (4-4-2): Schwarzer, Pantsil▌, Hughes, Hangeland, Konchesky, Dempsey, Murphy (Dacourt 76), Etuhu, Davies (Gera▌ 79), Zamora, Johnson (Nevland 87). Subs not used: Zuberbuhler, Kamara, Kallio, Baird.
12th	● Man City ....a	W 1–3	**Att:** 39,841. **Ref:** M Halsey — **Fulham** (4-4-2): Schwarzer, Pantsil, Hangeland, Hughes, Konchesky▌, Davies, Etuhu[1], Murphy (Dacourt 89), Dempsey[2] (Gera 86), Johnson, Zamora (Kamara 86). Subs not used: Zuberbuhler, Nevland, Stoor, Baird.
18th	● Middlesbrough ....a	D 0–0	**Att:** 30,389. **Ref:** P Walton — **Fulham** (4-4-2): Schwarzer, Pantsil, Hughes, Hangeland, Konchesky▌, Davies (Gera 70), Murphy, Etuhu, Dempsey, Johnson (Kamara 87), Zamora. Subs not used: Zuberbuhler, Nevland, Dacourt, Stoor, Baird.
25th	● Stoke ....h	W 1–0	**Att:** 25,069. **Ref:** L Mason — **Fulham** (4-4-2): Schwarzer, Pantsil, Hughes, Hangeland, Konchesky (Baird 82), Dempsey, Murphy, Etuhu, Gera, Zamora (Nevland▌[1] 20), Johnson (Kamara 34). Subs not used: Zuberbuhler, Dacourt, Gray, Stoor.

May

2nd	● Chelsea ....a	L 3–1	**Att:** 41,801. **Ref:** A Wiley — **Fulham** (4-4-2): Schwarzer, Pantsil, Hughes, Hangeland, Konchesky, Dempsey, Etuhu, Murphy▌, Gera, Zamora (Dacourt 76), Nevland[1] (Kamara 35). Subs not used: Zuberbuhler, Gray, Stoor, Baird, Smalling.
9th	● Aston Villa...........................h	W 3–1	**Att:** 25,660. **Ref:** M Halsey — **Fulham** (4-4-2): Schwarzer, Pantsil, Hughes, Hangeland, Konchesky, Gera, Murphy▌[1], Etuhu (Dacourt 89), Dempsey (Gray 85), Kamara[2], Nevland (Zamora 83). Subs not used: Zuberbuhler, Stoor, Baird, Smalling.
16th	● Newcastle ....a	W 0–1	**Att:** 52,114. **Ref:** H Webb — **Fulham** (4-4-2): Schwarzer, Pantsil, Hughes, Hangeland, Konchesky, Dempsey▌, Etuhu, Murphy▌, Gera, Nevland▌ (Johnson 75), Kamara[1]. Subs not used: Zuberbuhler, Zamora, Dacourt, Gray, Kallio, Baird.
24th	● Everton ....h	L 0–2	**Att:** 25,497. **Ref:** M Riley — **Fulham** (4-4-2): Schwarzer, Pantsil, Hughes (Smalling 77), Hangeland, Konchesky, Dempsey, Murphy, Etuhu, Gera (Dacourt 73), Nevland (Zamora 68), Kamara. Subs not used: Zuberbuhler, Gray, Stoor, Baird.

● Barclays Premier League ● FA Cup ● Carling Cup ● UEFA Champions League ● UEFA Cup   ▌ Yellow Card ▌ Red Card

Zoltan Gera scores in spectacular fashion in the stunning 2–0 victory over champions Manchester United at Craven Cottage

FULHAM

BARCLAYS PREMIER LEAGUE GOALKEEPER STATS

Player	Minutes on pitch	Appearances	Match starts	Completed matches	Sub appearances	Subbed off	Saved with feet	Punched	Parried	Tipped over	Fumbled	Tipped round	Caught	Blocked	Clean sheets	Goals conceded	Minutes since conceding	Save %	Saved	Resulting in goals	Opposition miss	Yellow cards	Red cards
Mark Schwarzer	3607	38	38	38	0	0	1	24	32	10	0	15	144	0	15	34	5	87.27	1	1	0	0	0

SAVES BREAKDOWN header spans Saved with feet to Blocked. *PENALTIES* header spans Saved to Opposition miss.

BARCLAYS PREMIER LEAGUE OUTFIELD PLAYER STATS

Player	Minutes on pitch	Appearances	Match starts	Completed matches	Substitute appearances	Subbed off	Goals scored	Minutes since scoring	Assists	Shots on target	Shots off target	Crosses	Defensive clearances	Defensive blocks	Fouls committed	Free-kicks won	Caught offside	Yellow cards	Red cards
Leon Andreasen	56	6	0	0	6	0	0	-	0	1	0	0	0	1	2	2	0	1	0
Chris Baird	302	10	3	2	7	1	0	-	0	0	0	2	2	1	1	2	0	0	0
Wayne Brown	7	1	0	0	1	0	0	-	0	0	0	0	0	0	0	0	0	0	0
Jimmy Bullard	1625	18	18	12	0	6	2	328	3	35	17	36	1	1	10	32	2	1	0
Olivier Dacourt	172	9	0	0	9	0	0	-	0	1	1	1	0	0	2	3	0	0	0
Simon Davies	3045	33	33	26	0	7	2	374	5	16	23	54	9	4	39	24	3	2	0
Clint Dempsey	2728	35	28	20	7	8	7	563	2	36	32	10	7	2	35	42	4	5	0
Dickson Etuhu	1781	21	19	14	2	5	1	597	0	3	7	0	8	8	20	3	0	1	0
Zoltan Gera	1827	32	20	11	12	9	2	504	1	19	19	18	4	2	26	25	0	2	0
Julian Gray	7	1	0	0	1	0	0	-	0	0	0	0	0	0	0	0	0	0	0
Brede Hangeland	3511	37	37	37	0	0	1	3395	2	6	7	1	56	19	30	24	0	3	0
Aaron Hughes	3572	38	38	36	0	2	0	-	0	0	0	3	58	21	8	20	0	0	0
Andrew Johnson	2701	31	30	22	1	7	7	463	4	40	15	17	2	4	30	31	31	1	1
Toni Kallio	186	3	2	1	1	1	0	-	0	0	0	1	0	0	4	0	0	0	0
Diomansy Kamara	477	12	3	3	9	0	4	148	1	9	3	3	0	0	10	8	4	0	0
Paul Konchesky	3404	36	36	35	0	1	1	1668	1	9	2	51	17	10	15	15	2	5	0
Robert Milsom	13	1	0	0	1	0	0	-	0	0	0	0	0	0	0	0	0	0	0
Danny Murphy	3481	38	38	27	0	11	5	275	5	14	15	16	10	5	45	36	0	8	0
Erik Nevland	525	21	4	0	17	4	4	257	2	9	5	4	1	0	10	4	7	2	0
John Pantsil	3463	37	37	34	0	3	0	-	0	1	8	42	29	13	42	30	1	7	0
Ki-Hyeon Seol	203	4	2	0	2	2	1	195	0	3	3	6	0	0	9	1	4	1	0
Chris Smalling	16	1	0	0	1	0	0	-	0	0	0	0	0	0	0	0	0	0	0
Fredrik Stoor	60	2	0	0	2	0	0	-	0	0	0	1	0	0	0	0	0	0	0
Andranik Teymourian	13	1	0	0	1	0	0	-	0	0	0	0	0	0	1	0	0	1	0
Bobby Zamora	2826	35	32	16	3	16	2	775	6	30	40	19	10	3	77	42	30	1	0

actim

BARCLAYS PREMIER LEAGUE

SEASON TOTALS

Goals scored	39
Goals conceded	34
Clean sheets	15
Shots on target	232
Shots off target	197
Shots per goal	11.00
Pens awarded	5
Pens scored	5
Pens conceded	2
Offsides	88
Corners	192
Crosses	285
Players used	26
Fouls committed	416
Free-kicks won	353

CARDS RECEIVED

41 **1**

SEQUENCES

Wins	2
(on four occasions)	
Losses	3
(20/09/08–04/10/08)	
Draws	4
(22/11/08–13/12/08)	
Undefeated	9
(09/11/08–28/12/08)	
Without win	5
(20/09/08–26/10/08)	
Undefeated home	9
(18/10/08–22/02/09)	
Undefeated away	4
(on two occasions)	
Without scoring	2
(on four occasions)	
Without conceding	3
(13/12/08–26/12/08)	
Scoring	4
(25/04/09–16/05/09)	
Conceding	4
(on two occasions)	

SEASON INFORMATION
Highest Position: 7
Lowest Position: 17
Average goals scored per game: 1.03
Average goals conceded per game: 0.89

League position at the end of each week

League position at the end of: August 14, September 15, October 14, November 10, December 9, January 9, February 8, March 9, April 7, May 7

MATCH RECORDS

Goals scored per match

		W	D	L	Pts
Failed to score	16	0	8	8	8
Scored 1 goal	10	3	2	5	11
Scored 2 goals	7	6	1	0	19
Scored 3 goals	5	5	0	0	15
Scored 4+ goals	0	0	0	0	0

Goals conceded per match

		W	D	L	Pts
Clean sheet	15	7	8	0	29
Conceded 1 goal	15	7	2	6	23
Conceded 2 goals	5	0	1	4	1
Conceded 3 goals	3	0	0	3	0
Conceded 4+ goals	0	0	0	0	0

GOALS SCORED/CONCEDED PER FIVE-MINUTE INTERVALS

Goals For	2	3	3	1	3	2	1	0	4	2	1	6	1	2	2	1	1	4
Goals Against	1	3	2	0	1	2	0	0	4	1	2	2	3	1	1	1	6	4
Mins	5	10	15	20	25	30	35	40	45	50	55	60	65	70	75	80	85	90

QUICK-FIRE GOALS

From the start of a match
Clint Dempsey
(v Blackburn) 1:36

By a substitute after coming on
Diomansy Kamara
(v Bolton) 4:19

LAST-GASP GOALS

From the start of a match
Clint Dempsey
(v Chelsea) 88:59

By a substitute after coming on
Erik Nevland
(v Portsmouth) 17:30

GOAL DETAILS

How the goals were struck

SCORED		CONCEDED
29	Right foot	19
9	Left foot	11
1	Headers	4
0	Others	0

How the goals were struck

SCORED		CONCEDED
27	Open play	26
2	Cross	3
4	Corner	2
5	Penalties	1
0	Direct from free-kick	1
1	Free-kick	1
0	Own goals	0

Distance from goal

SCORED		CONCEDED
14	6yds	15
21	18yds	15
4	18+yds	4

OFFICIAL FOOTBALL YEARBOOK OF THE ENGLISH & SCOTTISH LEAGUES 2009–2010   **81**

HULL CITY

CLUB SUMMARY

FORMED	1904
MANAGER	Phil Brown
GROUND	KC Stadium
CAPACITY	25,404
NICKNAME	The Tigers
WEBSITE	www.hullcityafc.net

The New Football Pools PLAYER OF THE SEASON — Michael Turner

OVERALL

P	W	D	L	F	A	GD
45	11	13	21	47	70	-23

BARCLAYS PREMIER LEAGUE

Pos	P	W	D	L	F	A	GD	Pts
17	38	8	11	19	39	64	-25	35

HOME

Pos	P	W	D	L	F	A	GD	Pts
20	19	3	5	11	18	36	-18	14

AWAY

Pos	P	W	D	L	F	A	GD	Pts
8	19	5	6	8	21	28	-7	21

CUP PROGRESS DETAILS

Competition	Round reached	Knocked out by
FA Cup	QF	Arsenal
Carling Cup	R2	Swansea

BIGGEST WIN (ALL COMPS)

25/10/08 3–0 v West Brom **PREM**

BIGGEST DEFEAT (ALL COMPS)

30/08/08 0–5 v Wigan **PREM**

THE PLAYER WITH THE MOST

Shots on target
Geovanni 46

Shots off target
Geovanni 40

Shots without scoring
Dean Marney 38

Assists
Bernard Mendy 6

Offsides
Daniel Cousin 21

Fouls
Ian Ashbee 50

Fouls without a card
Manucho 14

Free-kicks won
Geovanni 60

Defensive clearances
Michael Turner 102

actim INDEX
for the 2008/09 Barclays Premier League Season

Rank	Player	Pts
60	Michael Turner	379
143	Andy Dawson	269
158	Boaz Myhill	249
160	Sam Ricketts	248
162	Kamil Zayatte	247

ATTENDANCE RECORD

High	Low	Average
24,945	24,282	24,816
v Man Utd (24/05/2009)	v Wigan (30/08/2008)	

THE extraordinary story of Hull's first season in the Barclays Premier League was eventful to the last as they dramatically escaped relegation on the final day.

That Hull would end up in a battle to avoid the drop was predicted by many at the start of the campaign, but the manner of their eventual survival was remarkable.

Phil Brown's Tigers, buoyant after winning promotion from the Coca-Cola Championship via the play-offs, initially took to the top flight like a duck to water.

After 104 years in the lower divisions, Hull not only enjoyed rubbing shoulders with the elite, but looked quite capable of holding their own. Yet as fans started to dream of Europe, it all seemed too good to be be true, and so it proved.

Hull plummeted down the table in the second half of the season – a harsh reality check – and in the end only the weaknesses of others saved them. A final tally of 35 points would not have been enough in other seasons and Brown has several important issues to address over the summer.

Ultimately, however, the season can only be viewed as a success. The modest ambition of survival was achieved, even if it came in an unconventional manner.

The hard work was all done in the opening months of the campaign as Hull tore into their opponents with an attacking verve that few had anticipated. Fulham were beaten on the opening day and, a 5–0 thrashing by Wigan aside, a feelgood factor and lack of inhibition allowed momentum to build.

Brazilian playmaker Geovanni was grabbing all the headlines as he sealed priceless wins with two stunning strikes, one in a momentous victory over Arsenal at the Emirates Stadium, the other securing a second notable scalp against Tottenham.

Spirits were not dampened by back-to-back losses to Chelsea and Manchester United and points kept coming until mid-December when they claimed a superb 2–2 draw at Liverpool's Anfield.

Opponents were clearly taken aback by Hull's confidence and determination, and few who saw their Anfield heroics would have believed they were about to nosedive into a relegation scrap.

Hull hit the buffers after slumping 4–1 to Sunderland on 22nd December and so poor was their showing at Manchester

The hard work was all done in the opening months of the campaign

City on Boxing Day, that manager Brown took the unusual step of keeping his men on the field to deliver a few home truths at half-time in front of the travelling Tigers support. They eventually lost that game 5–1 and went into a freefall that was partly masked by a run to the quarter-finals of the FA Cup. The £5million record signing of Jimmy Bullard in January was meant to provide the spark for the rest of the campaign, but the move was a disaster. Bullard was injured on his debut at West Ham and soon after was in the United States for a season-ending knee operation.

Marlon King's loan move from Wigan also ended in acrimonious circumstances after a bust-up with Brown, and Hull were unable to arrest the slide.

A goalless draw at Chelsea and a last-gasp win at Fulham with an injury-time winner raised spirits, but the slump continued and the fall-out from a fiery FA Cup defeat to Arsenal proved a distraction.

Brown also began to attract plenty of criticism, not least as many began to pinpoint his Eastlands dressing-down as the turning point of the Tigers' whole campaign. Brown remained adamant it had been the right thing to do – as a shock tactic it had short-term benefits – but it was a moment that came back to haunt him with every poor result. Its significance was probably overstated but, given the team's inability to rouse themselves after that day, it was an incident destined for infamy.

Yet, despite collecting only three points from their last 10 games, Hull had just enough to cling on and Brown, not the shy or retiring type, led the celebrations on the pitch. Their awful form in the second half of the campaign does not inspire hope going into the 2009/10 season, but their survival could well provide the boost needed to revive their fortunes.

CLOCKWISE FROM ABOVE: Daniel Cousin scores in Hull's famous shock win at Arsenal's Emirates Stadium in September; Paul McShane celebrates his goal in the draw at Anfield; a dejected Boaz Myhill after losing to Aston Villa

HULL CITY

August

| 16th | ● Fulham ....h | W 2–1 |

Att: 24,525. **Ref:** P Walton — **Hull** (4-5-1): Myhill, Ricketts▌, Turner, Gardner, Dawson▌, Garcia (Fagan▌ 74), Ashbee, Boateng, Barmby (Halmosi 62), Geovanni', King (Folan' 70). Subs not used: Duke, Windass, Mendy, Marney.

| 23rd | ● Blackburn ....a | D 1–1 |

Att: 23,439. **Ref:** S Attwell — **Hull** (4-4-2): Myhill, Ricketts, Turner, Gardner, Dawson (Mendy 58), Garcia' (Barmby 78), Ashbee▌, Marney, Fagan, Geovanni (Folan 65), King. Subs not used: Brown, Windass, Duke, Halmosi.

| 26th | ● Swansea................a | L 2–1 |

Att: 8,622. **Ref:** M Russell — **Hull** (4-4-2): Duke, Brown▌, Mendy▌, Doyle, Cooper (Turner 91), Barmby (Featherstone 72), Hughes, France, Halmosi▌, Folan, Windass' (King 62). Subs not used: Atkinson, Garcia, Welsh, Warner.

| 30th | ● Wigan ....h | L 0–5 |

Att: 24,282. **Ref:** M Jones — **Hull** (4-4-1-1): Myhill, Ricketts, Brown, Turner, Dawson (Mendy 71), Fagan, Ashbee▌, Marney, Garcia (Barmby 60), Geovanni (Windass 56), Folan. Subs not used: Duke, Hughes, Halmosi, Cooper.

September

| 13th | ● Newcastle.............a | W 1–2 |

Att: 50,242. **Ref:** A Marriner — **Hull** (4-4-2): Myhill, McShane, Turner, Gardner, Dawson, Mendy (Folan▌ 73), Marney (Hughes 78), Ashbee, Halmosi▌, King² (Zayatte 83), Fagan. Subs not used: Duke, Windass, Geovanni, Ricketts.

| 21st | ● Everton ....h | D 2–2 |

Att: 24,845. **Ref:** L Mason — **Hull** (4-4-2): Myhill, McShane, Turner', Zayatte, Dawson, Mendy (Garcia 77), Ashbee, Marney, Halmosi, Cousin (Folan 69), King (Boateng 81). Subs not used: Duke, Geovanni, Hughes, Ricketts.

| 27th | ● Arsenal ....a | W 1–2 |

Att: 60,037. **Ref:** A Wiley — **Hull** (4-4-2): Myhill, McShane, Zayatte, Turner, Dawson, Marney, Boateng (Garcia 76), Geovanni' (Hughes 72), Ashbee, Cousin' (Mendy 80), King. Subs not used: Duke, Halmosi, Folan, Ricketts.

October

| 5th | ● Tottenham..............a | W 0–1 |

Att: 36,062. **Ref:** R Styles — **Hull** (4-3-3): Myhill, McShane, Turner, Zayatte, Dawson, Marney, Ashbee▌, Boateng▌, Geovanni' (Halmosi 71), King (Folan 81), Cousin (Mendy 60). Subs not used: Hughes, Duke, Garcia, Ricketts.

| 19th | ● West Ham ....h | W 1–0 |

Att: 24,896. **Ref:** C Foy — **Hull** (4-3-1-2): Myhill, McShane, Zayatte▌, Turner', Marney, Ashbee, Boateng (Hughes 72), Geovanni (Halmosi 73), Cousin (Garcia 82), King. Subs not used: Duke, Mendy, Folan, Ricketts.

| 25th | ● West Brom ....a | W 0–3 |

Att: 26,323. **Ref:** L Probert — **Hull** (4-3-3): Myhill, McShane, Zayatte', Turner, Dawson (Ricketts▌ 10), Marney, Ashbee▌ (Hughes 75), Boateng, Cousin, King', Geovanni' (Garcia 78). Subs not used: Duke, Mendy, Halmosi, Folan.

| 29th | ● Chelsea ....h | L 0–3 |

Att: 24,906. **Ref:** A Marriner — **Hull** (4-3-1-2): Myhill, McShane, Turner, Zayatte, Dawson, Marney (Garcia 71), Ashbee, Boateng (Halmosi 62), Geovanni, King (Windass 84), Cousin. Subs not used: Duke, Hughes, Mendy, Ricketts.

November

| 1st | ● Man Utd ....a | L 4–3 |

Att: 75,398. **Ref:** M Dean — **Hull** (4-3-1-2): Myhill, McShane, Turner▌, Zayatte, Dawson, Marney, Hughes (Mendy▌' 59), Boateng (Halmosi 63), Geovanni', King (Halmosi 63). Cousin' . Subs not used: Duke, Barmby, Garcia, Ricketts.

| 8th | ● Bolton ....h | L 0–1 |

Att: 24,903. **Ref:** A Wiley — **Hull** (4-3-3): Myhill, McShane, Turner, Zayatte, Dawson▌ (Ricketts 64), Boateng (Folan 73), Ashbee, Marney, Geovanni, King, Cousin (Mendy 54). Subs not used: Duke, Barmby, Garcia, Halmosi.

| 16th | ● Man City ....h | D 2–2 |

Att: 24,902. **Ref:** P Dowd — **Hull** (4-3-1-2): Myhill, McShane▌, Turner, Zayatte, Ricketts, Boateng (Halmosi 85), Ashbee, Marney▌, Geovanni', Cousin' (Barmby 76), King. Subs not used: Duke, Doyle, Garcia, Folan, Giannakopoulos.

| 22nd | ● Portsmouth ....a | D 2–2 |

Att: 20,240. **Ref:** S Attwell — **Hull** (4-3-1-2): Myhill, McShane, Turner', Zayatte, Ricketts, Marney (Giannakopoulos 82), Ashbee, Boateng (Halmosi 72), Geovanni, King (Windass 72), Cousin. Subs not used: Duke, Doyle, Barmby, Garcia.

| 29th | ● Stoke ....a | D 1–1 |

Att: 27,500. **Ref:** K Stroud — **Hull** (4-4-1-1): Myhill▌, McShane, Turner, Zayatte▌, Ricketts, Marney, Boateng (Cousin 78), Ashbee, Barmby (Halmosi 69), Geovanni (Garcia 90), King'. Subs not used: Duke, Windass▌, Mendy, Giannakopoulos.

December

| 6th | ● Middlesbrough ....h | W 2–1 |

Att: 24,912. **Ref:** S Tanner — **Hull** (4-4-1-1): Myhill, McShane, Turner, Zayatte, Ricketts, Boateng, Ashbee▌, Marney (Cousin 61), Barmby (Mendy 61), Geovanni (Halmosi 86), King'. Subs not used: Duke, Windass, Garcia, Giannakopoulos.

| 13th | ● Liverpool ....a | D 2–2 |

Att: 43,835. **Ref:** A Wiley — **Hull** (4-4-1-1): Myhill, McShane▌' (Marney▌ 27), Zayatte, Turner, Ricketts, Mendy, Ashbee, Boateng▌ (Halmosi 66), Geovanni, Barmby (Windass 77), King. Subs not used: Warner, Garcia, Cousin, Giannakopoulos.

| 20th | ● Sunderland ....h | L 1–4 |

Att: 24,917. **Ref:** M Riley — **Hull** (4-4-2): Myhill, Mendy, Turner, Zayatte, Ricketts▌, Garcia (Cousin 57), Ashbee, Boateng▌ (Halmosi 81), Geovanni, Barmby' (Giannakopoulos 68), King▌. Subs not used: Duke, Doyle, Windass, Marney.

| 26th | ● Man City ....a | L 5–1 |

Att: 45,196. **Ref:** A Marriner — **Hull** (4-4-2): Myhill, Mendy▌, Zayatte▌, Turner, McShane, Boateng (Doyle 34), Geovanni▌ (Cousin 70), Ashbee, Marney, Windass (Fagan▌ 46), King. Subs not used: Duke, Barmby, Hughes, Halmosi.

| 30th | ● Aston Villa............h | L 0–1 |

Att: 24,727. **Ref:** S Bennett — **Hull** (4-4-1-1): Myhill, McShane, Turner, Zayatte▌, Ricketts, Mendy, Garcia (Fagan 89), Ashbee, Halmosi, Barmby (Hughes 85), Cousin (King 69). Subs not used: Duke, Doyle, Geovanni, Giannakopoulos.

January

| 3rd | ● Newcastle.............h | D 0–0 |

Att: 20,557. **Ref:** C Foy — **Hull** (4-5-1): Duke, Doyle, Turner, McShane▌, Ricketts, Fagan▌ (Halmosi 73), Giannakopoulos▌, Boateng, Marney, Geovanni▌, Cousin (King 73). Subs not used: Ashbee, France, Zayatte, Warner, Featherstone.

| 10th | ● Everton ....a | L 2–0 |

Att: 37,527. **Ref:** M Atkinson — **Hull** (4-4-1-1): Myhill, McShane (Halmosi 79), Zayatte▌, Turner, Ricketts▌, Mendy▌, Ashbee, Marney (Fagan▌ 54), Geovanni (Cousin 66), Barmby, King. Subs not used: Duke, Doyle, France, Boateng.

| 14th | ● Newcastle.............a | W 0–1 |

Att: 31,380. **Ref:** P Dowd — **Hull** (4-5-1): Duke, Doyle, McShane, Zayatte, Ricketts▌, Fagan▌ (Mendy 74), Halmosi, Boateng (Ashbee 67), France, Garcia, Cousin' (Folan 86). Subs not used: Warner, Featherstone, Giannakopoulos, Atkinson.

| 17th | ● Arsenal ....h | L 1–3 |

Att: 24,924. **Ref:** A Wiley — **Hull** (4-4-1-1): Myhill, Doyle, Turner, Ricketts, Kilbane▌, Mendy, France (Fagan 83), Ashbee▌, Halmosi (Manucho 53), Geovanni (Garcia 87), Cousin'. Subs not used: Duke, Dawson, Folan, Giannakopoulos.

| 24th | ● Millwall ....h | W 2–0 |

Att: 18,639. **Ref:** S Attwell — **Hull** (4-4-2): Warner, Ricketts, Turner', Zayatte, Dawson, Garcia, Ashbee', Marney, Halmosi (Featherstone 66), Cousin, Manucho (Folan▌ 75). Subs not used: Duke, Doyle, Geovanni, France, Mendy.

| 28th | ● West Ham ....a | L 2–0 |

Att: 34,340. **Ref:** H Webb — **Hull** (4-3-1-2): Duke, Ricketts, Turner, Zayatte, Dawson, Marney▌ (Mendy 73), Ashbee, Kilbane, Geovanni (Bullard 53), Cousin, Manucho (Fagan 53). Subs not used: Myhill, Garcia, Halmosi, Folan.

| 31st | ● West Brom ....h | D 2–2 |

Att: 24,879. **Ref:** P Walton — **Hull** (4-5-1): Duke, Ricketts, Turner, Zayatte, Dawson▌, Mendy▌', Garcia (Folan 81), Ashbee, Marney, Kilbane, Fagan'. Subs not used: Myhill, Doyle, Geovanni, Hughes, France, Manucho.

February

| 7th | ● Chelsea ....a | D 0–0 |

Att: 41,802. **Ref:** L Mason — **Hull** (4-4-1-1): Duke, Ricketts, Turner, Zayatte, Dawson, Garcia▌, Ashbee▌, Marney, Kilbane, Geovanni (France 81), Fagan. Subs not used: Myhill, Doyle, Barmby, Hughes, Halmosi, Manucho.

| 14th | ● Sheff Utd............a | D 1–1 |

Att: 22,283. **Ref:** A Marriner — **Hull** (4-4-1-1): Myhill, Ricketts, Turner▌, Gardner, Dawson, Mendy▌ (France 88), Marney, Zayatte', Garcia (Manucho 79), Ashbee (Barmby 73), Cousin. Subs not used: Warner, Doyle, Halmosi, Featherstone.

| 23rd | ● Tottenham ....h | L 1–2 |

Att: 24,742. **Ref:** L Probert — **Hull** (4-4-2): Duke, Ricketts, Turner', Gardner, Dawson▌, Marney, Ashbee▌, Zayatte (Geovanni 87), Kilbane, Garcia (Manucho 79), Cousin (Mendy 67). Subs not used: Myhill, Doyle, Barmby, Halmosi.

● Barclays Premier League ● FA Cup ● Carling Cup ● UEFA Champions League ● UEFA Cup

▌ Yellow Card ▌ Red Card

RESULTS 2008/09

| 26th | ● Sheff Utd...........................h | W 2–1 | **Att:** 17,239. **Ref:** P Walton — **Hull** (4-4-2): Myhill, Doyle, Turner, Zayatte, Ricketts, Mendy, France, Marney▌, Halmosi¹, Barmby (Garcia 73), Folan (Manucho 65). Subs not used: Warner, Geovanni, Cousin, Featherstone, Gardner. |

March

1st	● Blackburn ....h	L 1–2	**Att:** 24,612. **Ref:** M Atkinson — **Hull** (4-4-1-1): Duke, Doyle (Fagan 67), Turner▌, Zayatte, Dawson▌, Mendy, Ashbee¹, Marney▌, Kilbane (Cousin 53), Geovanni (Barmby 53), Garcia. Subs not used: Myhill, Halmosi, Manucho, Gardner.
4th	● Fulham ....a	W 0–1	**Att:** 23,051. **Ref:** M Jones — **Hull** (4-4-2): Duke, Zayatte, Turner, Gardner, Kilbane, Mendy (Garcia 89), Ashbee, Ricketts, Geovanni▌ (Barmby 90), Fagan, Cousin (Manucho¹ 76). Subs not used: Myhill, Hughes, France, Halmosi.
14th	● Newcastle ....h	D 1–1	**Att:** 24,914. **Ref:** H Webb — **Hull** (4-4-1-1): Duke, Ricketts, Turner, Gardner, Kilbane, Mendy (Barmby 80), Ashbee, Zayatte▌, Geovanni¹, Fagan▌ (Garcia 70), Cousin (Manucho 54). Subs not used: Myhill, Dawson, Hughes, Halmosi.
17th	● Arsenal ....a	L 2–1	**Att:** 55,641. **Ref:** M Riley — **Hull** (4-3-3): Myhill▌, Ricketts, Gardner, Zayatte, Dawson▌, Ashbee (Hughes 46), Barmby¹ (France▌ 76), Geovanni, Fagan, Manucho▌, Halmosi▌ (Mendy 67). Subs not used: Duke, Garcia, Folan, Featherstone.
22nd	● Wigan ....a	L 1–0	**Att:** 17,689. **Ref:** A Marriner — **Hull** (4-4-2): Duke, Ricketts▌, Zayatte (Folan 61), Turner, Dawson (Garcia 38), Mendy▌, Marney, Kilbane, Geovanni, Manucho, Fagan▌ (Halmosi 82). Subs not used: Myhill, Doyle, Barmby, France.

April

4th	● Portsmouth ....h	D 0–0	**Att:** 24,802. **Ref:** C Foy — **Hull** (4-4-2): Duke, Ricketts (Folan 85), Zayatte, Turner, Dawson, Mendy, Ashbee, Barmby (Marney 74), Geovanni, Manucho, Fagan (Kilbane 71). Subs not used: Myhill, Garcia, Halmosi, Featherstone.
11th	● Middlesbrough ....a	L 3–1	**Att:** 32,255. **Ref:** P Dowd — **Hull** (4-5-1): Duke, Ricketts▌, Zayatte, Turner, Dawson, Fagan (Boateng▌ 71), Mendy (Marney 46), Ashbee▌, Barmby (Folan 62), Geovanni, Manucho¹. Subs not used: Myhill, Halmosi, Kilbane, Featherstone.
18th	● Sunderland ....a	L 1–0	**Att:** 42,855. **Ref:** M Dean — **Hull** (4-5-1): Myhill, Ricketts, Zayatte, Turner▌, Dawson, Fagan▌, Geovanni (Mendy 74), Boateng (Barmby 77), Marney (Folan 68), Kilbane, Manucho. Subs not used: Duke, Doyle, Halmosi, Cousin.
25th	● Liverpool ....h	L 1–3	**Att:** 24,942. **Ref:** M Atkinson — **Hull** (4-5-1): Myhill, Ricketts, Zayatte, Turner, Kilbane, Fagan▌ (Mendy 62), Boateng (Manucho 79), Marney▌, Geovanni¹, Barmby▌ (Cousin 62), Folan▌. Subs not used: Duke, Hughes, Garcia, Halmosi.

May

4th	● Aston Villa...........................a	L 1–0	**Att:** 39,607. **Ref:** M Dean — **Hull** (4-4-1-1): Myhill, Ricketts, Turner, Zayatte▌, Dawson, Garcia, Boateng▌, Ashbee (Marney 9), Kilbane (Manucho 73), Geovanni (Barmby 46), Cousin. Subs not used: Duke, Doyle, Halmosi, Featherstone.
9th	● Stoke ....h	L 1–2	**Att:** 24,932. **Ref:** H Webb — **Hull** (4-4-1-1): Myhill, Ricketts, Turner, Zayatte (Geovanni 67), Dawson¹, Garcia (Mendy 60), Boateng, Kilbane, Barmby, Fagan, Cousin (Manucho 60). Subs not used: Duke, Hughes, Halmosi, Marney.
16th	● Bolton ....a	D 1–1	**Att:** 25,085. **Ref:** P Walton — **Hull** (4-4-1-1): Myhill, Ricketts, Turner, Kilbane, Dawson, Garcia, Fagan¹, Boateng▌, Geovanni (Cousin 77), Manucho (Halmosi 83). Subs not used: Duke, Doyle, Hughes, Cooper.
24th	● Man Utd ....h	L 0–1	**Att:** 24,945. **Ref:** A Wiley — **Hull** (4-4-1-1): Myhill, Ricketts, Turner, Kilbane, Dawson, Garcia (Cousin 81), Marney▌, Boateng, Barmby▌ (Mendy 68), Geovanni (Folan 54), Fagan. Subs not used: Duke, Hughes, Halmosi, Zayatte.

● Barclays Premier League ● FA Cup ● Carling Cup ● UEFA Champions League ● UEFA Cup   ▌ Yellow Card ▌ Red Card

Hull boss Phil Brown celebrates as his team stay in the Barclays Premier League despite losing their last game of the season

HULL CITY

BARCLAYS PREMIER LEAGUE GOALKEEPER STATS

Player	Minutes on pitch	Appearances	Match starts	Completed matches	Sub appearances	Subbed off	Saved with feet	Punched	Parried	Tipped over	Fumbled	Tipped round	Caught	Blocked	Clean sheets	Goals conceded	Minutes since conceding	Save %	Saved	Resulting in goals	Opposition miss	Yellow cards	Red cards
Matt Duke 961	10	10	10	0	0	1	6	10	3	0	5	32	0	3	13	5	81.94	1	1	0	0	0
Boaz Myhill............2686	28	28	28	0	0	1	14	27	7	0	6	86	0	3	51	72	73.44	0	1	0	1	0

Header note: SAVES BREAKDOWN; PENALTIES

BARCLAYS PREMIER LEAGUE OUTFIELD PLAYER STATS

Player	Minutes on pitch	Appearances	Match starts	Completed matches	Substitute appearances	Subbed off	Goals scored	Minutes since scoring	Assists	Shots on target	Shots off target	Crosses	Defensive clearances	Defensive blocks	Fouls committed	Free-kicks won	Caught offside	Yellow cards	Red cards
Ian Ashbee 2858	31	31	29	0	2	1	408	1	6	17	11	35	13	50	27	1	10	0
Nick Barmby............1161	21	13	2	8	11	1	803	1	6	9	13	1	3	13	5	2	2	0
George Boateng............1761	23	21	8	2	13	0	-	1	10	6	14	7	4	42	32	0	6	0
Wayne Brown............95	1	1	1	0	0	0	-	0	0	0	1	4	0	1	1	0	0	0
Jimmy Bullard 40	1	0	0	1	0	0	328	0	2	0	1	0	0	1	0	0	0	0
Daniel Cousin............1667	27	18	7	9	11	4	588	1	22	16	19	3	0	25	27	21	1	0
Andy Dawson............2161	25	25	20	0	5	1	195	3	10	3	75	17	8	32	27	0	7	0
Nathan Doyle............225	3	2	1	1	1	0	-	0	1	0	6	1	1	0	4	0	0	0
Craig Fagan............1521	22	15	10	7	5	3	144	3	9	11	32	0	2	44	23	16	7	0
Caleb Folan............457	15	2	1	13	0	1	446	0	2	1	2	1	0	10	4	10	1	1
Ryan France............96	2	1	0	1	1	0	-	0	0	0	0	1	0	0	1	0	0	0
Richard Garcia............1237	23	13	4	10	9	1	1124	2	7	6	10	3	0	14	24	2	2	0
Anthony Gardner............576	6	6	6	0	0	0	-	0	0	1	1	11	4	7	2	0	0	0
Geovanni............2651	34	32	13	2	19	8	232	1	46	40	56	4	0	28	60	18	2	0
Stelios Giannakopoulos 40	2	0	0	2	0	0	-	0	0	0	0	0	0	0	1	0	0	0
Peter Halmosi 628	18	4	3	14	1	0	-	1	4	0	18	4	3	6	13	3	1	0
Bryan Hughes............149	6	1	0	5	1	0	-	0	0	0	0	0	0	1	0	0	0	0
Kevin Kilbane............1404	16	15	13	1	2	0	-	0	6	4	26	10	2	11	18	1	5	0
Marlon King 1709	20	19	12	1	7	5	354	2	22	12	42	1	0	26	16	39	1	0
Manucho 718	13	6	4	7	2	2	347	0	11	12	4	5	0	14	9	7	0	0
Dean Marney 2532	31	26	18	5	7	0	-	4	18	20	63	8	5	35	19	1	5	1
Paul McShane............1539	17	17	15	0	2	1	361	0	2	0	34	27	10	18	18	0	2	0
Bernard Mendy............1706	28	15	10	13	5	2	702	6	8	10	58	12	4	30	20	14	5	0
Sam Ricketts 2688	29	27	25	2	1	0	-	1	1	4	75	36	10	32	32	0	6	1
Michael Turner 3647	38	38	38	0	0	4	1236	0	15	22	2	102	34	44	38	1	3	0
Dean Windass 132	5	1	0	4	1	1	69	0	2	0	0	0	0	3	5	1	2	0
Kamil Zayatte............2914	32	31	28	1	3	1	2471	1	1	9	3	54	18	48	40	0	7	0

SEASON TOTALS

Goals scored	39
Goals conceded	64
Clean sheets	6
Shots on target	212
Shots off target	203
Shots per goal	10.64
Pens awarded	3
Pens scored	3
Pens conceded	3
Offsides	137
Corners	188
Crosses	566
Players used	29
Fouls committed	536
Free-kicks won	473

CARDS RECEIVED

72   3

SEQUENCES

Wins 4
(27/09/08–25/10/08)
Losses 6
(20/12/08–28/01/09)
Draws 3
(16/11/08–29/11/08)
Undefeated 6
(13/09/08–25/10/08)
Without win 11
(13/12/08–01/03/09)
Undefeated home 2
(on three occasions)
Undefeated away 5
(23/08/08–25/10/08)
Without scoring 2
(on two occasions)
Without conceding 3
(05/10/08–25/10/08)
Scoring 7
(16/11/08–26/12/08)
Conceding 15
(29/10/08–31/01/09)

SEASON INFORMATION

Highest Position: 2
Lowest Position: 18
Average goals scored per game: 1.03
Average goals conceded per game: 1.68

League position at the end of each week

(League position at the end of — August 12, September 6, October 5, November 6, December 8, January 11, February 13, March 13, April 17, May 17)

MATCH RECORDS

Goals scored per match

		W	D	L	Pts
Failed to score	12	0	2	10	2
Scored 1 goal	15	3	4	8	13
Scored 2 goals	9	4	5	0	17
Scored 3 goals	2	1	0	1	3
Scored 4+ goals	0	0	0	0	0

Goals conceded per match

		W	D	L	Pts
Clean sheet	6	4	2	0	14
Conceded 1 goal	14	4	4	6	16
Conceded 2 goals	10	0	5	5	5
Conceded 3 goals	4	0	0	4	0
Conceded 4+ goals	4	0	0	4	0

QUICK-FIRE GOALS

From the start of a match
Sam Ricketts (v Wigan) 4:24

By a substitute after coming on
Bernard Mendy (v Man Utd) 10:38

LAST-GASP GOALS

From the start of a match
Andy Dawson (v Stoke) 94:56

By a substitute after coming on
Craig Fagan (v Man City) 34:20

GOAL DETAILS

How the goals were struck

SCORED		CONCEDED
18	Right foot	32
7	Left foot	23
13	Headers	9
1	Others	0

How the goals were struck

SCORED		CONCEDED
15	Open play	33
9	Cross	17
4	Corner	5
3	Penalties	2
3	Direct from free-kick	2
2	Free-kick	1
3	Own goals	4

Distance from goal

SCORED		CONCEDED
17	6yds	24
17	18yds	30
5	18+yds	10

GOALS SCORED/CONCEDED PER FIVE-MINUTE INTERVALS

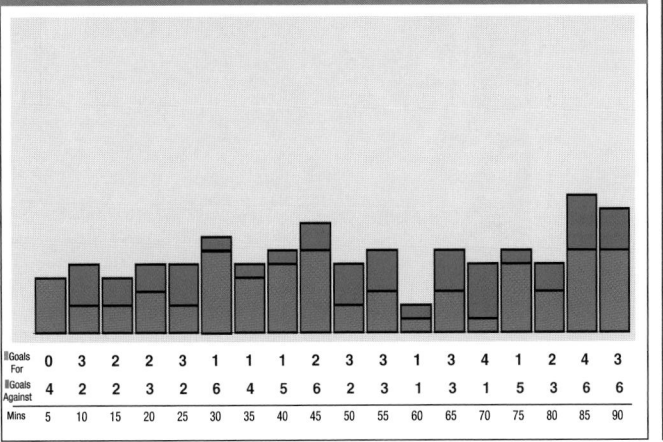

Mins	5	10	15	20	25	30	35	40	45	50	55	60	65	70	75	80	85	90
Goals For	0	3	2	2	3	1	1	1	2	3	3	1	3	4	1	2	4	3
Goals Against	4	2	2	3	2	6	4	5	6	2	3	1	3	1	5	3	6	6

CLUB SUMMARY

FORMED	1892
MANAGER	Rafael Benitez
GROUND	Anfield
CAPACITY	45,362
NICKNAME	The Reds
WEBSITE	www.liverpoolfc.tv

The New Football Pools PLAYER OF THE SEASON — Steven Gerrard

OVERALL

P	W	D	L	F	A	GD
55	34	16	5	106	46	60

BARCLAYS PREMIER LEAGUE

Pos	P	W	D	L	F	A	GD	Pts
2	38	25	11	2	77	27	50	86

HOME

Pos	P	W	D	L	F	A	GD	Pts
2	19	12	7	0	41	13	28	43

AWAY

Pos	P	W	D	L	F	A	GD	Pts
2	19	13	4	2	36	14	22	43

CUP PROGRESS DETAILS

Competition	Round reached	Knocked out by
FA Cup	R4	Everton
Champions League	QF	Chelsea
Carling Cup	R4	Tottenham

BIGGEST WIN (ALL COMPS)

22/03/09 5–0 v Aston Villa **PREM**

BIGGEST DEFEAT (ALL COMPS)

12/11/08 2–4 v Tottenham **LC4**

THE PLAYER WITH THE MOST

Shots on target		
Steven Gerrard		54
Shots off target		
Steven Gerrard		61
Shots without scoring		
Javier Mascherano		27
Assists		
Steven Gerrard		10
Offsides		
Dirk Kuyt		26
Fouls		
Javier Mascherano		41
Fouls without a card		
Dirk Kuyt		24
Free-kicks won		
Alvaro Arbeloa		42
Defensive clearances		
Jamie Carragher		36

actim INDEX for the 2008/09 Barclays Premier League Season

Rank	Player	Pts
2	Dirk Kuyt	655
6	Jose Reina	573
8	Jamie Carragher	552
9	Steven Gerrard	540
27	Alvaro Arbeloa	437

ATTENDANCE RECORD

High	Low	Average
44,424	41,169	43,611
v Arsenal (21/04/2009)	v West Ham (01/12/2008)	

CLOCKWISE FROM TOP: Xabi Alonso and Dirk Kuyt celebrate a goal in their thrilling 4–4 Champions League semi-final draw against Chelsea; skipper Steven Gerrard is mobbed by teammates during the 4–1 win at Manchester United; Rafael Benitez shouts orders from the touchline; Fernando Torres scores in the Barclays Premier League win at home to Chelsea

ANOTHER season gone, another year without the title. But Liverpool this time at least kept the battle going until the final days of the season.

Before Christmas they were top, and they went until the 1st November reverse at Spurs before tasting defeat in any competition, a 16-match unbeaten start to the campaign. The good form continued after that, apart from a Carling Cup defeat – also at Spurs – later in the month. They put together another 16-match unbeaten run and were still top at the turn of the year.

But critics will point to manager Rafael Benitez's public criticism of Manchester United and Sir Alex Ferguson 24 hours before an away game at determined Stoke in early January as the time their title race started to go off the rails. If Liverpool had won at the Brittania Stadium, they would have been 11 points ahead of the champions before United faced Chelsea the following day. But Liverpool only managed a 0–0 draw, with Steven Gerrard hitting the post in the final minutes, and the troubles began.

It is easy to say that Benitez's rant caused his players to lose sight of their goal and galvanised United. But most players are not moved by such matters and it is more likely that a collective loss of form, Fernando Torres' persistent knocks and bruises and a failure to kill off opponents contributed more to the problems that soon swamped Liverpool.

They had already wasted home points with stuttering draws against Stoke, Fulham, West Ham and Hull before being held at Stoke. Those were the results that eventually killed the title ambitions of the red half of Merseyside. They went on to draw with Everton – who also knocked them out of the FA Cup – at Anfield, then at Wigan and next at home to Manchester City. By the end of February they had also lost at Middlesbrough, and the title was already slipping away. Manchester United systematically dismantled the lesser sides in the Barclays Premier League, home and away; Liverpool failed to do that and drew far too many matches for comfort.

But they beat Chelsea twice, did a memorable double over United – including a 4–1 win at Old Trafford – and

produced two stunning victories over Spanish giants Real Madrid in the last 16 of the Champions League.

This was a team that could, maybe should, have won the title and stopped United from equalling their own proud record of 18 top-flight crowns.

Despite their earlier slips, the Reds' form in the closing months of the campaign – from March onwards – was simply breathtaking. They scored three times or more in six successive games – a club record – and when Torres and Gerrard were together they were an irresistible combination.

The 4–4 draw at Chelsea in the Champions League quarter-final second leg was arguably the classic match of the season and an attempt to make up for the 3–1 first-leg reverse from Anfield. Benitez's side needed a miracle at Stamford Bridge, and they looked on their way to just that when Fabio Aurelio and Xabi Alonso put them 2–0 up. Chelsea came back to lead 3–2, but the Reds somehow got a goal in front yet again before a late equaliser from Frank Lampard finally killed them off.

Just seven days later they shared eight goals again, this time with Arsenal, Liverpool finding a late leveller of their own thanks to Yossi Benayoun's goal some four minutes into stoppage time.

Aston Villa, Blackburn and Newcastle were then clinically taken apart as the goals and points mounted.

But, with Manchester United ahead in the table entering the last few weeks, Liverpool could only hope for a mistake or a small chink in the Old Trafford armour. Surely someone could give Fergie's men a game, like Liverpool had done so remarkably with that demolition at Old Trafford in March? Liverpool had shown the Barclays Premier League that United were not unbeatable, but nobody else really met their challenge, apart from Fulham who caught them spectacularly on an off day at Craven Cottage.

But that was it. Liverpool kept winning, but then so did United, and the rest is history. Despite their best points haul since the Premier League was formed in 1992/93, with the Red Devils having now won as many titles as the Merseyside giants, a first league crown in 20 years is a must in 2009/10.

> **The Reds' form in the closing months of the campaign was absolutely breathtaking**

LIVERPOOL

August

13th ● Standard Liège ....a — D 0–0 — **Att:** 25,000. **Ref:** T Ovrebo — **Liverpool** (4-4-2): Reina, Arbeloa, Dossena, Carragher, Agger, Alonso, Plessis, Benayoun, Kuyt (El Zhar 83), Keane (Gerrard 67), Torres. Subs not used: Cavalieri, Hyypia, Voronin, Pennant, Insua.

16th ● Sunderland ....a — W 0–1 — **Att:** 43,259. **Ref:** A Wiley — **Liverpool** (4-4-2): Reina, Arbeloa, Carragher, Hyypia, Dossena, Kuyt, Gerrard, Plessis (Alonso 46), Benayoun (Aurelio 81), Keane (El Zhar 77), Torres. Subs not used: Cavalieri, Agger, Ngog, Skrtel.

23rd ● Middlesbrough ....h — W 2–1 — **Att:** 43,168. **Ref:** M Riley — **Liverpool** (4-4-2): Reina, Arbeloa (El Zhar 83), Carragher, Skrtel, Dossena (Aurelio 75), Kuyt, Gerrard, Alonso, Benayoun (Babel 65), Keane, Torres. Subs not used: Cavalieri, Agger, Ngog, Plessis.

27th ● Standard Liège ....h — W 1–0 — **Att:** 43,889. **Ref:** M Busacca — **Liverpool** (4-4-2): Reina, Arbeloa, Carragher, Skrtel, Aurelio, Kuyt, Gerrard, Alonso, Benayoun (Babel 61), Keane (El Zhar 83), Torres (Plessis 120). Subs not used: Cavalieri, Dossena, Agger, Spearing.

31st ● Aston Villa...........................a — D 0–0 — **Att:** 41,647. **Ref:** M Atkinson — **Liverpool** (4-4-2): Reina, Arbeloa, Carragher, Skrtel, Dossena, Kuyt (Aurelio 70), Alonso, Mascherano, Lucas, Keane (Benayoun 79), Torres (Ngog 30). Subs not used: Cavalieri, Agger, Babel, El Zhar.

September

13th ● Man Utd ....h — W 2–1 — **Att:** 44,192. **Ref:** H Webb — **Liverpool** (4-4-2): Reina, Arbeloa, Skrtel, Carragher, Aurelio, Benayoun (Gerrard 68), Alonso, Mascherano (Hyypia 87), Riera (Babel 71), Kuyt, Keane. Subs not used: Cavalieri, Dossena, Torres, Ngog.

16th ● Marseille ....a — W 1–2 — **Att:** 45,000. **Ref:** K Plautz — **Liverpool** (4-3-3): Reina, Arbeloa, Skrtel, Carragher, Dossena, Gerrard (Benayoun 69), Mascherano, Lucas, Kuyt (Keane 86), Torres (Riera 64), Babel. Subs not used: Cavalieri, Agger, Alonso, Degen.

20th ● Stoke ....h — D 0–0 — **Att:** 43,931. **Ref:** A Marriner — **Liverpool** (4-4-1-1): Reina, Arbeloa, Carragher, Skrtel, Dossena, Kuyt, Gerrard, Alonso, Riera (Babel 65), Keane (Benayoun 73), Torres. Subs not used: Cavalieri, Agger, Mascherano, Lucas, Degen.

23rd ● Crewe ....h — W 2–1 — **Att:** 28,591. **Ref:** M Oliver — **Liverpool** (4-4-2): Cavalieri, Degen (Carragher 73), Hyypia, Agger, Insua, Pennant, Lucas, Plessis, El Zhar (Keane 87), Babel, Ngog (Torres 66). Subs not used: Gulacsi, Dossena, Agger, Skrtel.

27th ● Everton ....a — W 0–2 — **Att:** 39,574. **Ref:** M Riley — **Liverpool** (4-4-2): Reina, Arbeloa, Carragher, Skrtel, Dossena, Kuyt, Alonso (Lucas 86), Gerrard, Riera (Aurelio 67), Torres, Keane (Pennant 86). Subs not used: Cavalieri, Hyypia, Agger, Babel.

October

1st ● PSV ....h — W 3–1 — **Att:** 41,097. **Ref:** F Brych — **Liverpool** (4-4-2): Reina, Arbeloa, Skrtel, Carragher, Aurelio, Kuyt, Gerrard (Babel 81), Alonso, Riera (Benayoun 68), Lucas 75). Subs not used: Cavalieri, Dossena, Agger, Mascherano.

5th ● Man City ....a — W 2–3 — **Att:** 47,280. **Ref:** P Walton — **Liverpool** (4-1-4-1): Reina, Arbeloa, Skrtel, Carragher, Aurelio (Dossena 70), Mascherano (Keane 71), Kuyt, Gerrard, Alonso, Riera (Benayoun 81), Torres. Subs not used: Cavalieri, Agger, Babel, Lucas.

18th ● Wigan ....h — W 3–2 — **Att:** 43,868. **Ref:** A Wiley — **Liverpool** (4-4-2): Reina, Arbeloa (Benayoun 79), Carragher, Agger, Dossena (El Zhar 78), Pennant, Gerrard, Alonso, Riera, Keane (Hyypia 90), Kuyt. Subs not used: Cavalieri, Lucas, Insua, Ngog.

22nd ● Atletico Madrid ....a — D 1–1 — **Att:** 44,500. **Ref:** C Bo Larsen — **Liverpool** (4-2-3-1): Reina, Arbeloa, Carragher, Agger, Dossena, Mascherano, Alonso (Lucas 75), Benayoun, Gerrard (Babel 61), Riera, Keane (Kuyt 53). Subs not used: Cavalieri, Aurelio, Pennant, Darby.

26th ● Chelsea ....a — W 0–1 — **Att:** 41,705. **Ref:** H Webb — **Liverpool** (4-2-3-1): Reina, Arbeloa, Carragher, Agger, Aurelio, Alonso, Mascherano, Kuyt (Lucas 88), Gerrard, Riera (Hyypia 90), Keane (Babel 60). Subs not used: Cavalieri, Dossena, Benayoun, Pennant.

29th ● Portsmouth ....h — W 1–0 — **Att:** 43,378. **Ref:** S Tanner — **Liverpool** (4-4-1-1): Reina, Arbeloa, Hyypia, Carragher, Aurelio, Pennant (Benayoun 63), Alonso, Lucas, Babel (Riera 71), Gerrard (Keane 90), Kuyt. Subs not used: Cavalieri, Dossena, Agger, Mascherano.

November

1st ● Tottenham...........................a — L 2–1 — **Att:** 36,183. **Ref:** P Dowd — **Liverpool** (4-4-1-1): Reina, Arbeloa, Carragher, Agger, Dossena, Kuyt, Mascherano, Alonso, Riera (Benayoun 78), Gerrard, Keane (Babel 66). Subs not used: Cavalieri, Hyypia, Aurelio, Lucas, El Zhar.

4th ● Atletico Madrid ....h — D 1–1 — **Att:** 42,010. **Ref:** M Hansson — **Liverpool** (4-2-3-1): Reina, Arbeloa, Carragher, Agger, Aurelio, Mascherano (Lucas 77), Alonso, Kuyt, Gerrard, Riera (Babel 61), Keane (Ngog 71). Subs not used: Cavalieri, Dossena, Benayoun, Degen.

8th ● West Brom ....h — W 3–0 — **Att:** 43,451. **Ref:** P Walton — **Liverpool** (4-4-2): Reina, Arbeloa, Agger, Carragher, Aurelio, Benayoun, Mascherano, Gerrard (Alonso 80), Riera (Babel 65), Keane (Torres 72), Kuyt. Subs not used: Cavalieri, Hyypia, Insua, El Zhar.

12th ● Tottenham..........................a — L 4–2 — **Att:** 33,242. **Ref:** M Riley — **Liverpool** (4-4-2): Cavalieri, Dossena, Hyypia, Agger, Degen (Darby 84), Babel, Lucas, Ngog, Plessis (Alonso 66), Torres (Insua 56), El Zhar. Subs not used: Gulacsi, Riera, Benayoun, Carragher.

15th ● Bolton ....a — W 0–2 — **Att:** 24,893. **Ref:** R Styles — **Liverpool** (4-2-3-1): Reina, Carragher, Hyypia, Agger, Aurelio, Alonso, Mascherano, Kuyt (Lucas 84), Gerrard, Riera (Benayoun 89), Keane (Torres 59). Subs not used: Cavalieri, Dossena, Babel, Darby.

22nd ● Fulham ....h — D 0–0 — **Att:** 43,589. **Ref:** M Halsey — **Liverpool** (4-2-3-1): Reina, Arbeloa, Carragher, Agger, Aurelio, Kuyt (El Zhar 81), Lucas, Mascherano (Alonso 64), Riera (Babel 78), Keane, Torres. Subs not used: Cavalieri, Dossena, Hyypia, Benayoun.

26th ● Marseille ....h — W 1–0 — **Att:** 40,024. **Ref:** O Benquerenca — **Liverpool** (4-2-3-1): Reina, Arbeloa, Carragher, Agger, Aurelio (Dossena 46), Mascherano, Alonso, Kuyt (Lucas 85), Gerrard, Riera (Benayoun 63), Torres. Subs not used: Cavalieri, Keane, Babel, Kelly.

December

1st ● West Ham ....h — D 0–0 — **Att:** 41,169. **Ref:** P Walton — **Liverpool** (4-4-2): Reina, Arbeloa, Carragher, Hyypia, Dossena, Benayoun, Gerrard, Alonso, Riera (Babel 78), Kuyt, Keane (Ngog 66). Subs not used: Cavalieri, Agger, Mascherano, Lucas, Insua.

6th ● Blackburn ....a — W 1–3 — **Att:** 26,920. **Ref:** A Marriner — **Liverpool** (4-4-1-1): Reina, Arbeloa, Carragher, Hyypia, Insua, Benayoun (Riera 87), Mascherano (Lucas 83), Alonso, Babel (El Zhar 64), Gerrard, Kuyt. Subs not used: Cavalieri, Dossena, Agger, Keane.

9th ● PSV ....a — W 1–3 — **Att:** 35,000. **Ref:** N Ivanov — **Liverpool** (4-2-3-1): Cavalieri, Arbeloa (Darby 69), Carragher (Kelly 81), Agger, Dossena, Mascherano, Lucas, Babel, Ngog, Riera (Spearing 76), Keane. Subs not used: Reina, Gerrard, Alonso, Benayoun.

13th ● Hull ....h — D 2–2 — **Att:** 43,835. **Ref:** A Wiley — **Liverpool** (4-2-3-1): Reina, Arbeloa, Hyypia, Carragher, Dossena, Mascherano (Lucas 87), Alonso, Benayoun (El Zhar 74), Gerrard, Riera (Babel 82), Kuyt. Subs not used: Cavalieri, Agger, Keane, Ngog.

21st ● Arsenal ....a — D 1–1 — **Att:** 60,094. **Ref:** H Webb — **Liverpool** (4-4-1-1): Reina, Arbeloa, Carragher, Agger, Insua, Kuyt, Lucas (Ngog 88), Alonso, Riera (Babel 71), Gerrard, Keane (El Zhar 81). Subs not used: Cavalieri, Hyypia, Benayoun, Plessis.

26th ● Bolton ....h — W 3–0 — **Att:** 43,548. **Ref:** A Wiley — **Liverpool** (4-4-2): Reina, Carragher, Hyypia, Agger, Insua, Benayoun, Gerrard (Lucas 73), Alonso, Riera (El Zhar 69), Keane (Kuyt (Ngog 76). Subs not used: Cavalieri, Babel, Mascherano, Darby.

28th ● Newcastle ....a — W 1–5 — **Att:** 52,114. **Ref:** M Halsey — **Liverpool** (4-4-1-1): Reina, Carragher, Hyypia, Agger, Insua, Benayoun (Alonso 60), Mascherano, Lucas, Babel, Gerrard (Ngog 70), Kuyt (Skrtel 79). Subs not used: Cavalieri, Keane, Riera, El Zhar.

January

3rd ● Preston ....a — W 0–2 — **Att:** 23,046. **Ref:** M Atkinson — **Liverpool** (4-2-3-1): Cavalieri, Carragher, Hyypia, Agger, Insua, Alonso (Lucas 46), Mascherano (Aurelio 83), Babel, Gerrard, Riera, Keane (Torres 73). Subs not used: Reina, Ngog, El Zhar, Skrtel.

10th ● Stoke ....a — D 0–0 — **Att:** 27,500. **Ref:** L Mason — **Liverpool** (4-4-1-1): Reina, Carragher, Hyypia, Skrtel, Aurelio, Benayoun (Babel 76), Lucas, Mascherano, Riera (Torres 60), Gerrard, Kuyt. Subs not used: Cavalieri, Dossena, Keane, Plessis, El Zhar.

● Barclays Premier League ● FA Cup ● Carling Cup ● UEFA Champions League ● UEFA Cup

▌Yellow Card ▌Red Card

19th	● Everton ....h	D 1–1	**Att:** 44,382. **Ref:** H Webb — **Liverpool** (4-4-2): Reina, Carragher, Hyypia, Skrtel, Aurelio, Kuyt, Gerrard¹, Alonso, Riera (Babel 89), Keane (Benayoun 67), Torres (Lucas 85). Subs not used: Cavalieri, Dossena, Arbeloa, Mascherano.	
25th	● Everton ....h	D 1–1	**Att:** 43,524. **Ref:** S Bennett — **Liverpool** (4-4-1-1): Reina, Arbeloa, Skrtel, Carragher▮, Dossena, Kuyt, Alonso▮, Mascherano, Babel (Riera 75), Gerrard¹, Torres. Subs not used: Cavalieri, Hyypia, Aurelio, Benayoun, Lucas, Ngog.	
28th	● Wigan ....a	D 1–1	**Att:** 21,237. **Ref:** P Dowd — **Liverpool** (4-4-2): Reina, Arbeloa, Skrtel, Carragher, Aurelio, Benayoun¹ (Kuyt 75), Lucas, Mascherano, Babel, Gerrard (Keane 84), Torres (Riera 72). Subs not used: Cavalieri, Dossena, Agger, Alonso.	

February

1st	● Chelsea ....h	W 2–0	**Att:** 44,174. **Ref:** M Riley — **Liverpool** (4-4-1-1): Reina, Arbeloa▮, Carragher, Skrtel, Aurelio, Kuyt, Alonso▮, Mascherano▮ (Babel 83), Riera (Benayoun 74), Gerrard▮, Torres² (Ngog 90). Subs not used: Cavalieri, Dossena, Agger, Lucas.	
4th	● Everton ....a	L 1–0	**Att:** 37,918. **Ref:** A Wiley — **Liverpool** (4-5-1): Reina, Dossena, Carragher, Skrtel, Arbeloa, Kuyt, Alonso▮, Gerrard (Benayoun 16), Lucas▮, Riera (Mascherano 80), Torres (Babel 101). Subs not used: Cavalieri, Hyypia, Agger, El Zhar.	
7th	● Portsmouth ....a	W 2–3	**Att:** 20,524. **Ref:** H Webb — **Liverpool** (4-3-3): Reina, Carragher, Skrtel, Agger, Dossena (Alonso 67), Arbeloa, Mascherano, Aurelio¹, Babel (Torres¹ 76), Ngog (Kuyt¹ 56), Benayoun. Subs not used: Cavalieri, Hyypia, Riera, El Zhar.	
22nd	● Man City ....h	D 1–1	**Att:** 44,259. **Ref:** P Dowd — **Liverpool** (4-4-2): Reina, Arbeloa, Carragher, Skrtel, Dossena (Aurelio 76), Benayoun, Mascherano (Babel 83), Lucas, Riera (El Zhar▮ 63), Torres, Kuyt¹. Subs not used: Cavalieri, Hyypia, Ngog, Spearing.	
25th	● Real Madrid ....a	W 0–1	**Att:** 85,000. **Ref:** R Rosetti — **Liverpool** (4-4-2): Reina, Arbeloa, Skrtel, Carragher, Aurelio, Benayoun¹, Alonso, Mascherano▮, Riera▮ (Gerrard 88), Torres▮ (Babel 61), Kuyt (Lucas 90). Subs not used: Cavalieri, Dossena, Hyypia, Ngog.	
28th	● Middlesbrough ....a	L 2–0	**Att:** 33,724. **Ref:** R Styles — **Liverpool** (4-2-3-1): Reina, Carragher (Benayoun 71), Hyypia, Skrtel, Aurelio, Alonso, Mascherano, Kuyt, Gerrard (Lucas 76), Babel, El Zhar (Ngog 68). Subs not used: Cavalieri, Dossena, Riera, Darby.	

March

3rd	● Sunderland ....h	W 2–0	**Att:** 41,587. **Ref:** M Halsey — **Liverpool** (4-4-2): Reina, Mascherano, Skrtel, Carragher, Insua, Benayoun¹ (El Zhar 90), Gerrard (Babel 82), Alonso, Riera, Kuyt, Ngog▮¹ (Lucas 70). Subs not used: Cavalieri, Dossena, Hyypia, Aurelio.	
10th	● Real Madrid ....h	W 4–0	**Att:** 42,550. **Ref:** F De Bleeckere — **Liverpool** (4-2-3-1): Reina, Arbeloa, Skrtel, Carragher, Aurelio, Alonso (Lucas 60), Mascherano▮, Kuyt, Gerrard▮² (Spearing 74), Babel, Torres¹ (Dossena▮ 83). Subs not used: Cavalieri, Hyypia, Ngog, Kelly.	
14th	● Man Utd ....a	W 1–4	**Att:** 75,569. **Ref:** A Wiley — **Liverpool** (4-2-3-1): Reina, Carragher▮, Skrtel▮, Hyypia, Aurelio¹, Mascherano▮, Lucas, Kuyt, Gerrard¹ (El Zhar 90), Riera (Dossena¹ 67), Torres¹ (Babel 81). Subs not used: Cavalieri, Insua, Ngog, Arbeloa.	
22nd	● Aston Villa...............h	W 5–0	**Att:** 44,131. **Ref:** M Atkinson — **Liverpool** (4-2-3-1): Reina, Arbeloa (Agger 76), Carragher, Skrtel, Aurelio, Mascherano, Alonso (Lucas 66), Gerrard▮³ (Ngog 80), Kuyt¹, Riera¹, Torres. Subs not used: Cavalieri, Dossena, Hyypia, El Zhar.	

April

4th	● Fulham ....a	W 0–1	**Att:** 25,661. **Ref:** S Bennett — **Liverpool** (4-2-3-1): Reina, Arbeloa, Carragher, Skrtel▮, Insua, Alonso, Lucas, Kuyt (Benayoun¹ 76), Gerrard (Agger 90), Dossena (Babel▮ 65), Torres. Subs not used: Cavalieri, Riera, Mascherano, Ngog.	
8th	● Chelsea ....h	L 1–3	**Att:** 42,543. **Ref:** C Bo Larsen — **Liverpool** (4-4-2): Reina, Arbeloa, Carragher, Skrtel, Aurelio▮ (Dossena 75), Kuyt, Lucas (Babel 79), Alonso, Riera (Benayoun 67), Gerrard, Torres¹. Subs not used: Cavalieri, Hyypia, Agger, Ngog.	
11th	● Blackburn ....h	W 4–0	**Att:** 43,466. **Ref:** M Riley — **Liverpool** (4-4-2): Reina, Arbeloa, Carragher, Agger▮, Insua, Benayoun, Mascherano, Alonso▮ (Lucas 87), Riera, Torres² (El Zhar 74), Kuyt (Ngog¹ 84). Subs not used: Cavalieri, Dossena, Gerrard, Skrtel.	
14th	● Chelsea ....a	D 4–4	**Att:** 38,286. **Ref:** L Medina Cantalejo — **Liverpool** (4-3-3): Reina, Arbeloa▮ (Babel 85), Carragher, Skrtel, Aurelio¹, Lucas¹, Mascherano (Riera 69), Alonso¹, Kuyt¹, Torres (Ngog 80), Benayoun¹. Subs not used: Cavalieri, Dossena, Hyypia, Agger.	
21st	● Arsenal ....h	D 4–4	**Att:** 44,424. **Ref:** H Webb — **Liverpool** (4-2-3-1): Reina, Arbeloa, Carragher, Agger, Aurelio, Alonso, Mascherano, Benayoun², Kuyt (El Zhar 86), Riera (Babel 74), Torres². Subs not used: Cavalieri, Dossena, Lucas, Ngog, Skrtel.	
25th	● Hull ....a	W 1–3	**Att:** 24,942. **Ref:** M Atkinson — **Liverpool** (4-5-1): Reina, Arbeloa▮, Carragher, Skrtel, Insua, Kuyt² (Dossena 90), Alonso¹, Mascherano (El Zhar 84), Benayoun (Agger 87), Lucas, Torres. Subs not used: Cavalieri, Riera, Aurelio, Ngog.	

May

3rd	● Newcastle ....h	W 3–0	**Att:** 44,121. **Ref:** P Dowd — **Liverpool** (4-2-3-1): Reina, Arbeloa, Carragher, Agger, Aurelio, Alonso (Lucas¹ 80), Mascherano (Ngog 89), Benayoun¹, Gerrard, Riera (Babel 63), Kuyt¹. Subs not used: Cavalieri, Dossena, El Zhar, Skrtel.	
9th	● West Ham...............a	W 0–3	**Att:** 34,951. **Ref:** A Wiley — **Liverpool** (4-4-2): Reina, Arbeloa, Skrtel, Carragher, Aurelio▮ (Insua 54), Benayoun (Dossena 82), Mascherano▮, Lucas, Gerrard², Kuyt, Torres (Babel¹ 72). Subs not used: Cavalieri, Hyypia, Ngog, Degen.	
17th	● West Brom ....a	W 0–2	**Att:** 26,138. **Ref:** M Atkinson — **Liverpool** (4-2-3-1): Reina, Arbeloa, Agger, Carragher, Insua, Lucas, Mascherano (Alonso 51), Kuyt¹, Gerrard¹, Benayoun (Ngog 73), Torres¹ (Babel 68). Subs not used: Cavalieri, Dossena, Riera, Skrtel.	
24th	● Tottenham ....h	W 3–1	**Att:** 43,937. **Ref:** P Walton — **Liverpool** (4-2-3-1): Reina, Carragher, Agger, Skrtel, Aurelio, Mascherano, Alonso, Kuyt (Riera 66), Gerrard (Hyypia 84), Benayoun¹, Torres¹ (Ngog 78). Subs not used: Cavalieri, Lucas, Insua, Degen.	

● Barclays Premier League ● FA Cup ● Carling Cup ● UEFA Champions League ● UEFA Cup   ▮ Yellow Card ▌ Red Card

LIVERPOOL

BARCLAYS PREMIER LEAGUE GOALKEEPER STATS

Player	Minutes on pitch	Appearances	Match starts	Completed matches	Sub appearances	Subbed off	Saved with feet	Punched	Parried	Tipped over	Fumbled	Tipped round	Caught	Blocked	Clean sheets	Goals conceded	Minutes since conceding	Save %	Saved	Resulting in goals	Opposition miss	Yellow cards	Red cards
								SAVES BREAKDOWN												PENALTIES			
Jose Reina 3617	38	38	38	0	0	2	15	13	3	0	5	119	0	20	27	16	85.33	0	2	0	0	0

BARCLAYS PREMIER LEAGUE OUTFIELD PLAYER STATS

Player	Minutes on pitch	Appearances	Match starts	Completed matches	Substitute appearances	Subbed off	Goals scored	Minutes since scoring	Assists	Shots on target	Shots off target	Crosses	Defensive clearances	Defensive blocks	Fouls committed	Free-kicks won	Caught offside	Yellow cards	Red cards
Daniel Agger 1456	18	15	15	3	0	1	395	2	7	11	1	23	3	10	15	2	2	0
Xabi Alonso 2713	33	27	23	6	4	3	268	6	23	32	30	12	1	28	41	0	5	0
Alvaro Arbeloa 2718	29	29	26	0	3	1	1603	2	5	1	53	18	3	38	42	3	8	0
Fabio Aurelio 1837	24	19	17	5	2	2	451	4	10	9	41	5	0	16	6	1	1	0
Ryan Babel 933	27	6	3	21	3	3	34	1	10	5	4	1	0	11	19	2	2	0
Yossi Benayoun 1989	32	21	9	11	12	8	12	5	23	21	24	3	1	15	18	8	0	0
Jamie Carragher 3593	38	38	37	0	1	0	-	2	2	4	16	36	16	29	28	0	4	0
Andrea Dossena 1098	16	12	7	4	5	1	83	0	3	2	50	6	1	13	8	3	2	0
Nabil El Zhar 294	15	1	0	14	1	0	-	1	3	5	6	0	0	4	4	3	3	0
Steven Gerrard 2751	31	30	19	1	11	16	151	10	54	61	81	9	3	24	33	5	5	0
Sami Hyypia 1171	16	12	12	4	0	1	447	0	6	8	0	16	2	10	4	1	1	0
Emiliano Insua 892	10	9	9	1	0	0	-	0	2	5	12	8	0	9	3	1	0	0
Robbie Keane 1310	19	16	4	3	12	5	16	3	15	7	22	0	1	18	14	13	2	0
Dirk Kuyt 3326	38	36	25	2	11	12	96	8	49	39	42	12	0	24	20	26	0	0
Leiva Lucas 1387	25	13	12	12	1	1	196	2	10	10	1	4	0	35	20	2	2	0
Javier Mascherano 2401	27	27	17	0	10	0	-	1	13	14	13	2	1	41	32	2	6	0
David Ngog 359	14	2	0	12	2	2	41	2	6	3	2	0	1	5	1	2	1	0
Jermaine Pennant 170	3	2	1	1	1	0	-	1	0	0	12	0	0	2	2	0	0	0
Damien Plessis 45	1	1	0	0	1	0	-	0	0	0	0	0	0	0	0	0	0	0
Albert Riera 1946	28	24	4	4	20	3	321	4	18	26	58	11	2	33	41	6	1	0
Martin Skrtel 1918	21	20	20	1	0	0	-	2	7	6	2	30	6	24	26	0	4	0
Fernando Torres 1822	24	20	11	4	9	14	48	5	44	33	11	3	1	35	35	19	1	0

SEASON TOTALS

Goals scored	77
Goals conceded	27
Clean sheets	20
Shots on target	310
Shots off target	302
Shots per goal	7.95
Pens awarded	6
Pens scored	5
Pens conceded	2
Offsides	99
Corners	271
Crosses	481
Players used	23
Fouls committed	425
Free-kicks won	424

CARDS RECEIVED

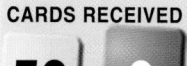

50   **0**

SEQUENCES

Wins	5
(on three occasions)	
Losses	
(–)	
Draws	3
(10/01/09–28/01/09)	
Undefeated	15
(08/11/08–22/02/09)	
Without win	3
(10/01/09–28/01/09)	
Undefeated home	
(all season)	
Undefeated away	7
(15/11/08–07/02/09)	
Without scoring	2
(22/11/08–01/12/08)	
Without conceding	4
(08/11/08–01/12/08)	
Scoring	11
(03/03/09–24/05/09)	
Conceding	3
(on two occasions)	

SEASON INFORMATION

Highest Position: 1
Lowest Position: 9
Average goals scored per game: 2.03
Average goals conceded per game: 0.71

League position at the end of each week

League position at the end of: August 2, September 2, October 1, November 2, December 1, January 3, February 3, March 2, April 2, May 2

MATCH RECORDS

Goals scored per match

	W	D	L	Pts
Failed to score	6	0	5	1	5
Scored 1 goal	9	4	4	1	16
Scored 2 goals	8	7	1	0	22
Scored 3 goals	10	10	0	0	30
Scored 4+ goals	5	4	1	0	13

Goals conceded per match

	W	D	L	Pts
Clean sheet	20	15	5	0	50
Conceded 1 goal	11	7	4	0	25
Conceded 2 goals	6	3	1	2	10
Conceded 3 goals	0	0	0	0	0
Conceded 4+ goals	1	0	1	0	1

QUICK-FIRE GOALS

From the start of a match
Steven Gerrard
(v West Ham) 1:16

By a substitute after coming on
David Ngog
(v Blackburn) 5:31

LAST-GASP GOALS

From the start of a match
Steven Gerrard
(v Blackburn) 94:29

By a substitute after coming on
Dirk Kuyt
(v Portsmouth) 28:08

GOAL DETAILS

How the goals were struck

SCORED		CONCEDED
50	Right foot	15
11	Left foot	5
14	Headers	6
2	Others	1

How the goals were struck

SCORED		CONCEDED
48	Open play	14
10	Cross	2
5	Corner	2
5	Penalties	2
2	Direct from free-kick	1
3	Free-kick	3
4	Own goals	3

Distance from goal

SCORED		CONCEDED
25	6yds	8
43	18yds	16
9	18+yds	3

GOALS SCORED/CONCEDED PER FIVE-MINUTE INTERVALS

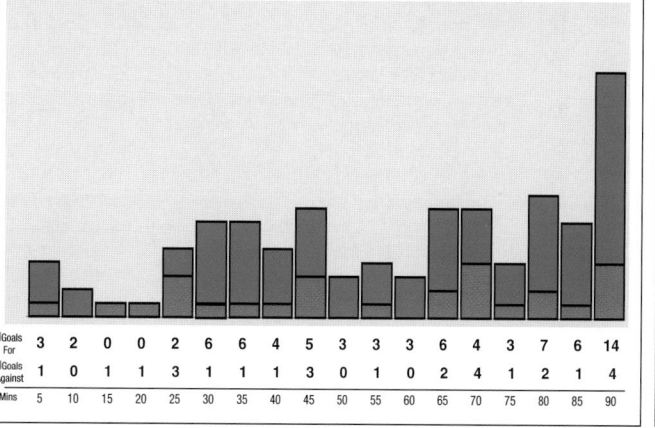

Goals For	3	2	0	0	2	6	6	4	5	3	3	3	6	4	3	7	6	14
Goals Against	1	0	1	1	3	1	1	1	3	0	1	0	2	4	1	2	1	4
Mins	5	10	15	20	25	30	35	40	45	50	55	60	65	70	75	80	85	90

MANCHESTER CITY

CLUB SUMMARY

FORMED	1880
MANAGER	Mark Hughes
GROUND	City of Manchester Stadium
CAPACITY	48,000
NICKNAME	The Blues
WEBSITE	www.mcfc.co.uk

The New Football Pools PLAYER OF THE SEASON

Stephen Ireland

OVERALL

P	W	D	L	F	A	GD
55	24	8	23	82	72	10

BARCLAYS PREMIER LEAGUE

Pos	P	W	D	L	F	A	GD	Pts
10	38	15	5	18	58	50	8	50

HOME

Pos	P	W	D	L	F	A	GD	Pts
3	19	13	0	6	40	18	22	39

AWAY

Pos	P	W	D	L	F	A	GD	Pts
17	19	2	5	12	18	32	-14	11

CUP PROGRESS DETAILS

Competition	Round reached	Knocked out by
FA Cup	R3	Nottm Forest
UEFA Cup	QF	Hamburg
Carling Cup	R2	Brighton

BIGGEST WIN (ALL COMPS)

21/09/08 6-0 v Portsmouth **PREM**

BIGGEST DEFEAT (ALL COMPS)

03/01/09 0-3 v Nottm Forest **FAC3**

THE PLAYER WITH THE MOST

Shots on target
Robinho 62

Shots off target
Robinho 39

Shots without scoring
Nigel De Jong 10

Assists
Stephen Ireland 9

Offsides
Craig Bellamy 29

Fouls
Vincent Kompany 60

Fouls without a card
Wayne Bridge 12

Free-kicks won
Shaun Wright-Phillips 61

Defensive clearances
Richard Dunne 58

actim INDEX for the 2008/09 Barclays Premier League Season

Rank	Player	Pts
21	Stephen Ireland	466
24	Robinho	450
56	Shay Given	382
74	Richard Dunne	362
117	Vincent Kompany	305

ATTENDANCE RECORD

High	Low	Average
47,331	36,635	42,900

v Chelsea (13/09/2008) v West Ham (24/08/2008)

THERE is no doubt the most significant moment of the season for Manchester City did not involve a ball being kicked.

On one mad September day, which stretched right up until the midnight hour, the Blues were at the centre of a storm which threatens to throw the Barclays Premier League off its axis.

The merits of having Thaksin Shinawatra as an owner were debatable at the best of times. A huge cash windfall from Abu Dhabi swept the disgraced former Thai prime minister out of his City powerbase and set in motion a chain of events, the full consequence of which may not be fully realised for some years.

An immediate consequence of the Abu Dhabi United Group taking over the stewardship of this most parochial of big-city clubs was to buy Robinho. The fee, at £32.5million, was a British record. It was a statement of intent from people who mean business.

An even more lucrative offer was prepared for another Brazilian, Kaka, during the January transfer window. The figures were astounding, yet City did not get their man. The bruising reaction that followed ensures a few lessons will be learned. There is no doubt, though, that the Blues are a club on the march, even if inconsistency remained a byword throughout a campaign that began in the UEFA Cup on 17th July in the Faroe Islands.

In total, City played 16 matches in the competition and the run to the quarter-finals included some major highlights. Although German side Schalke fell below the standards of some previous seasons, winning in Gelsenkirchen is not easy for any opposition side. For City to do so by 2-0 in the group stage was an achievement worth noting.

City progressed to the last eight, but eventually came unstuck against another German opponent, this time SV Hamburg. Despite a dream start, with a first-minute goal courtesy of Stephen Ireland in the first leg, the Bundesliga outfit progressed 4-3 on aggregate.

That the UEFA Cup should be remembered more fondly than either of the domestic cup competitions is not saying much. If beating Schalke was a high, the 3-0 FA Cup loss to Nottingham Forest at Eastlands was a pretty significant low as silverware continued to prove elusive.

'Ireland is now maturing into a top-class attacking midfield star'

However, it is league form on which manager Mark Hughes will be judged. On home soil City were excellent – only Manchester United managed more wins than the Blues' 13. Yet on their travels, Hughes' men struggled. Defeat at lowly West Bromwich Albion left them in the bottom three over Christmas, and their only away-day triumphs took place at Sunderland in August and Everton in May.

Little surprise, therefore, that moments to cherish from an up-and-down domestic campaign all came within the confines of City's own stadium. Six goals against Portsmouth and Robinho's hat-trick in the hammering of Stoke both figure high on that list, as does the three-goal triumph over Arsenal.

The second half of the season was not quite so productive. Robinho's 12-game barren run ended against West Brom in April, but his goals were unable to guide City any higher than 10th spot in the table, one down on 12 months previously.

Not that there is any need to worry. The positives outweigh the negatives, coming in the form of Shaun Wright-Phillips, back where he made his name after a spell at Chelsea, and a quartet of excellent new arrivals in the form of Shay Given, Pablo Zabaleta, Nigel de Jong and Vincent Kompany. Then there is Stephen Ireland, unrivalled winner of City's Player of the Season prize, who is maturing into a top-class attacking midfield star.

More importantly, City have, in Hughes, a manager with vision and focus, a fact recognised by the owners, who have adopted a welcome pragmatic view to football life.

Success might take longer than the more demanding Blues supporter would hope. However, with a little patience and a couple of significant signings in defence and attack, the dreams of those who have waited so long for the glory days to come back may end up being fulfilled.

CLOCKWISE FROM ABOVE: Robinho opens with a goal against Chelsea; City fans pay homage to their Brazilian star and the club's Abu Dhabi owners; Stephen Ireland scores against Arsenal; Mark Hughes is left frustrated by another poor display

MANCHESTER CITY

July

17th ● EB Streymur ....a W 0–2 **Att:** 3,000. **Ref:** N Petignat — **Man City** (4-4-2): Hart, Onuoha, Dunne, Richards, Ball, Ireland, Hamann¹, Johnson▊, Petrov¹, Vassell, Jo. Subs not used: Schmeichel, Corluka, Gelson, Elano, Evans, Mwaruwari, Castillo.

31st ● EB Streymur ....h W 2–0 **Att:** 7,334. **Ref:** A Constantin — **Man City** (4-4-2): Hart, Corluka, Dunne, Richards, Ball, Gelson (Hamann 62), Johnson, Elano, Petrov¹ (Etuhu 69), Vassell¹, Sturridge (Evans 70). Subs not used: Schmeichel, Onuoha, Ireland, Bianchi.

August

14th ● FC Midtjylland ....h L 0–1 **Att:** 17,200. **Ref:** B Rafati — **Man City** (4-4-2): Hart, Corluka▊, Richards, Dunne, Ben-Haim, Elano, Johnson, Gelson, Petrov, Caicedo, Sturridge. Subs not used: Schmeichel, Ball, Onuoha, Ireland, Hamann, Bojinov, Etuhu.

17th ● Aston Villa............................a L 4–2 **Att:** 39,955. **Ref:** P Dowd — **Man City** (4-4-1-1): Hart, Corluka¹, Richards, Ben-Haim▊, Garrido, Etuhu, Gelson (Ireland 81), Johnson, Petrov, Elano¹, Evans (Sturridge 81). Subs not used: Schmeichel, Ball, Onuoha, Caicedo, Hamann.

24th ● West Ham ....h W 3–0 **Att:** 36,635. **Ref:** H Webb — **Man City** (4-4-1-1): Hart, Corluka, Richards (Hamann 54), Ben-Haim, Ball, Ireland, Kompany, Johnson, Petrov (Etuhu 77), Elano² (Evans 77), Sturridge¹. Subs not used: Schmeichel, Garrido, Gelson, Caicedo.

28th ● FC Midtjylland.....................a W 0–1 **Att:** 9,552. **Ref:** R Malek — **Man City** (4-4-2): Hart, Ben-Haim (Hamann 58), Richards▊, Dunne, Ball, Corluka, Johnson, Ireland, Petrov, Elano▊ (Sturridge 57), Jo (Evans 80). Subs not used: Schmeichel, Garrido, Gelson, Caicedo.

31st ● Sunderland ....a W 0–3 **Att:** 39,622. **Ref:** C Foy — **Man City** (4-4-1-1): Hart, Corluka, Richards▊ (Ben-Haim 46), Dunne, Ball, Ireland¹, Hamann, Johnson (Gelson 81), Kompany▊, Wright-Phillips² (Elano 85), Jo. Subs not used: Schmeichel, Garrido, Evans, Sturridge.

September

13th ● Chelsea ....h L 1–3 **Att:** 47,331. **Ref:** M Halsey — **Man City** (4-4-2): Hart, Zabaleta, Richards, Dunne, Ball (Sturridge 84), Wright-Phillips, Hamann (Gelson 61), Kompany, Ireland, Robinho¹, Jo. Subs not used: Schmeichel, Elano, Garrido, Evans, Ben-Haim.

18th ● Omonia Nicosia ....a W 1–2 **Att:** 15,907. **Ref:** 154949 — **Man City:** Hart, Zabaleta, Richards, Dunne, Garrido▊, Kompany (Gelson 84), Wright-Phillips, Ireland, Elano (Hamann 85), Robinho▊, Jo² (Sturridge 76). Subs not used: Schmeichel, Ball, Ben-Haim, Evans.

21st ● Portsmouth ....h W 6–0 **Att:** 40,238. **Ref:** A Wiley — **Man City** (4-4-2): Hart, Zabaleta, Richards, Dunne¹, Garrido, Kompany, Wright-Phillips¹, Ireland (Gelson¹ 77), Elano, Robinho¹ (Sturridge 85), Jo¹ (Evans¹ 71). Subs not used: Schmeichel, Ball, Hamann, Ben-Haim.

24th ● Brighton ....a D 2–2 **Att:** 8,729. **Ref:** A D'Urso — **Man City** (4-4-2): Schmeichel, Zabaleta, Dunne, Ben-Haim, Ball, Kompany, Ireland¹, Johnson (Elano 102), Gelson¹, Sturridge (Evans 60), Jo (Caicedo 91). Subs not used: Hart, Garrido, Hamann, Logan.

28th ● Wigan ....a L 2–1 **Att:** 18,214. **Ref:** S Bennett — **Man City** (4-2-3-1): Hart, Zabaleta, Richards▊, Dunne, Garrido, Kompany▊¹ (Fernandes 90), Elano (Sturridge 84), Wright-Phillips, Ireland, Robinho▊, Jo (Evans 74). Subs not used: Schmeichel, Ball, Ben-Haim, Hamann.

October

2nd ● Omonia Nicosia ....h W 2–1 **Att:** 25,304. **Ref:** S Ennjimi — **Man City** (4-4-2): Hart, Zabaleta, Richards, Ben-Haim▊, Garrido, Wright-Phillips¹, Ireland, Kompany (Hamann 66), Elano¹, Robinho (Petrov 70), Jo (Evans 67). Subs not used: Schmeichel, Ball, Fernandes, Sturridge.

5th ● Liverpool ....h L 2–3 **Att:** 47,280. **Ref:** P Walton — **Man City** (4-4-1-1): Hart, Zabaleta▊, Dunne▊, Richards, Garrido¹, Wright-Phillips, Ireland¹, Kompany, Elano (Petrov 85), Robinho (Evans 80), Jo (Fernandes 70). Subs not used: Schmeichel, Hamann, Ben-Haim, Sturridge.

20th ● Newcastle ....a D 2–2 **Att:** 45,908. **Ref:** R Styles — **Man City** (4-4-2): Hart, Richards (Onuoha 58), Ben-Haim, Dunne, Garrido▊ (Sturridge 83), Wright-Phillips, Kompany▊, Hamann (Evans 64), Ireland▊, Jo, Robinho¹. Subs not used: Schmeichel, Elano, Fernandes, Berti.

26th ● Stoke ....h W 3–0 **Att:** 44,624. **Ref:** S Tanner — **Man City** (4-4-2): Hart, Richards, Dunne (Fernandes 76), Ben-Haim, Garrido (Onuoha 70), Wright-Phillips, Ireland, Kompany▊, Elano, Robinho³, Evans (Sturridge 42). Subs not used: Schmeichel, Caicedo, Hamann, Berti.

29th ● Middlesbrough ....a L 2–0 **Att:** 25,731. **Ref:** L Mason — **Man City** (4-1-1-1): Hart, Ben-Haim, Richards, Dunne, Onuoha, Kompany▊, Wright-Phillips, Ireland▊, Elano (Fernandes 67), Robinho▊, Sturridge (Evans 77). Subs not used: Schmeichel, Jo, Garrido, Hamann, Berti.

November

2nd ● Bolton ....a L 2–0 **Att:** 21,095. **Ref:** M Riley — **Man City** (4-4-2): Hart, Zabaleta▊, Dunne, Ben-Haim, Richards, Wright-Phillips, Kompany, Ireland, Elano (Hamann 69), Evans (Sturridge 69), Robinho. Subs not used: Schmeichel, Onuoha, Garrido, Fernandes, Caicedo.

6th ● FC Twente ....h W 3–2 **Att:** 21,247. **Ref:** N Ivanov — **Man City** (4-4-2): Hart, Zabaleta▊, Richards, Dunne, Garrido, Wright-Phillips¹, Ireland, Fernandes, Vassell (Elano 66), Robinho¹, Jo (Mwaruwari¹ 59). Subs not used: Schmeichel, Onuoha, Ben-Haim, Hamann, Evans.

9th ● Tottenham...........................h L 1–2 **Att:** 41,893. **Ref:** M Dean — **Man City** (4-4-2): Hart, Zabaleta, Richards, Dunne▊, Garrido, Wright-Phillips, Ireland, Fernandes▊▊, Vassell (Hamann 31), Robinho¹, Mwaruwari. Subs not used: Schmeichel, Onuoha, Elano, Jo, Evans, Ben-Haim.

16th ● Hull ....a D 2–2 **Att:** 24,902. **Ref:** P Dowd — **Man City** (4-3-3): Hart (Schmeichel 19), Zabaleta, Richards, Ben-Haim▊, Garrido, Wright-Phillips▊, Kompany, Ireland¹² (Mwaruwari (Jo 76), Robinho, Vassell. Subs not used: Onuoha, Ball, Hamann, Elano, Evans.

22nd ● Arsenal ....h W 3–0 **Att:** 44,878. **Ref:** A Wiley — **Man City** (4-4-2): Hart, Zabaleta, Richards, Dunne, Garrido, Wright-Phillips, Ireland¹, Kompany, Vassell (Elano 73), Robinho¹ (Hamann 82), Mwaruwari (Sturridge¹ 88). Subs not used: Schmeichel, Onuoha, Evans, Ben-Haim.

27th ● Schalke 04 ....a W 0–2 **Att:** 54,142. **Ref:** A Tudor — **Man City** (4-4-2): Hart, Richards▊, Kompany, Dunne, Garrido (Ball 46), Wright-Phillips, Hamann, Ireland▊¹, Vassell, Mwaruwari¹ (Jo 84), Sturridge. Subs not used: Schmeichel, Evans, Ben-Haim, Berti, Logan.

30th ● Man Utd ....h L 0–1 **Att:** 47,320. **Ref:** H Webb — **Man City** (4-4-2): Hart, Richards (Sturridge 76), Kompany, Dunne, Garrido, Wright-Phillips, Ireland▊, Hamann (Elano 46), Vassell▊ (Zabaleta 46), Robinho, Mwaruwari. Subs not used: Schmeichel, Ball, Jo, Ben-Haim.

December

3rd ● PSG ....h D 0–0 **Att:** 25,626. **Ref:** B Duarte Paixao — **Man City** (4-4-2): Hart, Zabaleta, Dunne, Ben-Haim, Garrido, Sturridge, Ireland, Kompany, Vassell (Hamann 76), Elano (Mwaruwari 49), Jo (Evans 65). Subs not used: Schmeichel, Logan, Berti, Caicedo.

6th ● Fulham ....a D 1–1 **Att:** 24,012. **Ref:** R Styles — **Man City** (4-4-1-1): Hart, Zabaleta, Dunne, Ben-Haim, Ball, Wright-Phillips, Kompany, Hamann, Vassell, Ireland▊, Mwaruwari (Evans 77). Subs not used: Schmeichel, Berti, Onuoha, Logan, Jo, Caicedo.

13th ● Everton ....h L 0–1 **Att:** 41,344. **Ref:** M Halsey — **Man City** (4-3-3): Hart, Zabaleta, Richards, Dunne, Ball, Kompany, Elano, Wright-Phillips, Mwaruwari (Jo 46), Robinho (Vassell 82). Subs not used: Schmeichel, Onuoha, Fernandes, Hamann, Ben-Haim.

18th ● Racing Santander.................a L 3–1 **Att:** 18,360. **Ref:** S Gumienny — **Man City** (4-2-3-1): Schmeichel, Zabaleta▊, Richards, Ben-Haim▊, Garrido, Hamann▊, Fernandes, Vassell, Elano▊ (Kompany 60), Robinho (Ireland 46), Evans (Caicedo¹ 75). Subs not used: Hart, Onuoha, Ball, Logan.

21st ● West Brom ....a L 2–1 **Att:** 25,010. **Ref:** C Foy — **Man City** (4-4-2): Hart, Zabaleta, Richards, Dunne▊, Ball, Wright-Phillips, Ireland, Kompany, Fernandes, Mwaruwari (Caicedo 58), Vassell. Subs not used: Schmeichel, Onuoha, Garrido, Clayton, Johnson, Evans.

26th ● Hull ....h W 5–1 **Att:** 45,196. **Ref:** A Marriner — **Man City** (4-4-2): Hart, Zabaleta, Dunne, Richards (Onuoha 46), Ball, Wright-Phillips, Ireland¹ (Fernandes 85), Kompany, Elano, Robinho² (Caicedo² 58), Caicedo² (Jo 46). Subs not used: Schmeichel, Vassell, Garrido, Sturridge.

28th ● Blackburn ....a D 2–2 **Att:** 25,200. **Ref:** H Webb — **Man City** (4-3-3): Hart, Zabaleta, Onuoha (Richards 64), Dunne, Ball, Ireland▊, Kompany, Elano (Vassell 71), Wright-Phillips, Caicedo (Sturridge¹ 71), Robinho¹. Subs not used: Schmeichel, Jo, Garrido, Fernandes.

● Barclays Premier League ● FA Cup ● Carling Cup ● UEFA Champions League ● UEFA Cup ▊ Yellow Card ▍ Red Card

RESULTS 2008/09

January

3rd	● Nottm Forest........................h	L 0–3	**Att:** 31,869. **Ref:** L Probert — **Man City** (4-4-2): Hart, Zabaleta, Richards, Dunne▌, Ball, Elano, Fernandes (Hamann 60), Kompany, Wright-Phillips (Vassell 24), Caicedo (Jo 70), Sturridge. Subs not used: Schmeichel, Garrido, Clayton, Berti.
17th	● Wigan ....h	W 1–0	**Att:** 41,262. **Ref:** L Mason — **Man City** (5-3-2): Hart, Zabaleta[1], Onuoha, Dunne▌, Richards, Bridge, Wright-Phillips, Kompany, Elano, Robinho▌, Sturridge (Garrido 62). Subs not used: Schmeichel, Vassell, Jo, Fernandes, Caicedo, Weiss.
28th	● Newcastle ....h	W 2–1	**Att:** 42,280. **Ref:** M Jones — **Man City** (4-4-2): Hart, Richards, Onuoha, Kompany, Bridge, Zabaleta (Fernandes 82), Ireland, De Jong (Elano 78), Wright-Phillips[1] (Caicedo 90), Robinho, Bellamy[1]. Subs not used: Schmeichel, Vassell, Jo, Garrido.
31st	● Stoke ....a	L 1–0	**Att:** 27,236. **Ref:** M Atkinson — **Man City** (4-5-1): Hart, Richards, Kompany, Onuoha, Bridge, Wright-Phillips, De Jong (Caicedo 72), Zabaleta (Elano▌ 55), Ireland, Bellamy, Robinho. Subs not used: Schmeichel, Fernandes, Garrido, Jo, Vassell.

February

7th	● Middlesbrough ....h	W 1–0	**Att:** 40,588. **Ref:** A Marriner — **Man City** (4-3-3): Given, Richards, Onuoha, Kompany, Bridge, Zabaleta, De Jong, Ireland, Wright-Phillips, Bellamy[1], Robinho (Caicedo 83). Subs not used: Hart, Elano, Vassell, Garrido, Fernandes, Evans.
14th	● Portsmouth ....a	L 2–0	**Att:** 20,018. **Ref:** L Probert — **Man City** (4-3-3): Given, Logan, Kompany, Onuoha, Bridge, Zabaleta (Evans 78), De Jong▌, Ireland▌, Elano, Bellamy▌, Robinho (Caicedo 66). Subs not used: Hart, Garrido, Fernandes, Berti, Weiss.
19th	● FC Copenhagen ....a	D 2–2	**Att:** 30,159. **Ref:** P Kralovec — **Man City** (4-3-2-1): Given, Onuoha[1], Richards[1], Dunne, Bridge, Zabaleta, Kompany, Ireland[1], Wright-Phillips, Robinho (Caicedo 89), Bellamy▌. Subs not used: Hart, Elano, Vassell, Garrido, Evans, Weiss.
22nd	● Liverpool ....a	D 1–1	**Att:** 44,259. **Ref:** P Dowd — **Man City** (4-3-3): Given, Richards, Dunne▌, Onuoha, Bridge, Zabaleta, De Jong, Kompany▌, Ireland, Bellamy, Robinho (Caicedo 88). Subs not used: Hart, Garrido, Vassell, Evans, Elano, Weiss.
26th	● FC Copenhagen ....h	W 2–1	**Att:** 26,018. **Ref:** S Dereli — **Man City** (4-4-2): Given, Zabaleta (Elano 82), Onuoha, Dunne, Richards, Bridge, Robinho, Bellamy[2]. Subs not used: Hart, Garrido, Berti, Vassell, Caicedo, Evans.

March

1st	● West Ham..........................a	L 1–0	**Att:** 34,562. **Ref:** M Dean — **Man City** (4-3-3): Given, Richards (Caicedo 15), Onuoha, Dunne, Bridge, Zabaleta, De Jong (Bojinov 89), Kompany▌, Ireland▌, Robinho. Subs not used: Hart, Vassell, Garrido, Berti.
4th	● Aston Villa ....h	W 2–0	**Att:** 40,137. **Ref:** C Foy — **Man City** (4-5-1): Given, Zabaleta, Onuoha, Dunne, Bridge, Wright-Phillips[1], Ireland, Kompany, De Jong (Fernandes 47), Elano[1] (Bojinov 83), Caicedo▌ (Evans 74). Subs not used: Hart, Vassell, Garrido, Berti.
12th	● AaB...................................h	W 2–0	**Att:** 24,502. **Ref:** A Hamer — **Man City** (4-4-1-1): Given, Richards, Onuoha, Dunne, Bridge, Wright-Phillips[1] (Etuhu 87), Zabaleta, Ireland, Elano▌, Robinho, Caicedo[1] (Evans 63). Subs not used: Hart, Vassell, Garrido, Fernandes, Berti.
15th	● Chelsea ....a	L 1–0	**Att:** 41,810. **Ref:** M Riley — **Man City** (4-4-1-1): Given, Richards, Onuoha, Dunne, Bridge, Wright-Phillips, Ireland, Zabaleta, Elano▌ (Etuhu 66), Robinho (Bojinov 81), Caicedo (Evans▌ 54). Subs not used: Hart, Garrido, Fernandes, Berti.
19th	● AaB...................................a	L 2–0	**Att:** 10,734. **Ref:** S Lannoy — **Man City** (4-4-2): Given, Richards, Dunne, Bridge (Garrido 55), Wright-Phillips[1], Zabaleta, Kompany▌ (Elano 107), Ireland, Robinho (Caicedo 96), Evans. Subs not used: Hart, Berti, Fernandes, Etuhu.
22nd	● Sunderland ....h	W 1–0	**Att:** 43,017. **Ref:** S Tanner — **Man City** (4-5-1): Given, Richards[1] (Garrido 83), Onuoha, Dunne, Zabaleta, Wright-Phillips▌, Elano, De Jong, Kompany (Fernandes▌ 84), Robinho, Bojinov▌ (Bellamy 65). Subs not used: Hart, Evans, Etuhu, Berti.

April

4th	● Arsenal ....a	L 2–0	**Att:** 60,097. **Ref:** H Webb — **Man City** (4-4-2): Given, Richards, Onuoha, Dunne▌, Bridge (Fernandes 17), Wright-Phillips, Zabaleta▌, De Jong▌, Kompany (Elano 38), Robinho (Sturridge 76), Bellamy. Subs not used: Hart, Bojinov, Garrido, Mwaruwari.
9th	● Hamburg.............................a	L 3–1	**Att:** 50,500. **Ref:** O Benquerenca — **Man City** (4-3-3): Given▌, Richards, Dunne, Onuoha, Bridge (Garrido 46), Wright-Phillips (Fernandes 83), Zabaleta, Ireland[1], Bellamy[1], Robinho (Mwaruwari 62), Bellamy▌, Robinho. Subs not used: Hart, Elano, Petrov, Berti.
12th	● Fulham..............................h	L 1–3	**Att:** 39,841. **Ref:** M Halsey — **Man City** (4-5-1): Given, Richards, Onuoha, Dunne, Garrido, Etuhu (Sturridge 64), Zabaleta, Ireland[1], De Jong, Petrov (Robinho 63), Bojinov (Evans 55). Subs not used: Hart, Elano, Fernandes, McGivern.
16th	● Hamburg............................h	W 2–1	**Att:** 47,009. **Ref:** N Rizzoli — **Man City** (4-4-2): Given, Richards, Onuoha, Dunne▌, Bridge, Zabaleta (Fernandes 77), Kompany▌, Ireland, Elano[1] (Sturridge 84), Robinho, Caicedo[1]. Subs not used: Hart, Garrido, Petrov, Evans, Logan.
19th	● West Brom ....h	W 4–2	**Att:** 40,072. **Ref:** M Jones — **Man City** (4-3-3): Given, Zabaleta, Onuoha[1], Dunne, Bridge, De Jong, Kompany▌, Ireland, Elano[1] (Fernandes 74), Caicedo (Sturridge[1] 58), Robinho[1] (Petrov 84). Subs not used: Hart, Richards, Garrido, Evans.
25th	● Everton ....a	W 1–2	**Att:** 37,791. **Ref:** A Wiley — **Man City** (4-2-3-1): Given, Richards (Fernandes 57), Onuoha, Dunne, Bridge, De Jong, Kompany, Elano▌ (Evans 88), Ireland[1], Robinho[1], Caicedo (Petrov 84). Subs not used: Hart, Bojinov, Garrido, Berti.

May

2nd	● Blackburn ....h	W 3–1	**Att:** 43,967. **Ref:** M Dean — **Man City** (4-3-3): Given, Richards, Onuoha, Dunne, Bridge, De Jong▌, Kompany, Ireland, Elano[1] (Petrov 78), Caicedo▌ (Bojinov 62), Robinho[1]. Subs not used: Hart, Garrido, Fernandes, Evans, Berti.
10th	● Man Utd ....a	L 2–0	**Att:** 75,464. **Ref:** C Foy — **Man City** (4-5-1): Given, Richards, Onuoha, Dunne, Bridge, Elano, Ireland▌, Kompany, De Jong (Petrov 73), Robinho (Evans 89), Caicedo (Bojinov 63). Subs not used: Hart, Zabaleta, Fernandes, Berti.
16th	● Tottenham..........................a	L 2–1	**Att:** 36,000. **Ref:** M Halsey — **Man City** (4-2-3-1): Given, Richards, Dunne, Onuoha, Bridge, Kompany, De Jong, Ireland, Elano (Zabaleta▌ 32), Petrov (Bojinov[1] 61), Caicedo (Mwaruwari 61). Subs not used: Hart, Fernandes, Sturridge, Berti.
24th	● Bolton ....h	W 1–0	**Att:** 47,202. **Ref:** M Clattenburg — **Man City** (4-3-3): Given, Richards, Onuoha, Dunne, Bridge (Berti 84), De Jong, Ireland (Weiss 71), Kompany (Zabaleta 82), Wright-Phillips, Caicedo[1], Robinho. Subs not used: Hart, Bojinov, Petrov, Mwaruwari.

● Barclays Premier League ● FA Cup ● Carling Cup ● UEFA Champions League ● UEFA Cup   ▌Yellow Card ▌Red Card

BARCLAYS PREMIER LEAGUE GOALKEEPER STATS

Player	Minutes on pitch	Appearances	Match starts	Completed matches	Sub appearances	Subbed off	Saved with feet	Punched	Parried	Tipped over	Fumbled	Tipped round	Caught	Blocked	Clean sheets	Goals conceded	Minutes since conceding	Save %	Saved	Resulting in goals	Opposition miss	Yellow cards	Red cards
Shay Given	1430	15	15	15	0	0	0	9	18	1	0	3	49	0	4	18	101	59.56	1	1	0	0	0
Joe Hart	2126	23	23	22	0	1	1	10	11	4	0	4	77	0	6	31	43	78.26	0	2	0	0	0
Kasper Schmeichel	81	1	0	0	1	0	0	1	0	0	0	0	6	0	0	1	-	87.50	0	0	0	0	0

BARCLAYS PREMIER LEAGUE OUTFIELD PLAYER STATS

Player	Minutes on pitch	Appearances	Match starts	Completed matches	Substitute appearances	Subbed off	Goals scored	Minutes since scoring	Assists	Shots on target	Shots off target	Crosses	Defensive clearances	Defensive blocks	Fouls committed	Free-kicks won	Caught offside	Yellow cards	Red cards
Michael Ball	758	8	8	7	0	1	0	-	1	2	0	16	6	4	6	1	0	0	0
Craig Bellamy	674	8	7	6	1	1	3	236	0	7	3	5	0	0	2	5	5	1	0
Tal Ben-Haim	817	9	8	8	1	0	0	-	0	2	4	1	13	3	9	13	0	2	0
Glauber Berti	8	1	0	0	1	0	0	-	0	0	0	0	1	0	0	0	0	0	0
Valeri Bojinov	243	8	2	0	6	2	1	29	1	4	4	0	0	0	4	4	2	1	0
Wayne Bridge	1446	16	16	14	0	2	0	-	0	2	2	11	4	7	11	7	1	0	0
Felipe Caicedo	863	17	10	1	7	9	5	86	0	18	13	1	8	1	12	6	7	2	0
Vedran Corluka	292	3	3	3	0	0	1	3341	0	1	1	6	4	0	4	4	0	0	0
Nigel De Jong	1415	16	16	11	0	5	0	-	1	2	8	1	7	4	20	24	0	3	0
Richard Dunne	2886	31	31	28	0	1	1	2678	0	3	3	0	58	30	40	9	0	4	2
Elano	1961	28	21	9	7	12	6	157	4	24	24	31	5	2	14	36	1	3	0
Kelvin Etuhu	208	4	2	1	2	1	0	-	0	1	2	0	0	0	1	1	0	0	0
Ched Evans	462	16	3	0	13	3	1	350	1	6	6	3	2	1	11	3	5	1	0
Gelson Fernandes	555	17	3	1	14	1	1	423	0	3	1	0	0	0	14	6	0	3	1
Javier Garrido	1059	13	11	9	2	2	1	735	2	2	1	21	6	2	8	5	1	1	0
Dietmar Hamann	507	9	5	2	4	3	0	-	0	1	1	2	4	1	5	13	0	0	0
Stephen Ireland	3219	35	34	31	1	3	9	404	9	30	30	16	13	8	45	34	9	8	0
Jo	617	9	6	3	3	3	1	379	2	5	3	3	0	0	6	10	1	0	0
Michael Johnson	279	3	3	2	0	1	0	-	1	1	0	1	0	0	1	8	0	0	0
Vincent Kompany	3179	34	34	30	0	4	1	2770	1	14	10	2	19	3	60	37	0	8	0
Shaleum Logan	94	1	1	1	0	0	0	-	0	0	0	0	0	0	1	0	1	0	0
Benjani Mwaruwari	576	8	7	2	1	5	1	209	1	2	8	2	0	0	12	4	10	0	0
Nedum Onuoha	1991	23	20	19	3	1	1	556	1	4	1	1	22	10	15	16	0	1	0
Martin Petrov	370	9	4	1	5	3	0	-	0	4	3	20	1	0	3	6	1	0	0
Micah Richards	2851	34	33	25	1	8	1	653	1	7	8	7	24	13	29	24	4	2	0
Robinho	2760	31	30	19	1	11	14	249	5	62	39	15	0	0	41	50	15	3	0
Daniel Sturridge	497	16	3	1	13	2	4	1	2	12	7	4	1	0	5	9	2	0	0
Darius Vassell	474	8	6	3	2	3	0	-	1	4	0	7	0	0	13	8	3	1	0
Vladimir Weiss	22	1	0	0	1	0	0	-	0	0	0	0	0	0	0	1	0	0	0
Shaun Wright-Phillips	2565	27	27	25	0	2	5	384	5	38	28	25	7	2	30	61	6	3	0
Pablo Zabaleta	2507	29	26	22	3	3	1	1195	2	8	10	30	23	6	35	33	1	3	1

actim

SEASON TOTALS

Goals scored	58
Goals conceded	50
Clean sheets	10
Shots on target	269
Shots off target	220
Shots per goal	8.43
Pens awarded	7
Pens scored	6
Pens conceded	4
Offsides	74
Corners	212
Crosses	231
Players used	34
Fouls committed	456
Free-kicks won	449

CARDS RECEIVED

50 4

SEQUENCES

Wins	3
(19/04/09–02/05/09)	
Losses	3
(29/10/08–09/11/08)	
Draws	
(–)	
Undefeated	4
(26/12/08–28/01/09)	
Without win	4
(on two occasions)	
Undefeated home	6
(26/12/08–22/03/09)	
Undefeated away	2
(16/11/08–06/12/08)	
Without scoring	2
(29/10/08–02/11/08)	
Without conceding	2
(24/08/08–31/08/08)	
Scoring	9
(17/08/08–26/10/08)	
Conceding	7
(04/04/09–16/05/09)	

SEASON INFORMATION
Highest Position: 3
Lowest Position: 18
Average goals scored per game: 1.53
Average goals conceded per game: 1.32

League position at the end of each week

League position at the end of: August 3, September 8, October 8, November 14, December 13, January 10, February 10, March 10, April 9, May 10

MATCH RECORDS

Goals scored per match

		W	D	L	Pts
Failed to score	10	0	0	10	0
Scored 1 goal	12	4	2	6	14
Scored 2 goals	8	3	3	2	12
Scored 3 goals	5	5	0	0	15
Scored 4+ goals	3	3	0	0	9

Goals conceded per match

		W	D	L	Pts
Clean sheet	10	10	0	0	30
Conceded 1 goal	11	4	2	5	14
Conceded 2 goals	13	1	3	9	6
Conceded 3 goals	3	0	0	3	0
Conceded 4+ goals	1	0	0	1	0

GOALS SCORED/CONCEDED PER FIVE-MINUTE INTERVALS

Goals For	0	3	5	4	3	4	2	2	5	2	4	5	3	2	1	3	2	8
Goals Against	0	1	1	4	0	3	1	1	5	3	4	2	2	5	4	4	3	7
Mins	5	10	15	20	25	30	35	40	45	50	55	60	65	70	75	80	85	90

QUICK-FIRE GOALS

From the start of a match
Benjani Mwaruwari (v Fulham) 5:42

By a substitute after coming on
Daniel Sturridge (v Arsenal) 3:44

LAST-GASP GOALS

From the start of a match
Robinho (v Blackburn) 93:36

By a substitute after coming on
Daniel Sturridge (v West Brom) 36:09

GOAL DETAILS

How the goals were struck

SCORED		CONCEDED
36	Right foot	30
19	Left foot	11
3	Headers	9
0	Others	0

How the goals were struck

SCORED		CONCEDED
38	Open play	31
8	Cross	5
2	Corner	4
6	Penalties	3
2	Direct from free-kick	3
2	Free-kick	2
0	Own goals	2

Distance from goal

SCORED		CONCEDED
17	6yds	25
36	18yds	19
5	18+yds	6

MANCHESTER UNITED

CLUB SUMMARY

FORMED	1878
MANAGER	Sir Alex Ferguson
GROUND	Old Trafford
CAPACITY	76,212
NICKNAME	The Red Devils
WEBSITE	www.manutd.com

The New **Football Pools** PLAYER OF THE SEASON — Nemanja Vidic

OVERALL
P	W	D	L	F	A	GD
66	44	15	7	119	46	73

BARCLAYS PREMIER LEAGUE
Pos	P	W	D	L	F	A	GD	Pts
1	38	28	6	4	68	24	44	90

HOME
Pos	P	W	D	L	F	A	GD	Pts
1	19	16	2	1	43	13	30	50

AWAY
Pos	P	W	D	L	F	A	GD	Pts
3	19	12	4	3	25	11	14	40

CUP PROGRESS DETAILS
Competition	Round reached	Knocked out by
FA Cup	SF	Everton
Champions League	Final	Barcelona
Carling Cup	Won	–

BIGGEST WIN (ALL COMPS)
15/11/08 5–0 v Stoke **PREM**

BIGGEST DEFEAT (ALL COMPS)
14/03/09 1–4 v Liverpool **PREM**

THE PLAYER WITH THE MOST
Shots on target
Cristiano Ronaldo 115
Shots off target
Cristiano Ronaldo 51
Shots without scoring
Anderson 18
Assists
Dimitar Berbatov 10
Offsides
Wayne Rooney 31
Fouls
Nemanja Vidic 39
Fouls without a card
Anderson 16
Free-kicks won
Cristiano Ronaldo 77
Defensive clearances
Nemanja Vidic 45

actim INDEX for the 2008/09 Barclays Premier League Season

Rank	Player	Pts
4	Dimitar Berbatov	586
10	Nemanja Vidic	540
11	Cristiano Ronaldo	517
15	Edwin van der Sar	481
36	Wayne Rooney	423

ATTENDANCE RECORD
High	Low	Average
75,569	73,917	75,304
v Liverpool (14/03/2009)	v Wigan (14/01/2009)	

CLOCKWISE FROM TOP: Rio Ferdinand lifts the Club World Cup trophy; Edwin van der Sar and Cristiano Ronaldo share the pain of United's defeat in the Champions League final; Nemanja Vidic shows his aerial prowess against Porto; Wayne Rooney slots the ball into the net in the home win against Tottenham

MANCHESTER UNITED continue to set the standards others have to match. Despite losing the UEFA Champions League final at the end of the campaign, another Barclays Premier League title and victory in the Club World Cup means that 2008/09 can only be viewed as yet another success for Sir Alex Ferguson and his men.

Those three seasons in the doldrums earlier in this decade have given way to an unprecedented period of glory for the Old Trafford outfit. Indeed, had referee Mike Riley decided Phil Jagielka's second-half shove of Danny Welbeck in their FA Cup semi-final against Everton was worthy of a penalty, United might well have played in every round of every competition they entered.

Given the way that things turned out, it is hard to believe now that Ferguson's men began the defence of their title with a goalless draw against a Newcastle outfit destined for relegation. In fact, United were still stuttering when they headed to Japan for a date at the Club World Cup, fearing the gap to Liverpool and Chelsea would be too wide by the time they returned.

Not for the first time, the battles the Red Devils had left behind as they were being crowned world champions would have a seismic effect on the league title.

In Yokohama, Ferguson famously declared, 'I wouldn't sell them a virus', when speculation about a deal being done with Real Madrid to sell Cristiano Ronaldo reached fever pitch. Back home, Rafael Benitez and Luiz Felipe Scolari were the ones catching a cold. Neither Chelsea nor Liverpool could take three points from either of their two matches while United were overseas, so when Carlos Tevez converted late on to hand the Red Devils a Boxing Day win at Stoke, the momentum began to swing.

Three points at the Britannia Stadium was the start of an 11-match winning run, the clean sheet number six in a tally that would reach a Barclays Premier League record 14 before Blackburn ended it on 21st February.

A week later, Ben Foster's penalty shoot-out heroics against Tottenham helped to bring more silverware to Old Trafford as the League Cup was won.

That Wembley glory was followed by a victory at Newcastle and an FA Cup win at Fulham. Suddenly, after the doubts, the major topic of conversation was whether United could wrap up the title before April.

One sunny March morning brought not so much a jolt as a beating so soundly handed out, it raised genuine questions about United's ability to stay the full course. All those players who had produced so much for so long, who were getting an air of indestructibility, fell like skittles in a bowling alley. Liverpool's 4–1 win at Old Trafford put the race for the Barclays Premier League back on the boil, with the Merseyside club suddenly looking like possible champions.

After that incredible result, the football world awaited a response. United put in an uncharacteristically poor display at Fulham and were beaten again. The wobble continued through the international break and into a home game against Aston Villa. With 10 minutes remaining, the hosts were behind. But Cristiano Ronaldo, returning to the form that saw him crowned Ballon D'Or winner for 2008, levelled brilliantly before an unknown 17-year-old Federico Macheda curled home an injury-time winner.

It was the pivotal moment, as the next time United dropped points was the day they only needed one to complete a Barclays Premier League hat-trick.

As ever at Old Trafford, talking points abound. Ronaldo is usually the centre of attention. However, Tevez battled for the headlines as talk over his likely exit grew stronger, culminating in an admission he was probably heading elsewhere. But the squad Ferguson has put together is a strong and formidable one, well capable of withstanding significant losses.

How they recover from surrendering their Champions League title to Barcelona, beaten 2–0 in the final, remains to be seen. A night when United's bright stars were outshone has certainly given Ferguson food for thought. But it has never been wise to write off the Scot and his team. Contrary to Ferguson's theory in 2005, no one is expecting to see him in a deckchair on Torquay beach any time soon.

> ❝ **When Carlos Tevez handed the Red Devils a win at Stoke, the momentum began to swing** ❞

MANCHESTER UNITED

RESULTS 2008/09

August

10th ● Portsmouth ....n **D 0–0** **Att:** 84,808. **Ref:** P Walton — Man Utd (5-4-1): Van der Sar, Neville▯ (Brown 66), Ferdinand, Vidic▯, Evra, Fletcher, O'Shea (Carrick 66), Scholes, Giggs, Nani (Campbell 79), Tevez. Subs not used: Kuszczak, Evans, Possebon, Rafael (Won 3–0 on pens)

17th ● Newcastle ....h **D 1–1** **Att:** 75,512. **Ref:** M Riley — Man Utd (4-4-2): Van der Sar, Brown▯, Vidic, Ferdinand, Evra, Fletcher▯, Carrick (O'Shea 25), Scholes, Giggs, Nani, Rooney▯. Subs not used: Kuszczak, Neville, Evans, Gibson.

25th ● Portsmouth ....a **W 0–1** **Att:** 20,540. **Ref:** C Foy — Man Utd (4-4-2): Van der Sar, Brown▯, Ferdinand, Vidic, O'Shea, Fletcher▯¹, Anderson (Possebon 76), Scholes, Evra, Rooney, Tevez. Subs not used: Kuszczak, Neville, Fabio, Rafael, Gibson, Campbell.

29th ● Zenit St Petersburg ....h **L 1–2** **Att:** 18,500. **Ref:** C Bo Larsen —Man Utd (4-4-2): Van der Sar, Neville (Brown 76), Ferdinand, Vidic▯, Evra, Fletcher (O'Shea 60), Anderson▯ (Park 60), Scholes▯, Nani, Rooney, Tevez▯. Subs not used: Kuszczak, Gibson, Campbell, Possebon.

September

13th ● Liverpool ....a **L 2–1** **Att:** 44,192. **Ref:** H Webb — Man Utd (4-4-1-1): Van der Sar, Brown, Ferdinand, Vidic▯, Evra, Rooney, Scholes (Hargreaves 66), Carrick (Giggs 46), Anderson (Nani▯ 78), Tevez▯, Berbatov. Subs not used: Kuszczak, Evans, O'Shea, Fletcher.

17th ● Villarreal ....h **D 0–0** **Att:** 74,944. **Ref:** W Stark — Man Utd (4-4-2): Van der Sar, Neville, Ferdinand, Evans, Evra, Nani, Hargreaves (Anderson 62), Fletcher, Park (Ronaldo 62), Rooney, Tevez▯ (Giggs 81). Subs not used: Foster, Brown, Vidic, O'Shea.

21st ● Chelsea ....a **D 1–1** **Att:** 41,760. **Ref:** M Riley — Man Utd (4-4-2): Van der Sar (Kuszczak 32), Neville▯, Ferdinand▯, Evans, Evra▯, Fletcher, Hargreaves, Scholes▯ (Ronaldo▯ 55), Park¹ (O'Shea 75), Berbatov▯, Rooney▯. Subs not used: Brown, Giggs, Nani, Tevez.

23rd ● Middlesbrough ....h **W 3–1** **Att:** 53,729. **Ref:** A Marriner — Man Utd (4-4-2): Amos, Rafael, Vidic, Brown, O'Shea, Nani¹, Possebon (Gibson 72), Anderson, Giggs¹ (Manucho 84), Welbeck, Ronaldo¹ (Tevez 61). Subs not used: Zieler, Cleverley, Gray, Eckersley.

27th ● Bolton ....h **W 2–0** **Att:** 75,484. **Ref:** R Styles — Man Utd (4-4-2): Van der Sar, Neville, Ferdinand, Vidic, Evra, Ronaldo¹ (Nani 80), Fletcher, Anderson (Scholes 71), Park, Tevez (Rooney▯ 71), Berbatov. Subs not used: Amos, Giggs, O'Shea, Evans.

30th ● AaB ....a **W 0–3** **Att:** 10,346. **Ref:** O Benquerenca — Man Utd (4-4-2): Van der Sar, Rafael (Brown 66), Ferdinand, Vidic, Evra, Ronaldo, Scholes (Giggs 16), O'Shea, Nani, Berbatov² (Rooney▯ 59). Subs not used: Amos, Anderson, Park, Evans.

October

4th ● Blackburn ....a **W 0–2** **Att:** 27,321. **Ref:** S Bennett — Man Utd (4-4-2): Van der Sar, Brown¹, Ferdinand, Vidic, Evra (O'Shea 71), Ronaldo, Fletcher▯, Anderson, Giggs (Tevez 66), Berbatov, Rooney¹ (Park 77). Subs not used: Amos, Nani, Rafael, Evans.

18th ● West Brom ....h **W 4–0** **Att:** 75,451. **Ref:** M Halsey — Man Utd (4-4-2): Van der Sar, Rafael (Neville 65), Ferdinand, Vidic, Evra (O'Shea 36), Ronaldo¹, Fletcher, Giggs, Park (Nani¹ 70), Berbatov¹, Rooney¹. Subs not used: Kuszczak, Brown, Evans, Gibson.

21st ● Celtic..................................h **W 3–0** **Att:** 74,655. **Ref:** F De Bleeckere — Man Utd (4-4-2): Van der Sar, Neville (Brown 59), Evans, Vidic, O'Shea, Ronaldo (Park 82), Fletcher, Anderson, Nani, Berbatov² (Tevez 60), Rooney¹. Subs not used: Kuszczak, Giggs, Rafael, Gibson.

25th ● Everton ....a **D 1–1** **Att:** 36,069. **Ref:** A Wiley — Man Utd (4-4-2): Van der Sar, Brown¹, Ferdinand, Vidic▯, Evra, Ronaldo, Fletcher¹ (Tevez 78), Giggs, Park (Anderson 67), Berbatov, Rooney▯ (Nani 71). Subs not used: Kuszczak, Neville, O'Shea, Evans.

29th ● West Ham...........................h **W 2–0** **Att:** 75,397. **Ref:** P Walton — Man Utd (4-4-2): Kuszczak, Rafael (Neville 81), Ferdinand, Vidic, Evra▯, Ronaldo², Fletcher (Carrick 69), Anderson, Nani (Rooney 70), Tevez, Berbatov. Subs not used: Foster, Giggs, Park, O'Shea.

November

1st ● Hull ....h **W 4–3** **Att:** 75,398. **Ref:** M Dean — Man Utd (4-4-2): Van der Sar, Neville, Ferdinand, Vidic¹, Evra, Ronaldo², Carrick¹ (Giggs 72), Anderson (O'Shea 88), Nani (Tevez¹ 64), Berbatov, Rooney▯. Subs not used: Foster, Park, Rafael, Fletcher.

5th ● Celtic..................................a **D 1–1** **Att:** 58,903. **Ref:** T Ovrebo — Man Utd (4-4-2): Foster, Rafael (Evra 66), Ferdinand, Vidic, O'Shea, Ronaldo, Fletcher, Carrick, Nani¹ (Berbatov 46), Tevez (Rooney 71), Giggs¹. Subs not used: Kuszczak, Anderson, Park, Evans.

8th ● Arsenal ....a **L 2–1** **Att:** 60,106. **Ref:** H Webb — Man Utd (4-4-2): Van der Sar, Neville (Rafael¹ 63), Ferdinand, Vidic, Evra▯, Ronaldo, Anderson (Giggs 72), Carrick▯, Park, Rooney (Tevez 77), Berbatov. Subs not used: Kuszczak, Nani, O'Shea, Evans.

11th ● QPR ....h **W 1–0** **Att:** 62,539. **Ref:** P Dowd — Man Utd (4-3-3): Kuszczak, Rafael, Neville, Vidic (Welbeck 89), Evans, O'Shea, Gibson, Possebon (Welbeck 72), Anderson, Nani, Tevez¹, Park. Subs not used: Foster, Carrick, Manucho, Cleverley, Gray.

15th ● Stoke ....h **W 5–0** **Att:** 75,369. **Ref:** P Walton — Man Utd (4-4-2): Van der Sar, O'Shea, Vidic, Evans, Evra▯, Ronaldo², Carrick¹, Fletcher (Gibson 63), Park (Welbeck¹ 63), Tevez (Manucho 74), Berbatov¹. Subs not used: Foster, Anderson, Nani, Rafael.

22nd ● Aston Villa...........................a **D 0–0** **Att:** 42,585. **Ref:** C Foy — Man Utd (4-4-2): Van der Sar, O'Shea, Ferdinand, Vidic, Evra, Ronaldo (Anderson 82), Park, Carrick, Giggs, Rooney, Tevez (Nani 71). Subs not used: Kuszczak, Welbeck, Evans, Gibson, Rafael.

25th ● Villarreal ....a **D 0–0** **Att:** 26,000. **Ref:** R Rosetti — Man Utd (4-4-1-1): Kuszczak, O'Shea, Ferdinand, Evans, Evra▯, Ronaldo▯, Fletcher (Gibson 80), Carrick (Tevez 86), Nani (Park 85), Anderson, Rooney. Subs not used: Foster, Giggs, Vidic, Rafael.

30th ● Man City ....a **W 0–1** **Att:** 47,320. **Ref:** H Webb — Man Utd (4-4-2): Van der Sar, Rafael▯, Ferdinand, Vidic, Evra▯, Ronaldo▯▯, Carrick▯, Fletcher▯, Park (O'Shea 90), Rooney¹, Berbatov (Giggs 83). Subs not used: Foster, Anderson, Nani, Evans, Tevez.

December

3rd ● Blackburn ....h **W 5–3** **Att:** 53,997. **Ref:** A Wiley — Man Utd (4-4-2): Foster, Rafael, Neville, Evans, O'Shea (Evra 66), Nani¹, Gibson, Possebon (Scholes 66), Anderson, Giggs (Manucho 71), Tevez⁴. Subs not used: Kuszczak, Park, Vidic, Welbeck.

6th ● Sunderland ....h **W 1–0** **Att:** 75,400. **Ref:** M Halsey — Man Utd (4-4-2): Van der Sar, Rafael, Ferdinand, Vidic¹, Evra, Park (Tevez 57), Fletcher (Anderson 68), Carrick, Ronaldo (Giggs 68), Berbatov, Rooney▯. Subs not used: Kuszczak, Neville, Nani, Evans.

10th ● AaB ....h **D 2–2** **Att:** 74,382. **Ref:** L Duhamel — Man Utd (4-4-2): Van der Sar, Rafael, Neville (Rafael 76), O'Shea, Evans, Nani, Gibson, Anderson, Giggs (Scholes 46), Rooney¹, Tevez¹. Subs not used: Foster, Vidic, Fletcher, Possebon.

13th ● Tottenham ....a **D 0–0** **Att:** 35,882. **Ref:** M Dean — Man Utd (4-4-2): Van der Sar, Rafael▯, Ferdinand, Vidic, O'Shea, Park, Fletcher (Scholes 69), Carrick, Ronaldo, Berbatov, Tevez (Giggs 69). Subs not used: Kuszczak, Neville, Anderson, Evans.

18th ● Gamba Osaka ....n **W 3–5** **Att:** 67,618. **Ref:** B Archundia Tellez — Man Utd (4-4-1-1): Van der Sar, Neville, Ferdinand, Vidic¹ (Evans 69), Evra, Nani, Anderson, Scholes (Fletcher¹ 67), Ronaldo¹, Giggs, Tevez (Rooney▯ 73). Subs not used: Kuszczak, Rafael, O'Shea, Carrick, Gibson, Park, Welbeck, Amos.

21st ● Liga Deportiva ....n **W 0–1** **Att:** 62,619. **Ref:** R Irmatov — Man Utd (4-4-2): Van der Sar, Rafael (Neville 85), Ferdinand, Vidic▯, Evra, Ronaldo, Carrick, Anderson¹ (Fletcher 87), Park, Tevez (Evans 51), Rooney¹. Subs not used: Kuszczak, Berbatov, Giggs, Nani, Scholes, Welbeck, O'Shea, Gibson, Amos.

26th ● Stoke ....a **W 0–1** **Att:** 27,500. **Ref:** C Foy — Man Utd (4-4-2): Van der Sar, Neville▯, Evans▯, Vidic, O'Shea (Berbatov 64), Ronaldo, Scholes (Carrick 90), Fletcher, Giggs, Rooney, Tevez¹. Subs not used: Kuszczak, Park, Welbeck, Rafael, Gibson.

29th ● Middlesbrough ....h **W 1–0** **Att:** 75,294. **Ref:** M Atkinson — Man Utd (4-4-2): Van der Sar, Rafael (Neville 62), Vidic, Evans, O'Shea, Park▯, Fletcher (Scholes▯ 62), Carrick, Ronaldo (Giggs 84), Rooney, Berbatov¹. Subs not used: Kuszczak, Welbeck, Gibson, Possebon.

● Barclays Premier League ● FA Cup ● Carling Cup ● UEFA Champions League ● World Club Challenge ○ FA Community Shield ○ European Super Cup

▯ Yellow Card ▮ Red Card

RESULTS 2008/09

January

4th ● Southampton ....a **W 0–3** **Att:** 31,901. **Ref:** M Riley — **Man Utd** (4-4-2): Van der Sar, Neville, Evans▪, Vidic, O'Shea▪, Nani¹, Anderson, Carrick (Gibson¹ 56), Giggs (Possebon 56), Welbeck¹ (Rooney 63), Berbatov. Subs not used: Kuszczak, Park, Rafael, Fletcher.

7th ● Derby ....a **L 1–0** **Att:** 30,194. **Ref:** P Dowd — **Man Utd** (4-4-2): Kuszczak, Rafael, Vidic, Evans, O'Shea, Anderson (Carrick 74), Scholes (Ronaldo 63), Gibson, Nani, Tevez, Welbeck (Rooney 63). Subs not used: Amos, Giggs, Fletcher, Possebon.

11th ● Chelsea ....h **W 3–0** **Att:** 75,455. **Ref:** H Webb — **Man Utd** (4-4-2): Van der Sar, Neville, Vidic¹, Evans, Evra (O'Shea 66), Ronaldo▪, Fletcher, Giggs (Carrick 79), Park▪, Berbatov¹, Rooney▪¹. Subs not used: Kuszczak, Anderson, Scholes, Welbeck, Tevez.

14th ● Wigan ....h **W 1–0** **Att:** 73,917. **Ref:** S Bennett — **Man Utd** (4-4-2): Van der Sar, Rafael, Vidic, Evans, O'Shea, Ronaldo, Scholes (Fletcher 85), Carrick, Nani (Anderson 59), Berbatov, Rooney¹ (Tevez 8). Subs not used: Kuszczak, Neville, Park, Welbeck.

17th ● Bolton ....a **W 0–1** **Att:** 26,021. **Ref:** A Marriner — **Man Utd** (4-4-2): Van der Sar, Neville, Vidic, Evans, O'Shea▪, Fletcher (Giggs 69), Carrick, Anderson (Scholes 69), Ronaldo, Tevez, Berbatov¹. Subs not used: Kuszczak, Park, Nani, Welbeck, Chester.

20th ● Derby ....h **W 4–2** **Att:** 73,374. **Ref:** M Dean — **Man Utd** (4-4-2): Foster, Rafael (Fletcher¹ 42), Neville (Chester 67), Evans, O'Shea¹, Nani¹, Gibson, Anderson, Giggs (Ronaldo¹ 58), Welbeck, Tevez¹. Subs not used: Kuszczak, Tosic, Scholes, Possebon.

24th ● Tottenham ....h **W 2–1** **Att:** 75,014. **Ref:** P Walton — **Man Utd** (4-4-2): Foster, O'Shea, Neville, Vidic▪, Rafael (Eckersley 53), Welbeck (Fletcher 86), Carrick, Scholes¹, Ronaldo (Tosic 72), Berbatov¹, Tevez▪. Subs not used: Kuszczak, Giggs, Possebon, Chester.

27th ● West Brom ....a **W 0–5** **Att:** 26,105. **Ref:** R Styles — **Man Utd** (4-4-2): Van der Sar, Neville (Eckersley 71), Ferdinand (Brown 70), Vidic▪, O'Shea, Park▪, Carrick▪, Giggs, Ronaldo², Berbatov¹ (Tosic 77), Tevez¹. Subs not used: Kuszczak, Scholes, Fletcher, Gibson.

31st ● Everton ....h **W 1–0** **Att:** 75,399. **Ref:** M Halsey — **Man Utd** (4-4-2): Van der Sar, Neville (Brown 56), Ferdinand, Vidic, O'Shea, Ronaldo¹, Carrick, Fletcher (Giggs 75), Park, Berbatov, Tevez. Subs not used: Kuszczak, Welbeck, Rafael, Gibson, Eckersley.

February

8th ● West Ham ....a **W 0–1** **Att:** 34,958. **Ref:** P Dowd — **Man Utd** (4-4-2): Van der Sar, R Rafael, Ferdinand, Vidic▪, O'Shea, Ronaldo, Scholes, Carrick, Giggs¹, Tevez (Park 87), Berbatov. Subs not used: Foster, Nani, Welbeck, Fabio, Fletcher, Eckersley.

15th ● Derby ....a **W 1–4** **Att:** 32,103. **Ref:** A Wiley — **Man Utd** (4-4-2): Foster, Rafael, Ferdinand, Evans, O'Shea (Evans 55), Park (Welbeck¹ 55), Fletcher, Gibson¹, Nani¹, Giggs, Ronaldo¹ (Possebon 72). Subs not used: Kuszczak, Vidic, Scholes, Tevez.

18th ● Fulham ....h **W 3–0** **Att:** 75,437. **Ref:** A Marriner — **Man Utd** (4-4-2): Van der Sar, O'Shea (Evans 62), Ferdinand, Vidic, Evra, Ronaldo, Carrick (Gibson 69), Scholes¹, Park▪, Berbatov¹ (Rooney¹ 61), Tevez. Subs not used: Kuszczak, Nani, Rafael, Fletcher.

21st ● Blackburn ....h **W 2–1** **Att:** 75,000. **Ref:** H Webb — **Man Utd** (4-4-2): Kuszczak, Rafael, Ferdinand, Evans (Vidic 64), Evra, Ronaldo▪¹, Carrick, Scholes (Giggs 82), Nani (Tevez 64), Rooney¹, Berbatov▪. Subs not used: Foster, Welbeck, Fabio, Fletcher.

24th ● Inter Milan.....................a **D 0–0** **Att:** 84,000. **Ref:** L Medina Cantalejo — **Man Utd** (4-3-3): Van der Sar, O'Shea, Ferdinand, Evans, Fletcher▪, Carrick, Giggs, Park (Rooney¹ 83), Berbatov, Ronaldo. Subs not used: Foster, Nani, Scholes, Rafael, Gibson, Tevez.

March

1st ● Tottenham ....n **D 0–0** **Att:** 88,217. **Ref:** C Foy — **Man Utd** (4-4-2): Foster, O'Shea▪ (Vidic 76), Evans, Ferdinand, Evra, Ronaldo▪, Scholes▪, Gibson (Giggs 91), Nani, Tevez, Welbeck (Anderson 56). Subs not used: Kuszczak, Park, Possebon, Eckersley. AET; Man Utd win 4-2 on penalties

4th ● Newcastle ....a **W 1–2** **Att:** 51,636. **Ref:** S Bennett — **Man Utd** (4-4-2): Van der Sar, O'Shea, Ferdinand▪, Vidic▪, Evra, Ronaldo, Fletcher, Carrick, Park, Berbatov¹ (Giggs 90), Rooney¹. Subs not used: Foster, Anderson, Scholes, Evans, Tevez, Eckersley.

7th ● Fulham ....a **W 0–4** **Att:** 24,662. **Ref:** S Bennett — **Man Utd** (4-4-2): Van der Sar, O'Shea (Eckersley 52), Ferdinand (Evans 46), Vidic, Evra, Fletcher, Carrick, Anderson, Park¹, Rooney¹ (Welbeck 64), Tevez². Subs not used: Foster, Berbatov, Giggs, Scholes.

11th ● Inter Milan.....................h **W 2–0** **Att:** 74,769. **Ref:** W Stark — **Man Utd** (4-4-2): Van der Sar, O'Shea, Ferdinand, Vidic¹, Evra, Ronaldo¹, Carrick, Scholes (Anderson 70), Giggs, Rooney▪ (Park 84), Berbatov. Subs not used: Foster, Evans, Fletcher, Gibson, Tevez.

14th ● Liverpool ....h **L 1–4** **Att:** 75,569. **Ref:** A Wiley — **Man Utd** (4-4-2): Van der Sar▪, O'Shea, Ferdinand▪, Vidic▪, Evra, Ronaldo¹, Carrick (Giggs 74), Anderson (Scholes 73), Park (Berbatov 74), Rooney, Tevez. Subs not used: Foster, Nani, Evans, Fletcher.

21st ● Fulham ....a **L 2–0** **Att:** 25,652. **Ref:** P Dowd — **Man Utd** (4-4-2): Van der Sar, O'Shea (Tevez 70), Evans▪, Ferdinand, Evra▪, Ronaldo▪, Fletcher, Scholes▪▪, Park, Giggs, Berbatov (Rooney▪▪ 46). Subs not used: Foster, Neville, Anderson, Carrick, Rafael.

April

5th ● Aston Villa.....................h **W 3–2** **Att:** 75,409. **Ref:** M Riley — **Man Utd** (4-4-2): Van der Sar, Neville, O'Shea, Evans, Evra, Nani (Macheda¹ 61), Carrick, Fletcher, Ronaldo², Giggs, Tevez (Welbeck 87). Subs not used: Foster, Park, Gibson, Martin, Eckersley.

7th ● FC Porto ....h **D 2–2** **Att:** 74,517. **Ref:** K Plautz — **Man Utd** (4-3-3): Van der Sar, O'Shea, Vidic, Evans (Neville 72), Evra, Fletcher, Carrick, Scholes (Tevez¹ 72), Ronaldo, Rooney¹, Park (Giggs 58). Subs not used: Foster, Eckersley, Nani, Macheda.

11th ● Sunderland ....a **W 1–2** **Att:** 45,408. **Ref:** R Styles — **Man Utd** (4-4-2): Foster, Neville¹, Evans, Vidic, O'Shea, Park (Welbeck 69), Carrick, Scholes¹, Rooney▪, Berbatov (Macheda¹ 75), Tevez (Anderson 82). Subs not used: Kuszczak, Evra, Giggs, Nani.

15th ● FC Porto ....a **W 0–1** **Att:** 50,000. **Ref:** M Busacca — **Man Utd** (4-3-3): Van der Sar, O'Shea, Ferdinand, Vidic▪, Evra▪, Giggs, Carrick, Anderson (Scholes 78), Rooney, Berbatov (Nani 68), Ronaldo¹. Subs not used: Foster, Neville, Evans, Tevez, Macheda.

19th ● Everton ....n **D 0–0** **Att:** 88,141. **Ref:** M Riley — **Man Utd** (4-4-2): Foster, Rafael, Ferdinand, Vidic, Fabio (Evra 63), Welbeck, Gibson, Anderson, Park (Scholes¹ 67), Tevez▪, Macheda (Berbatov 91). Subs not used: Kuszczak, Neville, Nani, Evans. AET; Everton win 4-2 on penalties

22nd ● Portsmouth ....h **W 2–0** **Att:** 74,895. **Ref:** P Walton — **Man Utd** (4-4-2): Van der Sar, Neville (J O'Shea 43 (Rafael 52)), Vidic¹, Evans, Evra, Fletcher, Scholes, Anderson (Carrick¹ 76), Giggs, Ronaldo, Rooney¹. Subs not used: Kuszczak, Berbatov, Nani, Tevez.

25th ● Tottenham ....h **W 5–2** **Att:** 75,458. **Ref:** H Webb — **Man Utd** (4-4-2): Van der Sar, Rafael (O'Shea 70), Ferdinand, Vidic, Evra, Ronaldo¹², Carrick, Fletcher (Welbeck▪ 61), Nani (Tevez¹ 46), Berbatov¹, Rooney². Subs not used: Foster, Anderson, Evans, Macheda.

29th ● Arsenal ....h **W 1–0** **Att:** 74,733. **Ref:** C Bo Larsen — **Man Utd** (4-3-2-1): Van der Sar, O'Shea¹, Ferdinand (Evans 87), Vidic, Evra, Fletcher, Carrick, Anderson (Giggs 66), Ronaldo, Tevez▪ (Berbatov 66), Rooney. Subs not used: Foster, Park, Scholes, Rafael.

May

2nd ● Middlesbrough ....a **W 0–2** **Att:** 33,767. **Ref:** M Halsey — **Man Utd** (4-4-2): Foster, O'Shea, Vidic, Evans, Evra (Rafael 78), Park¹ (Nani 74), Scholes, Giggs¹, Rooney, Berbatov, Macheda▪ (Tevez 55). Subs not used: Kuszczak, Ronaldo, Anderson, Gibson.

5th ● Arsenal ....a **W 1–3** **Att:** 59,867. **Ref:** R Rosetti — **Man Utd** (4-4-1-1): Van der Sar, O'Shea, Ferdinand, Vidic, Evra (Rafael 65), Fletcher▪, Carrick, Anderson (Giggs 63), Park¹, Ronaldo², Rooney (Berbatov 66). Subs not used: Kuszczak, Evans, Scholes, Tevez.

10th ● Man City ....h **W 2–0** **Att:** 75,464. **Ref:** C Foy — **Man Utd** (4-4-2): Van der Sar, Neville, Vidic, Evans (O'Shea 71), Evra, Ronaldo▪ (Scholes 58), Fletcher▪, Giggs, Park (Rooney 58), Berbatov, Tevez¹. Subs not used: Kuszczak, Neville, Carrick, Nani.

13th ● Wigan ....a **W 1–2** **Att:** 21,286. **Ref:** R Styles — **Man Utd** (4-3-3): Van der Sar, O'Shea, Vidic, Evans, Evra, Carrick¹, Scholes (Giggs 75), Anderson (Tevez¹ 58), Ronaldo, Berbatov (Park 89), Rooney. Subs not used: Kuszczak, Neville, Nani, Rafael.

16th ● Arsenal ....h **D 0–0** **Att:** 75,468. **Ref:** M Dean — **Man Utd** (4-5-1): Van der Sar, O'Shea, Vidic, Evans, Evra, Ronaldo, Fletcher, Carrick, Giggs, Rooney (Anderson 90), Tevez (Park 67). Subs not used: Kuszczak, Neville, Berbatov, Scholes, Rafael.

24th ● Hull ....a **W 0–1** **Att:** 24,945. **Ref:** A Wiley — **Man Utd** (4-4-2): Kuszczak, Rafael (Eckersley 60), Neville, Brown, De Laet (Possebon 79), Nani, Fletcher, Gibson▪¹ (Welbeck (Tosic 87), Martin, Macheda. Subs not used: Amos, Evans, Drinkwater, James.

27th ● Barcelona ....n **L 2–0** **Att:** 72,700. **Ref:** M Busacca — **Man Utd** (4-3-3): Van der Sar, O'Shea, Ferdinand, Vidic▪, Evra, Anderson (Tevez 46), Carrick, Giggs (Scholes▪ 75), Park (Berbatov 66), Ronaldo▪, Rooney. Subs not used: Kuszczak, Rafael, Evans, Nani.

● Barclays Premier League ● FA Cup ● Carling Cup ● UEFA Champions League ● World Club Challenge ● FA Community Shield ● European Super Cup

MANCHESTER UNITED

BARCLAYS PREMIER LEAGUE GOALKEEPER STATS

Player	Minutes on pitch	Appearances	Match starts	Completed matches	Sub appearances	Subbed off	Saves: Saved with feet	Punched	Parried	Tipped over	Fumbled	Tipped round	Caught	Blocked	Clean sheets	Goals conceded	Minutes since conceding	Save %	Penalties: Saved	Resulting in goals	Opposition miss	Yellow cards	Red cards
Ben Foster	190	2	2	0	0	0	1	1	1	0	0	0	4	0	1	1	134	88.89	0	0	0	0	0
Tomasz Kuszczak	352	4	3	3	1	0	3	1	1	0	0	0	16	0	2	2	161	91.30	0	0	0	0	0
Edwin van der Sar	3070	33	33	32	0	1	1	15	10	3	0	6	90	1	22	21	165	85.81	0	3	0	1	0

BARCLAYS PREMIER LEAGUE OUTFIELD PLAYER STATS

Player	Minutes on pitch	Appearances	Match starts	Completed matches	Substitute appearances	Subbed off	Goals scored	Minutes since scoring	Assists	Shots on target	Shots off target	Crosses	Defensive clearances	Defensive blocks	Fouls committed	Free-kicks won	Caught offside	Yellow cards	Red cards
Anderson	978	17	11	2	6	9	0	-	0	12	6	6	1	1	16	12	1	0	0
Dimitar Berbatov	2664	32	30	23	2	7	9	296	10	29	14	11	7	1	32	48	19	2	0
Wes Brown	632	8	6	6	2	0	1	316	0	1	1	11	4	1	11	12	0	3	0
Fraizer Campbell	80	1	1	0	0	1	0	161	0	3	0	0	0	0	4	2	1	0	0
Michael Carrick	2152	28	24	19	4	5	4	104	7	21	15	12	12	6	13	23	0	3	0
Rafael Da Silva	1113	16	12	7	4	5	1	924	0	4	2	26	1	4	25	16	0	2	0
Ritchie De Laet	80	1	1	0	0	1	0	-	0	0	1	1	3	0	0	1	0	0	0
Richard Eckersley	56	2	0	0	0	0	0	-	0	0	1	0	0	0	0	0	0	0	0
Jonathan Evans	1499	17	16	14	1	2	0	-	0	2	0	2	11	7	9	17	0	2	0
Patrice Evra	2540	28	28	24	0	4	0	-	2	1	5	40	15	6	24	47	5	6	0
Rio Ferdinand	2258	24	24	23	0	1	0	-	0	5	2	4	21	18	12	16	0	3	0
Darren Fletcher	2155	26	25	16	1	9	3	1567	0	12	11	24	12	3	28	17	0	4	0
Darron Gibson	150	3	1	1	2	0	1	72	0	1	3	1	1	0	3	0	0	1	0
Ryan Giggs	1613	28	15	12	13	3	2	282	8	12	8	52	6	1	14	19	0	0	0
Owen Hargreaves	124	2	1	1	1	0	0	-	0	0	3	0	0	0	2	1	0	0	0
Federico Macheda	206	4	2	0	2	1	2	170	1	3	3	0	0	0	3	4	1	2	0
Manucho	18	1	0	0	1	0	0	347	0	2	0	0	0	0	0	0	0	0	0
Lee Martin	96	1	1	1	0	0	0	-	0	0	0	1	0	0	1	4	0	0	0
Nani	579	13	7	1	6	6	1	531	4	5	11	17	0	1	11	13	2	1	0
Gary Neville	1132	16	13	9	3	4	0	-	0	1	2	6	6	2	13	8	1	3	0
John O'Shea	2105	30	20	16	10	4	0	-	3	4	1	12	14	8	22	8	1	1	0
Ji-Sung Park	1804	25	21	11	4	10	2	114	3	22	10	23	0	1	18	37	3	4	0
Rodrigo Possebon	64	3	0	0	3	0	0	-	0	0	0	0	0	0	0	0	0	0	0
Cristiano Ronaldo	2886	33	31	25	2	5	18	234	6	115	51	69	3	1	15	77	21	6	1
Wayne Rooney	2388	30	25	19	5	5	12	344	7	65	43	53	8	1	28	19	31	3	0
Paul Scholes	1331	21	14	7	7	6	2	411	2	15	14	1	1	1	17	6	0	3	0
Carlos Tevez	1960	29	18	10	11	8	5	102	4	29	25	10	0	1	24	20	13	3	0
Zoran Tosic	23	2	0	0	2	0	0	-	0	0	0	1	0	0	1	0	0	0	0
Nemanja Vidic	3142	34	33	31	1	0	4	1186	1	13	12	0	45	22	39	30	0	5	2
Danny Welbeck	127	3	1	0	2	1	1	105	0	3	1	1	2	0	0	1	0	0	0

actim

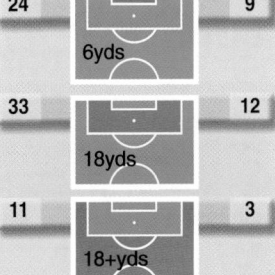

BARCLAYS PREMIER LEAGUE

SEASON TOTALS

Goals scored	68
Goals conceded	24
Clean sheets	24
Shots on target	376
Shots off target	246
Shots per goal	9.15
Pens awarded	4
Pens scored	4
Pens conceded	3
Offsides	98
Corners	260
Crosses	384
Players used	33
Fouls committed	384
Free-kicks won	472

CARDS RECEIVED

64 **5**

SEQUENCES

Wins	11
(26/12/08–04/03/09)	
Losses	2
(14/03/09–21/03/09)	
Draws	
(–)	
Undefeated	16
(15/11/08–04/03/09)	
Without win	2
(on two occasions)	
Undefeated home	13
(17/08/08–21/02/09)	
Undefeated away	8
(22/11/08–04/03/09)	
Without scoring	
(–)	
Without conceding	14
(15/11/08–18/02/09)	
Scoring	12
(on two occasions)	
Conceding	6
(21/02/09–11/04/09)	

League position at the end of each week

League position at the end of

August 9, September 11, October 6, November 3, December 3, January 1, February 1, March 1, April 1, May 1

SEASON INFORMATION
Highest Position: 1
Lowest Position: 15
Average goals scored per game: 1.79
Average goals conceded per game: 0.63

MATCH RECORDS

Goals scored per match

	W	D	L	Pts
Failed to score	4	0	3	1	3
Scored 1 goal	16	10	3	3	33
Scored 2 goals	10	10	0	0	30
Scored 3 goals	3	3	0	0	9
Scored 4+ goals	5	5	0	0	15

Goals conceded per match

	W	D	L	Pts
Clean sheet	24	21	3	0	66
Conceded 1 goal	7	4	3	0	15
Conceded 2 goals	5	2	0	3	6
Conceded 3 goals	1	1	0	0	3
Conceded 4+ goals	1	0	0	1	0

GOALS SCORED/CONCEDED PER FIVE-MINUTE INTERVALS

Goals For	4	1	3	4	7	3	2	0	7	1	1	7	6	4	3	4	3	8
Goals Against	0	1	0	1	3	5	2	0	1	1	1	1	1	1	0	3	1	2
Mins	5	10	15	20	25	30	35	40	45	50	55	60	65	70	75	80	85	90

QUICK-FIRE GOALS

From the start of a match
Wayne Rooney (v Wigan) 0:54

By a substitute after coming on
Federico Macheda (v Sunderland) 1:01

LAST-GASP GOALS

From the start of a match
Federico Macheda (v Aston Villa) 92:04

By a substitute after coming on
Federico Macheda (v Aston Villa) 31:19

GOAL DETAILS

How the goals were struck

SCORED		CONCEDED
46	Right foot	11
15	Left foot	6
7	Headers	6
0	Others	1

How the goals were struck

SCORED		CONCEDED
47	Open play	13
8	Cross	2
4	Corner	1
4	Penalties	3
3	Direct from free-kick	1
2	Free-kick	3
0	Own goals	1

Distance from goal

SCORED		CONCEDED
24	6yds	9
33	18yds	12
11	18+yds	3

MIDDLESBROUGH

CLUB SUMMARY

FORMED	1876
MANAGER	Gareth Southgate
GROUND	Riverside Stadium
CAPACITY	35,049
NICKNAME	Boro
WEBSITE	www.mfc.co.uk

The New Football Pools PLAYER OF THE SEASON — **Stewart Downing**

OVERALL

P	W	D	L	F	A	GD
45	11	12	22	42	66	-24

BARCLAYS PREMIER LEAGUE

Pos	P	W	D	L	F	A	GD	Pts
19	38	7	11	20	28	57	-29	32

HOME

Pos	P	W	D	L	F	A	GD	Pts
16	19	5	9	5	17	20	-3	24

AWAY

Pos	P	W	D	L	F	A	GD	Pts
20	19	2	2	15	11	37	-26	8

CUP PROGRESS DETAILS

Competition	Round reached	Knocked out by
FA Cup	QF	Everton
Carling Cup	R3	Man Utd

BIGGEST WIN (ALL COMPS)
26/08/08 5–1 v Yeovil **LC2**

BIGGEST DEFEAT (ALL COMPS)
18/10/08 0–5 v Chelsea **PREM**

THE PLAYER WITH THE MOST

Shots on target
Afonso Alves 54

Shots off target
Stewart Downing 37

Shots without scoring
Stewart Downing 70

Assists
Stewart Downing 4

Offsides
Marlon King 66

Fouls
Tuncay Sanli 38

Fouls without a card
Stewart Downing 17

Free-kicks won
Tuncay Sanli 59

Defensive clearances
Robert Huth 39

actim INDEX — for the 2008/09 Barclays Premier League Season

Rank	Player	Pts
110	Marlon King	313
134	Gary O'Neil	284
164	David Wheater	242
166	Tuncay Sanli	241
175	Stewart Downing	235

ATTENDANCE RECORD

High	Low	Average
33,767	24,020	28,429
v Man Utd (02/05/2009)	v Wigan (21/02/2009)	

MIDDLESBROUGH'S 11-year stay in the Barclays Premier League eventually came to an end at Upton Park on the final day of the season.

However, a 2–1 defeat by West Ham simply confirmed what had looked inevitable for several months.

Having finished 13th at the end of the previous campaign – Gareth Southgate's second in charge – Boro felt they were ready to take the next step in their mission to establish themselves as top-10 regulars. But anticipating the financial difficulties which would affect many of their counterparts, they adopted a frugal transfer policy and decided instead to rely on the products of their renowned Academy.

Ultimately, it was a gamble which did not pay off. Boro played an expansive brand of football, but were made to pay for fraility at one end of the pitch and their profligacy at the other, where record signing Afonso Alves never lived up to his £12.7million price tag and the much-travelled Mido packed his bags once again and headed for Wigan on loan.

In addition, they found themselves engaged in a tug of war over star winger Stewart Downing as Tottenham attempted to prise the talented England international away from his home-town club. Chairman Steve Gibson dug his heels in and refused to let the 24-year-old leave, and was equally uncompromising over Portsmouth's prolonged interest in Gary O'Neil. To their credit, both men knuckled down and produced some of their best form for the club, but in the final analysis it was all in vain.

Boro started encouragingly with a 2–1 home win over Tottenham and were unfortunate to lose by the same score at Liverpool when a late Steven Gerrard-inspired fightback cancelled out and then overhauled Mido's 70th-minute strike. Victory over Stoke came as some compensation and everything in the garden looked rosy for a brief moment.

However, they won only three of their next nine league games, which included an excellent 2–1 victory at Aston Villa. But it was then that the wheels really started to come off.

A 3–1 home defeat by Bolton on 22nd November started the alarm bells ringing, and a 2–1 reverse at Hull a fortnight later confirmed the downward trend.

> **Gibson has always given his managers the chance to prove themselves**

Indeed, they went 14 games without a victory before, remarkably, severely denting Liverpool's title challenge with an unexpected 2–0 home win on 28th February.

However, it was to prove a rare occurrence and the revenge they gained over Hull on 11th April was the second and last success of the final 26 games as they plummeted into the bottom three and never really looked like escaping.

Their form in the League was in stark contrast to that in the FA Cup, where they reached the last eight for the fourth successive season. Non-League Barrow, Wolves and West Ham were despatched to set up a quarter-final showdown with Everton at Goodison Park. Local-born defender David Wheater put the Teessiders ahead, but goals from Marouane Fellaini and Louis Saha within six second-half minutes ended Boro's dreams of reaching Wembley as the Toffees marched on towards the final.

But cup disappointment was to turn to league agony as the decline continued unabated.

Their fate was effectively sealed within the space of six days when, after losing 3–1 at Newcastle in what seemed a must-win game against their relegation rivals, they could only manage a home draw with Aston Villa. That left them with a mathematical chance of survival, albeit a slim one, but even final-day defeats for the Magpies and Hull could not prevent Middlesbrough from slipping back into the Coca-Cola Championship.

All the signs are that Southgate will be in charge of Boro on the opening day of the 2009/10 season, which may surprise some of football's more ruthless chairmen. But Gibson has always given his managers the opportunity to prove themselves, and Southgate looks likely to be handed at least one chance to propel Boro back to the top flight.

CLOCKWISE FROM ABOVE: Boro players watch on in horror as they concede a goal at Newcastle in a key game in the final weeks of the season; David Wheater shows the pain of relegation; Jérémie Aliadière celebrates scoring in a draw with Arsenal

MIDDLESBROUGH

August

16th ● Tottenham ....h   W 2–1   **Att:** 32,623. **Ref:** M Atkinson — **Middlesbrough** (4-4-2): Jones, Wheater[1], Huth, Pogatetz, Taylor, Aliadière, Shawky, O'Neil, Downing, Alves (Mido[1] 82), Sanli (Digard[1] 72). Subs not used: Turnbull, Emnes, Johnson, Williams, Grounds.

23rd ● Liverpool ....a   L 2–1   **Att:** 43,168. **Ref:** M Riley — **Middlesbrough** (4-4-2): Turnbull, Wheater, Huth, Pogatetz, Taylor (Hoyte 75), Aliadière, O'Neil, Shawky, Downing, Alves (Mido[1] 60), Sanli (Digard 87). Subs not used: Emnes, Johnson, Williams.

26th ● Yeovil ....h   W 5–1   **Att:** 15,651. **Ref:** S Mathieson — **Middlesbrough** (4-4-2): Turnbull, Hoyte, Riggott, Pogatetz (Williams 74), Grounds, Aliadière[1] (O'Neil 60), Digard[1], Shawky (Walker 60), Johnson[1], Emnes[1], Mido[1]. Subs not used: Steele, Downing, Sanli, Alves.

30th ● Stoke ....h   W 2–1   **Att:** 27,627. **Ref:** M Dean — **Middlesbrough** (4-4-2): Turnbull, Hoyte (Taylor 72), Wheater, Huth[1], Pogatetz, Aliadière, Shawky (Digard 61), O'Neil[1], Downing, Alves[1] (Mido 76), Sanli[1]. Subs not used: Steele, Riggott, Emnes, Johnson.

September

13th ● Portsmouth ....a   L 2–1   **Att:** 19,425. **Ref:** S Attwell — **Middlesbrough** (4-4-2): Turnbull, Hoyte, Huth, Riggott, Pogatetz, Aliadière, O'Neil, Digard (Taylor 70), Downing, Alves, Mido[1] (Johnson 84). Subs not used: Jones, Wheater, Porritt, Walker, Craddock.

20th ● Sunderland ....a   L 2–0   **Att:** 38,388. **Ref:** H Webb — **Middlesbrough** (4-4-1-1): Turnbull, Wheater, Huth[1], Pogatetz, Taylor, Aliadière, O'Neil[1], Digard (Shawky[1] 68), Downing, Johnson (Hoyte 68), Alves. Subs not used: Jones, Riggott, Arca, Emnes.

23rd ● Man Utd ....a   L 3–1   **Att:** 53,729. **Ref:** A Marriner — **Middlesbrough** (4-5-1): Jones, Hoyte, Wheater, Pogatetz[1], Taylor, Downing, Digard (Riggott 72), O'Neil, Shawky (Johnson[1] 46), Aliadière, Alves (Emnes 85). Subs not used: Turnbull, Arca, Walker, Craddock.

27th ● West Brom ....h   L 0–1   **Att:** 26,248. **Ref:** C Foy — **Middlesbrough** (4-4-2): Turnbull, Hoyte, Huth, Wheater, Taylor[1], Aliadière (Johnson 60), O'Neil, Shawky (Digard 60), Downing, Alves, Mido[1]. Subs not used: Jones, Riggott, Emnes, Bennett, Walker.

October

4th ● Wigan ....a   W 0–1   **Att:** 16,806. **Ref:** M Atkinson — **Middlesbrough** (4-4-2): Turnbull, Hoyte, Wheater, Riggott, Grounds, Aliadière[1], O'Neil, Shawky (Digard 58), Downing, Alves (A Johnson 79), Mido. Subs not used: Jones, Emnes, J Johnson, Walker, Craddock.

18th ● Chelsea ....h   L 0–5   **Att:** 29,221. **Ref:** P Dowd — **Middlesbrough** (4-4-1-1): Turnbull, Grounds (J Johnson 54), Wheater, Riggott, Taylor, Aliadière, Shawky (Digard 65), O'Neil, A Johnson (Alves[1] 65), Downing, Mido. Subs not used: Jones, Emnes, Bennett, Walker.

25th ● Blackburn ....a   D 1–1   **Att:** 17,606. **Ref:** M Dean — **Middlesbrough** (4-4-2): Turnbull, Wheater[1], Riggott, Pogatetz, Taylor, Aliadière, O'Neil, Digard, Downing, Alves[1], Sanli (Emnes 85). Subs not used: Jones, Shawky, A Johnson, J Johnson, Grounds.

29th ● Man City ....h   W 2–0   **Att:** 25,731. **Ref:** L Mason — **Middlesbrough** (4-4-2): Turnbull, Wheater, Riggott, Pogatetz, Taylor, Aliadière, O'Neil[1], Digard (Arca 75), Downing (A Johnson 83), Sanli, Alves[1]. Subs not used: Jones, Emnes, J Johnson, Grounds, Walker.

November

1st ● West Ham ....h   D 1–1   **Att:** 25,164. **Ref:** A Marriner — **Middlesbrough** (4-4-2): Turnbull, Wheater[1] (Hoyte 46), Riggott[1], Pogatetz, Taylor, Aliadière, O'Neil, Digard (Arca[1] 56), Downing, Sanli, Alves (Mido[1] 67). Subs not used: Jones, Emnes, Johnson, Grounds.

9th ● Aston Villa ....a   W 1–2   **Att:** 36,672. **Ref:** R Styles — **Middlesbrough** (4-4-1-1): Turnbull, Hoyte, Pogatetz, Riggott, Taylor, Aliadière[1], Digard, O'Neil, Downing, Sanli[2], Alves (Arca[1] 83). Subs not used: Jones, Emnes, Johnson, Wheater, Grounds, Walker.

16th ● Everton ....a   D 1–1   **Att:** 31,063. **Ref:** H Webb — **Middlesbrough** (4-4-2): Turnbull, Hoyte, Riggott (Wheater 52), Pogatetz[1], Taylor, O'Neil[1], Digard[1], Arca (Johnson 69), Downing, Alves (Emnes 84), Sanli. Subs not used: Jones, Franks, Grounds, Walker.

22nd ● Bolton ....h   L 1–3   **Att:** 24,487. **Ref:** M Atkinson — **Middlesbrough** (4-4-2): Turnbull, Hoyte, Wheater, Pogatetz[1][1], Taylor (Arca 76), Aliadière (Johnson 58), O'Neil, Digard[1], Downing, Alves (Emnes 75), Sanli. Subs not used: Jones, Hines, Grounds, Walker.

29th ● Newcastle ....h   D 0–0   **Att:** 32,160. **Ref:** A Wiley — **Middlesbrough** (4-4-2): Turnbull, Hoyte, Wheater, Pogatetz, Taylor, Aliadière (Mido 77), Arca[1], Digard, Downing, Sanli, Alves. Subs not used: Jones, Emnes, Johnson, Hines, Grounds, Walker.

December

6th ● Hull ....a   L 2–1   **Att:** 24,912. **Ref:** S Tanner — **Middlesbrough** (4-4-2): Turnbull, Hoyte, Wheater[1], Pogatetz, Taylor, Aliadière, Arca, Digard (Hines 87), Downing, Sanli[1][1], Alves. Subs not used: Jones, Emnes, Johnson, McMahon, Grounds, Walker.

13th ● Arsenal ....h   D 1–1   **Att:** 27,320. **Ref:** P Walton — **Middlesbrough** (4-4-2): Turnbull, McMahon, Riggott, Huth, Pogatetz, Johnson (Emnes 90), Digard (Shawky 90), Arca, Downing, Sanli, Aliadière[1]. Subs not used: Jones, Alves, Bates, Hines, Grounds.

20th ● Fulham ....a   L 3–0   **Att:** 23,722. **Ref:** K Stroud — **Middlesbrough** (4-4-2): Turnbull, McMahon[1], Riggott, Huth (Taylor 85), Pogatetz, Johnson (Emnes 80), Shawky, Arca[1] (Mido 46), Downing, Aliadière, Sanli. Subs not used: Jones, Alves, Wheater, Walker.

26th ● Everton ....h   L 0–1   **Att:** 30,253. **Ref:** M Riley — **Middlesbrough** (4-4-2): Turnbull, McMahon[1], Riggott[1], Pogatetz, Taylor[1], Aliadière (Johnson 70), O'Neil (Emnes 85), Arca[1], Downing, Sanli (Alves 54), Mido. Subs not used: Jones, Huth, Wheater, Walker.

29th ● Man Utd ....a   L 1–0   **Att:** 75,294. **Ref:** M Atkinson — **Middlesbrough** (4-5-1): Turnbull, Bates, Riggott, Wheater, Pogatetz, Aliadière (Emnes 76), O'Neil, Arca, Downing, Sanli, Alves. Subs not used: Jones, Taylor, Huth, Shawky, Porritt, Walker.

January

3rd ● Barrow ....h   W 2–1   **Att:** 25,132. **Ref:** M Dean — **Middlesbrough** (4-4-2): Jones, McMahon, Wheater, Huth, Pogatetz, Johnson, Walker, Digard[1], Downing, Alves[2], Aliadière (M Emnes 34 (Mido 84)), M Emnes (Mido 84). Subs not used: Turnbull, Taylor, Riggott, Sanli, Bates.

10th ● Sunderland ....h   D 1–1   **Att:** 29,310. **Ref:** P Dowd — **Middlesbrough** (4-5-1): Turnbull, McMahon, Riggott, Wheater, Pogatetz, Sanli, Digard (Bates 65), Walker (Johnson 47), Arca, Downing, Alves[1] (Mido 86). Subs not used: Jones, Taylor, Emnes, Huth.

17th ● West Brom ....h   L 3–0   **Att:** 25,557. **Ref:** M Halsey — **Middlesbrough** (4-4-1-1): Turnbull, McMahon (Bates 70), Wheater, Riggott (Huth[1] 36), Taylor, O'Neil (Mido 57), Digard[1], Shawky[1], Downing, Sanli, Alves. Subs not used: Jones, Emnes, Johnson, Bennett.

24th ● Wolverhampton ....a   W 1–2   **Att:** 18,013. **Ref:** R Styles — **Middlesbrough** (4-4-2): Jones, Bates, Wheater, Riggott, Taylor (McMahon 7), O'Neil[1], Sanli, Shawky (Hoyte 46), Johnson, Downing, Alves[1] (Emnes[1] 70). Subs not used: Porritt, Bennett, Turnbull, Craddock.

28th ● Chelsea ....a   L 2–0   **Att:** 40,280. **Ref:** L Probert — **Middlesbrough** (4-5-1): Turnbull, McMahon, Wheater, Riggott[1], Pogatetz, Johnson, O'Neil, Shawky[1] (Sanli 64), Bates, Downing, King (Alves 64). Subs not used: Jones, Taylor, Emnes, Huth, Arca.

31st ● Blackburn ....h   D 0–0   **Att:** 24,303. **Ref:** C Foy — **Middlesbrough** (4-4-2): Jones, Wheater, Riggott, Huth, Pogatetz, Johnson, Bates, Walker, Downing, King (Emnes 65), Sanli (Alves 65). Subs not used: Turnbull, Hoyte, Shawky, Arca, McMahon.

February

7th ● Man City ....a   L 1–0   **Att:** 40,588. **Ref:** A Marriner — **Middlesbrough** (4-4-2): Jones, Wheater, Riggott (Hoyte 68), Huth, Pogatetz, Johnson (Sanli 74), Bates, Digard (O'Neil[1] 60), Downing, Alves, King. Subs not used: Turnbull, Emnes, Shawky, Arca.

14th ● West Ham ....a   D 1–1   **Att:** 33,658. **Ref:** P Walton — **Middlesbrough** (4-5-1): Jones, Hoyte, Huth, Wheater, Pogatetz, Johnson, O'Neil[1], Digard, Arca (Walker 77), Downing[1], Alves (Sanli 74). Subs not used: Turnbull, Emnes, Bates, McMahon, Bennett.

21st ● Wigan ....h   D 0–0   **Att:** 24,020. **Ref:** M Dean — **Middlesbrough** (4-4-1-1): Jones, Hoyte, Wheater, Huth, Pogatetz, O'Neil[1], Digard (Walker 23), Arca (Aliadière 52), Johnson (Sanli 62), Downing, Alves[1]. Subs not used: Turnbull, Emnes, Bates, McMahon.

● Barclays Premier League ● FA Cup ● Carling Cup ● UEFA Champions League ● UEFA Cup   ▌Yellow Card ▌Red Card

RESULTS 2008/09

| 25th | ● West Ham...........................h | W 2–0 | **Att:** 15,602. **Ref:** S Bennett — **Middlesbrough** (4-4-2): Jones, Hoyte, Wheater, Huth, Pogatetz, O'Neil▌, Bates, Arca (Walker 88), Downing¹, Sanli¹ (Johnson 81), Aliadière (Emnes 67). Subs not used: Turnbull, Taylor, Alves, McMahon. |
| 28th | ● Liverpool.............................h | W 2–0 | **Att:** 33,724. **Ref:** R Styles — **Middlesbrough** (4-4-2): Jones, Hoyte, Wheater, Huth, Pogatetz, O'Neil, Bates▌, Arca (Walker 88), Downing, Sanli¹ (Johnson 79), Aliadière (King 68). Subs not used: Turnbull, Taylor, Emnes, Alves. |

March

4th	● Tottenham...........................a	L 4–0	**Att:** 35,761. **Ref:** H Webb — **Middlesbrough** (4-4-2): Jones, Hoyte (Johnson 70), Wheater, Huth (Taylor 46), Pogatetz▌, O'Neil, Bates, Arca, Downing, Aliadière (King 53), Sanli. Subs not used: Turnbull, Emnes, Alves, Walker.
8th	● Everton.............................a	L 2–1	**Att:** 37,856. **Ref:** M Halsey — **Middlesbrough** (4-4-1-1): Jones, Hoyte, Huth, Wheater¹, Pogatetz, O'Neil, Arca, Bates (Johnson 72), Downing, Sanli, Aliadière (Emnes 68). Subs not used: Turnbull, Taylor, McMahon, Franks, Walker.
14th	● Portsmouth..........................h	D 1–1	**Att:** 24,281. **Ref:** M Atkinson — **Middlesbrough** (4-4-2): Jones, McMahon, Wheater, Huth, Pogatetz (Taylor 46), Aliadière (Johnson 58), Arca (Alves 71), Bates▌, Downing, Sanli, King¹. Subs not used: Turnbull, Emnes, Shawky, Walker.
21st	● Stoke ....a	L 1–0	**Att:** 26,442. **Ref:** L Mason — **Middlesbrough** (4-4-2): Jones, McMahon (Hoyte 80), Wheater, Huth, Taylor (Johnson 86), O'Neil, Shawky, Pogatetz▌, Downing, Sanli, King (Alves 55). Subs not used: Turnbull, Emnes, Arca, Grounds.

April

4th	● Bolton..............................a	L 4–1	**Att:** 20,819. **Ref:** A Wiley — **Middlesbrough** (5-3-2): Jones, Hoyte, Wheater, Huth, Pogatetz (Taylor 36), Downing, O'Neil▌, Sanli, Bates, Aliadière (Emnes 74), Alves. Subs not used: Turnbull, Shawky, King, McMahon, Walker.
11th	● Hull ....h	W 3–1	**Att:** 32,255. **Ref:** P Dowd — **Middlesbrough** (4-1-2-12): Jones, McMahon, Wheater, Huth, Taylor¹, Bates▌, Aliadière (Emnes 90), Downing, Sanli▌, Alves (Johnson 77), King¹. Subs not used: Turnbull, Hoyte, Shawky, Riggott, Walker.
18th	● Fulham ....h	D 0–0	**Att:** 30,389. **Ref:** P Walton — **Middlesbrough** (4-4-2): Jones, McMahon▌, Wheater, Huth, Taylor, Aliadière, Sanli▌, Bates, Downing, King, Alves (Johnson 83). Subs not used: Turnbull, Hoyte, Riggott, Digard, Emnes, Shawky.
26th	● Arsenal ....a	L 2–0	**Att:** 60,089. **Ref:** C Foy — **Middlesbrough** (4-4-2): Jones, McMahon (Digard 73), Wheater, Huth, Taylor, O'Neil, Bates, Sanli, Downing, Aliadière (Emnes 86), King (Johnson 61). Subs not used: Turnbull, Hoyte, Alves, Grounds.

May

2nd	● Man Utd ....h	L 0–2	**Att:** 33,767. **Ref:** M Halsey — **Middlesbrough** (4-4-2): Jones, McMahon (Digard 55), Wheater, Huth▌, Hoyte, O'Neil (Emnes 70), Sanli, Bates, Downing, King (Alves 55), Aliadière. Subs not used: Turnbull, Arca, Johnson, Grounds.
11th	● Newcastle...........................a	L 3–1	**Att:** 51,252. **Ref:** M Dean — **Middlesbrough** (4-4-2): Jones, Hoyte, Bates▌, Huth▌, Taylor (Johnson 76), Downing, O'Neil, Shawky (Aliadière 69), Sanli, Emnes, Alves (King 36). Subs not used: Turnbull, Arca, McMahon, Grounds.
16th	● Aston Villa.........................h	D 1–1	**Att:** 27,261. **Ref:** M Riley — **Middlesbrough** (4-4-2): Jones, Bates, Wheater, Huth, Hoyte, O'Neil (Walker 72), Johnson, Arca, Downing (King 23), Sanli¹, Emnes. Subs not used: Turnbull, Taylor, Shawky, McMahon, Grounds.
24th	● West Ham...........................a	L 2–1	**Att:** 34,007. **Ref:** H Webb — **Middlesbrough** (4-4-1-1): Jones, McMahon (Bennett 46), Wheater, Huth, Hoyte, O'Neil▌, Bates, Arca (Walker 46), Johnson, Sanli, Emnes (Franks 81). Subs not used: Turnbull, Shawky, Williams, Grounds.

● Barclays Premier League ● FA Cup ● Carling Cup ● UEFA Champions League ● UEFA Cup

▌ Yellow Card ▌ Red Card

Middlesbrough players including David Wheater (left) leave the pitch dejected after their match against West Ham on the final day

BARCLAYS PREMIER LEAGUE GOALKEEPER STATS

Player	Minutes on pitch	Appearances	Match starts	Completed matches	Sub appearances	Subbed off	Saved with feet	Punched	Parried	Tipped over	Fumbled	Tipped round	Caught	Blocked	Clean sheets	Goals conceded	Minutes since conceding	Save %	Saved	Resulting in goals	Opposition miss	Yellow cards	Red cards
Brad Jones	1537	16	16	16	0	0	1	13	14	5	0	4	55	0	4	23	37	80.17	0	0	0	0	0
Ross Turnbull	2095	22	22	22	0	0	3	11	22	5	0	5	75	1	3	34	12	78.75	0	2	0	0	0

BARCLAYS PREMIER LEAGUE OUTFIELD PLAYER STATS

Player	Minutes on pitch	Appearances	Match starts	Completed matches	Substitute appearances	Subbed off	Goals scored	Minutes since scoring	Assists	Shots on target	Shots off target	Crosses	Defensive clearances	Defensive blocks	Fouls committed	Free-kicks won	Caught offside	Yellow cards	Red cards
Jérémie Aliadière	2376	29	27	16	2	11	2	1008	2	17	9	19	4	0	26	30	11	1	0
Afonso Alves	2278	31	24	12	7	12	4	791	3	54	35	2	8	1	29	45	29	2	0
Julio Arca	1227	18	14	8	4	6	0	–	0	2	10	3	2	1	21	12	0	5	0
Matthew Bates	1466	17	15	14	2	0	1	642	0	2	3	4	4	5	17	13	1	4	1
Joe Bennett	49	1	0	0	1	0	0	–	0	1	2	0	0	1	0	0	0	0	0
Didier Digard	1356	23	15	5	8	9	0	–	2	5	9	6	6	2	20	17	0	3	1
Stewart Downing	3447	37	37	35	0	2	0	–	4	33	37	148	16	5	17	24	8	0	0
Marvin Emnes	444	15	3	2	12	1	0	–	0	3	3	3	1	0	5	5	7	0	0
Jonathan Franks	13	1	0	0	1	0	0	–	0	0	0	0	0	0	0	0	0	0	0
Jonathan Grounds	151	2	2	1	0	1	0	–	0	0	0	0	2	3	0	0	0	0	0
Seb Hines	6	1	0	0	1	0	0	–	0	0	0	0	0	0	0	0	0	0	0
Justin Hoyte	1714	22	17	15	5	2	0	–	1	3	0	18	4	3	9	7	1	0	0
Robert Huth	2210	24	23	21	1	2	0	–	0	2	9	1	39	30	36	33	0	5	0
Adam Johnson	1197	26	10	4	16	6	0	–	0	5	8	14	0	1	6	27	0	1	0
John Johnson	38	1	0	0	1	0	0	–	0	0	0	0	0	0	1	0	0	0	0
Marlon King	891	13	9	4	4	5	2	354	0	3	5	4	4	0	11	14	27	1	0
Tony McMahon	1096	13	13	8	0	5	0	–	2	2	3	16	3	3	25	16	0	3	0
Mido	664	13	5	4	8	1	4	199	0	9	8	2	5	2	22	12	13	3	0
Gary O'Neil	2615	29	28	24	1	4	4	45	1	24	8	43	11	6	31	32	4	8	0
Emanuel Pogatetz	2466	27	27	25	0	2	1	1432	0	1	4	3	20	13	25	26	0	4	0
Chris Riggott	1490	17	17	14	0	3	0	–	0	2	1	0	26	19	16	12	0	3	0
Tuncay Sanli	2819	33	30	24	3	6	7	180	4	33	28	8	6	1	38	59	17	4	0
Mohamed Shawky	894	13	11	5	2	6	0	–	0	4	6	0	2	1	21	16	0	3	0
Andrew Taylor	2052	26	20	16	6	4	0	–	0	6	2	14	9	2	7	20	0	3	0
Joshua Walker	298	6	2	1	4	1	0	–	0	0	1	0	1	2	2	2	0	0	0
David Wheater	2948	32	31	29	1	1	1	2877	2	8	16	3	32	20	35	22	1	2	1

SEASON TOTALS

Goals scored	28
Goals conceded	57
Clean sheets	7
Shots on target	219
Shots off target	207
Shots per goal	15.21
Pens awarded	3
Pens scored	1
Pens conceded	2
Offsides	119
Corners	173
Crosses	313
Players used	28
Fouls committed	420
Free-kicks won	452

CARDS RECEIVED

55 **3**

SEQUENCES

Wins	(–)
Losses	3
(on four occasions)	
Draws	(–)
Undefeated	5
(25/10/08-16/11/08)	
Without win	14
(16/11/08-21/02/09)	
Undefeated home	7
(10/01/09-18/04/09)	
Undefeated away	4
(04/10/08-16/11/08)	
Without scoring	5
(17/01/09-21/02/09)	
Without conceding	2
(21/02/09-28/02/09)	
Scoring	6
(25/10/08-22/11/08)	
Conceding	8
(06/12/08-28/01/09)	

SEASON INFORMATION
Highest Position: 4
Lowest Position: 19
Average goals scored per game: 0.74
Average goals conceded per game: 1.50

League position at the end of each week

League position at the end of: August 6, September 16, October 9, November 12, December 17, January 19, February 17, March 19, April 19, May 19

MATCH RECORDS

Goals scored per match

		W	D	L	Pts
Failed to score	17	0	4	13	4
Scored 1 goal	15	1	7	7	10
Scored 2 goals	5	5	0	0	15
Scored 3 goals	1	1	0	0	3
Scored 4+ goals	0	0	0	0	0

Goals conceded per match

		W	D	L	Pts
Clean sheet	7	3	4	0	13
Conceded 1 goal	16	4	7	5	19
Conceded 2 goals	8	0	0	8	0
Conceded 3 goals	5	0	0	5	0
Conceded 4+ goals	2	0	0	2	0

GOALS SCORED/CONCEDED PER FIVE-MINUTE INTERVALS

Goals For	2	1	1	0	1	2	2	2	1	1	1	0	1	1	2	2	2	6
Goals Against	1	6	2	1	2	2	1	2	2	0	8	5	2	4	2	3	7	7
Mins	5	10	15	20	25	30	35	40	45	50	55	60	65	70	75	80	85	90

QUICK-FIRE GOALS

From the start of a match
Tuncay Sanli (v Hull) 2:48

By a substitute after coming on
Mido (v Tottenham) 4:03

LAST-GASP GOALS

From the start of a match
Gary O'Neil (v Man City) 93:56

By a substitute after coming on
Mido (v West Ham) 16:38

GOAL DETAILS

How the goals were struck

SCORED		CONCEDED
17	Right foot	30
9	Left foot	11
1	Headers	11
1	Others	5

How the goals were struck

SCORED		CONCEDED
18	Open play	36
4	Cross	3
2	Corner	6
1	Penalties	2
1	Direct from free-kick	1
0	Free-kick	3
2	Own goals	6

Distance from goal

SCORED		CONCEDED
6	6yds	22
20	18yds	30
2	18+yds	5

NEWCASTLE UNITED

CLUB SUMMARY

FORMED	1892
MANAGER	TBC
GROUND	St James' Park
CAPACITY	52,387
NICKNAME	The Magpies
WEBSITE	www.nufc.co.uk

The New Football Pools PLAYER OF THE SEASON — Sebastian Bassong

OVERALL

P	W	D	L	F	A	GD
42	8	14	20	44	64	-20

BARCLAYS PREMIER LEAGUE

Pos	P	W	D	L	F	A	GD	Pts
18	38	7	13	18	40	59	-19	34

HOME

Pos	P	W	D	L	F	A	GD	Pts
18	19	5	7	7	24	29	-5	22

AWAY

Pos	P	W	D	L	F	A	GD	Pts
16	19	2	6	11	16	30	-14	12

CUP PROGRESS DETAILS

Competition	Round reached	Knocked out by
FA Cup	R3	Hull
Carling Cup	R3	Tottenham

BIGGEST WIN (ALL COMPS)

14/12/08 3–0 v Portsmouth **PREM**

BIGGEST DEFEAT (ALL COMPS)

28/12/08 1–5 v Liverpool **PREM**

THE PLAYER WITH THE MOST

Shots on target	
Obafemi Martins	29
Shots off target	
Obafemi Martins	34
Shots without scoring	
Kevin Nolan	41
Assists	
Jonas Gutierrez	4
Offsides	
Obafemi Martins	16
Fouls	
Shola Ameobi	53
Fouls without a card	
Mark Viduka	10
Free-kicks won	
Jonas Gutierrez	89
Defensive clearances	
Fabricio Coloccini	56

actim INDEX — for the 2008/09 Barclays Premier League Season

Rank	Player	Pts
106	Steven Taylor	316
135	Damien Duff	280
148	Fabricio Coloccini	261
176	Jose Enrique	235
186	Michael Owen	226

ATTENDANCE RECORD

High	Low	Average
52,114	44,567	48,750
v Liverpool (28/12/2008)	v Aston Villa (03/11/2008)	

CLOCKWISE FROM TOP: A dejected Steven Taylor feels the pain of relegation at Villa Park; Obafemi Martins scores the second in a 3–0 win at Portsmouth; Joey Barton is sent off as Newcastle lose at Liverpool in May; Alan Shearer returns to St James' Park

AND it all started so well. When Kevin Keegan's Newcastle left Old Trafford with their heads held high on 17th August, there was genuine optimism on Tyneside that a corner had been turned.

Without the injured Michael Owen – that was to become something of a theme – Obafemi Martins' header had given the Magpies a lead which Darren Fletcher cancelled out, but Manchester United could not force their way past a Newcastle side for whom Argentinian winger Jonas Gutierrez looked a real find in the opening league game of the season.

Fast forward nine months or so and the mood in the black-and-white corner of a traumatised north-east could hardly be darker. Four managers, seven wins, an owner who tried and failed to offload the club and, ultimately, relegation tell the tale of a campaign which started on its downward spiral before August was out.

Like any compelling saga, the 2008/09 season had its heroes and villains. It began with the face-off between Keegan and executive director Dennis Wise and ended with Alan Shearer returning to the club and overseeing their humiliating relegation.

Keegan's departure was in protest at his lack of influence over the club's transfer dealings. The Magpies hero had reluctantly agreed to the sale of midfielder James Milner to Aston Villa in anticipation of wholesale signings, but was eventually presented with only Xisco and Ignacio Gonzalez, and suddenly the club was in turmoil.

The locals revolted after a 2–1 home defeat by newly-promoted Hull, prompting owner Mike Ashley to put the club up for sale just four games into the campaign.

Coach Chris Hughton was appointed caretaker manager as the club sought a replacement for Keegan but, having seen their overtures rejected by a series of contenders, Ashley sprang a surprise by handing Joe Kinnear the reins for what proved to be an equally turbulent few months. The former Wimbledon boss announced himself by launching a colourful salvo at his critics among the media before presiding over a run of four wins in 18 league games, only to succumb once again to the heart problems which had previously resulted in a four-year hiatus in his career.

Hughton got the nod for a second time

> ## The campaign started on a downward spiral before August was out

and, having recorded his first victory at West Brom on 7th February, hours after Kinnear had been rushed to hospital in the West Midlands, the plan was to leave him in charge until Kinnear returned to work.

However, once it emerged that Kinnear would not be back before the end of the season, Ashley turned to a second Tyneside hero in a desperate attempt to stem the tide.

Shearer was brought in on an eight-game mission, seemingly with nothing to lose. If he kept the club in the Barclays Premier League, his status would only be enhanced. If he failed, it was perceived that little of the blame could be attached to him.

His first game was at home to Chelsea and a regulation 2–0 win for the Blues spoilt the homecoming party.

Shearer claimed his first point courtesy of a late Andy Carroll equaliser at Stoke next time out and, having seen his side lose to the only goal at Tottenham, targeted home wins against Portsmouth, Middlesbrough and Fulham. Those key fixtures yielded just four points – a draw with Portsmouth and a win against Boro – and so the battle came down to 90 minutes at Aston Villa on the final day of the season.

Fittingly for a club that bears the scars of so many self-inflicted wounds, a Damien Duff own goal ultimately condemned Newcastle to the drop. A point would have been enough to keep them up, but now the Magpies face a season outside of the top flight for the first time since 1992/93.

NEWCASTLE UNITED

RESULTS 2008/09

August

17th ● Man Utd ....a **D 1–1** **Att:** 75,512. **Ref:** M Riley — **Newcastle** (4-4-1-1): Given, Beye, S Taylor, Coloccini, N'Zogbia, Milner, Butt, Guthrie, Gutierrez, Duff, Martins⌐. Subs not used: Harper, Jose Enrique, Bassong, Smith, Geremi, Edgar, Donaldson.

23rd ● Bolton ....h **W 1–0** **Att:** 47,711. **Ref:** S Bennett — **Newcastle** (4-4-2): Given, Beye, S Taylor, Coloccini, N'Zogbia, Milner, Butt, Guthrie, Gutierrez, Martins (Owen¹ 53), Duff (Geremi 46). Subs not used: Harper, Jose Enrique, Bassong, Smith, Edgar.

26th ● Coventry ....a **W 2–3** **Att:** 19,249. **Ref:** T Bates — **Newcastle** (4-5-1): Given, Beye, Coloccini, Bassong, Jose Enrique, Milner¹, Geremi (Owen¹ 75), Butt, Guthrie, N'Zogbia, Gutierrez. Subs not used: Harper, S Taylor, Edgar, Tozer, Donaldson, Ranger.

30th ● Arsenal ....a **L 3–0** **Att:** 60,067. **Ref:** R Styles — **Newcastle** (4-4-2): Given⌐, Coloccini⌐, Jose Enrique (Bassong 44), S Taylor, Gutierrez (Barton 89), Guthrie, Butt, Beye (Edgar 89), N'Zogbia, Owen, Ameobi. Subs not used: Harper, Tozer, Donaldson, Ranger.

September

13th ● Hull ....h **L 1–2** **Att:** 50,242. **Ref:** A Marriner — **Newcastle** (4-4-2): Given, Edgar (Bassong 68), S Taylor, Coloccini, N'Zogbia, Geremi, Butt, Guthrie⌐, Xisco¹, Owen, Ameobi (Gonzalez 61). Subs not used: Harper, Cacapa, Danquah, Doninger, Donaldson.

20th ● West Ham ....a **L 3–1** **Att:** 34,743. **Ref:** P Dowd — **Newcastle** (4-4-2): Given, Edgar (Bassong 59), S Taylor⌐, Coloccini, N'Zogbia⌐, Geremi, Cacapa (Gonzalez 81), Butt, Duff, Owen¹, Xisco. Subs not used: Harper, Ameobi, Tozer, Doninger, Donaldson.

24th ● Tottenham ....h **L 1–2** **Att:** 20,577. **Ref:** C Foy — **Newcastle** (4-2-3-1): Given, Beye, S Taylor, Coloccini, Bassong, Cacapa (Edgar 72), Butt⌐, N'Zogbia, Owen¹, Duff (Xisco 72), Martins. Subs not used: Harper, Ameobi, Tozer, Doninger, Donaldson.

27th ● Blackburn ....h **L 1–2** **Att:** 44,935. **Ref:** S Tanner — **Newcastle** (4-4-2): Given, Bassong, S Taylor, Coloccini, Cacapa, Geremi (Ameobi 71), Butt, Duff, N'Zogbia (Edgar 82), Xisco, Owen¹. Subs not used: Harper, Tozer, Doninger, Donaldson, Ranger.

October

5th ● Everton ....a **D 2–2** **Att:** 33,805. **Ref:** H Webb — **Newcastle** (4-4-2): Given, S Taylor¹, Coloccini, Cacapa, Jose Enrique (Bassong 39), Geremi⌐ (Ameobi 75), Butt⌐, Guthrie, N'Zogbia⌐, Owen, Duff¹. Subs not used: Harper, Xisco, Edgar, Doninger, Donaldson.

20th ● Man City ....h **D 2–2** **Att:** 45,908. **Ref:** R Styles — **Newcastle** (4-4-2): Given, Beye⌐, S Taylor, Coloccini, Bassong, Geremi, Guthrie, Butt, Duff, Martins (N'Zogbia 72), Ameobi¹ (Carroll 79). Subs not used: Harper, Cacapa, Jose Enrique, Xisco, Edgar.

25th ● Sunderland ....a **L 2–1** **Att:** 47,936. **Ref:** M Riley — **Newcastle** (4-4-2): Given, Beye, S Taylor, Coloccini, Bassong (Jose Enrique 84), Geremi (Gutierrez 73), Guthrie⌐, Butt⌐ (Barton 85), Duff, Ameobi¹, Martins. Subs not used: Harper, Cacapa, N'Zogbia, Xisco.

28th ● West Brom ....h **W 2–1** **Att:** 45,801. **Ref:** M Dean — **Newcastle** (4-4-2): Given, Beye, S Taylor, Coloccini, Jose Enrique, Duff, Guthrie, Barton¹, Gutierrez (Geremi 70), Martins¹ (Xisco 77), Ameobi (Carroll 90). Subs not used: Harper, Bassong, N'Zogbia, Edgar.

November

3rd ● Aston Villa ....h **W 2–0** **Att:** 44,567. **Ref:** S Bennett — **Newcastle** (4-4-2): Given, Beye⌐, Coloccini, S Taylor, Jose Enrique, Gutierrez, Barton⌐, Butt, Duff, Martins⌐ (Cacapa 88), Ameobi (Owen 90). Subs not used: Harper, Guthrie, Bassong, Geremi.

9th ● Fulham ....a **L 2–1** **Att:** 24,740. **Ref:** M Atkinson — **Newcastle** (4-4-2): Given, Beye⌐, Coloccini⌐, Cacapa, Jose Enrique, Gutierrez (Owen 70), Butt, Barton, Duff, Martins, Ameobi¹. Subs not used: Harper, Guthrie, Bassong, N'Zogbia, Geremi, Carroll.

15th ● Wigan ....h **D 2–2** **Att:** 47,657. **Ref:** A Marriner — **Newcastle** (4-4-2): Given, Beye¹, Bassong, Coloccini, Jose Enrique (N'Zogbia 68), Gutierrez (Owen¹ 68), Barton (Guthrie 16), Butt, Duff, Ameobi, Martins⌐. Subs not used: Harper, Cacapa, Geremi, Carroll.

22nd ● Chelsea ....a **D 0–0** **Att:** 41,660. **Ref:** P Dowd — **Newcastle** (4-4-2): Given, Beye, Coloccini, Bassong, Jose Enrique, Gutierrez⌐ (N'Zogbia 76), Guthrie⌐, Butt, Duff, Martins (Ameobi 61), Owen. Subs not used: Harper, Cacapa, Edgar, LuaLua, Carroll.

29th ● Middlesbrough ....a **D 0–0** **Att:** 32,160. **Ref:** A Wiley — **Newcastle** (4-4-2): Given, Beye, Coloccini, Bassong⌐, Jose Enrique, Gutierrez, Guthrie, Butt, N'Zobgia, Martins (Viduka 65), Owen. Subs not used: Harper, Cacapa, Geremi, S Taylor, Edgar, Carroll.

December

6th ● Stoke ....h **D 2–2** **Att:** 47,422. **Ref:** M Riley — **Newcastle** (4-4-2): Given, Beye, Coloccini, Bassong, Jose Enrique, N'Zogbia, Geremi (Cacapa 82), Guthrie (S Taylor 46), Gutierrez, Owen², Martins (Viduka 74). Subs not used: Harper, Xisco, Edgar, Carroll.

14th ● Portsmouth ....a **W 0–3** **Att:** 19,416. **Ref:** C Foy — **Newcastle** (4-4-2): Given, Beye, Bassong, Coloccini, Jose Enrique, Gutierrez⌐, Butt, Guthrie¹, N'Zogbia, Martins¹ (Ameobi 79), Owen¹. Subs not used: Harper, Cacapa, Duff, Geremi, S Taylor, Viduka.

21st ● Tottenham ....h **W 2–1** **Att:** 47,982. **Ref:** A Marriner — **Newcastle** (4-4-2): Given, Beye, Bassong, Coloccini, Jose Enrique⌐ (Duff⌐ 88), Gutierrez⌐, Guthrie, Butt, N'Zogbia¹, Ameobi (Viduka 30), Owen. Subs not used: Harper, Cacapa, Edgar, Geremi, Carroll.

26th ● Wigan ....a **L 2–1** **Att:** 20,266. **Ref:** M Dean — **Newcastle** (4-4-2): Given, Beye (S Taylor 38), Coloccini, Bassong⌐, N'Zogbia, Gutierrez, Butt⌐, Guthrie¹, Duff, Owen (Edgar 77), Viduka (Carroll⌐ 68). Subs not used: Harper, Xisco, Geremi, LuaLua.

28th ● Liverpool ....h **L 1–5** **Att:** 52,114. **Ref:** M Halsey — **Newcastle** (4-4-1-1): Given⌐, Edgar¹, S Taylor⌐, Coloccini, Jose Enrique (Ameobi 46), Gutierrez, Guthrie, Butt (Geremi 56), N'Zogbia, Duff, Owen (LuaLua 79). Subs not used: Harper, Xisco, Kadar, Carroll.

January

3rd ● Hull ....a **D 0–0** **Att:** 20,557. **Ref:** C Foy — **Newcastle** (4-4-2): Given, Coloccini, Bassong, S Taylor, Jose Enrique, Duff, Guthrie, Butt⌐, N'Zogbia (Gutierrez⌐ 36), Owen, Carroll. Subs not used: Harper, Xisco, Geremi, Kadar, Edgar, LuaLua.

10th ● West Ham ....h **D 2–2** **Att:** 47,571. **Ref:** A Wiley — **Newcastle** (4-4-2): Given, S Taylor, Coloccini, Bassong, Jose Enrique, Gutierrez, Guthrie⌐, Geremi (N'Zogbia 62), Duff, Owen¹, Carroll¹. Subs not used: Harper, Xisco, Kadar, Edgar, LuaLua, Donaldson.

14th ● Hull ....h **L 0–1** **Att:** 31,380. **Ref:** P Dowd — **Newcastle** (4-4-2): Given, Edgar, Bassong, Coloccini⌐, N'Zogbia, Gutierrez (LuaLua 82), Butt, Guthrie, Duff, Owen, Xisco (Carroll 76). Subs not used: Harper, S Taylor, Kadar, Donaldson, Ranger.

17th ● Blackburn ....a **L 3–0** **Att:** 25,583. **Ref:** R Styles — **Newcastle** (4-4-2): Given, Edgar¹, Coloccini, Jose Enrique, Duff (Gutierrez 79), Guthrie, Butt⌐⌐, N'Zogbia (Barton⌐ 74), Carroll, Owen. Subs not used: Harper, Xisco, S Taylor, Kadar, LuaLua.

28th ● Man City ....a **L 2–1** **Att:** 42,280. **Ref:** M Jones — **Newcastle** (4-4-2): Harper, Edgar, S Taylor⌐, Bassong, Jose Enrique, Geremi (LuaLua 90), Barton (Lovenkrands 64), Coloccini, Duff, Owen (Gutierrez⌐ 19), Carroll¹. Subs not used: Forster, Xisco, Donaldson, Inman.

February

1st ● Sunderland ....h **D 1–1** **Att:** 52,084. **Ref:** H Webb — **Newcastle** (4-4-2): Harper, S Taylor, Bassong, Coloccini (Edgar 90), Jose Enrique, Gutierrez, Butt⌐, Nolan, Duff⌐, Carroll (Lovenkrands 82), Ameobi¹. Subs not used: Krul, Xisco, Geremi, LuaLua, Donaldson.

7th ● West Brom ....a **W 2–3** **Att:** 25,817. **Ref:** C Foy — **Newcastle** (4-4-2): Harper, S Taylor¹, Bassong, Coloccini, Jose Enrique, R Taylor⌐, Nolan⌐, Butt, Duff¹, Ameobi (Viduka 80), Lovenkrands¹ (Xisco 90). Subs not used: Forster, Cacapa, Smith, Geremi, Edgar.

22nd ● Everton ....h **D 0–0** **Att:** 47,683. **Ref:** L Mason — **Newcastle** (4-4-2): Harper, S Taylor, Bassong, Coloccini, Jose Enrique, R Taylor, Butt, Nolan⌐, Duff (Gutierrez 46), Ameobi (Martins 58), Lovenkrands (Smith 77). Subs not used: Krul, Cacapa, Geremi, Viduka.

March

1st ● Bolton ....a **L 1–0** **Att:** 20,763. **Ref:** A Wiley — **Newcastle** (4-4-2): Harper, S Taylor, Coloccini, Bassong, Jose Enrique, Gutierrez⌐, R Taylor⌐, Butt⌐ (Geremi 66), Lovenkrands, Ameobi, Martins (Viduka 78). Subs not used: Forster, Cacapa, Smith, Edgar, Carroll.

● Barclays Premier League ● FA Cup ● Carling Cup ● UEFA Champions League ● UEFA Cup   ⌐ Yellow Card ⌐ Red Card

RESULTS 2008/09

4th	● Man Utd ....h	L 1–2	**Att:** 51,636. **Ref:** S Bennett — **Newcastle** (4-4-2): Harper, S Taylor▌, Coloccini, Bassong, Jose Enrique, Lovenkrands¹, R Taylor (Carroll 77), Geremi, Gutierrez▌, Martins, Smith (LuaLua 82). Subs not used: Krul, Cacapa, Butt, Ameobi, Edgar.
14th	● Hull ....a	D 1–1	**Att:** 24,914. **Ref:** H Webb — **Newcastle** (4-4-2): Harper, S Taylor¹, Coloccini▌, Bassong, Jose Enrique, Smith▌ (R Taylor 75), Butt, Geremi▌, Gutierrez, Owen (Ameobi 73), Martins. Subs not used: Forster, Duff, Lovenkrands, Edgar, Carroll.
21st	● Arsenal ....h	L 1–3	**Att:** 49,972. **Ref:** M Halsey — **Newcastle** (4-4-1-1): Harper, S Taylor (Owen 65), Coloccini, Bassong (Beye 38), Jose Enrique, R Taylor, Butt, Nolan, Duff, Lovenkrands (Ameobi 79), Martins¹. Subs not used: Krul, Smith, Gutierrez, Geremi.

April

4th	● Chelsea ....h	L 0–2	**Att:** 52,112. **Ref:** R Styles — **Newcastle** (4-4-2): Harper, R Taylor, Beye, Coloccini, Jose Enrique, Gutierrez, Nolan (Guthrie 69), Butt, Lovenkrands (Duff 44), Owen, Martins (Carroll 81). Subs not used: Forster, Smith, Geremi, Edgar.
11th	● Stoke ....a	D 1–1	**Att:** 27,500. **Ref:** C Foy — **Newcastle** (4-4-2): Harper, Edgar, Bassong▌, Beye, R Taylor ▌, Guthrie (Gutierrez 63), Nolan, Butt, Duff, Owen, Ameobi (Carroll¹ 70). Subs not used: Krul, Coloccini, Smith, Geremi, Ranger.
19th	● Tottenham ....a	L 1–0	**Att:** 35,850. **Ref:** M Halsey — **Newcastle** (4-4-2): Harper, R Taylor▌, S Taylor▌ (Smith 46), Bassong, Beye, Duff, Nolan (Viduka 61), Butt, Gutierrez, Owen, Carroll (Martins 60). Subs not used: Krul, Guthrie, Ameobi, Edgar.
27th	● Portsmouth ....h	D 0–0	**Att:** 47,481. **Ref:** M Riley — **Newcastle** (4-3-3): Harper, Beye, Coloccini, Bassong▌, Jose Enrique (Guthrie 28), Smith, Butt (Gutierrez 71), Duff, Viduka (Carroll¹ 64), Martins, Owen. Subs not used: Krul, Barton, Lovenkrands, Edgar.

May

3rd	● Liverpool ....a	L 3–0	**Att:** 44,121. **Ref:** P Dowd — **Newcastle** (4-2-3-1): Harper, Beye, Coloccini▌, Bassong, Duff, Smith▌, Butt, Martins (Owen 80), Barton▌, Lovenkrands (Gutierrez 46), Viduka (Nolan 80). Subs not used: Krul, Guthrie, Edgar, Carroll.
11th	● Middlesbrough ....h	W 3–1	**Att:** 51,252. **Ref:** M Dean — **Newcastle** (4-4-2): Harper, Beye, S Taylor¹, Bassong, Duff▌, Guthrie, Butt▌, Nolan▌, Gutierrez (Lovenkrands¹ 65), Owen (Martins¹ 70), Viduka (Carroll 87). Subs not used: Krul, Coloccini, R Taylor, LuaLua.
16th	● Fulham ....h	L 0–1	**Att:** 52,114. **Ref:** H Webb — **Newcastle** (4-4-2): Harper, Beye, S Taylor, Bassong▌, Duff, Guthrie (R Taylor 62), Butt, Nolan, Gutierrez (Lovenkrands 76), Martins, Viduka (Carroll 80). Subs not used: Krul, Coloccini, Smith, Ameobi.
24th	● Aston Villa...........................a	L 1–0	**Att:** 42,585. **Ref:** C Foy — **Newcastle** (4-4-2): Harper, Coloccini, S Taylor▌, Edgar▌, Duff, Guthrie, Nolan (Owen 66), Butt, Lovenkrands (Jose Enrique 57), Viduka (Ameobi 75), Martins. Subs not used: Krul, Smith, Gutierrez, R Taylor.

● Barclays Premier League ● FA Cup ● Carling Cup ● UEFA Champions League ● UEFA Cup   ▌Yellow Card ▌Red Card

Newcastle United manager Alan Shearer watches his team drop out of the Barclays Premier League with defeat at Aston Villa

NEWCASTLE UNITED

BARCLAYS PREMIER LEAGUE GOALKEEPER STATS

Player	Minutes on pitch	Appearances	Match starts	Completed matches	Sub appearances	Subbed off	SAVES BREAKDOWN								Clean sheets	Goals conceded	Minutes since conceding	Save %	PENALTIES			Yellow cards	Red cards
							Saved with feet	Punched	Parried	Tipped over	Fumbled	Tipped round	Caught	Blocked					Saved	Resulting in goals	Opposition miss		
Shay Given	2092	22	22	22	0	0	1	9	21	2	0	9	55	0	4	37	101	65.19	1	8	0	2	0
Steve Harper	1532	16	16	16	0	0	2	11	13	7	0	2	52	1	2	22	59	80.87	0	0	0	0	0

BARCLAYS PREMIER LEAGUE OUTFIELD PLAYER STATS

Player	Minutes on pitch	Appearances	Match starts	Completed matches	Substitute appearances	Subbed off	Goals scored	Minutes since scoring	Assists	Shots on target	Shots off target	Crosses	Defensive clearances	Defensive blocks	Fouls committed	Free-kicks won	Caught offside	Yellow cards	Red cards
Shola Ameobi	1338	22	14	6	8	8	4	396	4	19	18	9	3	0	53	28	12	1	0
Joey Barton	471	9	6	3	3	2	1	450	1	2	2	4	2	0	9	12	0	2	1
Sebastien Bassong	2527	30	26	22	4	2	0	–	0	3	9		32	14	22	26	0	3	2
Habib Beye	1998	23	22	19	1	2	0	–	1	2		12	7	7	20	19	0	3	1
Nicky Butt	3035	33	33	28	0	4	0	–	1	9	13	22	30	10	48	43	1	7	1
Claudio Cacapa	385	6	4	3	2	1	0	–	1	1	1	0	4	0	3	6	0	0	0
Andrew Carroll	588	14	5	3	9	2	3	128	1	7	10	1	3	0	13	11	3	2	0
Fabricio Coloccini	3239	34	34	33	0	1	0	–	0	1	5	3	56	18	28	27	0	4	0
Damien Duff	2610	30	28	25	2	3	2	950	2	20	5	88	3	2	16	34	5	4	0
David Edgar	647	11	7	4	4	2	1	438	1	1	0	1	7	5	12	3	0	2	1
Geremi	1076	15	11	5	4	6	0	–	3	8	8	56	7	1	12	13	2	2	0
Nacho Gonzalez	47	2	0	0	2	0	0	–	0	0	0	0	0	0	0	0	0	0	0
Danny Guthrie	2055	24	21	17	3	3	2	699	3	14	7	27	4	2	16	25	1	3	1
Jonas Gutierrez	2308	30	23	16	7	7	0	–	4	11	7	47	6	5	26	89	1	6	0
Jose Enrique	2078	26	24	18	2	6	0	–	2	1	3	27	12	7	9	19	0	1	0
Peter Lovenkrands	686	12	8	2	4	6	3	84	0	11	4	9	1	0	4	10	3	0	0
Kazenga LuaLua	31	3	0	0	3	0	0	–	0	1	0	0	0	0	0	1	0	0	0
Obafemi Martins	1859	24	21	10	3	11	8	213	3	29	34	25	2	3	14	30	16	1	0
James Milner	191	2	2	2	0	0	0	602	0	5	2	8	0	2	1	4	1	0	0
Charles N'Zogbia	1397	18	14	12	4	2	1	708	2	13	7	35	2	0	25	20	1	2	0
Kevin Nolan	828	11	10	6	1	3	0	–	1	4	4	2	3	1	10	2	1	2	1
Michael Owen	2003	28	21	16	7	5	8	784	0	22	12	5	0	0	5	33	10	0	0
Alan Smith	410	6	4	2	2	2	0	–	0	1	3	1	1	0	12	0	0	2	0
Ryan Taylor	804	10	8	7	2	1	0	1252	1	2	7	38	1	2	14	7	0	4	0
Steven Taylor	2417	27	25	23	2	2	4	277	1	11	4	5	31	26	27	18	3	6	0
Mark Viduka	639	12	6	0	6	6	0	–	2	4	5	1	2	1	10	8	7	0	0
Xisco	308	5	3	3	2	0	1	225	0	3	3	2	0	0	4	2	3	0	0

SEASON TOTALS

Goals scored	40
Goals conceded	59
Clean sheets	7
Shots on target	201
Shots off target	169
Shots per goal	9.25
Pens awarded	5
Pens scored	4
Pens conceded	9
Offsides	70
Corners	169
Crosses	437
Players used	29
Fouls committed	414
Free-kicks won	502

CARDS RECEIVED

59 **8**

SEQUENCES

Wins	2
(on two occasions)	
Losses	4
(30/08/08–27/09/08)	
Draws	4
(15/11/08–06/12/08)	
Undefeated	6
(15/11/08–21/12/08)	
Without win	10
(22/02/09–03/05/09)	
Undefeated home	6
(20/10/08–21/12/08)	
Undefeated away	3
(22/11/08–14/12/08)	
Without scoring	3
(19/04/09–03/05/09)	
Without conceding	2
(22/11/08–29/11/08)	
Scoring	10
(13/09/08–15/11/08)	
Conceding	8
(on two occasions)	

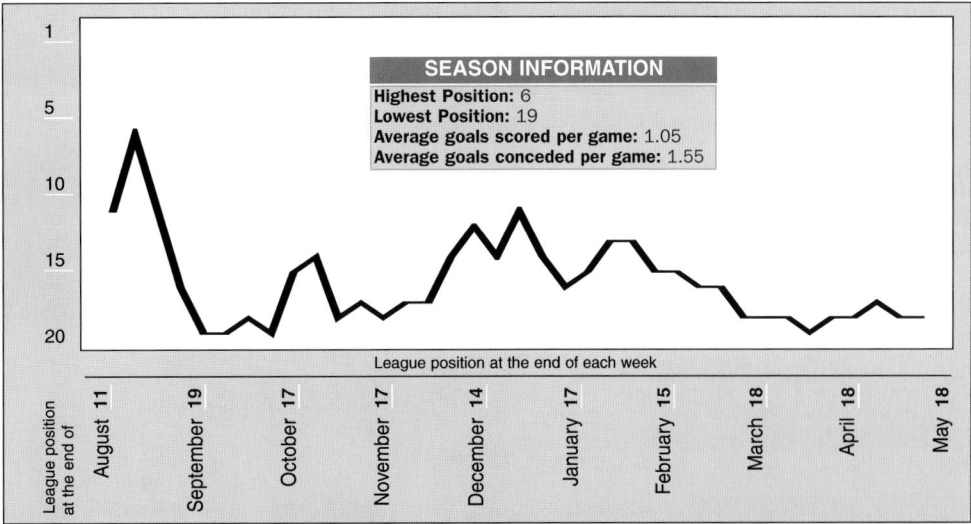

SEASON INFORMATION
Highest Position: 6
Lowest Position: 19
Average goals scored per game: 1.05
Average goals conceded per game: 1.55

League position at the end of each week

League position at the end of: August 11, September 19, October 17, November 17, December 14, January 17, February 15, March 18, April 18, May 18

MATCH RECORDS

Goals scored per match

		W	D	L	Pts
Failed to score	12	0	4	8	4
Scored 1 goal	15	1	4	10	7
Scored 2 goals	8	3	5	0	14
Scored 3 goals	3	3	0	0	9
Scored 4+ goals	0	0	0	0	0

Goals conceded per match

		W	D	L	Pts
Clean sheet	7	3	4	0	13
Conceded 1 goal	11	3	4	4	13
Conceded 2 goals	14	1	5	8	8
Conceded 3 goals	5	0	0	5	0
Conceded 4+ goals	1	0	0	1	0

GOALS SCORED/CONCEDED PER FIVE-MINUTE INTERVALS

Goals For	1	5	1	1	2	1	0	1	5	1	2	3	1	2	2	3	4	5
Goals Against	3	2	1	5	4	4	6	3	3	2	3	5	4	4	3	2	0	5
Mins	5	10	15	20	25	30	35	40	45	50	55	60	65	70	75	80	85	90

QUICK-FIRE GOALS

From the start of a match
Damien Duff
(v West Brom) 1:02

By a substitute after coming on
Obafemi Martins
(v Middlesbrough) 1:05

LAST-GASP GOALS

From the start of a match
Damien Duff (v Tottenham)
89:54

By a substitute after coming on
Peter Lovenkrands
(v Middlesbrough) 20:38

GOAL DETAILS

How the goals were struck

SCORED		CONCEDED
23	Right foot	30
7	Left foot	19
10	Headers	10
0	Others	0

How the goals were struck

SCORED		CONCEDED
22	Open play	32
9	Cross	7
4	Corner	4
4	Penalties	8
0	Direct from free-kick	2
0	Free-kick	4
1	Own goals	2

Distance from goal

SCORED		CONCEDED
18	6yds	20
20	18yds	32
2	18+yds	7

PORTSMOUTH

CLUB SUMMARY

FORMED	1898
MANAGER	TBC
GROUND	Fratton Park
CAPACITY	20,600
NICKNAME	Pompey
WEBSITE	www.pompeyfc.co.uk

The New Football Pools PLAYER OF THE SEASON — Nadir Belhadj

OVERALL

P	W	D	L	F	A	GD
49	13	15	21	51	73	-22

BARCLAYS PREMIER LEAGUE

Pos	P	W	D	L	F	A	GD	Pts
14	38	10	11	17	38	57	-19	41

HOME

Pos	P	W	D	L	F	A	GD	Pts
13	19	8	3	8	26	29	-3	27

AWAY

Pos	P	W	D	L	F	A	GD	Pts
15	19	2	8	9	12	28	-16	14

CUP PROGRESS DETAILS

Competition	Round reached	Knocked out by
FA Cup	R4	Swansea
UEFA Cup	Group stage	–
Carling Cup	R3	Chelsea

BIGGEST WIN (ALL COMPS)
3–0 on two occasions

BIGGEST DEFEAT (ALL COMPS)
21/09/08 0–6 v Man City **PREM**

THE PLAYER WITH THE MOST

Shots on target
Peter Crouch 43

Shots off target
Peter Crouch 43

Shots without scoring
Papa Bouba Diop 17

Assists
Peter Crouch 5

Offsides
Peter Crouch 26

Fouls
Papa Bouba Diop 46

Fouls without a card
Armand Traore............................... 7

Free-kicks won
Peter Crouch 40

Defensive clearances
Sylvain Distin............................... 66

actim INDEX for the 2008/09 Barclays Premier League Season

Rank	Player	Pts
50	Peter Crouch	392
58	David James	381
61	Sylvain Distin	377
79	Sol Campbell	356
109	Glen Johnson	314

ATTENDANCE RECORD

High	Low	Average
20,540	18,111	19,830
v Man Utd (25/08/2008)	v Blackburn (30/11/2008)	

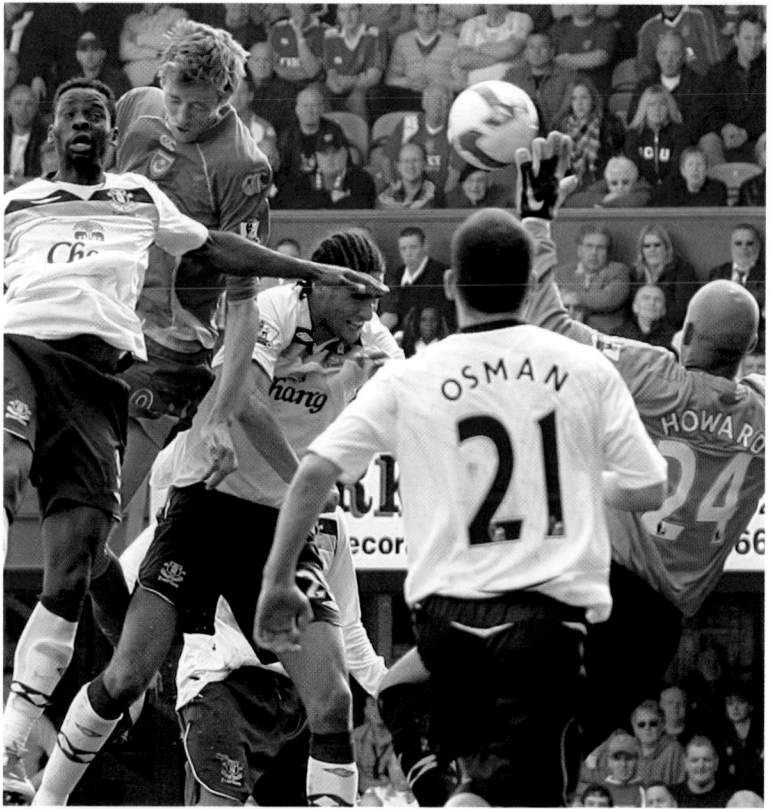

CLOCKWISE FROM TOP: Peter Crouch heads in his second of the afternoon in a home win over Everton; veteran David James guards the posts; Tony Adams looks forlorn after seeing his side knocked out of the FA Cup at the fourth-round stage by Swansea; Glen Johnson fires in a superb goal against Hull

PORTSMOUTH had three managers over the course of a season in which they limped over the finishing line to ensure survival in the Barclays Premier League.

The start of the campaign was a time of optimism, the club's previous match having been the FA Cup final win over Cardiff, a historic victory for the club and a first trophy for boss Harry Redknapp. Ahead of the season, there were even those who wondered if their FA Cup glory could be the precursor to a push for European qualification through the Barclays Premier League.

But Pompey were not helped by a tricky start to the season, with defeats to Chelsea and Manchester United in their opening two matches. However, it looked like business as usual when they went up to Goodison Park and convincingly beat Everton.

Getting thrashed at Manchester City, with Robinho running riot in a 6–0 win for Mark Hughes' men, was a setback but there were still hopes of turning the season around. After all, the England squads selected by boss Fabio Capello pointed to the quality available to Redknapp. David James was the country's first-choice goalkeeper, while Glen Johnson, Peter Crouch and Jermain Defoe were also options.

The turning point came when top-flight rivals Tottenham sacked Juande Ramos and approached Pompey about recruiting their manager. Spurs were bottom and had two points from eight games and felt they needed Redknapp's golden touch. After turning down the chance to manage Newcastle, mainly due to the distance away from his family home on the south coast, Redknapp felt this opportunity was perfect.

Redknapp, predictably, galvanised Spurs' season, while Pompey were left to pick up the pieces. 'We tried everything we could to keep Harry at Portsmouth, but he made it clear that despite the great success he had here at Fratton Park, apparently Spurs was one of the only clubs he would consider leaving for,' said chief executive Peter Storrie.

Portsmouth decided to promote from within and Tony Adams, Redknapp's assistant for two years, became the club's new boss. The appointment raised some concerns as the former Arsenal captain's managerial record included a relegation at Wycombe, and he faced a tough task in replacing a club legend.

Redknapp had had the total respect of his squad. He rescued most of them and turned their careers around, while Adams was a rookie who had to raise morale and salvage something from the season. He was also not helped by financial insecurity at the club, with Redknapp suggesting on his departure that owner Alexandre Gaydamak was looking to sell. January was a disaster for Adams as he wanted to keep his best players, only to see Defoe and Lassana Diarra sold during the transfer window. The manager had his midfield general taken away from him, with Diarra going to Real Madrid, and also the man who provided the goals, with Defoe returning to Spurs – who had sold him to Pompey just 12 months previously.

As results failed to improve, Adams' tenure was ended after just 22 matches and three months. His final game was against Liverpool at Fratton Park, a match in which Pompey were ahead with five minutes to go. But Fernando Torres came off the bench to set up the equaliser and then grab the winner for Rafael Benitez's men, with Adams later admitting that he was not decisive enough and should have moved quicker to protect his side's lead.

With the club deep in trouble, former Nottingham Forest boss Paul Hart was put in charge on a temporary basis and a change of fortunes followed, as so often happens when a new manager comes in. In Hart's first 11 games, Pompey only lost to Chelsea, Manchester United and Arsenal.

Steady improvement was the key with wins against Manchester City, Everton and Bolton adding much-needed points to Portsmouth's tally as their rivals continued to struggle. Safety was assured even before they beat Sunderland 3–1 in their penultimate match of the season, with the win taking them above the 40-point mark.

The club has still to decide on a permanent successor to Adams, but the club's future is looking healthy with billionaire businessman Dr Sulaiman Al Fahim set to buy out Gaydamak.

> **As results failed to improve, Adams' tenure was ended after 22 matches and three months**

PORTSMOUTH

August

10th ● Man Utd ....n D 0–0 **Att:** 84,808. **Ref:** P Walton — **Portsmouth** (4-4-2): James, Johnson, Campbell, Distin▌, Hreidarsson (Lauren 79), Diop, Pedro Mendes, (Mvuemba 75), Diarra, Kranjcar (Utaka 60), Crouch, Defoe. Subs not used: Ashdown, Sahar, Cranie, Traore (Lost 0–3 on pens)

17th ● Chelsea ....a L 4–0 **Att:** 41,468. **Ref:** M Dean — **Portsmouth** (4-4-2): James▌, Kaboul, Campbell, Distin, Hreidarsson, Johnson, Diarra (Mvuemba 68), Diop, Kranjcar (Thomas 73), Defoe, Crouch. Subs not used: Ashdown, Lauren, Utaka, Cranie, Traore.

25th ● Man Utd ....h L 0–1 **Att:** 20,540. **Ref:** C Foy — **Portsmouth** (3-5-2): James, Kaboul, Campbell, Distin, Johnson, Diop▌, Davis (Utaka 66), Diarra, Traore (Thomas 56), Crouch, Defoe▌. Subs not used: Ashdown, Lauren, Hreidarsson, Mvuemba, Sahar.

30th ● Everton ....a W 0–3 **Att:** 34,418. **Ref:** M Halsey — **Portsmouth** (4-4-2): James, Johnson[1], Kaboul, Campbell, Distin, Diop, Davis (Mvuemba 90), Diarra, Traore (Hreidarsson 77), Crouch, Defoe[2] (Utaka 76). Subs not used: Ashdown, Lauren, Sahar, D Traore.

September

13th ● Middlesbrough ....h W 2–1 **Att:** 19,425. **Ref:** S Attwell — **Portsmouth** (3-5-2): James, Kaboul (Belhadj 46), Campbell, Distin, Johnson▌, Diop (Utaka 46), Davis, Diarra, Traore (Hreidarsson 84), Crouch, Defoe[2]. Subs not used: Ashdown, Nugent, Pamarot, Mvuemba.

18th ● Guimaraes ....h W 2–0 **Att:** 19,612. **Ref:** K Kircher — **Portsmouth** (4-4-2): James, Johnson, Campbell, Distin, Belhadj, Utaka (Diop 73), Diarra[1], Davis, Traore (Hreidarsson 90), Crouch (Kanu 90), Defoe[1]. Subs not used: Ashdown, Kaboul, Mvuemba, Little.

21st ● Man City ....a L 6–0 **Att:** 40,238. **Ref:** A Wiley — **Portsmouth** (4-4-2): James, Johnson (Pamarot 82), Distin, Campbell, Belhadj, Diarra▌, Davis (Diop 33), Kaboul (Utaka 46), Traore, Crouch, Defoe. Subs not used: Ashdown, Hreidarsson, Mvuemba, Kanu.

24th ● Chelsea ....h L 0–4 **Att:** 15,339. **Ref:** S Bennett — **Portsmouth** (4-5-1): James, Johnson▌, Pamarot, Distin, Hreidarsson▌, Utaka, Mvuemba, Kaboul, Hughes▌ (Wilson 80), Belhadj (A Traore 69), Crouch (Kanu 69). Subs not used: Ashdown, Defoe, D Traore, Little.

28th ● Tottenham ....h W 2–0 **Att:** 20,352. **Ref:** M Dean — **Portsmouth** (4-4-2): James, Johnson, Campbell, Distin, Belhadj▌, Little (Utaka 61), Diarra▌▌, Hughes▌, Traore, Crouch▌, Defoe[1] (Kaboul 89). Subs not used: Ashdown, Hreidarsson, Pamarot, Mvuemba, Kanu.

October

2nd ● Guimaraes ....a D 2–2 **Att:** 18,000. **Ref:** S Dereli — **Portsmouth** (4-4-2): James, Johnson, Distin, Campbell, Pamarot, Davis (Mvuemba 73), Diarra, Hughes (Belhadj 99), Traore, Crouch[2], Defoe (Kaboul 106). Subs not used: Ashdown, Hreidarsson, Little, Kanu.

5th ● Stoke ....h W 2–1 **Att:** 19,248. **Ref:** A Marriner — **Portsmouth** (4-4-2): James, Johnson, Campbell, Distin, Belhadj, Diop, Davis, Hughes, Traore (Hreidarsson 90), Crouch[1], Defoe[1]. Subs not used: Ashdown, Little, Kanu, Kaboul, Mvuemba, Pamarot.

18th ● Aston Villa........................a D 0–0 **Att:** 37,660. **Ref:** M Riley — **Portsmouth** (4-4-2): James, Johnson▌, Campbell, Distin, Traore (Belhadj 78), Little (Utaka 71), Davis▌, Diop▌, Pamarot, Defoe (Mvuemba 82), Crouch. Subs not used: Ashdown, Hreidarsson, Thomas, Kanu.

23rd ● Braga ....a L 3–0 **Att:** 12,000. **Ref:** D Ceferin — **Portsmouth** (4-4-2): James, Campbell, Pamarot▌, Traore (Kanu 62), Distin, Davis, Diop, Hreidarsson (Belhadj▌ 46), Little, Defoe, Crouch. Subs not used: Ashdown, Utaka, Mvuemba, Hughes, Wilson.

26th ● Fulham ....h D 1–1 **Att:** 19,233. **Ref:** M Halsey — **Portsmouth** (4-4-2): James, Pamarot, Kaboul, Distin, Belhadj, Diop, Diarra (Mvuemba 83), Hughes, A Traore (Kranjcar 84), Crouch[1], Defoe. Subs not used: Ashdown, Hreidarsson, Utaka, Kanu, D Traore

29th ● Liverpool ....a L 1–0 **Att:** 43,378. **Ref:** S Tanner — **Portsmouth** (4-5-1): James, Pamarot, Kaboul, Distin, Belhadj, Utaka (Defoe 85), Davis, Diop▌, Diarra (Hughes 80), Traore (Kranjcar 64), Crouch. Subs not used: Ashdown, Kanu, Hreidarsson.

November

1st ● Wigan ....h L 1–2 **Att:** 18,416. **Ref:** P Walton — **Portsmouth** (4-4-2): James, Johnson, Campbell, Distin, Belhadj (Pamarot 90), Diop (Utaka 73), Diarra, Davis, Traore (Kranjcar[1] 46), Crouch, Defoe. Subs not used: Ashdown, Kaboul, Hughes, Kanu.

8th ● Sunderland ....a W 1–2 **Att:** 37,712. **Ref:** S Bennett — **Portsmouth** (4-4-2): James, Johnson, Campbell, Distin, Belhadj[1], Pamarot, Davis, Diarra▌, Kranjcar (Utaka 75), Defoe[1] (Hughes 90), Crouch (Kanu 69). Subs not used: Ashdown, Kaboul, Diop, Traore.

15th ● West Ham ....a D 0–0 **Att:** 32,328. **Ref:** M Atkinson — **Portsmouth** (4-4-2): James, Johnson, Kaboul, Distin, Pamarot▌, Diop, Davis, Diarra (Traore 19), Belhadj, Crouch (Kanu 75), Defoe. Subs not used: Ashdown, Hreidarsson, Nugent, Mvuemba, Hughes.

22nd ● Hull ....h D 2–2 **Att:** 20,240. **Ref:** S Attwell — **Portsmouth** (4-4-2): James, Johnson[1], Kaboul, Distin, Pamarot, Diop▌, Davis▌, Hughes (Nugent 58), Belhadj (Traore 58), Crouch[1], Utaka (Kanu 74). Subs not used: Ashdown, Hreidarsson, Mvuemba, Little.

27th ● AC Milan ....h D 2–2 **Att:** 20,403. **Ref:** S Gumienny — **Portsmouth** (4-4-2): James, Johnson, Kaboul[1], Distin, Belhadj, Little (Mvuemba 66), Diop, Hughes▌, Traore, Crouch, Kanu[1] (Davis 81). Subs not used: Ashdown, Hreidarsson, Pamarot, Wilson.

30th ● Blackburn ....h W 3–2 **Att:** 18,111. **Ref:** M Halsey — **Portsmouth** (4-4-2): James, Johnson, Distin, Pamarot, Belhadj, Little (Kranjcar 46), Diop, Hughes, Traore (Davis[1] 76), Crouch[1] (Kanu 69), Defoe[1]. Subs not used: Ashdown, Hreidarsson, Mvuemba, Nugent.

December

4th ● Wolfsburg ....a L 3–2 **Att:** 21,015. **Ref:** I Bebek — **Portsmouth** (4-4-1-1): James, Johnson, Campbell, Distin, Belhadj (Pamarot▌ 46), Mvuemba[1] (Crouch 66), Davis, Hughes, Traore, Kranjcar (Kanu 77), Defoe▌▌. Subs not used: Ashdown, Hreidarsson, Diop, Little.

7th ● West Brom ....a D 1–1 **Att:** 24,964. **Ref:** M Dean — **Portsmouth** (4-3-1-2): James, Johnson▌, Campbell, Distin, Pamarot, Davis, Diop▌, Belhadj (Little 46), Kranjcar, Defoe, Crouch[1] (Kanu 90). Subs not used: Ashdown, Hreidarsson, Nugent, Mvuemba, Mills.

14th ● Newcastle ....h L 0–3 **Att:** 19,416. **Ref:** C Foy — **Portsmouth** (4-4-2): James▌, Pamarot, Campbell, Distin▌, Belhadj, Mvuemba (Traore 58), Davis▌, Hughes (Kanu 70), Kranjcar, Crouch, Defoe▌. Subs not used: Ashdown, Lauren, Hreidarsson, Nugent, Wilson.

17th ● Heerenveen ....h W 3–0 **Att:** 19,612. **Ref:** R Havrilla — **Portsmouth** (4-4-2): James, Wilson, Pamarot, Hreidarsson[1], Belhadj, Mvuemba, Diop (Davis 84), Hughes, Traore (Little 63), Crouch[2], Kanu. Subs not used: James, Defoe, Distin, Kranjcar.

20th ● Bolton ....a L 2–1 **Att:** 19,884. **Ref:** M Atkinson — **Portsmouth** (4-4-2): James, Pamarot, Campbell, Distin, Hreidarsson, Diop (Nugent 75), Davis, Hughes (Diarra 63), Kranjcar, Defoe▌, Crouch[1]. Subs not used: Ashdown, Little, Kanu, Traore, Wilson.

26th ● West Ham ....h L 1–4 **Att:** 20,102. **Ref:** S Bennett — **Portsmouth** (4-4-2): James, Wilson▌, Campbell, Distin, Belhadj[1], Little (Traore 71), Davis, Hughes, Kranjcar, Crouch, Defoe (Kanu 73). Subs not used: Ashdown, Hreidarsson, Diop, Nugent, Pamarot.

28th ● Arsenal ....a L 1–0 **Att:** 60,092. **Ref:** A Wiley — **Portsmouth** (4-5-1): James, Wilson, Campbell, Distin, Belhadj, Nugent (Defoe 88), Diop (Pamarot 90), Davis, Hughes▌ (Mvuemba 50), Kranjcar, Crouch. Subs not used: Ashdown, Hreidarsson, Little, Kanu.

January

3rd ● Bristol City ....h D 0–0 **Att:** 14,446. **Ref:** P Dowd — **Portsmouth** (4-1-4-1): James, Wilson, Distin, Campbell, Belhadj▌, Cranie (Pamarot 82), Nugent, Mvuemba, Davis, Kranjcar, Crouch. Subs not used: Begovic, Little, Kanu, Lauren, Hreidarsson, Traore.

13th ● Bristol City ....a W 0–2 **Att:** 14,302. **Ref:** M Jones — **Portsmouth** (4-4-1-1): James, Johnson▌, Distin, Campbell, Kaboul▌, Wilson, Nugent (Utaka 66), Traore (Hreidarsson 86), Belhadj, Kranjcar (Kanu 90). Subs not used: Begovic, Pamarot, Mvuemba, Little.

18th ● Tottenham ....a D 1–1 **Att:** 36,011. **Ref:** S Bennett — **Portsmouth** (4-5-1): James, Johnson, Campbell, Distin, Belhadj, Nugent[1] (Utaka 73), Davis▌, Kaboul▌ (Wilson 88), Kranjcar (Hreidarsson 90), Traore, Crouch. Subs not used: Begovic, Pamarot, Little, Kanu.

24th ● Swansea ....h L 0–2 **Att:** 17,357. **Ref:** A Marriner — **Portsmouth** (4-4-1-1): James, Cranie, Campbell, Distin▌, Belhadj▌, Nugent (Kanu 46), Hughes (Kaboul 84), Davis, Traore (Hreidarsson 46), Pennant, Crouch. Subs not used: Begovic, Pamarot, Utaka, Mvuemba.

● Barclays Premier League ● FA Cup ● Carling Cup ● UEFA Champions League ● UEFA Cup ● FA Community Shield   ▌ Yellow Card ▌▌ Red Card

BARCLAYS PREMIER LEAGUE

RESULTS 2008/09

27th	● Aston Villa............................h	L 0–1	**Att:** 19,073. **Ref:** P Walton — **Portsmouth** (4-4-2): James, Johnson▮, Campbell (Kaboul 46), Distin, Hreidarsson, Pennant, Davis, Mullins, Belhadj▮, Crouch, Kanu (Utaka 74). Subs not used: Begovic, Nugent, Pamarot, Mvuemba, Traore.	
31st	● Fulham ....a	L 3–1	**Att:** 23,722. **Ref:** A Wiley — **Portsmouth** (4-4-2): James, Johnson, Kaboul (Pamarot 76), Distin, Hreidarsson, Pennant, Davis, Mullins▮, Traore (Utaka 63), Kanu (Nugent¹ 46), Crouch. Subs not used: Begovic, Lauren, Mvuemba, Little.	

February
7th	● Liverpool ....h	L 2–3	**Att:** 20,524. **Ref:** H Webb — **Portsmouth** (4-4-2): James, Johnson, Campbell, Distin, Hreidarsson▮, Basinas, Davis, Mullins (Kranjcar 46), Belhadj, Crouch, Nugent¹. Subs not used: Begovic, Lauren, Mvuemba, Pamarot, Kanu, Gekas.	
14th	● Man City ....h	W 2–0	**Att:** 20,018. **Ref:** L Probert — **Portsmouth** (4-4-2): James, Johnson¹, Campbell, Distin, Hreidarsson▮¹, Pennant (Belhadj 86), Basinas (Mullins 67), Davis, Kranjcar, Crouch, Nugent. Subs not used: Begovic, Pamarot, Utaka, Kanu, Gekas.	
21st	● Stoke ....a	D 2–2	**Att:** 26,354. **Ref:** M Jones — **Portsmouth** (4-4-2): James, Johnson▮, Campbell, Distin, Hreidarsson▮, Pennant, Basinas (Mullins 71), Davis▮, Kranjcar¹ (Kanu 89), Crouch, Nugent (Belhadj 89). Subs not used: Begovic, Kaboul, Pamarot, Utaka.	

March
3rd	● Chelsea ....h	L 0–1	**Att:** 20,326. **Ref:** P Dowd — **Portsmouth** (4-4-2): James, Johnson, Campbell, Distin, Hreidarsson, Pennant (Utaka 70), Mullins, Davis, Kranjcar, Crouch, Nugent. Subs not used: Begovic, Kanu, Kaboul, Pamarot, Basinas, Belhadj.	
14th	● Middlesbrough ....a	D 1–1	**Att:** 24,281. **Ref:** M Atkinson — **Portsmouth** (4-4-2): James, Johnson▮, Campbell, Distin, Hreidarsson, Pennant (Belhadj▮ 36), Davis, Mullins, Kranjcar (Pamarot 90), Crouch¹, Nugent▮ (Hughes 70). Subs not used: Begovic, Kaboul, Utaka, Kanu.	
21st	● Everton ....h	W 2–1	**Att:** 20,388. **Ref:** P Walton — **Portsmouth** (4-4-1-1): James, Kaboul▮, Campbell, Distin, Hreidarsson▮, Johnson, Davis, Mullins, Nugent (Kanu 74), Kranjcar, Crouch². Subs not used: Begovic, Pamarot, Utaka, Hughes, Basinas, Belhadj.	

April
4th	● Hull ....a	D 0–0	**Att:** 24,802. **Ref:** C Foy — **Portsmouth** (4-4-1-1): James, Kaboul, Campbell, Distin, Hreidarsson, Johnson▮, Mullins, Hughes, Nugent (Kanu 64), Kranjcar (Belhadj 76), Crouch▮. Subs not used: Begovic, Pennant, Basinas, Pamarot, Utaka.	
11th	● West Brom ....h	D 2–2	**Att:** 20,376. **Ref:** M Dean — **Portsmouth** (4-5-1): James, Kaboul▮, Campbell, Distin, Hreidarsson▮, Pennant (Gekas 90), Mullins, Hughes, Nugent (Kanu▮ 64), Kranjcar▮, Crouch. Subs not used: Begovic, Pamarot, Utaka, Basinas.	
18th	● Bolton ....h	W 1–0	**Att:** 20,158. **Ref:** P Dowd — **Portsmouth** (4-4-1-1): James, Kaboul (Pennant 90), Campbell, Distin▮, Hreidarsson, Johnson, Davis, Mullins, Nugent (Kanu¹ 71), Kranjcar▮ (Belhadj 77), Crouch. Subs not used: Begovic, Pamarot, Utaka, Hughes.	
22nd	● Man Utd ....a	L 2–0	**Att:** 74,895. **Ref:** P Walton — **Portsmouth** (4-4-2): James, Johnson, Campbell, Distin, Hreidarsson, Davis, Mullins, Hughes, Belhadj, Nugent (Pennant 46), Crouch. Subs not used: Begovic, Pamarot, Utaka, Cranie, Kanu, Basinas.	
27th	● Newcastle ....a	D 0–0	**Att:** 47,481. **Ref:** M Riley — **Portsmouth** (4-1-4-1): James, Johnson▮, Campbell, Distin, Hreidarsson▮, Davis, Belhadj, Hughes, Mullins, Nugent (Pennant 65), Crouch. Subs not used: Begovic, Pamarot, Utaka, Cranie, Kanu, Basinas.	

May
2nd	● Arsenal ....h	L 0–3	**Att:** 20,418. **Ref:** L Mason — **Portsmouth** (4-5-1): James, Pamarot▮, Campbell, Distin, Hreidarsson (Kanu 46), Pennant (Utaka 46), Davis▮, Hughes, Mullins, Belhadj, Crouch. Subs not used: Begovic, Primus, Nugent, Basinas, Cranie.	
9th	● Blackburn ....a	L 2–0	**Att:** 24,234. **Ref:** M Riley — **Portsmouth** (4-5-1): James, Kaboul (Pennant 64), Campbell, Distin, Hreidarsson, Johnson▮, Hughes (Kanu 53), Davis, Mullins, Belhadj (Utaka 53), Crouch. Subs not used: Begovic, Nugent, Basinas, Cranie.	
18th	● Sunderland ....h	W 3–1	**Att:** 20,398. **Ref:** A Wiley — **Portsmouth** (4-4-2): Begovic, Johnson, Campbell, Distin, Hreidarsson, Utaka▮, Davis, Mullins, Hughes (Traore¹ 46), Kanu (Kaboul 46), Crouch (Primus 90). Subs not used: Ashdown, Nugent, Basinas, Belhadj.	
24th	● Wigan ....a	L 1–0	**Att:** 17,696. **Ref:** P Dowd — **Portsmouth** (4-4-1-1): Begovic, Kaboul (Kanu 72), Campbell, Distin, Hreidarsson▮, Pennant (Thomas▮ 72), Hughes▮, Mullins, Traore, Utaka, Crouch▮. Subs not used: Ashdown, Primus, Pamarot, Cranie, Basinas.	

● Barclays Premier League ● FA Cup ● Carling Cup ● UEFA Champions League ● UEFA Cup ● FA Community Shield   ▮ Yellow Card ▮ Red Card

Sean Davis and Nadir Belhadj enjoy a goal against Bolton; Sol Campbell shakes off Sunderland's Steed Malbranque

PORTSMOUTH

BARCLAYS PREMIER LEAGUE GOALKEEPER STATS

Player	Minutes on pitch	Appearances	Match starts	Completed matches	Sub appearances	Subbed off	SAVES BREAKDOWN Saved with feet	Punched	Parried	Tipped over	Fumbled	Tipped round	Caught	Blocked	Clean sheets	Goals conceded	Minutes since conceding	Save %	PENALTIES Saved	Resulting in goals	Opposition miss	Yellow cards	Red cards
Asmir Begovic 190	2	2	2	0	0	0	0	2	1	0	0	12	0	0	2	68	88.24	0	0	0	0	0
David James.................3430	36	36	36	0	0	4	18	18	5	0	12	148	1	8	55	36	79.17	1	6	0	2	0

BARCLAYS PREMIER LEAGUE OUTFIELD PLAYER STATS

Player	Minutes on pitch	Appearances	Match starts	Completed matches	Substitute appearances	Subbed off	Goals scored	Minutes since scoring	Assists	Shots on target	Shots off target	Crosses	Defensive clearances	Defensive blocks	Fouls committed	Free-kicks won	Caught offside	Yellow cards	Red cards
Angelos Basinas 233	3	3	1	0	2	0	-	0	1	1	2	1	1	4	2	0	0	0
Nadir Belhadj 2048	29	21	16	8	4	2	927	3	8	9	53	8	5	26	19	0	3	1
Sol Campbell 3004	32	32	31	0	1	0	-	0	3	1	0	52	33	20	32	0	1	0
Peter Crouch...........................3543	38	38	33	0	5	11	873	5	43	43	7	36	0	45	40	26	3	0
Sean Davis 2868	32	31	27	1	3	1	1925	2	16	9	23	11	6	46	15	1	6	1
Jermain Defoe 1575	19	17	12	2	5	7	136	4	40	26	9	0	0	12	21	30	4	0
Lassana Diarra 941	12	11	6	1	4	0	-	0	7	3	6	1	1	23	15	0	4	1
Papa Bouba Diop 1394	16	15	11	1	4	0	-	0	5	12	3	4	1	46	28	1	5	0
Sylvain Distin 3620	38	38	38	0	0	0	-	0	2	2	4	66	23	20	17	0	2	0
Theofanis Gekas 7	1	0	0	1	0	0	-	0	0	0	0	0	0	0	0	0	0	0
Hermann Hreidarsson 1792	23	19	18	4	1	2	1211	1	3	10	11	15	4	28	23	0	7	0
Richard Hughes 1434	20	17	11	3	6	0	-	0	5	4	7	8	2	25	14	0	3	0
Glen Johnson...........................2737	29	29	27	0	1	3	967	4	26	17	44	23	11	30	35	0	9	1
Younes Kaboul 1537	20	17	10	3	7	1	345	2	5	12	14	10	5	18	11	0	3	0
Nwankwo Kanu 489	17	3	0	14	3	1	171	1	3	1	1	3	0	9	7	3	1	0
Niko Kranjcar 1625	21	16	9	5	7	3	111	3	27	18	21	1	0	20	23	2	2	0
Glen Little 300	5	4	0	1	4	0	-	1	1	0	15	3	0	3	5	1	0	0
Hayden Mullins.........................1431	17	15	14	2	1	0	1831	0	4	8	7	5	2	14	9	0	1	0
Arnold Mvuemba..........................157	6	1	0	5	1	0	-	0	1	1	0	0	0	2	0	0	0	0
David Nugent 1102	16	13	3	3	10	3	773	1	12	11	7	3	0	14	17	7	1	0
Noe Pamarot...........................1075	16	11	10	5	0	0	-	0	0	3	8	8	2	7	8	0	1	1
Jermaine Pennant 797	13	9	3	4	6	0	-	3	2	3	37	0	1	2	18	1	0	0
Linvoy Primus 5	1	0	0	1	0	0	-	0	0	0	0	0	0	0	0	0	0	0
Jerome Thomas 77	3	0	0	3	0	0	-	0	1	0	1	0	0	3	4	0	1	0
Armand Traore 1325	19	14	4	5	10	1	101	1	7	9	33	0	0	7	11	1	0	0
John Utaka 770	18	4	2	14	2	1	129	2	8	6	17	1	0	8	16	3	1	0
Marc Wilson 198	3	2	2	1	0	0	-	0	0	1	3	1	1	1	0	0	1	0

SEASON TOTALS

Goals scored	38
Goals conceded	57
Clean sheets	8
Shots on target	230
Shots off target	210
Shots per goal	11.58
Pens awarded	4
Pens scored	2
Pens conceded	7
Offsides	76
Corners	196
Crosses	333
Players used	29
Fouls committed	433
Free-kicks won	397

CARDS RECEIVED

61 **5**

SEQUENCES

Wins	2
(on two occasions)	
Losses	4
(14/12/08–28/12/08)	
Draws	2
(on three occasions)	
Undefeated	5
(on two occasions)	
Without win	9
(07/12/08–07/02/09)	
Undefeated home	4
(13/09/08–26/10/08)	
Undefeated away	3
(on two occasions)	
Without scoring	4
(22/04/09–09/05/09)	
Without conceding	
(–)	
Scoring	4
(31/01/09–21/02/09)	
Conceding	11
(22/11/08–07/02/09)	

SEASON INFORMATION

Highest Position: 6
Lowest Position: 20
Average goals scored per game: 1.00
Average goals conceded per game: 1.50

League position at the end of each week

League position at the end of: August 16 | September 9 | October 7 | November 8 | December 12 | January 15 | February 16 | March 15 | April 14 | May 14

MATCH RECORDS

Goals scored per match

		W	D	L	Pts
Failed to score	16	0	4	12	4
Scored 1 goal	9	1	4	4	7
Scored 2 goals	10	6	3	1	21
Scored 3 goals	3	3	0	0	9
Scored 4+ goals	0	0	0	0	0

Goals conceded per match

		W	D	L	Pts
Clean sheet	8	4	4	0	16
Conceded 1 goal	15	5	4	6	19
Conceded 2 goals	8	1	3	4	6
Conceded 3 goals	4	0	0	4	0
Conceded 4+ goals	3	0	0	3	0

QUICK-FIRE GOALS

From the start of a match
Nadir Belhadj (v West Ham) 7:05

By a substitute after coming on
Sean Davis (v Blackburn) 2:52

LAST-GASP GOALS

From the start of a match
Jermain Defoe (v Sunderland) 90:55

By a substitute after coming on
Armand Traore (v Sunderland) 42:14

GOAL DETAILS

How the goals were struck

SCORED		CONCEDED
18	Right foot	36
11	Left foot	12
9	Headers	9
0	Others	0

How the goals were struck

SCORED		CONCEDED
26	Open play	39
1	Cross	5
3	Corner	3
2	Penalties	6
1	Direct from free-kick	2
3	Free-kick	2
2	Own goals	0

Distance from goal

SCORED		CONCEDED
15	6yds	21
16	18yds	32
7	18+yds	4

GOALS SCORED/CONCEDED PER FIVE-MINUTE INTERVALS

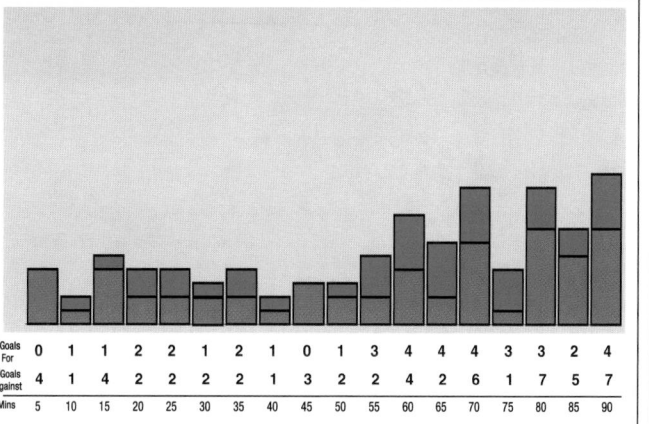

Goals For	0	1	1	2	1	2	1	0	1	3	4	4	4	3	3	2	4
Goals Against	4	1	4	2	2	2	1	3	2	2	4	2	6	1	7	5	7
Mins	5	10	15	20	25	30	35	40	45	50	55	60	65	70	75	80	85	90

STOKE CITY

CLUB SUMMARY

FORMED	1863
MANAGER	Tony Pulis
GROUND	Britannia Stadium
CAPACITY	28,218
NICKNAME	The Potters
WEBSITE	www.stokecityfc.com

The New Football Pools PLAYER OF THE SEASON — Rory Delap

OVERALL

P	W	D	L	F	A	GD
43	14	10	19	45	62	-17

BARCLAYS PREMIER LEAGUE

Pos	P	W	D	L	F	A	GD	Pts
12	38	12	9	17	38	55	-17	45

HOME

Pos	P	W	D	L	F	A	GD	Pts
8	19	10	5	4	22	15	7	35

AWAY

Pos	P	W	D	L	F	A	GD	Pts
18	19	2	4	13	16	40	-24	10

CUP PROGRESS DETAILS

Competition	Round reached	Knocked out by
FA Cup	R3	Hartlepool
Carling Cup	QF	Derby

BIGGEST WIN (ALL COMPS)

2–0 on four occasions

BIGGEST DEFEAT (ALL COMPS)

15/11/08 0–5 v Man Utd **PREM**

THE PLAYER WITH THE MOST

Shots on target
Ricardo Fuller 23
Shots off target
Ricardo Fuller 31
Shots without scoring
Salif Diao 10
Assists
Rory Delap 5
Offsides
Ricardo Fuller 19
Fouls
Ricardo Fuller 59
Fouls without a card
Danny Pugh 13
Free-kicks won
Ricardo Fuller 42
Defensive clearances
Abdoulaye Faye 46

actim INDEX for the 2008/09 Barclays Premier League Season

Rank	Player	Pts
46	Abdoulaye Faye	401
48	Thomas Sorensen	400
62	Ryan Shawcross	376
115	Danny Higginbotham	308
141	Ricardo Fuller	270

ATTENDANCE RECORD

High	Low	Average
27,500	25,287	26,960
v Aston Villa (23/08/2008)	v Fulham (13/12/2008)	

CLOCKWISE FROM TOP: January signing James Beattie makes his presence felt against Bolton; Rory Delap takes a long throw leading to Seyi Olofinjana's goal in a 2–1 victory over Arsenal at the Britannia Stadium; Danny Higginbotham slots home a crucial penalty in the 2–1 win against Tottenham

FEW outside the Potteries gave Barclays Premier League new boys Stoke any chance of avoiding the drop as they started the season as the bookies' favourites for a swift return to the Coca-Cola Championship.

But avoid it they did and by a comfortable margin thanks to a string of superb results against clubs with much greater resources. It was an outcome that seemed unlikely before Christmas as wins proved hard to come by, and the only headlines being made were related to the long throws of Rory Delap.

Stoke claimed a fine win over Villa in their second game, but that looked a flash in the pan as they had just four points after seven games and only 20 after 20. Yet there were also two hugely encouraging goalless draws with title-chasing Liverpool, and most opponents made it abundantly clear that they did not relish tackling them.

Initially, Delap's throws were the key reason. They were the talking point ahead of every game – and for good reason. Defences were unaccustomed to dealing with such high balls as the Irishman delivered into the box and it worked to devastating effect in the home game against Arsenal. The Gunners' defence struggled with Delap all afternoon when they visited the Britannia Stadium in November and both Stoke's goals in their 2–1 win came in the chaos following a mighty throw-in.

Having this weapon gave Stoke confidence that they could achieve results at the highest level, and this grew to such an extent over the season that, by May, few were talking about throw-ins.

When Stoke won at Hull to guarantee another season of Barclays Premier League football, they had proved themselves a solid all-round team. Manager Tony Pulis fashioned a side that was difficult to beat, especially at home, where the Potters' vocal supporters were voted the loudest in the League in a poll conducted by Sky Sports.

Working in partnership with chairman Peter Coates and chief executive Tony Scholes, Pulis proved his worth in the transfer market with £27million invested during the season. The arrivals of James Beattie and Matthew Etherington from Sheffield United and West Ham respectively in the January transfer window were cases in point. Both had top-flight experience and that nous helped Stoke get good results and ultimately survive, with Beattie grabbing an impressive seven goals during his four months at the club.

Scholes has nothing but praise for the work done by Pulis and said: 'The chairman has shown he will back the club and Tony has shown he will spend the money well. We brought in a lot of new players and Tony galvanised team spirit. He has done a magnificent job. We were tipped to go down, but Tony and the players proved a lot of people wrong.

'I am delighted for everyone at the club and everyone who lives in this area. We all share in that delight and we should all celebrate, although we will soon have to think about the challenges that the 2009/10 season will bring.'

Keeping a large group of players sweet when they are not in the team is historically a tough job. But team spirit, thanks to Pulis' stewardship, played an important part in the Potters' success, according to midfielder Glenn Whelan. 'Everyone gets on with each other and because of that the team did really well,' said the Republic of Ireland international. 'We have a big squad and we all know you have to take your opportunity when it comes along. The manager did some good business in the transfer market and I am sure he will be looking to do some more ahead of next season.'

> **Pulis fashioned a side that was difficult to beat, especially on home soil**

STOKE CITY

August

16th ● Bolton ....a | L 3–1 | **Att:** 22,717. **Ref:** C Foy — **Stoke** (4-4-2): Sorensen, Wilkinson (Dickinson 76), Cort, Shawcross, Griffin, Delap, Olofinjana▌, Whelan (Lawrence▌ 56), Cresswell, Kitson, Sidibe (Fuller▌ 65). Subs not used: Simonsen, Pericard, Diao, Am Faye.

23rd ● Aston Villa..............h | W 3–2 | **Att:** 27,500. **Ref:** M Halsey — **Stoke** (4-4-2): Sorensen, Griffin, Cort, Ab Faye, Dickinson, Lawrence[1], Olofinjana, Delap, Am Faye (Diao 72), Kitson (Sidibe[1] 76), Fuller[1] (Cresswell 87). Subs not used: Simonsen, Shawcross, Wilkinson, Whelan.

26th ● Cheltenham ....a | W 2–3 | **Att:** 3,600. **Ref:** D Deadman — **Stoke** (4-4-2): Simonsen, Wilkinson (Shotton 90), Buxton, Shawcross, Dickinson (D Phillips 79), Cresswell[1], Diao (Matteo 75), Whelan[1], Pugh, Parkin[1], Pericard[1]. Subs not used: De Laet, J Phillips, Wedderburn.

30th ● Middlesbrough ....a | L 2–1 | **Att:** 27,627. **Ref:** M Dean — **Stoke** (4-4-2): Sorensen, Griffin[1], Cort, Ab Faye, Dickinson (Wilkinson) 67), Lawrence[1], Olofinjana, Am Faye▌, Delap, Kitson (Cresswell 83), Fuller▌ (Sidibe 74). Subs not used: Simonsen, Whelan, Diao, Buxton.

September

14th ● Everton ....h | L 2–3 | **Att:** 27,415. **Ref:** A Wiley — **Stoke** (4-4-2): Sorensen, Griffin, Sonko, Cort, Higginbotham, Lawrence (Cresswell 86), Ab Faye[1] (Tonge 81), Olofinjana[1], Delap, Kitson (Sidibe 81), Fuller▌. Subs not used: Simonsen, Whelan, Shawcross, Wilkinson.

20th ● Liverpool ....a | D 0–0 | **Att:** 43,931. **Ref:** A Marriner — **Stoke** (4-4-1-1): Sorensen, Griffin, Ab Faye, Sonko (Cort 22), Higginbotham, Lawrence (Cresswell 66), Olofinjana, Diao, Delap, Kitson (Fuller[1] 78), Sidibe. Subs not used: Simonsen, Whelan, Tonge, Wilkinson.

23rd ● Reading ....h | D 2–2 | **Att:** 9,141. **Ref:** L Probert — **Stoke** (4-4-2): Simonsen, Wilkinson, Shawcross, Higginbotham (Cort 101), Dickinson, Lawrence, Buxton, Whelan[1], Cresswell (Fuller 78), Sidibe[1] (Phillips 63), Pericard[1]. Subs not used: Sorensen, De Laet, Davies, Wedderburn.

27th ● Chelsea ....h | L 0–2 | **Att:** 27,500. **Ref:** M Atkinson — **Stoke** (4-4-2): Sorensen, Griffin[1], Cort, Ab Faye, Higginbotham, Lawrence (Tonge 65) Diao, Olofinjana, Cresswell▌, Kitson (Fuller 52) Sidibe (Am Faye 81). Subs not used: Simonsen, Whelan, Soares, Sonko.

October

5th ● Portsmouth ....a | L 2–1 | **Att:** 19,248. **Ref:** A Marriner — **Stoke** (4-4-2): Simonsen[1], Griffin, Cort, Ab Faye, Higginbotham, Delap (Cresswell 74) Olofinjana▌, Am Faye[1], Tonge (Soares 65), Fuller[1], Kitson (Sidibe 61). Subs not used: Whelan, Shawcross, Wilkinson, Sonko.

19th ● Tottenham ....h | W 2–1 | **Att:** 27,500. **Ref:** L Mason — **Stoke** (4-4-2): Sorensen (Simonsen 66), Griffin, Ab Faye▌, Sonko (Shawcross 83) Higginbotham[1], Soares, Olofinjana, Diao, Delap[1], Sidibe, Kitson (Fuller 56). Subs not used: Whelan, Cresswell, Am Faye, Tonge.

26th ● Man City ....a | L 3–0 | **Att:** 44,624. **Ref:** S Tanner — **Stoke** (4-4-2): Sorensen, Griffin, Ab Faye, Shawcross, Higginbotham, Soares (Cresswell 69) Olofinjana, Diao (Whelan 76), Delap, Fuller, Sidibe (Kitson 66). Subs not used: Simonsen, Cort, Am Faye, Wilkinson.

29th ● Sunderland ....h | W 1–0 | **Att:** 26,731. **Ref:** C Foy — **Stoke** (4-4-2): Sorensen, Griffin, Ab Faye▌, Shawcross, Higginbotham, Soares (Tonge 69) Olofinjana (Am Faye 87), Diao▌, Delap, Sidibe, Fuller[1] (Kitson 90). Subs not used: Simonsen, Pericard, Wilkinson, Sonko.

November

1st ● Arsenal ....h | W 2–1 | **Att:** 26,704. **Ref:** R Styles — **Stoke** (4-4-2): Sorensen, Griffin, Ab Faye, Shawcross, Higginbotham▌, Am Faye, Olofinjana[1], Diao (Whelan 78), Delap▌, Fuller[1] (Cresswell 86), Sidibe▌ (Kitson 90). Subs not used: Simonsen, Soares, Wilkinson, Sonko.

8th ● Wigan ....a | D 0–0 | **Att:** 15,881. **Ref:** M Riley — **Stoke** (4-1-3-2): Sorensen, Griffin, Ab Faye, Shawcross▌, Higginbotham, Diao, Olofinjana (Whelan 86), Am Faye (Cresswell 84), Delap, Fuller▌, Sidibe (Kitson 47). Subs not used: Simonsen, Cort, Tonge, Wilkinson.

11th ● Rotherham ....h | W 2–0 | **Att:** 13,731. **Ref:** M Halsey — **Stoke** (4-4-2): Simonsen, Wilkinson, Cort, Shawcross, Dickinson, Pugh[1], Whelan[1], Olofinjana (Am Faye 58), Cresswell, Kitson, Pericard (Fuller 73). Subs not used: Sorensen, Delap, Phillips, Sonko, Wedderburn.

15th ● Man Utd ....a | L 5–0 | **Att:** 75,369. **Ref:** P Walton — **Stoke** (4-4-2): Sorensen, Griffin (Wilkinson 79), Ab Faye, Shawcross, Higginbotham, Olofinjana (Cresswell 31), Diao, Am Faye, Delap▌, Fuller▌ (Kitson 68), Sidibe. Subs not used: Simonsen, Cort, Whelan, Tonge.

22nd ● West Brom ....h | W 1–0 | **Att:** 26,613. **Ref:** L Mason — **Stoke** (4-4-2): Sorensen, Griffin, Ab Faye, Shawcross (Cort 80), Higginbotham, Soares (Tonge▌ 65) Am Faye, Diao, Delap, Kitson (Cresswell 11), Sidibe[1]. Subs not used: Simonsen, Olofinjana, Whelan, Wilkinson.

29th ● Hull ....a | D 1–1 | **Att:** 27,500. **Ref:** K Stroud — **Stoke** (4-4-2): Sorensen, Griffin▌, Ab Faye, Cort, Higginbotham, Soares (Tonge 62), Am Faye, Diao▌, Delap, Sidibe, Fuller[1]. Subs not used: Simonsen, Olofinjana, Whelan, Cresswell, Dickinson, Sonko.

December

2nd ● Derby ....h | L 0–1 | **Att:** 22,034. **Ref:** R Styles — **Stoke** (4-4-2): Simonsen, Griffin, Cort, Sonko, Higginbotham, Delap, Olofinjana (Pugh 81), Whelan, Cresswell, Sidibe, Fuller. Subs not used: Sorensen, Pericard, Ab Faye, Davies, Am Faye, Dickinson.

6th ● Newcastle ....a | D 2–2 | **Att:** 47,422. **Ref:** M Riley — **Stoke** (4-4-2): Sorensen, Griffin, Sonko, Ab Faye▌, Higginbotham, Delap (Fuller 57) Diao (Whelan 21), Pugh, Cresswell, Sidibe[1]. Subs not used: Simonsen, Olofinjana, Cort, Davies.

13th ● Fulham ....h | D 0–0 | **Att:** 25,287. **Ref:** S Attwell — **Stoke** (4-4-2): Sorensen, Wilkinson, Ab Faye, Sonko, Higginbotham, Delap (Tonge 61) Am Faye, Whelan, Pugh (Pericard 68), Sidibe (Cresswell 5), Fuller▌. Subs not used: Simonsen, Olofinjana, Cort, Davies.

20th ● Blackburn ....a | L 3–0 | **Att:** 23,004. **Ref:** P Walton — **Stoke** (4-4-2): Simonsen, Shawcross, Sonko, Ab Faye, Higginbotham, Delap (Soares 59) Whelan, Am Faye▌ (Olofinjana 75), Cresswell▌, Pericard (Tonge 59) Fuller. Subs not used: Sorensen, Pugh, Davies, Wilkinson.

26th ● Man Utd ....h | L 0–1 | **Att:** 27,500. **Ref:** C Foy — **Stoke** (4-4-2): Sorensen, Wilkinson▌, Ab Faye, Shawcross, Higginbotham, Delap (Davies 74) Whelan▌, Am Faye (Olofinjana 89), Pugh, Cresswell▌ (Pericard 90), Fuller▌. Subs not used: Simonsen, Lawrence, Tonge, Sonko.

28th ● West Ham ....a | L 2–1 | **Att:** 34,477. **Ref:** M Jones — **Stoke** (4-4-2): Sorensen, Griffin (Davies 58) Ab Faye[1], Shawcross, Higginbotham▌, Olofinjana▌, Whelan, Pugh (Pericard 53) Cresswell, Fuller▌. Subs not used: Simonsen, Lawrence, Soares, Tonge, Sonko.

January

3rd ● Hartlepool ....a | L 2–0 | **Att:** 5,367. **Ref:** M Halsey — **Stoke** (4-5-1): Simonsen, Davies (Wilkinson 71) Shawcross, Sonko, Dickinson, Soares (Lawrence 54) Olofinjana (Kitson 54) Whelan, Tonge, Delap, Pericard. Subs not used: Sorensen, Higginbotham, Diao, Ab Faye.

10th ● Liverpool ....h | D 0–0 | **Att:** 27,500. **Ref:** L Mason — **Stoke** (4-4-2): Sorensen, Wilkinson, Ab Faye, Shawcross, Higginbotham, Delap, Am Faye, Whelan, Etherington▌ (Lawrence 78), Kitson (Pugh 89) Cresswell. Subs not used: Simonsen, Griffin, Olofinjana, Tonge, Sonko.

17th ● Chelsea ....a | L 2–1 | **Att:** 41,788. **Ref:** P Walton — **Stoke** (4-4-2): Sorensen, Wilkinson, Shawcross, Ab Faye, Higginbotham (Griffin 34) Delap[1], Whelan▌, Am Faye▌ (Pugh 28) Etherington (Kitson) 83), Beattie, Cresswell. Subs not used: Simonsen, Olofinjana, Lawrence, Sonko.

27th ● Tottenham ....a | L 3–1 | **Att:** 36,072. **Ref:** M Riley — **Stoke** (4-5-1): Sorensen, Wilkinson (Griffin 46), Shawcross, Ab Faye (Sonko 46) Higginbotham▌, Delap, Am Faye (Fuller 49) Whelan▌, Etherington, Cresswell▌, Beattie[1]. Subs not used: Simonsen, Lawrence, Kitson, Pugh.

31st ● Man City ....h | W 1–0 | **Att:** 27,236. **Ref:** M Atkinson — **Stoke** (4-4-2): Sorensen, Wilkinson▌, Shawcross, Ab Faye, Pugh, Delap▌, Whelan, Am Faye (Griffin 78) Etherington (Sonko 86) Beattie[1], Fuller (Cresswell 46). Subs not used: Simonsen, Olofinjana, Lawrence, Kitson.

February

7th ● Sunderland ....a | L 2–0 | **Att:** 38,350. **Ref:** R Styles — **Stoke** (4-4-2): Sorensen, Wilkinson (Pugh 18) Shawcross (Sonko 26) Ab Faye, Kelly, Cresswell, Whelan, Diao▌, Etherington▌, Fuller (Camara 30), Beattie. Subs not used: Simonsen, Olofinjana, Lawrence, Kitson.

21st ● Portsmouth ....h | D 2–2 | **Att:** 26,354. **Ref:** M Jones — **Stoke** (4-4-2): Sorensen, Wilkinson, Shawcross, Ab Faye, Higginbotham, Lawrence[1] (Tonge 66) Diao, Am Faye, Pugh, Sidibe (Cresswell 84) Beattie[2]. Subs not used: Simonsen, Whelan, Kitson, Camara, Sonko.

● Barclays Premier League ● FA Cup ● Carling Cup ● UEFA Champions League ○ UEFA Cup | ▌ Yellow Card ▌ Red Card

RESULTS 2008/09

March

1st	● Aston Villa...........................a	D 2–2	**Att:** 39,641. **Ref:** H Webb — **Stoke** (3-4-3): Sorensen (Simonsen 46), Shawcross▪, Sonko, Higginbotham, Wilkinson, Diao, Am Faye (Whelan¹ 64), Pugh (Fuller 54), Lawrence, Beattie, Sidibe. Subs not used: Cort, Cresswell, Kelly, Camara.	
4th	● Bolton ....h	W 2–0	**Att:** 26,319. **Ref:** M Dean — **Stoke** (4-4-2): Sorensen, Wilkinson (Sonko 72), Shawcross, Ab Faye, Higginbotham, Lawrence▪, Whelan, Diao (Am Faye 66), Delap, Sidibe (Fuller¹ 56), Beattie¹. Subs not used: Simonsen, Pugh, Tonge, Camara.	
14th	● Everton ....a	L 3–1	**Att:** 36,396. **Ref:** A Marriner — **Stoke** (4-4-2): Sorensen, Wilkinson, Ab Faye, Shawcross¹, Higginbotham, Lawrence▪ (Camara 80), Whelan, Diao, Delap (Etherington 68), Beattie, Sidibe (Fuller 53). Subs not used: Simonsen, Am Faye, Camara, Sonko.	
21st	● Middlesbrough ....h	W 1–0	**Att:** 26,442. **Ref:** L Mason — **Stoke** (4-4-2): Sorensen, Wilkinson (Kelly 46), Shawcross¹, Ab Faye, Higginbotham, Lawrence (Sidibe 83), Diao▪ (Etherington 51), Whelan▪, Delap, Beattie▪, Fuller▪. Subs not used: Simonsen, Am Faye, Camara, Sonko.	

April

4th	● West Brom ....a	W 0–2	**Att:** 26,277. **Ref:** M Atkinson — **Stoke** (4-4-2): Sorensen, Wilkinson, Shawcross, Ab Faye▪, Higginbotham, Lawrence (Pugh 74), Delap, Whelan, Etherington, Fuller¹ (Olofinjana 88), Beattie¹ (Cresswell 78). Subs not used: Simonsen, Kelly, Camara, Sonko.	
11th	● Newcastle ....h	D 1–1	**Att:** 27,500. **Ref:** C Foy — **Stoke** (4-4-2): Sorensen, Wilkinson▪ (Kelly 90), Shawcross, Ab Faye¹, Higginbotham, Lawrence▪, Delap, Whelan, Etherington▪ (Pugh 80), Fuller▪, Beattie (Cresswell 73). Subs not used: Simonsen, Olofinjana, Tonge, Sonko.	
18th	● Blackburn ....h	W 1–0	**Att:** 27,500. **Ref:** H Webb — **Stoke** (4-4-2): Sorensen, Wilkinson▪ (Kelly 50), Ab Faye▪, Shawcross, Higginbotham, Lawrence¹, Whelan, Delap, Etherington (Sonko 87), Beattie (Cresswell 86), Fuller▪. Subs not used: Simonsen, Olofinjana, Pugh, Camara.	
25th	● Fulham ....a	L 1–0	**Att:** 25,069. **Ref:** L Mason — **Stoke** (4-4-2): Sorensen, Kelly (Sonko 83), Shawcross▪, Ab Faye, Pugh (Dickinson 87), Lawrence▪, Whelan, Delap, Etherington, Fuller, Cresswell (Camara 83). Subs not used: Simonsen, Olofinjana, Cort, Tonge.	

May

2nd	● West Ham ....h	L 0–1	**Att:** 27,500. **Ref:** P Walton — **Stoke** (4-4-2): Sorensen, Wilkinson (Sonko 88), Ab Faye, Shawcross▪, Pugh (Olofinjana 73), Lawrence▪, Delap▪, Whelan, Etherington, Fuller, Beattie (Camara 72). Subs not used: Simonsen, Cresswell, Kelly, Tonge.	
9th	● Hull ....a	W 1–2	**Att:** 24,932. **Ref:** H Webb — **Stoke** (4-4-2): Sorensen, Wilkinson, Shawcross, Ab Faye, Cort, Lawrence¹, Delap, Whelan, Etherington (Pugh 85), Beattie (Cresswell 78), Fuller¹ (Kelly 90). Subs not used: Simonsen, Olofinjana, Camara, Sonko.	
16th	● Wigan ....h	W 2–0	**Att:** 25,641. **Ref:** L Probert — **Stoke** (4-4-2): Sorensen, Shawcross, Ab Faye, Cort (Pugh 46), Wilkinson, Lawrence, Delap, Whelan, Etherington (Diao 76), Beattie¹ (Cresswell 86), Fuller¹. Subs not used: Simonsen, Olofinjana, Kelly, Tonge.	
24th	● Arsenal ....a	L 4–1	**Att:** 60,082. **Ref:** M Atkinson — **Stoke** (4-4-2): Simonsen (Sorensen 21), Wilkinson, Shawcross, Ab Faye, Dickinson, Lawrence, Diao (Pugh 64), Whelan, Delap, Beattie, Fuller¹ (Cresswell 69). Subs not used: Olofinjana, Kelly, Tonge, Sonko.	

● Barclays Premier League ● FA Cup ● Carling Cup ● UEFA Champions League ● UEFA Cup   ▪ Yellow Card ▮ Red Card

Stoke's Salif Diao and Andy Wilkinson attempt to stop Arsenal's Andrey Arshavin at the Emirates Stadium in May

STOKE CITY

BARCLAYS PREMIER LEAGUE GOALKEEPER STATS

Player	Minutes on pitch	Appearances	Match starts	Completed matches	Sub appearances	Subbed off	SAVES BREAKDOWN								Clean sheets	Goals conceded	Minutes since conceding	Save %	PENALTIES			Yellow cards	Red cards
							Saved with feet	Punched	Parried	Tipped over	Fumbled	Tipped round	Caught	Blocked					Saved	Resulting in goals	Opposition miss		
Steve Simonsen 296	296	5	3	2	2	1	1	2	3	0	0	1	16	0	1	8	10	74.19	0	1	0	1	0
Thomas Sorensen 3357	3357	36	35	33	1	2	1	18	21	5	0	10	153	0	12	47	170	81.57	0	1	1	0	0

BARCLAYS PREMIER LEAGUE OUTFIELD PLAYER STATS

Player	Minutes on pitch	Appearances	Match starts	Completed matches	Substitute appearances	Subbed off	Goals scored	Minutes since scoring	Assists	Shots on target	Shots off target	Crosses	Defensive clearances	Defensive blocks	Fouls committed	Free-kicks won	Caught offside	Yellow cards	Red cards
James Beattie	1443	16	16	10	0	6	7	106	3	16	12	7	5	0	35	30	5	1	0
Henri Camara	118	4	0	0	4	0	0	345	0	1	2	0	1	0	0	0	0	0	0
Leon Cort	902	11	9	8	2	1	0	-	0	6	2	0	16	7	3	9	1	0	0
Richard Cresswell	1557	30	11	9	19	2	0	-	0	3	6	10	12	2	22	16	9	6	0
Andrew Davies	58	2	0	0	2	0	0	-	0	0	0	0	0	0	0	0	0	0	0
Rory Delap	3036	34	34	27	0	6	2	1197	5	11	14	19	12	3	40	18	3	3	1
Salif Diao	1552	20	18	12	2	6	0	-	0	3	7	1	11	4	41	5	0	4	0
Carl Dickinson	286	5	3	2	2	1	0	-	1	0	0	3	2	0	1	1	0	0	0
Matthew Etherington	1107	14	12	4	2	7	0	1467	3	2	4	20	0	1	4	13	4	3	1
Abdoulaye Faye	3403	36	36	34	0	2	3	642	0	9	7	2	46	29	23	18	0	6	0
Amdy Faye	1478	21	18	8	3	9	0	-	0	1	6	2	3	2	22	5	0	3	1
Ricardo Fuller	2474	34	25	14	9	10	11	41	2	23	31	10	1	0	59	42	19	10	1
Andy Griffin	1712	20	17	15	3	2	0	-	0	0	1	19	9	10	19	15	0	4	0
Danny Higginbotham	2625	28	28	27	0	1	1	2224	3	5	6	37	24	12	13	11	4	3	0
Stephen Kelly	288	6	2	1	4	1	0	-	0	0	0	1	2	0	2	3	0	0	0
Dave Kitson	818	16	10	1	6	9	0	-	1	2	7	5	5	1	14	23	1	2	0
Liam Lawrence	1636	20	18	11	2	7	3	214	3	10	7	64	4	3	18	24	2	8	0
Seyi Olofinjana	1323	18	14	11	4	3	2	294	0	6	4	2	5	4	20	15	0	3	0
Vincent Pericard	132	4	1	0	3	1	0	-	0	0	1	0	0	0	2	1	1	0	0
Danny Pugh	1012	17	9	4	8	5	0	-	0	0	6	5	5	1	13	14	0	0	0
Ryan Shawcross	2618	29	28	26	1	2	3	781	1	11	12	6	35	32	32	23	3	4	0
Mamady Sidibe	1426	22	17	8	5	9	3	343	1	10	5	3	8	0	35	28	7	1	0
Tom Soares	435	7	5	1	2	4	0	-	1	4	2	11	0	0	3	9	1	0	0
Ibrahima Sonko	766	14	7	5	7	2	0	-	0	0	3	0	18	4	5	4	0	0	0
Michael Tonge	310	10	1	0	9	1	0	-	0	2	2	4	0	0	4	0	0	1	0
Glenn Whelan	2137	26	21	20	5	1	1	1059	2	9	21	16	10	8	28	18	0	4	0
Andy Wilkinson	1659	22	20	11	2	8	0	-	0	2	0	6	15	7	19	6	1	7	1

actim / BARCLAYS PREMIER LEAGUE

SEASON TOTALS

Goals scored	38
Goals conceded	55
Clean sheets	12
Shots on target	136
Shots off target	168
Shots per goal	8.00
Pens awarded	6
Pens scored	5
Pens conceded	3
Offsides	60
Corners	177
Crosses	253
Players used	29
Fouls committed	478
Free-kicks won	372

CARDS RECEIVED

73   5

SEQUENCES

Wins	2
(on three occasions)	
Losses	3
(20/12/08–28/12/08)	
Draws	3
(29/11/08–13/12/08)	
Undefeated	4
(on two occasions)	
Without win	9
(29/11/08–27/01/09)	
Undefeated home	7
(10/01/09–18/04/09)	
Undefeated away	
(–)	
Without scoring	3
(13/12/08–26/12/08)	
Without conceding	2
(21/03/09–04/04/09)	
Scoring	8
(21/02/09–18/04/09)	
Conceding	4
(on two occasions)	

SEASON INFORMATION
Highest Position: 11
Lowest Position: 19
Average goals scored per game: 1.00
Average goals conceded per game: 1.45

League position at the end of each week

League position at the end of: August 15, September 18, October 15, November 13, December 18, January 16, February 18, March 16, April 12, May 12

MATCH RECORDS

Goals scored per match

	W	D	L	Pts
Failed to score	12	0	4	8	4
Scored 1 goal	15	5	2	8	17
Scored 2 goals	10	6	3	1	21
Scored 3 goals	1	1	0	0	3
Scored 4+ goals	0	0	0	0	0

Goals conceded per match

	W	D	L	Pts
Clean sheet	12	8	4	0	28
Conceded 1 goal	8	3	2	3	11
Conceded 2 goals	10	1	3	6	6
Conceded 3 goals	6	0	0	6	0
Conceded 4+ goals	2	0	0	2	0

QUICK-FIRE GOALS

From the start of a match
Ricardo Fuller
(v West Brom) 1:50

By a substitute after coming on
Ricardo Fuller (v Bolton)
17:10

LAST-GASP GOALS

From the start of a match
Mamady Sidibe
(v Aston Villa) 93:31

By a substitute after coming on
Ricardo Fuller
(v Bolton) 28:01

GOAL DETAILS

How the goals were struck

SCORED		CONCEDED
16	Right foot	30
5	Left foot	15
16	Headers	9
1	Others	1

How the goals were struck

SCORED		CONCEDED
24	Open play	35
3	Cross	7
3	Corner	1
5	Penalties	2
0	Direct from free-kick	4
1	Free-kick	4
2	Own goals	2

Distance from goal

SCORED		CONCEDED
16	6yds	12
19	18yds	34
3	18+yds	9

GOALS SCORED/CONCEDED PER FIVE-MINUTE INTERVALS

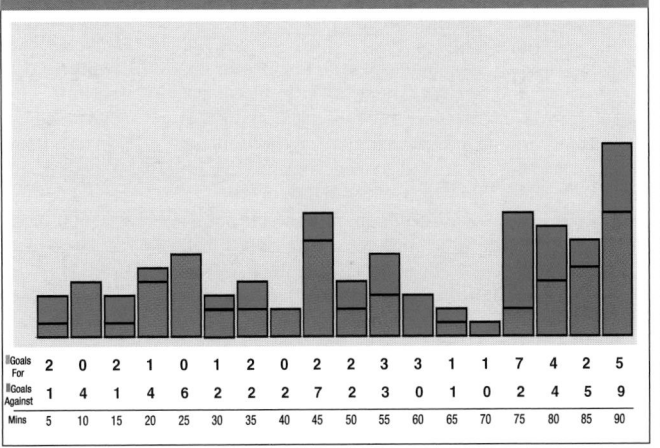

Goals For	2	0	2	1	0	1	2	0	2	2	3	3	1	1	7	4	2	5
Goals Against	1	4	1	4	6	2	2	2	7	2	3	0	1	0	2	4	5	9
Mins	5	10	15	20	25	30	35	40	45	50	55	60	65	70	75	80	85	90

CLUB SUMMARY

FORMED	1879
MANAGER	Steve Bruce
GROUND	Stadium of Light
CAPACITY	48,353
NICKNAME	The Black Cats
WEBSITE	www.safc.com

The New
Football Pools
PLAYER OF THE SEASON

Steed Malbranque

OVERALL

P	W	D	L	F	A	GD
44	11	11	22	42	62	-20

BARCLAYS PREMIER LEAGUE

Pos	P	W	D	L	F	A	GD	Pts
16	38	9	9	20	34	54	-20	36

HOME

Pos	P	W	D	L	F	A	GD	Pts
19	19	6	3	10	21	25	-4	21

AWAY

Pos	P	W	D	L	F	A	GD	Pts
14	19	3	6	10	13	29	-16	15

CUP PROGRESS DETAILS

Competition	Round reached	Knocked out by
FA Cup	R4	Blackburn
Carling Cup	R4	Blackburn

BIGGEST WIN (ALL COMPS)
13/12/08 4–0 v West Brom **PREM**

BIGGEST DEFEAT (ALL COMPS)
01/11/08 0–5 v Chelsea **PREM**

THE PLAYER WITH THE MOST

Shots on target
Djibril Cisse 53

Shots off target
Djibril Cisse 48

Shots without scoring
Phillip Bardsley 16

Assists
Steed Malbranque 9

Offsides
Djibril Cisse 56

Fouls
Kieran Richardson 41

Fouls without a card
Carlos Edwards 11

Free-kicks won
Steed Malbranque 47

Defensive clearances
Danny Collins 61

actim INDEX for the 2008/09 Barclays Premier League Season

Rank	Player	Pts
81	Danny Collins	352
101	Kenwyne Jones	323
108	Anton Ferdinand	314
136	Steed Malbranque	279
138	Djibril Cisse	278

ATTENDANCE RECORD

High	Low	Average
47,936	35,222	40,168

v Newcastle (25/10/2008) v West Ham (23/11/2008)

THERE were delirious celebrations at the Stadium of Light as final whistles around the country brought Barclays Premier League safety to Wearside on the last day of the season.

Sunderland's continued presence in the top flight was greeted even more enthusiastically than the demise of rivals Newcastle and Middlesbrough, as a club which has endured a yo-yo existence in recent years avoided further heartache. But when the dust settles on an eventful campaign, chairman Niall Quinn will make a slightly more sober appraisal of the 2008/09 season. The bottom line is that the Black Cats retained their Barclays Premier League status with just 36 points – three fewer than they had managed 12 months earlier – and having recorded just nine wins. Perhaps more worryingly for a club that thrives on its passionate support, Sunderland were also beaten at the Stadium of Light, where they had claimed 30 of their 39 points during the previous campaign, on 10 occasions.

The season had started with great optimism with manager Roy Keane having taken his spending during his two years at the helm to very nearly £80million by adding the likes of Anton Ferdinand, Teemu Tainio, Steed Malbranque, Pascal Chimbonda, George McCartney and David Healy to his squad.

A narrow 1–0 home defeat by Liverpool on the opening day did little to dampen the level of expectation with the club looking to build upon a solid 15th place in 2007/08. Loan signing Djibril Cisse gave them the lift-off they had been hoping for with a late strike to claim a 2–1 win at Tottenham a week later, and the ball was rolling.

A 3–0 home defeat by Manchester City and a penalty shoot-out victory over lowly Northampton in the League Cup third round left Keane scratching his head, but the season was ignited in spectacular style on 25th October. Kieran Richardson's blistering free-kick secured a precious 2–1 derby victory over Newcastle, Sunderland's first at home in the League since April 1980, although the joy was short lived.

Keane was furious at a 1–0 defeat at Stoke, which was followed by a 5–0 humiliation at Chelsea on 1st November, and suddenly his future on Wearside was placed in doubt. The final straw came four

> ## Their final 13 games of the season would bring them just one win

weeks later when a 4–1 thumping by Bolton at the Stadium of Light was the trigger for the former Manchester United skipper to stand down.

Quinn turned to first-team coach Ricky Sbragia on an interim basis and, having seen the Black Cats narrowly suffer defeat against United at Old Trafford in the caretaker manager's first game in charge, the chairman was delighted to see him secure successive victories over West Brom and Hull. A draw at Blackburn was then enough to persuade the chairman that he had the right man for the job on a permanent basis. Sbragia was appointed on the 28th December and, although he led Sunderland to an FA Cup third-round win over former club Bolton, he had to wait until 27th January for another three-point haul, a 1–0 win against Fulham.

When Stoke left the Stadium of Light on the wrong end of a 2–0 scoreline on 7th February, the Black Cats were looking towards the top half of the table rather than over their shoulders. But their final 13 games of the season would bring them just one more win and only six points as they slipped back to the very brink of relegation.

They went into the closing-day clash with Chelsea knowing defeat, coupled with wins for Hull and Newcastle, would send them down, although in the event all three lost.

With safety secured, Sbragia, having won only three of the 19 games for which he was in permanent control, decided to call it a day in order to allow the club to draft in a 'bigger name'. However, he insists he has no regrets about taking the job. He said: 'When you get an offer to manage Sunderland, you can't refuse it.'

The bigger name that Sbragia said was required at the Stadium of Light was installed within two weeks, Steve Bruce leaving Wigan to become Sunderland's third boss in seven months in early June.

CLOCKWISE FROM ABOVE: Sunderland score the decider in a crucial game against Stoke; Djibril Cisse celebrates his goal during a 2–1 win over rivals Newcastle; Ricky Sbragia cheers from the touchline as his side beats Hull at the KC Stadium

SUNDERLAND

RESULTS 2008/09

August
16th ● Liverpool ....h **L 0–1** **Att:** 43,259. **Ref:** A Wiley — **Sunderland** (4-4-2): Gordon, Chimbonda, Nosworthy, Collins, Bardsley, Malbranque (Edwards 73), Tainio (Whitehead 57), Reid, Richardson, Diouf (Chopra 81), Murphy. Subs not used: Ward, Leadbitter, Higginbotham, Stokes.

23rd ● Tottenham ....a **W 1–2** **Att:** 36,064. **Ref:** M Dean — **Sunderland** (4-4-2): Gordon, Bardsley, Nosworthy, Higginbotham, Collins, Malbranque▮, Whitehead, Reid (Miller 87), Richardson▮¹ (Cisse¹ 65) Diouf, Murphy. Subs not used: Ward, Chopra, Leadbitter, Healy, Stokes.

27th ● Nottm Forest.........................a **W 1–2** **Att:** 9,198. **Ref:** I Williamson — **Sunderland** (4-4-2): Gordon, Chimbonda▮, Nosworthy, Collins, Bardsley¹, Malbranque (Miller 19), Whitehead (Leadbitter 57), Reid, Murphy (Healy▮ 62), Diouf, Cisse. Subs not used: Ward, Edwards, Higginbotham, Stokes.

31st ● Man City ....h **L 0–3** **Att:** 39,622. **Ref:** C Foy — **Sunderland** (4-4-2): Gordon, Bardsley▮, Nosworthy, Collins, Chimbonda▮, Malbranque, Leadbitter (Murphy 60), Reid, Richardson▮, Cisse (Stokes 60), Diouf (Healy▮ 60). Subs not used: Ward, Miller, Yorke, Higginbotham.

September
13th ● Wigan ....a **D 1–1** **Att:** 18,015. **Ref:** R Styles — **Sunderland** (4-4-2): Gordon, Chimbonda, Nosworthy, Ferdinand, McCartney, Malbranque (Murphy 76), Whitehead, Tainio, Richardson, Cisse, Diouf▮. Subs not used: Fulop, Bardsley, Collins, Leadbitter, Reid, Healy.

20th ● Middlesbrough ....h **W 2–0** **Att:** 38,388. **Ref:** H Webb — **Sunderland** (4-4-2): Gordon, Chimbonda, Ferdinand, Nosworthy, McCartney, Malbranque, Whitehead, Tainio (Chopra▮² 45), Richardson▮, Cisse (Murphy 69), Diouf (Reid 68). Subs not used: Fulop, Bardsley, Collins, Leadbitter.

23rd ● Northampton.......................h **D 2–2** **Att:** 21,082. **Ref:** T Bates — **Sunderland** (4-4-2): Fulop, Bardsley, Nosworthy, Ferdinand, Collins, Edwards (Richardson 46), Leadbitter (Stokes² 78), Whitehead, Reid, Healy (Chopra 46), Murphy▮. Subs not used: Colgan, Miller, Yorke, Chimbonda.

27th ● Aston Villa............................a **L 2–1** **Att:** 38,706. **Ref:** P Walton — **Sunderland** (4-4-2): Gordon, Chimbonda, Ferdinand, Collins, McCartney▮, Malbranque, Whitehead, Richardson (Stokes 79), Miller (Reid 59), Cisse¹, Diouf (Murphy 59). Subs not used: Fulop, Chopra, Healy, Henderson.

October
4th ● Arsenal ....h **D 1–1** **Att:** 40,199. **Ref:** L Mason — **Sunderland** (4-5-1): Gordon, Chimbonda, Ferdinand, Collins, McCartney, Malbranque (Chopra 87), Whitehead▮, Yorke▮ (Leadbitter¹ 84), Reid, Richardson▮, Cisse (Murphy 88). Subs not used: Fulop, Bardsley, Diouf, Healy.

18th ● Fulham ....a **D 0–0** **Att:** 25,116. **Ref:** K Stroud — **Sunderland** (4-4-2): Gordon, Chimbonda, Nosworthy, Collins, McCartney, Malbranque▮, Leadbitter (Reid 62), Whitehead, Richardson, Cisse (Murphy 84), Chopra (Healy 69). Subs not used: Fulop, Bardsley, Tainio, Diouf.

25th ● Newcastle ....h **W 2–1** **Att:** 47,936. **Ref:** M Riley — **Sunderland** (4-4-2): Fulop, Chimbonda, Ferdinand, Collins, McCartney, Malbranque (Tainio 87), Whitehead, Yorke (Jones 57), Richardson¹, Cisse▮¹, Diouf (Reid 90). Subs not used: Colgan, Bardsley, Chopra, Leadbitter.

29th ● Stoke ....a **L 1–0** **Att:** 26,731. **Ref:** C Foy — **Sunderland** (4-4-2): Fulop, Bardsley, Ferdinand, Collins, McCartney, Malbranque▮ (Reid 75), Whitehead, Yorke (Jones 46), Richardson, Diouf, Cisse (Chopra 62). Subs not used: Colgan, Tainio, Nosworthy, Leadbitter.

November
1st ● Chelsea ....a **L 5–0** **Att:** 41,693. **Ref:** M Atkinson — **Sunderland** (4-4-2): Fulop, Chimbonda, Nosworthy, Ferdinand, McCartney, Malbranque (Henderson 46), Whitehead, Tainio▮, Richardson, Waghorn (Diouf 46), Jones (Cisse 58). Subs not used: Colgan, Bardsley, Reid, Meyler.

8th ● Portsmouth ....h **L 1–2** **Att:** 37,712. **Ref:** S Bennett — **Sunderland** (4-4-2): Fulop, Bardsley, Ferdinand, Nosworthy, Collins▮, Malbranque (Leadbitter 80), Whitehead▮, Reid (Healy 80), Richardson, Cisse¹, Murphy (Diouf 46). Subs not used: Colgan, Tainio, Miller, Henderson.

12th ● Blackburn ....h **L 1–2** **Att:** 18,555. **Ref:** R Styles — **Sunderland** (4-4-2): Fulop, Bardsley, Nosworthy, Ferdinand, Collins, Henderson (Leadbitter▮ 80), Whitehead, Richardson, Malbranque (Reid 71), Cisse, Jones¹ (Murphy 80). Subs not used: Colgan, Tainio, Kay.

15th ● Blackburn ....a **W 1–2** **Att:** 21,798. **Ref:** S Tanner — **Sunderland** (4-4-2): Fulop, Bardsley, Ferdinand▮, Nosworthy, Collins▮, Tainio (Reid 53), Whitehead, Richardson, Malbranque (Leadbitter 83), Cisse¹ (Yorke 83), Jones▮. Subs not used: Colgan, Diouf, Murphy, Henderson.

23rd ● West Ham ....h **L 0–1** **Att:** 35,222. **Ref:** M Dean — **Sunderland** (4-4-2): Fulop, Bardsley, Nosworthy, Ferdinand, Collins, Malbranque (Edwards 66), Whitehead, Reid▮ (Murphy 66), Richardson, Jones (Diouf 81), Cisse. Subs not used: Colgan, Tainio, Colback, Henderson.

29th ● Bolton ....h **L 1–4** **Att:** 35,457. **Ref:** C Foy — **Sunderland** (4-4-2): Gordon, Bardsley▮, Nosworthy▮, Collins, Chimbonda▮, Malbranque (Tainio 62), Whitehead, Richardson▮ (Leadbitter 46), Reid (Miller 63), Cisse¹, Jones. Subs not used: Fulop, Diouf, Murphy, Ferdinand.

December
6th ● Man Utd ....a **L 1–0** **Att:** 75,400. **Ref:** M Halsey — **Sunderland** (4-1-4-1): Fulop, Chimbonda, Ferdinand, Collins, Bardsley, Yorke (Tainio 60), Whitehead (Edwards 76), Reid, Diouf, Cisse (Jones 69), Malbranque. Subs not used: Colgan, Nosworthy, Murphy, Leadbitter.

13th ● West Brom ....h **W 4–0** **Att:** 36,280. **Ref:** L Mason — **Sunderland** (4-4-2): Fulop, Bardsley, Ferdinand▮, Nosworthy, Collins, Malbranque (Edwards 59), Tainio, Richardson, Reid¹ (Leadbitter 79), Cisse¹, Jones². Subs not used: Colgan, Diouf, Miller, Murphy, Yorke.

20th ● Hull ....a **W 1–4** **Att:** 24,917. **Ref:** M Riley — **Sunderland** (4-4-2): Fulop, Bardsley, Nosworthy, Ferdinand, Collins, Malbranque¹, Tainio (Leadbitter 79), Richardson▮ (Edwards 89), Reid (Whitehead 74), Jones¹, Cisse¹. Subs not used: Colgan, Murphy, Yorke, Healy.

26th ● Blackburn ....h **D 0–0** **Att:** 44,680. **Ref:** M Atkinson — **Sunderland** (4-4-2): Fulop, Bardsley, Nosworthy, Ferdinand, Collins, Malbranque, Tainio (Whitehead 62), Richardson (Leadbitter 81), Reid, Cisse (Murphy 80), Jones. Subs not used: Colgan, Edwards, Diouf, Chimbonda.

28th ● Everton ....a **L 3–0** **Att:** 39,146. **Ref:** R Styles — **Sunderland** (4-4-2): Fulop, Whitehead▮, Nosworthy, Collins, Bardsley▮, Malbranque▮ (Edwards 46), Tainio▮ (Yorke 75), Richardson, Murphy, Cisse (Healy 75), Jones. Subs not used: Colgan, Colback, Henderson, Prica.

January
3rd ● Bolton ....h **W 2–1** **Att:** 20,685. **Ref:** S Bennett — **Sunderland** (4-4-2): Fulop, Chimbonda, Nosworthy, Ferdinand, Collins, Edwards (Reid 82), Whitehead▮, Richardson (Tainio▮ 78), Diouf, Jones¹, Cisse¹. Subs not used: Colgan, Miller, Chopra, Yorke, Healy.

10th ● Middlesbrough ....a **D 1–1** **Att:** 29,310. **Ref:** P Dowd — **Sunderland** (4-4-2): Fulop, Chimbonda, Nosworthy▮, Ferdinand, Collins, Malbranque▮ (Edwards 54), Whitehead, Richardson▮ (Healy 80), Diouf (Reid 67), Cisse, Jones▮¹. Subs not used: Colgan, Tainio, Murphy, Yorke.

17th ● Aston Villa............................h **L 1–2** **Att:** 40,350. **Ref:** M Dean — **Sunderland** (4-4-2): Fulop, Chimbonda, Nosworthy▮ (McShane 46), Ferdinand, Collins¹ (Bardsley 62), Edwards, Tainio▮, Whitehead, Diouf (Reid 81), Cisse▮, Jones. Subs not used: Colgan, Chopra, Leadbitter, Healy.

24th ● Blackburn ....h **D 0–0** **Att:** 22,634. **Ref:** L Probert — **Sunderland** (4-4-2): Fulop, Chimbonda, Ferdinand, Collins, Bardsley (McCartney 65), Edwards, Leadbitter, Malbranque, Reid, Healy (Jones 67), Chopra. Subs not used: Colgan, Cisse, Diouf, Murphy, Yorke.

27th ● Fulham ....h **W 1–0** **Att:** 36,539. **Ref:** M Halsey — **Sunderland** (4-4-2): Fulop, Bardsley, Ferdinand, Collins, McCartney (McShane 70), Malbranque, Whitehead, Tainio (Leadbitter 81), Reid (Edwards 75), Cisse, Jones¹. Subs not used: Colgan, Diouf, Chopra, Healy.

February
1st ● Newcastle ....a **D 1–1** **Att:** 52,084. **Ref:** H Webb — **Sunderland** (4-4-2): Fulop, Bardsley▮, Ferdinand▮, Collins, McCartney▮, Edwards (Reid 71), Whitehead, Richardson▮, Malbranque (Leadbitter 90), Cisse¹ (Chopra 55), Jones. Subs not used: Colgan, Murphy, Healy.

4th ● Blackburn ....a **L 2–1** **Att:** 10,112. **Ref:** P Dowd — **Sunderland** (4-4-2): Gordon, Kay▮ (Bardsley 56), Ferdinand, Collins, McCartney (Luscombe 106), Edwards, Leadbitter▮, Reid, Malbranque (Yorke 76), Healy¹, Murphy. Subs not used: Colgan, Whitehead, Richardson, Colback.

7th ● Stoke ....h **W 2–0** **Att:** 38,350. **Ref:** R Styles — **Sunderland** (4-4-2): Fulop, Bardsley▮, Ferdinand, Collins▮, McCartney, Malbranque (Edwards 70), Whitehead, Richardson, Reid (Murphy 82), Jones¹, Cisse (Healy¹ 86). Subs not used: Gordon, Ben-Haim, Leadbitter, Davenport.

● Barclays Premier League ● FA Cup ● Carling Cup ● UEFA Champions League ● UEFA Cup   ▮ Yellow Card ▮ Red Card

RESULTS 2008/09

21st	● Arsenal ....a	D 0–0	**Att:** 60,104. **Ref:** A Wiley — **Sunderland** (4-4-1-1): Fulop, Ben-Haim, Ferdinand, Collins, McCartney▮, Malbranque, Whitehead, Tainio (Leadbitter 76), Reid (Murphy 78), Richardson▮, Jones (Edwards 88). Subs not used: Gordon, Davenport, Healy, McShane.	

March

3rd	● Liverpool ....a	L 2–0	**Att:** 41,587. **Ref:** M Halsey — **Sunderland** (4-5-1): Fulop, Ben-Haim, Ferdinand, Collins, McCartney, Malbranque (Edwards 81), Whitehead▮, Reid, Leadbitter (Cisse 62), Richardson, Jones (Murphy 76). Subs not used: Gordon, Bardsley, Davenport, Healy.
7th	● Tottenham ....h	D 1–1	**Att:** 37,894. **Ref:** P Dowd — **Sunderland** (4-4-2): Fulop, Bardsley▮, Ben-Haim, Collins, McCartney▮, Malbranque, Whitehead, Richardson▮ (Leadbitter 83), Reid (Edwards 82), Jones, Cisse (Murphy 73). Subs not used: Gordon, Davenport, Healy, McShane.
14th	● Wigan ....h	L 1–2	**Att:** 39,266. **Ref:** M Dean — **Sunderland** (4-4-2): Fulop, Bardsley, Ben-Haim (Healy 77), Collins, McCartney, Malbranque (Edwards 63), Whitehead, Leadbitter▮, Reid (Murphy 60), Jones, Cisse. Subs not used: Gordon, Yorke, Davenport, McShane.
22nd	● Man City ....a	L 1–0	**Att:** 43,017. **Ref:** S Tanner — **Sunderland** (4-4-1-1): Fulop, Bardsley▮, Collins, Ferdinand▮, McCartney▮, Edwards, Whitehead, Leadbitter▮, Murphy (Davenport 16), Malbranque (Reid▮ 72), Jones (Cisse 72). Subs not used: Gordon, Yorke, Healy, McShane.

April

4th	● West Ham ....a	L 2–0	**Att:** 34,761. **Ref:** M Jones — **Sunderland** (4-4-2): Gordon, Bardsley, Ferdinand, Ben-Haim, Collins, Malbranque (Edwards 75), Whitehead▮, Richardson, Leadbitter, Cisse, Murphy (Jones 54). Subs not used: Fulop, Nosworthy, Reid, Healy, McShane.
11th	● Man Utd ....h	L 1–2	**Att:** 45,408. **Ref:** R Styles — **Sunderland** (4-4-2): Gordon, Bardsley, Ferdinand▮, Davenport (McShane 73), Collins, Edwards, Leadbitter, Tainio (Yorke 85), Reid (Murphy 80), Cisse, Jones▮. Subs not used: Fulop, Malbranque, Ben-Haim, Colback.
18th	● Hull ....h	W 1–0	**Att:** 42,855. **Ref:** M Dean — **Sunderland** (4-4-2): Gordon, Bardsley, Davenport, Ferdinand, Collins, Edwards (Malbranque 78), Leadbitter, Tainio, Reid (Richardson▮ 76), Cisse▮ (Murphy 90), Jones. Subs not used: Fulop, Ben-Haim, Yorke, McShane.
25th	● West Brom ....a	L 3–0	**Att:** 26,256. **Ref:** M Halsey — **Sunderland** (4-4-2): Fulop, Bardsley▮, Davenport, Ferdinand, Collins, Edwards (Malbranque 54), Tainio (Healy 87), Reid (Whitehead 52), Richardson, Cisse, Jones. Subs not used: Colgan, Murphy, Leadbitter, McShane.

May

3rd	● Everton ....h	L 0–2	**Att:** 41,313. **Ref:** M Atkinson — **Sunderland** (4-4-2): Fulop, Bardsley▮, Davenport▮, Ferdinand, Collins, Malbranque (Edwards 83), Whitehead, Leadbitter▮, Richardson, Cisse (Healy 63), Jones. Subs not used: Colgan, Tainio, Ben-Haim, Murphy, McShane.
9th	● Bolton ....a	D 0–0	**Att:** 24,005. **Ref:** R Styles — **Sunderland** (4-2-3-1): Fulop, Bardsley, Davenport, Ferdinand, Collins, Whitehead, Tainio (Reid 80), Malbranque, Leadbitter, Richardson, Jones (Cisse 72). Subs not used: Colgan, Edwards, Murphy, Healy, McShane.
18th	● Portsmouth ....a	L 3–1	**Att:** 20,398. **Ref:** A Wiley — **Sunderland** (4-5-1): Fulop, Bardsley, Davenport, Ferdinand, Collins, Tainio (Cisse 80), Malbranque (Edwards 54), Whitehead, Leadbitter (Murphy 85), Richardson, Jones▮. Subs not used: Colgan, Reid, Healy, McShane.
24th	● Chelsea ....h	L 2–3	**Att:** 42,468. **Ref:** M Halsey — **Sunderland** (4-5-1): Fulop, Bardsley▮, Davenport, Ferdinand, Collins, Malbranque (Healy 78), Whitehead, Tainio (Reid 65), Leadbitter, Richardson▮ (Murphy 87), Jones▮. Subs not used: Colgan, Edwards, Cisse, McShane.

● Barclays Premier League ● FA Cup ● Carling Cup ● UEFA Champions League ● UEFA Cup   ▮ Yellow Card ▮ Red Card

Steed Malbranque and Phillip Bardsley win the ball ahead of Portsmouth's John Utaka during the match at Fratton Park

SUNDERLAND

BARCLAYS PREMIER LEAGUE GOALKEEPER STATS

Player	Minutes on pitch	Appearances	Match starts	Completed matches	Sub appearances	Subbed off	Saved with feet	Punched	Parried	Tipped over	Fumbled	Tipped round	Caught	Blocked	Clean sheets	Goals conceded	Minutes since conceding	Save %	Saved	Resulting in goals	Opposition miss	Yellow cards	Red cards
Marton Fulop	2472	26	26	26	0	0	1	15	12	4	0	7	91	0	6	37	8	78.11	1	3	0	1	0
Craig Gordon	1141	12	12	12	0	0	2	18	2	0	2		26	0	3	17	116	74.63	0	0	1	0	0

BARCLAYS PREMIER LEAGUE OUTFIELD PLAYER STATS

Player	Minutes on pitch	Appearances	Match starts	Completed matches	Substitute appearances	Subbed off	Goals scored	Minutes since scoring	Assists	Shots on target	Shots off target	Crosses	Defensive clearances	Defensive blocks	Fouls committed	Free-kicks won	Caught offside	Yellow cards	Red cards
Phillip Bardsley	2607	28	27	27	1	0	0	-	0	6	10	47	19	13	38	33	1	11	0
Tal Ben-Haim	463	5	5	4	0	1	0	-	0	0	0	5	4	3	5	4	0	0	0
Pascal Chimbonda	1226	13	13	13	0	0	0	-	0	0	1	17	14	6	5	19	0	2	0
Michael Chopra	210	6	1	0	5	1	2	150	0	4	4	2	1	0	5	1	1	1	0
Djibril Cisse	2631	35	29	15	6	14	10	243	1	53	48	23	4	1	11	34	56	3	0
Danny Collins	3300	35	35	34	0	1	1	1587	2	5	5	23	61	24	30	24	0	3	0
Calum Davenport	730	8	7	6	1	1	0	1198	1	1	2	2	6	5	10	3	0	2	0
El-Hadji Diouf	994	14	11	4	3	7	0	883	0	3	3	19	7	5	16	24	5	1	0
Carlos Edwards	864	22	6	3	16	3	0	-	1	3	8	20	2	0	11	13	1	0	0
Anton Ferdinand	2953	31	31	31	0	0	0	-	0	1	2	0	47	28	16	17	0	5	0
David Healy	180	10	0	0	10	0	1	70	1	2	1	3	0	0	7	1	0	1	0
Jordan Henderson	45	1	0	0	1	0	0	-	0	0	0	0	0	0	0	0	0	0	0
Danny Higginbotham	94	1	1	1	0	0	0	2224	0	0	1	0	0	1	0	1	1	0	0
Kenwyne Jones	2416	29	25	19	4	6	10	4	2	37	18	2	8	3	22	32	9	2	0
Grant Leadbitter	1217	23	12	8	11	4	2	817	1	14	14	20	5	4	9	13	1	2	0
Steed Malbranque	2775	36	34	12	2	22	1	1397	9	13	13	42	11	2	37	47	3	5	0
George McCartney	1412	16	16	14	0	1	0	-	0	1	0	32	8	11	11	18	0	4	1
Paul McShane	76	3	0	0	3	0	0	361	0	0	0	0	1	0	1	1	0	0	0
Liam Miller	96	3	1	0	2	1	0	-	0	1	1	1	0	1	2	1	0	0	0
Daryl Murphy	699	23	6	3	17	3	0	-	1	4	3	8	4	0	7	4	1	0	0
Nyron Nosworthy	1477	16	16	15	0	1	0	-	0	0	1	0	25	16	20	12	0	3	0
Andy Reid	1899	32	20	6	12	14	1	1030	5	19	15	106	6	6	20	22	0	2	0
Kieran Richardson	2818	32	31	23	1	8	4	34	2	28	30	35	7	9	41	24	10	11	0
Anthony Stokes	49	2	0	0	2	0	0	-	0	0	1	0	0	0	2	0	1	0	0
Teemu Tainio	1475	21	18	5	3	13	0	-	1	5	3	4	11	1	16	14	0	4	0
Martyn Waghorn	45	1	1	0	0	0	0	-	0	0	0	0	0	0	0	1	0	0	0
Dean Whitehead	2964	34	30	29	4	1	0	-	0	10	3	13	36	11	33	44	1	5	0
Dwight Yorke	283	7	4	0	3	4	0	-	0	0	0	0	1	0	4	2	0	1	0

SEASON TOTALS

Goals scored	34
Goals conceded	54
Clean sheets	9
Shots on target	210
Shots off target	187
Shots per goal	11.68
Pens awarded	1
Pens scored	1
Pens conceded	5
Offsides	91
Corners	175
Crosses	424
Players used	30
Fouls committed	380
Free-kicks won	416

CARDS RECEIVED

68 | 1

SEQUENCES

Wins	2
(13/12/08-20/12/08)	
Losses	4
(14/03/09-11/04/09)	
Draws	2
(04/10/08-18/10/08)	
Undefeated	4
(27/01/09-21/02/09)	
Without win	7
(21/02/09-11/04/09)	
Undefeated home	3
(on two occasions)	
Undefeated away	3
(10/01/09-21/02/09)	
Without scoring	3
(25/04/09-09/05/09)	
Without conceding	2
(07/02/09-21/02/09)	
Scoring	5
(10/01/09-07/02/09)	
Conceding	8
(25/10/08-06/12/08)	

SEASON INFORMATION

Highest Position: 5
Lowest Position: 19
Average goals scored per game: 0.89
Average goals conceded per game: 1.42

League position at the end of each week

League position at the end of:
August 18, September 13, October 10, November 18, December 15, January 13, February 11, March 14, April 16, May 16

MATCH RECORDS

Goals scored per match

		W	D	L	Pts
Failed to score	16	0	4	12	4
Scored 1 goal	14	2	5	7	11
Scored 2 goals	6	5	0	1	15
Scored 3 goals	0	0	0	0	0
Scored 4+ goals	2	2	0	0	6

Goals conceded per match

		W	D	L	Pts
Clean sheet	9	5	4	0	19
Conceded 1 goal	14	4	5	5	17
Conceded 2 goals	8	0	0	8	0
Conceded 3 goals	5	0	0	5	0
Conceded 4+ goals	2	0	0	2	0

QUICK-FIRE GOALS

From the start of a match
Kieran Richardson (v Tottenham) 2:11

By a substitute after coming on
Grant Leadbitter (v Arsenal) 1:50

LAST-GASP GOALS

From the start of a match
David Healy (v Stoke) 93:52

By a substitute after coming on
Michael Chopra (v Middlesbrough) 47:28

GOAL DETAILS

How the goals were struck

SCORED		CONCEDED
19	Right foot	31
6	Left foot	12
9	Headers	10
0	Others	1

How the goals were struck

SCORED		CONCEDED
22	Open play	36
6	Cross	8
1	Corner	2
1	Penalties	3
1	Direct from free-kick	2
1	Free-kick	1
2	Own goals	2

Distance from goal

SCORED		CONCEDED
17	6yds	23
12	18yds	25
5	18+yds	6

GOALS SCORED/CONCEDED PER FIVE-MINUTE INTERVALS

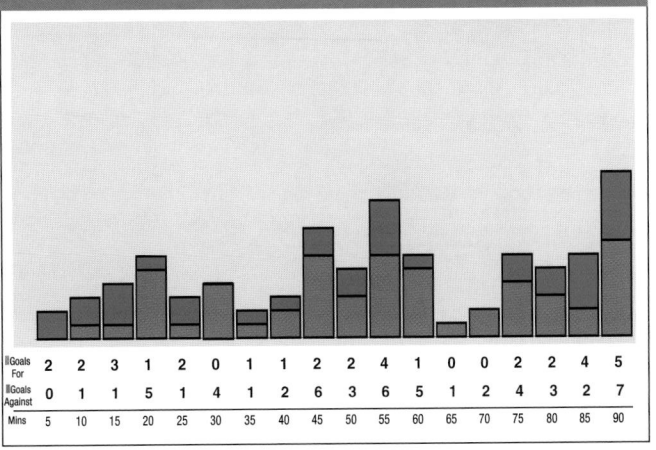

Goals For	2	2	3	1	2	0	1	1	2	2	4	1	0	0	2	2	4	5
Goals Against	0	1	1	5	1	4	1	2	6	3	6	5	1	2	4	3	2	7
Mins	5	10	15	20	25	30	35	40	45	50	55	60	65	70	75	80	85	90

TOTTENHAM HOTSPUR

CLUB SUMMARY

FORMED	1882
MANAGER	Harry Redknapp
GROUND	White Hart Lane
CAPACITY	36,236
NICKNAME	Spurs
WEBSITE	www.tottenhamhotspur.com

The New Football Pools PLAYER OF THE SEASON — Aaron Lennon

OVERALL

P	W	D	L	F	A	GD
54	22	13	19	74	65	9

BARCLAYS PREMIER LEAGUE

Pos	P	W	D	L	F	A	GD	Pts
8	38	14	9	15	45	45	0	51

HOME

Pos	P	W	D	L	F	A	GD	Pts
7	19	10	5	4	21	10	11	35

AWAY

Pos	P	W	D	L	F	A	GD	Pts
11	19	4	4	11	24	35	-11	16

CUP PROGRESS DETAILS

Competition	Round reached	Knocked out by
FA Cup	R4	Man Utd
UEFA Cup	R-32	Shakhtar Donetsk
Carling Cup	Final	Man Utd

BIGGEST WIN (ALL COMPS)
4–0 on two occasions

BIGGEST DEFEAT (ALL COMPS)
25/04/09 2–5 v Man Utd **PREM**

THE PLAYER WITH THE MOST

Shots on target	
David Bentley	41
Shots off target	
Luka Modric	23
Shots without scoring	
Tom Huddlestone	33
Assists	
Luka Modric	9
Offsides	
Darren Bent	26
Fouls	
Jermaine Jenas	44
Fouls without a card	
Jermain Defoe	5
Free-kicks won	
Luka Modric	55
Defensive clearances	
Jonathan Woodgate	37

actim INDEX for the 2008/09 Barclays Premier League Season

Rank	Player	Pts
14	Robbie Keane	482
33	Vedran Corluka	425
39	Aaron Lennon	411
43	Heurelho Gomes	408
72	Jermaine Jenas	364

ATTENDANCE RECORD

High	Low	Average
36,183	35,507	35,929
v Liverpool (01/11/2008)	v Bolton (26/10/2008)	

CLOCKWISE FROM TOP: Spurs' players come to terms with their League Cup final defeat to Manchester United; Harry Redknapp welcomes Robbie Keane back to White Hart Lane; Tottenham's big names feel the pain of a home defeat to Hull; Roman Pavlyuchenko scores in the win against Liverpool

AS HARRY Redknapp kept reminding everybody, Tottenham were bottom of the Barclays Premier League and only had two points from eight games when he arrived at the club in October.

The Juande Ramos era at the club had been brief and eventful. The Spaniard ended a nine-year trophy drought, but then lost the dressing room and only won three league games after the success at Wembley in picking up the League Cup in 2007/08. The extent of the problems Ramos had was illustrated by three dismissals in his final two games, with the lack of discipline highlighted later by chairman Daniel Levy as a sign of how deep the crisis was.

Redknapp arrived towards the end of October and turned the club's fortunes around. Ramos was a disciplinarian and his regime was strict, while Redknapp's way was to motivate players by telling them how good they are and putting an arm around their shoulders when needed.

'Treat them as I like to be treated myself,' Redknapp explained. 'I treat them with respect when they deserve it. If they step out of line you come down on them.'

Spurs waited less than 24 hours for the win they had been craving, a simple victory over Bolton. However, nothing was straightforward about the clash against Arsenal three days later. David Bentley put them ahead from 50 yards, but Arsenal were 4–2 ahead with a minute left to play. Cue Jermaine Jenas to offer hope. Cue Aaron Lennon to grab a dramatic stoppage-time equaliser. Cue pandemonium in the away end at the Emirates Stadium.

That was typical of Redknapp's start at Spurs. They also snatched a last-gasp victory over Liverpool despite being second best for the whole match.

With the bottom of the table being so tight, Spurs were still in the thick of the relegation battle despite their positive results. There were suggestions they were too good to go down, but within the club there was a feeling that the dogfight could go down to the wire.

Redknapp's reputation is for being a shrewd operator in the transfer market and he was busy during the January window, bringing Pascal Chimbonda, Jermain Defoe and Robbie Keane back to the club. All three had departed in the previous year.

The key signings, however, were Carlo Cudicini and Wilson Palacios. Cudicini hardly played, but his presence brought the

> ❝ **Cudicini's presence brought the best out of Heurelho Gomes** ❞

best out of Heurelho Gomes, the Brazilian keeper who had made a series of high-profile blunders at the start of the campaign. Gomes could well have departed in January, but Redknapp stuck with the summer signing and was rewarded with man-of-the-match displays.

Palacios added muscle to the midfield, a box-to-box grafter, and that also allowed Luka Modric to express himself as Spurs' playmaker. 'The fans love him – he's aggressive, he can play, he's got everything,' was how Redknapp described Palacios. 'Wilson is a good player and he will only get better for us.'

After struggling with the physical side of English football at the start of the campaign, Modric eventually became the cornerstone of Spurs' attack. 'He's the type of lad you look to build your team around. If you can get him on the ball, things can happen,' Redknapp said.

Things started happening for Spurs after Christmas. They reached the League Cup final again, but were beaten by Manchester United via a penalty shoot-out.

There was no hangover to the defeat and Spurs remained in the hunt for a European place and had an outside chance of qualification heading into the final week of the season. Under Redknapp they had only lost once at White Hart Lane in all competitions and, incredibly, they only conceded 10 league goals at home all season, a new club record.

TOTTENHAM HOTSPUR

August

16th ● Middlesbrough ....a **L 2–1** **Att:** 32,623. **Ref:** M Atkinson — **Tottenham** (4-4-1-1): Gomes, Zokora, Dawson, Woodgate, Assou-Ekotto (O'Hara 76), Lennon (Bale 65), Jenas▌, Modric, Bentley▌, Giovani (Berbatov 65), Bent. Subs not used: Cesar, Huddlestone, Gunter, King.

23rd ● Sunderland ....h **L 1–2** **Att:** 36,064. **Ref:** M Dean — **Tottenham** (4-1-4-1): Gomes, Zokora, King, Woodgate, Assou-Ekotto (Huddlestone 56), Modric, Lennon (Giovanni 56), Jenas▌, Bentley▌, Bale▌, Bent. Subs not used: Cesar, Gilberto, Gunter, O'Hara.

31st ● Chelsea ....a **D 1–1** **Att:** 41,790. **Ref:** H Webb — **Tottenham** (4-4-1-1): Gomes, Zokora, Woodgate, King, Gunter (Huddleston 62), Bent'ley (O'Hara 72), Jenas, Modric, Bale, Giovani (Lennon 59), Bent. Subs not used: Cesar, Gilberto, Dawson, Assou-Ekotto.

September

15th ● Aston Villa..........................h **L 1–2** **Att:** 36,075. **Ref:** S Bennett — **Tottenham** (4-4-2): Gomes, Corluka, Woodgate, Dawson▌ (Giovani 62), Bale, Lennon, Zokora (Bent'ley 46), Huddlestone, Modric (Jenas 29), Pavlyuchenko, Bent. Subs not used: Cesar, Gilberto, Campbell, O'Hara.

18th ● Wisla Krakow ....h **W 2–1** **Att:** 35,751. **Ref:** L Cortez Batista — **Tottenham** (4-4-2): Gomes, Gunter (O'Hara▌ 57), Woodgate, King, Bale, Bent'ley, Jenas, Zokora, Lennon (Campbell 57), Giovani (Assou-Ekotto 70), Bent. Subs not used: Cesar, Huddlestone, Gilberto, Dawson.

21st ● Wigan ....h **D 0–0** **Att:** 35,808. **Ref:** S Tanner — **Tottenham** (4-4-2): Gomes, Zokora, Woodgate, Corluka▌, Assou-Ekotto, Bentley (Lennon 64), Jenas, O'Hara▌, Bale (Huddleston 80), Bent, Pavlyuchenko (Campbell 46). Subs not used: Cesar, Gilberto, Gunter, Giovani.

24th ● Newcastle ....a **W 1–2** **Att:** 20,577. **Ref:** C Foy — **Tottenham** (4-5-1): Gomes, Corluka▌, King, Woodgate, Assou-Ekotto, Lennon (Campbell 62), Jenas, Zokora▌, O'Hara▌, Bale (Giovani▌ 53), Pavlyuchenko▌ (Modric 75). Subs not used: Cesar, Huddlestone, Bent, Gilberto.

28th ● Portsmouth ....a **L 2–0** **Att:** 20,352. **Ref:** M Dean — **Tottenham** (4-5-1): Gomes, Corluka, Dawson, Woodgate▌, Assou-Ekotto, Bentley, Jenas, Zokora (Giovani 58), O'Hara▌, Gilberto (Lennon▌ 46), Pavlyuchenko (Bent 73). Subs not used: Cesar, Huddlestone, Modric, Gunter.

October

2nd ● Wisla Krakow ....a **D 1–1** **Att:** 15,000. **Ref:** A Tudor — **Tottenham** (4-4-2): Gomes, Gunter, King, Woodgate▌, Bale▌, Lennon▌ (Dawson 88), Zokora▌, Jenas, Modric▌ (Huddlestone 77), Campbell (O'Hara 68), Bent. Subs not used: Cesar, Bentley, Giovani, Assou-Ekotto.

5th ● Hull ....h **L 0–1** **Att:** 36,062. **Ref:** R Styles — **Tottenham** (4-4-2): Gomes, Gunter (Bentley▌ 55), Corluka, Woodgate, Bale, Lennon▌ (Giovani 74), Jenas▌, Zokora, Modric, Pavlyuchenko (Bent 35), Campbell▌. Subs not used: Cesar, Dawson, O'Hara, Assou-Ekotto.

19th ● Stoke ....a **L 2–1** **Att:** 27,500. **Ref:** L Mason — **Tottenham** (4-5-1): Gomes, Hutton, Woodgate▌, Corluka (Dawson▌ 77), Bale▌, Lennon, Zokora, Jenas, Modric, Bent'ley (Pavlyuchenko 59), Bent. Subs not used: Cesar, Huddlestone, Campbell, O'Hara, Assou-Ekotto.

23rd ● Udinese ....a **L 2–0** **Att:** 22,000. **Ref:** F Brych — **Tottenham** (4-5-1): Gomes▌, Hutton, King, Woodgate (Giovani 64), Assou-Ekotto (Modric 46), Lennon, Zokora, Jenas, O'Hara▌▌, Bale▌, Bent. Subs not used: Cesar, Dawson, Gilberto, Gunter, Campbell.

26th ● Bolton ....h **W 2–0** **Att:** 35,507. **Ref:** A Marriner — **Tottenham** (4-4-2): Gomes, Hutton, Corluka, King, Assou-Ekotto, Bent'ley, Jenas, Huddlestone, Modric, O'Hara (Lennon 70), Pavlyuchenko▌ (Bent 67). Subs not used: Cesar, Zokora, Gunter, Giovani, Campbell.

29th ● Arsenal ....a **D 4–4** **Att:** 60,043. **Ref:** M Atkinson — **Tottenham** (4-5-1): Gomes, Hutton (Gunter 79), Corluka, Woodgate, Assou-Ekotto▌, Bent'ley, Modric, Jenas▌▌, Huddlestone▌, Bale (Lennon▌ 55), Pavlyuchenko (Bent 65). Subs not used: Cesar, Zokora, Campbell, O'Hara.

November

1st ● Liverpool ....h **W 2–1** **Att:** 36,183. **Ref:** P Dowd — **Tottenham** (4-4-1-1): Gomes, Corluka, King▌, Woodgate, Assou-Ekotto (Hutton 46), Bentley, Zokora, Huddlestone, O'Hara (Pavlyuchenko▌ 46), Modric (Lennon 75), Bent. Subs not used: Cesar, Bale, Gunter, Campbell.

6th ● Dinamo Zagreb...................h **W 4–0** **Att:** 32,788. **Ref:** F Fautrel — **Tottenham** (4-4-2): Gomes, Hutton, Woodgate (Gunter 85), Dawson, Bale, Bent'ley (Bostock 79), Zokora, Huddlestone▌, Lennon, Modric (Campbell 75), Bent. Subs not used: Cesar, Gilberto, Dervite, Assou-Ekotto.

9th ● Man City ....a **W 1–2** **Att:** 41,893. **Ref:** M Dean — **Tottenham** (4-4-1-1): Gomes, Corluka, Woodgate, King▌, Assou-Ekotto▌, Bent'ley, Huddlestone, Zokora▌, Jenas, Modric (Lennon 71), Bent. Subs not used: Cesar, Hutton, Pavlyuchenko, Campbell, Dawson, O'Hara.

12th ● Liverpool ....h **W 4–2** **Att:** 33,242. **Ref:** M Riley — **Tottenham** (4-4-2): Gomes (Cesar 74), Hutton, Dawson, Corluka, Bale, Lennon, Zokora, Huddlestone, Pavlyuchenko[2] (Boateng 90), Campbell[2] (Bent 90). Subs not used: Bentley, Modric, Gunter, Rocha.

15th ● Fulham ....a **L 2–1** **Att:** 25,139. **Ref:** A Wiley — **Tottenham** (4-4-2): Gomes, Corluka, Woodgate, King, Bale, Bentley, Jenas, Huddlestone (Pavlyuchenko 45), Zokora, Modric (Lennon 45), Bent (Campbell[1] 71). Subs not used: Cesar, Hutton, Dawson, Assou-Ekotto.

23rd ● Blackburn ....h **W 1–0** **Att:** 35,903. **Ref:** H Webb — **Tottenham** (4-4-2): Gomes, Corluka, Woodgate, King, Assou-Ekotto, Bentley▌ (O'Hara 86), Jenas▌, Huddlestone, Lennon, Pavlyuchenko▌ (Campbell 74), Bent. Subs not used: Cesar, Bale, Zokora, Gunter, Dawson.

27th ● NEC ....a **W 0–1** **Att:** 12,500. **Ref:** C Muniz Fernandez — **Tottenham** (4-4-2): Gomes, Gunter, Dawson, Woodgate, Bale, Bentley (Mason 90), Zokora, Huddlestone, O'Hara▌, Bent (Lennon 71), Campbell (Obika 83). Subs not used: Cesar, Assou-Ekotto, Bostock, Smith.

30th ● Everton ....h **L 0–1** **Att:** 35,742. **Ref:** S Bennett — **Tottenham** (4-4-2): Gomes, Corluka, Woodgate, King, Assou-Ekotto▌ (Bale 68), Lennon, Zokora, Huddlestone (Boateng 76), Bentley, Bent (Campbell 62), Pavlyuchenko. Subs not used: Cesar, Gunter, Dawson, O'Hara.

December

3rd ● Watford ....a **W 1–2** **Att:** 16,501. **Ref:** P Dowd — **Tottenham** (4-4-2): Gomes, Corluka, Dawson, Woodgate, Assou-Ekotto▌, Zokora, Lennon, Jenas, O'Hara, Pavlyuchenko▌, Campbell (Bent▌ 65). Subs not used: Cesar, Bale, Bentley, Huddlestone, Gunter, Boateng.

8th ● West Ham...........................a **W 0–2** **Att:** 34,277. **Ref:** C Foy — **Tottenham** (4-4-1-1): Gomes, Corluka, Woodgate, King▌, Assou-Ekotto, Lennon, Zokora, Jenas, Bentley (O'Hara▌ 81), Modric, Pavlyuchenko (Bent 54). Subs not used: Cesar, Bale, Huddlestone, Dawson, Boateng.

13th ● Man Utd ....h **D 0–0** **Att:** 35,882. **Ref:** M Dean — **Tottenham** (4-4-1-1): Gomes, Corluka, Dawson, Woodgate (Huddlestone▌ 10), Assou-Ekotto, Lennon, Zokora, Jenas (O'Hara 62), Bentley, Modric, Pavlyuchenko (Bent 54). Subs not used: Cesar, Bale, Gunter, Boateng.

18th ● Spartak Moscow.................h **D 2–2** **Att:** 28,906. **Ref:** P Proenca — **Tottenham** (4-4-2): Gomes, Gunter, Zokora, Dawson, Gilberto (Lennon 46), Bentley, Huddlestone▌, O'Hara, Bale, Modric▌, Campbell. Subs not used: Cesar, Assou-Ekotto, Bostock, Parrett, Dervite, Obika.

21st ● Newcastle ....a **L 2–1** **Att:** 47,982. **Ref:** A Marriner — **Tottenham** (4-4-2): Gomes, Corluka, King, Dawson, Assou-Ekotto, Bentley, Zokora, Huddlestone▌, Lennon, Pavlyuchenko (Campbell 64), Modric▌[1]. Subs not used: Cesar, Bale, Gunter, Taarabt, Boateng, O'Hara.

26th ● Fulham ....h **D 0–0** **Att:** 35,866. **Ref:** P Walton — **Tottenham** (4-4-1-1): Gomes, Corluka, Dawson, King, Assou-Ekotto, Lennon, Zokora, Huddlestone (Jenas 20), Bentley (Campbell 58), Modric, Bent (Pavlyuchenko 72). Subs not used: Cesar, Bale, O'Hara, Woodgate.

28th ● West Brom........................a **L 2–0** **Att:** 26,344. **Ref:** S Tanner — **Tottenham** (4-4-2): Gomes, Corluka, Dawson▌, Woodgate, Assou-Ekotto▌, Lennon, Zokora (Campbell 86), Jenas▌, Bentley (O'Hara 69), Modric (Bale 75), Bent. Subs not used: Cesar, Gunter, Taarabt, Obika.

January

2nd ● Wigan ....h **W 3–1** **Att:** 34,040. **Ref:** A Wiley — **Tottenham** (4-4-2): Gomes, Corluka, Woodgate, Dawson, Bale, Bentley, Modric▌ (Lennon 90), Zokora, O'Hara, Bent (Campbell 27), Pavlyuchenko[2]. Subs not used: Alnwick, Ghaly, Gunter, Taarabt, Boateng.

6th ● Burnley ....h **W 4–1** **Att:** 31,377. **Ref:** M Atkinson — **Tottenham** (4-4-2): Gomes, Corluka, Dawson[1], Woodgate, Bale, Lennon, Modric, Zokora, Bentley (O'Hara[1] 46), Pavlyuchenko[1], Campbell. Subs not used: Alnwick, Gunter, Giovani, Taarabt, Boateng, Rocha.

11th ● Wigan ....a **L 1–0** **Att:** 17,500. **Ref:** A Marriner — **Tottenham** (5-3-2): Gomes, Corluka, Dawson (Jenas 79), Woodgate▌, King, Bale▌, Zokora▌, Modric (Lennon 57), O'Hara, Pavlyuchenko (Bent 53), Defoe. Subs not used: Cesar, Bentley, Huddlestone, Campbell.

● Barclays Premier League ● FA Cup ● Carling Cup ● UEFA Champions League ● UEFA Cup

▌ Yellow Card ▌ Red Card

RESULTS 2008/09

18th	● Portsmouth	h	D 1–1	**Att:** 36,011. **Ref:** S Bennett — **Tottenham** (4-3-1-2): Gomes, Corluka, Woodgate, King (Dawson 44), Bale (Bentley 68), Lennon, Zokora, O'Hara, Modric, Pavlyuchenko (Bent 28), Defoe[1]. Subs not used: Alnwick, Huddlestone, Campbell, Taarabt.
21st	● Burnley	a	L 3–2	**Att:** 19,533. **Ref:** M Halsey — **Tottenham** (4-4-1-1): Alnwick, Gunter (Taarabt 95), Woodgate, Dawson, Assou-Ekotto, Bentley▌, Zokora, Huddlestone, O'Hara (Bale 62), Modric (Pavlyuchenko[1] 65), Defoe[1]. Subs not used: Cesar, Giovani, Campbell, Rocha.
24th	● Man Utd	a	L 2–1	**Att:** 75,014. **Ref:** P Walton — **Tottenham** (4-4-1-1): Alnwick, Gunter, Corluka, Dawson, Assou-Ekotto, Bentley (Defoe 72), Huddlestone, Zokora, Bale (Taarabt 67), Modric (Giovani 46), Pavlyuchenko[1]. Subs not used: Gomes, Gilberto, Rocha, Dervite.
27th	● Stoke	h	W 3–1	**Att:** 36,072. **Ref:** M Riley — **Tottenham** (4-4-2): Cudicini, Corluka, Dawson[1], Woodgate▌, Assou-Ekotto, Lennon[1] (Huddlestone 90), Zokora, Modric, Bentley▌, Pavlyuchenko (Campbell 90), Defoe[1]. Subs not used: Alnwick, Bale, Taarabt, Rocha, Giovani.
31st	● Bolton	a	L 3–2	**Att:** 21,575. **Ref:** P Dowd — **Tottenham** (4-4-1-1): Cudicini, Corluka (Chimbonda 67), Dawson▌, Woodgate, Assou-Ekotto, Bent[2]ley, Zokora (Jenas 46), Palacios, Lennon, Modric (Bent 46), Pavlyuchenko. Subs not used: Alnwick, Bale, Huddlestone, Campbell.

February

8th	● Arsenal	h	D 0–0	**Att:** 36,021. **Ref:** M Dean — **Tottenham** (4-4-2): Cudicini, Corluka (Chimbonda 74), Dawson, Woodgate, Assou-Ekotto, Lennon (Taarabt 87), Jenas, Palacios, Modric▌, Pavlyuchenko (Bent 64), Keane. Subs not used: Gomes, Bale, Zokora, Huddlestone.
19th	● Shakhtar Donetsk	a	L 2–0	**Att:** 25,000. **Ref:** T Einwaller — **Tottenham** (4-3-2-1): Gomes, Gunter, Huddlestone, Dawson, Chimbonda, Jenas, Zokora, Parrett (Bostock 89), Bentley, Giovani (Bent 69), Campbell. Subs not used: Jansson, Gilberto, Smith, Mason, Obika.
23rd	● Hull	a	W 1–2	**Att:** 24,742. **Ref:** L Probert — **Tottenham** (4-4-2): Cudicini, Corluka, Woodgate[1] (Dawson 89), King, Assou-Ekotto, Lennon[1] (Zokora 87), Jenas, Palacios, Modric▌, Keane, Bent (Pavlyuchenko 72). Subs not used: Gomes, Bentley, Huddlestone, Chimbonda.
26th	● Shakhtar Donetsk	h	D 1–1	**Att:** 30,595. **Ref:** P Tagliavento — **Tottenham** (4-4-2): Gomes, Gunter, Chimbonda, Huddlestone, Gilberto (Bostock 77), Giovani[1], Palacios▌, O'Hara▌ (Parrett 71), Bale, Campbell, Obika. Subs not used: Jansson, Butcher, Smith, Mason, Townsend.

March

1st	● Man Utd	n	D 0–0	**Att:** 88,217. **Ref:** C Foy — **Tottenham** (4-4-2): Gomes, Corluka, Dawson, King, Assou-Ekotto, Lennon (Bentley 102), Jenas (Bale 98), Zokora, Modric, Bent, Pavlyuchenko (O'Hara 65). Subs not used: Alnwick, Huddlestone, Gunter, Taarabt. AET; Man Utd won 4-1 on pens
4th	● Middlesbrough	h	W 4–0	**Att:** 35,761. **Ref:** H Webb — **Tottenham** (4-4-2): Gomes, Zokora, Dawson, Woodgate, Assou-Ekotto, Lennon[2], Palacios, Jenas (Huddlestone 64), Modric (O'Hara 73), Pavlyuchenko[1] (Bent 53), Keane[1]. Subs not used: Cudicini, Bentley, Chimbonda, Corluka.
7th	● Sunderland	a	D 1–1	**Att:** 37,894. **Ref:** P Dowd — **Tottenham** (4-4-2): Gomes, Corluka (Pavlyuchenko 83), Woodgate▌, King, Chimbonda, Lennon, Jenas (Huddlestone 63), Palacios (Bentley 72), Modric, Bent, Keane[1]. Subs not used: Cudicini, Zokora, Dawson, O'Hara.
15th	● Aston Villa	a	W 1–2	**Att:** 41,205. **Ref:** S Bennett — **Tottenham** (4-4-2): Gomes, Zokora (Corluka 35), King, Woodgate, Assou-Ekotto, Lennon, Jenas[1], Palacios, Modric[1] (O'Hara 82), Bent[1], Keane▌. Subs not used: Cudicini, Bentley, Huddlestone, Pavlyuchenko, Dawson.
21st	● Chelsea	h	W 1–0	**Att:** 36,034. **Ref:** M Dean — **Tottenham** (4-4-2): Gomes, Corluka, Woodgate, King, Assou-Ekotto, Lennon (Zokora 90), Jenas, Palacios▌, Modric▌[1] (O'Hara 87), Bent, Keane. Subs not used: Cudicini, Bentley, Huddlestone, Pavlyuchenko, Dawson.

April

4th	● Blackburn	a	L 2–1	**Att:** 21,891. **Ref:** P Walton — **Tottenham** (4-4-2): Gomes, Corluka, Woodgate, King, Assou-Ekotto, Lennon (Zokora 83), Jenas, Palacios▌▌, Modric, Bent, Keane[1]. Subs not used: Cudicini, Bentley, Huddlestone, Pavlyuchenko, Dawson, Chimbonda.
11th	● West Ham	h	W 1–0	**Att:** 35,969. **Ref:** M Atkinson — **Tottenham** (4-4-2): Gomes, Corluka, Woodgate, King, Assou-Ekotto, Lennon, Huddlestone, Jenas (Zokora▌ 46), Modric, Bent (Pavlyuchenko[1] 56), Keane. Subs not used: Cudicini, Bale, Bentley, Dawson, Chimbonda.
19th	● Newcastle	h	W 1–0	**Att:** 35,850. **Ref:** M Halsey — **Tottenham** (4-4-2): Gomes, Corluka, Dawson (Hutton 33), Woodgate, Assou-Ekotto▌, Lennon, Palacios, Huddlestone, Modric, Keane, Bent[1] (Defoe 75). Subs not used: Cudicini, Bale, Zokora, Bentley, Campbell.
25th	● Man Utd	a	L 5–2	**Att:** 75,458. **Ref:** H Webb — **Tottenham** (4-4-2): Gomes▌, Corluka, Woodgate▌, King, Assou-Ekotto, Lennon, Palacios, Jenas▌, Modric[1] (Bale 86), Keane (Huddlestone 87), Bent[1]. Subs not used: Cudicini, Hutton, Zokora, Bentley, Chimbonda.

May

2nd	● West Brom	h	W 1–0	**Att:** 35,836. **Ref:** R Styles — **Tottenham** (4-4-2): Gomes, Corluka, Woodgate, King, Assou-Ekotto, Lennon, Palacios▌, Jenas[1], Modric, Pavlyuchenko (Defoe 65), Keane. Subs not used: Cudicini, Hutton, Bale, Zokora, Bentley, Huddlestone.
9th	● Everton	a	D 0–0	**Att:** 36,646. **Ref:** L Mason — **Tottenham** (4-4-2): Gomes, Corluka, King, Woodgate, Bale, Hutton▌, Huddlestone, Jenas▌, Modric (Pavlyuchenko▌ 81), Keane, Defoe. Subs not used: Cudicini, Bentley, Gunter, Campbell, Chimbonda, Rose.
16th	● Man City	h	W 2–1	**Att:** 36,000. **Ref:** M Halsey — **Tottenham** (4-1-3-2): Gomes, Corluka, Woodgate (Hutton 46), King, Assou-Ekotto, Huddlestone, Keane[1], Jenas (Zokora 67), Modric, Pavlyuchenko (Campbell 70), Defoe[1]. Subs not used: Cudicini, Bale, Bentley, Chimbonda.
24th	● Liverpool	a	L 3–1	**Att:** 43,937. **Ref:** P Walton — **Tottenham** (4-4-2): Gomes, Hutton, Corluka▌, King, Assou-Ekotto, Modric, Zokora, Jenas (Bentley 40), Bale (Bent 78), Defoe (Pavlyuchenko 70), Keane[1]. Subs not used: Cudicini, Gunter, Campbell, Chimbonda.

● Barclays Premier League ● FA Cup ● Carling Cup ● UEFA Champions League ● UEFA Cup   ▌Yellow Card ▐ Red Card

Jermaine Jenas celebrates a goal with his Spurs teammates; Jermain Defoe takes on Manchester City's Micah Richards

TOTTENHAM HOTSPUR

BARCLAYS PREMIER LEAGUE GOALKEEPER STATS

Player	Minutes on pitch	Appearances	Match starts	Completed matches	Sub appearances	Subbed off	Saved with feet	Punched	Parried	Tipped over	Fumbled	Tipped round	Caught	Blocked	Clean sheets	Goals conceded	Minutes since conceding	Save %	Saved	Resulting in goals	Opposition miss	Yellow cards	Red cards
							SAVES BREAKDOWN													**PENALTIES**			
Carlo Cudicini 383	4	4	4	0	0	0	3	0	1	0	0	11	0	1	5	70	75.00	0	0	0	0	0
Heurelho Gomes 3251	34	34	34	0	0	1	33	30	6	0	15	114	1	12	40	29	83.47	0	3	1	1	0

BARCLAYS PREMIER LEAGUE OUTFIELD PLAYER STATS

Player	Minutes on pitch	Appearances	Match starts	Completed matches	Substitute appearances	Subbed off	Goals scored	Minutes since scoring	Assists	Shots on target	Shots off target	Crosses	Defensive clearances	Defensive blocks	Fouls committed	Free-kicks won	Caught offside	Yellow cards	Red cards
Benoit Assou-Ekotto 2562	29	29	23	0	4	0	-	1	4	4	28	8	9	25	39	1	3	2
Gareth Bale.................................1051	16	12	7	4	4	0	-	0	8	11	36	8	4	6	20	0	2	1
Darren Bent 2315	33	21	15	12	6	12	81	2	35	21	5	13	0	33	22	26	1	0
David Bentley 1929	25	20	13	5	7	1	1249	3	41	21	105	2	0	22	35	2	4	0
Dimitar Berbatov 29	1	0	0	1	0	0	296	0	0	0	1	0	0	1	1	0	0	0
Kevin-Prince Boateng 20	1	0	0	1	0	0	-	0	0	0	0	0	0	2	0	0	0	0
Fraizer Campbell...........................315	10	1	1	9	0	1	161	1	4	5	3	0	0	8	5	2	1	0
Pascal Chimbonda 143	3	1	1	2	0	0	-	1	0	0	4	1	0	0	2	0	0	0
Vedran Corluka 3139	34	33	29	1	4	0	3341	3	4	4	11	20	15	28	29	0	3	0
Michael Dawson 1208	16	13	9	3	3	1	395	1	4	1	0	28	11	14	16	1	3	1
Jermain Defoe..............................590	8	6	5	2	1	3	136	1	10	6	3	2	0	5	7	10	0	0
Gilberto 45	1	1	0	0	1	0	-	0	0	0	0	0	0	1	1	0	0	0
Dos Santos Giovani 252	6	2	0	4	2	0	-	0	3	3	4	0	0	4	3	0	0	0
Chris Gunter 135	3	2	0	1	2	0	-	0	0	0	2	1	0	0	3	0	0	0
Tom Huddlestone 1426	22	14	11	8	3	0	-	2	20	13	11	21	5	28	8	0	3	0
Alan Hutton 628	8	5	4	3	1	0	-	1	2	0	5	2	0	1	9	1	2	0
Jermaine Jenas 2659	32	28	22	4	6	4	253	3	18	11	9	16	10	44	27	2	7	0
Robbie Keane............................1329	14	14	13	0	1	5	16	3	14	9	6	5	2	9	21	4	1	0
Ledley King...............................2232	24	24	23	0	1	1	1402	0	7	6	0	27	17	17	13	0	2	0
Aaron Lennon 2680	35	26	18	9	8	5	769	6	29	15	55	0	0	23	44	3	2	0
Luka Modric 2921	34	34	22	0	12	3	419	9	35	23	30	2	0	23	55	8	5	0
Jamie O'Hara 652	15	6	4	9	2	1	289	0	4	9	16	2	1	10	1	2	2	0
Wilson Palacios 1016	11	11	9	0	1	0	-	1	9	4	1	1	1	31	18	0	3	1
Roman Pavlyuchenko 1531	28	19	3	9	16	5	207	1	24	22	0	3	2	32	28	19	1	0
Adel Taarabt....................................8	1	0	0	1	0	0	-	0	0	1	0	0	0	0	0	0	0	0
Jonathan Woodgate..................3112	34	34	31	0	3	1	1001	0	4	10	0	37	20	29	20	1	6	0
Didier Zokora 2188	29	24	19	5	5	0	-	0	2	4	7	6	3	34	19	0	4	0

SEASON TOTALS

Goals scored	45
Goals conceded	45
Clean sheets	13
Shots on target	281
Shots off target	203
Shots per goal	10.76
Pens awarded	3
Pens scored	3
Pens conceded	4
Offsides	82
Corners	222
Crosses	342
Players used	29
Fouls committed	429
Free-kicks won	462

CARDS RECEIVED

56 **5**

SEQUENCES

Wins	2
(on four occasions)	
Losses	3
(28/09/08-19/10/08)	
Draws	
(−)	
Undefeated	6
(08/02/09-21/03/09)	
Without win	8
(16/08/08-19/10/08)	
Undefeated home	11
(13/12/08-16/05/09)	
Undefeated away	3
(23/02/09-15/03/09)	
Without scoring	3
(on two occasions)	
Without conceding	2
(on three occasions)	
Scoring	10
(23/02/09-02/05/09)	
Conceding	5
(28/12/08-31/01/09)	

SEASON INFORMATION

Highest Position: 7
Lowest Position: 20
Average goals scored per game: 1.18
Average goals conceded per game: 1.18

League position at the end of each week

League position at the end of: August 19, September 20, October 20, November 16, December 16, January 14, February 14, March 11, April 10, May 8

MATCH RECORDS

Goals scored per match

		W	D	L	Pts
Failed to score	10	0	5	5	5
Scored 1 goal	16	5	3	8	18
Scored 2 goals	9	7	0	2	21
Scored 3 goals	1	1	0	0	3
Scored 4+ goals	2	2	1	0	4

Goals conceded per match

		W	D	L	Pts
Clean sheet	13	8	5	0	29
Conceded 1 goal	12	6	3	3	21
Conceded 2 goals	9	0	0	9	0
Conceded 3 goals	2	0	0	2	0
Conceded 4+ goals	2	0	1	1	1

QUICK-FIRE GOALS

From the start of a match
Jermaine Jenas (v Aston Villa) 4:09

By a substitute after coming on
Darren Bent (v Arsenal) 1:20

LAST-GASP GOALS

From the start of a match
Aaron Lennon (v Arsenal) 93:18

By a substitute after coming on
Roman Pavlyuchenko (v Liverpool) 45:06

GOAL DETAILS

How the goals were struck

SCORED		CONCEDED
25	Right foot	25
13	Left foot	9
7	Headers	11
0	Others	0

How the goals were struck

SCORED		CONCEDED
35	Open play	30
4	Cross	3
1	Corner	4
3	Penalties	3
0	Direct from free-kick	1
0	Free-kick	2
2	Own goals	2

Distance from goal

SCORED		CONCEDED
11	6yds	19
30	18yds	21
4	18+yds	5

GOALS SCORED/CONCEDED PER FIVE-MINUTE INTERVALS

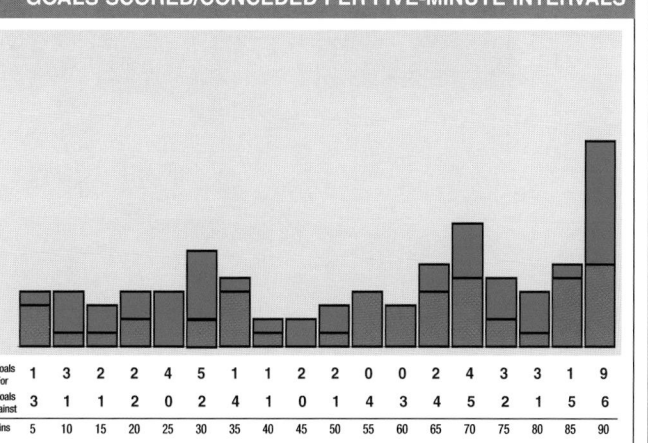

Goals For	1	3	2	2	4	5	1	1	2	2	0	0	2	4	3	3	1	9
Goals Against	3	1	1	2	0	2	4	1	0	1	4	3	4	5	2	1	5	6
Mins	5	10	15	20	25	30	35	40	45	50	55	60	65	70	75	80	85	90

WEST BROMWICH ALBION

CLUB SUMMARY

FORMED	1878
MANAGER	Tony Mowbray
GROUND	The Hawthorns
CAPACITY	27,877
NICKNAME	The Baggies
WEBSITE	www.wbafc.co.uk

The New **Football Pools** PLAYER OF THE SEASON — **Chris Brunt**

OVERALL

P	W	D	L	F	A	GD
43	9	10	24	43	76	-33

BARCLAYS PREMIER LEAGUE

Pos	P	W	D	L	F	A	GD	Pts
20	38	8	8	22	36	67	-31	32

HOME

Pos	P	W	D	L	F	A	GD	Pts
17	19	7	3	9	26	33	-7	24

AWAY

Pos	P	W	D	L	F	A	GD	Pts
19	19	1	5	13	10	34	-24	8

CUP PROGRESS DETAILS

Competition	Round reached	Knocked out by
FA Cup	R4	Burnley
Carling Cup	R2	Hartlepool

BIGGEST WIN (ALL COMPS)
3–0 on two occasions

BIGGEST DEFEAT (ALL COMPS)
27/01/09 0–5 v Man Utd **PREM**

THE PLAYER WITH THE MOST

Shots on target		
Marc-Antoine Fortuné		32
Shots off target		
Chris Brunt		38
Shots without scoring		
Borja Valero		25
Assists		
Marc-Antoine Fortuné		4
Offsides		
Marc-Antoine Fortuné		26
Fouls		
Gianni Zuiverloon		54
Fouls without a card		
Marc-Antoine Fortuné		15
Free-kicks won		
Jonathan Greening		50
Defensive clearances		
Jonas Olsson		48

actim INDEX
for the 2008/09 Barclays Premier League Season

Rank	Player	Pts
93	Scott Carson	335
121	Jonas Olsson	302
125	Jonathan Greening	296
126	Paul Robinson	295
132	Robert Koren	288

ATTENDANCE RECORD

High	Low	Average
26,344	24,741	25,828

v Tottenham (28/12/2008) v Wigan (09/05/2009)

CLOCKWISE FROM TOP: Chris Brunt celebrates scoring against Wigan in May; Scott Carson shows his dismay after conceding yet again in a tough season for West Brom; Tony Mowbray gives instructions from the touchline; Juan Carlos Menseguez fires the ball home in the 3–0 win over Sunderland

WEST BROM lived up to their reputation of being a yo-yo club as they were relegated from the Barclays Premier League for the third time in seven seasons.

The Baggies had been impressive in securing the Coca-Cola Championship title 12 months ago with a brand of attacking football which produced more than 100 goals. But they lasted only one campaign in the top flight, while their fellow promoted clubs Stoke City and Hull City survived – the latter on the final day – for another crack amongst the elite.

Albion reached the lofty heights of eighth spot in early October after back-to-back wins but, from that point on, the season became one of constant struggle. A three-month spell from mid-January without a league win effectively sealed their fate.

Baggies boss Tony Mowbray refused to compromise his beliefs with Albion often enjoying as much possession as their opponents and their football being pleasing on their eye. But in the final analysis, major failings in both penalty boxes led to their downfall.

Too often West Brom lacked a killer touch in their opponents' area and were hit by the loss of Ishmael Miller with a long-term knee injury before Christmas, just as he was beginning to hit form with three goals in seven games. Only on-loan striker Marc-Antoine Fortuné threatened to provide a solution in this department during the second half of the campaign, but the likes of Luke Moore and Roman Bednar were major flops.

The biggest headache for Mowbray was the shocking defensive frailties of his side, a particularly galling situation given that his own distinguished and lengthy playing career was spent in that role for nearly two decades. At times Albion's defending was embarrassing with too many sides being gifted soft and sloppy goals via schoolboy errors rather than having to work for to create them. West Brom did suffer a string of injuries in this department, but that was still no excuse for the unforced mistakes that became an unwanted trademark.

The Baggies were also chronically short of players with proven Barclays Premier League experience, with only skipper Jonathan Greening and Paul Robinson – members of the side that avoided relegation under Bryan Robson in 2004/05 – falling into that category.

West Brom often looked lightweight, and club-record signing Borja Valero struggled to come to terms with the physical demands of the fast and frantic Barclays Premier League.

Mowbray's immediate future looks secure – unless he decides the time is right to quit – and he has retained the faith of the majority of the Baggies followers.

But the Baggies boss will have to sell from within his current squad if he is to rebuild, with no new funds being made available, and he has been told he must reduce his senior playing staff from 31 to 20 players. Publicly at least, Mowbray has always maintained he will work within the parameters placed before him by chairman Jeremy Peace.

Captain Greening had already pledged his future to the club before relegation was confirmed in the penultimate game against Liverpool, but it remains to be seen whether other key players will follow suit.

Midfield duo James Morrison – a transfer target for Bolton in January – and Robert Koren plus centre-back Jonas Olsson are likely to be targeted by top-flight clubs keen to profit from Albion's relegation. Scotland international Morrison, a key man since joining from Middlesbrough, was one of Albion's most consistent performers before a heel problem curtailed his involvement in the final few games. Olsson has already indicated his desire to remain in the top flight and has been linked with the likes of Everton and local rivals Aston Villa, who need a dominant defender after the retirement of Martin Laursen.

But, no matter which players decide to leave or remain at The Hawthorns, Mowbray will not compromise his dogmatic belief in playing a passing and fluent style of football. That might get his team back into the Barclays Premier League, but staying there could again be a problem.

> ## A three-month spell from mid-January without a win effectively sealed their fate

WEST BROMWICH ALBION

August

16th ● Arsenal ....a   L 1–0   **Att:** 60,071. **Ref:** H Webb — **West Brom** (4-5-1): Carson, Hoefkens, Barnett, Meite, Robinson, Brunt (Beattie 80), Morrison, Greening, Kim, Cech (MacDonald 68), Miller (Bednar 74). Subs not used: Kiely, Dorrans, Pele, Martis.

23rd ● Everton ....h   L 1–2   **Att:** 26,190. **Ref:** R Styles —West Brom (4-5-1): Carson, Zuiverloon, Meite, Barnett, Robinson, Morrison, Kim (MacDonald 71), Koren (Bednar' 70), Greening, Brunt, Miller (Beattie 80). Subs not used: Kiely, Hoefkens, Cech, Pele.

26th ● Hartlepool ....a   L 3–1   **Att:** 3,387. **Ref:** M Haywood —West Brom (4-4-2): Kiely, Hoefkens, Barnett, Meite, Cech, Koren' (Pele 94) Greening, Borja Valero, Brunt (MacDonald 46), Bednar (Beattie 64), Moore. Subs not used: Dorrans, Carson, Slusarski, Martis.

30th ● Bolton ....a   D 0–0   **Att:** 20,387. **Ref:** K Stroud —West Brom (4-4-1-1): Carson, Zuiverloon, Meite (Hoefkens 46), Barnett, Robinson, Borja Valero (Cech 58), Koren (MacDonald 70), Greening, Morrison, Kim, Miller. Subs not used: Kiely, Bednar, Brunt, Moore.

September

13th ● West Ham ....h   W 3–2   **Att:** 26,213. **Ref:** L Probert —West Brom (4-1-4-1): Carson, Hoefkens, Barnett, Olsson, Robinson, Morrison' (Kim 64), Koren, Greening, Brunt', Borja Valero (Moore 64) Bednar' (Cech 86). Subs not used: Kiely, Beattie, MacDonald, Donk.

21st ● Aston Villa...............h   L 1–2   **Att:** 26,011. **Ref:** M Dean —West Brom (4-5-1): Carson, Zuiverloon, Barnett, Olsson, Robinson, Borja Valero (Moore 57), Morrison', Koren, Greening, Brunt (Kim 20), Bednar (Miller 57). Subs not used: Kiely, Hoefkens, Cech, Donk.

27th ● Middlesbrough ....a   W 0–1   **Att:** 26,248. **Ref:** C Foy —West Brom (4-5-1): Carson, Zuiverloon, Donk, Olsson', Robinson, Borja Valero, Morrison (Cech 76), Koren, Greening, Kim (S MacDonald 4 (Miller 46)), Bednar, S MacDonald (Miller 46). Subs not used: Kiely, Barnett, Moore, Pele.

October

4th ● Fulham ....h   W 1–0   **Att:** 25,708. **Ref:** P Dowd —West Brom (4-4-2): Carson, Zuiverloon, Donk, Olsson, Robinson, Morrison (Cech 79), Koren, Greening, Borja Valero, Miller (Moore 64), Bednar'. Subs not used: Kiely, Hoefkens, Barnett, MacDonald, Pele.

18th ● Man Utd ....a   L 4–0   **Att:** 75,451. **Ref:** M Halsey —West Brom (4-5-1): Carson, Zuiverloon, Donk, Olsson, Robinson, Morrison, Koren (Moore 72), Borja Valero, Greening, Brunt, Bednar (Miller 53). Subs not used: Kiely, Hoefkens, Cech, Barnett, MacDonald.

25th ● Hull ....h   L 0–3   **Att:** 26,323. **Ref:** L Probert —West Brom (4-4-2): Carson, Zuiverloon, Donk, Olsson, Robinson, Morrison (Moore 80), Greening, Koren (Brunt 80), Borja Valero, Miller (MacDonald 80), Bednar. Subs not used: Kiely, Hoefkens, Cech, Barnett.

28th ● Newcastle ....a   L 2–1   **Att:** 45,801. **Ref:** M Dean —West Brom (4-5-1): Carson, Zuiverloon, Donk, Olsson, Robinson, Koren, Morrison, Brunt (Miller' 54), Borja Valero, Greening, Bednar (Moore' 67). Subs not used: Kiely, Hoefkens, Cech, MacDonald, Pele.

November

1st ● Blackburn ....h   D 2–2   **Att:** 24,976. **Ref:** M Jones —West Brom (4-4-2): Carson, Zuiverloon, Donk (Hoefkens 46), Olsson, Robinson, Koren, Greening, Morrison (Brunt 69), Borja Valero, Bednar', Miller' (Moore 80). Subs not used: Kiely, Cech, Kim, Pele.

8th ● Liverpool..................a   L 3–0   **Att:** 43,451. **Ref:** P Walton —West Brom (4-4-2): Carson, Zuiverloon, Olsson, Donk, Robinson, Koren, Borja Valero, Greening, Kim (Filipe Teixeira 56), Bednar (Moore 56), Miller (Brunt 71). Subs not used: Kiely, Hoefkens, Dorrans, Pele.

15th ● Chelsea ....a   L 0–3   **Att:** 26,322. **Ref:** S Bennett —West Brom (4-4-2): Carson, Zuiverloon, Meite (Donk 68), Olsson, Robinson, Koren, Morrison (Filipe Teixeira 58), Greening, Borja Valero, Miller, Bednar (Kim 46). Subs not used: Kiely, Cech, Brunt, Moore.

22nd ● Stoke ....a   L 1–0   **Att:** 26,613. **Ref:** L Mason —West Brom (4-5-1): Carson, Zuiverloon, Meite, Olsson, Robinson, Greening, Borja Valero (Bednar 86), Kim (Filipe Teixeira 57), Brunt, Koren, Miller. Subs not used: Kiely, Cech, Barnett, Moore, Donk.

29th ● Wigan ....a   L 2–1   **Att:** 17,054. **Ref:** P Dowd —West Brom (4-5-1): Carson, Zuiverloon, Meite, Olsson, Robinson, Morrison (Moore 89), Koren, Greening, Borja Valero, Brunt (Bednar 89), Miller'. Subs not used: Kiely, Cech, Barnett, Kim, Filipe Teixeira.

December

7th ● Portsmouth ....h   D 1–1   **Att:** 24,964. **Ref:** M Dean —West Brom (4-5-1): Carson, Zuiverloon, Meite, Olsson, Robinson, Morrison, Borja Valero (Bednar 67), Greening', Koren, Brunt, Miller (Moore 76). Subs not used: Kiely, Cech, Barnett, Kim, Filipe Teixeira.

13th ● Sunderland ....a   L 4–0   **Att:** 36,280. **Ref:** L Mason —West Brom (4-4-2): Carson', Zuiverloon, Olsson, Meite, Robinson', Brunt (Kim 46), Borja Valero, Koren, Morrison (Bednar 46), Greening, Moore (Beattie 68). Subs not used: Kiely, Cech, Barnett, Filipe Teixeira.

21st ● Man City ....h   W 2–1   **Att:** 25,010. **Ref:** C Foy —West Brom (4-4-2): Carson, Zuiverloon, Meite, Olsson, Robinson', Morrison, Koren, Greening (Brunt 83), Kim (Dorrans 64), Bednar', Moore' (Beattie 73). Subs not used: Kiely, Hoefkens, Barnett, Pele.

26th ● Chelsea ....a   L 2–0   **Att:** 43,417. **Ref:** R Styles —West Brom (4-5-1): Carson, Zuiverloon, Meite (Barnett 27), Olsson, Robinson, Morrison, Koren, Greening, Kim (Bednar 69), Brunt, Beattie (Moore 60). Subs not used: Kiely, Cech, Dorrans, Borja Valero.

28th ● Tottenham ....h   W 2–0   **Att:** 26,344. **Ref:** S Tanner —West Brom (4-3-1-2): Carson, Zuiverloon (Hoefkens 72), Olsson, Barnett, Cech, Morrison, Greening, Brunt (Dorrans 65), Borja Valero (Beattie' 80), Bednar', Moore. Subs not used: Kiely, Kim, MacDonald, Donk.

January

3rd ● Peterborough ....h   D 1–1   **Att:** 18,659. **Ref:** K Friend —West Brom (4-4-2): Carson, Hoefkens, Olsson', Barnett, Cech, Koren (Simpson 46), Greening, Borja Valero, Morrison (Dorrans 70), Bednar (Beattie 76). Subs not used: Kiely, Robinson, Kim, Donk.

10th ● Aston Villa...............a   L 2–1   **Att:** 41,757. **Ref:** S Bennett —West Brom (4-4-1-1): Carson, Hoefkens, Barnett, Olsson, Robinson, Morrison' (Brunt 65) Koren, Greening, Borja Valero (Kim 77), Simpson, Moore (Bednar' 46). Subs not used: Kiely, Cech, Beattie, Donk.

13th ● Peterborough ....a   W 0–2   **Att:** 10,735. **Ref:** A D'Urso —West Brom (4-4-2): Carson, Hoefkens, Barnett, Donk, Robinson', Kim (Borja Valero 80), Koren, Greening, Filipe Teixeira (Dorrans 65), Bednar, Simpson' (Beattie 71). Subs not used: Kiely, Brunt, Moore, Pele.

17th ● Middlesbrough ....h   W 3–0   **Att:** 25,557. **Ref:** M Halsey —West Brom (4-3-1-2): Carson, Hoefkens, Barnett (Pele 39), Donk, Robinson, Borja Valero, Greening, Brunt', Koren², Simpson (Moore 77), Fortuné (Beattie 69). Subs not used: Kiely, Cech, Kim, Filipe Teixeira.

24th ● Burnley ....h   D 2–2   **Att:** 18,294. **Ref:** M Dean —West Brom (4-3-1-2): Carson, Hoefkens, Pele, Donk (Zuiverloon 72), Robinson, Kim', Greening (Borja Valero 40), Filipe Teixeira (Brunt 71), Koren', Simpson, Bednar. Subs not used: Kiely, Cech, Dorrans, Fortuné.

27th ● Man Utd ....h   L 0–5   **Att:** 26,105. **Ref:** R Styles —West Brom (4-4-2): Carson', Hoefkens, Pele, Donk', Robinson, Zuiverloon (Morrison 64), Borja Valero, Koren', Brunt, Simpson (Bednar 64), Fortuné (Cech 46). Subs not used: Kiely, Kim, Dorrans, Filipe Teixeira.

31st ● Hull ....a   D 2–2   **Att:** 24,879. **Ref:** P Walton —West Brom (4-4-2): Carson, Hoefkens, Donk, Meite, Robinson', Morrison' (Kim 76), Borja Valero (Pele 88), Brunt', Fortuné (Bednar 75), Simpson'. Subs not used: Kiely, Hoefkens, Cech, Filipe Teixeira.

February

3rd ● Burnley ....a   L 3–1   **Att:** 6,635. **Ref:** M Jones —West Brom (4-4-2): Carson, Zuiverloon', Donk, Pele, Cech, Kim, Dorrans, Simpson (Brunt 36), Filipe Teixeira (Hoefkens 57), Fortuné (Bednar 46), Koren, Martis, Morrison.

7th ● Newcastle ....h   L 2–3   **Att:** 25,817. **Ref:** C Foy —West Brom (4-4-1-1): Carson, Hoefkens, Barnett, Meite, Robinson, Kim (Filipe Teixeira 46), Koren', Borja Valero (Moore 84), Brunt (Bednar 46), Morrison, Fortuné². Subs not used: Kiely, Cech, Pele, Mulumbu.

22nd ● Fulham ....a   L 2–0   **Att:** 22,394. **Ref:** M Atkinson —West Brom (4-4-2): Carson, Zuiverloon, Meite, Barnett, Robinson', Morrison (Menseguez 77), Koren, Borja Valero, Filipe Teixeira (Brunt 50), Fortuné (Bednar 81), Simpson. Subs not used: Kiely, Cech, Moore, Martis.

● Barclays Premier League   ● FA Cup   ● Carling Cup   ● UEFA Champions League   ● UEFA Cup   ▮ Yellow Card ▮ Red Card

RESULTS 2008/09

28th ● Everton ....a | L 2–0 | **Att:** 33,898. **Ref:** S Bennett —West Brom (4-4-2): Carson, Zuiverloon, Meite, Donk, Robinson, Morrison, Koren, Borja Valero (Greening▊ 53), Brunt, Simpson (Moore 57), Fortuné (Filipe Teixeira 89). Subs not used: Kiely, Hoefkens, Cech, Menseguez.

March
3rd ● Arsenal ....h | L 1–3 | **Att:** 26,244. **Ref:** S Tanner —West Brom (4-4-2): Carson, Zuiverloon, Meite▊, Donk▊, Robinson, Morrison (Menseguez 72), Greening, Koren▊, Brunt▊[1] (Filipe Teixeira 72), Moore, Fortuné. Subs not used: Kiely, Hoefkens, Cech, Kim, Borja Valero.

16th ● West Ham ....a | D 0–0 | **Att:** 30,842. **Ref:** M Halsey —West Brom (4-5-1): Carson, Zuiverloon, Martis, Olsson▊, Robinson, Morrison (Filipe Teixeira 88), Koren, Dorrans, Greening, Brunt (Simpson 80), Fortuné (Moore 80). Subs not used: Kiely, Hoefkens, Cech, Bednar.

21st ● Bolton ....h | D 1–1 | **Att:** 25,530. **Ref:** H Webb —West Brom (4-4-2): Carson, Zuiverloon (Borja Valero 74), Martis, Olsson, Robinson (Dorrans 74), Morrison, Koren, Greening▊, Brunt, Fortuné, Simpson (Bednar▊ 57). Subs not used: Kiely, Cech, Moore, Filipe Teixeira.

April
4th ● Stoke ....h | L 0–2 | **Att:** 26,277. **Ref:** M Atkinson —West Brom (4-4-2): Carson, Zuiverloon, Martis, Olsson▊, Robinson (Bednar 60), Morrison, Greening▊ (Koren 60), Borja Valero, Brunt, Fortuné, Simpson (Filipe Teixeira 60). Subs not used: Kiely, Hoefkens, Moore, Dorrans.

11th ● Portsmouth ....a | D 2–2 | **Att:** 20,376. **Ref:** M Dean —West Brom (4-5-1): Carson, Zuiverloon (Hoefkens 77), Meite, Olsson, Robinson, Morrison (Woods 75), Greening[1], Koren, Dorrans[1], Brunt[1] (Mulumbu 81), Fortuné. Subs not used: Kiely, Menseguez, Borja Valero, Simpson.

19th ● Man City ....a | L 4–2 | **Att:** 40,072. **Ref:** M Jones —West Brom (4-5-1): Carson▊, Zuiverloon, Meite, Olsson, Robinson, Morrison▊ (Mulumbu 66), Greening, Koren (Simpson 62), Dorrans (Borja Valero 62), Brunt[2], Fortuné. Subs not used: Kiely, Filipe Teixeira, Donk, Wood.

25th ● Sunderland ....h | W 3–0 | **Att:** 26,256. **Ref:** M Halsey —West Brom (4-4-2): Carson, Zuiverloon, Meite (Martis 46), Olsson[1], Robinson, Koren, Dorrans (Menseguez[1] 64), Greening, Brunt[1], Simpson (Mulumbu 46), Fortuné. Subs not used: Kiely, Filipe Teixeira, Borja Valero, Wood.

May
2nd ● Tottenham ....a | L 1–0 | **Att:** 35,836. **Ref:** R Styles —West Brom (4-4-2): Carson, Zuiverloon, Martis, Olsson, Robinson (Simpson 58), Koren, Borja Valero (Filipe Teixeira 77), Greening, Brunt, Mulumbu▊ (Menseguez 68), Fortuné. Subs not used: Kiely, Bednar, Kim, Donk.

9th ● Wigan ....h | W 3–1 | **Att:** 24,741. **Ref:** P Walton —West Brom (4-4-1-1): Kiely, Zuiverloon, Martis, Olsson, Cech (Donk 74), Brunt[1], Dorrans (Mulumbu 55), Greening, Borja Valero[1], Menseguez (Simpson 87), Fortuné[2]. Subs not used: Allsopp, Bednar, Kim, Filipe Teixeira.

17th ● Liverpool ....h | L 0–2 | **Att:** 26,138. **Ref:** M Atkinson —West Brom (4-4-1-1): Kiely, Zuiverloon, Martis (Borja Valero 56), Olsson▊, Donk, Brunt, Mulumbu (Moore 68), Greening▊, Koren, Menseguez, Fortuné. Subs not used: Carson, Filipe Teixeira, Meite, Simpson, Wood.

24th ● Blackburn ....a | D 0–0 | **Att:** 28,389. **Ref:** M Jones —West Brom (4-4-1-1): Kiely, Zuiverloon, Donk, Olsson, Robinson, Koren, Borja Valero▊ (Kim 83), Greening, Brunt, Menseguez (Wood 90), Fortuné. Subs not used: Carson, Moore, Simpson, Downing, Sawyers.

● Barclays Premier League ● FA Cup ● Carling Cup ● UEFA Champions League ● UEFA Cup   ▊ Yellow Card ▊ Red Card

West Brom's Marc-Antoine Fortuné takes on Blackburn's Benni McCarthy during the game at Ewood Park in May

WEST BROMWICH ALBION

BARCLAYS PREMIER LEAGUE GOALKEEPER STATS

Player	Minutes on pitch	Appearances	Match starts	Completed matches	Sub appearances	Subbed off	SAVES BREAKDOWN								Clean sheets	Goals conceded	Minutes since conceding	Save %	PENALTIES			Yellow cards	Red cards
							Saved with feet	Punched	Parried	Tipped over	Fumbled	Tipped round	Caught	Blocked					Saved	Resulting in goals	Opposition miss		
Scott Carson	3325	35	35	35	0	0	3	19	35	5	0	8	136	0	7	64	53	76.73	0	4	0	3	0
Dean Kiely	288	3	3	3	0	0	1	0	4	1	0	3	2	0	1	3	124	78.57	0	0	0	0	0

BARCLAYS PREMIER LEAGUE OUTFIELD PLAYER STATS

Player	Minutes on pitch	Appearances	Match starts	Completed matches	Substitute appearances	Subbed off	Goals scored	Minutes since scoring	Assists	Shots on target	Shots off target	Crosses	Defensive clearances	Defensive blocks	Fouls committed	Free-kicks won	Caught offside	Yellow cards	Red cards
Leon Barnett	967	11	10	9	1	1	0	-	1	0	3	1	12	14	9	16	1	1	0
Craig Beattie	170	7	1	0	6	1	1	24	0	2	3	1	0	0	5	0	2	0	0
Roman Bednar	1323	26	12	6	14	6	6	240	1	24	13	10	4	0	36	18	20	6	0
Borja Valero	2398	30	27	15	3	12	0	-	3	14	11	17	2	3	27	29	4	5	0
Chris Brunt	2493	34	28	18	6	10	8	226	3	31	38	78	8	2	25	12	1	3	0
Marek Cech	363	8	3	1	5	2	0	-	1	1	1	1	2	0	3	5	0	0	0
Ryan Donk	1320	16	14	13	2	1	0	-	1	4	3	0	20	11	21	7	0	4	0
Graham Dorrans	455	8	5	2	3	3	0	-	2	1	1	0	0	0	7	7	0	1	0
Filipe Teixeira	288	10	1	0	9	1	0	-	1	1	8	5	0	0	2	8	0	0	0
Marc-Antoine Fortuné	1492	17	17	11	0	6	4	212	4	32	12	11	5	0	15	30	26	0	0
Jonathan Greening	3134	34	33	31	1	2	2	619	1	10	14	62	22	3	36	50	3	7	0
Carl Hoefkens	705	10	6	6	4	0	0	-	0	0	0	14	4	6	11	6	0	0	0
Do-heon Kim	804	16	9	2	7	7	0	-	0	8	5	2	0	0	9	9	0	1	0
Robert Koren	3147	35	34	29	1	5	2	1353	3	29	19	21	7	4	15	37	1	3	0
Sherjill MacDonald	124	5	0	0	5	1	0	-	0	1	1	0	0	0	2	1	0	2	0
Shelton Martis	586	7	6	5	1	1	0	-	0	2	3	0	8	4	8	4	0	0	0
Abdoulaye Meite	1515	18	18	14	0	0	0	-	0	1	4	1	18	13	20	14	2	3	0
Juan Carlos Menseguez	366	7	3	1	4	2	1	304	0	4	3	3	0	0	1	7	0	0	0
Ishmael Miller	1074	15	11	4	4	7	3	122	2	26	13	8	1	0	18	21	15	2	0
Luke Moore	739	21	5	2	16	3	1	373	0	10	4	1	0	0	16	9	9	1	0
James Morrison	2456	30	29	14	1	15	3	885	4	31	27	25	6	4	16	31	7	5	0
Youssouf Mulumbu	271	6	2	0	4	2	0	-	0	0	0	0	0	1	6	1	0	1	0
Jonas Olsson	2665	28	28	28	0	0	2	438	0	6	7	0	48	26	31	24	1	7	0
Pedro Pele	156	3	1	1	2	0	0	-	0	0	2	0	5	2	0	0	0	0	0
Paul Robinson	3177	35	35	31	0	3	0	-	1	3	3	35	34	15	36	39	0	7	1
Jay Simpson	742	13	9	3	4	6	1	450	0	8	4	3	1	0	5	12	1	0	0
Chris Wood	22	2	0	0	2	0	0	-	0	0	1	0	0	0	0	1	0	0	0
Gianni Zuiverloon	3045	33	33	29	0	4	0	-	2	5	9	35	18	10	54	40	1	5	0

actim | BARCLAYS PREMIER LEAGUE

SEASON TOTALS

Goals scored	36
Goals conceded	67
Clean sheets	8
Shots on target	255
Shots off target	212
Shots per goal	12.97
Pens awarded	5
Pens scored	3
Pens conceded	4
Offsides	95
Corners	232
Crosses	337
Players used	30
Fouls committed	434
Free-kicks won	440

CARDS RECEIVED

67   1

SEQUENCES

Wins	2
(27/09/08-04/10/08)	
Losses	4
(on two occasions)	
Draws	2
(16/03/09-21/03/09)	
Undefeated	2
(on three occasions)	
Without win	11
(27/01/09-19/04/09)	
Undefeated home	4
(07/12/08-17/01/09)	
Undefeated away	2
(on two occasions)	
Without scoring	3
(08/11/08-22/11/08)	
Without conceding	2
(27/09/08-04/10/08)	
Scoring	4
(13/09/08-04/10/08)	
Conceding	12
(18/10/08-26/12/08)	

SEASON INFORMATION

Highest Position: 8
Lowest Position: 20
Average goals scored per game: 0.95
Average goals conceded per game: 1.76

League position at the end of each week

League position at the end of: August 20, September 12, October 16, November 20, December 20, January 20, February 20, March 20, April 20, May 20

MATCH RECORDS

Goals scored per match

		W	D	L	Pts
Failed to score	17	0	3	14	3
Scored 1 goal	10	2	2	6	8
Scored 2 goals	7	2	3	2	9
Scored 3 goals	4	4	0	0	12
Scored 4+ goals	0	0	0	0	0

Goals conceded per match

		W	D	L	Pts
Clean sheet	8	5	3	0	18
Conceded 1 goal	7	2	2	3	8
Conceded 2 goals	14	1	3	10	6
Conceded 3 goals	5	0	0	5	0
Conceded 4+ goals	3	0	0	3	0

QUICK-FIRE GOALS

From the start of a match
James Morrison
(v West Ham) 2:16

By a substitute after coming on
Ishmael Miller
(v Newcastle) 11:17

LAST-GASP GOALS

From the start of a match
Craig Beattie
(v Tottenham) 93:26

By a substitute after coming on
Juan Carlos Menseguez
(v Sunderland) 24:48

GOAL DETAILS

How the goals were struck

SCORED		CONCEDED
15	Right foot	31
16	Left foot	21
4	Headers	15
1	Others	0

How the goals were struck

SCORED		CONCEDED
21	Open play	47
4	Cross	6
3	Corner	5
3	Penalties	4
3	Direct from free-kick	2
0	Free-kick	3
2	Own goals	0

Distance from goal

SCORED		CONCEDED
8	6yds	24
23	18yds	33
5	18+yds	10

GOALS SCORED/CONCEDED PER FIVE-MINUTE INTERVALS

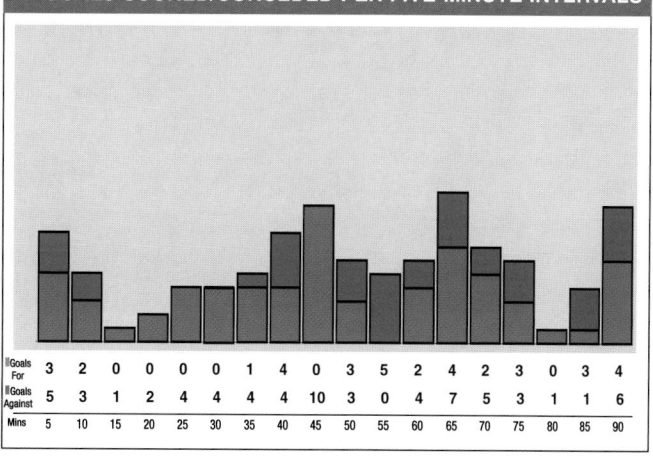

Mins	5	10	15	20	25	30	35	40	45	50	55	60	65	70	75	80	85	90
Goals For	3	2	0	0	0	0	1	4	0	3	5	2	4	2	3	0	3	4
Goals Against	5	3	1	2	4	4	4	4	10	3	0	4	7	5	3	1	1	6

CLUB SUMMARY

FORMED	1895
MANAGER	Gianfranco Zola
GROUND	Upton Park
CAPACITY	35,089
NICKNAME	The Hammers
WEBSITE	www.whufc.co.uk

The New Football Pools PLAYER OF THE SEASON — Scott Parker

OVERALL

P	W	D	L	F	A	GD
44	17	10	17	52	50	2

BARCLAYS PREMIER LEAGUE

Pos	P	W	D	L	F	A	GD	Pts
9	38	14	9	15	42	45	-3	51

HOME

Pos	P	W	D	L	F	A	GD	Pts
11	19	9	2	8	23	22	1	29

AWAY

Pos	P	W	D	L	F	A	GD	Pts
7	19	5	7	7	19	23	-4	22

CUP PROGRESS DETAILS

Competition	Round reached	Knocked out by
FA Cup	R5	Middlesbrough
Carling Cup	R3	Watford

BIGGEST WIN (ALL COMPS)
4–1 on two occasions

BIGGEST DEFEAT (ALL COMPS)
0–3 on two occasions

THE PLAYER WITH THE MOST

Shots on target
Carlton Cole 46

Shots off target
Carlton Cole 29

Shots without scoring
Luis Boa Morte 21

Assists
Carlton Cole 5

Offsides
Carlton Cole 28

Fouls
Carlton Cole 65

Fouls without a card
Diego Tristan 9

Free-kicks won
Valon Behrami 70

Defensive clearances
Matthew Upson 60

actim INDEX — for the 2008/09 Barclays Premier League Season

Rank	Player	Pts
32	Robert Green	431
45	Matthew Upson	402
66	Herita Ilunga	372
68	Lucas Neill	370
92	Carlton Cole	336

ATTENDANCE RECORD

High	Low	Average
34,958	30,842	33,700
v Man Utd (08/02/2009)	v West Brom (16/03/2009)	

CLOCKWISE FROM TOP: West Ham's players enjoy a 4–1 win at Portsmouth on Boxing Day; boss Gianfranco Zola offers some words of advice to striker Carlton Cole; Jack Collison scores the only goal in a home win against Manchester City; Diego Tristan fires home a free-kick against Stoke

THE West Ham story over the last three seasons could have been penned by the script-writers over at Albert Square as the club lurched from one crisis to another.

With sacked managers, inelligible players, court cases, dreadful football and potential bankruptcy to deal with, life has certainly not been a bed of roses at Upton Park.

When manager Alan Curbishley walked out in protest at the club's transfer policy early in the season, it appeared to be just the latest setback at a club ready to implode. The 'Tevez affair' with Sheffield United was still alive and the looming recession was threatening to wipe the club's Icelandic owners clean off the financial map. Life was gloomy indeed.

But Curbishley's departure, and that of George McCartney to Sunderland which had sparked his exit, proved to be just the change West Ham needed. From a chaotic start to the season the Hammers finished the campaign in ninth place and in buoyant mood. While they just missed out on Europa League qualification, there is genuine excitement about what lies ahead.

Curbishley was replaced by Gianfranco Zola, an untested manager but a man whose footballing philosophy is closely aligned to West Ham's traditions, and assistant Steve Clarke. Zola not only understood the structure he was coming into, with technical director Gianluca Nani responsible for talent identification, but he relished it.

Zola could concentrate on coaching, and the dour, unimaginative football that had been the curse of Curbishley's regime – partly due to injuries, partly due to a natural conservatism – was replaced by a style which was both more palettable and more effective.

At first it was a little too gung-ho, but Zola and Clarke soon helped instil the right balance, with England internationals Robert Green, Matthew Upson, Scott Parker and the newly-capped Carlton Cole providing the spine of the team. At their best the Hammers scored goals for fun – banging four past Blackburn and Portsmouth and three past Newcastle and Middlesbrough – but they also earned impressive away draws at Arsenal, Chelsea and Liverpool.

Despite the sale of Craig Bellamy, West

> ## West Ham launched a determined push for Europe in the new year

Ham launched a determined push for Europe in the new year with an eight-game unbeaten run, featuring six wins and two draws. In the end, Europe just eluded the Hammers as their squad was stretched by injuries, but that came with its own silver lining as Zola tapped into the next generation of academy graduates.

Jack Collison, James Tomkins and Junior Stanislas all featured frequently in the second half of the season and provided a glimpse into a promising future at Upton Park. Zola believes they could even match the vintage which produced Rio Ferdinand, Frank Lampard and Joe Cole.

Zola succeeded where even Jose Mourinho failed by turning Carlton Cole into an England player, while defender Upson and goalkeeper Green ended the season in Fabio Capello's plans.

And McCartney's departure hardly seemed to matter as Herita Ilunga, the Congolese left-back brought in on a loan deal, enjoyed an impressive season to earn a permanent move from Toulouse.

Along the way the Sheffield United case was finally settled. It was not cheap but, pending any possible individual actions from ex-Blades players or management, it was over.

And, while the club could still be sold, Zola and Clarke – two Chelsea boys who found a home in the East End – ensured that West Ham were able to give their fans something to cheer once again.

WEST HAM UNITED

RESULTS 2008/09

August

16th ● Wigan ....h W 2–1 **Att:** 32,758. **Ref:** S Bennett — **West Ham** (4-4-2): Green, Behrami, Davenport▌, Upson, Neill, Faubert (Boa Morte 86), Parker▌ (Mullins 72), Noble, Etherington, Ashton² (Sears 73), Cole. Subs not used: Lastuvka, Reid, Bowyer, Spence.

24th ● Man City ....a L 3–0 **Att:** 36,635. **Ref:** H Webb — **West Ham** (4-4-2): Green, Behrami▌, Davenport, Upson, Neill, Faubert, Noble▌, Parker, Etherington (Boa Morte 74), Ashton, Cole (F Sears 31 (Mullins 46)), F Sears (Mullins 46). Subs not used: Lastuvka, Reid, Bowyer, Spence.

27th ● Macclesfield ....h W 4–1 **Att:** 10,055. **Ref:** C Penton — **West Ham** (4-4-2): Green, Behrami (Hines¹ 27), Davenport, Upson, McCartney (Reid¹ 55), Faubert, Mullins, Bowyer¹, Boa Morte▌, Sears (Cole¹ 58), Ashton. Subs not used: Lastuvka, Parker, Widdowson, Spence.

30th ● Blackburn ....h W 4–1 **Att:** 32,905. **Ref:** M Riley — **West Ham** (4-4-2): Green, Behrami, Davenport¹, Upson, Neill, Faubert (McCartney 60), Parker, Noble (Mullins 81), Etherington, Cole¹, Ashton (Bellamy▌ 69). Subs not used: Lastuvka, Boa Morte, Reid, Sears.

September

13th ● West Brom ....a L 3–2 **Att:** 26,213. **Ref:** L Probert — **West Ham** (4-4-2): Green, Neill¹, Davenport, Upson, Ilunga, Behrami (Faubert 65), Parker, Noble¹, Boa Morte (Etherington 79), Ashton (Di Michele▌ 19), Cole. Subs not used: Lastuvka, Bellamy, Mullins, Tomkins.

20th ● Newcastle ....h W 3–1 **Att:** 34,743. **Ref:** P Dowd — **West Ham** (4-4-2): Green, Behrami, Upson, Neill▌, Ilunga, Faubert, Noble, Parker (Mullins 72), Etherington¹ (Boa Morte 73), Di Michele², Cole (Sears 87). Subs not used: Lastuvka, Lopez, Davenport, Reid.

23rd ● Watford ....a L 1–0 **Att:** 12,914. **Ref:** P Walton — **West Ham** (3-5-2): Lastuvka, Neill, Lopez, Upson, Etherington, Boa Morte (Parker 62), Noble, Mullins, Faubert, Di Michele (Reid 71), Sears. Subs not used: Green, Ilunga, Behrami, Collison, Stanislas.

27th ● Fulham ....a W 1–2 **Att:** 23,946. **Ref:** A Marriner — **West Ham** (4-3-3): Green, Faubert, Neill, Upson, Ilunga, Behrami, Parker▌ (Boa Morte 90), Noble, Etherington¹ (Mullins 80), Cole¹, Di Michele (Bellamy 74). Subs not used: Lastuvka, Lopez, Davenport, Sears.

October

5th ● Bolton ....h L 1–3 **Att:** 33,715. **Ref:** M Dean — **West Ham** (4-3-2-1): Green, Faubert▌, Neill, Upson, Ilunga, Behrami, Parker▌, Noble▌, Di Michele (Bellamy 54), Etherington (Sears 79), Cole¹. Subs not used: Lastuvka, Lopez, Boa Morte, Mullins, Davenport.

19th ● Hull ....a L 1–0 **Att:** 24,896. **Ref:** C Foy — **West Ham** (4-4-2): Green, Faubert (Di Michele 73), Neill, Upson, Ilunga▌, Behrami, Parker, Noble, Etherington (Sears 83), Bellamy, Cole. Subs not used: Lastuvka, Lopez, Boa Morte, Mullins, Reid.

26th ● Arsenal ....h L 0–2 **Att:** 34,802. **Ref:** P Dowd — **West Ham** (4-3-2-1): Green, Faubert▌, Collins, Upson, Ilunga, Mullins, Parker▌ (Boa Morte 77), Bowyer (Sears 89), Di Michele (Etherington 78), Bellamy, Cole▌. Subs not used: Lastuvka, Lopez, Davenport, Collison.

29th ● Man Utd ....a L 2–0 **Att:** 75,397. **Ref:** P Walton — **West Ham** (4-4-2): Green, Faubert, Collins▌, Upson, Ilunga, Behrami (Boa Morte 44), Bowyer (Sears 69), Mullins, Etherington (Collison▌ 46), Di Michele, Bellamy. Subs not used: Lastuvka, Lopez, Davenport, Reid.

November

1st ● Middlesbrough ....a D 1–1 **Att:** 25,164. **Ref:** A Marriner — **West Ham** (4-4-2): Green, Neill▌, Collins, Upson, Ilunga, Faubert, Collison▌, Mullins¹, Boa Morte▌ (Bowyer 84), Bellamy▌, Sears (Etherington 73). Subs not used: Walker, Lopez, Tristan, Tomkins, Di Michele.

8th ● Everton ....h L 1–3 **Att:** 33,961. **Ref:** M Halsey — **West Ham** (4-3-3): Green, Neill, Collins, Upson (Collison¹ 18), Ilunga, Faubert, Parker (Di Michele 87), Bowyer, Sears, Bellamy, Boa Morte (Etherington 57). Subs not used: Lastuvka, Lopez, Mullins, Reid.

15th ● Portsmouth ....h D 0–0 **Att:** 32,328. **Ref:** M Atkinson — **West Ham** (4-3-3): Green, Neill, Collins, Upson, Ilunga (Faubert 61), Behrami, Parker (Mullins 75), Collison, Sears (Etherington 46), Cole, Bellamy. Subs not used: Lastuvka, Davenport, Bowyer, Di Michele.

23rd ● Sunderland ....a W 0–1 **Att:** 35,222. **Ref:** M Dean — **West Ham** (4-4-2): Green, Neill, Collins, Upson, Ilunga, Faubert (Boa Morte 76), Parker, Bowyer▌ (Mullins 61), Behrami¹, Bellamy (Di Michele 87), Cole. Subs not used: Lastuvka, Davenport, Collison, Sears.

December

1st ● Liverpool ....a D 0–0 **Att:** 41,169. **Ref:** P Walton — **West Ham** (4-4-2): Green, Neill, Collins, Upson, Ilunga, Faubert (Boa Morte 86), Parker, Mullins▌, Behrami, Bellamy, Cole. Subs not used: Lastuvka, Tristan, Davenport, Collison, Di Michele.

8th ● Tottenham ....h L 0–2 **Att:** 34,277. **Ref:** C Foy — **West Ham** (4-4-2): Green, Neill, Collins, Upson, Ilunga, Behrami▌, Mullins (Di Michele 73), Parker (Tristan 83), Faubert (Noble▌ 58), Cole, Bellamy. Subs not used: Lastuvka, Boa Morte, Davenport, Collison.

14th ● Chelsea ....a D 1–1 **Att:** 41,675. **Ref:** M Riley — **West Ham** (4-4-2): Green, Neill, Upson, Davenport, Ilunga, Collison (Boa Morte 87), Parker, Noble (Mullins 72), Behrami, Bellamy▌ (Di Michele 90), Cole▌. Subs not used: Lastuvka, Faubert, Tristan, Sears.

20th ● Aston Villa ....a L 0–1 **Att:** 31,353. **Ref:** M Halsey — **West Ham** (4-4-2): Green, Neill▌, Davenport, Upson, Ilunga, Collison (Tristan 84), Noble, Parker (Mullins 46), Behrami (Bowyer 57), Bellamy▌, Cole. Subs not used: Lastuvka, Boa Morte, Faubert, Di Michele.

26th ● Portsmouth ....a W 1–4 **Att:** 20,102. **Ref:** S Bennett — **West Ham** (4-4-2): Green, Neill (Faubert 46), Davenport, Upson, Ilunga, Collison¹, Noble▌ (Boa Morte 73), Parker▌, Behrami▌, Cole¹ (Tristan 87), Bellamy². Subs not used: Lastuvka, Mullins, Collins, Di Michele.

28th ● Stoke ....h W 2–1 **Att:** 34,477. **Ref:** M Jones — **West Ham** (4-4-2): Green, Faubert, Collins, Upson, Ilunga, Behrami, Parker (Mullins 77), Collison (Tristan¹ 77), Boa Morte▌, Di Michele▌ (Spector 89), Cole¹. Subs not used: Lastuvka, Bowyer, Sears, Ngala.

January

3rd ● Barnsley ....h W 3–0 **Att:** 28,869. **Ref:** M Oliver — **West Ham** (4-4-2): Green, Faubert▌, Collins, Tomkins, Ilunga¹, Collison (Dyer 70), Noble¹, Mullins▌, Boa Morte (Etherington 66), Bellamy, Cole¹ (Tristan 75). Subs not used: Lastuvka, Spector, Bowyer, Di Michele.

10th ● Newcastle ....a D 2–2 **Att:** 47,571. **Ref:** A Wiley — **West Ham** (4-4-2): Green, Neill, Collins, Upson, Ilunga, Behrami, Parker, Noble (Mullins 86), Collison (Boa Morte 76), Cole¹, Bellamy¹ (Di Michele 81). Subs not used: Stech, Faubert, Tristan, Tomkins.

18th ● Fulham ....h W 3–1 **Att:** 31,818. **Ref:** P Dowd — **West Ham** (4-4-2): Green, Neill, Collins, Upson, Ilunga, Behrami, Parker, Noble¹ (Faubert 81), Collison (Mullins 83), Cole¹, Di Michele¹ (Dyer 87). Subs not used: Stech, Boa Morte, Tristan, Sears.

24th ● Hartlepool ....a W 0–2 **Att:** 6,849. **Ref:** L Mason — **West Ham** (4-4-2): Green, Faubert, Collins▌, Tomkins, Ilunga▌, Behrami¹, Parker, Noble¹, Collison (Boa Morte 64), Cole¹ (Sears 78), Di Michele (Mullins 75). Subs not used: Stech, Neill, Spector, Tristan.

28th ● Hull ....h W 2–0 **Att:** 34,340. **Ref:** H Webb — **West Ham** (4-3-1-2): Green, Neill, Collins, Upson, Ilunga, Behrami, Parker, Collison (Faubert 71), Noble (Boa Morte 84), Di Michele¹ (Nsereko 86), Cole¹. Subs not used: Lastuvka, Tristan, Tomkins, Sears.

31st ● Arsenal ....a D 0–0 **Att:** 60,109. **Ref:** S Bennett — **West Ham** (4-4-2): Green, Neill▌, Collins▌, Upson, Ilunga, Behrami, Parker, Noble (Nsereko 70), Collison, Cole, Di Michele (Boa Morte 83). Subs not used: Lastuvka, Lopez, Spector, Tristan, Sears.

February

8th ● Man Utd ....h L 0–1 **Att:** 34,958. **Ref:** P Dowd — **West Ham** (4-4-2): Green, Neill▌, Collins, Upson, Ilunga, Behrami (Tristan 87), Parker, Noble (Nsereko 77), Collison, Cole, Di Michele. Subs not used: Lastuvka, Boa Morte, Kovac, Spector, Sears.

14th ● Middlesbrough ....h D 1–1 **Att:** 33,658. **Ref:** P Walton — **West Ham** (4-4-2): Green, Neill, Collins, Upson, Ilunga¹, Collison, Parker, Noble▌ (Nsereko 74), Boa Morte (Sears 49), Di Michele▌, Cole (Tristan 33). Subs not used: Lastuvka, Lopez, Kovac, Spector.

21st ● Bolton ....a L 2–1 **Att:** 21,245. **Ref:** S Tanner — **West Ham** (4-4-1-1): Green, Spector (Sears 85), Collins (Tomkins 16), Upson▌, Ilunga, Behrami, Parker¹, Noble▌, Collison (Nsereko 62), Cole, Di Michele. Subs not used: Lastuvka, Lopez, Kovac, Tristan.

RESULTS 2008/09

| 25th | ● Middlesbrough ....a | L 2–0 | **Att:** 15,602. **Ref:** S Bennett — **West Ham** (4-4-2): Green, Neill, Tomkins, Upson, Ilunga, Behrami▮, Parker, Noble (Collison 56), Kovac (Tristan 69), Cole, Sears (Di Michele 57). Subs not used: Lastuvka, Lopez, Nsereko, Spector. |

March
1st	● Man City ....h	W 1–0	**Att:** 34,562. **Ref:** M Dean — **West Ham** (4-3-1-2): Green, Neill, Tomkins, Upson, Ilunga, Behrami (Nsereko 43), Parker▮, Collison¹, Kovac▮ (Spector 83), Di Michele (Lopez 87), Cole. Subs not used: Lastuvka, Sears, Stanislas, Payne.
4th	● Wigan ....a	W 0–1	**Att:** 14,169. **Ref:** S Attwell — **West Ham** (4-4-2): Green, Neill▮, Tomkins, Upson, Ilunga, Collison (Spector 78), Noble▮, Parker▮ (Lopez 88), Kovac, Di Michele (Nsereko▮ 75), Cole▮▮¹. Subs not used: Lastuvka, Sears, Payne, Stanislas.
16th	● West Brom ....h	D 0–0	**Att:** 30,842. **Ref:** M Halsey — **West Ham** (4-4-2): Green, Neill, Tomkins, Upson (Spector 29), Ilunga, Noble (Boa Morte 82), Kovac, Parker, Nsereko▮ (Stanislas 68), Di Michele, Sears. Subs not used: Lastuvka, Lopez, Tristan, Payne.
21st	● Blackburn ....a	D 1–1	**Att:** 21,672. **Ref:** C Foy — **West Ham** (4-4-2): Green, Neill, Tomkins, Spector, Ilunga, Noble¹, Parker▮, Kovac, Boa Morte (Lopez 79), Tristan (Payne 90), Di Michele (Dyer 82). Subs not used: Lastuvka, Sears, N'Gala, Stanislas.

April
4th	● Sunderland ....h	W 2–0	**Att:** 34,761. **Ref:** M Jones — **West Ham** (4-3-1-2): Green, Neill, Tomkins¹, Upson, Ilunga▮, Noble, Spector (Collins 73), Stanislas¹ (Lopez 90), Boa Morte, Di Michele (Dyer 81), Tristan. Subs not used: Lastuvka, Nsereko, Sears, Payne.
11th	● Tottenham ....a	L 1–0	**Att:** 35,969. **Ref:** M Atkinson — **West Ham** (4-4-2): Green, Collins▮, Tomkins (Nsereko 81), Upson, Ilunga, Stanislas, Neill▮, Noble▮, Boa Morte▮ (Dyer 71), Tristan (Sears 85), Di Michele▮. Subs not used: Lastuvka, Lopez, Payne, N'Gala.
18th	● Aston Villa.............a	D 1–1	**Att:** 39,534. **Ref:** R Styles — **West Ham** (4-1-2-12): Green, Tomkins, Upson▮, Collins (Dyer 33), Ilunga, Neill, Boa Morte▮, Stanislas (Nsereko 74), Noble▮, Di Michele (Sears 81), Tristan¹. Subs not used: Lastuvka, Lopez, Payne, Hines.
25th	● Chelsea ....h	L 0–1	**Att:** 34,749. **Ref:** M Dean — **West Ham** (4-3-1-2): Green, Tomkins, Upson, Ilunga, Boa Morte (Nsereko 72), Noble, Stanislas▮, Dyer (Sears 61), Tristan, Di Michele (Kovac 61). Subs not used: Lastuvka, Lopez, Spector, Payne.

May
2nd	● Stoke ....a	W 0–1	**Att:** 27,500. **Ref:** P Walton — **West Ham** (4-4-2): Green, Neill▮, Tomkins, Upson, Ilunga, Stanislas, Noble (Lopez 87), Kovac, Boa Morte▮ (Collison 82), Tristan¹, Di Michele (Sears 89). Subs not used: Lastuvka, Spector, Payne, Hines.
9th	● Liverpool.............h	L 0–3	**Att:** 34,951. **Ref:** A Wiley — **West Ham** (4-4-2): Green, Neill, Tomkins, Upson, Ilunga, Boa Morte▮ (Payne 80), Noble, Kovac▮, Stanislas (Collison 59), Di Michele▮ (Sears 70), Tristan. Subs not used: Lastuvka, Lopez, Nsereko, Spector.
16th	● Everton ....a	L 3–1	**Att:** 38,501. **Ref:** P Dowd — **West Ham** (4-4-2): Green, Neill, Tomkins▮, Upson, Ilunga, Collison, Noble, Kovac¹ (Stanislas 67), Boa Morte▮, Tristan (Cole 46), Di Michele (Spector▮ 46). Subs not used: Kurucz, Lopez, Nsereko, Payne.
24th	● Middlesbrough ....h	W 2–1	**Att:** 34,007. **Ref:** H Webb — **West Ham** (4-3-3): Green, Spector, Neill, Upson, Ilunga, Noble (Dyer 53), Kovac, Collison (Di Michele 72), Boa Morte, Cole¹ (Tristan 63), Stanislas¹. Subs not used: Lastuvka, Lopez, Nsereko, Payne.

● Barclays Premier League ● FA Cup ● Carling Cup ● UEFA Champions League ● UEFA Cup   ▮ Yellow Card ▮ Red Card

David Di Michele and Chelsea's John Terry fight for possession in the 1–0 defeat at Upton Park

WEST HAM UNITED

BARCLAYS PREMIER LEAGUE GOALKEEPER STATS

Player	Minutes on pitch	Appearances	Match starts	Completed matches	Sub appearances	Subbed off	SAVES BREAKDOWN Saved with feet	Punched	Parried	Tipped over	Fumbled	Tipped round	Caught	Blocked	Clean sheets	Goals conceded	Minutes since conceding	Save %	PENALTIES Saved	Resulting in goals	Opposition miss	Yellow cards	Red cards
Robert Green 3647		38	38	38	0	0	2	22	24	7	0	17	144	0	10	45	45	83.08	2	3	1	0	0

BARCLAYS PREMIER LEAGUE OUTFIELD PLAYER STATS

Player	Minutes on pitch	Appearances	Match starts	Completed matches	Substitute appearances	Subbed off	Goals scored	Minutes since scoring	Assists	Shots on target	Shots off target	Crosses	Defensive clearances	Defensive blocks	Fouls committed	Free-kicks won	Caught offside	Yellow cards	Red cards
Dean Ashton 265		4	4	1	0	3	2	256	0	3	4	2	0	1	6	3	6	0	0
Valon Behrami 2120		24	24	19	0	5	1	1217	3	11	9	3	9	3	42	70	0	4	0
Craig Bellamy 1301		16	13	10	3	3	5	236	0	30	21	27	0	0	17	20	24	5	0
Luis Boa Morte................1331		27	13	5	14	8	0	-	3	10	11	12	4	1	35	32	1	7	0
Lee Bowyer 364		6	4	1	2	3	0	-	0	3	1	0	0	0	8	4	0	1	0
Carlton Cole 2358		27	26	20	1	4	10	30	5	46	29	6	23	2	65	37	28	3	2
James Collins..................1503		18	17	15	1	2	0	-	0	4	3	1	37	19	11	7	1	3	0
Jack Collison 1542		20	16	7	4	9	3	317	1	13	6	5	2	4	14	16	2	2	0
Calum Davenport 679		7	7	7	0	0	1	1198	2	3	6	0	25	7	5	5	1	1	0
David Di Michele 1989		30	22	6	8	16	4	1224	4	29	28	6	1	0	18	10	22	4	0
Kieron Dyer 226		7	1	0	6	1	0	-	1	6	2	0	0	0	4	1	1	0	0
Matthew Etherington 769		13	8	2	5	6	2	1467	1	3	1	15	0	1	5	11	1	1	0
Julien Faubert 1458		20	15	9	5	6	0	-	2	5	9	19	4	8	16	14	1	2	0
Herita Ilunga 3319		35	35	34	0	1	0	-	2	3	2	9	31	15	20	29	6	2	0
Radoslav Kovac 767		9	8	6	1	2	1	140	0	2	5	0	4	5	16	9	0	2	0
Walter Lopez 48		5	0	0	5	0	0	-	0	2	0	1	0	0	0	0	0	0	0
George McCartney 36		1	0	0	1	0	0	-	0	0	0	0	0	0	0	0	0	0	0
Hayden Mullins 738		17	5	4	12	1	0	1831	0	1	0	4	2	7	7	0	1	0	
Lucas Neill 3210		34	34	33	0	1	1	2879	0	7	4	8	33	18	42	22	1	8	0
Mark Noble 2465		29	28	16	1	11	3	779	5	20	12	35	6	4	29	27	7	8	1
Savio Nsereko 283		10	1	0	9	1	0	-	1	3	4	2	0	0	8	5	5	2	0
Scott Parker 2505		28	28	18	0	10	1	403	4	10	10	5	9	17	37	48	1	8	0
Josh Payne 18		2	0	0	2	0	0	-	0	0	0	0	1	0	1	0	0	0	0
Freddie Sears 506		17	4	1	13	3	0	-	0	5	1	4	0	0	0	8	5	0	0
Jonathan Spector 496		9	4	2	5	2	0	-	1	0	0	2	4	4	5	7	0	1	0
Junior Stanislas 665		9	7	4	2	3	2	37	1	10	5	6	0	1	2	3	3	1	0
James Tomkins................1071		12	11	9	1	1	1	551	0	2	4	1	20	7	7	5	0	0	1
Diego Tristan 793		14	8	5	6	3	3	240	1	11	8	0	6	1	9	11	16	0	0
Matthew Upson 3408		37	37	35	0	2	0	-	1	3	6	1	60	32	27	35	0	2	0

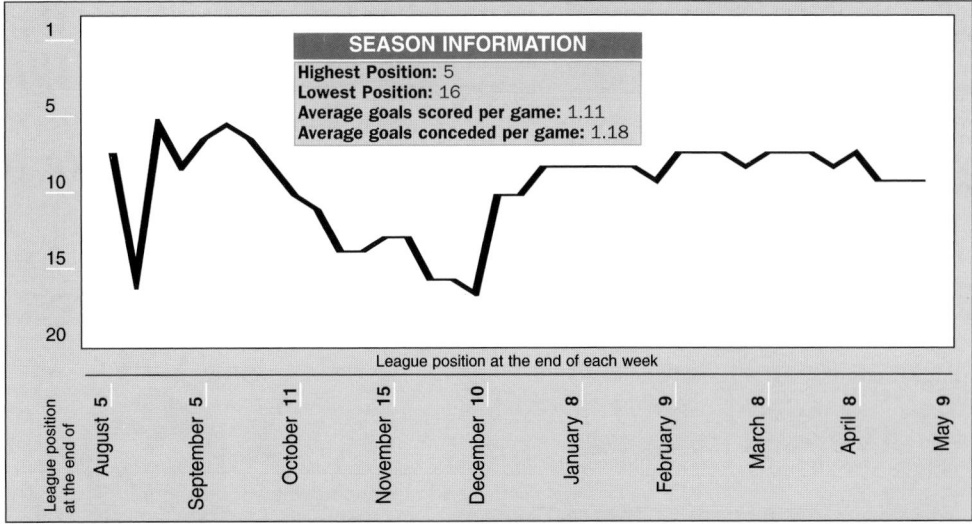

SEASON TOTALS

Goals scored	42
Goals conceded	45
Clean sheets	10
Shots on target	246
Shots off target	192
Shots per goal	10.43
Pens awarded	3
Pens scored	1
Pens conceded	6
Offsides	132
Corners	191
Crosses	173
Players used	30
Fouls committed	457
Free-kicks won	461

CARDS RECEIVED

68 **4**

SEQUENCES

Wins	2
(on four occasions)	
Losses	4
(05/10/08-29/10/08)	
Draws	2
(16/03/09-21/03/09)	
Undefeated	6
(26/12/08-31/01/09)	
Without win	7
(05/10/08-15/11/08)	
Undefeated home	3
(on three occasions)	
Undefeated away	7
(01/11/08-31/01/09)	
Without scoring	3
(19/10/08-29/10/08)	
Without conceding	3
(on two occasions)	
Scoring	5
(on two occasions)	
Conceding	12
(16/08/08-08/11/08)	

SEASON INFORMATION

Highest Position: 5
Lowest Position: 16
Average goals scored per game: 1.11
Average goals conceded per game: 1.18

League position at the end of each week

League position at the end of:
August 5, September 5, October 11, November 15, December 10, January 8, February 9, March 8, April 8, May 9

MATCH RECORDS

Goals scored per match

		W	D	L	Pts
Failed to score	14	0	4	10	4
Scored 1 goal	12	4	4	4	16
Scored 2 goals	8	6	1	1	19
Scored 3 goals	2	2	0	0	6
Scored 4+ goals	2	2	0	0	6

Goals conceded per match

		W	D	L	Pts
Clean sheet	10	6	4	0	22
Conceded 1 goal	17	8	4	5	28
Conceded 2 goals	5	0	1	4	1
Conceded 3 goals	6	0	0	6	0
Conceded 4+ goals	0	0	0	0	0

GOALS SCORED/CONCEDED PER FIVE-MINUTE INTERVALS

Goals For	1	3	1	3	2	2	7	1	3	0	5	2	1	4	1	1	2	3
Goals Against	3	2	3	1	2	2	1	3	0	3	4	1	3	3	1	4	5	4
Mins	5	10	15	20	25	30	35	40	45	50	55	60	65	70	75	80	85	90

QUICK-FIRE GOALS

From the start of a match
Dean Ashton (v Wigan)
2:59

By a substitute after coming on
Diego Tristan (v Stoke)
11:20

LAST-GASP GOALS

From the start of a match
Carlton Cole (v Blackburn)
94:56

By a substitute after coming on
Jack Collison (v Everton)
45:24

GOAL DETAILS

How the goals were struck

SCORED		CONCEDED
29	Right foot	24
9	Left foot	14
3	Headers	6
1	Others	1

How the goals were struck

SCORED		CONCEDED
32	Open play	31
2	Cross	4
4	Corner	2
1	Penalties	3
1	Direct from free-kick	3
1	Free-kick	0
1	Own goals	2

Distance from goal

SCORED		CONCEDED
16	6yds	11
23	18yds	29
3	18+yds	5

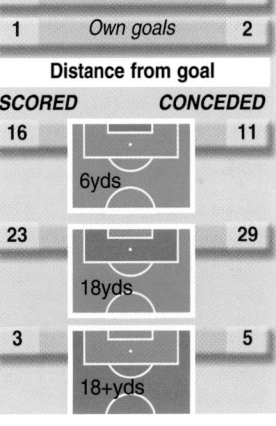

WIGAN ATHLETIC

CLUB SUMMARY

FORMED	1932
MANAGER	TBC
GROUND	DW Stadium
CAPACITY	25,138
NICKNAME	The Latics
WEBSITE	www.wiganathletic.co.uk

The New Football Pools PLAYER OF THE SEASON — Antonio Valencia

OVERALL
P	W	D	L	F	A	GD
42	14	9	19	43	52	-9

BARCLAYS PREMIER LEAGUE
Pos	P	W	D	L	F	A	GD	Pts
11	38	12	9	17	34	45	-11	45

HOME
Pos	P	W	D	L	F	A	GD	Pts
12	19	8	5	6	17	18	-1	29

AWAY
Pos	P	W	D	L	F	A	GD	Pts
10	19	4	4	11	17	27	-10	16

CUP PROGRESS DETAILS
Competition	Round reached	Knocked out by
FA Cup	R3	Tottenham
Carling Cup	R4	Arsenal

BIGGEST WIN (ALL COMPS)
30/08/08 5–0 v Hull **PREM**

BIGGEST DEFEAT (ALL COMPS)
0–4 on two occasions

THE PLAYER WITH THE MOST
Shots on target	
Amr Zaki	30
Shots off target	
Amr Zaki	37
Shots without scoring	
Paul Scharner	25
Assists	
Antonio Valencia	5
Offsides	
Mido	27
Fouls	
Lee Cattermole	59
Fouls without a card	
Hugo Rodallega	11
Free-kicks won	
Amr Zaki	67
Defensive clearances	
Titus Bramble	70

actim INDEX for the 2008/09 Barclays Premier League Season

Rank	Player	Pts
84	Titus Bramble	350
97	Antonio Valencia	328
105	Chris Kirkland	319
114	Mario Melchiot	308
124	Maynor Figueroa	300

ATTENDANCE RECORD
High	Low	Average
22,954	14,169	18,350
v Arsenal (11/04/2009)	v West Ham (04/03/2009)	

STEVE BRUCE once again proved his credentials after masterminding another superb season for Wigan, and his successor will have a tough act to follow after the popular boss agreed to become Sunderland's new manager shortly after the season had ended.

The former Birmingham chief took over at the JJB Stadium in November 2007 with the club in fear of relegation. Bruce helped them survive that scare, and they enjoyed a much more successful 2008/09.

Many Latics fans would have considered simply preserving the club's top-flight status as an achievement this term, but Wigan were not content to settle for that, and heading into the final eight weeks of the campaign, they were in the running to qualify for Europe. An appearance in next season's UEFA Europa League would have been a historic feat but, despite missing out, Wigan will still head into 2009/10 with high expectations.

Their activity in the 2008 summer transfer market proved significant, with the capture of England Under-21 midfielder Lee Cattermole and the loan signing of Amr Zaki proving particularly inspired.

The latter, brought in from Egyptian club El Zamalek, had an immediate impact and was the Barclays Premier League's leading goalscorer heading into November. He scored eight goals in his first 11 league matches, with two goals in the 5–0 victory over newcomers Hull and a couple – one a memorable volley – in the 3–2 defeat at Liverpool.

Zaki was the talk of the top flight, with both Chelsea and Liverpool linked with a move for the striker, and Bruce was lauded for having the vision to sign the player. Unfortunately, the Egyptian's form was to suffer something of a slump, not helped by injuries and, with the player also struggling to adapt to the travelling back and forth involved in playing for his country, his impact following the turn of the year was nowhere near as impressive.

A run-in with the club over his late arrival back from international duty coincided with a difficult patch for Wigan. After beating Tottenham in mid-January to go seventh in the table, they began to struggle.

Midfield lynchpin Wilson Palacios was sold to Spurs for a fee of around

> ## Heading into the final eight weeks, the Latics were in the hunt to qualify for Europe

£14million and powerful striker Emile Heskey left for Aston Villa. Although Bruce brought in Mido on loan from Middlesbrough, Ben Watson for £2million from Crystal Palace, striker Hugo Rodallega from Mexican side Necaxa and effectively swapped Ryan Taylor for Newcastle's Charles N'Zogbia, the rhythm of the side was disrupted during a testing run of fixtures. They did not win for eight matches and that inflicted fatal damage on their European ambitions.

Wigan did, however, secure their top-flight status earlier than they might have expected. A 1–0 victory over Hull in late March, courtesy of a Watson strike, took them to 41 points and Bruce breathed a sigh of relief, although his fears about his players easing up proved to be well founded.

'I had it at Birmingham in my second year,' he recalled. 'We were in the top six all year and then we got to the magical mark and everyone then relaxed and started thinking about next season.'

Results tailed off and, although that was a disappointment, the club knew that their mission had been accomplished. Bruce's acquisitions, especially young Cattermole, had been key men, while Antonio Valencia enjoyed a superb season.

Bruce's reputation had once again been enhanced and, after Ricky Sbragia stepped down from his position at Sunderland following the climax of the campaign, the Black Cats immediately identified the Northumberland-born Latics boss as their man. A deal was agreed in early June, with Bruce bidding farewell to Wigan for the second time, after a brief spell in charge at the JJB Stadium in 2000/01. He left to begin a new adventure, but he did so with Wigan – who looked set to name Roberto Martinez as their new boss at the time of going to press – in superb shape.

CLOCKWISE FROM ABOVE: Amr Zaki slots home the only goal of the game in a hard-fought victory at Bolton; Maynor Figueroa reacts after grabbing the winning goal against Tottenham; Antonio Valencia scores in the 3–0 home win over Blackburn

WIGAN ATHLETIC

RESULTS 2008/09

August
16th	● West Ham	.........a	L 2–1	**Att:** 32,758. **Ref:** S Bennett — **Wigan** (4-4-2): Kirkland, Melchiot (De Ridder 83), Scharner (Koumas 83), Boyce, Figueroa, Valencia, Cattermole (Sibierski 85), Palacios▌, Kapo, Heskey, Zaki¹. Subs not used: Pollitt, Kilbane, Brown, Bramble.
24th	● Chelsea	.........h	L 0–1	**Att:** 18,139. **Ref:** A Wiley — **Wigan** (4-4-2): Pollitt, Melchiot (Camara 85), Boyce, Bramble, Figueroa, Valencia, Cattermole▌, Palacios (Kapo 80), Koumas (De Ridder 46), Heskey, Zaki. Subs not used: Nash, Sibierski, Kilbane, Brown.
26th	● Notts County	.........h	W 4–0	**Att:** 4,100. **Ref:** C Webster — **Wigan** (4-4-2): Nash, Montrose, Bramble, Boyce, Figueroa, De Ridder, Valencia (Kupisz¹ 63), Brown, Kilbane (Bouaouzan 70), Camara², Heskey (Zaki¹ 46). Subs not used: Pollitt, Palacios, Cattermole, Cywka.
30th	● Hull	.........a	W 0–5	**Att:** 24,282. **Ref:** M Jones — **Wigan** (4-4-2): Kirkland, Melchiot, Boyce, Bramble, Figueroa, Valencia¹, Palacios, Cattermole (Kapo 79), Kilbane (Brown 56), Heskey¹ (Camara 85), Zaki². Subs not used: Pollitt, Koumas, De Ridder, Kupisz.

September
13th	● Sunderland	.........h	D 1–1	**Att:** 18,015. **Ref:** R Styles — **Wigan** (4-4-2): Kirkland, Melchiot, Boyce, Bramble, Figueroa, Valencia, Cattermole▌, Palacios (Kapo 64), Kilbane (Koumas 56), Zaki¹ (Scharner 90), Heskey. Subs not used: Pollitt, Brown, De Ridder, Camara.
21st	● Tottenham	.........a	D 0–0	**Att:** 35,808. **Ref:** S Tanner — **Wigan** (4-4-2): Kirkland, Figueroa, Boyce▌, Bramble, Melchiot, Valencia, Scharner, Palacios▌, Koumas (Kapo 72), Zaki (Camara 82), Heskey. Subs not used: Kingson, Pollitt, Taylor, Kilbane, De Ridder.
24th	● Ipswich	.........a	W 1–4	**Att:** 13,803. **Ref:** M Dean — **Wigan** (4-4-2): Kirkland, Cattermole¹, Boyce, Bramble, Kilbane, Valencia, Scharner¹▌, Palacios (De Ridder 71), Kapo¹, Heskey (Camara¹ 75), Zaki (Koumas 82). Subs not used: Pollitt, Taylor, Kupisz, Figueroa.
28th	● Man City	.........h	W 2–1	**Att:** 18,214. **Ref:** S Bennett — **Wigan** (4-4-2): Kirkland, Melchiot▌, Bramble, Boyce, Figueroa, Valencia¹▌, Palacios, Cattermole (Brown▌ 53), Kapo, Heskey, Zaki¹. Subs not used: Pollitt, Scharner, Kilbane, De Ridder, Camara, Koumas.

October
4th	● Middlesbrough	.........h	L 0–1	**Att:** 16,806. **Ref:** M Atkinson — **Wigan** (4-4-2): Kirkland, Melchiot, Bramble, Scharner▌, Figueroa, Valencia, Cattermole▌, Palacios (De Ridder 85), Kapo (Koumas 67), Zaki▌ (Camara 81), Heskey. Subs not used: Pollitt, Taylor, Kilbane, Brown.
18th	● Liverpool	.........a	L 3–2	**Att:** 43,868. **Ref:** A Wiley — **Wigan** (4-4-2): Kirkland, Melchiot, Scharner, Bramble, Figueroa, Valencia▌, Cattermole, Palacios (Koumas 90), Kapo (Brown 82), De Ridder (Kilbane 79), Zaki². Subs not used: Pollitt, Taylor, Boyce, Camara.
26th	● Aston Villa	.........h	L 0–4	**Att:** 20,249. **Ref:** M Jones — **Wigan** (4-4-2): Kirkland, Boyce, Bramble, Scharner, Figueroa, De Ridder (Taylor 81), Palacios▌, Cattermole (Brown 81), Kapo (Koumas 46), Zaki, Heskey. Subs not used: Pollitt, Kilbane, Camara, Cywka.
29th	● Fulham	.........a	L 2–0	**Att:** 22,500. **Ref:** H Webb — **Wigan** (4-4-2): Kirkland, Boyce, Scharner, Figueroa (Koumas 62), Palacios (Camara 80), Cattermole▌ (De Ridder 80), Kilbane▌, Melchiot, Valencia, Heskey, Zaki. Subs not used: Pollitt, Taylor, Brown, Bramble.

November
1st	● Portsmouth	.........a	W 1–2	**Att:** 18,416. **Ref:** P Walton — **Wigan** (4-4-2): Kirkland, Melchiot, Bramble▌, Boyce, Figueroa▌, Valencia, Palacios, Cattermole▌, Koumas, Heskey¹, Zaki¹ (Camara 89). Subs not used: Pollitt, Taylor, Scharner, Kilbane, Brown, De Ridder.
8th	● Stoke	.........h	D 0–0	**Att:** 15,881. **Ref:** M Riley — **Wigan** (4-4-2): Kirkland, Melchiot, Boyce, Bramble▌, Figueroa, Valencia, Palacios, Cattermole, Koumas, Heskey (Camara 57), Zaki. Subs not used: Pollitt, Kingson, Scharner, Kilbane, Brown, De Ridder.
11th	● Arsenal	.........a	L 3–0	**Att:** 59,665. **Ref:** S Tanner — **Wigan** (4-4-2): Kirkland, Cattermole (Brown 67), Boyce, Bramble, Melchiot, Valencia, Koumas (Camara 58), Palacios, De Ridder, Figueroa, Zaki. Subs not used: Kingson, Taylor, Scharner, Kilbane, Cywka.
15th	● Newcastle	.........a	D 2–2	**Att:** 47,657. **Ref:** A Marriner — **Wigan** (4-3-3): Kirkland, Taylor¹ (De Ridder 81), Bramble¹▌, Boyce▌, Figueroa, Scharner, Cattermole, Palacios▌, Kapo (Brown 90), Camara (Kilbane 90), Valencia. Subs not used: Pollitt, Cywka, Kupisz, Routledge.
24th	● Everton	.........h	W 1–0	**Att:** 18,344. **Ref:** R Styles — **Wigan** (4-4-2): Kirkland, Taylor, Bramble, Scharner, Valencia, Palacios, Brown, Kapo (Camara¹ 46), Heskey. Subs not used: Pollitt, Kilbane, Koumas, De Ridder, Cywka, Routledge.
29th	● West Brom	.........h	W 2–1	**Att:** 17,054. **Ref:** P Dowd — **Wigan** (4-4-2): Kirkland, Taylor (Melchiot 70), Bramble, Boyce¹, Figueroa (Kilbane 81), Valencia, Brown (Koumas 60), Cattermole, Palacios, Heskey, Camara¹. Subs not used: Pollitt, Kingson, De Ridder, Cywka.

December
6th	● Arsenal	.........a	L 1–0	**Att:** 59,317. **Ref:** S Bennett — **Wigan** (4-4-2): Kirkland, Taylor, Boyce (Kilbane 63), Bramble, Figueroa▌, Valencia, Palacios▌, Cattermole (Koumas 77), Melchiot, Heskey, Camara (Zaki 66). Subs not used: Kingson, Brown, De Ridder, Kapo.
13th	● Blackburn	.........h	W 3–0	**Att:** 18,003. **Ref:** H Webb — **Wigan** (4-4-2): Kirkland, Melchiot (Kilbane 79), Bramble, Scharner, Figueroa, Valencia¹ (De Ridder 87), Cattermole¹, Brown▌, Taylor, Zaki, Heskey¹ (Camara 83). Subs not used: Pollitt, Kingson, Koumas, Cywka.
26th	● Newcastle	.........h	W 2–1	**Att:** 20,266. **Ref:** M Dean — **Wigan** (4-4-2): Kirkland, Melchiot, Bramble, Scharner, Valencia, Cattermole▌, Palacios▌ (Kilbane 90), Taylor¹ (Brown 71), Heskey (Camara 85), Zaki¹. Subs not used: Pollitt, Koumas, Boyce, De Ridder.
28th	● Bolton	.........a	W 0–1	**Att:** 23,726. **Ref:** P Dowd — **Wigan** (4-4-2): Pollitt, Melchiot, Scharner, Bramble, Figueroa, Valencia, Cattermole▌, Palacios▌, Taylor▌ (Kilbane 86), Heskey (Camara 33), Zaki¹ (Brown 90). Subs not used: Kingson, Koumas, Boyce, De Ridder.

January
2nd	● Tottenham	.........a	L 3–1	**Att:** 34,040. **Ref:** A Wiley — **Wigan** (4-5-1): Kingson▌, Boyce, Bramble, Scharner (Figueroa 73), Kilbane, Valencia, De Ridder (Cywka 74), Brown, Palacios▌, Kapo (Edman 84), Camara¹. Subs not used: Pollitt, Taylor, Routledge, Holt.
11th	● Tottenham	.........h	W 1–0	**Att:** 17,500. **Ref:** A Marriner — **Wigan** (4-4-2): Kirkland, Melchiot, Scharner▌, Bramble, Figueroa¹, Valencia, Cattermole▌, Palacios▌, Heskey, Zaki. Subs not used: Pollitt, Edman, Kilbane, Brown, Boyce, De Ridder, Camara.
14th	● Man Utd	.........a	L 1–0	**Att:** 73,917. **Ref:** S Bennett — **Wigan** (4-4-2): Kirkland, Melchiot, Scharner▌, Bramble▌, Figueroa, Valencia, Cattermole (Kapo 88), Palacios, Taylor (De Ridder 81), Zaki (Camara 75), Heskey. Subs not used: Kingson, Edman, Brown, Boyce.
17th	● Man City	.........a	L 1–0	**Att:** 41,262. **Ref:** L Mason — **Wigan** (4-4-2): Kirkland▌, Melchiot, Bramble▌ (Camara 87), Scharner, Figueroa (Kapo 74), Valencia, Palacios▌, Cattermole▌, Taylor (De Ridder 58), Heskey, Zaki. Subs not used: Kingson, Edman, Brown, Boyce.
28th	● Liverpool	.........h	D 1–1	**Att:** 21,237. **Ref:** P Dowd — **Wigan** (4-4-2): Pollitt, Melchiot, Boyce, Scharner, Figueroa▌, De Ridder (Koumas 63), Brown, Cattermole, Taylor (Camara 80), Zaki (Rodallega 46), Mido¹. Subs not used: Kingson, Edman, Watson, Kapo.
31st	● Aston Villa	.........a	D 0–0	**Att:** 41,766. **Ref:** R Styles — **Wigan** (4-5-1): Kirkland, Melchiot, Bramble, Boyce, Figueroa, De Ridder (Rodallega 46), Scharner (Watson 77), Brown▌, Koumas, Mido. Subs not used: Pollitt, Edman, Cywka, Kapo, Camara.

February
7th	● Fulham	.........h	D 0–0	**Att:** 16,499. **Ref:** L Probert — **Wigan** (4-4-2): Kirkland, Melchiot, Scharner, Bramble, Figueroa▌, Valencia (Watson 18), Brown (Koumas 19), Cattermole, N'Zogbia, Mido (Zaki 42), Rodallega. Subs not used: Pollitt, Edman, Boyce, De Ridder.
21st	● Middlesbrough	.........a	D 0–0	**Att:** 24,020. **Ref:** M Dean — **Wigan** (4-4-1-1): Kirkland, Melchiot, Boyce, Bramble, Watson▌, Brown, Cattermole▌, N'Zogbia, Kapo▌ (Rodallega 61), Zaki▌ (Sibierski 75). Subs not used: Kingson, Edman, Koumas, Cywka, Routledge.
28th	● Chelsea	.........a	L 2–1	**Att:** 40,714. **Ref:** L Probert — **Wigan** (4-3-3): Kirkland, Melchiot, Bramble, Boyce, Figueroa, Cattermole▌ (Rodallega 69), Brown, Scharner, Kapo¹, Zaki (Sibierski 89), N'Zogbia▌. Subs not used: Kingson, Edman, Kupisz, Routledge, Holt.

● Barclays Premier League ● FA Cup ● Carling Cup ● UEFA Champions League ● UEFA Cup   ▌ Yellow Card ▐ Red Card

RESULTS 2008/09

March

4th	● West Ham ....h	L 0–1	**Att:** 14,169. **Ref:** S Attwell — **Wigan** (4-4-2): Kirkland, Melchiot, Boyce, Bramble (Watson 78), Figueroa, Valencia▌, Brown▌ (Scharner 64), Cattermole▌, N'Zogbia, Mido, Zaki (Rodallega 64). Subs not used: Pollitt, Edman, Sibierski, Kapo.
14th	● Sunderland ....a	W 1–2	**Att:** 39,266. **Ref:** M Dean — **Wigan** (4-5-1): Kirkland, Melchiot, Bramble, Boyce, Figueroa, Scharner, Valencia, Watson¹, Brown▌, N'Zogbia¹, Mido (Zaki 84). Subs not used: Pollitt, Edman, Kapo, Koumas, Rodallega, De Ridder.
22nd	● Hull ....h	W 1–0	**Att:** 17,689. **Ref:** A Marriner — **Wigan** (4-4-1-1): Kirkland, Melchiot, Bramble▌, Boyce, Figueroa, Watson¹, Brown, Scharner (Kapo 77), N'Zogbia (De Ridder 46), Rodallega, Mido (Zaki 72). Subs not used: Kingson, Pollitt, Edman, Cho.

April

5th	● Everton ....a	L 4–0	**Att:** 34,427. **Ref:** P Dowd — **Wigan** (4-2-3-1): Kirkland, Melchiot▌, Bramble▌, Boyce, Figueroa, Watson, Brown▌ (Rodallega 46), Valencia (De Ridder 71), Scharner, N'Zogbia, Mido. Subs not used: Kingson, Edman, Sibierski, Koumas, Kapo.
11th	● Arsenal ....h	L 1–4	**Att:** 22,954. **Ref:** A Wiley — **Wigan** (4-4-1-1): Kirkland, Melchiot, Boyce▌, Bramble▌, Figueroa, Valencia, Watson (Koumas 85), Brown▌ (De Ridder 78), Rodallega, Scharner, Mido¹ (Kapo 58). Subs not used: Pollitt, Kingson, Sibierski, Edman.
26th	● Blackburn ....a	L 2–0	**Att:** 25,019. **Ref:** P Walton — **Wigan** (4-4-2): Kirkland, Boyce, Scharner, Bramble, Figueroa (Kapo 78), Valencia, Watson (De Ridder 78), Cattermole, N'Zogbia, Mido (Zaki 46), Rodallega. Subs not used: Pollitt, Edman, Koumas, Brown.

May

2nd	● Bolton ....h	D 0–0	**Att:** 18,655. **Ref:** M Jones — **Wigan** (4-4-2): Kirkland, Melchiot (Boyce 46), Bramble, Scharner (Edman 53), Figueroa, Valencia, Brown, Cattermole▌, N'Zogbia, Rodallega, Mido▌ (Zaki 75). Subs not used: Pollitt, Watson, De Ridder, Koumas.
9th	● West Brom ....a	L 3–1	**Att:** 24,741. **Ref:** P Walton — **Wigan** (4-4-2): Kirkland (Kingson 10), Melchiot, Bramble, Scharner, Figueroa, Valencia, Cattermole, Brown, N'Zogbia (A Zaki 70 (De Ridder 81)), Kapo, Rodallega¹. Subs not used: Edman, Watson, Koumas, Boyce.
13th	● Man Utd ....h	L 1–2	**Att:** 21,286. **Ref:** R Styles — **Wigan** (4-4-1-1): Kingson, Melchiot, Boyce, Bramble, Figueroa, Valencia, Cattermole, Scharner, Brown, N'Zogbia (Mido 82), Rodallega¹. Subs not used: Pollitt, Edman, Watson, Koumas, De Ridder, Kapo.
16th	● Stoke ....a	L 2–0	**Att:** 25,641. **Ref:** L Probert — **Wigan** (4-1-4-1): Kingson, Melchiot, Boyce, Bramble, Figueroa (Edman 81), Scharner, Cho (Watson 58), Brown (Mido 73), Cattermole, N'Zogbia, Rodallega. Subs not used: Pollitt, Koumas, De Ridder, McManaman.
24th	● Portsmouth ....h	W 1–0	**Att:** 17,696. **Ref:** P Dowd — **Wigan** (4-4-1-1): Kingson, Melchiot, Boyce, Bramble, Figueroa, Valencia, Cattermole, Brown, N'Zogbia (McManaman 78), De Ridder (Routledge 90), Rodallega¹. Subs not used: Pollitt, Edman, Cho, Watson, Kupisz.

● Barclays Premier League ● FA Cup ● Carling Cup ● UEFA Champions League ● UEFA Cup   ▌Yellow Card ▌Red Card

Colombian striker Hugo Rodallega scores his first goal in English football direct from a free-kick at the Hawthorns in May

BARCLAYS PREMIER LEAGUE GOALKEEPER STATS

Player	Minutes on pitch	Appearances	Match starts	Completed matches	Sub appearances	Subbed off	Saved with feet	Punched	Parried	Tipped over	Fumbled	Tipped round	Caught	Blocked	Clean sheets	Goals conceded	Minutes since conceding	Save %	Saved	Resulting in goals	Opposition miss	Yellow cards	Red cards
Richard Kingson	374	4	3	3	1	0	0	1	3	0	0	3	14	0	1	7	112	75.00	1	0	0	0	0
Chris Kirkland	2989	32	32	31	0	1	2	9	19	9	0	5	81	0	11	36	1	77.91	0	2	0	1	0
Mike Pollitt	289	3	3	3	0	0	0	2	0	1	0	2	5	0	1	2	54	84.62	0	0	0	0	0

BARCLAYS PREMIER LEAGUE OUTFIELD PLAYER STATS

Player	Minutes on pitch	Appearances	Match starts	Completed matches	Substitute appearances	Subbed off	Goals scored	Minutes since scoring	Assists	Shots on target	Shots off target	Crosses	Defensive clearances	Defensive blocks	Fouls committed	Free-kicks won	Caught offside	Yellow cards	Red cards
Emmerson Boyce	2473	27	26	24	1	1	1	1375	0	5	6	2	25	11	18	9	0	3	1
Titus Bramble	3336	35	35	33	0	2	1	2287	1	6	13	6	70	26	30	28	0	8	0
Michael Brown	1640	25	18	12	7	6	0	-	1	2	10	7	1	1	36	16	0	7	0
Henri Camara	536	17	3	1	14	2	2	345	1	6	4	4	0	0	3	2	9	0	0
Lee Cattermole	2973	33	33	23	0	8	1	1578	2	7	17	8	11	4	59	29	2	11	2
Won-Hee Cho	58	1	1	0	0	1	0	-	0	1	1	0	0	0	1	1	0	0	0
Daniel De Ridder	640	18	5	0	13	5	0	-	1	7	7	24	1	0	5	13	0	0	0
Erik Edman	53	2	0	0	2	0	0	-	0	0	0	2	0	0	1	0	0	0	0
Maynor Figueroa	3555	38	38	33	0	5	1	1687	2	16	17	37	22	5	39	42	1	4	0
Emile Heskey	1775	20	20	15	0	5	3	294	2	12	14	3	11	0	15	24	16	0	0
Olivier Kapo	970	19	10	4	9	6	1	185	0	9	13	9	4	0	8	9	10	1	0
Kevin Kilbane	312	10	3	1	7	2	0	-	1	0	2	8	1	0	2	0	1	1	0
Jason Koumas	731	16	5	3	11	2	0	-	2	10	7	36	3	0	1	12	1	0	0
Callum McManaman	15	1	0	0	1	0	0	-	0	0	0	1	0	0	0	0	0	0	0
Mario Melchiot	3110	34	33	29	1	4	0	-	1	10	3	27	29	7	13	34	1	2	0
Mido	801	12	10	4	2	6	2	199	0	8	7	4	0	0	20	14	14	1	0
Charles N'Zogbia	1146	13	13	9	0	4	1	708	1	10	8	29	1	0	18	17	2	1	0
Wilson Palacios	1934	21	21	15	0	6	0	-	1	20	13	15	7	3	39	27	1	9	0
Hugo Rodallega	1072	15	9	6	6	9	3	68	0	18	19	7	1	0	11	11	9	0	0
Jonathon Routledge	4	1	0	0	1	0	0	-	0	0	0	0	0	0	0	0	0	0	0
Paul Scharner	2545	29	27	23	2	4	0	-	2	9	16	8	27	9	31	32	5	3	0
Antoine Sibierski	32	3	0	0	3	0	0	-	0	0	0	0	0	0	0	0	0	0	0
Ryan Taylor	929	12	11	4	1	7	2	1252	1	9	10	37	0	4	10	3	1	1	0
Antonio Valencia	2847	31	31	27	0	3	3	1422	5	21	20	88	9	2	40	50	10	4	1
Ben Watson	706	10	6	4	4	2	2	312	0	9	10	13	1	1	9	7	0	1	0
Amr Zaki	2174	29	22	11	7	11	10	797	1	30	37	21	2	1	31	67	19	3	0

SEASON TOTALS

Goals scored	34
Goals conceded	45
Clean sheets	13
Shots on target	227
Shots off target	255
Shots per goal	14.18
Pens awarded	5
Pens scored	5
Pens conceded	3
Offsides	101
Corners	217
Crosses	399
Players used	29
Fouls committed	441
Free-kicks won	453

CARDS RECEIVED

61 **4**

SEASON INFORMATION

Highest Position: 7
Lowest Position: 19
Average goals scored per game: 0.89
Average goals conceded per game: 1.18

League position at the end of each week

League position at the end of: August 13, September 10, October 18, November 11, December 7, January 7, February 7, March 7, April 11, May 11

SEQUENCES

Wins	4
(13/12/08–11/01/09)	
Losses	4
(04/10/08–29/10/08)	
Draws	4
(28/01/09–21/02/09)	
Undefeated	5
(01/11/08–29/11/08)	
Without win	8
(14/01/09–04/03/09)	
Undefeated home	8
(08/11/08–07/02/09)	
Undefeated away	2
(on three occasions)	
Without scoring	3
(31/01/09–21/02/09)	
Without conceding	3
(31/01/09–21/02/09)	
Scoring	4
(13/12/08–11/01/09)	
Conceding	6
(28/09/08–01/11/08)	

MATCH RECORDS

Goals scored per match

		W	D	L	Pts
Failed to score	17	0	6	11	6
Scored 1 goal	12	5	2	5	17
Scored 2 goals	7	5	1	1	16
Scored 3 goals	1	1	0	0	3
Scored 4+ goals	1	1	0	0	3

Goals conceded per match

		W	D	L	Pts
Clean sheet	13	7	6	0	27
Conceded 1 goal	13	5	2	6	17
Conceded 2 goals	7	0	1	6	1
Conceded 3 goals	2	0	0	2	0
Conceded 4+ goals	3	0	0	3	0

QUICK-FIRE GOALS

From the start of a match
Ryan Taylor (v Newcastle) 2:38

By a substitute after coming on
Henri Camara (v Everton) 5:05

LAST-GASP GOALS

From the start of a match
Emile Heskey (v Portsmouth) 91:11

By a substitute after coming on
Henri Camara (v Everton) 5:05

GOAL DETAILS

How the goals were struck

SCORED		CONCEDED
23	Right foot	26
8	Left foot	12
3	Headers	7
0	Others	0

How the goals were struck

SCORED		CONCEDED
20	Open play	33
2	Cross	3
4	Corner	3
5	Penalties	2
2	Direct from free-kick	1
0	Free-kick	2
1	Own goals	1

Distance from goal

SCORED		CONCEDED
11	6yds	17
17	18yds	24
6	18+yds	4

GOALS SCORED/CONCEDED PER FIVE-MINUTE INTERVALS

Goals For	2	1	3	3	0	4	1	0	4	1	1	0	2	1	1	2	4	4
Goals Against	3	2	2	1	3	1	1	1	3	2	2	4	4	1	2	3	2	8
Mins	5	10	15	20	25	30	35	40	45	50	55	60	65	70	75	80	85	90

COCA-COLA CHAMPIONSHIP STATISTICS 2008/09

Player of the season
Sylvan Ebanks-Blake (Wolves)

Manager of the season
Mick McCarthy (Wolves)

The player with the most...

Shots on target	
Jordi Gomez (Swansea)	70
Shots off target	
Jordi Gomez (Swansea)	60
Shots without scoring	
Mark Gower (Swansea)	45
Shots per goal	
Adam Lallana (Southampton)	66
Assists	
Michael Kightly (Wolves)	19
Offsides	
Tamas Priskin (Watford)	57
Fouls	
Rory Fallon (Plymouth), Chris Iwelumo (Wolves)	93
Fouls without a card	
Ross Jenkins (Watford)	33
Free-kicks won	
Jordi Gomez (Swansea)	121
Penalties scored	
Ross McCormack (Cardiff)	9
Goals scored direct from free-kicks	
Daniel Fox (Coventry)	4
Saves made	
Andy Lonergan (Preston)	300
Defensive clearances	
Youl Mawene (Preston)	109
Defensive blocks	
Liam Fontaine (Bristol City)	37

The team with the most...

Shots on target	Ipswich	337
Shots off target	Burnley	284
Shots per goal	Southampton	12.7
Corners	Reading	360
Fouls	Barnsley	670
Woodwork strikes	Reading, Ipswich, Wolves	18
Offsides	Norwich	184
Penalties conceded	Norwich	11
Yellow cards	Coventry	85
Red cards	Birmingham, Burnley, Norwich	6

TOTALS 2008/09

Goals	
Total	1350
Home	767
Away	767
Cards	
Yellow	1574
Average per game	2.85
Red	92
Average per game	0.17
Attendances	
Total	9,875,953

AN EFFICIENT brand of football brought its rewards as Wolves returned to the promised land as Coca-Cola Championship champions while three former Barclays Premier League sides dropped out of the Football League's top tier.

Five years after a season-long spell in the Premier League, Wolves, managed by Mick McCarthy, swept to the title thanks to a brilliant start to the campaign. Birmingham followed their midlands rivals into the top flight after beating Reading 2–1 at the Madejski Stadium on the final day of the regular season. At the other end of the table, Charlton, Southampton and Norwich endured miserable campaigns which culminated in relegation to Coca-Cola League One.

Wolves topped the table at the end of August, September, October and, by 30th November, were six points clear of Birmingham after 15 wins and just three defeats in the opening 20 games. Wolves were seven points clear at the end of 2008, and continued in pole position despite a run of just one win in nine matches – including a 1–0 loss at Reading in January, which saw the Royals cut the gap to two points.

Wolves claimed 23 points from a possible 30 in March and April to clinch the title at Barnsley – one of McCarthy's former clubs – with a game to spare. It was a result that led to mixed emotions for McCarthy as Barnsley spiralled towards the drop zone.

The Tykes, however, survived courtesy of a final-day win at Plymouth, while Norwich's chances were wiped out by a 4–2 loss at Charlton on 3rd May. Glenn Roeder – one of 10 managerial departures during the season – had left Carrow Road on 14th January with the Canaries 21st in the table. However, fortunes did not improve under Bryan Gunn and relegation was confirmed after Barnsley, whose season was marred by the horrific head injury suffered by Iain Hume, won in Devon.

The fate of Charlton and Southampton was decided in advance of the finale. The Addicks – who dropped out of the Premier League at the end of the 2006/07 season – and manager Alan Pardew parted company on 22nd November after a record of just four wins in the opening 18 fixtures of the campaign had left the club languishing in the drop zone. Pardew's successor, Phil Parkinson, could not stop the rot, with just four more wins before the end of the campaign, and Charlton dropped into the third tier for the first time in 29 years.

Southampton, a Premier League club until 2005 when their 27-year top-flight stint ended, also fell a division. Their last-ditch bid for survival was rendered meaningless once their holding company entered administration. With the Saints – who parted company with Jan Poortvliet in January – in the drop zone with two games remaining, the Football League ruled the club and the holding company were 'inextricably linked' and the south-coast club were consigned to relegation.

> **The teams vying for the automatic promotion places stuttered with the end in sight**

At the other end of the table, the teams vying for the automatic promotion places stuttered with the end in sight and the race for second place went to the death.

Birmingham and Reading faced each other at the Madejski Stadium for the second automatic promotion spot, with the Blues winning the match – leaving Sheffield United's failure to beat Crystal Palace immaterial – and thus returning to the Premier League.

Elsewhere, QPR parted company with two managers – Iain Dowie becoming the Championship's first managerial departure on 24th October and Paulo Sousa following on 9th April – as the team's performances failed to match the great expectations of their billionaire owners.

Established managers Adrian Boothroyd, Colin Calderwood and Paul Jewell left Watford, Nottingham Forest and Derby, while Simon Grayson departed Blackpool for League One Leeds.

Perhaps the most dramatic managerial change, however, was at Ipswich as Jim Magilton was replaced by Roy Keane in April. The Irishman's early days at Portman Road will be a key ingredient of what promises to be another compelling Championship season in 2009/10.

FINAL COCA-COLA CHAMPIONSHIP TABLE

		P	W	D	L	F	A	W	D	L	F	A	GD	Pts
			HOME					**AWAY**						
1	WOLVES	46	15	5	3	44	21	12	4	7	36	31	28	90
2	BIRMINGHAM	46	14	5	4	30	17	9	9	5	24	20	17	83
3	Sheffield Utd	46	12	6	5	35	22	10	8	5	29	17	25	80
4	Reading	46	12	5	6	40	17	9	9	5	32	23	32	77
5	BURNLEY	46	14	5	4	42	23	7	8	8	30	37	12	76
6	Preston	46	16	3	4	39	20	5	8	10	27	34	12	74
7	Cardiff	46	14	5	4	40	23	5	12	6	25	30	12	74
8	Swansea	46	11	9	3	40	22	5	11	7	23	28	13	68
9	Ipswich	46	8	9	6	30	26	9	6	8	32	27	9	66
10	Bristol City	46	7	13	3	30	23	8	3	12	24	31	0	61
11	QPR	46	12	7	4	28	19	3	9	11	14	25	-2	61
12	Sheffield W	46	11	6	6	26	14	5	7	11	25	44	-7	61
13	Watford	46	11	6	6	42	32	5	4	14	26	40	-4	58
14	Doncaster	46	9	5	9	16	18	8	2	13	26	35	-11	58
15	Crystal Palace*	46	9	8	6	26	19	6	4	13	26	36	-3	56
16	Blackpool	46	5	8	10	25	33	8	9	6	22	25	-11	56
17	Coventry	46	8	8	7	26	26	5	7	11	21	32	-11	54
18	Derby	46	9	7	7	31	26	5	5	13	24	41	-12	54
19	Nottm Forest	46	8	7	8	27	28	5	7	11	23	37	-15	53
20	Barnsley	46	8	7	8	28	24	5	6	12	17	34	-13	52
21	Plymouth	46	7	5	11	31	35	6	7	10	13	22	-13	51
22	Norwich	46	9	5	9	35	28	3	5	15	22	42	-13	46
23	Southampton	46	4	10	9	23	29	6	5	12	23	40	-23	45
24	Charlton	46	6	8	9	33	38	2	7	14	19	36	-22	39

* 1 point deducted

LEE CARSLEY (BIRMINGHAM)

MICHAEL DUFF (BURNLEY)

NICK BAILEY (CHARLTON)

PLAY-OFF REVIEW

OWEN COYLE'S Burnley secured promotion to the Barclays Premier League following a 1–0 victory over Sheffield United in the Championship play-off final.

The Clarets, among the founder members of the Football League, are back in the top flight for the first time since 1976 courtesy of Wade Elliott's 13th-minute strike at Wembley. Burnley stepped up when it counted most to land the estimated £60million booty for reaching the promised land. Elliott's long-range winner was worthy of any Premier League ground – and certainly lit up a packed Wembley. It was quite a way to sign off for the summer as Burnley clinched victory in their 61st game of the season, having also reached the semi-finals of the League Cup.

Coyle's side, who booked a play-off berth thanks to a final-day victory over Bristol City, reached Wembley following a 3–0 aggregate win over Reading. Graham Alexander's 84th-minute penalty – after Andre Bikey had pulled back Steve Thompson – handed Coyle's men a narrow first-leg advantage at Turf Moor. Bikey was booked for his indiscretion and was then shown a straight red card in the closing stages after kicking out at Robbie Blake. Superb goals from Martin Paterson and Thompson then sealed victory at the Madejski Stadium.

Sheffield United had a tougher test against Alan Irvine's Preston, who scraped into the play-offs ahead of Cardiff on goal difference. Sean St Ledger had put Preston ahead in the first leg at Deepdale but Brian Howard ensured a 1–1 draw. Greg Halford's strike settled matters at Bramall Lane, but Wembley would prove a step too far for Kevin Blackwell's men.

The Wolves squad enjoy the moment after claiming the Championship title following a successful season in which they led the table from start to finish

SEASON REVIEW

COCA-COLA CHAMPIONSHIP FIXTURES AND RESULTS

Away →

Home	BARNSLEY	BIRMINGHAM	BLACKPOOL	BRISTOL CITY	BURNLEY	CARDIFF	CHARLTON	COVENTRY	CRYSTAL P	DERBY	DONCASTER	IPSWICH	NORWICH	NOTTM FOREST	PLYMOUTH	PRESTON	QPR	READING	SHEFF UTD	SHEFF WED	SOUTHAMPTON	SWANSEA	WATFORD	WOLVES
BARNSLEY	–	1-1	0-1	0-0	3-2	0-1	0-0	1-2	3-1	2-0	4-1	1-2	0-0	1-1	2-0	1-1	2-1	0-1	1-2	2-1	0-1	1-3	2-1	1-1
BIRMINGHAM	2-0	–	0-1	1-0	1-1	1-1	3-2	0-1	1-0	1-0	1-0	2-1	1-1	2-0	1-1	1-2	1-0	1-3	1-0	3-1	1-0	0-0	3-2	2-0
BLACKPOOL	1-0	2-0	–	0-1	0-1	1-1	2-0	1-1	2-2	3-2	2-3	0-1	2-0	1-1	0-1	1-3	0-3	2-2	1-3	0-2	1-1	1-1	0-2	2-2
BRISTOL CITY	2-0	1-2	0-0	–	1-2	1-1	2-1	2-0	1-0	1-1	4-1	1-1	1-0	2-2	2-2	1-1	1-1	1-4	0-0	1-1	2-0	0-0	1-1	2-2
BURNLEY	1-2	1-1	2-0	4-0	–	2-2	2-1	1-1	4-2	3-0	0-0	0-3	2-0	5-0	0-0	3-1	1-0	1-0	1-0	2-4	3-2	0-2	3-2	1-0
CARDIFF	3-1	1-2	2-0	0-0	3-1	–	2-0	2-1	2-1	4-1	3-0	0-3	2-2	2-0	1-0	2-0	0-2	0-3	2-0	2-1	2-2	2-1	2-1	1-2
CHARLTON	1-3	0-0	2-2	0-2	1-1	2-2	–	1-2	1-0	2-2	1-2	2-1	4-2	0-2	2-0	0-0	2-2	4-2	2-5	1-2	0-0	2-0	2-3	1-3
COVENTRY	1-1	1-0	2-1	0-3	1-3	0-2	0-0	–	0-2	1-1	1-0	2-2	2-0	2-2	0-1	0-0	1-0	0-0	1-2	2-0	4-1	1-1	2-3	2-1
CRYSTAL P	3-0	0-0	0-1	4-2	0-0	0-2	1-1	1-1	–	1-0	2-1	1-4	3-1	1-2	1-2	2-1	0-0	0-0	0-0	1-1	3-0	0-0	2-2	0-1
DERBY	0-0	1-1	4-1	2-1	1-1	1-1	1-0	2-1	1-2	–	0-1	0-1	3-1	1-1	2-1	2-2	0-2	0-2	2-1	3-0	0-1	2-2	1-0	2-3
DONCASTER	0-1	0-2	0-0	1-0	2-1	1-1	0-1	1-0	2-0	2-1	–	1-0	1-1	0-0	1-0	0-2	2-0	0-1	0-2	1-0	0-2	0-0	1-2	0-1
IPSWICH	3-0	0-1	1-1	3-1	1-1	1-2	1-1	2-1	1-1	2-0	1-3	–	3-2	2-1	0-0	1-2	2-0	1-1	1-1	0-3	0-0	2-2	0-0	0-2
NORWICH	4-0	1-1	1-1	1-2	2-0	1-0	1-2	1-2	1-2	2-0	2-3	1-0	–	2-3	1-2	0-2	1-0	0-1	2-2	2-3	2-0	2-3	2-0	5-2
NOTTM FOREST	1-0	1-1	0-0	3-2	1-2	0-1	0-0	1-0	0-2	1-3	2-4	1-1	1-2	–	2-0	2-1	2-2	0-0	0-1	2-1	3-1	1-1	3-2	0-1
PLYMOUTH	1-2	0-1	1-2	0-2	1-2	2-1	2-2	4-0	1-3	0-3	0-3	1-3	1-2	1-0	–	1-0	1-1	2-2	2-2	4-0	2-0	0-1	2-1	2-2
PRESTON	2-1	1-0	0-1	2-0	2-1	6-0	2-1	2-1	2-0	2-0	1-0	3-2	1-0	2-1	1-1	–	2-1	2-1	0-0	1-1	2-3	0-2	2-0	1-3
QPR	2-1	1-0	1-1	2-1	1-2	1-1	2-1	1-1	0-0	0-2	2-0	1-3	0-1	2-1	0-0	3-2	–	0-0	0-1	3-2	4-1	1-0	0-0	1-0
READING	0-0	1-2	1-0	0-2	3-1	1-1	2-2	3-1	4-2	3-0	2-1	0-1	2-0	0-1	2-0	0-0	0-0	–	0-1	6-0	1-2	4-0	4-0	1-0
SHEFF UTD	2-1	2-1	2-2	3-0	2-3	0-0	3-1	1-1	2-2	4-2	0-1	2-0	0-0	2-0	1-0	3-0	2-0	1-3	–	1-2	0-0	1-0	2-1	1-3
SHEFF WED	0-1	1-1	1-1	0-0	4-1	0-1	4-1	0-1	2-0	0-1	1-0	0-0	3-2	1-0	0-1	1-1	1-0	1-2	1-0	–	2-0	0-0	2-0	0-1
SOUTHAMPTON	0-0	1-2	0-1	0-1	2-2	1-0	2-3	1-1	1-1	1-1	1-2	2-2	2-0	0-2	0-0	3-1	0-1	1-1	1-2	1-1	–	2-2	0-3	1-2
SWANSEA	2-2	2-3	0-1	1-0	1-1	2-2	1-1	0-0	1-3	1-1	3-1	3-0	2-1	3-1	1-0	4-1	0-0	2-0	1-1	1-1	3-0	–	3-1	3-1
WATFORD	1-1	0-1	3-4	2-4	3-0	2-2	1-0	2-1	2-0	3-1	1-1	2-1	2-1	1-2	2-1	3-0	2-2	0-2	2-2	2-2	2-0	2-2	–	2-3
WOLVES	2-0	1-1	2-0	2-0	2-0	2-2	2-1	2-1	2-1	3-0	1-0	0-0	3-3	5-1	0-1	1-3	1-0	0-3	1-1	4-1	3-0	2-1	3-1	–

SYLVAN EBANKS-BLAKE (WOLVES)

LEADING SCORERS

Player	(Team)	Goals
Sylvan Ebanks-Blake	(Wolves)	25
Jason Scotland	(Swansea)	21
Ross McCormack	(Cardiff)	21
Kevin Doyle	(Reading)	18
Tommy Smith	(Watford)	17
Rob Hulse	(Derby)	15
Chris Iwelumo	(Wolves)	14
Kevin Phillips	(Birmingham)	14
Marcus Tudgay	(Sheffield W)	14
Nick Bailey	(Charlton)	13
Dexter Blackstock	(QPR)	13

2 for Nottingham Forest

ON THE CLOCK COCA-COLA CHAMPIONSHIP

FROM THE START OF A MATCH

Quickest goal
Nicky Maynard 0:23
(Bristol City v Watford)

Quickest card
Nick Carle 0:41
(Crystal Palace v Derby)

Last-gasp goal
Francis Jeffers 96:12
(Sheffield W v Watford)

BY A SUBSTITUTE

Quickest goal
Jonathan Macken 0:48
(Barnsley v Cardiff)

Quickest card
Jonathan Stead 1:34
(Sheffield Utd v Birmingham)

Substitute being substituted
Stephen McPhee 5:21
(Blackpool v Sheffield W)

PADDY KENNY (SHEFFIELD UTD)

LEADING GOALKEEPERS

Player	(Team)	Clean Sheets
Paddy Kenny	(Sheffield Utd)	19
Radek Cerny	(QPR)	19
Brian Jensen	(Burnley)	19
Adriano Basso	(Bristol City)	17
Maik Taylor	(Birmingham)	16
Neil Sullivan	(Doncaster)	16
Marcus Hahnemann	(Reading)	15
Julian Speroni	(Crystal Palace)	15
Richard Wright	(Ipswich)	14
Andy Lonergan	(Preston)	14
Lee Grant	(Sheffield W)	13
Dorus De Vries	(Swansea)	13
Keiren Westwood	(Coventry)	13
Romain Larrieu	(Plymouth)	12
Paul Rachubka	(Blackpool)	12

DISCIPLINARY RECORDS

Player	Team	Fouls	Y	R
Karl Henry	Wolves	78	12	0
Darel Russell	Norwich	74	8	2
Liam Rosenior	Reading	29	8	2
Clarke Carlisle	Burnley	44	9	1
Leon Britton	Swansea	47	9	1
Matthew Lawrence	Crystal Palace	23	9	1
Bradley Orr	Bristol City	47	10	0
James Perch	Nottm Forest	43	10	0
Jon Harley	Watford	51	10	0
Lloyd James	Southampton	36	10	0
Daniel Fox	Coventry	26	8	1
Mikele Leigertwood	QPR	66	8	1
Richard Wellens	Doncaster	45	8	1
Shaun Derry	Crystal Palace	40	8	1
Stephen Jordan	Burnley	45	8	1
Aron Gunnarsson	Coventry	70	9	0
Louis Carey	Bristol City	44	9	0
Nick Bailey	Charlton	47	9	0
Stephen Foster	Barnsley	49	9	0
Darren Moore	Barnsley	62	7	1

PLAYER WITH THE MOST...

Shots on target
Jordi Gomez (Swansea)	70
David McGoldrick (Southampton)	64
Jason Scotland (Swansea)	62
Sylvan Ebanks-Blake (Wolves)	61
Kris Commons (Derby)	59
Jonathan Stead (Ipswich)	57

Shots off target
Jordi Gomez (Swansea)	60
David McGoldrick (Southampton)	54
Hameur Bouazza (Birmingham)	51
Jay Bothroyd (Cardiff)	47
Martin Woods (Doncaster)	45
Kris Commons (Derby)	43

Shots without scoring
Mark Gower (Swansea)	45
Darren Ambrose (Charlton)	41
Luke Summerfield (Plymouth)	31
James O'Connor (Sheffield W)	28
Lloyd Sam (Charlton)	27
Bradley Orr (Bristol City)	26

Assists
Michael Kightly (Wolves)	19
Stephen Hunt (Reading)	17
Ross Wallace (Preston)	14
Robbie Blake (Burnley)	12
Jimmy Kebe (Reading)	11
Wayne Routledge (QPR)	9

Offsides
Tamas Priskin (Watford)	57
Deon Burton (Charlton)	54
Leroy Lita (Reading)	53
Martin Paterson (Burnley)	52
Kevin Lisbie (Ipswich)	49
Dudley Campbell (Blackpool)	48

Fouls commited
Rory Fallon (Plymouth)	93
Chris Iwelumo (Wolves)	93
Jon Parkin (Preston)	91
Jonathan Macken (Barnsley)	82
Darius Henderson (Sheffield Utd)	81
Marcus Tudgay (Sheffield W)	80

TEAM STATISTICS

Club	Played	Shots on	Shots off	Corners	Hit woodwork	Caught offside	Offside trap	Fouls	Yellow cards	Red cards	Pens awarded	Pens con
Barnsley	46	266	239	218	9	173	69	**670**	76	5	7 (4)	7
Birmingham	46	229	251	235	12	183	141	583	66	**6**	1 (1)	2
Blackpool	46	256	237	238	6	159	98	528	73	5	6 (6)	7
Bristol City	46	329	249	252	6	177	101	597	65	1	6 (3)	3
Burnley	46	294	**284**	281	9	144	177	584	68	**6**	8 (8)	8
Cardiff	46	279	249	286	5	122	143	432	42	5	**16 (12)**	4
Charlton	46	266	259	216	12	162	146	585	73	3	6 (4)	10
Coventry	46	264	240	247	14	152	188	570	**85**	2	6 (4)	5
Crystal Palace	46	215	204	244	9	116	169	600	78	5	4 (4)	7
Derby	46	298	257	276	13	119	227	514	49	2	3 (2)	4
Doncaster	46	230	222	226	5	160	115	485	57	2	5 (4)	5
Ipswich	46	**337**	252	265	**18**	173	112	568	74	4	5 (4)	5
Norwich	46	263	273	279	15	**184**	130	495	57	**6**	5 (4)	**11**
Nottm Forest	46	242	202	269	9	115	150	598	80	4	1 (1)	8
Plymouth	46	209	222	209	10	138	127	572	61	3	4 (4)	5
Preston	46	260	263	261	9	110	139	547	58	3	6 (6)	6
QPR	46	225	218	237	10	132	138	572	66	4	3 (1)	5
Reading	46	228	205	**360**	**18**	119	136	549	63	5	7 (5)	3
Sheffield Utd	46	295	254	294	11	168	93	600	57	5	10 (10)	6
Sheffield W	46	254	233	254	9	176	167	530	55	5	5 (4)	7
Southampton	46	318	261	279	11	129	**253**	549	83	4	7 (3)	9
Swansea	46	314	242	284	11	119	128	488	68	2	7 (6)	6
Watford	46	226	179	258	14	154	148	584	56	1	6 (4)	9
Wolves	46	294	224	272	**18**	129	210	630	64	4	10 (8)	2

Offside trap – number of times a side has caught the opposition offside. **Pens awarded** (scored in brackets). **Pens con** – number of penalties awarded to opposition. **Bold** – biggest total

Total league games played this season: **552** • Home wins: **239** (43%) • Away wins: **151** (27%)
• Draws: **162** (29%) • Average goals scored per match **2.4**

SEASON REVIEW

SYLVAN EBANKS-BLAKE was crowned the king of the 2008/09 Coca-Cola Championship Actim Index having led the standings for the majority of the season.

The 23-year-old came through the youth system at Manchester United but made his name at Plymouth, netting 21 goals in 56 league games to earn a mid-season move to Wolves in 2007/08. Mick McCarthy's side were denied a play-off berth on goal difference during that campaign but they were not to be thwarted this time around as 25 goals in 41 games from the frontman helped secure the Championship title. The

marksman finished with 753 points – 46 clear of Watford's Tommy Smith in second place – with his goals coming from just 61 shots on target.

Kevin Doyle was denied the runner-up spot in the final week after accumulating just one point in Reading's loss to Birmingham. The Republic of Ireland striker can, however, be pleased with his haul of 18 goals in 3,650 minutes – a goal every 200 minutes. He also narrowly avoided dropping behind team-mate Stephen Hunt, who had a final total of 684 points.

Smith was the highest-ranked midfielder on the Actim Index, with his best individual

match score coming with a 46-point return against Swansea in February. This added to an impressive 17 goals and nine assists, while Hunt finished as one of the division's top providers, assisting in 17 goals.

The teams promoted or in the play-offs dominated the upper echelons of the standings with only four players from outside that group earning a place in the top 20. Relegated Charlton's Nicky Bailey sealed a season-high 20th position overall on the final day of the season, scoring 13 goals from midfield in 43 games. He also supplied seven assists and 53 crosses to cap a fine individual campaign.

Actim player rankings for the 2008/09 Coca-Cola Championship season

	Name	Team	Index Score		Name	Team	Index Score		Name	Team	Index Score
1	Sylvan Ebanks-Blake	Wolves	753	34	Julian Speroni	Crystal P	495	67	Lee Croft	Norwich	434
2	Tommy Smith	Watford	707	35	Radek Cerny	QPR	492	68	Sebastian Larsson	Birmingham	425
3	Kevin Doyle	Reading	689	36	Robbie Blake	Burnley	492	69	Clarke Carlisle	Burnley	425
4	Stephen Hunt	Reading	684	37	Liam Fontaine	Bristol City	490	70	Stephen Ward	Wolves	424
5	Jason Scotland	Swansea	643	38	Paul McKenna	Preston	482	71	Joe Ledley	Cardiff	419
6	Graham Alexander	Burnley	638	39	Tamas Priskin	Watford	482	72	Richard Wood	Sheffield W	418
7	Andy Lonergan	Preston	622	40	Paul Rachubka	Blackpool	481	73	Paul Gallagher	Plymouth	416
8	Maik Taylor	Birmingham	604	41	Neil Sullivan	Doncaster	480	74	Clinton Morrison	Coventry	416
9	Martin Paterson	Burnley	604	42	Ross Wallace	Preston	476	75	Chris Barker	Plymouth	414
10	Ross McCormack	Cardiff	590	43	Daniel Fox	Coventry	476	76	Dexter Blackstock	QPR	413
11	Michael Kightly	Wolves	587	44	Michael McIndoe	Bristol City	475	77	David Jones	Wolves	410
12	Brian Jensen	Burnley	580	45	Jimmy Kebe	Reading	471	78	Mark Hudson	Charlton	409
13	Kevin Foley	Wolves	569	46	Chris Armstrong	Reading	470	79	Jose Fonte	Crystal P	406
14	Wade Elliott	Burnley	565	47	Shaun Barker	Blackpool	469	80	Garry Monk	Swansea	403
15	Paddy Kenny	Sheffield Utd	559	48	Lee Johnson	Bristol City	466	81	Jay Bothroyd	Cardiff	402
16	Stephen Quinn	Sheffield Utd	557	49	David Marshall	Norwich	465	82	Wes Morgan	Nottm Forest	402
17	Liam Rosenior	Reading	554	50	Karl Henry	Wolves	465	83	Chris McCann	Burnley	401
18	Sean St Ledger	Preston	553	51	Youl Mawene	Preston	464	84	Noel Hunt	Reading	399
19	Chris Iwelumo	Wolves	545	52	Matthew Kilgallon	Sheffield Utd	459	85	Angel Rangel	Swansea	399
20	Nick Bailey	Charlton	545	53	Rob Hulse	Derby	459	86	Clint Hill	Crystal P	398
21	Kyle Naughton	Sheffield Utd	545	54	Kevin Phillips	Birmingham	457	87	Jonathan Macken	Barnsley	397
22	Adriano Basso	Bristol City	544	55	Damion Stewart	QPR	456	88	Jamie McAllister	Bristol City	393
23	Richard Wright	Ipswich	532	56	Romain Larrieu	Plymouth	455	89	Heinz Muller	Barnsley	392
24	Chris Eagles	Burnley	520	57	Marcus Hahnemann	Reading	455	90	Marcel Seip	Plymouth	391
25	Roger Johnson	Cardiff	518	58	Andrew Surman	Southampton	454	91	David McGoldrick	Southampton	390
26	Jamal C-Ryce	Barnsley	518	59	Lee Carsley	Birmingham	450	92	Pablo Counago	Ipswich	390
27	Keiren Westwood	Coventry	517	60	Tommy Spurr	Sheffield W	449	93	Darius Henderson	Sheffield Utd	390
28	Ashley Williams	Swansea	515	61	Steven Caldwell	Burnley	444	94	Bradley Orr	Bristol City	385
29	Chris Cohen	Nottm Forest	509	62	Wayne Hennessey	Wolves	443	95	Greg Halford	Sheffield Utd	384
30	Billy Jones	Preston	506	63	Kelvin Davis	Southampton	443	96	Kevin McNaughton	Cardiff	384
31	Marcus Tudgay	Sheffield W	504	64	Chris Morgan	Sheffield Utd	441	97	Jon Parkin	Preston	382
32	Jordi Gomez	Swansea	503	65	Gary Naysmith	Sheffield Utd	440	98	Elliott Ward	Coventry	381
33	Lee Grant	Sheffield W	496	66	Dorus De Vries	Swansea	439	99	Adrian Mariappa	Watford	380
								100	Scott Loach	Watford	378

LEADING PLAYERS IN THE ACTIM INDEX BY POSITION

TOP 5 GOALKEEPERS

Name	Index Score	Overall Index Rank	Team
Andy Lonergan	622	7	Preston
Maik Taylor	604	8	Birmingham
Brian Jensen	580	12	Burnley
Paddy Kenny	559	15	Sheffield Utd
Adriano Basso	544	22	Bristol City

TOP 5 DEFENDERS

Name	Index Score	Overall Index Rank	Team
Graham Alexander	638	6	Burnley
Kevin Foley	569	13	Wolves
Liam Rosenior	554	17	Reading
Sean St Ledger	553	18	Preston
Kyle Naughton	545	21	Sheffield Utd

TOP 5 MIDFIELDERS

Name	Index Score	Overall Index Rank	Team
Tommy Smith	707	2	Watford
Stephen Hunt	684	4	Reading
Michael Kightly	587	11	Wolves
Wade Elliott	565	14	Burnley
Stephen Quinn	557	16	Sheffield Utd

TOP 5 STRIKERS

Name	Index Score	Overall Index Rank	Team
Sylvan Ebanks-Blake	753	1	Wolves
Kevin Doyle	689	3	Reading
Jason Scotland	643	5	Swansea
Martin Paterson	604	9	Burnley
Ross McCormack	590	10	Cardiff

BEST INDIVIDUAL MATCH SCORES

Deon Burton	Charlton	75
03/05/2009: Charlton 4–2 Norwich		
Chris Iwelumo	Wolves	65
20/09/2008: Preston 1–3 Wolves		
Billy Sharp	Sheffield Utd	65
16/08/2008: Sheffield Utd 3–0 QPR		
Noel Hunt	Reading	64
16/09/2008: Reading 6–0 Sheff Wed		
Leon Clarke	Sheffield W	64
28/02/2009: Burnley 2–4 Sheffield W		
Kevin Doyle	Reading	63
30/08/2008: Reading 4–2 Crystal Palace		
Sylvan Ebanks-Blake	Wolves	61
03/02/2009: Wolves 3–3 Norwich		
Leroy Lita	Norwich	61
21/10/2008: Norwich 5–2 Wolves		
Ross McCormack	Cardiff	60
13/04/2009: Cardiff 3–1 Burnley		
Luke Varney	Charlton	60
23/08/2008: Charlton 4–2 Reading		
Jason Euell	Southampton	60
03/03/2009: Ipswich 0–3 Southampton		
Marcus Tudgay	Sheffield W	59
09/08/2008: Sheffield W 4–1 Burnley		
Kevin Doyle	Reading	57
16/09/2008: Reading 6–0 Sheffield W		
Fitz Hall	QPR	57
09/08/2008: QPR 2–1 Barnsley		
Kevin Doyle	Reading	56
01/11/2008: Bristol City 1–4 Reading		
Chris Iwelumo	Wolves	55
25/11/2008: Sheffield Utd 1–3 Wolves		

ACTIM INDEX TEAM OF THE SEASON

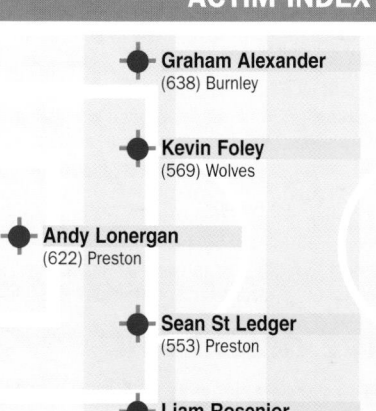

Graham Alexander (638) Burnley

Stephen Hunt (684) Reading

Kevin Foley (569) Wolves

Wade Elliott (565) Burnley

Kevin Doyle (689) Reading

Andy Lonergan (622) Preston

Sean St Ledger (553) Preston

Tommy Smith (707) Watford

Sylvan Ebanks-Blake (753) Wolves

Liam Rosenior (554) Reading

Michael Kightly (587) Wolves

TOP RANK BY CLUB

	SCORE	RANK	POSITON
Barnsley J Campbell-Ryce	518	26	Midfielder
Birmingham Maik Taylor	604	8	Goalkeeper
Blackpool Paul Rachubka	481	40	Goalkeeper
Bristol City Adriano Basso	544	22	Goalkeeper
Burnley Graham Alexander	638	6	Defender
Cardiff Ross McCormack	590	10	Striker
Charlton Nick Bailey	545	20	Midfielder
Coventry Keiren Westwood	517	27	Goalkeeper
Crystal Palace Julian Speroni	495	34	Goalkeeper
Derby Rob Hulse	459	53	Striker
Doncaster Neil Sullivan	480	41	Goalkeeper
Ipswich Richard Wright	532	23	Goalkeeper
Norwich David Marshall	465	49	Goalkeeper
Nottm Forest Chris Cohen	509	29	Midfielder
Plymouth Romain Larrieu	455	56	Goalkeeper
Preston Andy Lonergan	622	7	Goalkeeper
QPR Radek Cerny	492	35	Goalkeeper
Reading Kevin Doyle	689	3	Striker
Sheffield Utd Paddy Kenny	559	15	Goalkeeper
Sheffield W Marcus Tudgay	504	31	Striker
Southampton Andrew Surman	454	58	Midfielder
Swansea Jason Scotland	643	5	Striker
Watford Tommy Smith	707	2	Midfielder
Wolves Sylvan Ebanks-Blake	753	1	Striker

CLUB SUMMARY

FORMED	1887
MANAGER	Simon Davey
GROUND	Oakwell Stadium
CAPACITY	23,000
NICKNAME	The Tykes
WEBSITE	www.barnsleyfc.co.uk

The New Football Pools PLAYER OF THE SEASON — Bobby Hassell

OVERALL

P	W	D	L	F	A	GD
48	13	13	22	45	63	-18

COCA-COLA CHAMPIONSHIP

Pos	P	W	D	L	F	A	GD	Pts
20	46	13	13	20	45	58	-13	52

HOME

Pos	P	W	D	L	F	A	GD	Pts
19	23	8	7	8	28	24	4	31

AWAY

Pos	P	W	D	L	F	A	GD	Pts
19	23	5	6	12	17	34	-17	21

CUP PROGRESS DETAILS

Competition	Round reached	Knocked out by
FA Cup	R3	West Ham
Carling Cup	R1	Crewe

BIGGEST WIN (ALL COMPS)
04/10/08 4–1 v Doncaster **FLC**

BIGGEST DEFEAT (ALL COMPS)
17/01/09 0–4 v Norwich **FLC**

THE PLAYER WITH THE MOST

Shots on target
Jamal Campbell-Ryce 41

Shots off target
Anderson De Silva 30

Shots without scoring
Hugo Colace, Bobby Hassell 21

Assists
Jon Macken 4

Offsides
Jon Macken 40

Fouls
Jon Macken 82

Fouls without a card
Daniel Bogdanovic 25

Free-kicks won
Jamal Campbell-Ryce 58

Defensive clearances
Darren Moore 69

actim INDEX — for the 2008/09 Coca-Cola Championship Season

Rank	Player	Pts
26	Jamal Campbell-Ryce	518
87	Jon Macken	397
89	Heinz Muller	392
104	Stephen Foster	370
125	Robert Kozluk	348

ATTENDANCE RECORD

High	Low	Average
19,681	10,678	13,189
v Nottm F (04/04/2009)	v Burnley (24/11/2008)	

BARNSLEY had the Oakwell faithful chewing their fingernails for a third successive season before a last-day win ensured another narrow escape.

A section of Tykes fans, finally losing patience with manager Simon Davey and his cosmopolitan squad, called for the Welshman to go as tension mounted during the run-in.

Davey had added overseas players Hugo Colace and Mounir El Haimour to his extensive international collection in the close season and spent £1.2million on Canada international Iain Hume, but Barnsley won just one of their opening 10 league matches.

In mitigation, Davey lost Hume to a horrific injury in the South Yorkshire derby defeat to Sheffield United in November, with the forward fracturing his skull following a collision with the elbow of the Blades' defender Chris Morgan. Hume spent a night in the high dependency unit of a Manchester hospital due to internal bleeding.

Morgan's mere booking for the challenge angered the Tykes, but the game's authorities decided not to punish him further, concluding they could 'only bring additional charges in the most exceptional cases'. Local Barnsley Central MP Eric Illsley actually tabled a parliamentary Early Day Motion calling for the Football Association to review its decision on the matter.

On the field, an encouraging Boxing Day win at Burnley saw Davey's side climb to 15th in the table, but five straight defeats in January sent the

Defenders Darren Moore and Stephen Foster celebrate beating local rivals Sheffield Wednesday

Tykes plummeting to the lower reaches of the table once again.

Davey called for reinforcements and club owner Patrick Cryne responded with a series of signings. Striker Daniel Bogdanovic was brought in permanently, while his Malta international teammate Michael Mifsud, Fulham midfielder

Andranik Teymourian and Liverpool winger Adam Hammill were drafted in on loan.

Results improved and by March Barnsley were holding their heads above water. The Tykes lost just four of their last 13 league matches, but just could not climb clear of trouble or appease disgruntled fans.

Davey cursed his luck and complained that his side had been letting too many one-goal leads slip in the closing stages of games, but even the win at relegation rivals Plymouth on the final day did little to improve his relationship with some supporters.

> ## Five defeats in January sent the Tykes plummeting

August

9th	● QPR ....a	L 2–1	**Att:** 14,964. **Ref:** N Swarbrick — **Scorers:** Hume. **Dismissed:** Van Homoet
12th	● Crewe ....a	L 2–0	**Att:** 2,492. **Ref:** A Taylor — **Booked:** Kozluk, Foster, Leon, Leon
16th	● Coventry ....h	L 1–2	**Att:** 12,987. **Ref:** S Bratt — **Scorers:** Howard. **Booked:** Hume, Macken, Foster, Howard. **Dismissed:** Hume
23rd	● Birmingham ....a	L 2–0	**Att:** 17,413. **Ref:** R Beeby — **Booked:** Howard
30th	● Derby ....h	W 2–0	**Att:** 14,223. **Ref:** G Salisbury — **Scorers:** Foster, Hume. **Booked:** Foster, Howard

September

13th	● Blackpool ....a	L 1–0	**Att:** 8,363. **Ref:** T Bates — **Booked:** Foster, Odejayi, Moore
16th	● Cardiff ....h	L 0–1	**Att:** 11,282. **Ref:** G Laws — **Booked:** Campbell-Ryce, Howard, Kozluk
20th	● Southampton ....a	D 0–0	**Att:** 14,836. **Ref:** A D'Urso — **Booked:** Colace
27th	● Norwich...............................h	D 0–0	**Att:** 12,324. **Ref:** N Miller — **Booked:** Colace
30th	● Ipswich ....a	L 3–0	**Att:** 18,177. **Ref:** K Friend — **Booked:** De Silva, Moore

October

4th	● Doncaster ....h	W 4–1	**Att:** 15,086. **Ref:** S Tanner — **Scorers:** Campbell-Ryce, Foster, Hume, Macken.
			Booked: Kozluk, Guedes, Devaney, Rigters. **Dismissed:** Moore
18th	● Crystal Palace ....a	L 3–0	**Att:** 16,494. **Ref:** T Bates — **Booked:** Muller
21st	● Sheff Wed...........................h	W 2–1	**Att:** 17,784. **Ref:** P Crossley — **Scorers:** Campbell-Ryce, Hume. **Booked:** Guedes, Hume
25th	● Bristol City ....h	D 0–0	**Att:** 11,551. **Ref:** M Russell — **Booked:** Kozluk
28th	● Doncaster ....a	W 0–1	**Att:** 13,251. **Ref:** A Wiley — **Scorers:** Macken. **Booked:** Colace

November

1st	● Charlton ....a	W 1–3	**Att:** 21,527. **Ref:** N Swarbrick — **Scorers:** Macken[2], Moore. **Booked:** Foster, De Silva
8th	● Sheff Utd ....h	L 1–2	**Att:** 19,002. **Ref:** A D'Urso — **Scorers:** Odejayi. **Booked:** Campbell-Ryce. **Dismissed:** De Silva
15th	● Watford ....h	W 2–1	**Att:** 11,285. **Ref:** C Webster — **Scorers:** Foster, Mostto.
22nd	● Preston ....a	L 2–1	**Att:** 12,153. **Ref:** A Hall — **Scorers:** Campbell-Ryce. **Booked:** Leon, Colace, Hassell
24th	● Burnley ....h	W 3–2	**Att:** 10,678. **Ref:** N Miller — **Scorers:** Campbell-Ryce, Leon, Macken. **Booked:** Foster
29th	● Nottm Forest.......................a	L 1–0	**Att:** 24,974. **Ref:** P Crossley

December

6th	● Reading ....h	L 0–1	**Att:** 11,938. **Ref:** C Oliver — **Booked:** Foster, Macken
9th	● Swansea.............................a	D 2–2	**Att:** 11,442. **Ref:** G Horwood — **Scorers:** Campbell-Ryce, Macken. **Booked:** Hassell
13th	● Wolverhampton...................a	L 2–0	**Att:** 22,399. **Ref:** G Salisbury — **Booked:** Campbell-Ryce, Colace
20th	● Plymouth.............................h	W 2–0	**Att:** 10,944. **Ref:** D Whitestone — **Scorers:** Campbell-Ryce, De Silva. **Booked:** Foster, Van Homoet, Campbell-Ryce
26th	● Burnley ....a	W 1–2	**Att:** 16,580. **Ref:** S Mathieson — **Scorers:** Campbell-Ryce, Cureton. **Booked:** Moore
28th	● Preston ....h	D 1–1	**Att:** 13,851. **Ref:** A Taylor — **Scorers:** Cureton. **Booked:** Van Homoet, Foster, Cureton

January

3rd	● West Ham...........................a	L 3–0	**Att:** 28,869. **Ref:** M Oliver — **Booked:** Odejayi, El Haimour, Colace
10th	● Southampton ....h	L 0–1	**Att:** 11,789. **Ref:** T Bates
17th	● Norwich...............................a	L 4–0	**Att:** 24,685. **Ref:** S Hooper — **Booked:** Leon, Kozluk, Van Homoet
27th	● Ipswich ....h	L 1–2	**Att:** 11,183. **Ref:** C Boyeson — **Scorers:** Bogdanovic.
31st	● Bristol City ....a	L 2–0	**Att:** 15,667. **Ref:** T Kettle — **Booked:** Odejayi, Guedes

February

17th	● Sheff Wed...........................a	W 0–1	**Att:** 25,820. **Ref:** R Booth — **Scorers:** Campbell-Ryce. **Booked:** Campbell-Ryce, Van Homoet, Mifsud, Moore
21st	● Charlton ....h	D 0–0	**Att:** 11,668. **Ref:** M Oliver
28th	● QPR ....h	W 2–1	**Att:** 11,614. **Ref:** R Shoebridge — **Scorers:** Bogdanovic, De Silva. **Booked:** De Silva

March

3rd	● Cardiff ....a	L 3–1	**Att:** 15,902. **Ref:** P Miller — **Scorers:** Macken. **Booked:** Teymourian, Foster. **Dismissed:** Teymourian
10th	● Birmingham ....h	D 1–1	**Att:** 11,299. **Ref:** G Horwood — **Scorers:** Mifsud. **Booked:** Hassell
14th	● Blackpool ....h	L 0–1	**Att:** 12,228. **Ref:** C Webster — **Booked:** El Haimour, Moore
17th	● Crystal Palace ....h	W 3–1	**Att:** 10,885. **Ref:** G Salisbury — **Scorers:** Campbell-Ryce, Mifsud, Hills OG. **Booked:** Kozluk
21st	● Derby ....a	D 0–0	**Att:** 32,277. **Ref:** A Penn

April

4th	● Nottm Forest.......................h	D 1–1	**Att:** 19,681. **Ref:** L Probert — **Scorers:** Campbell-Ryce. **Booked:** Macken, Colace, Moore, Campbell-Ryce
7th	● Sheff Utd ....a	L 2–1	**Att:** 27,061. **Ref:** G Hegley — **Scorers:** Bogdanovic. **Booked:** De Silva, Campbell-Ryce
11th	● Watford ....a	D 1–1	**Att:** 16,052. **Ref:** D Whitestone — **Scorers:** Macken. **Booked:** Mifsud
13th	● Swansea.............................h	L 1–3	**Att:** 11,788. **Ref:** D Foster — **Scorers:** Bogdanovic. **Booked:** Campbell-Ryce, Hammill, Hassell, De Silva
18th	● Reading ....h	D 0–0	**Att:** 19,420. **Ref:** R Beeby — **Booked:** Moore
21st	● Coventry ....a	D 1–1	**Att:** 15,035. **Ref:** S Cook — **Scorers:** Bogdanovic. **Booked:** Colace, De Silva
25th	● Wolverhampton...................h	D 1–1	**Att:** 18,288. **Ref:** K Friend — **Scorers:** Macken. **Booked:** Guedes

May

3rd	● Plymouth.............................a	W 1–2	**Att:** 14,529. **Ref:** C Penton — **Scorers:** Campbell-Ryce, Hammill.

● Coca-Cola Championship/Play-Offs ● FA Cup ● Carling Cup

BARNSLEY

CHAMPIONSHIP GOALKEEPER STATS

Player	Minutes on pitch	Appearances	Match starts	Completed matches	Sub appearances	Subbed off	SAVES BREAKDOWN Saved with feet	Punched	Parried	Tipped over	Fumbled	Tipped round	Caught	Blocked	Clean sheets	Goals conceded	Minutes since conceding	Save %	PENALTIES Saved	Resulting in goals	Opposition miss	Yellow cards	Red cards
Heinz Muller 3454		36	36	36	0	0	3	21	35	8	0	15	123	0	8	47	27	81.35	0	5	0	1	0
Luke Steele 962		10	10	10	0	0	0	5	10	1	0	5	38	1	2	11	84	84.51	1	1	0	0	0

CHAMPIONSHIP OUTFIELD PLAYER STATS

Player	Minutes on pitch	Appearances	Match starts	Completed matches	Substitute appearances	Subbed off	Goals scored	Minutes since scoring	Assists	Shots on target	Shots off target	Crosses	Defensive clearances	Defensive blocks	Fouls committed	Free-kicks won	Caught offside	Yellow cards	Red cards
Daniel Bogdanovic...............1035		16	13	2	3	11	5	248	1	12	4	12	1	0	25	12	14	0	0
Jacob Butterfield 117		3	0	0	3	0	0	-	0	0	2	2	0	0	2	2	0	0	0
Jamal Campbell-Ryce 3673		40	39	35	1	4	11	47	3	41	22	90	3	3	31	58	3	8	0
Hugo Colace...............2970		34	30	26	4	4	0	-	0	11	10	3	30	6	50	12	4	7	0
Michael Coulson 15		2	0	0	2	0	0	-	0	0	0	0	0	0	1	0	0	0	0
Jamie Cureton...............644		8	7	4	1	3	2	137	1	8	4	3	0	0	2	5	20	1	0
Anderson De Silva 2924		32	32	27	0	4	2	1015	3	25	30	6	15	5	66	37	0	6	1
Martin Devaney 1565		26	16	9	10	7	0	-	1	6	14	33	11	2	30	26	7	1	0
Mounir El Haimour 758		16	8	3	8	5	0	-	0	2	6	17	4	3	6	11	0	1	0
Stephen Foster...............3651		38	38	38	0	0	3	2146	0	10	8	8	35	13	49	26	3	9	0
Dennis Souza Guedes 3035		33	32	29	1	3	0	-	1	4	5	1	59	14	51	41	0	4	0
Adam Hammill...............894		14	9	3	5	6	1	54	1	17	10	28	0	1	6	22	2	1	0
Bobby Hassell...............3340		40	34	29	6	5	0	-	1	9	12	57	29	9	25	23	0	4	0
Brian Howard...............672		7	7	7	0	0	1	103	0	7	8	13	4	0	16	19	2	4	0
Iain Hume 1232		15	15	7	0	7	4	369	1	12	8	13	1	0	14	18	14	2	1
Robert Kozluk...............3416		37	36	34	1	2	0	-	3	4	8	49	25	11	38	44	3	5	0
Diego Leon...............1268		19	15	4	4	11	1	414	1	14	18	37	0	0	16	16	1	2	0
Jon Macken 3524		45	37	18	8	19	6	121	4	40	27	16	4	0	82	55	40	3	0
Michael Mifsud...............1061		15	11	7	4	4	2	410	1	16	9	3	0	0	10	15	27	2	0
Darren Moore...............3471		38	37	35	1	1	1	2237	1	3	3	1	69	14	62	42	2	7	0
Miguel Mostto 313		9	2	1	7	1	1	190	0	3	4	0	2	0	3	3	1	0	0
Reuben Noble-Lazarus 15		2	0	0	2	0	0	-	0	0	0	0	0	0	0	0	0	0	0
Kayode Odejayi...............1055		28	7	4	21	3	1	629	0	10	4	5	5	0	24	23	19	2	0
Maceo Rigters 529		19	4	0	15	4	0	-	0	5	6	1	0	1	12	8	6	1	0
Gary Teale 210		3	2	1	1	1	0	1409	0	0	10	1	0	0	1	0	0	0	0
Andranik Teymourian 880		11	10	6	1	3	0	-	0	3	11	14	4	0	17	26	0	1	1
Marciano Van Homoet 1349		17	14	11	3	2	0	-	0	2	3	17	5	3	29	18	3	4	1
Simon Whaley 323		4	4	2	0	2	0	1127	1	1	3	11	0	0	2	3	2	0	0

SEASON TOTALS

Goals scored	45
Goals conceded	58
Clean sheets	10
Shots on target	266
Shots off target	239
Shots per goal	11.22
Pens awarded	7
Pens scored	4
Pens conceded	7
Offsides	173
Corners	218
Crosses	450
Players used	30
Fouls committed	670
Free-kicks won	576

CARDS RECEIVED

76   5

SEQUENCES

Wins	2
(on two occasions)	
Losses	4
(10/01/09-31/01/09)	
Draws	3
(18/04/09-25/04/09)	
Undefeated	4
(on two occasions)	
Without win	8
(21/03/09-25/04/09)	
Undefeated home	4
(27/09/08-25/10/08)	
Undefeated away	4
(11/04/09-03/05/09)	
Without scoring	5
(13/09/08-30/09/08)	
Without conceding	2
(on three occasions)	
Scoring	6
(28/10/08-24/11/08)	
Conceding	9
(01/11/08-13/12/08)	

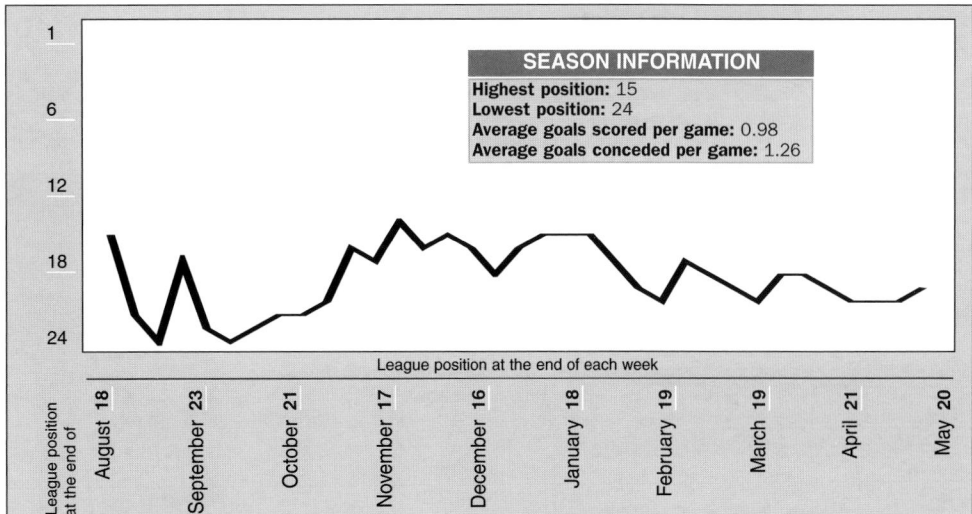

SEASON INFORMATION

Highest position: 15
Lowest position: 24
Average goals scored per game: 0.98
Average goals conceded per game: 1.26

League position at the end of each week

League position at the end of: August 18, September 23, October 21, November 17, December 16, January 18, February 19, March 19, April 21, May 20

MATCH RECORDS

Goals scored per match

		W	D	L	Pts
Failed to score	18	0	6	12	6
Scored 1 goal	16	2	6	8	12
Scored 2 goals	8	7	1	0	22
Scored 3 goals	3	3	0	0	9
Scored 4+ goals	1	1	0	0	3

Goals conceded per match

		W	D	L	Pts
Clean Sheet	10	4	6	0	18
Conceded 1 goal	20	8	6	6	30
Conceded 2 goals	11	1	1	9	4
Conceded 3 goals	4	0	0	4	0
Conceded 4+ goals	1	0	0	1	0

QUICK-FIRE GOALS

From the start of a match
Jonathan Macken
(v Charlton) 2:02

By a substitute after coming on
Jonathan Macken
(v Cardiff) 0:48

LAST-GASP GOALS

From the start of a match
Jamal Campbell-Ryce
(v Plymouth) 90:40

By a substitute after coming on
Diego Leon (v Burnley)
40:47

GOAL DETAILS

How the goals were struck

SCORED		CONCEDED
27	Right foot	32
10	Left foot	16
8	Headers	9
0	Others	1

How the goals were struck

SCORED		CONCEDED
29	Open play	39
3	Cross	5
3	Corner	3
4	Penalties	6
0	Direct from free-kick	1
5	Free-kick	3
1	Own goals	1

Distance from goal

SCORED		CONCEDED
12	6yds	14
28	18yds	37
5	18+yds	7

GOALS SCORED/CONCEDED PER FIVE-MINUTE INTERVALS

	5	10	15	20	25	30	35	40	45	50	55	60	65	70	75	80	85	90
Goals For	3	2	0	3	1	1	2	3	3	5	3	3	2	3	4	0	3	4
Goals Against	2	3	5	3	2	1	2	3	2	0	2	1	2	9	4	2	5	10
Mins	5	10	15	20	25	30	35	40	45	50	55	60	65	70	75	80	85	90

BIRMINGHAM CITY

CLUB SUMMARY

FORMED	1875
MANAGER	Alex McLeish
GROUND	St Andrew's
CAPACITY	30,079
NICKNAME	Blues
WEBSITE	www.bcfc.com

The New Football Pools PLAYER OF THE SEASON — Franck Queudrue

OVERALL

P	W	D	L	F	A	GD
49	24	14	11	58	41	17

COCA-COLA CHAMPIONSHIP

Pos	P	W	D	L	F	A	GD	Pts
2	46	23	14	9	54	37	17	83

HOME

Pos	P	W	D	L	F	A	GD	Pts
5	23	14	5	4	30	17	13	47

AWAY

Pos	P	W	D	L	F	A	GD	Pts
4	23	9	9	5	24	20	4	36

CUP PROGRESS DETAILS

Competition	Round reached	Knocked out by
FA Cup	R3	Wolverhampton
Carling Cup	R2	Southampton

BIGGEST WIN (ALL COMPS)
13/08/08 4–0 v Wycombe **LC1**

BIGGEST DEFEAT (ALL COMPS)
20/12/08 1–3 v Reading **FLC**

THE PLAYER WITH THE MOST

Shots on target	
Kevin Phillips	43
Shots off target	
Cameron Jerome	32
Shots without scoring	
Radhi Jaidi	21
Assists	
Sebastian Larsson	6
Offsides	
Cameron Jerome	40
Fouls	
Lee Carsley	65
Fouls without a card	
Carlos Costly	6
Free-kicks won	
Liam Ridgewell	92
Defensive clearances	
Radhi Jaidi	71

actim INDEX
for the 2008/09 Coca-Cola Championship Season

Rank	Player	Pts
8	Maik Taylor	604
54	Kevin Phillips	457
59	Lee Carsley	450
68	Sebastian Larsson	425
101	Liam Ridgewell	377

ATTENDANCE RECORD

High	Low	Average
25,935	15,330	19,081
v Wolves (06/04/2009)	v Derby (27/01/2009)	

THERE has rarely been a dull campaign at St Andrew's during recent times, and the 2008/09 season was yet another rollercoaster.

After the joy of a second promotion to the Barclays Premier League in 2006/07, the nightmare of a second relegation back down to the Coca-Cola Championship followed in 2007/08. Boss Alex McLeish was set the task of guiding the Blues to England's top flight for the third time in seven years, in what was his first full season at the helm.

Chairman David Gold admitted he did not care how, and in that respect you could say it was 'job done', but what happened in between was anything but straightforward.

Pre-season favourites Birmingham raced into the automatic promotion places after just their third game, and there they stayed until a 3–1 home defeat to Reading on 20th

December saw Steve Coppell's side leapfrog them into the top two.

Despite their success, it was already proving to be a tough campaign. It was obvious that if the Blues

> ## "Promotion was won with a mix of youth and experience"

were to gain promotion, they would not do it in the same manner as their rivals, with hard-working, defensive displays the order of the day rather than free-flowing, attacking football. While McLeish had a wealth of attacking options at his disposal, he chose to concentrate on making his team difficult to beat as they sought promotion. And this, combined with a winter slump on the pitch, resulted in unrest in the stands and dwindling attendances at St Andrew's.

But City, having never slipped lower than third, regained second spot in mid-February and, with a host of injuries, entered the final straight.

Despite briefly threatening Wolves for top spot, McLeish and his charges were made to endure a nervy final day at Reading before clinching second place and an automatic return to England's elite.

Promotion was won with a mix of youth and experience, with the likes of Lee Carsley, Kevin Phillips, Franck Queudrue, Liam Ridgewell and Lee Bowyer each proving inspirational. And, in Keith Fahey, Sebastian Larsson and James McFadden they have the quality to put up a real fight in the Premier League, although some investment will be needed.

The 2009/10 season will be a challenge but, for the time being, the Blues can simply look forward to another crack at the Premier League.

Alex McLeish and Radhi Jaidi celebrate promotion

RESULTS 2008/09

August

9th	● Sheff Utd ....h	W 1–0	**Att:** 24,019. **Ref:** K Stroud — **Scorers:** Phillips. **Booked:** Parnaby, Carsley
13th	● Wycombe ....a	W 0–4	**Att:** 2,735. **Ref:** A D'Urso — **Scorers:** Jerome, Larsson, Nafti, Owusu-Abeyie
16th	● Southampton ....a	W 1–2	**Att:** 18,925. **Ref:** C Penton — **Scorers:** O'Connor, Phillips.
23rd	● Barnsley ....h	W 2–0	**Att:** 17,413. **Ref:** R Beeby — **Scorers:** O'Connor, Phillips. **Booked:** Carsley
26th	● Southampton ....a	L 2–0	**Att:** 11,331. **Ref:** G Hegley — **Booked:** Mutch, Ridgewell
30th	● Norwich.............................a	D 1–1	**Att:** 24,229. **Ref:** J Moss — **Scorers:** Larsson. **Booked:** Larsson

September

13th	● Doncaster ....h	W 1–0	**Att:** 18,165. **Ref:** G Ward — **Scorers:** Jerome. **Booked:** Larsson, McFadden. **Dismissed:** Nafti
16th	● Bristol City ....a	W 1–2	**Att:** 18,456. **Ref:** K Friend — **Scorers:** Jerome, Carey OG. **Booked:** Agustien, Taylor, Larsson
20th	● Blackpool ....h	L 0–1	**Att:** 20,983. **Ref:** M Russell
27th	● Cardiff ....a	W 1–2	**Att:** 18,304. **Ref:** M Jones — **Scorers:** McFadden, Owusu-Abeyie. **Booked:** Parnaby
30th	● Derby ....a	D 1–1	**Att:** 29,743. **Ref:** M Oliver — **Scorers:** Owusu-Abeyie.

October

4th	● QPR ....h	W 1–0	**Att:** 18,498. **Ref:** A D'Urso — **Scorers:** Phillips. **Booked:** Ridgewell
18th	● Burnley ....a	D 1–1	**Att:** 13,809. **Ref:** L Probert — **Scorers:** Jerome. **Booked:** McFadden
21st	● Crystal Palace ....h	W 1–0	**Att:** 17,706. **Ref:** N Miller — **Scorers:** O'Connor.
25th	● Sheff Wed........................h	W 3–1	**Att:** 17,300. **Ref:** P Taylor — **Scorers:** O'Connor[2], Phillips. **Booked:** Larsson, McFadden
28th	● QPR ....a	L 1–0	**Att:** 13,594. **Ref:** S Attwell — **Booked:** Wilson, Queudrue

November

3rd	● Coventry ....h	L 0–1	**Att:** 17,215. **Ref:** T Bates
8th	● Nottm Forest.....................a	D 1–1	**Att:** 21,415. **Ref:** P Dowd — **Scorers:** McFadden. **Booked:** Quashie, Jaidi, Agustien, Jerome
15th	● Charlton ....h	W 3–2	**Att:** 20,071. **Ref:** K Hill — **Scorers:** McFadden, Phillips, Queudrue. **Booked:** Quashie, McFadden, Ridgewell. **Dismissed:** Quashie
21st	● Swansea ....a	W 2–3	**Att:** 16,956. **Ref:** A Taylor — **Scorers:** Bent, Phillips[2]. **Booked:** Bent
25th	● Ipswich ....h	W 2–1	**Att:** 15,689. **Ref:** R Shoebridge — **Scorers:** Phillips, Ridgewell.
29th	● Wolverhampton.................a	D 1–1	**Att:** 26,329. **Ref:** P Taylor — **Scorers:** Jerome. **Booked:** Quashie, Carsley, Nafti, Jerome

December

6th	● Watford ....h	W 3–2	**Att:** 18,174. **Ref:** S Mathieson — **Scorers:** Bent, Jerome, Phillips. **Booked:** Queudrue
9th	● Plymouth...........................a	W 0–1	**Att:** 10,446. **Ref:** K Wright — **Scorers:** Carsley.
13th	● Preston ....a	L 1–0	**Att:** 10,943. **Ref:** C Oliver — **Booked:** Ridgewell, Queudrue, Quashie
20th	● Reading ....h	L 1–3	**Att:** 19,695. **Ref:** M Dean — **Scorers:** Phillips. **Booked:** Queudrue
26th	● Ipswich ....a	W 0–1	**Att:** 23,536. **Ref:** I Williamson — **Scorers:** McFadden. **Booked:** Parnaby, Ridgewell
28th	● Swansea ....h	D 0–0	**Att:** 21,836. **Ref:** M Riley — **Booked:** Murphy, Parnaby, Carsley. **Dismissed:** Murphy

January

13th	● Wolverhampton.................h	L 0–2	**Att:** 22,232. **Ref:** H Webb — **Booked:** Quashie, Jaidi
17th	● Cardiff ....h	D 1–1	**Att:** 19,853. **Ref:** M Jones — **Scorers:** Bowyer. **Booked:** Ridgewell
24th	● Blackpool ....a	L 2–0	**Att:** 8,105. **Ref:** S Tanner — **Booked:** Maik Taylor
27th	● Derby ....h	W 1–0	**Att:** 15,330. **Ref:** G Salisbury — **Scorers:** Carsley. **Booked:** Ridgewell, Bowyer
31st	● Sheff Wed........................a	D 1–1	**Att:** 18,409. **Ref:** P Crossley — **Scorers:** Phillips. **Booked:** Taylor, Murphy

February

7th	● Burnley ....h	D 1–1	**Att:** 16,763. **Ref:** K Stroud — **Scorers:** Phillips. **Booked:** Bowyer, Ridgewell
14th	● Nottm Forest.....................h	W 2–0	**Att:** 17,631. **Ref:** G Laws — **Scorers:** Bent, Fahey. **Booked:** Bowyer
21st	● Coventry ....a	L 1–0	**Att:** 22,637. **Ref:** C Oliver — **Booked:** Bowyer, Larsson
24th	● Crystal Palace ....a	D 0–0	**Att:** 12,847. **Ref:** P Taylor — **Booked:** Bowyer

March

1st	● Sheff Utd ....a	L 2–1	**Att:** 24,232. **Ref:** L Mason — **Scorers:** Morgan OG. **Booked:** Bouazza, Carr, Carsley
4th	● Bristol City ....h	W 1–0	**Att:** 17,551. **Ref:** J Moss — **Scorers:** Queudrue.
7th	● Southampton ....h	W 1–0	**Att:** 16,735. **Ref:** M Atkinson — **Scorers:** Fahey.
10th	● Barnsley ....a	D 1–1	**Att:** 11,299. **Ref:** G Horwood — **Scorers:** Taylor. **Booked:** Carr, Johnson
14th	● Doncaster ....a	W 0–2	**Att:** 11,482. **Ref:** P Walton — **Scorers:** Bouazza, Jerome.
21st	● Norwich.............................h	D 1–1	**Att:** 18,159. **Ref:** M Haywood — **Scorers:** Jerome.

April

6th	● Wolverhampton.................h	W 2–0	**Att:** 25,935. **Ref:** M Halsey — **Scorers:** Jerome, O'Connor. **Dismissed:** Carsley
11th	● Charlton ....a	D 0–0	**Att:** 20,022. **Ref:** L Probert — **Booked:** Murphy, Jaidi
13th	● Plymouth...........................h	D 1–1	**Att:** 19,323. **Ref:** M Oliver — **Scorers:** Queudrue. **Booked:** Jaidi, Jerome, Johnson. **Dismissed:** Maik Taylor
18th	● Watford ....a	W 0–1	**Att:** 16,180. **Ref:** T Bates — **Scorers:** Jerome.
25th	● Preston ....h	L 1–2	**Att:** 24,825. **Ref:** P Dowd — **Scorers:** Fahey. **Booked:** Queudrue, Bowyer, Jaidi. **Dismissed:** Bowyer

May

| 3rd | ● Reading ....a | W 1–2 | **Att:** 24,011. **Ref:** H Webb — **Scorers:** Fahey, Phillips. **Booked:** Jaidi, Phillips, Traore. |

● Coca-Cola Championship/Play-Offs ● FA Cup ● Carling Cup

BIRMINGHAM CITY

CHAMPIONSHIP GOALKEEPER STATS

Player	Minutes on pitch	Appearances	Match starts	Completed matches	Sub appearances	Subbed off	Saved with feet	Punched	Parried	Tipped over	Fumbled	Tipped round	Caught	Blocked	Clean sheets	Goals conceded	Minutes since conceding	Save %	Saved	Resulting in goals	Opposition miss	Yellow cards	Red cards
Colin Doyle	174	2	1	1	1	0	0	0	1	2	0	1	6	0	1	1	-	90.91	0	1	0	0	0
Maik Taylor	4255	45	45	44	0	0	2	13	15	5	0	12	211	1	17	36	36	87.84	0	1	0	1	1

CHAMPIONSHIP OUTFIELD PLAYER STATS

Player	Minutes on pitch	Appearances	Match starts	Completed matches	Substitute appearances	Subbed off	Goals scored	Minutes since scoring	Assists	Shots on target	Shots off target	Crosses	Defensive clearances	Defensive blocks	Fouls committed	Free-kicks won	Caught offside	Yellow cards	Red cards
Kemy Agustien	1141	18	13	6	5	7	0	-	0	3	2	4	3	0	11	11	1	2	0
Marcus Bent	1807	33	16	7	17	9	3	435	2	15	17	7	4	2	23	34	22	1	0
Hameur Bouazza	928	16	9	5	7	4	1	199	2	7	11	31	1	3	18	4	9	1	0
Lee Bowyer	1604	17	17	16	0	0	1	1507	2	7	14	11	3	4	28	34	3	6	1
Stephen Carr	1255	13	13	13	0	0	0	-	0	0	1	20	8	2	11	13	1	2	0
Lee Carsley	3638	41	41	34	0	6	2	1040	1	12	15	11	46	12	65	46	1	5	1
Carlos Costly	343	8	3	0	5	3	0	-	0	2	4	4	1	0	6	9	13	0	0
Ulises De la Cruz	24	1	0	0	1	0	0	-	0	0	0	0	0	0	0	0	0	0	0
Keith Fahey	1410	19	15	12	4	3	4	79	1	14	6	11	6	0	5	13	1	0	0
Nicky Hunt	856	11	9	8	2	1	0	-	2	0	0	14	4	0	5	8	0	0	0
Radhi Jaidi	2894	30	30	30	0	0	0	-	0	8	13	1	71	16	53	39	2	5	0
Cameron Jerome	2600	43	25	8	18	17	9	141	0	25	32	21	7	1	52	46	40	3	0
Damien Johnson	749	9	8	7	1	1	0	-	0	0	1	4	3	1	14	6	0	2	0
Stephen Kelly	285	5	2	1	3	1	0	-	0	0	0	7	4	1	2	3	0	0	0
Sebastian Larsson	3260	38	35	26	3	3	1	2946	6	19	29	135	12	5	53	34	2	5	0
James McFadden	2236	30	22	15	8	7	4	603	4	21	19	59	3	2	28	50	25	4	0
Gary McSheffrey	296	6	3	1	3	2	0	-	0	3	6	7	0	1	4	5	0	0	0
David Murphy	2642	30	28	25	2	2	0	-	3	1	5	24	10	4	26	33	2	3	1
Mehdi Nafti	606	11	6	2	5	3	0	-	0	3	2	4	1	3	12	6	0	1	1
Garry O'Connor	935	16	10	4	6	6	6	287	2	12	11	4	1	4	17	18	0	0	0
Quincy Owusu-Abeyie	1092	19	12	4	7	8	2	866	2	11	7	28	4	1	3	16	0	0	0
Stuart Parnaby	1628	21	19	14	2	5	0	-	1	1	0	16	11	3	19	15	1	4	0
Kevin Phillips	2184	36	24	11	12	13	14	12	2	43	23	4	0	1	19	34	34	1	0
Nigel Quashie	744	10	8	5	2	2	0	-	1	5	2	8	3	0	16	10	2	4	1
Franck Queudrue	2087	25	23	12	2	11	3	227	1	8	12	33	35	7	29	31	0	5	0
Liam Ridgewell	3401	36	36	35	0	1	1	1658	0	3	6	5	61	8	43	92	1	7	0
Scott Sinclair	763	14	8	4	6	4	0	-	1	8	23	0	1	3	17	4	0	0	0
Martin Taylor	2222	24	23	23	1	0	1	106	0	1	5	0	37	5	24	24	1	2	0
Djimi Traore	202	3	2	2	1	0	0	-	0	0	0	7	2	0	4	1	0	1	0
Jared Wilson	87	1	0	0	1	0	0	-	0	0	0	2	2	0	2	0	0	1	0

SEASON TOTALS

Goals scored	54
Goals conceded	37
Clean sheets	17
Shots on target	229
Shots off target	251
Shots per goal	8.89
Pens awarded	1
Pens scored	1
Pens conceded	2
Offsides	183
Corners	235
Crosses	502
Players used	32
Fouls committed	583
Free-kicks won	658

CARDS RECEIVED

66   **6**

SEQUENCES

Wins	3
(on two occasions)	
Losses	2
(28/10/08–03/11/08)	
Draws	2
(on two occasions)	
Undefeated	9
(04/03/09–18/04/09)	
Without win	3
(on three occasions)	
Undefeated home	10
(28/12/08–13/04/09)	
Undefeated away	7
(09/08/08–18/10/08)	
Without scoring	2
(on two occasions)	
Without conceding	2
(on three occasions)	
Scoring	7
(on two occasions)	
Conceding	9
(25/10/08–06/12/08)	

League position at the end of each week

League position at the end of:
August 3, September 2, October 2, November 2, December 3, January 3, February 2, March 2, April 2, May 2

SEASON INFORMATION

Highest position: 1
Lowest position: 7
Average goals scored per game: 1.17
Average goals conceded per game: 0.80

MATCH RECORDS

Goals scored per match

	W	D	L	Pts
Failed to score	9	0	3	6	3
Scored 1 goal	24	10	11	3	41
Scored 2 goals	9	9	0	0	27
Scored 3 goals	4	4	0	0	12
Scored 4+ goals	0	0	0	0	0

Goals conceded per match

	W	D	L	Pts
Clean sheet	17	14	3	0	45
Conceded 1 goal	22	6	11	5	29
Conceded 2 goals	6	3	0	3	9
Conceded 3 goals	1	0	0	1	0
Conceded 4+ goals	0	0	0	0	0

QUICK-FIRE GOALS

From the start of a match
James McFadden
(v Cardiff) 4:30

By a substitute after coming on
Kevin Phillips
(v Southampton) 0:50

LAST-GASP GOALS

From the start of a match
Lee Bowyer
(v Cardiff) 93:34

By a substitute after coming on
Kevin Phillips
(v Sheff Utd) 27:37

GOAL DETAILS

How the goals were struck

SCORED		CONCEDED
27	Right foot	17
11	Left foot	11
15	Headers	9
1	Others	0

How the goals were struck

SCORED		CONCEDED
35	Open play	17
9	Cross	6
3	Corner	4
1	Penalties	2
0	Direct from free-kick	3
4	Free-kick	4
2	Own goals	1

Distance from goal

SCORED		CONCEDED
19	6yds	19
28	18yds	10
7	18+yds	8

GOALS SCORED/CONCEDED PER FIVE-MINUTE INTERVALS

Goals For	1	3	6	3	1	1	0	5	7	5	1	4	2	1	4	3	2	5
Goals Against	3	1	3	0	2	2	0	1	3	2	4	1	2	2	1	1	4	5
Mins	5	10	15	20	25	30	35	40	45	50	55	60	65	70	75	80	85	90

CLUB SUMMARY

FORMED	1887
MANAGER	Ian Holloway
GROUND	Bloomfield Road
CAPACITY	9,650
NICKNAME	The Tangerines
WEBSITE	www.blackpoolfc.co.uk

The New **Football Pools**
PLAYER OF THE SEASON

Paul Rachubka

OVERALL

P	W	D	L	F	A	GD
48	13	17	18	47	61	-14

COCA-COLA CHAMPIONSHIP

Pos	P	W	D	L	F	A	GD	Pts
16	46	13	17	16	47	58	-11	56

HOME

Pos	P	W	D	L	F	A	GD	Pts
23	23	5	8	10	25	33	-8	23

AWAY

Pos	P	W	D	L	F	A	GD	Pts
6	23	8	9	6	22	25	-3	33

CUP PROGRESS DETAILS

Competition	Round reached	Knocked out by
FA Cup	R3	Torquay
Carling Cup	R1	Macclesfield

BIGGEST WIN (ALL COMPS)

2–0 on three occasions

BIGGEST DEFEAT (ALL COMPS)

18/02/09 1–4 v Derby FLC

THE PLAYER WITH THE MOST

Shots on target
Ben Burgess 23
Shots off target
Ben Burgess 29
Shots without scoring
Claus Bech Jorgensen 20
Assists
Gary Taylor-Fletcher 5
Offsides
Dudley Campbell 48
Fouls
Ben Burgess 55
Fouls without a card
Lee Hughes 5
Free-kicks won
Shaun Barker 53
Defensive clearances
Shaun Barker 71

actim INDEX for the 2008/09 Coca-Cola Championship Season

Rank	Player	Pts
40	Paul Rachubka	481
47	Shaun Barker	469
111	Rob Edwards	362
141	Gary Taylor-Fletcher	324
148	Ian Evatt	317

ATTENDANCE RECORD

High	Low	Average
9,643	6,648	7,843
v Preston (16/11/2008)	v Charlton (06/12/2008)	

THE MAGNITUDE of Blackpool's achievement in avoiding relegation was summed up when Tony Parkes rated the feat alongside winning the Barclays Premier League title with Blackburn back in 1995.

Parkes – a coach at Ewood Park 14 years ago – ended the season with his reputation enhanced further after steering the club to safety with the help of right-hand man Steve Thompson.

However, soon after the end of the campaign, he left the club, with the charismatic former QPR, Leicester, Plymouth and Bristol Rovers boss Ian Holloway taking over.

Parkes had been handed the reins until the end of the season after Simon Grayson walked out on the club shortly before the

The brief was simple: keep Blackpool in the Championship

turn of the year to join his former club Leeds. The brief was simple: keep Blackpool in the Coca-Cola Championship, and the

mission was accomplished as the Lancashire outfit marched to safety with a fine run of form during the closing weeks of the campaign. They lost just one of their last 10 games and finished their 2008/09

campaign on a high by winning 1–0 away at Swansea. DJ Campbell was the goal hero at the Liberty Stadium with his ninth strike in 20 starts since joining the club on loan from Leicester in January.

Despite eventually deciding to depart, Parkes believes that finishing some 10 points above the Championship relegation zone was an outstanding achievement for a club of Blackpool's size – and believes they could have set their targets much higher had they found their form a little earlier.

'It ranks as highly as winning the Premier League,' said Parkes. 'It is also up there with any of the six occasions I took over as caretaker manager at Blackburn. The end of the season came a bit too soon for us really, otherwise we might have been in the play-offs! To lose only one of the last 10 games really was a great achievement by the team. I am very proud.'

Holloway must now build on Parkes' success, and will be looking to make an impact after his spell at Leicester ended in disaster as he oversaw the Foxes being relegated to the third tier for the first time in 2007/08.

Chairman Karl Oyston said: 'We are delighted to welcome Ian to Bloomfield Road. He is a professional and thorough person who ticked all the boxes and has an excellent track record. He is hungry to take the club forward.'

Keith Southern (right) celebrates scoring Blackpool's second goal in a 2–0 defeat of Birmingham

August

9th	● Bristol City ....h	L 0–1	**Att:** 8,244. **Ref:** G Laws — **Booked:** Camara
12th	● Macclesfield ....a	L 2–0	**Att:** 1,631. **Ref:** M Haywood — **Booked:** Edwards. **Dismissed:** Southern
16th	● Norwich.........................a	D 1–1	**Att:** 23,727. **Ref:** K Friend — **Scorers:** Burgess. **Booked:** Hammill, Evatt, Camara, Taylor-Fletcher
23rd	● Sheff Utd ....h	L 1–3	**Att:** 8,611. **Ref:** S Mathieson — **Scorers:** Kabba. **Booked:** Hammill
30th	● Southampton ....a	W 0–1	**Att:** 15,629. **Ref:** A Marriner — **Scorers:** Burgess. **Booked:** Camara, Burgess

September

13th	● Barnsley ....h	W 1–0	**Att:** 8,363. **Ref:** T Bates — **Scorers:** Kabba. **Booked:** Taylor-Fletcher, Kabba, Vaughan
16th	● Burnley ....a	L 2–0	**Att:** 13,752. **Ref:** J Moss
20th	● Birmingham ....a	W 0–1	**Att:** 20,983. **Ref:** M Russell — **Scorers:** Taylor-Fletcher. **Booked:** Camara
27th	● Coventry ....h	D 1–1	**Att:** 8,462. **Ref:** M Oliver — **Scorers:** Burgess
30th	● QPR ....a	D 1–1	**Att:** 12,500. **Ref:** G Hegley — **Scorers:** Taylor-Fletcher

October

4th	● Cardiff............................h	D 1–1	**Att:** 7,328. **Ref:** N Miller — **Scorers:** Gow. **Booked:** Vaughan
18th	● Doncaster ....a	D 0–0	**Att:** 11,342. **Ref:** D Drysdale — **Booked:** Gow
21st	● Derby ....h	W 3–2	**Att:** 7,267. **Ref:** A Hall — **Scorers:** Burgess, Gow, Taylor-Fletcher
25th	● Crystal Palace ....h	D 2–2	**Att:** 7,597. **Ref:** A Taylor — **Scorers:** Burgess, Evatt. **Booked:** Evatt
28th	● Cardiff............................a	L 2–0	**Att:** 17,570. **Ref:** R Shoebridge — **Booked:** Barker, Evatt

November

1st	● Watford ....a	W 3–4	**Att:** 13,517. **Ref:** R East — **Scorers:** Burgess, Gow, Southern, Taylor-Fletcher. **Booked:** Southern, Taylor-Fletcher, Hammill, Gow
8th	● Ipswich ....h	L 0–1	**Att:** 7,349. **Ref:** C Webster — **Booked:** Southern, Fox
16th	● Preston ....h	L 1–3	**Att:** 9,643. **Ref:** M Dean — **Scorers:** Hammill. **Booked:** Barker, Hammill, Hendrie
22nd	● Wolverhampton...............a	L 2–0	**Att:** 22,044. **Ref:** A D'Urso — **Booked:** Hendrie, Evatt
25th	● Sheff Wed......................h	L 0–2	**Att:** 7,054. **Ref:** C Boyeson —
29th	● Plymouth........................a	W 1–2	**Att:** 9,969. **Ref:** T Kettle — **Scorers:** Dickinson[2]

December

6th	● Charlton ....h	W 2–0	**Att:** 6,648. **Ref:** M Jones — **Scorers:** Dickinson[2]. **Booked:** Evatt
9th	● Reading ....a	L 1–0	**Att:** 16,514. **Ref:** J Singh — **Booked:** Edwards, Taylor-Fletcher. **Dismissed:** Hendrie
13th	● Nottm Forest..................a	D 0–0	**Att:** 19,103. **Ref:** P Miller — **Booked:** Baptiste, Barker, Fox, Reid
20th	● Swansea........................h	D 1–1	**Att:** 7,007. **Ref:** D Deadman — **Scorers:** Gow. **Booked:** Fox
26th	● Sheff Wed......................a	D 1–1	**Att:** 25,044. **Ref:** M Oliver — **Scorers:** Gow. **Booked:** Reid, Southern, Dickinson, Taylor-Fletcher
29th	● Wolverhampton...............h	D 2–2	**Att:** 8,906. **Ref:** K Friend — **Scorers:** Edwards, Taylor-Fletcher. **Booked:** Martin

January

3rd	● Torquay ....a	L 1–0	**Att:** 3,654. **Ref:** A Penn — **Booked:** Barker, Harte, Evatt
17th	● Coventry ....a	L 2–1	**Att:** 15,551. **Ref:** C Pawson — **Scorers:** Campbell. **Booked:** Southern, O'Donovan
24th	● Birmingham ....h	W 2–0	**Att:** 8,105. **Ref:** S Tanner — **Scorers:** Campbell, Southern. **Booked:** O'Donovan, Campbell. **Dismissed:** Jorgensen
27th	● QPR ....h	L 0–3	**Att:** 6,656. **Ref:** G Laws
31st	● Crystal Palace ....a	W 0–1	**Att:** 13,810. **Ref:** A Marriner — **Scorers:** Campbell. **Booked:** Taylor-Fletcher. **Dismissed:** Rachubka

February

7th	● Doncaster ....h	L 2–3	**Att:** 7,452. **Ref:** A Taylor — **Scorers:** Campbell, Vaughan. **Booked:** O'Donovan. **Dismissed:** Adam
14th	● Ipswich ....a	D 1–1	**Att:** 19,299. **Ref:** P Crossley — **Scorers:** Baptiste. **Booked:** Vaughan, O'Donovan
18th	● Derby ....a	L 4–1	**Att:** 26,834. **Ref:** D Whitestone — **Scorers:** Edwards. **Booked:** Barker, Baptiste
21st	● Watford ....h	L 0–2	**Att:** 7,451. **Ref:** J Moss — **Booked:** O'Donovan
28th	● Bristol City ....a	D 0–0	**Att:** 16,855. **Ref:** F Graham — **Booked:** Ormerod, Adam

March

3rd	● Burnley ....h	L 0–1	**Att:** 7,679. **Ref:** L Mason — **Booked:** Barker, Crainey, Jorgensen
7th	● Norwich.........................h	W 2–0	**Att:** 7,505. **Ref:** C Oliver — **Scorers:** Adam, Ormerod. **Booked:** Adam, Ormerod
10th	● Sheff Utd ....a	D 2–2	**Att:** 25,273. **Ref:** R Booth — **Scorers:** Blackman, Campbell. **Booked:** Barker, Rachubka
14th	● Barnsley ....a	W 0–1	**Att:** 12,228. **Ref:** C Webster — **Scorers:** Small. **Booked:** Edwards, Small, Adam
21st	● Southampton ....h	D 1–1	**Att:** 7,947. **Ref:** D Foster — **Scorers:** Campbell. **Booked:** Mahon, Edwards, Barker

April

4th	● Plymouth........................h	L 0–1	**Att:** 8,103. **Ref:** M Haywood — **Booked:** Crainey
11th	● Preston ....a	W 0–1	**Att:** 21,273. **Ref:** A D'Urso — **Scorers:** Adam. **Booked:** Adam
13th	● Reading ....h	D 2–2	**Att:** 7,722. **Ref:** K Wright — **Scorers:** Campbell, Southern. **Booked:** Baptiste
18th	● Charlton ....a	D 2–2	**Att:** 19,615. **Ref:** M Russell — **Scorers:** Campbell, Hughes
25th	● Nottm Forest..................h	D 1–1	**Att:** 9,279. **Ref:** J Moss — **Scorers:** Ormerod. **Booked:** Adam, Crainey. **Dismissed:** Evatt

May

| 3rd | ● Swansea........................a | W 0–1 | **Att:** 16,316. **Ref:** C Boyeson — **Scorers:** Campbell. **Booked:** Ormerod |

● Coca-Cola Championship/Play-Offs ● FA Cup ● Carling Cup

BLACKPOOL

CHAMPIONSHIP GOALKEEPER STATS

Player	Minutes on pitch	Appearances	Match starts	Completed matches	Sub appearances	Subbed off	SAVES BREAKDOWN								Clean sheets	Goals conceded	Minutes since conceding	Save %	PENALTIES			Yellow cards	Red cards
							Saved with feet	Punched	Parried	Tipped over	Fumbled	Tipped round	Caught	Blocked					Saved	Resulting in goals	Opposition miss		
Matthew Gilks 474	5	4	4	1	0	0	2	1	1	0	0	24	0	1	10	8	73.68	0	0	0	0	0
Paul Rachubka 3915	42	42	41	0	0	3	18	23	6	0	15	166	2	13	48	180	83.04	1	6	0	1	1

CHAMPIONSHIP OUTFIELD PLAYER STATS

Player	Minutes on pitch	Appearances	Match starts	Completed matches	Substitute appearances	Subbed off	Goals scored	Minutes since scoring	Assists	Shots on target	Shots off target	Crosses	Defensive clearances	Defensive blocks	Fouls committed	Free-kicks won	Caught offside	Yellow cards	Red cards
Charlie Adam 1194	13	13	10	0	2	2	432	1	13	25	43	13	3	31	28	0	5	1
Sone Aluko 5	1	0	0	1	0	0	-	0	0	0	0	0	0	0	0	0	0	0
Alex Baptiste 1976	21	21	19	0	2	1	1388	1	1	0	14	35	11	10	18	0	3	0
Shaun Barker 4019	43	42	42	1	0	0	-	1	11	7	18	71	26	38	53	2	7	0
Nick Blackman 191	5	2	0	3	2	0	115	0	3	0	0	0	0	3	2	0	0	0
Marlon Broomes 9	1	0	0	1	0	0	-	0	0	0	0	0	0	0	0	0	0	0
Ben Burgess 2268	29	25	17	4	8	6	916	3	23	29	11	18	1	55	25	21	1	0
Mohammed Camara 1288	14	14	11	0	3	0	-	0	2	1	26	14	4	14	10	0	4	0
Dudley Campbell 1852	20	20	16	0	4	9	83	0	17	11	10	0	0	31	33	48	1	0
Danny Coid...................1305	18	13	11	5	2	0	-	0	0	5	3	22	11	3	4	11	0	0
Stephen Crainey 1473	17	15	15	2	0	0	-	0	5	3	26	21	7	13	10	0	3	0
Liam Dickinson 484	7	5	2	2	3	4	407	0	9	10	5	6	0	7	8	13	1	0
Rob Edwards 3338	36	35	34	1	1	2	620	0	7	4	3	68	20	36	35	2	3	0
Ian Evatt 3051	33	33	31	0	1	1	1834	1	5	10	2	69	27	34	34	2	5	1
David Fox 1451	22	15	10	7	5	0	-	1	8	4	30	2	1	15	6	0	3	0
Alan Gow 1028	17	10	7	7	3	5	940	0	19	15	16	1	1	15	19	13	2	0
Adam Hammill 1338	22	14	8	8	6	1	54	2	16	21	76	5	1	15	41	5	4	0
Ian Harte 330	4	4	2	0	2	0	-	0	1	3	16	3	2	4	0	0	0	0
Lee Hendrie 412	6	5	3	1	1	0	-	1	2	4	6	1	0	8	4	0	2	1
Lee Hughes 171	3	2	0	1	2	1	1	0	4	1	2	1	0	5	0	1	0	0
Claus Bech Jorgensen 2061	32	21	14	11	6	0	-	1	10	10	34	19	5	18	28	0	1	1
Steven Kabba 1143	17	12	8	5	4	2	856	0	15	6	9	0	0	24	20	14	1	0
Alan Mahon 57	1	1	0	0	1	0	-	0	1	0	2	0	0	2	1	0	1	0
Paul Marshall 15	2	1	0	1	1	0	-	0	0	0	0	0	0	0	0	0	0	0
Joe Martin 966	15	10	8	5	2	0	-	2	1	3	29	12	1	11	14	0	1	0
Stephen McPhee...............106	5	0	0	5	1	0	-	0	1	2	1	0	0	1	0	1	0	0
Danny Mitchley 9	2	0	0	2	0	0	-	0	0	0	0	0	0	0	0	1	0	0
Daniel Nardiello 35	2	0	0	2	0	0	-	0	2	0	1	0	0	1	1	0	0	0
Kristian Nemeth 35	1	0	0	1	0	0	-	0	0	0	0	0	0	0	0	0	0	0
Roy O'Donovan 950	12	11	4	1	7	0	-	0	7	5	16	3	3	15	11	5	5	0
Brett Ormerod 804	15	7	2	8	5	2	149	1	6	2	16	3	2	8	8	12	3	0
Graeme Owens 261	8	0	0	7	1	0	-	0	2	3	8	0	0	1	0	0	1	0
Zeshan Rehman 71	3	0	0	3	0	0	-	0	0	0	1	1	0	1	0	0	0	0
Kyel Reid 637	7	7	6	0	1	0	9	1	7	5	38	0	1	9	14	3	2	0
Wade Small 318	5	4	1	1	3	1	247	0	2	2	10	1	0	1	4	0	1	0
Keith Southern 3108	35	34	27	1	7	3	349	3	16	16	8	39	6	32	33	3	4	0
Gary Taylor-Fletcher 3123	38	34	21	4	13	5	1169	5	23	25	53	18	3	49	39	10	6	0
David Vaughan 2490	33	26	16	7	10	1	1195	2	17	9	43	7	0	15	28	2	3	0
Simon Walton 20	1	0	0	1	0	0	-	0	0	0	0	0	0	0	0	0	0	0
Jermaine Wright 258	3	3	2	0	1	0	-	0	0	0	2	3	1	1	0	0	0	0

SEASON TOTALS

Goals scored	47
Goals conceded	58
Clean sheets	13
Shots on target	256
Shots off target	237
Shots per goal	10.49
Pens awarded	6
Pens scored	6
Pens conceded	7
Offsides	159
Corners	238
Crosses	600
Players used	42
Fouls committed	528
Free-kicks won	550

CARDS RECEIVED

73 **5**

SEQUENCES

Wins	2
(on two occasions)	
Losses	4
(08/11/08–25/11/08)	
Draws	4
(on two occasions)	
Undefeated	7
(20/09/08–25/10/08)	
Without win	6
(09/12/08–17/01/09)	
Undefeated home	5
(13/09/08–25/10/08)	
Undefeated away	6
(28/02/09–03/05/09)	
Without scoring	3
(21/02/09–03/03/09)	
Without conceding	2
(30/08/08–13/09/08)	
Scoring	5
(on two occasions)	
Conceding	9
(21/10/08–29/11/08)	

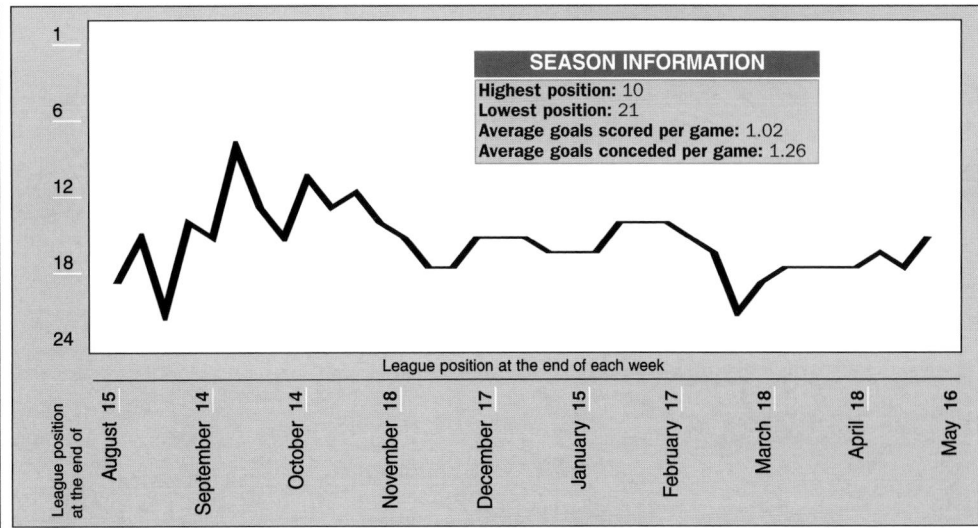

SEASON INFORMATION
Highest position: 10
Lowest position: 21
Average goals scored per game: 1.02
Average goals conceded per game: 1.26

League position at the end of each week

League position at the end of: August 15, September 14, October 14, November 18, December 17, January 15, February 17, March 18, April 18, May 16

MATCH RECORDS

Goals scored per match

		W	D	L	Pts
Failed to score	14	0	3	11	3
Scored 1 goal	20	7	9	4	30
Scored 2 goals	10	4	5	1	17
Scored 3 goals	1	1	0	0	3
Scored 4+ goals	1	1	0	0	3

Goals conceded per match

		W	D	L	Pts
Clean Sheet	13	10	3	0	33
Conceded 1 goal	15	1	9	5	12
Conceded 2 goals	12	1	5	6	8
Conceded 3 goals	5	1	0	4	3
Conceded 4+ goals	1	0	0	1	0

GOALS SCORED/CONCEDED PER FIVE-MINUTE INTERVALS

Goals For	0	2	3	3	1	2	3	1	5	5	3	3	2	3	3	1	3	4
Goals Against	3	3	0	1	2	4	1	1	1	4	5	4	2	8	3	5	4	7
Mins	5	10	15	20	25	30	35	40	45	50	55	60	65	70	75	80	85	90

QUICK-FIRE GOALS

From the start of a match
Danny Coid (v Sheff Utd)
4:49

By a substitute after coming on
Liam Dickinson
(v Plymouth) 3:01

LAST-GASP GOALS

From the start of a match
Alan Gow (v Cardiff)
94:53

By a substitute after coming on
Alan Gow (v Swansea)
28:13

GOAL DETAILS

How the goals were struck

SCORED		CONCEDED
29	Right foot	28
14	Left foot	16
4	Headers	14
0	Others	0

How the goals were struck

SCORED		CONCEDED
32	Open play	32
6	Cross	10
1	Corner	5
6	Penalties	6
0	Direct from free-kick	2
2	Free-kick	2
0	Own goals	1

Distance from goal

SCORED		CONCEDED
11	6yds	19
28	18yds	31
8	18+yds	8

CLUB SUMMARY

FORMED	1897
MANAGER	Gary Johnson
GROUND	Ashton Gate
CAPACITY	21,479
NICKNAME	The Robins
WEBSITE	www.bcfc.co.uk

The New Football Pools PLAYER OF THE SEASON — Louis Carey

OVERALL

P	W	D	L	F	A	GD
50	16	17	17	57	59	-2

COCA-COLA CHAMPIONSHIP

Pos	P	W	D	L	F	A	GD	Pts
10	46	15	16	15	54	54	0	61

HOME

Pos	P	W	D	L	F	A	GD	Pts
13	23	7	13	3	30	23	7	34

AWAY

Pos	P	W	D	L	F	A	GD	Pts
9	23	8	3	12	24	31	-7	27

CUP PROGRESS DETAILS

Competition	Round reached	Knocked out by
FA Cup	R3	Portsmouth
Carling Cup	R2	Crewe

BIGGEST WIN (ALL COMPS)

20/09/08 4–1 v Doncaster **FLC**

BIGGEST DEFEAT (ALL COMPS)

03/05/09 4–0 v Burnley **FLC**

THE PLAYER WITH THE MOST

Shots on target
Michael McIndoe 50

Shots off target
Michael McIndoe 35

Shots without scoring
Louis Carey 14

Assists
Michael McIndoe 7

Offsides
Nicky Maynard..................................... 45

Fouls
Dele Adebola...................................... 70

Fouls without a card
Lee Trundle 14

Free-kicks won
Gavin Williams 57

Defensive clearances
Liam Fontaine 64

actim INDEX for the 2008/09 Coca-Cola Championship Season

Rank	Player	Pts
22	Adriano Basso	544
37	Liam Fontaine	490
44	Michael McIndoe	475
48	Lee Johnson	466
88	Jamie McAllister	393

ATTENDANCE RECORD

High	Low	Average
18,456	15,304	16,816
v Birmingham (16/09/2008)	v Charlton (03/02/2009)	

THE 2007/08 play-off finalists found the Coca-Cola Championship a much tougher division this time around.

Expectations were perhaps unrealistically high at Ashton Gate after City came within a whisker of promotion to the Premier League on their return to the second tier.

The Robins started the campaign well, losing just one of their opening seven league fixtures. But, after managing to record successive victories only once – against struggling duo Norwich and Charlton in October – and enduring a run of eight games without a win prior to Christmas, Gary Johnson's side were languishing in mid-table going into the new year.

It looked like repeating the success of the previous campaign would be well beyond City, but one defeat in 11 matches up to the start of March, including a five-game winning run, propelled them right back into contention to reach the play-offs.

However, just when it mattered most, the Robins had their worst run of the 2008/09 season. After a morale-boosting 2–0 victory at Reading on 21st February, City won just once more in their remaining 12 matches.

Despite their inability to win, City's top-six aspirations were not extinguished until defeat by a solitary goal at Swansea in mid-April.

Johnson's side finished in 10th place and the manager was quick to point to the Robins' home form as the reason behind their failure to mount a serious challenge for promotion. They only lost

Dele Adebola scores in a 2–0 win at Reading

three games at Ashton Gate, but 13 draws – more than any other team in the Championship – speaks volumes about City's inability to finish off visiting teams.

Johnson himself admitted that scoring more than one goal in home games had been a problem, and the Robins scored more than two goals at home just once – when they beat Doncaster 4–1 in September.

Johnson has vowed to match the ambitions and commitment of his chairman Steve Lansdown with performances on the pitch next season. Lansdown has sold off millions of pounds worth of shares in his stockbroker business, Hargreaves Lansdown, to fund the building of the club's new 30,000-seater stadium at nearby Ashton Vale.

He has also promised that the investment will not affect the financial support he gives to Johnson as City again pursue promotion.

> **When it mattered most, the Robins had their worst run**

RESULTS 2008/09

August
9th	● Blackpool ....a	W 0–1	**Att:** 8,244. **Ref:** G Laws — **Scorers:** Brooker. **Booked:** Skuse, Orr, Weale
12th	● Peterborough ....h	W 2–1	**Att:** 5,684. **Ref:** P Taylor — **Scorers:** Brooker, Carey. **Booked:** McIndoe, McAllister, Carey
16th	● Derby ....h	D 1–1	**Att:** 16,389. **Ref:** S Attwell — **Scorers:** Maynard
23rd	● Coventry ....a	W 0–3	**Att:** 17,994. **Ref:** P Dowd — **Scorers:** Adebola, Brooker, McIndoe. **Booked:** Johnson
26th	● Crewe ....a	L 2–1	**Att:** 3,227. **Ref:** A Hall — **Scorers:** Wilson
30th	● QPR ....h	D 1–1	**Att:** 17,543. **Ref:** D Deadman — **Scorers:** Adebola. **Booked:** Orr, Sproule

September
13th	● Cardiff ....a	D 0–0	**Att:** 19,312. **Ref:** P Walton — **Booked:** Sproule
16th	● Birmingham ....h	L 1–2	**Att:** 18,456. **Ref:** K Friend — **Scorers:** Trundle. **Booked:** Carey
20th	● Doncaster ....h	W 4–1	**Att:** 15,960. **Ref:** J Singh — **Scorers:** Maynard, McIndoe[2], Sproule. **Booked:** Orr, Carey
27th	● Wolverhampton..................a	L 2–0	**Att:** 24,324. **Ref:** P Crossley — **Booked:** Skuse
30th	● Plymouth...........................h	D 2–2	**Att:** 17,489. **Ref:** I Williamson — **Scorers:** Akinde, Noble. **Booked:** Johnson, Sproule

October
4th	● Sheff Utd ....a	L 3–0	**Att:** 24,712. **Ref:** K Stroud — **Booked:** McAllister, Orr
18th	● Norwich............................h	W 1–0	**Att:** 16,791. **Ref:** A Hall — **Scorers:** McCombe. **Booked:** Orr, Maynard
21st	● Charlton ....a	W 0–2	**Att:** 21,207. **Ref:** C Penton — **Scorers:** Trundle, Williams
25th	● Barnsley ....a	D 0–0	**Att:** 11,551. **Ref:** M Russell — **Booked:** Elliott, McAllister
28th	● Sheff Utd ....h	D 0–0	**Att:** 16,798. **Ref:** R Styles — **Booked:** Elliott, Williams

November
1st	● Reading ....h	L 1–4	**Att:** 18,296. **Ref:** J Moss — **Scorers:** John. **Booked:** Maynard
8th	● Southampton ....a	W 0–1	**Att:** 14,535. **Ref:** A Penn — **Scorers:** Johnson. **Booked:** Williams
15th	● Nottm Forest.....................h	D 2–2	**Att:** 17,440. **Ref:** G Horwood — **Scorers:** Elliott, Fontaine
22nd	● Crystal Palace ....a	L 4–2	**Att:** 14,599. **Ref:** G Hegley — **Scorers:** Adebola, Maynard. **Booked:** Sproule
25th	● Watford ....h	D 1–1	**Att:** 15,551. **Ref:** N Swarbrick — **Scorers:** Maynard. **Booked:** McAllister
29th	● Preston ....a	L 2–0	**Att:** 11,161. **Ref:** R Beeby — **Booked:** Maynard

December
6th	● Swansea............................h	D 0–0	**Att:** 16,405. **Ref:** L Mason — **Booked:** McIndoe, Carey, Maynard
10th	● Ipswich ....a	L 3–1	**Att:** 17,749. **Ref:** P Taylor — **Scorers:** John. **Booked:** Carey, Sproule
13th	● Sheff Wed.........................h	D 0–0	**Att:** 15,542. **Ref:** R Shoebridge
20th	● Burnley ....h	L 1–2	**Att:** 16,108. **Ref:** R Booth — **Scorers:** Maynard
26th	● Watford ....a	W 2–4	**Att:** 15,527. **Ref:** F Graham — **Scorers:** Adebola, Elliott, Maynard[2]. **Booked:** Carey, Fontaine, Adebola
28th	● Crystal Palace ....h	W 1–0	**Att:** 18,265. **Ref:** A Penn — **Scorers:** Maynard.

January
3rd	● Portsmouth ....a	D 0–0	**Att:** 14,446. **Ref:** P Dowd — **Booked:** John
13th	● Portsmouth ....h	L 0–2	**Att:** 14,302. **Ref:** M Jones — **Booked:** Johnson
17th	● Wolverhampton..................a	D 2–2	**Att:** 16,749. **Ref:** M Haywood — **Scorers:** Adebola, Maynard. **Booked:** Sproule
27th	● Plymouth...........................a	W 0–2	**Att:** 11,438. **Ref:** P Taylor — **Scorers:** Fontaine, McIndoe. **Booked:** McAllister, Carey, Orr
31st	● Barnsley ....h	W 2–0	**Att:** 15,667. **Ref:** T Kettle — **Scorers:** McIndoe, Williams

February
3rd	● Charlton ....h	W 2–1	**Att:** 15,304. **Ref:** K Friend — **Scorers:** Adebola[2]
7th	● Norwich............................a	W 1–2	**Att:** 24,691. **Ref:** A D'Urso — **Scorers:** Orr, Skuse
14th	● Southampton ....h	W 2–0	**Att:** 17,000. **Ref:** M Oliver — **Scorers:** Adebola, Sproule. **Booked:** Fontaine, Orr, Williams
17th	● Doncaster ....a	L 1–0	**Att:** 10,928. **Ref:** C Oliver — **Booked:** Orr, McIndoe, Carey
21st	● Reading ....a	W 0–2	**Att:** 22,462. **Ref:** A Penn — **Scorers:** Adebola, Skuse. **Booked:** Williams
28th	● Blackpool ....h	D 0–0	**Att:** 16,855. **Ref:** F Graham

March
4th	● Birmingham ....a	L 1–0	**Att:** 17,551. **Ref:** J Moss — **Booked:** Williams, Carey, Johnson
7th	● Derby ....a	L 2–1	**Att:** 30,824. **Ref:** K Stroud — **Scorers:** Williams
10th	● Coventry ....h	W 2–0	**Att:** 15,706. **Ref:** P Crossley — **Scorers:** Johnson, McAllister. **Booked:** Carey
15th	● Cardiff ....h	D 1–1	**Att:** 17,487. **Ref:** L Mason — **Scorers:** Maynard. **Booked:** Maynard, Orr, Skuse
21st	● QPR ....a	L 2–1	**Att:** 14,059. **Ref:** G Hegley — **Scorers:** McIndoe. **Booked:** Adebola, Basso

April
4th	● Preston ....h	D 1–1	**Att:** 16,596. **Ref:** T Bates — **Scorers:** Maynard
11th	● Nottm Forest.....................a	L 3–2	**Att:** 22,776. **Ref:** C Webster — **Scorers:** Adebola, Sproule. **Booked:** McAllister, Sproule, Orr. **Dismissed:** McAllister
13th	● Ipswich ....h	D 1–1	**Att:** 16,430. **Ref:** A Taylor — **Scorers:** Elliott. **Booked:** McCombe
18th	● Swansea............................a	L 1–0	**Att:** 15,327. **Ref:** L Mason — **Booked:** McCombe, Adebola, Johnson, Sproule
25th	● Sheff Wed.........................h	D 1–1	**Att:** 17,486. **Ref:** A D'Urso — **Scorers:** Johnson. **Booked:** McAllister

May
3rd	● Burnley ....a	L 4–0	**Att:** 18,005. **Ref:** C Oliver — **Booked:** McAllister, Elliott

● Coca-Cola Championship/Play-Offs ● FA Cup ● Carling Cup

CHAMPIONSHIP GOALKEEPER STATS

Player	Minutes on pitch	Appearances	Match starts	Completed matches	Sub appearances	Subbed off	Saved with feet	Punched	Parried	Tipped over	Fumbled	Tipped round	Caught	Blocked	Clean sheets	Goals conceded	Minutes since conceding	Save %	Saved	Resulting in goals	Opposition miss	Yellow cards	Red cards
Adriano Basso 3914	43	43	40	0	3	0	16	23	10	0	14	225	0	17	47	7	86.05	0	2	0	1	0
Stephen Henderson..........89	1	0	0	1	0	0	2	1	1	0	0	1	0	0	1	-	83.33	0	1	0	0	0
Chris Weale 396	5	3	3	2	0	0	1	0	0	0	3	14	0	1	6	26	76.92	0	0	0	1	0

Saves breakdown / Penalties

CHAMPIONSHIP OUTFIELD PLAYER STATS

Player	Minutes on pitch	Appearances	Match starts	Completed matches	Substitute appearances	Subbed off	Goals scored	Minutes since scoring	Assists	Shots on target	Shots off target	Crosses	Defensive clearances	Defensive blocks	Fouls committed	Free-kicks won	Caught offside	Yellow cards	Red cards
Dele Adebola 2875	39	32	14	7	18	10	317	7	33	32	8	12	1	70	51	31	3	0
John Akinde 254	7	1	0	6	1	1	236	0	3	2	1	3	0	4	4	4	0	0
Steve Brooker...............................90	4	0	0	4	0	2	25	0	2	1	3	0	0	4	1	0	0	0
Louis Carey 2610	28	28	26	0	2	0	-	0	5	9	5	41	12	44	29	1	9	0
Marvin Elliott 2319	28	24	22	4	2	3	330	0	17	18	3	11	6	39	37	1	3	0
Liam Fontaine 3887	42	41	40	1	1	0	1586	2	14	12	10	64	37	53	35	1	2	0
Izzy Iriekpen 475	9	4	4	5	0	0	-	0	2	1	0	7	4	6	8	0	0	0
Stern John 1281	24	13	5	11	8	2	861	2	23	14	3	9	1	13	32	20	0	0
Lee Johnson................................4050	44	43	35	1	8	3	165	2	26	10	80	9	2	30	28	2	4	0
Nicky Maynard 3087	43	34	17	9	17	11	444	4	46	33	12	4	0	44	47	45	5	0
Jamie McAllister 3195	35	35	26	0	8	1	647	3	6	10	49	38	14	40	31	1	7	1
Jamie McCombe 2115	28	24	20	4	4	1	1927	0	9	9	1	44	15	35	17	0	2	0
Michael McIndoe 4072	45	43	38	2	5	6	534	7	50	35	133	11	3	29	43	36	2	0
Scott Murray 62	3	0	0	3	0	0	-	0	0	0	2	0	0	0	1	1	0	0
David Noble 416	9	5	0	4	5	1	409	1	3	1	7	0	0	1	9	1	0	0
Bradley Orr 3421	38	37	32	1	5	1	1285	3	10	16	54	39	14	47	25	2	10	0
Cole Skuse 2622	33	29	21	4	8	2	863	1	16	5	8	15	8	25	19	1	3	0
Ivan Sproule 2045	38	18	5	20	13	3	236	4	20	13	42	3	2	34	30	9	8	0
Peter Styvar 262	10	2	0	8	2	0	-	1	2	1	2	3	0	10	4	6	0	0
Lee Trundle 692	19	4	1	15	3	2	426	0	9	2	6	1	1	14	12	6	0	0
Andy Webster 277	5	2	2	3	0	0	-	0	0	1	0	5	0	8	3	0	0	0
Gavin Williams 2207	35	24	9	11	15	3	447	1	29	18	29	6	6	39	57	7	5	0
Brian Wilson 1606	20	17	14	3	3	0	-	3	4	6	10	20	5	12	6	1	0	0
James Wilson 58	2	0	0	2	0	0	-	0	0	0	0	0	0	0	0	0	0	0

SEASON TOTALS

Goals scored	54
Goals conceded	54
Clean sheets	17
Shots on target	329
Shots off target	249
Shots per goal	10.70
Pens awarded	6
Pens scored	3
Pens conceded	3
Offsides	177
Corners	252
Crosses	468
Players used	27
Fouls committed	597
Free-kicks won	539

CARDS RECEIVED

65 1

SEQUENCES

Wins	5
(27/01/09–14/02/09)	
Losses	2
(04/03/09–07/03/09)	
Draws	2
(on two occasions)	
Undefeated	8
(26/12/08–14/02/09)	
Without win	8
(on two occasions)	
Undefeated home	11
(28/12/08–25/04/09)	
Undefeated away	4
(13/12/08–07/02/09)	
Without scoring	2
(on four occasions)	
Without conceding	4
(18/10/08–28/10/08)	
Scoring	9
(20/12/08–14/02/09)	
Conceding	5
(16/09/08–04/10/08)	

SEASON INFORMATION

Highest Position: 3
Lowest Position: 18
Average goals scored per game: 1.17
Average goals conceded per game: 1.17

League position at the end of each week

League position at the end of: August 4, September 10, October 8, November 14, December 12, January 11, February 5, March 9, April 10, May 10

MATCH RECORDS

Goals scored per match

		W	D	L	Pts
Failed to score	13	0	6	7	6
Scored 1 goal	17	4	7	6	19
Scored 2 goals	13	8	3	2	27
Scored 3 goals	1	1	0	0	3
Scored 4+ goals	2	2	0	0	6

Goals conceded per match

		W	D	L	Pts
Clean sheet	17	11	6	0	39
Conceded 1 goal	13	3	7	3	16
Conceded 2 goals	10	1	3	6	6
Conceded 3 goals	3	0	0	3	0
Conceded 4+ goals	3	0	0	3	0

GOALS SCORED/CONCEDED PER FIVE-MINUTE INTERVALS

Goals For	3	0	2	1	3	3	1	1	2	4	6	3	4	1	5	6	1	8
Goals Against	2	2	4	4	3	2	1	0	4	4	5	3	3	4	2	2	3	6
Mins	5	10	15	20	25	30	35	40	45	50	55	60	65	70	75	80	85	90

QUICK-FIRE GOALS

From the start of a match
Nicky Maynard (v Watford)
0:23

By a substitute after coming on
David Noble (v Plymouth)
7:12

LAST-GASP GOALS

From the start of a match
Stern John (v Reading)
92:46

By a substitute after coming on
Ivan Sproule
(v Southampton) 32:42

GOAL DETAILS

How the goals were struck

SCORED		CONCEDED
31	Right foot	27
17	Left foot	16
6	Headers	11
0	Others	0

How the goals were struck

SCORED		CONCEDED
41	Open play	31
5	Cross	3
1	Corner	7
3	Penalties	3
0	Direct from free-kick	3
4	Free-kick	3
0	Own goals	4

Distance from goal

SCORED		CONCEDED
23	6yds	23
21	18yds	23
10	18+yds	8

BURNLEY

CLUB SUMMARY

FORMED	1882
MANAGER	Owen Coyle
GROUND	Turf Moor
CAPACITY	22,619
NICKNAME	The Clarets
WEBSITE	www.burnleyfootballclub.co.uk

The New Football Pools PLAYER OF THE SEASON

Robbie Blake

OVERALL

P	W	D	L	F	A	GD
61	31	16	14	96	74	22

COCA-COLA CHAMPIONSHIP

Pos	P	W	D	L	F	A	GD	Pts
5	46	21	13	12	72	60	12	76

HOME

Pos	P	W	D	L	F	A	GD	Pts
3	23	14	5	4	42	23	19	47

AWAY

Pos	P	W	D	L	F	A	GD	Pts
7	23	7	8	8	30	37	-7	29

CUP PROGRESS DETAILS

Competition	Round reached	Knocked out by
FA Cup	R5	Arsenal
Carling Cup	SF	Tottenham

BIGGEST WIN (ALL COMPS)
14/03/09 5–0 v Nottingham Forest **FLC**

BIGGEST DEFEAT (ALL COMPS)
1–4 on two occasions

THE PLAYER WITH THE MOST

Shots on target	
Martin Paterson	46
Shots off target	
Chris McCann	40
Shots without scoring	
Rhys Williams	9
Assists	
Robbie Blake	12
Offsides	
Martin Paterson	52
Fouls	
Martin Paterson	71
Fouls without a card	
Jay Rodriguez	14
Free-kicks won	
Chris McCann	66
Defensive clearances	
Clarke Carlisle	65

actim INDEX for the 2008/09 Coca-Cola Championship Season

Rank	Player	Pts
6	Graham Alexander	638
9	Martin Paterson	604
12	Brian Jensen	580
14	Wade Elliott	565
24	Chris Eagles	520

ATTENDANCE RECORD

High	Low	Average
18,005	10,032	13,082

v Bristol City (03/05/2009) v Plymouth (30/08/2008)

Burnley players are presented with the Coca-Cola Championship play-off final trophy

BURNLEY capped an incredible season with victory at Wembley in the Coca-Cola Championship play-off final to return to the top flight of English football for the first time in 33 years.

The Lancastrians will be the smallest town to grace the Barclays Premier League after Wade Elliott's superb 25-yard effort earned them a 1–0 win over Sheffield United. The game at Wembley was the Clarets' 61st in all competitions, which included a superb run in the League Cup, where only two late Tottenham goals in extra-time denied them a place in the final.

Burnley also reached the fifth round of the FA Cup, where they fell to another north London club in the shape of Arsenal.

But along the way the Clarets showed they will be able to cope with life in the Premier League. Fulham, Chelsea and Arsenal were all knocked out of the League Cup by Burnley in a run dubbed 'capital punishment' by the

Press. Tottenham were also beaten 3–0 at Turf Moor after 90 minutes in the second leg of the semi-final, but goals from Roman Pavlyuchenko and Jermain Defoe after 118 and 120 minutes helped Spurs scrape through 6–4 on aggregate. In the FA Cup, top-flight team West Brom were also beaten in an FA Cup fourth-round replay.

The Clarets' successes were based on a small squad, emphasised by the fact that 37-year-old defender Graham Alexander appeared in all 61 games. Keeping the likes of Elliott, Steven Caldwell, Chris Eagles and the mercurial Robbie Blake will be pivotal to Burley's chances next season.

Owen Coyle is now looking forward to pitting his wits against the best, despite being installed as one of the favourites to take over as Celtic boss early in the summer.

> ## The Clarets showed they can cope with life in the top flight

RESULTS 2008/09

August
9th	● Sheff Wed..................a	L 4–1	**Att:** 23,793. **Ref:** C Oliver — **Scorers:** Paterson. **Booked:** Blake
12th	● Bury ....a	W 0–2	**Att:** 4,276. **Ref:** S Mathieson — **Scorers:** Paterson[2]
16th	● Ipswich ....h	L 0–3	**Att:** 11,312. **Ref:** T Bates
23rd	● Crystal Palace ....a	D 0–0	**Att:** 14,071. **Ref:** I Williamson — **Booked:** Paterson, McDonald, Carlisle
26th	● Oldham ....h	W 3–0	**Att:** 5,528. **Ref:** A Penn — **Scorers:** McCann, Paterson[2]. **Booked:** Elliott
30th	● Plymouth................h	D 0–0	**Att:** 10,032. **Ref:** M Oliver — **Booked:** Eagles. **Dismissed:** Eagles

September
13th	● Nottm Forest............a	W 1–2	**Att:** 20,504. **Ref:** C Penton — **Scorers:** Alexander[2]. **Booked:** Anderson, Elliott
16th	● Blackpool ....h	W 2–0	**Att:** 13,752. **Ref:** J Moss — **Scorers:** Alexander, Paterson
20th	● Swansea..................a	D 1–1	**Att:** 13,299. **Ref:** A Hall — **Scorers:** Gudjonsson. **Booked:** McDonald, Jordan, Carlisle, Caldwell
23rd	● Fulham ....h	W 1–0	**Att:** 7,119. **Ref:** M Jones — **Scorers:** Rodriguez
27th	● Preston ....h	W 3–1	**Att:** 16,276. **Ref:** L Mason — **Scorers:** Caldwell, Eagles, Gudjonsson
30th	● Watford ....h	W 3–2	**Att:** 10,033. **Ref:** S Bratt — **Scorers:** Alexander, Elliott, Paterson

October
4th	● Reading ....a	L 3–1	**Att:** 18,621. **Ref:** K Friend — **Scorers:** McCann. **Booked:** Paterson, Caldwell, Jordan. **Dismissed:** Jordan
18th	● Birmingham ....h	D 1–1	**Att:** 13,809. **Ref:** L Probert — **Scorers:** McCann. **Booked:** Thompson, Carlisle
21st	● Coventry ....a	W 1–3	**Att:** 14,621. **Ref:** M Thorpe — **Scorers:** Blake, Duff, Eagles. **Booked:** Duff, Kalvenes, Blake
25th	● Charlton ....a	D 1–1	**Att:** 21,884. **Ref:** R Shoebridge — **Scorers:** Thompson. **Booked:** Elliott
28th	● Reading ....h	W 1–0	**Att:** 11,538. **Ref:** M Haywood — **Scorers:** Blake

November
1st	● Norwich....................h	W 2–0	**Att:** 11,353. **Ref:** G Laws — **Scorers:** Eagles[2]. **Booked:** Gudjonsson, Thompson, Caldwell
8th	● Wolverhampton...........a	L 2–0	**Att:** 23,711. **Ref:** D Deadman — **Booked:** Jordan, Jensen, Carlisle, Blake, McCann, McDonald. **Dismissed:** Carlisle
12th	● Chelsea ....a	D 1–1	**Att:** 41,369. **Ref:** K Stroud — **Scorers:** Akinbiyi. **Booked:** Caldwell, Akinbiyi, Eagles. **Dismissed:** Caldwell (Won 5–4 on pens)
15th	● QPR ....a	W 1–2	**Att:** 13,226. **Ref:** K Woolmer — **Scorers:** Blake, Mahon. **Booked:** Gudjonsson, Jordan, McDonald
22nd	● Doncaster ....h	D 0–0	**Att:** 12,173. **Ref:** S Bennett — **Booked:** Thompson, Gudjonsson, Akinbiyi. **Dismissed:** Thompson
24th	● Barnsley ....a	L 3–2	**Att:** 10,678. **Ref:** N Miller — **Scorers:** Paterson[2]. **Booked:** Carlisle, Eagles, Paterson
29th	● Derby ....h	W 3–0	**Att:** 11,552. **Ref:** S Tanner — **Scorers:** McDonald, Paterson[2]. **Booked:** Carlisle

December
2nd	● Arsenal ....h	W 2–0	**Att:** 19,045. **Ref:** A Marriner — **Scorers:** McDonald.
6th	● Sheff Utd ....a	W 2–3	**Att:** 24,702. **Ref:** A Taylor — **Scorers:** Alexander, Eagles, Paterson. **Booked:** Elliott, Jordan
9th	● Cardiff ....h	D 2–2	**Att:** 11,230. **Ref:** C Webster — **Scorers:** Blake, Thompson. **Booked:** Gudjonsson
13th	● Southampton ....h	W 3–2	**Att:** 11,229. **Ref:** P Dowd — **Scorers:** Gudjonsson[2], Perry OG. **Booked:** Carlisle, Thompson
20th	● Bristol City ....a	W 1–2	**Att:** 16,108. **Ref:** R Booth — **Scorers:** Paterson, Thompson
26th	● Barnsley ....h	L 1–2	**Att:** 16,580. **Ref:** S Mathieson — **Scorers:** McCann. **Booked:** Jordan
28th	● Doncaster ....a	L 2–1	**Att:** 14,020. **Ref:** T Kettle — **Scorers:** Paterson. **Booked:** Jordan, Carlisle. **Dismissed:** Caldwell

January
3rd	● QPR ....a	D 0–0	**Att:** 8,896. **Ref:** T Bates
6th	● Tottenham ....a	L 4–1	**Att:** 31,377. **Ref:** M Atkinson — **Scorers:** Paterson. **Booked:** Jordan, Duff
10th	● Swansea...................h	L 0–2	**Att:** 13,740. **Ref:** M Oliver — **Booked:** Elliott. **Dismissed:** Duff
13th	● QPR ....h	W 2–1	**Att:** 3,760. **Ref:** C Webster — **Scorers:** Rodriguez, Thompson. **Booked:** Caldwell, Mahon (AET)
17th	● Preston ....a	L 2–1	**Att:** 15,692. **Ref:** P Taylor — **Scorers:** Blake
21st	● Tottenham ....h	W 3–2	**Att:** 19,533. **Ref:** M Halsey — **Scorers:** Blake, McCann, Rodriguez. **Booked:** McCann, Duff (AET)
24th	● West Brom ....a	D 2–2	**Att:** 18,294. **Ref:** M Dean — **Scorers:** Alexander, Paterson
27th	● Watford ....a	L 3–0	**Att:** 13,193. **Ref:** J Linington — **Booked:** Kalvenes
31st	● Charlton ....h	W 2–1	**Att:** 14,404. **Ref:** R Beeby — **Scorers:** Thompson[2]

February
3rd	● West Brom ....h	W 3–1	**Att:** 6,635. **Ref:** M Jones — **Scorers:** Elliott, Thompson. **Booked:** Caldwell
7th	● Birmingham ....a	D 1–1	**Att:** 16,763. **Ref:** K Stroud — **Scorers:** Paterson. **Booked:** Thompson, Kalvenes
14th	● Wolverhampton...........h	W 1–0	**Att:** 13,515. **Ref:** C Oliver — **Scorers:** McCann
17th	● Coventry ....h	D 1–1	**Att:** 14,595. **Ref:** D Foster — **Scorers:** Eagles
21st	● Norwich....................a	D 1–1	**Att:** 24,363. **Ref:** K Friend — **Scorers:** Thompson. **Booked:** Duff
28th	● Sheff Wed.................h	L 2–4	**Att:** 12,449. **Ref:** A D'Urso — **Scorers:** Eagles, McCann. **Booked:** Jordan

March
3rd	● Blackpool ....a	W 0–1	**Att:** 7,679. **Ref:** L Mason — **Scorers:** Kalvenes. **Booked:** Kalvenes, McDonald
8th	● Arsenal ....a	L 3–0	**Att:** 57,454. **Ref:** C Foy — **Booked:** McDonald
11th	● Crystal Palace ....h	W 4–2	**Att:** 10,312. **Ref:** C Boyeson — **Scorers:** Alexander, Carlisle, Rodriguez, Thompson
14th	● Nottm Forest.............h	W 5–0	**Att:** 13,055. **Ref:** D Whitestone — **Scorers:** Blake, Carlisle, Elliott, Gudjonsson, Rodriguez
17th	● Ipswich ....h	D 1–1	**Att:** 18,745. **Ref:** R Shoebridge — **Scorers:** Elliott. **Booked:** Paterson
21st	● Plymouth..................a	W 1–2	**Att:** 11,246. **Ref:** R Booth — **Scorers:** Blake, Caldwell. **Booked:** Williams

April
4th	● Derby ....a	D 1–1	**Att:** 33,010. **Ref:** G Hegley — **Scorers:** McCann. **Booked:** Paterson
11th	● QPR ....h	W 1–0	**Att:** 15,058. **Ref:** M Haywood — **Scorers:** Carlisle. **Booked:** Kalvenes
13th	● Cardiff ....a	L 3–1	**Att:** 19,379. **Ref:** L Probert — **Scorers:** Blake. **Booked:** Kalvenes, Carlisle, Elliott, Williams
20th	● Sheff Utd ....h	W 1–0	**Att:** 14,884. **Ref:** G Laws — **Scorers:** Paterson
25th	● Southampton ....a	D 2–2	**Att:** 23,927. **Ref:** M Jones — **Scorers:** Alexander, Carlisle. **Booked:** Paterson, Alexander, Caldwell

May
3rd	● Bristol City ....h	W 4–0	**Att:** 18,005. **Ref:** C Oliver — **Scorers:** Alexander[2], Elliott, Gudjonsson. **Booked:** Williams
9th	● Reading ....h	W 1–0	**Att:** 18,853. **Ref:** M Atkinson — **Scorers:** Alexander
12th	● Reading ....a	W 0–2	**Att:** 19,909. **Ref:** M Riley — **Scorers:** Paterson, Thompson. **Booked:** Kalvenes, Elliott
25th	● Sheff Utd ....n	W 1–0	**Att:** 80,518. **Ref:** M Dean — **Scorers:** Elliott. **Booked:** Kalvenes, Carlisle

● Coca-Cola Championship/Play-Offs ● FA Cup ● Carling Cup

CHAMPIONSHIP GOALKEEPER STATS

Player	Minutes on pitch	Appearances	Match starts	Completed matches	Sub appearances	Subbed off	Saved with feet	Punched	Parried	Tipped over	Fumbled	Tipped round	Caught	Blocked	Clean sheets	Goals conceded	Minutes since conceding	Save %	Saved	Resulting in goals	Opposition miss	Yellow cards	Red cards
Brian Jensen	4308	45	45	45	0	0	4	22	23	14	0	14	171	1	13	56	148	81.76	1	7	0	1	0
Diego Penny	95	1	1	1	0	0	0	0	1	0	0	1	1	0	0	4	28	42.86	0	0	0	0	0

CHAMPIONSHIP OUTFIELD PLAYER STATS

Player	Minutes on pitch	Appearances	Match starts	Completed matches	Substitute appearances	Subbed off	Goals scored	Minutes since scoring	Assists	Shots on target	Shots off target	Crosses	Defensive clearances	Defensive blocks	Fouls committed	Free-kicks won	Caught offside	Yellow cards	Red cards
Ade Akinbiyi	249	11	1	0	10	1	0	-	0	1	1	0	0	0	7	3	5	1	0
Graham Alexander	4368	46	46	44	0	2	9	16	5	15	16	46	30	11	40	33	0	1	0
Russell Anderson	382	4	4	4	0	0	0	-	0	1	0	1	3	0	4	2	0	1	0
Robbie Blake	2905	46	33	10	13	23	8	284	12	44	23	78	1	1	17	51	10	3	0
Steven Caldwell	4205	45	45	44	0	1	2	657	2	9	20	0	64	18	55	43	0	4	1
Clarke Carlisle	3382	36	36	34	0	2	4	91	2	11	16	2	65	15	44	42	3	9	1
Michael Duff	2036	27	22	19	5	3	1	1479	0	4	4	12	22	11	30	19	0	2	1
Chris Eagles	2963	43	30	19	13	11	7	785	6	44	30	85	6	1	14	65	13	3	1
Wade Elliott	3725	42	41	33	1	8	4	16	8	21	22	130	13	2	55	39	11	5	0
Joey Gudjonsson	2072	39	20	10	19	10	6	7	2	22	26	7	14	4	17	32	4	4	0
Stephen Jordan	2508	27	26	25	1	1	0	-	0	1	3	24	21	6	45	13	1	8	1
Christian Kalvenes	1897	21	21	17	0	4	1	967	0	3	1	22	11	2	29	23	1	6	0
Alex MacDonald	38	3	0	0	3	0	0	-	0	0	0	0	1	0	0	0	0	0	0
Alan Mahon	191	8	0	0	8	0	1	220	1	1	2	2	0	0	3	1	0	0	0
Chris McCann	4108	44	44	39	0	5	6	515	3	39	40	25	16	3	54	66	5	1	0
Kevin McDonald	1032	25	9	2	16	7	1	554	1	8	8	6	3	1	13	7	1	5	0
Martin Paterson	3374	43	39	15	4	24	12	229	4	46	27	32	4	0	71	52	52	6	0
Jay Rodriguez	696	25	2	0	23	2	2	363	0	9	12	1	1	0	14	14	14	0	0
Steven Thompson	1985	34	23	3	11	20	7	28	2	14	25	9	18	0	47	35	24	5	1
Remco van der Schaaf	60	1	1	0	0	1	0	-	0	0	0	0	0	0	0	0	0	0	0
Rhys Williams	1573	17	17	15	0	2	0	-	1	1	8	8	13	2	23	21	0	3	0

SEASON TOTALS

Goals scored	72
Goals conceded	60
Clean sheets	13
Shots on target	294
Shots off target	284
Shots per goal	8.03
Pens awarded	8
Pens scored	8
Pens conceded	8
Offsides	144
Corners	282
Crosses	496
Players used	23
Fouls committed	584
Free-kicks won	567

CARDS RECEIVED

68 **6**

SEQUENCES

Wins	3
(03/03/09–14/03/09)	
Losses	5
(26/12/08–27/01/09)	
Draws	2
(on two occasions)	
Undefeated	7
(23/08/08–30/09/08)	
Without win	5
(26/12/08–27/01/09)	
Undefeated home	11
(30/08/08–13/12/08)	
Undefeated away	6
(07/02/09–04/04/09)	
Without scoring	3
(16/08/08–30/08/08)	
Without conceding	2
(23/08/08–30/08/08)	
Scoring	17
(31/01/09–03/05/09)	
Conceding	11
(06/12/08–07/02/09)	

SEASON INFORMATION

Highest position: 4
Lowest position: 24
Average goals scored per game: 1.57
Average goals conceded per game: 1.30

League position at the end of each week

League position at the end of

August 23 · September 4 · October 5 · November 5 · December 5 · January 9 · February 8 · March 5 · April 6 · May 5

MATCH RECORDS

Goals scored per match

		W	D	L	Pts
Failed to score	7	0	3	4	3
Scored 1 goal	19	5	8	6	23
Scored 2 goals	11	7	2	2	23
Scored 3 goals	6	6	0	0	18
Scored 4+ goals	3	3	0	0	9

Goals conceded per match

		W	D	L	Pts
Clean sheet	13	10	3	0	33
Conceded 1 goal	15	7	8	0	29
Conceded 2 goals	11	4	2	5	14
Conceded 3 goals	5	0	0	5	0
Conceded 4+ goals	2	0	0	2	0

GOALS SCORED/CONCEDED PER FIVE-MINUTE INTERVALS

Goals For	2	4	4	4	5	0	3	4	3	2	5	6	2	4	2	8	5	9
Goals Against	4	2	2	5	1	2	4	5	5	3	5	0	3	2	3	4	3	7
Mins	5	10	15	20	25	30	35	40	45	50	55	60	65	70	75	80	85	90

QUICK-FIRE GOALS

From the start of a match
Martin Paterson
(v Birmingham) 2:15

By a substitute after coming on
Joey Gudjonsson
(v Nottm Forest) 3:37

LAST-GASP GOALS

From the start of a match
Chris Eagles
(v Preston) 94:01

By a substitute after coming on
Jay Rodriguez
(v Nottm Forest) 47:54

GOAL DETAILS

How the goals were struck

SCORED		CONCEDED
42	Right foot	40
16	Left foot	13
14	Headers	6
0	Others	1

How the goals were struck

SCORED		CONCEDED
38	Open play	42
9	Cross	4
6	Corner	2
8	Penalties	7
2	Direct from free-kick	1
8	Free-kick	2
1	Own goals	2

Distance from goal

SCORED		CONCEDED
28	6yds	18
32	18yds	37
12	18+yds	5

CARDIFF CITY

CLUB SUMMARY

FORMED	1899
MANAGER	Dave Jones
GROUND	Cardiff City Stadium
CAPACITY	27,000
NICKNAME	The Bluebirds
WEBSITE	www.cardiffcityfc.co.uk

The New Football Pools PLAYER OF THE SEASON — Roger Johnson

OVERALL

P	W	D	L	F	A	GD
52	22	18	12	71	60	11

COCA-COLA CHAMPIONSHIP

Pos	P	W	D	L	F	A	GD	Pts
7	46	19	17	10	65	53	12	74

HOME

Pos	P	W	D	L	F	A	GD	Pts
4	23	14	5	4	40	23	17	47

AWAY

Pos	P	W	D	L	F	A	GD	Pts
8	23	5	12	6	25	30	-5	27

CUP PROGRESS DETAILS

Competition	Round reached	Knocked out by
FA Cup	R4	Arsenal
Carling Cup	R3	Swansea

BIGGEST WIN (ALL COMPS)
08/04/09 4–1 v Derby **FLC**

BIGGEST DEFEAT (ALL COMPS)
18/04/09 0–6 v Preston **FLC**

THE PLAYER WITH THE MOST

Shots on target
Jay Bothroyd 52

Shots off target
Jay Bothroyd 47

Shots without scoring
Stephen McPhail 21

Assists
Paul Parry 5

Offsides
Michael Chopra 33

Fouls
Jay Bothroyd 67

Fouls without a card
Paul Parry 21

Free-kicks won
Jay Bothroyd 90

Defensive clearances
Roger Johnson 75

actim INDEX for the 2008/09 Coca-Cola Championship Season

Rank	Player	Pts
10	Ross McCormack	590
25	Roger Johnson	518
71	Joe Ledley	419
81	Jay Bothroyd	402
96	Kevin McNaughton	384

ATTENDANCE RECORD

High	Low	Average
20,156	15,902	18,044
v Swansea (05/04/2009)	v Barnsley (03/03/2009)	

CARDIFF will look back on the 2008/09 season with a huge sense of disappointment, despite the club securing their highest Football League finish for 38 years.

The Bluebirds were pipped to a play-off place by Preston on the final day with both teams level on points and goal difference, but with North End having scored one more goal throughout the course of the campaign.

In a strange turn of events, it was Preston who had torn Cardiff apart 6–0 on a freak Saturday four games from the end of the season. Had it been 'just' five goals then Dave Jones' side would have been facing Sheffield United in the play-offs instead.

It was a bitter pill to swallow for a side who, in the build-up to that game,

were just four points adrift of the two automatic promotion places with a game in hand, and eight points clear of the others just below the top six. Their fate was sealed by a haul of just one point from a possible 12 in the closing stages of the season.

Cardiff had occupied a play-off place for the

> **The Bluebirds were pipped to a play-off place by Preston**

majority of the campaign, occasionally flirting with those in the top two.

The conclusion to a season that harboured so much promise even as late as mid-April, left a sour taste in what should have been a joyous final few weeks at the club's Ninian Park home.

After 99 years at their famous old ground, fans were hoping to say one last goodbye in a play-off semi-final. Instead, the final game at Ninian Park proved to be a rather embarrassing 3–0 defeat to Ipswich.

Despite missing out on the play-offs, manager Jones has, in the wake of calls for his head, been assured of his future by chairman Peter Ridsdale.

The club has rightly pointed to the progress made in recent years under Jones, both on and off the pitch, but he knows this season should have delivered more.

The challenge now must lie in keeping hold of the club's star players. Joe Ledley looks set for a move away from his roots, while Ross McCormack and Roger Johnson have also attracted attention.

With their 27,000 all-seater stadium set to open in time for the new season, a state-of-the-art training facility and a reasonably sound financial footing, maybe it is time for the Bluebirds' fans to look back at the progress made in recent years and not just at the failure of their final four games.

Ross McCormack's goal tally was important for Cardiff

August

9th	● Southampton ....h	W 2–1	**Att:** 19,749. **Ref:** S Mathieson — **Scorers:** R. Johnson, Thompson. **Booked:** Loovens
12th	● Bournemouth ....a	W 1–2	**Att:** 3,399. **Ref:** G Horwood — **Scorers:** Parry[2]
16th	● Doncaster ....a	D 1–1	**Att:** 11,873. **Ref:** M Halsey — **Scorers:** McCormack. **Booked:** McPhail
23rd	● Norwich..............................h	D 2–2	**Att:** 18,032. **Ref:** A Taylor — **Scorers:** McCormack[2]
26th	● Milton Keynes Dons ....h	W 2–1	**Att:** 6,334. **Ref:** R Shoebridge — **Scorers:** McCormack, Whittingham
30th	● Sheff Utd ....a	D 0–0	**Att:** 29,226. **Ref:** C Webster

September

13th	● Bristol City ....h	D 0–0	**Att:** 19,312. **Ref:** P Walton
16th	● Barnsley ....a	W 0–1	**Att:** 11,282. **Ref:** G Laws — **Scorers:** Whittingham
20th	● Derby ....a	D 1–1	**Att:** 28,007. **Ref:** M Haywood — **Scorers:** McCormack
23rd	● Swansea.............................a	L 1–0	**Att:** 17,411. **Ref:** A Wiley — **Booked:** Ledley, McPhail, Whittingham, McCormack, Comminges. **Dismissed:** McPhail
27th	● Birmingham ....h	L 1–2	**Att:** 18,304. **Ref:** M Jones — **Scorers:** McCormack. **Booked:** Comminges
30th	● Coventry ....h	W 2–1	**Att:** 16,312. **Ref:** R East — **Scorers:** Bothroyd, McCormack

October

4th	● Blackpool ....a	D 1–1	**Att:** 7,328. **Ref:** N Miller — **Scorers:** Parry. **Booked:** Comminges
18th	● Charlton ....h	W 2–0	**Att:** 17,310. **Ref:** K Friend — **Scorers:** McCormack[2]. **Booked:** Bothroyd
21st	● Watford ....a	D 2–2	**Att:** 13,461. **Ref:** R Beeby — **Scorers:** Bothroyd. **Booked:** Rae
25th	● Nottm Forest......................a	W 0–1	**Att:** 19,468. **Ref:** K Stroud — **Scorers:** McCormack. **Booked:** Kennedy, McCormack
28th	● Blackpool ....h	W 2–0	**Att:** 17,570. **Ref:** R Shoebridge — **Scorers:** McCormack, Whittingham. **Booked:** Purse

November

1st	● Wolverhampton...................h	L 1–2	**Att:** 17,734. **Ref:** S Tanner — **Scorers:** McCormack
8th	● QPR ....a	L 1–0	**Att:** 13,347. **Ref:** L Probert — **Booked:** McPhail, Comminges. **Dismissed:** Purse, Comminges
15th	● Crystal Palace ....h	W 2–1	**Att:** 17,478. **Ref:** J Moss — **Scorers:** Chopra, Ledley. **Booked:** Whittingham
22nd	● Plymouth............................a	L 2–1	**Att:** 11,438. **Ref:** P Taylor — **Scorers:** Chopra. **Booked:** Rae
25th	● Reading ....h	D 2–2	**Att:** 17,154. **Ref:** P Walton — **Scorers:** McCormack, Routledge. **Booked:** Bothroyd
30th	● Swansea.............................a	D 2–2	**Att:** 18,053. **Ref:** M Atkinson — **Scorers:** Ledley, McCormack. **Booked:** R. Johnson, McPhail, Routledge

December

6th	● Preston ....h	W 2–0	**Att:** 16,560. **Ref:** A D'Urso — **Scorers:** Chopra, R. Johnson
9th	● Burnley ....a	D 2–2	**Att:** 11,230. **Ref:** C Webster — **Scorers:** Bothroyd, Routledge. **Booked:** Routledge
13th	● Ipswich ....a	W 1–2	**Att:** 19,665. **Ref:** A Woolmer — **Scorers:** Bothroyd, Gyepes
20th	● Sheff Wed ....h	W 2–0	**Att:** 17,600. **Ref:** K Friend — **Scorers:** Chopra, R. Johnson
26th	● Reading ....a	D 1–1	**Att:** 22,770. **Ref:** A Hall — **Scorers:** Chopra. **Booked:** Chopra, R. Johnson
28th	● Plymouth............................h	W 1–0	**Att:** 19,145. **Ref:** S Attwell — **Scorers:** Bothroyd. **Booked:** R. Johnson

January

3rd	● Reading ....h	W 2–0	**Att:** 12,448. **Ref:** A Taylor — **Scorers:** Ledley, McCormack
17th	● Birmingham ....a	D 1–1	**Att:** 19,853. **Ref:** M Jones — **Scorers:** Ledley. **Booked:** Rae, Kennedy
25th	● Arsenal ....h	D 0–0	**Att:** 20,079. **Ref:** M Atkinson
28th	● Coventry ....a	W 0–2	**Att:** 14,922. **Ref:** T Bates — **Scorers:** Bothroyd, McCormack
31st	● Nottm Forest......................h	W 2–0	**Att:** 18,779. **Ref:** G Hegley — **Scorers:** Bothroyd, Parry. **Booked:** Gyepes, Bothroyd

February

16th	● Arsenal ....a	L 4–0	**Att:** 57,237. **Ref:** M Halsey
22nd	● Wolverhampton...................a	D 2–2	**Att:** 22,093. **Ref:** D Deadman — **Scorers:** Chopra, R. Johnson
25th	● QPR ....h	D 0–0	**Att:** 17,340. **Ref:** R East
28th	● Southampton ....a	L 1–0	**Att:** 18,526. **Ref:** K Wright

March

3rd	● Barnsley ....h	W 3–1	**Att:** 15,902. **Ref:** P Miller — **Scorers:** Chopra, Ledley, Whittingham. **Booked:** E. Johnson
7th	● Doncaster ....h	W 3–0	**Att:** 17,821. **Ref:** G Hegley — **Scorers:** Bothroyd, Chopra, E. Johnson
10th	● Norwich..............................a	L 2–0	**Att:** 23,706. **Ref:** T Kettle
15th	● Bristol City ....a	D 1–1	**Att:** 17,487. **Ref:** L Mason — **Scorers:** McCormack. **Booked:** Ledley, R. Johnson
18th	● Watford ....h	W 2–1	**Att:** 17,899. **Ref:** A Hall — **Scorers:** Bothroyd, McCormack. **Booked:** McNaughton, McCormack
22nd	● Sheff Utd ....h	L 0–3	**Att:** 17,942. **Ref:** P Taylor — **Booked:** Comminges, Rae. **Dismissed:** Gyepes, McCormack

April

5th	● Swansea.............................h	D 2–2	**Att:** 20,156. **Ref:** M Dean — **Scorers:** Chopra, McCormack
8th	● Derby ....h	W 4–1	**Att:** 18,403. **Ref:** N Swarbrick — **Scorers:** Bothroyd, E. Johnson, R. Johnson, Rae
11th	● Crystal Palace ....a	W 0–2	**Att:** 14,814. **Ref:** R Booth — **Scorers:** McCormack[2]. **Booked:** Bothroyd, Rae
13th	● Burnley ....h	W 3–1	**Att:** 19,379. **Ref:** L Probert — **Scorers:** Bothroyd, McCormack[2]. **Booked:** Kennedy
18th	● Preston ....a	L 6–0	**Att:** 13,692. **Ref:** K Stroud — **Booked:** Rae
21st	● Charlton ....a	D 2–2	**Att:** 19,390. **Ref:** I Williamson — **Scorers:** Burke, Gyepes. **Booked:** Bothroyd, Ledley
25th	● Ipswich ....h	L 0–3	**Att:** 19,129. **Ref:** S Mathieson — **Booked:** McNaughton, Gyepes

May

3rd	● Sheff Wed ....a	L 1–0	**Att:** 30,658. **Ref:** P Crossley — **Booked:** Chopra, McNaughton

● Coca-Cola Championship/Play-Offs ● FA Cup ● Carling Cup

CHAMPIONSHIP GOALKEEPER STATS

Player	Minutes on pitch	Appearances	Match starts	Completed matches	Sub appearances	Subbed off	SAVES BREAKDOWN Saved with feet	Punched	Parried	Tipped over	Fumbled	Tipped round	Caught	Blocked	Clean sheets	Goals conceded	Minutes since conceding	Save %	PENALTIES Saved	Resulting in goals	Opposition miss	Yellow cards	Red cards
Peter Enckelman 1068		12	11	11	1	0	0	4	8	1	0	2	35	0	5	11	191	82.54	0	0	0	0	0
Tom Heaton 2001		21	21	20	0	1	0	7	6	1	0	1	58	0	6	21	24	77.66	0	0	1	0	0
Dimi Konstantopoulos 573		6	6	6	0	0	0	2	3	0	0	1	14	0	2	6	3	62.50	0	1	0	0	0
Stuart Taylor 773		8	8	8	0	0	0	5	3	1	0	4	18	1	1	15	39	68.75	0	2	0	0	0

CHAMPIONSHIP OUTFIELD PLAYER STATS

Player	Minutes on pitch	Appearances	Match starts	Completed matches	Substitute appearances	Subbed off	Goals scored	Minutes since scoring	Assists	Shots on target	Shots off target	Crosses	Defensive clearances	Defensive blocks	Fouls committed	Free-kicks won	Caught offside	Yellow cards	Red cards
Darcy Blake 405		7	4	3	3	1	0	-	1	0	1	5	1	0	2	6	0	0	0
Jay Bothroyd 3013		39	35	18	4	17	12	379	5	52	47	13	20	1	67	90	30	5	0
Chris Burke 848		14	8	3	6	5	1	185	2	6	1	32	0	1	7	25	2	0	0
Tony Capaldi 284		3	3	2	0	1	0	-	0	0	0	2	2	0	2	2	0	0	0
Michael Chopra 1941		27	23	11	4	12	9	433	2	25	22	10	0	0	20	42	33	2	0
Miguel Comminges 1597		30	10	6	20	3	0	-	2	1	18	9	5	12	17	0	4	1
Gabor Gyepes 2422		27	25	23	2	1	2	101	0	5	9	0	46	3	16	23	0	2	1
Eddie Johnson 943		30	5	3	25	2	2	88	4	9	10	1	5	0	10	24	7	1	0
Roger Johnson 4262		45	45	43	0	2	5	508	3	27	24	7	75	16	27	65	3	4	0
Mark Kennedy 3100		36	35	27	1	8	0	-	0	1	5	56	22	11	26	23	1	3	0
Joe Ledley 3689		40	40	35	0	5	4	1155	2	20	22	25	9	4	28	63	3	2	0
Glenn Loovens 94		1	1	1	0	0	0	-	0	0	1	0	3	1	3	0	0	1	0
Ross McCormack...........2917		38	32	21	6	10	21	282	1	45	34	49	2	0	26	49	20	2	1
Kevin McNaughton 3462		39	39	31	0	8	0	-	1	3	5	27	16	5	22	53	0	3	0
Stephen McPhail 2681		32	27	25	5	1	0	-	2	10	11	15	5	3	34	35	3	3	1
Quincy Owusu-Abeyie 177		5	0	0	5	0	0	866	0	2	2	10	0	0	1	4	1	0	0
Paul Parry 3043		40	33	18	7	15	2	1029	5	12	16	88	11	2	21	20	18	0	0
Darren Purse 1919		23	21	19	2	1	0	-	0	4	3	2	35	9	29	26	0	1	1
Gavin Rae 3757		41	39	37	2	2	1	596	3	22	17	8	14	7	59	34	1	6	0
Wayne Routledge 864		9	9	9	0	0	2	1660	5	6	3	34	0	0	10	22	1	2	0
Riccardo Scimeca 184		4	2	1	2	0	0	-	1	0	0	0	0	0	2	2	0	0	0
Steven Thompson 112		4	0	0	3	1	0	28	0	0	1	0	0	0	2	0	0	0	0
Peter Whittingham 2121		33	23	12	10	11	3	576	5	24	15	67	6	2	6	18	2	1	0

SEASON TOTALS

Goals scored	65
Goals conceded	53
Clean sheets	14
Shots on target	279
Shots off target	249
Shots per goal	8.12
Pens awarded	16
Pens scored	12
Pens conceded	4
Offsides	122
Corners	287
Crosses	470
Players used	27
Fouls committed	432
Free-kicks won	650

CARDS RECEIVED

42   5

SEQUENCES

Wins	3
(08/04/09–13/04/09)	
Losses	2
(on two occasions)	
Draws	4
(16/08/08–13/09/08)	
Undefeated	13
(25/11/08–25/02/09)	
Without win	4
(on two occasions)	
Undefeated home	10
(15/11/08–18/03/09)	
Undefeated away	8
(09/08/08–25/10/08)	
Without scoring	2
(on three occasions)	
Without conceding	3
(30/08/08–16/09/08)	
Scoring	14
(15/11/08–22/02/09)	
Conceding	6
(on two occasions)	

League position at the end of each week

League position at the end of:
August 12, September 7, October 3, November 6, December 4, January 6, February 6, March 6, April 5, May 7

SEASON INFORMATION

Highest position: 4
Lowest position: 13
Average goals scored per game: 1.41
Average goals conceded per game: 1.15

MATCH RECORDS

Goals scored per match

		W	D	L	Pts
Failed to score	10	0	3	7	3
Scored 1 goal	12	3	6	3	15
Scored 2 goals	20	12	8	0	44
Scored 3 goals	3	3	0	0	9
Scored 4+ goals	1	1	0	0	3

Goals conceded per match

		W	D	L	Pts
Clean sheet	14	11	3	0	36
Conceded 1 goal	17	8	6	3	30
Conceded 2 goals	12	0	8	4	8
Conceded 3 goals	2	0	0	2	0
Conceded 4+ goals	1	0	0	1	0

QUICK-FIRE GOALS

From the start of a match
Ross McCormack
(v Norwich) 2:12

By a substitute after coming on
Eddie Johnson
(v Derby) 14:07

LAST-GASP GOALS

From the start of a match
Ross McCormack
(v Watford) 96:04

By a substitute after coming on
Michael Chopra
(v Preston) 39:16

GOAL DETAILS

How the goals were struck

SCORED		CONCEDED
37	Right foot	33
23	Left foot	10
5	Headers	9
0	Others	1

How the goals were struck

SCORED		CONCEDED
35	Open play	36
7	Cross	5
5	Corner	5
12	Penalties	3
2	Direct from free-kick	0
4	Free-kick	1
0	Own goals	3

Distance from goal

SCORED		CONCEDED
14	6yds	21
48	18yds	28
3	18+yds	4

GOALS SCORED/CONCEDED PER FIVE-MINUTE INTERVALS

Goals For	2	3	2	4	1	3	4	0	5	4	4	1	6	2	3	2	6	13
Goals Against	3	2	4	3	2	1	2	2	5	3	3	0	2	1	3	4	3	10
Mins	5	10	15	20	25	30	35	40	45	50	55	60	65	70	75	80	85	90

CHARLTON ATHLETIC

CLUB SUMMARY

FORMED	1905
MANAGER	Phil Parkinson
GROUND	The Valley
CAPACITY	27,111
NICKNAME	The Addicks
WEBSITE	www.cafc.co.uk

The New Football Pools PLAYER OF THE SEASON — Nicky Bailey

OVERALL

P	W	D	L	F	A	GD
50	9	16	25	55	78	-23

COCA-COLA CHAMPIONSHIP

Pos	P	W	D	L	F	A	GD	Pts
24	46	8	15	23	52	74	-22	39

HOME

Pos	P	W	D	L	F	A	GD	Pts
22	23	6	8	9	33	38	-5	26

AWAY

Pos	P	W	D	L	F	A	GD	Pts
24	23	2	7	14	19	36	-17	13

CUP PROGRESS DETAILS

Competition	Round reached	Knocked out by
FA Cup	R4	Sheff Utd
Carling Cup	R1	Yeovil

BIGGEST WIN (ALL COMPS)
4–2 on two occasions

BIGGEST DEFEAT (ALL COMPS)
22/11/08 2–5 v Sheffield United **FLC**

THE PLAYER WITH THE MOST

Shots on target
Nick Bailey 34
Shots off target
Hameur Bouazza 40
Shots without scoring
Lloyd Sam 27
Assists
Lloyd Sam 9
Offsides
Deon Burton 28
Fouls
Mark Hudson 58
Fouls without a card
Matt Holland 18
Free-kicks won
Nick Bailey 64
Defensive clearances
Mark Hudson 83

actim INDEX for the 2008/09 Coca-Cola Championship Season

Rank	Player	Pts
20	Nick Bailey	.545
78	Mark Hudson	.409
200	Kelly Youga	.282
202	Danny Butterfield	.281
239	Lloyd Sam	.249

ATTENDANCE RECORD

High	Low	Average
24,553	19,215	20,894
v Nottm Forest (10/01/2009)	v Preston (21/03/2009)	

Charlton's players come to terms with relegation

CHARLTON continued their dramatic fall from grace as they tumbled into Coca-Cola League One following a dreadful 2008/09 season.

When Alan Pardew took over in 2007, the Addicks were still in with a fighting chance of staying in the top flight. When he left, just under two years later, they were on their way to the third tier. Where a couple of years ago, Manchester United and Arsenal were visitors to The Valley, next season Yeovil and Brentford will provide the opposition.

At the start of the campaign, Pardew was confident of a play-off push. With little money to spend, the Addicks boss had decided to let top-scorer Chris Iwelumo move to Wolves in order to fund his rebuilding. But while the Scotland international's goals helped fire Wolves to the title, Charlton hit reverse.

How different the story could have been had Dubai-based Zabeel Investments completed their proposed takeover in October. The promise of a mega-cash windfall saw Pardew admit he was 'picking his dream team'. But Zabeel pulled out, blaming the credit crunch and, six weeks later, following the 5–2 home defeat by Sheffield United which left them in the drop zone, Pardew was gone.

His assistant, Phil Parkinson, took over but could not stop the rot. The eight-game winless run which did for Pardew eventually became a club-record 18 matches without a victory. Parkinson was still given the job on a permanent basis, but the club's reliance on loanees, who came and went with varying degrees of success, meant he could never find a settled side – the Addicks used a total of 39 players all season.

The winless streak finally came to an end with the visit of London rivals Crystal Palace at the end of January, Matt Spring providing a fleeting highlight in a dismal campaign with the only goal of the match. But relegation, which looked a formality from the turn of the year, was confirmed with a 2–2 draw at home to Blackpool. Not for the first time during the 2008/09 season they got in front in a game but just could not stay ahead.

One of their scorers on that afternoon, exciting midfielder Jonjo Shelvey, at least offers a glimmer of hope. If the Addicks can keep the Barclays Premier League vultures at bay, the 17-year-old provides their best chance of emulating Leicester by bouncing straight back.

> **Phil Parkinson took over, but could not stop the rot**

August

9th	● Swansea ....h	W 2–0	**Att:** 21,675. **Ref:** R Beeby — **Scorers:** Gray, Hudson
12th	● Yeovil ....h	L 0–1	**Att:** 6,239. **Ref:** P Miller
16th	● Watford ....a	L 1–0	**Att:** 14,413. **Ref:** I Williamson — **Dismissed:** Youga
23rd	● Reading ....h	W 4–2	**Att:** 20,020. **Ref:** L Mason — **Scorers:** Bouazza, Gray, Holland, Varney. **Booked:** Bouazza
30th	● Preston ....a	L 2–1	**Att:** 12,089. **Ref:** C Oliver — **Scorers:** Gray. **Booked:** Bailey, Ambrose

September

13th	● Wolverhampton ....h	L 1–3	**Att:** 21,547. **Ref:** A Taylor — **Scorers:** Bailey. **Booked:** Sam, Youga, Bailey, Fortune
16th	● Doncaster ....a	W 0–1	**Att:** 10,483. **Ref:** N Miller — **Scorers:** Gray
20th	● Nottm Forest.......................a	D 0–0	**Att:** 18,771. **Ref:** K Evans — **Booked:** Youga, Bailey
27th	● Sheff Wed ....h	L 1–2	**Att:** 20,278. **Ref:** D Whitestone — **Scorers:** Varney. **Booked:** Varney
30th	● Crystal Palace ....a	L 1–0	**Att:** 16,358. **Ref:** M Russell

October

4th	● Ipswich ....h	W 2–1	**Att:** 20,643. **Ref:** G Hegley — **Scorers:** Bailey, Volz OG. **Booked:** Bouazza, Gray
18th	● Cardiff ....a	L 2–0	**Att:** 17,310. **Ref:** K Friend — **Booked:** Hudson, Bouazza. **Dismissed:** Semedo, Hudson
21st	● Bristol City ....a	L 0–2	**Att:** 21,207. **Ref:** C Penton
25th	● Burnley ....h	D 1–1	**Att:** 21,884. **Ref:** R Shoebridge — **Scorers:** Todorov. **Booked:** Basey
28th	● Ipswich ....a	D 1–1	**Att:** 20,352. **Ref:** K Wright — **Scorers:** Bailey. **Booked:** Youga, Cranie

November

1st	● Barnsley ....h	L 1–3	**Att:** 21,527. **Ref:** N Swarbrick — **Scorers:** Hudson. **Booked:** Varney
8th	● Plymouth............................a	D 2–2	**Att:** 10,716. **Ref:** A Hall — **Scorers:** Gray, Youga. **Booked:** Youga, Bailey, Hudson
15th	● Birmingham ....a	L 3–2	**Att:** 20,071. **Ref:** K Hill — **Scorers:** Bouazza, Gray. **Booked:** Sam, Hudson
22nd	● Sheff Utd ....h	L 2–5	**Att:** 20,328. **Ref:** S Tanner — **Scorers:** Bouazza, Primus. **Booked:** Semedo
25th	● QPR ....a	L 2–1	**Att:** 12,286. **Ref:** K Stroud — **Scorers:** Racon. **Booked:** Hudson
29th	● Southampton ....h	D 0–0	**Att:** 20,831. **Ref:** S Mathieson — **Booked:** McEveley

December

6th	● Blackpool ....a	L 2–0	**Att:** 6,648. **Ref:** M Jones
9th	● Coventry ....h	L 1–2	**Att:** 20,427. **Ref:** D Whitestone — **Scorers:** Burton. **Booked:** Bouazza, Fortune, Cranie
15th	● Derby ....h	D 2–2	**Att:** 20,989. **Ref:** A D'Urso — **Scorers:** Gray, Waghorn
20th	● Norwich..............................a	L 1–0	**Att:** 23,827. **Ref:** M Haywood — **Booked:** Elliot, Burton
26th	● QPR ....h	D 2–2	**Att:** 21,023. **Ref:** P Taylor — **Scorers:** Bailey[2]. **Booked:** McEveley, Cranie, Semedo
28th	● Sheff Utd ....a	L 3–1	**Att:** 24,717. **Ref:** C Webster — **Scorers:** Bouazza. **Booked:** Burton, Bailey, Hudson, Cranie, McEveley

January

3rd	● Norwich..............................h	D 1–1	**Att:** 12,615. **Ref:** S Tanner — **Scorers:** Shelvey
10th	● Nottm Forest.......................h	L 0–2	**Att:** 24,553. **Ref:** A Woolmer — **Booked:** Murty
13th	● Norwich..............................a	W 0–1	**Att:** 13,997. **Ref:** C Oliver — **Booked:** Ambrose
17th	● Sheff Wed ....a	L 4–1	**Att:** 28,766. **Ref:** D Deadman — **Scorers:** Spring. **Booked:** Spring, Randolph
24th	● Sheff Utd ....a	L 2–1	**Att:** 15,957. **Ref:** T Bates — **Scorers:** Dickson. **Booked:** Dickson
27th	● Crystal Palace ....h	W 1–0	**Att:** 20,627. **Ref:** S Attwell — **Scorers:** Spring. **Booked:** Youga, Dickson
31st	● Burnley ....a	L 2–1	**Att:** 14,404. **Ref:** R Beeby — **Scorers:** Bailey. **Booked:** Kandol

February

3rd	● Bristol City ....a	L 2–1	**Att:** 15,304. **Ref:** K Friend — **Scorers:** Soares. **Booked:** Racon, Spring, Elliot
14th	● Plymouth............................h	W 2–0	**Att:** 21,876. **Ref:** T Kettle — **Scorers:** Bailey, Racon. **Booked:** Dickson, Soares, Burton
21st	● Barnsley ....a	D 0–0	**Att:** 11,668. **Ref:** M Oliver
28th	● Swansea ....a	D 1–1	**Att:** 15,053. **Ref:** K Stroud — **Scorers:** Bailey. **Booked:** Murty, Shelvey, Spring, Bailey, Dickson

March

3rd	● Doncaster ....h	L 1–2	**Att:** 20,815. **Ref:** R Styles — **Scorers:** Bailey. **Booked:** Racon, Ambrose
7th	● Watford ....h	L 2–3	**Att:** 20,052. **Ref:** A Penn — **Scorers:** Kandol[2]
10th	● Reading ....a	D 2–2	**Att:** 17,875. **Ref:** A Taylor — **Scorers:** Bailey, Hudson. **Booked:** Kandol
14th	● Wolverhampton ....a	L 2–1	**Att:** 24,319. **Ref:** G Laws — **Scorers:** Zhi
21st	● Preston ....h	D 0–0	**Att:** 19,215. **Ref:** D Deadman

April

4th	● Southampton ....a	W 2–3	**Att:** 27,228. **Ref:** J Moss — **Scorers:** Bailey, Racon, Shelvey. **Booked:** Hudson, Kandol, Shelvey, Elliot
11th	● Birmingham ....h	D 0–0	**Att:** 20,022. **Ref:** L Probert — **Booked:** Bailey
13th	● Coventry ....a	D 0–0	**Att:** 16,121. **Ref:** C Boyeson — **Booked:** Sam
18th	● Blackpool ....h	D 2–2	**Att:** 19,615. **Ref:** M Russell — **Scorers:** Burton, Shelvey. **Booked:** Hudson, Youga
21st	● Cardiff ....h	D 2–2	**Att:** 19,390. **Ref:** I Williamson — **Scorers:** Bailey, Shelvey. **Booked:** Butterfield, Zhi, Bailey
25th	● Derby ....a	L 1–0	**Att:** 31,541. **Ref:** F Graham — **Booked:** Bailey

May

3rd	● Norwich..............................h	W 4–2	**Att:** 22,020. **Ref:** R Booth — **Scorers:** Bailey, Burton[3]. **Booked:** Shelvey, Youga.

● Coca-Cola Championship/Play-Offs ● FA Cup ● Carling Cup

CHARLTON ATHLETIC

CHAMPIONSHIP GOALKEEPER STATS

Player	Minutes on pitch	Appearances	Match starts	Completed matches	Sub appearances	Subbed off	SAVES BREAKDOWN Saved with feet	Punched	Parried	Tipped over	Fumbled	Tipped round	Caught	Blocked	Clean sheets	Goals conceded	Minutes since conceding	Save %	PENALTIES Saved	Resulting in goals	Opposition miss	Yellow cards	Red cards
Robert Elliot	2215	23	23	23	0	0	0	12	14	2	0	5	80	0	6	33	35	77.55	1	4	0	3	0
Darren Randolph	96	1	1	1	0	0	0	1	3	0	0	0	8	0	0	4	0	76.47	0	1	0	1	0
Nicky Weaver	2105	22	22	22	0	0	4	12	23	2	0	5	66	0	4	37	44	75.33	1	2	1	0	0

CHAMPIONSHIP OUTFIELD PLAYER STATS

Player	Minutes on pitch	Appearances	Match starts	Completed matches	Substitute appearances	Subbed off	Goals scored	Minutes since scoring	Assists	Shots on target	Shots off target	Crosses	Defensive clearances	Defensive blocks	Fouls committed	Free-kicks won	Caught offside	Yellow cards	Red cards
Darren Ambrose	1004	21	9	5	12	4	0	-	0	13	11	22	2	1	8	11	1	2	0
Nick Bailey	4048	43	43	42	0	1	13	92	7	34	26	53	34	12	47	64	1	9	0
Grant Basey	1117	19	10	9	9	1	0	-	3	3	4	31	12	3	6	16	1	1	0
Hameur Bouazza	2107	25	22	19	3	3	4	199	2	24	40	47	2	1	26	20	20	4	0
Deon Burton	1161	20	12	6	8	6	5	44	0	15	10	5	8	0	31	17	28	3	0
Danny Butterfield	1135	12	12	11	0	1	0	1617	0	2	3	15	4	7	10	6	0	1	0
Martin Cranie	1661	19	19	13	0	6	0	-	0	1	1	17	12	7	19	10	0	4	0
Chris Dickson	849	21	6	3	15	3	0	-	0	13	8	5	1	0	20	14	14	3	0
Jonathan Fortune	1561	17	17	15	0	2	0	-	1	0	0	8	19	9	13	14	0	2	0
Keith Gillespie	338	6	4	1	2	3	0	-	0	4	1	19	7	0	0	6	0	0	0
Andy Gray	1954	27	21	13	6	8	7	482	0	17	7	0	7	1	45	43	21	1	0
Matt Holland	2107	34	18	15	16	3	1	2007	1	6	11	8	10	8	18	23	0	0	0
Mark Hudson	4086	43	43	41	0	1	3	861	0	16	14	1	83	28	58	30	4	7	1
Tresor Kandol	1014	13	10	8	3	2	2	668	0	15	9	3	5	0	36	12	23	3	0
James McEveley	493	6	6	5	0	1	0	-	0	1	0	9	6	1	7	2	1	3	0
Izale McLeod	141	2	2	1	0	1	0	-	0	2	1	2	0	0	5	3	0	0	0
Yassin Moutaouakil	854	11	9	6	2	3	0	-	0	1	1	22	4	4	2	11	0	0	0
Graeme Murty	681	8	8	5	0	2	0	-	0	1	1	6	6	2	5	13	0	1	0
Linvoy Primus	878	10	10	8	0	2	1	173	0	3	4	1	8	6	7	7	0	0	0
Therry Racon	1750	19	19	16	0	3	3	597	1	11	8	5	2	3	30	30	0	2	0
Lloyd Sam	2640	38	28	9	10	19	0	-	9	8	19	51	3	1	37	38	6	3	0
Jose Vitor Semedo	1138	18	12	4	6	7	0	-	2	1	3	6	4	4	15	25	0	2	1
Jonjo Shelvey	1182	16	14	8	2	6	3	245	1	18	26	24	2	0	15	3	3	3	0
Tom Soares	853	11	10	5	1	5	1	562	2	6	2	6	3	0	12	11	1	1	0
Chris Solly	87	1	0	0	1	0	0	-	0	0	0	0	0	0	0	0	0	0	0
Matthew Spring	1050	13	12	7	1	5	2	876	1	6	8	15	2	1	15	9	0	3	0
Jerome Thomas	78	1	1	0	0	1	0	-	0	0	0	0	0	0	0	2	4	1	0
Svetoslav Todorov	445	13	2	0	11	2	1	274	0	3	3	0	1	0	9	3	2	0	0
Tamer Tuna	30	2	0	0	2	0	0	-	0	0	0	0	0	0	0	0	0	0	0
Luke Varney	1536	18	16	15	2	1	2	1037	0	17	17	7	3	1	20	28	23	2	0
Martyn Waghorn	367	7	4	0	3	4	1	197	0	6	2	3	0	0	2	2	3	0	0
Scott Wagstaff	36	2	0	0	2	0	0	-	0	1	0	0	0	0	0	0	0	0	0
Darren Ward	1442	16	16	14	0	2	0	1594	0	2	4	0	21	9	16	9	1	0	0
Josh Wright	156	2	2	0	0	2	0	-	0	1	3	2	1	0	2	3	0	0	0
Kelly Youga	2972	33	32	27	1	4	1	1851	0	5	4	20	33	7	35	53	0	7	1
Zheng Zhi	1019	13	11	6	2	5	1	730	1	10	8	5	4	3	15	15	5	1	0

SEASON TOTALS

Goals scored	52
Goals conceded	74
Clean sheets	10
Shots on target	266
Shots off target	259
Shots per goal	10.10
Pens awarded	6
Pens scored	4
Pens conceded	10
Offsides	162
Corners	216
Crosses	418
Players used	39
Fouls committed	585
Free-kicks won	570

CARDS RECEIVED

73 3

SEQUENCES

Wins	(−)
Losses	3
(15/11/08–25/11/08)	
Draws	4
(11/04/09–21/04/09)	
Undefeated	6
(21/03/09–21/04/09)	
Without win	18
(18/10/08–17/01/09)	
Undefeated home	2
(09/08/08–23/08/08)	
Undefeated away	3
(21/02/09–10/03/09)	
Without scoring	2
(on three occasions)	
Without conceding	2
(on three occasions)	
Scoring	7
(25/10/08–25/11/08)	
Conceding	12
(27/09/08–25/11/08)	

SEASON INFORMATION

Highest position: 8
Lowest position: 24
Average goals scored per game: 1.13
Average goals conceded per game: 1.61

League position at the end of each week

League position at the end of

August 11 · September 17 · October 20 · November 22 · December 24 · January 24 · February 24 · March 24 · April 24 · May 24

MATCH RECORDS

Goals scored per match

		W	D	L	Pts
Failed to score	14	0	6	8	6
Scored 1 goal	17	2	3	12	9
Scored 2 goals	12	3	6	3	15
Scored 3 goals	1	1	0	0	3
Scored 4+ goals	2	2	0	0	6

Goals conceded per match

		W	D	L	Pts
Clean sheet	10	4	6	0	18
Conceded 1 goal	8	1	3	4	6
Conceded 2 goals	21	3	6	12	15
Conceded 3 goals	5	0	0	5	0
Conceded 4+ goals	2	0	0	2	0

QUICK-FIRE GOALS

From the start of a match
Nick Bailey
(v Wolverhampton) 2:06

By a substitute after coming on
Svetoslav Todorov
(v Burnley) 30:10

LAST-GASP GOALS

From the start of a match
Andy Gray
(v Plymouth) 91:13

By a substitute after coming on
Svetoslav Todorov
(v Burnley) 30:10

GOAL DETAILS

How the goals were struck

SCORED		CONCEDED
25	Right foot	41
11	Left foot	19
15	Headers	14
1	Others	0

How the goals were struck

SCORED		CONCEDED
31	Open play	43
5	Cross	3
5	Corner	9
4	Penalties	7
1	Direct from free-kick	5
5	Free-kick	5
1	Own goals	2

Distance from goal

SCORED		CONCEDED
19	6yds	27
24	18yds	38
9	18+yds	9

GOALS SCORED/CONCEDED PER FIVE-MINUTE INTERVALS

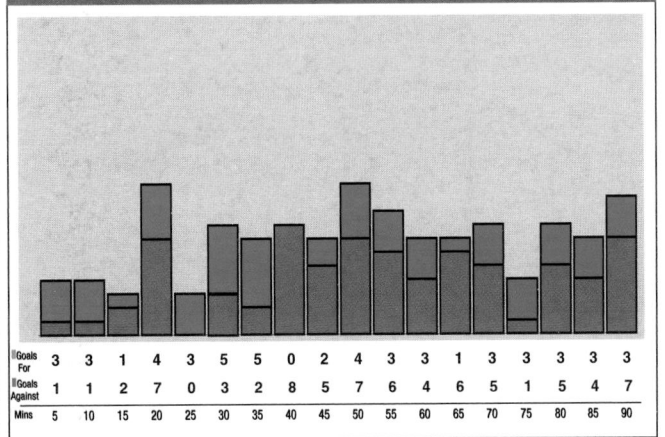

Goals For	3	3	1	4	3	5	5	0	2	4	3	3	1	3	3	3	3	3
Goals Against	1	1	2	7	0	3	2	8	5	7	6	4	6	5	1	5	4	7
Mins	5	10	15	20	25	30	35	40	45	50	55	60	65	70	75	80	85	90

COVENTRY CITY

CLUB SUMMARY

FORMED	1883
MANAGER	Chris Coleman
GROUND	Ricoh Arena
CAPACITY	32,609
NICKNAME	The Sky Blues
WEBSITE	www.ccfc.co.uk

The New **Football Pools** PLAYER OF THE SEASON — Aron Gunnarsson

OVERALL

P	W	D	L	F	A	GD
53	17	16	20	58	66	-8

COCA-COLA CHAMPIONSHIP

Pos	P	W	D	L	F	A	GD	Pts
17	46	13	15	18	47	58	-11	54

HOME

Pos	P	W	D	L	F	A	GD	Pts
17	23	8	8	7	26	26	0	32

AWAY

Pos	P	W	D	L	F	A	GD	Pts
16	23	5	7	11	21	32	-11	22

CUP PROGRESS DETAILS

Competition	Round reached	Knocked out by
FA Cup	QF	Chelsea
Carling Cup	R2	Newcastle

BIGGEST WIN (ALL COMPS)

04/10/08 4–1 v Southampton **FLC**

BIGGEST DEFEAT (ALL COMPS)

11/04/09 0–4 v Plymouth **FLC**

THE PLAYER WITH THE MOST

Shots on target	
Freddy Eastwood	45
Shots off target	
Freddy Eastwood	33
Shots without scoring	
Isaac Osbourne, Ben Turner	8
Assists	
Daniel Fox	5
Offsides	
Clinton Morrison	47
Fouls	
Aron Gunnarsson	70
Fouls without a card	
David Bell	9
Free-kicks won	
Aron Gunnarsson	74
Defensive clearances	
Elliott Ward	94

actim INDEX for the 2008/09 Coca-Cola Championship Season

Rank	Player	Pts
27	Keiren Westwood	517
43	Daniel Fox	476
74	Clinton Morrison	416
98	Elliott Ward	381
103	Scott Dann	371

ATTENDANCE RECORD

High	Low	Average
22,637	14,621	17,408
v Birmingham (21/02/2009)	v Burnley (21/10/2008)	

A masked Leon Best scored the winner in the FA Cup fifth-round tie against Blackburn

CHRIS COLEMAN'S first full season in charge brought improvement for Coventry.

Coleman took over in February 2008, and the Sky Blues only stayed in the Coca-Cola Championship by the skin of their teeth at the end of that season. City easily avoided a relegation battle this time around, finishing closer to mid-table than the bottom three.

Coleman's progress has been steady and he may have achieved a mid-table finish had it not been for a glut of injuries towards the end of the campaign.

Scott Dann, Stephen Wright, Jordan Henderson, David Bell and Leon McKenzie all had their seasons prematurely ended, while James McPake, Kevin Thornton and Leon Best – who wore a mask to protect a broken cheekbone – struggled for many weeks with niggling problems. It exposed the lack of strength in depth within the squad, and Coleman has received the backing of chairman Ray Ranson to address the problem in the summer.

But much of what City could achieve next time

around will depend on the players they can keep at the club, not who they bring in. Goalkeeper Keiren Westwood has attracted the interest of Barclays Premier League clubs, while Coventry rejected a bid from Newcastle for highly-rated left-back Dan Fox in January. Both players were included in the PFA Championship Team of the Season – the first time the Sky Blues have featured in the end-of-season vote.

Ranson will now expect further progress, but there were signs in 2008/09 that City could live with the best in the division. Champions Wolves and promoted Birmingham were beaten at the Ricoh Arena, while top-six finishers Reading and Preston also failed to win at the Sky Blues' home.

City took Newcastle to extra-time in the League Cup in August before losing 3–2, and knocked Blackburn out of the FA Cup in February to reach the quarter-final stage.

> **City easily avoided a relegation battle this time around**

RESULTS 2008/09

August
9th	● Norwich.....................h	W 2–0	**Att:** 22,607. **Ref:** C Webster — **Scorers:** McKenzie, Ward. **Booked:** McKenzie
13th	● Aldershot ....h	W 3–1	**Att:** 9,293. **Ref:** J Singh — **Scorers:** Morrison, Simpson[2]. **Booked:** Gunnarsson, Wright
16th	● Barnsley ....a	W 1–2	**Att:** 12,987. **Ref:** S Bratt — **Scorers:** Eastwood, Gray. **Booked:** Eastwood, Morrison, McKenzie
23rd	● Bristol City ....h	L 0–3	**Att:** 17,994. **Ref:** P Dowd — **Booked:** Morrison, Fox, Beuzelin
26th	● Newcastle ....h	L 2–3	**Att:** 19,249. **Ref:** T Bates — **Scorers:** Dann, Morrison. **Booked:** Hall, Fox. (AET)
30th	● Doncaster ....a	L 1–0	**Att:** 11,806. **Ref:** R Shoebridge

September
13th	● Preston ....h	D 0–0	**Att:** 16,544. **Ref:** G Hegley
16th	● Sheff Utd ....a	D 1–1	**Att:** 24,130. **Ref:** D Deadman — **Scorers:** Tabb. **Booked:** Osbourne, Dann, Mifsud
20th	● QPR ....h	W 1–0	**Att:** 16,718. **Ref:** D Whitestone — **Scorers:** Ward. **Booked:** Tabb, Doyle, Ward, Osbourne
27th	● Blackpool ....a	D 1–1	**Att:** 8,462. **Ref:** M Oliver — **Scorers:** Eastwood. **Booked:** Tabb, Fox
30th	● Cardiff ....a	L 2–1	**Att:** 16,312. **Ref:** R East — **Scorers:** Dann. **Booked:** Gunnarsson, McKenzie

October
4th	● Southampton ....h	W 4–1	**Att:** 15,518. **Ref:** M Jones — **Scorers:** Best, McKenzie, Tabb[2]. **Booked:** Best
18th	● Wolverhampton.....................a	L 2–1	**Att:** 25,893. **Ref:** S Bennett — **Scorers:** Mifsud. **Booked:** Doyle, Eastwood, Tabb, Fox, Best
21st	● Burnley ....h	L 1–3	**Att:** 14,621. **Ref:** M Thorpe — **Scorers:** Ward. **Booked:** Osbourne, Doyle, Simpson, Beuzelin
25th	● Derby ....a	D 1–1	**Att:** 18,430. **Ref:** I Williamson — **Scorers:** Morrison. **Booked:** Gunnarsson, Dann
28th	● Southampton ....a	D 1–1	**Att:** 14,226. **Ref:** F Graham — **Scorers:** Morrison

November
3rd	● Birmingham ....a	W 0–1	**Att:** 17,215. **Ref:** T Bates — **Scorers:** Morrison. **Booked:** Dann, Tabb
8th	● Crystal Palace ....h	L 0–2	**Att:** 16,883. **Ref:** C Oliver — **Booked:** Gunnarsson
15th	● Plymouth.....................h	L 0–1	**Att:** 18,528. **Ref:** N Miller — **Booked:** Gunnarsson, Osbourne, Dann
22nd	● Sheff Wed ....h	W 0–1	**Att:** 16,119. **Ref:** K Friend — **Scorers:** Morrison. **Booked:** Ward, Eastwood, Wright
25th	● Swansea.....................h	D 1–1	**Att:** 15,149. **Ref:** M Haywood — **Scorers:** Fox. **Booked:** Fox, Beuzelin

December
1st	● Reading ....a	L 3–1	**Att:** 16,803. **Ref:** K Wright — **Scorers:** Fox. **Booked:** Gunnarsson
6th	● Nottm Forest.....................h	D 2–2	**Att:** 17,542. **Ref:** N Swarbrick — **Scorers:** Morrison, Ward. **Booked:** Beuzelin, Doyle
9th	● Charlton ....a	W 1–2	**Att:** 20,427. **Ref:** D Whitestone — **Scorers:** Morrison, Simpson. **Booked:** Fox, Simpson
13th	● Watford ....a	L 2–1	**Att:** 14,075. **Ref:** J Moss — **Scorers:** Morrison
20th	● Ipswich ....h	D 2–2	**Att:** 15,598. **Ref:** R Styles — **Scorers:** Eastwood, Morrison
26th	● Swansea.....................a	D 0–0	**Att:** 17,603. **Ref:** S Tanner — **Booked:** Wright, Gunnarsson, Westwood, Beuzelin
28th	● Sheff Wed.....................h	W 2–0	**Att:** 19,602. **Ref:** G Laws — **Scorers:** Morrison, Simpson

January
3rd	● Kidderminster ....h	W 2–0	**Att:** 13,652. **Ref:** M Haywood — **Scorers:** Best, McKenzie
10th	● QPR ....a	D 1–1	**Att:** 13,330. **Ref:** K Stroud — **Scorers:** Fox. **Booked:** Wright, Fox, Gunnarsson, Westwood. **Dismissed:** Wright
17th	● Blackpool ....h	W 2–1	**Att:** 15,551. **Ref:** C Pawson — **Scorers:** Beuzelin, Mifsud. **Booked:** Gunnarsson
24th	● Torquay ....a	W 0–1	**Att:** 6,018. **Ref:** K Friend — **Scorers:** Ward. **Booked:** Gunnarsson
28th	● Cardiff ....h	L 0–2	**Att:** 14,922. **Ref:** T Bates
31st	● Derby ....a	L 2–1	**Att:** 29,710. **Ref:** M Jones — **Scorers:** Doyle

February
7th	● Wolverhampton.....................h	W 2–1	**Att:** 21,167. **Ref:** M Oliver — **Scorers:** Doyle, McKenzie. **Booked:** Wright
14th	● Blackburn ....a	D 2–2	**Att:** 15,053. **Ref:** S Tanner — **Scorers:** Doyle, Gunnarsson. **Booked:** Beuzelin, Best, Eastwood
17th	● Burnley ....a	D 1–1	**Att:** 14,595. **Ref:** D Foster — **Scorers:** Best. **Booked:** Dann
21st	● Birmingham ....h	W 1–0	**Att:** 22,637. **Ref:** C Oliver — **Scorers:** Dann. **Booked:** Morrison
24th	● Blackburn ....h	W 1–0	**Att:** 22,793. **Ref:** M Riley — **Scorers:** Best. **Booked:** Gunnarsson, Ward, Westwood
28th	● Norwich.....................a	W 1–2	**Att:** 24,450. **Ref:** P Taylor — **Scorers:** Fox, Henderson. **Booked:** Dann

March
4th	● Sheff Utd ....h	L 1–2	**Att:** 16,300. **Ref:** K Wright — **Scorers:** Dann. **Booked:** Westwood, Gunnarsson, Dann
7th	● Chelsea ....h	L 0–2	**Att:** 31,407. **Ref:** S Bennett — **Booked:** Beuzelin
10th	● Bristol City ....a	L 2–0	**Att:** 15,706. **Ref:** P Crossley — **Booked:** Morrison, McPake
14th	● Preston ....a	L 2–1	**Att:** 13,251. **Ref:** K Friend — **Scorers:** Morrison. **Booked:** Henderson, Beuzelin
21st	● Doncaster ....h	W 1–0	**Att:** 18,498. **Ref:** R Beeby — **Scorers:** Bell. **Booked:** Henderson, Wright, Morrison

April
4th	● Reading ....h	D 0–0	**Att:** 17,218. **Ref:** T Kettle — **Booked:** Turner, Wright, Fox, Morrison
7th	● Crystal Palace ....a	D 1–1	**Att:** 12,898. **Ref:** F Graham — **Scorers:** Gunnarsson. **Booked:** Osbourne
11th	● Plymouth.....................a	L 4–0	**Att:** 12,568. **Ref:** C Oliver — **Booked:** Dann, Doyle, Morrison, Fox
13th	● Charlton ....h	D 0–0	**Att:** 16,121. **Ref:** C Boyeson
18th	● Nottm Forest.....................a	L 1–0	**Att:** 27,856. **Ref:** S Tanner — **Booked:** Doyle, Osbourne
21st	● Barnsley ....h	D 1–1	**Att:** 15,035. **Ref:** S Cook — **Scorers:** Ward. **Booked:** Simpson, Ward
25th	● Watford ....h	L 2–3	**Att:** 17,195. **Ref:** R Booth — **Scorers:** Eastwood, Simpson. **Booked:** Hall, Turner. **Dismissed:** Fox

May
3rd	● Ipswich ....a	L 2–1	**Att:** 27,225. **Ref:** G Laws — **Scorers:** Morrison. **Booked:** Morrison

● Coca-Cola Championship/Play-Offs ● FA Cup ● Carling Cup

COVENTRY CITY

CHAMPIONSHIP GOALKEEPER STATS

Player	Minutes on pitch	Appearances	Match starts	Completed matches	Sub appearances	Subbed off	SAVES BREAKDOWN								Clean sheets	Goals conceded	Minutes since conceding	Save %	PENALTIES			Yellow cards	Red cards
							Saved with feet	Punched	Parried	Tipped over	Fumbled	Tipped round	Caught	Blocked					Saved	Resulting in goals	Opposition miss		
Andy Marshall	121	2	0	0	2	0	0	1	0	0	0	1	5	0	0	7	-	53.33	0	0	0	0	0
Keiren Westwood	4287	46	46	44	0	2	0	14	31	12	0	8	211	1	11	51	73	85.22	2	3	0	3	0

CHAMPIONSHIP OUTFIELD PLAYER STATS

Player	Minutes on pitch	Appearances	Match starts	Completed matches	Substitute appearances	Subbed off	Goals scored	Minutes since scoring	Assists	Shots on target	Shots off target	Crosses	Defensive clearances	Defensive blocks	Fouls committed	Free-kicks won	Caught offside	Yellow cards	Red cards
David Bell	780	9	8	6	1	2	1	75	1	5	6	21	0	0	9	6	1	0	0
Leon Best	1535	31	16	3	15	13	2	458	1	14	18	14	1	2	44	28	23	2	0
Guillaume Beuzelin	2735	35	28	21	7	7	1	1209	4	6	13	19	16	3	45	28	0	6	0
Ashley Cain	117	5	0	0	5	0	0	-	0	1	1	8	0	0	3	1	0	0	0
Scott Dann	2896	31	31	29	0	2	3	667	0	10	12	5	89	30	35	23	1	8	0
Michael Doyle	3133	37	34	26	3	8	2	1187	0	21	19	27	7	13	45	26	0	6	0
Freddy Eastwood	3329	46	37	20	9	17	4	185	4	45	33	37	1	2	41	25	27	3	0
Daniel Fox	3659	39	39	36	0	2	5	726	5	25	8	151	30	14	26	23	0	8	1
Jermaine Grandison	69	2	0	0	2	0	0	-	0	0	0	0	0	0	0	0	0	0	0
Julian Gray	252	3	3	1	0	2	1	108	0	1	1	10	1	0	1	0	0	0	0
Aron Gunnarsson	3525	40	38	34	2	4	1	481	1	14	20	35	18	18	70	74	2	9	0
Marcus Hall	1552	23	15	14	8	1	0	-	1	0	1	21	25	11	6	8	2	1	0
Jordan Henderson	850	10	9	6	1	3	1	501	2	6	6	36	2	2	10	4	2	2	0
Leon McKenzie	1033	19	10	5	9	7	3	57	2	5	11	43	1	0	22	22	17	3	0
James McPake	276	4	3	2	1	1	0	-	0	2	0	0	5	0	8	4	0	1	0
Michael Mifsud	1780	26	19	10	7	9	2	410	1	19	13	32	4	4	14	28	14	1	0
Clinton Morrison	3800	45	40	30	5	10	10	15	4	42	30	42	24	5	54	44	47	8	0
Isaac Osbourne	2008	25	20	17	5	3	0	-	1	4	4	42	33	16	23	19	0	6	0
Lee Sawyer	103	2	1	1	1	0	0	-	0	0	0	0	0	0	0	3	0	0	0
Robbie Simpson	1638	33	14	8	19	6	3	121	1	16	20	31	5	2	22	41	11	3	0
Jay Tabb	1825	22	21	15	1	6	3	1697	1	11	7	24	1	1	15	46	2	4	0
Kevin Thornton	179	4	1	0	3	1	0	-	0	2	0	0	0	0	3	3	1	0	0
Ben Turner	2187	24	22	22	2	0	0	-	0	4	4	8	46	25	29	20	0	2	0
Adam Walker	26	2	0	0	2	0	0	-	0	0	0	0	1	0	0	0	0	0	0
Elliott Ward	3056	33	33	31	0	2	5	145	0	11	12	8	94	33	25	26	2	3	0
Stephen Wright	1509	17	17	14	0	2	0	-	1	0	1	8	30	9	21	18	0	6	1
Curtis Wynter	95	1	1	1	0	0	0	-	0	0	0	2	0	0	0	0	0	0	0

SEASON TOTALS

Goals scored	47
Goals conceded	58
Clean sheets	11
Shots on target	264
Shots off target	240
Shots per goal	10.72
Pens awarded	6
Pens scored	4
Pens conceded	5
Offsides	152
Corners	247
Crosses	625
Players used	29
Fouls committed	570
Free-kicks won	533

CARDS RECEIVED

85 **2**

SEQUENCES

Wins	2
(on two occasions)	
Losses	3
(04/03/09–14/03/09)	
Draws	2
(13/09/08–16/09/08)	
Undefeated	5
(20/12/08–17/01/09)	
Without win	8
(04/04/09–03/05/09)	
Undefeated home	5
(25/11/08–17/01/09)	
Undefeated away	3
(28/10/08–22/11/08)	
Without scoring	3
(on two occasions)	
Without conceding	2
(on two occasions)	
Scoring	10
(16/09/08–03/11/08)	
Conceding	7
(27/09/08–28/10/08)	

SEASON INFORMATION

Highest position: 3
Lowest position: 18
Average goals scored per game: 1.02
Average goals conceded per game: 1.26

League position at the end of each week

League position at the end of: August 13, September 13, October 16, November 16, December 14, January 14, February 14, March 14, April 15, May 17

MATCH RECORDS

Goals scored per match

		W	D	L	Pts
Failed to score	12	0	4	8	4
Scored 1 goal	23	5	9	9	24
Scored 2 goals	10	7	2	1	23
Scored 3 goals	0	0	0	0	0
Scored 4+ goals	1	1	0	0	3

Goals conceded per match

		W	D	L	Pts
Clean sheet	11	7	4	0	25
Conceded 1 goal	18	6	9	3	27
Conceded 2 goals	12	0	2	10	2
Conceded 3 goals	4	0	0	4	0
Conceded 4+ goals	1	0	0	1	0

QUICK-FIRE GOALS

From the start of a match
Clinton Morrison
(v Ipswich) 0:37

By a substitute after coming on
Leon McKenzie
(v Norwich) 16:00

LAST-GASP GOALS

From the start of a match
Elliott Ward (v Barnsley) 93:48

By a substitute after coming on
Clinton Morrison (v Derby) 22:04

GOAL DETAILS

How the goals were struck

SCORED		CONCEDED
26	Right foot	27
14	Left foot	18
7	Headers	13
0	Others	0

How the goals were struck

SCORED		CONCEDED
31	Open play	35
4	Cross	13
3	Corner	1
4	Penalties	3
5	Direct from free-kick	2
0	Free-kick	3
0	Own goals	1

Distance from goal

SCORED		CONCEDED
21	6yds	19
19	18yds	32
7	18+yds	7

GOALS SCORED/CONCEDED PER FIVE-MINUTE INTERVALS

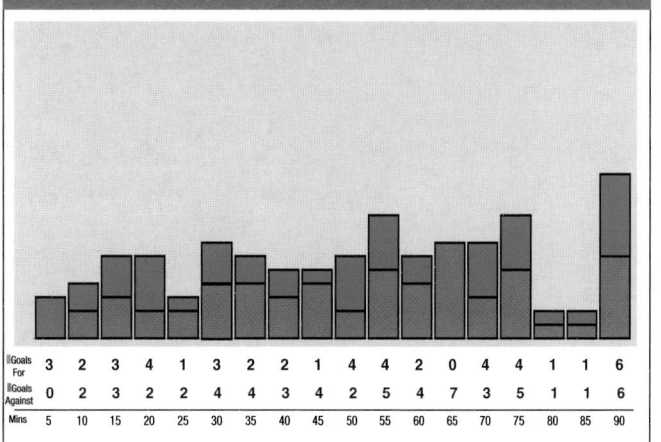

Goals For	3	2	3	4	1	3	2	2	1	4	4	2	0	4	4	1	1	6
Goals Against	0	2	3	2	2	4	4	3	4	2	5	4	7	3	5	1	1	6
Mins	5	10	15	20	25	30	35	40	45	50	55	60	65	70	75	80	85	90

CLUB SUMMARY

FORMED	1905
MANAGER	Neil Warnock
GROUND	Selhurst Park
CAPACITY	26,400
NICKNAME	The Eagles
WEBSITE	www.cpfc.co.uk

The New Football Pools PLAYER OF THE SEASON — Julian Speroni

OVERALL

P	W	D	L	F	A	GD
51	17	13	21	59	65	-6

COCA-COLA CHAMPIONSHIP

Pos	P	W	D	L	F	A	GD	Pts
15	46	15	12	19	52	55	-3	56

HOME

Pos	P	W	D	L	F	A	GD	Pts
12	23	9	8	6	26	19	7	34

AWAY

Pos	P	W	D	L	F	A	GD	Pts
15	23	6	4	13	26	36	-10	22

CUP PROGRESS DETAILS

Competition	Round reached	Knocked out by
FA Cup	R4	Watford
Carling Cup	R2	Leeds

BIGGEST WIN (ALL COMPS)
3–0 on two occasions

BIGGEST DEFEAT (ALL COMPS)
26/08/08 0–4 v Leeds LC2

THE PLAYER WITH THE MOST

Shots on target	
Shefki Kuqi	34
Shots off target	
Paul Ifill	20
Shots without scoring	
Shaun Derry	18
Assists	
Paul Ifill	4
Offsides	
Shefki Kuqi	23
Fouls	
Clint Hill	69
Fouls without a card	
Anthony Stokes	10
Free-kicks won	
Jose Fonte	47
Defensive clearances	
Clint Hill	42

actim INDEX for the 2008/09 Coca-Cola Championship Season

Rank	Player	Pts
34	Julian Speroni	495
79	Jose Fonte	406
86	Clint Hill	398
143	Nick Carle	323
145	Shefki Kuqi	322

ATTENDANCE RECORD

High	Low	Average
22,824	12,847	15,220
v Sheff Utd (03/05/2009)	v Birmingham (24/02/2009)	

NEIL WARNOCK has promised better next season after his Crystal Palace side meandered through the campaign without troubling either end of the table.

'Transitional' was the buzzword at Selhurst Park as the Eagles, who were never in relegation trouble and yet always way below the play-off zone, look to a brighter future.

Warnock is planning major summer surgery to his squad to supplement the talented youngsters who will carry the hopes of Palace fans next term.

Teenage frontmen Victor Moses and Sean Scannell have a full season under their belts, while this year saw the emergence of talented 18-year-old right-back Nathanial Clyne.

Kieron Cadogan, James Comley and Nathanial

Pinney are the next batch of rookies off the production line and have already made their debuts.

Palace's problems during 2008/09 were in front of goal, with £600,000 summer signing Alan Lee finding the net just three times before being farmed out on loan to Norwich. Loanees

'Transitional' was the buzzword at Selhurst Park

Anthony Stokes and Jose Fonte fared no better, scoring just once between them, while Craig Beattie's temporary spell promised much until he was recalled by West Brom.

Palace's top scorer was actually Shefki Kuqi, who hit 10 goals despite Warnock trying all season to sell the high-earning Finland international.

The January sale of midfielder Ben Watson also hit Palace hard. The 23-year-old was frozen out by Warnock after snubbing a new contract, but his recall to the team coincided with their best run of the campaign – five wins from seven games before Christmas.

When, around the same time, Beattie left and star defender Paddy McCarthy was ruled out for four months through injury, any faint hopes of a late play-off push disappeared.

Warnock did at least try to keep the interest levels up by continuing his crusade against what he saw as poor refereeing – even bringing out a laptop computer in one post-match briefing to illustrate how a penalty decision had gone against his side.

Warnock's enthusiasm for the game remains undimmed. So much so that the 60-year-old recently ended speculation he was ready to retire by signing a contract extension until 2011.

Palace were deducted a point after the end of the season due to fielding the ineligible Rui Fonte in the last game of the campaign.

Neil Warnock oversaw his first full season at Palace

RESULTS 2008/09

August
9th	● Watford ....h	D 0–0	**Att:** 15,614. **Ref:** M Jones — **Booked:** Lawrence, Derry
12th	● Hereford ....h	W 2–1	**Att:** 3,094. **Ref:** T Kettle — **Scorers:** Carle, Oster
16th	● Preston ....a	L 2–0	**Att:** 14,225. **Ref:** K Woolmer — **Booked:** Hill, Hills
23rd	● Burnley ....h	D 0–0	**Att:** 14,071. **Ref:** I Williamson — **Booked:** Scowcroft, Derry, McCarthy, Hill, J Fonte
26th	● Leeds ....a	L 4–0	**Att:** 10,765. **Ref:** K Friend
30th	● Reading ....a	L 4–2	**Att:** 20,441. **Ref:** C Penton — **Scorers:** Carle, Soares. **Booked:** Carle

September
13th	● Swansea..................h	W 2–0	**Att:** 14,621. **Ref:** L Mason — **Scorers:** Carle, Watson. **Booked:** Derry
16th	● Wolverhampton..................a	L 2–1	**Att:** 22,200. **Ref:** S Mathieson — **Scorers:** Ifill. **Booked:** Hill, Lawrence
20th	● Plymouth..................h	L 1–2	**Att:** 14,209. **Ref:** N Swarbrick — **Scorers:** McCarthy. **Booked:** J Fonte, Griffit
27th	● Ipswich ....a	D 1–1	**Att:** 19,032. **Ref:** D Deadman — **Scorers:** Moses. **Booked:** Watson, Beattie
30th	● Charlton ....h	W 1–0	**Att:** 16,358. **Ref:** M Russell — **Scorers:** Beattie

October
4th	● Nottm Forest..................a	W 0–2	**Att:** 22,811. **Ref:** R Beeby — **Scorers:** Ifill, Kuqi. **Booked:** Carle, Derry, Watson
18th	● Barnsley ....h	W 3–0	**Att:** 16,494. **Ref:** T Bates — **Scorers:** Kuqi, Watson[2]
21st	● Birmingham ....a	L 1–0	**Att:** 17,706. **Ref:** N Miller — **Booked:** Lawrence
25th	● Blackpool ....a	D 2–2	**Att:** 7,597. **Ref:** A Taylor — **Scorers:** Beattie, Ifill. **Booked:** McCarthy
28th	● Nottm Forest..................h	L 1–2	**Att:** 15,162. **Ref:** A D'Urso — **Scorers:** Kuqi. **Booked:** Derry, McCarthy

November
1st	● Sheff Wed..................h	D 1–1	**Att:** 14,650. **Ref:** K Wright — **Scorers:** Watson. **Booked:** Watson
8th	● Coventry ....a	W 0–2	**Att:** 16,883. **Ref:** C Oliver — **Scorers:** Hill, Watson
15th	● Cardiff ....a	L 2–1	**Att:** 17,478. **Ref:** J Moss — **Scorers:** Scannell. **Dismissed:** Lawrence
22nd	● Bristol City ....h	W 4–2	**Att:** 14,599. **Ref:** G Hegley — **Scorers:** Beattie, J Fonte, Oster, Scannell
25th	● Norwich..................a	W 1–2	**Att:** 24,034. **Ref:** D Whitestone — **Scorers:** Beattie, Oster. **Booked:** Watson, Oster
29th	● QPR ....h	D 0–0	**Att:** 16,411. **Ref:** R Styles — **Booked:** Carle

December
6th	● Derby ....a	W 1–2	**Att:** 27,203. **Ref:** M Oliver — **Scorers:** Kuqi, McCarthy. **Booked:** Speroni
8th	● Southampton ....h	W 3–0	**Att:** 13,799. **Ref:** D Deadman — **Scorers:** Beattie, Ifill, Kuqi. **Booked:** Hill
13th	● Doncaster ....h	W 2–1	**Att:** 13,811. **Ref:** A Hall — **Scorers:** Kuqi, Lee
20th	● Sheff Utd ....a	D 2–2	**Att:** 23,045. **Ref:** P Taylor — **Scorers:** Carle, McCarthy. **Booked:** Derry, Kuqi, Hill
26th	● Norwich..................h	W 3–1	**Att:** 17,180. **Ref:** K Stroud — **Scorers:** Butterfield, J Fonte[2]. **Booked:** Derry, Oster, Carle, J Fonte
28th	● Bristol City ....a	L 1–0	**Att:** 18,265. **Ref:** A Penn — **Booked:** Butterfield, J Fonte

January
3rd	● Leicester..................a	D 0–0	**Att:** 15,976. **Ref:** G Laws — **Booked:** J Fonte
14th	● Leicester..................h	W 2–1	**Att:** 6,023. **Ref:** S Tanner — **Scorers:** Ifill, Scannell
17th	● Ipswich ....h	L 1–4	**Att:** 15,348. **Ref:** C Penton — **Scorers:** Lee. **Booked:** Ifill
24th	● Watford ....a	L 4–3	**Att:** 10,006. **Ref:** M Oliver — **Scorers:** Hill, Ifill[2]. **Booked:** J Fonte, Lee, Danns
27th	● Charlton ....a	L 1–0	**Att:** 20,627. **Ref:** S Attwell — **Booked:** Kuqi, Carle, Moses
31st	● Blackpool ....h	L 0–1	**Att:** 13,810. **Ref:** A Marriner — **Booked:** J Fonte

February
17th	● Plymouth..................a	W 1–3	**Att:** 10,710. **Ref:** R Shoebridge — **Scorers:** Danns, Lee, Oster
21st	● Sheff Wed..................a	L 2–0	**Att:** 22,687. **Ref:** C Webster — **Booked:** Clyne, Lawrence
24th	● Birmingham ....h	D 0–0	**Att:** 12,847. **Ref:** P Taylor — **Booked:** J Fonte, Lee
28th	● Watford ....a	L 2–0	**Att:** 15,529. **Ref:** G Hegley — **Booked:** Butterfield, Lee

March
3rd	● Wolverhampton..................h	L 0–1	**Att:** 14,907. **Ref:** G Horwood — **Booked:** Scannell, Lawrence
7th	● Preston ....h	W 2–1	**Att:** 16,340. **Ref:** R Booth — **Scorers:** Danns, Stokes. **Booked:** Davis
11th	● Burnley ....a	L 4–2	**Att:** 10,312. **Ref:** C Boyeson — **Scorers:** Kuqi, Carlisle OG. **Booked:** Danns, J Fonte, Lee
14th	● Swansea..................a	W 1–3	**Att:** 13,663. **Ref:** R East — **Scorers:** J Fonte, Kuqi, Moses. **Booked:** Hills, Danns, Clyne, Speroni
17th	● Barnsley ....a	L 3–1	**Att:** 10,885. **Ref:** G Salisbury — **Scorers:** Kuqi. **Booked:** Kuqi
21st	● Reading ....h	D 0–0	**Att:** 14,567. **Ref:** A D'Urso

April
4th	● QPR ....a	D 0–0	**Att:** 15,234. **Ref:** S Mathieson — **Booked:** Hill, Davis, Lawrence, Moses
7th	● Coventry ....h	D 1–1	**Att:** 12,898. **Ref:** F Graham — **Scorers:** Cadogan. **Booked:** Derry, Davis
11th	● Cardiff ....h	L 0–2	**Att:** 14,814. **Ref:** R Booth — **Booked:** Hill, R Fonte
13th	● Southampton ....a	L 1–0	**Att:** 23,220. **Ref:** M Russell — **Booked:** R Fonte, Lawrence
18th	● Derby ....h	W 1–0	**Att:** 14,736. **Ref:** K Woolmer — **Scorers:** Kuqi. **Booked:** Carle, Moses, Hill, Lawrence. **Dismissed:** Moses
25th	● Doncaster ....a	L 2–0	**Att:** 12,031. **Ref:** A Taylor — **Booked:** Danns

May
3rd	● Sheff Utd ....h	D 0–0	**Att:** 22,824. **Ref:** C Foy — **Booked:** Lawrence, Ertl

● Coca-Cola Championship/Play-Offs ● FA Cup ● Carling Cup

CRYSTAL PALACE

CHAMPIONSHIP GOALKEEPER STATS

Player	Minutes on pitch	Appearances	Match starts	Completed matches	Sub appearances	Subbed off	Saved with feet	Punched	Parried	Tipped over	Fumbled	Tipped round	Caught	Blocked	Clean sheets	Goals conceded	Minutes since conceding	Save %	Saved	Resulting in goals	Opposition miss	Yellow cards	Red cards
Darryl Flahavan	97	1	1	1	0	0	0	0	1	0	0	0	2	0	0	2	43	60.00	1	1	0	0	0
Julian Speroni	4335	45	45	45	0	0	2	11	31	8	0	10	140	0	14	53	116	79.30	0	5	0	2	0

CHAMPIONSHIP OUTFIELD PLAYER STATS

Player	Minutes on pitch	Appearances	Match starts	Completed matches	Substitute appearances	Subbed off	Goals scored	Minutes since scoring	Assists	Shots on target	Shots off target	Crosses	Defensive clearances	Defensive blocks	Fouls committed	Free-kicks won	Caught offside	Yellow cards	Red cards
Calvin Andrew	259	7	1	1	6	0	0	-	0	2	1	2	3	0	5	7	2	0	0
Craig Beattie	1290	15	15	8	0	7	5	243	2	10	14	9	4	0	19	26	18	1	0
Danny Butterfield	1848	26	17	16	9	1	1	1617	0	3	6	30	13	8	21	20	0	2	0
Kieron Cadogan	115	4	0	0	4	0	1	104	0	1	1	0	0	0	1	0	0	0	0
Nick Carle	3003	37	35	17	2	17	3	1251	3	16	17	19	3	1	56	29	3	6	1
Nathanial Clyne	2424	26	25	25	1	0	0	-	1	2	1	13	5	3	19	26	1	2	0
James Comley	195	4	1	1	3	0	0	-	0	0	0	0	1	0	3	0	0	0	0
Neil Danns	1449	20	14	12	6	2	2	799	0	8	9	2	6	1	26	16	1	3	0
Claude Davis	640	7	7	6	0	1	0	-	0	0	0	0	3	3	9	5	0	3	0
Shaun Derry	3369	39	35	29	4	5	0	-	0	6	12	7	14	4	40	21	0	8	1
Kieran Djilali	300	6	2	1	4	1	0	-	1	1	1	0	0	0	1	5	0	0	0
Johannes Ertl	417	12	3	3	9	0	0	-	0	0	5	0	3	0	4	2	0	1	0
Carl Fletcher	43	3	0	0	3	0	0	1208	0	0	2	0	1	0	0	0	0	0	0
Jose Fonte	3497	38	36	34	2	2	4	505	1	4	6	0	30	12	63	47	1	7	0
Rui Fonte	514	10	5	0	5	5	0	-	0	4	1	1	2	0	5	4	3	2	0
Leandre Griffit	175	5	2	0	3	2	0	-	0	1	0	1	0	0	4	3	0	1	0
Clint Hill	4087	43	43	42	0	1	1	2737	3	8	9	13	42	9	69	27	1	8	0
Lee Hills	799	14	8	4	6	4	0	-	0	6	3	6	2	0	5	6	0	2	0
Paul Ifill	2385	33	27	14	6	13	4	1076	4	25	20	12	2	0	34	26	22	1	0
Shefki Kuqi	2161	35	20	11	15	9	10	198	1	34	20	6	12	1	38	28	23	3	0
Matthew Lawrence	2760	32	28	25	4	2	0	-	0	0	0	9	25	10	23	32	0	9	1
Alan Lee	1032	16	10	4	6	6	3	46	1	8	4	2	4	0	32	19	5	3	0
Patrick McCarthy	2259	27	25	21	2	4	3	592	2	6	4	0	31	9	36	20	1	3	0
Victor Moses	1794	27	19	9	8	9	2	715	1	16	17	16	1	1	15	37	11	3	1
John Oster	2314	31	27	11	4	16	3	626	2	10	13	41	7	1	17	16	6	2	0
Nathanial Pinney	5	1	0	0	1	0	0	-	0	0	0	0	0	0	0	0	0	0	0
Sean Scannell	1399	25	16	4	9	12	2	1016	1	10	6	0	0	0	15	7	3	1	0
James Scowcroft	446	10	5	2	5	2	0	-	0	3	5	1	3	0	11	13	2	1	1
Tom Soares	381	4	4	4	0	0	1	562	0	2	2	2	1	1	6	3	0	0	0
Anthony Stokes	984	13	11	3	2	8	1	918	0	14	10	6	1	0	10	8	9	0	0
Simon Thomas	18	1	0	0	1	0	0	-	0	0	0	0	0	0	0	0	2	0	0
Ben Watson	1660	18	18	17	0	1	5	550	2	15	15	29	9	1	14	7	2	4	0
Rhoys Wiggins	95	1	1	1	0	0	0	-	0	0	0	0	0	0	1	4	0	0	0

SEASON TOTALS

Goals scored	52
Goals conceded	55
Clean sheets	14
Shots on target	215
Shots off target	204
Shots per goal	8.06
Pens awarded	4
Pens scored	4
Pens conceded	7
Offsides	116
Corners	244
Crosses	227
Players used	35
Fouls committed	600
Free-kicks won	474

CARDS RECEIVED

78 **5**

SEQUENCES

Wins	3
(on two occasions)	
Losses	4
(28/12/08–31/01/09)	
Draws	3
(21/03/09–07/04/09)	
Undefeated	8
(22/11/08–26/12/08)	
Without win	6
(17/03/09–13/04/09)	
Undefeated home	6
(01/11/08–26/12/08)	
Undefeated away	3
(25/11/08–20/12/08)	
Without scoring	4
(21/02/09–03/03/09)	
Without conceding	3
(30/09/08–18/10/08)	
Scoring	8
(30/08/08–18/10/08)	
Conceding	9
(13/12/08–21/02/09)	

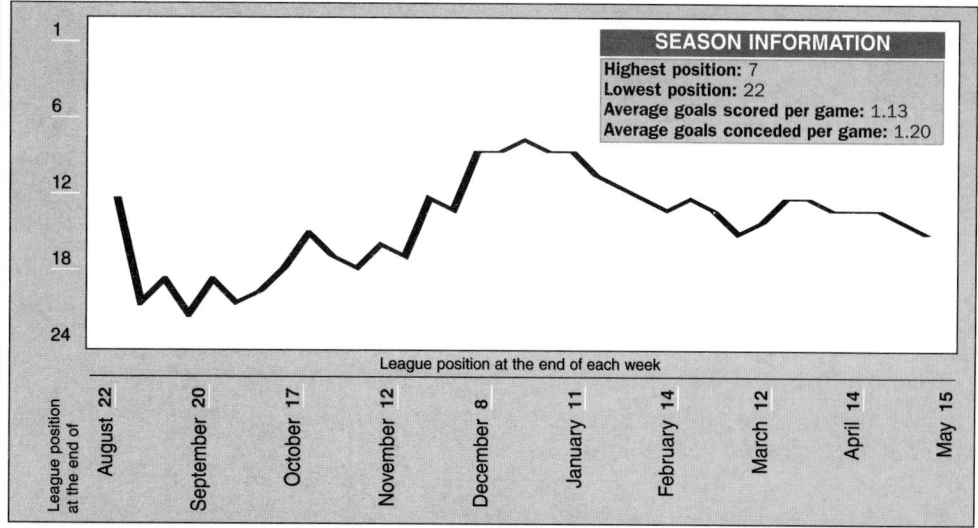

League position at the end of each week

SEASON INFORMATION
Highest position: 7
Lowest position: 22
Average goals scored per game: 1.13
Average goals conceded per game: 1.20

MATCH RECORDS

Goals scored per match

		W	D	L	Pts
Failed to score	18	0	7	11	7
Scored 1 goal	11	2	3	6	9
Scored 2 goals	11	7	2	2	23
Scored 3 goals	5	5	0	0	15
Scored 4+ goals	1	1	0	0	3

Goals conceded per match

		W	D	L	Pts
Clean Sheet	14	7	7	0	28
Conceded 1 goal	16	7	3	6	24
Conceded 2 goals	12	1	2	9	5
Conceded 3 goals	1	0	0	1	0
Conceded 4+ goals	3	0	0	3	0

GOALS SCORED/CONCEDED PER FIVE-MINUTE INTERVALS

Goals For	2	4	3	0	4	5	6	3	1	3	2	1	6	1	4	0	3	4
Goals Against	2	1	2	3	4	4	2	1	5	1	2	3	2	6	5	1	2	9
Mins	5	10	15	20	25	30	35	40	45	50	55	60	65	70	75	80	85	90

QUICK-FIRE GOALS

From the start of a match
Patrick McCarthy
(v Derby) 2:31

By a substitute after coming on
Shefki Kuqi
(v Barnsley) 8:02

LAST-GASP GOALS

From the start of a match
Nick Carle (v Sheff Utd)
94:22

By a substitute after coming on
Alan Lee (v Doncaster)
62:15

GOAL DETAILS

How the goals were struck

SCORED		CONCEDED
32	Right foot	29
12	Left foot	15
7	Headers	9
1	Others	2

How the goals were struck

SCORED		CONCEDED
40	Open play	33
2	Cross	5
2	Corner	3
4	Penalties	6
2	Direct from free-kick	2
1	Free-kick	3
1	Own goals	3

Distance from goal

SCORED		CONCEDED
13	6yds	21
33	18yds	29
6	18+yds	5

OFFICIAL FOOTBALL YEARBOOK OF THE ENGLISH & SCOTTISH LEAGUES 2009–2010 **201**

DERBY COUNTY

CLUB SUMMARY

FORMED	1884
MANAGER	Nigel Clough
GROUND	Pride Park
CAPACITY	33,597
NICKNAME	The Rams
WEBSITE	www.dcfc.co.uk

The New Football Pools PLAYER OF THE SEASON — Rob Hulse

OVERALL

P	W	D	L	F	A	GD
57	22	13	22	78	84	-6

COCA-COLA CHAMPIONSHIP

Pos	P	W	D	L	F	A	GD	Pts
18	46	14	12	20	55	67	-12	54

HOME

Pos	P	W	D	L	F	A	GD	Pts
14	23	9	7	7	31	26	5	34

AWAY

Pos	P	W	D	L	F	A	GD	Pts
20	23	5	5	13	24	41	-17	20

CUP PROGRESS DETAILS

Competition	Round reached	Knocked out by
FA Cup	R5	Man Utd
Carling Cup	SF	Man Utd

BIGGEST WIN (ALL COMPS)
4–1 on two occasions

BIGGEST DEFEAT (ALL COMPS)
1–4 on two occasions

THE PLAYER WITH THE MOST

Shots on target	
Kris Commons	59
Shots off target	
Rob Hulse	43
Shots without scoring	
James Tomkins	4
Assists	
Kris Commons	8
Offsides	
Rob Hulse	48
Fouls	
Rob Hulse	58
Fouls without a card	
Steve Davies, Nathan Ellington	17
Free-kicks won	
Rob Hulse	78
Defensive clearances	
Lewin Nyatanga	39

actim INDEX for the 2008/09 Coca-Cola Championship Season

Rank	Player	Pts
53	Rob Hulse	459
122	Paul Connolly	349
129	Kris Commons	344
136	Martin Albrechtsen	328
161	Stephen Bywater	306

ATTENDANCE RECORD

High	Low	Average
33,079	25,534	29,440
v Wolves (13/04/2009)	v Preston (25/11/2008)	

IT WAS an up and down season for Derby. The club began 2008/09 still wounded following their disastrous term in the top flight, but the Rams' swagger returned when the son of a club legend replaced Paul Jewell as manager in January.

The campaign featured four games against Derby's east midlands rivals Nottingham Forest and three matches with Barclays Premier League champions Manchester United, and included a League Cup semi-final and a battle against relegation.

It took five league matches for Derby to win a game after being relegated from the Premier League with an all-time low points total of 11 – after winning only one top-flight encounter. Almost a year to the day after recording that home win over Newcastle, on 17th September 2008, the Rams finally won again in the League when Sheffield United visited Pride Park.

A huge weight was lifted from the club's shoulders, but it did not bring the expected upturn in league form as Jewell's side saved their best performances for the League Cup.

Leeds and Stoke were beaten as Derby reached a major cup semi-final for the first time since 1976, but it was not enough to keep Jewell in his job as he left the club following the 1–0 home defeat to Ipswich on 28th December.

Manchester United were their opponents in the last four and, under the guidance of academy manager David Lowe, the Rams deservedly beat the reigning English, European and world champions 1–0

Nigel Clough was appointed Derby manager

in the first leg at Pride Park. However, United would go on to reach the final – and eventually lift the trophy – after winning the return leg 4–2 at Old Trafford to claim a 4–3 aggregate victory.

Nigel Clough was in charge for the game at Old Trafford after agreeing to follow in the footsteps of his father, Brian, who led

the Rams to the title in 1971/72. Soon into his tenure, Clough Jr led the Rams to their first win at his former club Forest since 1971 in an FA Cup-replay win that set up another clash with Manchester United.

Derby went on to finally secure their Coca-Cola Championship status with a win over Charlton on the penultimate weekend of the campaign.

Wholesale changes are planned at Pride Park over the summer and Clough has stated that he plans to bring six new players into the club in a bid to build a squad that can challenge at the top end of the table.

> **Clough led the Rams to their first win at Forest since 1971**

RESULTS 2008/09

August
9th	● Doncaster ....h	L 0–1	**Att:** 33,010. **Ref:** A D'Urso	
12th	● Lincoln City ....h	W 3–1	**Att:** 10,091. **Ref:** C Oliver — **Scorers:** Ellington[3]. **Booked:** Mears (AET)	
16th	● Bristol City ....a	D 1–1	**Att:** 16,389. **Ref:** S Attwell — **Scorers:** Green. **Booked:** Green	
23rd	● Southampton ....h	L 0–1	**Att:** 27,032. **Ref:** G Laws	
26th	● Preston ....a	W 0–1	**Att:** 8,037. **Ref:** J Moss — **Scorers:** Green. **Booked:** Addison, Leacock, Villa	
30th	● Barnsley ....a	L 2–0	**Att:** 14,223. **Ref:** G Salisbury — **Booked:** Addison	

September
13th	● Sheff Utd ....h	W 2–1	**Att:** 28,473. **Ref:** C Foy — **Scorers:** Hulse, Kilgallon OG. **Booked:** Leacock	
16th	● Swansea.............................a	D 1–1	**Att:** 14,003. **Ref:** A Penn — **Scorers:** Pearson. **Booked:** Connolly, McEveley	
20th	● Cardiff ....h	D 1–1	**Att:** 28,007. **Ref:** M Haywood — **Scorers:** Albrechtsen	
27th	● QPR ....a	W 0–2	**Att:** 14,311. **Ref:** A Taylor — **Scorers:** Albrechtsen, Villa. **Booked:** Leacock	
30th	● Birmingham ....h	D 1–1	**Att:** 29,743. **Ref:** M Oliver — **Scorers:** Davies. **Booked:** Connolly, Leacock, Addison	

October
4th	● Norwich..............................a	W 1–2	**Att:** 24,771. **Ref:** D Deadman — **Scorers:** Ellington, Hulse. **Booked:** Leacock, Hulse, Kazmierczak, Stewart .**Dismissed:** Carroll	
18th	● Plymouth.............................h	W 2–1	**Att:** 28,495. **Ref:** C Webster — **Scorers:** Green, Hulse	
21st	● Blackpool ....a	L 3–2	**Att:** 7,267. **Ref:** A Hall — **Scorers:** Commons, Sterjovski. **Booked:** Hulse, Sterjovski	
25th	● Coventry ....a	D 1–1	**Att:** 18,430. **Ref:** I Williamson — **Scorers:** Hulse. **Booked:** Addison, Commons	
28th	● Norwich..............................h	W 3–1	**Att:** 26,621. **Ref:** N Swarbrick — **Scorers:** Green, Hulse, Kazmierczak	

November
2nd	● Nottm Forest......................h	D 1–1	**Att:** 33,010. **Ref:** S Attwell — **Scorers:** Villa. **Booked:** Addison, Leacock, Nyatanga	
4th	● Brighton ....a	W 1–4	**Att:** 6,625. **Ref:** K Friend — **Scorers:** Ellington, Villa[3]. **Booked:** Addison, Nyatanga	
8th	● Reading ....a	L 3–0	**Att:** 18,724. **Ref:** D Mattison	
11th	● Leeds ....h	W 2–1	**Att:** 18,540. **Ref:** G Laws — **Scorers:** Ellington, Villa. **Booked:** Davis	
15th	● Sheff Wed...........................h	W 3–0	**Att:** 30,111. **Ref:** K Stroud — **Scorers:** Addison, Commons, Stewart. **Booked:** Villa	
22nd	● Ipswich ....a	L 2–0	**Att:** 20,239. **Ref:** M Russell — **Booked:** Nyatanga, Connolly	
25th	● Preston ....h	D 2–2	**Att:** 25,534. **Ref:** K Woolmer — **Scorers:** Hulse, Stewart. **Booked:** Addison	
29th	● Burnley ....a	L 3–0	**Att:** 11,552. **Ref:** S Tanner — **Booked:** Green, Varney	

December
2nd	● Stoke ....a	W 0–1	**Att:** 22,034. **Ref:** R Styles — **Scorers:** Ellington. **Booked:** Addison, Powell	
6th	● Crystal Palace ....h	L 1–2	**Att:** 27,203. **Ref:** M Oliver — **Scorers:** Varney. **Booked:** Tomkins	
9th	● Wolverhampton...................a	L 3–0	**Att:** 21,326. **Ref:** G Hegley	
15th	● Charlton ....a	D 2–2	**Att:** 20,989. **Ref:** A D'Urso — **Scorers:** Ellington[2]. **Booked:** Powell, Connolly	
20th	● Watford ....h	W 1–0	**Att:** 27,833. **Ref:** C Boyeson — **Scorers:** Hulse	
26th	● Preston ....a	L 2–0	**Att:** 13,896. **Ref:** K Friend	
28th	● Ipswich ....h	L 0–1	**Att:** 28,358. **Ref:** K Stroud — **Booked:** Nyatanga, Stewart. **Dismissed:** Stewart	

January
3rd	● Forest Green ....a	W 3–4	**Att:** 4,836. **Ref:** P Taylor — **Scorers:** Albrechtsen, Davies, Green, Hulse. **Booked:** Commons, Hulse, Davies	
7th	● Man Utd ....h	W 1–0	**Att:** 30,194. **Ref:** P Dowd — **Scorers:** Commons. **Booked:** Teale, Connolly	
17th	● QPR ....h	L 0–2	**Att:** 28,390. **Ref:** K Wright — **Booked:** Camara, Todd	
20th	● Man Utd ....a	L 4–2	**Att:** 73,374. **Ref:** M Dean — **Scorers:** Barnes. **Booked:** Addison, Green, Carroll	
23rd	● Nottm Forest......................h	D 1–1	**Att:** 32,035. **Ref:** H Webb — **Scorers:** Hulse. **Booked:** Connolly	
27th	● Birmingham ....a	L 1–0	**Att:** 15,330. **Ref:** G Salisbury — **Booked:** Connolly	
31st	● Coventry ....h	W 2–1	**Att:** 29,710. **Ref:** M Jones — **Scorers:** Commons, Hulse. **Booked:** Savage	

February
4th	● Nottm Forest......................a	W 2–3	**Att:** 29,001. **Ref:** C Foy — **Scorers:** Commons, Green, Hulse. **Booked:** Bywater, Nyatanga	
7th	● Plymouth.............................a	W 0–3	**Att:** 10,893. **Ref:** S Cook — **Scorers:** Hulse, Teale[2]	
15th	● Man Utd ....h	L 1–4	**Att:** 32,103. **Ref:** A Wiley — **Scorers:** Addison. **Booked:** Connolly	
18th	● Blackpool ....h	W 4–1	**Att:** 26,834. **Ref:** D Whitestone — **Scorers:** Barazite, Commons[2], Green. **Booked:** McEveley	
21st	● Nottm Forest......................a	W 1–3	**Att:** 29,140. **Ref:** A Marriner — **Scorers:** Davies, Hulse, Nyatanga	
27th	● Doncaster ....a	L 2–1	**Att:** 14,435. **Ref:** R Booth — **Scorers:** Savage	

March
3rd	● Swansea.............................h	D 2–2	**Att:** 26,691. **Ref:** P Crossley — **Scorers:** Porter[2]. **Booked:** McEveley	
7th	● Bristol City ....h	W 2–1	**Att:** 30,824. **Ref:** K Stroud — **Scorers:** Hulse, Porter. **Booked:** Todd	
10th	● Southampton ....a	D 1–1	**Att:** 17,567. **Ref:** K Friend — **Scorers:** Davies	
14th	● Sheff Utd ....a	L 4–2	**Att:** 27,565. **Ref:** I Williamson — **Scorers:** Bannan, Hulse. **Booked:** Eustace, Todd, Hulse	
21st	● Barnsley ....h	D 0–0	**Att:** 32,277. **Ref:** A Penn — **Booked:** Connolly	

April
4th	● Burnley ....h	D 1–1	**Att:** 33,010. **Ref:** G Hegley — **Scorers:** Connolly. **Booked:** Bannan	
8th	● Cardiff ....a	L 4–1	**Att:** 18,403. **Ref:** N Swarbrick — **Scorers:** Johnson OG	
11th	● Sheff Wed...........................a	W 0–1	**Att:** 24,392. **Ref:** S Tanner — **Scorers:** Hulse. **Booked:** Hulse, Bywater	
13th	● Wolverhampton...................h	L 2–3	**Att:** 33,079. **Ref:** P Taylor — **Scorers:** Kazmierczak, Sterjovski	
18th	● Crystal Palace ....a	L 1–0	**Att:** 14,736. **Ref:** K Woolmer — **Booked:** Sterjovski, Teale	
21st	● Reading ....h	L 0–2	**Att:** 31,345. **Ref:** C Webster — **Booked:** Bannan	
25th	● Charlton ....h	W 1–0	**Att:** 31,541. **Ref:** F Graham — **Scorers:** Hulse. **Booked:** Commons	

May
3rd	● Watford ....a	L 3–1	**Att:** 16,131. **Ref:** S Mathieson — **Scorers:** Eustace	

● Coca-Cola Championship/Play-Offs ● FA Cup ● Carling Cup

DERBY COUNTY

CHAMPIONSHIP GOALKEEPER STATS

Player	Minutes on pitch	Appearances	Match starts	Completed matches	Sub appearances	Subbed off	Saves Breakdown								Clean sheets	Goals conceded	Minutes since conceding	Save %	Penalties			Yellow cards	Red cards
							Saved with feet	Punched	Parried	Tipped over	Fumbled	Tipped round	Caught	Blocked					Saved	Resulting in goals	Opposition miss		
Stephen Bywater	2916	31	30	30	1	0	1	12	13	7	0	3	93	1	5	47	54	73.89	0	2	0	1	0
Roy Carroll	1486	16	16	15	0	0	1	1	5	3	0	4	45	0	2	20	62	75.00	0	2	0	0	1

CHAMPIONSHIP OUTFIELD PLAYER STATS

Player	Minutes on pitch	Appearances	Match starts	Completed matches	Substitute appearances	Subbed off	Goals scored	Minutes since scoring	Assists	Shots on target	Shots off target	Crosses	Defensive clearances	Defensive blocks	Fouls committed	Free-kicks won	Caught offside	Yellow cards	Red cards
Miles Addison	2562	28	28	25	0	3	1	1265	0	16	16	3	22	2	53	14	0	5	0
Martin Albrechtsen	3202	35	35	32	0	3	2	2450	1	7	6	13	33	14	11	31	0	0	0
Barry Bannan	620	10	6	3	4	3	1	597	1	4	1	12	1	0	4	4	0	2	0
Nacer Barazite	1974	30	21	11	9	10	1	339	6	15	19	53	5	0	13	25	2	0	0
Giles Barnes	144	3	1	0	2	1	0	-	0	0	2	0	0	0	0	1	0	0	0
Mohammed Camara	98	1	1	1	0	0	0	-	0	0	0	0	0	0	2	0	0	1	0
Kris Commons	2802	34	30	17	4	13	5	767	8	59	43	140	1	6	23	55	9	2	0
Paul Connolly	3769	40	39	39	1	0	1	674	0	2	1	41	29	4	44	22	0	6	0
Steve Davies	971	19	8	4	11	4	3	191	3	21	19	9	2	0	17	13	8	0	0
Claude Davis	509	8	6	3	2	3	0	-	0	1	0	1	6	4	15	8	0	0	0
Mark Dudley	9	1	0	0	1	0	0	-	0	0	0	0	1	1	0	0	0	0	0
Nathan Ellington	1411	27	13	6	14	7	3	229	2	16	20	22	4	0	17	22	6	0	0
John Eustace	599	9	6	4	3	2	1	11	0	7	4	4	5	2	13	8	0	1	0
Paul Green	2750	29	29	27	0	2	4	279	3	22	17	14	13	2	22	33	1	2	0
Rob Hulse	3731	44	42	27	2	15	15	119	3	50	43	15	10	1	58	78	48	4	0
Przemyslaw Kazmierczak	1055	22	12	5	10	7	2	15	1	12	10	23	3	1	16	6	4	1	0
Dean Leacock	994	11	10	9	1	1	0	-	0	0	1	2	13	7	15	13	0	5	0
Jay McEveley	1235	15	13	11	2	2	0	-	0	2	0	12	11	3	10	8	0	3	0
Tyrone Mears	288	3	3	3	0	0	0	-	0	0	0	2	0	1	2	1	0	0	0
Lewin Nyatanga	2669	30	27	24	3	3	1	1285	0	4	1	8	39	11	35	24	1	3	0
Mark O'Brien	28	1	0	0	1	0	0	-	0	0	0	0	1	1	0	0	0	0	0
Stephen Pearson	709	12	8	2	4	6	1	638	0	2	0	4	0	3	8	7	2	0	0
Andrejs Pereplotkins	110	2	2	0	0	2	0	-	0	1	1	1	0	0	2	3	0	0	0
Chris Porter	264	5	3	2	2	1	3	44	0	4	3	0	1	0	6	5	7	0	0
Darren Powell	468	6	5	3	1	2	0	-	0	2	0	0	9	3	7	12	0	1	0
Robbie Savage	1939	22	20	18	2	2	1	1178	2	4	5	14	1	3	18	26	0	1	0
Mile Sterjovski	723	15	6	1	9	5	2	119	1	3	4	10	1	1	12	10	1	2	0
Jordan Stewart	2464	26	26	25	0	0	2	996	1	6	5	62	21	11	14	29	2	2	1
Alan Stubbs	57	1	1	0	0	1	0	-	0	0	0	0	1	0	0	0	0	0	0
Gary Teale	2045	25	24	17	1	7	1	1409	7	20	15	53	4	2	5	19	5	1	0
Andy Todd	821	11	7	6	4	1	0	-	0	0	1	3	12	5	15	5	0	3	0
James Tomkins	542	7	5	5	2	0	0	-	0	2	2	0	5	3	7	7	0	1	0
Luke Varney	826	10	9	5	1	4	1	1037	0	8	7	8	3	1	17	13	10	1	0
Emanuel Villa	1315	30	12	5	18	7	2	636	1	8	10	3	11	0	29	17	13	1	0
Ruben Zadkovich	177	5	2	1	3	1	0	-	0	0	1	0	0	0	3	0	0	0	0

SEASON TOTALS

Goals scored	55
Goals conceded	67
Clean sheets	7
Shots on target	298
Shots off target	257
Shots per goal	10.09
Pens awarded	3
Pens scored	2
Pens conceded	4
Offsides	119
Corners	277
Crosses	532
Players used	37
Fouls committed	514
Free-kicks won	528

CARDS RECEIVED

49   2

SEQUENCES

Wins	4
(31/01/09–21/02/09)	
Losses	4
(26/12/08–27/01/09)	
Draws	2
(16/09/08–20/09/08)	
Undefeated	7
(13/09/08–18/10/08)	
Without win	6
(22/11/08–15/12/08)	
Undefeated home	8
(13/09/08–25/11/08)	
Undefeated away	3
(16/09/08–04/10/08)	
Without scoring	4
(26/12/08–27/01/09)	
Without conceding	
(–)	
Scoring	11
(13/09/08–02/11/08)	
Conceding	8
(30/09/08–08/11/08)	

SEASON INFORMATION

Highest position: 10
Lowest position: 24
Average goals scored per game: 1.20
Average goals conceded per game: 1.46

League position at the end of each week

League position at the end of

August 24 | September 18 | October 10 | November 14 | December 18 | January 22 | February 22 | March 17 | April 16 | May 18

MATCH RECORDS

Goals scored per match

		W	D	L	Pts
Failed to score	14	0	1	13	1
Scored 1 goal	15	3	8	4	17
Scored 2 goals	12	6	3	3	21
Scored 3 goals	4	4	0	0	12
Scored 4+ goals	1	1	0	0	3

Goals conceded per match

		W	D	L	Pts
Clean sheet	7	6	1	0	19
Conceded 1 goal	21	8	8	5	32
Conceded 2 goals	10	0	3	7	3
Conceded 3 goals	6	0	0	6	0
Conceded 4+ goals	2	0	0	2	0

GOALS SCORED/CONCEDED PER FIVE-MINUTE INTERVALS

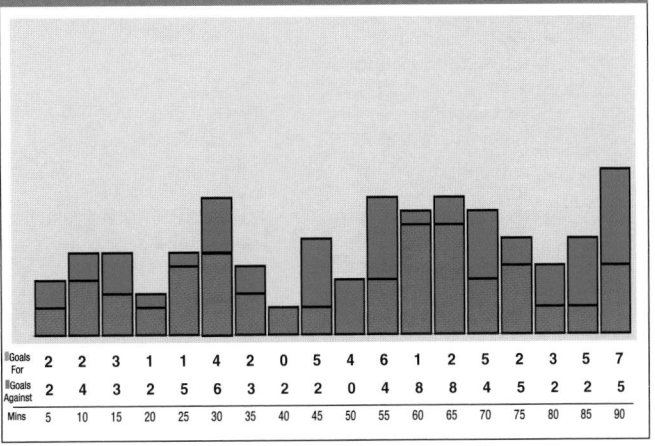

Goals For	2	2	3	1	1	4	2	0	5	4	6	1	2	5	2	3	5	7
Goals Against	2	4	3	2	5	6	3	2	2	0	4	8	8	4	5	2	2	5
Mins	5	10	15	20	25	30	35	40	45	50	55	60	65	70	75	80	85	90

QUICK-FIRE GOALS

From the start of a match
Chris Porter (v Bristol City) 0:52

By a substitute after coming on
Przemyslaw Kazmierczak (v Norwich) 3:29

LAST-GASP GOALS

From the start of a match
Nathan Ellington (v Charlton) 94:03

By a substitute after coming on
Emanuel Villa (v Nottm Forest) 36:45

GOAL DETAILS

How the goals were struck

SCORED		CONCEDED
20	Right foot	39
21	Left foot	13
13	Headers	14
1	Others	1

How the goals were struck

SCORED		CONCEDED
28	Open play	36
12	Cross	15
2	Corner	4
2	Penalties	4
3	Direct from free-kick	0
6	Free-kick	7
2	Own goals	1

Distance from goal

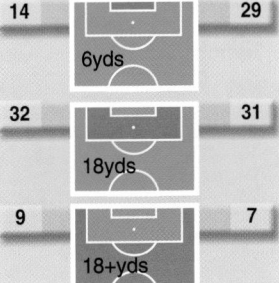

SCORED		CONCEDED
14	6yds	29
32	18yds	31
9	18+yds	7

CLUB SUMMARY

FORMED	1879
MANAGER	Sean O'Driscoll
GROUND	Keepmoat Stadium
CAPACITY	15,000
NICKNAME	Rovers
WEBSITE	www.doncasterroversfc.co.uk

The New Football Pools PLAYER OF THE SEASON — Matthew Mills

OVERALL

P	W	D	L	F	A	GD
51	18	9	24	46	57	-11

COCA-COLA CHAMPIONSHIP

Pos	P	W	D	L	F	A	GD	Pts
14	46	17	7	22	42	53	-11	58

HOME

Pos	P	W	D	L	F	A	GD	Pts
18	23	9	5	9	16	18	-2	32

AWAY

Pos	P	W	D	L	F	A	GD	Pts
11	23	8	2	13	26	35	-9	26

CUP PROGRESS DETAILS

Competition	Round reached	Knocked out by
FA Cup	R4	Aston Villa
Carling Cup	R1	Notts County

BIGGEST WIN (ALL COMPS)

20/01/09 3–0 v Cheltenham **FAC3R**

BIGGEST DEFEAT (ALL COMPS)

20/09/08 1–4 v Bristol City **FLC**

THE PLAYER WITH THE MOST

Shots on target	
Richie Wellens	30
Shots off target	
Martin Woods	45
Shots without scoring	
Jason Price	32
Assists	
James Coppinger	5
Offsides	
Lewis Guy	37
Fouls	
Martin Woods	60
Fouls without a card	
Adam Lockwood	10
Free-kicks won	
Richie Wellens	85
Defensive clearances	
Matthew Mills	46

actim INDEX for the 2008/09 Coca-Cola Championship Season

Rank	Player	Pts
41	Neil Sullivan	480
105	James Coppinger	367
110	James Chambers	362
120	Matthew Mills	352
126	Paul Heffernan	348

ATTENDANCE RECORD

High	Low	Average
14,823	9,534	11,964

v Sheff Wed (14/02/2009) v Swansea (01/11/2008)

Richie Wellens' goal in the 4–2 win over Forest helped start a run of four wins

A STUNNING haul of 31 points from a possible 39 in the 74 days after Christmas ensured that Doncaster secured their place in the Coca-Cola Championship for at least another season.

Having earned their promotion via the play-offs during 2007/08, Sean O'Driscoll's men looked set to make an instant return to League One when they sat rock-bottom of the table on Christmas Day with just 18 points to their name. But a run of 10 victories from their next 13 outings, including spirited 1–0 wins over both South Yorkshire rivals Sheffield United and Sheffield Wednesday, saw them gradually climb their way up the table and away from the danger zone.

How they would have fared with a genuine goalscorer is unknown, with Paul Heffernan the only Rovers player to reach double figures as they scored just 16 goals at home and 42 in total. The majority of the remainder of their goals came from the cultured midfield trio of captain Brian Stock and playmakers James Coppinger and Richie Wellens, while there were also valuable contributions

DONCASTER ROVERS

from Lewis Guy and Martin Woods.

James Hayter – Rovers' goal hero at Wembley last season – did not open his account until 4th April, but went on to score four times as the season came to its conclusion, with one of those goals coming in a comprehensive 3–0 win at Plymouth which sealed their survival.

They also enjoyed a number of other notable successes on their travels, including a 4–2 win at Nottingham Forest on Boxing Day and an opening-day victory at Derby's Pride Park.

O'Driscoll deserves enormous credit for building his side on a limited budget, with strikers Dean Shiels and Steve Brooker the only additions to the squad that cost any money.

The highlight of their cup campaigns came as they held Aston Villa to a goalless draw in the fourth round of the FA Cup before losing 3–1 at Villa Park in the replay.

' They sat rock-bottom of the table on Christmas Day '

RESULTS 2008/09

August
9th	● Derby ....a	W 0–1	**Att:** 33,010. **Ref:** A D'Urso — **Scorers:** Guy. **Booked:** Stock, Taylor
12th	● Notts County........................a	L 1–0	**Att:** 3,272. **Ref:** M Oliver — **Booked:** Chambers, Hird, Van Nieuwstadt (AET)
16th	● Cardiff..................................h	D 1–1	**Att:** 11,873. **Ref:** M Halsey — **Scorers:** Guy
23rd	● QPR ....a	L 2–0	**Att:** 15,536. **Ref:** M Thorpe
30th	● Coventry ....h	W 1–0	**Att:** 11,806. **Ref:** R Shoebridge — **Scorers:** Wellens

September
13th	● Birmingham ....a	L 1–0	**Att:** 18,165. **Ref:** G Ward — **Booked:** Stock
16th	● Charlton ....h	L 0–1	**Att:** 10,483. **Ref:** N Miller — **Booked:** Wellens
20th	● Bristol City ....a	L 4–1	**Att:** 15,960. **Ref:** J Singh — **Scorers:** Wellens. **Booked:** Stock, Sullivan
27th	● Southampton ....h	L 0–2	**Att:** 10,867. **Ref:** M Russell
30th	● Sheff Utd ....h	L 0–2	**Att:** 14,242. **Ref:** T Bates — **Booked:** Price

October
4th	● Barnsley ....a	L 4–1	**Att:** 15,086. **Ref:** S Tanner — **Scorers:** Stock. **Booked:** O'Connor, Wellens
18th	● Blackpool ....h	D 0–0	**Att:** 11,342. **Ref:** D Drysdale — **Booked:** Mills, Stock
21st	● Reading ....a	L 2–1	**Att:** 17,294. **Ref:** D Deadman — **Scorers:** Van Nieuwstadt. **Booked:** Chambers, Stock
25th	● Norwich................................a	L 2–1	**Att:** 24,543. **Ref:** C Penton — **Scorers:** Stock. **Booked:** Roberts, Price
28th	● Barnsley ....h	L 0–1	**Att:** 13,251. **Ref:** A Wiley — **Booked:** L Guy

November
1st	● Swansea...............................h	D 0–0	**Att:** 9,534. **Ref:** K Stroud — **Booked:** Wilson, Stock
8th	● Sheff Wed............................a	L 1–0	**Att:** 20,872. **Ref:** L Mason
15th	● Ipswich ....h	W 1–0	**Att:** 10,823. **Ref:** K Friend — **Scorers:** Martis. **Booked:** Mills, Heffernan
22nd	● Burnley ....a	D 0–0	**Att:** 12,173. **Ref:** S Bennett — **Booked:** Mills, M. Woods
25th	● Nottm Forest........................h	D 0–0	**Att:** 12,612. **Ref:** A Penn — **Booked:** Chambers, M. Woods
29th	● Watford ....a	D 1–1	**Att:** 14,008. **Ref:** I Williamson — **Scorers:** Brooker. **Booked:** Chambers, Martis, M. Woods

December
6th	● Plymouth..............................h	W 1–0	**Att:** 10,187. **Ref:** R Beeby — **Scorers:** Stock. **Booked:** M. Woods, Mills
9th	● Preston ....a	L 1–0	**Att:** 13,152. **Ref:** G Laws
13th	● Crystal Palace ....a	L 2–1	**Att:** 13,811. **Ref:** A Hall — **Scorers:** Heffernan. **Booked:** Elliott, M. Woods
20th	● Wolverhampton...................h	L 0–1	**Att:** 13,669. **Ref:** K Wright
26th	● Nottm Forest........................a	W 2–4	**Att:** 26,501. **Ref:** P Dowd — **Scorers:** Heffernan[2], Wellens, M. Woods. **Booked:** Stock, Wilson, Hird
28th	● Burnley ....h	W 2–1	**Att:** 14,020. **Ref:** T Kettle — **Scorers:** Coppinger, Stock. **Booked:** Heffernan

January
13th	● Cheltenham ....a	D 0–0	**Att:** 4,417. **Ref:** N Swarbrick
17th	● Southampton ....a	W 1–2	**Att:** 15,837. **Ref:** A Woolmer — **Scorers:** Coppinger, M. Woods. **Booked:** Chambers, M. Woods
20th	● Cheltenham ....h	W 3–0	**Att:** 5,345. **Ref:** S Attwell — **Scorers:** Hird, Stock[2]
24th	● Aston Villa...........................h	D 0–0	**Att:** 13,517. **Ref:** M Halsey
27th	● Sheff Utd ....a	W 0–1	**Att:** 26,555. **Ref:** A Wiley — **Scorers:** O'Connor. **Booked:** M. Woods
30th	● Norwich................................h	D 1–1	**Att:** 12,384. **Ref:** M Oliver — **Scorers:** Heffernan

February
4th	● Aston Villa...........................a	L 3–1	**Att:** 24,203. **Ref:** L Mason — **Scorers:** Price. **Booked:** Hird
7th	● Blackpool ....a	W 2–3	**Att:** 7,452. **Ref:** A Taylor — **Scorers:** Coppinger, Hird, Stock
14th	● Sheff Wed............................h	W 1–0	**Att:** 14,823. **Ref:** N Swarbrick — **Scorers:** Heffernan. **Booked:** Wellens
17th	● Bristol City ....h	W 1–0	**Att:** 10,928. **Ref:** C Oliver — **Scorers:** Heffernan
21st	● Swansea...............................a	L 3–1	**Att:** 16,161. **Ref:** S Mathieson — **Scorers:** Coppinger. **Booked:** Chambers, Wellens, Price. **Dismissed:** Wellens
27th	● Derby ....h	W 2–1	**Att:** 14,435. **Ref:** R Booth — **Scorers:** Heffernan, Wilson

March
3rd	● Charlton ....a	W 1–2	**Att:** 20,815. **Ref:** R Styles — **Scorers:** Coppinger, Stock. **Booked:** Chambers, Coppinger, Spicer
7th	● Cardiff..................................a	L 3–0	**Att:** 17,821. **Ref:** G Hegley — **Booked:** Mills
10th	● QPR ....h	W 2–0	**Att:** 10,223. **Ref:** C Webster — **Scorers:** Heffernan, Stewart OG. **Booked:** Mills
14th	● Birmingham ....h	L 0–2	**Att:** 11,482. **Ref:** P Walton
17th	● Reading ....h	L 0–1	**Att:** 10,393. **Ref:** P Taylor — **Booked:** Shiels
21st	● Coventry ....a	L 1–0	**Att:** 18,498. **Ref:** R Beeby — **Booked:** Wellens

April
4th	● Watford ....h	L 1–2	**Att:** 12,126. **Ref:** G Laws — **Scorers:** Hayter. **Booked:** LuaLua
11th	● Ipswich ....a	W 1–3	**Att:** 19,918. **Ref:** K Stroud — **Scorers:** Hayter, Heffernan, Roberts. **Booked:** Mills, Shiels, Wellens
13th	● Preston ....h	L 0–2	**Att:** 11,648. **Ref:** I Williamson — **Booked:** Hayter, Wellens
18th	● Plymouth..............................a	W 0–3	**Att:** 11,100. **Ref:** P Crossley — **Scorers:** Hayter, Heffernan, Spicer. **Booked:** Spicer
25th	● Crystal Palace ....h	W 2–0	**Att:** 12,031. **Ref:** A Taylor — **Scorers:** Hayter, Shiels. **Booked:** Wellens

May
3rd	● Wolverhampton...................a	L 1–0	**Att:** 28,252. **Ref:** R Beeby

● Coca-Cola Championship/Play-Offs ● FA Cup ● Carling Cup

DONCASTER ROVERS

CHAMPIONSHIP GOALKEEPER STATS

Player	Minutes on pitch	Appearances	Match starts	Completed matches	Sub appearances	Subbed off	Saved with feet	Punched	Parried	Tipped over	Fumbled	Tipped round	Caught	Blocked	Clean sheets	Goals conceded	Minutes since conceding	Save %	Saved	Resulting in goals	Opposition miss	Yellow cards	Red cards
											SAVES BREAKDOWN								PENALTIES				
Neil Sullivan 4400	46	46	45	0	1	3	15	8	18	0	11	140	0	14	53	1	78.71	1	4	0	1	0
Gary Woods......................4	1	0	0	1	0	0	0	0	0	0	0	0	0	0	1	0	-	0	0	0	0	0

CHAMPIONSHIP OUTFIELD PLAYER STATS

Player	Minutes on pitch	Appearances	Match starts	Completed matches	Substitute appearances	Subbed off	Goals scored	Minutes since scoring	Assists	Shots on target	Shots off target	Crosses	Defensive clearances	Defensive blocks	Fouls committed	Free-kicks won	Caught offside	Yellow cards	Red cards
Tomi Ameobi 18	1	0	0	1	0	0	-	0	0	0	0	0	0	2	0	1	0	0
Steve Brooker..........................30	1	0	0	1	0	1	25	0	2	0	0	0	0	0	0	0	0	0
Darren Byfield 428	15	3	2	12	1	0	-	0	8	4	0	2	0	9	6	3	0	0
James Chambers 3163	37	34	31	3	3	0	-	1	0	5	25	32	10	36	37	3	6	0
James Coppinger.....................2574	32	29	17	3	12	5	349	5	23	17	43	3	1	13	46	16	1	0
Stuart Elliott 340	9	3	1	6	3	0	-	0	4	0	0	0	0	7	4	6	1	0
Waide Fairhurst 64	3	0	0	3	0	0	-	1	0	0	0	0	0	0	1	0	0	0
Gordon Greer 13	1	0	0	1	0	0	-	0	0	0	0	0	0	0	0	0	0	0
Lewis Guy 1765	29	19	2	10	17	2	1625	2	12	12	6	2	1	9	21	37	1	0
James Hayter 1526	27	13	7	14	6	4	112	0	12	12	0	4	0	14	20	10	1	0
Paul Heffernan 1834	28	19	5	9	14	10	24	4	22	15	4	10	0	15	26	23	2	0
Sam Hird 3130	37	33	29	4	4	1	1107	0	7	3	0	22	3	20	21	2	1	0
Adam Lockwood 1214	22	12	8	10	4	0	-	0	0	2	0	13	6	10	18	0	0	0
Kazenga LuaLua 183	4	2	0	2	2	0	-	1	3	1	0	0	0	5	6	1	1	0
Shelton Martis 422	5	5	4	0	1	1	287	0	2	0	0	3	0	8	2	0	1	0
Matthew Mills 3759	41	41	38	0	2	0	-	2	6	11	4	46	14	36	38	1	7	1
James O'Connor 3047	32	31	31	1	0	1	527	0	6	2	28	18	3	15	17	1	1	0
Jason Price.............................1137	22	11	4	11	7	0	-	0	16	16	3	2	2	32	33	21	3	0
Gareth Roberts........................2615	32	27	24	5	5	1	451	1	1	4	33	5	1	16	23	3	1	0
Dean Shiels 652	12	6	3	6	3	1	100	0	10	4	3	0	0	6	7	4	2	0
John Spicer 2448	30	26	16	4	10	1	269	2	15	6	16	10	1	25	15	4	2	0
Brian Stock.............................3255	36	36	29	0	7	6	187	3	16	19	30	14	3	51	70	2	7	0
Gareth Taylor 1027	17	11	2	6	9	0	-	0	6	9	0	5	0	25	12	16	1	0
Jos Van Nieuwstadt 912	16	9	8	7	1	0	782	0	1	1	0	13	6	5	0	0	0	0
Richie Wellens 3562	39	39	29	0	9	3	1823	4	30	26	17	7	0	45	85	2	8	1
Mark Wilson 1389	22	15	7	7	8	1	585	0	7	4	5	5	0	19	11	1	2	0
Martin Woods 3374	41	36	30	5	6	2	1745	3	25	45	76	11	1	60	38	3	7	0

actim

Coca-Cola CHAMPIONSHIP

SEASON TOTALS

Goals scored	42
Goals conceded	53
Clean sheets	14
Shots on target	230
Shots off target	222
Shots per goal	10.76
Pens awarded	5
Pens scored	4
Pens conceded	5
Offsides	160
Corners	226
Crosses	294
Players used	29
Fouls committed	485
Free-kicks won	570

CARDS RECEIVED

57 **2**

SEQUENCES

Wins	4
(26/12/08-27/01/09)	
Losses	6
(13/09/08-04/10/08)	
Draws	3
(22/11/08-29/11/08)	
Undefeated	8
(26/12/08-17/02/09)	
Without win	12
(13/09/08-08/11/08)	
Undefeated home	6
(28/12/08-10/03/09)	
Undefeated away	4
(26/12/08-07/02/09)	
Without scoring	3
(on two occasions)	
Without conceding	3
(15/11/08-25/11/08)	
Scoring	11
(26/12/08-03/03/09)	
Conceding	6
(on three occasions)	

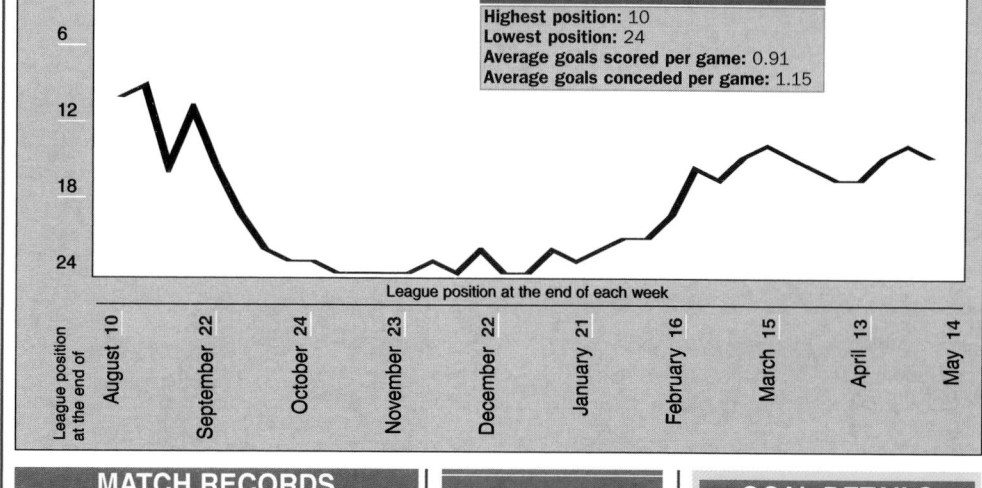

SEASON INFORMATION
Highest position: 10
Lowest position: 24
Average goals scored per game: 0.91
Average goals conceded per game: 1.15

League position at the end of each week

League position at the end of — August 10, September 22, October 24, November 23, December 22, January 21, February 16, March 15, April 13, May 14

MATCH RECORDS

Goals scored per match

		W	D	L	Pts
Failed to score	19	0	4	15	4
Scored 1 goal	17	7	3	7	24
Scored 2 goals	6	6	0	0	18
Scored 3 goals	3	3	0	0	9
Scored 4+ goals	1	1	0	0	3

Goals conceded per match

		W	D	L	Pts
Clean sheet	14	10	4	0	34
Conceded 1 goal	17	5	3	9	18
Conceded 2 goals	11	2	0	9	6
Conceded 3 goals	2	0	0	2	0
Conceded 4+ goals	2	0	0	2	0

QUICK-FIRE GOALS

From the start of a match
Paul Heffernan
(v Bristol City) 3:58

By a substitute after coming on
James Hayter
(v Ipswich) 2:16

LAST-GASP GOALS

From the start of a match
James Hayter
(v Ipswich) 84:39

By a substitute after coming on
James Hayter
(v Plymouth) 11:36

GOAL DETAILS

How the goals were struck

SCORED		CONCEDED
20	Right foot	24
11	Left foot	14
11	Headers	13
0	Others	2

How the goals were struck

SCORED		CONCEDED
26	Open play	35
7	Cross	4
1	Corner	1
4	Penalties	4
1	Direct from free-kick	1
2	Free-kick	4
1	Own goals	4

Distance from goal

SCORED		CONCEDED
17	6yds	18
19	18yds	28
6	18+yds	7

GOALS SCORED/CONCEDED PER FIVE-MINUTE INTERVALS

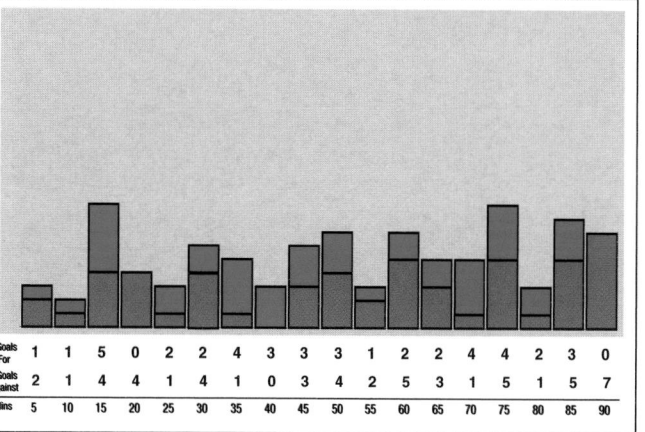

Goals For	1	1	5	0	2	2	4	3	3	3	1	2	2	4	4	2	3	0
Goals Against	2	1	4	4	1	4	1	0	3	4	2	5	3	1	5	1	5	7
Mins	5	10	15	20	25	30	35	40	45	50	55	60	65	70	75	80	85	90

IPSWICH TOWN

CLUB SUMMARY

FORMED	1878
MANAGER	Roy Keane
GROUND	Portman Road
CAPACITY	30,311
NICKNAME	The Tractor Boys
WEBSITE	www.itfc.co.uk

The New **Football Pools** PLAYER OF THE SEASON — Richard Wright

OVERALL

P	W	D	L	F	A	GD
51	20	15	16	73	62	11

COCA-COLA CHAMPIONSHIP

Pos	P	W	D	L	F	A	GD	Pts
9	46	17	15	14	62	53	9	66

HOME

Pos	P	W	D	L	F	A	GD	Pts
15	23	8	9	6	30	26	4	33

AWAY

Pos	P	W	D	L	F	A	GD	Pts
5	23	9	6	8	32	27	5	33

CUP PROGRESS DETAILS

Competition	Round reached	Knocked out by
FA Cup	R4	Chelsea
Carling Cup	R3	Wigan

BIGGEST WIN (ALL COMPS)

4–1 on two occasions

BIGGEST DEFEAT (ALL COMPS)

24/09/08 1–4 v Wigan **LC3**

THE PLAYER WITH THE MOST

Shots on target	
Jonathan Stead	57
Shots off target	
Jonathan Stead	39
Shots without scoring	
Gareth McAuley	25
Assists	
Jonathan Stead	7
Offsides	
Kevin Lisbie	49
Fouls	
David Norris	57
Fouls without a card	
Kevin Lisbie	25
Free-kicks won	
Pablo Counago	61
Defensive clearances	
Gareth McAuley	64

actim INDEX for the 2008/09 Coca-Cola Championship Season

Rank	Player	Pts
23	Richard Wright	532
92	Pablo Counago	390
115	Jonathan Stead	356
116	David Wright	355
117	Gareth McAuley	353

ATTENDANCE RECORD

High	Low	Average
28,274	17,749	20,961
v Norwich (19/04/2009)	v Bristol City (10/12/2008)	

ROY KEANE may only have been in charge for the final two games of Ipswich's season, but his appointment was undoubtedly the major talking point of the entire campaign.

Expectations of a promotion charge were high at Portman Road, but an ultimately disappointing mid-table position led to the dismissal of Jim Magilton and the surprise arrival of Keane.

Magilton had been handed funds by owner Marcus Evans and the summer arrivals of Richard Wright, Pim Balkestein, Ben Thatcher, Gareth McAuley, Ivan Campo, Moritz Volz, Kevin Lisbie and Jon Stead all pointed towards a play-off position at the least. But a 2–1 home defeat by Preston on the opening day dampened

Midfielder David Norris caused national outrage in November when he celebrated his winner at Blackpool with a gesture which was interpreted as a show of support for his

Roy Keane became Ipswich's manager in late April

' Expectations for 2009/10 will be at an all-time high '

the optimism in Suffolk and a lack of consistency was to curtail any chance of Magilton establishing Town in the top six.

friend, former Plymouth keeper Luke McCormick, who had been jailed for causing death by dangerous driving.

Norris was fined by the club, but he soon found himself back in the side as Magilton came under fire following a 2–0 defeat at rivals Norwich, while an FA Cup away trip to Chelsea allowed a break from league action. Alex Bruce's strike ensured Town went in at half-time level, but ultimately two free-kicks from Michael Ballack and Frank Lampard helped Chelsea to a 3–1 win.

The January transfer window saw another seven-figure fee splashed out on Luciano Civelli. However, the Argentinian winger was soon ruled out by a knee injury, and a terrible performance in a 3–0 defeat to Southampton in March left the club off the play-off pace.

Magilton was sacked soon after, following the appointment of Simon Clegg as the new chief executive, and Keane was quickly handed the task of re-establishing Town in the Barclays Premier League.

After a press conference which put the club back in the limelight, Keane masterminded a hugely impressive 3–0 win at play-off chasing Cardiff in his first game in charge.

With 13 players out of contract at the end of the season, and the promise of cash, Keane faces a spell of rebuilding at the club. Undoubtedly, Ipswich's expectations for 2009/10 will be at an all-time high.

RESULTS 2008/09

August

9th	● Preston ....h	L 1–2	**Att:** 22,307. **Ref:** P Taylor — **Scorers:** Lisbie
12th	● Leyton Orient ....h	W 4–1	**Att:** 1,477. **Ref:** G Ward — **Scorers:** Haynes[2], Lee, Miller. **Booked:** Bruce, Norris
16th	● Burnley ....a	W 0–3	**Att:** 11,312. **Ref:** T Bates — **Scorers:** Lisbie, Trotter, Jordan OG. **Booked:** Shumulikoski
23rd	● Wolverhampton..................h	L 0–2	**Att:** 21,483. **Ref:** S Tanner — **Booked:** Shumulikoski, Counago. **Dismissed:** Bruce
26th	● Colchester ....h	W 2–1	**Att:** 17,084. **Ref:** R Beeby — **Scorers:** Counago, Lisbie. **Booked:** Quinn, Casement
30th	● Watford ....a	L 2–1	**Att:** 16,345. **Ref:** L Probert — **Scorers:** Counago. **Booked:** Campo, Volz

September

13th	● Reading ....h	W 2–0	**Att:** 21,366. **Ref:** K Hill — **Scorers:** Stead, Walters. **Booked:** Garvan
17th	● Southampton ....a	D 2–2	**Att:** 14,916. **Ref:** P Crossley — **Scorers:** Garvan, Quinn. **Booked:** Volz, Garvan, Walters, Balkestein
20th	● Sheff Wed........................a	D 0–0	**Att:** 17,198. **Ref:** M Jones
24th	● Wigan ....h	L 1–4	**Att:** 13,803. **Ref:** M Dean — **Scorers:** Walters. **Booked:** Volz
27th	● Crystal Palace ....h	D 1–1	**Att:** 19,032. **Ref:** D Deadman — **Scorers:** Stead. **Booked:** Bruce, Miller
30th	● Barnsley ....h	W 3–0	**Att:** 18,177. **Ref:** K Friend — **Scorers:** Campo, Garvan, Stead

October

4th	● Charlton ....a	L 2–1	**Att:** 20,643. **Ref:** G Hegley — **Scorers:** Cranie OG
18th	● Swansea..........................h	D 2–2	**Att:** 20,026. **Ref:** J Moss — **Scorers:** Counago[2]. **Booked:** Stead, Naylor, Campo
21st	● Nottm Forest......................a	D 1–1	**Att:** 19,455. **Ref:** G Laws — **Scorers:** Miller. **Booked:** D Wright
25th	● Plymouth..........................a	W 1–3	**Att:** 12,294. **Ref:** P Miller — **Scorers:** Garvan[2], Lisbie. **Booked:** McAuley, Volz, Garvan, Norris. **Dismissed:** Norris
28th	● Charlton ....h	D 1–1	**Att:** 20,352. **Ref:** K Wright — **Scorers:** Garvan. **Booked:** Stead

November

1st	● QPR ....h	W 2–0	**Att:** 20,966. **Ref:** T Kettle — **Scorers:** Stead[2]. **Booked:** Garvan
8th	● Blackpool ....a	W 0–1	**Att:** 7,349. **Ref:** C Webster — **Scorers:** Norris. **Booked:** Norris
15th	● Doncaster ....a	L 1–0	**Att:** 10,823. **Ref:** K Friend — **Booked:** Volz, Bruce
22nd	● Derby ....h	W 2–0	**Att:** 20,239. **Ref:** M Russell — **Scorers:** Counago, Walters. **Booked:** Naylor
25th	● Birmingham ....a	L 2–1	**Att:** 15,689. **Ref:** R Shoebridge — **Scorers:** Bruce. **Booked:** Naylor
29th	● Sheff Utd ....h	D 1–1	**Att:** 19,785. **Ref:** D Whitestone — **Scorers:** Miller. **Booked:** Norris, Quinn

December

7th	● Norwich............................a	L 2–0	**Att:** 25,472. **Ref:** L Probert — **Booked:** D Wright, Walters, Shumulikoski
10th	● Bristol City ....h	W 3–1	**Att:** 17,749. **Ref:** P Taylor — **Scorers:** Counago, Walters, Fontaine OG. **Booked:** Volz, Counago, Shumulikoski. **Dismissed:** Bruce
13th	● Cardiff ....h	L 1–2	**Att:** 19,665. **Ref:** A Woolmer — **Scorers:** Stead. **Booked:** Thatcher, Garvan, Balkestein. **Dismissed:** Thatcher
20th	● Coventry ....a	D 2–2	**Att:** 15,598. **Ref:** R Styles — **Scorers:** Lisbie[2]. **Booked:** Miller, Quinn
26th	● Birmingham ....h	L 0–1	**Att:** 23,536. **Ref:** I Williamson — **Booked:** Quinn, Volz, Miller
28th	● Derby ....a	W 0–1	**Att:** 28,358. **Ref:** K Stroud — **Scorers:** Walters. **Booked:** McAuley, Campo

January

3rd	● Chesterfield ....h	W 3–0	**Att:** 12,524. **Ref:** K Hill — **Scorers:** Counago, Stead, Walters. **Booked:** Shumulikoski
10th	● Sheff Wed........................h	D 1–1	**Att:** 22,213. **Ref:** G Horwood — **Scorers:** Counago. **Booked:** Campo
17th	● Crystal Palace ....a	W 1–4	**Att:** 15,348. **Ref:** C Penton — **Scorers:** Garvan, Lisbie, Norris, Hill OG. **Booked:** Miller, McAuley
24th	● Chelsea ....a	L 3–1	**Att:** 41,137. **Ref:** A Wiley — **Scorers:** Bruce. **Booked:** Bruce, Garvan, Norris
27th	● Barnsley ....a	W 1–2	**Att:** 11,183. **Ref:** C Boyeson — **Scorers:** Stead[2]
31st	● Plymouth..........................h	D 0–0	**Att:** 20,333. **Ref:** D Deadman — **Booked:** McAuley

February

7th	● Swansea..........................a	L 3–0	**Att:** 14,020. **Ref:** K Wright — **Booked:** Norris, Quinn
14th	● Blackpool ....h	D 1–1	**Att:** 19,299. **Ref:** P Crossley — **Scorers:** Miller. **Booked:** Thatcher
18th	● Nottm Forest......................h	W 2–1	**Att:** 19,930. **Ref:** M Atkinson — **Scorers:** Wright, Perch OG. **Booked:** Stead, Counago, Norris
21st	● QPR ....a	W 1–3	**Att:** 13,904. **Ref:** S Attwell — **Scorers:** Counago, Stead, Walters. **Booked:** Thatcher
28th	● Preston ....a	L 3–2	**Att:** 12,709. **Ref:** S Tanner — **Scorers:** Miller[2]. **Booked:** Norris, McAuley

March

3rd	● Southampton ....h	L 0–3	**Att:** 20,040. **Ref:** A D'Urso
10th	● Wolverhampton..................a	D 0–0	**Att:** 22,227. **Ref:** G Salisbury — **Booked:** Thatcher, Norris, Quinn, D Wright
14th	● Reading ....a	W 0–1	**Att:** 20,592. **Ref:** M Oliver — **Scorers:** Stead. **Booked:** Thatcher, Garvan
17th	● Burnley ....h	D 1–1	**Att:** 18,745. **Ref:** R Shoebridge — **Booked:** Giovani
21st	● Watford ....h	D 0–0	**Att:** 21,434. **Ref:** C Webster — **Booked:** Counago, Campo

April

4th	● Sheff Utd ....a	L 2–0	**Att:** 25,315. **Ref:** N Miller — **Booked:** Quinn, Thatcher
11th	● Doncaster ....h	L 1–3	**Att:** 19,918. **Ref:** K Stroud — **Scorers:** Garvan
13th	● Bristol City ....a	D 1–1	**Att:** 16,430. **Ref:** A Taylor — **Scorers:** Giovani. **Booked:** Balkestein
19th	● Norwich............................h	W 3–2	**Att:** 28,274. **Ref:** N Swarbrick — **Scorers:** Giovani, Quinn, Stead. **Booked:** Counago, Bruce, Haynes
25th	● Cardiff ....a	W 0–3	**Att:** 19,129. **Ref:** S Mathieson — **Scorers:** Counago, Norris, Stead. **Booked:** Giovani, Haynes

May

| 3rd | ● Coventry ....h | W 2–1 | **Att:** 27,225. **Ref:** G Laws — **Scorers:** Counago, Giovani |

● Coca-Cola Championship/Play-Offs ● FA Cup ● Carling Cup

IPSWICH TOWN

CHAMPIONSHIP GOALKEEPER STATS

Player	Minutes on pitch	Appearances	Match starts	Completed matches	Sub appearances	Subbed off	Saved with feet	Punched	Parried	Tipped over	Fumbled	Tipped round	Caught	Blocked	Clean sheets	Goals conceded	Minutes since conceding	Save %	Saved	Resulting in goals	Opposition miss	Yellow cards	Red cards
Richard Wright	4407	46	46	46	0	0	2	10	22	12	0	17	173	0	13	53	15	81.91	1	4	0	0	0

CHAMPIONSHIP OUTFIELD PLAYER STATS

Player	Minutes on pitch	Appearances	Match starts	Completed matches	Substitute appearances	Subbed off	Goals scored	Minutes since scoring	Assists	Shots on target	Shots off target	Crosses	Defensive clearances	Defensive blocks	Fouls committed	Free-kicks won	Caught offside	Yellow cards	Red cards
Darren Ambrose	582	9	6	3	3	3	0	-	1	15	2	19	0	0	3	4	0	0	0
Pim Balkestein	1641	20	15	15	5	0	0	-	0	6	7	5	28	7	14	16	0	3	0
Dean Bowditch	18	1	0	0	1	0	0	-	0	0	0	0	0	0	0	0	0	0	0
Alex Bruce	2273	25	25	22	0	1	1	1634	0	4	6	22	47	14	19	26	0	3	2
Ivan Campo	1323	17	14	10	3	4	1	1127	1	5	6	8	17	9	22	27	0	5	0
Luciano Civelli	646	8	8	4	0	4	0	-	1	7	2	16	4	0	7	8	3	0	0
Pablo Counago	2651	44	26	8	18	18	9	52	6	35	19	4	1	0	42	61	39	5	0
Owen Garvan	2380	37	22	17	15	5	7	276	1	17	17	41	14	2	28	19	5	6	0
Dos Santos Giovani	524	8	6	3	2	3	4	42	1	6	3	2	3	0	1	12	1	1	0
Dan Harding	97	1	1	1	0	0	0	-	0	0	0	0	0	0	0	1	0	0	0
Danny Haynes	975	24	8	2	16	6	0	-	1	5	15	28	1	2	10	8	5	2	0
Alan Lee	171	3	2	1	1	0	0	46	1	3	2	1	0	0	4	3	0	0	0
Kevin Lisbie	2428	41	24	11	17	13	6	1067	3	34	15	11	2	1	25	43	49	0	0
Gareth McAuley	3277	35	35	34	0	1	0	-	3	10	15	5	64	13	45	29	3	5	0
Tommy Miller	2458	32	26	20	6	6	5	448	2	19	9	22	14	1	43	20	1	4	0
Richard Naylor	1966	23	20	20	3	0	0	-	0	1	6	3	37	12	18	18	1	3	0
David Norris	3147	37	35	25	2	9	3	141	3	31	17	29	12	1	57	58	18	7	1
Jaime Peters	225	3	2	1	1	0	0	-	0	0	0	6	1	2	2	5	1	0	0
Alan Quinn	2526	34	28	17	6	11	2	115	2	30	24	41	11	2	43	37	2	6	0
Jordan Rhodes	39	2	0	0	2	0	0	-	0	0	1	0	0	0	0	1	0	0	0
Matthew Richards	95	1	1	1	0	0	0	-	0	0	0	0	0	0	0	1	0	0	0
Veliche Shumulikoski	2010	26	22	16	4	6	0	-	0	11	9	2	14	4	27	18	3	4	0
Tommy Smith	193	2	2	2	0	0	0	-	0	0	1	0	4	3	3	0	0	0	0
Jonathan Stead	2342	39	26	7	13	19	12	101	7	57	39	33	11	1	35	33	24	3	0
Ben Thatcher	1815	20	20	17	0	2	0	-	1	1	4	14	15	5	32	17	0	6	1
Liam Trotter	179	3	2	0	1	2	1	146	0	1	1	2	1	1	2	0	0	0	0
Moritz Volz	1903	22	20	18	2	2	0	-	0	2	4	31	19	5	30	15	0	6	0
Jonathan Walters	2850	36	30	20	6	10	5	286	5	31	22	63	14	1	23	36	12	2	0
Connor Wickham	52	2	0	0	2	0	0	-	0	0	0	0	0	0	0	0	1	0	0
David Wright	3148	34	34	32	0	2	1	797	1	4	6	60	26	10	34	32	4	3	0

actim

SEASON TOTALS

Goals scored	62
Goals conceded	53
Clean sheets	13
Shots on target	337
Shots off target	252
Shots per goal	9.50
Pens awarded	5
Pens scored	4
Pens conceded	5
Offsides	173
Corners	265
Crosses	468
Players used	31
Fouls committed	568
Free-kicks won	561

CARDS RECEIVED

74 4

SEQUENCES

Wins	3
(19/04/09–03/05/09)	
Losses	2
(on two occasions)	
Draws	3
(17/09/08–27/09/08)	
Undefeated	6
(18/10/08–08/11/08)	
Without win	5
(17/03/09–13/04/09)	
Undefeated home	9
(13/09/08–10/12/08)	
Undefeated away	4
(20/12/08–27/01/09)	
Without scoring	2
(on three occasions)	
Without conceding	2
(on three occasions)	
Scoring	9
(27/09/08–08/11/08)	
Conceding	7
(25/11/08–26/12/08)	

SEASON INFORMATION

Highest position: 8
Lowest position: 19
Average goals scored per game: 1.35
Average goals conceded per game: 1.15

League position at the end of each week

League position at the end of: August 17, September 11, October 13, November 11, December 10, January 10, February 10, March 10, April 9, May 9

MATCH RECORDS

Goals scored per match

		W	D	L	Pts
Failed to score	11	0	4	7	4
Scored 1 goal	17	3	8	6	17
Scored 2 goals	10	6	3	1	21
Scored 3 goals	7	7	0	0	21
Scored 4+ goals	1	1	0	0	3

Goals conceded per match

		W	D	L	Pts
Clean sheet	13	9	4	0	31
Conceded 1 goal	17	7	8	2	29
Conceded 2 goals	12	1	3	8	6
Conceded 3 goals	4	0	0	4	0
Conceded 4+ goals	0	0	0	0	0

QUICK-FIRE GOALS

From the start of a match
Kevin Lisbie
(v Preston) 1:36

By a substitute after coming on
Kevin Lisbie
(v Crystal Palace) 4:06

LAST-GASP GOALS

From the start of a match
Dos Santos Giovani
(v Bristol City) 93:55

By a substitute after coming on
Jonathan Stead
(v Cardiff) 63:15

GOAL DETAILS

How the goals were struck

SCORED		CONCEDED
34	Right foot	23
17	Left foot	17
11	Headers	13
0	Others	0

How the goals were struck

SCORED		CONCEDED
39	Open play	28
7	Cross	10
4	Corner	1
4	Penalties	4
3	Direct from free-kick	2
0	Free-kick	7
5	Own goals	1

Distance from goal

SCORED		CONCEDED
19	6yds	20
32	18yds	24
11	18+yds	9

GOALS SCORED/CONCEDED PER FIVE-MINUTE INTERVALS

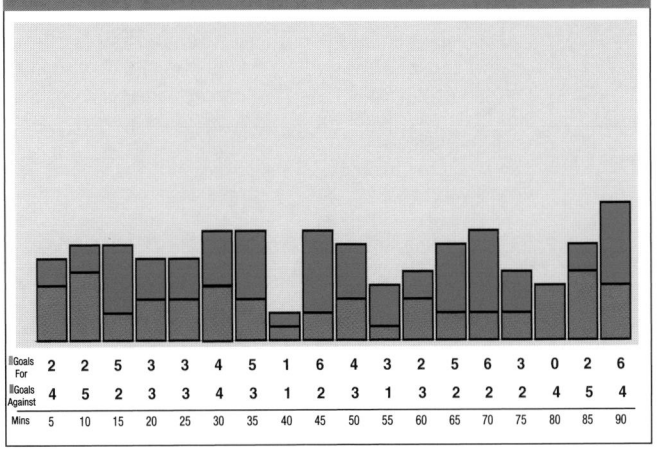

Goals For	2	2	5	3	3	4	5	1	6	4	3	2	5	6	3	0	2	6
Goals Against	4	5	2	3	3	4	3	1	2	3	1	3	2	2	2	4	5	4
Mins	5	10	15	20	25	30	35	40	45	50	55	60	65	70	75	80	85	90

NORWICH CITY

CLUB SUMMARY

FORMED	1902
MANAGER	Bryan Gunn
GROUND	Carrow Road
CAPACITY	26,034
NICKNAME	The Canaries
WEBSITE	www.canaries.co.uk

The New Football Pools PLAYER OF THE SEASON — Lee Croft

OVERALL

P	W	D	L	F	A	GD
49	12	11	26	58	73	-15

COCA-COLA CHAMPIONSHIP

Pos	P	W	D	L	F	A	GD	Pts
22	46	12	10	24	57	70	-13	46

HOME

Pos	P	W	D	L	F	A	GD	Pts
16	23	9	5	9	35	28	7	32

AWAY

Pos	P	W	D	L	F	A	GD	Pts
23	23	3	5	15	22	42	-20	14

CUP PROGRESS DETAILS

Competition	Round reached	Knocked out by
FA Cup	R3	Charlton
Carling Cup	R1	Milton Keynes Dons

BIGGEST WIN (ALL COMPS)
17/01/09 4–0 v Barnsley **FLC**

BIGGEST DEFEAT (ALL COMPS)
03/05/09 2–4 v Charlton **FLC**

THE PLAYER WITH THE MOST

Shots on target
Darel Russell 35

Shots off target
Matthew Pattison 27

Shots without scoring
Alan Gow 20

Assists
David Bell 7

Offsides
Leroy Lita.. 48

Fouls
Darel Russell 74

Fouls without a card
Antoine Sibierski 20

Free-kicks won
Lee Croft 64

Defensive clearances
Gary Doherty.. 75

actim INDEX for the 2008/09 Coca-Cola Championship Season

Rank	Player	Pts
49	David Marshall	465
67	Lee Croft	434
113	Sammy Clingan	359
140	Gary Doherty	324
162	Jon Otsemobor	305

ATTENDANCE RECORD

High	Low	Average
25,487	23,225	24,543
v Watford (13/04/2009)	v Preston (08/11/2008)	

A SECOND successive season of struggle for Norwich ended in relegation as the Canaries slid into the third tier for the first time since 1959/60.

Expectations were high at the start of the season after manager Glenn Roeder had steered the club away from trouble to stay up in his first six months in charge.

However, supporters were unhappy with the decision to allow cult hero Darren Huckerby to leave on a free transfer, while promising youngsters Chris Martin and Michael Spillane were sent to Luton on season-long loans.

Roeder's side got off to a poor start, failing to pick up a win until the middle of September and crashing out of the League Cup to Coca-Cola League One side Milton Keynes Dons.

The signing of Reading striker Leroy Lita on loan in October provided a boost, and his hat-trick saw eventual champions Wolves hammered 5–2. Lita would score seven times in his 16 games for the club and, despite returning to the Royals in January, would finish as the club's top scorer.

Rivals Ipswich were beaten 2–0 at the start of December, but it proved another false dawn as the Canaries continued to struggle at the foot of the table and, following an FA Cup defeat to Charlton, Roeder was sacked.

Bryan Gunn – a hero at the club during 12 seasons as a player – stepped up to take control until the end of the 2008/09 campaign and immediately tasted success as Barnsley were beaten 4–0 in his first game in charge.

Gary Doherty holds his head following Norwich's relegation

Gunn brought in a host of loan players, including forwards Chris Killen, Alan Gow and Alan Lee, but saw the Canaries win just four more games as they slid towards relegation.

Rivals Ipswich hit a nail into their coffin at the end of April when a rather debatable penalty saw Gunn's side lose 3–2, while Reading beat City 2–0 in the last game of the campaign at Carrow Road.

The Canaries entered the final day of the season knowing that a win at already-relegated Charlton, coupled with a Barnsley defeat, could see them save their Championship status, but Gunn saw his side humiliated at The Valley. City were 3–0 down inside 30 minutes and had their fate confirmed with a 4–2 defeat.

With more than 18,000 season tickets already sold, City will be a force in League One, but Gunn – who is now the manager on a permanent basis – will be expected to deliver immediate promotion.

> **Ipswich hit a nail into their coffin at the end of April**

August

9th	● Coventry ....a	L 2–0	**Att:** 22,607. **Ref:** C Webster — **Booked:** Stefanovic, Fotheringham
12th	● Milton Keynes Dons ....a	L 1–0	**Att:** 6,261. **Ref:** M Thorpe
16th	● Blackpool ....h	D 1–1	**Att:** 23,727. **Ref:** K Friend — **Scorers:** Russell. **Booked:** Russell
23rd	● Cardiff ....a	D 2–2	**Att:** 18,032. **Ref:** A Taylor — **Scorers:** Lupoli[2]
30th	● Birmingham ....h	D 1–1	**Att:** 24,229. **Ref:** J Moss — **Scorers:** Russell. **Booked:** Kennedy, Russell

September

13th	● Plymouth............................a	W 1–2	**Att:** 11,185. **Ref:** A Woolmer — **Scorers:** Lupoli, Sibierski. **Booked:** Omozusi, Lupoli
17th	● QPR ....h	L 0–1	**Att:** 24,249. **Ref:** R Shoebridge — **Booked:** Fotheringham, Lupoli
20th	● Sheff Utd ....h	W 1–0	**Att:** 24,175. **Ref:** P Crossley — **Scorers:** Croft
27th	● Barnsley ....a	D 0–0	**Att:** 12,324. **Ref:** N Miller
30th	● Southampton ....a	L 2–0	**Att:** 14,480. **Ref:** R Beeby — **Booked:** Fotheringham, Croft. **Dismissed:** Stefanovic

October

4th	● Derby ....h	L 1–2	**Att:** 24,771. **Ref:** D Deadman — **Scorers:** Clingan. **Booked:** Russell
18th	● Bristol City ....a	L 1–0	**Att:** 16,791. **Ref:** A Hall — **Booked:** Bertrand, Russell
21st	● Wolverhampton...................h	W 5–2	**Att:** 24,351. **Ref:** G Horwood — **Scorers:** Croft, Lita[3], Ikeme OG. **Booked:** Lita
25th	● Doncaster ....h	W 2–1	**Att:** 24,543. **Ref:** C Penton — **Scorers:** Lita, Sibierski. **Booked:** Clingan, Omozusi, Bell, Stefanovic, Lita
28th	● Derby ....a	L 3–1	**Att:** 26,621. **Ref:** N Swarbrick — **Scorers:** Kennedy

November

1st	● Burnley ....a	L 2–0	**Att:** 11,353. **Ref:** G Laws
8th	● Preston ....h	D 2–2	**Att:** 23,225. **Ref:** P Taylor — **Scorers:** Kennedy, Lita. **Booked:** Bell, Lita. **Dismissed:** Russell
15th	● Swansea............................h	L 2–3	**Att:** 24,262. **Ref:** G Hegley — **Scorers:** Lupoli, Rangel OG
22nd	● Nottm Forest......................a	W 1–2	**Att:** 18,566. **Ref:** M Oliver — **Scorers:** Pattison, Cohen OG. **Booked:** Pattison. **Dismissed:** Doherty
25th	● Crystal Palace ....h	L 1–2	**Att:** 24,034. **Ref:** D Whitestone — **Scorers:** Pattison
29th	● Sheff Wed..........................a	L 3–2	**Att:** 18,883. **Ref:** T Bates — **Scorers:** Clingan, Lita. **Dismissed:** Kennedy

December

7th	● Ipswich ....h	W 2–0	**Att:** 25,472. **Ref:** L Probert — **Scorers:** Croft, Pattison. **Booked:** Clingan
10th	● Watford ....a	L 2–1	**Att:** 13,268. **Ref:** P Crossley — **Scorers:** Croft. **Booked:** Doherty, Otsemobor
13th	● Reading ....a	L 2–0	**Att:** 19,382. **Ref:** T Kettle — **Booked:** Bertrand
20th	● Charlton ....h	W 1–0	**Att:** 23,827. **Ref:** M Haywood — **Scorers:** Lita. **Booked:** Lita
26th	● Crystal Palace ....a	L 3–1	**Att:** 17,180. **Ref:** K Stroud — **Scorers:** Doherty. **Booked:** Fotheringham
28th	● Nottm Forest......................h	L 2–3	**Att:** 25,475. **Ref:** J Moss — **Scorers:** Breckin OG, Garner OG. **Booked:** Croft, Russell

January

3rd	● Charlton ....a	D 1–1	**Att:** 12,615. **Ref:** S Tanner — **Scorers:** Lupoli. **Booked:** Drury
10th	● Sheff Utd ....a	L 1–0	**Att:** 27,267. **Ref:** M Halsey
13th	● Charlton ....h	L 0–1	**Att:** 13,997. **Ref:** C Oliver — **Booked:** Doherty
17th	● Barnsley ....h	W 4–0	**Att:** 24,685. **Ref:** S Hooper — **Scorers:** Clingan, Cureton, Hoolahan, Russell
27th	● Southampton ....h	D 2–2	**Att:** 25,271. **Ref:** L Mason — **Scorers:** Fotheringham, Hoolahan. **Booked:** Doherty, Croft
30th	● Doncaster ....a	D 1–1	**Att:** 12,384. **Ref:** M Oliver — **Scorers:** Grounds. **Booked:** Fotheringham

February

3rd	● Wolverhampton...................a	D 3–3	**Att:** 21,654. **Ref:** K Woolmer — **Scorers:** Cort, Croft, Doherty. **Booked:** Croft
7th	● Bristol City ....h	L 1–2	**Att:** 24,691. **Ref:** A D'Urso — **Scorers:** Grounds. **Dismissed:** Doherty
14th	● Preston ....a	L 1–0	**Att:** 12,033. **Ref:** R Shoebridge — **Booked:** Grounds, Shackell
21st	● Burnley ....h	D 1–1	**Att:** 24,363. **Ref:** K Friend — **Scorers:** Cureton
28th	● Coventry ....h	L 1–2	**Att:** 24,450. **Ref:** P Taylor — **Scorers:** Grounds. **Booked:** Clingan, Russell

March

3rd	● QPR ....a	W 0–1	**Att:** 13,533. **Ref:** G Scott — **Scorers:** Russell. **Booked:** Bertrand, Croft
7th	● Blackpool ....a	L 2–0	**Att:** 7,505. **Ref:** C Oliver — **Booked:** Doherty
10th	● Cardiff ....h	W 2–0	**Att:** 23,706. **Ref:** T Kettle — **Scorers:** McDonald, Mooney. **Booked:** Mooney
14th	● Plymouth............................h	W 1–0	**Att:** 25,064. **Ref:** F Graham — **Scorers:** Mooney. **Booked:** Doherty, Mooney, Russell. **Dismissed:** Russell
21st	● Birmingham ....a	D 1–1	**Att:** 18,159. **Ref:** M Haywood — **Scorers:** Clingan. **Booked:** Lee, Marshall

April

4th	● Sheff Wed..........................h	L 0–1	**Att:** 25,385. **Ref:** M Russell — **Booked:** Mooney
11th	● Swansea............................a	L 2–1	**Att:** 15,783. **Ref:** G Salisbury — **Scorers:** Lee. **Booked:** Russell, Lee
13th	● Watford ....h	W 2–0	**Att:** 25,487. **Ref:** S Tanner — **Scorers:** Doherty, Rose OG. **Booked:** Shackell, Lee
19th	● Ipswich ....a	L 3–2	**Att:** 28,274. **Ref:** N Swarbrick — **Scorers:** Clingan, Mooney. **Booked:** Gow
27th	● Reading ....h	L 0–2	**Att:** 25,041. **Ref:** C Oliver — **Booked:** Lee

May

| 3rd | ● Charlton ....a | L 4–2 | **Att:** 22,020. **Ref:** R Booth — **Scorers:** Clingan, Lee. **Booked:** Lappin, Shackell |

● Coca-Cola Championship/Play-Offs ● FA Cup ● Carling Cup

NORWICH CITY

CHAMPIONSHIP GOALKEEPER STATS

Player	Minutes on pitch	Appearances	Match starts	Completed matches	Sub appearances	Subbed off	Saved with feet	Punched	Parried	Tipped over	Fumbled	Tipped round	Caught	Blocked	Clean sheets	Goals conceded	Minutes since conceding	Save %	Saved	Resulting in goals	Opposition miss	Yellow cards	Red cards
David Marshall	4416	46	46	46	0	0	0	19	40	4	0	9	189	1	9	70	44	78.85	1	10	0	1	0

CHAMPIONSHIP OUTFIELD PLAYER STATS

Player	Minutes on pitch	Appearances	Match starts	Completed matches	Substitute appearances	Subbed off	Goals scored	Minutes since scoring	Assists	Shots on target	Shots off target	Crosses	Defensive clearances	Defensive blocks	Fouls committed	Free-kicks won	Caught offside	Yellow cards	Red cards
David Bell	1245	19	12	8	7	4	0	75	7	7	5	89	9	0	9	6	6	2	0
Ryan Bertrand	3425	38	37	33	1	4	0	-	0	4	13	69	31	7	32	48	3	3	0
David Carney	466	9	4	1	5	3	0	-	0	1	1	16	1	0	1	3	2	0	0
Sammy Clingan	3806	40	40	38	0	2	6	35	6	16	25	79	26	7	24	35	0	3	0
Carl Cort	740	12	7	3	5	4	1	547	0	5	8	3	10	1	15	6	8	0	0
Lee Croft	3205	41	34	18	7	16	5	984	3	16	13	170	2	1	51	64	19	5	0
Jamie Cureton	1094	22	10	1	12	9	2	137	1	13	12	15	0	0	6	7	22	0	0
Luke Daley	56	3	0	0	3	0	0	-	0	0	0	1	0	0	1	1	0	0	0
Gary Doherty	3049	34	32	29	2	1	3	302	1	10	7	2	75	17	38	21	1	4	2
Adam Drury	818	11	10	6	1	4	0	-	1	1	1	27	14	1	6	8	0	0	0
Mark Fotheringham	2083	27	20	16	7	4	1	471	4	12	8	29	9	1	19	16	3	5	0
Alan Gow	799	13	8	4	5	4	0	940	1	4	16	20	2	0	13	15	6	1	0
Jonathan Grounds	1386	16	14	14	2	0	3	230	1	5	8	16	32	3	11	13	0	1	0
Wesley Hoolahan	2260	32	27	10	5	17	2	754	3	19	16	75	5	1	13	62	3	0	0
John Kennedy	1423	16	15	12	1	2	2	489	0	4	3	3	40	11	21	15	0	1	1
Christopher Killen	79	4	0	0	4	0	0	-	0	1	0	0	0	0	2	3	0	0	0
Omar Koroma	202	5	2	0	3	2	0	-	0	4	1	3	2	0	0	3	3	0	0
Simon Lappin	381	5	4	3	1	1	0	-	0	1	4	11	0	1	8	1	0	1	0
Alan Lee	610	7	6	6	1	0	2	46	1	6	6	1	4	0	21	19	4	4	0
Adrian Leijer	110	4	1	0	3	1	0	-	0	0	0	0	1	0	1	1	0	0	0
Leroy Lita	1517	16	16	15	0	1	9	336	1	24	23	10	1	0	23	35	48	4	0
Arturo Lupoli	611	17	7	0	10	7	4	70	1	13	13	3	0	0	7	11	11	2	0
Cody McDonald	242	7	1	1	6	0	1	225	0	3	5	0	0	0	4	5	1	0	0
David Mooney	790	9	8	7	1	1	3	182	0	12	9	8	1	0	10	4	15	3	0
Elliot Omozusi	1859	21	20	18	1	2	0	-	0	1	1	17	24	5	17	13	0	2	0
Jon Otsemobor	3429	37	35	34	2	1	0	-	1	5	9	72	31	11	12	23	0	1	0
Matthew Pattison	1601	24	18	10	6	8	3	437	2	20	27	21	7	3	9	26	3	3	0
Darel Russell	3061	38	31	26	7	3	4	784	1	35	21	22	21	3	74	53	14	8	2
Jason Shackell	1382	15	15	13	0	2	0	-	1	10	5	4	41	9	12	11	2	3	0
Antoine Sibierski	1033	15	13	6	2	7	2	262	1	10	9	4	1	1	20	28	10	0	0
Korey Smith	112	2	1	1	1	0	0	-	0	0	1	0	0	0	0	3	0	0	0
Dejan Stefanovic	1028	12	12	10	0	1	0	-	1	1	3	3	20	5	14	7	0	2	1

actim

SEASON TOTALS

Goals scored	57
Goals conceded	70
Clean sheets	9
Shots on target	263
Shots off target	273
Shots per goal	9.40
Pens awarded	5
Pens scored	4
Pens conceded	11
Offsides	184
Corners	279
Crosses	793
Players used	33
Fouls committed	495
Free-kicks won	571

CARDS RECEIVED

57 **6**

SEQUENCES

Wins	2
(on two occasions)	
Losses	3
(on three occasions)	
Draws	3
(on two occasions)	
Undefeated	4
(on two occasions)	
Without win	7
(27/01/09–28/02/09)	
Undefeated home	3
(21/10/08–08/11/08)	
Undefeated away	3
(23/08/08–27/09/08)	
Without scoring	2
(27/09/08–30/09/08)	
Without conceding	2
(on two occasions)	
Scoring	7
(08/11/08–10/12/08)	
Conceding	12
(30/09/08–29/11/08)	

SEASON INFORMATION

Highest position: 11
Lowest position: 23
Average goals scored per game: 1.24
Average goals conceded per game: 1.52

League position at the end of each week

League position at the end of: August 19, September 19, October 18, November 19, December 20, January 19, February 22, March 20, April 20, May 22

MATCH RECORDS

Goals scored per match

		W	D	L	Pts
Failed to score	12	0	1	11	1
Scored 1 goal	17	4	5	8	17
Scored 2 goals	14	6	3	5	21
Scored 3 goals	1	0	1	0	1
Scored 4+ goals	2	2	0	0	6

Goals conceded per match

		W	D	L	Pts
Clean sheet	9	8	1	0	25
Conceded 1 goal	13	3	5	5	14
Conceded 2 goals	16	1	3	12	6
Conceded 3 goals	7	0	1	6	1
Conceded 4+ goals	1	0	0	1	0

QUICK-FIRE GOALS

From the start of a match
Leroy Lita (v Preston) 13:16

By a substitute after coming on
Arturo Lupoli (v Cardiff) 3:17

LAST-GASP GOALS

From the start of a match
Leroy Lita (v Doncaster) 92:08

By a substitute after coming on
Cody McDonald (v Cardiff) 16:23

GOAL DETAILS

How the goals were struck

SCORED		CONCEDED
27	Right foot	40
12	Left foot	14
17	Headers	16
1	Others	0

How the goals were struck

SCORED		CONCEDED
27	Open play	39
5	Cross	15
7	Corner	2
4	Penalties	10
2	Direct from free-kick	0
6	Free-kick	4
6	Own goals	0

Distance from goal

SCORED		CONCEDED
20	6yds	20
30	18yds	40
7	18+yds	10

GOALS SCORED/CONCEDED PER FIVE-MINUTE INTERVALS

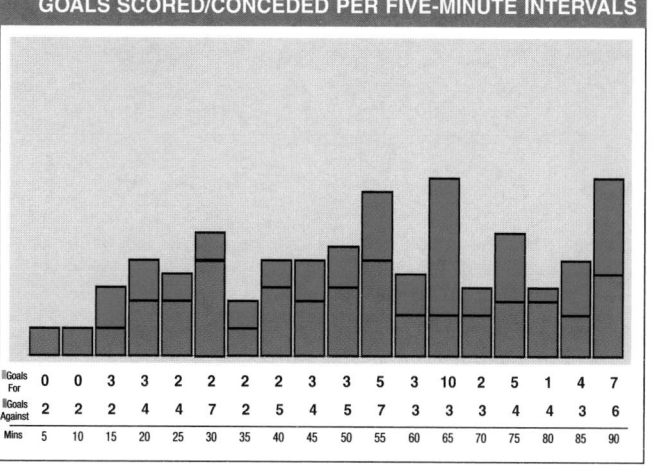

Goals For	0	0	3	3	2	2	2	2	3	3	5	3	10	2	5	1	4	7
Goals Against	2	2	2	4	4	7	2	5	4	5	7	3	3	3	4	4	3	6
Mins	5	10	15	20	25	30	35	40	45	50	55	60	65	70	75	80	85	90

NOTTINGHAM FOREST

CLUB SUMMARY

FORMED	1865
MANAGER	Billy Davies
GROUND	City Ground
CAPACITY	30,602
NICKNAME	The Reds
WEBSITE	www.nottinghamforest.co.uk

The New Football Pools PLAYER OF THE SEASON — Chris Cohen

OVERALL

P	W	D	L	F	A	GD
51	15	15	21	61	71	-10

COCA-COLA CHAMPIONSHIP

Pos	P	W	D	L	F	A	GD	Pts
19	46	13	14	19	50	65	-15	53

HOME

Pos	P	W	D	L	F	A	GD	Pts
20	23	8	7	8	27	28	-1	31

AWAY

Pos	P	W	D	L	F	A	GD	Pts
17	23	5	7	11	23	37	-14	22

CUP PROGRESS DETAILS

Competition	Round reached	Knocked out by
FA Cup	R4	Derby
Carling Cup	R2	Sunderland

BIGGEST WIN (ALL COMPS)

13/08/08 4–0 v Morecambe **LC1**

BIGGEST DEFEAT (ALL COMPS)

14/03/09 0–5 v Burnley **FLC**

THE PLAYER WITH THE MOST

Shots on target	
Robert Earnshaw	39
Shots off target	
Robert Earnshaw	32
Shots without scoring	
Guy Moussi	10
Assists	
Chris Cohen	6
Offsides	
Robert Earnshaw	38
Fouls	
Chris Cohen	77
Fouls without a card	
Gary McSheffrey	8
Free-kicks won	
Chris Cohen	60
Defensive clearances	
Wes Morgan	76

actim INDEX for the 2008/09 Coca-Cola Championship Season

Rank	Player	Pts
29	Chris Cohen	509
76	Dexter Blackstock	413
82	Wes Morgan	402
133	Robert Earnshaw	340
135	Lewis McGugan	329

ATTENDANCE RECORD

High	Low	Average
29,140	17,568	22,299
v Derby (21/02/2009)	v Preston (03/03/2009)	

Forest's players celebrate their final goal of the 3–0 win at Manchester City

WHEN Billy Davies arrived at the City Ground at the turn of the year, Nottingham Forest were only above the relegation zone by the virtue of goal difference and one of the favourites to drop down into Coca-Cola League One.

However, with just a single match still to spare, Norwich's defeat to Reading ensured Forest would still be playing Championship football in 2009/10.

Forest may have ultimately secured their Championship status by virtue of results elsewhere, but that should not take anything away from the good work done by Davies since arriving at the club, following the dismissal of Colin Calderwood on Boxing Day.

The benchmark was set with a 3–0 victory at Manchester City in the third round of the FA Cup in Davies' first game in charge, and Forest built on that shock result.

Victories over relegation rivals Charlton and Plymouth followed to kick-start Forest's survival bid, and a sensational 1–0 win at promotion-chasing Reading at the end of

February sent a message that the City Ground club were determined to stay in the division.

Consecutive defeats to Watford, Burnley and Wolves in March sent Forest into the relegation zone, but they showed grit and determination to pull themselves out of trouble once again.

After earning a 1–1 draw with Barnsley at the start of April, they embarked upon a six-match unbeaten run that secured their survival.

With a difficult season behind them, Forest and manager Davies are now determined to build in the summer ahead of the new campaign.

'This has been too close for comfort for a club of this size, let's not be kidded,' said Davies. 'The competition will be fierce and we've got to be ready for a very difficult season. We've started touching base with agents and making contact with clubs as we look to build for the 2009/10 season.'

> **Forest and Davies are determined to build in the summer**

RESULTS 2008/09

August

10th	● Reading ....h	D 0–0	**Att:** 21,571. **Ref:** S Attwell — **Booked:** McGugan			
13th	● Morecambe........................h	W 4–0	**Att:** 4,030. **Ref:** C Boyeson — **Scorers:** Cohen, Earnshaw[2], Newbold. **Booked:** Martin			
16th	● Swansea............................a	L 3–1	**Att:** 16,611. **Ref:** P Taylor — **Scorers:** Perch. **Booked:** Moussi, Bennett			
23rd	● Watford ....h	W 3–2	**Att:** 20,005. **Ref:** M Haywood — **Scorers:** Earnshaw, Martin, Tyson			
27th	● Sunderland ....h	L 1–2	**Att:** 9,198. **Ref:** I Williamson — **Scorers:** Earnshaw. **Booked:** Cohen, Bennett (AET)			
30th	● Wolverhampton..................a	L 5–1	**Att:** 25,301. **Ref:** G Hegley — **Scorers:** Foley OG. **Booked:** Chambers, Bennett			

September

13th	● Burnley ....h	L 1–2	**Att:** 20,504. **Ref:** C Penton — **Scorers:** Earnshaw			
16th	● Preston ....a	L 2–1	**Att:** 13,145. **Ref:** C Webster — **Scorers:** Mawene OG. **Booked:** Morgan			
20th	● Charlton ....h	D 0–0	**Att:** 18,771. **Ref:** K Evans — **Booked:** Chambers, Wilson, Thornhill. **Dismissed:** Thornhill			
27th	● Plymouth...........................a	L 1–0	**Att:** 12,594. **Ref:** K Wright — **Booked:** Perch, Morgan, Cole. **Dismissed:** Morgan			
30th	● Sheff Wed.........................a	L 1–0	**Att:** 20,823. **Ref:** A D'Urso			

October

4th	● Crystal Palace ....h	L 0–2	**Att:** 22,811. **Ref:** R Beeby — **Booked:** Tyson, Thornhill, Cole			
18th	● QPR ....a	L 2–1	**Att:** 15,122. **Ref:** F Graham — **Scorers:** McGugan. **Booked:** Tyson, McCleary			
21st	● Ipswich ....h	D 1–1	**Att:** 19,455. **Ref:** G Laws — **Scorers:** McCleary. **Booked:** Cole			
25th	● Cardiff...............................h	L 0–1	**Att:** 19,468. **Ref:** K Stroud			
28th	● Crystal Palace ....a	W 1–2	**Att:** 15,162. **Ref:** A D'Urso — **Scorers:** Cohen, Thornhill. **Booked:** Tyson			

November

2nd	● Derby ....a	D 1–1	**Att:** 33,010. **Ref:** S Attwell — **Scorers:** Villa OG. **Booked:** Fletcher, Garner, Lynch, Camp, Perch. **Dismissed:** McGugan			
8th	● Birmingham ....h	D 1–1	**Att:** 21,415. **Ref:** P Dowd — **Scorers:** Perch. **Booked:** Perch			
15th	● Bristol City ....a	D 2–2	**Att:** 17,440. **Ref:** G Horwood — **Scorers:** Garner, Tyson			
22nd	● Norwich............................h	L 1–2	**Att:** 18,566. **Ref:** M Oliver — **Scorers:** Anderson. **Booked:** Cohen			
25th	● Doncaster ....a	D 0–0	**Att:** 12,612. **Ref:** A Penn — **Booked:** Garner			
29th	● Barnsley ....h	W 1–0	**Att:** 24,974. **Ref:** P Crossley — **Scorers:** Garner. **Booked:** Garner, Tyson			

December

6th	● Coventry ....a	D 2–2	**Att:** 17,542. **Ref:** N Swarbrick — **Scorers:** Earnshaw, Garner			
9th	● Sheff Utd ....h	L 0–1	**Att:** 19,541. **Ref:** G Salisbury — **Booked:** Perch			
13th	● Blackpool ....h	D 0–0	**Att:** 19,103. **Ref:** P Miller — **Booked:** Perch			
20th	● Southampton ....a	W 0–2	**Att:** 26,580. **Ref:** I Williamson — **Scorers:** Garner, Morgan. **Booked:** Cohen, Moloney			
26th	● Doncaster ....h	L 2–4	**Att:** 26,501. **Ref:** P Dowd — **Scorers:** Garner, Hird OG. **Booked:** Garner, Perch, Davies, Moloney			
28th	● Norwich............................a	W 2–3	**Att:** 25,475. **Ref:** J Moss — **Scorers:** Earnshaw, McGugan, Thornhill. **Booked:** Perch, Heath, Breckin, Chambers			

January

3rd	● Man City ....a	W 0–3	**Att:** 31,869. **Ref:** L Probert — **Scorers:** Earnshaw, Garner, Tyson			
10th	● Charlton ....a	W 0–2	**Att:** 24,553. **Ref:** A Woolmer — **Scorers:** Earnshaw, Tyson			
17th	● Plymouth...........................h	W 2–0	**Att:** 20,392. **Ref:** K Stroud — **Scorers:** Anderson, Earnshaw. **Booked:** Morgan, Anderson, Perch, Tyson			
23rd	● Derby ....a	D 1–1	**Att:** 32,035. **Ref:** H Webb — **Scorers:** Earnshaw. **Booked:** McCleary, Cohen			
27th	● Sheff Wed.........................h	W 2–1	**Att:** 22,618. **Ref:** S Mathieson — **Scorers:** Chambers, Tyson. **Booked:** Breckin, Garner			
31st	● Cardiff...............................a	L 2–0	**Att:** 18,779. **Ref:** G Hegley — **Booked:** Wilson, Breckin			

February

4th	● Derby ....h	L 2–3	**Att:** 29,001. **Ref:** C Foy — **Scorers:** Cohen, Tyson. **Booked:** McGugan			
7th	● QPR ....h	D 2–2	**Att:** 25,859. **Ref:** D Deadman — **Scorers:** Cohen, McGugan. **Booked:** Moloney, Newbold, McCleary, Morgan			
14th	● Birmingham ....a	L 2–0	**Att:** 17,631. **Ref:** G Laws — **Booked:** Perch			
18th	● Ipswich ....a	L 2–1	**Att:** 19,930. **Ref:** M Atkinson — **Scorers:** Tyson. **Booked:** Morgan, Moloney			
21st	● Derby ....h	L 1–3	**Att:** 29,140. **Ref:** A Marriner — **Scorers:** Earnshaw. **Booked:** Chambers, Perch			
28th	● Reading ....a	W 0–1	**Att:** 21,196. **Ref:** N Swarbrick — **Scorers:** McGugan. **Booked:** Earnshaw, Morgan			

March

3rd	● Preston ....h	W 2–1	**Att:** 17,568. **Ref:** P Walton — **Scorers:** Earnshaw[2]. **Booked:** Chambers, McCleary			
7th	● Swansea............................h	D 1–1	**Att:** 20,475. **Ref:** J Moss — **Scorers:** McGugan. **Booked:** Osbourne, Breckin, Lynch			
10th	● Watford ....a	L 2–1	**Att:** 14,730. **Ref:** M Haywood — **Scorers:** Thornhill. **Booked:** Tyson			
14th	● Burnley ....a	L 5–0	**Att:** 13,055. **Ref:** D Whitestone — **Booked:** Cohen, Garner			
21st	● Wolverhampton..................h	L 0–1	**Att:** 24,510. **Ref:** P Crossley — **Booked:** Gunter, Anderson, Lynch			

April

4th	● Barnsley ....a	D 1–1	**Att:** 19,681. **Ref:** L Probert — **Scorers:** Earnshaw. **Booked:** Cohen			
11th	● Bristol City ....h	W 3–2	**Att:** 22,776. **Ref:** C Webster — **Scorers:** Blackstock, Earnshaw, Garner. **Booked:** Blackstock, Garner			
13th	● Sheff Utd ....a	D 0–0	**Att:** 28,374. **Ref:** M Jones — **Booked:** Breckin, Cohen, Morgan. **Dismissed:** Wilson			
18th	● Coventry ....h	W 1–0	**Att:** 27,856. **Ref:** S Tanner — **Scorers:** Perch. **Booked:** McGugan			
25th	● Blackpool ....a	D 1–1	**Att:** 9,279. **Ref:** J Moss — **Scorers:** Blackstock. **Booked:** Chambers, Garner			

May

3rd	● Southampton ....h	W 3–1	**Att:** 29,008. **Ref:** K Stroud — **Scorers:** Chambers, Earnshaw, Garner			

● Coca-Cola Championship/Play-Offs ● FA Cup ● Carling Cup

NOTTINGHAM FOREST

CHAMPIONSHIP GOALKEEPER STATS

Player	Minutes on pitch	Appearances	Match starts	Completed matches	Sub appearances	Subbed off	SAVES BREAKDOWN								Clean sheets	Goals conceded	Minutes since conceding	Save %	PENALTIES			Yellow cards	Red cards
							Saved with feet	Punched	Parried	Tipped over	Fumbled	Tipped round	Caught	Blocked					Saved	Resulting in goals	Opposition miss		
Lee Camp	1446	15	15	15	0	0	1	2	12	2	0	5	50	0	4	18	24	76.04	2	2	0	1	0
Paul Smith	2697	28	28	28	0	0	2	11	18	9	0	3	85	0	7	43	78	75.14	1	2	0	0	0
Iain Turner	290	3	3	3	0	0	0	3	1	2	0	0	10	0	0	4	18	80.00	1	0	0	0	0

CHAMPIONSHIP OUTFIELD PLAYER STATS

Player	Minutes on pitch	Appearances	Match starts	Completed matches	Substitute appearances	Subbed off	Goals scored	Minutes since scoring	Assists	Shots on target	Shots off target	Crosses	Defensive clearances	Defensive blocks	Fouls committed	Free-kicks won	Caught offside	Yellow cards	Red cards
Paul Anderson	2063	26	24	14	2	10	2	644	1	22	9	46	2	3	18	32	2	2	0
Julian Bennett	956	12	10	7	2	3	0	-	0	3	5	10	10	2	15	13	1	2	0
Dexter Blackstock	490	6	6	4	0	2	2	130	1	3	4	0	3	1	15	12	3	1	0
Ian Breckin	1651	23	17	15	6	2	0	-	0	0	1	1	43	6	15	11	0	5	0
Mark Byrne	5	1	0	0	1	0	0	-	0	0	0	0	0	0	0	0	0	0	0
Luke Chambers	3076	39	32	27	7	5	2	6	3	9	10	26	35	4	42	26	1	6	0
Chris Cohen	3908	41	41	38	0	3	2	1349	6	31	12	124	28	3	77	60	12	5	0
Andrew Cole	523	10	5	3	5	2	0	-	0	6	3	2	0	0	9	1	3	3	0
Arron Davies	524	13	3	0	10	3	0	-	0	1	1	0	0	1	2	8	0	1	0
Robert Earnshaw	2392	32	26	13	6	13	12	0	0	39	32	4	2	1	22	19	38	1	0
Carl Fletcher	339	5	4	2	1	2	0	1208	0	1	0	0	4	2	6	5	0	1	0
Joe Garner	1824	28	19	7	9	12	7	20	1	28	18	8	10	1	45	60	5	8	0
Chris Gunter	769	8	8	8	0	0	0	-	0	2	1	8	3	0	2	15	0	1	0
Joe Heath	812	10	9	5	1	4	0	-	0	2	0	14	8	2	7	8	0	1	0
Joel Lynch	1839	23	20	15	3	3	0	-	2	1	1	26	14	10	16	22	1	3	0
Lee Martin	817	13	9	3	4	6	1	711	1	4	6	29	0	0	7	10	11	0	0
Garath McCleary	1903	39	14	6	25	8	1	1358	3	11	12	28	3	1	21	18	3	3	0
Lewis McGugan	2418	33	25	15	8	9	5	494	4	20	18	63	14	4	24	43	2	2	1
Gary McSheffrey	310	4	4	1	0	3	0	-	1	2	5	10	1	0	8	5	1	0	0
Brendan Moloney	829	12	9	5	3	4	0	-	0	1	1	4	1	2	12	9	0	4	0
Wes Morgan	4039	42	42	40	0	1	1	1892	0	5	2	2	76	25	77	42	0	7	1
Guy Moussi	1228	15	14	9	1	5	0	-	1	7	3	7	5	2	17	20	0	1	0
Adam Newbold	131	4	0	0	4	0	0	-	0	0	0	0	0	0	4	0	2	1	0
Isaiah Osbourne	661	8	7	4	1	2	0	-	1	3	6	1	6	1	6	8	0	1	0
James Perch	3368	37	36	32	1	4	3	141	0	5	16	7	30	9	43	48	2	10	0
James Reid	5	1	0	0	1	0	0	-	0	0	0	0	0	0	0	0	0	0	0
Emile Sinclair	72	3	0	0	3	0	0	-	0	0	0	1	1	0	0	0	1	0	0
Matt Thornhill	1307	24	13	7	11	5	3	97	1	11	6	12	5	1	12	10	1	2	1
Nathan Tyson	2685	35	28	22	7	6	5	452	4	23	24	43	3	0	42	50	25	6	0
Kelvin Wilson	3169	36	35	31	1	3	0	-	1	2	3	6	54	11	34	35	1	2	1

SEASON TOTALS

Goals scored	50
Goals conceded	65
Clean sheets	11
Shots on target	242
Shots off target	202
Shots per goal	8.88
Pens awarded	1
Pens scored	1
Pens conceded	8
Offsides	115
Corners	268
Crosses	487
Players used	33
Fouls committed	598
Free-kicks won	598

CARDS RECEIVED

80 **4**

SEQUENCES

Wins	4
(28/12/08–27/01/09)	
Losses	4
(27/09/08–18/10/08)	
Draws	3
(02/11/08–15/11/08)	
Undefeated	6
(04/04/09–03/05/09)	
Without win	10
(30/08/08–25/10/08)	
Undefeated home	3
(on two occasions)	
Undefeated away	8
(28/10/08–10/01/09)	
Without scoring	4
(20/09/08–04/10/08)	
Without conceding	2
(on four occasions)	
Scoring	6
(20/12/08–27/01/09)	
Conceding	11
(27/09/08–22/11/08)	

SEASON INFORMATION

Highest position: 14
Lowest position: 24
Average goals scored per game: 1.09
Average goals conceded per game: 1.41

League position at the end of each week

League position at the end of: August 16 · September 24 · October 23 · November 24 · December 21 · January 17 · February 21 · March 22 · April 20 · May 19

MATCH RECORDS

Goals scored per match

		W	D	L	Pts
Failed to score	14	0	5	9	5
Scored 1 goal	18	3	6	9	15
Scored 2 goals	10	6	3	1	21
Scored 3 goals	4	4	0	0	12
Scored 4+ goals	0	0	0	0	0

Goals conceded per match

		W	D	L	Pts
Clean sheet	11	6	5	0	23
Conceded 1 goal	15	4	6	5	18
Conceded 2 goals	15	3	3	9	12
Conceded 3 goals	2	0	0	2	0
Conceded 4+ goals	3	0	0	3	0

QUICK-FIRE GOALS

From the start of a match
Paul Smith (v Swansea) 8:09

By a substitute after coming on
Nathan Tyson (v Watford) 3:42

LAST-GASP GOALS

From the start of a match
Robert Earnshaw (v Southampton) 91:52

By a substitute after coming on
Joe Garner (v Southampton) 27:08

GOAL DETAILS

How the goals were struck

SCORED		CONCEDED
26	Right foot	34
9	Left foot	17
12	Headers	13
3	Others	1

How the goals were struck

SCORED		CONCEDED
25	Open play	39
9	Cross	3
1	Corner	6
1	Penalties	4
2	Direct from free-kick	2
8	Free-kick	5
4	Own goals	6

Distance from goal

SCORED		CONCEDED
19	6yds	23
25	18yds	31
6	18+yds	11

GOALS SCORED/CONCEDED PER FIVE-MINUTE INTERVALS

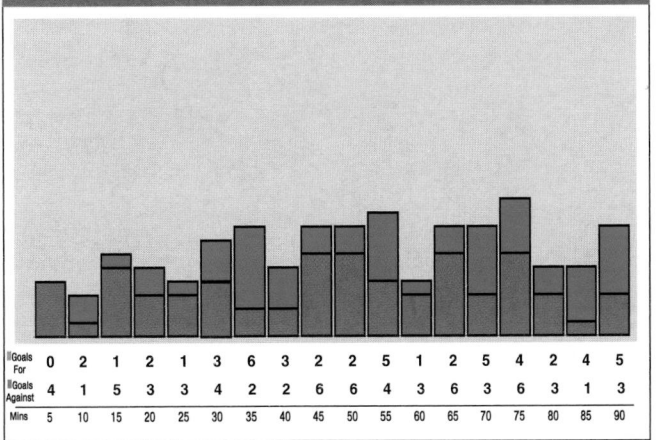

Goals For	0	2	1	2	1	3	6	3	2	2	5	1	2	5	4	2	4	5
Goals Against	4	1	5	3	3	4	2	2	6	6	4	3	6	3	6	3	1	3
Mins	5	10	15	20	25	30	35	40	45	50	55	60	65	70	75	80	85	90

PLYMOUTH ARGYLE

CLUB SUMMARY

FORMED	1886
MANAGER	Paul Sturrock
GROUND	Home Park
CAPACITY	21,118
NICKNAME	The Pilgrims
WEBSITE	www.pafc.co.uk

The New Football Pools PLAYER OF THE SEASON — Romain Larrieu

OVERALL

P	W	D	L	F	A	GD
48	13	12	23	45	62	-17

COCA-COLA CHAMPIONSHIP

Pos	P	W	D	L	F	A	GD	Pts
21	46	13	12	21	44	57	-13	51

HOME

Pos	P	W	D	L	F	A	GD	Pts
21	23	7	5	11	31	35	-4	26

AWAY

Pos	P	W	D	L	F	A	GD	Pts
12	23	6	7	10	13	22	-9	25

CUP PROGRESS DETAILS

Competition	Round reached	Knocked out by
FA Cup	R3	Arsenal
Carling Cup	R1	Luton

BIGGEST WIN (ALL COMPS)
4–0 on two occasions

BIGGEST DEFEAT (ALL COMPS)
0–3 on two occasions

THE PLAYER WITH THE MOST

Shots on target	
Paul Gallagher	52
Shots off target	
Paul Gallagher	38
Shots without scoring	
Chris Clark	22
Assists	
Rory Fallon	7
Offsides	
Paul Gallagher	26
Fouls	
Rory Fallon	93
Fouls without a card	
Jason Puncheon	10
Free-kicks won	
Rory Fallon	81
Defensive clearances	
Marcel Seip	46

actim INDEX for the 2008/09 Coca-Cola Championship Season

Rank	Player	Pts
56	Romain Larrieu	455
73	Paul Gallagher	416
75	Chris Barker	414
90	Marcel Seip	391
131	Jamie Mackie	341

ATTENDANCE RECORD

High	Low	Average
15,197	9,203	11,533

v Southampton (26/12/2008) v Swansea (23/08/2008)

PLYMOUTH will be more than satisfied to have survived the drop after what turned into a rather tough campaign at Home Park.

The signs were not good when it took Paul Sturrock's men until 6th September to register a win in any competition, with a 3–1 defeat at Coca-Cola League Two Luton in the League Cup the low point of a difficult start.

That September win over Watford sparked a run of three straight victories, which would prove to be the best run of the season for the Devon outfit.

At the turn of the year, Argyle were 15th in the table with nine wins from their 26 games, and nine points clear of the drop zone. At that time they had managed four wins on the road, despite netting just

nine goals on their travels, and they continued to be troubled by inconsistency in displays and results as the season progressed. In

fact, they went on a run of just one win in 16 games until the end of February, which left them three points ahead of the bottom three in the table. However, the on-loan

> ## When the pressure was on, Argyle came up trumps

Blackburn Rovers striker, Paul Gallagher – who ended the season as Plymouth's top scorer – bagged the only goal as they stunned leaders Wolves at Molineux at the end of February and, three days later, another win over Watford gave them breathing space.

But three defeats in a row at the end of March saw Argyle again slump too close to the relegation places for their liking, and gave hope to fans of Norwich, Southampton and Charlton that they could be reeled in.

Yet again though, when the pressure was on, Argyle came up trumps and a 1–0 win at Blackpool followed by a superb 4–0 thumping of Coventry – when all the goals came before half-time – and a 1–1 draw at promotion-bound Birmingham in the next three games saw them to the brink of safety with the magical 50-point mark achieved.

As it was, that was enough for them to be secure, so the fact that they claimed just one more point in three games before the season ended mattered little – although back-to-back home defeats to Doncaster and Barnsley hardly bodes well for the future.

Sturrock's plans for next season may again depend on his movements in the loan market, with Gallagher and Manchester United duo Craig Cathcart and David Gray integral to their eventual survival during 2008/09.

Paul Gallagher scores in a 2–1 win at Crystal Palace

RESULTS 2008/09

August
9th	● Wolverhampton...................h	D 2–2	**Att:** 14,789. **Ref:** K Friend — **Scorers:** Fallon, Seip. **Booked:** Seip, Barker, Fallon
12th	● Luton...................a	L 2–0	**Att:** 2,682. **Ref:** R Shoebridge — **Booked:** Walton
16th	● Reading ....a	L 2–0	**Att:** 19,202. **Ref:** R Beeby
23rd	● Swansea...................h	L 0–1	**Att:** 9,203. **Ref:** A D'Urso — **Booked:** Summerfield
30th	● Burnley ....a	D 0–0	**Att:** 10,032. **Ref:** M Oliver — **Booked:** Gallagher

September
13th	● Norwich...................h	L 1–2	**Att:** 11,185. **Ref:** A Woolmer — **Scorers:** Gallagher. **Booked:** Timar, Walton. **Dismissed:** Timar
16th	● Watford ....a	W 1–2	**Att:** 13,237. **Ref:** C Penton — **Scorers:** Duguid, Summerfield. **Booked:** Paterson, Doumbe
20th	● Crystal Palace ....a	W 1–2	**Att:** 14,209. **Ref:** N Swarbrick — **Scorers:** Gallagher². **Booked:** Doumbe, Gallagher
27th	● Nottm Forest...................h	W 1–0	**Att:** 12,594. **Ref:** K Wright — **Scorers:** Fallon. **Booked:** Seip
30th	● Bristol City ....a	D 2–2	**Att:** 17,489. **Ref:** I Williamson — **Scorers:** Fallon, Mackie. **Booked:** Fallon

October
4th	● Sheff Wed...................h	W 4–0	**Att:** 10,795. **Ref:** R East — **Scorers:** Gallagher, Mackie, Seip, Beevers OG
18th	● Derby ....a	L 2–1	**Att:** 28,495. **Ref:** C Webster — **Scorers:** Gallagher
21st	● Preston ....h	W 1–0	**Att:** 9,824. **Ref:** A Penn — **Scorers:** Fallon. **Booked:** Fallon
25th	● Ipswich ....h	L 1–3	**Att:** 12,294. **Ref:** P Miller — **Scorers:** Cathcart. **Booked:** Duguid, Cathcart, Fallon, Seip, Noone, McNamee
28th	● Sheff Wed...................a	W 0–1	**Att:** 16,515. **Ref:** G Laws — **Scorers:** MacLean. **Booked:** McNamee, Gallagher

November
1st	● Sheff Utd ....a	L 2–0	**Att:** 25,601. **Ref:** S Mathieson — **Booked:** Doumbe, Gallagher
8th	● Charlton ....h	D 2–2	**Att:** 10,716. **Ref:** A Hall — **Scorers:** Doumbe, Mpenza. **Booked:** Summerfield, Gallagher
15th	● Coventry ....a	W 0–1	**Att:** 18,528. **Ref:** N Miller — **Scorers:** Noone. **Booked:** Mackie, Clark
22nd	● Cardiff...................h	W 2–1	**Att:** 11,438. **Ref:** P Taylor — **Scorers:** Gallagher, Mpenza. **Booked:** Summerfield
25th	● Southampton ....a	D 0–0	**Att:** 14,895. **Ref:** A D'Urso — **Booked:** Doumbe
29th	● Blackpool ....h	L 1–2	**Att:** 9,969. **Ref:** T Kettle — **Scorers:** Gallagher

December
6th	● Doncaster ....a	L 1–0	**Att:** 10,187. **Ref:** R Beeby — **Booked:** MacLean
9th	● Birmingham ....h	L 0–1	**Att:** 10,446. **Ref:** K Wright — **Booked:** Fallon
13th	● QPR ....h	D 1–1	**Att:** 10,747. **Ref:** K Friend — **Scorers:** MacLean. **Booked:** Walton
20th	● Barnsley ....a	L 2–0	**Att:** 10,944. **Ref:** D Whitestone — **Booked:** MacLean. **Dismissed:** Walton
26th	● Southampton ....h	W 2–0	**Att:** 15,197. **Ref:** R East — **Scorers:** Fallon, Summerfield. **Booked:** MacLean
28th	● Cardiff...................a	L 1–0	**Att:** 19,145. **Ref:** S Attwell — **Booked:** Mackie. **Dismissed:** McNamee

January
3rd	● Arsenal ....a	L 3–1	**Att:** 59,424. **Ref:** M Jones — **Scorers:** Duguid. **Booked:** Duguid
17th	● Nottm Forest...................a	L 2–0	**Att:** 20,392. **Ref:** K Stroud — **Booked:** Barker, Mpenza, Duguid
27th	● Bristol City ....h	L 0–2	**Att:** 11,438. **Ref:** P Taylor
31st	● Ipswich ....a	D 0–0	**Att:** 20,333. **Ref:** D Deadman — **Booked:** Mackie, McNamee

February
3rd	● Preston ....a	D 1–1	**Att:** 10,660. **Ref:** A Haines — **Scorers:** Mackie. **Booked:** Doumbe, Clark, Fallon
7th	● Derby ....h	L 0–3	**Att:** 10,893. **Ref:** S Cook
14th	● Charlton ....a	L 2–0	**Att:** 21,876. **Ref:** T Kettle — **Booked:** Larrieu, Duguid, Gallagher
17th	● Crystal Palace ....h	L 1–3	**Att:** 10,710. **Ref:** R Shoebridge — **Scorers:** Sawyer. **Booked:** MacLean
21st	● Sheff Utd ....h	D 2–2	**Att:** 10,044. **Ref:** A Woolmer — **Scorers:** Fletcher, Gallagher. **Booked:** Sawyer
28th	● Wolverhampton...................a	W 0–1	**Att:** 25,710. **Ref:** C Boyeson — **Scorers:** Gallagher

March
3rd	● Watford ....h	W 2–1	**Att:** 9,529. **Ref:** N Miller — **Scorers:** Gallagher²
7th	● Reading ....h	D 2–2	**Att:** 14,014. **Ref:** A Bates — **Scorers:** Gallagher, Mackie
10th	● Swansea...................a	L 1–0	**Att:** 13,103. **Ref:** I Williamson — **Booked:** Judge, Gray, Duguid, C Fletcher, Barnes, Sawyer
14th	● Norwich...................a	L 1–0	**Att:** 25,064. **Ref:** F Graham — **Booked:** Seip
21st	● Burnley ....h	L 1–2	**Att:** 11,246. **Ref:** R Booth — **Scorers:** Judge

April
4th	● Blackpool ....a	W 0–1	**Att:** 8,103. **Ref:** M Haywood — **Scorers:** Sawyer
11th	● Coventry ....h	W 4–0	**Att:** 12,568. **Ref:** C Oliver — **Scorers:** Barnes, Judge, Mackie, Seip
13th	● Birmingham ....a	D 1–1	**Att:** 19,323. **Ref:** M Oliver — **Scorers:** Gallagher. **Booked:** Barnes, Gray, Fletcher
18th	● Doncaster ....h	L 0–3	**Att:** 11,100. **Ref:** P Crossley
25th	● QPR ....a	D 0–0	**Att:** 14,779. **Ref:** N Miller — **Booked:** Judge, Fletcher

May
| 3rd | ● Barnsley ....h | L 1–2 | **Att:** 14,529. **Ref:** C Penton — **Scorers:** Sawyer |

● Coca-Cola Championship/Play-Offs ● FA Cup ● Carling Cup

PLYMOUTH ARGYLE

CHAMPIONSHIP GOALKEEPER STATS

Player	Minutes on pitch	Appearances	Match starts	Completed matches	Sub appearances	Subbed off	Saved with feet	Punched	Parried	Tipped over	Fumbled	Tipped round	Caught	Blocked	Clean sheets	Goals conceded	Minutes since conceding	Save %	Saved	Resulting in goals	Opposition miss	Yellow cards	Red cards
Romain Larrieu	3928	41	41	41	0	0	1	25	21	14	0	12	156	1	12	50	47	82.21	1	4	0	1	0
Graham Stack	475	5	5	5	0	0	0	4	7	2	0	5	10	0	1	7	35	80.00	0	0	0	0	0

Column groups above: SAVES BREAKDOWN (Saved with feet through Blocked); PENALTIES (Saved, Resulting in goals, Opposition miss).

CHAMPIONSHIP OUTFIELD PLAYER STATS

Player	Minutes on pitch	Appearances	Match starts	Completed matches	Substitute appearances	Subbed off	Goals scored	Minutes since scoring	Assists	Shots on target	Shots off target	Crosses	Defensive clearances	Defensive blocks	Fouls committed	Free-kicks won	Caught offside	Yellow cards	Red cards
Chris Barker	3628	40	38	33	2	5	0	-	1	1	2	16	41	23	20	26	0	2	0
Ashley Barnes	1047	15	12	4	3	8	1	376	1	7	7	0	4	0	34	23	18	2	0
Craig Cathcart	2734	31	30	26	1	4	1	2028	0	2	3	2	34	14	23	20	0	1	0
Chris Clark	2833	36	30	22	6	8	0	-	3	13	9	71	9	6	17	22	4	2	0
George Donnelly	43	2	0	0	2	0	0	-	0	0	3	0	0	0	1	0	0	0	0
Roudolphe Douala	69	2	1	0	1	1	0	-	0	2	0	0	0	0	0	0	1	0	0
Mathias Doumbe	1913	24	21	14	3	7	1	893	0	1	3	15	20	11	32	24	0	5	0
Karl Duguid	3661	39	39	38	0	1	1	3157	1	7	12	13	41	9	33	41	3	4	0
Jermaine Easter	199	4	2	1	2	1	0	-	0	1	1	0	0	0	4	4	4	0	0
Rory Fallon	2671	44	26	19	18	7	5	928	7	20	20	2	23	1	93	81	23	6	0
Carl Fletcher	1258	13	13	13	0	0	1	1208	0	6	6	4	1	1	12	8	0	3	0
Yoann Folly	679	11	6	4	5	2	0	-	0	0	3	1	6	2	3	8	0	0	0
Paul Gallagher	3306	40	36	20	4	16	13	350	4	52	38	58	12	0	38	31	26	6	0
David Gray	1354	14	14	14	0	0	0	-	0	0	4	7	7	3	18	9	0	2	0
Alan Judge	1300	17	15	5	2	10	2	403	1	11	17	23	2	0	8	25	0	2	0
Steven MacLean	1088	21	11	5	10	6	2	386	1	8	3	2	4	0	34	23	16	4	0
Jamie Mackie	3165	43	35	20	8	15	5	384	1	32	18	21	1	0	40	57	24	3	0
Nicolas Marin	163	6	1	0	5	1	0	-	0	0	1	4	0	0	4	4	3	0	0
David McNamee	528	10	5	1	5	3	0	-	1	0	0	2	7	1	12	5	0	3	1
Emile Mpenza	320	9	3	0	6	3	2	145	0	5	1	1	2	1	1	2	6	1	0
Craig Noone	598	21	3	0	18	3	1	507	2	7	8	17	2	1	10	21	4	1	0
James Paterson	749	17	7	1	10	6	0	-	0	2	4	10	3	1	11	10	0	1	0
Jason Puncheon	408	6	5	3	1	2	0	-	0	4	6	13	1	0	10	6	2	0	0
Gary Sawyer	1247	13	13	12	0	1	3	84	2	3	3	12	7	1	7	9	1	2	0
Marcel Seip	3914	41	41	40	0	1	3	451	0	9	15	2	46	16	44	25	1	4	0
Luke Summerfield	2502	29	28	19	1	9	2	363	3	11	20	47	5	4	25	22	2	3	0
Krisztian Timar	1399	21	13	12	8	0	0	-	0	1	8	0	29	6	21	11	0	1	1
Simon Walton	1053	13	12	9	1	2	0	-	0	4	7	4	6	1	16	8	0	2	1

actim⊞

SEASON TOTALS

Goals scored	44
Goals conceded	57
Clean sheets	13
Shots on target	209
Shots off target	222
Shots per goal	9.80
Pens awarded	4
Pens scored	4
Pens conceded	5
Offsides	138
Corners	208
Crosses	347
Players used	30
Fouls committed	572
Free-kicks won	532

CARDS RECEIVED

61 **3**

SEQUENCES

Wins	3
(16/09/08–27/09/08)	
Losses	3
(on four occasions)	
Draws	2
(31/01/09–03/02/09)	
Undefeated	5
(16/09/08–04/10/08)	
Without win	9
(28/12/08–21/02/09)	
Undefeated home	3
(on two occasions)	
Undefeated away	4
(30/08/08–30/09/08)	
Without scoring	4
(28/12/08–31/01/09)	
Without conceding	2
(04/04/09–11/04/09)	
Scoring	10
(13/09/08–28/10/08)	
Conceding	5
(on three occasions)	

SEASON INFORMATION

Highest position: 7
Lowest position: 24
Average goals scored per game: 0.96
Average goals conceded per game: 1.24

League position at the end of each week

League position at the end of: August 21, September 12, October 9, November 7, December 15, January 16, February 20, March 21, April 19, May 21

MATCH RECORDS

Goals scored per match

		W	D	L	Pts
Failed to score	18	0	4	14	4
Scored 1 goal	16	6	3	7	21
Scored 2 goals	10	5	5	0	20
Scored 3 goals	0	0	0	0	0
Scored 4+ goals	2	2	0	0	6

Goals conceded per match

		W	D	L	Pts
Clean sheet	13	9	4	0	31
Conceded 1 goal	13	4	3	6	15
Conceded 2 goals	16	0	5	11	5
Conceded 3 goals	4	0	0	4	0
Conceded 4+ goals	0	0	0	0	0

GOALS SCORED/CONCEDED PER FIVE-MINUTE INTERVALS

Goals For	1	3	4	4	2	6	1	4	2	1	2	2	0	3	2	1	1	5
Goals Against	0	0	3	3	3	2	3	2	6	6	4	3	5	2	1	5	4	5
Mins	5	10	15	20	25	30	35	40	45	50	55	60	65	70	75	80	85	90

QUICK-FIRE GOALS

From the start of a match
Paul Gallagher
(v Wolverhampton) 0:39

By a substitute after coming on
Emile Mpenza
(v Charlton) 1:04

LAST-GASP GOALS

From the start of a match
Emile Mpenza
(v Charlton) 93:51

By a substitute after coming on
Craig Noone
(v Coventry) 19:12

GOAL DETAILS

How the goals were struck

SCORED		CONCEDED
24	Right foot	36
11	Left foot	10
8	Headers	11
1	Others	0

How the goals were struck

SCORED		CONCEDED
25	Open play	37
2	Cross	5
9	Corner	8
4	Penalties	4
0	Direct from free-kick	1
3	Free-kick	2
1	Own goals	0

Distance from goal

SCORED		CONCEDED
18	6yds	22
20	18yds	25
6	18+yds	10

PRESTON NORTH END

CLUB SUMMARY

FORMED	1881
MANAGER	Alan Irvine
GROUND	Deepdale
CAPACITY	22,226
NICKNAME	The Lilywhites
WEBSITE	www.pnefc.net

The New **Football Pools** PLAYER OF THE SEASON — **Jon Parkin**

OVERALL

P	W	D	L	F	A	GD
51	22	12	17	69	59	10

COCA-COLA CHAMPIONSHIP

Pos	P	W	D	L	F	A	GD	Pts
6	46	21	11	14	66	54	12	74

HOME

Pos	P	W	D	L	F	A	GD	Pts
1	23	16	3	4	39	20	19	51

AWAY

Pos	P	W	D	L	F	A	GD	Pts
13	23	5	8	10	27	34	-7	23

CUP PROGRESS DETAILS

Competition	Round reached	Knocked out by
FA Cup	R3	Liverpool
Carling Cup	R2	Derby

BIGGEST WIN (ALL COMPS)
18/04/09 6–0 v Cardiff **FLC**

BIGGEST DEFEAT (ALL COMPS)
27/01/09 1–4 v Swansea **FLC**

THE PLAYER WITH THE MOST

Shots on target
Jon Parkin 48

Shots off target
Jon Parkin 34

Shots without scoring
Darren Carter 13

Assists
Ross Wallace... 14

Offsides
Jon Parkin 36

Fouls
Jon Parkin 91

Fouls without a card
Jay McEveley 6

Free-kicks won
Sean St Ledger 82

Defensive clearances
Youl Mawene 109

actim INDEX — for the 2008/09 Coca-Cola Championship Season

Rank	Player	Pts
7	Andy Lonergan	622
18	Sean St Ledger	553
30	Billy Jones	506
38	Paul McKenna	482
42	Ross Wallace	476

ATTENDANCE RECORD

High	Low	Average
21,273	10,558	13,426
v Blackpool (11/04/2009)	v Swansea (30/09/2008)	

PRESTON failed to end their 48-year wait for a return to the top flight of English football, but there was undeniable progress at the famous Lancashire outfit.

Having spent the previous season fighting relegation, Alan Irvine's men reached the Coca-Cola Championship play-off semi-finals after a dramatic final-day victory over QPR. The 2–1 success, coupled with Cardiff's 1–0 defeat at Sheffield Wednesday, meant the Lilywhites leapfrogged Dave Jones' men into sixth position in the table. It was achieved by virtue of having scored one more goal than the Welshmen, who ultimately paid a heavy price for their 6–0 thumping at Deepdale on 18th April.

North End failed to progress via the play-offs as Sheffield United secured an aggregate 2–1 success, but merely making the top six confirmed the strides Irvine's men had made.

It must be remembered that Preston were in danger of sliding into League One when Irvine quit his 'brilliant job' as David Moyes' assistant at Everton to replace Paul Simpson in November 2007. For the likeable Irvine, who had never previously managed, it was some leap of faith. But the 50-year-old Glaswegian stopped the rot at Deepdale, re-establishing belief and easily guiding his side away from danger.

Few pundits, however, could have predicted the progress made in 2008/09 – and all on a shoestring budget. Preston won four and drew two of their opening six games to signal their intentions for

Preston's players celebrate after a dramatic win at promotion-chasing Birmingham in late April

the months ahead. However, they were soon brought down to earth by a 3–1 home defeat to eventual champions Wolves. That was the first of four successive losses, highlighting North End's weakness away from Deepdale.

Loan signings Jon Parkin and Ross Wallace, which were made permanent,

quickly impressed and gave Irvine's side some real ammunition in attack. Parkin, nicknamed 'The Beast', became a cult figure among Preston fans with a number of crucial goals, including winning goals against Doncaster, Birmingham and Norwich.

Homegrown goalkeeper Andy Lonergan and highly-rated centre-back Sean St Ledger also enhanced their reputations with a series of stunning displays.

The biggest problem was transferring their formidable home form on to the road to leave Irvine in no doubt as to where the improvement must come next season.

> **Parkin, nicknamed 'The Beast', became a cult figure**

RESULTS 2008/09

August

9th	● Ipswich ....a	W 1–2	**Att:** 22,307. **Ref:** P Taylor — **Scorers:** McKenna, Whaley. **Booked:** Mellor
12th	● Chesterfield ....h	W 2–0	**Att:** 5,150. **Ref:** G Laws — **Scorers:** Mellor²
16th	● Crystal Palace ....h	W 2–0	**Att:** 14,225. **Ref:** K Woolmer — **Scorers:** Chaplow, Nicholson
23rd	● Sheff Wed................a	D 1–1	**Att:** 17,963. **Ref:** M Russell — **Scorers:** Chaplow. **Booked:** Hill
26th	● Derby ....h	L 0–1	**Att:** 8,037. **Ref:** J Moss
30th	● Charlton ....h	W 2–1	**Att:** 12,089. **Ref:** C Oliver — **Scorers:** Mellor, Nicholson. **Booked:** Mawene, Hart

September

13th	● Coventry ....a	D 0–0	**Att:** 16,544. **Ref:** G Hegley
16th	● Nottm Forest............h	W 2–1	**Att:** 13,145. **Ref:** C Webster — **Scorers:** Mawene, Mellor
20th	● Wolverhampton.........h	L 1–3	**Att:** 17,567. **Ref:** M Atkinson — **Scorers:** Mellor. **Booked:** Carter
27th	● Burnley ....a	L 3–1	**Att:** 16,276. **Ref:** L Mason — **Scorers:** Nicholson. **Booked:** Sedgwick, Carter, McKenna, Nicholson, Mellor. **Dismissed:** Davidson
30th	● Swansea ....h	L 0–2	**Att:** 10,558. **Ref:** C Boyeson

October

4th	● Watford ....a	L 2–1	**Att:** 14,087. **Ref:** K Wright — **Scorers:** St. Ledger. **Booked:** St. Ledger, C. Brown
18th	● Reading ....h	W 2–1	**Att:** 12,316. **Ref:** N Miller — **Scorers:** Elliott, Ingimarsson OG. **Booked:** Wallace, Sedgwick
21st	● Plymouth..................a	L 1–0	**Att:** 9,824. **Ref:** A Penn — **Booked:** Mawene
25th	● Sheff Utd ....a	L 1–0	**Att:** 24,445. **Ref:** D Whitestone — **Booked:** Nicholson, Parkin, Jones
28th	● Watford ....h	W 2–0	**Att:** 11,234. **Ref:** M Oliver — **Scorers:** Jones, Wallace

November

1st	● Southampton ....h	L 2–3	**Att:** 11,508. **Ref:** M Haywood — **Scorers:** Elliott, Jones
8th	● Norwich....................a	D 2–2	**Att:** 23,225. **Ref:** P Taylor — **Scorers:** C. Brown, Mellor
16th	● Blackpool ....a	W 1–3	**Att:** 9,643. **Ref:** M Dean — **Scorers:** C. Brown², Mellor. **Booked:** Mellor, C. Brown
22nd	● Barnsley ....h	W 2–1	**Att:** 12,153. **Ref:** A Hall — **Scorers:** Chaplow, St. Ledger. **Booked:** Davidson, Sedgwick
25th	● Derby ....h	D 2–2	**Att:** 25,534. **Ref:** K Woolmer — **Scorers:** Davidson, Mellor
29th	● Bristol City ....h	W 2–0	**Att:** 11,161. **Ref:** R Beeby — **Scorers:** Elliott, Wallace. **Booked:** Wallace

December

6th	● Cardiff.....................a	L 2–0	**Att:** 16,560. **Ref:** A D'Urso — **Booked:** Davidson, Parkin
9th	● Doncaster ....h	W 1–0	**Att:** 13,152. **Ref:** G Laws — **Scorers:** Parkin. **Booked:** Chaplow
13th	● Birmingham ....h	W 1–0	**Att:** 10,943. **Ref:** C Oliver — **Scorers:** Parkin
20th	● QRP ....a	L 3–2	**Att:** 14,103. **Ref:** A Wiley — **Scorers:** Davidson, Sedgwick. **Booked:** Sedgwick
26th	● Derby ....h	W 2–0	**Att:** 13,896. **Ref:** K Friend — **Scorers:** Parkin, St. Ledger. **Booked:** St. Ledger
28th	● Barnsley ....a	D 1–1	**Att:** 13,851. **Ref:** A Taylor — **Scorers:** Wallace. **Booked:** Jones

January

3rd	● Liverpool ....h	L 0–2	**Att:** 23,046. **Ref:** M Atkinson — **Booked:** Chaplow
10th	● Wolverhampton.........a	W 1–3	**Att:** 26,138. **Ref:** C Webster — **Scorers:** Elliott², St. Ledger. **Booked:** Nolan, Elliott
17th	● Burnley ....h	W 2–1	**Att:** 15,692. **Ref:** P Taylor — **Scorers:** Davidson, Mellor. **Booked:** McKenna, Wallace, Sedgwick
27th	● Swansea..................a	L 4–1	**Att:** 14,774. **Ref:** P Gibbs — **Scorers:** C. Brown. **Booked:** McKenna, Wallace, Mawene
31st	● Sheff Utd ....h	D 0–0	**Att:** 14,889. **Ref:** S Mathieson — **Booked:** Parkin

February

3rd	● Plymouth..................h	D 1–1	**Att:** 10,660. **Ref:** A Haines — **Scorers:** Parkin
7th	● Reading ....a	D 0–0	**Att:** 19,570. **Ref:** M Jones — **Booked:** St. Ledger, Wallace, Parkin
14th	● Norwich...................h	W 1–0	**Att:** 12,033. **Ref:** R Shoebridge — **Scorers:** Parkin. **Booked:** McKenna
21st	● Southampton ....a	L 3–1	**Att:** 14,790. **Ref:** P Miller — **Scorers:** Wallace. **Booked:** Chaplow
28th	● Ipswich ....h	W 3–2	**Att:** 12,709. **Ref:** S Tanner — **Scorers:** Davidson, Elliott, Parkin. **Booked:** Parkin, Elliott, McKenna, Davidson, Chaplow

March

3rd	● Nottm Forest............a	L 2–1	**Att:** 17,568. **Ref:** P Walton — **Scorers:** Parkin
7th	● Crystal Palace ....a	L 2–1	**Att:** 16,340. **Ref:** R Booth — **Scorers:** Jones
10th	● Sheff Wed................h	D 1–1	**Att:** 12,381. **Ref:** A Penn — **Scorers:** Parkin
14th	● Coventry ....h	W 2–1	**Att:** 13,251. **Ref:** K Friend — **Scorers:** Parkin, Turner OG. **Booked:** Parkin
21st	● Charlton ....a	D 0–0	**Att:** 19,215. **Ref:** D Deadman

April

4th	● Bristol City ....a	D 1–1	**Att:** 16,596. **Ref:** T Bates — **Scorers:** Mawene. **Booked:** Mawene
11th	● Blackpool ....h	L 0–1	**Att:** 21,273. **Ref:** A D'Urso
13th	● Doncaster ....a	W 0–2	**Att:** 11,648. **Ref:** I Williamson — **Scorers:** C. Brown, Mellor. **Booked:** Mellor, Wallace
18th	● Cardiff.....................h	W 6–0	**Att:** 13,692. **Ref:** K Stroud — **Scorers:** C. Brown, Mellor, Parkin, Williamson, Kennedy OG. **Booked:** Williamson, Parkin
25th	● Birmingham ....a	W 1–2	**Att:** 24,825. **Ref:** P Dowd — **Scorers:** McKenna, Wallace. **Booked:** Parkin, Wallace. **Dismissed:** Williamson, Wallace

May

3rd	● QPR ....h	W 2–1	**Att:** 18,264. **Ref:** M Oliver — **Scorers:** Parkin, St. Ledger. **Booked:** Jones, St. Ledger
8th	● Sheff Utd ....h	D 1–1	**Att:** 19,840. **Ref:** A Marriner — **Scorers:** St. Ledger. **Booked:** Carter
11th	● Sheff Utd ....a	L 1–0	**Att:** 26,354. **Ref:** A Wiley — **Booked:** Wallace, Parkin

● Coca-Cola Championship/Play-Offs ● FA Cup ● Carling Cup

PRESTON NORTH END

CHAMPIONSHIP GOALKEEPER STATS

Player	Minutes on pitch	Appearances	Match starts	Completed matches	Sub appearances	Subbed off	Saved with feet	Punched	Parried	Tipped Over	Fumbled	Tipped Round	Caught	Blocked	Clean Sheets	Goals conceded	Minutes since conceding	Save %	Saved	Resulting in goals	Opposition miss	Yellow cards	Red cards
									SAVES BREAKDOWN										PENALTIES				
Andy Lonergan	4399	46	46	46	0	0	2	33	26	14	0	28	192	3	13	54	38	84.75	1	5	0	0	0

CHAMPIONSHIP OUTFIELD PLAYER STATS

Player	Minutes on pitch	Appearances	Match starts	Completed matches	Substitute appearances	Subbed off	Goals scored	Minutes since scoring	Assists	Shots on target	Shots off target	Crosses	Defensive clearances	Defensive blocks	Fouls committed	Free-kicks won	Caught offside	Yellow cards	Red cards
Wayne Brown	570	6	6	6	0	0	0	-	0	0	1	4	16	5	2	7	0	0	0
Chris Brown	1670	30	15	8	15	7	6	87	1	14	15	6	7	1	53	24	10	2	0
Darren Carter	898	18	8	5	10	3	0	-	2	8	5	12	2	2	19	11	0	2	0
Richard Chaplow	1929	25	21	12	4	9	3	1287	1	11	12	24	6	5	42	25	2	3	0
Liam Chilvers	4	1	0	0	1	0	0	-	0	0	0	0	0	0	0	0	0	0	0
Callum Davidson	1656	20	18	16	2	2	4	285	1	3	2	21	21	8	19	10	1	3	1
Andrew Davies	399	5	5	3	0	2	0	-	0	0	2	1	7	6	4	6	0	0	0
Stephen Elliott	2244	37	23	7	14	16	6	605	1	21	25	16	3	0	27	19	14	2	0
Michael Hart	435	6	5	4	1	1	0	-	0	0	0	8	3	2	3	2	1	1	0
Karl Hawley	77	5	0	0	5	0	0	-	0	0	0	1	0	0	1	2	0	0	0
Matthew Hill	97	1	1	1	0	0	0	-	0	0	0	0	0	0	1	0	0	1	0
Jason Jarrett	45	3	0	0	3	0	0	-	0	0	0	0	0	0	1	2	0	0	0
Billy Jones	4134	44	44	43	0	1	3	928	2	12	17	65	24	20	30	31	0	3	0
Youl Mawene	3707	41	38	37	1	1	2	503	0	5	13	6	109	26	42	30	0	4	0
James McEveley	667	7	7	7	0	0	0	-	0	1	1	10	7	2	6	2	0	0	0
Paul McKenna	4083	44	44	37	0	7	2	123	5	18	15	59	29	6	54	59	2	5	0
Neil Mellor	1907	33	20	7	13	13	10	185	2	42	26	43	0	0	19	24	29	4	0
Barry Nicholson	2591	37	27	18	10	9	3	1939	1	13	13	51	5	3	21	12	0	2	0
Eddie Nolan	1943	21	18	18	3	0	0	-	1	4	5	45	21	8	10	17	2	1	0
Jon Parkin	2723	39	30	18	9	12	11	53	5	48	34	10	12	3	91	41	36	8	0
Chris Sedgwick	3280	40	38	18	2	20	1	1509	6	12	20	91	35	2	28	31	6	5	0
Sean St Ledger	4311	46	46	44	0	2	5	20	0	11	17	12	87	23	40	82	2	4	0
Ross Wallace	3239	39	34	30	5	4	5	0	14	26	30	170	3	5	21	41	4	7	1
Simon Whaley	838	21	7	4	14	3	1	1127	0	10	9	54	1	1	5	10	1	0	0
Lee Williamson	423	5	5	3	0	2	1	68	0	1	1	0	2	1	8	3	0	1	1

Coca-Cola CHAMPIONSHIP

SEASON TOTALS

Goals scored	66
Goals conceded	54
Clean sheets	13
Shots on target	260
Shots off target	263
Shots per goal	7.92
Pens awarded	6
Pens scored	6
Pens conceded	6
Offsides	110
Corners	261
Crosses	709
Players used	26
Fouls committed	547
Free-kicks won	501

CARDS RECEIVED

58   3

SEQUENCES

Wins	4
(13/04/09–03/05/09)	
Losses	4
(20/09/08–04/10/08)	
Draws	3
(31/01/09–07/02/09)	
Undefeated	6
(09/08/08–16/09/08)	
Without win	4
(on two occasions)	
Undefeated home	12
(22/11/08–14/03/09)	
Undefeated away	4
(21/03/09–03/05/09)	
Without scoring	2
(21/10/08–25/10/08)	
Without conceding	2
(on three occasions)	
Scoring	8
(09/12/08–27/01/09)	
Conceding	8
(16/09/08–25/10/08)	

SEASON INFORMATION

Highest Position: 2
Lowest Position: 15
Average goals scored per game: 1.43
Average goals conceded per game: 1.17

League position at the end of each week

League position at the end of: August 2, September 9, October 12, November 9, December 7, January 5, February 5, March 7, April 7, May 6

MATCH RECORDS

Goals scored per match

		W	D	L	Pts
Failed to score	9	0	4	5	4
Scored 1 goal	15	3	5	7	14
Scored 2 goals	18	14	2	2	44
Scored 3 goals	3	3	0	0	9
Scored 4+ goals	1	1	0	0	3

Goals conceded per match

		W	D	L	Pts
Clean sheet	13	9	4	0	31
Conceded 1 goal	19	11	5	3	38
Conceded 2 goals	8	1	2	5	5
Conceded 3 goals	5	0	0	5	0
Conceded 4+ goals	1	0	0	1	0

QUICK-FIRE GOALS

From the start of a match
Chris Brown
(v Norwich) 1:58

By a substitute after coming on
Neil Mellor
(v Burnley) 1:27

LAST-GASP GOALS

From the start of a match
Neil Mellor
(v Wolves) 94:10

By a substitute after coming on
Neil Mellor
(v Norwich) 21:47

GOAL DETAILS

How the goals were struck

SCORED		CONCEDED
33	Right foot	32
19	Left foot	11
14	Headers	11
0	Others	0

How the goals were struck

SCORED		CONCEDED
34	Open play	29
14	Cross	7
5	Corner	5
6	Penalties	5
2	Direct from free-kick	2
2	Free-kick	5
3	Own goals	1

Distance from goal

SCORED		CONCEDED
24	6yds	17
32	18yds	26
10	18+yds	11

GOALS SCORED/CONCEDED PER FIVE-MINUTE INTERVALS

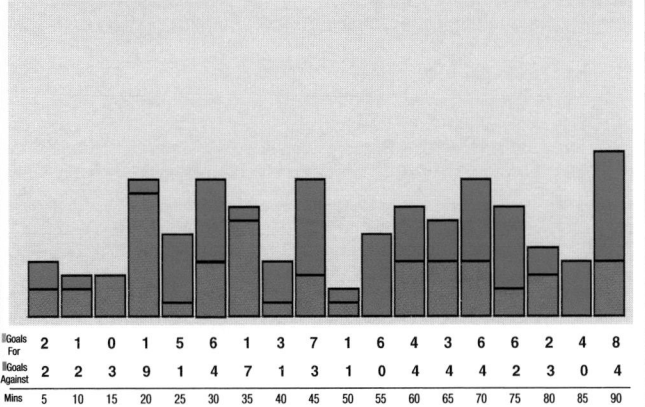

	Mins	5	10	15	20	25	30	35	40	45	50	55	60	65	70	75	80	85	90
Goals For		2	1	0	1	5	6	1	3	7	1	6	4	3	6	6	2	4	8
Goals Against		2	2	3	9	1	4	7	1	3	1	0	4	4	4	2	3	0	4

CLUB SUMMARY

FORMED	1882
MANAGER	Jim Magilton
GROUND	Loftus Road
CAPACITY	18,420
NICKNAME	The R's
WEBSITE	www.qprfc.co.uk

The New Football Pools PLAYER OF THE SEASON — Damion Stewart

OVERALL
P	W	D	L	F	A	GD
52	18	17	17	51	49	2

COCA-COLA CHAMPIONSHIP
Pos	P	W	D	L	F	A	GD	Pts
11	46	15	16	15	42	44	-2	61

HOME
Pos	P	W	D	L	F	A	GD	Pts
6	23	12	7	4	28	19	9	43

AWAY
Pos	P	W	D	L	F	A	GD	Pts
22	23	3	9	11	14	25	-11	18

CUP PROGRESS DETAILS
Competition	Round reached	Knocked out by
FA Cup	R3	Burnley
Carling Cup	R4	Man Utd

BIGGEST WIN (ALL COMPS)
26/08/08 4–0 v Carlisle **LC2**

BIGGEST DEFEAT (ALL COMPS)
0–3 on two occasions

THE PLAYER WITH THE MOST
Shots on target	
Dexter Blackstock	31
Shots off target	
Dexter Blackstock	27
Shots without scoring	
Daniel Parejo	16
Assists	
Lee Cook	4
Offsides	
Dexter Blackstock	33
Fouls	
Dexter Blackstock	68
Fouls without a card	
Damiano Tommasi	16
Free-kicks won	
Samuel Di Carmine	44
Defensive clearances	
Damion Stewart	50

actim INDEX — for the 2008/09 Coca-Cola Championship Season

Rank	Player	Pts
35	Radek Cerny	492
55	Damion Stewart	456
124	Wayne Routledge	349
165	Mikele Leigertwood	302
169	Damien Delaney	299

ATTENDANCE RECORD
High	Low	Average
17,120	12,286	14,090
v Reading (31/01/2009)	v Charlton (25/11/2008)	

Wayne Routledge celebrates after scoring in QPR's 2–0 win at Derby

QPR were installed among the pre-season promotion favourites, but the rich London club were soon to realise money is not everything.

Backed by billionaires Bernie Ecclestone and Lakshmi Mittal, as well as millionaire chairman Flavio Briatore, hopes were understandably high at Loftus Road at the start of the 2008/09 season. But 46 matches and three managers later, 11th place was all they had to show for a turbulent campaign.

When Iain Dowie was brought in to replace the outgoing Luigi De Canio as manager in the summer, all seemed rosy in the Loftus Road garden.

But the first signs of unease came when, rather than recruiting prosaic Dowie targets – such as Palace's Ben Watson – Real Madrid's teenage midfielder Daniel Parejo was drafted in. Reports emerged suggesting that

Dowie had clashed with Briatore over the club's transfer policy – which saw sporting director Gianni Paladini identify targets – even before the season began.

By mid-October, the R's were in ninth place having

won more games than they had lost, as well as having beaten Aston Villa in the League Cup.

But on Friday 24th October, Dowie was sacked. His contract had

been terminated after just 15 games, with rumours implying that Briatore's influence had stretched to picking the team.

Gareth Ainsworth was placed in caretaker charge until, with great fanfare, former Portugal midfielder Paulo Sousa took the reins. But injuries hit Rangers hard and, after a bright start under Sousa, their play-off aims fizzled out.

All season, Rangers looked laboured in front of goal, which made the decision to let top scorer Dexter Blackstock join Nottingham Forest on loan all the more baffling. Sousa admitted as much, and his services were promptly dispensed with.

The R's announced Jim Magilton as their new boss in June.

> **All season, Rangers looked laboured in front of goal**

RESULTS 2008/09

August

9th	● Barnsley ....h	W 2–1	**Att:** 14,964. **Ref:** N Swarbrick — **Scorers:** Hall[2]. **Booked:** Cook
12th	● Swindon ....a	W 2–3	**Att:** 7,230. **Ref:** R Beeby — **Scorers:** Balanta, Blackstock, Delaney. **Booked:** Connolly, Ledesma, Balanta
16th	● Sheff Utd ....a	L 3–0	**Att:** 25,273. **Ref:** G Laws — **Booked:** Delaney
23rd	● Doncaster ....h	W 2–0	**Att:** 15,536. **Ref:** M Thorpe — **Scorers:** Blackstock, Ledesma. **Booked:** Ledesma, Parejo
26th	● Carlisle ....h	W 4–0	**Att:** 8,021. **Ref:** K Hill — **Scorers:** Ledesma[3], Stewart. **Booked:** Delaney
30th	● Bristol City ....a	D 1–1	**Att:** 17,543. **Ref:** D Deadman — **Scorers:** Blackstock. **Booked:** Ledesma, Cook, Rowlands, Blackstock. **Dismissed:** Ledesma

September

14th	● Southampton ....h	W 4–1	**Att:** 13,770. **Ref:** K Friend — **Scorers:** Agyemang, Blackstock[2], Stewart. **Booked:** Leigertwood, Delaney
17th	● Norwich...........................a	W 0–1	**Att:** 24,249. **Ref:** R Shoebridge — **Scorers:** Rowlands. **Booked:** Connolly, Blackstock. **Dismissed:** Connolly
20th	● Coventry ....a	L 1–0	**Att:** 16,718. **Ref:** D Whitestone — **Booked:** Mahon
24th	● Aston Villa........................a	W 0–1	**Att:** 21,541. **Ref:** L Mason — **Scorers:** Stewart. **Booked:** Delaney
27th	● Derby ....h	L 0–2	**Att:** 14,311. **Ref:** A Taylor — **Booked:** Ledesma
30th	● Blackpool ....h	D 1–1	**Att:** 12,500. **Ref:** G Hegley — **Scorers:** Blackstock. **Booked:** Leigertwood

October

4th	● Birmingham ....a	L 1–0	**Att:** 18,498. **Ref:** A D'Urso — **Booked:** Leigertwood
18th	● Nottm Forest......................h	W 2–1	**Att:** 15,122. **Ref:** F Graham — **Scorers:** Balanta, Buzsaky. **Booked:** Blackstock, Cook
21st	● Swansea...........................a	D 0–0	**Att:** 13,475. **Ref:** T Bates — **Booked:** Rowlands, Delaney, Buzsaky, Leigertwood, Stewart, Connolly
25th	● Reading ....a	D 0–0	**Att:** 20,571. **Ref:** C Foy — **Booked:** Parejo
28th	● Birmingham ....h	W 1–0	**Att:** 13,594. **Ref:** S Attwell — **Scorers:** Di Carmine. **Booked:** Cerny, Ledesma **Dismissed:** Leigertwood

November

1st	● Ipswich ....a	L 2–0	**Att:** 20,966. **Ref:** T Kettle — **Booked:** Di Carmine
8th	● Cardiff...........................h	W 1–0	**Att:** 13,347. **Ref:** L Probert — **Scorers:** Mahon. **Booked:** Agyemang
11th	● Man Utd ....a	L 1–0	**Att:** 62,539. **Ref:** P Dowd
15th	● Burnley ....h	L 1–2	**Att:** 13,226. **Ref:** K Woolmer — **Scorers:** Blackstock. **Booked:** Ramage
22nd	● Watford ....a	L 3–0	**Att:** 16,201. **Ref:** A Penn — **Booked:** Mahon, Ledesma, Stewart. **Dismissed:** Hall
25th	● Charlton ....h	W 2–1	**Att:** 12,286. **Ref:** K Stroud — **Scorers:** Blackstock[2]. **Booked:** Leigertwood, Delaney, Ephraim
29th	● Crystal Palace ....a	D 0–0	**Att:** 16,411. **Ref:** R Styles — **Booked:** Ephraim, Delaney

December

6th	● Wolverhampton...................h	W 1–0	**Att:** 13,416. **Ref:** I Williamson — **Scorers:** Rowlands. **Booked:** Rowlands
9th	● Sheff Wed ....a	L 1–0	**Att:** 14,792. **Ref:** N Miller
13th	● Plymouth..........................a	D 1–1	**Att:** 10,747. **Ref:** K Friend — **Scorers:** Helguson. **Booked:** Ramage, Helguson
20th	● Preston ....h	W 3–2	**Att:** 14,103. **Ref:** A Wiley — **Scorers:** Blackstock, Helguson[2]. **Booked:** Delaney
26th	● Charlton ....a	D 2–2	**Att:** 21,023. **Ref:** P Taylor — **Scorers:** Blackstock, Cook. **Booked:** Alberti, Cook, Connolly
28th	● Watford ....h	D 0–0	**Att:** 16,196. **Ref:** C Penton — **Booked:** Ramage, Rowlands, Helguson

January

3rd	● Burnley ....h	D 0–0	**Att:** 8,896. **Ref:** T Bates
10th	● Coventry ....h	D 1–1	**Att:** 13,330. **Ref:** K Stroud — **Scorers:** Blackstock. **Booked:** Routledge, Helguson
13th	● Burnley ....a	L 2–1	**Att:** 3,760. **Ref:** C Webster — **Scorers:** Di Carmine. **Booked:** Delaney, Alberti. (AET)
17th	● Derby ....a	W 0–2	**Att:** 28,390. **Ref:** K Wright — **Scorers:** Leigertwood, Routledge
27th	● Blackpool ....a	W 0–3	**Att:** 6,656. **Ref:** G Laws — **Scorers:** Ephraim, Helguson. **Booked:** Cook, Routledge
31st	● Reading ....h	D 0–0	**Att:** 17,120. **Ref:** J Moss — **Booked:** Helguson

February

7th	● Nottm Forest......................a	D 2–2	**Att:** 25,859. **Ref:** D Deadman — **Scorers:** Alberti[2]
21st	● Ipswich ....h	L 1–3	**Att:** 13,904. **Ref:** S Attwell — **Scorers:** Di Carmine
25th	● Cardiff...........................a	D 0–0	**Att:** 17,340. **Ref:** R East — **Booked:** Miller, Alberti
28th	● Barnsley ....a	L 2–1	**Att:** 11,614. **Ref:** R Shoebridge — **Scorers:** Delaney

March

3rd	● Norwich...........................h	L 0–1	**Att:** 13,533. **Ref:** G Scott
7th	● Sheff Utd ....h	D 0–0	**Att:** 13,718. **Ref:** N Swarbrick — **Booked:** Stewart
10th	● Doncaster ....a	L 2–0	**Att:** 10,223. **Ref:** C Webster — **Booked:** Leigertwood
14th	● Southampton ....a	D 0–0	**Att:** 18,691. **Ref:** M Jones — **Booked:** Gorkss, Stewart
17th	● Swansea...........................h	W 1–0	**Att:** 12,288. **Ref:** G Horwood — **Scorers:** Leigertwood. **Booked:** Leigertwood
21st	● Bristol City ....h	W 2–1	**Att:** 14,059. **Ref:** G Hegley — **Scorers:** Lopez, Taarabt. **Booked:** Taarabt

April

4th	● Crystal Palace ....h	D 0–0	**Att:** 15,234. **Ref:** S Mathieson
11th	● Burnley ....a	L 1–0	**Att:** 15,058. **Ref:** M Haywood
13th	● Sheff Wed ....h	W 3–2	**Att:** 13,742. **Ref:** D Deadman — **Scorers:** Mahon, Stewart, Vine. **Booked:** Taarabt, Cook
18th	● Wolverhampton...................a	L 1–0	**Att:** 27,511. **Ref:** J Moss — **Booked:** Lopez.
25th	● Plymouth..........................h	D 0–0	**Att:** 14,779. **Ref:** N Miller

May

3rd	● Preston ....a	L 2–1	**Att:** 18,264. **Ref:** M Oliver — **Scorers:** Agyemang. **Booked:** Leigertwood, Connolly

● Coca-Cola Championship/Play-Offs ● FA Cup ● Carling Cup

QUEENS PARK RANGERS

CHAMPIONSHIP GOALKEEPER STATS

Player	Minutes on pitch	Appearances	Match starts	Completed matches	Sub appearances	Subbed off	SAVES BREAKDOWN Saved with feet	Punched	Parried	Tipped over	Fumbled	Tipped round	Caught	Blocked	Clean sheets	Goals conceded	Minutes since conceding	Save %	PENALTIES Saved	Resulting in goals	Opposition miss	Yellow cards	Red cards
Lee Camp	385	4	4	4	0	0	0	1	1	0	0	3	8	1	2	5	24	36.11	0	1	0	0	0
Radek Cerny	4027	42	42	42	0	0	1	36	16	3	0	17	150	1	16	39	20	85.17	0	4	0	1	0

CHAMPIONSHIP OUTFIELD PLAYER STATS

Player	Minutes on pitch	Appearances	Match starts	Completed matches	Substitute appearances	Subbed off	Goals scored	Minutes since scoring	Assists	Shots on target	Shots off target	Crosses	Defensive clearances	Defensive blocks	Fouls committed	Free-kicks won	Caught offside	Yellow cards	Red cards
Patrick Agyemang	1213	20	11	6	9	5	2	18	0	14	8	8	6	0	10	13	11	1	0
Matteo Alberti	526	12	6	1	6	5	2	384	1	5	2	7	1	0	11	8	2	2	0
Angelo Balanta	262	10	2	0	8	2	1	145	0	2	1	0	0	1	2	4	2	0	0
Dexter Blackstock	2543	36	26	20	10	6	11	130	0	31	27	3	15	1	68	40	33	3	0
Akos Buzsaky	571	11	5	2	6	3	1	354	0	5	3	8	1	0	3	13	0	1	0
Matthew Connolly	2935	35	31	27	4	3	0	-	1	5	4	3	30	10	24	18	0	4	1
Lee Cook	2528	34	28	14	6	14	1	895	4	16	14	69	2	1	22	38	9	6	0
Damien Delaney	3350	37	35	31	2	4	1	649	2	4	10	25	20	7	45	29	4	6	0
Samuel Di Carmine	1283	27	15	2	12	13	2	556	1	17	2	3	0	0	22	44	16	1	0
Hogan Ephraim	1724	27	16	10	11	6	1	675	1	12	6	16	0	1	17	16	2	2	0
Antonio German	71	3	0	0	3	0	0	-	0	1	1	0	0	0	0	1	1	0	0
Kaspars Gorkss	2892	31	30	28	1	2	0	-	0	3	4	3	27	13	31	16	1	1	0
Fitz Hall	1650	24	18	14	6	3	2	1620	0	3	1	4	32	13	12	15	0	0	1
Heidar Helguson	1477	20	13	8	5	7	5	729	1	17	25	3	10	0	24	35	29	4	0
Emanuel Jorge Ledesma	942	17	11	3	6	7	1	733	1	12	15	16	0	0	16	22	4	5	1
Mikele Leigertwood	3508	42	36	32	6	3	2	573	4	20	22	12	24	12	66	31	2	8	1
Jordi Lopez	701	10	7	3	3	4	1	204	1	8	6	15	2	0	13	14	1	1	0
Gavin Mahon	2703	35	29	18	6	11	2	277	0	6	4	5	35	6	24	26	0	2	0
Liam Miller	738	13	11	1	2	10	0	-	0	2	1	5	1	1	14	8	0	1	0
Daniel Parejo	893	14	10	3	4	7	0	-	1	6	10	13	3	1	8	17	2	2	0
Peter Ramage	2819	31	30	25	1	5	0	-	1	2	2	11	15	8	19	22	0	3	0
Romone Rose	80	2	0	0	2	0	0	-	0	1	3	1	0	0	0	1	0	0	0
Wayne Routledge	1780	19	18	18	1	0	1	1660	4	7	8	18	0	0	21	43	3	2	0
Martin Rowlands	1907	24	20	17	4	3	2	618	3	10	20	31	4	0	25	27	1	4	0
Damion Stewart	3546	37	37	37	0	0	2	198	0	6	3	3	50	23	49	23	1	4	0
Adel Taarabt	463	7	5	3	2	2	1	271	0	4	11	5	0	0	2	16	4	2	0
Damiano Tommasi	441	7	5	2	2	3	0	-	2	1	3	5	0	0	16	5	0	0	0
Rowan Vine	306	5	3	1	2	2	1	196	1	5	2	4	0	1	6	4	4	0	0

SEASON TOTALS

Goals scored	42
Goals conceded	44
Clean sheets	18
Shots on target	225
Shots off target	218
Shots per goal	10.55
Pens awarded	3
Pens scored	1
Pens conceded	5
Offsides	132
Corners	237
Crosses	294
Players used	30
Fouls committed	572
Free-kicks won	560

CARDS RECEIVED

66   4

SEQUENCES

Wins	2
(on three occasions)	
Losses	2
(on two occasions)	
Draws	3
(26/12/08–10/01/09)	
Undefeated	9
(13/12/08–07/02/09)	
Without win	9
(31/01/09–14/03/09)	
Undefeated home	6
(on two occasions)	
Undefeated away	6
(13/12/08–25/02/09)	
Without scoring	4
(03/03/09–14/03/09)	
Without conceding	3
(on two occasions)	
Scoring	4
(23/08/08–17/09/08)	
Conceding	5
(20/09/08–18/10/08)	

League position at the end of each week

SEASON INFORMATION
Highest position: 4
Lowest position: 17
Average goals scored per game: 0.91
Average goals conceded per game: 0.96

League position at the end of: August 9 | September 8 | October 7 | November 10 | December 9 | January 7 | February 11 | March 11 | April 11 | May 11

MATCH RECORDS

Goals scored per match

		W	D	L	Pts
Failed to score	21	0	10	11	10
Scored 1 goal	13	5	4	4	19
Scored 2 goals	8	6	2	0	20
Scored 3 goals	3	3	0	0	9
Scored 4+ goals	1	1	0	0	3

Goals conceded per match

		W	D	L	Pts
Clean sheet	18	8	10	0	34
Conceded 1 goal	15	5	4	6	19
Conceded 2 goals	10	2	2	6	8
Conceded 3 goals	3	0	0	3	0
Conceded 4+ goals	0	0	0	0	0

QUICK-FIRE GOALS

From the start of a match
Dexter Blackstock
(v Southampton) 0:44

By a substitute after coming on
Rowan Vine
(v Sheff Wed) 5:42

LAST-GASP GOALS

From the start of a match
Patrick Agyemang
(v Southampton) 90:58

By a substitute after coming on
Hogan Ephraim
(v Blackpool) 36:52

GOAL DETAILS

How the goals were struck

SCORED		CONCEDED
23	Right foot	20
7	Left foot	11
11	Headers	13
1	Others	0

How the goals were struck

SCORED		CONCEDED
27	Open play	24
5	Cross	5
2	Corner	6
1	Penalties	5
1	Direct from free-kick	2
6	Free-kick	0
0	Own goals	2

Distance from goal

SCORED		CONCEDED
17	6yds	16
19	18yds	24
6	18+yds	4

GOALS SCORED/CONCEDED PER FIVE-MINUTE INTERVALS

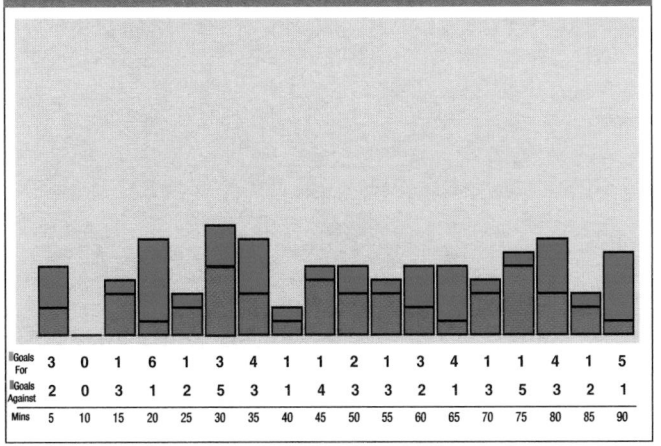

Goals For	3	0	1	6	1	3	4	1	1	2	1	3	4	1	1	4	1	5
Goals Against	2	0	3	1	2	5	3	1	4	3	3	2	1	3	5	3	2	1
Mins	5	10	15	20	25	30	35	40	45	50	55	60	65	70	75	80	85	90

CLUB SUMMARY

FORMED	1871
MANAGER	Brendan Rodgers
GROUND	Madejski Stadium
CAPACITY	24,200
NICKNAME	The Royals
WEBSITE	www.readingfc.co.uk

The New Football Pools PLAYER OF THE SEASON — Chris Armstrong

OVERALL

P	W	D	L	F	A	GD
52	23	15	14	81	49	32

COCA-COLA CHAMPIONSHIP

Pos	P	W	D	L	F	A	GD	Pts
4	46	21	14	11	72	40	32	77

HOME

Pos	P	W	D	L	F	A	GD	Pts
9	23	12	5	6	40	17	23	41

AWAY

Pos	P	W	D	L	F	A	GD	Pts
3	23	9	9	5	32	23	9	36

CUP PROGRESS DETAILS

Competition	Round reached	Knocked out by
FA Cup	R3	Cardiff
Carling Cup	R3	Stoke

BIGGEST WIN (ALL COMPS)
16/09/08 6–0 v Sheffield W **FLC**

BIGGEST DEFEAT (ALL COMPS)
23/08/08 2–4 v Charlton **FLC**

THE PLAYER WITH THE MOST

Shots on target	
Kevin Doyle	43
Shots off target	
Kevin Doyle	27
Shots without scoring	
Michael Duberry	10
Assists	
Stephen Hunt	17
Offsides	
Kevin Doyle	31
Fouls	
Stephen Hunt	45
Fouls without a card	
Dave Kitson	24
Free-kicks won	
Stephen Hunt	75
Defensive clearances	
Andre Bikey	52

actim INDEX for the 2008/09 Coca-Cola Championship Season

Rank	Player	Pts
3	Kevin Doyle	689
4	Stephen Hunt	684
17	Liam Rosenior	554
45	Jimmy Kebe	471
46	Chris Armstrong	470

ATTENDANCE RECORD

High	Low	Average
24,011	16,514	19,942
v Birmingham (03/05/2009)	v Blackpool (09/12/2008)	

STEVE COPPELL'S side looked certain to return to the Barclays Premier League for the majority of the season, but capitulated in the final three months to fall off the pace.

The Royals' final home win of the season came way back in January and, after Birmingham secured automatic promotion with a win at the Madejski Stadium on the final day of the season, Coppell's side were destined for a play-off place.

After losing Nicky Shorey and Dave Kitson in the close season, Coppell managed to hold on to Kevin Doyle and Stephen Hunt through the transfer window, and saw the pair lead an early charge up the table. Doyle hit hat-tricks in back-to-back home games as the Royals

> **Coppell celebrated his 1,000th game as a boss with a win**

sought a quick return to the Barclays Premier League, while Hunt had registered 18 assists by the end of January.

A fine 3–1 win at Birmingham at the end of December saw Reading move into the top two for the first time and they looked set for automatic promotion. They then beat

eventual champions Wolves at home at the end of January – but, incredibly, would not pick up another victory at the Madejski in their final nine games.

A dismal run of results saw the formerly rampant Royals score just eight times in 14 games as they slipped to fifth place, with even a play-off place looking in doubt.

Coppell celebrated his 1,000th game as a boss with a win at Doncaster, while Kitson and Glen Little – members of the side who romped to the title in 2005/06 – returned on loan. Despite the Royals' loss of form, a top-six finish was assured following back-to-back wins at Derby and Norwich.

Indeed, going into that final game of the season against Birmingham, the Royals still had a chance of stealing a top-two spot thanks to their superior goal difference. However, a 2–1 win for the Blues ended their dreams of automatic promotion and meant the Royals faced a play-off tie against Burnley.

Ultimately, their season was to end in failure as a 1–0 defeat at Turf Moor – which saw Andre Bikey sent off – was followed by another home defeat, as Owen Coyle's side won 2–0 in Berkshire.

Coppell resigned shortly after the game, with the club's former youth-team coach, Brendan Rodgers, brought in from Watford and charged with the task of leading the Royals back to the Barclays Premier League in 2009/10.

Jay Tabb in action in Reading's play-off semi-final defeat

RESULTS 2008/09

August

10th	● Nottm Forest	a	D 0–0	**Att:** 21,571. **Ref:** S Attwell — **Booked:** Kebe
12th	● Dag & Red	a	W 1–2	**Att:** 2,360. **Ref:** A Penn — **Scorers:** Henry, N. Hunt
16th	● Plymouth	h	W 2–0	**Att:** 19,202. **Ref:** R Beeby — **Scorers:** Sonko[2]
23rd	● Charlton	a	L 4–2	**Att:** 20,020. **Ref:** L Mason — **Scorers:** S. Hunt, Sonko. **Booked:** Sonko, N. Hunt
26th	● Luton	a	W 5–1	**Att:** 7,498. **Ref:** D Whitestone — **Scorers:** Henry, N. Hunt, S. Hunt, Karacan, Pearce. **Booked:** N. Hunt
30th	● Crystal Palace	h	W 4–2	**Att:** 20,441. **Ref:** C Penton — **Scorers:** Doyle[3], Harper. **Booked:** Karacan, Doyle

September

13th	● Ipswich	a	L 2–0	**Att:** 21,366. **Ref:** K Hill — **Booked:** Karacan, S. Hunt
16th	● Sheff Wed	h	W 6–0	**Att:** 18,159. **Ref:** A Woolmer — **Scorers:** Bikey, Doyle[3], N. Hunt[2]
20th	● Watford	a	D 2–2	**Att:** 14,761. **Ref:** S Attwell — **Scorers:** S. Hunt, Eustace OG. **Booked:** Karacan, Armstrong, Long, Bikey
23rd	● Stoke	a	D 2–2	**Att:** 9,141. **Ref:** L Probert — **Scorers:** Henry[2]. **Booked:** Bikey, Cisse, Henry (Lost 4–3 on pens)
27th	● Swansea	h	W 4–0	**Att:** 20,093. **Ref:** S Mathieson — **Scorers:** Doyle[2], N. Hunt, S. Hunt. **Booked:** Gunnarsson
30th	● Wolverhampton	a	W 0–3	**Att:** 24,302. **Ref:** R Shoebridge — **Scorers:** Bikey, Cisse, Hennessey OG

October

4th	● Burnley	h	W 3–1	**Att:** 18,621. **Ref:** K Friend — **Scorers:** S. Hunt, N. Hunt, Long. **Booked:** Armstrong
18th	● Preston	a	L 2–1	**Att:** 12,316. **Ref:** N Miller — **Scorers:** S. Hunt
21st	● Doncaster	a	W 2–1	**Att:** 17,294. **Ref:** D Deadman — **Scorers:** Bikey, Doyle. **Booked:** Doyle
25th	● QPR	h	D 0–0	**Att:** 20,571. **Ref:** C Foy — **Booked:** Rosenior
28th	● Burnley	a	L 1–0	**Att:** 11,538. **Ref:** M Haywood

November

1st	● Bristol City	a	W 1–4	**Att:** 18,296. **Ref:** J Moss — **Scorers:** Cisse, Doyle[2], N. Hunt. **Booked:** Ingimarsson, Doyle, Rosenior
8th	● Derby	h	W 3–0	**Att:** 18,724. **Ref:** D Mattison — **Scorers:** Doyle[2], N. Hunt
15th	● Sheff Utd	a	W 0–2	**Att:** 25,065. **Ref:** M Oliver — **Scorers:** Cisse, Doyle. **Booked:** Kebe, Bikey, Armstrong
22nd	● Southampton	h	L 1–2	**Att:** 23,121. **Ref:** L Probert — **Scorers:** Kebe. **Booked:** Matejovsky
25th	● Cardiff	a	D 2–2	**Att:** 17,154. **Ref:** P Walton — **Scorers:** Doyle, Gunnarsson. **Dismissed:** Bikey

December

1st	● Coventry	h	W 3–1	**Att:** 16,803. **Ref:** K Wright — **Scorers:** Cisse, N. Hunt[2]. **Booked:** S. Hunt
6th	● Barnsley	a	W 0–1	**Att:** 11,938. **Ref:** C Oliver — **Scorers:** Gunnarsson. **Booked:** Cisse. **Dismissed:** Kebe
9th	● Blackpool	h	W 1–0	**Att:** 16,514. **Ref:** J Singh — **Scorers:** Ingimarsson. **Booked:** Gunnarsson
13th	● Norwich	h	W 2–0	**Att:** 19,382. **Ref:** T Kettle — **Scorers:** S. Hunt, Long. **Booked:** Harper
20th	● Birmingham	a	W 1–3	**Att:** 19,695. **Ref:** M Dean — **Scorers:** Cisse, Doyle, N. Hunt. **Booked:** Rosenior, Federici
26th	● Cardiff	h	D 1–1	**Att:** 22,770. **Ref:** A Hall — **Scorers:** Federici. **Booked:** N. Hunt, Armstrong
28th	● Southampton	a	D 1–1	**Att:** 20,142. **Ref:** P Crossley — **Scorers:** Long. **Booked:** Doyle, Matejovsky, Long

January

3rd	● Cardiff	a	L 2–0	**Att:** 12,448. **Ref:** A Taylor — **Booked:** Bikey
9th	● Watford	h	W 4–0	**Att:** 18,072. **Ref:** A D'Urso — **Scorers:** Armstrong, Doyle, N. Hunt, Lita
17th	● Swansea	a	L 2–0	**Att:** 15,197. **Ref:** F Graham — **Booked:** Rosenior, S. Hunt
27th	● Wolverhampton	h	W 1–0	**Att:** 23,009. **Ref:** R Booth — **Scorers:** Collins OG. **Booked:** Gunnarsson
31st	● QPR	a	D 0–0	**Att:** 17,120. **Ref:** J Moss — **Booked:** S. Hunt, Duberry

February

7th	● Preston	h	D 0–0	**Att:** 19,570. **Ref:** M Jones — **Booked:** Matejovsky
21st	● Bristol City	h	L 0–2	**Att:** 22,462. **Ref:** A Penn — **Booked:** Harper
28th	● Nottm Forest	h	L 0–1	**Att:** 21,196. **Ref:** N Swarbrick — **Booked:** Pearce

March

3rd	● Sheff Wed	a	W 1–2	**Att:** 19,268. **Ref:** A Hall — **Scorers:** Doyle, Long. **Booked:** Rosenior, N. Hunt
7th	● Plymouth	a	D 2–2	**Att:** 14,014. **Ref:** A Bates — **Scorers:** Kebe, Pearce. **Booked:** Rosenior
10th	● Charlton	h	D 2–2	**Att:** 17,875. **Ref:** A Taylor — **Scorers:** Long[2]. **Booked:** Long, Armstrong
14th	● Ipswich	h	L 0–1	**Att:** 20,592. **Ref:** M Oliver
17th	● Doncaster	a	W 0–1	**Att:** 10,393. **Ref:** P Taylor — **Scorers:** Kitson. **Booked:** Matejovsky, S. Hunt
21st	● Crystal Palace	a	D 0–0	**Att:** 14,567. **Ref:** A D'Urso — **Booked:** S. Hunt, Rosenior, Doyle

April

4th	● Coventry	a	D 0–0	**Att:** 17,218. **Ref:** T Kettle — **Booked:** Harper, Bikey, Tabb
10th	● Sheff Utd	h	L 0–1	**Att:** 20,756. **Ref:** K Friend — **Booked:** Armstrong, Duberry
13th	● Blackpool	a	D 2–2	**Att:** 7,722. **Ref:** K Wright — **Scorers:** N. Hunt, Karacan. **Booked:** Karacan, N. Hunt
18th	● Barnsley	h	D 0–0	**Att:** 19,420. **Ref:** R Beeby — **Booked:** Bikey, Duberry
21st	● Derby	a	W 0–2	**Att:** 31,345. **Ref:** C Webster — **Scorers:** Kitson, Long
27th	● Norwich	a	W 0–2	**Att:** 25,041. **Ref:** C Oliver — **Scorers:** Long[2]. **Booked:** Rosenior, Cisse, Matejovsky

May

3rd	● Birmingham	h	L 1–2	**Att:** 24,011. **Ref:** H Webb — **Scorers:** Matejovsky
9th	● Burnley	a	L 1–0	**Att:** 18,853. **Ref:** M Atkinson — **Booked:** Matejovsky, Bikey. **Dismissed:** Bikey
12th	● Burnley	h	L 0–2	**Att:** 19,909. **Ref:** M Riley — **Booked:** Duberry, Kitson

● Coca-Cola Championship/Play-Offs ● FA Cup ● Carling Cup

READING

CHAMPIONSHIP GOALKEEPER STATS

Player	Minutes on pitch	Appearances	Match starts	Completed matches	Sub appearances	Subbed off	SAVES BREAKDOWN								Clean sheets	Goals conceded	Minutes since conceding	Save %	PENALTIES			Yellow cards	Red cards
							Saved with feet	Punched	Parried	Tipped over	Tipped round	Fumbled	Caught	Blocked					Saved	Resulting in goals	Opposition miss		
Adam Federici	1367	14	14	14	1	0	0	3	3	0	0	3	57	0	6	13	10	83.54	0	0	0	1	0
Marcus Hahnemann	3039	32	32	31	0	1	3	8	15	9	0	10	149	0	16	27	37	87.78	0	3	0	0	0

CHAMPIONSHIP OUTFIELD PLAYER STATS

Player	Minutes on pitch	Appearances	Match starts	Completed matches	Substitute appearances	Subbed off	Goals scored	Minutes since scoring	Assists	Shots on target	Shots off target	Crosses	Defensive clearances	Defensive blocks	Fouls committed	Free-kicks won	Caught offside	Yellow cards	Red cards
Chris Armstrong	3742	40	40	36	0	4	1	1577	3	3	8	65	20	8	40	39	2	6	0
Andre Bikey	2170	25	23	22	2	1	3	1564	0	9	7	7	52	12	45	35	2	4	1
Kalifa Cisse	2295	36	24	14	12	10	5	1101	1	17	11	3	13	3	28	10	0	2	0
Bobby Convey	315	6	3	1	3	2	0	-	1	0	4	6	0	0	2	3	0	0	0
Kevin Doyle	3630	41	39	30	2	9	18	588	3	43	27	49	9	5	30	74	31	5	0
Michael Duberry	2526	27	27	26	0	1	0	-	0	3	7	0	39	11	38	30	1	3	0
Brynjar Gunnarsson	1418	27	13	5	14	8	2	783	0	6	5	4	8	1	16	13	0	3	0
Dan Harding	248	3	3	2	1	0	0	-	0	0	0	4	0	1	0	1	0	0	0
James Harper	2621	34	28	20	6	8	1	2316	2	9	9	19	15	5	31	21	3	3	0
James Henry	266	7	3	0	4	3	0	-	1	0	1	15	0	0	3	2	1	0	0
Noel Hunt	2111	37	27	5	10	22	11	136	3	29	22	35	14	1	32	33	28	4	0
Stephen Hunt	3993	46	41	37	5	4	6	1838	17	17	24	174	10	7	45	75	13	6	0
Ivar Ingimarsson	2478	26	26	26	0	0	1	645	0	7	5	3	40	7	31	17	0	1	0
Jem Karacan	1285	15	15	7	0	8	1	412	2	2	2	10	5	0	12	14	0	4	0
Jimmy Kebe	3408	41	38	25	3	13	2	673	11	23	24	68	7	0	35	40	12	2	1
Julian Kelly	445	7	4	4	3	0	0	-	0	0	1	15	3	0	1	4	0	0	0
Dave Kitson	886	10	9	7	1	2	2	224	1	16	9	5	4	1	24	21	2	0	0
Leroy Lita	622	10	6	4	4	2	1	336	0	8	7	3	1	0	15	10	5	0	0
Glen Little	436	8	5	1	3	4	0	-	0	1	1	14	0	0	3	3	0	0	0
Shane Long	1592	37	11	7	26	4	9	114	2	14	13	18	8	0	37	30	18	3	0
Marek Matejovsky	1232	22	11	7	11	4	1	36	1	6	5	23	0	1	24	14	0	5	0
Alex Pearce	1229	16	13	11	3	2	1	251	1	3	3	1	14	2	16	19	0	1	0
Liam Rosenior	3958	42	42	41	0	1	0	-	6	3	6	82	37	15	29	29	1	8	2
Ibrahima Sonko	277	3	3	3	0	0	3	37	0	3	0	0	10	3	3	2	0	1	1
Jay Tabb	647	9	6	4	3	2	0	1697	1	3	5	4	0	0	8	12	0	1	0

Coca-Cola CHAMPIONSHIP

SEASON TOTALS

Goals scored	72
Goals conceded	40
Clean sheets	21
Shots on target	228
Shots off target	205
Shots per goal	6.03
Pens awarded	7
Pens scored	5
Pens conceded	3
Offsides	119
Corners	360
Crosses	627
Players used	27
Fouls committed	549
Free-kicks won	562

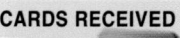

CARDS RECEIVED

63 5

SEQUENCES

Wins	5
(01/12/08–20/12/08)	
Losses	2
(21/02/09–28/02/09)	
Draws	2
(on four occasions)	
Undefeated	9
(25/11/08–09/01/09)	
Without win	5
(21/03/09–18/04/09)	
Undefeated home	9
(10/08/08–08/11/08)	
Undefeated away	6
(01/11/08–28/12/08)	
Without scoring	4
(31/01/09–28/02/09)	
Without conceding	3
(on four occasions)	
Scoring	13
(01/11/08–09/01/09)	
Conceding	6
(21/02/09–14/03/09)	

SEASON INFORMATION
Highest position: 2
Lowest position: 14
Average goals scored per game: 1.57
Average goals conceded per game: 0.87

League position at the end of each week

League position at the end of: August 6, September 3, October 4, November 3, December 2, January 2, February 3, March 3, April 4, May 4

MATCH RECORDS
Goals scored per match

	W	D	L	Pts
Failed to score	14	0	7	7	7
Scored 1 goal	9	4	2	3	14
Scored 2 goals	13	7	5	1	26
Scored 3 goals	5	5	0	0	15
Scored 4+ goals	5	5	0	0	15

Goals conceded per match

	W	D	L	Pts
Clean sheet	21	14	7	0	49
Conceded 1 goal	12	6	2	4	20
Conceded 2 goals	12	1	5	6	8
Conceded 3 goals	0	0	0	0	0
Conceded 4+ goals	1	0	0	1	0

QUICK-FIRE GOALS
From the start of a match
Noel Hunt (v Burnley) 3:54
By a substitute after coming on
Shane Long (v Sheff Wed) 2:42

LAST-GASP GOALS
From the start of a match
Adam Federici (v Cardiff) 95:38
By a substitute after coming on
Shane Long (v Burnley) 38:27

GOAL DETAILS
How the goals were struck
SCORED		CONCEDED
28	Right foot	19
16	Left foot	14
26	Headers	7
2	Others	0

How the goals were struck
SCORED		CONCEDED
38	Open play	25
14	Cross	6
9	Corner	1
5	Penalties	3
1	Direct from free-kick	1
2	Free-kick	3
3	Own goals	1

Distance from goal
SCORED		CONCEDED
34	6yds	17
34	18yds	16
4	18+yds	7

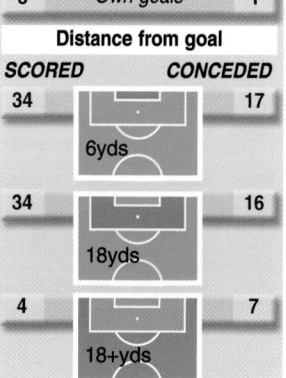

GOALS SCORED/CONCEDED PER FIVE-MINUTE INTERVALS

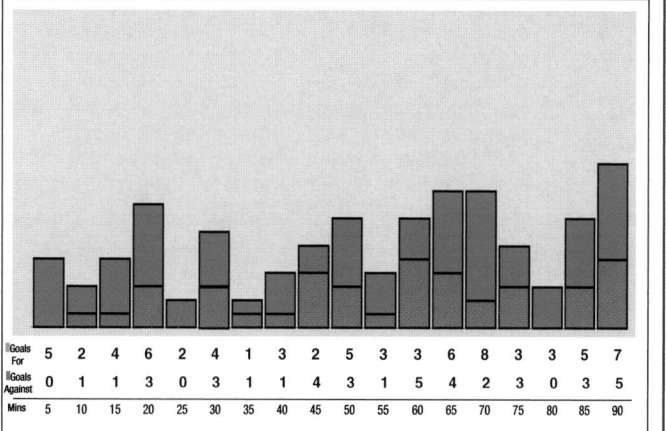

Goals For	5	2	4	6	2	4	1	3	2	5	3	3	6	8	3	3	5	7
Goals Against	0	1	1	3	0	3	1	1	4	3	1	5	4	2	3	0	3	5
Mins	5	10	15	20	25	30	35	40	45	50	55	60	65	70	75	80	85	90

SHEFFIELD UNITED

CLUB SUMMARY

FORMED	1889
MANAGER	Kevin Blackwell
GROUND	Bramall Lane
CAPACITY	30,945
NICKNAME	The Blades
WEBSITE	www.sufc.co.uk

The New Football Pools PLAYER OF THE SEASON — Kyle Naughton

OVERALL

P	W	D	L	F	A	GD
56	27	16	13	79	54	25

COCA-COLA CHAMPIONSHIP

Pos	P	W	D	L	F	A	GD	Pts
3	46	22	14	10	64	39	25	80

HOME

Pos	P	W	D	L	F	A	GD	Pts
8	23	12	6	5	35	22	13	42

AWAY

Pos	P	W	D	L	F	A	GD	Pts
2	23	10	8	5	29	17	12	38

CUP PROGRESS DETAILS

Competition	Round reached	Knocked out by
FA Cup	R5	Hull
Carling Cup	R3	Arsenal

BIGGEST WIN (ALL COMPS)

22/11/08 5–2 v Charlton **FLC**

BIGGEST DEFEAT (ALL COMPS)

23/09/08 0–6 v Arsenal **LC3**

THE PLAYER WITH THE MOST

Shots on target
Darius Henderson 39

Shots off target
James Beattie 33

Shots without scoring
Anthony Stokes 19

Assists
David Cotterill 7

Offsides
Danny Webber 29

Fouls
Darius Henderson 81

Fouls without a card
Billy Sharp 19

Free-kicks won
Stephen Quinn 88

Defensive clearances
Chris Morgan 69

actim INDEX for the 2008/09 Coca-Cola Championship Season

Rank	Player	Pts
15	Patrick Kenny	559
16	Stephen Quinn	557
21	Kyle Naughton	545
52	Matthew Kilgallon	459
64	Chris Morgan	441

ATTENDANCE RECORD

High	Low	Average
30,786	23,045	26,023
v Sheff Wed (07/02/2009)	v Crystal Palace (20/12/2008)	

A SEASON of progress for Sheffield United ended in heartbreak as they were pipped to promotion by Burnley.

The Blades embarked on a fine late run of just two defeats in their last 15 games and finished only three points outside the automatic promotion places. A third-place finish then gave them an advantageous draw in the play-offs and initially they made good use of it, overcoming Preston 2–1 on aggregate, with goals from Brian Howard and Greg Halford.

But the Blades were disappointing in the final and, despite a couple of penalty appeals, they were unable to seriously trouble Burnley, who ran out 1–0 winners at Wembley.

It was a second play-off final defeat in four years for manager Kevin Blackwell, who was a loser with Leeds in 2006, but it should not wholly detract from what was a positive season at Bramall Lane.

Finishing five places and 14 points better off than a year ago, United managed 10 wins away from home, a record bettered only by champions Wolves, but more tellingly they lost five times at home, a statistic that ultimately hamstrung their chances of finishing in the top two.

Blackwell did well to cope with the mid-season sale of top scorer James Beattie to Stoke, in particular with his decision to employ loan defender Halford as a striker. Halford grabbed eight goals during the course of the season, but outscored all of the club's other forwards, with Darius Henderson (seven) and Danny Webber (six) coming the closest.

A dejected Nick Montgomery after the play-off final

Despite those helpful contributions, Beattie remained their top scorer until the end of the season.

A back injury cruelly curtailed veteran midfielder Gary Speed's season in November, forcing the former Wales international to concentrate on coaching. But again Blackwell juggled his pack to good effect, with mid-season signing Howard and Stephen Quinn taking over in the middle of the park.

The most promising aspect of the season for the Blades faithful, though, was the emergence of exciting defensive duo Kyle Naughton and Kyle Walker. Naughton has already earned England Under-21 honours, although his own goal – which was later proved not to have crossed the line – contributed to the club being knocked out of the FA Cup in the fifth round by Hull.

Their League Cup campaign also ended in despair with a 6–0 thrashing by a vibrant young Arsenal side.

 **Kevin Blackwell juggled his pack to good effect**

RESULTS 2008/09

August

9th	● Birmingham ....a	L 1–0	**Att:** 24,019. **Ref:** K Stroud — **Booked:** Stead
13th	● Port Vale ....h	W 3–1	**Att:** 7,694. **Ref:** K Friend — **Scorers:** Hendrie, Quinn, Webber. **Booked:** Geary
16th	● QPR ....h	W 3–0	**Att:** 25,273. **Ref:** G Laws — **Scorers:** Sharp³. **Booked:** Halford
23rd	● Blackpool ....a	W 1–3	**Att:** 8,611. **Ref:** S Mathieson — **Scorers:** Halford, Quinn, Speed. **Booked:** Henderson
27th	● Huddersfield ....a	W 1–2	**Att:** 9,552. **Ref:** N Miller — **Scorers:** Henderson, Naughton. **Booked:** Henderson, Jihai
30th	● Cardiff ....h	D 0–0	**Att:** 29,226. **Ref:** C Webster

September

13th	● Derby ....a	L 2–1	**Att:** 28,473. **Ref:** C Foy — **Scorers:** Henderson. **Booked:** Montgomery, Morgan, Quinn, J. Beattie
16th	● Coventry ....h	D 1–1	**Att:** 24,130. **Ref:** D Deadman — **Scorers:** Sharp. **Booked:** Quinn. **Dismissed:** Jihai
20th	● Norwich ....a	L 1–0	**Att:** 24,175. **Ref:** P Crossley — **Booked:** Halford, Speed
23rd	● Arsenal ....a	L 6–0	**Att:** 56,632. **Ref:** P Dowd — **Booked:** Halford
27th	● Watford ....h	W 2–1	**Att:** 24,427. **Ref:** M Halsey — **Scorers:** J. Beattie, Speed
30th	● Doncaster ....a	W 0–2	**Att:** 14,242. **Ref:** T Bates — **Scorers:** Quinn, Roberts OG. **Booked:** Quinn, Halford

October

4th	● Bristol City ....h	W 3–0	**Att:** 24,712. **Ref:** K Stroud — **Scorers:** J. Beattie², Fontaine OG. **Booked:** Quinn
19th	● Sheff Wed ....a	L 1–0	**Att:** 30,441. **Ref:** M Dean — **Booked:** Speed, Naysmith, Ehiogu. **Dismissed:** Kilgallon
21st	● Southampton ....h	D 0–0	**Att:** 25,642. **Ref:** C Oliver — **Booked:** Webber
25th	● Preston ....h	W 1–0	**Att:** 24,445. **Ref:** D Whitestone — **Scorers:** Ehiogu. **Booked:** Naughton, Kenny, Howard
28th	● Bristol City ....a	D 0–0	**Att:** 16,798. **Ref:** R Styles — **Booked:** Ehiogu, Howard

November

1st	● Plymouth ....h	W 2–0	**Att:** 25,601. **Ref:** S Mathieson — **Scorers:** J. Beattie²
8th	● Barnsley ....a	W 1–2	**Att:** 19,002. **Ref:** A D'Urso — **Scorers:** J. Beattie². **Booked:** Morgan, J. Beattie, Kenny. **Dismissed:** Ehiogu
15th	● Reading ....h	L 0–2	**Att:** 25,065. **Ref:** M Oliver — **Booked:** Stokes
22nd	● Charlton ....a	W 2–5	**Att:** 20,328. **Ref:** S Tanner — **Scorers:** J. Beattie, Kilgallon, Quinn, Speed, Youga OG
25th	● Wolverhampton ....h	L 1–3	**Att:** 27,111. **Ref:** G Laws — **Scorers:** Spring
29th	● Ipswich ....a	D 1–1	**Att:** 19,785. **Ref:** D Whitestone — **Scorers:** J. Beattie

December

6th	● Burnley ....h	L 2–3	**Att:** 24,702. **Ref:** A Taylor — **Scorers:** J. Beattie, Quinn. **Booked:** Naysmith, Naughton
9th	● Nottm Forest ....a	W 0–1	**Att:** 19,541. **Ref:** G Salisbury — **Scorers:** Howard. **Booked:** Naysmith
13th	● Swansea ....a	D 1–1	**Att:** 14,744. **Ref:** A Marriner — **Scorers:** Morgan. **Booked:** Howard. **Dismissed:** Henderson
20th	● Crystal Palace ....h	D 2–2	**Att:** 23,045. **Ref:** P Taylor — **Scorers:** J. Beattie, Dyer. **Booked:** Montgomery, Morgan, Kilgallon
26th	● Wolverhampton ....a	D 1–1	**Att:** 27,106. **Ref:** T Bates — **Scorers:** J. Beattie. **Booked:** Dyer
28th	● Charlton ....h	W 3–1	**Att:** 24,717. **Ref:** C Webster — **Scorers:** Quinn², Webber. **Booked:** Howard

January

10th	● Norwich ....h	W 1–0	**Att:** 27,267. **Ref:** M Halsey — **Scorers:** Henderson. **Booked:** Howard
13th	● Leyton Orient ....a	W 1–4	**Att:** 4,527. **Ref:** I Williamson — **Scorers:** J. Beattie³, Naughton, Sharp. **Booked:** Sharp, Morgan
17th	● Watford ....a	W 0–2	**Att:** 14,555. **Ref:** K Friend — **Scorers:** Henderson, Webber. **Booked:** Quinn
24th	● Charlton ....h	W 2–1	**Att:** 15,957. **Ref:** T Bates — **Scorers:** Hendrie, Webber
27th	● Doncaster ....h	L 0–1	**Att:** 26,555. **Ref:** A Wiley — **Booked:** Quinn, Henderson
31st	● Preston ....a	D 0–0	**Att:** 14,889. **Ref:** S Mathieson — **Booked:** Henderson

February

3rd	● Southampton ....a	W 1–2	**Att:** 13,257. **Ref:** L Probert — **Scorers:** Halford, Ward. **Dismissed:** Henderson
7th	● Sheff Wed ....h	L 1–2	**Att:** 30,786. **Ref:** M Halsey — **Scorers:** Lupoli
14th	● Hull ....h	D 1–1	**Att:** 22,283. **Ref:** A Marriner — **Scorers:** Halford
21st	● Plymouth ....a	D 2–2	**Att:** 10,044. **Ref:** A Woolmer — **Scorers:** Halford, Webber. **Booked:** Webber, Morgan, C. Beattie
26th	● Hull ....a	L 2–1	**Att:** 17,239. **Ref:** P Walton — **Scorers:** Sharp. **Booked:** Naughton, Sharp

March

1st	● Birmingham ....h	W 2–1	**Att:** 24,232. **Ref:** L Mason — **Scorers:** Cotterill, Webber. **Booked:** Montgomery, Quinn, Naughton
4th	● Coventry ....a	W 1–2	**Att:** 16,300. **Ref:** K Wright — **Scorers:** Bromby, Morgan. **Booked:** Montgomery
7th	● QPR ....a	D 0–0	**Att:** 13,718. **Ref:** N Swarbrick
10th	● Blackpool ....h	D 2–2	**Att:** 25,273. **Ref:** R Booth — **Scorers:** Cotterill, Coid OG
14th	● Derby ....h	W 4–2	**Att:** 27,565. **Ref:** I Williamson — **Scorers:** C. Beattie, Henderson², Naughton. **Booked:** O'Toole
22nd	● Cardiff ....a	W 0–3	**Att:** 17,942. **Ref:** P Taylor — **Scorers:** Cotterill, Quinn, Ward. **Booked:** Halford, Naughton, Montgomery

April

4th	● Ipswich ....h	W 2–0	**Att:** 25,315. **Ref:** N Miller — **Scorers:** Halford, Henderson. **Booked:** Naysmith, Bromby
7th	● Barnsley ....h	W 2–1	**Att:** 27,061. **Ref:** G Hegley — **Scorers:** Lupoli, O'Toole. **Booked:** O'Toole
10th	● Reading ....a	W 0–1	**Att:** 20,756. **Ref:** K Friend — **Scorers:** Howard. **Booked:** Howard
13th	● Nottm Forest ....h	D 0–0	**Att:** 28,374. **Ref:** M Jones — **Booked:** Bromby
20th	● Burnley ....a	L 1–0	**Att:** 14,884. **Ref:** G Laws
25th	● Swansea ....h	W 1–0	**Att:** 28,010. **Ref:** R Styles — **Scorers:** Cotterill. **Booked:** Kilgallon

May

3rd	● Crystal Palace ....a	D 0–0	**Att:** 22,824. **Ref:** C Foy
8th	● Preston ....a	D 1–1	**Att:** 19,840. **Ref:** A Marriner — **Scorers:** Howard. **Booked:** Kilgallon, Montgomery, Lupoli
11th	● Preston ....h	W 1–0	**Att:** 26,354. **Ref:** A Wiley — **Scorers:** Halford. **Booked:** Quinn, Cotterill
25th	● Burnley ....n	L 1–0	**Att:** 80,518. **Ref:** M Dean — **Booked:** Ward, Lupoli. **Dismissed:** Ward

● Coca-Cola Championship/Play-Offs ● FA Cup ● Carling Cup

CHAMPIONSHIP GOALKEEPER STATS

Player	Minutes on pitch	Appearances	Match starts	Completed matches	Sub appearances	Subbed off	Saved with feet	Punched	Parried	Tipped over	Fumbled	Tipped round	Caught	Blocked	Clean sheets	Goals conceded	Minutes since conceding	Save %	Saved	Resulting in goals	Opposition miss	Yellow cards	Red cards
Ian Bennett 189	2	2	2	0	0	0	0	0	0	0	1	3	0	0	2	62	71.43	0	0	0	0	0
Paddy Kenny 4239	44	44	44	0	0	1	4	29	5	0	7	162	0	19	37	265	84.96	2	3	1	2	0

Columns under SAVES BREAKDOWN: Saved with feet, Punched, Parried, Tipped over, Fumbled, Tipped round, Caught, Blocked.
Columns under PENALTIES: Saved, Resulting in goals, Opposition miss.

CHAMPIONSHIP OUTFIELD PLAYER STATS

Player	Minutes on pitch	Appearances	Match starts	Completed matches	Substitute appearances	Subbed off	Goals scored	Minutes since scoring	Assists	Shots on target	Shots off target	Crosses	Defensive clearances	Defensive blocks	Fouls committed	Free-kicks won	Caught offside	Yellow cards	Red cards
James Beattie 1964	23	21	15	2	6	12	167	3	38	33	10	7	2	39	31	19	2	0
Craig Beattie 406	13	1	0	12	1	1	243	1	9	9	1	1	0	6	10	6	1	0
Leigh Bromby 675	12	6	4	6	2	1	322	0	3	4	2	15	3	10	1	1	2	0
David Cotterill 1460	24	17	4	7	13	4	153	7	7	8	73	2	3	11	26	2	0	0
Nathan Dyer 307	7	3	2	4	1	1	320	0	1	1	4	0	0	4	4	2	1	0
Ugo Ehiogu 1022	16	11	10	5	1	1	412	2	2	5	0	15	10	16	9	3	2	1
Derek Geary 5	1	0	0	1	0	0	-	0	0	0	0	0	0	0	0	0	0	0
Keith Gillespie 4	1	0	0	1	0	0	-	0	0	0	0	0	0	0	0	0	0	0
Greg Halford 2859	41	31	17	10	14	4	659	5	19	16	64	19	2	34	23	10	4	0
Darius Henderson 2368	32	25	19	7	6	6	637	4	39	23	11	12	2	81	37	25	3	2
Lee Hendrie 104	5	0	0	5	0	0	-	0	0	2	5	0	0	1	3	1	0	0
Brian Howard 1983	26	22	13	4	9	4	103	3	16	16	24	4	2	40	43	4	6	0
Sun Jihai 1045	12	11	9	1	2	0	-	0	1	1	12	2	1	13	14	0	0	1
Matthew Kilgallon 3719	40	39	37	1	2	1	2521	2	4	7	16	43	15	33	21	3	2	1
Arturo Lupoli 211	9	2	0	7	2	2	70	0	5	3	0	0	0	1	1	2	0	0
Nick Montgomery 2524	28	26	25	2	1	0	-	1	4	5	12	16	6	55	38	0	5	0
Chris Morgan 3785	41	40	38	1	2	2	1114	0	13	14	2	69	11	50	37	4	4	0
Kyle Naughton 3753	40	39	38	1	1	1	875	3	12	5	79	28	9	31	49	0	4	0
Gary Naysmith 3482	39	37	34	2	3	0	-	2	1	0	39	26	10	38	20	0	4	0
John-Joe O'Toole 510	9	5	4	4	1	1	180	0	3	4	2	4	0	20	11	1	2	0
Stephen Quinn 3945	43	43	35	0	8	7	340	2	35	28	100	10	3	35	88	11	7	0
Billy Sharp 1397	22	17	3	5	14	4	952	1	19	16	28	0	0	19	25	23	0	0
Gary Speed 1501	17	17	15	0	2	3	77	1	9	9	5	19	1	24	13	0	2	0
Matthew Spring 806	11	8	5	3	3	1	876	0	5	10	3	2	7	8	1	0	0	0
Jonathan Stead 12	1	0	0	1	0	0	101	0	0	0	0	0	0	2	0	0	1	0
Anthony Stokes 530	12	5	0	7	5	0	918	1	10	9	6	0	0	4	6	6	1	0
Michael Tonge 385	4	4	3	0	1	0	-	1	2	2	6	1	0	2	1	1	0	0
Kyle Walker 191	2	2	2	0	0	0	-	0	0	0	2	0	0	1	3	0	0	0
Jamie Ward 942	16	7	1	9	6	2	644	1	15	14	7	0	0	10	12	14	0	0
Danny Webber 2062	36	21	4	15	17	4	190	2	26	15	28	0	1	13	9	29	2	0

actim

SEASON TOTALS

Goals scored	64
Goals conceded	39
Clean sheets	19
Shots on target	295
Shots off target	254
Shots per goal	8.58
Pens awarded	10
Pens scored	10
Pens conceded	6
Offsides	168
Corners	294
Crosses	548
Players used	32
Fouls committed	600
Free-kicks won	547

CARDS RECEIVED

57   5

SEQUENCES

Wins 5
(14/03/09–10/04/09)
Losses
(–)
Draws 3
(13/12/08–26/12/08)
Undefeated 11
(21/02/09–13/04/09)
Without win 4
(30/08/08–20/09/08)
Undefeated home 8
(on two occasions)
Undefeated away 15
(28/10/08–10/04/09)
Without scoring 2
(on three occasions)
Without conceding 4
(21/10/08–01/11/08)
Scoring 11
(22/11/08–17/01/09)
Conceding 6
(08/11/08–06/12/08)

SEASON INFORMATION
Highest Position: 3
Lowest Position: 21
Average goals scored per game: 1.39
Average goals conceded per game: 0.85

League position at the end of each week

League position at the end of — August 5, September 6, October 6, November 4, December 6, January 4, February 7, March 4, April 3, May 3

MATCH RECORDS
Goals scored per match

		W	D	L	Pts
Failed to score	13	0	7	6	7
Scored 1 goal	12	5	4	3	19
Scored 2 goals	14	10	3	1	33
Scored 3 goals	5	5	0	0	15
Scored 4+ goals	2	2	0	0	6

Goals conceded per match

		W	D	L	Pts
Clean Sheet	19	12	7	0	43
Conceded 1 goal	17	8	4	5	28
Conceded 2 goals	8	2	3	3	9
Conceded 3 goals	2	0	0	2	0
Conceded 4+ goals	0	0	0	0	0

QUICK-FIRE GOALS
From the start of a match
Gary Speed (v Watford) 0:40
By a substitute after coming on
Jamie Ward (v Cardiff) 5:10

LAST-GASP GOALS
From the start of a match
Craig Beattie (v Derby) 94:36
By a substitute after coming on
Matthew Spring (v Wolves) 64:22

GOAL DETAILS
How the goals were struck

SCORED		CONCEDED
31	Right foot	20
18	Left foot	10
15	Headers	8
0	Others	1

How the goals were struck

SCORED		CONCEDED
32	Open play	19
8	Cross	10
4	Corner	4
10	Penalties	3
3	Direct from free-kick	0
3	Free-kick	1
4	Own goals	2

Distance from goal

SCORED		CONCEDED
28	6yds	9
32	18yds	25
4	18+yds	5

GOALS SCORED/CONCEDED PER FIVE-MINUTE INTERVALS

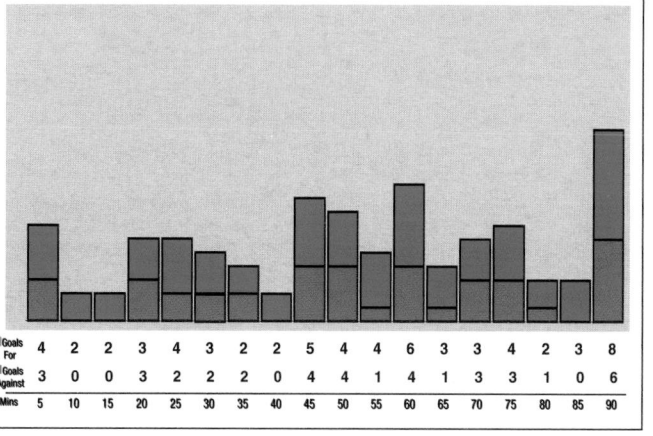

Goals For	4	2	2	3	4	3	2	2	5	4	4	6	3	3	4	2	3	8
Goals Against	3	0	0	3	2	2	2	0	4	4	1	4	1	3	3	1	0	6
Mins	5	10	15	20	25	30	35	40	45	50	55	60	65	70	75	80	85	90

SHEFFIELD WEDNESDAY

CLUB SUMMARY

FORMED	1867
MANAGER	Brian Laws
GROUND	Hillsborough
CAPACITY	39,859
NICKNAME	The Owls
WEBSITE	www.swfc.co.uk

The New Football Pools PLAYER OF THE SEASON — Marcus Tudgay

OVERALL
P	W	D	L	F	A	GD	
48	16	14	18	54	62	-8	

COCA-COLA CHAMPIONSHIP
Pos	P	W	D	L	F	A	GD	Pts
12	46	16	13	17	51	58	-7	61

HOME
Pos	P	W	D	L	F	A	GD	Pts
10	23	11	6	6	26	14	12	39

AWAY
Pos	P	W	D	L	F	A	GD	Pts
18	23	5	7	11	25	44	-19	22

CUP PROGRESS DETAILS
Competition	Round reached	Knocked out by
FA Cup	R3	Fulham
Carling Cup	R1	Rotherham

BIGGEST WIN (ALL COMPS)
4–1 on two occasions

BIGGEST DEFEAT (ALL COMPS)
16/09/08 0–6 v Reading **FLC**

THE PLAYER WITH THE MOST
Shots on target	
Marcus Tudgay	48
Shots off target	
Marcus Tudgay	38
Shots without scoring	
James O'Connor	28
Assists	
Etienne Esajas	4
Offsides	
Leon Clarke	46
Fouls	
Marcus Tudgay	80
Fouls without a card	
Richard Hinds	12
Free-kicks won	
Marcus Tudgay	65
Defensive clearances	
Richard Wood	57

actim INDEX for the 2008/09 Coca-Cola Championship Season

Rank	Player	Pts
31	Marcus Tudgay	504
33	Lee Grant	496
60	Tommy Spurr	449
72	Richard Wood	418
106	Sean McAllister	365

ATTENDANCE RECORD
High	Low	Average
30,658	14,792	21,542
v Cardiff (03/05/2009)	v QPR (09/12/2008)	

Wednesday players celebrate Steve Watson's winning goal against rivals United

THE 2008/9 season will be best remembered by Wednesday fans for a derby double and a boardroom revolution.

The Owls steered well clear of relegation trouble thanks to an impressive home record while, off the field, Wednesday were transformed by the arrival of a new chairman and chief executive, who implemented a refreshing fan-friendly doctrine.

A club that had been hamstrung by boardroom bickering was suddenly united when Lee Strafford and Nick Parker were brought in. The pair have since instigated a three-year plan to get the Owls back to the Barclays Premier League, with the coming season marking the 10th anniversary of the club's relegation from the top flight.

However, when fans look back at the 2008/09 campaign, it will be the two wins over the Blades that stand out. Veteran Steve Watson's volley clinched a 1–0 win at Hillsborough, and a stunning strike from Marcus Tudgay ensured Brian Laws' side were the first to record a Steel City derby double in 95 years.

Some of the football played at home by the Owls was enough to remind the faithful of past glories. Fans returned to Hillsborough in increasing numbers during the second half of the season and will look towards the next campaign with renewed optimism.

Laws has been given an increased budget to strengthen his squad in the summer and hopes to supplement a young side with experienced players in key areas. The 2008/09 season saw the emergence of homegrown academy graduates such as Sean McAllister, Mark Beevers and, more recently, Luke Boden, while Tudgay was a revelation.

Other highlights of the campaign included the Owls sticking four goals past Burnley in each of their league encounters, while a last-day win over Cardiff prompted Laws to target a play-off finish in 2009/10.

> **Fans returned to Hillsborough in increasing numbers**

RESULTS 2008/09

August
9th	● Burnley ....h	W 4–1	**Att:** 23,793. **Ref:** C Oliver — **Scorers:** Sodje², Tudgay². **Booked:** O'Connor, Beevers
12th	● Rotherham ....h	D 2–2	**Att:** 16,298. **Ref:** N Miller — **Scorers:** Esajas (Lost 5–3 on pens)
16th	● Wolverhampton...........a	L 4–1	**Att:** 22,491. **Ref:** M Jones — **Scorers:** Esajas
23rd	● Preston ....h	D 1–1	**Att:** 17,963. **Ref:** M Russell — **Scorers:** McAllister. **Booked:** Burton, Esajas
30th	● Swansea..................a	D 1–1	**Att:** 16,702. **Ref:** K Friend — **Scorers:** Watson. **Booked:** Burton, McAllister, McMahon

September
13th	● Watford ....h	W 2–0	**Att:** 17,066. **Ref:** G Salisbury — **Scorers:** Spurr, Tudgay. **Booked:** Watson, Wood
16th	● Reading ....a	L 6–0	**Att:** 18,159. **Ref:** A Woolmer — **Booked:** Gilbert
20th	● Ipswich ....h	D 0–0	**Att:** 17,198. **Ref:** M Jones
27th	● Charlton ....a	W 1–2	**Att:** 20,278. **Ref:** D Whitestone — **Scorers:** Small, Tudgay. **Booked:** McMahon, O'Connor, Tudgay
30th	● Nottm Forest.............h	W 1–0	**Att:** 20,823. **Ref:** A D'Urso — **Scorers:** Esajas. **Booked:** McAllister

October
4th	● Plymouth..................a	L 4–0	**Att:** 10,795. **Ref:** R East
19th	● Sheff Utd ....h	W 1–0	**Att:** 30,441. **Ref:** M Dean — **Scorers:** Watson. **Booked:** O'Connor, Johnson, Sodje. **Dismissed:** Johnson
21st	● Barnsley ....a	L 2–1	**Att:** 17,784. **Ref:** P Crossley — **Scorers:** Clarke. **Booked:** Beevers, Gilbert. **Dismissed:** McMahon
25th	● Birmingham ....a	L 3–1	**Att:** 17,300. **Ref:** P Taylor — **Scorers:** Esajas. **Booked:** Smith, Buxton. **Dismissed:** Smith
28th	● Plymouth..................h	L 0–1	**Att:** 16,515. **Ref:** G Laws

November
1st	● Crystal Palace ....a	D 1–1	**Att:** 14,650. **Ref:** K Wright — **Scorers:** Clarke
8th	● Doncaster ....h	W 1–0	**Att:** 20,872. **Ref:** L Mason — **Scorers:** Clarke
15th	● Derby ....a	L 3–0	**Att:** 30,111. **Ref:** K Stroud — **Booked:** Sodje
22nd	● Coventry ....h	L 0–1	**Att:** 16,119. **Ref:** K Friend — **Booked:** Johnson
25th	● Blackpool ....a	W 0–2	**Att:** 7,054. **Ref:** C Boyeson — **Scorers:** Burton, Tudgay
29th	● Norwich...................h	W 3–2	**Att:** 18,883. **Ref:** T Bates — **Scorers:** Clarke, McMahon, Tudgay. **Booked:** McMahon

December
6th	● Southampton ....a	D 1–1	**Att:** 15,440. **Ref:** G Hegley — **Scorers:** Tudgay. **Booked:** Tudgay
9th	● QPR ....h	W 1–0	**Att:** 14,792. **Ref:** N Miller — **Scorers:** Clarke. **Booked:** Grant
13th	● Bristol City ....h	D 0–0	**Att:** 15,542. **Ref:** R Shoebridge
20th	● Cardiff ....a	L 2–0	**Att:** 17,600. **Ref:** K Friend — **Booked:** Buxton, McAllister
26th	● Blackpool ....h	D 1–1	**Att:** 25,044. **Ref:** M Oliver — **Scorers:** Slusarski. **Booked:** Buxton, O'Connor
28th	● Coventry ....a	L 2–0	**Att:** 19,602. **Ref:** G Laws

January
3rd	● Fulham ....h	L 1–2	**Att:** 18,377. **Ref:** L Mason — **Scorers:** Spurr. **Booked:** O'Connor
10th	● Ipswich ....a	D 1–1	**Att:** 22,213. **Ref:** G Horwood — **Scorers:** Watson
17th	● Charlton ....h	W 4–1	**Att:** 28,766. **Ref:** D Deadman — **Scorers:** Jeffers, Potter, Tudgay². **Booked:** Johnson, Wood, Jeffers, Boden
27th	● Nottm Forest.............a	L 2–1	**Att:** 22,618. **Ref:** S Mathieson — **Scorers:** Johnson. **Booked:** Buxton. **Dismissed:** Jeffers
31st	● Birmingham ....h	D 1–1	**Att:** 18,409. **Ref:** P Crossley — **Scorers:** Buxton

February
7th	● Sheff Utd ....a	W 1–2	**Att:** 30,786. **Ref:** M Halsey — **Scorers:** Spurr, Tudgay. **Booked:** Beevers, O'Connor, Potter
14th	● Doncaster ....a	L 1–0	**Att:** 14,823. **Ref:** N Swarbrick — **Booked:** O'Connor, Buxton
17th	● Barnsley ....h	L 0–1	**Att:** 25,820. **Ref:** R Booth — **Booked:** Johnson
21st	● Crystal Palace ....h	W 2–0	**Att:** 22,687. **Ref:** C Webster — **Scorers:** Clarke, McAllister. **Booked:** Jeffers, Johnson
28th	● Burnley ....a	W 2–4	**Att:** 12,449. **Ref:** A D'Urso — **Scorers:** Clarke², Tudgay². **Booked:** Clarke

March
3rd	● Reading ....h	L 1–2	**Att:** 19,268. **Ref:** A Hall — **Scorers:** McAllister. **Booked:** Clarke
7th	● Wolverhampton...........h	L 0–1	**Att:** 23,703. **Ref:** S Mathieson
10th	● Preston ....a	D 1–1	**Att:** 12,381. **Ref:** A Penn — **Scorers:** Jeffers
14th	● Watford ....a	D 2–2	**Att:** 16,294. **Ref:** A Woolmer — **Scorers:** Jeffers, Tudgay. **Booked:** Jeffers, Wood
21st	● Swansea..................h	D 0–0	**Att:** 22,564. **Ref:** M Jones — **Booked:** Potter, Varney

April
4th	● Norwich...................a	W 0–1	**Att:** 25,385. **Ref:** M Russell — **Scorers:** Johnson. **Booked:** Wood, Spurr. **Dismissed:** Spurr
11th	● Derby ....h	L 0–1	**Att:** 24,392. **Ref:** S Tanner — **Booked:** O'Connor
13th	● QPR ....a	L 3–2	**Att:** 13,742. **Ref:** D Deadman — **Scorers:** Tudgay, Mahon OG. **Booked:** Varney, Beevers
18th	● Southampton ....h	W 2–0	**Att:** 24,145. **Ref:** R Shoebridge — **Scorers:** Varney²
25th	● Bristol City ....a	D 1–1	**Att:** 17,486. **Ref:** A D'Urso — **Scorers:** Potter

May
3rd	● Cardiff ....h	W 1–0	**Att:** 30,658. **Ref:** P Crossley — **Scorers:** Johnson. **Booked:** Johnson

● Coca-Cola Championship/Play-Offs ● FA Cup ● Carling Cup

SHEFFIELD WEDNESDAY

CHAMPIONSHIP GOALKEEPER STATS

Player	Minutes on pitch	Appearances	Match starts	Completed matches	Sub appearances	Subbed off	SAVES BREAKDOWN Saved with feet	Punched	Parried	Tipped over	Fumbled	Tipped round	Caught	Blocked	Clean sheets	Goals conceded	Minutes since conceding	Save %	PENALTIES Saved	Resulting in goals	Opposition miss	Yellow cards	Red cards
Lee Grant	4397	46	46	46	0	0	2	24	27	10	0	11	132	0	13	58	168	78.03	1	6	0	1	0

CHAMPIONSHIP OUTFIELD PLAYER STATS

Player	Minutes on pitch	Appearances	Match starts	Completed matches	Substitute appearances	Subbed off	Goals scored	Minutes since scoring	Assists	Shots on target	Shots off target	Crosses	Defensive clearances	Defensive blocks	Fouls committed	Free-kicks won	Caught offside	Yellow cards	Red cards
Mark Beevers	3006	34	30	30	4	0	0	-	0	1	4	1	51	18	27	23	0	4	0
Luke Boden	423	12	2	2	10	0	0	-	0	1	1	6	2	0	8	2	0	1	0
Deon Burton	1006	17	9	4	8	5	1	44	2	8	15	4	3	0	25	13	26	2	0
Lewis Buxton	3009	32	32	31	0	1	1	1475	1	4	4	42	33	3	26	24	0	5	0
Leon Clarke	2003	29	20	12	9	8	8	366	3	33	21	12	2	0	37	19	46	2	0
Etienne Esajas	1387	22	8	4	14	4	0	765	4	18	18	28	1	3	15	18	2	1	0
Peter Gilbert	763	8	8	8	0	0	0	-	0	0	0	8	4	1	6	7	0	2	0
Michael Gray	1090	13	13	6	0	7	0	1335	2	10	8	38	1	3	4	14	3	0	0
Richard Hinds	1204	14	13	12	1	1	0	-	0	1	2	3	19	7	12	17	2	0	0
Francis Jeffers	1646	31	20	2	11	17	3	357	2	16	13	8	0	1	16	19	31	3	1
Jermaine Johnson	2656	37	29	8	8	20	3	24	3	35	35	63	3	0	40	56	16	6	1
Rocky Lekaj	34	2	0	0	2	0	0	-	0	0	0	1	0	0	1	0	0	0	0
Sean McAllister	3376	40	37	28	3	9	3	837	2	11	13	21	10	4	26	31	1	3	0
Tony McMahon	1319	15	14	13	1	0	1	43	0	7	5	30	6	6	17	17	2	3	1
Nathan Modest	74	4	1	0	3	1	0	-	0	0	0	0	0	0	1	0	0	0	0
James O'Connor	3301	41	35	27	6	8	0	-	1	18	10	21	10	4	52	27	2	7	0
Darren Potter	1599	17	17	15	0	2	2	103	0	8	12	34	6	1	18	10	1	2	0
Frank Simek	390	6	4	3	2	1	0	-	0	0	0	6	4	2	3	3	0	0	0
Bartosz Slusarski	406	7	4	2	3	2	1	134	0	2	3	9	0	0	7	5	3	0	0
Wade Small	715	19	6	0	13	6	1	247	0	4	4	14	1	0	5	11	1	0	0
Jimmy Smith	474	12	3	1	9	1	0	-	0	2	2	1	2	0	6	3	0	1	0
Akpo Sodje	283	11	2	0	9	2	2	267	1	3	7	1	4	0	7	8	5	2	0
Tommy Spurr	3890	41	41	39	0	1	2	1405	0	6	6	31	22	11	32	31	1	1	0
Marcus Tudgay	3938	42	42	40	0	2	14	329	3	48	38	19	37	6	80	65	21	2	0
Luke Varney	346	4	3	3	1	0	2	1037	0	4	3	9	1	0	6	7	12	2	0
Steve Watson	1544	22	15	12	7	3	3	48	2	11	6	22	12	5	12	21	0	1	0
Richard Wood	3893	42	42	39	0	3	0	-	1	2	3	1	57	19	41	27	1	4	0

SEASON TOTALS

Goals scored	51
Goals conceded	58
Clean sheets	13
Shots on target	254
Shots off target	233
Shots per goal	9.55
Pens awarded	5
Pens scored	4
Pens conceded	7
Offsides	176
Corners	254
Crosses	434
Players used	28
Fouls committed	530
Free-kicks won	491

CARDS RECEIVED

55 **5**

SEQUENCES

Wins	2
(on three occasions)	
Losses	3
(21/10/08–28/10/08)	
Draws	3
(10/03/09–21/03/09)	
Undefeated	5
(25/11/08–13/12/08)	
Without win	5
(on two occasions)	
Undefeated home	6
(09/08/08–19/10/08)	
Undefeated away	4
(28/02/09–04/04/09)	
Without scoring	2
(on four occasions)	
Without conceding	2
(on two occasions)	
Scoring	5
(on two occasions)	
Conceding	10
(20/12/08–17/02/09)	

SEASON INFORMATION

Highest position: 5
Lowest position: 17
Average goals scored per game: 1.11
Average goals conceded per game: 1.26

League position at the end of each week

League position at the end of: August 14, September 5, October 15, November 15, December 13, January 13, February 12, March 13, April 12, May 12

MATCH RECORDS

Goals scored per match

		W	D	L	Pts
Failed to score	14	0	3	11	3
Scored 1 goal	20	6	9	5	27
Scored 2 goals	8	6	1	1	19
Scored 3 goals	1	1	0	0	3
Scored 4+ goals	3	3	0	0	9

Goals conceded per match

		W	D	L	Pts
Clean sheet	13	10	3	0	33
Conceded 1 goal	19	4	9	6	21
Conceded 2 goals	8	2	1	5	7
Conceded 3 goals	3	0	0	3	0
Conceded 4+ goals	3	0	0	3	0

GOALS SCORED/CONCEDED PER FIVE-MINUTE INTERVALS

Goals For	3	1	2	5	2	3	2	2	3	2	6	1	3	3	4	2	1	6
Goals Against	4	2	5	1	3	3	3	3	3	3	4	4	6	2	2	1	3	6
Mins	5	10	15	20	25	30	35	40	45	50	55	60	65	70	75	80	85	90

QUICK-FIRE GOALS

From the start of a match
Marcus Tudgay
(v Burnley) 0:31

By a substitute after coming on
Steve Watson
(v Swansea) 1:13

LAST-GASP GOALS

From the start of a match
Francis Jeffers
(v Watford) 96:12

By a substitute after coming on
Leon Clarke
(v Crystal Palace) 27:47

GOAL DETAILS

How the goals were struck

SCORED		CONCEDED
26	Right foot	26
15	Left foot	13
10	Headers	18
0	Others	1

How the goals were struck

SCORED		CONCEDED
33	Open play	34
4	Cross	7
5	Corner	2
4	Penalties	6
1	Direct from free-kick	0
3	Free-kick	7
1	Own goals	2

Distance from goal

SCORED		CONCEDED
16	6yds	21
25	18yds	30
10	18+yds	7

SOUTHAMPTON

CLUB SUMMARY

FORMED	1885
MANAGER	Mark Wotte
GROUND	St Mary's Stadium
CAPACITY	32,551
NICKNAME	The Saints
WEBSITE	www.saintsfc.co.uk

The New Football Pools PLAYER OF THE SEASON

Kelvin Davis

OVERALL

P	W	D	L	F	A	GD
50	12	15	23	52	76	-24

COCA-COLA CHAMPIONSHIP

Pos	P	W	D	L	F	A	GD	Pts
23	46	10	15	21	46	69	-23	45

HOME

Pos	P	W	D	L	F	A	GD	Pts
24	23	4	10	9	23	29	-6	22

AWAY

Pos	P	W	D	L	F	A	GD	Pts
14	23	6	5	12	23	40	-17	23

CUP PROGRESS DETAILS

Competition	Round reached	Knocked out by
FA Cup	R3	Man Utd
Carling Cup	R3	Rotherham

BIGGEST WIN (ALL COMPS)

03/03/09 3–0 v Ipswich **FLC**

BIGGEST DEFEAT (ALL COMPS)

1–4 on two occasions

THE PLAYER WITH THE MOST

Shots on target
David McGoldrick 64

Shots off target
David McGoldrick 54

Shots without scoring
Simon Gillett 22

Assists
Andrew Surman 6

Offsides
Jason Euell 26

Fouls
David McGoldrick 56

Fouls without a card
J Mills, M Paterson, T Pekhart, J Thomson.... 5

Free-kicks won
Chris Perry 46

Defensive clearances
Chris Perry 72

actim INDEX
for the 2008/09 Coca-Cola Championship Season

Rank	Player	Pts
58	Andrew Surman	454
63	Kelvin Davis	443
91	David McGoldrick	390
121	Chris Perry	349
150	Lloyd James	316

ATTENDANCE RECORD

High	Low	Average
27,228	13,257	17,849
v Charlton (04/04/2009)	v Sheff Utd (03/02/2009)	

SOUTHAMPTON'S season began with promises of total football and a push for promotion but ended in relegation, a points deduction and possible extinction.

The Saints will kick off next term in Coca-Cola League One on minus 10 points after plc chairman Rupert Lowe put the club's holding company into administration. But starting the 2009/10 season at all would be a success for the 2003 FA Cup finalists, who are desperately looking for a buyer to avoid going bust.

Lowe was the predictable scapegoat having returned to the south-coast club in May 2008, two years after being ousted as chairman. Lowe immediately chose to part company with their interim boss Nigel Pearson, who had saved the Saints

'Lowe decided to go Dutch, bringing in Jan Poortvliet'

from relegation on the final day of 2007/08. The club's board decided to go Dutch, bringing in Jan Poortvliet as head coach, assisted by countryman Mark Wotte.

Poortvliet – who played in the 1978 World Cup final – talked up his squad's chances of promotion, but cost-cutting meant big earners such as Stern John and Nathan Dyer were loaned out to Bristol City and Swansea respectively. In came rookies Adam Lallana, Simon Gillett and Lloyd James alongside old heads Chris Perry, Paul Wotton and Jason Euell.

Unfortunately, they very quickly fell down into the relegation zone, from where they never emerged.

Poortvliet's reliance on a 4-3-3 formation drew criticism as his side won just once in their first 14 home games and he walked away from St Mary's in January.

Wotte took the reins and successive wins over Preston, Cardiff and Ipswich offered brief hope of another great escape on the south coast. But, away from the pitch, Saints were in meltdown and Lowe's final act was to place Southampton Leisure Holdings plc into the hands of administrators.

Southampton argued that, because the club itself was not in administration, they should avoid the mandatory 10-point deduction. The Football League disagreed.

The sight of club legend Lawrie McMenemy shaking collection tins in a bid to keep the club alive prior to their final home game of the 2008/09 season sums up an awful period in the Saints' history.

The subsequent 2–2 draw with Burnley meant relegation was confirmed, so the points penalty will be carried over to the 2009/10 season.

The Saints concede another goal in a 3–0 loss at Wolves

August

9th	● Cardiff ....a	L 2–1	**Att:** 19,749. **Ref:** S Mathieson — **Scorers:** McGoldrick	
12th	● Exeter ....a	W 1–3	**Att:** 6,471. **Ref:** F Graham — **Scorers:** Holmes, McGoldrick[2]. **Booked:** Schneiderlin, James	
16th	● Birmingham ....h	L 1–2	**Att:** 18,925. **Ref:** C Penton — **Scorers:** Perry	
23rd	● Derby ....a	W 0–1	**Att:** 27,032. **Ref:** G Laws — **Scorers:** McGoldrick. **Booked:** Svensson	
26th	● Birmingham ....h	W 2–0	**Att:** 11,331. **Ref:** G Hegley — **Scorers:** Holmes, Lallana	
30th	● Blackpool ....h	L 0–1	**Att:** 15,629. **Ref:** A Marriner — **Booked:** Surman, Gillett, James, Svensson	

September

14th	● QPR ....a	L 4–1	**Att:** 13,770. **Ref:** K Friend — **Scorers:** Lallana. **Booked:** Schneiderlin, Dyer. **Dismissed:** Lancashire
17th	● Ipswich ....h	D 2–2	**Att:** 14,916. **Ref:** P Crossley — **Scorers:** Pekhart, Surman
20th	● Barnsley ....h	D 0–0	**Att:** 14,836. **Ref:** A D'Urso — **Booked:** Surman, Gillett
23rd	● Rotherham ....a	L 3–1	**Att:** 5,147. **Ref:** R Shoebridge — **Scorers:** John. **Booked:** Svensson
27th	● Doncaster ....a	W 0–2	**Att:** 10,867. **Ref:** M Russell — **Scorers:** Surman, Mills OG
30th	● Norwich ....h	W 2–0	**Att:** 14,480. **Ref:** R Beeby — **Scorers:** McGoldrick, Robertson

October

4th	● Coventry ....a	L 4–1	**Att:** 15,518. **Ref:** M Jones — **Scorers:** Surman. **Booked:** Davis, James
18th	● Watford ....h	L 0–3	**Att:** 17,454. **Ref:** T Kettle — **Booked:** McGoldrick
21st	● Sheff Utd ....a	D 0–0	**Att:** 25,642. **Ref:** C Oliver — **Booked:** Surman, Lancashire. **Dismissed:** Lancashire
25th	● Swansea ....a	L 3–0	**Att:** 15,564. **Ref:** P Walton — **Booked:** James, Gillett
28th	● Coventry ....h	D 1–1	**Att:** 14,226. **Ref:** F Graham — **Scorers:** McGoldrick. **Booked:** Schneiderlin, Wotton, James

November

1st	● Preston ....a	W 2–3	**Att:** 11,508. **Ref:** M Haywood — **Scorers:** McGoldrick, Pearce, Surman. **Booked:** McGoldrick
8th	● Bristol City ....h	L 0–1	**Att:** 14,535. **Ref:** A Penn — **Booked:** Cork
15th	● Wolverhampton..................h	L 1–2	**Att:** 17,812. **Ref:** L Mason — **Scorers:** Pearce. **Booked:** Lancashire, Surman, Skacel. **Dismissed:** Euell
22nd	● Reading ....a	W 1–2	**Att:** 23,121. **Ref:** L Probert — **Scorers:** Wright-Phillips[2]. **Booked:** Wright-Phillips, James, Lallana
25th	● Plymouth..........................h	D 0–0	**Att:** 14,895. **Ref:** A D'Urso
29th	● Charlton ....a	D 0–0	**Att:** 20,831. **Ref:** S Mathieson — **Booked:** Robertson

December

6th	● Sheff Wed ....h	D 1–1	**Att:** 15,440. **Ref:** G Hegley — **Scorers:** Wright-Phillips
8th	● Crystal Palace ....a	L 3–0	**Att:** 13,799. **Ref:** D Deadman — **Booked:** Perry
13th	● Burnley ....a	L 3–2	**Att:** 11,229. **Ref:** P Dowd — **Scorers:** Skacel, Surman. **Booked:** James, Pearce, Skacel
20th	● Nottm Forest......................h	L 0–2	**Att:** 26,580. **Ref:** I Williamson — **Booked:** Lallana, Cork, Skacel, Perry
26th	● Plymouth..........................a	L 2–0	**Att:** 15,197. **Ref:** R East — **Booked:** Davis, Lancashire, Skacel
28th	● Reading ....h	D 1–1	**Att:** 20,142. **Ref:** P Crossley — **Scorers:** McGoldrick. **Booked:** Smith, Cork, McGoldrick, Gobern

January

4th	● Man Utd ....h	L 0–3	**Att:** 31,901. **Ref:** M Riley — **Booked:** Skacel, James. **Dismissed:** Paterson
10th	● Barnsley ....a	W 0–1	**Att:** 11,789. **Ref:** T Bates — **Scorers:** McGoldrick. **Booked:** Molyneux, James
17th	● Doncaster ....h	L 1–2	**Att:** 15,837. **Ref:** A Woolmer — **Scorers:** Saganowski. **Booked:** Surman, Saeijs, Wright-Phillips
27th	● Norwich..........................a	D 2–2	**Att:** 25,271. **Ref:** L Mason — **Scorers:** McLaggon, Saganowski. **Booked:** Gillett, Lallana, Wotton, Saganowski
31st	● Swansea ....h	D 2–2	**Att:** 17,623. **Ref:** S Tanner — **Scorers:** Saganowski[2]. **Booked:** Molyneux, Surman, Saganowski. **Dismissed:** Molyneux

February

3rd	● Sheff Utd ....h	L 1–2	**Att:** 13,257. **Ref:** L Probert — **Scorers:** Surman. **Booked:** Saeijs, Perry, Schneiderlin
14th	● Bristol City ....a	L 2–0	**Att:** 17,000. **Ref:** M Oliver — **Booked:** Skacel, Surman, Schneiderlin
21st	● Preston ....h	W 3–1	**Att:** 14,790. **Ref:** P Miller — **Scorers:** Saganowski[2], Surman. **Booked:** Euell
28th	● Cardiff ....h	W 1–0	**Att:** 18,526. **Ref:** K Wright — **Scorers:** McGoldrick. **Booked:** Euell

March

3rd	● Ipswich ....a	W 0–3	**Att:** 20,040. **Ref:** A D'Urso — **Scorers:** Euell[2], Paterson. **Booked:** Gillett, Schneiderlin
7th	● Birmingham ....a	L 1–0	**Att:** 16,735. **Ref:** M Atkinson — **Booked:** McGoldrick, Saeijs, Liptak
10th	● Derby ....h	D 1–1	**Att:** 17,567. **Ref:** K Friend — **Scorers:** Perry
14th	● QPR ....h	D 0–0	**Att:** 18,691. **Ref:** M Jones — **Booked:** James, McGoldrick
21st	● Blackpool ....a	D 1–1	**Att:** 7,947. **Ref:** D Foster — **Scorers:** McGoldrick. **Booked:** Saeijs, Perry, McGoldrick

April

4th	● Charlton ....h	L 2–3	**Att:** 27,228. **Ref:** J Moss — **Scorers:** McGoldrick, Wright-Phillips. **Booked:** Wotton
7th	● Watford ....a	D 2–2	**Att:** 16,066. **Ref:** C Penton — **Scorers:** Saeijs[2]. **Booked:** Skacel
10th	● Wolverhampton..................a	L 3–0	**Att:** 24,636. **Ref:** A Taylor — **Booked:** Smith, Perry
13th	● Crystal Palace ....h	W 1–0	**Att:** 23,220. **Ref:** M Russell — **Scorers:** McGoldrick
18th	● Sheff Wed ....a	L 2–0	**Att:** 24,145. **Ref:** R Shoebridge — **Booked:** James
25th	● Burnley ....h	D 2–2	**Att:** 23,927. **Ref:** M Jones — **Scorers:** McGoldrick, Wright-Phillips. **Booked:** Wotton, McGoldrick, Perry, Saeijs

May

3rd	● Nottm Forest......................a	L 3–1	**Att:** 29,008. **Ref:** K Stroud — **Scorers:** Wright-Phillips. **Booked:** James

● Coca-Cola Championship/Play-Offs ● FA Cup ● Carling Cup

SOUTHAMPTON

CHAMPIONSHIP GOALKEEPER STATS

Player	Minutes on pitch	Appearances	Match starts	Completed matches	Sub appearances	Subbed off	Saved with feet	Punched	Parried	Tipped over	Fumbled	Tipped round	Caught	Blocked	Clean sheets	Goals conceded	Minutes since conceding	Save %	Saved	Resulting in goals	Opposition miss	Yellow cards	Red cards
Kelvin Davis	4391	46	46	46	0	0	3	14	26	12	0	20	147	0	12	69	0	76.61	4	5	0	2	0

Saves Breakdown columns: Saved with feet, Punched, Parried, Tipped over, Fumbled, Tipped round, Caught, Blocked. Penalties columns: Saved, Resulting in goals, Opposition miss.

CHAMPIONSHIP OUTFIELD PLAYER STATS

Player	Minutes on pitch	Appearances	Match starts	Completed matches	Substitute appearances	Subbed off	Goals scored	Minutes since scoring	Assists	Shots on target	Shots off target	Crosses	Defensive clearances	Defensive blocks	Fouls committed	Free-kicks won	Caught offside	Yellow cards	Red cards
Jack Cork	2119	23	22	22	1	0	0	-	0	5	2	7	18	5	10	24	0	3	0
Nathan Dyer	223	4	1	0	3	1	0	320	0	1	2	1	0	0	4	4	0	1	0
Jason Euell	1762	24	18	13	6	4	2	907	2	13	24	11	7	1	36	31	26	2	1
Romain Gasmi	66	4	0	0	4	0	0	-	0	1	0	0	0	0	1	0	0	0	0
Simon Gillett	2065	27	23	17	4	6	0	-	2	15	7	32	8	4	36	20	5	5	0
Oscar Gobern	374	6	4	2	2	2	0	-	1	4	3	5	1	2	5	2	3	1	0
Lee Holmes	741	11	11	3	0	8	0	-	2	10	7	11	1	0	4	6	3	0	0
Lloyd James	3684	41	40	35	1	5	0	-	3	7	6	94	34	7	36	40	0	10	0
Stern John	269	7	4	0	3	4	0	861	0	1	7	0	1	0	4	4	7	0	0
Adam Lallana	3196	40	34	25	6	9	1	2760	3	36	30	22	9	3	33	40	4	3	0
Oliver Lancashire	854	11	10	7	1	1	0	-	0	0	4	1	22	4	11	14	0	3	2
Zoltan Liptak	54	7	0	0	7	0	0	-	0	0	0	0	0	0	2	2	0	1	0
David McGoldrick	4084	46	45	33	1	12	12	143	1	64	54	27	30	0	56	31	22	7	0
Kayne McLaggon	264	7	1	0	6	1	1	153	1	3	1	3	1	1	2	10	2	0	0
Joseph Mills	588	8	6	4	2	2	0	-	0	1	3	4	1	2	5	11	0	0	0
Lee Molyneux	342	4	4	3	0	0	0	-	0	1	1	2	2	0	8	3	1	2	1
Matthew Paterson	288	11	1	0	10	1	1	56	0	6	1	5	1	0	5	1	4	0	0
Alex Pearce	641	9	6	5	3	1	2	251	0	2	0	1	8	3	9	8	0	1	0
Tomas Pekhart	353	9	2	1	7	1	1	313	0	4	2	0	2	0	5	8	5	0	0
Chris Perry	3658	40	38	37	2	1	2	897	0	6	6	0	72	17	39	46	0	6	0
Jordan Robertson	613	10	8	2	6	1	1	584	0	5	7	11	1	0	10	5	7	1	0
Jan Paul Saeijs	1897	20	20	19	0	1	2	467	0	9	4	3	47	11	26	34	0	5	0
Marek Saganowski	1424	19	14	7	5	7	6	895	0	21	14	7	1	0	14	20	13	2	0
Morgan Schneiderlin	1905	30	23	8	7	15	0	-	0	4	10	10	4	3	38	19	0	5	0
Rudi Skacel	2575	28	28	25	0	3	1	1480	0	17	9	45	9	13	31	32	2	6	0
Ryan Smith	642	13	7	2	6	5	0	-	1	4	3	14	0	0	4	13	1	2	0
Andrew Surman	4150	44	44	41	0	3	7	1273	6	38	24	73	21	6	54	39	6	7	0
Michael Svensson	380	4	4	4	0	0	0	-	0	0	1	0	9	1	4	3	0	2	0
Jake Thomson	542	10	6	0	4	6	0	-	1	0	1	21	1	2	5	2	2	0	0
Jamie White	126	3	2	0	1	2	0	-	0	1	0	0	0	0	1	1	0	0	0
Paul Wotton	1861	29	18	13	11	5	0	-	0	6	7	4	13	3	31	19	0	4	0
Bradley Wright-Phillips	1932	33	16	6	17	10	6	56	2	34	20	29	2	0	20	12	16	2	0

actim

SEASON TOTALS

Goals scored	46
Goals conceded	69
Clean sheets	12
Shots on target	318
Shots off target	261
Shots per goal	12.59
Pens awarded	7
Pens scored	3
Pens conceded	9
Offsides	129
Corners	279
Crosses	444
Players used	33
Fouls committed	549
Free-kicks won	520

CARDS RECEIVED

83   4

SEQUENCES

Wins	3
(21/02/09–03/03/09)	
Losses	4
(08/12/08–26/12/08)	
Draws	3
(on two occasions)	
Undefeated	4
(on two occasions)	
Without win	8
(25/11/08–28/12/08)	
Undefeated home	4
(21/02/09–14/03/09)	
Undefeated away	3
(01/11/08–29/11/08)	
Without scoring	3
(18/10/08–25/10/08)	
Without conceding	3
(20/09/08–30/09/08)	
Scoring	6
(28/12/08–03/02/09)	
Conceding	6
(on three occasions)	

SEASON INFORMATION

Highest position: 17
Lowest position: 24
Average goals scored per game: 1.00
Average goals conceded per game: 1.50

League position at the end of each week

League position at the end of: August 20, September 16, October 22, November 20, December 23, January 23, February 23, March 23, April 23, May 23

MATCH RECORDS

Goals scored per match

		W	D	L	Pts
Failed to score	16	0	5	11	5
Scored 1 goal	17	4	5	8	17
Scored 2 goals	10	3	5	2	14
Scored 3 goals	3	3	0	0	9
Scored 4+ goals	0	0	0	0	0

Goals conceded per match

		W	D	L	Pts
Clean sheet	12	7	5	0	26
Conceded 1 goal	10	2	5	3	11
Conceded 2 goals	15	1	5	9	8
Conceded 3 goals	7	0	0	7	0
Conceded 4+ goals	2	0	0	2	0

GOALS SCORED/CONCEDED PER FIVE-MINUTE INTERVALS

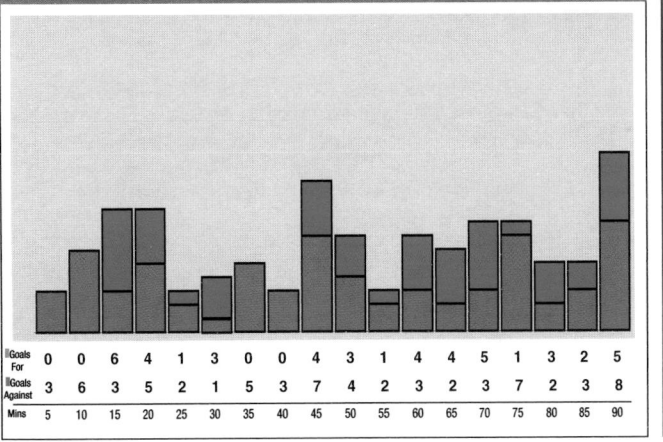

Goals For	0	0	6	4	1	3	0	0	4	3	1	4	4	5	1	3	2	5
Goals Against	3	6	3	5	2	1	5	3	7	4	2	3	2	3	7	2	3	8
Mins	5	10	15	20	25	30	35	40	45	50	55	60	65	70	75	80	85	90

QUICK-FIRE GOALS

From the start of a match
Chris Perry
(v Burnley) 3:54

By a substitute after coming on
Matthew Paterson
(v Ipswich) 1:10

LAST-GASP GOALS

From the start of a match
Marek Saganowski
(v Doncaster) 90:28

By a substitute after coming on
Marek Saganowski
(v Norwich) 32:51

GOAL DETAILS

How the goals were struck

SCORED		CONCEDED
26	Right foot	39
11	Left foot	16
9	Headers	14
0	Others	0

How the goals were struck

SCORED		CONCEDED
32	Open play	48
4	Cross	5
4	Corner	5
3	Penalties	5
1	Direct from free-kick	0
1	Free-kick	5
1	Own goals	1

Distance from goal

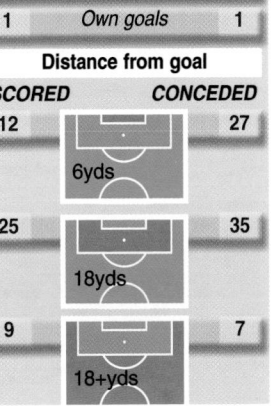

SCORED		CONCEDED
12	6yds	27
25	18yds	35
9	18+yds	7

SWANSEA CITY

CLUB SUMMARY

FORMED	1912
MANAGER	Roberto Martinez
GROUND	Liberty Stadium
CAPACITY	20,532
NICKNAME	The Swans
WEBSITE	www.swanseacity.net

The New Football Pools PLAYER OF THE SEASON — Jordi Gomez

OVERALL

P	W	D	L	F	A	GD
54	21	21	12	74	56	18

COCA-COLA CHAMPIONSHIP

Pos	P	W	D	L	F	A	GD	Pts
8	46	16	20	10	63	50	13	68

HOME

Pos	P	W	D	L	F	A	GD	Pts
7	23	11	9	3	40	22	18	42

AWAY

Pos	P	W	D	L	F	A	GD	Pts
10	23	5	11	7	23	28	-5	26

CUP PROGRESS DETAILS

Competition	Round reached	Knocked out by
FA Cup	R5	Fulham
Carling Cup	R4	Watford

BIGGEST WIN (ALL COMPS)
27/01/09 4-1 v Preston FLC

BIGGEST DEFEAT (ALL COMPS)
27/09/08 0–4 v Reading FLC

THE PLAYER WITH THE MOST

Shots on target	
Jordi Gomez	70
Shots off target	
Jordi Gomez	60
Shots without scoring	
Mark Gower	45
Assists	
Jason Scotland	8
Offsides	
Jason Scotland	37
Fouls	
Darren Pratley	54
Fouls without a card	
Owain Tudur Jones	7
Free-kicks won	
Jordi Gomez	121
Defensive clearances	
Ashley Williams	59

actim INDEX for the 2008/09 Coca-Cola Championship Season

Rank	Player	Pts
5	Jason Scotland	643
28	Ashley Williams	515
32	Jordi Gomez	503
66	Dorus De Vries	439
80	Garry Monk	403

ATTENDANCE RECORD

High	Low	Average
18,053	11,442	15,187
v Cardiff (30/11/2008)	v Barnsley (09/12/2008)	

Jason Scotland celebrates after scoring in the FA Cup win at Portsmouth

THE SWANS took to the Coca-Cola Championship like a duck to water, looking set for a venture into the play-offs until the penultimate weekend of the season.

After guiding Swansea into the second tier of English football for the first time in 24 years, boss Roberto Martinez further enhanced his reputation, as the Welshmen made their mark in the Championship.

Their attractive brand of passing football ensured they finished eighth and their promotion hopes were dashed only when they were beaten by Sheffield United in their final away game.

The club's profile was raised further by a 2–0 FA Cup win at top-flight side Portsmouth in January, with Nathan Dyer and Jason Scotland on the scoresheet. They also managed a 2–1 success against Hull City in the League Cup in August, with Jordi Gomez and

Gorka Pintado guiding them to a win that set them up for the season.

Martinez's charges almost caused an upset in the FA Cup fifth round, but were forced to settle for a draw against Fulham before losing the replay at Craven Cottage.

Spanish boss Martinez had been shrewd in the transfer market, with on-loan Espanyol playmaker Gomez crowned Player of the Season and the likes of fellow loanee Dyer also becoming a fans' favourite.

Swansea hope to sign Gomez on a permanent deal this summer, but they are sure to face stiff competition for the Spanish player's signature.

They will also hope to keep hold of Trinidad striker Scotland, who scored 24 goals in all competitions in 2008/09 and is one of the most sought-after strikers outside the top flight.

City lost just three times at home, with the Liberty Stadium becoming a real fortress, and their superb season led to Martinez being linked with Scottish giants Celtic. However, at the time of going to press, Martinez looked set to become the new boss of Barclays Premier League side Wigan.

> **'The Welshmen made their mark in the Championship'**

RESULTS 2008/09

August

9th	● Charlton ....a	L 2–0	**Att:** 21,675. **Ref:** R Beeby — **Booked:** Bodde, Monk **Dismissed:** Monk
12th	● Brentford......................h	W 2–0	**Att:** 5,366. **Ref:** S Bratt — **Scorers:** MacDonald². **Booked:** Brandy
16th	● Nottm Forest.................h	W 3–1	**Att:** 16,611. **Ref:** P Taylor — **Scorers:** Bodde, Pintado, Smith OG. **Booked:** Pratley, Bodde
23rd	● Plymouth........................a	W 0–1	**Att:** 9,203. **Ref:** A D'Urso — **Scorers:** Scotland. **Booked:** Britton
26th	● Hull................................h	W 2–1	**Att:** 8,622. **Ref:** M Russell — **Scorers:** Gomez, Pintado. **Booked:** Bauza (AET)
30th	● Sheff Wed ....h	D 1–1	**Att:** 16,702. **Ref:** K Friend — **Scorers:** Bodde

September

13th	● Crystal Palace ....a	L 2–0	**Att:** 14,621. **Ref:** L Mason — **Booked:** Painter, Pratley, Bodde
16th	● Derby ....h	D 1–1	**Att:** 14,003. **Ref:** A Penn — **Scorers:** Williams
20th	● Burnley ....h	D 1–1	**Att:** 13,299. **Ref:** A Hall — **Scorers:** Bodde. **Booked:** Orlandi, Gower
23rd	● Cardiff ....h	W 1–0	**Att:** 17,411. **Ref:** A Wiley — **Scorers:** Gomez. **Booked:** Gomez
27th	● Reading ....a	L 4–0	**Att:** 20,093. **Ref:** S Mathieson — **Booked:** Bodde
30th	● Preston ....a	W 0–2	**Att:** 10,558. **Ref:** C Boyeson — **Scorers:** Bodde, Gomez

October

4th	● Wolverhampton.............h	W 3–1	**Att:** 17,556. **Ref:** T Kettle — **Scorers:** Gomez, Scotland². **Booked:** Painter, Gomez, Orlandi, Scotland
18th	● Ipswich ....a	D 2–2	**Att:** 20,026. **Ref:** J Moss — **Scorers:** Bodde, Gomez. **Booked:** Rangel, Pratley
21st	● QPR ....h	D 0–0	**Att:** 13,475. **Ref:** T Bates
25th	● Southampton ....h	W 3–0	**Att:** 15,564. **Ref:** P Walton — **Scorers:** Butler, Gomez, Pratley. **Booked:** Gomez
28th	● Wolverhampton.............a	L 2–1	**Att:** 21,988. **Ref:** R Beeby — **Scorers:** Pratley

November

1st	● Doncaster......................a	D 0–0	**Att:** 9,534. **Ref:** K Stroud — **Booked:** Bodde, Pratley
9th	● Watford ....h	W 3–1	**Att:** 13,891. **Ref:** R Shoebridge — **Scorers:** Bauza, Bodde, Scotland. **Booked:** Britton, Gomez
11th	● Watford ....h	L 0–1	**Att:** 9,549. **Ref:** A D'Urso — **Booked:** Tudur Jones, Pintado
15th	● Norwich.........................h	W 2–3	**Att:** 24,262. **Ref:** G Hegley — **Scorers:** Bodde, Pratley, Scotland. **Booked:** Bodde
21st	● Birmingham ....h	L 2–3	**Att:** 16,956. **Ref:** A Taylor — **Scorers:** Gomez, Jaidi OG. **Booked:** Gomez
25th	● Coventry ....a	D 1–1	**Att:** 15,149. **Ref:** M Haywood — **Scorers:** Gomez
30th	● Cardiff ....h	D 2–2	**Att:** 18,053. **Ref:** M Atkinson — **Scorers:** Pintado, Pratley. **Booked:** Bessone, Pratley, Britton. **Dismissed:** Britton

December

6th	● Bristol City ....a	D 0–0	**Att:** 16,405. **Ref:** L Mason — **Booked:** Williams, Gomez, Butler
9th	● Barnsley ....h	D 2–2	**Att:** 11,442. **Ref:** G Horwood — **Scorers:** Scotland². **Booked:** Rangel, Britton, Monk
13th	● Sheff Utd ....h	D 1–1	**Att:** 14,744. **Ref:** A Marriner — **Scorers:** Scotland
20th	● Blackpool ....a	D 1–1	**Att:** 7,007. **Ref:** D Deadman — **Scorers:** Scotland. **Booked:** Butler
26th	● Coventry ....h	D 0–0	**Att:** 17,603. **Ref:** S Tanner — **Booked:** Butler
28th	● Birmingham ....a	D 0–0	**Att:** 21,836. **Ref:** M Riley — **Booked:** Pintado, Monk

January

10th	● Burnley ....a	W 0–2	**Att:** 13,740. **Ref:** M Oliver — **Scorers:** Scotland². **Booked:** Britton
13th	● Histon ....a	W 1–2	**Att:** 2,821. **Ref:** P Crossley — **Scorers:** Bauza, Pintado
17th	● Reading ....h	W 2–0	**Att:** 15,197. **Ref:** F Graham — **Scorers:** Orlandi, Scotland. **Booked:** Scotland, Tate
24th	● Portsmouth....................a	W 0–2	**Att:** 17,357. **Ref:** A Marriner — **Scorers:** Dyer, Scotland. **Booked:** Pratley, Tate, Rangel, Britton
27th	● Preston ....h	W 4–1	**Att:** 14,774. **Ref:** P Gibbs — **Scorers:** Bauza, Gomez, Scotland, Tate. **Booked:** Rangel
31st	● Southampton ....a	D 2–2	**Att:** 17,623. **Ref:** S Tanner — **Scorers:** Gomez, Pintado. **Booked:** Gomez

February

7th	● Ipswich ....h	W 3–0	**Att:** 14,020. **Ref:** K Wright — **Scorers:** Gomez, Scotland². **Booked:** Tate
14th	● Fulham ....h	D 1–1	**Att:** 16,573. **Ref:** H Webb — **Scorers:** Scotland. **Booked:** Williams
17th	● Watford ....a	L 2–0	**Att:** 13,727. **Ref:** A Taylor — **Booked:** Britton, Serran
21st	● Doncaster......................h	W 3–1	**Att:** 16,161. **Ref:** S Mathieson — **Scorers:** Gomez², Scotland. **Booked:** Gomez, Rangel
24th	● Fulham ....a	L 2–1	**Att:** 12,316. **Ref:** M Halsey — **Scorers:** Scotland. **Booked:** Bauza
28th	● Charlton ....h	D 1–1	**Att:** 15,053. **Ref:** K Stroud — **Scorers:** Dyer. **Booked:** Bauza, Serran, Rangel

March

3rd	● Derby ....a	D 2–2	**Att:** 26,691. **Ref:** P Crossley — **Scorers:** Pintado, Rangel. **Booked:** Allen, Dyer
7th	● Nottm Forest.................a	D 1–1	**Att:** 20,475. **Ref:** J Moss — **Scorers:** Scotland. **Booked:** Britton, Allen
10th	● Plymouth........................h	W 1–0	**Att:** 13,103. **Ref:** I Williamson — **Scorers:** Scotland. **Booked:** Gomez, Serran
14th	● Crystal Palace ....h	L 1–3	**Att:** 13,663. **Ref:** R East — **Scorers:** Pintado
17th	● QPR ....a	L 1–0	**Att:** 12,288. **Ref:** G Horwood — **Booked:** Pratley
21st	● Sheff Wed ....a	D 0–0	**Att:** 22,564. **Ref:** M Jones — **Booked:** Williams

April

5th	● Cardiff ....a	D 2–2	**Att:** 20,156. **Ref:** M Dean — **Scorers:** Allen, Dyer. **Booked:** Allen
11th	● Norwich.........................h	W 2–1	**Att:** 15,783. **Ref:** G Salisbury — **Scorers:** Scotland². **Booked:** Britton, Williams, Tate, Bessone
13th	● Barnsley ....a	W 1–3	**Att:** 11,788. **Ref:** D Foster — **Scorers:** Gomez, Scotland, Williams. **Booked:** Britton, De Vries
18th	● Bristol City ....h	W 1–0	**Att:** 15,327. **Ref:** L Mason — **Scorers:** Monk. **Booked:** MacDonald
25th	● Sheff Utd ....a	L 1–0	**Att:** 28,010. **Ref:** R Styles — **Booked:** Allen

May

3rd	● Blackpool ....h	L 0–1	**Att:** 16,316. **Ref:** C Boyeson — **Booked:** Tate

● Coca-Cola Championship/Play-Offs ● FA Cup ● Carling Cup

SWANSEA CITY

CHAMPIONSHIP GOALKEEPER STATS

Player	Minutes on pitch	Appearances	Match starts	Completed matches	Sub appearances	Subbed off	Saved with feet	Punched	Parried	Tipped over	Fumbled	Tipped round	Caught	Blocked	Clean sheets	Goals conceded	Minutes since conceding	Save %	Saved	Resulting in goals	Opposition miss	Yellow cards	Red cards
Dorus De Vries	3754	40	40	39	0	1	3	18	32	4	0	12	107	0	12	42	83	80.91	0	5	0	1	0
Dimi Konstantopoulos	382	4	4	4	0	0	1	2	0	0	0	0	17	0	1	6	3	62.50	1	0	0	0	0
Artur Krysiak	191	2	2	2	0	0	0	1	0	1	0	1	8	0	1	2	38	84.62	0	0	0	0	0

CHAMPIONSHIP OUTFIELD PLAYER STATS

Player	Minutes on pitch	Appearances	Match starts	Completed matches	Substitute appearances	Subbed off	Goals scored	Minutes since scoring	Assists	Shots on target	Shots off target	Crosses	Defensive clearances	Defensive blocks	Fouls committed	Free-kicks won	Caught offside	Yellow cards	Red cards
Joe Allen	1503	23	17	6	6	11	1	294	1	7	7	2	3	0	19	34	0	4	0
Guillem Bauza	661	15	4	1	11	3	2	369	3	9	5	2	3	1	10	9	6	1	0
Federico Bessone	1160	14	13	10	1	3	0	-	2	0	0	12	5	2	15	10	0	2	0
Ferrie Bodde	1562	17	17	16	0	1	7	81	2	19	18	4	14	3	38	13	0	6	0
Febian Brandy	191	14	0	0	14	0	0	-	0	2	2	0	0	0	2	9	2	0	0
Leon Britton	3801	43	42	32	1	9	0	-	1	6	6	3	8	3	47	80	1	9	1
Thomas Butler	1846	29	20	12	9	8	1	1127	1	23	18	16	0	0	9	28	7	3	0
Matthew Collins	207	3	2	1	1	1	0	-	0	0	2	1	0	0	3	4	0	0	0
Nathan Dyer	1167	17	13	3	4	10	2	320	2	8	2	6	0	0	9	27	4	1	0
Bessone Fede	24	1	0	0	1	0	0	-	0	0	0	0	0	0	1	0	0	0	0
Jordi Gomez	3678	44	38	33	6	5	12	344	5	70	60	53	12	2	42	121	12	8	0
Mark Gower	2728	36	32	12	4	20	0	-	4	27	18	54	4	2	15	24	8	1	0
Shaun MacDonald	191	5	2	0	3	2	0	-	1	0	4	5	1	0	1	5	0	1	0
Garry Monk	3719	40	40	38	0	1	1	165	0	2	6	0	42	15	34	41	0	3	1
Stephen O'Halloran	133	2	2	1	0	1	0	-	0	0	0	1	0	0	0	1	0	0	0
Andrea Orlandi	571	11	6	2	5	4	1	414	3	6	4	7	1	0	6	14	6	2	0
Marcos Painter	983	11	11	9	0	2	0	-	0	2	2	5	7	4	13	14	0	2	0
Gorka Pintado	1537	40	9	3	31	6	5	265	0	20	9	7	4	0	18	19	23	1	0
Darren Pratley	2978	37	33	24	4	9	4	1515	4	25	24	7	18	4	54	75	5	6	0
Angel Rangel	3733	40	39	37	1	2	1	766	4	11	13	25	20	9	39	37	4	5	0
Jason Scotland	3524	45	39	22	6	17	21	295	8	62	28	5	0	1	25	43	37	2	0
Albert Serran	1064	13	10	10	3	0	0	-	1	0	0	2	11	0	21	11	0	3	0
Alan Tate	2156	25	21	18	4	3	1	1348	2	7	5	4	19	9	19	18	1	4	0
Owain Tudur Jones	457	9	4	3	5	1	0	-	0	0	3	1	1	2	7	5	1	0	0
Ashley Williams	4398	46	46	46	0	0	2	377	1	8	5	1	59	23	41	26	2	3	0

actim

SEASON TOTALS

Goals scored	63
Goals conceded	50
Clean sheets	14
Shots on target	314
Shots off target	242
Shots per goal	8.83
Pens awarded	7
Pens scored	6
Pens conceded	6
Offsides	119
Corners	283
Crosses	220
Players used	28
Fouls committed	488
Free-kicks won	686

CARDS RECEIVED

68 **2**

SEQUENCES

Wins	3
(on two occaisons)	
Losses	2
(on two occaisons)	
Draws	8
(25/11/08–28/12/08)	
Undefeated	13
(25/11/08–07/02/09)	
Without win	9
(21/11/08–28/12/08)	
Undefeated home	10
(30/11/08–10/03/09)	
Undefeated away	8
(01/11/08–31/01/09)	
Without scoring	2
(on three occaisons)	
Without conceding	4
(26/12/08–17/01/09)	
Scoring	6
(21/02/09–14/03/09)	
Conceding	5
(on three occaisons)	

SEASON INFORMATION

Highest position: 6
Lowest position: 23
Average goals scored per game: 1.37
Average goals conceded per game: 1.09

League position at the end of each week

League position at the end of

August 7 | September 15 | October 11 | November 8 | December 11 | January 8 | February 9 | March 8 | April 8 | May 8

MATCH RECORDS

Goals scored per match

		W	D	L	Pts
Failed to score	13	0	6	7	6
Scored 1 goal	13	3	8	2	17
Scored 2 goals	11	4	6	1	18
Scored 3 goals	8	8	0	0	24
Scored 4+ goals	1	1	0	0	3

Goals conceded per match

		W	D	L	Pts
Clean sheet	14	8	6	0	30
Conceded 1 goal	18	7	8	3	29
Conceded 2 goals	11	1	6	4	9
Conceded 3 goals	2	0	0	2	0
Conceded 4+ goals	1	0	0	1	0

GOALS SCORED/CONCEDED PER FIVE-MINUTE INTERVALS

Goals For	5	1	2	2	1	3	3	2	6	5	1	4	3	7	4	3	1	10
Goals Against	1	0	3	3	1	4	4	2	4	4	2	3	3	2	2	3	3	6
Mins	5	10	15	20	25	30	35	40	45	50	55	60	65	70	75	80	85	90

QUICK-FIRE GOALS

From the start of a match
Jordi Gomez
(v Wolverhampton) 0:26

By a substitute after coming on
Gorka Pintado
(v Cardiff) 2:47

LAST-GASP GOALS

From the start of a match
Jason Scotland
(v Barnsley) 93:32

By a substitute after coming on
Guillem Bauza
(v Preston) 58:30

GOAL DETAILS

How the goals were struck

SCORED		CONCEDED
40	Right foot	29
18	Left foot	9
5	Headers	12
0	Others	0

How the goals were struck

SCORED		CONCEDED
43	Open play	31
3	Cross	5
4	Corner	3
6	Penalties	5
2	Direct from free-kick	2
3	Free-kick	3
2	Own goals	1

Distance from goal

SCORED		CONCEDED
17	6yds	16
34	18yds	30
12	18+yds	4

CLUB SUMMARY

FORMED	1881
MANAGER	TBC
GROUND	Vicarage Road
CAPACITY	19,920
NICKNAME	The Hornets
WEBSITE	www.watfordfc.com

The New Football Pools PLAYER OF THE SEASON — Tommy Smith

OVERALL

P	W	D	L	F	A	GD
54	22	10	22	80	81	-1

COCA-COLA CHAMPIONSHIP

Pos	P	W	D	L	F	A	GD	Pts
13	46	16	10	20	68	72	-4	58

HOME

Pos	P	W	D	L	F	A	GD	Pts
11	23	11	6	6	42	32	10	39

AWAY

Pos	P	W	D	L	F	A	GD	Pts
21	23	5	4	14	26	40	-14	19

CUP PROGRESS DETAILS

Competition	Round reached	Knocked out by
FA Cup	R5	Chelsea
Carling Cup	QF	Tottenham

BIGGEST WIN (ALL COMPS)
3–0 on three occasions

BIGGEST DEFEAT (ALL COMPS)
09/01/09 0–4 v Reading **FLC**

THE PLAYER WITH THE MOST

Shots on target	
Tamas Priskin	41
Shots off target	
Jobi McAnuff	25
Shots without scoring	
Jack Cork	15
Assists	
Tommy Smith	9
Offsides	
Tamas Priskin	57
Fouls	
Tamas Priskin	71
Fouls without a card	
Ross Jenkins	33
Free-kicks won	
Tommy Smith	68
Defensive clearances	
Jay DeMerit	45

actim INDEX for the 2008/09 Coca-Cola Championship Season

Rank	Player	Pts
2	Tommy Smith	707
39	Tamas Priskin	482
99	Adrian Mariappa	380
100	Scott Loach	378
109	Jobi McAnuff	363

ATTENDANCE RECORD

High	Low	Average
16,386	13,193	14,858
v Wolves (25/10/2008)	v Burnley (27/01/2009)	

A SACKING, a resignation, Extraordinary General Meetings, a new chairman and the return of Graham Taylor and Elton John.

It was certainly a turbulent 12 months for Watford, who could face even more ups and downs in 2009/10 after boss Brendan Rodgers quit for Reading in June.

Adrian Boothroyd had led the club to a place in the play-offs in May 2008, where they fell at the semi-final stage to Hull City, but the summer saw the loss of a number of key personnel. Giant defender Danny Shittu was sold to Barclays Premier League side Bolton Wanderers for a fee of £2million, while forward Darius Henderson joined Championship rivals Sheffield United. Record signing Nathan Ellington was loaned to Derby after just one poor season with the Hornets, while left-back Jordan Stewart joined him at Pride Park as the Vicarage Road club attempted to cut costs.

Despite the exodus, Boothroyd started the season well, with just one defeat in August, but a run of one win in 11 led to his departure following a loss to Blackpool, which left the club in the drop zone.

Chairman Graham Simpson appointed Chelsea reserve-team manager Rodgers as the new man to lead the Hornets away from danger, but himself resigned within a week after fellow board members called an EGM to discuss his running of the club.

While club legends Taylor and John returned as non-executive director and honorary life president

Tommy Smith was Watford's top goalscorer

respectively, Rodgers was inspiring an improvement in displays and results.

Tottenham earned a narrow 2–1 win in the League Cup quarter-finals while Rodgers' old club Chelsea arrived in February for an FA Cup tie. Guus Hiddink led his side to a 3–1 win, but the Hornets were by now a much-improved outfit.

Rodgers also continued to focus on balancing the finances, allowing Leigh Bromby, John-Joe O'Toole and Lee Williamson to leave on loan.

There was also success in the January transfer window with centre-half Mike Williamson proving a big hit after arriving from League Two side Wycombe, while midfielder Don Cowie looked a bargain at £50,000 from Inverness.

A run of five wins from six games heading into March pulled the club away from danger but, just after the end of the campaign, Rodgers took up the chance to return to his former club, Reading.

> **On the field, Rodgers set about a revolution in style**

August

9th	● Crystal Palace ....a	D 0–0	**Att:** 15,614. **Ref:** M Jones — **Booked:** L. Williamson
12th	● Bristol Rovers ....h	W 1–0	**Att:** 5,574. **Ref:** D Whitestone — **Scorers:** Hoskins
16th	● Charlton ....h	W 1–0	**Att:** 14,413. **Ref:** I Williamson — **Booked:** Eustace, Harley, Francis, McAnuff
23rd	● Nottm Forest......................a	L 3–2	**Att:** 20,005. **Ref:** M Haywood — **Scorers:** Smith[2]
26th	● Darlington ....h	W 2–1	**Att:** 5,236. **Ref:** F Graham — **Scorers:** Francis, O'Toole. **Booked:** O'Toole, Ainsworth. (AET)
30th	● Ipswich ....h	W 2–1	**Att:** 16,345. **Ref:** L Probert — **Scorers:** Eustace, O'Toole. **Booked:** Eustace, McAnuff

September

13th	● Sheff Wed..........................a	L 2–0	**Att:** 17,066. **Ref:** G Salisbury — **Booked:** Bromby, Harley
16th	● Plymouth............................h	L 1–2	**Att:** 13,237. **Ref:** C Penton — **Scorers:** O'Toole. **Booked:** Smith
20th	● Reading ....h	D 2–2	**Att:** 14,761. **Ref:** S Attwell — **Scorers:** O'Toole, Smith. **Booked:** McAnuff, Hoskins, O'Toole, Harley
23rd	● West Ham ....h	W 1–0	**Att:** 12,914. **Ref:** P Walton — **Scorers:** Mullins OG. **Booked:** Jenkins
27th	● Sheff Utd ....a	L 2–1	**Att:** 24,427. **Ref:** M Halsey — **Scorers:** O'Toole
30th	● Burnley ....a	L 3–2	**Att:** 10,033. **Ref:** S Bratt — **Scorers:** Hoskins[2]

October

4th	● Preston ....h	W 2–1	**Att:** 14,087. **Ref:** K Wright — **Scorers:** Harley, Smith.
18th	● Southampton ....a	W 0–3	**Att:** 17,454. **Ref:** T Kettle — **Scorers:** Eustace, Priskin[2]. **Booked:** Lee, Eustace, L. Williamson, Harley
21st	● Cardiff ....h	D 2–2	**Att:** 13,461. **Ref:** R Beeby — **Scorers:** Hoskins, O'Toole. **Dismissed:** Priskin
25th	● Wolverhampton...................h	L 2–3	**Att:** 16,386. **Ref:** K Woolmer — **Scorers:** O'Toole, Rasiak. **Booked:** Eustace
28th	● Preston ....a	L 2–0	**Att:** 11,234. **Ref:** M Oliver

November

1st	● Blackpool ....h	L 3–4	**Att:** 13,517. **Ref:** R East — **Scorers:** Hoskins, Rasiak, Smith. **Booked:** Harley
9th	● Swansea.............................a	L 3–1	**Att:** 13,891. **Ref:** R Shoebridge — **Scorers:** L. Williamson. **Booked:** Smith, O'Toole, L. Williamson, Eustace
11th	● Swansea.............................a	W 0–1	**Att:** 9,549. **Ref:** A D'Urso — **Scorers:** L. Williamson. **Booked:** Priskin, Bromby, Mariappa, L. Williamson
15th	● Barnsley ....a	L 2–1	**Att:** 11,285. **Ref:** C Webster — **Scorers:** Smith.
22nd	● QPR ....h	W 3–0	**Att:** 16,201. **Ref:** A Penn — **Scorers:** Smith, Ward, L. Williamson. **Booked:** Harley
25th	● Bristol City ....a	D 1–1	**Att:** 15,551. **Ref:** N Swarbrick — **Scorers:** Smith. **Booked:** DeMerit, L. Williamson
29th	● Doncaster ....h	D 1–1	**Att:** 14,008. **Ref:** I Williamson — **Scorers:** Smith. **Booked:** Harley, Bridcutt, Priskin, O'Toole, L. Williamson

December

3rd	● Tottenham ....h	L 1–2	**Att:** 16,501. **Ref:** P Dowd — **Scorers:** Priskin. **Booked:** McAnuff, Priskin
6th	● Birmingham ....a	L 3–2	**Att:** 18,174. **Ref:** S Mathieson — **Scorers:** Jenkins, Priskin
10th	● Norwich..............................h	W 2–1	**Att:** 13,268. **Ref:** P Crossley — **Scorers:** Priskin, Smith. **Booked:** L. Williamson
13th	● Coventry ....h	W 2–1	**Att:** 14,075. **Ref:** J Moss — **Scorers:** O'Toole, Smith. **Booked:** Priskin
20th	● Derby ....a	L 1–0	**Att:** 27,833. **Ref:** C Boyeson
26th	● Bristol City ....h	L 2–4	**Att:** 15,527. **Ref:** F Graham — **Scorers:** Rasiak, Elliott OG
28th	● QPR ....a	D 0–0	**Att:** 16,196. **Ref:** C Penton — **Booked:** Mariappa, Rasiak, DeMerit, Harley

January

3rd	● Scunthorpe ....h	W 1–0	**Att:** 8,690. **Ref:** K Wright — **Scorers:** Rasiak. **Booked:** O'Toole
9th	● Reading ....a	L 4–0	**Att:** 18,072. **Ref:** A D'Urso
17th	● Sheff Utd ....h	L 0–2	**Att:** 14,555. **Ref:** K Friend — **Booked:** Harley
24th	● Crystal Palace ....h	W 4–3	**Att:** 10,006. **Ref:** M Oliver — **Scorers:** Cork, DeMerit, Hoskins, Rasiak
27th	● Burnley ....h	W 3–0	**Att:** 13,193. **Ref:** J Linington — **Scorers:** McAnuff, Priskin[2]. **Booked:** Hoyte
31st	● Wolverhampton...................a	L 3–1	**Att:** 23,571. **Ref:** N Miller — **Scorers:** Mariappa. **Booked:** Hoyte, M. Williamson

February

14th	● Chelsea ....h	L 1–3	**Att:** 16,851. **Ref:** M Dean — **Scorers:** Priskin. **Booked:** O'Toole
17th	● Swansea.............................h	W 2–0	**Att:** 13,727. **Ref:** A Taylor — **Scorers:** Priskin, Smith. **Booked:** Cowie, L. Williamson
21st	● Blackpool ....a	W 0–2	**Att:** 7,451. **Ref:** J Moss — **Scorers:** Priskin, M. Williamson. **Booked:** M. Williamson, Priskin
28th	● Crystal Palace ....h	W 2–0	**Att:** 15,529. **Ref:** G Hegley — **Scorers:** Cowie, Fonte OG

March

3rd	● Plymouth............................a	L 2–1	**Att:** 9,529. **Ref:** N Miller — **Scorers:** Smith. **Booked:** M. Williamson
7th	● Charlton ....a	W 2–3	**Att:** 20,052. **Ref:** A Penn — **Scorers:** Cowie, Priskin, Rasiak
10th	● Nottm Forest......................h	W 2–1	**Att:** 14,730. **Ref:** M Haywood — **Scorers:** Priskin, Rasiak. **Booked:** Harley
14th	● Sheff Wed..........................h	D 2–2	**Att:** 16,294. **Ref:** A Woolmer — **Scorers:** McAnuff, Beevers OG. **Booked:** M. Williamson, McAnuff
18th	● Cardiff ....a	L 2–1	**Att:** 17,899. **Ref:** A Hall — **Scorers:** Smith. **Booked:** Cork, Mariappa, McAnuff, DeMerit
21st	● Ipswich ....a	D 0–0	**Att:** 21,434. **Ref:** C Webster

April

4th	● Doncaster ....a	W 1–2	**Att:** 12,126. **Ref:** G Laws — **Scorers:** Cowie, Hird OG
7th	● Southampton ....h	D 2–2	**Att:** 16,066. **Ref:** C Penton — **Scorers:** Cauna, Priskin
11th	● Barnsley ....h	D 1–1	**Att:** 16,052. **Ref:** D Whitestone — **Scorers:** Smith
13th	● Norwich..............................a	L 2–0	**Att:** 25,487. **Ref:** S Tanner — **Booked:** Cork
18th	● Birmingham ....h	L 0–1	**Att:** 16,180. **Ref:** T Bates
25th	● Coventry ....a	W 2–3	**Att:** 17,195. **Ref:** R Booth — **Scorers:** Priskin, Rasiak, Smith

May

3rd	● Derby ....h	W 3–1	**Att:** 16,131. **Ref:** S Mathieson — **Scorers:** McAnuff, Rasiak[2]. **Booked:** Doyley

● Coca-Cola Championship/Play-Offs   ● FA Cup   ● Carling Cup

WATFORD

CHAMPIONSHIP GOALKEEPER STATS

Player	Minutes on pitch	Appearances	Match starts	Completed matches	Sub appearances	Subbed off	SAVES BREAKDOWN								Clean sheets	Goals conceded	Minutes since conceding	Save %	PENALTIES			Yellow cards	Red cards
							Saved with feet	Punched	Parried	Tipped over	Fumbled	Tipped round	Caught	Blocked					Saved	Resulting in goals	Opposition miss		
Richard Lee	940	10	9	9	1	0	1	0	8	0	0	3	48	0	1	21	24	74.39	3	1	0	1	0
Scott Loach	2881	31	30	29	1	1	3	6	21	6	0	10	152	0	8	43	11	82.16	0	4	0	0	0
Mart Poom	577	7	7	6	0	1	0	2	1	1	0	0	22	0	2	8	25	77.14	0	1	0	0	0

CHAMPIONSHIP OUTFIELD PLAYER STATS

Player	Minutes on pitch	Appearances	Match starts	Completed matches	Substitute appearances	Subbed off	Goals scored	Minutes since scoring	Assists	Shots on target	Shots off target	Crosses	Defensive clearances	Defensive blocks	Fouls committed	Free-kicks won	Caught offside	Yellow cards	Red cards
Lionel Ainsworth	193	7	1	0	6	1	0	-	0	0	2	9	0	0	1	1	2	0	0
Alhassan Bangura	24	2	0	0	2	0	0	-	0	0	0	0	0	0	0	0	0	0	0
Liam Bridcutt	322	6	4	0	2	4	0	-	1	1	0	0	3	1	7	2	0	1	0
Leigh Bromby	1822	22	19	18	3	1	0	322	0	1	4	3	45	4	14	15	0	1	0
Aleksandrs Cauna	157	5	2	0	3	2	1	116	0	4	0	6	0	0	2	1	0	0	0
Jack Cork	1767	19	18	17	1	1	0	-	1	5	10	12	7	2	27	25	1	2	0
Don Cowie	864	10	10	6	0	4	3	17	1	11	8	15	1	0	2	6	3	1	0
Jay DeMerit	2920	32	31	28	1	3	0	-	0	1	4	4	45	16	22	37	0	3	0
Lloyd Doyley	3315	37	35	32	2	3	0	-	1	0	4	16	27	10	28	20	0	1	0
John Eustace	1331	17	14	10	3	4	2	11	0	6	6	1	8	5	27	26	0	5	0
Damien Francis	68	4	0	0	4	0	0	-	0	0	0	0	0	0	1	3	0	1	0
Jon Harley	3002	37	32	25	5	7	1	2165	3	9	7	37	14	7	51	38	9	10	0
Liam Henderson	87	5	0	0	5	0	0	-	0	1	0	1	0	0	3	2	0	0	0
Lee Hodson	27	1	0	0	1	0	0	-	0	0	0	1	0	0	0	0	0	0	0
Will Hoskins	1732	32	16	7	16	9	4	886	3	16	12	20	9	1	24	19	27	1	0
Gavin Hoyte	524	7	6	3	1	3	0	-	0	0	0	5	10	1	7	1	0	2	0
Ross Jenkins	2610	29	28	23	1	5	1	2148	0	6	4	24	16	6	33	23	0	0	0
Adrian Mariappa	3543	39	37	35	2	2	1	1549	1	1	3	14	39	11	44	40	1	2	0
Jobi McAnuff	3171	40	34	26	6	8	3	81	8	27	25	82	3	4	35	53	4	5	0
John-Joe O'Toole	1383	22	14	9	8	5	7	180	0	14	7	5	8	3	21	18	1	3	0
Jordan Parkes	45	1	1	0	0	1	0	-	0	0	0	2	1	1	0	0	0	0	0
Tamas Priskin	2704	36	32	14	4	17	12	111	3	41	21	18	14	3	71	56	57	3	1
Grzegorz Rasiak	1372	21	12	8	9	4	8	54	2	22	19	20	8	0	30	16	14	1	0
Theo Robinson	51	3	0	0	3	0	0	-	0	1	0	0	0	0	0	0	3	0	0
Danny Rose	346	7	3	0	4	4	0	-	0	1	2	5	0	1	8	8	1	0	0
Mathew Sadler	1335	15	15	11	0	0	0	-	1	0	0	12	22	2	8	10	2	0	0
Tommy Smith	4093	44	43	41	1	2	17	131	9	35	19	112	3	1	37	68	27	2	0
Sam Sodje	95	1	1	1	0	0	0	-	0	0	0	0	4	0	2	2	0	0	0
Andrei Stepanov	7	1	0	0	1	0	0	-	0	0	0	0	0	0	0	0	0	0	0
Darren Ward	852	9	9	8	0	1	1	1594	1	0	3	1	0	24	3	7	12	0	0
Lee Williamson	2434	34	26	18	8	8	2	68	2	14	18	49	7	0	41	40	0	7	0
Mike Williamson	1632	17	17	17	0	0	0	1291	0	5	3	1	41	10	29	15	2	4	0
Lewis Young	49	1	0	0	1	0	0	-	0	1	0	0	0	0	0	1	0	0	0

SEASON TOTALS

Goals scored	68
Goals conceded	72
Clean sheets	10
Shots on target	226
Shots off target	179
Shots per goal	5.96
Pens awarded	6
Pens scored	4
Pens conceded	9
Offsides	154
Corners	258
Crosses	474
Players used	36
Fouls committed	584
Free-kicks won	571

CARDS RECEIVED

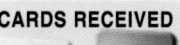

56 **1**

SEQUENCES

Wins	3
(17/02/09–28/02/09)	
Losses	5
(25/10/08–15/11/08)	
Draws	2
(on two occasions)	
Undefeated	4
(21/03/09–11/04/09)	
Without win	6
(21/10/08–15/11/08)	
Undefeated home	7
(27/01/09–11/04/09)	
Undefeated away	2
(21/03/09–04/04/09)	
Without scoring	3
(28/12/08–17/01/09)	
Without conceding	3
(17/02/09–28/02/09)	
Scoring	10
(27/01/09–18/03/09)	
Conceding	8
(23/08/08–04/10/08)	

SEASON INFORMATION

Highest position: 7
Lowest position: 22
Average goals scored per game: 1.48
Average goals conceded per game: 1.57

League position at the end of each week

League position at the end of: August 8, September 21, October 19, November 21, December 19, January 20, February 18, March 16, April 15, May 13

MATCH RECORDS

Goals scored per match

		W	D	L	Pts
Failed to score	10	0	3	7	3
Scored 1 goal	11	1	3	7	6
Scored 2 goals	18	9	4	5	31
Scored 3 goals	7	6	0	1	18
Scored 4+ goals	0	0	0	0	0

Goals conceded per match

		W	D	L	Pts
Clean sheet	10	7	3	0	24
Conceded 1 goal	12	7	3	2	24
Conceded 2 goals	15	2	4	9	10
Conceded 3 goals	6	0	0	6	0
Conceded 4+ goals	3	0	0	3	0

QUICK-FIRE GOALS

From the start of a match
Jobi McAnuff (v Burnley)
1:20

By a substitute after coming on
Tamas Priskin (v Burnley)
1:35

LAST-GASP GOALS

From the start of a match
Tamas Priskin
(v Burnley) 93:26

By a substitute after coming on
John-Joe O'Toole
(v Ipswich) 41:14

GOAL DETAILS

How the goals were struck

SCORED		CONCEDED
39	Right foot	35
15	Left foot	22
13	Headers	13
1	Others	2

How the goals were struck

SCORED		CONCEDED
40	Open play	42
13	Cross	15
6	Corner	4
4	Penalties	6
0	Direct from free-kick	2
1	Free-kick	1
4	Own goals	2

Distance from goal

SCORED		CONCEDED
31	6yds	22
32	18yds	39
5	18+yds	11

GOALS SCORED/CONCEDED PER FIVE-MINUTE INTERVALS

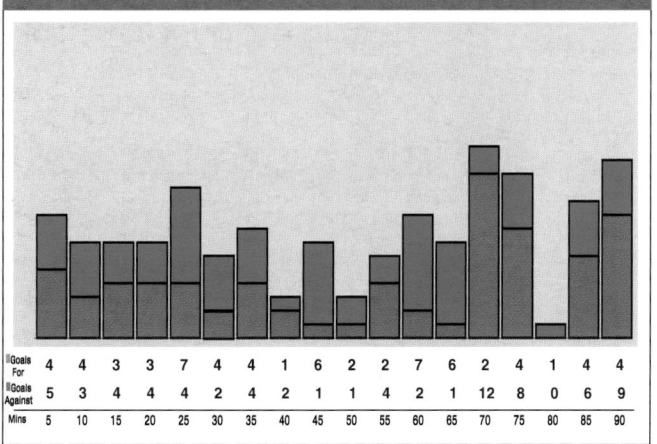

Goals For	4	4	3	3	7	4	4	1	6	2	2	7	6	2	4	1	4	4
Goals Against	5	3	4	4	4	2	4	2	1	1	4	2	1	12	8	0	6	9
Mins	5	10	15	20	25	30	35	40	45	50	55	60	65	70	75	80	85	90

CLUB SUMMARY

FORMED	1877
MANAGER	Mick McCarthy
GROUND	Molineux
CAPACITY	28,525
NICKNAME	Wolves
WEBSITE	www.wolves.co.uk

The New Football Pools PLAYER OF THE SEASON — Sylvan Ebanks-Blake

OVERALL

P	W	D	L	F	A	GD
50	29	10	11	86	56	30

COCA-COLA CHAMPIONSHIP

Pos	P	W	D	L	F	A	GD	Pts
1	46	27	9	10	80	52	28	90

HOME

Pos	P	W	D	L	F	A	GD	Pts
2	23	15	5	3	44	21	23	50

AWAY

Pos	P	W	D	L	F	A	GD	Pts
1	23	12	4	7	36	31	5	40

CUP PROGRESS DETAILS

Competition	Round reached	Knocked out by
FA Cup	R4	Middlesbrough
Carling Cup	R2	Rotherham

BIGGEST WIN (ALL COMPS)

30/08/08 5–1 v Nottm Forest **FLC**

BIGGEST DEFEAT (ALL COMPS)

21/10/08 2–5 v Norwich **FLC**

THE PLAYER WITH THE MOST

Shots on target	
Sylvan Ebanks-Blake	61
Shots off target	
Michael Kightly	36
Shots without scoring	
Karl Henry	22
Assists	
Michael Kightly	19
Offsides	
Andrew Keogh	35
Fouls	
Chris Iwelumo	93
Fouls without a card	
Matthew Jarvis	19
Free-kicks won	
Karl Henry	54
Defensive clearances	
Neill Collins	37

actim INDEX

for the 2008/09 Coca-Cola Championship Season

Rank	Player	Pts
1	Sylvan Ebanks-Blake	753
11	Michael Kightly	587
13	Kevin Foley	569
19	Chris Iwelumo	545
50	Karl Henry	465

ATTENDANCE RECORD

High	Low	Average
28,252	21,326	24,153
v Doncaster (03/05/2009)	v Derby (09/12/2008)	

PERHAPS only the most optimistic of the Black Country's inhabitants would have successfully predicted how Wolves' season was to pan out.

Having missed out on the play-off places in the 2007/08 season by the slenderest of margins, Mick McCarthy's charges took the division by storm, eventually lifting the Coca-Cola Championship trophy after leading the pack for the whole campaign.

Three years in the making, McCarthy's side was built on youth and hunger. Sylvan Ebanks-Blake once again scooped the Championship's Golden Boot award, taking a place in the PFA's Championship Team of the Season in the process, alongside the impressive Michael Kightly and Richard Stearman.

' Mick McCarthy's charges took the division by storm '

Unlike their midlands rivals, Birmingham, who also secured automatic promotion to the Premier League, Wolves did it largely by scoring a hatful of goals. They were the division's leading scorers both at home (44) and away (36) throughout the course of the campaign, although they conceded 52 goals – 15 more than Alex McLeish's Blues.

The men in gold and black started the league season as they meant to go on, entering the automatic promotion places following their third league game of the season – and there they stayed until 3rd May.

They were seven points clear at the summit going into Christmas Day, but a case of new year jitters soon struck as they subsequently won just two of their next 13 games. Fortunately, almost all of their rivals were stumbling at the same time.

But McCarthy's side recaptured their form at the start of March. A 2–0 loss to closest rivals Birmingham set nerves jangling, but Wolves ran out comfortable winners by seven points in the end.

Chief executive Jez Moxey and chairman Steve Morgan have vowed to act on the lessons learned from the club's last venture among England's big boys, in 2003/04, and invest the funds necessary to help Wolves stay in the Premier League for an extended period.

With players such as Ebanks-Blake, Kightly, Wayne Hennessey, Christophe Berra and Kevin Foley, among others, they already have a strong base from which to start.

Whether the club and McCarthy can prove the doubters wrong remains to be seen, but they will certainly give it a good go and will not just tag along for the ride.

Wolves were worthy winners of the Championship title

August

9th	● Plymouth............................a	D 2–2	**Att:** 14,789. **Ref:** K Friend — **Scorers:** Kightly, Vokes. **Booked:** Kightly, Iwelumo
12th	● Accrington Stanley ....h	W 3–2	**Att:** 9,424. **Ref:** J Moss — **Scorers:** Davies, Iwelumo². **Booked:** Keogh (AET)
16th	● Sheff Wed ....h	W 4–1	**Att:** 22,491. **Ref:** M Jones — **Scorers:** Ebanks-Blake, D. Edwards, Iwelumo². **Booked:** Jones
23rd	● Ipswich ....a	W 0–2	**Att:** 21,483. **Ref:** S Tanner — **Scorers:** Ebanks-Blake, D. Edwards. **Booked:** Henry, D. Edwards
26th	● Rotherham ....a	D 0–0	**Att:** 5,404. **Ref:** N Swarbrick — (Lost 3–4 on pens)
30th	● Nottm Forest.....................h	W 5–1	**Att:** 25,301. **Ref:** G Hegley — **Scorers:** Iwelumo, Jones, Kightly², Morgan OG

September

13th	● Charlton ....a	W 1–3	**Att:** 21,547. **Ref:** A Taylor — **Scorers:** Ebanks-Blake, Vokes². **Booked:** Jones
16th	● Crystal Palace ....h	W 2–1	**Att:** 22,200. **Ref:** S Mathieson — **Scorers:** Ebanks-Blake, Keogh. **Booked:** Foley, Ebanks-Blake
20th	● Preston ....a	W 1–3	**Att:** 17,567. **Ref:** M Atkinson — **Scorers:** Iwelumo³. **Booked:** Jones, Kightly
27th	● Bristol City ....h	W 2–0	**Att:** 24,324. **Ref:** P Crossley — **Scorers:** Ebanks-Blake, Kightly. **Booked:** Kightly
30th	● Reading ....h	L 0–3	**Att:** 24,302. **Ref:** R Shoebridge — **Booked:** Stearman

October

4th	● Swansea...........................a	L 3–1	**Att:** 17,556. **Ref:** T Kettle — **Scorers:** Keogh. **Booked:** Keogh
18th	● Coventry ....h	W 2–1	**Att:** 25,893. **Ref:** S Bennett — **Scorers:** Ebanks-Blake, Kightly. **Booked:** Kightly, Foley, Henry, Iwelumo
21st	● Norwich ....a	L 5–2	**Att:** 24,351. **Ref:** G Horwood — **Scorers:** Collins, Ebanks-Blake. **Booked:** Stearman, Henry. **Dismissed:** Stearman
25th	● Watford ....a	W 2–3	**Att:** 16,386. **Ref:** K Woolmer — **Scorers:** Gray, Iwelumo, Jones. **Booked:** Henry, Collins, Iwelumo
28th	● Swansea...........................h	W 2–1	**Att:** 21,988. **Ref:** R Beeby — **Scorers:** Ebanks-Blake²

November

1st	● Cardiff ....a	W 1–2	**Att:** 17,734. **Ref:** S Tanner — **Scorers:** Ebanks-Blake, Iwelumo
8th	● Burnley ....h	W 2–0	**Att:** 23,711. **Ref:** D Deadman — **Scorers:** Kightly². **Booked:** Jones
15th	● Southampton ....a	W 1–2	**Att:** 17,812. **Ref:** L Mason — **Scorers:** Iwelumo, Jones. **Booked:** Mancienne, Henry
22nd	● Blackpool ....h	W 2–0	**Att:** 22,044. **Ref:** A D'Urso — **Scorers:** Iwelumo². **Booked:** D. Edwards
25th	● Sheff Utd ....a	W 1–3	**Att:** 27,111. **Ref:** G Laws — **Scorers:** Ebanks-Blake, Iwelumo². **Booked:** Foley, Ebanks-Blake, Hennessey
29th	● Birmingham ....h	D 1–1	**Att:** 26,329. **Ref:** P Taylor — **Scorers:** Ebanks-Blake. **Booked:** Iwelumo, Stearman

December

6th	● QPR ....a	L 1–0	**Att:** 13,416. **Ref:** I Williamson — **Booked:** Mancienne
9th	● Derby ....h	W 3–0	**Att:** 21,326. **Ref:** G Hegley — **Scorers:** Ebanks-Blake², D. Edwards
13th	● Barnsley ....h	W 2–0	**Att:** 22,399. **Ref:** G Salisbury — **Scorers:** Foley, Hassell OG
20th	● Doncaster ....a	W 0–1	**Att:** 13,669. **Ref:** K Wright — **Scorers:** Collins. **Booked:** Kightly, Collins
26th	● Sheff Utd ....h	D 1–1	**Att:** 27,106. **Ref:** T Bates — **Scorers:** Collins. **Booked:** D. Edwards, Henry
29th	● Blackpool ....a	D 2–2	**Att:** 8,906. **Ref:** K Friend — **Scorers:** Ebanks-Blake, Jarvis. **Booked:** Stearman, Jones, S. Ward

January

10th	● Preston ....h	L 1–3	**Att:** 26,138. **Ref:** C Webster — **Scorers:** Ebanks-Blake.
13th	● Birmingham ....a	W 0–2	**Att:** 22,232. **Ref:** H Webb — **Scorers:** Keogh, Vokes. **Booked:** Stearman
17th	● Bristol City ....a	D 2–2	**Att:** 16,749. **Ref:** M Haywood — **Scorers:** Collins, Jarvis. **Booked:** Stearman
24th	● Middlesbrough ....h	L 1–2	**Att:** 18,013. **Ref:** R Styles — **Scorers:** Vokes. **Booked:** Jones
27th	● Reading ....a	L 1–0	**Att:** 23,009. **Ref:** R Booth — **Booked:** S. Ward
31st	● Watford ....h	W 3–1	**Att:** 23,571. **Ref:** N Miller — **Scorers:** Ebanks-Blake, Keogh, Vokes. **Booked:** Henry, S. Ward

February

3rd	● Norwich...........................h	D 3–3	**Att:** 21,654. **Ref:** K Woolmer — **Scorers:** Ebanks-Blake. **Booked:** Henry
7th	● Coventry ....a	L 2–1	**Att:** 21,167. **Ref:** M Oliver — **Scorers:** Vokes. **Booked:** S. Ward, Henry
14th	● Burnley ....a	L 1–0	**Att:** 13,515. **Ref:** C Oliver
22nd	● Cardiff ....h	D 2–2	**Att:** 22,093. **Ref:** D Deadman — **Scorers:** Ebanks-Blake, Konstantopoulos OG. **Booked:** Berra
28th	● Plymouth..........................h	L 0–1	**Att:** 25,710. **Ref:** C Boyeson — **Booked:** Henry

March

3rd	● Crystal Palace ....a	W 0–1	**Att:** 14,907. **Ref:** G Horwood — **Scorers:** Ebanks-Blake³. **Booked:** Berra, Craddock, Hill, Henry
7th	● Sheff Wed ....a	W 0–1	**Att:** 23,703. **Ref:** S Mathieson — **Scorers:** Ebanks-Blake. **Booked:** Hill, Keogh, Stearman
10th	● Ipswich ....h	D 0–0	**Att:** 22,227. **Ref:** G Salisbury — **Booked:** Craddock
14th	● Charlton ....h	W 2–1	**Att:** 24,319. **Ref:** G Laws — **Scorers:** Ebanks-Blake, Iwelumo. **Booked:** Kightly
21st	● Nottm Forest.....................a	W 0–1	**Att:** 24,510. **Ref:** P Crossley — **Scorers:** Kightly. **Booked:** Berra, Kightly

April

6th	● Birmingham ....a	L 2–0	**Att:** 25,935. **Ref:** M Halsey — **Booked:** Henry
10th	● Southampton ....h	W 3–0	**Att:** 24,636. **Ref:** A Taylor — **Scorers:** Craddock, Jones, Vokes. **Booked:** Berra
13th	● Derby ....a	W 2–3	**Att:** 33,079. **Ref:** P Taylor — **Scorers:** Jarvis, Keogh. **Booked:** Keogh
18th	● QPR ....h	W 1–0	**Att:** 27,511. **Ref:** J Moss — **Scorers:** Ebanks-Blake. **Booked:** S. Ward
25th	● Barnsley ....a	D 1–1	**Att:** 18,288. **Ref:** K Friend — **Scorers:** Reid. **Booked:** D. Edwards

May

3rd	● Doncaster ....h	W 1–0	**Att:** 28,252. **Ref:** R Beeby — **Scorers:** Stearman

● Coca-Cola Championship/Play-Offs ● FA Cup ● Carling Cup

WOLVERHAMPTON WANDERERS

CHAMPIONSHIP GOALKEEPER STATS

Player	Minutes on pitch	Appearances	Match starts	Completed matches	Sub appearances	Subbed off	SAVES BREAKDOWN								Clean sheets	Goals conceded	Minutes since conceding	Save %	PENALTIES			Yellow cards	Red cards
							Saved with feet	Punched	Parried	Tipped over	Fumbled	Tipped round	Caught	Blocked					Saved	Resulting in goals	Opposition miss		
Wayne Hennessey	3297	35	34	33	1	0	5	19	16	2	0	7	106	1	11	34	128	82.20	0	0	0	1	1
Carl Ikeme	1093	12	12	11	0	1	0	4	5	2	0	2	40	0	4	18	33	76.00	0	1	1	0	0

CHAMPIONSHIP OUTFIELD PLAYER STATS

Player	Minutes on pitch	Appearances	Match starts	Completed matches	Substitute appearances	Subbed off	Goals scored	Minutes since scoring	Assists	Shots on target	Shots off target	Crosses	Defensive clearances	Defensive blocks	Fouls committed	Free-kicks won	Caught offside	Yellow cards	Red cards
Christophe Berra	1430	15	15	15	0	0	0	-	1	4	5	1	13	9	26	17	1	4	0
Neill Collins	2027	23	20	19	3	0	4	146	0	6	10	2	37	12	22	14	0	2	1
Jody Craddock	1533	17	17	16	0	1	1	466	0	1	2	0	19	5	26	10	0	2	0
Sylvan Ebanks-Blake	3449	41	41	17	0	24	25	77	5	61	28	14	0	2	60	49	19	2	0
David Edwards	2317	44	23	16	21	7	3	1579	2	17	20	18	9	1	30	30	2	4	0
Carlos Edwards	414	6	5	0	1	5	0	-	3	1	1	5	1	0	3	6	2	0	0
George Elokobi	261	4	3	2	1	1	0	-	0	2	0	4	2	1	2	3	0	0	0
Kevin Foley	4286	45	45	44	0	1	1	2102	2	7	5	62	30	4	20	27	0	3	0
George Friend	348	6	4	1	2	3	0	-	0	1	2	1	0	1	2	2	1	0	0
Michael Gray	371	8	4	1	4	3	1	1335	0	1	1	13	1	1	1	2	0	0	0
Marlon Harewood	243	5	2	1	3	1	0	-	1	0	2	0	0	0	10	2	5	0	0
Ashley Hemmings	54	2	0	0	2	0	0	-	0	0	0	0	0	0	0	0	0	0	0
Karl Henry	4048	43	42	41	1	1	0	-	2	12	10	8	15	8	78	54	0	12	0
Matthew Hill	1058	13	13	7	0	6	0	-	1	1	4	12	2		22	20	0	2	0
Chris Iwelumo	2235	31	25	11	6	13	14	173	4	34	16	2	9	2	93	32	30	4	1
Matthew Jarvis	1954	28	21	8	7	13	3	268	8	19	15	53	4	0	3	19	7	0	0
David Jones	2816	34	31	24	3	7	4	238	3	24	20	39	16	2	44	22	1	5	0
Andrew Keogh	2264	42	21	11	21	10	5	262	5	24	24	13	11	1	28	25	35	3	0
Michael Kightly	3325	38	37	21	1	16	8	17	19	41	36	96	6	2	40	53	15	7	0
Michael Mancienne	816	10	8	8	2	0	0	-	0	0	0	0	8	9	15	5	0	2	0
Nigel Quashie	245	3	3	1	0	2	0	-	0	4	1	2	1	0	2	3	0	0	0
Kyel Reid	299	8	3	0	5	3	0	9	2	4	2	11	1	0	3	11	0	0	0
Jason Shackell	435	12	3	1	9	2	0	-	0	0	0	0	5	1	5	7	0	0	0
Richard Stearman	3043	37	32	30	5	1	1	1	1	7	12	0	35	16	46	44	2	6	1
Sam Vokes	992	36	4	0	32	4	6	233	1	20	8	3	4	0	13	11	7	0	0
Darren Ward	31	1	0	0	1	0	0	-	0	0	0	0	0	1	0	0	0	0	0
Stephen Ward	3511	42	38	28	4	10	0	-	3	2	5	48	18	7	34	42	2	5	0

Coca-Cola CHAMPIONSHIP

SEASON TOTALS

Goals scored	80
Goals conceded	52
Clean sheets	14
Shots on target	294
Shots off target	224
Shots per goal	6.47
Pens awarded	10
Pens scored	8
Pens conceded	2
Offsides	129
Corners	272
Crosses	401
Players used	30
Fouls committed	630
Free-kicks won	515

CARDS RECEIVED

64   4

SEQUENCES

Wins	7
(on two occasions)	
Losses	2
(on two occasions)	
Draws	2
(26/12/08–29/12/08)	
Undefeated	8
(on two occasions)	
Without win	5
(on two occasions)	
Undefeated home	8
(18/10/08–26/12/08)	
Undefeated away	4
(on two occasions)	
Without scoring	
(–)	
Without conceding	3
(on two occasions)	
Scoring	11
(04/10/08–29/11/08)	
Conceding	11
(26/12/08–28/02/09)	

SEASON INFORMATION

Highest position: 1
Lowest position: 15
Average goals scored per game: 1.74
Average goals conceded per game: 1.13

League position at the end of each week

(chart: League position at the end of — positions 1, 6, 12, 18, 24 against months August 1 to May 1)

MATCH RECORDS

Goals scored per match

		W	D	L	Pts
Failed to score	7	0	1	6	1
Scored 1 goal	12	6	3	3	21
Scored 2 goals	16	11	4	1	37
Scored 3 goals	9	8	1	0	25
Scored 4+ goals	2	2	0	0	6

Goals conceded per match

		W	D	L	Pts
Clean sheet	14	13	1	0	40
Conceded 1 goal	19	12	3	4	39
Conceded 2 goals	8	2	4	2	10
Conceded 3 goals	4	0	1	3	1
Conceded 4+ goals	1	0	0	1	0

GOALS SCORED/CONCEDED PER FIVE-MINUTE INTERVALS

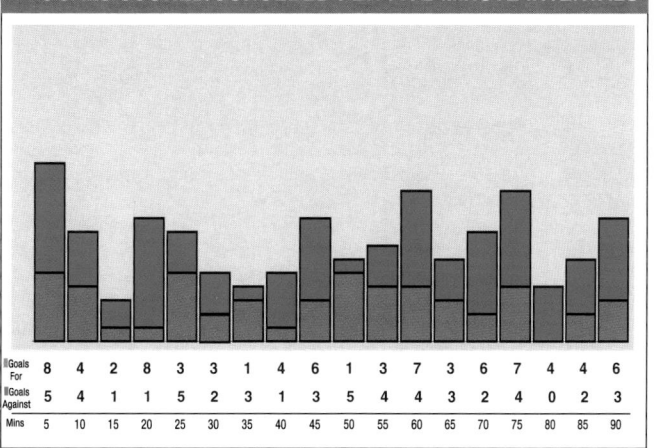

Goals For	8	4	2	8	3	3	1	4	6	1	3	7	3	6	7	4	4	6	
Goals Against	5	4	1	1	5	2	3	1	3	5	4	4	3	2	4	0	2	3	
Mins	5	10	15	20	25	30	35	40	45	50	55	60	65	70	75	80	85	90	

QUICK-FIRE GOALS

From the start of a match
Sylvan Ebanks-Blake
(v Crystal Palace) 0:33

By a substitute after coming on
Sam Vokes
(v Plymouth) 1:08

LAST-GASP GOALS

From the start of a match
Richard Stearman
(v Doncaster) 91:16

By a substitute after coming on
Kyel Reid
(v Barnsley) 38:57

GOAL DETAILS

How the goals were struck

SCORED		CONCEDED
44	Right foot	27
12	Left foot	15
20	Headers	6
4	Others	4

How the goals were struck

SCORED		CONCEDED
49	Open play	36
12	Cross	3
4	Corner	5
8	Penalties	1
1	Direct from free-kick	1
3	Free-kick	2
3	Own goals	4

Distance from goal

SCORED		CONCEDED
34	6yds	22
41	18yds	24
5	18+yds	6

COCA-COLA LEAGUE 1 STATISTICS 2008/09

Player of the season
Matty Fryatt (Leicester)
Manager of the season
Darren Ferguson (Peterborough)

The player with the most...

Shots on target
Matty Fryatt (Leicester) **98**
Shots off target
Jermaine Beckford (Leeds)..................... **73**
Shots without scoring
Robbie Williams (Huddersfield).............. **40**
Shots per goal
Simon Hackney (Colchester/Carlisle) **42**
Assists
Robert Snodgrass (Leeds) **16**
Offsides
Lee Hughes (Oldham) **87**
Fouls
Steve Howard (Leicester) **116**
Fouls without a card
Paul Connor (Cheltenham) **47**
Free-kicks won
Gary Roberts (Yeovil)............................ **111**
Penalties scored
Simon Cox (Swindon).............................
Joel Porter (Hartlepool) **6**
Goals scored direct from free-kicks
Danny Jackman (Northampton)..............
Grant McCann (Scunthorpe) **6**
Defensive clearances
Steve Elliott (Bristol Rovers).................. **120**
Defensive blocks
Mark Hughes (Northampton) **47**

The team with the most...

Shots on target	Scunthorpe	364
Shots off target	Peterborough	335
Shots per goal	Hereford	11.1
Corners	Leicester	297
Fouls	Millwall	662
Woodwork strikes	Leeds	19
Offsides	Leicester	182
Penalties conceded	Oldham	11
Yellow cards	Millwall	96
Red cards	Cheltenham	10

TOTALS 2008/09

Goals	
Total	1516
Home	838
Away	678
Cards	
Yellow	1528
Average per game	2.77
Red	94
Average per game	0.17
Attendances	
Total	4,170,344

FOR SO long it appeared that Leicester would stroll to the Coca-Cola League One title unchallenged, but a late-season wobble, along with the form of Peterborough, made it an interesting final few weeks. Although Nigel Pearson's side did ultimately manage to get their hands on the trophy and secure an instant return to the second tier, they were made to work hard for it by the Posh, who also succeeded in moving out of the division as they claimed back-to-back promotions.

The Foxes, powered by the 27 goals of Matty Fryatt and the craft of experienced midfielder Matt Oakley, reached the summit on 22nd November and never surrendered their position at the top. They were 12 points clear on 7th March, a lead that was reduced to just a solitary point a month later. However, they regained their composure and clinched promotion with a 2–0 win at Southend. Fittingly, a brace from striker Fryatt confirmed their success – but he was not the only lethal marksman to ply his trade in the division.

Six players scored 20 goals or more in League One with Swindon's Simon Cox and Rickie Lambert of Bristol Rovers each grabbing 29. Despite a series of injuries, Leeds' Jermaine Beckford joined Fryatt on 27 goals, while Scunthorpe's Gary Hooper (24) and Peterborough's Craig Mackail-Smith (23) were also in hot scoring form.

The 47 goals shared between Peterborough duo Mackail-Smith and Aaron Mclean were a key reason behind the London Road club's move up to the Coca-Cola Championship under the astute guidance of manager Darren Ferguson.

Another side promoted this time last year, the MK Dons, also enjoyed a fine campaign under rookie boss Roberto Di Matteo and finished in a play-off spot while Leeds, the pre-season favourites, finished in fourth.

Manager Gary McAllister paid the price for a disappointing first half of the season at Elland Road and was replaced by Simon Grayson, who oversaw a renaissance after Christmas. McAllister was one of 15 managers to part company with their clubs during the season, with Stan Ternent (Huddersfield), John Ward (Carlisle) and John Sheridan (Oldham) all notably paying the price for failing to sustain a promotion challenge.

Carlisle, in particular, were expected to be challenging at the right end of the table following play-off heartbreak the previous

> **The Foxes were powered by the 27 goals of Matty Fryatt and the craft of Matt Oakley**

term, but instead they had to wait until the final day to beat the drop, when a 2–0 win over Millwall, saw them avoid relegation against all the odds. Despite that result, Millwall enjoyed a fine year, finishing in fifth as manager Kenny Jackett recaptured the spirit of the club and transformed them into one of the best teams in the division.

The top six was completed by Scunthorpe, who provided the most dramatic moment of the season. Nigel Adkins' side led Tranmere by two points in the race for sixth place going into the final weekend as both sides were pitted against each other for the last remaining play-off spot. The Iron looked doomed as they trailed 1–0 with only two minutes remaining, but captain Cliff Byrne headed home a priceless equaliser to end Tranmere's dreams.

Stockport endured a testing season following their promotion to the division. Led by Jim Gannon, County were sitting in eighth at the turn of the year before financial problems saw a fire sale of some of their brightest stars, and, following a decision to enter administration – which also saw them docked 10 points – Gannon was made redundant by the club in May.

At the bottom of the table, Hereford were the first side to be relegated, a move that saw chairman Graham Turner step down as manager, while Cheltenham soon followed despite a rousing finish under Martin Allen.

Crewe were made to pay for a poor start and also slipped into Coca-Cola League Two, while Northampton, who were outside the drop zone going into the final game, joined them following defeat at Leeds.

One of the stories of the season came at Yeovil, who defied the odds to avoid relegation, thanks to a vital draw with Hereford late in the season when on-loan goalkeeper Chris Weale nodded home an equaliser five minutes into injury-time.

FINAL COCA-COLA LEAGUE 1 TABLE

			HOME				AWAY						
		P	W	D	L	F	A	W	D	L	F	A	GD	Pts
1	LEICESTER	46	13	9	1	41	16	14	6	3	43	23	45	96
2	PETERBOROUGH	46	14	6	3	41	22	12	5	6	37	32	24	89
3	MK Dons	46	12	4	7	42	25	14	5	4	41	22	36	87
4	Leeds	46	17	2	4	49	20	9	4	10	28	29	28	84
5	Millwall	46	13	4	6	30	21	12	3	8	33	32	10	82
6	SCUNTHORPE	46	13	5	5	44	24	9	5	9	38	39	19	76
7	Tranmere	46	15	5	3	41	20	6	6	11	21	29	13	74
8	Southend	46	13	2	8	29	20	8	6	9	29	41	-3	71
9	Huddersfield	46	9	8	6	32	28	9	6	8	30	37	-3	68
10	Oldham	46	9	9	5	35	24	7	8	8	31	41	1	65
11	Bristol Rovers	46	11	4	8	44	29	6	8	9	35	32	18	63
12	Colchester	46	7	4	12	21	24	11	5	7	37	34	0	63
13	Walsall	46	10	3	10	34	36	7	7	9	27	30	-5	61
14	Leyton Orient	46	6	6	11	24	33	9	5	9	21	24	-12	56
15	Swindon	46	8	7	8	37	34	4	10	9	31	37	-3	53
16	Brighton	46	6	6	11	32	40	7	7	9	23	30	-15	52
17	Yeovil	46	6	10	7	26	29	6	5	12	15	37	-25	51
18	Stockport*	46	9	7	7	34	28	7	5	11	25	29	2	50
19	Hartlepool	46	8	7	8	45	40	5	4	14	21	39	-13	50
20	Carlisle	46	8	7	8	36	32	4	7	12	20	37	-13	50
21	Northampton	46	8	8	7	38	29	4	5	14	23	36	-4	49
22	Crewe	46	8	4	11	30	38	4	6	13	29	44	-23	46
23	Cheltenham	46	7	6	10	30	38	2	6	15	21	53	-40	39
24	Hereford	46	6	4	13	23	28	3	3	17	19	51	-37	34

* 10 points deducted

GEORGE BOYD (PETERBOROUGH)

JONATHAN DOUGLAS (LEEDS)

TOM POPE (CREWE)

PLAY-OFF REVIEW

SCUNTHORPE secured promotion with a dramatic play-off final win over Millwall.

With their support heavily outnumbered at a scorching Wembley, Nigel Adkins' side came from behind to earn an instant return to the Coca-Cola Championship with a 3–2 win. Matt Sparrow – in his testimonial season – fired Scunthorpe into an early lead, only for Gary Alexander's quick-fire brace to put Millwall in the driving seat. But Sparrow levelled matters before Martyn Woolford – a pre-season signing from York – scored the most important goal of his career to win the game five minutes from time.

Millwall's place in the final was secured after two bruising encounters with Leeds. They opened up a narrow first-leg lead, with Neil Harris' 117th goal for the club setting up a 1–0 win. That proved to be decisive on a rain-soaked night at Elland Road in the second leg. Roared on by a crowd of 37,036 – the biggest in the Football League during the season – Leeds overcame a missed penalty from Jermaine Beckford to take the lead through Luciano Becchio. But Millwall clung on and finished the stronger, with Nadjim Abdou's equaliser making sure of their trip to Wembley.

Scunthorpe were made to work even harder for their place in the final, relying on a penalty shoot-out and the brilliance of Joe Murphy to see them past MK Dons. In the first game at Glanford Park, Woolford's backheel put the Iron ahead only for Aaron Wilbraham to level. That is how it turned out to be, with both sides cancelling each other out until Murphy saved shoot-out efforts from Jason Puncheon and Jude Stirling, while Tore André Flo hit his against the crossbar.

Leicester made an immediate return to the Championship as they stormed to the Coca-Cola League One title under new manager Nigel Pearson

COCA-COLA LEAGUE 1 FIXTURES AND RESULTS

Home \ Away

Home	BRIGHTON	BRISTOL RVRS	CARLISLE	CHELTENHAM	COLCHESTER	CREWE	HARTLEPOOL	HEREFORD	HUDDERSFIELD	LEEDS UTD	LEICESTER	LEYTON ORIENT	MILLWALL	MK DONS	NORTHAMPTON	OLDHAM	PETERBORO	SCUNTHORPE	SOUTHEND	STOCKPORT	SWINDON	TRANMERE	WALSALL	YEOVIL
BRIGHTON	–	1-1	0-2	3-3	1-2	0-4	2-1	0-0	0-1	0-2	3-2	0-0	4-1	2-4	1-1	3-1	2-4	1-4	1-3	1-0	2-3	0-0	0-1	5-0
BRISTOL RVRS	1-2	–	2-3	3-2	0-0	0-0	4-1	6-1	1-2	2-2	0-1	2-1	4-2	1-2	1-0	2-0	0-1	1-2	4-2	2-0	2-2	2-0	1-3	3-0
CARLISLE	3-1	1-1	–	1-0	0-2	4-2	0-1	1-2	3-0	0-2	1-2	1-3	2-0	3-2	1-1	1-1	3-3	1-1	2-1	1-2	1-1	1-2	1-1	4-1
CHELTENHAM	2-2	2-1	1-1	–	4-3	1-0	2-0	2-3	1-2	1-0	0-4	0-1	1-3	3-5	0-1	1-1	3-6	1-2	0-0	2-2	2-0	1-0	1-0	1-0
COLCHESTER	0-1	0-1	5-0	3-1	–	0-1	1-1	1-2	0-0	0-1	0-1	1-0	1-2	0-3	2-1	2-2	0-0	0-1	1-0	3-2	0-1	0-1	0-2	1-0
CREWE	1-2	1-1	1-2	1-2	2-0	–	0-0	2-1	3-1	2-3	0-3	0-2	2-2	1-3	0-3	1-1	3-2	3-4	0-3	1-0	2-1	2-1	2-1	2-0
HARTLEPOOL	1-0	1-1	2-2	4-1	4-2	1-4	–	4-2	5-3	0-1	2-2	0-1	2-3	1-3	2-0	3-3	1-2	2-3	3-0	0-1	3-3	2-1	2-2	0-0
HEREFORD	1-2	0-3	1-0	3-0	0-2	2-0	1-1	–	0-1	2-0	1-3	2-0	0-1	0-2	5-0	0-1	0-1	1-1	1-2	2-0	3-0	2-1	0-0	1-2
HUDDERSFIELD	2-2	1-1	1-0	2-2	2-2	3-2	1-1	2-0	–	1-0	2-3	0-1	1-2	1-3	3-2	1-1	1-0	2-0	0-1	0-1	2-1	1-2	0-0	1-0
LEEDS UTD	3-1	2-2	0-2	2-0	1-2	5-2	4-1	1-0	1-2	–	1-1	2-1	2-0	2-0	3-0	0-2	3-1	3-2	2-0	1-0	1-0	3-1	3-0	4-0
LEICESTER	0-0	2-1	2-2	4-0	1-1	2-1	1-0	2-1	4-2	1-0	–	3-0	0-1	2-0	0-0	0-1	4-0	2-2	3-0	1-1	3-1	3-2	2-2	0-1
LEYTON ORIENT	2-1	1-2	0-1	2-1	1-0	1-0	2-1	1-1	2-2	1-3	0-0	–	1-2	1-3	2-1	2-3	2-2	1-1	0-3	1-2	0-1	0-1	0-1	0-1
MILLWALL	1-0	3-2	1-0	2-0	0-1	0-0	2-0	1-0	2-1	3-1	0-1	2-1	–	0-4	1-2	2-3	2-0	1-1	1-0	1-1	1-1	1-0	3-1	1-1
MK DONS	2-0	2-1	3-1	3-1	1-1	2-2	3-1	3-0	1-1	3-1	2-2	1-2	0-1	–	1-0	6-2	1-2	0-2	2-0	1-2	1-2	1-2	1-0	3-0
NORTHAMPTON	2-2	0-0	1-0	4-2	1-2	5-1	1-0	2-1	1-2	1-2	0-0	0-1	0-1	1-0	–	1-1	3-3	2-3	4-0	3-4	1-1	1-1	0-2	3-0
OLDHAM	1-1	0-2	0-0	4-0	0-1	1-1	2-1	4-0	1-1	1-1	1-1	1-1	4-3	2-0	2-1	–	1-2	3-0	1-1	3-1	0-0	3-2	3-2	0-2
PETERBORO	0-0	5-4	1-0	1-1	2-1	4-2	1-2	2-0	4-0	2-0	3-0	1-0	0-0	1-0	2-2	2-2	–	2-1	1-2	1-0	2-2	2-2	1-0	1-3
SCUNTHORPE	2-0	0-2	2-1	3-0	3-0	3-0	3-0	1-2	1-2	1-2	2-1	3-2	0-1	4-4	2-0	1-0	1-1	–	1-1	2-1	3-3	1-1	1-1	2-0
SOUTHEND	0-2	1-0	3-0	2-0	3-3	0-1	3-2	1-0	0-1	1-0	0-2	3-0	0-1	0-2	1-2	1-0	0-2	1-1	–	1-1	2-1	2-1	2-0	0-1
STOCKPORT	2-0	3-1	3-0	1-0	1-2	4-3	2-1	4-1	1-1	1-3	0-0	0-1	2-2	0-1	1-1	3-1	1-3	0-3	3-1	–	1-1	0-0	1-2	0-0
SWINDON	0-2	2-1	1-1	2-2	1-3	0-0	0-1	3-0	1-3	1-3	2-2	0-1	1-2	1-1	2-1	2-0	2-2	4-2	3-0	1-1	–	3-1	3-2	2-3
TRANMERE	1-0	2-0	4-1	2-0	3-4	2-0	1-0	2-1	3-1	2-1	2-0	0-0	1-3	1-1	4-1	0-1	1-1	2-0	2-2	2-1	1-0	–	2-1	1-1
WALSALL	3-0	0-5	2-1	1-1	2-0	1-1	2-3	1-1	2-3	1-0	1-4	0-2	1-2	0-3	3-1	1-2	2-1	2-1	5-2	1-0	2-1	0-1	–	2-0
YEOVIL	1-1	2-2	1-1	1-1	0-2	3-2	2-3	2-2	1-0	1-1	0-2	2-0	0-0	1-0	2-2	0-1	1-2	1-2	2-4	1-0	1-0	1-1	1-1	–

SIMON COX (SWINDON)

LEADING SCORERS

Player	(Team)	Goals
Simon Cox	(Swindon)	29
Rickie Lambert	(Bristol R)	29
Jermaine Beckford	(Leeds)	27
Matty Fryatt	(Leicester)	27
Gary Hooper	(Scunthorpe)	24
Craig Mackail-Smith	(Peterborough)	23
Lee Hughes	(Oldham)	18
Aaron Mclean	(Peterborough)	18
Joel Porter	(Hartlepool)	18
Paul Hayes	(Scunthorpe)	17
Aaron Wilbraham	(MK Dons)	16
Danny Graham	(Carlisle)	15
Lloyd Owusu	(Brighton)	15

7 for Cheltenham, 1 for Yeovil

ON THE CLOCK COCA-COLA LEAGUE 1

FROM THE START OF A MATCH

Quickest goal
Dominic Blizzard 0:11
(Stockport v Hereford)

Quickest card
■ Billy Clarke 0:54
(Northampton v Leicester)

Last-gasp goal
Max-Alain Gradel 96:05
(Leicester v MK Dons)

BY A SUBSTITUTE

Quickest goal
Kevin Gallen 0:51
(MK Dons v Tranmere)

Quickest card
■ Ben May 1:15
(Scunthorpe v Millwall)

Substitute being substituted
Johnnie Jackson 3:25
(Colchester v Scunthorpe)

DANNY COYNE (TRANMERE)

LEADING GOALKEEPERS

Player	(Team)	Clean sheets
Danny Coyne	(Tranmere)	20
David Forde	(Millwall)	19
Joe Lewis	(Peterborough)	18
Willy Gueret	(MK Dons)	16
Joe Murphy	(Scunthorpe)	15
Casper Ankergren	(Leeds)	13
Steve Phillips	(Bristol R)	13
Clayton Ince	(Walsall)	12
David Martin	(Leicester)	12
Steve Mildenhall	(Southend)	12
Michel Kuipers	(Brighton)	11
Glenn Morris	(Leyton Orient)	9
Owain Fon Williams	(Stockport)	9
Scott Brown	(Cheltenham)	8
Alex Smithies	(Huddersfield)	7

DISCIPLINARY RECORDS

Player	Team	Fouls	Y	R
Jim Goodwin	Huddersfield	63	14	0
Gary Roberts	Yeovil	36	9	2
Lee Hughes	Oldham	76	10	1
Adam Virgo	Brighton	41	8	2
Alan Navarro	MK Dons	43	11	0
Lee Peltier	Yeovil	40	11	0
Steve Howard	Leicester	116	11	0
Terrell Forbes	Yeovil	58	9	1
Ian Goodison	Tranmere	22	7	2
Andy Monkhouse	Hartlepool	64	10	0
Dean Hammond	Colchester	49	10	0
Fabian Delph	Leeds	40	10	0
Andrew Whing	Brighton	26	8	1
Cliff Byrne	Scunthorpe	52	8	1
Gary Alexander	Millwall	61	8	1
Jason Demetriou	Leyton Orient	35	8	1
Miguel Angel Llera	MK Dons	48	8	1
Anthony Grant	Southend	44	9	0
Ben Clark	Hartlepool	50	9	0
Charlie Lee	Peterborough	38	9	0

PLAYER WITH THE MOST...

Shots on target

Matty Fryatt (Leicester)	98
Rickie Lambert (Bristol R)	82
Gary Hooper (Scunthorpe)	77
George Boyd (Peterborough)	76
Steve Howard (Leicester)	69
Craig Mackail-Smith (Peterborough)	68

Shots off target

Jermaine Beckford (Leeds)	73
Rickie Lambert (Bristol R)	71
Craig Mackail-Smith (Peterborough)	66
Simon Cox (Swindon)	60
George Boyd (Peterborough)	59
Steve Howard (Leicester)	59

Shots without scoring

Robbie Williams (Huddersfield)	40
Sofiene Zaaboub (Walsall)	33
Anthony McNamee (Swindon)	31
Ryan Jarvis (Leyton Orient)	29
Paul Coutts (Peterborough)	28
Matt Done (Hereford)	26

Assists

Robert Snodgrass (Leeds)	16
Steve Howard (Leicester)	14
Rickie Lambert (Bristol R)	13
George Boyd (Peterborough)	11
Stuart Campbell (Bristol R)	11
Grant McCann (Scunthorpe)	11

Offsides

Matty Fryatt (Leicester)	86
Craig Mackail-Smith (Peterborough)	76
Gary Hooper (Scunthorpe)	73
Simon Cox (Swindon)	70
Jabo Ibehre (Walsall)	67
Nicky Forster (Brighton)	48

Fouls commited

Steve Howard (Leicester)	116
Bas Savage (Tranmere)	93
Adebayo Akinfenwa (Northampton)	86
Jabo Ibehre (Walsall)	84
Clive Platt (Colchester)	77
Luciano Becchio (Leeds)	75

TEAM STATISTICS

Club	Played	Shots on	Shots off	Corners	Hit woodwork	Caught offside	Offside Trap	Fouls	Yellow cards	Red cards	Pens awarded	Pens con
Brighton	46	213	224	259	16	149	141	544	90	5	7 (5)	9
Bristol Rovers	46	267	227	219	13	84	119	488	45	3	6 (5)	4
Carlisle	46	241	230	246	7	131	68	526	55	4	5 (4)	4
Cheltenham	46	229	192	233	10	156	195	532	55	**10**	8 (7)	8
Colchester	46	207	222	217	12	132	188	579	79	1	3 (3)	4
Crewe	46	275	242	226	10	122	99	370	35	3	4 (4)	4
Hartlepool	46	236	243	240	11	167	89	529	73	3	9 (**8**)	5
Hereford	46	228	239	233	8	124	138	389	41	3	6 (5)	10
Huddersfield	46	255	276	286	7	149	153	613	77	3	3 (1)	7
Leeds	46	330	320	250	**19**	119	115	503	67	5	5 (1)	1
Leicester	46	356	273	**297**	15	**182**	119	538	63	1	8 (7)	5
Leyton Orient	46	221	235	258	8	96	**241**	456	48	2	**11** (6)	8
Millwall	46	231	226	245	10	132	148	**662**	**96**	8	5 (5)	7
MK Dons	46	327	210	271	15	113	129	543	83	5	7 (4)	7
Northampton	46	261	275	236	17	104	175	581	56	5	4 (4)	5
Oldham	46	303	274	273	15	173	138	510	72	5	6 (6)	**11**
Peterborough	46	324	**335**	291	16	162	117	520	55	1	9 (5)	4
Scunthorpe	46	**364**	299	280	13	141	193	569	59	4	9 (7)	4
Southend	46	285	242	223	8	158	117	554	74	5	5 (4)	10
Stockport	46	244	184	287	10	117	53	430	31	0	2 (1)	5
Swindon	46	212	251	282	15	130	158	535	68	2	10 (**8**)	3
Tranmere	46	218	250	256	5	135	126	511	67	5	4 (4)	4
Walsall	46	203	205	226	12	144	154	516	49	4	3 (3)	6
Yeovil	46	172	180	228	9	175	122	561	86	7	3 (0)	7

Offside trap – number of times a side has caught the opposition offside. **Pens awarded** (scored in brackets). **Pens con** – number of penalties awarded to opposition. **Bold** – biggest total

Total league games played this season: **552** • Home wins: **236** (43%) •Away wins: **179** (32%)
•Draws: **137** (25%) • Average goals scored per match **2.7**

RUSSELL SLADE was Brighton's saviour as the Seagulls performed a final-day escape act. The former Yeovil manager was drafted in after Micky Adams' second spell in charge ended, and soon the south-coast club was some eight points adrift of safety.

However, five wins and a draw from their last seven games ensured the Seagulls, who have had more than their fair share of last-day drama in recent years, narrowly beat the drop.

Victories at Hereford and Colchester kick-started the survival bid and Oldham and Bristol Rovers were also dispatched to set up a nerve-jangling final game against Stockport – managed by Jim Gannon, who had turned down the Brighton job in March.

Nicky Forster was the hero, the striker climbing off the bench to tuck away the winner and secure their Coca-Cola League One status.

CLUB SUMMARY

FORMED	1901
MANAGER	Russell Slade
GROUND	Withdean Stadium
CAPACITY	8,850
NICKNAME	The Seagulls
WEBSITE	www.seagulls.co.uk

The New Football Pools PLAYER OF THE SEASON — Andrew Whing

OVERALL
P	W	D	L	F	A	GD
57	16	19	22	72	84	-12

COCA-COLA FOOTBALL LEAGUE ONE
Pos	P	W	D	L	F	A	GD	Pts
16	46	13	13	20	55	70	-15	52

HOME
Pos	P	W	D	L	F	A	GD	Pts
22	23	6	6	11	32	40	-8	24

AWAY
Pos	P	W	D	L	F	A	GD	Pts
13	23	7	7	9	23	30	-7	28

CUP PROGRESS DETAILS
Competition	Round reached	Knocked out by
FA Cup	R1	Hartlepool
JP Trophy	Area Final	Luton
Carling Cup	R3	Derby

BIGGEST WIN (ALL COMPS)
14/03/09 5–0 v Yeovil **FL1**

BIGGEST DEFEAT (ALL COMPS)
28/02/09 0–4 v Crewe **FL1**

ATTENDANCE RECORD
High	Low	Average
8,618	5,035	6,092

v Stockport (02/05/2009)   v Southend (10/03/2009)

RESULTS 2008/09

August
9th	Crewe	a	W 1–2	Att: 4,557 — **Scorers:** Forster, Virgo. **Booked:** Forster
12th	Barnet	h	W 4–0	Att: 2,571 — **Scorers:** Forster, Richards, Virgo². **Booked:** Whing, Murray. **Dismissed:** Murray
16th	Bristol Rovers	h	D 1–1	Att: 6,210 — **Scorers:** Forster. **Booked:** Hart, Elphick
22nd	Southend	a	W 0–2	Att: 7,976 — **Scorers:** Forster, Murray. **Booked:** Kuipers, Elphick, Forster
30th	Leyton Orient	h	D 0–0	Att: 6,675 — **Booked:** Virgo

September
2nd	Northampton	a	W 0–1	Att: 2,047 — **Scorers:** McLeod. **Booked:** Livermore
6th	Scunthorpe	h	L 1–4	Att: 5,529 — **Scorers:** Robinson. **Booked:** Livermore, Elphick
13th	Yeovil	a	D 1–1	Att: 4,451 — **Scorers:** Forster. **Booked:** Anyinsah, Whing, Murray. **Dismissed:** Anyinsah
20th	Walsall	h	L 0–1	Att: 5,679 — **Booked:** Virgo
24th	Man City	h	D 2–2	Att: 8,729 — **Scorers:** Anyinsah, Murray. **Booked:** Livermore, El-Abd (AET – W 5–3 on pens)
27th	Northampton	a	D 2–2	Att: 5,389 — **Scorers:** Murray². **Booked:** Hawkins, Whing, Richards, Murray, Forster

October
4th	Cheltenham	h	D 3–3	Att: 5,859 — **Scorers:** Murray³. **Booked:** Elphick, Thornton, Savage
7th	Leyton Orient	h	D 2–2	Att: 2,157 — **Scorers:** Anyinsah, Virgo. **Booked:** Hawkins, Robinson (Won 5–4 on pens)
11th	Leeds	a	L 3–1	Att: 22,726 — **Scorers:** Murray. **Booked:** Livermore, Hawkins, Elphick, Virgo, Thomson
18th	Hereford	h	D 0–0	Att: 5,608 — **Booked:** El-Abd
21st	Peterborough	a	D 0–0	Att: 5,772 — **Booked:** Savage, Murray
25th	Hartlepool	a	L 1–0	Att: 3,962
28th	Leicester	h	W 3–2	Att: 6,282 — **Scorers:** Johnson², Hobbs OG. **Booked:** Savage, Richards, Elphick

November
1st	Millwall	h	W 4–1	Att: 5,973 — **Scorers:** Cox, Johnson, Murray². **Booked:** Virgo, Johnson
4th	Derby	h	L 1–4	Att: 6,625 — **Scorers:** Elphick
8th	Hartlepool	h	D 3–3	Att: 2,545 — **Scorers:** Cox, Fraser, McLeod
12th	Swindon	h	W 2–0	Att: 2,234 — **Scorers:** Forster, Livermore. **Booked:** Livermore
15th	Carlisle	a	L 3–1	Att: 5,333 — **Scorers:** Richards. **Booked:** Livermore
18th	Hartlepool	a	L 2–1	Att: 3,288 — **Scorers:** Forster. **Booked:** Cox, Cook
22nd	Huddersfield	h	L 0–1	Att: 6,461 — **Booked:** Thomson
25th	Stockport	a	L 2–0	Att: 5,201

December
6th	Oldham	a	D 1–1	Att: 4,803 — **Scorers:** Murray. **Booked:** Virgo, Whing. **Dismissed:** Virgo
12th	MK Dons	h	L 2–4	Att: 5,691 — **Scorers:** Johnson². **Booked:** Thomson, Cox, Hawkins, El-Abd
16th	Shrewsbury	a	D 0–0	Att: 4,052 — **Booked:** Elphick, Virgo, Hinshelwood (Won 5–4 on pens)
20th	Tranmere	a	L 1–0	Att: 4,885 — **Booked:** El-Abd, Cox, Johnson
26th	Colchester	h	L 1–2	Att: 6,299 — **Scorers:** Forster. **Booked:** Cox, Fraser
28th	Swindon	a	W 0–2	Att: 8,438 — **Scorers:** Forster². **Booked:** Virgo, Fraser

January
17th	Leeds	h	L 0–2	Att: 7,096 — **Booked:** El-Abd, Fraser
20th	Luton	h	D 0–0	Att: 6,127 — **Booked:** Mayo
24th	Cheltenham	a	D 2–2	Att: 3,597 — **Scorers:** Forster, Hinshelwood. **Booked:** Hinshelwood, Fraser, Whing, Livermore, Elphick
27th	Leicester	a	D 0–0	Att: 17,410
31st	Hartlepool	h	W 2–1	Att: 5,784 — **Scorers:** Andrew, Forster. **Booked:** Elphick

February
10th	Peterborough	h	L 2–4	Att: 5,087 — **Scorers:** Davies, McNulty. **Booked:** Virgo, Jarrett
14th	Carlisle	h	L 0–2	Att: 5,529 — **Booked:** Forster, Virgo
17th	Luton	a	D 1–1	Att: 8,711 — **Scorers:** Forster. **Booked:** Jarrett. **Dismissed:** Livermore (Lost 3–4 on pens)
21st	Millwall	a	W 0–1	Att: 9,226 — **Scorers:** Virgo. **Booked:** Jarrett
24th	Northampton	h	D 1–1	Att: 5,062 — **Scorers:** Elphick. **Dismissed:** Virgo
28th	Crewe	h	L 0–4	Att: 6,366 — **Booked:** McNulty, Cox

March
7th	Leyton Orient	a	L 2–1	Att: 5,885 — **Scorers:** Heath. **Booked:** Jarrett, Whing, Bangura, Owusu
10th	Southend	h	L 1–3	Att: 5,035 — **Scorers:** Owusu. **Booked:** Cox
14th	Yeovil	h	W 5–0	Att: 6,291 — **Scorers:** Cox², Forster², Murray
17th	Walsall	a	L 3–0	Att: 3,549 — **Booked:** Heath, Borrowdale
21st	Scunthorpe	a	L 2–0	Att: 4,404 — **Booked:** Elphick, Bangura, Davies. **Dismissed:** Heath
28th	Tranmere	h	D 0–0	Att: 5,819

April
4th	MK Dons	a	L 2–0	Att: 15,842 — **Booked:** Loft, Whing, Fraser
7th	Hereford	a	W 1–2	Att: 2,033 — **Scorers:** Fraser, Owusu. **Booked:** Davies, Whing
11th	Swindon	h	L 2–3	Att: 6,549 — **Scorers:** Dicker, Virgo. **Booked:** Kuipers, Borrowdale
13th	Colchester	a	W 0–1	Att: 4,873 — **Scorers:** Owusu. **Booked:** Loft
18th	Oldham	h	W 3–1	Att: 6,618 — **Scorers:** Cox, Owusu². **Booked:** Whing, Owusu, Hart. **Dismissed:** Whing
21st	Bristol Rovers	a	W 1–2	Att: 6,193 — **Scorers:** Andrew, Owusu. **Booked:** Hinshelwood, Kuipers
25th	Huddersfield	a	D 2–2	Att: 14,740 — **Scorers:** Andrew, Owusu. **Booked:** Fraser

May
2nd	Stockport	h	W 1–0	Att: 8,618 — **Scorers:** Forster. **Booked:** Owusu, McLeod

● Coca-Cola League 1/Play-Offs ● FA Cup ● Carling Cup ● Johnstone's Paint Trophy

LEAGUE ONE GOALKEEPER STATS

Player	Appearances	Match starts	Completed matches	Sub appearances	Subbed off	Clean sheets	Yellow cards	Red cards
Mikkel Andersen	5	5	5	0	0	0	0	0
Michel Kuipers	28	28	28	0	0	8	3	0
John Sullivan	13	13	13	0	0	2	0	0

LEAGUE ONE OUTFIELD PLAYER STATS

Player	Appearances	Match starts	Completed matches	Substitute appearances	Subbed off	Goals scored	Yellow cards	Red cards
Calvin Andrew	9	3	2	6	1	3	0	0
Joe Anyinsah	11	10	6	1	3	0	1	1
Alhassan Bangura	6	6	4	0	2	0	2	0
Chris Birchall	9	8	3	1	5	0	0	0
Gary Borrowdale	12	11	9	1	2	0	2	0
Sebastien Carole	12	5	2	7	3	0	0	0
Steve Cook	2	0	0	2	0	0	0	0
Dean Cox	40	32	18	8	14	4	5	0
Craig Davies	16	10	8	6	2	1	2	0
Gary Dicker	9	9	9	0	0	1	0	0
Jonny Dixon	1	0	0	1	0	0	0	0
Adam El-Abd	31	25	21	6	4	0	4	0
Tommy Elphick	39	38	35	1	3	1	9	0
Stuart Fleetwood	11	5	1	6	4	0	0	0
Nicky Forster	30	26	20	4	6	12	4	0
Tommy Fraser	27	18	10	9	8	1	6	0
Gary Hart	11	7	1	4	6	0	2	0
Colin Hawkins	17	17	15	0	2	0	3	0
Matt Heath	6	6	4	0	1	1	1	1
Adam Hinshelwood	14	11	9	3	2	1	2	0
Jason Jarrett	13	11	9	2	2	0	3	0
Bradley Johnson	10	10	9	0	1	5	2	0
David Livermore	16	12	7	4	5	0	4	0
Doug Loft	12	7	4	5	3	0	2	0
Joel Lynch	2	0	0	2	0	0	0	0
Kerry Mayo	2	0	0	2	0	0	0	0
Kevin McLeod	21	11	2	10	9	0	1	0
Jim McNulty	5	5	5	0	0	1	1	0
Glenn Murray	23	18	15	5	3	11	3	0
Lloyd Owusu	14	13	6	1	7	7	3	0
Matthew Richards	23	23	23	0	0	1	2	0
Jake Robinson	5	0	0	5	0	1	0	0
Robbie Savage	6	6	2	0	4	0	3	0
Steven Thomson	17	17	17	0	0	0	3	0
Kevin Thornton	12	4	2	8	2	0	1	0
Adam Virgo	36	36	32	0	2	3	8	2
Andrew Whing	40	40	35	0	4	0	8	1

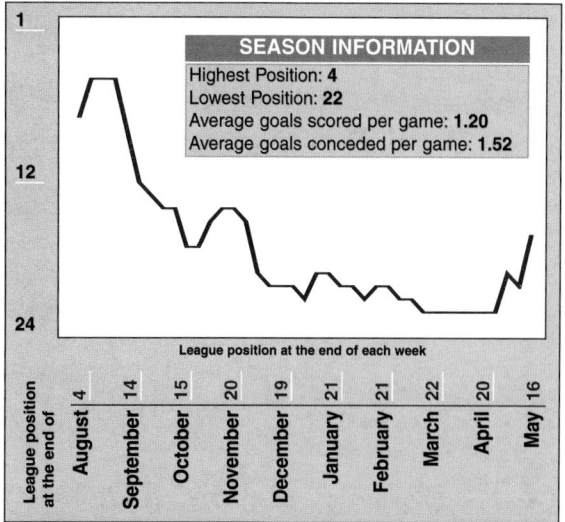

SEASON INFORMATION
Highest Position: **4**
Lowest Position: **22**
Average goals scored per game: **1.20**
Average goals conceded per game: **1.52**

League position at the end of each week

League position at the end of: August 4, September 14, October 15, November 20, December 19, January 21, February 21, March 22, April 20, May 16

LONGEST SEQUENCES

Wins (13/04/09–21/04/09)	3	Undefeated home (04/10/08–01/11/08)	4
Losses (on three occasions)	3	Undefeated away (09/08/08–27/09/08)	4
Draws (on three occasions)	2	Without scoring (17/03/09–04/04/09)	4
Undefeated (13/04/09–02/05/09)	5	Without conceding (on two occasions)	2
Without win (30/08/08–25/10/08)	10	Scoring (07/04/09–02/05/09)	7

CARDS RECEIVED

90   5

QUICK-FIRE GOALS

From the start of a match
Glenn Murray (v Cheltenham) 0:49

By a substitute after coming on
Calvin Andrew (v Bristol Rovers) 5:08

GOALS SCORED/CONCEDED PER FIVE-MINUTE INTERVALS

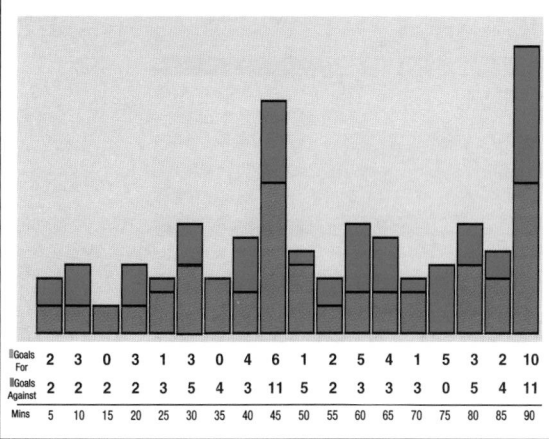

	Mins	5	10	15	20	25	30	35	40	45	50	55	60	65	70	75	80	85	90
Goals For		2	3	0	3	1	3	0	4	6	1	2	5	4	1	5	3	2	10
Goals Against		2	2	2	2	3	5	4	3	11	5	2	3	3	3	0	5	4	11

BRISTOL ROVERS

ROVERS' progress under manager Paul Trollope continued as the Pirates finished in the top half of the table. It was a big improvement on the previous season's 16th-place finish and a real feat considering the defence's injury problems.

Danny Coles was sidelined after suffering cruciate ligament damage while Ryan Green, Aaron Lescott, Joe Jacobson, Steve Elliott and Byron Anthony were also missing.

Director of football Lennie Lawrence has already intimated that the play-offs are the target for the 2009/10 campaign, but keeping hold of the prolific Rickie Lambert will be pivotal to those ambitions after the striker hit 29 goals during the season.

The club's proposed £30million-plus redevelopment of the Memorial Stadium is expected to begin during the coming season.

CLUB SUMMARY

FORMED	1883
MANAGER	Paul Trollope
GROUND	Memorial Stadium
CAPACITY	9,400
NICKNAME	The Pirates
WEBSITE	www.bristolrovers.co.uk

The New **Football Pools** PLAYER OF THE SEASON

Rickie Lambert

OVERALL
P	W	D	L	F	A	GD
49	17	12	20	79	66	13

COCA-COLA FOOTBALL LEAGUE ONE
Pos	P	W	D	L	F	A	GD	Pts
11	46	17	12	17	79	61	18	63

HOME
Pos	P	W	D	L	F	A	GD	Pts
9	23	11	4	8	44	29	15	37

AWAY
Pos	P	W	D	L	F	A	GD	Pts
14	23	6	8	9	35	32	3	26

CUP PROGRESS DETAILS
Competition	Round reached	Knocked out by
FA Cup	R1	Bournemouth
JP Trophy	R1	Bournemouth
Carling Cup	R1	Watford

BIGGEST WIN (ALL COMPS)
23/08/08 6–1 v Hereford **FL1**

BIGGEST DEFEAT (ALL COMPS)
02/09/08 0–3 v Bournemouth **FLTS1**

ATTENDANCE RECORD
High	Low	Average
10,293	5,870	7,171
v Leeds (07/03/2009)	v Crewe (27/09/2008)	

RESULTS 2008/09

August
9th	● Carlisle	h	L 2–3	**Att:** 8,285 — **Scorers:** Lambert, Williams
12th	● Watford	a	L 1–0	**Att:** 5,574
16th	● Brighton	a	D 1–1	**Att:** 6,210 — **Scorers:** Lambert. **Booked:** Campbell, Lambert
23rd	● Hereford	h	W 6–1	**Att:** 6,735 — **Scorers:** Duffy², Hughes, Lambert², Lines. **Booked:** Pipe
30th	● Leeds	a	D 2–2	**Att:** 21,024 — **Scorers:** Duffy, Lambert

September
2nd	● Bournemouth	a	L 3–0	**Att:** 2,220 — **Booked:** Anthony
6th	● Peterborough	a	L 5–4	**Att:** 4,876 — **Scorers:** Elliott, Hughes, Lambert, Blackett OG
13th	● Walsall	h	L 1–2	**Att:** 6,609 — **Scorers:** Elliott. **Booked:** Hughes. **Dismissed:** Anthony
16th	● Cheltenham	a	L 2–1	**Att:** 4,546 — **Scorers:** Lambert. **Booked:** Elliott, Lambert
20th	● Yeovil	a	D 2–2	**Att:** 5,748 — **Scorers:** Kuffour, Lambert. **Booked:** Campbell
27th	● Crewe	h	D 0–0	**Att:** 5,870 —**Booked:** Hinton

October
4th	● Colchester	a	W 0–1	**Att:** 4,811 — **Scorers:** Lambert. **Booked:** Lambert, Disley
11th	● Leyton Orient	h	W 2–1	**Att:** 6,425 — **Scorers:** Coles, Hinton. **Booked:** Pipe
18th	● Huddersfield	a	D 1–1	**Att:** 13,779 — **Scorers:** Lambert. **Booked:** Pipe
21st	● Oldham	h	W 2–0	**Att:** 6,379 — **Scorers:** Lambert, Lines. **Booked:** Pipe
25th	● Southend	h	W 4–2	**Att:** 7,055 — **Scorers:** Lambert⁴

November
1st	● Leicester	a	L 2–1	**Att:** 18,941 — **Scorers:** Kuffour. **Booked:** Kuffour, Phillips
8th	● Bournemouth	a	L 1–0	**Att:** 3,935 — **Booked:** Lines, Anthony, Phillips, Hughes. **Dismissed:** Anthony
14th	● Scunthorpe	h	L 1–2	**Att:** 7,173 — **Scorers:** Lambert
22nd	● Swindon	h	D 2–2	**Att:** 8,016 — **Scorers:** Lambert, Lines. **Booked:** R. Green, Lines
25th	● Hartlepool	a	D 1–1	**Att:** 3,171 — **Scorers:** Hughes

December
6th	● Millwall	a	L 3–2	**Att:** 8,123 — **Scorers:** Kuffour, Lambert. **Booked:** Anthony
13th	● Tranmere	h	W 2–0	**Att:** 6,217 — **Scorers:** Kuffour, Lines
20th	● Stockport	a	L 3–1	**Att:** 5,364 — **Scorers:** Disley. **Booked:** Lescott, Pipe
26th	● MK Dons	h	L 1–2	**Att:** 9,002 — **Scorers:** Kuffour. **Booked:** Anthony
28th	● Northampton	a	D 0–0	**Att:** 5,557 — **Booked:** Lescott, Lines, Hughes

January
17th	● Leyton Orient	a	W 1–2	**Att:** 4,262 — **Scorers:** Duffy, Hughes. **Booked:** Elliott, R. Green
24th	● Colchester	h	D 0–0	**Att:** 6,634 — **Booked:** Kuffour
27th	● Cheltenham	h	W 3–2	**Att:** 6,600 — **Scorers:** Duffy, Lambert²
31st	● Southend	a	L 1–0	**Att:** 7,234 —**Booked:** Phillips

February
14th	● Scunthorpe	a	W 0–2	**Att:** 4,156 — **Scorers:** Duffy, Kuffour
17th	● Yeovil	h	W 3–0	**Att:** 8,049 — **Scorers:** Duffy, Lambert, Pipe. **Booked:** Pipe
21st	● Leicester	h	L 0–1	**Att:** 9,138
24th	● Oldham	a	W 0–2	**Att:** 3,745 — **Scorers:** Anthony, Duffy
28th	● Carlisle	a	D 1–1	**Att:** 5,343 — **Scorers:** Hughes

March
7th	● Leeds	h	D 2–2	**Att:** 10,293 — **Scorers:** Hughes, Kuffour. **Booked:** Campbell, R. Green, Lambert
10th	● Hereford	a	W 0–3	**Att:** 3,199 — **Scorers:** Lambert³
14th	● Walsall	a	W 0–5	**Att:** 5,169 — **Scorers:** Disley, Duffy², Lescott²
17th	● Crewe	a	D 1–1	**Att:** 3,879 — **Scorers:** Duffy. **Booked:** Disley
21st	● Peterborough	h	L 0–1	**Att:** 7,103
28th	● Stockport	h	W 2–0	**Att:** 6,214 — **Scorers:** Anthony, Lambert. **Booked:** Jacobson
31st	● Huddersfield	h	L 1–2	**Att:** 6,286 — **Scorers:** Kuffour.

April
5th	● Tranmere	a	L 2–0	**Att:** 8,119 — **Booked:** Hughes, Disley
10th	● Northampton	h	W 1–0	**Att:** 6,666 — **Scorers:** Kuffour. **Booked:** Hughes
13th	● MK Dons	a	L 2–1	**Att:** 10,251 — **Scorers:** Elliott. **Booked:** Anthony, Campbell
18th	● Millwall	h	W 4–2	**Att:** 6,618 — **Scorers:** Disley, Kuffour, Lambert². **Booked:** Anthony, Elliott. **Dismissed:** Elliott
21st	● Brighton	h	L 1–2	**Att:** 6,193 — **Scorers:** Lambert. **Booked:** Kuffour, Phillips, Pipe, Campbell
25th	● Swindon	a	L 2–1	**Att:** 10,977 — **Scorers:** Duffy

May
2nd	● Hartlepool	h	W 4–1	**Att:** 7,363 — **Scorers:** Duffy, Kuffour, Lambert, Lescott

● Coca-Cola League 1/Play-Offs ● FA Cup ● Carling Cup ● Johnstone's Paint Trophy

LEAGUE ONE GOALKEEPER STATS

Player	Appearances	Match starts	Completed matches	Sub appearances	Subbed off	Clean sheets	Yellow cards	Red cards
Steve Phillips	46	46	46	0	0	13	3	0

LEAGUE ONE OUTFIELD PLAYER STATS

Player	Appearances	Match starts	Completed matches	Substitute appearances	Subbed off	Goals scored	Yellow cards	Red cards
Byron Anthony	30	29	27	1	1	2	4	1
Stuart Campbell	44	42	42	2	0	0	5	0
Danny Coles	5	5	3	0	2	1	0	0
Craig Disley	44	33	27	11	6	3	3	0
Darryl Duffy	43	28	11	15	17	13	0	0
Steve Elliott	39	39	37	0	1	3	3	1
Ryan Green	26	23	22	3	1	0	3	0
Craig Hinton	25	19	18	6	1	1	1	0
Jeff Hughes	43	43	23	0	20	6	4	0
Ben Hunt	12	0	0	12	0	0	0	0
Joe Jacobson	22	6	4	16	2	0	1	0
Jo Kuffour	41	26	14	15	12	11	3	0
Rickie Lambert	45	43	36	2	7	29	4	0
Aaron Lescott	44	43	38	1	5	3	2	0
Chris Lines	45	44	32	1	11	4	2	1
David Pipe	39	36	23	3	13	1	7	0
Charles Reece	1	1	0	0	1	0	0	0
Sean Rigg	8	0	0	8	0	0	0	0
Andrew Williams	4	0	0	4	0	1	0	0

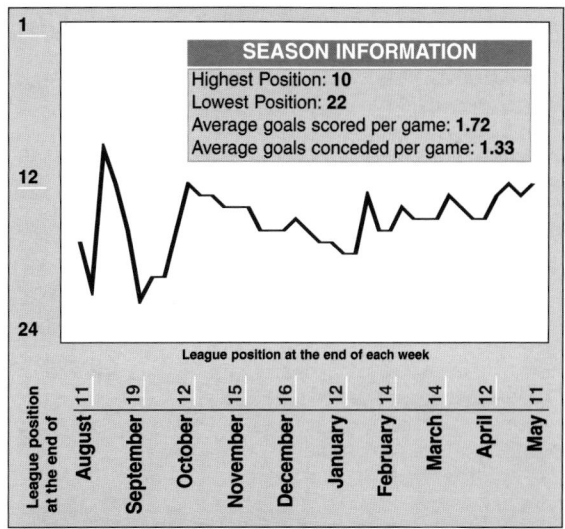

SEASON INFORMATION

Highest Position: **10**
Lowest Position: **22**
Average goals scored per game: **1.72**
Average goals conceded per game: **1.33**

League position at the end of each week

League position at the end of	August 11	September 19	October 12	November 15	December 16	January 12	February 14	March 14	April 12	May 11

LONGEST SEQUENCES

Wins (on four occasions)	2	Undefeated home (27/09/08–25/10/08)	4
Losses (06/09/08–16/09/08)	3	Undefeated away (14/02/09–17/03/09)	6
Draws (on three occasions)	2	Without scoring (–)	
Undefeated (20/09/08–25/10/08)	7	Without conceding (on three occasions)	2
Without win (30/08/08–27/09/08)	6	Scoring (04/10/08–26/12/08)	13

CARDS RECEIVED

45   **3**

QUICK-FIRE GOALS

From the start of a match
Darryl Duffy (v Walsall) 2:16

By a substitute after coming on
Jo Kuffour (v Yeovil) 2:00

GOALS SCORED/CONCEDED PER FIVE-MINUTE INTERVALS

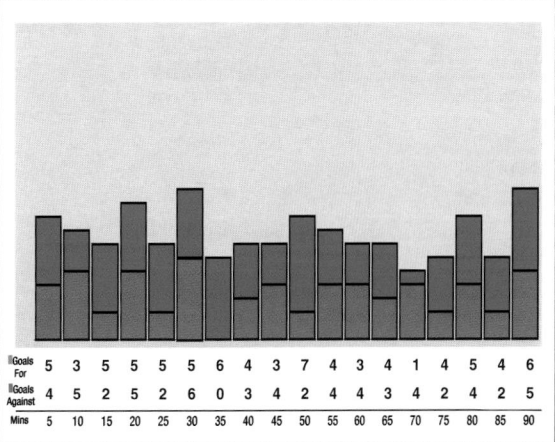

Goals For	5	3	5	5	5	6	4	3	7	4	3	4	1	4	5	4	6
Goals Against	4	5	2	5	2	6	0	3	4	2	4	4	3	4	2	4	2	5
Mins	5	10	15	20	25	30	35	40	45	50	55	60	65	70	75	80	85	90

CARLISLE UNITED

AFTER the heartbreaking 2007/08 play-off semi-final defeat at the hands of Leeds, John Ward's Carlisle went into the new season determined to emulate the previous term's achievements.

Boosted by the return of local hero Michael Bridges on a season-long loan from Hull, the Cumbrians started well, winning four and drawing one of their opening five fixtures as Danny Graham scored six goals.

However, the season soon turned sour, and after a nine-game winless streak, boss Ward was replaced by his assistant Greg Abbott with the team languishing in 20th position.

Graham continued his fine scoring form, registering 15 league goals, but the Cumbrians were forced to rely on a dramatic 2–0 final-day victory over Millwall to ensure their Coca-Cola League One survival.

CLUB SUMMARY

FORMED	1903
MANAGER	Greg Abbott
GROUND	Brunton Park
CAPACITY	16,651
NICKNAME	The Cumbrians
WEBSITE	www.carlisleunited.co.uk

Cleveland Taylor
PLAYER OF THE SEASON

OVERALL
P	W	D	L	F	A	GD
52	14	16	22	62	78	-16

COCA-COLA FOOTBALL LEAGUE ONE
Pos	P	W	D	L	F	A	GD	Pts
20	46	12	14	20	56	69	-13	50

HOME
Pos	P	W	D	L	F	A	GD	Pts
16	23	8	7	8	36	32	4	31

AWAY
Pos	P	W	D	L	F	A	GD	Pts
19	23	4	7	12	20	37	-17	19

CUP PROGRESS DETAILS
Competition	Round reached	Knocked out by
FA Cup	R2	Crewe
JP Trophy	R2	Rochdale
Carling Cup	R2	QPR

BIGGEST WIN (ALL COMPS)
30/08/08 4–1 v Yeovil **FL1**

BIGGEST DEFEAT (ALL COMPS)
25/10/08 0–5 v Colchester **FL1**

ATTENDANCE RECORD
High	Low	Average
12,148	4,223	6,268
v Leeds (20/09/2008)	v Hereford (24/03/2009)	

RESULTS 2008/09

August
9th	● Bristol Rovers	..a	W 2–3	Att: 8,285 — **Scorers:** Bridge-Wilkinson, Carlton[2]. **Booked:** Thirlwell
12th	● Shrewsbury	......a	W 0–1	Att: 3,337 — **Scorers:** Murphy
16th	● Crewe	.............h	W 4–2	Att: 6,919 — **Scorers:** Dobie, Graham[2], Hackney
23rd	● Leyton Orient	....a	D 0–0	Att: 3,803 — **Booked:** Bridge-Wilkinson, Thirlwell, Bridges. **Dismissed:** Dobie
26th	● QPR	...............a	L 4–0	Att: 8,021
30th	● Yeovil	.................h	W 4–1	Att: 6,286 — **Scorers:** Graham[3], Madine

September
6th	● Southend	...........h	W 2–1	Att: 6,561 — **Scorers:** Graham, Taylor. **Booked:** Raven, Thirlwell, Horwood
13th	● Scunthorpe	......a	L 2–1	Att: 5,188 — **Scorers:** Carlton
20th	● Leeds	.................h	L 0–2	Att: 12,148
27th	● Walsall	...............a	L 2–1	Att: 4,830 — **Scorers:** Bridge-Wilkinson. **Booked:** Thirlwell, Myrie-Williams

October
4th	● Tranmere	...........h	L 1–2	Att: 6,093 — **Scorers:** Graham. **Booked:** Thirlwell
7th	● Rochdale	..........a	D 2–2	Att: 1,608 — **Scorers:** Bridges, Madine (Won 4–3 on pens)
11th	● MK Dons	...........a	L 3–1	Att: 11,194 — **Scorers:** Graham
18th	● Peterborough	....h	D 3–3	Att: 6,074 — **Scorers:** Graham[2], Kavanagh. **Booked:** Horwood, Keogh
21st	● Hereford	...........a	L 1–0	Att: 2,300 — **Dismissed:** Keogh
25th	● Colchester	.......a	L 5–0	Att: 5,152 — **Booked:** Gowling
28th	● Hartlepool	.......h	L 0–1	Att: 5,637 — **Booked:** Dobie

November
1st	● Stockport	.........a	L 3–0	Att: 6,301
8th	● Grays Athletic	..h	D 1–1	Att: 3,921 — **Scorers:** Madine
15th	● Brighton	.............h	W 3–1	Att: 5,333 — **Scorers:** Bridge-Wilkinson[2], Taylor. **Booked:** Keogh, C. Taylor
22nd	● Cheltenham	......h	W 1–0	Att: 5,374 — **Scorers:** Kavanagh. **Booked:** Kavanagh
25th	● Millwall	..............a	L 1–0	Att: 6,828 — **Booked:** Keogh
29th	● Grays Athletic	..a	W 0–2	Att: 1,217 — **Scorers:** Graham, Kavanagh. **Booked:** Kavanagh

December
3rd	● Crewe	.............h	L 0–2	Att: 2,755
6th	● Swindon	...........a	D 1–1	Att: 6,787 — **Scorers:** Thirlwell
13th	● Leicester	...........h	L 1–2	Att: 7,085 — **Scorers:** Graham. **Booked:** Krul, Bridges, C. Taylor
20th	● Northampton	....a	L 1–0	Att: 4,673 — **Booked:** Bridges
26th	● Huddersfield	......h	W 3–0	Att: 7,883 — **Scorers:** Bridges, Graham, Kavanagh
28th	● Oldham	............a	D 0–0	Att: 6,254

January
10th	● Leeds	.................a	W 0–2	Att: 22,411 — **Scorers:** Bridges, Graham. **Booked:** J. Smith, Thirlwell, Graham, Kavanagh
17th	● MK Dons	.........h	W 3–2	Att: 6,298 — **Scorers:** Anyinsah, Graham, Thirlwell. **Booked:** Graham, Liddle, Kavanagh, Livesey
24th	● Tranmere	.......a	L 4–1	Att: 5,924 — **Scorers:** Graham
27th	● Hartlepool	.......a	D 2–2	Att: 3,765 — **Scorers:** Bridge-Wilkinson, Taylor. **Booked:** Kavanagh, Anyinsah, Graham
31st	● Colchester	.......h	L 0–2	Att: 5,745 — **Booked:** Kavanagh

February
10th	● Walsall	..............h	D 1–1	Att: 4,502 — **Scorers:** Thirlwell
14th	● Brighton	...........a	W 0–2	Att: 5,529 — **Scorers:** Anyinsah, Keogh. **Booked:** Kane, Murphy, Anyinsah, Bridges
21st	● Stockport	.........h	L 1–2	Att: 5,930 — **Scorers:** Neal. **Booked:** Kane
24th	● Peterborough	....a	L 1–0	Att: 5,103
28th	● Bristol Rovers	..h	D 1–1	Att: 5,343 — **Scorers:** Kavanagh. **Booked:** Keogh

March
3rd	● Crewe	.............a	W 1–2	Att: 3,759 — **Scorers:** Anyinsah, Taylor. **Booked:** Raven, Kavanagh
7th	● Yeovil	.................a	D 1–1	Att: 3,892 — **Scorers:** Bridges. **Booked:** Raven
10th	● Leyton Orient	....h	L 1–3	Att: 4,536 — **Scorers:** Dobie.
14th	● Scunthorpe	......h	D 1–1	Att: 4,867 — **Scorers:** Anyinsah. **Booked:** Kane
21st	● Southend	...........a	L 3–0	Att: 7,789 — **Booked:** Murphy, C. Taylor, Kavanagh
24th	● Hereford	...........h	L 1–2	Att: 4,223 — **Scorers:** Bridges. **Booked:** Kavanagh, G. Taylor
28th	● Northampton	....h	D 1–1	Att: 5,254 — **Scorers:** Neal. **Booked:** Morris

April
4th	● Leicester	...........a	D 2–2	Att: 20,159 — **Scorers:** Bridges, Dobie
10th	● Oldham	............h	D 1–1	Att: 6,635 — **Scorers:** Bridges. **Booked:** Keogh, Kavanagh
13th	● Huddersfield	......a	L 1–0	Att: 12,309
18th	● Swindon	...........h	D 1–1	Att: 5,959 — **Scorers:** Bridges. **Booked:** Lumsdon
25th	● Cheltenham	......a	D 1–1	Att: 4,290 — **Scorers:** Harte. **Booked:** Horwood. **Dismissed:** Horwood, Bridges

May
2nd	● Millwall	..............h	W 2–0	Att: 9,470 — **Scorers:** Kavanagh, Thirlwell. **Booked:** Murphy

● Coca-Cola League 1/Play-Offs ● FA Cup ● Carling Cup ● Johnstone's Paint Trophy

LEAGUE ONE GOALKEEPER STATS

Player	Appearances	Match starts	Completed matches	Sub appearances	Subbed off	Clean sheets	Yellow cards	Red cards
Ben Alnwick	6	6	6	0	0	0	0	0
Tim Krul	9	9	9	0	0	4	1	0
Ben Williams	31	31	31	0	0	3	0	0

LEAGUE ONE OUTFIELD PLAYER STATS

Player	Appearances	Match starts	Completed matches	Substitute appearances	Subbed off	Goals scored	Yellow cards	Red cards
Joe Anyinsah	19	16	7	3	9	4	2	0
Chris Birchall	2	0	0	2	0	0	0	0
Marc Bridge-Wilkinson	23	20	14	3	6	5	1	0
Michael Bridges	30	12	5	18	6	7	4	1
Michael Burns	1	0	0	1	0	0	0	0
Darren Campion	2	2	1	0	1	0	0	0
Danny Carlton	12	12	4	0	8	3	0	0
Scott Dobie	30	11	2	19	8	3	1	1
Josh Gowling	4	3	3	1	0	0	1	0
Danny Graham	44	39	24	5	15	15	3	0
Simon Hackney	22	16	9	6	7	1	0	0
Ian Harte	3	3	3	0	0	1	0	0
Evan Horwood	24	22	17	2	4	0	3	1
Luke Joyce	7	4	2	3	2	0	0	0
Tony Kane	9	6	6	3	0	0	3	0
Graham Kavanagh	34	34	32	0	2	5	9	0
Richard Keogh	32	31	30	1	0	1	5	1
Michael Liddle	22	21	19	1	2	0	1	0
Danny Livesey	27	27	27	0	0	0	1	0
Chris Lumsdon	6	4	1	2	3	0	1	0
Gary Madine	14	0	0	14	0	1	0	0
Ian Morris	6	4	3	2	1	0	1	0
Peter Murphy	28	27	25	1	2	0	3	0
Jennison Myrie-Williams	8	1	0	7	1	0	1	0
Lewis Neal	16	15	9	1	6	2	0	0
David Raven	41	41	39	0	2	0	3	0
Gavin Rothery	1	0	0	1	0	0	0	0
Grant Smith	1	1	0	0	1	0	0	0
Jeff Smith	16	11	5	5	6	0	1	0
Cleveland Taylor	42	37	26	5	11	3	3	0
Gareth Taylor	5	5	2	0	3	1	1	0
Paul Thirlwell	34	33	29	1	4	4	6	0
John Welsh	4	2	2	2	0	0	0	0

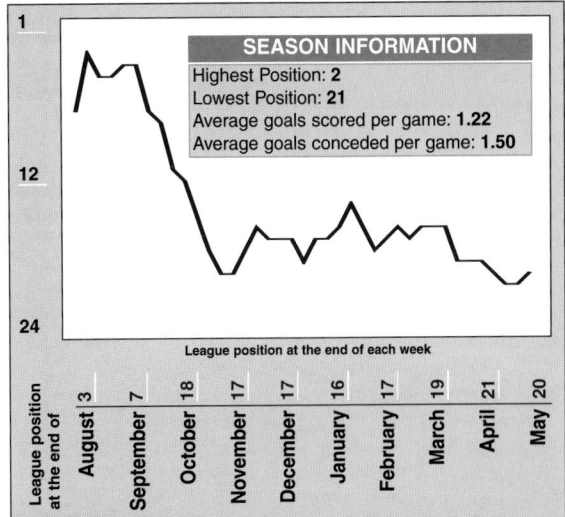

SEASON INFORMATION
Highest Position: **2**
Lowest Position: **21**
Average goals scored per game: **1.22**
Average goals conceded per game: **1.50**

League position at the end of each week

LONGEST SEQUENCES

Wins (on four occasions)	2	Undefeated home (09/08/08–06/09/08)	4
Losses (13/09/08–11/10/08)	5	Undefeated away (on four occasions)	2
Draws (28/03/09–10/04/09)	3	Without scoring (21/10/08–01/11/08)	4
Undefeated (09/08/08–06/09/08)	5	Without conceding (26/12/08–10/01/09)	3
Without win (07/03/09–25/04/09)	11	Scoring (28/02/09–14/03/09)	5

CARDS RECEIVED

55   4

QUICK-FIRE GOALS

From the start of a match
Danny Graham (v MK Dons) 3:20

By a substitute after coming on
Gary Madine (v Yeovil) 4:45

GOALS SCORED/CONCEDED PER FIVE-MINUTE INTERVALS

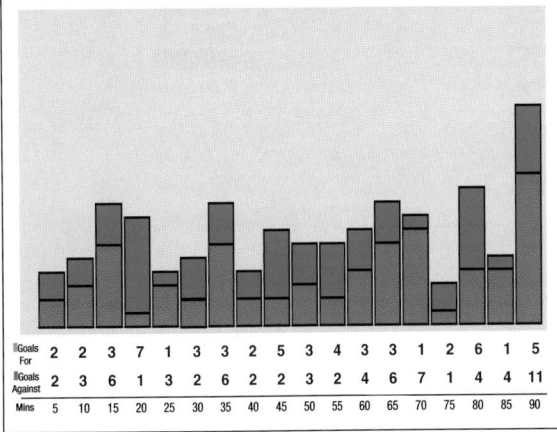

Goals For	2	2	3	7	1	3	3	2	5	3	4	3	3	1	2	6	1	5
Goals Against	2	3	6	1	3	2	6	2	2	3	2	4	6	7	1	4	4	11
Mins	5	10	15	20	25	30	35	40	45	50	55	60	65	70	75	80	85	90

CHELTENHAM TOWN

CHELTENHAM fans will not want to look back on the 2008/09 season in a hurry. The Robins went into the campaign with high hopes of a strong mid-table finish, having avoided relegation for the two previous years since their promotion.

However, the club lost five of their opening six matches and manager Keith Downing departed 'by mutual consent' in September. Martin Allen took over the reins but could not reverse the slump and, despite using 50 different players, Cheltenham were relegated back to Coca-Cola League Two.

The club have also struggled financially and were forced to offload several key players in an attempt to stave off administration. Whaddon Road has been renamed Abbey Business Stadium, with many fans now unsure of what to expect in 2009/10.

CLUB SUMMARY

FORMED	1892
MANAGER	Martin Allen
GROUND	Abbey Business Stadium
CAPACITY	7,066
NICKNAME	The Robins
WEBSITE	www.ctfc.com

PLAYER OF THE SEASON — **David Bird**

OVERALL

P	W	D	L	F	A	GD
54	12	14	28	61	103	-42

COCA-COLA FOOTBALL LEAGUE ONE

Pos	P	W	D	L	F	A	GD	Pts
23	46	9	12	25	51	91	-40	39

HOME

Pos	P	W	D	L	F	A	GD	Pts
20	23	7	6	10	30	38	-8	27

AWAY

Pos	P	W	D	L	F	A	GD	Pts
23	23	2	6	15	21	53	-32	12

CUP PROGRESS DETAILS

Competition	Round reached	Knocked out by
FA Cup	R3	Doncaster
JP Trophy	R2	Walsall
Carling Cup	R2	Stoke

BIGGEST WIN (ALL COMPS)
2–0 on two occasions

BIGGEST DEFEAT (ALL COMPS)
0–4 on three occasions

ATTENDANCE RECORD

High	Low	Average
5,726	2,845	3,854
v Leeds (01/11/2008)	v Tranmere (17/03/2009)	

RESULTS 2008/09

August
9th	● Northampton	a	L 4–2	Att: 4,716 — **Scorers:** Townsend, Gyepes OG. **Booked:** J. Gill
12th	● Southend	a	W 0–1	Att: 2,998 — **Scorers:** Gill. **Booked:** J. Gill, Connor (AET)
16th	● Swindon	h	W 2–0	Att: 4,975 — **Scorers:** Gill, Myrie–Williams. **Booked:** B. Gill **Dismissed:** B. Gill
23rd	● Oldham	a	L 4–0	Att: 4,673
26th	● Stoke	h	L 2–3	Att: 3,600 — **Scorers:** Russell, Vincent. **Booked:** Armstrong
30th	● Leicester	h	L 0–4	Att: 5,344 — **Booked:** Vincent, J. Gill

September
6th	● Huddersfield	h	L 1–2	Att: 3,587 — **Scorers:** Owusu. **Booked:** Caines, Hayles
12th	● Hartlepool	a	L 4–1	Att: 3,637 — **Scorers:** Owusu
16th	● Bristol Rovers	.h	W 2–1	Att: 4,546 — **Scorers:** Hayles². **Booked:** Murray, Caines, Low, Vincent
20th	● Millwall	a	L 2–0	Att: 8,009 — **Booked:** Owusu. **Dismissed:** Hayles
27th	● Stockport	h	D 2–2	Att: 3,796 — **Scorers:** Fleetwood, Payne. **Booked:** Townsend

October
4th	● Brighton	a	D 3–3	Att: 5,859 — **Scorers:** Gallinagh, Murray². **Booked:** Russell, Payne. **Dismissed:** Payne
7th	● Walsall	h	L 1–2	Att: 1,741 — **Scorers:** Low. **Booked:** Lindegaard
11th	● Colchester	h	W 4–3	Att: 3,580 — **Scorers:** Fleetwood, Hayles, Kenton, Owusu. **Booked:** Diallo
18th	● Scunthorpe	h	L 1–2	Att: 3,682 — **Scorers:** Connor. **Booked:** Wesolowski, Kenton
21st	● Tranmere	a	L 2–0	Att: 4,535 — **Booked:** Ridley
25th	● MK Dons	a	L 3–1	Att: 8,190 — **Booked:** Caines, Payne, Owusu, Westlake. **Dismissed:** Owusu

November
1st	● Leeds	h	L 0–1	Att: 5,726 — **Booked:** Diallo
8th	● Oldham	h	D 2–2	Att: 2,585 — **Scorers:** Murray, Owusu. **Booked:** Montrose
15th	● Hereford	a	L 3–0	Att: 3,761
18th	● Oldham	h	W 0–1	Att: 2,552 — **Scorers:** Montrose. **Booked:** Montrose
22nd	● Carlisle	a	L 1–0	Att: 5,374 — **Booked:** Vincent
25th	● Southend	h	D 0–0	Att: 2,908
29th	● Morecambe	a	A–A	Att: 1,984 — **Scorers:** Hayles. **Booked:** Brown

December
2nd	● Morecambe	a	W 2–3	Att: 1,758 — **Scorers:** Finnigan, Vincent². **Booked:** Payne, Diallo
6th	● Crewe	h	W 1–0	Att: 4,052 — **Scorers:** Diallo
13th	● Leyton Orient	a	W 1–2	Att: 4,510 — **Scorers:** Hayles, Westlake. **Booked:** Vincent, Payne. **Dismissed:** Vincent
20th	● Walsall	h	D 0–0	Att: 3,656
26th	● Yeovil	a	D 1–1	Att: 4,989 — **Scorers:** Vincent. **Booked:** Lindegaard
28th	● Peterborough	h	L 3–6	Att: 3,976 — **Scorers:** Hammond, Owusu, Vincent. **Booked:** Ridley. **Dismissed:** Hayles

January
13th	● Doncaster	h	D 0–0	Att: 4,417 — **Booked:** Lindegaard, Owusu
17th	● Colchester	a	L 3–1	Att: 4,183 — **Scorers:** Westwood. **Booked:** Montrose, Finnigan. **Dismissed:** Finnigan
20th	● Doncaster	a	L 3–0	Att: 5,345 — **Booked:** Vincent
24th	● Brighton	h	D 2–2	Att: 3,597 — **Scorers:** Westlake, Westwood. **Booked:** Russell
27th	● Bristol Rovers	a	L 3–2	Att: 6,600 — **Scorers:** Owusu, Vincent. **Booked:** Westlake
31st	● MK Dons	h	L 3–5	Att: 3,681 — **Scorers:** Spencer³. **Booked:** Owusu. **Dismissed:** Spencer

February
14th	● Hereford	h	L 2–3	Att: 4,660 — **Scorers:** Owusu². **Booked:** Westwood. **Dismissed:** Ridley
17th	● Stockport	a	L 1–0	Att: 5,041 — **Booked:** Westlake
21st	● Leeds	a	L 2–0	Att: 20,131 — **Booked:** Townsend
24th	● Millwall	h	L 1–3	Att: 2,942 — **Scorers:** Duffy OG. **Booked:** Finnigan
28th	● Northampton	h	L 0–1	Att: 3,495

March
3rd	● Swindon	a	D 2–2	Att: 6,293 — **Scorers:** Hammond²
7th	● Leicester	a	L 4–0	Att: 18,939 — **Booked:** Gallinagh
14th	● Hartlepool	h	W 2–0	Att: 2,945 — **Scorers:** Bignall, Hammond. **Booked:** Brown
17th	● Tranmere	h	W 1–0	Att: 2,845 — **Scorers:** Bird
21st	● Huddersfield	a	D 2–2	Att: 11,516 — **Scorers:** Constantine, Hammond. **Booked:** Brown. **Dismissed:** Low
24th	● Oldham	h	D 1–1	Att: 2,992 — **Scorers:** Artus. **Booked:** Wright, Diallo
28th	● Walsall	a	D 1–1	Att: 4,101 — **Scorers:** Artus. **Booked:** Townsend, Berchiche

April
4th	● Leyton Orient	h	L 0–1	Att: 3,594 — **Booked:** Hammond
10th	● Peterborough	a	D 1–1	Att: 9,817 — **Scorers:** Hutton
13th	● Yeovil	h	W 1–0	Att: 3,775 — **Scorers:** Artus. **Booked:** Diallo, Antonio
18th	● Crewe	a	L 2–1	Att: 4,542 — **Scorers:** Connor, Finnigan. **Booked:** Artus, Finnigan
25th	● Carlisle	h	D 1–1	Att: 4,290 — **Scorers:** Diallo. **Booked:** Townsend, Watkins, Artus, Ridley.
28th	● Scunthorpe	a	L 3–0	Att: 3,635 — **Booked:** Artus, Berchiche

May
2nd	● Southend	a	L 2–0	Att: 8,192 — **Booked:** Berchiche

● Coca-Cola League 1/Play-Offs ● FA Cup ● Carling Cup ● Johnstone's Paint Trophy

LEAGUE ONE GOALKEEPER STATS

Player	Appearances	Match starts	Completed matches	Sub appearances	Subbed off	Clean sheets	Yellow cards	Red cards
Scott P Brown	35	35	35	0	0	7	2	0
Shane Higgs	10	10	10	0	0	0	0	0
Will Puddy	1	1	1	0	0	0	0	0

LEAGUE ONE OUTFIELD PLAYER STATS

Player	Appearances	Match starts	Completed matches	Substitute appearances	Subbed off	Goals scored	Yellow cards	Red cards
Michail Antonio	9	7	2	2	5	0	1	0
Craig Armstrong	5	3	0	2	3	0	0	0
Frankie Artus	9	9	8	0	1	3	3	0
Yuri Berchiche	7	7	4	0	3	0	3	0
Nicholas Bignall	13	8	4	5	4	1	0	0
David Bird	27	24	18	3	6	1	0	0
Gavin Caines	8	5	5	3	0	1	2	0
Paul Connor	25	18	10	7	8	2	0	0
Leon Constantine	6	4	2	2	2	1	0	0
Drissa Diallo	27	27	24	0	3	2	4	0
Shane Duff	20	18	16	2	2	0	0	0
Jack Durrant	4	0	0	4	0	0	0	0
Josh Emery	1	0	0	1	0	0	0	0
John Finnigan	17	13	2	4	10	1	3	1
Stuart Fleetwood	6	6	2	0	4	2	0	0
Andy Gallinagh	39	30	25	9	5	1	1	0
Ben Gill	5	0	0	5	0	1	1	1
Jeremy Gill	6	6	6	0	0	0	2	0
Elvis Hammond	22	17	7	5	10	5	1	0
Jonathan Hayes	6	3	1	3	2	0	0	0
Barry Hayles	12	11	4	1	5	4	1	2
Kyle Haynes	4	2	0	2	2	0	0	0
Ashley Hemmings	1	0	0	1	0	0	0	0
David Hutton	7	5	4	2	1	1	0	0
Darren Kenton	13	13	10	0	3	1	1	0
Aaron Ledgister	1	0	0	1	0	0	0	0
Jake Lee	3	2	0	1	2	0	0	0
Theo Lewis	2	0	0	2	0	0	0	0
Andy Lindegaard	15	11	9	4	2	0	1	0
Joshua Low	14	13	7	1	5	0	1	1
Lewis Montrose	5	5	2	0	3	0	1	0
Scott Murray	13	12	9	1	3	2	1	0
Jennison Myrie-Williams	5	5	4	0	1	1	0	0
Lloyd Owusu	22	16	10	6	5	7	3	1
Josh Payne	11	9	4	2	4	1	3	1
Lee Ridley	27	24	21	3	2	0	3	1
Lathanial Rowe-Turner	1	1	1	0	0	0	0	0
Alex Russell	23	19	18	4	1	0	2	0
Dean Sinclair	3	2	1	1	1	0	0	0
Damian Spencer	14	5	1	9	3	3	0	1
Michael Townsend	26	23	22	3	1	1	4	0
Ashley Vincent	29	16	10	13	5	3	4	1
Marley Watkins	12	4	3	8	1	0	1	0
James Wesolowski	4	4	3	0	1	0	1	0
Ian Westlake	22	22	21	0	1	2	3	0
Chris Westwood	9	9	9	0	0	2	1	0
Alan Wright	23	22	19	1	3	0	1	0

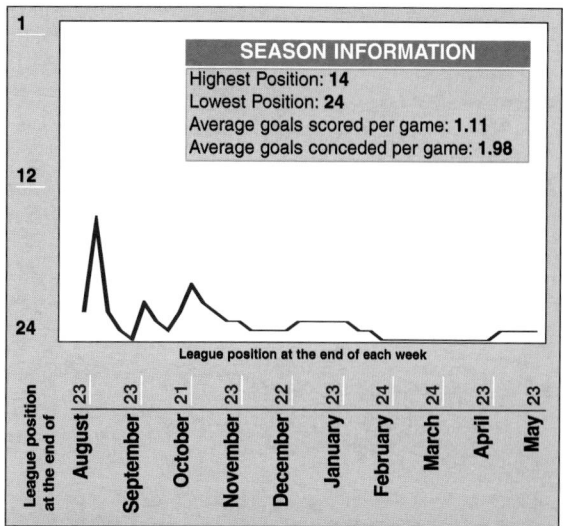

SEASON INFORMATION
Highest Position: **14**
Lowest Position: **24**
Average goals scored per game: **1.11**
Average goals conceded per game: **1.98**

League position at the end of each week

LONGEST SEQUENCES

Wins	2	Undefeated home	3
(on three occasions)		(16/09/08–11/10/08)	
Losses	7	Undefeated away	4
(27/01/09–28/02/09)		(21/03/09–18/04/09)	
Draws	3	Without scoring	4
(21/03/09–28/03/09)		(01/11/08–25/11/08)	
Undefeated	5	Without conceding	2
(on two occasions)		(on two occasions)	
Without win	14	Scoring	7
(20/12/08–07/03/09)		(26/12/08–14/02/09)	

CARDS RECEIVED

55 10

QUICK-FIRE GOALS

From the start of a match
Scott Murray (v Brighton) 1:58

By a substitute after coming on
John Finnigan (v Crewe) 3:40

GOALS SCORED/CONCEDED PER FIVE-MINUTE INTERVALS

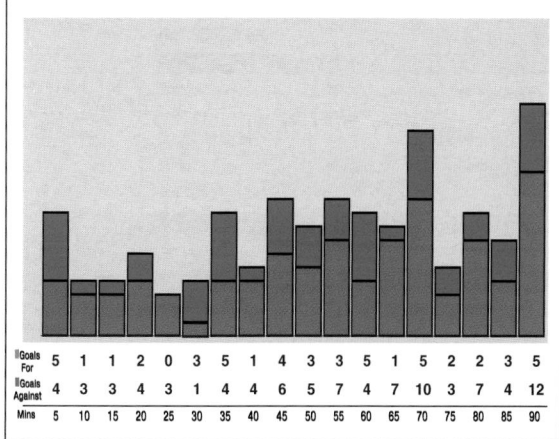

Goals For	5	1	1	2	0	3	5	1	4	3	3	5	1	5	2	2	3	5
Goals Against	4	3	4	3	1	4	4	6	5	7	4	7	10	3	7	4	12	
Mins	5	10	15	20	25	30	35	40	45	50	55	60	65	70	75	80	85	90

COLCHESTER UNITED

COLCHESTER flirted with relegation and promotion before finding their level somewhere in between during a topsy-turvy season in Essex.

A miserable start, which saw them fail to register a win in their first six games at their new Weston Homes Community Stadium, left the U's in the drop zone and accounted for the departure of manager Geraint Williams.

Paul Lambert was recruited in October and oversaw a major improvement, with a nine-game unbeaten run around the turn of the year prompting talk of a late push for the play-offs.

In the end they fell short, but a 12th-place finish offers hope of a successful campaign next time. Lambert will make changes, but Pat Baldwin looks solid at the back, Mark Yeates continues to impress in midfield and Steven Gillespie will hope for an injury-free season.

CLUB SUMMARY

FORMED	1937
MANAGER	Paul Lambert
GROUND	Community Stadium
CAPACITY	10,000
NICKNAME	The U's
WEBSITE	www.cu-fc.com

The New Football Pools PLAYER OF THE SEASON

Dean Hammond

OVERALL

P	W	D	L	F	A	GD
53	22	9	22	63	62	1

COCA-COLA FOOTBALL LEAGUE ONE

Pos	P	W	D	L	F	A	GD	Pts
12	46	18	9	19	58	58	0	63

HOME

Pos	P	W	D	L	F	A	GD	Pts
21	23	7	4	12	21	24	-3	25

AWAY

Pos	P	W	D	L	F	A	GD	Pts
5	23	11	5	7	37	34	3	38

CUP PROGRESS DETAILS

Competition	Round reached	Knocked out by
FA Cup	R1	Leyton Orient
JP Trophy	SF	Luton
Carling Cup	R2	Ipswich

BIGGEST WIN (ALL COMPS)

25/10/08 5–0 v Carlisle **FL1**

BIGGEST DEFEAT (ALL COMPS)

0–3 on two occasions

ATTENDANCE RECORD

High	Low	Average
9,559	3,179	5,084

v Leeds (04/04/2009)   v Stockport (24/02/2009)

RESULTS 2008/09

August
9th	● Hartlepool	a	L 4–2	Att: 3,831 — Scorers: Gillespie²
12th	● Gillingham	a	W 0–1	Att: 2,566 — Scorers: Heath. Booked: Reid, Heath
16th	● Huddersfield	h	D 0–0	Att: 5,340 — Booked: M. Lockwood
23rd	● Swindon	a	W 1–3	Att: 7,031 — Scorers: Jackson, Vernon, Wasiu. Booked: Wordsworth, Izzet
26th	● Ipswich	a	L 2–1	Att: 17,084 — Scorers: Gillespie. Booked: Coyne
30th	● Oldham	h	D 2–2	Att: 4,708 — Scorers: Yeates². Booked: White, Yeates, Wordsworth, Perkins

September
2nd	● Millwall	a	W 0–1	Att: 2,456 — Scorers: Perkins. Booked: White, Elito
13th	● Crewe	a	L 2–0	Att: 3,510 — Booked: Ifil, Heath, Platt, Hammond. Dismissed: Gillespie
20th	● MK Dons	h	L 0–3	Att: 4,888
26th	● Tranmere	a	W 3–4	Att: 5,713 — Scorers: Jackson, Perkins, Platt, Yeates. Booked: Gerken, Hammond
30th	● Leicester	h	L 0–1	Att: 5,133 — Booked: Platt

October
4th	● Bristol Rovers	h	L 0–1	Att: 4,811 — Booked: Reid
7th	● Gillingham	a	W 0–1	Att: 1,557 — Scorers: Yeates
11th	● Cheltenham	a	L 4–3	Att: 3,580 — Scorers: Jackson, Wordsworth². Booked: Yeates, Borrowdale, Heath
18th	● Stockport	a	W 1–2	Att: 6,025 — Scorers: Perkins, Platt. Booked: Hammond, Reid, Jackson, Wordsworth
21st	● Millwall	h	L 1–2	Att: 5,506 — Scorers: Izzet. Booked: Hammond, White
25th	● Carlisle	h	W 5–0	Att: 5,152 — Scorers: Hammond, Perkins, Wasiu, Yeates²

November
1st	● Southend	a	D 3–3	Att: 8,920 — Scorers: Jackson, Wordsworth, Yeates. Booked: Coyne, Hammond, Jackson, Wordsworth, A. Wasiu
4th	● Bournemouth	a	W 0–1	Att: 2,275 — Scorers: Williams. Booked: Ifil, Heath
8th	● Leyton Orient	h	L 0–1	Att: 4,600 — Booked: Platt, Yeates
15th	● Walsall	h	L 0–2	Att: 4,071
22nd	● Peterborough	a	L 2–1	Att: 7,401 — Scorers: Platt. Booked: Jackson, Wordsworth
25th	● Yeovil	h	W 1–0	Att: 3,214 — Scorers: Easter. Booked: Hammond, Easter
29th	● Northampton	a	W 1–2	Att: 4,833 — Scorers: Platt, Reid. Booked: Baldwin, Platt, Easter

December
6th	● Hereford	h	L 1–2	Att: 4,794 — Scorers: Easter. Booked: Hammond
13th	● Leeds	a	W 1–2	Att: 19,625 — Scorers: Hammond, Yeates. Booked: Reid
16th	● Luton	a	L 1–0	Att: 2,638 — Booked: Wordsworth, Maybury
20th	● Scunthorpe	h	D 0–0	Att: 4,606 — Booked: Yeates
26th	● Brighton	a	W 1–2	Att: 6,299 — Scorers: Vernon, Hinshelwood OG. Booked: Tierney
28th	● Leyton Orient	h	W 1–0	Att: 6,290 — Scorers: Gillespie. Booked: Tierney, Izzet, Maybury

January
12th	● MK Dons	a	D 1–1	Att: 8,408 — Scorers: Platt. Booked: Izzet
17th	● Cheltenham	h	W 3–1	Att: 4,183 — Scorers: Gillespie, Hammond, Yeates. Booked: Gillespie
24th	● Bristol Rovers	a	D 0–0	Att: 6,634 — Booked: Tierney, Wordsworth, Izzet, Platt
27th	● Northampton	h	W 2–1	Att: 3,973 — Scorers: Vernon, Yeates. Booked: Baldwin
31st	● Carlisle	a	W 0–2	Att: 5,745 — Scorers: Perkins, Livesey OG. Booked: Izzet

February
10th	● Tranmere	h	L 0–1	Att: 3,588 — Booked: Gobern, Reid
14th	● Walsall	a	L 2–0	Att: 3,719
21st	● Southend	h	L 0–1	Att: 8,651 — Booked: Maybury, Hammond
24th	● Stockport	h	W 1–0	Att: 3,179 — Scorers: Tierney. Booked: Platt
28th	● Hartlepool	h	D 1–1	Att: 5,158 — Scorers: Vernon. Booked: Maybury

March
3rd	● Huddersfield	a	D 2–2	Att: 10,580 — Scorers: Hammond². Booked: Platt, Hackney, Hammond, Maybury
7th	● Oldham	a	W 0–1	Att: 4,591 — Scorers: Platt. Booked: Izzet, Gillespie
10th	● Swindon	h	W 3–2	Att: 3,827 — Scorers: Perkins, Platt²
14th	● Crewe	h	L 0–1	Att: 4,907 — Booked: Izzet
21st	● Leicester	a	D 1–1	Att: 20,218 — Scorers: Yeates. Booked: Platt
28th	● Scunthorpe	a	L 3–0	Att: 4,304 — Booked: Yeates
31st	● Millwall	a	W 0–1	Att: 8,071 — Scorers: Platt. Booked: Baldwin, Trotman, Maybury, Tierney

April
4th	● Leeds	h	L 0–1	Att: 9,559 — Booked: Izzet, Hackney
11th	● Leyton Orient	a	L 2–1	Att: 4,685 — Scorers: Platt. Booked: Hammond
13th	● Brighton	h	L 0–1	Att: 4,873 — Booked: Coyne
18th	● Hereford	a	W 0–2	Att: 2,100 — Scorers: Yeates, Beckwith OG. Booked: Coyne
25th	● Peterborough	h	L 0–1	Att: 6,532 — Booked: Gerken, Tierney, Platt

May
2nd	● Yeovil	a	W 0–2	Att: 5,237 — Scorers: Vincent, Yeates. Booked: Jackson

● Coca-Cola League 1/Play-Offs   ● FA Cup   ● Carling Cup   ● Johnstone's Paint Trophy

LEAGUE ONE GOALKEEPER STATS

Player	Appearances	Match starts	Completed matches	Sub appearances	Subbed off	Clean sheets	Yellow cards	Red cards
Mark Cousins 9	9	9	0	0	2	0	0	
Dean Gerken 21	21	21	0	0	5	2	0	
Jimmy Walker 16	16	16	0	0	5	0	0	

LEAGUE ONE OUTFIELD PLAYER STATS

Player	Appearances	Match starts	Completed matches	Substitute appearances	Subbed off	Goals scored	Yellow cards	Red cards
Pat Baldwin.....................35	35	34	0	1	0	3	0	
Gary Borrowdale 4	4	4	0	0	0	1	0	
Sam Corcoran 1	0	0	1	0	0	0	0	
Chris Coyne 19	17	16	2	1	0	3	0	
Jermaine Easter 5	5	4	0	1	2	2	0	
Medy Elito 5	0	0	5	0	0	0	0	
Steven Gillespie 17	8	0	9	7	4	2	1	
Lewis Gobern 12	5	0	7	5	0	1	0	
Jamie Guy 4	1	0	3	1	0	0	0	
Simon Hackney 17	11	3	6	8	0	2	0	
Dean Hammond 41	38	36	3	2	5	10	0	
Karl Hawley 4	4	2	0	2	0	0	0	
Matt Heath 14	11	9	3	2	0	2	0	
Lee Hills 2	1	0	1	1	0	0	0	
Philip Ifil 6	5	3	1	2	0	1	0	
Kemal Izzet 43	39	23	4	16	1	8	0	
Johnnie Jackson 29	22	18	7	4	4	4	0	
Matthew Lockwood.........5	5	5	0	0	0	1	0	
Alan Maybury 25	25	23	0	2	0	5	0	
David Perkins 38	35	23	3	12	5	1	0	
Clive Platt 43	39	25	4	14	10	8	0	
Paul Reid........................26	25	22	1	3	1	4	0	
Marc Tierney 26	26	26	0	0	1	5	0	
Neal Trotman 6	5	5	1	0	0	1	0	
Scott Vernon 33	15	5	18	10	4	0	0	
Ashley Vincent 6	5	2	1	3	1	0	0	
Akanni-Sunday Wasiu 15	3	1	12	2	2	1	0	
John White.....................26	19	15	7	4	0	2	0	
Sam Williams 1	1	1	0	0	0	0	0	
Anthony Wordsworth 30	9	4	21	5	3	6	0	
Mark Yeates 43	42	29	1	13	12	4	0	

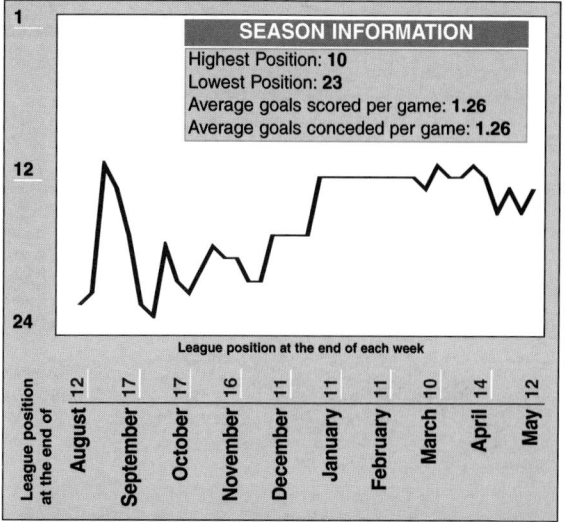

SEASON INFORMATION
Highest Position: **10**
Lowest Position: **23**
Average goals scored per game: **1.26**
Average goals conceded per game: **1.26**

League position at the end of each week

League position at the end of: August 12, September 17, October 17, November 16, December 11, January 11, February 11, March 10, April 14, May 12

LONGEST SEQUENCES

Wins (on two occasions)	2	Undefeated home (20/12/08–27/01/09)	4
Losses (on three occasions)	3	Undefeated away (29/11/08–31/01/09)	6
Draws (28/02/09–03/03/09)	2	Without scoring (10/02/09–21/02/09)	3
Undefeated (13/12/08–31/01/09)	9	Without conceding (–)	
Without win (on four occasions)	3	Scoring (11/10/08–01/11/08)	5

CARDS RECEIVED

79   1

QUICK-FIRE GOALS

From the start of a match
Clive Platt (v Oldham) 1:06

By a substitute after coming on
Akanni-Sunday Wasiu (v Swindon) 3:51

GOALS SCORED/CONCEDED PER FIVE-MINUTE INTERVALS

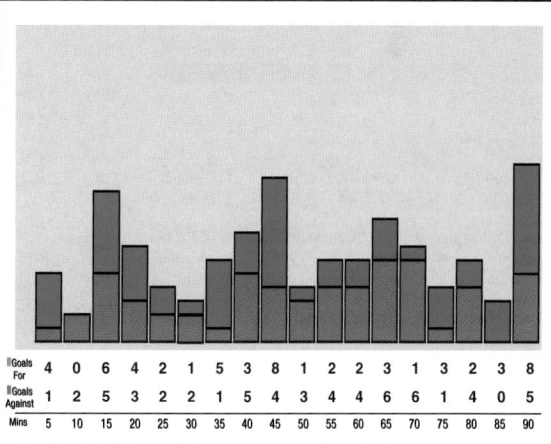

Goals For	4	0	6	4	2	1	5	3	8	1	2	2	3	1	3	2	3	8
Goals Against	1	2	5	3	2	2	1	5	4	3	4	4	6	6	1	4	0	5
Mins	5	10	15	20	25	30	35	40	45	50	55	60	65	70	75	80	85	90

OFFICIAL FOOTBALL YEARBOOK OF THE ENGLISH & SCOTTISH LEAGUES 2009–2010   **275**

CREWE ALEXANDRA

GUDJON THORDARSON was unable to prevent Crewe from falling into the bottom tier for the first time in 15 years. The Railwaymen were relegated from Coca-Cola League One on the final day of the season following a 3–0 home defeat to Leicester.

It had looked as though Thordarson would keep the club up following an impressive start after his arrival at the turn of the year. The Icelander inherited a side that was seven points adrift at the foot of the table, but he inspired eight wins in his first 13 games and lifted Crewe clear of the bottom four.

However, after a 1–0 win at Colchester in mid-March, results took a turn for the worse and Thordarson's side failed to win any of their last 10 matches. Despite a poor season, Crewe will see themselves as one of the favourites for promotion from League Two during 2009/10.

CLUB SUMMARY

FORMED	1877
MANAGER	Gudjon Thordarson
GROUND	Gresty Road
CAPACITY	10,046
NICKNAME	The Railwaymen
WEBSITE	www.crewealex.net

The New **Football Pools** PLAYER OF THE SEASON — John Brayford

OVERALL
P	W	D	L	F	A	GD
55	17	11	27	74	91	-17

COCA-COLA FOOTBALL LEAGUE ONE
Pos	P	W	D	L	F	A	GD	Pts
22	46	12	10	24	59	82	-23	46

HOME
Pos	P	W	D	L	F	A	GD	Pts
19	23	8	4	11	30	38	-8	28

AWAY
Pos	P	W	D	L	F	A	GD	Pts
21	23	4	6	13	29	44	-15	18

CUP PROGRESS DETAILS
Competition	Round reached	Knocked out by
FA Cup	R3	Millwall
JP Trophy	R2	Tranmere
Carling Cup	R3	Liverpool

BIGGEST WIN (ALL COMPS)
28/02/09 4–0 v Brighton **FL1**

BIGGEST DEFEAT (ALL COMPS)
24/01/09 1–5 v Northampton **FL1**

ATTENDANCE RECORD
High	Low	Average
7,138	3,432	4,537
v Leeds (21/03/2009)	v Yeovil (24/02/2009)	

RESULTS 2008/09

August
9th	● Brighton ....h	L 1–2	Att: 4,557 — Scorers: Zola. Booked: O'Connor
12th	● Barnsley..........h	W 2–0	Att: 2,492 — Scorers: Elding, O'Connor
16th	● Carlisle..............a	L 4–2	Att: 6,919 — Scorers: McCready, Pope. Booked: Pope
23rd	● Walsall ....h	W 2–1	Att: 4,160 — Scorers: Elding, Grant. Booked: O'Connor
26th	● Bristol City ....h	W 2–1	Att: 3,227 — Scorers: Elding, Moore
30th	● Hereford...........a	L 2–0	Att: 2,894

September
2nd	● Macclesfield ....h	W 3–0	Att: 2,463 — Scorers: Jones, O'Donnell, Schumacher. Booked: Rix
6th	● Leeds ....a	L 5–2	Att: 20,075 — Scorers: Bopp, Zola. Booked: Baudet
13th	● Colchester ....h	W 2–0	Att: 3,510 — Scorers: O'Connor, Pope
20th	● Southend ....h	L 3–4	Att: 3,574 — Scorers: O'Connor, Pope, Zola
23rd	● Liverpool ....a	L 2–1	Att: 28,591 — Scorers: O'Connor
27th	● Bristol Rovers ..a	D 0–0	Att: 5,870

October
4th	● Northampton ....h	L 1–3	Att: 3,977 — Scorers: Pope. Booked: O'Connor
6th	● Tranmere ....a	L 1–0	Att: 2,626
11th	● Scunthorpe ....a	L 3–0	Att: 4,790 — Booked: Schumacher
18th	● MK Dons ....h	D 2–2	Att: 4,055 — Scorers: Miller, O'Hanlon OG
21st	● Yeovil ....a	L 3–2	Att: 3,536 — Scorers: Miller, Moore. Booked: Zola, O'Connor
24th	● Tranmere ....a	L 2–0	Att: 5,790 — Booked: Miller. Dismissed: Jones
28th	● Peterborough ....h	D 1–1	Att: 3,699 — Scorers: Pope

November
1st	● Huddersfield......a	L 3–2	Att: 11,679 — Scorers: Donaldson[2]
8th	● Ebbsfleet Unitedh	W 1–0	Att: 2,593 — Scorers: Donaldson. Booked: O'Donnell, Grant
15th	● Leyton Orient ...h	L 0–2	Att: 3,872 — Booked: Grant, O'Connor
22nd	● Stockport ....h	L 0–3	Att: 5,337 — Booked: Jones
25th	● Leicester ....a	L 2–1	Att: 16,961 — Scorers: Zola

December
3rd	● Carlisle..............a	W 0–2	Att: 2,755 — Scorers: Miller[2]
6th	● Cheltenham ......a	L 1–0	Att: 4,052
13th	● Swindon ....h	W 1–0	Att: 3,941 — Scorers: Miller
20th	● Millwall ....a	D 0–0	Att: 9,018
26th	● Oldham ....h	L 0–3	Att: 5,780
28th	● Hartlepool ....h	W 1–4	Att: 3,877 — Scorers: Brayford, Miller, Murphy, Nelson OG

January
3rd	● Millwall ....a	D 2–2	Att: 5,754 — Scorers: Lawrence, Shelley. Booked: Brayford, Donaldson
13th	● Millwall ....h	L 2–3	Att: 3,060 — Scorers: Miller, Murphy
17th	● Scunthorpe ....h	W 3–2	Att: 3,811 — Scorers: Donaldson, O'Connor, O'Donnell. Booked: O'Connor
24th	● Northampton .....a	L 5–1	Att: 4,675 — Scorers: Daniel. Booked: Carrington, Daniel, O'Connor. Dismissed: Baudet
27th	● Peterborough ....a	L 4–2	Att: 5,782 — Scorers: Pope[2]
31st	● Tranmere ....h	W 2–1	Att: 4,936 — Scorers: Carrington, Grant. Booked: Donaldson, Grant

February
14th	● Leyton Orient ....a	L 1–0	Att: 3,705 — Booked: Baudet, Jones
17th	● Southend ....a	W 0–1	Att: 6,614 — Scorers: Jones
21st	● Huddersfield......h	W 3–1	Att: 5,056 — Scorers: Donaldson, Moore, Pope. Booked: M. Broomes
24th	● Yeovil ....h	W 2–0	Att: 3,432 — Scorers: Brayford, Donaldson. Booked: Pope
28th	● Brighton ....a	W 0–4	Att: 6,366 — Scorers: Jones[2], Schumacher, Sigurdsson. Booked: Daniel, Baudet

March
3rd	● Carlisle..............h	L 1–2	Att: 3,759 — Scorers: Donaldson. Booked: Baudet
7th	● Hereford...........h	W 2–1	Att: 5,195 — Scorers: Jones[2]. Booked: Zola
10th	● Walsall ....a	D 1–1	Att: 3,604 — Scorers: Schumacher
14th	● Colchester ....a	D 1–0	Att: 4,907 — Scorers: Zola. Booked: Sigurdsson, Brayford
17th	● Bristol Rovers ..h	D 1–1	Att: 3,879 — Scorers: Lawrence
21st	● Leeds ....h	L 2–3	Att: 7,138 — Scorers: Pope[2]. Booked: Jones. Dismissed: Jones
24th	● MK Dons ....a	D 2–2	Att: 8,454 — Scorers: Carrington, Sigurdsson. Booked: Grant, Brayford, Pope
28th	● Millwall ....h	L 0–1	Att: 4,680 — Booked: Baudet, Donaldson

April
4th	● Swindon ....a	D 0–0	Att: 7,165
11th	● Hartlepool ....h	D 0–0	Att: 4,477
13th	● Oldham ....a	D 1–1	Att: 4,334 — Scorers: Moore. Booked: Baudet
18th	● Cheltenham ......h	L 1–2	Att: 4,542 — Scorers: Sigurdsson.
24th	● Stockport ....a	L 4–3	Att: 7,134 — Scorers: Jones, Lawrence, McManus

May
2nd	● Leicester ....h	L 0–3	Att: 6,982

● Coca-Cola League 1/Play-Offs ● FA Cup ● Carling Cup ● Johnstone's Paint Trophy

LEAGUE ONE GOALKEEPER STATS

Player	Appearances	Match starts	Completed matches	Sub appearances	Subbed off	Clean sheets	Yellow cards	Red cards
Steve Collis	18	18	18	0	0	2	0	0
John Ruddy	19	19	19	0	0	6	0	0
Stuart Tomlinson	9	9	9	0	0	2	0	0

LEAGUE ONE OUTFIELD PLAYER STATS

Player	Appearances	Match starts	Completed matches	Substitute appearances	Subbed off	Goals scored	Yellow cards	Red cards
George Abbey	7	4	2	3	2	0	0	0
James Bailey	24	24	17	0	7	0	0	0
Julien Baudet	35	35	28	0	6	0	6	1
Eugen Bopp	7	4	0	3	4	1	0	0
John Brayford	36	34	34	2	0	2	2	0
Marlon Broomes	19	19	17	0	2	0	1	0
Mark Carrington	17	12	8	5	4	2	1	0
Colin Daniel	13	9	5	4	4	1	2	0
Clayton Donaldson	37	28	20	9	8	6	2	0
Anthony Elding	16	10	2	6	8	1	0	0
Joel Grant	28	19	10	9	9	2	3	0
Stuart Green	2	2	1	0	1	0	0	0
Billy Jones	38	38	34	0	2	6	3	2
Dennis Lawrence	26	26	24	0	2	2	0	0
Kenny Lunt	3	2	2	1	0	0	0	0
Chris McCready	5	4	2	1	2	1	0	0
Scott McManus	6	3	1	3	2	1	0	0
Shaun Miller	33	18	14	15	4	4	1	0
Byron Moore	36	22	13	14	9	3	0	0
Luke Murphy	9	3	1	6	2	1	0	0
Michael O'Connor	23	23	19	0	4	3	7	0
Daniel O'Donnell	24	22	20	2	2	1	0	0
Tom Pope	26	17	8	9	9	10	3	0
Ben Rix	4	1	0	3	1	0	0	0
Steven Schumacher	15	8	6	7	2	2	1	0
Alan Sheehan	3	3	2	0	1	0	0	0
Danny Shelley	3	3	0	0	3	0	0	0
Gylfi Sigurdsson	15	14	14	1	0	3	1	0
Ashley Westwood	2	0	0	2	0	0	0	0
Dan Woodards	37	35	30	2	5	0	0	0
Calvin Zola	27	18	7	9	11	5	2	0

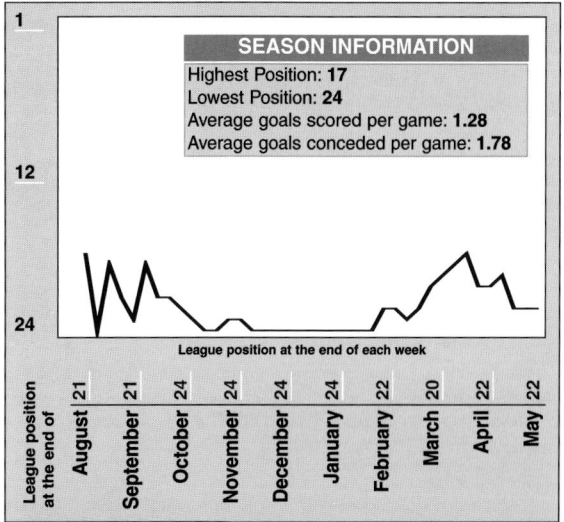

SEASON INFORMATION
Highest Position: 17
Lowest Position: 24
Average goals scored per game: 1.28
Average goals conceded per game: 1.78

League position at the end of each week

League position at the end of	August 21	September 21	October 24	November 24	December 24	January 24	February 22	March 20	April 22	May 22

LONGEST SEQUENCES

Wins (17/02/09–28/02/09)	4	Undefeated home (17/01/09–24/02/09)	4
Losses (01/11/08–06/12/08)	5	Undefeated away (17/02/09–13/04/09)	7
Draws (04/04/09–13/04/09)	3	Without scoring (28/03/09–11/04/09)	3
Undefeated (on two occasions)	4	Without conceding (on three occasions)	2
Without win (20/09/08–06/12/08)	13	Scoring (17/02/09–24/03/09)	11

CARDS RECEIVED

35   3

QUICK-FIRE GOALS

From the start of a match
Tom Pope (v Peterborough) 1:04

By a substitute after coming on
Byron Moore (v Yeovil) 1:57

GOALS SCORED/CONCEDED PER FIVE-MINUTE INTERVALS

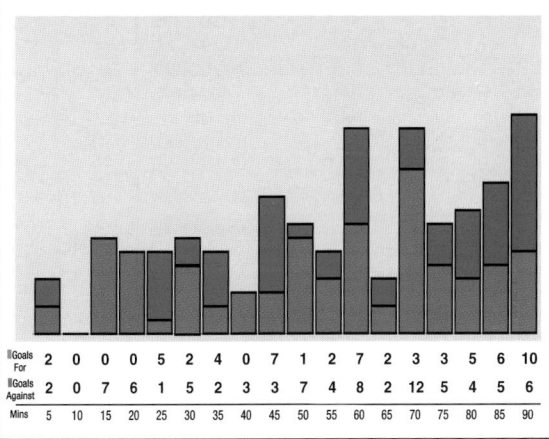

Goals For	2	0	0	5	2	4	0	7	1	2	7	2	3	3	5	6	10	
Goals Against	2	0	7	6	1	5	2	3	3	7	4	8	2	12	5	4	5	6
Mins	5	10	15	20	25	30	35	40	45	50	55	60	65	70	75	80	85	90

HARTLEPOOL UNITED

HARTLEPOOL'S season started with a bang and ended with a whimper as they escaped relegation on the last day.

Hopes of a successful campaign were high after Colchester were thumped 4–2 by a James Brown-inspired Pools on the opening day, but a season-ending knee injury to the exciting forward was a contributing factor in what turned out to be a disappointing campaign.

Boss Danny Wilson departed in December but, under director of sport Chris Turner, Pools' best display came in the FA Cup as they claimed a 2–0 win against Barclays Premier League side Stoke, adding to a 3–1 League Cup success against West Brom.

Joel Porter, who scored 18 league goals, will not be at Victoria Park next season after joining Gold Coast United, but Adam Boyd has returned, offering fresh hope for next term.

CLUB SUMMARY

FORMED	1908
MANAGER	Chris Turner
GROUND	Victoria Park
CAPACITY	7,691
NICKNAME	The Pools
WEBSITE	www.hartlepoolunited.co.uk

The New **Football Pools** PLAYER OF THE SEASON — **Joel Porter**

OVERALL
P	W	D	L	F	A	GD
55	18	12	25	84	94	-10

COCA-COLA FOOTBALL LEAGUE ONE
Pos	P	W	D	L	F	A	GD	Pts
19	46	13	11	22	66	79	-13	50

HOME
Pos	P	W	D	L	F	A	GD	Pts
15	23	8	7	8	45	40	5	31

AWAY
Pos	P	W	D	L	F	A	GD	Pts
20	23	5	4	14	21	39	-18	19

CUP PROGRESS DETAILS
Competition	Round reached	Knocked out by
FA Cup	R4	West Ham
JP Trophy	R1	Leicester
Carling Cup	R3	Leeds

BIGGEST WIN (ALL COMPS)
12/09/08 4–1 v Cheltenham FL1

BIGGEST DEFEAT (ALL COMPS)
1–4 on three occasions

ATTENDANCE RECORD
High	Low	Average
6,402	3,033	3,835
v Leeds (25/04/2009)	v Tranmere (03/03/2009)	

RESULTS 2008/09

August
9th	● Colchester	........h	W 4–2	**Att:** 3,831 — **Scorers:** Boland, Brown[2], Jones. **Booked:** Nelson
12th	● Scunthorpe	......h	W 3–0	**Att:** 2,076 — **Scorers:** Brown, Foley, Porter
16th	● Tranmere	..........a	L 1–0	**Att:** 5,418
23rd	● Stockport	..........h	L 0–1	**Att:** 3,945 — **Booked:** Jones, Liddle, Humphreys
26th	● West Brom	.......h	W 3–1	**Att:** 3,387 — **Scorers:** Barker, Foley, Porter (AET)
30th	● Peterborough	..a	W 1–2	**Att:** 5,728 — **Scorers:** Barker, Monkhouse. **Booked:** Monkhouse, Liddle

September
2nd	● Leicester	.........h	L 0–3	**Att:** 2,807
6th	● Millwall	..............a	L 2–0	**Att:** 7,207 — **Booked:** Liddle, Porter
12th	● Cheltenham	...h	W 4–1	**Att:** 3,637 — **Scorers:** Brown, Mackay, Monkhouse, Gallinagh OG
20th	● Oldham	...........h	D 3–3	**Att:** 4,507 — **Scorers:** Monkhouse, Porter, Sweeney. **Booked:** Sweeney
23rd	● Leeds	..............a	L 3–2	**Att:** 14,599 — **Scorers:** Monkhouse, Porter. **Booked:** Collins
27th	● Leicester	.........a	L 1–0	**Att:** 18,578 — **Booked:** Monkhouse

October
3rd	● Swindon	...........h	D 3–3	**Att:** 4,018 — **Scorers:** Porter[3]. **Booked:** McCunnie
10th	● Northampton	....a	L 1–0	**Att:** 5,277 — **Booked:** Jones
18th	● Walsall	..............a	W 2–3	**Att:** 4,142 — **Scorers:** Brown, Robson, Sweeney. **Booked:** Sweeney, Jones, Brown
21st	● Huddersfield	.....h	W 5–3	**Att:** 3,771 — **Scorers:** Brown, Kyle[2], Porter[2]. **Booked:** Monkhouse, Kyle, Clark
25th	● Brighton	...........h	W 1–0	**Att:** 3,962 — **Scorers:** Kyle. **Booked:** Sweeney
28th	● Carlisle	..............a	W 0–1	**Att:** 5,637 — **Scorers:** Brown. **Booked:** Brown

November
1st	● Leyton Orient	...a	L 1–0	**Att:** 3,638 — **Booked:** Kyle, Monkhouse
8th	● Brighton	...........a	D 3–3	**Att:** 2,545 — **Scorers:** Brown, Monkhouse, Hawkins OG.
15th	● MK Dons	.........h	L 1–3	**Att:** 4,021 — **Scorers:** O'Hanlon OG. **Booked:** Collins, Clark. **Dismissed:** Collins
18th	● Brighton	...........h	W 2–1	**Att:** 3,288 — **Scorers:** Liddle, Porter. **Booked:** Porter
22nd	● Leeds	..............a	L 4–1	**Att:** 21,182 — **Scorers:** Porter
25th	● Bristol Rovers	..h	D 1–1	**Att:** 3,171 — **Scorers:** Nelson
29th	● Fleetwood Town	a	W 2–3	**Att:** 3,280 — **Scorers:** Mackay[2], Porter. **Booked:** Liddle, Lee-Barrett

December
6th	● Yeovil	...............h	D 0–0	**Att:** 3,393 — **Booked:** Robson, Jones
13th	● Hereford	...........a	D 1–1	**Att:** 2,490 — **Scorers:** Beckwith OG. **Booked:** Liddle, Robson, Kyle
19th	● Southend	.........h	W 3–0	**Att:** 3,123 — **Scorers:** Kyle[2], Robson. **Booked:** Collins
26th	● Scunthorpe	......a	L 3–0	**Att:** 5,347 — **Booked:** Rowell, Kyle
28th	● Crewe	..............h	L 1–4	**Att:** 3,877 — **Scorers:** Porter

January
3rd	● Stoke	...............h	W 2–0	**Att:** 5,367 — **Scorers:** Foley, Nelson
12th	● Oldham	...........a	L 2–1	**Att:** 4,211 — **Scorers:** Lomax OG
16th	● Northampton	....h	W 2–0	**Att:** 3,814 — **Scorers:** Porter[2]. **Booked:** Lee-Barrett
24th	● West Ham	.......a	L 0–2	**Att:** 6,849
27th	● Carlisle	..............h	D 2–2	**Att:** 3,765 — **Scorers:** Monkhouse, Porter. **Booked:** Monkhouse, Robson, Clark
31st	● Brighton	...........a	L 2–1	**Att:** 5,784 — **Scorers:** Nelson. **Booked:** Nelson

February
3rd	● Huddersfield	.....a	D 1–1	**Att:** 9,294 — **Scorers:** Jones. **Booked:** Clark, Robson. **Dismissed:** Nardiello
7th	● Walsall	..............h	D 2–2	**Att:** 3,286 — **Scorers:** Porter, Gerrard OG. **Booked:** Clark, Robson, Humphreys
14th	● MK Dons	.........a	L 3–1	**Att:** 8,657 — **Scorers:** Lange. **Booked:** Henderson
17th	● Leicester	.........h	D 2–2	**Att:** 4,068 — **Scorers:** Monkhouse, Porter **Booked:** Collins, Humphreys, Monkhouse
21st	● Leyton Orient	...h	L 0–1	**Att:** 3,678 — **Booked:** Guy
24th	● Swindon	...........a	W 0–1	**Att:** 6,010 — **Scorers:** Clark. **Booked:** Monkhouse
28th	● Colchester	........a	D 1–1	**Att:** 5,158 — **Scorers:** Nelson. **Booked:** Monkhouse, Jones, Clark, Nelson

March
3rd	● Tranmere	..........h	W 2–1	**Att:** 3,033 — **Scorers:** Clark, Nelson
7th	● Peterborough	...h	L 1–2	**Att:** 3,722 — **Scorers:** Monkhouse. **Booked:** Nelson, Porter
10th	● Stockport	..........a	L 2–1	**Att:** 4,790 — **Scorers:** Mackay. **Booked:** Clark, Sweeney, Humphreys
14th	● Cheltenham	......a	L 2–0	**Att:** 2,945 — **Booked:** Monkhouse, Sweeney
21st	● Millwall	..............h	L 2–3	**Att:** 3,601 — **Scorers:** Sweeney[2]. **Booked:** Sweeney, Collins
27th	● Southend	.........a	L 3–2	**Att:** 7,227 — **Scorers:** Jones, Porter. **Booked:** Monkhouse, Clark, Nelson, Nardiello. **Dismissed:** Lee-Barrett

April
4th	● Hereford	...........h	W 4–2	**Att:** 3,579 — **Scorers:** Collins, Porter[2], Sweeney. **Booked:** Nelson, Collins
11th	● Crewe	..............a	D 0–0	**Att:** 4,477
13th	● Scunthorpe	......h	L 2–3	**Att:** 3,998 — **Scorers:** Nardiello, Nelson
18th	● Yeovil	...............a	W 2–3	**Att:** 4,232 — **Scorers:** Nardiello, Porter[2]. **Booked:** Collins, Jones, Clark
25th	● Leeds	..............h	L 0–1	**Att:** 6,402 — **Booked:** Collins, Jones

May
2nd	● Bristol Rovers	..a	L 4–1	**Att:** 7,363 — **Scorers:** Nardiello. **Booked:** Jones

● Coca-Cola League 1/Play-Offs ● FA Cup ● Carling Cup ● Johnstone's Paint Trophy

LEAGUE ONE GOALKEEPER STATS

Player	Appearances	Match starts	Completed matches	Sub appearances	Subbed off	Clean sheets	Yellow cards	Red cards
Jan Budtz	10	9	9	1	0	3	0	0
Arran Lee-Barrett	37	37	36	0	0	4	1	1

LEAGUE ONE OUTFIELD PLAYER STATS

Player	Appearances	Match starts	Completed matches	Substitute appearances	Subbed off	Goals scored	Yellow cards	Red cards
Richard Barker	8	0	0	8	0	1	0	0
Willie Boland	3	3	1	0	2	1	0	0
James Brown	18	18	12	0	6	6	2	0
Ben Clark	35	35	31	0	4	2	9	0
Sam Collins	40	40	38	0	1	1	7	1
David Foley	23	4	0	19	4	0	0	0
Lewis Guy	4	4	3	0	1	0	1	0
Liam Henderson	8	2	1	6	1	0	1	0
Ritchie Humphreys	45	39	35	6	4	0	4	0
Ritchie Jones	36	36	23	0	13	3	8	0
Kevin Kyle	15	15	14	0	1	5	4	0
Rune Lange	3	2	2	1	0	1	0	0
Gary Liddle	43	37	36	6	1	0	4	0
Michael Mackay	23	9	4	14	5	2	0	0
Jamie McCunnie	15	10	8	5	2	0	1	0
Andy Monkhouse	44	41	26	3	15	6	10	0
Daniel Nardiello	12	8	4	4	3	3	1	1
Michael Nelson	46	46	43	0	3	5	6	0
Keigan Parker	9	9	5	0	4	0	0	0
Joel Porter	38	37	19	1	18	18	2	0
Alan Power	4	0	0	0	0	0	0	0
Matty Robson	29	14	11	15	3	2	5	0
Jonny Rowell	6	3	1	3	0	0	1	0
Joe Skarz	7	5	5	2	0	0	0	0
Antony Sweeney	44	43	37	1	6	5	6	0

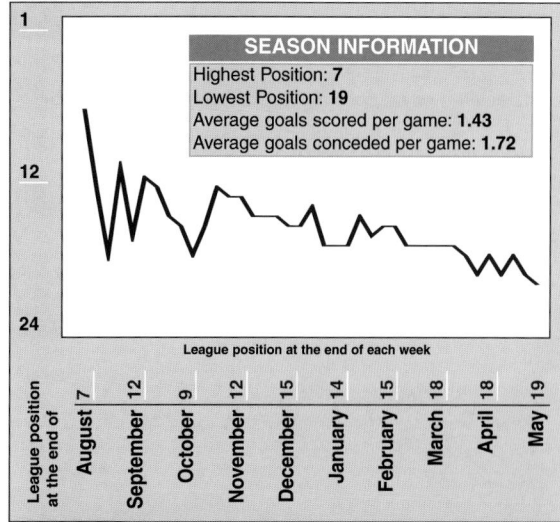

SEASON INFORMATION
Highest Position: **7**
Lowest Position: **19**
Average goals scored per game: **1.43**
Average goals conceded per game: **1.72**

League position at the end of each week

LONGEST SEQUENCES

Wins (18/10/08–28/10/08)	4	Undefeated home (12/09/08–25/10/08)	5	
Losses (07/03/09–27/03/09)	5	Undefeated away (on three occasions)	2	
Draws (25/11/08–13/12/08)	3	Without scoring (on two occasions)	2	
Undefeated (on two occasions)	4	Without conceding (25/10/08–28/10/08)	2	
Without win (27/01/09–21/02/09)	7	Scoring (28/12/08–17/02/09)	9	

CARDS RECEIVED

73 **3**

QUICK-FIRE GOALS

From the start of a match
Kevin Kyle (v Southend) 3:59

By a substitute after coming on
Richard Barker (v Peterborough) 0:48

GOALS SCORED/CONCEDED PER FIVE-MINUTE INTERVALS

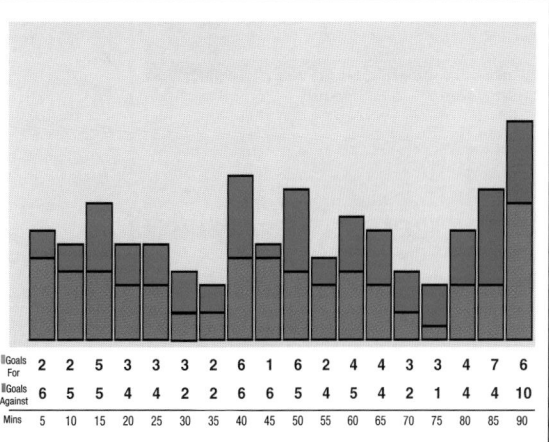

Goals For	2	2	5	3	3	3	2	6	1	6	2	4	4	3	3	4	7	6
Goals Against	6	5	5	4	4	2	2	6	6	5	4	5	4	2	1	4	4	10
Mins	5	10	15	20	25	30	35	40	45	50	55	60	65	70	75	80	85	90

HEREFORD endured a tough introduction to life in England's third tier in 2008/09.

Having secured automatic promotion predominantly on the back of Graham Turner's success in the loan market, the Bulls boss looked to take the same approach to safeguard the club's survival. However, the plan hit problems and Turner struggled to bring in the calibre of players required, while a series of injuries also did not help matters.

After an astonishing 14 years in charge at Edgar Street, Turner – also the club's chairman – quit as manager to become director of football and appointed former assistant John Trewick for the final two games.

With Trewick in charge and a sound financial footing, Bulls fans will look ahead with optimism, but whether they can push for promotion remains to be seen.

CLUB SUMMARY

FORMED	1924
MANAGER	John Trewick
GROUND	Edgar Street
CAPACITY	8,843
NICKNAME	The Bulls
WEBSITE	www.herefordunited.co.uk

The New Football Pools PLAYER OF THE SEASON — **Steve Guinan**

OVERALL

	P	W	D	L	F	A	GD
	50	9	8	33	45	85	-40

COCA-COLA FOOTBALL LEAGUE ONE

Pos	P	W	D	L	F	A	GD	Pts
24	46	9	7	30	42	79	-37	34

HOME

Pos	P	W	D	L	F	A	GD	Pts
24	23	6	4	13	23	28	-5	22

AWAY

Pos	P	W	D	L	F	A	GD	Pts
24	23	3	3	17	19	51	-32	12

CUP PROGRESS DETAILS

Competition	Round reached	Knocked out by
FA Cup	R1	Dag & Red
JP Trophy	R2	Swindon
Carling Cup	R1	Crystal Palace

BIGGEST WIN (ALL COMPS)

17/01/09 5–0 v Oldham **FL1**

BIGGEST DEFEAT (ALL COMPS)

23/08/08 1–6 v Bristol Rovers **FL1**

ATTENDANCE RECORD

High	Low	Average
6,120	2,033	3,270
v Leeds (17/02/2009)	v Brighton (07/04/2009)	

RESULTS 2008/09

August
9th	● Leyton Orient	a	L 2–1	**Att:** 4,727 — **Scorers:** Beckwith
12th	● Crystal Palace	a	L 2–1	**Att:** 3,094 — **Scorers:** Ashikodi. **Booked:** Ashikodi
16th	● Yeovil	h	L 1–2	**Att:** 3,476 — **Scorers:** Hudson-Odoi
23rd	● Bristol Rovers	a	L 6–1	**Att:** 6,735 — **Scorers:** Guinan. **Booked:** Oji
30th	● Crewe	h	W 2–0	**Att:** 2,894 — **Scorers:** Hudson-Odoi, O'Leary

September
5th	● Swindon	h	D 1–1	**Att:** 4,061 — **Scorers:** Hudson-Odoi
13th	● Southend	a	L 1–0	**Att:** 6,393
20th	● Scunthorpe	h	L 1–2	**Att:** 3,004 — **Scorers:** Chadwick
27th	● Leeds	a	L 1–0	**Att:** 25,676 — **Booked:** O'Leary, Broadhurst

October
4th	● Walsall	h	D 0–0	**Att:** 3,900
7th	● Swindon	h	L 1–2	**Att:** 1,458 — **Scorers:** Done
12th	● Oldham	a	L 4–0	**Att:** 5,468 — **Booked:** O'Leary. **Dismissed:** O'Leary
18th	● Brighton	a	D 0–0	**Att:** 5,608 — **Booked:** Broadhurst, Diagouraga, N'Gotty
21st	● Carlisle	h	W 1–0	**Att:** 2,300 — **Scorers:** Williams. **Booked:** Guinan
25th	● Stockport	h	L 0–1	**Att:** 3,210
28th	● Millwall	a	L 1–0	**Att:** 9,071 — **Booked:** Rose, Chadwick, Taylor. **Dismissed:** Chadwick

November
1st	● Peterborough	a	L 2–0	**Att:** 6,087 — **Booked:** Taylor, Beckwith
8th	● Dag & Red	h	D 0–0	**Att:** 1,825 — **Booked:** Broadhurst
15th	● Cheltenham	h	W 3–0	**Att:** 3,761 — **Scorers:** Guinan[2], Gwynne. **Booked:** Gwynne
18th	● Dag & Red	a	L 2–1	**Att:** 1,409 — **Scorers:** Taylor. **Booked:** Broadhurst
22nd	● Northampton	h	L 0–2	**Att:** 3,061 — **Booked:** Diagouraga
25th	● MK Dons	a	L 3–0	**Att:** 7,189 — **Booked:** Broadhurst

December
6th	● Colchester	a	W 1–2	**Att:** 4,794 — **Scorers:** Ainsworth, Guinan. **Booked:** Taylor, Williams
13th	● Hartlepool	h	D 1–1	**Att:** 2,490 — **Scorers:** Guinan
20th	● Huddersfield	a	L 2–0	**Att:** 13,070 — **Booked:** Taylor
26th	● Tranmere	h	D 2–2	**Att:** 3,495 — **Scorers:** Diagouraga, Guinan
28th	● Leicester	a	L 2–1	**Att:** 22,920 — **Scorers:** Broadhurst

January
17th	● Oldham	h	W 5–0	**Att:** 3,342 — **Scorers:** Ainsworth[2], Guinan[3]. **Booked:** Guinan
24th	● Walsall	a	D 1–1	**Att:** 4,438 — **Scorers:** Guinan. **Booked:** Rose, Taylor
27th	● Millwall	h	L 0–2	**Att:** 3,001 — **Booked:** Guinan
31st	● Stockport	a	L 4–1	**Att:** 5,586 — **Scorers:** Hewson. **Booked:** Hewson

February
14th	● Cheltenham	a	W 2–3	**Att:** 4,660 — **Scorers:** Brandy, Hewson[2].
17th	● Leeds	h	W 2–0	**Att:** 6,120 — **Scorers:** Brandy, Myrie-Williams. **Booked:** Diagouraga
21st	● Peterborough	h	L 0–1	**Att:** 3,217
28th	● Leyton Orient	h	W 2–1	**Att:** 3,286 — **Scorers:** Brandy, Guinan. **Booked:** Taylor, Hewson, Gulacsi

March
7th	● Crewe	a	L 2–1	**Att:** 5,195 — **Scorers:** Diagouraga. **Dismissed:** Hewson
10th	● Bristol Rovers	h	L 0–3	**Att:** 3,199 — **Booked:** Brandy, Johnson
14th	● Southend	h	L 0–1	**Att:** 2,663 — **Booked:** Gwynne, Hewson, Dennehy, Beckwith
17th	● Scunthorpe	a	L 3–0	**Att:** 3,672
21st	● Swindon	a	L 3–0	**Att:** 7,129
24th	● Carlisle	a	W 1–2	**Att:** 4,223 — **Scorers:** Guinan, Smith
28th	● Huddersfield	h	L 0–1	**Att:** 2,979 — **Booked:** Smith

April
4th	● Hartlepool	a	L 4–2	**Att:** 3,579 — **Scorers:** Brandy, Pugh. **Booked:** Taylor
7th	● Brighton	h	L 1–2	**Att:** 2,033 — **Scorers:** Taylor
11th	● Leicester	h	L 1–3	**Att:** 4,389 — **Scorers:** Guinan
13th	● Tranmere	a	L 2–1	**Att:** 5,945 — **Scorers:** Guinan. **Booked:** Diagouraga
18th	● Colchester	h	L 0–2	**Att:** 2,100 — **Booked:** Guinan. Hereford are relegated
21st	● Yeovil	a	D 2–2	**Att:** 3,780 — **Scorers:** Guinan, Myrie-Williams. **Booked:** Gwynne, Williams
25th	● Northampton	a	L 2–1	**Att:** 5,518 — **Scorers:** Williams

May
2nd	● MK Dons	h	L 0–1	**Att:** 3,224 — **Booked:** Gowling

● Coca-Cola League 1/Play-Offs ● FA Cup ● Carling Cup ● Johnstone's Paint Trophy

LEAGUE ONE GOALKEEPER STATS

Player	Appearances	Match starts	Completed matches	Sub appearances	Subbed off	Clean sheets	Yellow cards	Red cards
Peter Gulacsi	18	18	18	0	0	1	1	0
Matt Murray	3	3	2	0	1	1	0	0
Darren Randolph	13	13	13	0	0	4	0	0
Craig Samson	11	10	10	1	0	1	0	0
Jose Veiga	1	1	1	0	0	0	0	0
Chris Weale	1	1	1	0	0	0	0	0

LEAGUE ONE OUTFIELD PLAYER STATS

Player	Appearances	Match starts	Completed matches	Substitute appearances	Subbed off	Goals scored	Yellow cards	Red cards
Lionel Ainsworth	7	7	6	0	1	3	0	0
Godwin Antwi	5	5	3	0	2	0	0	0
Moses Ashikodi	6	4	0	2	4	0	0	0
Dean Beckwith	25	22	20	3	2	1	2	0
Febian Brandy	15	14	8	1	6	4	1	0
Karl Broadhurst	25	23	22	2	1	1	3	0
Nick Chadwick	10	5	1	5	3	1	1	0
Darren Dennehy	3	3	3	0	0	0	1	0
Toumani Diagouraga	45	45	43	0	2	2	4	0
Matt Done	36	24	14	12	10	0	0	0
Clint Easton	12	9	4	3	5	0	0	0
Josh Gowling	13	13	11	0	2	0	1	0
Stephen Guinan	43	40	36	3	4	15	4	0
Sam Gwynne	21	17	13	4	4	1	3	0
Sam Hewson	10	9	6	1	2	3	3	1
Bradley Hudson-Odoi	16	10	5	6	5	3	0	0
Richard Jackson	25	24	21	1	3	0	0	0
Simon Johnson	29	8	4	21	4	0	1	0
Craig Jones	3	1	0	2	1	0	0	0
Jack Macleod	6	2	1	4	1	0	0	0
Jennison Myrie-Williams	15	15	11	0	4	2	0	0
Bruno N'Gotty	8	8	7	0	1	0	1	0
Stephen O'Leary	15	11	6	4	4	1	2	1
Samuel Oji	4	4	4	0	0	0	1	0
Marc Pugh	9	8	2	1	6	1	0	0
Richard Rose	42	40	40	2	0	0	2	0
Ben Smith	37	29	24	8	5	1	1	0
Kris Taylor	39	38	36	1	2	1	7	0
Robbie Threlfall	3	3	3	0	0	0	0	0
Andrew Williams	26	19	10	7	9	2	2	0

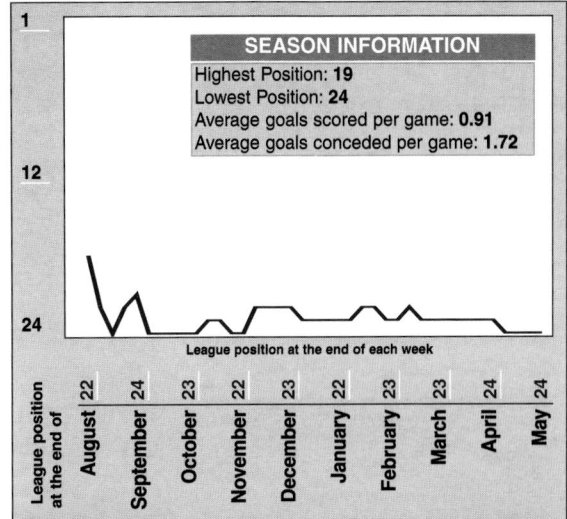

SEASON INFORMATION
Highest Position: **19**
Lowest Position: **24**
Average goals scored per game: **0.91**
Average goals conceded per game: **1.72**

League position at the end of each week

LONGEST SEQUENCES

Wins (14/02/09–17/02/09)	2	Undefeated home (13/12/08–17/01/09)	3
Losses (28/03/09–18/04/09)	6	Undefeated away (–)	
Draws (–)		Without scoring (on two occasions)	4
Undefeated (on five occasions)	2	Without conceding (18/10/08–21/10/08)	2
Without win (28/03/09–02/05/09)	9	Scoring (09/08/08–05/09/08)	5

CARDS RECEIVED

41   3

QUICK-FIRE GOALS

From the start of a match
Stephen Guinan (v Oldham) 2:21

By a substitute after coming on
Bradley Hudson-Odoi (v Yeovil) 16:56

GOALS SCORED/CONCEDED PER FIVE-MINUTE INTERVALS

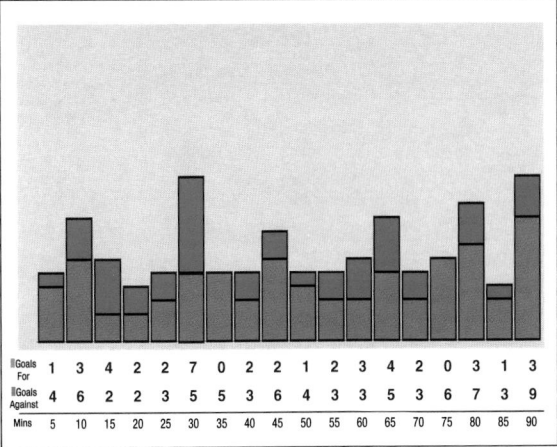

Goals For	1	3	4	2	2	7	0	2	2	1	2	3	4	2	0	3	1	3
Goals Against	4	6	2	2	3	5	5	3	6	4	3	3	5	3	6	7	3	9
Mins	5	10	15	20	25	30	35	40	45	50	55	60	65	70	75	80	85	90

HUDDERSFIELD TOWN

THE TERRIERS lost just one of their last nine matches but were never likely to force their way back into play-off contention once the club's centenary celebrations had fallen flat by the end of February.

Stan Ternent had been installed as manager in the summer, but was sacked in November. Academy coach Gerry Murphy embarked on his third stint as caretaker-manager and again worked wonders before the arrival of Lee Clark.

The new boss announced his intention to quickly establish Huddersfield as a Coca-Cola Championship force, and a run of just two defeats in nine games lifted Town to within four points of the top six.

But, after the high point of a 1–0 win over Leeds, the Terriers went seven matches without a win and, despite an impressive run-in, were out of contention for the play-offs.

CLUB SUMMARY

FORMED	1908
MANAGER	Lee Clark
GROUND	The Galpharm Stadium
CAPACITY	24,500
NICKNAME	The Terriers
WEBSITE	www.htafc.com

The New **Football Pools** PLAYER OF THE SEASON — **Gary Roberts**

OVERALL

P	W	D	L	F	A	GD
50	19	14	17	70	72	-2

COCA-COLA FOOTBALL LEAGUE ONE

Pos	P	W	D	L	F	A	GD	Pts
9	46	18	14	14	62	65	-3	68

HOME

Pos	P	W	D	L	F	A	GD	Pts
11	23	9	8	6	32	28	4	35

AWAY

Pos	P	W	D	L	F	A	GD	Pts
6	23	9	6	8	30	37	-7	33

CUP PROGRESS DETAILS

Competition	Round reached	Knocked out by
FA Cup	R1	Port Vale
JP Trophy	R2	Darlington
Carling Cup	R2	Sheff Utd

BIGGEST WIN (ALL COMPS)

12/08/08 4–0 v Bradford **LC1**

BIGGEST DEFEAT (ALL COMPS)

25/10/08 0–4 v Peterborough **FL1**

ATTENDANCE RECORD

High	Low	Average
20,928	9,294	13,298
v Leeds (14/02/2009)	v Hartlepool (03/02/2009)	

RESULTS 2008/09

August
9th	● Stockport	........h	D 1–1	Att: 15,578 — **Scorers:** Booth. **Booked:** Collins
12th	● Bradford	............h	W 4–0	Att: 8,932 — **Scorers:** Roberts², Williams, Worthington
16th	● Colchester	........a	D 0–0	Att: 5,340 — **Booked:** Goodwin, Williams, Cadamarteri
23rd	● MK Dons	..........h	L 1–3	Att: 13,189 — **Scorers:** Roberts. **Booked:** Butler, Lucketti
27th	● Sheff Utd	.........h	L 1–2	Att: 9,552 — **Scorers:** Flynn
30th	● Millwall	.............a	L 2–1	Att: 7,513 — **Scorers:** Dickinson
				Booked: Dickinson, Worthington, Lucketti, Flynn, Roberts

September
6th	● Cheltenham	......a	W 1–2	Att: 3,587 — **Scorers:** Clarke, Craney.
				Booked: Unsworth, Roberts, Craney, Parker
13th	● Tranmere	..........h	L 1–2	Att: 13,352 — **Scorers:** Dickinson. **Booked:** Worthington
20th	● Northampton	...h	W 3–2	Att: 12,414 — **Scorers:** Booth, Flynn². **Booked:** Dickinson
27th	● Oldham	...........a	D 1–1	Att: 7,418 — **Scorers:** Craney.
				Booked: Goodwin, Jevons, Dickinson, Worthington

October
4th	● Leicester	..........h	L 2–3	Att: 16,212 — **Scorers:** Dickinson, Roberts. **Booked:** Cadamarteri, Skarz
7th	● Darlington	........a	L 1–0	Att: 1,791 — **Booked:** Lucketti. **Dismissed:** Roberts
11th	● Swindon	...........a	W 1–3	Att: 7,071 — **Scorers:** Dickinson, Flynn, Roberts. **Booked:** Roberts
18th	● Bristol Rovers	..h	D 1–1	Att: 13,779 — **Scorers:** Flynn. **Booked:** Goodwin, Roberts, Jones
21st	● Hartlepool	........a	L 5–3	Att: 3,771 — **Scorers:** Craney, Dickinson². **Booked:** Craney, Dickinson
25th	● Peterborough	...a	L 4–0	Att: 7,064 — **Booked:** Goodwin, Worthington. **Dismissed:** Lucketti
28th	● Yeovil	................h	D 0–0	Att: 10,719

November
1st	● Crewe	...........h	W 3–2	Att: 11,679 — **Scorers:** Butler, Craney, Parker.
				Booked: Parker, Worthington. **Dismissed:** Parker
8th	● Port Vale	.........h	L 3–4	Att: 6,942 — **Scorers:** Collins, Craney, Williams
15th	● Leeds	...............a	W 1–2	Att: 32,028 — **Scorers:** Collins, Skarz. **Booked:** N. Clarke, Collins, Goodwin
22nd	● Brighton	...........a	W 0–1	Att: 6,461 — **Scorers:** Collins. **Booked:** Berrett, Holdsworth
25th	● Leyton Orient	...h	L 0–1	Att: 10,414 — **Booked:** Worthington

December
6th	● Walsall	.............h	W 2–1	Att: 11,827 — **Scorers:** Collins, Roberts.
				Booked: Goodwin, Cadamarteri, Berrett, Butler
13th	● Southend	.........a	W 0–1	Att: 8,382 — **Scorers:** Craney. **Booked:** Craney, Goodwin
20th	● Hereford	...........h	W 2–0	Att: 13,070 — **Scorers:** Clarke, Roberts. **Booked:** Holdsworth
26th	● Carlisle	.............a	L 3–0	Att: 7,883
28th	● Scunthorpe	......h	W 2–0	Att: 15,228 — **Scorers:** Goodwin, Roberts. **Booked:** Parker, Smithies

January
3rd	● Oldham	...........h	D 1–1	Att: 16,950 — **Scorers:** Collins
10th	● Northampton	...a	D 1–1	Att: 5,110 — **Scorers:** Jevons. **Booked:** Goodwin, Collins
17th	● Swindon	...........h	W 2–1	Att: 13,414 — **Scorers:** Butler, Collins
24th	● Leicester	..........a	L 4–2	Att: 21,311 — **Scorers:** Jevons, Parker.
				Booked: Goodwin, Roberts. **Dismissed:** Roberts
27th	● Yeovil	................a	L 1–0	Att: 3,703 — **Booked:** Craney
31st	● Peterborough	...h	W 1–0	Att: 14,480 — **Scorers:** Collins

February
3rd	● Hartlepool	........h	D 1–1	Att: 9,294 — **Scorers:** Nelson OG
14th	● Leeds	...............h	W 1–0	Att: 20,928 — **Scorers:** Clarke. **Booked:** Holdsworth
21st	● Crewe	...........a	L 3–1	Att: 5,056 — **Scorers:** Berrett. **Booked:** Williams
28th	● Stockport	..........a	D 1–1	Att: 7,739 — **Scorers:** Collins. **Booked:** N. Clarke, Goodwin

March
3rd	● Colchester	........h	D 2–2	Att: 10,580 — **Scorers:** Pilkington, Roberts. **Booked:** Goodwin, Lucketti
7th	● Millwall	.............h	L 1–2	Att: 13,196 — **Scorers:** Roberts. **Booked:** Lucketti
10th	● MK Dons	..........a	D 1–1	Att: 9,707 — **Scorers:** Butler
14th	● Tranmere	..........a	L 3–1	Att: 5,515 — **Scorers:** Booth. **Booked:** Collins, Lucketti, Pilkington
21st	● Cheltenham	......h	D 2–2	Att: 11,516 — **Scorers:** Butler, Cadamarteri. **Booked:** Goodwin, T. Clarke, Flynn
28th	● Hereford	...........a	W 0–1	Att: 2,979 — **Scorers:** Collins. **Booked:** T. Clarke
31st	● Bristol Rovers	..a	W 1–2	Att: 6,286 — **Scorers:** Cadamarteri, Pilkington. **Booked:** T. Clarke

April
4th	● Southend	.........h	L 0–1	Att: 12,203 — **Booked:** Butler, Flynn
10th	● Scunthorpe	......a	W 1–2	Att: 5,543 — **Scorers:** Clarke, Roberts.
				Booked: N. Clarke, Williams, Goodwin, Collins
13th	● Carlisle	.............h	W 1–0	Att: 12,309 — **Scorers:** Booth
18th	● Walsall	.............a	W 2–3	Att: 3,951 — **Scorers:** Booth², Kelly. **Booked:** Cadamarteri, Roberts, Goodwin
25th	● Brighton	...........h	D 2–2	Att: 14,740 — **Scorers:** Booth, Collins

May
2nd	● Leyton Orient	...a	D 1–1	Att: 5,371 — **Scorers:** Booth

● Coca-Cola League 1/Play-Offs ● FA Cup ● Carling Cup ● Johnstone's Paint Trophy

LEAGUE ONE GOALKEEPER STATS

Player	Appearances	Match starts	Completed matches	Sub appearances	Subbed off	Clean sheets	Yellow cards	Red cards
Simon Eastwood...............1	1	1	0	0	0	0	0
Matthew Glennon.............18	18	18	0	0	3	0	0
Alex Smithies...................27	27	27	0	0	7	1	0

LEAGUE ONE OUTFIELD PLAYER STATS

Player	Appearances	Match starts	Completed matches	Substitute appearances	Subbed off	Goals scored	Yellow cards	Red cards
Lionel Ainsworth 14	7	1	7	6	0	0	0
Luke Beckett 1	0	0	1	0	0	0	0
James Berrett 9	8	5	1	3	1	2	0
Andy Booth................................20	9	4	11	5	8	0	0
Daniel Broadbent 1	0	0	1	0	0	0	0
Andy Butler................................42	42	42	0	0	4	3	0
Danny Cadamarteri 32	24	19	8	5	2	4	0
Nathan Clarke............................38	38	38	0	0	3	3	0
Tom Clarke 15	11	11	4	0	1	3	0
Michael Collins...........................36	34	32	2	2	9	5	0
Ian Craney.................................34	23	14	11	9	5	4	0
Liam Dickinson 13	13	10	0	3	6	4	0
Michael Flynn............................25	18	14	7	4	4	3	0
Jim Goodwin 37	35	27	2	8	1	14	0
Andy Holdsworth........................34	30	29	4	1	0	3	0
Phil Jevons 23	12	3	11	9	2	1	0
Steve Jones 4	2	2	2	0	0	1	0
Lukas Jutkiewicz.........................7	6	0	1	6	0	0	0
Malvin Kamara 2	0	0	2	0	0	0	0
Martin Kelly 7	7	6	0	1	1	0	0
Chris Lucketti 13	12	11	1	0	0	5	1
Keigan Parker.............................20	14	2	6	11	2	3	1
Anthony Pilkington 16	16	13	0	3	2	1	0
Gary Roberts 43	43	34	0	8	9	6	1
Joe Skarz 9	9	7	0	2	1	1	0
David Unsworth..........................4	4	3	0	1	0	1	0
Dominik Werling 3	0	0	3	0	0	0	0
Robbie Williams 35	31	28	4	3	0	3	0
Jonathan Worthington..............19	12	6	7	6	0	6	0

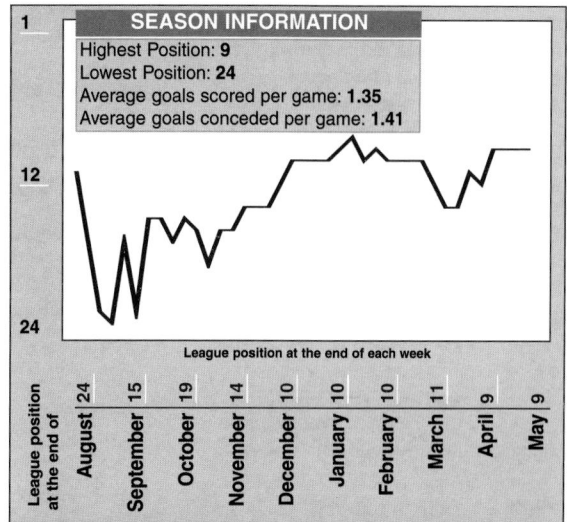

SEASON INFORMATION

Highest Position: **9**
Lowest Position: **24**
Average goals scored per game: **1.35**
Average goals conceded per game: **1.41**

League position at the end of each week

League position at the end of

August 24 | September 15 | October 19 | November 14 | December 10 | January 10 | February 10 | March 11 | April 9 | May 9

LONGEST SEQUENCES

Wins (on two occasions)	3	Undefeated home (06/12/08–03/03/09)	9
Losses (on two occasions)	2	Undefeated away (06/09/08–11/10/08)	3
Draws (on two occasions)	2	Without scoring (25/10/08–28/10/08)	2
Undefeated (10/04/09–02/05/09)	5	Without conceding (13/12/08–20/12/08)	2
Without win (21/02/09–21/03/09)	7	Scoring (31/01/09–31/03/09)	12

CARDS RECEIVED

77   3

QUICK-FIRE GOALS

From the start of a match
Phil Jevons (v Leicester) 5:10

By a substitute after coming on
Danny Cadamarteri (v Cheltenham) 8:41

GOALS SCORED/CONCEDED PER FIVE-MINUTE INTERVALS

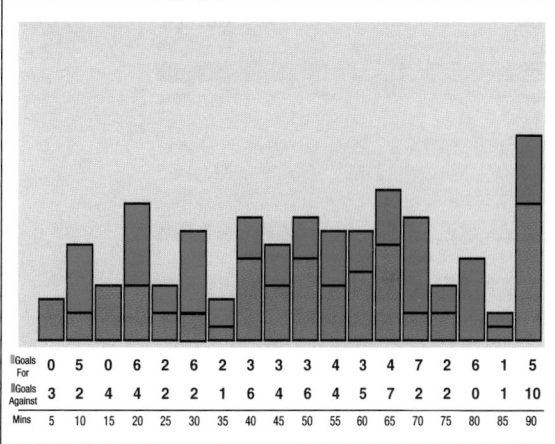

Goals For	0	5	0	6	2	6	2	3	3	3	4	3	4	7	2	6	1	5
Goals Against	3	2	4	4	2	2	1	6	4	6	4	5	7	2	2	0	1	10
Mins	5	10	15	20	25	30	35	40	45	50	55	60	65	70	75	80	85	90

LEEDS UNITED

LEEDS began the season as promotion favourites but lost out to Millwall in the play-off semi-finals and now face another campaign in Coca-Cola League One.

The fallen Yorkshire giants recovered from an awful run of form at the end of 2008 and the subsequent sacking of Gary McAllister, but ultimately fell short again under new boss Simon Grayson.

Leeds completed the season in fine style, especially at home, where they won 11 straight league games. Jermaine Beckford finished the season with 27 League goals and teenage midfielder Fabian Delph and left-back Ben Parker emerged as two fantastic prospects.

But 10 away defeats scuppered their automatic promotion chances, and their Wembley dreams were ended by a 2–1 aggregate defeat to the Lions.

CLUB SUMMARY

FORMED	1919
MANAGER	Simon Grayson
GROUND	Elland Road
CAPACITY	40,296
NICKNAME	The Whites
WEBSITE	www.leedsunited.com

The New Football Pools PLAYER OF THE SEASON — Fabian Delph

OVERALL

P	W	D	L	F	A	GD
57	31	8	18	101	66	35

COCA-COLA FOOTBALL LEAGUE ONE

Pos	P	W	D	L	F	A	GD	Pts
4	46	26	6	14	77	49	28	84

HOME

Pos	P	W	D	L	F	A	GD	Pts
1	23	17	2	4	49	20	29	53

AWAY

Pos	P	W	D	L	F	A	GD	Pts
9	23	9	4	10	28	29	-1	31

CUP PROGRESS DETAILS

Competition	Round reached	Knocked out by
FA Cup	R2	Histon
JP Trophy	R2	Rotherham
Carling Cup	R4	Derby

BIGGEST WIN (ALL COMPS)
4–0 on two occasions

BIGGEST DEFEAT (ALL COMPS)
08/10/08 2–4 v Rotherham **FLTN2**

ATTENDANCE RECORD

High	Low	Average
34,214	18,847	23,639

v Northampton (02/05/2009) v Yeovil (10/03/2009)

RESULTS 2008/09

August
9th	● Scunthorpe	.....a W 1–2	**Att:** 8,315 — **Scorers:** Beckford, Showunmi. **Booked:** Showunmi
12th	● Chester	...........a W 2–5	**Att:** 3,644 — **Scorers:** Beckford³, Robinson, Snodgrass. **Booked:** Delph, Richardson, Johnson
16th	● Oldham	...........h L 0–2	**Att:** 24,631 — **Booked:** Prutton
23rd	● Yeovil	...............a D 1–1	**Att:** 6,580 — **Scorers:** Becchio. **Booked:** Snodgrass, Becchio, Huntington, Beckford
26th	● Crystal Palace	..h W 4–0	**Att:** 10,765 — **Scorers:** Becchio, Beckford, Douglas, Showunmi
30th	● Bristol Rovers	..h D 2–2	**Att:** 21,024 — **Scorers:** Beckford²

September
2nd	● Bradford	...........h W 2–1	**Att:** 20,128 — **Scorers:** Becchio, Robinson. **Booked:** Snodgrass, Johnson
6th	● Crewe	.............h W 5–2	**Att:** 20,075 — **Scorers:** Beckford, Delph, Douglas, Robinson, Sheehan. **Booked:** Michalik, Delph. **Dismissed:** Michalik
13th	● Swindon	..........a W 1–3	**Att:** 13,001 — **Scorers:** Beckford², Kilkenny. **Booked:** Marques, Kilkenny, Beckford, Delph. **Dismissed:** Sheehan
20th	● Carlisle	............a W 0–2	**Att:** 12,148 — **Scorers:** Becchio, Beckford. **Booked:** Richardson
23rd	● Hartlepool	........h W 3–2	**Att:** 14,599 — **Scorers:** Robinson, Showunmi, Snodgrass
27th	● Hereford	...........h W 1–0	**Att:** 25,676 — **Scorers:** Robinson

October
4th	● Peterborough	....a L 2–0	**Att:** 13,191
8th	● Rotherham	........a L 4–2	**Att:** 4,658 — **Scorers:** Howson, Showunmi
11th	● Brighton	............h W 3–1	**Att:** 22,726 — **Scorers:** Becchio, Beckford². **Booked:** Kilkenny, Michalik, Beckford
18th	● Millwall	.............h L 3–1	**Att:** 13,041 — **Scorers:** Becchio, Beckford. **Booked:** Kilkenny, Becchio
21st	● Leyton Orient	...h W 2–1	**Att:** 18,990 — **Scorers:** Becchio, Purches OG
25th	● Walsall	...............h W 3–0	**Att:** 22,422 — **Scorers:** Becchio, Delph²
28th	● Southend	.........a L 1–0	**Att:** 10,132 — **Booked:** Michalik, Becchio, Robinson

November
1st	● Cheltenham	......a W 0–1	**Att:** 5,726 — **Scorers:** Becchio. **Booked:** Delph
7th	● Northampton	....h D 1–1	**Att:** 9,531 — **Scorers:** Robinson. **Booked:** White
11th	● Derby	..............a L 2–1	**Att:** 18,540 — **Scorers:** Becchio
15th	● Huddersfield	....h L 1–2	**Att:** 32,028 — **Scorers:** Snodgrass. **Booked:** Douglas, Robinson
17th	● Northampton	....a W 2–5	**Att:** 3,960 — **Scorers:** Beckford³, Howson, Parker. **Booked:** Michalik
22nd	● Hartlepool	........h W 4–1	**Att:** 21,182 — **Scorers:** Becchio, Beckford², Delph
25th	● Northampton	....a W 2–1	**Att:** 6,008 — **Scorers:** Beckford. **Booked:** Robinson, Delph, Douglas, Prutton
30th	● Histon	................a L 1–0	**Att:** 4,500

December
6th	● Tranmere	..........a L 2–1	**Att:** 8,700 — **Scorers:** Showunmi. **Booked:** Prutton, Telfer
13th	● Colchester	........h L 1–2	**Att:** 19,625 — **Scorers:** Snodgrass. **Booked:** Prutton. **Dismissed:** Prutton
20th	● MK Dons	...........a W 1–3	**Att:** 17,073 — **Scorers:** Snodgrass
26th	● Leicester	...........h D 1–1	**Att:** 33,580 — **Scorers:** Snodgrass. **Booked:** Marques
28th	● Stockport	.........a W 1–3	**Att:** 10,273 — **Scorers:** Becchio, Christie, Delph. **Booked:** Becchio, Sheehan, Douglas, Delph

January
10th	● Carlisle	...............h L 0–2	**Att:** 22,411
17th	● Brighton	............a W 0–2	**Att:** 7,096 — **Scorers:** Delph, Trundle. **Booked:** Douglas
24th	● Peterborough	...h W 3–1	**Att:** 22,766 — **Scorers:** Beckford², Howson. **Booked:** Delph
27th	● Southend	.........h W 2–0	**Att:** 20,392 — **Scorers:** Marques, Naylor
31st	● Walsall	...............a L 1–0	**Att:** 8,920

February
9th	● Millwall	.............h W 2–0	**Att:** 19,314 — **Scorers:** Beckford². **Booked:** Marques, Douglas, Beckford
14th	● Huddersfield	....a L 1–0	**Att:** 20,928 — **Booked:** Naylor, Delph
17th	● Hereford	...........a L 2–0	**Att:** 6,120 — **Booked:** C. Dickinson, Becchio
21st	● Cheltenham	......h W 2–0	**Att:** 20,131 — **Scorers:** Howson²
28th	● Scunthorpe	......h W 3–2	**Att:** 24,921 — **Scorers:** Beckford², Johnson. **Booked:** Johnson, Howson. **Dismissed:** Howson

March
2nd	● Oldham	............a D 1–1	**Att:** 7,835 — **Scorers:** Becchio. **Booked:** Becchio, Delph
7th	● Bristol Rovers	..a D 2–2	**Att:** 10,293 — **Scorers:** Becchio, Snodgrass. **Booked:** Becchio, Parker
10th	● Yeovil	...............h W 4–0	**Att:** 18,847 — **Scorers:** Beckford², Kilkenny
14th	● Swindon	...........h W 1–0	**Att:** 21,765 — **Scorers:** Beckford. **Booked:** Snodgrass, Beckford. **Dismissed:** Beckford
21st	● Crewe	.............a W 2–3	**Att:** 7,138 — **Scorers:** Becchio, Kilkenny, Snodgrass. **Booked:** Naylor, Ankergren, Snodgrass
28th	● MK Dons	...........h W 2–0	**Att:** 27,649 — **Scorers:** Beckford². **Booked:** Howson, Kilkenny

April
4th	● Colchester	........a W 0–1	**Att:** 9,559 — **Scorers:** Becchio. **Booked:** Naylor
7th	● Leyton Orient	...a D 2–2	**Att:** 6,943 — **Scorers:** Snodgrass². **Booked:** Delph, Dickinson, Robinson
11th	● Stockport	.........h W 2–0	**Att:** 24,967 — **Scorers:** Howson. **Booked:** Marques, Delph
13th	● Leicester	...........a L 1–0	**Att:** 27,507 — **Booked:** Becchio, Sodje
18th	● Tranmere	..........h W 3–1	**Att:** 24,360 — **Scorers:** Becchio, Beckford, Kilkenny
25th	● Hartlepool	........a W 0–1	**Att:** 6,402 — **Scorers:** Beckford. **Booked:** Robinson

May
2nd	● Northampton	....h W 3–0	**Att:** 34,214 — **Scorers:** Becchio, Beckford, Snodgrass
9th	● Millwall	.............a L 1–0	**Att:** 13,228 — **Booked:** Snodgrass, Delph
14th	● Millwall	.............h D 1–1	**Att:** 37,036 — **Scorers:** Becchio. **Booked:** Delph, Robinson, Ankergren, Beckford

● Coca-Cola League 1/Play-Offs ● FA Cup ● Carling Cup ● Johnstone's Paint Trophy

LEAGUE ONE GOALKEEPER STATS

Player	Appearances	Match starts	Completed matches	Sub appearances	Subbed off	Clean sheets	Yellow cards	Red cards
Casper Ankergren	33	33	33	0	0	13	1	0
David Lucas	13	13	13	0	0	2	0	0

LEAGUE ONE OUTFIELD PLAYER STATS

Player	Appearances	Match starts	Completed matches	Substitute appearances	Subbed off	Goals scored	Yellow cards	Red cards
Mansour Assoumani	1	1	1	0	0	0	0	0
Luciano Becchio	45	40	26	5	14	15	8	0
Jermaine Beckford	34	32	22	2	9	27	5	1
Malcolm Christie	4	1	0	3	1	1	0	0
Fabian Delph	42	40	36	2	4	6	10	0
Carl Dickinson	7	7	7	0	0	0	1	0
Liam Dickinson	8	4	0	4	4	0	1	0
Jonathan Douglas	43	42	38	1	4	1	5	0
Mike Grella	11	0	0	11	0	0	0	0
Jonathan Howson	40	26	19	14	6	4	2	1
Andy Hughes	27	18	10	9	8	0	0	0
Paul Huntington	4	4	4	0	0	0	1	0
Bradley Johnson	15	7	4	8	3	1	1	0
Neil Kilkenny	30	27	6	3	21	4	4	0
Rui Marques	32	32	30	0	2	1	4	0
Lubomir Michalik	19	15	13	4	1	0	3	1
Richard Naylor	22	22	22	0	0	1	3	0
Ben Parker	24	23	20	1	3	0	1	0
David Prutton	16	8	6	8	1	0	4	1
Frazer Richardson	23	21	20	2	1	0	1	0
Andy Robinson	32	20	10	12	10	2	5	0
Alan Sheehan	11	11	9	0	1	1	1	1
Enoch Showunmi	8	3	1	5	2	2	1	0
Robert Snodgrass	42	25	17	17	8	9	3	0
Sam Sodje	5	5	4	0	1	0	1	0
Paul Telfer	14	14	14	0	0	0	1	0
Lee Trundle	10	7	0	3	7	1	0	0
Aidan White	5	5	2	0	3	0	0	0

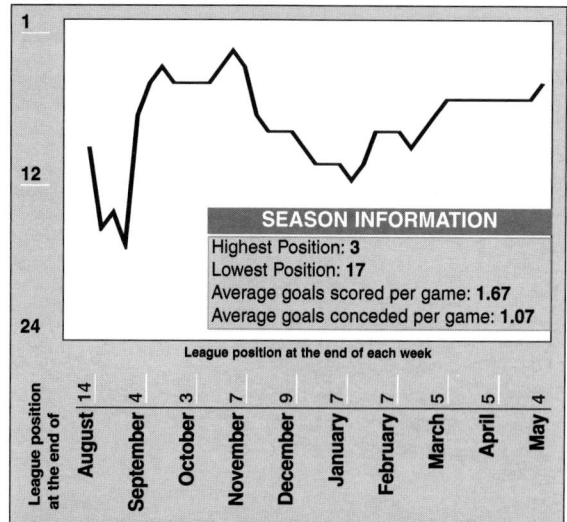

SEASON INFORMATION
Highest Position: **3**
Lowest Position: **17**
Average goals scored per game: **1.67**
Average goals conceded per game: **1.07**

League position at the end of each week

League position at the end of: August 14, September 4, October 3, November 7, December 9, January 7, February 7, March 5, April 5, May 4

LONGEST SEQUENCES

Wins (10/03/09–04/04/09)	5	Undefeated home (24/01/09–02/05/08)	11
Losses (25/11/08–20/12/08)	4	Undefeated away (02/03/09–07/04/09)	5
Draws (on two occasions)	2	Without scoring (14/02/09–17/02/09)	2
Undefeated (21/02/09–11/04/09)	11	Without conceding (20/09/08–27/09/08)	2
Without win (25/11/08–26/12/08)	5	Scoring (21/02/09–11/04/09)	11

CARDS RECEIVED

67   5

QUICK-FIRE GOALS

From the start of a match
Luciano Becchio (v Yeovil) 0:27

By a substitute after coming on
Jermaine Beckford (v Peterboro) 4:12

GOALS SCORED/CONCEDED PER FIVE-MINUTE INTERVALS

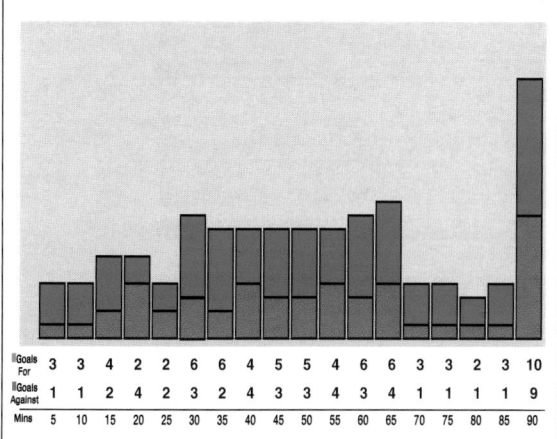

Goals For	3	3	4	2	2	6	6	4	5	5	4	6	6	3	3	2	3	10
Goals Against	1	1	2	4	2	3	2	4	3	3	4	3	4	1	1	1	1	9
Mins	5	10	15	20	25	30	35	40	45	50	55	60	65	70	75	80	85	90

LEICESTER'S first experience of English football's third tier lasted just a season as Nigel Pearson masterminded an immediate return to the Coca-Cola Championship by winning the League One title.

The Foxes dominated the division and were beaten just four times. They set a new club record of 23 league matches unbeaten between November and March.

Matty Fryatt scored 27 league goals and chairman Milan Mandaric has already stated that the club will not listen to any offers for the striker this summer. On-loan defenders Jack Hobbs and Wayne Brown have been signed on permanent deals for 2009/10 and Mandaric has vowed to strengthen the squad with further signings. Kerrea Gilbert, who had a season-long loan spell with the Foxes from Arsenal, is one such target.

CLUB SUMMARY

FORMED	1884
MANAGER	Nigel Pearson
GROUND	The Walkers Stadium
CAPACITY	32,500
NICKNAME	The Foxes
WEBSITE	www.lcfc.co.uk

The New **Football Pools** PLAYER OF THE SEASON

Steve Howard

OVERALL

P	W	D	L	F	A	GD
55	31	17	7	97	48	49

COCA-COLA FOOTBALL LEAGUE ONE

Pos	P	W	D	L	F	A	GD	Pts
1	46	27	15	4	84	39	45	96

HOME

Pos	P	W	D	L	F	A	GD	Pts
3	23	13	9	1	41	16	25	48

AWAY

Pos	P	W	D	L	F	A	GD	Pts
1	23	14	6	3	43	23	20	48

CUP PROGRESS DETAILS

Competition	Round reached	Knocked out by
FA Cup	R3	Crystal Palace
JP Trophy	FLTNQ	Rotherham
Carling Cup	R2	Fulham

BIGGEST WIN (ALL COMPS)
4–0 on three occasions

BIGGEST DEFEAT (ALL COMPS)
0–2 on three occasions

ATTENDANCE RECORD

High	Low	Average
30,542	16,378	20,340

v Scunthorpe (24/04/2009) v Stockport (03/03/2009)

RESULTS 2008/09

August
9th	● MK Dons	..........h W 2–0	**Att:** 23,351 — **Scorers:** Fryatt[2]
12th	● Stockport	..........h W 1–0	**Att:** 7,386 — **Scorers:** Howard. **Booked:** Dickov
16th	● Stockport	........a D 0–0	**Att:** 7,151 — **Booked:** Gradel
23rd	● Tranmere	......h W 3–1	**Att:** 17,798 — **Scorers:** Fryatt[2], Howard. **Booked:** Howard, Fryatt
27th	● Fulham	..............a L 3–2	**Att:** 7,584 — **Scorers:** Dickov, King
30th	● Cheltenham	......a W 0–4	**Att:** 5,344 — **Scorers:** Dyer[2], Fryatt, Oakley. **Booked:** Dickov, Dyer

September
2nd	● Hartlepool	........a W 0–3	**Att:** 2,807 — **Scorers:** Adams, Fryatt, Howard
13th	● Millwall	..........h L 0–1	**Att:** 19,591 — **Booked:** Gradel, Tunchev
20th	● Leyton Orient	....a W 1–3	**Att:** 6,448 — **Scorers:** Dyer, Fryatt, King. **Booked:** Morrison
23rd	● Lincoln City	.....h D 0–0	**Att:** 8,046 — **Booked:** Berner, Tunchev (Won 3–1 on pens)
27th	● Hartlepool	........h W 1–0	**Att:** 18,578 — **Scorers:** Oakley. **Booked:** Fryatt
30th	● Colchester	........a W 0–1	**Att:** 5,133 — **Scorers:** Dyer. **Booked:** Howard

October
4th	● Huddersfield	......a W 2–3	**Att:** 16,212 — **Scorers:** Dyer, Fryatt[2]. **Booked:** Gilbert, Howard, Tunchev
18th	● Oldham	............a D 1–1	**Att:** 8,901 — **Scorers:** Howard
21st	● Walsall	...........h D 2–2	**Att:** 17,178 — **Scorers:** King, Tunchev. **Booked:** Gradel
25th	● Northampton	....h D 0–0	**Att:** 22,795 — **Booked:** Mattock
28th	● Brighton	...........a L 3–2	**Att:** 6,282 — **Scorers:** Fryatt[2]. **Booked:** Kisnorbo, Howard, Berner

November
1st	● Bristol Rovers	..h W 2–1	**Att:** 18,941 — **Scorers:** Fryatt[2]. **Booked:** Hayles, Kisnorbo
4th	● Rotherham	........a L 2–0	**Att:** 4,255 — **Booked:** Hobbs
8th	● Stevenage	.......h W 3–0	**Att:** 7,586 — **Scorers:** Dyer, Fryatt, King
11th	● Yeovil	..............h W 1–0	**Att:** 16,528 — **Scorers:** Dyer. **Booked:** Berner
15th	● Swindon	...........a D 2–2	**Att:** 9,499 — **Scorers:** Fryatt, Oakley. **Booked:** Howard, Fryatt
22nd	● Scunthorpe	......a W 1–2	**Att:** 7,967 — **Scorers:** Dyer, King
25th	● Crewe	..............h W 2–1	**Att:** 16,961 — **Scorers:** Fryatt, King
29th	● Dag & Red	......h W 3–2	**Att:** 7,791 — **Scorers:** Fryatt[3]. **Booked:** Adams

December
6th	● Southend	........h W 3–0	**Att:** 16,836 — **Scorers:** Fryatt[3]
13th	● Carlisle	............a W 1–2	**Att:** 7,085 — **Scorers:** Davies, Howard. **Booked:** Davies
20th	● Peterborough	..h W 4–0	**Att:** 23,390 — **Scorers:** Fryatt, Howard, King, Morgan OG. **Booked:** P. Dickov
26th	● Leeds	..............a D 1–1	**Att:** 33,580 — **Scorers:** Oakley. **Booked:** Davies
28th	● Hereford	...........h W 2–1	**Att:** 22,920 — **Scorers:** Howard, King. **Booked:** Howard, Adams

January
3rd	● Crystal Palace	..h D 0–0	**Att:** 15,976
10th	● Leyton Orient	....h W 3–0	**Att:** 18,240 — **Scorers:** Davies, Dickov, Oakley
14th	● Crystal Palace	..a L 2–1	**Att:** 6,023 — **Scorers:** Gradel. **Booked:** Chambers, Gradel
19th	● Yeovil	..............a W 0–2	**Att:** 4,569 — **Scorers:** Howard, Mattock
24th	● Huddersfield	......h W 4–2	**Att:** 21,311 — **Scorers:** Berner, Fryatt, Hobbs, Morrison. **Booked:** Gilbert, Howard
27th	● Brighton	...........h D 0–0	**Att:** 17,410
31st	● Northampton	....a W 1–2	**Att:** 7,028 — **Scorers:** Dyer, Howard. **Booked:** Mattock

February
3rd	● Walsall	..............a W 1–4	**Att:** 5,634 — **Scorers:** Cleverley, Fryatt, Howard, King
7th	● Oldham	............h D 0–0	**Att:** 22,328
14th	● Swindon	...........h D 1–1	**Att:** 19,926 — **Scorers:** King. **Booked:** Morrison, Hobbs
17th	● Hartlepool	........a D 2–2	**Att:** 4,068 — **Scorers:** Howard[2]. **Booked:** Oakley, Fryatt, Morrison, King
21st	● Bristol Rovers	..a W 0–1	**Att:** 9,138 — **Scorers:** Fryatt. **Booked:** Bunn. **Dismissed:** Hobbs
28th	● MK Dons	.........a D 2–2	**Att:** 17,717 — **Scorers:** Fryatt, Gradel. **Booked:** Howard

March
3rd	● Stockport	..........h D 1–1	**Att:** 16,378 — **Scorers:** Gilbert. **Booked:** Oakley, Fryatt
7th	● Cheltenham	......h W 4–0	**Att:** 18,939 — **Scorers:** Cleverley, Fryatt, Howard, Oakley. **Booked:** Cleverley
11th	● Tranmere	.........a L 2–0	**Att:** 6,032
14th	● Millwall	............a W 0–1	**Att:** 13,261 — **Scorers:** Howard. **Booked:** Howard, Warner
21st	● Colchester	........h D 1–1	**Att:** 20,218 — **Scorers:** Dickov. **Booked:** Hayles
28th	● Peterborough	..a L 2–0	**Att:** 14,110 — **Booked:** Berner, Warner, Gradel, Hayles

April
4th	● Carlisle	............h D 2–2	**Att:** 20,159 — **Scorers:** Fryatt, Oakley
11th	● Hereford	...........a W 1–3	**Att:** 4,389 — **Scorers:** Dyer, Howard, Oakley. **Booked:** King, Dyer
13th	● Leeds	..............h W 1–0	**Att:** 27,507 — **Scorers:** Howard. **Booked:** Brown, Morrison, Oakley, Gradel, Howard
18th	● Southend	........a W 0–2	**Att:** 10,089 — **Scorers:** Fryatt[2]. **Booked:** Gradel, Fryatt, Oakley, Mattock
24th	● Scunthorpe	......h D 2–2	**Att:** 30,542 — **Scorers:** Morrison[2]. **Booked:** Howard, Powell, Edworthy

May
2nd	● Crewe	..............a W 0–3	**Att:** 6,982 — **Scorers:** Berner, Dyer, Fryatt

● Coca-Cola League 1/Play-Offs ● FA Cup ● Carling Cup ● Johnstone's Paint Trophy

LEAGUE ONE GOALKEEPER STATS

Player	Appearances	Match starts	Completed matches	Sub appearances	Subbed off	Clean sheets	Yellow cards	Red cards
Mark Bunn	3	3	3	0	0	1	1	0
Paul Henderson	6	6	6	0	0	3	0	0
David Martin	25	25	24	0	1	10	0	0
Carl Pentney	1	0	0	1	0	0	0	0
David Stockdale	8	8	8	0	0	4	0	0
Tony Warner	4	4	4	0	0	1	2	0

LEAGUE ONE OUTFIELD PLAYER STATS

Player	Appearances	Match starts	Completed matches	Substitute appearances	Subbed off	Goals scored	Yellow cards	Red cards
Nicky Adams	12	4	2	8	2	0	1	0
Astrit Ajdarevic	5	0	0	5	0	0	0	0
Bruno Berner	32	21	14	11	7	3	3	0
Wayne Brown	9	7	6	2	1	0	1	0
Dudley Campbell	7	2	1	5	1	0	0	0
Ashley Chambers	1	0	0	1	0	0	0	0
Tom Cleverley	15	10	8	5	2	2	1	0
Mark Davies	7	5	5	2	0	2	2	0
Paul Dickov	20	4	1	16	3	2	2	0
Lloyd Dyer	44	43	28	1	15	10	2	0
Marc Edworthy	5	5	1	0	4	0	1	0
Matty Fryatt	46	46	31	0	15	27	6	0
Kerrea Gilbert	34	33	26	1	7	1	2	0
Max-Alain Gradel	27	16	6	11	10	1	6	0
Barry Hayles	10	1	1	9	0	0	3	0
Jack Hobbs	44	39	37	5	1	1	1	1
Steve Howard	41	40	32	1	8	13	11	0
Andy King	45	45	43	0	2	9	2	0
Patrick Kisnorbo	8	5	5	3	0	0	0	0
Joe Mattock	31	25	15	6	10	1	3	0
Michael Morrison	35	32	30	3	2	3	4	0
Matt Oakley	45	45	42	0	3	8	4	0
Levi Porter	1	1	0	0	1	0	0	0
Chris Powell	17	12	8	5	4	0	1	0
Aleksandar Tunchev	20	19	16	1	3	1	2	0

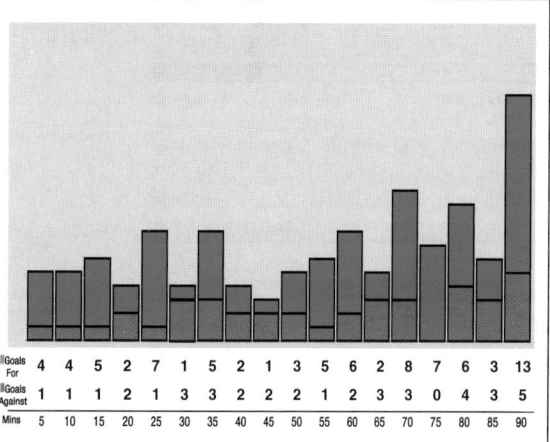

League position at the end of each week

SEASON INFORMATION

Highest Position: **1**
Lowest Position: **8**
Average goals scored per game: **1.83**
Average goals conceded per game: **0.85**

LONGEST SEQUENCES

Wins (22/11/08–20/12/08)	5	Undefeated home (09/08/08–23/08/08)	20
Losses (–)		Undefeated away (15/11/08–28/02/09)	10
Draws (on two occasions)	3	Without scoring (–)	
Undefeated (01/11/08–07/03/09)	23	Without conceding (on four occasions)	2
Without win (18/10/08–28/10/08)	4	Scoring (28/10/08–24/01/09)	14

CARDS RECEIVED

63 **1**

QUICK-FIRE GOALS

From the start of a match
Kerrea Gilbert (v Stockport) 1:34

By a substitute after coming on
Paul Dickov (v Colchester) 1:31

GOALS SCORED/CONCEDED PER FIVE-MINUTE INTERVALS

Goals For	4	4	5	2	7	1	5	2	1	3	5	6	2	8	7	6	3	13
Goals Against	1	1	1	2	1	3	3	2	2	2	1	2	3	3	0	4	3	5
Mins	5	10	15	20	25	30	35	40	45	50	55	60	65	70	75	80	85	90

A TURBULENT campaign, which saw the end of Martin Ling's six-year reign, concluded with a mid-table finish.

Ling was the sixth longest-serving manager in the League when he departed Brisbane Road on 18th January. A run of just five wins in the first 25 league fixtures of the season saw Orient slump to 21st in the table, and Ling and the club parted company by mutual consent after a streak of seven games without a win.

Geraint Williams was appointed as manager on 5th February and earned a point in a goalless draw at Tranmere in his first game. Williams won nine of his first 14 fixtures to make sure of survival.

Adam Boyd finished as top scorer, while loan players, including Simon Church from Reading, played their part. Williams has agreed a one-year extension and will stay on next season.

CLUB SUMMARY

FORMED	1881
MANAGER	Geraint Williams
GROUND	Brisbane Road
CAPACITY	9,271
NICKNAME	The O's
WEBSITE	www.leytonorient.com

The New Football Pools PLAYER OF THE SEASON — Jason Demetriou

OVERALL
P	W	D	L	F	A	GD
52	18	12	22	56	70	-14

COCA-COLA FOOTBALL LEAGUE ONE
Pos	P	W	D	L	F	A	GD	Pts
14	46	15	11	20	45	57	-12	56

HOME
Pos	P	W	D	L	F	A	GD	Pts
23	23	6	6	11	24	33	-9	24

AWAY
Pos	P	W	D	L	F	A	GD	Pts
8	23	9	5	9	21	24	-3	32

CUP PROGRESS DETAILS
Competition	Round reached	Knocked out by
FA Cup	R3	Sheff Utd
JP Trophy	R2	Brighton
Carling Cup	R1	Ipswich

BIGGEST WIN (ALL COMPS)
02/09/08 4–2 v Southend FLTS1

BIGGEST DEFEAT (ALL COMPS)
1–4 on two occasions

ATTENDANCE RECORD
High	Low	Average
6,951	3,381	4,692
v Millwall (22/11/2008)	v Peterborough (03/03/2009)	

RESULTS 2008/09

August
9th	○	Hereford	h	W 2–1	**Att:** 4,727 — **Scorers:** Boyd, Melligan
12th	○	Ipswich	a	L 4–1	**Att:** 1,477 — **Scorers:** Boyd. **Booked:** Thornton
16th	○	Peterborough	a	L 3–0	**Att:** 6,643 — **Booked:** Purches
23rd	○	Carlisle	h	D 0–0	**Att:** 3,803 — **Booked:** Demetriou
30th	○	Brighton	a	D 0–0	**Att:** 6,675 — **Booked:** Demetriou

September
2nd	○	Southend	a	W 2–4	**Att:** 3,499 — **Scorers:** Boyd, Chambers, Jarvis, Melligan. **Booked:** Palmer, Cave-Brown
6th	○	Walsall	a	W 0–2	**Att:** 4,838 — **Scorers:** Boyd, Terry
13th	○	Stockport	h	L 0–3	**Att:** 4,473 — **Booked:** Demetriou
20th	○	Leicester	h	L 1–3	**Att:** 6,448 — **Scorers:** Chambers
26th	○	Southend	a	L 3–0	**Att:** 9,261 — **Booked:** Saah, Chambers

October
4th	○	Scunthorpe	h	D 2–2	**Att:** 4,244 — **Scorers:** Boyd, Purches. **Booked:** Demetriou, Terry
7th	○	Brighton	a	D 2–2	**Att:** 2,157 — **Scorers:** Boyd, Jarvis. **Booked:** Jones (Lost 4–5 on pens)
11th	○	Bristol Rovers	a	L 2–1	**Att:** 6,425 — **Scorers:** Demetriou
18th	○	Tranmere	h	L 0–1	**Att:** 5,568
21st	○	Leeds	a	L 2–1	**Att:** 18,990 — **Scorers:** Morgan
25th	○	Yeovil	a	D 0–0	**Att:** 4,320 — **Booked:** Parkin
28th	○	MK Dons	h	L 1–2	**Att:** 3,869 — **Scorers:** Mkandawire

November
1st	○	Hartlepool	h	W 1–0	**Att:** 3,638 — **Scorers:** Boyd. **Booked:** Saah, Granville, Thornton
8th	●	Colchester	a	W 0–1	**Att:** 4,600 — **Scorers:** Demetriou
15th	○	Crewe	a	W 0–2	**Att:** 3,872 — **Scorers:** Boyd, Mkandawire. **Booked:** Saah
22nd	○	Millwall	h	D 0–0	**Att:** 6,951 — **Booked:** Melligan, Parkin
25th	○	Huddersfield	a	W 0–1	**Att:** 10,414 — **Scorers:** Boyd. **Booked:** Chambers
29th	●	Bradford	a	W 1–2	**Att:** 5,065 — **Scorers:** Demetriou, Granville. **Booked:** Granville, Chambers

December
6th	○	Northampton	a	D 1–1	**Att:** 5,039 — **Scorers:** Melligan. **Booked:** Demetriou
13th	○	Cheltenham	h	L 1–2	**Att:** 4,510 — **Scorers:** Boyd
20th	○	Oldham	a	D 1–1	**Att:** 6,839 — **Scorers:** Demetriou
26th	○	Swindon	h	L 1–2	**Att:** 4,349 — **Scorers:** Mkandawire. **Booked:** Mkandawire, Melligan, Granville
28th	○	Colchester	a	L 1–0	**Att:** 6,290 — **Booked:** Demetriou, Thornton, Jarvis, Chambers, Melligan, Cave-Brown. **Dismissed:** Thornton

January
10th	○	Leicester	a	L 3–0	**Att:** 18,240 — **Booked:** Mkandawire
13th	●	Sheff Utd	h	L 1–4	**Att:** 4,527 — **Scorers:** Melligan. **Booked:** Thornton, Parkin
17th	○	Bristol Rovers	h	L 1–2	**Att:** 4,262 — **Scorers:** Boyd. **Booked:** Parkin
20th	○	Southend	h	D 1–1	**Att:** 3,835 — **Scorers:** Boyd
24th	○	Scunthorpe	a	L 2–1	**Att:** 4,230 — **Scorers:** Morgan
27th	○	MK Dons	a	W 1–2	**Att:** 8,170 — **Scorers:** Morgan, Purches
31st	○	Yeovil	h	L 0–1	**Att:** 4,597 — **Booked:** Purches

February
7th	○	Tranmere	a	D 0–0	**Att:** 4,892 — **Booked:** Demetriou
14th	○	Crewe	h	W 1–0	**Att:** 3,705 — **Scorers:** Purches. **Booked:** Smith
21st	○	Hartlepool	a	W 0–1	**Att:** 3,678 — **Scorers:** Mkandawire. **Booked:** Spence, Jones
28th	○	Hereford	a	L 2–1	**Att:** 3,286 — **Scorers:** Mkandawire. **Booked:** Daniels

March
3rd	○	Peterborough	h	L 2–3	**Att:** 3,381 — **Scorers:** McGleish[2]
7th	○	Brighton	h	W 2–1	**Att:** 5,885 — **Scorers:** McGleish, Thornton. **Booked:** Chambers, Spence, Thornton
10th	○	Carlisle	a	W 1–3	**Att:** 4,536 — **Scorers:** Church, Daniels, McGleish
14th	○	Stockport	a	W 0–1	**Att:** 5,835 — **Scorers:** Church. **Booked:** Jones
21st	○	Walsall	h	L 0–1	**Att:** 3,969 — **Booked:** McGleish
28th	○	Oldham	h	W 2–1	**Att:** 4,034 — **Scorers:** Demetriou, McGleish. **Booked:** Daniels, Thelwell

April
4th	○	Cheltenham	a	W 0–1	**Att:** 3,594 — **Scorers:** Morgan. **Booked:** Daniels
7th	○	Leeds	h	D 2–2	**Att:** 6,943 — **Scorers:** Church, Thornton. **Booked:** Daniels, Demetriou. **Dismissed:** Demetriou
11th	○	Colchester	h	W 2–1	**Att:** 4,685 — **Scorers:** Daniels, Smith. **Booked:** Smith, Spence
13th	○	Swindon	a	W 0–1	**Att:** 7,735 — **Scorers:** Demetriou. **Booked:** Terry
18th	○	Northampton	h	L 1–3	**Att:** 4,665 — **Scorers:** Crowe OG
25th	○	Millwall	a	L 2–1	**Att:** 11,414 — **Scorers:** Church. **Booked:** Morgan

May
2nd	○	Huddersfield	h	D 1–1	**Att:** 5,371 — **Scorers:** Morgan

● Coca-Cola League 1/Play-Offs ● FA Cup ● Carling Cup ● Johnstone's Paint Trophy

LEAGUE ONE GOALKEEPER STATS

Player	Appearances	Match starts	Completed matches	Sub appearances	Subbed off	Clean sheets	Yellow cards	Red cards
Jamie Jones	20	20	20	0	0	6	2	0
Glenn Morris	26	26	26	0	0	8	0	0

LEAGUE ONE OUTFIELD PLAYER STATS

Player	Appearances	Match starts	Completed matches	Substitute appearances	Subbed off	Goals scored	Yellow cards	Red cards
Luke Ashworth	3	1	1	2	0	0	0	0
Harry Baker	4	2	0	2	2	0	0	0
Adam Boyd	33	27	17	6	10	9	0	0
Andrew Cave-Brown	13	10	6	3	4	0	1	0
Adam Chambers	33	33	32	0	1	1	4	0
Simon Church	13	12	6	1	6	4	0	0
Charlie Daniels	21	21	21	0	0	2	4	0
Simon Dawkins	11	2	0	9	2	0	0	0
Jason Demetriou	43	42	39	1	2	4	8	1
Danny Granville	12	12	8	0	4	0	2	0
Wayne Gray	16	6	2	10	4	0	0	0
Ryan Jarvis	31	15	7	16	8	0	1	0
Jack Jeffery	1	0	0	1	0	0	0	0
Scott McGleish	16	15	11	1	4	5	1	0
JJ Melligan	35	25	11	10	14	2	3	0
Tamika Mkandawire	36	36	35	0	1	5	2	0
Dean Morgan	32	18	8	14	10	5	1	0
Aiden Palmer	10	7	6	3	1	0	0	0
Sam Parkin	13	12	4	1	8	0	3	0
Loick Pires	6	0	0	6	0	0	0	0
Stephen Purches	42	42	40	0	2	3	3	0
Brian Saah	15	14	13	1	1	0	3	0
Jimmy Smith	16	15	10	1	5	1	2	0
Jordan Spence	20	20	20	0	0	0	3	0
Paul Terry	28	24	17	4	7	1	2	0
Alton Thelwell	28	23	21	5	2	0	1	0
Sean Thornton	30	26	22	4	3	2	3	1

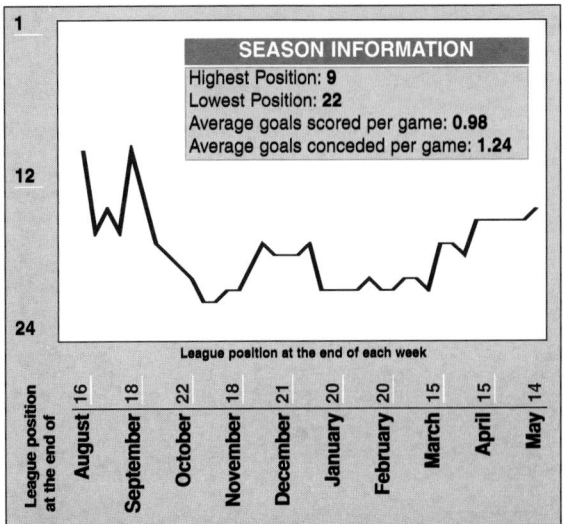

SEASON INFORMATION

Highest Position: **9**
Lowest Position: **22**
Average goals scored per game: **0.98**
Average goals conceded per game: **1.24**

League position at the end of each week

League position at the end of: August 16, September 18, October 22, November 18, December 21, January 20, February 20, March 15, April 15, May 14

LONGEST SEQUENCES

Wins (07/03/09–14/03/09)	3	Undefeated home (28/03/09–11/04/09)	3
Losses (26/12/08–17/01/09)	4	Undefeated away (25/10/08–20/12/08)	5
Draws (23/08/08–30/08/08)	2	Without scoring (16/08/08–30/08/08)	3
Undefeated (on two occasions)	5	Without conceding (01/11/08–25/11/08)	4
Without win (on two occasions)	9	Scoring (28/03/09–02/05/09)	8

CARDS RECEIVED

48   2

QUICK-FIRE GOALS

From the start of a match
Adam Boyd (v Huddersfield) 1:04

By a substitute after coming on
Adam Boyd (v Hartlepool) 5:33

GOALS SCORED/CONCEDED PER FIVE-MINUTE INTERVALS

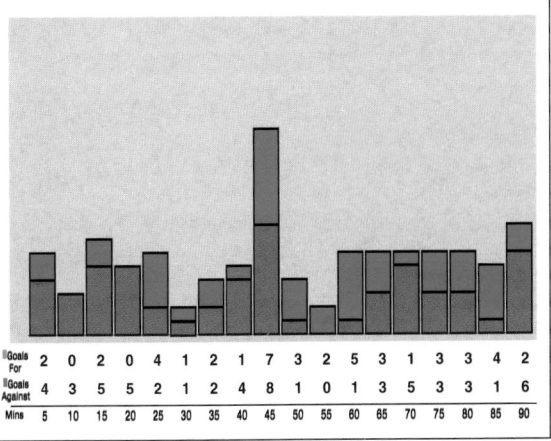

	Mins →	5	10	15	20	25	30	35	40	45	50	55	60	65	70	75	80	85	90
Goals For		2	0	2	0	4	1	2	1	7	3	2	5	3	1	3	3	4	2
Goals Against		4	3	5	5	2	1	2	4	8	1	0	1	3	5	3	3	1	6

MILLWALL were turned from relegation candidates into play-off finalists, but their season ended in Wembley heartbreak.

Kenny Jackett, who saved the Lions from the drop last term, steered them into fifth and an epic two-legged semi-final against Leeds.

Nadjim Abdou was the unlikely name added to Millwall folklore when his equaliser at Elland Road booked a place at Wembley. And 45,000 Lions fans were 45 minutes from the Coca-Cola Championship after Gary Alexander's double – the first a 30-yard strike – put them 2–1 up at half-time against Scunthorpe. But, when Alexander headed wide when it looked easier to score, the final turned Scunthorpe's way and Millwall were eventually beaten 3–2.

Neil Harris also had a season to remember, breaking Teddy Sheringham's goalscoring record for the Lions, which now stands at 117.

CLUB SUMMARY

FORMED	1885
MANAGER	Kenny Jackett
GROUND	The New Den
CAPACITY	20,146
NICKNAME	The Lions
WEBSITE	www.millwallfc.co.uk

The New Football Pools **PLAYER OF THE SEASON**

Andy Frampton

OVERALL

P	W	D	L	F	A	GD
56	29	9	18	78	65	13

COCA-COLA FOOTBALL LEAGUE ONE

Pos	P	W	D	L	F	A	GD	Pts
5	46	25	7	14	63	53	10	82

HOME

Pos	P	W	D	L	F	A	GD	Pts
6	23	13	4	6	30	21	9	43

AWAY

Pos	P	W	D	L	F	A	GD	Pts
4	23	12	3	8	33	32	1	39

CUP PROGRESS DETAILS

Competition	Round reached	Knocked out by
FA Cup	R4	Hull
JP Trophy	R1	Colchester
Carling Cup	R1	Northampton

BIGGEST WIN (ALL COMPS)
3–0 on two occasions

BIGGEST DEFEAT (ALL COMPS)
04/10/08 0–4 v Milton Keynes Dons **FL1**

ATTENDANCE RECORD

High	Low	Average
13,261	6,685	8,940
v Leicester (14/03/2009)	v Northampton (10/03/2009)	

RESULTS 2008/09

August
9th	● Oldham	a	L 4–3	**Att:** 5,367 — **Scorers:** Grabban, Kandol, Hazell OG. **Booked:** Abdou, Dunne, Whitbread. **Dismissed:** Robinson
12th	● Northampton	h	L 0–1	**Att:** 3,525 — **Booked:** Frampton, Grabban, Hackett
23rd	● Northampton	a	D 0–0	**Att:** 4,402 — **Booked:** Brkovic, Craig, Hackett
30th	● Bristol Rovers	a	L 4–2	**Att:** 6,618 — **Scorers:** Abdou[2]. **Booked:** Craig, Dunne, Barron. **Dismissed:** Alexander

September
2nd	● Colchester	h	L 0–1	**Att:** 2,456 — **Booked:** Fuseini, Hackett
6th	● Hartlepool	h	W 2–0	**Att:** 7,207 — **Scorers:** Alexander, Grabban
13th	● Leicester	a	W 0–1	**Att:** 19,591 — **Scorers:** Alexander. **Booked:** Alexander, Abdou, Craig, Whitbread. **Dismissed:** Kandol
20th	● Cheltenham	h	W 2–0	**Att:** 8,009 — **Scorers:** Alexander, Martin
28th	● Swindon	a	W 1–2	**Att:** 7,589 — **Scorers:** Easter, Grabban. **Booked:** Easter. **Dismissed:** Easter

October
4th	● MK Dons	h	L 0–4	**Att:** 9,871 — **Booked:** Martin, Abdou
11th	● Tranmere	a	W 1–3	**Att:** 5,863 — **Scorers:** Abdou, Kandol[2]. **Booked:** Craig, Hackett, Whitbread
18th	● Leeds	h	W 3–1	**Att:** 13,041 — **Scorers:** Harris[2], Martin. **Booked:** Alexander, Harris
21st	● Colchester	a	W 1–2	**Att:** 5,506 — **Scorers:** Grabban, Robinson. **Booked:** Laird, Hackett, Martin, Grabban
25th	● Scunthorpe	a	L 3–2	**Att:** 5,670 — **Scorers:** Craig, Harris. **Booked:** Whitbread
28th	● Hereford	h	W 1–0	**Att:** 9,071 — **Scorers:** Grabban. **Dismissed:** Abdou

November
1st	● Brighton	a	L 4–1	**Att:** 5,973 — **Scorers:** Kandol. **Booked:** Hackett, Kandol, Fuseini
8th	● Chester	a	W 0–3	**Att:** 1,932 — **Scorers:** Grabban, Grimes, Harris. **Booked:** Dunne, Grabban
15th	● Stockport	h	W 1–0	**Att:** 9,030 — **Scorers:** Martin. **Booked:** Grabban, Frampton, Craig, Martin
25th	● Carlisle	h	W 1–0	**Att:** 6,828 — **Scorers:** Kandol. **Booked:** Alexander, Robinson
29th	● Aldershot	h	W 3–0	**Att:** 6,159 — **Scorers:** Alexander[2], Grimes. **Booked:** Hackett, Craig, Laird

December
6th	● Bristol Rovers	h	W 3–2	**Att:** 8,123 — **Scorers:** Alexander, Kandol[2]. **Booked:** Dunne, Kandol, Abdou, A. Bolder
13th	● Walsall	a	W 1–2	**Att:** 3,790 — **Scorers:** Frampton, Harris. **Booked:** Robinson
20th	● Crewe	h	D 0–0	**Att:** 9,018 — **Booked:** Robinson, Grabban
26th	● Peterborough	a	L 1–0	**Att:** 9,351 — **Booked:** Martin. **Dismissed:** Craig
28th	● Yeovil	h	D 1–1	**Att:** 9,042 — **Scorers:** Robinson. **Booked:** A. Bolder, Barron, Forde

January
3rd	● Crewe	h	D 2–2	**Att:** 5,754 — **Scorers:** Frampton, Laird. **Booked:** Frampton, Laird, Kandol, Fuseini
6th	● Leyton Orient	a	D 0–0	**Att:** 6,951
13th	● Crewe	a	W 2–3	**Att:** 3,060 — **Scorers:** Barron, Harris, Whitbread. **Booked:** Barron
24th	● Hull	a	L 2–0	**Att:** 18,639 — **Booked:** Martin, Harris, Dunne, Grimes
27th	● Hereford	a	W 0–2	**Att:** 3,001 — **Scorers:** Craig, Laird. **Booked:** Robinson
31st	● Scunthorpe	h	L 1–2	**Att:** 8,868 — **Scorers:** Alexander. **Booked:** Laird

February
9th	● Leeds	a	L 2–0	**Att:** 19,314 — **Booked:** Bolder, Fuseini, Grimes
14th	● Stockport	a	D 2–2	**Att:** 5,461 — **Scorers:** McLeod[2]. **Booked:** Frampton, McLeod, Martin, Forde. **Dismissed:** Martin
17th	● Swindon	h	D 1–1	**Att:** 7,104 — **Scorers:** Henry. **Booked:** Grimes
21st	● Brighton	h	L 0–1	**Att:** 9,226 — **Booked:** Abdou, Whitbread, Craig

March
7th	● Huddersfield	a	W 1–2	**Att:** 13,196 — **Scorers:** Henry, Laird. **Booked:** Duffy, Alexander
10th	● Northampton	h	W 1–0	**Att:** 6,685 — **Scorers:** Alexander
14th	● Leicester	h	L 0–1	**Att:** 13,261 — **Booked:** Frampton
17th	● MK Dons	a	W 0–1	**Att:** 12,238 — **Scorers:** Laird. **Booked:** Laird, Alexander, Duffy, Henry
21st	● Hartlepool	a	W 2–3	**Att:** 3,601 — **Scorers:** Harris[3]. **Booked:** Frampton, Henry, Harris
28th	● Crewe	a	W 0–1	**Att:** 4,680 — **Scorers:** Price. **Booked:** Whitbread, Alexander, Bolder, Henry, Price
31st	● Colchester	h	L 0–1	**Att:** 8,071 — **Booked:** Whitbread, Grimes

April
4th	● Walsall	h	W 3–1	**Att:** 8,800 — **Scorers:** Alexander[2], Price
10th	● Yeovil	a	L 2–0	**Att:** 6,230 — **Booked:** Dunne, Martin, Laird. **Dismissed:** Dunne
13th	● Peterborough	h	W 2–0	**Att:** 10,518 — **Scorers:** Martin, Price. **Booked:** Alexander
18th	● Cheltenham	a	W 1–3	**Att:** 2,942 — **Scorers:** Grimes, Henry, Laird. **Booked:** Pericard
25th	● Leyton Orient	h	W 2–1	**Att:** 11,414 — **Scorers:** Alexander[2]. **Booked:** Abdou, Frampton

May
2nd	● Carlisle	a	L 2–0	**Att:** 9,470
9th	● Leeds	h	W 1–0	**Att:** 13,228 — **Scorers:** Harris. **Booked:** Martin
14th	● Leeds	a	W 0–1	**Att:** 37,036 — **Scorers:** Abdou. **Booked:** Bolder, Martin, Dunne, Craig, Abdou
24th	● Scunthorpe	n	L 2–3	**Att:** 59,661 — **Scorers:** Alexander[2]. **Booked:** Craig

● Coca-Cola League 1/Play-Offs ● FA Cup ● Carling Cup ● Johnstone's Paint Trophy

LEAGUE ONE GOALKEEPER STATS

Player	Appearances	Match starts	Completed matches	Sub appearances	Subbed off	Clean sheets	Yellow cards	Red cards
David Forde	46	46	46	0	0	16	2	0

LEAGUE ONE OUTFIELD PLAYER STATS

Player	Appearances	Match starts	Completed matches	Substitute appearances	Subbed off	Goals scored	Yellow cards	Red cards
Nadjim Abdou	36	31	26	5	4	3	7	1
Gary Alexander	35	29	23	6	5	11	8	1
Scott Barron	14	7	7	7	0	0	2	0
Marcus Bignot	1	1	1	0	0	0	0	0
Adam Bolder	28	28	23	0	5	0	4	0
Ahmet Brkovic	6	3	2	3	1	1	1	0
Tony Craig	44	43	42	1	0	2	7	1
Richard Duffy	12	11	4	1	7	0	2	0
Alan Dunne	24	20	17	4	2	0	4	1
Jermaine Easter	5	2	0	3	1	1	1	1
Adrian Forbes	2	0	0	2	0	0	0	0
Andy Frampton	37	32	29	5	3	1	7	0
Ali Fuseini	17	11	6	6	5	0	2	0
Lewis Grabban	31	29	14	2	15	6	3	0
Ashley Grimes	17	4	1	13	3	2	3	0
Chris Hackett	22	15	10	7	5	0	5	0
Neil Harris	35	20	13	15	7	9	4	0
James Henry	16	15	10	1	5	3	3	0
Tresor Kandol	18	16	7	2	8	8	2	1
Marc Laird	38	30	23	8	7	5	5	0
David Martin	44	37	19	7	17	4	8	1
Izale McLeod	7	5	2	2	3	2	1	0
Karl Moore	6	2	0	4	3	0	0	0
Gifton Noel-Williams	1	1	0	0	1	0	0	0
Vincent Pericard	2	2	1	0	1	0	1	0
Jason Price	8	6	5	2	1	3	1	0
Paul Robinson	26	26	23	0	2	2	5	1
Ryan Smith	1	0	0	1	0	0	0	0
Daniel Spiller	2	0	0	2	0	0	0	0
Zak Whitbread	38	34	32	4	2	0	9	0

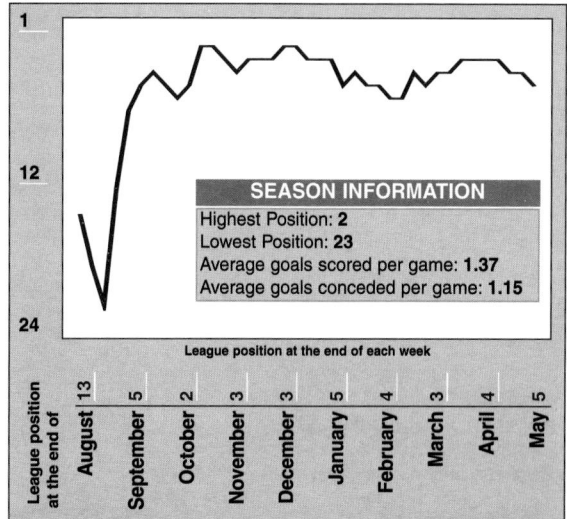

League position at the end of										
August 13	September 5	October 2	November 3	December 3	January 5	February 4	March 3	April 4	May 5	

SEASON INFORMATION
Highest Position: **2**
Lowest Position: **23**
Average goals scored per game: **1.37**
Average goals conceded per game: **1.15**

League position at the end of each week

LONGEST SEQUENCES

Wins (30/08/08–28/09/08)	5	Undefeated home (18/10/08–17/01/09)	8
Losses (31/01/09–09/02/09)	2	Undefeated away (14/02/09–28/03/09)	7
Draws (on two occasions)	2	Without scoring (20/12/08–26/12/08)	2
Undefeated (16/08/08–28/09/08)	7	Without conceding (on two occasions)	3
Without win (31/01/09–21/02/09)	5	Scoring (11/10/08–15/11/08)	7

CARDS RECEIVED

96 **8**

QUICK-FIRE GOALS

From the start of a match
Tresor Kandol (v Oldham) 0:13

By a substitute after coming on
David Martin (v Stockport) 11:20

GOALS SCORED/CONCEDED PER FIVE-MINUTE INTERVALS

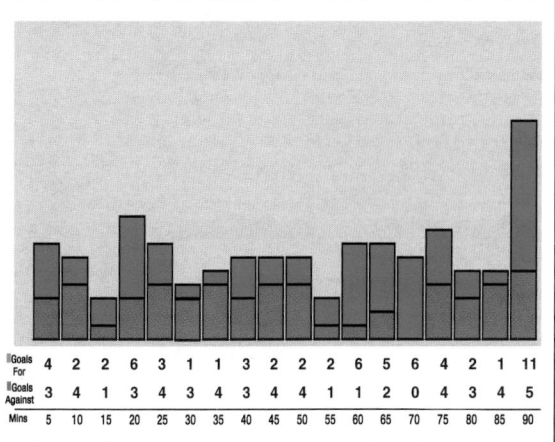

Goals For	4	2	2	6	3	1	1	3	2	2	2	6	5	6	4	2	1	11
Goals Against	3	4	1	3	4	3	4	3	4	4	1	1	2	0	4	3	4	5
Mins	5	10	15	20	25	30	35	40	45	50	55	60	65	70	75	80	85	90

MK DONS

AFTER losing manager Paul Ince and captain Keith Andrews to Blackburn in the close season, the MK Dons were set for a tough start to their first season back in Coca-Cola League One.

Eyebrows were raised when Roberto Di Matteo was installed as manager despite having no previous experience, but the Italian soon had the club on the charge.

With Sam Baldock – the club's first academy product from Milton Keynes – finding the net 12 times and Aaron Wilbraham scoring 16, the Dons were in with a shout of automatic promotion until the final weeks. But they had to settle for the play-offs and their semi-final against Scunthorpe went down to a penalty shoot-out, with Tore André Flo missing the vital spot-kick to condemn the Dons to at least another season in the third tier.

CLUB SUMMARY

FORMED	1889
MANAGER	Roberto Di Matteo
GROUND	stadium:mk
CAPACITY	22,000
NICKNAME	The Dons
WEBSITE	www.mkdons.com

The New Football Pools PLAYER OF THE SEASON — **Aaron Wilbraham**

OVERALL
P	W	D	L	F	A	GD
52	27	11	14	87	53	34

COCA-COLA FOOTBALL LEAGUE ONE
Pos	P	W	D	L	F	A	GD	Pts
3	46	26	9	11	83	47	36	87

HOME
Pos	P	W	D	L	F	A	GD	Pts
8	23	12	4	7	42	25	17	40

AWAY
Pos	P	W	D	L	F	A	GD	Pts
2	23	14	5	4	41	22	19	47

CUP PROGRESS DETAILS
Competition	Round reached	Knocked out by
FA Cup	R1	Bradford
JP Trophy	R2	Bournemouth
Carling Cup	R2	Cardiff

BIGGEST WIN (ALL COMPS)
14/03/09 6–2 v Oldham **FL1**

BIGGEST DEFEAT (ALL COMPS)
0–2 on four occasions

ATTENDANCE RECORD
High	Low	Average
17,717	6,931	10,551
v Leicester (28/02/2009)	v Stockport (21/10/2008)	

RESULTS 2008/09

August
9th	● Leicester	a	L 2–0	Att: 23,351 — **Booked:** O'Hanlon
12th	● Norwich	h	W 1–0	Att: 6,261 — **Scorers:** Baldock. **Booked:** Leven
16th	● Northampton	h	W 1–0	Att: 12,078 — **Scorers:** Wilbraham
23rd	● Huddersfield	a	W 1–3	Att: 13,189 — **Scorers:** Baldock, Leven, Stirling. **Booked:** Wright
26th	● Cardiff	a	L 2–1	Att: 6,334 — **Scorers:** O'Hanlon. **Booked:** Stirling
30th	● Swindon	h	L 1–2	Att: 8,846 — **Scorers:** Stirling. **Booked:** Regan, Gallen

September
6th	● Yeovil	h	W 3–0	Att: 7,959 — **Scorers:** Baldock, Leven[2]
13th	● Oldham	a	L 2–0	Att: 5,530
20th	● Colchester	a	W 0–3	Att: 4,888 — **Scorers:** Baldock[2], Wilbraham. **Booked:** Wilbraham
27th	● Peterborough	h	L 1–2	Att: 10,876 — **Scorers:** Gerba. **Booked:** Llera, Gueret, Navarro

October
4th	● Millwall	a	W 0–4	Att: 9,871 — **Scorers:** Baldock[2], O'Hanlon, Robinson OG. **Booked:** Chadwick, Leven, Wright, Baldock
7th	● Bournemouth	h	L 0–1	Att: 4,329 — **Booked:** Gallen. **Dismissed:** Belson
11th	● Carlisle	h	W 3–1	Att: 11,194 — **Scorers:** Leven[2], Llera. **Booked:** Llera
18th	● Crewe	a	D 2–2	Att: 4,055 — **Scorers:** Baldock, Chadwick. **Booked:** O'Hanlon
21st	● Stockport	h	L 1–2	Att: 6,931 — **Scorers:** Gerba. **Booked:** Leven, Cummings, Llera, Gallen, Navarro
25th	● Cheltenham	h	W 3–1	Att: 8,190 — **Scorers:** Baldock, Gerba[2]. **Booked:** Stirling. **Dismissed:** Gueret
28th	● Leyton Orient	a	W 1–2	Att: 3,869 — **Scorers:** Chadwick[2]. **Booked:** Gerba. **Dismissed:** Cummings

November
1st	● Tranmere	h	W 1–0	Att: 8,185 — **Scorers:** Gallen. **Booked:** Regan, Belson
8th	● Bradford	h	L 1–2	Att: 5,542 — **Scorers:** Johnson. **Booked:** Llera
15th	● Hartlepool	a	W 1–3	Att: 4,021 — **Scorers:** Lewington, Powell, Wright. **Booked:** Puncheon, Gerba
22nd	● Walsall	a	W 0–3	Att: 5,026 — **Scorers:** Gerba, Johnson, Wright. **Booked:** Johnson
25th	● Hereford	h	W 3–0	Att: 7,189 — **Scorers:** Johnson, Leven, Wright. **Booked:** Llera

December
6th	● Scunthorpe	h	L 0–2	Att: 11,550 — **Booked:** Baldock, Puncheon
12th	● Brighton	a	W 2–4	Att: 5,691 — **Scorers:** Johnson, Leven, Llera, Puncheon. **Booked:** Stirling, Navarro, Wilbraham, Puncheon
20th	● Leeds	h	W 3–1	Att: 17,073 — **Scorers:** O'Hanlon, Wilbraham[2]
26th	● Bristol Rovers	a	W 1–2	Att: 9,002 — **Scorers:** Wilbraham, Anthony OG. **Booked:** Llera, O'Hanlon, Navarro. **Dismissed:** Llera
28th	● Southend	h	W 2–0	Att: 10,432 — **Scorers:** Baldock, O'Hanlon. **Booked:** Navarro, O'Hanlon, Powell

January
12th	● Colchester	h	D 1–1	Att: 8,408 — **Scorers:** Wilbraham. **Booked:** Wilbraham, Johnson, Howell. **Dismissed:** Puncheon
17th	● Carlisle	a	L 3–2	Att: 6,298 — **Scorers:** Wilbraham[2]. **Booked:** Wilbraham, Navarro
20th	● Peterborough	a	D 0–0	Att: 8,982 — **Booked:** Llera, Chadwick, Navarro
27th	● Leyton Orient	h	L 1–2	Att: 8,170 — **Booked:** Chadwick
31st	● Cheltenham	a	W 3–5	Att: 3,681 — **Scorers:** Johnson[2], Wilbraham[3]. **Booked:** Gueret, Stirling, Puncheon

February
3rd	● Stockport	a	W 0–1	Att: 4,891 — **Scorers:** Wilbraham. **Booked:** Wilbraham, Regan
14th	● Hartlepool	h	W 3–1	Att: 8,657 — **Scorers:** Gerba[2], Lewington. **Booked:** Navarro, Llera
21st	● Tranmere	a	D 1–1	Att: 5,625 — **Scorers:** Leven. **Booked:** Navarro
28th	● Leicester	h	D 2–2	Att: 17,717 — **Scorers:** Leven[2]

March
7th	● Swindon	a	D 1–1	Att: 7,453 — **Scorers:** Wilbraham. **Booked:** Powell, Leven, Lewington. **Dismissed:** Lewington
10th	● Huddersfield	h	D 1–1	Att: 9,707 — **Scorers:** Baldock.
14th	● Oldham	h	W 6–2	Att: 10,621 — **Scorers:** Baldock[2], Gerba, Navarro, Puncheon, Wilbraham. **Booked:** Llera
17th	● Millwall	h	L 0–1	Att: 12,238 — **Booked:** Wilbraham
21st	● Yeovil	a	D 0–0	Att: 4,028 — **Booked:** Belson
24th	● Crewe	h	D 2–2	Att: 8,454 — **Scorers:** Puncheon, Wilbraham. **Booked:** Gueret, O'Hanlon, Howell, Leven
28th	● Leeds	a	L 2–0	Att: 27,649 — **Booked:** Leven, Regan, Puncheon, Johnson

April
4th	● Brighton	h	W 2–0	Att: 15,842 — **Scorers:** Gerba, Puncheon. **Booked:** Regan, Baldock, Gleeson
10th	● Southend	a	W 0–2	Att: 10,241 — **Scorers:** Wright[2]. **Booked:** Howell
13th	● Bristol Rovers	h	W 2–1	Att: 10,251 — **Scorers:** Chadwick, Gerba. **Booked:** Regan, Gueret, Navarro
18th	● Scunthorpe	a	W 0–1	Att: 4,873 — **Scorers:** Chadwick. **Booked:** Chadwick, Gueret, Baldock, Gleeson
25th	● Walsall	h	W 2–0	Att: 12,094 — **Booked:** Regan
28th	● Northampton	a	W 0–1	Att: 6,054 — **Scorers:** Wilbraham. **Booked:** Stirling, Navarro

May
2nd	● Hereford	a	W 0–1	Att: 3,224 — **Scorers:** Howell.
8th	● Scunthorpe	a	L 1–0	Att: 6,599 — **Scorers:** Wilbraham. **Booked:** Llera, Puncheon, Stirling
15th	● Scunthorpe	h	D 0–0	Att: 14,479 — **Booked:** Llera (Lost 6–7 on pens)

● Coca-Cola League 1/Play-Offs ● FA Cup ● Carling Cup ● Johnstone's Paint Trophy

actim

Coca-Cola
LEAGUE 1

LEAGUE ONE GOALKEEPER STATS

Player	Appearances	Match starts	Completed matches	Sub appearances	Subbed off	Clean sheets	Yellow cards	Red cards
Nathan Abbey	1	0	0	1	0	0	0	0
Willy Gueret	44	44	43	0	0	16	5	1
Lewis Price	2	2	2	0	0	0	0	0

LEAGUE ONE OUTFIELD PLAYER STATS

Player	Appearances	Match starts	Completed matches	Substitute appearances	Subbed off	Goals scored	Yellow cards	Red cards
Keith Andrews	1	1	1	0	0	0	0	0
Sam Baldock	40	32	20	8	12	12	4	0
Flavien Belson	13	9	4	4	5	0	2	0
Luke Chadwick	24	21	6	3	15	6	3	0
Adam Chicksen	1	0	0	1	0	0	0	0
Shaun Cummings	32	29	26	3	2	0	1	1
Tore André Flo	13	2	1	11	1	0	0	0
Kevin Gallen	6	1	0	5	1	1	2	0
Ali Gerba	24	16	5	8	11	10	2	0
Stephen Gleeson	5	5	5	0	0	0	2	0
Luke Howell	15	9	7	6	2	1	3	0
Jemal Johnson	33	19	10	14	9	5	3	0
Peter Leven	40	37	34	3	3	10	6	0
Dean Lewington	40	40	38	0	1	2	1	1
Miguel Angel Llera	34	34	28	0	5	2	8	1
Carl Magnay	2	0	0	2	0	0	0	0
Bondz N'Gala	3	1	1	2	0	0	0	0
Alan Navarro	38	32	30	6	2	1	10	0
Sean O'Hanlon	40	40	38	0	2	3	5	0
Daniel Powell	7	0	0	7	0	1	2	0
Jason Puncheon	27	26	17	1	8	4	5	1
Carl Regan	27	24	19	3	5	0	7	0
Jude Stirling	32	21	19	11	2	2	4	0
Florian Sturm	5	2	0	3	2	0	0	0
Danny Swailes	1	1	0	0	1	0	0	0
Aaron Wilbraham	33	29	22	4	7	16	6	0
Mark Wright	32	29	15	3	14	5	2	0

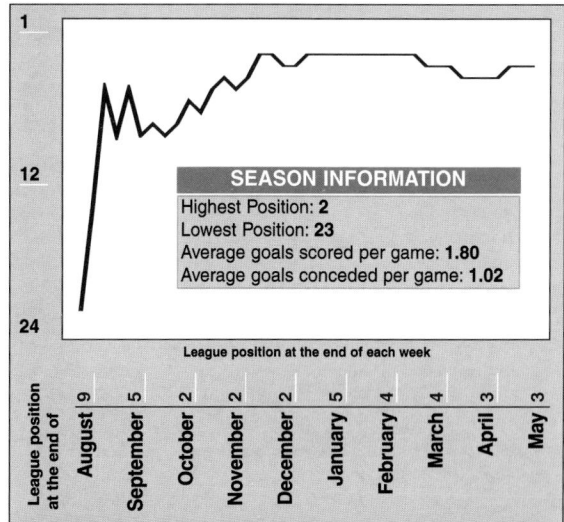

League position at the end of each week

League position at the end of: August 9, September 5, October 2, November 2, December 2, January 5, February 4, March 4, April 3, May 3

SEASON INFORMATION

Highest Position: **2**
Lowest Position: **23**
Average goals scored per game: **1.80**
Average goals conceded per game: **1.02**

LONGEST SEQUENCES

Wins (25/10/08–25/11/08)	6	Undefeated home (14/02/09–14/03/09)	4
Losses (–)		Undefeated away (20/09/08–26/12/08)	8
Draws (21/02/09–10/03/09)	4	Without scoring (17/03/09–21/03/09)	2
Undefeated (31/01/09–14/03/09)	8	Without conceding (on two occasions)	2
Without win (on three occasions)	4	Scoring (20/09/08–25/11/08)	12

CARDS RECEIVED

85   5

QUICK-FIRE GOALS

From the start of a match
Aaron Wilbraham (v Colchester) 1:38

By a substitute after coming on
Kevin Gallen (v Tranmere) 0:51

GOALS SCORED/CONCEDED PER FIVE-MINUTE INTERVALS

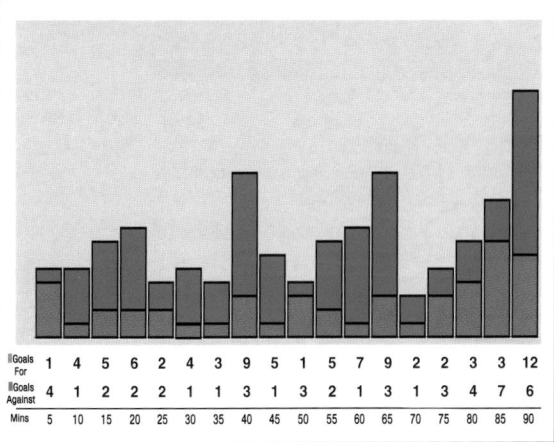

Goals For	1	4	5	6	2	4	3	9	5	1	5	7	9	2	2	3	3	12
Goals Against	4	1	2	2	2	1	1	3	1	3	2	1	3	1	3	4	7	6
Mins	5	10	15	20	25	30	35	40	45	50	55	60	65	70	75	80	85	90

NORTHAMPTON TOWN

NORTHAMPTON were left to rue a poor end to the season as Stuart Gray's side were relegated to Coca-Cola League Two after three years in the third tier. The Cobblers were 12th at Christmas, but won just five games in 2009 to plummet into the bottom four at the season's climax.

Gray's preparations were hampered in August by the sale of Mark Bunn to Blackburn and Gabor Gyepes to Cardiff, and the duo were not properly replaced.

Gray was forced to rely on loan signings as he operated on a shoestring budget, but relegation was confirmed on the final day of the season with a 3–0 defeat at Leeds.

Off the field, the club's long-standing attempts to develop Sixfields were again blocked by the council and the future looks bleak in terms of expansion.

CLUB SUMMARY

FORMED	1897
MANAGER	Stuart Gray
GROUND	Sixfields Stadium
CAPACITY	7,653
NICKNAME	The Cobblers
WEBSITE	www.ntfc.co.uk

The New Football Pools PLAYER OF THE SEASON

Mark Hughes

OVERALL

P	W	D	L	F	A	GD
52	14	15	23	69	75	-6

COCA-COLA FOOTBALL LEAGUE ONE

Pos	P	W	D	L	F	A	GD	Pts
21	46	12	13	21	61	65	-4	49

HOME

Pos	P	W	D	L	F	A	GD	Pts
14	23	8	8	7	38	29	9	32

AWAY

Pos	P	W	D	L	F	A	GD	Pts
22	23	4	5	14	23	36	-13	17

CUP PROGRESS DETAILS

Competition	Round reached	Knocked out by
FA Cup	R1	Leeds
JP Trophy	R1	Brighton
Carling Cup	R3	Sunderland

BIGGEST WIN (ALL COMPS)
24/01/09 5–1 v Crewe FL1

BIGGEST DEFEAT (ALL COMPS)
17/11/08 2–5 v Leeds FAC1R

ATTENDANCE RECORD

High	Low	Average
7,028	4,402	5,200
v Leicester (31/01/2009)	v Millwall (23/08/2008)	

RESULTS 2008/09

August
9th	● Cheltenham	......h W 4–2	**Att:** 4,716 — **Scorers:** Akinfenwa[2], Constantine, Doig.
			Booked: Guttridge, Gyepes, Gilligan
12th	● Millwall	..............a W 0–1	**Att:** 3,525 — **Scorers:** Crowe. **Booked:** Doig, Guttridge, Bunn
16th	● MK Dons	..........a L 1–0	**Att:** 12,078 — **Booked:** Guttridge, Coke
23rd	● Millwall	..............h D 0–0	**Att:** 4,402 — **Booked:** Osman, Little
26th	● Bolton	..............a W 1–2	**Att:** 7,136 — **Scorers:** Akinfenwa[2]
30th	● Tranmere	..........a L 4–1	**Att:** 5,034 — **Scorers:** Gilligan

September
2nd	● Brighton	..........h L 0–1	**Att:** 2,047
13th	● Peterborough	....h D 1–1	**Att:** 6,520 — **Scorers:** Larkin. **Booked:** Holt, Crowe. **Dismissed:** Crowe
16th	● Stockport	..........a D 1–1	**Att:** 4,974 — **Scorers:** Hawley. **Booked:** Guttridge, Coke, Hawley
20th	● Huddersfield	......a L 3–2	**Att:** 12,414 — **Scorers:** Davis, Goodwin OG
23rd	● Sunderland	........a D 2–2	**Att:** 21,082 — **Scorers:** Guttridge, Larkin. **Booked:** Davis (Lost 3–4 on pens)
27th	● Brighton	..........h D 2–2	**Att:** 5,389 — **Scorers:** Akinfenwa[2]

October
4th	● Crewe	..............a W 1–3	**Att:** 3,977 — **Scorers:** Akinfenwa, Jackman, Osman. **Booked:** Davis, Crowe
10th	● Hartlepool	........h W 1–0	**Att:** 5,277 — **Scorers:** Hawley. **Booked:** Gilligan, Akinfenwa, Hughes
18th	● Yeovil	..............h W 3–0	**Att:** 5,217 — **Scorers:** Akinfenwa, Crowe, Jackman
21st	● Swindon	..........a L 2–1	**Att:** 6,653 — **Scorers:** Coke. **Booked:** Hughes, Gilligan
25th	● Leicester	..........a D 0–0	**Att:** 22,795 — **Booked:** Doig

November
1st	● Walsall	..............a L 3–1	**Att:** 4,377 — **Scorers:** Constantine
7th	● Leeds	................a D 1–1	**Att:** 9,531 — **Scorers:** McGleish. **Booked:** Coke, Holt, Jackman.
			Dismissed: Coke
15th	● Oldham	............h L 0–1	**Att:** 5,067 — **Booked:** K. Walker
17th	● Leeds	................h L 2–5	**Att:** 3,960 — **Scorers:** Crowe[2]. **Booked:** Crowe
22nd	● Hereford	............a W 0–2	**Att:** 3,061 — **Scorers:** Gilligan, Jackman. **Booked:** Jackman, Davis
25th	● Leeds	................h W 2–1	**Att:** 6,008 — **Scorers:** Bignall, Davis
29th	● Colchester	........h L 1–2	**Att:** 4,833 — **Scorers:** Jackman. **Booked:** Guttridge, Coke

December
6th	● Leyton Orient	....h D 1–1	**Att:** 5,039 — **Scorers:** Davis.
13th	● Scunthorpe	......a D 4–4	**Att:** 3,976 — **Scorers:** Coke, Jackman[2], McGleish
20th	● Carlisle	..........h W 1–0	**Att:** 4,673 — **Scorers:** Crowe
26th	● Southend	..........a L 1–0	**Att:** 7,767 — **Booked:** Davis, Osman, K. Walker. **Dismissed:** Osman
28th	● Bristol Rovers	.h D 0–0	**Att:** 5,557

January
10th	● Huddersfield	....h D 1–1	**Att:** 5,110 — **Scorers:** Akinfenwa. **Dismissed:** Crowe
16th	● Hartlepool	........a L 2–0	**Att:** 3,814 — **Booked:** Akinfenwa
24th	● Crewe	..............h W 5–1	**Att:** 4,675 — **Scorers:** Clarke[3], Davis, Jackman. **Booked:** Doig
27th	● Colchester	........a L 2–1	**Att:** 3,973 — **Scorers:** Akinfenwa
			Booked: Hughes, Rodgers, Constantine. **Dismissed:** Rodgers
31st	● Leicester	..........h L 1–2	**Att:** 7,028 — **Scorers:** Constantine. **Booked:** Clarke, Davis

February
14th	● Oldham	............a L 2–1	**Att:** 4,629 — **Scorers:** Akinfenwa. **Booked:** Crowe, Doig
21st	● Walsall	..............h L 0–2	**Att:** 4,528
24th	● Brighton	..........a D 1–1	**Att:** 5,062 — **Scorers:** Gilligan. **Booked:** Doig, Dyer. **Dismissed:** Akinfenwa
28th	● Cheltenham	......a W 0–1	**Att:** 3,495 — **Scorers:** Crowe. **Booked:** Constantine, Rodgers

March
7th	● Tranmere	..........h D 1–1	**Att:** 4,546 — **Scorers:** Holt. **Booked:** Osman
10th	● Millwall	..............a L 1–0	**Att:** 6,685
14th	● Peterborough	....a L 1–0	**Att:** 8,881 — **Booked:** Osman, Crowe
21st	● Stockport	..........h W 4–0	**Att:** 4,814 — **Scorers:** Akinfenwa, Guttridge, Osman, Vernon.
			Booked: Osman, Hughes
24th	● Swindon	..........h L 3–4	**Att:** 5,025 — **Scorers:** Akinfenwa, Anya, Jackman. **Booked:** Crowe
28th	● Carlisle	..............a D 1–1	**Att:** 5,254 — **Scorers:** Guttridge. **Booked:** Dunn, Akinfenwa, Davis, Jackman
31st	● Yeovil	..............a L 1–0	**Att:** 3,884

April
10th	● Bristol Rovers	..a L 1–0	**Att:** 6,666
13th	● Southend	..........h L 2–3	**Att:** 5,190 — **Scorers:** Akinfenwa, Prijovic
18th	● Leyton Orient	....a W 1–3	**Att:** 4,665 — **Scorers:** Akinfenwa, Anya, Prijovic. **Booked:** Anya
21st	● Scunthorpe	......h D 3–3	**Att:** 4,416 — **Scorers:** Anya, Crowe, Hughes. **Booked:** Osman
25th	● Hereford	............h W 2–1	**Att:** 5,518 — **Scorers:** Crowe, Holt
28th	● MK Dons	..........h L 0–1	**Att:** 6,054 — **Booked:** Holt, Watts

May
2nd	● Leeds	................a L 3–0	**Att:** 34,214 — **Booked:** Dolman

● Coca-Cola League 1/Play-Offs ● FA Cup ● Carling Cup ● Johnstone's Paint Trophy

LEAGUE ONE GOALKEEPER STATS

Player	Appearances	Match starts	Completed matches	Sub appearances	Subbed off	Clean sheets	Yellow cards	Red cards
Mark Bunn	3	3	3	0	0	1	0	0
Chris Dunn	29	29	29	0	0	4	1	0
Frank Fielding	12	12	12	0	0	4	0	0
Ron-Robert Zieler	2	2	2	0	0	0	0	0

LEAGUE ONE OUTFIELD PLAYER STATS

Player	Appearances	Match starts	Completed matches	Substitute appearances	Subbed off	Goals scored	Yellow cards	Red cards
Adebayo Akinfenwa	33	29	15	4	13	13	3	1
Ikechi Anya	14	6	5	8	1	3	1	0
Joe Benjamin	4	0	0	4	0	0	0	0
Nicholas Bignall	5	1	0	4	1	1	0	0
Billy Clarke	5	5	2	0	3	3	1	0
Giles Coke	32	25	20	7	5	2	3	0
Leon Constantine	32	21	19	11	2	3	2	0
Jason Crowe	43	42	37	1	3	5	6	2
Liam Davis	29	21	11	8	10	4	5	0
Chris Doig	28	26	21	2	5	1	4	0
Liam Dolman	14	9	8	5	1	0	1	0
Alex Dyer	8	5	3	3	2	0	1	0
Ryan Gilligan	31	23	9	8	14	3	3	0
Luke Guttridge	25	23	12	2	11	2	4	0
Gabor Gyepes	2	2	2	0	0	0	1	0
Karl Hawley	11	11	9	0	2	2	1	0
Ian Henderson	3	0	0	3	0	0	0	0
Jared Hodgkiss	5	4	1	1	3	0	0	0
Andrew Holt	41	28	22	13	6	2	2	0
Mark Hughes	41	41	37	0	4	1	4	0
Danny Jackman	43	42	39	1	3	8	2	0
Colin Larkin	21	9	2	12	7	1	0	0
Mark Little	9	9	8	0	1	0	1	0
Carl Magnay	2	2	1	0	1	0	0	0
Scott McGleish	9	7	2	2	5	1	0	0
Abdul Osman	36	34	29	2	4	2	7	1
Aleksandar Prijovic	10	3	1	7	2	2	0	0
Paul Rodgers	11	9	6	2	2	0	3	1
Andy Todd	7	7	7	0	0	0	0	0
Scott Vernon	6	4	2	2	2	1	0	0
Kyle Walker	9	9	8	0	1	0	2	0
Adam Watts	5	3	3	2	0	0	1	0

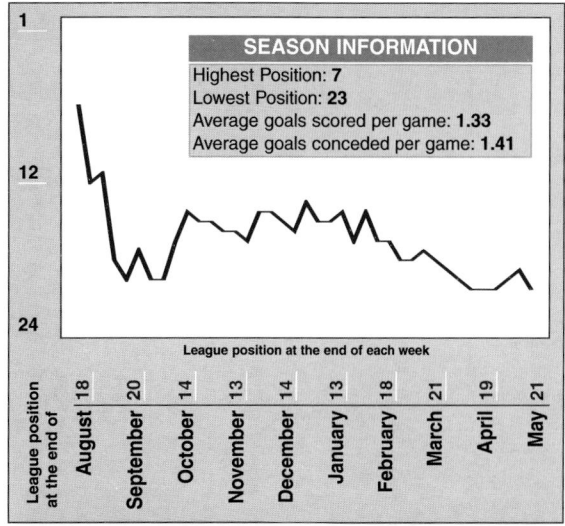

SEASON INFORMATION
Highest Position: **7**
Lowest Position: **23**
Average goals scored per game: **1.33**
Average goals conceded per game: **1.41**

League position at the end of each week

LONGEST SEQUENCES

Wins (04/10/08–18/10/08)	3	Undefeated home (09/08/08–18/10/08)	6
Losses (27/01/09–21/02/09)	4	Undefeated away (on two occasions)	2
Draws (on three occasions)	2	Without scoring (on five occasions)	2
Undefeated (27/09/08–18/10/08)	4	Without conceding (10/10/08–18/10/08)	2
Without win (16/08/08–27/09/08)	7	Scoring (30/08/08–21/10/08)	9

CARDS RECEIVED

59 **5**

QUICK-FIRE GOALS

From the start of a match
Liam Davis (v Leyton Orient) 1:09

By a substitute after coming on
Aleksandar Prijovic (v L Orient) 6:15

GOALS SCORED/CONCEDED PER FIVE-MINUTE INTERVALS

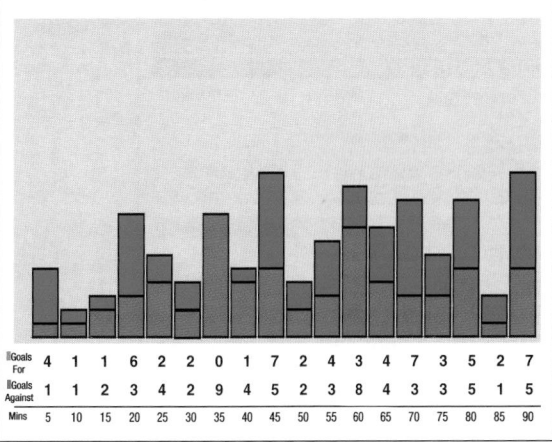

Goals For	4	1	1	6	2	2	0	1	7	2	4	3	4	7	3	5	2	7
Goals Against	1	1	2	3	4	2	9	4	5	2	3	8	4	3	3	5	1	5
Mins	5	10	15	20	25	30	35	40	45	50	55	60	65	70	75	80	85	90

DESPITE a wave of pre-season optimism and the January acquisition of striker Dean Windass, some high-profile departures and a disappointing run-in caused Oldham's promotion hopes to disappear.

A superb start to the campaign saw the Latics – under the leadership of John Sheridan – cement a place amongst the top six, enjoying a three-week spell at the summit in September.

However, a turning point came with the 6–2 defeat to promotion rivals MK Dons in March. Sheridan was relieved of his duties after that loss and Lee Hughes was loaned out to Blackpool as the Latics slumped to a 10th-place finish under caretaker boss Joe Royle.

But, after the appointment of Dave Penney as Sheridan's permanent successor, there is fresh reason for optimism as a new era begins at Boundary Park in 2009/10.

CLUB SUMMARY

FORMED	1895
MANAGER	Dave Penney
GROUND	Boundary Park
CAPACITY	13,595
NICKNAME	The Latics
WEBSITE	www.oldhamathletic.co.uk

The New Football Pools PLAYER OF THE SEASON

Reuben Hazell

OVERALL

P	W	D	L	F	A	GD
51	16	20	15	69	72	-3

COCA-COLA FOOTBALL LEAGUE ONE

Pos	P	W	D	L	F	A	GD	Pts
10	46	16	17	13	66	65	1	65

HOME

Pos	P	W	D	L	F	A	GD	Pts
10	23	9	9	5	35	24	11	36

AWAY

Pos	P	W	D	L	F	A	GD	Pts
11	23	7	8	8	31	41	-10	29

CUP PROGRESS DETAILS

Competition	Round reached	Knocked out by
FA Cup	R1	Cheltenham
JP Trophy	R1	Morecambe
Carling Cup	R2	Burnley

BIGGEST WIN (ALL COMPS)

23/08/08 4–0 v Cheltenham **FL1**

BIGGEST DEFEAT (ALL COMPS)

17/01/09 0–5 v Hereford **FL1**

ATTENDANCE RECORD

High	Low	Average
8,901	3,745	5,636
v Leicester (18/10/2008)	v Bristol Rovers (24/02/2009)	

RESULTS 2008/09

August

9th	● Millwall	h	W 4–3	Att: 5,367 — **Scorers:** Alessandra, Liddell[2], Taylor. **Booked:** O'Grady, Liddell, Taylor
12th	● Rochdale	a	D 0–0	Att: 5,786 — **Booked:** Hazell, Taylor. **Dismissed:** Davies (Won 4–1 on pens)
16th	● Leeds	a	W 0–2	Att: 24,631 — **Scorers:** Taylor[2]. **Booked:** Eardley, O'Grady
23rd	● Cheltenham	h	W 4–0	Att: 4,673 — **Scorers:** Hughes[3], Whitaker
26th	● Burnley	a	L 3–0	Att: 5,528 — **Booked:** Hazell
30th	● Colchester	a	D 2–2	Att: 4,708 — **Scorers:** Smalley, Taylor. **Booked:** Allott, Hughes

September

2nd	● Morecambe	h	D 1–1	Att: 2,016 — **Scorers:** Whitaker (Lost 5–4 on pens)
6th	● Tranmere	a	W 0–1	Att: 6,802 — **Scorers:** Hazell. **Booked:** Lomax, Crossley, Gregan, Eardley
13th	● MK Dons	h	W 2–0	Att: 5,530 — **Scorers:** Allott, Hughes. **Booked:** Gregan, Taylor
20th	● Hartlepool	a	D 3–3	Att: 4,507 — **Scorers:** Hughes, Taylor[2]. **Booked:** Hazell, Davies. **Dismissed:** Gregan
27th	● Huddersfield	h	D 1–1	Att: 7,418 — **Scorers:** Liddell. **Booked:** Lomax, Whitaker, Hughes

October

3rd	● Stockport	a	L 3–1	Att: 8,360 — **Scorers:** Liddell
12th	● Hereford	h	W 4–0	Att: 5,468 — **Scorers:** Hughes, Jones, Liddell, Whitaker. **Booked:** Hazell
18th	● Leicester	h	D 1–1	Att: 8,901 — **Scorers:** Whitaker. **Booked:** Whitaker, Hughes
21st	● Bristol Rovers	a	L 2–0	Att: 6,379 — **Booked:** Allott, Lomax, Gregan
25th	● Swindon	a	L 2–0	Att: 6,756 — **Booked:** Ormerod, Allott
28th	● Scunthorpe	h	W 3–0	Att: 6,057 — **Scorers:** Alessandra[3]. **Booked:** Hughes, Allott

November

1st	● Yeovil	h	L 0–2	Att: 5,318 — **Booked:** Jones, Hughes
8th	● Cheltenham	a	D 2–2	Att: 2,585 — **Scorers:** Taylor, Whitaker
15th	● Northampton	a	W 0–1	Att: 5,067 — **Scorers:** Liddell. **Booked:** Hughes, Byfield. **Dismissed:** Hughes
18th	● Cheltenham	h	L 0–1	Att: 2,552 — **Booked:** Hazell, Wolfenden
22nd	● Southend	a	W 1–2	Att: 7,041 — **Scorers:** Hughes, Taylor. **Booked:** Stam, Maher
25th	● Walsall	h	W 3–2	Att: 3,936 — **Scorers:** Allott, Hughes[2]

December

6th	● Brighton	h	D 1–1	Att: 4,803 — **Scorers:** Liddell. **Booked:** Hughes
13th	● Peterborough	a	D 2–2	Att: 6,219 — **Scorers:** Hughes[2]. **Booked:** Whitaker, Fleming, Eardley, Hughes
20th	● Leyton Orient	h	D 1–1	Att: 6,839 — **Scorers:** Liddell. **Booked:** Fleming
26th	● Crewe	a	W 0–3	Att: 5,780 — **Scorers:** Byfield, Hughes[2]. **Booked:** Hazell
28th	● Carlisle	h	D 0–0	Att: 6,254 — **Booked:** Maher

January

3rd	● Huddersfield	a	D 1–1	Att: 16,950 — **Scorers:** Allott. **Booked:** Hazell, Allott
12th	● Hartlepool	h	W 2–1	Att: 4,211 — **Scorers:** Hughes, Smalley
17th	● Hereford	a	L 5–0	Att: 3,342 — **Booked:** Eardley
24th	● Stockport	h	W 3–1	Att: 7,605 — **Scorers:** Hughes, Taylor, Whitaker
27th	● Scunthorpe	a	L 2–0	Att: 4,447 — **Booked:** Hazell, Smalley, Windass, Taylor
31st	● Swindon	h	D 0–0	Att: 4,712

February

7th	● Leicester	a	D 0–0	Att: 22,328 — **Booked:** Taylor, Hughes, Eardley. **Dismissed:** Fleming
14th	● Northampton	h	W 2–1	Att: 4,629 — **Scorers:** Hazell, Windass. **Booked:** Windass
21st	● Yeovil	a	D 2–2	Att: 4,150 — **Scorers:** Smalley, Forbes OG. **Booked:** Hazell, Gregan
24th	● Bristol Rovers	h	L 0–2	Att: 3,745
28th	● Millwall	a	W 2–3	Att: 8,551 — **Scorers:** Hughes, Smalley, Taylor. **Booked:** Smalley, Eardley

March

2nd	● Leeds	h	D 1–1	Att: 7,835 — **Scorers:** Hughes. **Booked:** Hazell, Hughes
7th	● Colchester	h	L 0–1	Att: 4,591 — **Booked:** Smalley
14th	● MK Dons	a	L 6–2	Att: 10,621 — **Scorers:** Hughes, Maher. **Booked:** Gregan, Taylor, Allott
21st	● Tranmere	h	L 0–2	Att: 7,489 — **Booked:** Stam. **Dismissed:** Stam
24th	● Cheltenham	a	D 1–1	Att: 2,992 — **Scorers:** Whitaker. **Booked:** Allott
28th	● Leyton Orient	a	L 2–1	Att: 4,034 — **Scorers:** Whitaker. **Booked:** Gregan, Westlake

April

4th	● Peterborough	h	L 1–2	Att: 5,083 — **Scorers:** Taylor
10th	● Carlisle	a	D 1–1	Att: 6,635 — **Scorers:** Eardley. **Booked:** Hazell. **Dismissed:** Jones
13th	● Crewe	h	D 1–1	Att: 4,334 — **Scorers:** Hazell
18th	● Brighton	a	L 3–1	Att: 6,618 — **Scorers:** Alessandra. **Booked:** Smalley, Allott, Taylor
25th	● Southend	h	D 1–1	Att: 4,830 — **Scorers:** Eardley. **Booked:** Westlake

May

2nd	● Walsall	a	W 1–2	Att: 4,807 — **Scorers:** Brooke, Smalley

● Coca-Cola League 1/Play-Offs ● FA Cup ● Carling Cup ● Johnstone's Paint Trophy

actim — Coca-Cola LEAGUE 1

LEAGUE ONE GOALKEEPER STATS

Player	Appearances	Match starts	Completed matches	Sub appearances	Subbed off	Clean sheets	Yellow cards	Red cards
Jan Budtz	3	3	3	0	0	0	0	0
Mark Crossley	21	21	20	0	1	7	1	0
Greg Fleming	18	17	16	1	0	3	1	1
Shane Supple	5	5	5	0	0	0	0	0

LEAGUE ONE OUTFIELD PLAYER STATS

Player	Appearances	Match starts	Completed matches	Substitute appearances	Subbed off	Goals scored	Yellow cards	Red cards
Lewis Alessandra	32	12	3	20	9	5	0	0
Mark Allott	45	44	39	1	5	3	8	0
Paul Black	3	2	0	1	2	0	0	0
Ryan Brooke	1	0	0	1	0	1	0	0
Darren Byfield	8	8	3	0	5	1	1	0
Richie Byrne	4	3	2	1	1	0	0	0
Craig Davies	12	5	3	7	2	0	1	0
Neal Eardley	34	31	30	3	1	2	6	0
Fabio Ferreira	1	0	0	1	0	0	0	0
Scott Golbourne	8	7	6	1	1	0	0	0
Sean Gregan	40	38	36	2	1	0	6	1
Reuben Hazell	43	43	43	0	0	3	8	0
Seb Hines	4	4	4	0	0	0	0	0
Lee Hughes	37	36	24	1	11	18	10	1
Daniel Jones	23	23	21	0	1	1	1	1
Steven Kabba	8	7	1	1	6	0	0	0
Kieran Lee	7	6	1	1	5	0	0	0
Andy Liddell	32	18	2	14	16	8	1	0
Kelvin Lomax	27	27	26	0	1	0	3	0
Kevin Maher	28	21	11	7	10	1	2	0
Chris O'Grady	13	3	1	10	2	0	2	0
Brett Ormerod	5	2	0	3	2	0	1	0
Deane Smalley	34	22	17	12	5	5	4	0
Stefan Stam	13	11	8	2	2	0	2	1
Chris Taylor	42	42	39	0	3	10	6	0
Ian Westlake	5	5	5	0	0	0	2	0
Danny Whitaker	39	30	24	9	6	6	3	0
Dean Windass	11	9	3	2	6	1	2	0
Matthew Wolfenden	5	1	0	4	1	0	0	0

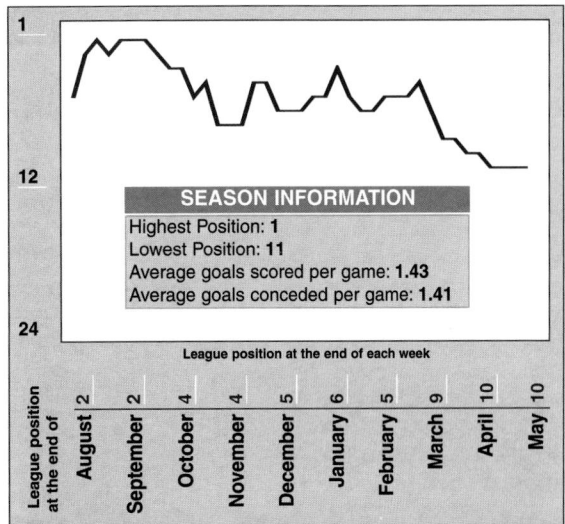

League position at the end of each week

SEASON INFORMATION
Highest Position: **1**
Lowest Position: **11**
Average goals scored per game: **1.43**
Average goals conceded per game: **1.41**

LONGEST SEQUENCES

Wins (09/08/08–23/08/08)	3	Undefeated home (25/11/08–14/02/09)	8
Losses (07/03/09–21/03/09)	3	Undefeated away (09/08/08–20/09/08)	5
Draws (06/12/08–20/12/08)	3	Without scoring (27/01/09–07/02/09)	3
Undefeated (15/11/08–12/01/09)	10	Without conceding (on four occasions)	2
Without win (02/03/09–25/04/09)	11	Scoring (09/08/08–18/10/08)	11

CARDS RECEIVED

72   5

QUICK-FIRE GOALS

From the start of a match
Andy Liddell (v Millwall) 2:13

By a substitute after coming on
Ryan Brooke (v Walsall) 2:22

GOALS SCORED/CONCEDED PER FIVE-MINUTE INTERVALS

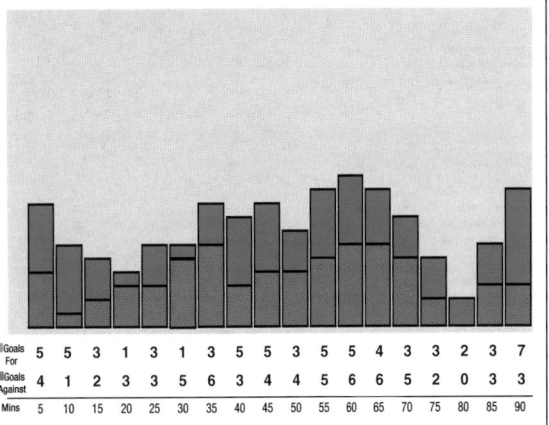

Goals For	5	5	3	1	3	1	3	5	5	3	5	5	4	3	3	2	3	7
Goals Against	4	1	2	3	3	5	6	3	4	4	5	6	6	5	2	0	3	3
Mins	5	10	15	20	25	30	35	40	45	50	55	60	65	70	75	80	85	90

PETERBOROUGH UNITED

SOME felt that Darren Ferguson was being overly optimistic when he predicted a second successive promotion last summer, but that confidence proved well placed as the Posh finished second in the table.

Ferguson kept faith with the majority of the side which came up from the basement division, adding just Paul Coutts, Russell Martin and Sergio Torres to his first-team squad.

However, with the front three of George Boyd, Aaron Mclean and Craig Mackail-Smith firing, the Posh soon found themselves in the promotion mix. That trio hit 55 goals between them in all competitions as Ferguson's side joined Leicester in the top two.

The key period of the season came in March and April when Peterborough picked up seven straight wins, and promotion was confirmed with a 1–0 win at Colchester.

CLUB SUMMARY

FORMED	1934
MANAGER	Darren Ferguson
GROUND	London Road
CAPACITY	15,314
NICKNAME	The Posh
WEBSITE	www.theposh.com

The New Football Pools PLAYER OF THE SEASON

George Boyd

OVERALL

P	W	D	L	F	A	GD
53	28	13	12	83	61	22

COCA-COLA FOOTBALL LEAGUE ONE

Pos	P	W	D	L	F	A	GD	Pts
2	46	26	11	9	78	54	24	89

HOME

Pos	P	W	D	L	F	A	GD	Pts
4	23	14	6	3	41	22	19	48

AWAY

Pos	P	W	D	L	F	A	GD	Pts
3	23	12	5	6	37	32	5	41

CUP PROGRESS DETAILS

Competition	Round reached	Knocked out by
FA Cup	R3	West Brom
JP Trophy	R2	Dag & Red
Carling Cup	R1	Bristol C

BIGGEST WIN (ALL COMPS)
25/10/08 4–0 v Huddersfield **FL1**

BIGGEST DEFEAT (ALL COMPS)
20/12/08 0–4 v Leicester **FL1**

ATTENDANCE RECORD

High	Low	Average
14,110	4,876	7,599
v Leicester (28/03/2009)	v Bristol Rovers (06/09/2008)	

RESULTS 2008/09

August
9th	● Southend	a	L 1–0	Att: 8,665 — **Booked:** Boyd, Lee, Williams
12th	● Bristol City	a	L 2–1	Att: 5,684 — **Scorers:** Boyd. **Booked:** Torres
16th	● Leyton Orient	h	W 3–0	Att: 6,643 — **Scorers:** Mackail-Smith², Mclean
23rd	● Scunthorpe	a	L 1–0	Att: 4,717
30th	● Hartlepool	h	L 1–2	Att: 5,728 — **Scorers:** Boyd. **Booked:** Hyde, Mclean

September
6th	● Bristol Rovers	h	W 5–4	Att: 4,876 — **Scorers:** Mackail-Smith³, Mclean, Rendell
13th	● Northampton	a	D 1–1	Att: 6,520 — **Scorers:** Boyd
20th	● Tranmere	h	D 2–2	Att: 5,735 — **Scorers:** Mackail-Smith, Zakuani. **Booked:** Lee, Morgan
27th	● MK Dons	a	W 1–2	Att: 10,876 — **Scorers:** Green, Mackail-Smith. **Booked:** Hyde

October
4th	● Leeds	h	W 2–0	Att: 13,191 — **Scorers:** Boyd, Mackail-Smith
7th	● Dag & Red	h	L 0–1	Att: 2,644
11th	● Walsall	a	W 1–2	Att: 4,792 — **Scorers:** Batt, Whelpdale. **Booked:** Charnock, Martin
18th	● Carlisle	a	D 3–3	Att: 6,074 — **Scorers:** Lee, Mackail-Smith². **Booked:** Boyd, Lee
21st	● Brighton	h	D 0–0	Att: 5,772 — **Booked:** Lee, Morgan, Mackail-Smith, Zakuani
25th	● Huddersfield	h	W 4–0	Att: 7,064 — **Scorers:** Boyd, Mclean², Whelpdale
28th	● Crewe	a	D 1–1	Att: 3,699 — **Scorers:** Mclean. **Booked:** Zakuani, Hyde

November
1st	● Hereford	h	W 2–0	Att: 6,087 — **Scorers:** Mackail-Smith². **Booked:** Lee, Batt
9th	● AFC Hornchurch	a	W 0–1	Att: 3,000 — **Scorers:** Mackail-Smith
15th	● Yeovil	a	W 0–1	Att: 4,001 — **Scorers:** Mclean. **Booked:** Keates, Batt
22nd	● Colchester	h	W 2–1	Att: 7,401 — **Scorers:** Boyd, Mackail-Smith. **Booked:** Morgan
25th	● Swindon	a	D 2–2	Att: 6,616 — **Scorers:** Batt, McGovern OG. **Booked:** Williams, Lewis, Lewis
29th	● Tranmere	h	D 0–0	Att: 5,980 — **Booked:** Williams

December
6th	● Stockport	a	W 1–3	Att: 6,148 — **Scorers:** Mackail-Smith, Raynes OG, Tunnicliffe OG. **Booked:** Boyd, Batt
9th	● Tranmere	a	W 1–2	Att: 3,139 — **Scorers:** Mackail-Smith, Mclean (AET)
13th	● Oldham	h	D 2–2	Att: 6,219 — **Scorers:** Mclean². **Booked:** Mclean, Morgan
20th	● Leicester	a	L 4–0	Att: 23,390 — **Booked:** Morgan
26th	● Millwall	h	W 1–0	Att: 9,351 — **Scorers:** Mclean. **Booked:** Lewis
28th	● Cheltenham	a	W 3–6	Att: 3,976 — **Scorers:** Boyd, Lee, Mackail-Smith, Mclean, Whelpdale, Wright OG

January
3rd	● West Brom	a	D 1–1	Att: 18,659 — **Scorers:** Mackail-Smith
13th	● West Brom	h	L 0–2	Att: 10,735
17th	● Walsall	h	W 1–0	Att: 5,705 — **Scorers:** Whelpdale
20th	● MK Dons	h	D 0–0	Att: 8,982 — **Booked:** Morgan, Whelpdale
24th	● Leeds	a	L 3–1	Att: 22,766 — **Scorers:** Mackail-Smith
27th	● Crewe	h	W 4–2	Att: 5,782 — **Scorers:** Boyd², Keates, Mclean
31st	● Huddersfield	a	L 1–0	Att: 14,480

February
10th	● Brighton	a	W 2–4	Att: 5,087 — **Scorers:** Keates, Mackail-Smith, Mclean². **Booked:** Lee
14th	● Yeovil	h	L 1–3	Att: 6,129 — **Scorers:** Mclean. **Booked:** Blanchett, Keates
17th	● Tranmere	a	D 1–1	Att: 4,862 — **Scorers:** Mackail-Smith. **Booked:** Zakuani, Coutts
21st	● Hereford	a	W 0–1	Att: 3,217 — **Scorers:** Mclean. **Booked:** Coutts, Lewis
24th	● Carlisle	h	W 1–0	Att: 5,103 — **Scorers:** Mclean. **Booked:** Chester
28th	● Southend	h	L 1–2	Att: 7,341 — **Scorers:** Keates. **Booked:** Keates, Boyd

March
3rd	● Leyton Orient	a	W 2–3	Att: 3,381 — **Scorers:** Martin, Torres, Whelpdale. **Booked:** Lee, Boyd, Williams
7th	● Hartlepool	a	W 1–2	Att: 3,722 — **Scorers:** Boyd, Keates
10th	● Scunthorpe	h	W 2–1	Att: 5,637 — **Scorers:** Mackail-Smith, Whelpdale. **Booked:** Torres
14th	● Northampton	h	W 1–0	Att: 8,881 — **Scorers:** Lee. **Dismissed:** Zakuani
21st	● Bristol Rovers	a	W 0–1	Att: 7,103 — **Scorers:** Mclean
28th	● Leicester	h	W 2–0	Att: 14,110 — **Scorers:** Lee, Whelpdale. **Booked:** Lee

April
4th	● Oldham	a	W 1–2	Att: 5,083 — **Scorers:** Mackail-Smith². **Booked:** Batt
10th	● Cheltenham	h	D 1–1	Att: 9,817 — **Scorers:** Mclean
13th	● Millwall	a	L 2–0	Att: 10,518 — **Booked:** Mclean, Lee
18th	● Stockport	h	W 1–0	Att: 8,333 — **Scorers:** Mackail-Smith. **Booked:** Coutts, Boyd
25th	● Colchester	a	W 0–1	Att: 6,532 — **Booked:** Whelpdale

May
2nd	● Swindon	h	D 2–2	Att: 10,886 — **Scorers:** Keates, Mackail-Smith

● Coca-Cola League 1/Play-Offs ● FA Cup ● Carling Cup ● Johnstone's Paint Trophy

LEAGUE ONE GOALKEEPER STATS

Player	Appearances	Match starts	Completed matches	Sub appearances	Subbed off	Clean sheets	Yellow cards	Red cards
Joe Lewis	46	46	45	0	1	16	3	0
James McKeown	1	0	0	1	0	0	0	0

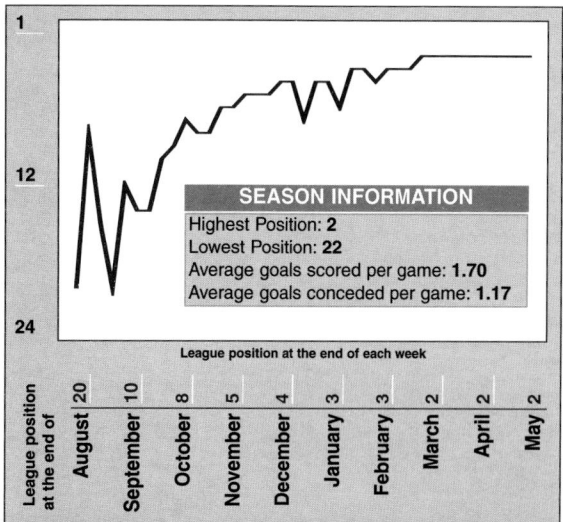

SEASON INFORMATION

Highest Position: **2**
Lowest Position: **22**
Average goals scored per game: **1.70**
Average goals conceded per game: **1.17**

League position at the end of each week

LEAGUE ONE OUTFIELD PLAYER STATS

Player	Appearances	Match starts	Completed matches	Substitute appearances	Subbed off	Goals scored	Yellow cards	Red cards
Shaun Batt	30	10	4	20	6	2	4	0
Shane Blackett	11	7	5	4	2	0	0	0
Daniel Blanchett	3	2	2	1	0	0	1	0
George Boyd	46	46	40	0	6	9	6	0
Kieran Charnock	2	2	1	0	1	0	1	0
James Chester	5	5	5	0	0	0	1	0
Paul Coutts	37	34	27	3	7	0	3	0
Andrew Crofts	9	4	3	5	1	0	0	0
Jamie Day	5	5	4	0	1	0	0	0
Lee Frecklington	7	2	0	5	2	0	0	0
Dominic Green	16	3	0	13	3	1	0	0
Liam Hatch	1	0	0	1	0	0	0	0
Micah Hyde	9	5	3	4	2	0	3	0
Dean Keates	38	37	33	1	4	5	3	0
Charlie Lee	44	39	31	5	8	5	9	0
Craig Mackail-Smith	46	43	36	3	7	23	1	0
Russell Martin	46	46	45	0	1	1	1	0
Aaron Mclean	42	39	34	3	5	18	3	0
Craig Morgan	27	26	25	1	1	0	5	0
Scott Rendell	3	2	1	1	1	1	0	0
Sergio Torres	15	10	2	5	8	1	1	0
Chris Westwood	16	10	8	6	2	0	0	0
Chris Whelpdale	39	29	11	10	18	7	2	0
Tom Williams	25	22	17	3	5	0	3	0
Ben Wright	1	0	0	1	0	0	0	0
Gabriel Zakuani	32	32	27	0	4	0	3	1

LONGEST SEQUENCES

Wins (03/03/09–04/04/09)	7	Undefeated home (06/09/08–27/01/09)	12
Losses (23/08/08–30/08/08)	2	Undefeated away (13/09/08–06/12/08)	8
Draws (on two occasions)	2	Without scoring (–)	
Undefeated (06/09/08–13/12/08)	16	Without conceding (14/03/09–28/03/09)	3
Without win (on seven occasions)	2	Scoring (10/02/09-10/04/09)	14

CARDS RECEIVED

54 **1**

QUICK-FIRE GOALS

From the start of a match
Shaun Batt (v Walsall) 1:10

By a substitute after coming on
Dominic Green (v MK Dons) 8:39

GOALS SCORED/CONCEDED PER FIVE-MINUTE INTERVALS

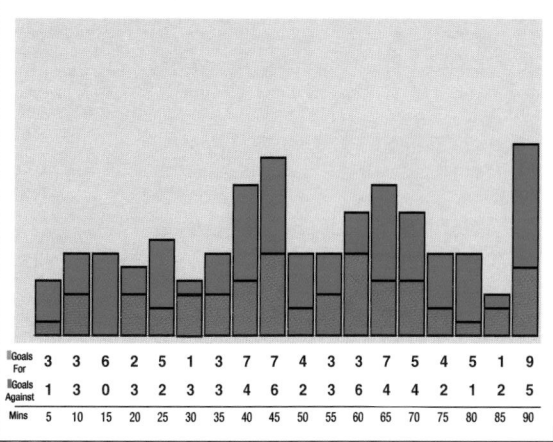

Goals For	3	3	6	2	5	1	3	7	7	4	3	3	7	5	4	5	1	9
Goals Against	1	3	0	3	2	3	3	4	6	2	3	6	4	4	2	1	2	5
Mins	5	10	15	20	25	30	35	40	45	50	55	60	65	70	75	80	85	90

OFFICIAL FOOTBALL YEARBOOK OF THE ENGLISH & SCOTTISH LEAGUES 2009–2010

SCUNTHORPE UNITED

SCUNTHORPE secured an instant return to the Coca-Cola Championship after one of the most dramatic finishes to the season possible.

Knowing that anything barring a defeat to Tranmere on the final day would see them make the play-offs, the Iron were heading for heartbreak until Cliff Byrne's 88th-minute header scraped them over the line at the expense of their visitors.

Nigel Adkins' side made the most of their second chance and went through to the play-off final after beating MK Dons on penalties – Joe Murphy the hero with two fine saves. At Wembley, a Matt Sparrow brace secured a 3–2 win over Millwall.

United embarked on a successful cup run too, reaching the Johnstone's Paint Trophy final, in which they were beaten 3–2 by Luton.

CLUB SUMMARY

FORMED	**1899**
MANAGER	**Nigel Adkins**
GROUND	**Glanford Park**
CAPACITY	**9,183**
NICKNAME	**The Iron**
WEBSITE	www.scunthorpe-united.co.uk

PLAYER OF THE SEASON

Gary Hooper

OVERALL

P	W	D	L	F	A	GD
60	31	12	17	105	77	28

COCA-COLA FOOTBALL LEAGUE ONE

Pos	P	W	D	L	F	A	GD	Pts
6	46	22	10	14	82	63	19	76

HOME

Pos	P	W	D	L	F	A	GD	Pts
5	23	13	5	5	44	24	20	44

AWAY

Pos	P	W	D	L	F	A	GD	Pts
7	23	9	5	9	38	39	-1	32

CUP PROGRESS DETAILS

Competition	Round reached	Knocked out by
FA Cup	R3	Watford
JP Trophy	Final	Luton
Carling Cup	R1	Hartlepool

BIGGEST WIN (ALL COMPS)
29/11/08 4–0 v Alfreton Town **FAC2**

BIGGEST DEFEAT (ALL COMPS)
0–3 on two occasions

ATTENDANCE RECORD

High	Low	Average
8,315	3,423	5,021
v Leeds (09/08/2008)	v Walsall (03/03/2009)	

RESULTS 2008/09

August
9th	● Leeds	h	L 1–2	**Att:** 8,315 — **Scorers:** Hooper. **Booked:** McCann, Milne
12th	● Hartlepool	a	L 3–0	**Att:** 2,076 — **Booked:** Wright
16th	● Walsall	a	L 2–1	**Att:** 4,162 — **Scorers:** Thompson. **Booked:** Byrne. **Dismissed:** Mirfin
23rd	● Peterborough	h	W 1–0	**Att:** 4,717 — **Scorers:** Hayes. **Booked:** Togwell
30th	● Stockport	a	W 0–3	**Att:** 6,348 — **Scorers:** Hooper², McCann

September
2nd	● Notts County	h	W 2–1	**Att:** 1,755 — **Scorers:** Hayes². **Booked:** McCann
6th	● Brighton	a	W 1–4	**Att:** 5,529 — **Scorers:** Hooper³, Woolford. **Booked:** Mirfin, Pearce
13th	● Carlisle	h	W 2–1	**Att:** 5,188 — **Scorers:** Hayes, Sparrow
20th	● Hereford	a	W 1–2	**Att:** 3,004 — **Scorers:** Hooper, Togwell. **Booked:** Iriekpen, McCann
27th	● Yeovil	h	W 2–0	**Att:** 4,829 — **Scorers:** Iriekpen, Forbes OG. **Booked:** Iriekpen

October
4th	● Leyton Orient	a	D 2–2	**Att:** 4,244 — **Scorers:** Hayes, Iriekpen. **Booked:** Hayes, Byrne. **Dismissed:** Murphy
7th	● Grimsby	h	W 2–1	**Att:** 4,844 — **Scorers:** Morris, Togwell. **Booked:** Togwell
11th	● Crewe	h	W 3–0	**Att:** 4,790 — **Scorers:** Hayes, Iriekpen, Woolford. **Booked:** Williams, Mirfin
18th	● Cheltenham	a	W 1–2	**Att:** 3,682 — **Scorers:** Hooper, Sparrow. **Booked:** Togwell, McCann, Byrne
21st	● Southend	h	D 1–1	**Att:** 4,324 — **Scorers:** Hayes. **Booked:** Sparrow
25th	● Millwall	h	W 3–2	**Att:** 5,670 — **Scorers:** Hayes, Hooper, Sparrow. **Booked:** Hooper, May
28th	● Oldham	a	L 3–0	**Att:** 6,057 — **Booked:** Iriekpen, Murphy

November
1st	● Swindon	h	D 3–3	**Att:** 4,744 — **Scorers:** Hayes, McCann, Woolford. **Booked:** Byrne
4th	● Rochdale	h	W 1–0	**Att:** 2,474 — **Scorers:** Mirfin. **Booked:** Togwell, Lea, Mirfin
8th	● Walsall	a	W 1–3	**Att:** 2,318 — **Scorers:** Hooper², Hurst. **Booked:** Woolford
14th	● Bristol Rovers	a	W 1–2	**Att:** 7,173 — **Scorers:** Iriekpen, McCann. **Booked:** Pearce, Togwell
22nd	● Leicester	h	L 1–2	**Att:** 7,967 — **Scorers:** Hayes
25th	● Tranmere	a	L 2–0	**Att:** 4,564 — **Booked:** Murphy, Togwell
29th	● Alfreton Town	h	W 4–0	**Att:** 4,249 — **Scorers:** Hooper², May, Togwell

December
6th	● MK Dons	a	W 0–2	**Att:** 11,550 — **Scorers:** Morris, Thompson. **Booked:** McCann
13th	● Northampton	h	D 4–4	**Att:** 3,976 — **Scorers:** Hooper², May². **Booked:** Sparrow, Togwell
16th	● Tranmere	h	W 2–1	**Att:** 2,669 — **Scorers:** Hayes, May
20th	● Colchester	a	D 0–0	**Att:** 4,606 — **Booked:** Wright
26th	● Hartlepool	h	W 3–0	**Att:** 5,347 — **Scorers:** Hayes, Hooper, McCann. **Booked:** May
28th	● Huddersfield	a	L 2–0	**Att:** 15,228 — **Booked:** Murphy, Sparrow

January
3rd	● Watford	a	L 1–0	**Att:** 8,690 — **Booked:** Byrne
13th	● Yeovil	a	W 1–2	**Att:** 3,275 — **Scorers:** Hooper, Togwell
17th	● Crewe	a	L 3–2	**Att:** 3,811 — **Scorers:** Hayes, O'Donnell OG. **Booked:** Thompson, Byrne
20th	● Rotherham	h	W 2–0	**Att:** 6,038 — **Scorers:** Pearce, Woolford. **Booked:** Sparrow, Pearce, Wright
24th	● Leyton Orient	h	W 2–1	**Att:** 4,230 — **Scorers:** Hayes, Thompson
27th	● Oldham	h	W 2–0	**Att:** 4,447 — **Scorers:** Hooper, McCann. **Booked:** McCann
31st	● Millwall	a	W 1–2	**Att:** 8,868 — **Scorers:** Hooper²

February
14th	● Bristol Rovers	h	L 0–2	**Att:** 4,156
17th	● Rotherham	a	W 0–1	**Att:** 6,555 — **Scorers:** Hooper. **Booked:** Wright
21st	● Swindon	a	L 4–2	**Att:** 6,852 — **Scorers:** Hooper, Lansbury. **Booked:** Mirfin, Byrne, Murphy. **Dismissed:** Byrne, Mirfin
24th	● Southend	a	L 2–0	**Att:** 6,028
28th	● Leeds	a	L 3–2	**Att:** 24,921 — **Scorers:** Hooper². **Booked:** Togwell, Pearce, McCann

March
3rd	● Walsall	h	D 1–1	**Att:** 3,423 — **Scorers:** Odejayi
7th	● Stockport	h	W 2–1	**Att:** 4,890 — **Scorers:** Hooper, Hurst. **Booked:** Lansbury, Trotter
10th	● Peterborough	a	L 2–1	**Att:** 5,637 — **Scorers:** Lansbury. **Booked:** Mills, Lansbury, Mirfin, Murphy
14th	● Carlisle	a	D 1–1	**Att:** 4,867 — **Scorers:** Hayes
17th	● Hereford	h	W 3–0	**Att:** 3,672 — **Scorers:** Hayes, Hooper, Hurst
21st	● Brighton	h	W 2–0	**Att:** 4,404 — **Scorers:** Hooper, McCann. **Booked:** Murphy
28th	● Colchester	h	W 3–0	**Att:** 4,304 — **Scorers:** Hooper², Lansbury

April
5th	● Luton	n	L 3–2	**Att:** 55,378 — **Scorers:** Hooper, McCann. **Booked:** Wright (AET)
10th	● Huddersfield	h	L 1–2	**Att:** 5,543 — **Scorers:** Woolford. **Booked:** Woolford, May, Togwell, Lansbury
13th	● Hartlepool	a	W 2–3	**Att:** 3,998 — **Scorers:** Hayes², McCann. **Booked:** Byrne
18th	● MK Dons	h	L 0–1	**Att:** 4,873 — **Booked:** Hayes
21st	● Northampton	a	D 3–3	**Att:** 4,416 — **Scorers:** McCann, Sparrow, Trotter. **Booked:** Wright
24th	● Leicester	a	D 2–2	**Att:** 30,542 — **Scorers:** Hayes, McCann. **Booked:** Byrne
28th	● Cheltenham	h	W 3–0	**Att:** 3,635 — **Scorers:** Byrne, Hayes, Lansbury. **Booked:** Hooper

May
2nd	● Tranmere	h	D 1–1	**Att:** 8,029 — **Scorers:** Byrne. **Booked:** McCann
8th	● MK Dons	h	D 1–1	**Att:** 6,599 — **Scorers:** Woolford. **Booked:** Togwell
15th	● MK Dons	a	D 0–0	**Att:** 14,479 — **Booked:** McCann, Byrne, Murphy (Won 7–6 on pens)
24th	● Millwall	n	W 3–2	**Att:** 59,661 — **Scorers:** Sparrow², Woolford. **Booked:** Togwell, Sparrow

● Coca-Cola League 1/Play-Offs ● FA Cup ● Carling Cup ● Johnstone's Paint Trophy

actim

LEAGUE ONE GOALKEEPER STATS

Player	Appearances	Match starts	Completed matches	Sub appearances	Subbed off	Clean sheets	Yellow cards	Red cards
Josh Lillis	5	4	4	1	0	1	0	0
Joe Murphy	42	42	41	0	0	12	6	1

LEAGUE ONE OUTFIELD PLAYER STATS

Player	Appearances	Match starts	Completed matches	Substitute appearances	Subbed off	Goals scored	Yellow cards	Red cards
Cliff Byrne	43	43	40	0	2	2	8	1
Andy Crosby	4	3	2	1	1	0	0	0
Jonathan Forte	8	1	0	7	1	0	0	0
Paul Hayes	44	39	18	5	21	17	2	0
Gary Hooper	45	45	28	0	17	24	2	0
Kevan Hurst	20	13	3	7	10	2	0	0
Izzy Iriekpen	16	14	14	2	0	4	3	0
Henri Lansbury	16	12	3	4	9	4	3	0
Ben May	23	5	3	18	2	2	3	0
Grant McCann	43	43	34	0	9	9	7	0
Joseph Mills	14	13	11	1	2	0	1	0
Kenny Milne	1	1	1	0	0	0	1	0
David Mirfin	33	32	27	1	3	0	4	2
Ian Morris	20	4	3	16	1	1	0	0
Kayode Odejayi	6	1	0	5	1	1	0	0
Krystian Pearce	39	36	32	3	4	0	3	0
Matt Sparrow	36	27	23	9	4	4	3	0
Garry Thompson	24	15	7	9	8	3	1	0
Sam Togwell	40	34	30	6	4	2	7	0
Liam Trotter	12	4	3	8	1	1	1	0
Marcus Williams	26	26	25	0	1	0	1	0
Martyn Woolford	39	32	14	7	18	4	1	0
Andrew Wright	28	17	15	11	2	0	2	0

SEASON INFORMATION
- Highest Position: **1**
- Lowest Position: **22**
- Average goals scored per game: **1.78**
- Average goals conceded per game: **1.37**

League position at the end of each week

League position at the end of: August 21, September 18, October 4, November 1, December 6, January 5, February 4, March 6, April 6, May 6

LONGEST SEQUENCES

Wins (23/08/08–27/09/08)	6	Undefeated home (23/08/08–01/11/08)	7
Losses (14/02/09–28/02/09)	4	Undefeated away (30/08/08–18/10/08)	5
Draws (02/05/09–15/05/09)	3	Without scoring (–)	
Undefeated (23/08/08–25/10/08)	11	Without conceding (17/03/09–28/03/09)	3
Without win (14/02/09–03/03/09)	5	Scoring (09/08/08–25/10/08)	13

CARDS RECEIVED
59 **4**

QUICK-FIRE GOALS
From the start of a match
Garry Thompson (v Walsall) 1:31

By a substitute after coming on
Matt Sparrow (v Carlisle) 3:02

GOALS SCORED/CONCEDED PER FIVE-MINUTE INTERVALS

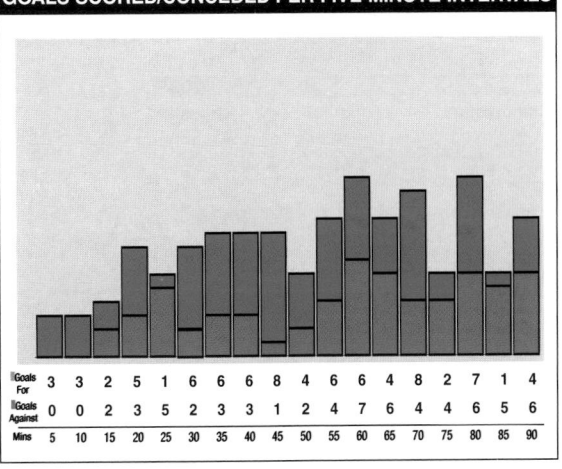

Goals For	3	3	2	5	1	6	6	6	8	4	6	6	4	8	2	7	1	4
Goals Against	0	0	2	3	5	2	3	3	1	2	4	7	6	4	4	6	5	6
Mins	5	10	15	20	25	30	35	40	45	50	55	60	65	70	75	80	85	90

SOUTHEND UNITED

SOUTHEND'S early-season form cost them dear as Steve Tilson's men ultimately fell short of a play-off place.

Seventh at the end of October, Southend did not win a league fixture in November and picked up just one in December: a 1–0 defeat of Northampton. The new year continued in the same vein as Southend slumped to 17th in the standings.

Successive home victories – over Bristol Rovers and Tranmere – lifted the gloom and were the start of a formidable run. Including those wins, the Shrimpers went on a run of 12 victories in 16 matches. However, even that streak left them behind their rivals in the play-off reckoning.

With a new stadium being constructed, Tilson must rely on his current crop of talent to push forward next season.

CLUB SUMMARY

FORMED	1906
MANAGER	Steve Tilson
GROUND	Roots Hall
CAPACITY	12,306
NICKNAME	The Shrimpers
WEBSITE	www.southendunited.co.uk

The New **Football Pools** PLAYER OF THE SEASON — **Peter Clarke**

OVERALL
P	W	D	L	F	A	GD
53	23	10	20	69	74	-5

COCA-COLA FOOTBALL LEAGUE ONE
Pos	P	W	D	L	F	A	GD	Pts
8	46	21	8	17	58	61	-3	71

HOME
Pos	P	W	D	L	F	A	GD	Pts
7	23	13	2	8	29	20	9	41

AWAY
Pos	P	W	D	L	F	A	GD	Pts
10	23	8	6	9	29	41	-12	30

CUP PROGRESS DETAILS
Competition	Round reached	Knocked out by
FA Cup	R3	Chelsea
JP Trophy	R1	Leyton Orient
Carling Cup	R1	Cheltenham

BIGGEST WIN (ALL COMPS)
3–0 on two occasions

BIGGEST DEFEAT (ALL COMPS)
30/08/08 2–5 v Walsall FL1

ATTENDANCE RECORD
High	Low	Average
10,241	6,028	7,850
v MK Dons (10/04/2009)	v Scunthorpe (24/02/2009)	

RESULTS 2008/09

August
9th	● Peterborough	....h	W 1–0	**Att:** 8,665 — **Scorers:** Clarke
12th	● Cheltenham	....h	L 0–1	**Att:** 2,998 — **Booked:** Moussa, Barnard (AET)
16th	● Millwall	..........a	D 1–1	**Att:** 8,114 — **Scorers:** Revell. **Booked:** Harding, Moussa, Clarke, Ademeno
22nd	● Brighton	...........h	L 0–2	**Att:** 7,976 — **Booked:** Revell, Clarke, Harding, Sawyer. **Dismissed:** Moussa
30th	● Walsall	..............a	L 5–2	**Att:** 3,843 — **Scorers:** Barnard, Robson-Kanu. **Booked:** Revell, Sawyer

September
2nd	● Leyton Orient	...h	L 2–4	**Att:** 3,499 — **Scorers:** Sawyer[2]. **Booked:** Grant, Barnard, Sawyer
6th	● Carlisle	..............a	L 2–1	**Att:** 6,561 — **Scorers:** Freedman. **Booked:** Robson-Kanu, Christophe
13th	● Hereford	............h	W 1–0	**Att:** 6,393 — **Scorers:** Barnard. **Booked:** Francis, Grant
20th	● Crewe	..............a	W 3–4	**Att:** 3,574 — **Scorers:** Freedman[2], Grant, Baudet OG. **Booked:** Betsy
26th	● Leyton Orient	...h	W 3–0	**Att:** 9,261 — **Scorers:** Barnard, Freedman, Sawyer. **Booked:** Barnard

October
4th	● Yeovil	................a	W 1–2	**Att:** 4,008 — **Scorers:** Barnard, Robson-Kanu. **Booked:** Christophe, McCormack, Harding
11th	● Stockport	..........h	D 1–1	**Att:** 7,125 — **Scorers:** Barnard. **Booked:** McCormack. **Dismissed:** Harding
18th	● Swindon	............h	W 2–1	**Att:** 7,965 — **Scorers:** Laurent, Revell. **Booked:** Laurent
21st	● Scunthorpe	......a	D 1–1	**Att:** 4,324 — **Scorers:** Barrett. **Booked:** Francis, Sankofa
25th	● Bristol Rovers	..a	L 4–2	**Att:** 7,055 — **Scorers:** Clarke, Laurent. **Booked:** Francis
28th	● Leeds	...............h	W 1–0	**Att:** 10,132 — **Scorers:** Harding

November
1st	● Colchester	........h	D 3–3	**Att:** 8,920 — **Scorers:** Christophe, Clarke, Laurent
8th	● AFC Telford	......a	D 2–2	**Att:** 3,631 — **Scorers:** Christophe, Laurent. **Booked:** Betsy
15th	● Tranmere	..........a	D 2–2	**Att:** 5,019 — **Scorers:** Betsy, Revell. **Booked:** Sawyer, Christophe. **Dismissed:** Laurent
18th	● AFC Telford	......h	W 2–0	**Att:** 4,415 — **Scorers:** Francis, Walker. **Booked:** Betsy, McCormack
22nd	● Oldham	..............a	L 1–2	**Att:** 7,041 — **Scorers:** Walker
25th	● Cheltenham	......a	D 0–0	**Att:** 2,908 — **Booked:** Harding
29th	● Luton	...............h	W 3–1	**Att:** 4,111 — **Scorers:** Stanislas[2], Walker

December
6th	● Leicester	...........a	L 3–0	**Att:** 16,836
13th	● Huddersfield	....h	L 0–1	**Att:** 8,382 — **Booked:** Milsom, McCormack
19th	● Hartlepool	.........a	L 3–0	**Att:** 3,123 — **Booked:** Barrett, Harding. **Dismissed:** Barrett
26th	● Northampton	...h	W 1–0	**Att:** 7,767 — **Scorers:** Stanislas. **Booked:** Milsom
28th	● MK Dons	..........a	L 2–0	**Att:** 10,432 — **Booked:** Grant, Freedman, Clarke

January
3rd	● Chelsea	............a	D 1–1	**Att:** 41,090 — **Scorers:** Clarke. **Booked:** McCormack, Grant
14th	● Chelsea	............h	L 1–4	**Att:** 11,314 — **Scorers:** Barrett
17th	● Stockport	..........a	L 3–1	**Att:** 5,762 — **Scorers:** Revell. **Booked:** Herd. **Dismissed:** Clarke
20th	● Leyton Orient	...a	D 1–1	**Att:** 3,835 — **Scorers:** Walker. **Booked:** Grant, Christophe, Barrett
24th	● Yeovil	................h	L 0–1	**Att:** 6,409 — **Booked:** Betsy, Walker
27th	● Leeds	...............a	L 2–0	**Att:** 20,392
31st	● Bristol Rovers	..h	W 1–0	**Att:** 7,234 — **Scorers:** Freedman. **Booked:** McCormack, Barrett

February
14th	● Tranmere	..........h	W 2–1	**Att:** 6,507 — **Scorers:** Betsy, Robinson
17th	● Crewe	..............h	L 0–1	**Att:** 6,614 — **Booked:** Francis, Dervite
21st	● Colchester	........a	W 3–1	**Att:** 8,651 — **Scorers:** Moussa. **Booked:** McCormack, Laurent, Barnard, Grant
24th	● Scunthorpe	......h	W 2–0	**Att:** 6,028 — **Scorers:** McCormack, Robinson. **Booked:** Barnard
28th	● Peterborough	....a	W 1–2	**Att:** 7,341 — **Scorers:** Christophe, Blackett OG. **Booked:** Christophe

March
3rd	● Millwall	..............h	L 0–1	**Att:** 7,620
7th	● Walsall	..............h	W 2–0	**Att:** 6,973 — **Scorers:** Betsy, Robinson. **Booked:** McCormack
10th	● Brighton	...........a	W 1–3	**Att:** 5,035 — **Scorers:** Barnard[2], Robinson. **Booked:** Sankofa, Dervite
14th	● Hereford	............a	W 0–1	**Att:** 2,663 — **Scorers:** Robinson. **Booked:** Dervite
17th	● Swindon	............a	L 3–0	**Att:** 6,269 — **Booked:** Sankofa, Christophe, Clarke
21st	● Carlisle	...............h	W 3–0	**Att:** 7,789 — **Scorers:** Clarke, McCormack, Scannell. **Booked:** Grant
27th	● Hartlepool	.........h	W 3–2	**Att:** 7,227 — **Scorers:** Barnard, Moussa, Robinson. **Booked:** Barnard, Francis

April
4th	● Huddersfield	......a	W 0–1	**Att:** 12,203 — **Scorers:** Barnard. **Booked:** Francis, Barnard, Grant
10th	● MK Dons	..........h	L 0–2	**Att:** 10,241 — **Booked:** Grant, McCormack
13th	● Northampton	....a	W 2–3	**Att:** 5,190 — **Scorers:** Barnard, Christophe, Robinson. **Booked:** Christophe, Clarke
18th	● Leicester	...........h	L 0–2	**Att:** 10,089
25th	● Oldham	..............a	D 1–1	**Att:** 4,830 — **Scorers:** Barnard. **Booked:** Grant, Dervite, McCormack, Clarke

May
2nd	● Cheltenham	......h	W 2–0	**Att:** 8,192 — **Scorers:** Barrett, Christophe. **Booked:** Grant, Barrett

● Coca-Cola League 1/Play-Offs   ● FA Cup   ● Carling Cup   ● Johnstone's Paint Trophy

LEAGUE ONE GOALKEEPER STATS

Player	Appearances	Match starts	Completed matches	Sub appearances	Subbed off	Clean sheets	Yellow cards	Red cards
Adam Federici 10	10	10	0	0	2	0	0	
Ian Joyce 3	2	2	1	0	1	0	0	
Steve Mildenhall 34	34	33	0	1	11	0	0	

LEAGUE ONE OUTFIELD PLAYER STATS

Player	Appearances	Match starts	Completed matches	Substitute appearances	Subbed off	Goals scored	Yellow cards	Red cards
Charles Ademeno 2	1	0	1	1	0	1	0
Nick Bailey...................................1	1	1	0	0	0	0	0
Lee Barnard 35	24	11	11	13	11	5	0
Adam Barrett 45	45	44	0	0	2	4	1
Kevin Betsy 41	28	19	13	9	3	2	0
Jean Francois Christophe...........33	29	23	4	6	4	7	0
Peter Clarke 43	43	42	0	0	4	6	1
Dorian Dervite 18	18	18	0	0	0	4	0
Liam Feeney 1	0	0	1	0	0	0	0
Simon Francis 45	37	36	8	1	0	6	0
Dougie Freedman 16	12	7	4	5	5	1	0
Paul Furlong 3	1	0	2	1	0	0	0
Anthony Grant 35	23	18	12	5	1	9	0
Dan Harding 19	19	17	0	1	1	5	1
Johnny Herd 6	5	5	1	0	0	1	0
Francis Laurent 21	10	0	11	9	3	2	1
Alan McCormack 34	26	21	8	5	2	8	0
Robert Milsom.............................6	6	5	0	1	0	2	0
Franck Moussa...........................26	25	23	1	1	2	1	1
Stuart O'Keefe.............................3	1	0	2	1	0	0	0
Alex Revell 23	19	7	4	12	4	2	0
Theo Robinson...........................21	20	14	1	6	7	0	0
Hal Robson-Kanu 14	12	7	2	5	2	1	0
Osei Sankofa 27	23	16	4	7	0	3	0
Lee Sawyer 12	11	2	1	9	1	3	0
Damian Scannell 19	6	0	13	6	1	0	0
Junior Stanislas 6	6	3	0	3	1	0	0
James Walker 17	9	4	8	5	2	1	0

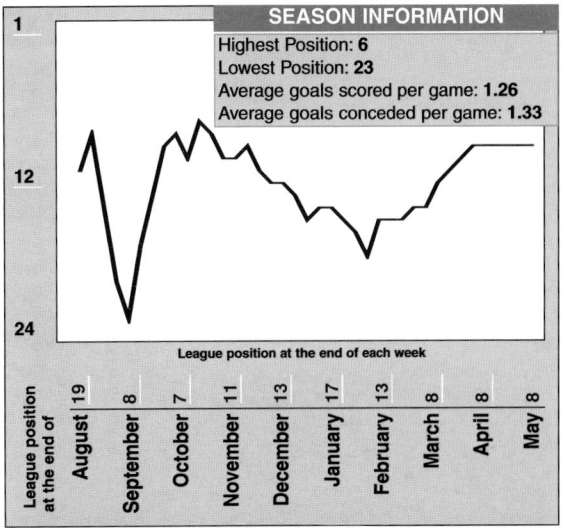

SEASON INFORMATION

Highest Position: **6**
Lowest Position: **23**
Average goals scored per game: **1.26**
Average goals conceded per game: **1.33**

League position at the end of each week

LONGEST SEQUENCES

Wins (13/09/08–04/10/08)	4	Undefeated home (13/09/08–01/11/08)	6
Losses (on two occasions)	3	Undefeated away (21/02/09–14/03/09)	4
Draws (01/11/08–15/11/08)	2	Without scoring (25/11/08–19/12/08)	4
Undefeated (13/09/08–21/10/08)	7	Without conceding (21/02/09–24/02/09)	2
Without win (01/11/08–19/12/08)	7	Scoring (30/08/08–22/11/08)	14

CARDS RECEIVED

74   **5**

QUICK-FIRE GOALS

From the start of a match
Lee Barnard (v Leyton Orient) 0:57

By a substitute after coming on
Francis Laurent (v Swindon) 3:57

GOALS SCORED/CONCEDED PER FIVE-MINUTE INTERVALS

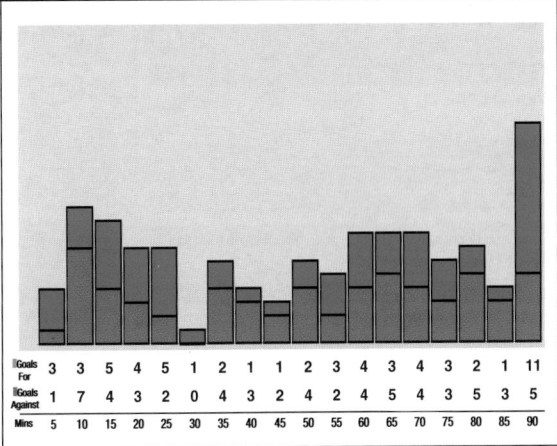

Goals For	3	3	5	4	5	1	2	1	1	2	3	4	3	4	3	2	1	11
Goals Against	1	7	4	3	2	0	4	3	2	4	2	4	5	4	3	5	3	5
Mins	5	10	15	20	25	30	35	40	45	50	55	60	65	70	75	80	85	90

STOCKPORT COUNTY

STOCKPORT looked a decent outside bet to reach the play-offs during the first half of the season, but finished the campaign just one point above the drop zone.

Fresh from their Coca-Cola League Two play-off final win, Jim Gannon's men seemed far from overawed in the third tier.

However, financial woes gradually hit home as defender Jim McNulty and midfielders Anthony Pilkington and Jason Taylor left the club in January to ease the burden.

Despite those sales, the cash finally ran out and the club was placed into administration in April, and docked 10 points as punishment. County fought hard to stave off administration, but their level of debt made it unavoidable.

Their plight was highlighted by Gannon being made redundant by the administrators just days after the end of the season.

CLUB SUMMARY

FORMED	1883
MANAGER	TBC
GROUND	Edgeley Park
CAPACITY	10,852
NICKNAME	The Hatters
WEBSITE	www.stockportcounty.com

The New Football Pools PLAYER OF THE SEASON — **Owain Fon Williams**

OVERALL

P	W	D	L	F	A	GD
53	18	14	21	67	62	5

COCA-COLA FOOTBALL LEAGUE ONE

Pos	P	W	D	L	F	A	GD	Pts
18	46	16	12	18	59	57	2	50

HOME

Pos	P	W	D	L	F	A	GD	Pts
12	23	9	7	7	34	28	6	34

AWAY

Pos	P	W	D	L	F	A	GD	Pts
15	23	7	5	11	25	29	-4	26

CUP PROGRESS DETAILS

Competition	Round reached	Knocked out by
FA Cup	R2	Gillingham
JP Trophy	R2	Bury
Carling Cup	R1	Leicester

BIGGEST WIN (ALL COMPS)
18/11/08 5-0 v Yeovil **FAC1R**

BIGGEST DEFEAT (ALL COMPS)
21/03/09 0-4 v Northampton **FL1**

ATTENDANCE RECORD

High	Low	Average
10,273	4,790	6,130
v Leeds (28/12/2008)	v Hartlepool (10/03/2009)	

RESULTS 2008/09

August
9th	● Huddersfield	a	D 1-1	Att: 15,578 — **Scorers:** Rowe. **Booked:** Raynes
12th	● Leicester	a	L 1-0	Att: 7,386 — **Dismissed:** McNeil
16th	● Leicester	h	D 0-0	Att: 7,151
23rd	● Hartlepool	a	W 0-1	Att: 3,945 — **Scorers:** Rowe
30th	● Scunthorpe	h	L 0-3	Att: 6,348

September
2nd	● Port Vale	h	W 1-0	Att: 2,290 — **Scorers:** McSweeney
13th	● Leyton Orient	a	W 0-3	Att: 4,473 — **Scorers:** McNulty, Raynes, Rowe. **Booked:** Raynes, McNulty
16th	● Northampton	h	D 1-1	Att: 4,974 — **Scorers:** McSweeney
20th	● Swindon	h	D 1-1	Att: 5,536 — **Scorers:** Gleeson. **Booked:** Gleeson
27th	● Cheltenham	a	D 2-2	Att: 3,796 — **Scorers:** Raynes, Thompson

October
3rd	● Oldham	h	W 3-1	Att: 8,360 — **Scorers:** Raynes, Thompson, Turnbull
7th	● Bury	a	L 1-0	Att: 2,384 — **Booked:** T. Rowe
11th	● Southend	a	D 1-1	Att: 7,125 — **Scorers:** McSweeney
18th	● Colchester	h	L 1-2	Att: 6,025 — **Scorers:** McNeil
21st	● MK Dons	a	W 1-2	Att: 6,931 — **Scorers:** Taylor, Lewington OG. **Booked:** T. Rowe, Turnbull
25th	● Hereford	a	W 0-1	Att: 3,210 — **Scorers:** Rowe. **Booked:** Kane
28th	● Tranmere	h	D 0-0	Att: 6,121

November
1st	● Carlisle	h	W 3-0	Att: 6,301 — **Scorers:** Baker², Gleeson. **Booked:** Gleeson
8th	● Yeovil	a	D 1-1	Att: 3,582 — **Scorers:** Davies. **Booked:** Raynes. **Dismissed:** Gleeson
15th	● Millwall	a	L 1-0	Att: 9,030 — **Booked:** Blizzard, Davies, Fon Williams, McSweeney, Tunnicliffe
18th	● Yeovil	h	W 5-0	Att: 3,260 — **Scorers:** Dicker, McNeil, Pilkington, Rose, Vincent
22nd	● Crewe	a	W 0-3	Att: 5,337 — **Scorers:** Davies, Pilkington, Thompson
25th	● Brighton	h	W 2-0	Att: 5,201 — **Scorers:** Blizzard, Davies
29th	● Gillingham	a	D 0-0	Att: 4,419

December
6th	● Peterborough	h	L 1-3	Att: 6,148 — **Scorers:** Pilkington
9th	● Gillingham	h	L 1-2	Att: 3,329 — **Scorers:** Gleeson
13th	● Yeovil	a	W 2-4	Att: 3,687 — **Scorers:** Baker, Mullins², Rowe. **Booked:** Rose, Baker
20th	● Bristol Rovers	h	W 3-1	Att: 5,364 — **Scorers:** Davies³. **Booked:** Blizzard
26th	● Walsall	a	L 1-0	Att: 5,496
28th	● Leeds	h	L 1-3	Att: 10,273 — **Scorers:** Mullins

January
13th	● Swindon	a	D 1-1	Att: 6,002 — **Scorers:** Pilkington. **Booked:** McNulty
17th	● Southend	h	W 3-1	Att: 5,762 — **Scorers:** Pilkington², Rowe
24th	● Oldham	a	L 3-1	Att: 7,605 — **Scorers:** Johnson
27th	● Tranmere	a	L 2-1	Att: 5,259 — **Scorers:** Johnson. **Booked:** Baker
31st	● Hereford	h	W 4-1	Att: 5,586 — **Scorers:** Blizzard, Mainwaring, McNeil, McSweeney

February
3rd	● MK Dons	h	L 0-1	Att: 4,891
14th	● Millwall	h	D 2-2	Att: 5,461 — **Scorers:** Johnson, McNeil. **Booked:** Fon Williams, Mullins
17th	● Cheltenham	h	W 1-0	Att: 5,041 — **Scorers:** Johnson
21st	● Carlisle	a	W 1-2	Att: 5,930 — **Scorers:** Blizzard, Rowe
24th	● Colchester	a	L 1-0	Att: 3,179
28th	● Huddersfield	h	D 1-1	Att: 7,739 — **Scorers:** Clarke OG

March
3rd	● Leicester	a	D 1-1	Att: 16,378 — **Scorers:** O'Grady
7th	● Scunthorpe	a	L 2-1	Att: 4,890 — **Scorers:** Raynes. **Booked:** Dicker, McNeil
10th	● Hartlepool	h	W 2-1	Att: 4,790 — **Scorers:** McSweeney, Vincent. **Booked:** Rose
14th	● Leyton Orient	h	L 0-1	Att: 5,835
21st	● Northampton	a	L 4-0	Att: 4,814 — **Booked:** McSweeney
28th	● Bristol Rovers	a	L 2-0	Att: 6,214

April
4th	● Yeovil	h	D 0-0	Att: 5,664 — **Booked:** Tansey
11th	● Leeds	a	L 1-0	Att: 24,967 — **Booked:** Halls
13th	● Walsall	h	L 1-2	Att: 5,274 — **Booked:** Tansey
18th	● Peterborough	a	L 1-0	Att: 8,333 — **Booked:** McSweeney, Turnbull
24th	● Crewe	h	W 4-3	Att: 7,134 — **Scorers:** Johnson², O'Grady, Vincent

May
2nd	● Brighton	a	L 1-0	Att: 8,618 — **Booked:** Turnbull, O'Grady, Johnson

● Coca-Cola League 1/Play-Offs ● FA Cup ● Carling Cup ● Johnstone's Paint Trophy

LEAGUE ONE GOALKEEPER STATS

Player	Appearances	Match starts	Completed matches	Sub appearances	Subbed off	Clean sheets	Yellow cards	Red cards
Owain Fon Williams	33	33	33	0	0	6	2	0
Fraser Forster	6	6	6	0	0	3	0	0
Conrad Logan	7	7	7	0	0	1	0	0

LEAGUE ONE OUTFIELD PLAYER STATS

Player	Appearances	Match starts	Completed matches	Substitute appearances	Subbed off	Goals scored	Yellow cards	Red cards
Carl Baker	22	15	2	7	13	3	2	0
Dominic Blizzard	31	30	26	1	4	3	2	0
Craig Davies	9	9	3	0	6	5	1	0
Gary Dicker	25	22	12	3	10	0	1	0
Paul Ennis	2	0	0	2	0	0	0	0
Tom Fisher	1	0	0	1	0	0	0	0
Jaroslaw Fojut	3	3	2	0	1	0	0	0
Stephen Gleeson	21	17	11	4	6	2	2	0
Andy Halls	5	4	3	1	1	0	1	0
Oli Johnson	24	9	6	15	3	6	1	0
Tony Kane	3	3	2	0	1	0	1	0
Matty Mainwaring	21	17	9	4	8	1	0	0
Matty McNeil	19	15	13	4	2	3	1	0
Jim McNulty	26	26	26	0	0	1	2	0
Leon McSweeney	36	28	18	8	10	4	3	0
David Mooney	2	2	0	0	2	0	0	0
Johnny Mullins	33	31	27	2	4	3	1	0
Chris O'Grady	18	17	15	1	2	2	1	0
Gareth Owen	8	8	7	0	1	0	0	0
Danny Pilkington	3	0	0	3	0	0	0	0
Anthony Pilkington	24	22	14	2	8	5	0	0
Michael Raynes	35	34	31	1	3	4	2	0
Michael Rose	27	23	15	4	8	0	2	0
Daniel Rowe	3	0	0	3	0	0	0	0
Tommy Rowe	44	42	36	2	6	7	1	0
Greg Tansey	12	9	6	3	3	1	1	0
Jason Taylor	8	5	5	3	0	1	0	0
Josh Thompson	9	6	6	3	0	0	0	0
Peter Thompson	19	12	8	7	4	3	0	0
Robbie Threlfall	2	1	0	1	1	0	0	0
James Tunnicliffe	30	27	23	3	4	0	1	0
Paul Turnbull	34	15	12	19	3	1	3	0
James Vincent	16	8	7	8	1	2	0	0

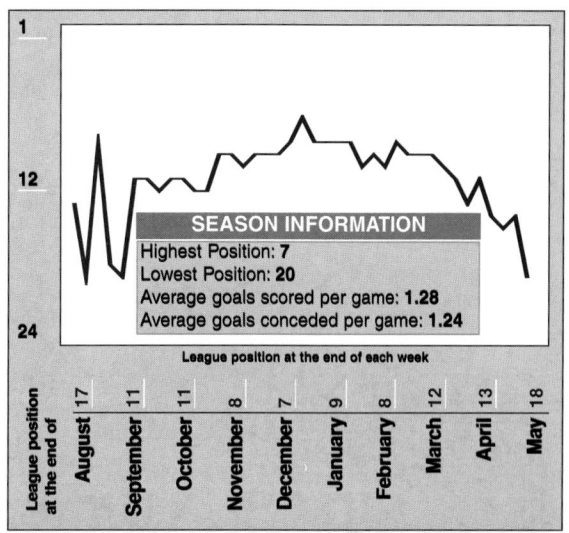

SEASON INFORMATION
Highest Position: **7**
Lowest Position: **20**
Average goals scored per game: **1.28**
Average goals conceded per game: **1.24**

League position at the end of each week

LONGEST SEQUENCES

Wins	2	Undefeated home	4
(on four occasions)		(14/02/09–10/03/09)	
Losses	3	Undefeated away	7
(on two occasions)		(09/08/08–25/10/08)	
Draws	3	Without scoring	5
(16/09/08–27/09/08)		(14/03/09–11/04/09)	
Undefeated	6	Without conceding	3
(13/09/08–11/10/08)		(25/10/08–01/11/08)	
Without win	7	Scoring	9
(14/03/09–18/04/09)		(13/09/08–25/10/08)	

CARDS RECEIVED

31 **0**

QUICK-FIRE GOALS

From the start of a match
Dominic Blizzard (v Hereford) 0:11

By a substitute after coming on
Leon McSweeney (v Southend) 1:25

GOALS SCORED/CONCEDED PER FIVE-MINUTE INTERVALS

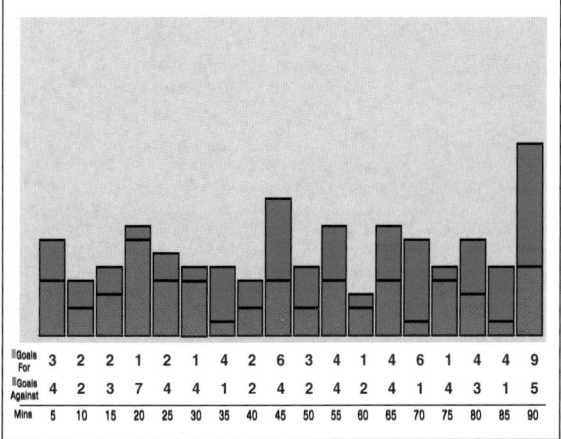

Goals For	3	2	2	1	2	1	4	2	6	3	4	1	4	6	1	4	4	9
Goals Against	4	2	3	7	4	4	1	2	4	2	4	2	4	1	4	3	1	5
Mins	5	10	15	20	25	30	35	40	45	50	55	60	65	70	75	80	85	90

OFFICIAL FOOTBALL YEARBOOK OF THE ENGLISH & SCOTTISH LEAGUES 2009–2010 **305**

THERE must have been a huge sigh of relief for everyone involved at Swindon when the 2008/09 season came to an end. The Robins only secured their Coca-Cola League One status with a victory over Bristol Rovers in their penultimate game, having flirted with the bottom four all season.

With Maurice Malpas in charge, Swindon began the season hoping to build on their mid-table finish in 2007/08. However, as poor league form was compounded by successive cup exits, most notably to Histon in the FA Cup, Malpas departed in November.

After a six-week wait, Danny Wilson was appointed and brought with him a breath of fresh air. He is planning big changes this summer, although top of his agenda must be keeping hold of top goalscorer Simon Cox, who enjoyed a spectacular campaign.

CLUB SUMMARY

FORMED	1881
MANAGER	Danny Wilson
GROUND	County Ground
CAPACITY	14,800
NICKNAME	The Robins
WEBSITE	www.swindontownfc.co.uk

PLAYER OF THE SEASON — Simon Cox

OVERALL

P	W	D	L	F	A	GD
51	13	18	20	74	80	-6

COCA-COLA FOOTBALL LEAGUE ONE

Pos	P	W	D	L	F	A	GD	Pts
15	46	12	17	17	68	71	-3	53

HOME

Pos	P	W	D	L	F	A	GD	Pts
17	23	8	7	8	37	34	3	31

AWAY

Pos	P	W	D	L	F	A	GD	Pts
18	23	4	10	9	31	37	-6	22

CUP PROGRESS DETAILS

Competition	Round reached	Knocked out by
FA Cup	R1	Histon
JP Trophy	QF	Brighton
Carling Cup	R1	QPR

BIGGEST WIN (ALL COMPS)
3–0 on two occasions

BIGGEST DEFEAT (ALL COMPS)
1–3 on three occasions

ATTENDANCE RECORD

High	Low	Average
13,001	6,002	7,499
v Leeds (13/09/2008)	v Stockport (13/01/2009)	

RESULTS 2008/09

August
9th	● Tranmere	.........h W 3–1	Att: 7,975 — Scorers: Cox, McGovern, Paynter. Booked: Timlin
12th	● QPR	.................h L 2–3	Att: 7,230 — Scorers: Cox, Paynter
16th	● Cheltenham	.....a L 2–0	Att: 4,975 — Booked: Aljofree
23rd	● Colchester	.......h L 1–3	Att: 7,031 — Scorers: Cox. Booked: Ifil
30th	● MK Dons	.........a W 1–2	Att: 8,846 — Scorers: Cox, Paynter. Booked: J. Smith

September
2nd	● Aldershot	.........a D 2–2	Att: 1,814 — Scorers: Cox, Ifil. Booked: Timlin (Won 7–6 on pens)
5th	● Hereford	............a D 1–1	Att: 4,061 — Scorers: Ifil. Booked: Ifil
13th	● Leeds	................h L 1–3	Att: 13,001 — Booked: Nalis, Cox, Marshall, Timlin
20th	● Stockport	.........a D 1–1	Att: 5,536 — Scorers: Easton. Booked: Aljofree, Amankwaah, J. Smith
28th	● Millwall	...........h L 1–2	Att: 7,589 — Scorers: Smith. Booked: Nalis, Cox

October
3rd	● Hartlepool	.....a D 3–3	Att: 4,018 — Scorers: Cox[3]. Booked: Casal
7th	● Hereford	............a W 1–2	Att: 1,458 — Scorers: Cox, Peacock. Booked: Cox
11th	● Huddersfield	....h L 1–3	Att: 7,071 — Scorers: Easton. Booked: Nalis, Timlin, Ifil, Easton
18th	● Southend	.........a L 2–1	Att: 7,965 — Scorers: Paynter. Booked: J. Smith
21st	● Northampton	...h W 2–1	Att: 6,653 — Scorers: Cox, Paynter
25th	● Oldham	.............h W 2–0	Att: 6,756 — Scorers: Morrison, Smith

November
1st	● Scunthorpe	......a D 3–3	Att: 4,744 — Scorers: Cox[3]. Booked: Aljofree, Pook
8th	● Histon	................a L 1–0	Att: 1,541 — Booked: Cox
12th	● Brighton	...........a L 2–0	Att: 2,234 — Booked: Pook, Cox
15th	● Leicester	...........h D 2–2	Att: 9,499 — Scorers: Corr, Cox. Booked: Kanyuka, Pook
22nd	● Bristol Rovers	..a D 2–2	Att: 8,016 — Scorers: Corr, Kanyuka. Booked: Corr, Morrison, Nalis
25th	● Peterborough	...h D 2–2	Att: 6,616 — Scorers: Cox, Smith
29th	● Walsall	..............a L 2–1	Att: 3,844 — Scorers: Paynter. Booked: Timlin, Kanyuka

December
6th	● Carlisle	...........h D 1–1	Att: 6,787 — Scorers: Murphy OG. Booked: Peacock, Cox, Aljofree
13th	● Crewe	..............a L 1–0	Att: 3,941 — Scorers: Ifil. Dismissed: Paynter
20th	● Yeovil	...............h L 2–3	Att: 7,072 — Scorers: McGovern, Timlin
26th	● Leyton Orient	....a W 1–2	Att: 4,349 — Scorers: Peacock, Smith. Booked: Timlin, McGovern, Peacock
28th	● Brighton	...........h L 0–2	Att: 8,438

January
13th	● Stockport	.........h D 1–1	Att: 6,002 — Scorers: Smith. Booked: Timlin
17th	● Huddersfield	....a L 2–1	Att: 13,414 — Scorers: Cox. Booked: Easton. Dismissed: Kanyuka
27th	● Walsall	..............h W 3–2	Att: 6,100 — Scorers: Amankwaah, Cox, Paynter
31st	● Oldham	.............a D 0–0	Att: 4,712 — Booked: Vincent, Paynter, H. Razak

February
14th	● Leicester	.........a D 1–1	Att: 19,926 — Scorers: Cox. Booked: Timlin
17th	● Millwall	.............a D 1–1	Att: 7,104 — Scorers: Paynter. Booked: Greer, J. Smith, Cox
21st	● Scunthorpe	......h W 4–2	Att: 6,852 — Scorers: Peacock, Robson-Kanu, Timlin, Wright OG. Booked: Kanyuka
24th	● Hartlepool	.......h L 0–1	Att: 6,010 — Booked: Paynter
28th	● Tranmere	.......a L 1–0	Att: 5,153 — Booked: Greer, Peacock

March
3rd	● Cheltenham	.....h D 2–2	Att: 6,293 — Scorers: Amankwaah, Robson-Kanu. Booked: Timlin
7th	● MK Dons	.........h D 1–1	Att: 7,453 — Scorers: Paynter
10th	● Colchester	.......a L 3–2	Att: 3,827 — Scorers: Cox, Robson-Kanu
14th	● Leeds	................a L 1–0	Att: 21,765 — Booked: Tudur Jones, Cox
17th	● Southend	.........h W 3–0	Att: 6,269 — Scorers: Cox[2], Robson-Kanu. Booked: Morrison
21st	● Hereford	............h W 3–0	Att: 7,129 — Scorers: Cox[2], Paynter
24th	● Northampton	...a W 3–4	Att: 5,025 — Scorers: Cox[3], Paynter. Booked: Morrison, P. Smith
28th	● Yeovil	...............a L 1–0	Att: 5,476 — Booked: J. Smith, Amankwaah

April
4th	● Crewe	..............h D 0–0	Att: 7,165 — Booked: Robson-Kanu, Tudur Jones, Vincent
11th	● Brighton	...........a W 2–3	Att: 6,549 — Scorers: Cox, Greer, Paynter. Booked: Tudur Jones, Timlin, Paynter, Cox
13th	● Leyton Orient	....h L 0–1	Att: 7,735 — Booked: Greer
18th	● Carlisle	..............a D 1–1	Att: 5,959 — Scorers: Tudur Jones. Booked: Paynter, Jean-Francois
25th	● Bristol Rovers	..h W 2–1	Att: 10,977 — Scorers: Cox[2]

May
2nd	● Peterborough	...a D 2–2	Att: 10,886 — Scorers: Cox[2]. Booked: Ifil

● Coca-Cola League 1/Play-Offs ● FA Cup ● Carling Cup ● Johnstone's Paint Trophy

LEAGUE ONE GOALKEEPER STATS

Player	Appearances	Match starts	Completed matches	Sub appearances	Subbed off	Clean sheets	Yellow cards	Red cards
Peter Brezovan	21	21	21	0	0	2	0	0
Phil Smith	25	25	25	0	0	3	1	0

LEAGUE ONE OUTFIELD PLAYER STATS

Player	Appearances	Match starts	Completed matches	Substitute appearances	Subbed off	Goals scored	Yellow cards	Red cards
Hasney Aljofree	18	17	16	1	1	0	4	0
Chris Allen	4	2	2	2	0	0	0	0
Kevin Amankwaah	31	26	21	5	5	2	2	0
Kasali Casal	5	4	2	1	2	0	1	0
Barry Corr	11	2	1	9	1	2	1	0
Simon Cox	45	45	43	0	2	29	6	0
Craig Easton	23	14	11	9	3	2	2	0
Gordon Greer	19	19	18	0	1	1	3	0
Jerel Ifil	30	28	28	2	0	1	5	0
Lescinel Jean-Francois	5	2	1	3	1	0	1	0
Ben Joyce	1	1	0	0	1	0	0	0
Patrick Kanyuka	16	16	11	0	4	1	3	1
Callum Kennedy	4	3	1	1	2	0	0	0
Lloyd Macklin	2	0	0	2	0	0	0	0
Mark Marshall	12	0	0	12	0	0	1	0
Jon-Paul McGovern	26	22	14	4	8	2	1	0
Anthony McNamee	43	30	15	13	15	0	0	0
Sean Morrison	20	18	16	2	2	1	3	0
Lilian Nalis	24	18	12	6	6	0	4	0
Billy Paynter	42	42	24	0	17	11	4	1
Lee Peacock	27	17	14	10	3	2	3	0
Michael Pook	14	11	9	3	2	0	2	0
Hamdi Razak	3	0	0	3	0	0	1	0
Hal Robson-Kanu	20	20	11	0	9	4	1	0
Jack Smith	38	34	32	4	2	5	5	0
Blair Sturrock	10	2	0	8	2	0	0	0
Michael Timlin	41	38	33	3	5	2	9	0
Owain Tudur Jones	11	11	7	0	4	1	3	0
Jamie Vincent	18	18	13	0	5	0	2	0

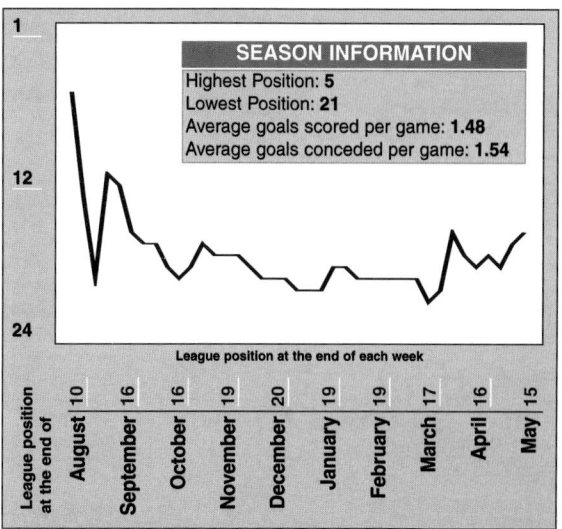

SEASON INFORMATION
Highest Position: **5**
Lowest Position: **21**
Average goals scored per game: **1.48**
Average goals conceded per game: **1.54**

League position at the end of each week

League position at the end of	August	September	October	November	December	January	February	March	April	May
	10	16	16	19	20	19	19	17	16	15

LONGEST SEQUENCES

Wins (on two occasions)	3	Undefeated home (21/10/08–06/12/08)	5
Losses (on five occasions)	2	Undefeated away (30/08/08–03/10/08)	4
Draws (01/11/08–25/11/08)	4	Without scoring (on two occasions)	2
Undefeated (21/10/08–25/11/08)	6	Without conceding (17/03/09–21/03/09)	2
Without win (01/11/08–20/12/08)	8	Scoring (23/08/08–06/12/08)	17

CARDS RECEIVED

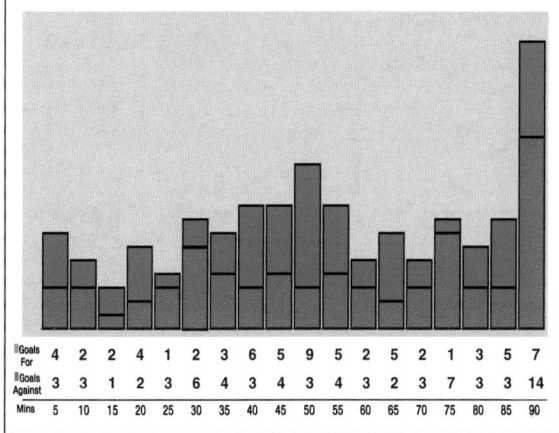

68 2

QUICK-FIRE GOALS

From the start of a match
Lee Peacock (v Leyton Orient) 0:43

By a substitute after coming on
Kevin Amankwaah (v Cheltenham) 2:01

GOALS SCORED/CONCEDED PER FIVE-MINUTE INTERVALS

Goals For	4	2	2	4	1	2	3	6	5	9	5	2	5	2	1	3	5	7
Goals Against	3	3	1	2	3	6	4	3	4	3	4	3	2	3	7	3	3	14
Mins	5	10	15	20	25	30	35	40	45	50	55	60	65	70	75	80	85	90

TRANMERE ROVERS

TRANMERE were cruelly denied a place in the play-offs on the final day of the season as a late equaliser from Scunthorpe's Cliff Byrne robbed them of victory. The 1–1 draw at Glanford Park ensured the Iron finished sixth, leaving the Prenton Park club with little to show for 10 months of blood, sweat and tears.

Despite limited resources, boss Ronnie Moore again ensured that Rovers were a force to be reckoned with in Coca-Cola League One. Ultimately, they were made to pay for their poor away form, which saw them lose 11 times on the road, in stark contrast to an outstanding home record.

Chris Greenacre quit Rovers for Australia's A-League at the end of the season, and Moore paid the ultimate price for his failure to make the play-offs when he was sacked in June.

CLUB SUMMARY

FORMED	1884
MANAGER	TBC
GROUND	Prenton Park
CAPACITY	16,567
NICKNAME	Rovers
WEBSITE	www.tranmererovers.co.uk

The New Football Pools PLAYER OF THE SEASON

Antony Kay

OVERALL

P	W	D	L	F	A	GD
55	25	13	17	68	55	13

COCA-COLA FOOTBALL LEAGUE ONE

Pos	P	W	D	L	F	A	GD	Pts
7	46	21	11	14	62	49	13	74

HOME

Pos	P	W	D	L	F	A	GD	Pts
2	23	15	5	3	41	20	21	50

AWAY

Pos	P	W	D	L	F	A	GD	Pts
16	23	6	6	11	21	29	-8	24

CUP PROGRESS DETAILS

Competition	Round reached	Knocked out by
FA Cup	R2	Peterborough
JP Trophy	SF	Scunthorpe
Carling Cup	R1	Grimsby

BIGGEST WIN (ALL COMPS)
4–1 on two occasions

BIGGEST DEFEAT (ALL COMPS)
1–3 on four occasions

ATTENDANCE RECORD

High	Low	Average
8,700	4,535	5,820
v Leeds (06/12/2008)	v Cheltenham (21/10/2008)	

RESULTS 2008/09

August
9th	● Swindon	a	L 3–1	Att: 7,975 — Scorers: Savage. Booked: Antwi
12th	● Grimsby	a	L 2–0	Att: 1,858
16th	● Hartlepool	h	W 1–0	Att: 5,418 — Scorers: Curran
23rd	● Leicester	a	L 3–1	Att: 17,798 — Scorers: Shuker. Booked: O'Callaghan
30th	● Northampton	h	W 4–1	Att: 5,034 — Scorers: Curran, Kay, Moore, Savage

September
2nd	● Accrington S	h	W 1–0	Att: 2,410 — Scorers: Sonko. Booked: Jennings
6th	● Oldham	h	L 0–1	Att: 6,802 — Booked: Kay, Curran, Chorley, Sonko, Jennings, Moore
13th	● Huddersfield	a	W 1–2	Att: 13,352 — Scorers: Shotton, Sonko. Booked: Goodison, Sonko
20th	● Peterborough	a	D 2–2	Att: 5,735 — Scorers: Greenacre². Booked: Goodison, Shotton, Jennings
26th	● Colchester	h	L 3–4	Att: 5,713 — Scorers: Kay, Shotton, An Taylor

October
4th	● Carlisle	a	W 1–2	Att: 6,093 — Scorers: Moore, Shotton. Booked: Kay, Sonko
6th	● Crewe	h	W 1–0	Att: 2,626 — Scorers: Shuker
11th	● Millwall	h	L 1–3	Att: 5,863 — Scorers: Savage
18th	● Leyton Orient	a	W 0–1	Att: 5,568 — Scorers: Shuker. Booked: Kay, Moore
21st	● Cheltenham	h	W 2–0	Att: 4,535 — Scorers: Savage, Sonko. Booked: Shotton, Jennings
24th	● Crewe	h	W 2–0	Att: 5,790 — Scorers: Jennings, Shuker. Booked: Shotton
28th	● Stockport	a	D 0–0	Att: 6,121 — Booked: An Taylor

November
1st	● MK Dons	a	L 1–0	Att: 8,185 — Booked: Chorley, Shotton
4th	● Morecambe	h	W 1–0	Att: 2,110 — Scorers: Shotton. Booked: Edds
8th	● Accrington S	a	D 0–0	Att: 2,126 — Booked: Savage
13th	● Accrington S	h	W 1–0	Att: 2,560 — Scorers: Shuker. Booked: Kay, Jennings
15th	● Southend	h	D 2–2	Att: 5,019 — Scorers: Moore, Savage. Booked: Kay, Jennings, Shotton
22nd	● Yeovil	a	L 1–0	Att: 3,445 — Booked: Savage, Barnett, Wilson, Chorley
25th	● Scunthorpe	h	W 2–0	Att: 4,564 — Scorers: Shotton, Sonko. Booked: Shotton, Moore, Savage
29th	● Peterborough	a	D 0–0	Att: 5,980 — Booked: Chorley, An Taylor

December
6th	● Leeds	h	W 2–1	Att: 8,700 — Scorers: Kay, Moore. Booked: Kay, Jennings
9th	● Peterborough	h	L 1–2	Att: 3,139 — Scorers: Kay (AET)
13th	● Bristol Rovers	a	L 2–0	Att: 6,217 — Booked: Goodison, Moore
16th	● Scunthorpe	a	L 2–1	Att: 2,669 — Scorers: Moore. Booked: Moore, Chorley, Johnson
20th	● Brighton	h	W 1–0	Att: 4,885 — Scorers: Kay
26th	● Hereford	a	D 2–2	Att: 3,495 — Scorers: Sonko². Booked: Johnson, An Taylor
28th	● Walsall	h	W 2–1	Att: 5,913 — Scorers: Goodison, Kay. Booked: Savage

January
17th	● Millwall	a	L 1–0	Att: 8,257 — Booked: Kay, Goodison, Chorley, Savage
24th	● Carlisle	h	W 4–1	Att: 5,924 — Scorers: Edds, Jennings, Moore²
27th	● Stockport	h	W 2–1	Att: 5,259 — Scorers: Edds, Moore. Booked: Goodison
31st	● Crewe	a	L 2–1	Att: 4,936 — Scorers: Kay. Booked: Shotton, Barnett, Chorley

February
7th	● Leyton Orient	h	D 0–0	Att: 4,892 — Booked: Chorley
10th	● Colchester	a	L 3–0	Att: 3,588 — Booked: Shotton. Booked: An Taylor, Barnett
14th	● Southend	a	L 2–1	Att: 6,507 — Scorers: Moore. Booked: Savage, Edds, Moore
17th	● Peterborough	h	D 1–1	Att: 4,862 — Booked: Barnett
21st	● MK Dons	h	D 1–1	Att: 5,625 — Scorers: Gornell
28th	● Swindon	h	W 1–0	Att: 5,153 — Scorers: Kay. Booked: Shotton. Dismissed: Goodison

March
3rd	● Hartlepool	a	L 2–1	Att: 3,033 — Scorers: Chorley
7th	● Northampton	a	D 1–1	Att: 4,546 — Scorers: Savage. Booked: Goodison, Mayor, An Taylor
11th	● Leicester	h	W 2–0	Att: 6,032 — Scorers: Jennings, Kay
14th	● Huddersfield	h	W 3–1	Att: 5,515 — Scorers: Kay², Savage
17th	● Cheltenham	a	L 1–0	Att: 2,845
21st	● Oldham	a	W 0–2	Att: 7,489 — Scorers: Barnett, Moore. Booked: Shotton, Moore
28th	● Brighton	a	D 0–0	Att: 5,819

April
5th	● Bristol Rovers	h	W 2–0	Att: 8,119 — Scorers: Cresswell, Moore. Booked: Savage, Goodison
11th	● Walsall	a	W 0–1	Att: 4,206 — Scorers: Savage
13th	● Hereford	h	W 2–1	Att: 5,945 — Scorers: Barnett, Savage. Dismissed: Goodison
18th	● Leeds	a	L 3–1	Att: 24,360 — Scorers: Sodje OG. Booked: Jennings
25th	● Yeovil	h	D 1–1	Att: 8,306 — Scorers: Kay. Booked: Barnett

May
2nd	● Scunthorpe	a	D 1–1	Att: 8,029 — Scorers: Curran Booked: Coyne, Edds, Jennings. Dismissed: Edds

● Coca-Cola League 1/Play-Offs ● FA Cup ● Carling Cup ● Johnstone's Paint Trophy

LEAGUE ONE GOALKEEPER STATS

Player	Appearances	Match starts	Completed matches	Sub appearances	Subbed off	Clean sheets	Yellow cards	Red cards
John Achterberg	7	7	7	0	0	1	0	0
Danny Coyne	39	39	39	0	0	14	1	0

LEAGUE ONE OUTFIELD PLAYER STATS

Player	Appearances	Match starts	Completed matches	Substitute appearances	Subbed off	Goals scored	Yellow cards	Red cards
Godwin Antwi	5	4	4	1	0	0	1	0
Charlie Barnett	29	25	17	4	8	3	4	0
Robbie Burns	2	0	0	2	0	0	0	0
Ben Chorley	45	45	45	0	0	1	6	0
Aaron Cresswell	13	8	7	5	1	1	0	0
Craig Curran	15	7	5	8	2	3	1	0
Gareth Edds	34	22	16	12	5	2	2	1
Ian Goodison	33	33	28	0	3	1	7	2
Terry Gornell	10	4	1	6	3	1	0	0
Chris Greenacre	13	6	2	7	4	2	0	0
Paul Henry	1	1	0	0	1	0	0	0
Danny Holmes	1	1	1	0	0	0	0	0
Steven Jennings	44	44	38	0	5	3	7	1
John Johnson	4	4	4	0	0	0	1	0
Antony Kay	44	44	42	0	2	11	6	0
Josh Macauley	1	0	0	1	0	0	0	0
Danny Mayor	3	3	2	0	1	0	1	0
Ian Moore	42	40	34	2	6	10	6	0
George O'Callaghan	6	4	0	2	4	0	1	0
Bas Savage	42	38	32	4	6	9	6	0
Ryan Shotton	33	33	33	0	0	5	9	0
Chris Shuker	28	23	15	5	8	3	0	0
Edrissa Sonko	38	29	19	9	10	5	3	0
Andy Taylor	39	38	36	1	1	1	4	1
Ash Taylor	1	0	0	1	0	0	0	0
Mark Wilson	5	4	3	1	1	0	1	0

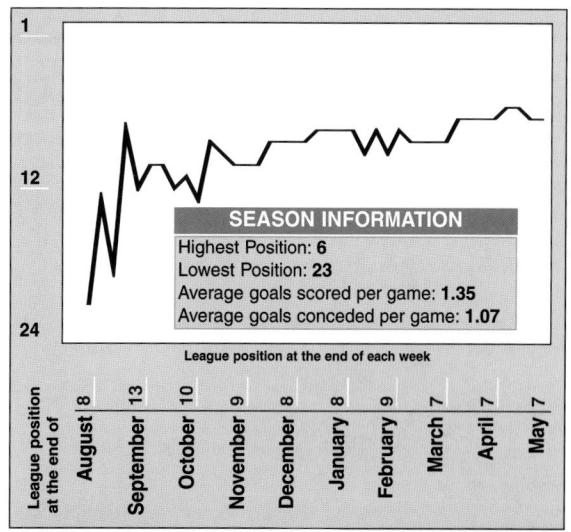

League position at the end of each week

SEASON INFORMATION
Highest Position: **6**
Lowest Position: **23**
Average goals scored per game: **1.35**
Average goals conceded per game: **1.07**

LONGEST SEQUENCES

Wins (on two occasions)	3	Undefeated home (21/10/08–25/04/09)	18
Losses (–)		Undefeated away (13/09/08–28/10/08)	5
Draws (on two occasions)	2	Without scoring (28/10/08–01/11/08)	2
Undefeated (21/03/09–13/04/09)	5	Without conceding (on two occasions)	4
Without win (28/10/08–22/11/08)	4	Scoring (10/02/09–14/03/09)	9

CARDS RECEIVED
67   **5**

QUICK-FIRE GOALS
From the start of a match
Ian Moore (v Carlisle) 0:49

By a substitute after coming on
Terry Gornell (v MK Dons) 1:55

GOALS SCORED/CONCEDED PER FIVE-MINUTE INTERVALS

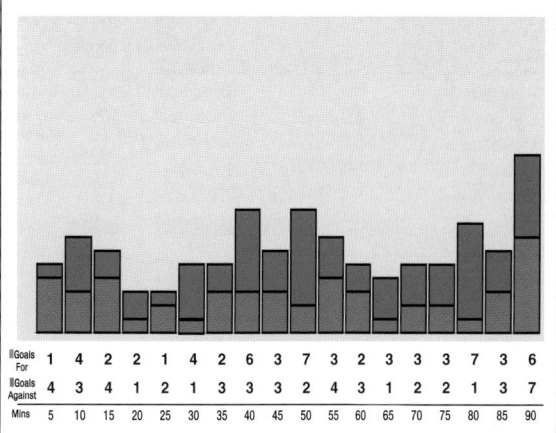

Goals For	1	4	2	2	1	4	2	6	3	7	3	2	3	3	3	7	3	6
Goals Against	4	3	4	1	2	1	3	3	3	2	4	3	1	2	2	1	3	7
Mins	5	10	15	20	25	30	35	40	45	50	55	60	65	70	75	80	85	90

WALSALL fans will probably look back on the 2008/09 season as having taken one step back and two steps forward.

The Saddlers went into the campaign with one eye on the play-off places having finished a healthy 12th just months earlier in their first season since promotion from Coca-Cola League Two. However, with the club 10 points adrift of the top six towards the end of 2008, the decision was taken to replace Jimmy Mullen with Chris Hutchings.

While results did improve slightly, supporters were aware of clear progress being made and optimism is rife again following what was another safe mid-table finish.

The development of striker Troy Deeney, among others, is a big plus point and focus will again be on the play-off places at the start of the 2009/10 season.

CLUB SUMMARY

FORMED	1888
MANAGER	Chris Hutchings
GROUND	Banks's Stadium
CAPACITY	11,300
NICKNAME	The Saddlers
WEBSITE	www.saddlers.co.uk

The New Football Pools
PLAYER OF THE SEASON

Clayton
Ince

OVERALL
P	W	D	L	F	A	GD
50	18	10	22	65	73	-8

COCA-COLA FOOTBALL LEAGUE ONE
Pos	P	W	D	L	F	A	GD	Pts
13	46	17	10	19	61	66	-5	61

HOME
Pos	P	W	D	L	F	A	GD	Pts
13	23	10	3	10	34	36	-2	33

AWAY
Pos	P	W	D	L	F	A	GD	Pts
12	23	7	7	9	27	30	-3	28

CUP PROGRESS DETAILS
Competition	Round reached	Knocked out by
FA Cup	R1	Scunthorpe
JP Trophy	FLTSQ	Luton
Carling Cup	R1	Darlington

BIGGEST WIN (ALL COMPS)
30/08/08 5–2 v Southend **FL1**

BIGGEST DEFEAT (ALL COMPS)
14/03/09 0–5 v Bristol Rovers **FL1**

ATTENDANCE RECORD
High	Low	Average
8,920	3,549	4,572
v Leeds (31/01/2009)	v Brighton (17/03/2009)	

RESULTS 2008/09

August
9th	● Yeovil	a	D 1–1	**Att:** 4,518 — **Scorers:** Ibehre
12th	● Darlington	h	L 1–2	**Att:** 2,702 — **Scorers:** Ricketts. **Booked:** Taundry, Hughes. **Dismissed:** Ricketts
16th	● Scunthorpe	h	W 2–1	**Att:** 4,162 — **Scorers:** Ibehre, Reich. **Booked:** Gerrard, Ibehre, Palmer
23rd	● Crewe	a	L 2–1	**Att:** 4,160 — **Scorers:** Hughes. **Booked:** Hughes, Ibehre, Reich, Palmer
30th	● Southend	h	W 5–2	**Att:** 3,843 — **Scorers:** Demontagnac[3], Reich, Grant OG. **Booked:** Demontagnac

September
6th	● Leyton Orient	h	L 0–2	**Att:** 4,838 — **Booked:** Reich, Ricketts
13th	● Bristol Rovers	a	W 1–3	**Att:** 6,609 — **Scorers:** Ricketts[2], Roberts. **Booked:** Ibehre, Ince, Weston
20th	● Brighton	a	W 0–1	**Att:** 5,679 — **Scorers:** Mattis. **Booked:** Ibehre, Ince **Dismissed:** Weston, Sansara
27th	● Carlisle	h	W 2–1	**Att:** 4,830 — **Scorers:** Ibehre, Mattis

October
4th	● Hereford	a	D 0–0	**Att:** 3,900 — **Booked:** Mattis
7th	● Cheltenham	a	W 1–2	**Att:** 1,741 — **Scorers:** Ibehre, Ricketts. **Booked:** Ricketts
11th	● Peterborough	h	L 1–2	**Att:** 4,792 — **Scorers:** Deeney. **Booked:** Hughes
18th	● Hartlepool	h	L 2–3	**Att:** 4,142 — **Scorers:** Ibehre, Ricketts. **Booked:** Taundry, Gerrard
21st	● Leicester	a	D 2–2	**Att:** 17,178 — **Scorers:** Nicholls, Ricketts
25th	● Leeds	a	L 3–0	**Att:** 22,422

November
1st	● Northampton	h	W 3–1	**Att:** 4,377 — **Scorers:** Deeney, Gerrard, Palmer. **Booked:** Deeney, Hughes
4th	● Luton	h	L 0–1	**Att:** 1,844 — **Booked:** Gerrard, Ibehre
8th	● Scunthorpe	h	L 1–3	**Att:** 2,318 — **Scorers:** Ricketts. **Booked:** Ricketts. **Dismissed:** Demontagnac
15th	● Colchester	a	W 0–2	**Att:** 4,071 — **Scorers:** Mattis, Ricketts
22nd	● MK Dons	h	L 0–3	**Att:** 5,026 — **Booked:** Weston
25th	● Oldham	a	L 3–2	**Att:** 3,936 — **Scorers:** Nicholls, Ricketts
29th	● Swindon	h	W 2–1	**Att:** 3,844 — **Scorers:** Nicholls, Ricketts. **Booked:** Nicholls

December
6th	● Huddersfield	a	L 2–1	**Att:** 11,827 — **Scorers:** Nicholls. **Booked:** Ricketts, Roberts, Weston
13th	● Millwall	h	L 1–2	**Att:** 3,790 — **Scorers:** Nicholls. **Booked:** Sansara
20th	● Cheltenham	a	D 0–0	**Att:** 3,656
26th	● Stockport	h	W 1–0	**Att:** 5,496 — **Scorers:** Weston. **Booked:** Weston, Mattis, Ricketts **Dismissed:** Ricketts
28th	● Tranmere	a	L 2–1	**Att:** 5,913 — **Scorers:** Reich. **Booked:** Sansara

January
17th	● Peterborough	a	L 1–0	**Att:** 5,705
24th	● Hereford	h	D 1–1	**Att:** 4,438 — **Scorers:** Deeney. **Booked:** Taundry
27th	● Swindon	a	L 3–2	**Att:** 6,100 — **Scorers:** Deeney, Ibehre
31st	● Leeds	h	W 1–0	**Att:** 8,920 — **Scorers:** Deeney. **Booked:** Palmer, Zaaboub, Mattis

February
3rd	● Leicester	h	L 1–4	**Att:** 5,634 — **Scorers:** Mattis
7th	● Hartlepool	a	D 2–2	**Att:** 3,286 — **Scorers:** Deeney, Williams. **Booked:** Mattis, Zaaboub
10th	● Carlisle	a	D 1–1	**Att:** 4,502 — **Scorers:** Ricketts
14th	● Colchester	h	W 2–0	**Att:** 3,719 — **Scorers:** Deeney, Ricketts
21st	● Northampton	a	W 0–2	**Att:** 4,528 — **Scorers:** Hughes, Ibehre
28th	● Yeovil	h	W 2–0	**Att:** 3,916 — **Scorers:** Deeney, Nicholls

March
3rd	● Scunthorpe	a	D 1–1	**Att:** 3,423 — **Scorers:** Deeney
7th	● Southend	a	L 2–0	**Att:** 6,973 — **Booked:** Zaaboub, Weston. **Dismissed:** Ricketts
10th	● Crewe	h	D 1–1	**Att:** 3,604 — **Scorers:** Deeney
14th	● Bristol Rovers	h	L 0–5	**Att:** 5,169
17th	● Brighton	h	W 3–0	**Att:** 3,549 — **Scorers:** Bradley, Deeney, Gerrard
21st	● Leyton Orient	a	W 0–1	**Att:** 3,969 — **Scorers:** Bradley. **Booked:** Weston, Deeney
28th	● Cheltenham	h	D 1–1	**Att:** 4,101 — **Scorers:** Townsend OG. **Booked:** Zaaboub

April
4th	● Millwall	a	L 3–1	**Att:** 8,800 — **Scorers:** Ibehre. **Booked:** Hughes, Nicholls
11th	● Tranmere	h	L 0–1	**Att:** 4,206
13th	● Stockport	a	W 1–2	**Att:** 5,274 — **Scorers:** Gerrard, Logan OG
18th	● Huddersfield	a	L 2–3	**Att:** 3,951 — **Scorers:** Ibehre[2]. **Booked:** Deeney, Weston
25th	● MK Dons	a	W 0–1	**Att:** 12,094 — **Scorers:** Ibehre. **Booked:** Zaaboub, Mattis, Gerrard

May
2nd	● Oldham	h	L 1–2	**Att:** 4,807 — **Scorers:** Deeney

● Coca-Cola League 1/Play-Offs ● FA Cup ● Carling Cup ● Johnstone's Paint Trophy

LEAGUE ONE GOALKEEPER STATS

Player	Appearances	Match starts	Completed matches	Sub appearances	Subbed off	Clean sheets	Yellow cards	Red cards
Rene Gilmartin 11	10	10	1	0	0	0	0
Clayton Ince 36	36	35	0	1	12	2	0

LEAGUE ONE OUTFIELD PLAYER STATS

Player	Appearances	Match starts	Completed matches	Substitute appearances	Subbed off	Goals scored	Yellow cards	Red cards
Sam Adkins 1	0	0	1	0	0	0	0
Paul Boertien 31	25	24	6	1	0	0	0
Mark Bradley 28	16	9	12	7	2	0	0
Josh Craddock 2	0	0	2	0	0	0	0
Richard Davies 3	0	0	3	0	0	0	0
Troy Deeney 45	37	26	8	11	12	3	0
Ishmel Demontagnac 10	2	2	8	0	3	1	0
Anthony Gerrard 42	42	39	0	3	3	3	0
William Grigg 1	0	0	1	0	0	0	0
Stephen Hughes 32	32	21	0	11	2	4	0
Jabo Ibehre.....................39	35	24	4	11	10	4	0
Dwayne Mattis 37	33	29	4	4	4	5	0
Alex Nicholls 45	38	22	7	16	6	2	0
Chris Palmer...................44	41	40	3	1	1	3	0
Marco Reich 19	9	5	10	4	3	2	0
Michael Ricketts............28	25	14	3	9	9	3	2
Stephen Roberts 15	15	11	0	4	1	1	0
Netan Sansara 10	7	5	3	1	0	2	1
Robin Shroot 5	0	0	5	0	0	0	0
Emmanuele Smith 26	22	21	4	1	0	0	0
Richard Taundry 38	27	23	11	4	0	2	0
Rhys Weston....................31	30	24	1	5	1	7	1
Sam Williams 5	0	0	5	0	1	0	0
Sofiene Zaaboub 29	24	11	5	13	0	5	0

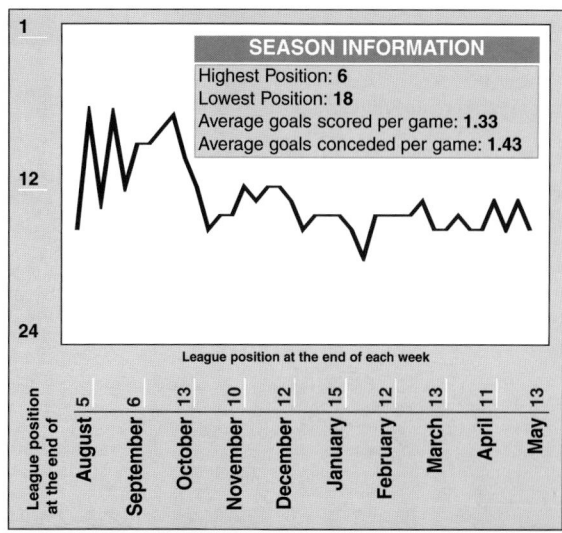

SEASON INFORMATION
Highest Position: **6**
Lowest Position: **18**
Average goals scored per game: **1.33**
Average goals conceded per game: **1.43**

League position at the end of each week

LONGEST SEQUENCES

Wins (on two occasions)	3	Undefeated home (on two occasions)	3
Losses (on five occasions)	2	Undefeated away (13/09/08–21/10/08)	4
Draws (07/02/09–10/02/09)	2	Without scoring (–)	
Undefeated (07/02/09–03/03/09)	6	Without conceding (14/02/09–28/02/09)	3
Without win (04/10/08–25/10/08)	5	Scoring (24/01/09–03/03/09)	10

CARDS RECEIVED

49   **4**

QUICK-FIRE GOALS
From the start of a match
Troy Deeney (v Oldham) 1:29

By a substitute after coming on
Jabo Ibehre (v Northampton) 13:54

GOALS SCORED/CONCEDED PER FIVE-MINUTE INTERVALS

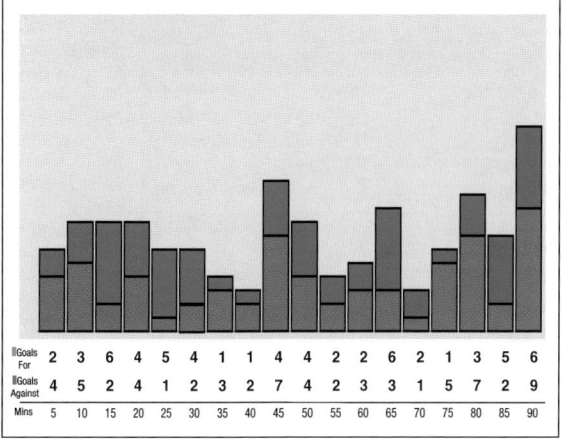

Goals For	2	3	6	4	5	4	1	1	4	4	2	2	6	2	1	3	5	6
Goals Against	4	5	2	4	1	2	3	2	7	4	2	3	3	1	5	7	2	9
Mins	5	10	15	20	25	30	35	40	45	50	55	60	65	70	75	80	85	90

TWO Yeovil stalwarts played their part in keeping the club in Coca-Cola League One. Former skipper Terry Skiverton took the managerial reins following the departure of Russell Slade, while Chris Weale – the club's goalkeeper when they secured two promotions earlier this decade – returned on loan from Bristol City and helped earn a vital late-season draw with Hereford by scoring a last-gasp equaliser.

Slade was relieved of his duties following a stunning 3–1 win at Peterborough, and Skiverton initially struggled to settle in as the Glovers went on an eight-game winless run.

However, buoyed by the loan signings of Weale and Tottenham striker Jon Obika – whose goals earned them seven points in three late-season games – the Somerset club secured their survival with a week to spare.

CLUB SUMMARY

FORMED	1895
MANAGER	Terry Skiverton
GROUND	Huish Park
CAPACITY	9,665
NICKNAME	The Glovers
WEBSITE	www.ytfc.net

Lee Peltier

OVERALL

P	W	D	L	F	A	GD
51	13	17	21	46	79	-33

COCA-COLA FOOTBALL LEAGUE ONE

Pos	P	W	D	L	F	A	GD	Pts
17	46	12	15	19	41	66	-25	51

HOME

Pos	P	W	D	L	F	A	GD	Pts
18	23	6	10	7	26	29	-3	28

AWAY

Pos	P	W	D	L	F	A	GD	Pts
17	23	6	5	12	15	37	-22	23

CUP PROGRESS DETAILS

Competition	Round reached	Knocked out by
FA Cup	R1	Stockport
JP Trophy	R1	Brentford
Carling Cup	R2	Middlesbrough

BIGGEST WIN (ALL COMPS)
14/02/09 3–1 v Peterborough **FL1**

BIGGEST DEFEAT (ALL COMPS)
0–5 on two occasions

ATTENDANCE RECORD

High	Low	Average
6,580	3,275	4,423
v Leeds (23/08/2008)	v Scunthorpe (13/01/2009)	

RESULTS 2008/09

August
9th	● Walsall	..........h	D 1-1	Att: 4,518 — **Scorers:** Tomlin
12th	● Charlton	..........a	W 0-1	Att: 6,239 — **Scorers:** Warne. **Booked:** Peltier
16th	● Hereford	..........a	W 1-2	Att: 3,476 — **Scorers:** Schofield, Warne. **Booked:** Begovic, Alcock
23rd	● Leeds	..........h	D 1-1	Att: 6,580 — **Scorers:** Owusu. **Booked:** Downes, Peltier, Warne, Forbes
26th	● Middlesbrough	..a	L 5-1	Att: 15,651 — **Scorers:** Tomlin. **Booked:** Bircham
30th	● Carlisle	..........a	L 4-1	Att: 6,286 — **Scorers:** Tomlin. **Booked:** Peltier, Warne, Bircham, Forbes

September
2nd	● Brentford	..........a	D 2-2	Att: 1,339 — **Scorers:** Bircham, Tomlin. **Booked:** Bircham, Roberts (Lost 2–4 on pens)
6th	● MK Dons	..........a	L 3-0	Att: 7,959 — **Booked:** Schofield
13th	● Brighton	..........h	D 1-1	Att: 4,451 — **Scorers:** Way. **Booked:** Way, Jones, Begovic, A. McCollin
20th	● Bristol Rovers	..h	D 2-2	Att: 5,748 — **Scorers:** Roberts, Skiverton. **Booked:** Skiverton
27th	● Scunthorpe	......a	L 2-0	Att: 4,829 — **Booked:** Roberts

October
4th	● Southend	..........h	L 1-2	Att: 4,008 — **Scorers:** Schofield. **Booked:** Jones, Peltier, Roberts. **Dismissed:** Roberts, Schofield
18th	● Northampton	....a	L 3-0	Att: 5,217 — **Booked:** Schofield. **Dismissed:** Forbes
21st	● Crewe	..........h	W 3-2	Att: 3,536 — **Scorers:** Schofield[2], Way. **Booked:** Owen, Schofield
25th	● Leyton Orient	...h	D 0-0	Att: 4,320 — **Booked:** Jones, Roberts
28th	● Huddersfield	......a	D 0-0	Att: 10,719 — **Booked:** Rendell, Brown

November
1st	● Oldham	..........a	W 0-2	Att: 5,318 — **Scorers:** Brown, Warne. **Booked:** Owen
8th	● Stockport	..........h	D 1-1	Att: 3,582 — **Scorers:** Skiverton
11th	● Leicester	..........a	L 1-0	Att: 16,528 — **Booked:** Downes
15th	● Peterborough	...h	L 0-1	Att: 4,001 — **Booked:** Warne, Peltier, Roberts, Schofield
18th	● Stockport	..........a	L 5-0	Att: 3,260 — **Booked:** Peltier, Alcock. **Dismissed:** Brown
22nd	● Tranmere	..........h	W 1-0	Att: 3,445 — **Scorers:** Skiverton. **Booked:** Tomlin, Roberts
25th	● Colchester	......a	L 1-0	Att: 3,214 — **Booked:** Forbes, Peltier

December
6th	● Hartlepool	..........a	D 0-0	Att: 3,393 — **Booked:** Downes
13th	● Stockport	..........h	L 2-4	Att: 3,687 — **Scorers:** Smith, Warne. **Booked:** Forbes
20th	● Swindon	..........a	W 2-3	Att: 7,072 — **Scorers:** Alcock, Peltier, Ifil OG. **Booked:** Peltier, Forbes, Roberts, Tomlin
26th	● Cheltenham	......h	D 1-1	Att: 4,989 — **Scorers:** Rodgers. **Booked:** Peltier, Rodgers
28th	● Millwall	..........a	D 1-1	Att: 9,042 — **Scorers:** Rodgers. **Booked:** Peltier

January
13th	● Scunthorpe	......h	L 1-2	Att: 3,275 — **Scorers:** McCollin. **Booked:** Smith. **Dismissed:** Skiverton
19th	● Leicester	..........h	L 0-2	Att: 4,569
24th	● Southend	..........a	W 0-1	Att: 6,409 — **Scorers:** Brown. **Booked:** Rodgers, Alcock. **Dismissed:** Downes
27th	● Huddersfield	......h	W 1-0	Att: 3,703 — **Scorers:** MacDonald. **Booked:** Forbes, Schofield
31st	● Leyton Orient	...a	W 0-1	Att: 4,597 — **Scorers:** Tomlin. **Booked:** Worthington

February
14th	● Peterborough	....a	W 1-3	Att: 6,129 — **Scorers:** Brown, MacDonald, Warne. **Booked:** Warne
17th	● Bristol Rovers	..a	L 3-0	Att: 8,049 — **Booked:** Smith
21st	● Oldham	..........h	D 2-2	Att: 4,150 — **Scorers:** Tomlin[2]. **Booked:** Peltier, Worthington
24th	● Crewe	..........a	L 2-0	Att: 3,432 — **Booked:** Peltier
28th	● Walsall	..........a	L 2-0	Att: 3,916 — **Booked:** Welsh, Worthington, Tomlin

March
7th	● Carlisle	..........h	D 1-1	Att: 3,892 — **Scorers:** Roberts. **Booked:** Welsh, Schofield
10th	● Leeds	..........a	L 4-0	Att: 18,847 — **Booked:** Downes, Roberts
14th	● Brighton	..........a	L 5-0	Att: 6,291 — **Booked:** Worthington, Warne, Wagenaar. **Dismissed:** Wagenaar
21st	● MK Dons	..........h	D 0-0	Att: 4,028 — **Booked:** Warne
28th	● Swindon	..........h	W 1-0	Att: 5,476 — **Scorers:** Obika. **Booked:** Forbes, Weale, Noble
31st	● Northampton	....h	W 1-0	Att: 3,884 — **Scorers:** Obika.

April
4th	● Stockport	..........a	D 0-0	Att: 5,664 — **Booked:** Hutchins
10th	● Millwall	..........h	W 2-0	Att: 6,230 — **Scorers:** Obika, Tomlin. **Booked:** Murtagh, Roberts, Rodgers
13th	● Cheltenham	......a	L 1-0	Att: 3,775 — **Booked:** Roberts, Forbes, Peltier. **Dismissed:** Roberts
18th	● Hartlepool	..........h	L 2-3	Att: 4,232 — **Scorers:** Tomlin, Townsend. **Booked:** Smith, Murtagh
21st	● Hereford	..........h	D 2-2	Att: 3,780 — **Scorers:** Rodgers, Weale. **Booked:** Townsend
25th	● Tranmere	..........a	D 1-1	Att: 8,306 — **Scorers:** Obika. **Booked:** Warne, Tomlin, Brown, Forbes, Alcock

May
2nd	● Colchester	..........h	L 0-2	Att: 5,237

● Coca-Cola League 1/Play-Offs ● FA Cup ● Carling Cup ● Johnstone's Paint Trophy

LEAGUE ONE GOALKEEPER STATS

Player	Appearances	Match starts	Completed matches	Sub appearances	Subbed off	Clean sheets	Yellow cards	Red cards
Asmir Begovic	14	14	14	0	0	3	2	0
Josh Wagenaar	23	22	21	1	0	6	1	1
Chris Weale*	10	10	9	0	1	4	1	0

*Weale scored 1 goal in 2008/09 season

LEAGUE ONE OUTFIELD PLAYER STATS

Player	Appearances	Match starts	Completed matches	Substitute appearances	Subbed off	Goals scored	Yellow cards	Red cards
Craig Alcock	30	25	21	5	4	1	3	0
Marc Bircham	3	3	2	0	1	0	1	0
Aaron Brown	23	16	14	7	2	3	2	0
James Dayton	2	0	0	2	0	0	0	0
Aidan Downes	24	15	4	9	10	0	4	1
Terrell Forbes	38	38	36	0	1	0	9	1
Danny Hutchins	9	8	7	1	1	0	1	0
Nathan Jones	21	14	14	7	0	0	3	0
Shaun MacDonald	4	4	3	0	1	2	0	0
Danny Maguire	1	1	0	0	1	0	0	0
Andre McCollin	11	0	0	11	0	1	1	0
Kieran Murtagh	26	16	14	10	2	0	2	0
David Noble	2	2	2	0	0	0	1	0
Gifton Noel-Williams	6	6	4	0	2	0	0	0
Jon Obika	10	10	8	0	2	4	0	0
Gareth Owen	7	7	7	0	0	0	2	0
Lloyd Owusu	4	0	0	4	0	1	0	0
Lee Peltier	35	34	32	1	2	1	11	0
Aleksandar Prijovic	4	4	0	0	4	0	0	0
Scott Rendell	5	5	3	0	2	0	1	0
Gary Roberts	30	27	22	3	3	2	9	2
Luke Rodgers	22	10	6	12	4	3	3	0
Danny Schofield	39	34	30	5	3	4	6	1
Terry Skiverton	25	25	21	0	3	2	1	1
Nathan Smith	33	32	31	1	1	1	3	0
Gavin Tomlin	42	29	13	13	16	7	4	0
Andros Townsend	10	10	5	0	5	1	1	0
Paul Warne	44	38	17	6	21	4	7	0
Darren Way	15	15	11	0	4	2	1	0
Andrew Welsh	37	23	7	14	16	0	2	0
Jonathan Worthington	9	9	9	0	0	0	4	0

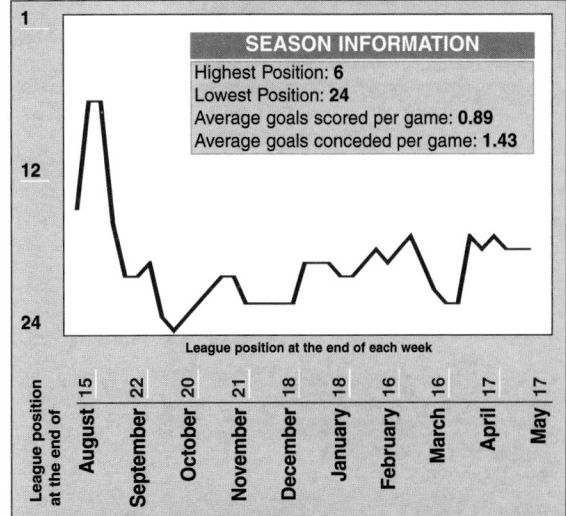

SEASON INFORMATION

Highest Position: **6**
Lowest Position: **24**
Average goals scored per game: **0.89**
Average goals conceded per game: **1.43**

League position at the end of each week

LONGEST SEQUENCES

Wins (24/01/09–14/02/09)	4	Undefeated home (27/01/09–10/04/09)	7
Losses (27/09/08–18/10/08)	3	Undefeated away (06/12/08–14/02/09)	6
Draws (on four occasions)	2	Without scoring (10/03/09–21/03/09)	3
Undefeated (21/03/09–10/04/09)	5	Without conceding (21/03/09–10/04/09)	5
Without win (on two occasions)	8	Scoring (13/12/08–13/01/09)	5

CARDS RECEIVED

86   **7**

QUICK-FIRE GOALS

From the start of a match
Aaron Brown (v Southend) 5:37

By a substitute after coming on
Luke Rodgers (v Hereford) 5:36

GOALS SCORED/CONCEDED PER FIVE-MINUTE INTERVALS

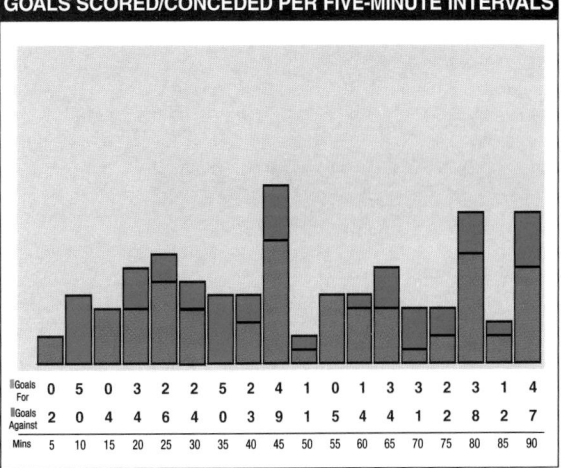

Goals For	0	5	0	3	2	2	5	2	4	1	0	1	3	3	2	3	1	4
Goals Against	2	0	4	4	6	4	0	3	9	1	5	4	4	1	2	8	2	7
Mins	5	10	15	20	25	30	35	40	45	50	55	60	65	70	75	80	85	90

SEASON REVIEW

COCA-COLA LEAGUE 2 STATISTICS 2008/09

Player of the season
Grant Holt (Shrewsbury)

Manager of the season
Paul Tisdale (Exeter)

The player with the most...

Shots on target	
Andy Bishop (Bury)	70

Shots off target	
Grant Holt (Shrewsbury)	72

Shots without scoring	
Gary Jones (Rochdale)	41

Shots per goal	
Sam Wood (Brentford)	41

Assists	
Sam Saunders (Dag & Red)	
Ryan Lowe (Chester)	12

Offsides	
Ryan Lowe (Chester)	97

Fouls	
Grant Holt (Shrewsbury)	123

Fouls without a card	
Barry Conlon (Bradford/Grimsby)	52

Free-kicks won	
Grant Holt (Shrewsbury)	110

Penalties scored	
Grant Holt (Shrewsbury)	10

Goals scored direct from free-kicks	
Ben Davies (Shrewsbury)	4

Defensive clearances	
Ian Sharps (Rotherham)	
David Artell (Morecambe)	88

Defensive blocks	
Simon King (Gillingham)	32

The team with the most...

Shots on target	Dag & Red	301
Shots off target	Rochdale	293
Shots per goal	Accrington	11.4
Corners	Dag & Red	341
Fouls	Shrewsbury	654
Woodwork strikes	Bradford, Exeter	16
Offsides	Chester	216
Penalties conceded	Chester	11
Yellow cards	Darlington	77
Red cards	Chesterfield	9

TOTALS 2008/09

Goals	
Total	1374
Home	776
Away	598

Cards	
Yellow	1402
Average per game	2.54
Red	93
Average per game	0.17

Attendances	
Total	2,304,675

AN EXCITING season at the top saw Brentford emerge as Coca-Cola League Two champions while Luton bowed out of the Football League after 92 years.

Under the guidance of Andy Scott, Brentford managed to finally break clear of Exeter and Wycombe, the latter having looked set to be crowned as champions for much of the season.

The Chairboys made a flying start to the campaign and did not taste defeat in the League until a 3–2 loss at Aldershot on 6th December. At the turn of the year they were eight points clear at the top of the table, but a poor spell of form saw them falter and Brentford took the initiative to charge to the title. The Bees lost just three of their final 19 games and clinched the title with a game to spare following a 3–1 win over Darlington.

While Brentford emerged as the best side in League Two, Exeter secured a second successive promotion by taking second place. The Grecians were tipped by many to struggle after winning the Conference play-off final the previous season, but Paul Tisdale and his side proved the doubters wrong in spectacular fashion. Exeter's promotion push was built on their superb home form and they turned St James Park into a fortress, winning 15 and drawing five of their 23 home games. A 1–0 win at Rotherham on the final day of the season saw Exeter clinch their place in Coca-Cola League One for 2009/10, while Wycombe recovered to take the third automatic spot by the narrowest of margins. The Chairboys lost 2–1 to Notts County on the final day, but Bury only managed to beat Accrington 1–0, meaning they missed out on automatic promotion by a single goal, having tied on 78 points.

While there was joy for Brentford, Exeter and Wycombe, there was despair for Luton following their relegation. The Hatters were always likely to struggle after being handed a 30-point deduction at the start of the season for failing to get a CVA to exit administration, and for financial irregularities. Mick Harford's side put up a brave fight in the League, and also gave the fans something to cheer about by beating Scunthorpe in the Johnstone's Paint Trophy final. However, ultimately they failed to overcome the points deficit and finished bottom of the table – the Hatters falling out of the League 21 years after winning the League Cup final against Arsenal at Wembley.

> The Bees lost three of their final 19 games and clinched the title with a game to spare

They will be joined in the Blue Square Premier in 2009/10 by Chester, who endured a turbulent campaign and were also relegated. Despite the return of Mark Wright as manager in November, the Blues were not helped by a transfer embargo and ultimately succumbed to the drop after five years back in the Football League. Their main rivals for the drop were Grimsby, who survived despite a dreadful start to the season which saw them wait until their 16th game, on 15th November, for their first league win.

Luton may have failed to overcome a points deficit, but Bournemouth and Rotherham had superb seasons despite each starting with 17-point deductions.

Jimmy Quinn took the reins at Bournemouth at the beginning of September and they wiped their points deficit out with a draw at Luton on 2nd December. The Cherries entered 2009 seven points from safety, and when Quinn departed, Eddie Howe became the youngest manager in the Football League at the age of 31. Howe galvanised the club and steered them clear of relegation with a 2–1 win over Grimsby in their last home game of the season, securing League Two football in 2009/10.

Rotherham manager Mark Robins performed an equally admirable job as he guided his side to safety in considerable style. The Millers made a flying start to the season, winning five of their first nine league games, with a resounding 4–1 victory over Grimsby on 4th October erasing the deficit. Rotherham eventually finished 19 points clear of the bottom two and were in contention for a play-off place at one stage. They eventually fell 11 points short of the top seven, but would have finished in fifth position had it not been for their points deduction.

Praise must also go to newly-promoted Aldershot Town who enjoyed a fine debut season in the Football League and finished in 15th place.

FINAL COCA-COLA LEAGUE 2 TABLE

			HOME					AWAY					
		P	W	D	L	F	A	W	D	L	F	A	GD	Pts
1	BRENTFORD	46	13	8	2	39	15	10	8	5	26	21	29	85
2	EXETER	46	13	5	5	36	25	9	8	6	29	25	15	79
3	WYCOMBE	46	11	9	3	32	16	9	9	5	22	17	21	78
4	Bury	46	14	4	5	36	19	7	11	5	27	24	20	78
5	GILLINGHAM	46	12	7	4	38	21	9	5	9	20	34	3	75
6	Rochdale	46	11	6	6	40	24	8	7	8	30	35	11	70
7	Shrewsbury	46	14	6	3	41	16	3	12	8	20	28	17	69
8	Dag & Red	46	12	3	8	44	24	7	8	8	33	29	24	68
9	Bradford	46	11	10	2	39	18	7	3	13	27	37	11	67
10	Chesterfield	46	8	8	7	32	28	8	7	8	30	29	5	63
11	Morecambe	46	9	9	5	29	24	6	9	8	24	32	-3	63
12	Darlington*	46	11	6	6	36	23	9	6	8	25	21	17	62
13	Lincoln City	46	6	11	6	26	22	8	6	9	27	30	1	59
14	Rotherham**	46	11	6	6	32	21	10	6	7	28	25	14	58
15	Aldershot	46	9	10	4	36	31	5	2	16	23	49	-21	54
16	Accrington Stanley	46	9	5	9	25	24	4	6	13	17	35	-17	50
17	Barnet	46	7	7	9	30	35	4	8	11	26	39	-18	48
18	Port Vale	46	6	6	11	23	33	7	3	13	21	33	-22	48
19	Notts County	46	6	6	11	22	31	5	8	10	27	38	-20	47
20	Macclesfield	46	7	4	12	23	37	6	4	13	22	40	-32	47
21	Bournemouth**	46	11	6	6	28	15	6	6	11	31	36	8	46
22	Grimsby	46	6	7	10	31	28	3	7	13	20	41	-18	41
23	Chester	46	4	7	12	24	34	4	6	13	19	47	-38	37
24	Luton***	46	7	8	8	34	34	6	9	8	24	31	-7	26

* 10 points deducted ** 17 points deducted *** 30 points deducted

**DAVID McCRACKEN
(WYCOMBE)**

**CHRIS DAGNALL
(ROCHDALE)**

**KEVIN ELLISON
(CHESTER)**

Brentford celebrate capturing the League Two title, the Bees having lost just seven games during their triumphant 2008/09 season

PLAY-OFF REVIEW

GILLINGHAM gained the ultimate revenge for their biggest defeat since the 1960s by securing play-off success with a 1–0 Wembley win over Shrewsbury.

The Shrews beat the Gills 7–0 in a league match in September but Simeon Jackson headed in a late goal to take the Priestfield Stadium club back to League One at the first attempt.

The semi-finals were both intriguing clashes. The Gills faced Rochdale over two legs and ground out a 0–0 draw in the first game at Spotland in a match short on clear-cut chances. But it was that man Jackson who fired them to Wembley in the second leg at Priestfield with goals 19 and 20 for the season. The first was a smart finish at the near post from Andy Barcham's low cross and, after Chris Dagnall had levelled, Jackson won the tie with a coolly-taken penalty.

Shrewsbury's clash with Bury was an amazing game. The first leg at the Prostar Stadium was dominated by the home side, but they lost it 1–0 after a freak own goal by Neil Ashton, which many blamed on goalkeeper Luke Daniels. Bury had the better of the second leg, but found Daniels in inspired form. He saved a penalty from Phil Jevons and, despite Shrewsbury being on the back foot, Kevin McIntyre drilled home late on to take the clash to extra-time.

Shrewsbury's Steve Leslie was sent off early in the extra period and Bury threw everything at the Shrews, but Daniels would not be beaten and the on-loan West Brom keeper then saved two more penalties to take his side to Wembley. But Paul Simpson's men would suffer defeat in the final for the second time in three years, with the Gills now looking forward to League One football in 2009/10.

COCA-COLA LEAGUE 2 FIXTURES AND RESULTS

Away teams are listed across the top; Home teams down the side.

Home \ Away	ACCRINGTON	ALDERSHOT	BARNET	BOURNEMOUTH	BRADFORD	BRENTFORD	BURY	CHESTER	CHESTERFIELD	DAG & RED	DARLINGTON	EXETER	GILLINGHAM	GRIMSBY	LINCOLN CITY	LUTON	MACCLESFIELD	MORECAMBE	NOTTS COUNTY	PORT VALE	ROCHDALE	ROTHERHAM	SHREWSBURY	WYCOMBE
ACCRINGTON	–	0-1	1-1	3-0	2-3	1-1	1-2	0-1	1-0	0-0	1-0	2-1	0-2	3-1	0-2	0-0	2-0	1-0	1-1	2-0	1-3	1-3	2-1	0-1
ALDERSHOT	3-1	–	1-1	1-1	3-2	1-1	3-3	2-2	1-1	1-2	2-1	1-0	2-1	2-2	2-0	2-1	1-1	0-2	2-2	1-0	2-4	0-1	0-0	3-2
BARNET	2-1	0-3	–	1-0	4-1	0-1	1-2	3-1	1-3	1-1	0-1	0-1	2-2	3-3	3-2	1-1	1-3	1-1	0-4	1-2	2-1	2-0	0-0	1-1
BOURNEMOUTH	1-0	2-0	0-2	–	4-1	0-1	2-0	1-0	1-1	2-1	3-1	1-1	1-1	2-1	0-1	1-1	0-0	0-1	0-0	4-0	0-0	1-0	1-0	3-1
BRADFORD	1-1	5-0	3-3	1-3	–	0-1	1-0	0-0	3-2	1-1	0-0	4-1	2-2	2-0	1-1	1-1	4-0	2-1	1-0	2-0	3-0	0-0	1-0	3-1
BRENTFORD	3-0	3-0	1-0	2-0	2-1	–	1-0	3-0	0-1	2-1	1-1	1-1	4-0	1-1	2-0	1-0	3-1	1-1	2-0	1-2	0-0	1-1	1-1	3-3
BURY	1-0	2-1	1-0	1-0	1-0	1-0	–	1-1	1-2	2-2	2-2	0-1	4-0	0-2	3-1	1-2	3-0	2-1	2-0	3-0	2-1	1-2	2-1	0-0
CHESTER	2-0	0-1	5-1	0-2	0-0	3-0	1-1	–	1-3	2-2	1-2	0-0	0-1	1-1	0-2	2-2	1-2	0-2	1-2	0-2	1-5	1-1	1-1	0-2
CHESTERFIELD	1-1	5-1	1-1	1-0	0-2	0-1	1-3	1-1	–	1-1	0-0	2-1	0-1	2-1	1-2	2-2	2-4	1-2	3-1	2-1	3-0	1-0	2-2	0-1
DAG & RED	0-0	3-1	2-0	0-1	3-0	3-1	1-3	6-0	3-0	–	0-1	1-2	2-0	4-0	0-3	2-1	2-1	0-2	6-1	1-1	3-2	1-1	1-2	0-1
DARLINGTON	3-0	2-0	2-2	2-1	2-1	1-3	2-2	1-2	0-0	3-0	–	1-2	1-0	2-0	5-1	1-2	0-0	1-0	2-1	1-2	1-1	0-1	1-1	1-2
EXETER	2-1	3-2	2-1	1-3	1-0	0-2	0-0	2-0	1-6	2-1	2-0	–	3-0	0-0	2-1	0-1	4-0	2-2	2-2	1-0	4-1	1-1	0-1	1-0
GILLINGHAM	1-0	4-4	0-2	1-0	0-2	1-1	0-0	2-0	2-1	2-1	1-1	1-0	–	3-0	1-2	0-1	3-1	5-0	2-2	1-0	1-1	4-0	2-2	1-1
GRIMSBY	0-1	1-0	0-1	3-3	1-3	0-1	1-2	1-3	0-1	1-1	1-2	3-0	1-0	–	5-1	2-2	0-0	2-3	0-1	3-0	0-0	3-0	1-0	1-1
LINCOLN CITY	5-1	0-2	2-0	3-3	0-0	2-2	2-1	1-1	3-1	1-3	0-1	0-1	2-0	1-1	–	0-0	1-1	1-1	0-1	1-1	0-1	0-0	1-0	1-0
LUTON	1-2	3-1	3-3	3-3	0-1	1-2	1-1	0-1	2-1	1-2	1-2	0-0	2-1	3-2	1-1	–	1-0	1-1	1-1	1-3	1-1	2-4	3-1	0-1
MACCLESFIELD	0-2	4-2	2-1	0-2	0-2	2-0	1-1	3-1	1-1	0-4	0-6	1-4	0-1	1-0	1-2	2-1	–	0-1	1-1	0-2	1-1	1-2	3-0	0-1
MORECAMBE	1-1	2-0	2-1	0-4	2-1	2-0	0-0	3-1	2-2	1-2	1-0	1-1	0-1	1-1	1-1	1-2	4-1	–	1-0	1-1	1-1	1-3	1-0	0-0
NOTTS COUNTY	1-1	2-1	2-0	1-1	3-1	1-1	0-1	1-2	0-1	0-3	0-0	2-1	0-1	0-2	0-1	0-2	1-1	1-0	–	4-2	1-2	0-3	2-2	0-2
PORT VALE	0-2	0-0	0-0	3-1	0-3	1-1	3-0	0-1	0-1	3-1	1-3	1-3	2-1	0-1	1-3	1-4	2-1	1-2	1-2	–	2-1	0-0	1-1	1-1
ROCHDALE	3-1	3-1	3-1	1-1	3-0	1-2	1-1	6-1	2-1	0-2	0-2	2-2	0-1	2-0	2-2	2-0	1-1	1-1	3-0	1-0	–	1-2	2-1	0-1
ROTHERHAM	0-0	1-2	3-4	1-0	0-2	0-0	1-1	3-1	3-0	1-1	0-1	0-1	2-0	4-1	1-0	2-0	3-2	2-1	1-0	2-2	2-1	–	1-2	0-1
SHREWSBURY	2-0	1-0	2-2	4-1	2-0	1-3	1-0	1-0	2-1	2-1	1-0	1-1	7-0	1-1	0-0	3-0	0-0	3-2	1-2	1-1	1-0	1-0	–	0-1
WYCOMBE	2-1	3-0	1-1	3-1	1-0	0-0	1-2	2-0	1-1	2-1	1-1	1-0	0-1	1-0	0-0	4-0	1-1	2-2	4-2	0-1	0-0	1-1	0-1	–

GRANT HOLT (SHREWSBURY)

LEADING SCORERS

Player	(Team)	Goals
Grant Holt	(Shrewsbury)	20
Jack Lester	(Chesterfield)	20
Paul Benson	(Dag & Red)	18
Reuben Reid	(Rotherham)	18
Billy Clarke	(Brentford)	17
	3 for Northampton, 8 for Darlington	
Simeon Jackson	(Gillingham)	17
Adam Le Fondre	(Rochdale)	17
John O'Flynn	(Barnet)	17
Brett Pitman	(Bournemouth)	17
Peter Thorne	(Bradford)	17
Andy Bishop	(Bury)	16
Ryan Lowe	(Chester)	16
Charlie MacDonald	(Brentford)	16

ON THE CLOCK COCA-COLA LEAGUE 2

FROM THE START OF A MATCH

Quickest goal
John O'Flynn 0:19
(Barnet v Accrington)

Quickest card
Jay Harris 0:11
(Chester v Brentford)

Last-gasp goal
Scott McGleish .... Pen **97:18**
(Wycombe v Darlington)

BY A SUBSTITUTE

Quickest goal
Danny North 0:43
(Grimsby v Chester)

Quickest card
Phil Jevons 1:16
(Bury v Rotherham)

Substitute being substituted
Jamie Lowry 3:29
(Chesterfield v Brentford)

BEN HAMER (BRENTFORD)

LEADING GOALKEEPERS

Player	(Team)	Clean sheets
Ben Hamer	(Brentford)	20
Simon Royce	(Gillingham)	18
Rhys Evans	(Bradford)	17
Shwan Jalal	(Bournemouth)	17
Luke Daniels	(Shrewsbury)	16
Andy Warrington	(Rotherham)	16
Paul Jones	(Exeter)	15
Kenny Arthur	(Accrington)	14
Rob Burch	(Lincoln)	14
Scott Shearer	(Wycombe)	14
Barry Roche	(Morecambe)	13
Wayne Brown	(Bury)	12
Tony Roberts	(Dag & Red)	12
Jonny Brain	(Macclesfield)	9
Dean Brill	(Luton)	9

DISCIPLINARY RECORDS

Player	Team	Fouls	Y	R
Ricky Ravenhill	Darlington	61	11	2
Alan White	Darlington	48	10	2
Stephen Dawson	Bury	49	11	1
Nathan Stanton	Rochdale	48	10	1
Tommy Doherty	Wycombe	43	8	2
Anthony Charles	Aldershot	63	11	0
Grant Holt	Shrewsbury	123	11	0
James Vaughan	Chester	49	11	0
Danny Hollands	Bournemouth	51	9	1
Efetobore Sodje	Bury	63	9	1
Jay Harris	Chester	49	9	1
Clark Keltie	Rochdale	42	10	0
John Thompson	Notts County	49	10	0
Barry Fuller	Gillingham	31	8	1
Jack Lester	Chesterfield	57	8	1
Matthew Flynn	Macclesfield	28	8	1
Alan Goodall	Chesterfield	25	6	2
Kieran Charnock	Accrington	59	9	0
Lee Bell	Macclesfield	61	9	0
Liam Hatch	Darlington	65	9	0

PLAYER WITH THE MOST...

Shots on target

Andy Bishop (Bury)	70
Brett Pitman (Bournemouth)	67
Jack Lester (Chesterfield)	65
Grant Holt (Shrewsbury)	63
Ben Davies (Shrewsbury)	60
Ben Strevens (Dag & Red)	56

Shots off target

Grant Holt (Shrewsbury)	72
Ryan Lowe (Chester)	60
Kevin Ellison (Chester)	56
James Ryan (Accrington)	51
Ben Davies (Shrewsbury)	45
Simeon Jackson (Gillingham)	45

Shots without scoring

Gary Jones (Rochdale)	41
Jamie Lowry (Chesterfield)	29
Steven Leslie (Shrewsbury)	28
Mark Hughes (Chester/Barnet)	26
Richie Partridge (Chester)	24
Clark Keltie (Rochdale)	23

Assists

Ryan Lowe (Chester)	12
Sam Saunders (Dag & Red)	12
Rossi Jarvis (Luton)	10
John Miles (Accrington)	10
John Nutter (Gillingham)	10
Elliott Bennett (Bury)	9

Offsides

Ryan Lowe (Chester)	97
Andy Bishop (Bury)	88
Jack Lester (Chesterfield)	85
Drewe Broughton (Rotherham)	75
Paul Mullin (Accrington/Bradford)	75
Simeon Jackson (Gillingham)	67

Fouls commited

Grant Holt (Shrewsbury)	123
Drewe Broughton (Rotherham)	103
Paul Mullin (Bradford)	91
Martin Gritton (Macclesf/Chesterfld)	88
Ben Strevens (Dag & Red)	79
Paul Linwood (Chester)	76

TEAM STATISTICS

Club	Played	Shots on	Shots off	Corners	Hit woodwork	Caught offside	Offside trap	Fouls	Yellow cards	Red cards	Pens awarded	Pens con
Accrington	46	239	238	265	13	152	**236**	548	61	2	5 (1)	10
Aldershot	46	244	244	275	14	170	184	510	58	2	9 (5)	9
Barnet	46	225	228	260	10	160	225	573	48	5	7 (3)	4
Bournemouth	46	300	228	239	12	151	109	579	64	3	4 (3)	4
Bradford	46	294	267	249	**16**	165	136	511	46	2	4 (3)	2
Brentford	46	233	215	274	8	120	116	509	50	4	10 (6)	6
Bury	46	268	207	263	14	196	99	491	57	3	8 (7)	8
Chester	46	172	260	218	12	**216**	149	618	76	7	4 (3)	**11**
Chesterfield	46	289	262	242	15	176	136	617	69	9	4 (3)	6
Dag & Red	46	**301**	258	**341**	15	158	220	454	48	1	3 (2)	3
Darlington	46	248	240	220	10	130	176	547	**77**	7	5 (5)	5
Exeter	46	209	210	231	**16**	151	129	479	43	2	10 (4)	10
Gillingham	46	244	219	247	9	135	161	538	60	3	7 (5)	5
Grimsby	46	224	248	269	9	170	130	528	66	5	4 (3)	6
Lincoln City	46	220	252	250	8	143	203	555	58	4	3 (3)	4
Luton	46	248	237	254	12	151	200	589	70	3	5 (5)	8
Macclesfield	46	204	209	179	12	167	117	567	62	5	6 (6)	4
Morecambe	46	239	231	220	8	159	170	558	50	1	1 (1)	6
Notts County	46	241	245	280	13	158	219	530	54	1	5 (4)	3
Port Vale	46	226	163	201	11	122	120	536	64	6	2 (1)	6
Rochdale	46	285	**293**	333	11	153	168	497	53	4	**12 (10)**	7
Rotherham	46	245	258	249	9	167	115	563	47	6	8 (6)	5
Shrewsbury	46	264	270	261	10	128	57	**654**	68	3	10 (**10**)	4
Wycombe	46	191	178	215	9	97	116	489	53	5	4 (4)	4

Offside trap – number of times a side has caught the opposition offside. **Pens awarded** (scored in brackets). **Pens con** – number of penalties awarded to opposition. **Bold** – biggest total

Total league games played this season: **552** • Home wins: **228** (41%) •Away wins: **160** (29%)
•Draws: **164** (30%) • Average goals scored per match **2.5**

OFFICIAL FOOTBALL YEARBOOK OF THE ENGLISH & SCOTTISH LEAGUES 2009–2010   **317**

ACCRINGTON STANLEY

IT WAS a season of highs and lows both on and off the pitch for Accrington.

Boss John Coleman, who became the Football League's longest-serving manager after Graham Turner stood down at Hereford, once again masterminded his side's survival on a shoestring budget.

Coleman's men kicked off the campaign with a disappointing home defeat to newly-promoted Aldershot before travelling to Wolves in what proved to be a thrilling League Cup encounter. After a pulsating game at Molineux, only a 106th-minute strike from Mark Davies separated the teams as Stanley fell to a valiant 3–2 defeat after extra-time.

But the club's record 16th-place finish was ultimately overshadowed by the uncertainty created by long-serving chairman Eric Whalley's decision to sell up and step down.

CLUB SUMMARY

FORMED	1891
MANAGER	John Coleman
GROUND	Fraser Eagle Stadium
CAPACITY	5,057
NICKNAME	The Stans
WEBSITE	www.accringtonstanley.co.uk

Jimmy Ryan — PLAYER OF THE SEASON

OVERALL
P	W	D	L	F	A	GD
50	13	12	25	44	64	-20

COCA-COLA FOOTBALL LEAGUE TWO
Pos	P	W	D	L	F	A	GD	Pts
16	46	13	11	22	42	59	-17	50

HOME
Pos	P	W	D	L	F	A	GD	Pts
16	23	9	5	9	25	24	1	32

AWAY
Pos	P	W	D	L	F	A	GD	Pts
21	23	4	6	13	17	35	-18	18

CUP PROGRESS DETAILS
Competition	Round reached	Knocked out by
FA Cup	R1	Tranmere
JP Trophy	R1	Tranmere
Carling Cup	R1	Wolverhampton

BIGGEST WIN (ALL COMPS)
15/11/08 3–0 v Bournemouth **FL2**

BIGGEST DEFEAT (ALL COMPS)
12/12/08 1–5 v Lincoln City **FL2**

ATTENDANCE RECORD
High	Low	Average
3,012	1,033	1,414
v Bradford (11/10/2008)	v Luton (24/02/2009)	

RESULTS 2008/09

August
9th	● Aldershot	.........h	L 0–1	**Att:** 1,805 — **Booked:** Murdock
12th	● Wolverhampton a	L 3–2	**Att:** 9,424 — **Scorers:** Craney, P. Mullin. **Booked:** Williams (AET)
16th	● Port Vale	.........a	W 0–2	**Att:** 6,643 — **Scorers:** Craney, P. Mullin. **Booked:** P. Mullin, Cavanagh
23rd	● Macclesfield	.....h	W 2–0	**Att:** 1,323 — **Scorers:** P. Mullin, Ryan
30th	● Gillingham	........a	L 1–0	**Att:** 4,733

September
2nd	● Tranmere	......a	L 1–0	**Att:** 2,410 — **Booked:** Williams
6th	● Exeter	...........a	L 2–1	**Att:** 3,930 — **Scorers:** Clarke. **Booked:** Arthur, Williams, Edwards
13th	● Notts County	....h	D 1–1	**Att:** 1,404 — **Booked:** Ryan
20th	● Darlington	........a	L 3–0	**Att:** 2,814 — **Booked:** Cavanagh, J. Mullin
28th	● Rochdale	..........h	L 1–3	**Att:** 2,417 — **Scorers:** Miles. **Booked:** Murdock, Cavanagh

October
4th	● Barnet	...............a	L 2–1	**Att:** 1,899 — **Scorers:** Murdock. **Booked:** Cavanagh, Murdock, P. Mullin, Gornell. **Dismissed:** Williams
11th	● Bradford	..........h	L 2–3	**Att:** 3,012 — **Scorers:** Gornell, Ryan. **Booked:** Cavanagh
18th	● Luton	...............a	W 1–2	**Att:** 5,492 — **Scorers:** Gornell, P. Mullin. **Booked:** Charnock, Griffiths, Gornell
21st	● Shrewsbury	......h	W 2–1	**Att:** 1,249 — **Scorers:** Gornell, P. Mullin. **Booked:** Ryan
25th	● Wycombe	..........h	L 0–1	**Att:** 1,217
28th	● Morecambe	......a	D 1–1	**Att:** 2,044 — **Scorers:** McStay OG. **Booked:** Williams

November
1st	● Dag & Red	........a	D 0–0	**Att:** 1,433
8th	● Tranmere	..........h	D 0–0	**Att:** 2,126 — **Booked:** Procter
13th	● Tranmere	..........a	L 1–0	**Att:** 2,560 — **Booked:** J. Mullin
15th	● Bournemouth	....h	W 3–0	**Att:** 1,152 — **Scorers:** Gornell, Griffiths, P. Mullin. **Booked:** Charnock
22nd	● Chesterfield	......a	D 1–1	**Att:** 3,215 — **Scorers:** Ryan, Miles, Edwards
29th	● Bury	...............h	L 1–2	**Att:** 2,093 — **Scorers:** Clarke. **Booked:** Blundell

December
12th	● Lincoln City	.....a	L 5–1	**Att:** 2,625 — **Scorers:** Miles. **Booked:** Charnock, Grant
20th	● Rotherham	........h	L 1–3	**Att:** 1,172 — **Scorers:** Procter
26th	● Chester	............a	L 2–0	**Att:** 2,223 — **Booked:** Miles
28th	● Grimsby	...........h	W 3–1	**Att:** 1,200 — **Scorers:** Clarke[3]

January
3rd	● Rochdale	..........a	L 3–1	**Att:** 3,126 — **Scorers:** Cavanagh. **Booked:** Procter, Charnock
17th	● Bradford	..........a	D 1–1	**Att:** 12,172 — **Scorers:** Ryan. **Booked:** Turner, P. Mullin, Edwards
24th	● Barnet	...............h	D 1–1	**Att:** 1,056 — **Scorers:** P. Mullin
27th	● Morecambe	......h	W 1–0	**Att:** 1,407 — **Scorers:** Ryan
31st	● Wycombe	..........a	L 2–1	**Att:** 6,166 — **Scorers:** P. Mullin

February
3rd	● Shrewsbury	......a	L 2–0	**Att:** 4,134
10th	● Brentford	..........h	D 1–1	**Att:** 1,111 — **Scorers:** Ryan. **Booked:** Charnock, Lindfield, Cavanagh
14th	● Bournemouth	....a	L 1–0	**Att:** 4,109 — **Booked:** Ryan, Procter, Bell
21st	● Dag & Red	........h	D 0–0	**Att:** 1,123
24th	● Luton	...............h	D 0–0	**Att:** 1,033
28th	● Aldershot	.........a	L 3–1	**Att:** 2,604 — **Scorers:** Lindfield. **Booked:** Edwards, Lindfield

March
7th	● Gillingham	........h	L 0–2	**Att:** 1,308
10th	● Macclesfield	.....a	W 0–2	**Att:** 1,746 — **Scorers:** Procter, Williams. **Booked:** Ryan
14th	● Notts County	....a	D 1–1	**Att:** 3,701 — **Scorers:** Ryan. **Booked:** Cavanagh, Turner, Lindfield
17th	● Port Vale	.........h	W 2–0	**Att:** 1,144 — **Scorers:** Procter, Ryan. **Booked:** Charnock, Cavanagh
21st	● Exeter	...............h	W 2–1	**Att:** 1,169 — **Scorers:** Lindfield, Miles. **Booked:** Lindfield
24th	● Darlington	........h	W 1–0	**Att:** 1,086 — **Scorers:** Ryan. **Booked:** Lindfield
28th	● Rotherham	........a	D 0–0	**Att:** 2,804

April
4th	● Lincoln City	.....h	L 0–2	**Att:** 1,139 — **Booked:** Edwards
11th	● Grimsby	...........a	W 0–1	**Att:** 6,453 — **Scorers:** Symes. **Booked:** Murdock, Cavanagh, Ryan
13th	● Chester	............h	L 0–1	**Att:** 1,100 — **Booked:** Lindfield
18th	● Brentford	..........a	L 3–0	**Att:** 7,135 — **Booked:** Charnock, Ryan, Arthur
25th	● Chesterfield	......h	W 1–0	**Att:** 1,795 — **Scorers:** Grant. **Booked:** Charnock

May
2nd	● Bury	...............a	L 1–0	**Att:** 7,515 — **Booked:** Procter, Charnock, Edwards. **Dismissed:** Procter

● Coca-Cola League 2/Play-Offs   ● FA Cup   ● Carling Cup   ● Johnstone's Paint Trophy

LEAGUE TWO GOALKEEPER STATS

Player	Appearances	Match starts	Completed matches	Sub appearances	Subbed off	Clean sheets	Yellow cards	Red cards
Kenny Arthur	42	42	42	0	0	13	2	0
Ian Dunbavin	4	4	4	0	0	0	0	0

LEAGUE TWO OUTFIELD PLAYER STATS

Player	Appearances	Match starts	Completed matches	Substitute appearances	Subbed off	Goals scored	Yellow cards	Red cards
James Bell	6	5	4	1	1	0	1	0
Gregg Blundell	2	2	1	0	1	0	1	0
Peter Cavanagh	29	28	28	1	0	1	9	0
Kieran Charnock	34	33	33	1	0	0	9	0
Jamie Clarke	15	12	6	3	6	5	0	0
Ian Craney	2	2	2	0	0	1	0	0
Phil Edwards	46	46	45	0	1	0	6	0
Terry Gornell	11	10	7	1	3	4	2	0
Robert Grant	15	6	4	9	2	1	1	0
Rostyn Griffiths	13	13	10	0	3	1	1	0
Kallum Higginbotham	12	5	2	7	3	0	0	0
Adam Kay	3	1	0	2	1	0	0	0
Chris King	27	27	24	0	3	0	0	0
John Kissock	5	5	2	0	3	0	0	0
Craig Lindfield	20	17	13	3	4	2	6	0
Craig Mahon	2	0	0	2	0	0	0	0
Sean McConville	5	2	0	3	2	0	0	0
John Miles	43	42	33	1	9	3	2	0
Paul Mullin	36	36	36	0	0	7	3	0
John Mullin	31	25	20	6	5	0	1	0
Colin Murdock	23	20	16	3	4	1	4	0
Peter Murphy	3	1	0	2	1	0	0	0
Folawiyo Onibuje	5	0	0	5	0	0	0	0
Andrew Procter	37	32	24	5	7	3	3	1
Leam Richardson	11	9	4	2	5	0	0	0
James Ryan	44	41	36	3	5	10	6	0
Andrew Smith	1	0	0	1	0	0	0	0
Michael Symes	7	7	7	0	0	1	0	0
Chris Turner	22	14	7	8	7	0	2	0
Robbie Williams	23	18	16	5	1	1	2	1
David Worrall	4	1	1	3	0	0	0	0

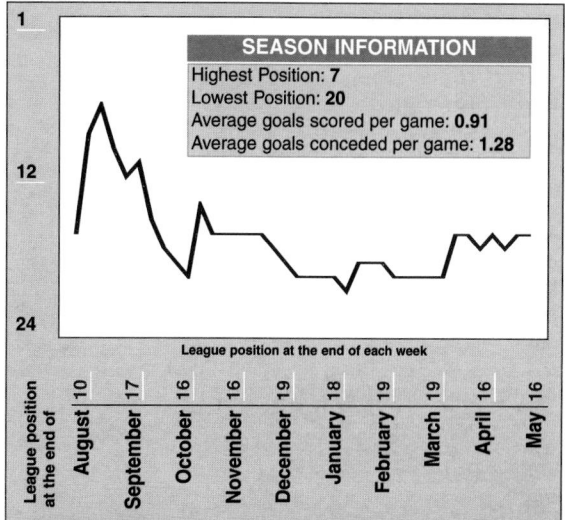

SEASON INFORMATION
Highest Position: **7**
Lowest Position: **20**
Average goals scored per game: **0.91**
Average goals conceded per game: **1.28**

League position at the end of each week

LONGEST SEQUENCES

Wins (17/03/09–24/03/09)	3	Undefeated home (28/12/08–24/02/09)	6
Losses (on two occasions)	4	Undefeated away (on two occasions)	4
Draws (on two occasions)	2	Without scoring (14/02/09–24/02/09)	3
Undefeated (10/03/09–28/03/09)	6	Without conceding (16/08/08–23/08/08)	2
Without win (31/01/09–07/03/09)	8	Scoring (28/12/08–31/01/09)	6

CARDS RECEIVED

61 **2**

QUICK-FIRE GOALS

From the start of a match
John Miles (v Rochdale) 1:05

By a substitute after coming on
Jamie Clarke (v Bury) 13:08

GOALS SCORED/CONCEDED PER FIVE-MINUTE INTERVALS

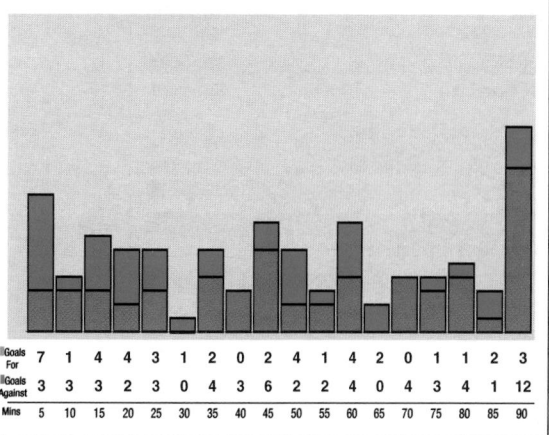

Goals For	7	1	4	4	3	1	2	0	2	4	1	4	2	0	1	1	2	3
Goals Against	3	3	3	2	3	0	4	3	6	2	2	4	0	4	3	4	1	12
Mins	5	10	15	20	25	30	35	40	45	50	55	60	65	70	75	80	85	90

AFC BOURNEMOUTH

BOURNEMOUTH manager Eddie Howe deserves immense credit for keeping the club in Coca-Cola League Two after they began the season on minus 17 points.

Howe, 31, became the youngest boss in the Football League after taking charge of the Cherries on New Year's Eve. Back then, the club were second from bottom and facing a massive fight to stave off the threat of relegation. Under the thoughtful leadership of Howe, the Dean Court side enjoyed a sparkling 2009, producing form befitting of promotion hopefuls.

They finished the season nine points above the drop zone but off-the-field problems were evident all season and continue to cast a dark shadow. The protracted sale of the club has yet to be completed, but Howe remains keen to continue his excellent work next term.

CLUB SUMMARY

FORMED	1899
MANAGER	Eddie Howe
GROUND	Dean Court
CAPACITY	10,770
NICKNAME	The Cherries
WEBSITE	www.afcb.co.uk

The New Football Pools PLAYER OF THE SEASON — Jason Pearce

OVERALL

P	W	D	L	F	A	GD
53	20	13	20	65	55	10

COCA-COLA FOOTBALL LEAGUE TWO

Pos	P	W	D	L	F	A	GD	Pts
21	46	17	12	17	59	51	8	46

HOME

Pos	P	W	D	L	F	A	GD	Pts
11	23	11	6	6	28	15	13	39

AWAY

Pos	P	W	D	L	F	A	GD	Pts
14	23	6	6	11	31	36	-5	24

CUP PROGRESS DETAILS

Competition	Round reached	Knocked out by
FA Cup	R2	Blyth Spartans
JP Trophy	FLTSQ	Colchester
Carling Cup	R1	Cardiff

BIGGEST WIN (ALL COMPS)

4–0 on two occasions

BIGGEST DEFEAT (ALL COMPS)

18/10/08 1–4 v Shrewsbury **FL2**

ATTENDANCE RECORD

High	Low	Average
9,008	3,068	4,931
v Grimsby (25/04/2009)	v Morecambe (25/11/2008)	

RESULTS 2008/09

August
9th	● Gillingham	.......h	D 1–1	Att: 5,377 — **Scorers:** Anderton. **Booked:** Pitman
12th	● Cardiff	..............h	L 1–2	Att: 3,399 — **Scorers:** Kuffour
16th	● Aldershot	..........a	D 1–1	Att: 4,564 — **Scorers:** Sappleton. **Booked:** Guyett
23rd	● Exeter	...............h	L 0–1	Att: 5,350 — **Booked:** Bradbury
30th	● Port Vale	.........a	L 3–1	Att: 6,048 — **Scorers:** Lindfield. **Booked:** Pearce

September
2nd	● Bristol Rovers	..h	W 3–0	Att: 2,220 — **Scorers:** Goulding, Hollands, Igoe
6th	● Notts County	....a	D 1–1	Att: 4,362 — **Scorers:** Pitman. **Booked:** Cummings, Wagstaff
13th	● Macclesfield	....h	W 1–0	Att: 3,922
20th	● Bradford	........a	W 1–3	Att: 12,824 — **Scorers:** Goulding, Hollands, Pearce. **Booked:** Hollands
27th	● Darlington	.......h	W 3–1	Att: 4,124 — **Scorers:** Bartley, Pitman, Austin OG. **Booked:** Cummings, Pearce, Pitman

October
4th	● Wycombe	.........a	L 3–1	Att: 5,005 — **Scorers:** Hollands. **Booked:** Bartley, Goulding, Pitman, Hollands
7th	● MK Dons	......a	W 0–1	Att: 4,329 — **Scorers:** Anderton. **Booked:** Bartley, Pitman, Bradbury, Cummings
11th	● Rotherham	.......h	D 0–0	Att: 4,530
18th	● Shrewsbury	......a	L 4–1	Att: 5,738 — **Scorers:** Pitman. **Booked:** Bradbury, Pearce, Ward. **Dismissed:** Ward
21st	● Dag & Red	......h	W 2–1	Att: 3,554 — **Scorers:** Bradbury, Pitman. **Booked:** Goulding, Bartley, Bradbury
25th	● Lincoln City	....h	L 0–1	Att: 4,464 — **Booked:** Hollands

November
1st	● Chesterfield	......h	D 1–1	Att: 4,082 — **Scorers:** Goodall OG
4th	● Colchester	.......h	L 0–1	Att: 2,275 — **Booked:** Bradbury
8th	● Bristol Rovers	..h	W 1–0	Att: 3,935 — **Scorers:** Pearce. **Booked:** Cummings, Anderton, Bradbury. **Dismissed:** Bradbury
15th	● Accrington S	....a	L 3–0	Att: 1,152 — **Booked:** Pitman, Hollands
21st	● Grimsby	..........a	D 3–3	Att: 4,353 — **Scorers:** Anderton, Bradbury[2]. **Booked:** Guyett. **Dismissed:** Guyett
25th	● Morecambe	.......h	D 0–0	Att: 3,068
29th	● Blyth Spartans	..h	D 0–0	Att: 4,165 — **Booked:** Bradbury, Molesley

December
2nd	● Luton	...............a	D 3–3	Att: 6,773 — **Scorers:** Molesley[2], Tubbs
6th	● Chester	............h	W 1–0	Att: 4,154 — **Scorers:** Anderton. **Booked:** Cooper, Pitman
13th	● Rochdale	........a	D 1–1	Att: 2,285 — **Scorers:** Bradbury. **Booked:** Hollands, Molesley
16th	● Blyth Spartans	..a	L 1–0	Att: 4,040 — **Booked:** Partington. **Dismissed:** Pitman
20th	● Bury	................h	W 2–0	Att: 3,479 — **Scorers:** Igoe, Partington. **Booked:** Bartley
26th	● Brentford	........a	L 2–0	Att: 6,450 — **Booked:** Partington, Bartley
28th	● Barnet	..............h	L 0–2	Att: 4,725 — **Booked:** Jalal

January
3rd	● Darlington	.......a	L 2–1	Att: 2,571 — **Scorers:** Hollands. **Booked:** Cooper
17th	● Rotherham	.......a	L 1–1	Att: 3,270 — **Booked:** Hollands, Pitman. **Dismissed:** Hollands
24th	● Wycombe	.........a	W 3–1	Att: 5,946 — **Scorers:** Pearce, Pitman, Thomson. **Booked:** Cooper
27th	● Luton	...............h	D 1–1	Att: 5,230 — **Scorers:** Hollands. **Booked:** Pearce, Cooper
31st	● Lincoln City	....a	D 3–3	Att: 3,634 — **Scorers:** Molesley, Pitman[2]. **Booked:** Pitman

February
7th	● Shrewsbury	......h	W 1–0	Att: 4,187 — **Scorers:** Pitman. **Booked:** Cooper
14th	● Accrington S	....h	W 1–0	Att: 4,109 — **Scorers:** Pitman. **Booked:** Thomson, Molesley
20th	● Chesterfield	......a	L 1–0	Att: 3,130 — **Booked:** Jalal, Goulding
24th	● Dag & Red	......a	W 0–1	Att: 1,602 — **Scorers:** Molesley
28th	● Gillingham	.......a	L 1–0	Att: 5,353 — **Booked:** Goulding, Fletcher, Robinson, Molesley

March
3rd	● Aldershot	..........h	W 2–0	Att: 4,556 — **Scorers:** Fletcher, Hollands. **Booked:** Robinson, Garry
7th	● Port Vale	.........h	D 0–0	Att: 5,924
10th	● Exeter	...............a	W 1–3	Att: 4,946 — **Scorers:** Hollands, Pitman[2]
14th	● Macclesfield	....a	W 0–2	Att: 1,589 — **Scorers:** Bradbury[2]. **Booked:** Cummings, Fletcher
17th	● Bradford	........h	W 4–1	Att: 4,847 — **Scorers:** Fletcher[2], Goulding[2]
21st	● Notts County	....h	L 0–1	Att: 5,510 — **Booked:** Cummings, Bartley
28th	● Bury	................a	L 1–0	Att: 2,762

April
4th	● Rochdale	........h	W 4–0	Att: 5,092 — **Scorers:** Feeney, Pitman[3]
11th	● Barnet	..............a	L 1–0	Att: 3,133 — **Booked:** Bradbury, Hollands, Goulding
13th	● Brentford	........h	L 0–1	Att: 8,168 — **Booked:** Fletcher, Hollands, Wiggins, Goulding
18th	● Chester	............a	W 0–2	Att: 3,349 — **Scorers:** Pitman, Robinson. **Booked:** Jalal, Hollands
25th	● Grimsby	..........h	W 2–1	Att: 9,008 — **Scorers:** Feeney, Fletcher. **Booked:** Fletcher

May
2nd	● Morecambe	......a	W 0–4	Att: 2,601 — **Scorers:** Feeney, Pitman[2], Ward

● Coca-Cola League 2/Play-Offs ● FA Cup ● Carling Cup ● Johnstone's Paint Trophy

actim

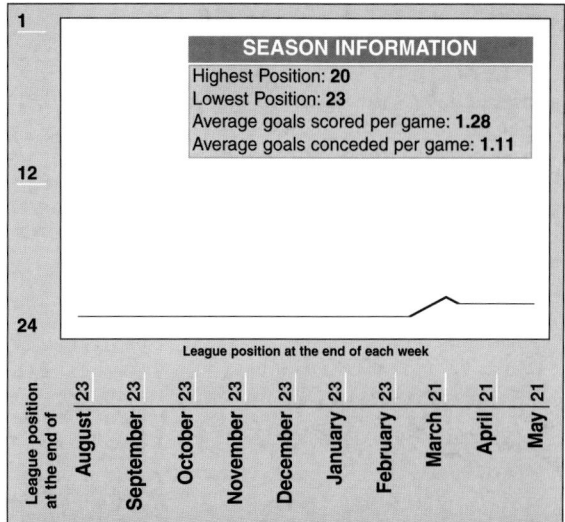

LEAGUE TWO GOALKEEPER STATS

Player	Appearances	Match starts	Completed matches	Sub appearances	Subbed off	Clean sheets	Yellow cards	Red cards
David Button	4	4	4	0	0	0	0	0
Shwan Jalal	41	41	41	0	0	13	3	0
Ryan Pryce	1	1	1	0	0	0	0	0

LEAGUE TWO OUTFIELD PLAYER STATS

Player	Appearances	Match starts	Completed matches	Substitute appearances	Subbed off	Goals scored	Yellow cards	Red cards
Darren Anderton	18	17	12	1	5	3	0	0
Marvin Bartley	33	27	15	6	12	1	5	0
Lee Bradbury	34	28	21	6	7	6	4	0
Alan Connell	12	6	3	6	3	0	0	0
Shaun Cooper	37	35	32	2	3	0	5	0
Warren Cummings	32	27	23	5	4	0	4	0
Liam Feeney	14	6	1	8	5	3	0	0
Steve Fletcher	21	19	11	2	8	4	4	0
Ryan Garry	25	21	15	4	6	0	1	0
Jeff Goulding	27	14	4	13	10	3	6	0
Scott Guyett	25	21	18	4	2	0	2	1
Danny Hollands	42	39	36	3	2	6	9	1
Sammy Igoe	28	22	8	6	14	1	0	0
Jo Kuffour	2	2	2	0	0	0	0	0
Craig Lindfield	3	1	1	2	0	1	0	0
Josh McQuoid	16	5	2	11	3	0	0	0
Mark Molesley	29	22	15	7	7	4	3	0
Joe Partington	11	6	3	5	3	1	1	0
Jason Pearce	44	44	43	0	1	2	4	0
Carl Pettefer	1	0	0	1	0	0	0	0
Brett Pitman	39	29	20	10	9	17	7	0
Carl Preston	2	2	0	0	2	0	0	0
Michael Rankine	3	3	1	0	2	0	0	0
Anton Robinson	17	16	15	1	1	1	2	0
Ricky Sappleton	3	1	0	2	1	1	0	0
Blair Sturrock	4	1	0	3	1	0	0	0
Michael Symes	5	3	1	2	2	0	0	0
Jake Thomson	6	6	2	0	4	1	1	0
Jason Tindall	2	0	0	2	0	0	0	0
Matthew Tubbs	8	6	5	2	1	1	0	0
Scott Wagstaff	5	3	1	2	2	0	1	0
Joel Ward	21	16	12	5	3	1	1	1
George Webb	1	0	0	1	0	0	0	0
Rhoys Wiggins	13	12	12	1	0	0	1	0

SEASON INFORMATION
Highest Position: **20**
Lowest Position: **23**
Average goals scored per game: **1.28**
Average goals conceded per game: **1.11**

League position at the end of each week

League position at the end of	August 23	September 23	October 23	November 23	December 23	January 23	February 23	March 21	April 21	May 21

LONGEST SEQUENCES

Wins	3	Undefeated home	7
(on two occasions)		(24/01/09–17/03/09)	
Losses	4	Undefeated away	3
(26/12/08–17/01/09)		(21/11/08–13/12/08)	
Draws	3	Without scoring	2
(21/11/08–02/12/08)		(on three occasions)	
Undefeated	6	Without conceding	2
(21/11/08–20/12/08)		(on two occasions)	
Without win	6	Scoring	5
(on two occasions)		(24/01/09–14/02/09)	

CARDS RECEIVED

64 **3**

QUICK-FIRE GOALS

From the start of a match
Brett Pitman (v Chester) 2:48

By a substitute after coming on
Brett Pitman (v Darlington) 10:18

GOALS SCORED/CONCEDED PER FIVE-MINUTE INTERVALS

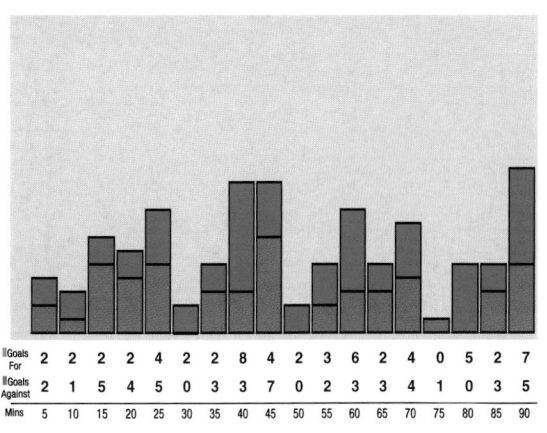

Goals For	2	2	2	2	4	2	2	8	4	2	3	6	2	4	0	5	2	7
Goals Against	2	1	5	4	5	0	3	3	7	0	2	3	3	4	1	0	3	5
Mins	5	10	15	20	25	30	35	40	45	50	55	60	65	70	75	80	85	90

AFTER winning promotion to the League with a record 101-point haul in 2007/08, Gary Waddock's side had good reason to be optimistic about their chances of another season of success.

However, victories over promotion hopefuls Bradford, Darlington and Gillingham in August and September alongside early-season defeats at lowly Luton, Notts County and Macclesfield set the tone for a campaign of inconsistency.

Their record of just four defeats at the Recreation Ground all season was in stark contrast to the 16 losses suffered in away games, and boss Waddock knows he will have to address his side's problems on the road if they are to mount a challenge next season.

Kirk Hudson and on-loan Reading midfielder Scott Davies were the star performers with 11 and 13 league goals respectively.

CLUB SUMMARY

FORMED	1926
MANAGER	Gary Waddock
GROUND	Recreation Ground
CAPACITY	7,100
NICKNAME	The Shots
WEBSITE	www.theshots.co.uk

The New **Football Pools** PLAYER OF THE SEASON — **Anthony Charles**

OVERALL

P	W	D	L	F	A	GD
51	15	14	22	66	89	-23

COCA-COLA FOOTBALL LEAGUE TWO

Pos	P	W	D	L	F	A	GD	Pts
15	46	14	12	20	59	80	-21	54

HOME

Pos	P	W	D	L	F	A	GD	Pts
13	23	9	10	4	36	31	5	37

AWAY

Pos	P	W	D	L	F	A	GD	Pts
23	23	5	2	16	23	49	-26	17

CUP PROGRESS DETAILS

Competition	Round reached	Knocked out by
FA Cup	R2	Millwall
JP Trophy	R1	Swindon
Carling Cup	R1	Coventry

BIGGEST WIN (ALL COMPS)

3–0 on two occasions

BIGGEST DEFEAT (ALL COMPS)

07/03/09 0–5 v Bradford FL2

ATTENDANCE RECORD

High	Low	Average
5,023	2,090	3,276
v Brentford (18/10/2008)	v Shrewsbury (10/03/2009)	

RESULTS 2008/09

August
9th	● Accrington S	....a W 0–1	Att: 1,805 — **Scorers:** Donnelly. **Booked:** Howell
13th	● Coventry	......a L 3–1	Att: 9,293 — **Scorers:** Morgan. **Booked:** Hylton
16th	● Bournemouth	...h D 1–1	Att: 4,564 — **Scorers:** Soares. **Booked:** Chalmers
23rd	● Shrewsbury	....a L 1–0	Att: 5,422 — **Booked:** Charles, Soares
30th	● Bradford	..........h W 3–2	Att: 3,805 — **Scorers:** Davies, Grant, Morgan. **Booked:** Chalmers

September
2nd	● Swindon	..........h D 2–2	Att: 1,814 — **Scorers:** Davies, Elvins. **Booked:** Newman, Blackburn (Lost 6–7 on pens)
6th	● Darlington	.......h W 2–1	Att: 3,460 — **Scorers:** Morgan, Soares
13th	● Luton	................a L 3–1	Att: 6,462 — **Scorers:** Grant. **Booked:** Morgan, Chalmers, Davies, Charles
20th	● Gillingham	......h W 2–1	Att: 4,198 — **Scorers:** Davies, Hudson. **Booked:** Morgan
27th	● Notts County	....a L 2–1	Att: 6,033 — **Scorers:** Charles. **Booked:** Morgan, Charles

October
4th	● Bury	.................h D 3–3	Att: 3,621 — **Scorers:** Davies, Elvins, Hylton. **Booked:** Hylton, Blackburn
11th	● Macclesfield	......a L 4–2	Att: 1,857 — **Scorers:** Hudson, Hylton. **Booked:** Charles
18th	● Brentford	..........h D 1–1	Att: 5,023 — **Scorers:** Davies. **Booked:** Blackburn, Howell, Hylton
22nd	● Chesterfield	.....a L 5–1	Att: 3,079 — **Scorers:** Hudson
25th	● Rochdale	.........a L 3–1	Att: 2,750 — **Scorers:** Morgan. **Booked:** Charles
28th	● Port Vale	.........h W 1–0	Att: 3,039 — **Scorers:** Soares

November
1st	● Morecambe	......a L 2–0	Att: 1,897
8th	● Rotherham	.......h D 1–1	Att: 2,632 — **Scorers:** Grant. **Booked:** Hylton
15th	● Exeter	...............h W 1–0	Att: 3,784 — **Scorers:** Grant. **Booked:** Hudson, Morgan. **Dismissed:** Hylton
18th	● Rotherham	.......a W 0–3	Att: 2,431 — **Scorers:** Hudson[2], Morgan. **Booked:** Straker
22nd	● Chester	..........a W 0–1	Att: 1,653 — **Scorers:** Morgan
25th	● Lincoln City	....h W 2–0	Att: 2,625 — **Scorers:** Davies, Sandell
29th	● Millwall	..........a L 3–0	Att: 6,159 — **Booked:** Davies

December
6th	● Wycombe	.........h W 3–2	Att: 3,915 — **Scorers:** Hudson[2], Hylton. **Booked:** Morgan
20th	● Grimsby	...........h D 2–2	Att: 3,605 — **Scorers:** Davies[2]. **Booked:** Day
26th	● Barnet	..............a W 0–3	Att: 2,729 — **Scorers:** Charles, Davies, Hylton. **Booked:** Harding
28th	● Dag & Red	......h L 1–2	Att: 3,697 — **Scorers:** Hudson

January
17th	● Macclesfield	......h D 1–1	Att: 3,018 — **Scorers:** Hudson. **Booked:** Hylton
20th	● Notts County	....h D 2–2	Att: 2,491 — **Scorers:** Davies, Harding
24th	● Bury	.................a L 2–1	Att: 2,558 — **Scorers:** Davies. **Booked:** Charles, Day, Harding
27th	● Brentford	.........a L 3–0	Att: 5,111 — **Booked:** Blackburn, Charles, Straker, Soares
31st	● Rochdale	..........h L 2–4	Att: 3,018 — **Scorers:** Davies, Morgan. **Booked:** Newman, Charles

February
14th	● Exeter	................a L 3–2	Att: 4,840 — **Scorers:** Harding, Robinson. **Booked:** Davies, Harding
17th	● Gillingham	........a D 4–4	Att: 5,974 — **Scorers:** Lindegaard, Sandell, Winfield, Bentley OG
21st	● Morecambe	......h L 0–2	Att: 2,872 — **Booked:** Soares, Lindegaard, Morgan
28th	● Accrington S	...h W 3–1	Att: 2,604 — **Scorers:** Hudson, Robinson[2]. **Booked:** Straker

March
3rd	● Bournemouth	...a L 2–0	Att: 4,556 — **Booked:** Cochrane
7th	● Bradford	..........a L 5–0	Att: 12,465
10th	● Shrewsbury	....h D 0–0	Att: 2,090 — **Booked:** Jaimez–Ruiz, Day
14th	● Luton	................h W 2–1	Att: 3,098 — **Scorers:** Davies, Hudson. **Booked:** Chalmers, Sandell, Winfield
17th	● Rotherham	.......a W 1–2	Att: 2,769 — **Scorers:** Grant[2]
21st	● Darlington	.......a L 2–0	Att: 2,532 — **Booked:** Winfield, Robinson
28th	● Grimsby	...........a L 1–0	Att: 7,095
31st	● Chesterfield	...h D 1–1	Att: 2,482 — **Scorers:** Robinson. **Booked:** Charles

April
4th	● Rotherham	.......h L 0–1	Att: 2,643 — **Booked:** Charles, Newman, Straker
7th	● Port Vale	.........a D 0–0	Att: 4,140 — **Booked:** Newman
11th	● Dag & Red	......a L 3–1	Att: 1,586 — **Scorers:** Hylton
13th	● Barnet	..............h D 1–1	Att: 2,597 — **Scorers:** Chalmers. **Booked:** Davies
18th	● Wycombe	.........a L 3–0	Att: 5,440 — **Booked:** Charles
25th	● Chester	...........h D 2–2	Att: 3,100 — **Scorers:** Hudson[2]. **Booked:** Soares, Hylton

May
| 2nd | ● Lincoln City | ......a W 0–2 | Att: 3,910 — **Scorers:** Davies, Grant. **Booked:** Chalmers |

● Coca-Cola League 2/Play-Offs ● FA Cup ● Carling Cup ● Johnstone's Paint Trophy

LEAGUE TWO GOALKEEPER STATS

Player	Appearances	Match starts	Completed matches	Sub appearances	Subbed off	Clean sheets	Yellow cards	Red cards
Nikki Bull	30	30	28	0	2	7	0	0
Mikhael Jaimez-Ruiz	14	13	13	1	0	2	1	0
Alex McCarthy	4	3	3	1	0	0	0	0

LEAGUE TWO OUTFIELD PLAYER STATS

Player	Appearances	Match starts	Completed matches	Substitute appearances	Subbed off	Goals scored	Yellow cards	Red cards
Chris Blackburn	36	36	35	0	1	0	3	0
Lewis Chalmers	23	19	14	4	5	1	5	0
Anthony Charles	41	41	40	0	1	2	11	0
Justin Cochrane	10	9	6	1	3	0	1	0
Scott Davies	41	37	35	4	2	13	3	0
Rhys Day	17	16	12	1	4	0	3	0
Scott Donnelly	20	12	4	8	8	1	0	0
Rob Elvins	15	7	3	8	4	1	0	0
John Grant	35	28	23	7	5	6	0	0
Ben Harding	29	29	26	0	3	2	3	0
Dean Howell	14	14	9	0	5	0	2	0
Kirk Hudson	43	35	29	8	6	11	1	0
Daniel Hylton	29	16	9	13	6	5	4	1
Andy Lindegaard	6	6	5	0	1	1	1	0
Junior Mendes	6	1	0	5	1	0	0	0
Marvin Morgan	32	22	11	10	11	5	6	0
Ricky Newman	17	10	6	7	3	0	3	1
Junior Osborne	8	8	7	0	1	0	0	0
Jake Robinson	19	19	13	0	6	4	1	0
Andrew Sandell	29	24	19	5	5	2	1	0
Louis Soares	35	30	25	5	5	3	4	0
Ben Starosta	3	3	2	0	0	0	0	0
Anthony Straker	32	29	27	3	2	0	3	0
Dave Winfield	10	9	8	1	1	1	2	0

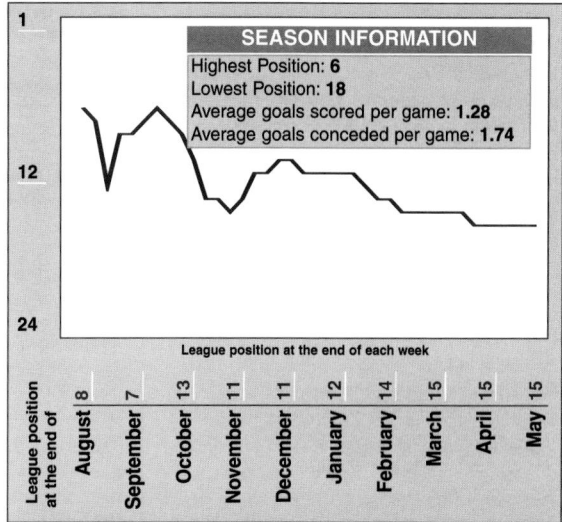

SEASON INFORMATION

Highest Position: **6**
Lowest Position: **18**
Average goals scored per game: **1.28**
Average goals conceded per game: **1.74**

LONGEST SEQUENCES

Wins (15/11/08–06/12/08)	4	Undefeated home (09/08/08–20/12/08)	12
Losses (24/01/09–14/02/09)	4	Undefeated away (22/11/08–26/12/08)	2
Draws (17/01/09–20/01/09)	2	Without scoring (03/03/09–10/03/09)	3
Undefeated (15/11/08–26/12/08)	6	Without conceding (15/11/08–25/11/08)	3
Without win (28/12/08–21/02/09)	9	Scoring (30/08/08–28/10/08)	11

CARDS RECEIVED

58   **2**

QUICK-FIRE GOALS

From the start of a match
Ben Harding (v Notts County) 5:23

By a substitute after coming on
Kirk Hudson (v Chesterfield) 4:20

GOALS SCORED/CONCEDED PER FIVE-MINUTE INTERVALS

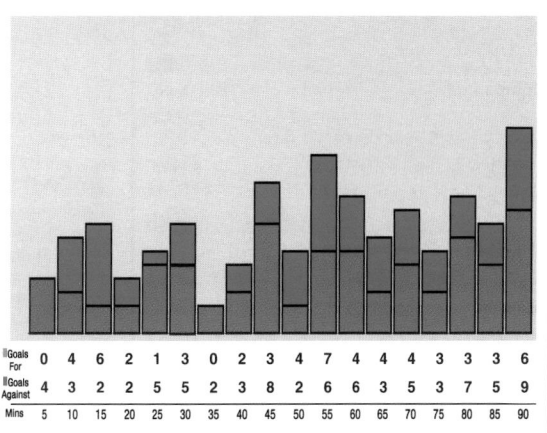

Goals For	0	4	6	2	1	3	0	2	3	4	7	4	4	4	3	3	3	6	
Goals Against	4	3	2	2	5	5	2	3	8	2	6	6	3	5	3	7	5	9	
Mins	5	10	15	20	25	30	35	40	45	50	55	60	65	70	75	80	85	90	

BARNET

IAN HENDON steered Barnet to Coca-Cola League Two safety as the Bees underwent a season of change. The former club captain took the reins from the long-serving Paul Fairclough, who moved into an advisory role following four years as manager.

Barnet were flirting with relegation on 16 points when the 37-year-old assumed control, but a haul of 32 points from his 24 games in charge helped them move clear.

John O'Flynn was a shining light during the campaign, scoring 18 goals in his first season with the club after signing from Cork City. Old-stager Paul Furlong also played his part, grabbing nine goals at the age of 40 after joining on loan from Southend in January.

The club, which opened a new FA-licensed Centre of Excellence during the season, were dumped out of all three Cups in the first round.

CLUB SUMMARY

FORMED	1888
MANAGER	Ian Hendon
GROUND	Underhill
CAPACITY	5,568
NICKNAME	The Bees
WEBSITE	www.barnetfc.com

The New **Football Pools** PLAYER OF THE SEASON — **John O'Flynn**

OVERALL
P	W	D	L	F	A	GD
50	11	16	23	61	86	-25

COCA-COLA FOOTBALL LEAGUE TWO
Pos	P	W	D	L	F	A	GD	Pts
17	46	11	15	20	56	74	-18	48

HOME
Pos	P	W	D	L	F	A	GD	Pts
19	23	7	7	9	30	35	-5	28

AWAY
Pos	P	W	D	L	F	A	GD	Pts
20	23	4	8	11	26	39	-13	20

CUP PROGRESS DETAILS
Competition	Round reached	Knocked out by
FA Cup	R1	Rochdale
JP Trophy	R1	Dag & Red
Carling Cup	R1	Brighton

BIGGEST WIN (ALL COMPS)
21/02/09 4–1 v Bradford **FL2**

BIGGEST DEFEAT (ALL COMPS)
30/08/08 1–5 v Chester **FL2**

ATTENDANCE RECORD
High	Low	Average
3,133	1,332	2,153

v Bournemouth (11/04/2009) v Rochdale (03/03/2009)

RESULTS 2008/09

August
9th	● Chesterfield ......h	L 1–3	Att: 2,237 — Scorers: Carew. Booked: Gillet
12th	● Brighton ....a	L 4–0	Att: 2,571 — Booked: Tabiri. Dismissed: Gillet
16th	● Rochdale ....a	L 3–1	Att: 2,442 — Scorers: Birchall
23rd	● Brentford ....h	L 0–1	Att: 2,815 — Booked: Leary, Thomas, Charles
30th	● Chester ....a	L 5–1	Att: 1,295 — Scorers: Akurang

September
2nd	● Dag & Red.......a	L 4–2	Att: 1,412 — Scorers: Birchall[2]. Booked: Thomas
6th	● Lincoln City .....a	L 2–0	Att: 3,417 — Booked: Carew
13th	● Morecambe .....h	D 1–1	Att: 1,776 — Scorers: Adomah. Booked: C. Akurang
20th	● Bury ....h	L 1–2	Att: 1,995 — Scorers: Adomah. Booked: C. Akurang
27th	● Grimsby ....a	W 0–1	Att: 3,713 — Scorers: Bishop. Booked: Gillet, Carew

October
4th	● Accrington S ....h	W 2–1	Att: 1,899 — Scorers: O'Flynn, Yakubu. Booked: C. Akurang
10th	● Dag & Red.......a	L 2–0	Att: 2,629 — Booked: Carew, Yakubu
18th	● Rotherham .....a	W 3–4	Att: 3,801 — Scorers: Adomah, Akurang[2], Medley. Booked: Gillet, Leary, Tabiri. Dismissed: Porter
21st	● Wycombe ....h	D 1–1	Att: 2,258 — Scorers: Deverdics. Booked: Leary
25th	● Exeter ....h	L 0–1	Att: 2,887
28th	● Shrewsbury .....a	D 2–2	Att: 5,163 — Scorers: O'Flynn[2]

November
1st	● Bradford ....a	D 3–3	Att: 12,510 — Scorers: Adomah, Nicolau, O'Flynn. Booked: Yakubu
8th	● Rochdale ....h	D 1–1	Att: 1,782 — Scorers: Yakubu. Booked: Gillet
15th	● Notts County ...h	L 0–4	Att: 1,934 — Booked: Townsend
18th	● Rochdale ....a	L 3–2	Att: 2,339 — Scorers: Adomah, O'Flynn. Booked: Deverdics, Bishop, Townsend. (AET)
22nd	● Macclesfield.....h	L 1–3	Att: 1,579 — Scorers: O'Flynn. Booked: Townsend
25th	● Port Vale ....a	D 0–0	Att: 4,617

December
6th	● Luton ....a	L 3–1	Att: 5,536 — Scorers: Ogogo. Booked: Ogogo, Leary, Gillet. Dismissed: Ogogo
13th	● Gillingham ....h	D 2–2	Att: 2,248 — Scorers: Leary, O'Flynn
20th	● Darlington ......a	D 2–2	Att: 2,770 — Scorers: O'Flynn, Yakubu. Booked: Leary
26th	● Aldershot ....h	L 0–3	Att: 2,729
28th	● Bournemouth ....a	W 0–2	Att: 4,725 — Scorers: Adomah[2]

January
10th	● Bury ....a	L 1–0	Att: 2,402
17th	● Dag & Red.......h	D 1–1	Att: 2,366 — Scorers: O'Flynn. Booked: Leary, Townsend, Bishop. Dismissed: Leary
24th	● Accrington S ....a	D 1–1	Att: 1,056 — Scorers: Furlong. Dismissed: Gillet
27th	● Shrewsbury .....h	D 0–0	Att: 1,568 — Booked: Nicolau, Furlong
31st	● Exeter ....a	L 2–1	Att: 4,145 — Scorers: Furlong. Booked: Bolasie

February
10th	● Grimsby ....h	D 3–3	Att: 1,554 — Scorers: Bolasie, Furlong, O'Flynn. Booked: Lockwood
14th	● Notts County ...a	L 2–0	Att: 3,830 — Booked: Hughes
21st	● Bradford ....h	W 4–1	Att: 2,445 — Scorers: Adomah, Bolasie, Devera, O'Flynn. Booked: Bolasie
28th	● Chesterfield .....a	D 1–1	Att: 3,068 — Scorers: Yakubu. Booked: Lockwood

March
3rd	● Rochdale ....h	W 2–1	Att: 1,332 — Scorers: Bolasie, O'Flynn
7th	● Chester ....h	W 3–1	Att: 2,085 — Scorers: Furlong, O'Flynn[2]
10th	● Brentford ....a	L 1–0	Att: 4,742 — Booked: Deverdics, Bolasie
14th	● Morecambe .....a	L 2–1	Att: 1,899 — Scorers: O'Flynn
21st	● Lincoln City .....h	W 3–2	Att: 1,979 — Scorers: Adomah, O'Flynn[2]. Booked: Breen, Lockwood
28th	● Darlington ......h	L 0–1	Att: 2,069 — Booked: Deverdics, Bishop, Lockwood
31st	● Wycombe ....a	D 1–1	Att: 4,066 — Scorers: Furlong

April
4th	● Gillingham ......a	W 0–2	Att: 6,033 — Scorers: Furlong, O'Flynn. Booked: Bolasie, Furlong, Deverdics
7th	● Rotherham ......h	W 2–0	Att: 1,508 — Scorers: Furlong[2]
11th	● Bournemouth ...h	W 1–0	Att: 3,133 — Scorers: Furlong. Booked: Furlong, Bishop
13th	● Aldershot ....a	D 1–1	Att: 2,597 — Scorers: Leary
18th	● Luton ....h	D 1–1	Att: 2,808 — Scorers: Birchall. Booked: Bolasie, Breen
25th	● Macclesfield.....a	L 2–1	Att: 1,619 — Scorers: Adomah. Booked: Hughes

May
2nd	● Port Vale ....h	L 1–2	Att: 2,305 — Scorers: Hart. Dismissed: Ogogo

● Coca-Cola League 2/Play-Offs ● FA Cup ● Carling Cup ● Johnstone's Paint Trophy

LEAGUE TWO GOALKEEPER STATS

Player	Appearances	Match starts	Completed matches	Sub appearances	Subbed off	Clean sheets	Yellow cards	Red cards
Rob Beckwith	5	5	5	0	0	1	0	0
Jake Cole	10	10	10	0	0	3	0	0
Lee Harrison	21	20	19	1	1	1	0	0
Ran Kadoch	12	11	10	1	1	2	0	0

LEAGUE TWO OUTFIELD PLAYER STATS

Player	Appearances	Match starts	Completed matches	Substitute appearances	Subbed off	Goals scored	Yellow cards	Red cards
Albert Adomah	45	45	38	0	7	9	0	0
Cliff Akurang	24	12	1	12	11	3	3	0
Adam Birchall	39	19	8	20	11	2	0	0
Neal Bishop	44	41	41	3	0	1	3	0
Tommy Black	5	5	1	0	4	0	0	0
Yannick Bolasie	20	17	13	3	4	3	5	0
Gary Breen	22	22	22	0	0	0	2	0
Ryan Burge	2	1	1	1	0	0	0	0
Ashley Carew	10	10	7	0	3	1	3	0
Elliot Charles	5	0	0	5	0	0	1	0
Jeremy De Magalhaes	4	4	4	0	0	0	0	0
Joe Devera	34	33	32	1	1	1	0	0
Nicky Deverdics	29	22	10	7	12	1	3	0
Paul Furlong	21	21	15	0	6	9	3	0
Kenny Gillet	32	28	27	4	0	0	4	1
Danny Hart	3	2	1	1	1	1	0	0
Mark Hughes	9	8	6	1	2	0	2	0
Michael Leary	28	24	19	4	4	2	6	1
Matthew Lockwood	12	12	11	0	1	0	4	0
Luke Medley	18	5	1	13	4	1	0	0
Paul Mitchell	3	3	1	0	2	0	0	0
Nicky Nicolau	21	12	8	9	4	1	1	0
John O'Flynn	34	32	19	2	13	17	0	0
Abu Ogogo	9	7	4	2	1	1	1	2
Max Porter	26	18	13	8	4	0	0	1
Kieron St Aimie	3	1	0	2	1	0	0	0
Joe Tabiri	7	4	2	3	2	0	1	0
Aswad Thomas	2	2	2	0	0	0	1	0
Michael Townsend	13	13	13	0	0	0	3	0
Ismail Yakubu	38	37	33	1	4	3	2	0

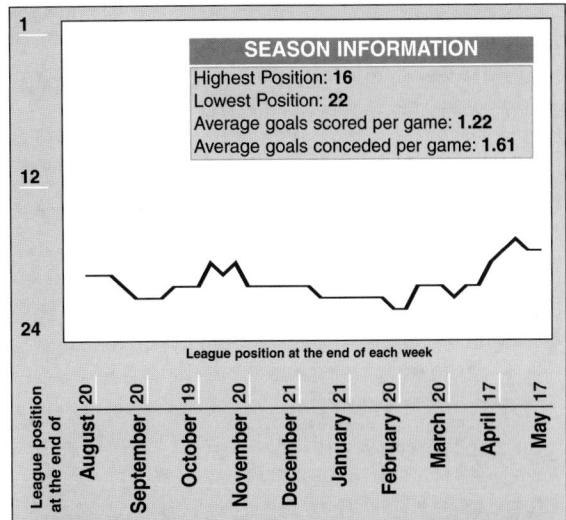

SEASON INFORMATION
Highest Position: **16**
Lowest Position: **22**
Average goals scored per game: **1.22**
Average goals conceded per game: **1.61**

League position at the end of each week

LONGEST SEQUENCES

Wins (04/04/09–11/04/09)	3	Undefeated home (17/01/09–21/03/09)	7
Losses (09/08/08–06/09/08)	5	Undefeated away (18/10/08–25/11/08)	4
Draws (17/01/09–27/01/09)	3	Without scoring (–)	
Undefeated (31/03/09–18/04/09)	6	Without conceding (04/04/09–11/04/09)	3
Without win (21/10/08–26/12/08)	11	Scoring (31/03/09–02/05/09)	8

CARDS RECEIVED

48 **5**

QUICK-FIRE GOALS

From the start of a match
John O'Flynn (v Accrington S) 0:19

By a substitute after coming on
Cliff Akurang (v Chester) 27:02

GOALS SCORED/CONCEDED PER FIVE-MINUTE INTERVALS

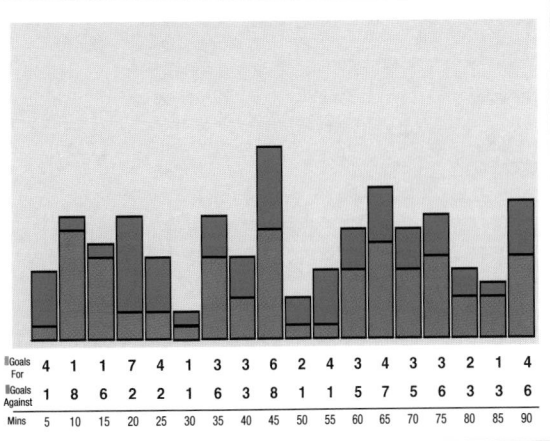

Goals For	4	1	1	7	4	1	3	3	6	2	4	3	4	3	3	2	1	4
Goals Against	1	8	6	2	2	1	6	3	8	1	1	5	7	5	6	3	3	6
Mins	5	10	15	20	25	30	35	40	45	50	55	60	65	70	75	80	85	90

BRADFORD CITY

BANTAMS fans must be wondering when their fortunes will change after another season of bitter disappointment.

Bradford launched the campaign as promotion favourites following the board's decision to hand Stuart McCall increased funds.

The manager, who had spent the previous season getting accustomed to the job, built a side that showed flashes of real quality this time around and they appeared well-placed to challenge for a top-two finish in February.

But the Bantams' challenge fell apart after a sequence of nine games without a win and McCall then hogged the spotlight following his announcement, in March, that he would quit should his side fail to make the play-offs.

Fan power later convinced McCall to stay and he will start all over again next season, albeit on a reduced budget.

CLUB SUMMARY

FORMED	1903
MANAGER	Stuart McCall
GROUND	Valley Parade
CAPACITY	25,136
NICKNAME	The Bantams
WEBSITE	www.bradfordcityfc.co.uk

The New **Football Pools**
PLAYER OF THE SEASON

Omar Daley

OVERALL
P	W	D	L	F	A	GD
50	19	13	18	70	64	6

COCA-COLA FOOTBALL LEAGUE TWO
Pos	P	W	D	L	F	A	GD	Pts
9	46	18	13	15	66	55	11	67

HOME
Pos	P	W	D	L	F	A	GD	Pts
5	23	11	10	2	39	18	21	43

AWAY
Pos	P	W	D	L	F	A	GD	Pts
15	23	7	3	13	27	37	-10	24

CUP PROGRESS DETAILS
Competition	Round reached	Knocked out by
FA Cup	R2	Leyton Orient
JP Trophy	R1	Leeds
Carling Cup	R1	Huddersfield

BIGGEST WIN (ALL COMPS)
07/03/09 5–0 v Aldershot **FL2**

BIGGEST DEFEAT (ALL COMPS)
12/08/08 0–4 v Huddersfield **LC1**

ATTENDANCE RECORD
High	Low	Average
14,038	11,908	12,704

v Notts Cnty (09/08/2008) v Macclesfield (03/03/2009)

RESULTS 2008/09

August
9th	● Notts County	...h	W 2–1	Att: 14,038 — Scorers: Thorne[2]. Booked: Arnison
12th	● Huddersfield	......a	L 4–0	Att: 8,932 — Booked: Daley, Bullock
16th	● Macclesfield	...a	W 0–2	Att: 2,556 — Scorers: Thorne[2]
23rd	● Rochdale	...h	W 2–0	Att: 13,154 — Scorers: Boulding, Thorne
30th	● Aldershot	.........a	L 3–2	Att: 3,805 — Scorers: Bullock, McLaren. Booked: Lee

September
2nd	● Leeds	..............a	L 2–1	Att: 20,128 — Scorers: Conlon. Booked: Colbeck, Nix, Daley
6th	● Port Vale	......a	W 0–2	Att: 7,273 — Scorers: Bullock, Thorne. Booked: Clarke, McLaren, Heckingbottom
13th	● Exeter	.............h	W 4–1	Att: 12,683 — Scorers: Boulding[2], Thorne[2]
20th	● Bournemouth	...h	L 1–3	Att: 12,824 — Scorers: Colbeck. Booked: McLaren, Colbeck, Daley
27th	● Shrewsbury	......a	L 2–0	Att: 6,517 — Booked: Furman

October
4th	● Luton	...............h	D 1–1	Att: 13,083 — Scorers: Conlon. Booked: Heckingbottom, Colbeck. Dismissed: Heckingbottom
11th	● Accrington S	...a	W 2–3	Att: 3,012 — Scorers: Boulding, Conlon, Thorne. Booked: Colbeck, Lee
18th	● Gillingham	......h	D 2–2	Att: 12,432 — Scorers: Colbeck, Thorne. Booked: O'Brien, Furman
20th	● Darlington	......a	L 2–1	Att: 3,034 — Scorers: Daley. Booked: Moncur, Daley
24th	● Grimsby	...........a	W 1–3	Att: 4,470 — Scorers: Boulding, Daley, Lee. Dismissed: M. Clarke
28th	● Bury	..................h	W 1–0	Att: 12,830 — Scorers: Conlo

November
1st	● Barnet	.............h	D 3–3	Att: 12,510 — Scorers: Conlon[2], Thorne. Booked: Moncur
8th	● MK Dons	......a	W 1–2	Att: 5,542 — Scorers: Daley, Lee
15th	● Wycombe	......a	L 1–0	Att: 5,002 — Booked: Lee
22nd	● Rotherham	......a	W 0–2	Att: 4,586 — Scorers: Law, O'Brien. Booked: M. Clarke
25th	● Chesterfield	...h	W 3–2	Att: 12,145 — Scorers: Boulding, Conlon, Lee
29th	● Leyton Orient	...h	L 1–2	Att: 5,065 — Scorers: Boulding. Booked: T. Clarke, Jones

December
6th	● Dag & Red	......h	D 1–1	Att: 12,145 — Scorers: Boulding
13th	● Brentford	.........a	L 2–1	Att: 4,339 — Scorers: Boulding
20th	● Chester	.........h	D 0–0	Att: 12,092 — Booked: Lee
26th	● Lincoln City	......a	D 0–0	Att: 6,156 — Booked: Arnison
28th	● Morecambe	...h	W 4–0	Att: 13,105 — Scorers: Boulding, Conlon, Law, McLaren. Booked: McLaren

January
3rd	● Shrewsbury	...h	D 0–0	Att: 12,877
17th	● Accrington S	...h	D 1–1	Att: 12,172 — Scorers: Conlon. Booked: Arnison
24th	● Luton	...............a	D 3–3	Att: 6,053 — Scorers: Conlon, Furman, McLaren. Booked: Law, Arnison, Thorne
27th	● Bury	..................a	L 1–0	Att: 4,112
31st	● Grimsby	...........h	W 2–0	Att: 12,816 — Scorers: Jones, Law

February
7th	● Gillingham	......a	W 0–2	Att: 4,866 — Scorers: Boulding, Daley. Booked: Lee
14th	● Wycombe	.........h	W 1–0	Att: 12,689 — Scorers: Jones
17th	● Darlington	......h	D 0–0	Att: 12,782
21st	● Barnet	.............a	L 4–1	Att: 2,445 — Scorers: Boulding. Booked: Furman
28th	● Notts County	...a	L 3–1	Att: 5,138 — Scorers: Thorne

March
3rd	● Macclesfield	...h	W 1–0	Att: 11,908 — Scorers: Furman. Booked: Furman
7th	● Aldershot	.........h	W 5–0	Att: 12,465 — Scorers: Conlon, Furman, Thorne[2], Day OG
10th	● Rochdale	.........a	L 3–0	Att: 5,500 — Booked: Colbeck, Arnison, Furman, Rehman, Law
14th	● Exeter	.............a	L 1–0	Att: 5,253 — Booked: Rehman
17th	● Bournemouth	...a	L 4–1	Att: 4,847 — Scorers: Clarke
21st	● Port Vale	......h	L 0–1	Att: 12,436 — Booked: Lee, Bullock
28th	● Chester	.........a	D 0–0	Att: 2,735 — Booked: Jones, Clarke, Furman

April
4th	● Brentford	.........h	D 1–1	Att: 12,832 — Scorers: Thorne. Booked: Mullin, McLaren
10th	● Morecambe	......a	L 2–1	Att: 4,546 — Scorers: Clarke. Booked: Colbeck, Clarke
13th	● Lincoln City	......h	D 2–2	Att: 12,932 — Scorers: Bullock
18th	● Dag & Red	........a	L 3–0	Att: 1,883
25th	● Rotherham	......h	W 3–0	Att: 13,242 — Scorers: Jones, Thorne[2]. Booked: Bullock

May
2nd	● Chesterfield	......a	W 0–2	Att: 3,859 — Scorers: Boulding, Furman

● Coca-Cola League 2/Play-Offs ● FA Cup ● Carling Cup ● Johnstone's Paint Trophy

LEAGUE TWO GOALKEEPER STATS

Player	Appearances	Match starts	Completed matches	Sub appearances	Subbed off	Clean sheets	Yellow cards	Red cards
Rhys Evans	45	45	45	0	0	17	0	0
Jon McLaughlan	1	1	1	0	0	1	0	0

LEAGUE TWO OUTFIELD PLAYER STATS

Player	Appearances	Match starts	Completed matches	Substitute appearances	Subbed off	Goals scored	Yellow cards	Red cards
Simon Ainge	1	1	1	0	0	0	0	0
Paul Arnison	27	25	22	2	3	0	5	0
Michael Boulding	44	35	19	9	16	12	0	0
Rory Boulding	1	1	0	0	1	0	0	0
Mark Bower	3	0	0	3	0	0	0	0
Chris Brandon	7	4	0	3	4	0	0	0
Lee Bullock	23	15	11	8	4	3	2	0
Matthew Clarke	42	42	40	0	1	2	4	1
Tom Clarke	6	4	3	2	1	0	0	0
Joe Colbeck	28	19	14	9	5	2	5	0
Barry Conlon	30	15	11	15	4	10	0	0
Omar Daley	28	26	16	2	10	3	2	0
Dean Furman	32	26	20	6	6	4	6	0
Keith Gillespie	3	2	0	1	2	0	0	0
Paul Heckingbottom	9	9	8	0	0	0	2	1
Steve Jones	27	25	18	2	7	3	1	0
Nicky Law	33	30	28	3	2	3	2	0
Graeme Lee	44	44	42	0	2	2	6	0
Paul McLaren	34	32	26	2	6	3	4	0
Thomas Moncur	14	11	10	3	1	0	2	0
Paul Mullin	6	5	5	1	0	0	1	0
Kyle Nix	16	6	3	10	3	0	0	0
Luke O'Brien	35	34	34	1	0	1	1	0
Chris O'Grady	2	0	0	2	0	0	0	0
Leon Osborne	2	1	0	1	1	0	0	0
Zeshan Rehman	17	16	14	1	2	0	2	0
Luke Sharry	1	0	0	1	0	0	0	0
Peter Thorne	37	32	19	5	13	17	1	0
Willy Topp	2	0	0	2	0	0	0	0

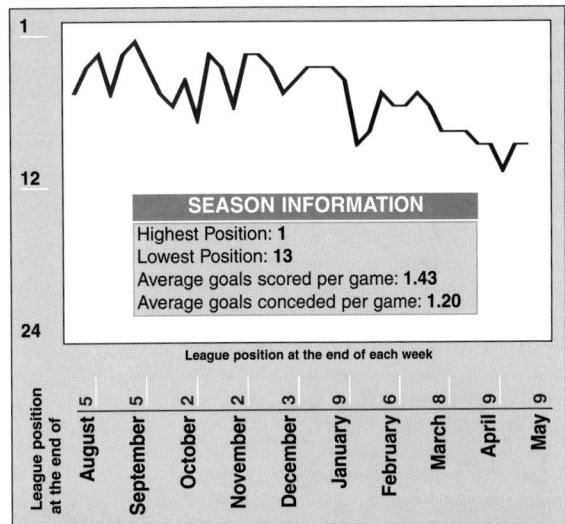

SEASON INFORMATION

Highest Position: **1**
Lowest Position: **13**
Average goals scored per game: **1.43**
Average goals conceded per game: **1.20**

League position at the end of each week

LONGEST SEQUENCES

Wins (on two occasions)	3	Undefeated home (04/10/08–07/03/09)	15
Losses (10/03/09–21/03/09)	4	Undefeated away (26/12/08–24/01/09)	2
Draws (03/01/09–24/01/09)	3	Without scoring (on three occasions)	2
Undefeated (20/12/08–24/01/09)	6	Without conceding (on two occasions)	4
Without win (10/03/09–18/04/09)	9	Scoring (on two occasions)	7

CARDS RECEIVED

46 **2**

QUICK-FIRE GOALS

From the start of a match
Peter Thorne (v Aldershot) 1:14

By a substitute after coming on
Barry Conlon (v Luton) 1:12

GOALS SCORED/CONCEDED PER FIVE-MINUTE INTERVALS

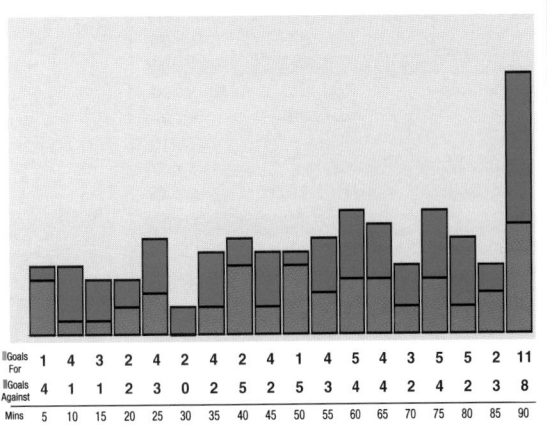

Goals For	1	4	3	2	4	2	4	2	4	1	4	5	4	3	5	5	2	11
Goals Against	4	1	1	2	3	0	2	5	2	5	3	4	4	2	4	2	3	8
Mins	5	10	15	20	25	30	35	40	45	50	55	60	65	70	75	80	85	90

BRENTFORD

BRENTFORD boss Andy Scott celebrated his first full season in management by guiding the west Londoners to the title. Scott cemented his reputation as one of the brightest young bosses in the country by dragging last season's mid-table also-rans to promotion in fine style.

Scott overhauled his squad by bringing in seven permanent signings and landing Reading duo Ben Hamer and Alan Bennett on season-long loans. Hamer was installed as first-choice goalkeeper while Bennett ended an impressive season wearing the captain's armband.

The only blot for the Bees was a series of injuries to their forwards. Both Nathan Elder and Damian Spencer suffered fractured cheekbones while Charlie MacDonald and Jordan Rhodes saw their campaigns ended prematurely through injury.

CLUB SUMMARY

FORMED	1889
MANAGER	Andy Scott
GROUND	Griffin Park
CAPACITY	12,763
NICKNAME	The Bees
WEBSITE	www.brentfordfc.co.uk

The New Football Pools PLAYER OF THE SEASON

Sam Wood

OVERALL
P	W	D	L	F	A	GD
51	24	18	9	73	45	28

COCA-COLA FOOTBALL LEAGUE TWO
Pos	P	W	D	L	F	A	GD	Pts
1	46	23	16	7	65	36	29	85

HOME
Pos	P	W	D	L	F	A	GD	Pts
2	23	13	8	2	39	15	24	47

AWAY
Pos	P	W	D	L	F	A	GD	Pts
1	23	10	8	5	26	21	5	38

CUP PROGRESS DETAILS
Competition	Round reached	Knocked out by
FA Cup	R2	Barrow
JP Trophy	R2	Luton
Carling Cup	R1	Swansea

BIGGEST WIN (ALL COMPS)
16/08/08 4–0 v Grimsby **FL2**

BIGGEST DEFEAT (ALL COMPS)
28/10/08 0–3 v Chester **FL2**

ATTENDANCE RECORD
High	Low	Average
10,642	3,733	5,707

v Wycombe (14/03/2009)   v Morecambe (21/10/2008)

RESULTS 2008/09

August
9th	● Bury	a	L 1–0	Att: 2,819
12th	● Swansea	a	L 2–0	Att: 5,366 — Booked: Johnson, Bean, Bennett. Dismissed: Bean
16th	● Grimsby	h	W 4–0	Att: 4,009 — Scorers: Elder, MacDonald[2], Poole
23rd	● Barnet	a	W 0–1	Att: 2,815 — Scorers: Poole. Booked: O'Connor, Elder, Bennett
30th	● Rotherham	h	D 0–0	Att: 4,381

September
2nd	● Yeovil	h	D 2–2	Att: 1,339 — Scorers: O'Connor, Poole (Won 4–2 on pens)
6th	● Dag & Red	h	W 2–1	Att: 4,519 — Scorers: Elder, MacDonald Booked: Newton. Dismissed: O'Connor
13th	● Wycombe	a	D 0–0	Att: 5,799
20th	● Lincoln City	h	D 1–1	Att: 4,557 — Scorers: Elder. Booked: M. Williams, Bean, Elder, Hamer
27th	● Chesterfield	a	W 0–1	Att: 3,188 — Scorers: Bean. Booked: Wilson, Elder

October
4th	● Macclesfield	h	W 1–0	Att: 4,773 — Scorers: MacDonald
7th	● Luton	a	D 2–2	Att: 2,029 — Scorers: Poole, Williams Booked: M. Williams, Poole, Hamer (Lost 3–4 on pens)
13th	● Notts County	a	D 1–1	Att: 6,012 — Scorers: Poole. Booked: Newton
18th	● Aldershot	a	D 1–1	Att: 5,023 — Scorers: Poole. Booked: Wright
21st	● Morecambe	h	W 3–1	Att: 3,733 — Scorers: Elder, MacDonald, Poole. Booked: Elder
25th	● Shrewsbury	h	D 1–1	Att: 5,362 — Scorers: MacDonald. Booked: Poole, Elder, Halls
28th	● Chester	a	L 3–0	Att: 1,301

November
1st	● Rochdale	h	L 1–2	Att: 4,291 — Scorers: Bowditch. Booked: Poole
9th	● Havant and W.	a	W 1–3	Att: 1,631 — Scorers: Elder, MacDonald, Williams. Booked: Newton
15th	● Port Vale	a	W 0–3	Att: 6,058 — Scorers: Bean, MacDonald, Osborne. Booked: Bennett, Phillips, Bowditch
22nd	● Darlington	h	D 1–1	Att: 4,837 — Scorers: Osborne. Booked: Osborne
25th	● Luton	a	W 0–1	Att: 5,248 — Scorers: Elder
28th	● Barrow	a	L 2–1	Att: 3,120 — Scorers: MacDonald. Booked: Bennett. Dismissed: Hamer

December
13th	● Bradford	h	W 2–1	Att: 4,339 — Scorers: Bean, Elder. Booked: O'Connor, Wood
20th	● Gillingham	a	D 1–1	Att: 5,521 — Scorers: MacDonald. Booked: M. Williams
26th	● Bournemouth	h	W 2–0	Att: 6,450 — Scorers: Bean[2]. Booked: Osborne
28th	● Exeter	a	W 0–2	Att: 6,791 — Scorers: MacDonald, Wood. Booked: Bennett, MacDonald

January
10th	● Lincoln City	a	D 2–2	Att: 3,932 — Scorers: Bean, Bowditch. Booked: Dickson
17th	● Notts County	h	D 1–1	Att: 5,465 — Scorers: Phillips. Booked: Wood. Dismissed: Elder
24th	● Macclesfield	a	L 2–0	Att: 1,942
27th	● Aldershot	h	W 3–0	Att: 5,111 — Scorers: Bean, MacDonald, Rhodes. Booked: Bean
31st	● Shrewsbury	a	W 1–3	Att: 5,674 — Scorers: Rhodes[3]. Booked: O'Connor

February
3rd	● Morecambe	a	L 2–0	Att: 1,253
7th	● Chester	h	W 3–0	Att: 4,719 — Scorers: MacDonald[3]
10th	● Accrington S	a	D 1–1	Att: 1,111 — Scorers: Rhodes. Booked: Newton
14th	● Port Vale	h	W 2–0	Att: 4,702 — Scorers: MacDonald, Osborne
21st	● Rochdale	a	W 1–2	Att: 3,412 — Scorers: MacDonald, Rhodes
28th	● Bury	h	W 1–0	Att: 6,597 — Scorers: Bean. Booked: MacDonald, Dickson

March
3rd	● Grimsby	a	W 0–1	Att: 3,001 — Scorers: MacDonald
7th	● Rotherham	a	D 0–0	Att: 3,406 — Booked: Dickson
10th	● Barnet	h	W 1–0	Att: 4,742 — Scorers: Bean.
14th	● Wycombe	h	D 3–3	Att: 10,642 — Scorers: Hunt, Rhodes, Williams. Booked: Bennett, Newton
17th	● Chesterfield	h	L 0–1	Att: 4,541
28th	● Gillingham	h	D 1–1	Att: 7,908 — Scorers: Hunt. Booked: Osborne, MacDonald

April
4th	● Bradford	a	D 1–1	Att: 12,832 — Scorers: Clarke. Booked: Bean, Dickson, Spencer, Clarke
11th	● Exeter	h	D 1–1	Att: 8,234 — Scorers: Clarke. Booked: Powell
13th	● Bournemouth	a	W 0–1	Att: 8,168 — Scorers: Clarke. Booked: Bean, Osborne. Dismissed: Powell
18th	● Accrington S	h	W 3–0	Att: 7,135 — Scorers: Clarke, Dickson, Williams
21st	● Dag & Red	a	L 3–1	Att: 3,537 — Scorers: Spencer. Booked: Dickson
25th	● Darlington	a	W 1–3	Att: 3,868 — Scorers: Bennett, Clarke[2]. Booked: Phillips, Halls

May
2nd	● Luton	h	W 2–0	Att: 10,223 — Scorers: Newton, Osborne. Booked: Newton

● Coca-Cola League 2/Play-Offs ● FA Cup ● Carling Cup ● Johnstone's Paint Trophy

actim

LEAGUE TWO GOALKEEPER STATS

Player	Appearances	Match starts	Completed matches	Sub appearances	Subbed off	Clean sheets	Yellow cards	Red cards
Mikkel Andersen	1	1	0	0	0	0	0	0
Simon Brown	1	0	0	1	0	0	0	0
Ben Hamer	45	45	44	0	1	20	1	0

LEAGUE TWO OUTFIELD PLAYER STATS

Player	Appearances	Match starts	Completed matches	Substitute appearances	Subbed off	Goals scored	Yellow cards	Red cards
Moses Ademola	8	0	0	8	0	0	0	0
Frankie Artus	1	0	0	1	0	0	0	0
Marcus Bean	44	43	39	1	4	9	4	0
Alan Bennett	44	44	42	0	2	1	4	0
Dean Bowditch	9	8	7	1	1	2	1	0
Billy Clarke	8	8	3	0	5	6	1	0
Alan Connell	2	1	1	1	0	0	0	0
Ryan Dickson	39	31	29	8	2	1	5	0
Nathan Elder	27	18	11	9	5	6	5	2
John Halls	23	22	19	1	3	0	2	0
David Hunt	20	10	10	10	0	2	0	0
Brett Johnson	10	7	6	3	1	0	0	0
Charlie MacDonald	38	38	32	0	6	16	3	0
Adam Newton	35	30	17	5	13	1	5	0
Kevin O'Connor	28	25	21	3	3	0	3	1
Karleigh Osborne	23	19	18	4	1	4	4	0
Craig Pead	6	5	4	1	1	0	0	0
Mark Phillips	32	28	26	4	2	1	2	0
Glenn Poole	26	18	5	8	13	5	2	0
Darren Powell	4	3	2	1	0	0	1	1
Jordan Rhodes	14	14	6	0	8	7	0	0
Damian Scannell	2	1	0	1	1	0	0	0
Gary Smith	4	2	1	2	1	0	0	0
Damian Spencer	5	3	1	2	2	1	1	0
Marvin Williams	34	21	10	13	11	0	2	0
Sam Williams	11	5	2	6	3	2	0	0
James Wilson	14	14	13	0	1	0	1	0
Sam Wood	40	37	29	3	8	1	2	0
Josh Wright	5	5	5	0	0	0	1	0

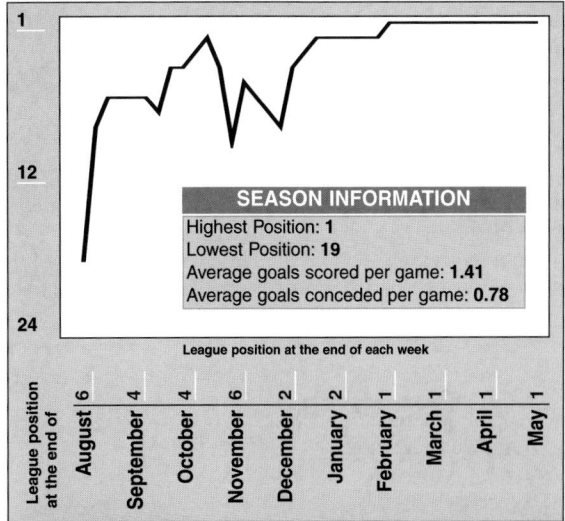

SEASON INFORMATION

Highest Position: **1**
Lowest Position: **19**
Average goals scored per game: **1.41**
Average goals conceded per game: **0.78**

League position at the end of each week

LONGEST SEQUENCES

Wins (14/02/09–03/03/09)	4	Undefeated home (22/11/08–14/03/09)	10
Losses (28/10/08–01/11/08)	2	Undefeated away (10/02/09–13/04/09)	6
Draws (28/03/09–11/04/09)	3	Without scoring (–)	
Undefeated (16/08/08–25/10/08)	12	Without conceding (28/02/09–10/03/09)	4
Without win (14/03/09–11/04/09)	5	Scoring (01/11/08–17/01/09)	10

CARDS RECEIVED

50 4

QUICK-FIRE GOALS

From the start of a match
Jordan Rhodes (v Shrewsbury) 1:29

By a substitute after coming on
Sam Williams (v Wycombe) 12:40

GOALS SCORED/CONCEDED PER FIVE-MINUTE INTERVALS

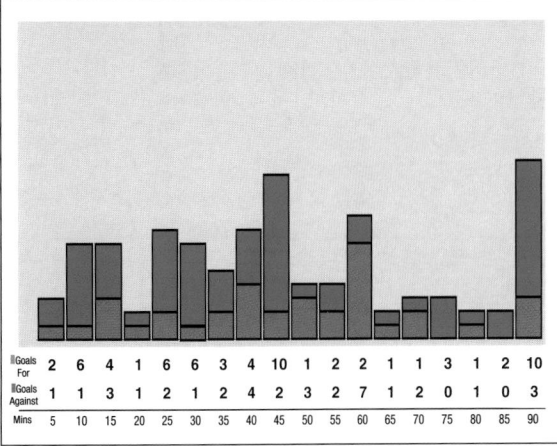

	Mins	5	10	15	20	25	30	35	40	45	50	55	60	65	70	75	80	85	90
Goals For		2	6	4	1	6	6	3	4	10	1	2	2	1	1	3	1	2	10
Goals Against		1	1	3	1	2	1	2	4	2	3	2	7	1	2	0	1	0	3

BURY

ONE OF the most successful seasons in Bury's recent history ended in despair as they were knocked out of the Coca-Cola League Two play-offs by Shrewsbury.

Alan Knill's men, who finished the regular season in fourth place and only missed out on automatic promotion by one goal, won the first leg 1–0 before going out on penalties after a 1–0 defeat in the reverse fixture at Gigg Lane.

Despite meeting an unfortunate end, Bury's season was still one of considerable triumph as they won the most home games in the division, 14. The Shakers also ended the season with a 12-game unbeaten run, although things could have been different had they won rather than drawn seven of those matches.

Andy Bishop was again a shining light, notching 17 goals to take his total for the club to 63 in three years.

CLUB SUMMARY

FORMED	1885
MANAGER	Alan Knill
GROUND	Gigg Lane
CAPACITY	11,669
NICKNAME	The Shakers
WEBSITE	www.buryfc.co.uk

The New **Football Pools** PLAYER OF THE SEASON

Andy Bishop

OVERALL
P	W	D	L	F	A	GD
52	23	15	14	65	48	17

COCA-COLA FOOTBALL LEAGUE TWO
Pos	P	W	D	L	F	A	GD	Pts
4	46	21	15	10	63	43	20	78

HOME
Pos	P	W	D	L	F	A	GD	Pts
3	23	14	4	5	36	19	17	46

AWAY
Pos	P	W	D	L	F	A	GD	Pts
6	23	7	11	5	27	24	3	32

CUP PROGRESS DETAILS
Competition	Round reached	Knocked out by
FA Cup	R1	Gillingham
JP Trophy	FLTNQ	Darlington
Carling Cup	R1	Burnley

BIGGEST WIN (ALL COMPS)
22/11/08 4–0 v Gillingham FL2

BIGGEST DEFEAT (ALL COMPS)
0–2 v on two occasions

ATTENDANCE RECORD
High	Low	Average
7,589	2,068	3,342
v Rochdale (07/03/2009)	v Gillingham (22/11/2008)	

RESULTS 2008/09

August
9th	● Brentford	.........h W 1–0	Att: 2,819 — **Scorers:** Bishop
12th	● Burnley	...........h L 0–2	Att: 4,276 — **Booked:** Futcher
16th	● Chesterfield	......a W 1–3	Att: 3,728 — **Scorers:** Futcher, Morrell, Sodje
23rd	● Morecambe	...h W 2–1	Att: 2,679 — **Scorers:** Scott, Artell OG. **Booked:** Dawson, Sodje
30th	● Rochdale	........a D 1–1	Att: 5,492 — **Scorers:** Russell OG

September
6th	● Chester	..........a D 1–1	Att: 2,327 — **Scorers:** Bishop. **Booked:** Morrell, Dawson, Jones
13th	● Lincoln City	.....h W 3–1	Att: 2,663 — **Scorers:** Bishop, Morrell, Sodje. **Booked:** Sodje, Dawson
20th	● Barnet	............a W 1–2	Att: 1,995 — **Scorers:** Bishop, Morrell. **Booked:** Barry-Murphy, Sodje
27th	● Wycombe	......h D 0–0	Att: 3,597

October
4th	● Aldershot	........a D 3–3	Att: 3,621 — **Scorers:** Bishop², Scott. **Booked:** Dawson, Brown, Scott
7th	● Stockport	........h W 1–0	Att: 2,384 — **Scorers:** Bishop. **Booked:** Barry-Murphy
11th	● Exeter	.............h L 0–1	Att: 3,220
18th	● Dag & Red	......a W 1–3	Att: 2,364 — **Scorers:** Bennett, Dawson, Jones. **Booked:** Sodje
21st	● Rotherham	.......h L 1–2	Att: 2,362 — **Scorers:** Scott
25th	● Luton	...............h L 1–2	Att: 3,052 — **Scorers:** Bishop. **Booked:** Scott
28th	● Bradford	...........a L 1–0	Att: 12,830 — **Booked:** Bishop, Dawson, Cresswell, Sodje

November
1st	● Notts County	...a W 0–1	Att: 4,391 — **Scorers:** Cresswell. **Booked:** Bennett
4th	● Darlington	........a L 1–0	Att: 1,651 — **Booked:** Barry-Murphy, Scott
8th	● Gillingham	.......h L 0–1	Att: 2,161 — **Booked:** Buchanan
15th	● Grimsby	...........h L 0–2	Att: 2,549
22nd	● Gillingham	.......h W 4–0	Att: 2,068 — **Scorers:** Bishop², Hurst². **Booked:** Dawson, Brown
29th	● Accrington S	....a W 1–2	Att: 2,093 — **Scorers:** Barry-Murphy, Jones. **Booked:** Sodje, Brown

December
6th	● Macclesfield	......a D 1–1	Att: 2,431 — **Scorers:** Dawson. **Booked:** Scott
13th	● Port Vale	........h W 3–0	Att: 2,651 — **Scorers:** Futcher, Hurst². **Booked:** Futcher
20th	● Bournemouth	....a L 2–0	Att: 3,479 — **Booked:** Scott
26th	● Darlington	.......h D 2–2	Att: 3,454 — **Scorers:** Bishop, Brown OG. **Booked:** Jones, Futcher, Dawson
28th	● Shrewsbury	......a L 1–0	Att: 7,127 — **Booked:** Dawson, Cresswell. **Dismissed:** Sodje

January
3rd	● Wycombe	.........a L 2–1	Att: 4,961 — **Scorers:** Williamson OG. **Booked:** Baker, Bennett
10th	● Barnet	.............h W 1–0	Att: 2,402 — **Scorers:** Jones
17th	● Exeter	...............a D 0–0	Att: 4,158 — **Booked:** Futcher
24th	● Aldershot	.........h W 2–1	Att: 2,558 — **Scorers:** Barry-Murphy, Morrell. **Booked:** Dawson, Bennett
27th	● Bradford	............h W 1–0	Att: 4,112 — **Scorers:** Morrell. **Booked:** Buchanan
31st	● Luton	................a W 1–2	Att: 5,545 — **Scorers:** Bishop, Morrell

February
7th	● Dag & Red	.......h D 2–2	Att: 2,530 — **Scorers:** Sodje². **Booked:** Sodje
14th	● Grimsby	...........a W 1–2	Att: 3,673 — **Scorers:** Bishop, Morrell. **Booked:** Jones, Hurst
21st	● Notts County	...h W 2–0	Att: 2,810 — **Scorers:** Bishop, Sodje
28th	● Brentford	.........a L 1–0	Att: 6,597 — **Booked:** Dawson. **Dismissed:** Dawson

March
3rd	● Chesterfield	......h L 1–2	Att: 2,077 — **Scorers:** Bishop
7th	● Rochdale	..........h W 2–1	Att: 7,589 — **Scorers:** Bennett, Jones
10th	● Morecambe	.....a D 0–0	Att: 2,165
14th	● Lincoln City	.....a D 1–1	Att: 3,642 — **Scorers:** Bishop. **Booked:** Cresswell, Bennett
21st	● Chester	............h D 1–1	Att: 3,049 — **Scorers:** Morrell. **Booked:** Buchanan. **Dismissed:** Cresswell
24th	● Rotherham	.......a D 1–1	Att: 2,890 — **Scorers:** Sodje. **Booked:** Jevons, Haslam
28th	● Bournemouth	....h W 1–0	Att: 2,762 — **Scorers:** Morrell

April
4th	● Port Vale	.........a D 1–1	Att: 5,763 — **Scorers:** Bennett. **Booked:** Sodje, Dawson, Haslam
10th	● Shrewsbury	......h W 2–1	Att: 4,850 — **Scorers:** Hurst, Jevons. **Booked:** Futcher, Sodje
13th	● Darlington	.......a D 2–2	Att: 2,927 — **Scorers:** Hurst, Sodje. **Booked:** Bishop, Buchanan, Welsh
18th	● Macclesfield	......h W 3–0	Att: 3,499 — **Scorers:** Bishop, Hurst². **Booked:** Futcher
25th	● Gillingham	........a D 0–0	Att: 8,360 — **Booked:** Welsh, Bennett

May
2nd	● Accrington S	...h W 1–0	Att: 7,515 — **Scorers:** Jevons
7th	● Shrewsbury	.....a W 0–1	Att: 8,429 — **Scorers:** Ashton OG. **Booked:** Sodje, Bishop
10th	● Shrewsbury	.....h L 0–1	Att: 7,673 — **Booked:** Bennett, Futcher, Dawson, Sodje. (lost 4-3 on pens)

● Coca-Cola League 2/Play-Offs ● FA Cup ● Carling Cup ● Johnstone's Paint Trophy

LEAGUE TWO GOALKEEPER STATS

Player	Appearances	Match starts	Completed matches	Sub appearances	Subbed off	Clean sheets	Yellow cards	Red cards
Cameron Belford	1	0	0	1	0	0	0	0
Wayne Brown	35	35	34	0	1	11	3	0
Mark Tyler	11	11	11	0	4	4	0	0

LEAGUE TWO OUTFIELD PLAYER STATS

Player	Appearances	Match starts	Completed matches	Substitute appearances	Subbed off	Goals scored	Yellow cards	Red cards
Richie Baker	22	6	5	16	1	0	1	0
Brian Barry-Murphy	42	41	39	1	2	2	1	0
Elliott Bennett	46	46	37	0	9	3	5	0
Andy Bishop	42	39	31	3	8	16	2	0
David Buchanan	46	46	46	0	0	0	3	0
Ryan Cresswell	25	19	18	6	0	1	3	1
Stephen Dawson	43	42	39	1	2	2	11	1
Ben Futcher	34	33	30	1	3	2	5	0
Steven Haslam	13	13	12	0	1	0	2	0
Dean Howell	3	0	0	3	0	0	0	0
Glynn Hurst	37	16	2	21	14	8	1	0
Phil Jevons	7	3	1	4	2	2	1	0
Mike Jones	46	46	24	0	22	4	3	0
Andrew Morrell	41	31	6	10	25	9	1	0
Chris O'Grady	6	3	2	3	1	0	0	0
Danny Racchi	21	0	0	21	0	0	0	0
Paul Scott	33	33	31	0	2	3	4	0
Efetobore Sodje	41	40	38	1	1	7	9	1
John Welsh	5	3	3	2	0	0	2	0

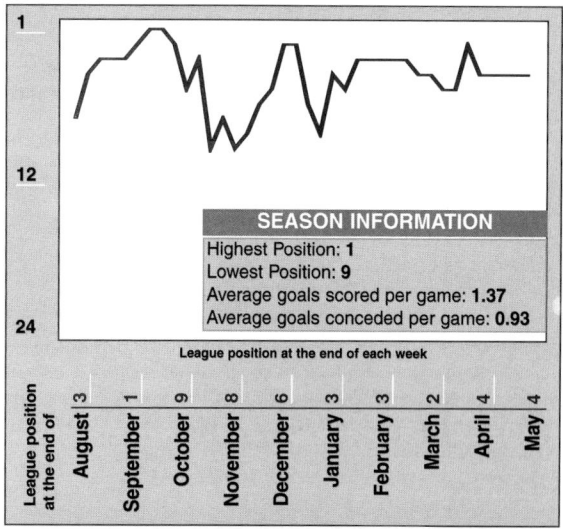

SEASON INFORMATION

Highest Position: **1**
Lowest Position: **9**
Average goals scored per game: **1.37**
Average goals conceded per game: **0.93**

League position at the end of each week

League position at the end of

August 3 | September 1 | October 9 | November 8 | December 6 | January 3 | February 3 | March 2 | April 4 | May 4

LONGEST SEQUENCES

Wins (on two occasions)	3	Undefeated home (22/11/08–21/02/09)	8
Losses (21/10/08–28/10/08)	3	Undefeated away (on two occasions)	6
Draws (10/03/09–24/03/09)	4	Without scoring (–)	
Undefeated (07/03/09–02/05/09)	12	Without conceding (18/04/09–02/05/09)	3
Without win (on two occasions)	4	Scoring (14/03/09–18/04/09)	8

CARDS RECEIVED

57 3

QUICK-FIRE GOALS

From the start of a match
Ben Futcher (v Port Vale) 1:43

By a substitute after coming on
Glynn Hurst (v Shrewsbury) 5:59

GOALS SCORED/CONCEDED PER FIVE-MINUTE INTERVALS

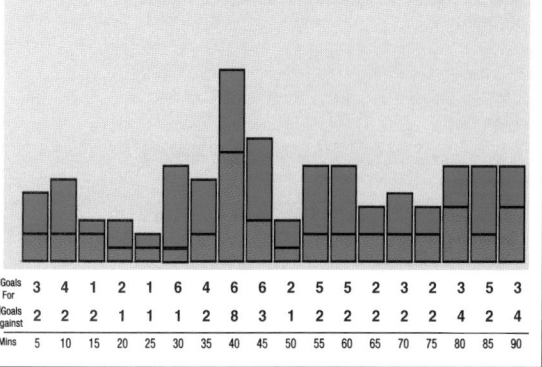

Goals For	3	4	1	2	1	6	4	6	6	2	5	5	2	3	2	3	5	3
Goals Against	2	2	2	1	1	1	2	8	3	1	2	2	2	2	2	4	2	4
Mins	5	10	15	20	25	30	35	40	45	50	55	60	65	70	75	80	85	90

FINANCIAL troubles, player unrest, a managerial departure, a transfer embargo and eventually relegation from the Football League capped a disastrous season.

After just two wins in their opening 15 games, coach Simon Davies was sacked, paving the way for the return of former manager Mark Wright for his third spell in charge of the club. However, the change did little to turn around City's ailing fortunes and, to compound matters, a transfer embargo following reports of unpaid wages prevented Wright from strengthening in January.

Damien Mozika, a summer signing from AS Nancy, proved to be a rare ray of light, but Chester eventually finished second bottom and dropped out of the League. Owner Stephen Vaughan is now desperately seeking a new buyer, with the club's future uncertain.

CLUB SUMMARY

FORMED	1885
MANAGER	Mark Wright
GROUND	Deva Stadium
CAPACITY	5,556
NICKNAME	The Seals
WEBSITE	www.chestercityfc.net

The New Football Pools PLAYER OF THE SEASON — Ryan Lowe

OVERALL

P	W	D	L	F	A	GD
49	8	14	27	46	90	-44

COCA-COLA FOOTBALL LEAGUE TWO

Pos	P	W	D	L	F	A	GD	Pts
23	46	8	13	25	43	81	-38	63

HOME

Pos	P	W	D	L	F	A	GD	Pts
24	23	4	7	12	24	34	-10	19

AWAY

Pos	P	W	D	L	F	A	GD	Pts
22	23	4	6	13	19	47	-28	18

CUP PROGRESS DETAILS

Competition	Round reached	Knocked out by
FA Cup	R1	Millwall
JP Trophy	R2	Morecambe
Carling Cup	R1	Leeds

BIGGEST WIN (ALL COMPS)
30/08/08 5–1 v Barnet **FL2**

BIGGEST DEFEAT (ALL COMPS)
09/08/08 0–6 v Dag & Red **FL2**

ATTENDANCE RECORD

High	Low	Average
3,349	1,235	1,972

v Bournemouth (18/04/2009) v Rotherham (10/03/2009)

RESULTS 2008/09

August
9th	● Dag & Red	a	L 6–0	Att: 1,434 — **Booked:** Mozika
12th	● Leeds	h	L 2–5	Att: 3,644 — **Scorers:** Lowe². **Booked:** Mozika, J. Vaughan
16th	● Wycombe	h	L 0–2	Att: 1,419 — **Booked:** Mozika, Lowe, Wilson
23rd	● Rotherham	a	L 3–1	Att: 3,462 — **Scorers:** Ellison. **Booked:** J. Vaughan
30th	● Barnet	h	W 5–1	Att: 1,295 — **Scorers:** Ellison, Linwood, Lowe², Roberts

September
6th	● Bury	h	D 1–1	Att: 2,327 — **Scorers:** Mozika. **Booked:** Hughes, J. Vaughan
13th	● Grimsby	a	W 1–3	Att: 2,950 — **Scorers:** Ellison³
21st	● Shrewsbury	h	D 1–1	Att: 2,891 — **Scorers:** McManus. **Booked:** Mozika, Ellison
27th	● Luton	a	D 1–1	Att: 5,731 — **Scorers:** McManus
				Booked: McManus, Roberts. **Dismissed:** Roberts

October
4th	● Lincoln City	h	L 0–2	Att: 1,962 — **Booked:** Linwood, J. Vaughan
7th	● Morecambe	h	D 1–1	Att: 926 — **Scorers:** Ellison (Lost 1–3 on pens)
11th	● Chesterfield	a	D 1–1	Att: 3,042 — **Scorers:** Linwood. **Booked:** Harris, Lowe, S. Vaughan
19th	● Port Vale	h	L 1–2	Att: 3,102 — **Scorers:** Lowe. **Booked:** S. Vaughan, Hughes, Roberts
21st	● Rochdale	a	L 6–1	Att: 2,162 — **Scorers:** McArdle OG. **Dismissed:** Rule
25th	● Gillingham	a	L 2–0	Att: 4,852 — **Booked:** Harris, J. Vaughan
28th	● Brentford	h	W 3–0	Att: 1,301 — **Scorers:** Lowe², Roberts. **Booked:** Harris

November
1st	● Exeter	a	L 2–0	Att: 4,448 — **Booked:** Roberts, Harris, Hughes
8th	● Millwall	h	L 0–3	Att: 1,932 — **Booked:** J. Vaughan
15th	● Morecambe	h	L 1–2	Att: 1,647 — **Scorers:** Johnson.
				Booked: Linwood, Wilson, Partridge. **Dismissed:** Ellison
22nd	● Aldershot	h	L 0–1	Att: 1,653
25th	● Darlington	a	W 1–2	Att: 2,416 — **Scorers:** Kelly, Lowe. **Booked:** Harris

December
6th	● Bournemouth	a	L 1–0	Att: 4,154 — **Booked:** J. Vaughan, Wilson
13th	● Notts County	h	W 2–0	Att: 1,767 — **Scorers:** Lowe, Roberts. **Booked:** Roberts
20th	● Bradford	a	D 0–0	Att: 12,092 — **Booked:** J. Vaughan, Mozika
26th	● Accrington S	h	W 2–0	Att: 2,223 — **Scorers:** Lowe². **Booked:** Wilson
28th	● Macclesfield	a	L 3–1	Att: 2,219 — **Scorers:** Lowe

January
13th	● Luton	h	D 2–2	Att: 1,652 — **Scorers:** Ellison, Lowe. **Booked:** J. Vaughan, Wilson, Kelly
17th	● Chesterfield	h	L 1–3	Att: 1,806 — **Scorers:** Mozika. **Booked:** Linwood
24th	● Lincoln City	a	D 1–1	Att: 3,760 — **Scorers:** Barry. **Booked:** Mozika, Dinning, Rule, Ellison
27th	● Port Vale	a	L 3–0	Att: 4,448 — **Booked:** Rule, Roberts, Barry, Dinning. **Dismissed:** Wilson, Rule
31st	● Gillingham	h	L 0–1	Att: 1,541 — **Booked:** Hughes, Harris

February
3rd	● Rochdale	h	L 0–2	Att: 1,357 — **Booked:** Kelly
7th	● Brentford	a	L 3–0	Att: 4,719
14th	● Morecambe	a	L 3–1	Att: 1,795 — **Scorers:** Wilson. **Booked:** Rule, Harris, Linwood
17th	● Shrewsbury	a	L 1–0	Att: 6,133 — **Booked:** J. Vaughan, Partridge
21st	● Exeter	h	D 0–0	Att: 1,640 — **Booked:** J. Vaughan
28th	● Dag & Red	h	D 2–2	Att: 1,416 — **Scorers:** Mannix, Roberts. **Booked:** Barry

March
3rd	● Wycombe	a	L 2–0	Att: 3,713
7th	● Barnet	a	L 3–1	Att: 2,085 — **Scorers:** Ellison. **Booked:** Harris, J. Vaughan, Linwood
10th	● Rotherham	h	L 1–5	Att: 1,235 — **Scorers:** Ellison. **Booked:** Harris
14th	● Grimsby	h	D 1–1	Att: 2,836 — **Scorers:** Lowe. **Booked:** Ellison, Rule, Barry
21st	● Bury	a	D 1–1	Att: 3,049 — **Scorers:** Lowe. **Booked:** Mannix
28th	● Bradford	h	D 0–0	Att: 2,735 — **Booked:** Linwood, Ellison

April
4th	● Notts County	a	W 1–2	Att: 4,025 — **Scorers:** Lowe, Mannix. **Booked:** Rutherford, Mannix
11th	● Macclesfield	h	L 0–2	Att: 2,248
13th	● Accrington S	a	W 0–1	Att: 1,100 — **Scorers:** Lowe. **Booked:** Linwood
18th	● Bournemouth	h	L 0–2	Att: 3,349 — **Scorers:** Spencer, Wilson, J. Vaughan
25th	● Aldershot	a	D 2–2	Att: 3,100 — **Scorers:** Ellans, Lowe. **Booked:** Owen, Lowe

May
2nd	● Darlington	h	L 1–2	Att: 1,945 — **Scorers:** Miller OG. **Booked:** Kelly

● Coca-Cola League 2/Play-Offs ● FA Cup ● Carling Cup ● Johnstone's Paint Trophy

LEAGUE TWO GOALKEEPER STATS

Player	Appearances	Match starts	Completed matches	Sub appearances	Subbed off	Clean sheets	Yellow cards	Red cards
John Danby	41	41	40	0	1	7	0	0
James Spencer	5	5	5	0	0	1	1	0

LEAGUE TWO OUTFIELD PLAYER STATS

Player	Appearances	Match starts	Completed matches	Substitute appearances	Subbed off	Goals scored	Yellow cards	Red cards
Anthony Barry	43	38	32	5	6	1	3	0
Paul Butler	1	1	1	0	0	0	0	0
Tony Dinning	4	3	0	1	2	0	2	1
Lloyd Ellans	4	2	1	2	1	1	0	0
Kevin Ellison	39	39	32	0	6	8	4	1
Jay Harris	31	24	18	7	5	0	9	1
Mark Hughes	26	25	24	1	1	0	4	0
Eddie Johnson	10	7	2	3	5	1	0	0
Ben Jones	15	2	0	13	2	0	0	0
Shaun Kelly	27	23	18	4	5	1	3	0
Paul Linwood	43	43	41	0	2	2	7	0
Ryan Lowe	45	45	35	0	10	16	3	0
David Mannix	13	10	4	3	6	2	2	0
Paul McManus	8	6	0	2	6	2	1	0
Damien Mozika	22	21	18	1	3	2	5	0
James Owen	7	4	3	3	1	0	1	0
Richie Partridge	28	15	2	13	13	0	2	0
Chris Platt	1	0	0	1	0	0	0	0
Kevin Roberts	44	44	42	0	1	4	5	1
Glenn Rule	22	18	11	4	5	0	4	2
Paul Rutherford	19	5	2	14	3	0	1	0
Paul Smith	5	0	0	5	0	0	0	0
Paul Taylor	9	2	2	7	0	0	0	0
James Vaughan	41	41	40	0	1	0	11	0
Stephen Vaughan	9	8	7	1	1	0	2	0
Laurence Wilson	34	34	29	0	4	1	6	1

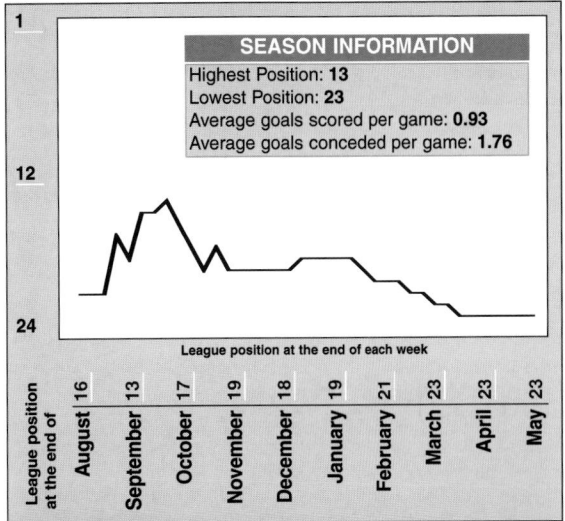

SEASON INFORMATION
Highest Position: **13**
Lowest Position: **23**
Average goals scored per game: **0.93**
Average goals conceded per game: **1.76**

League position at the end of each week

LONGEST SEQUENCES

Wins (–)		Undefeated home (on two occasions)	3
Losses (27/01/09–17/02/09)	6	Undefeated away (on two occasions)	3
Draws (14/03/09–28/03/09)	3	Without scoring (27/01/09–07/02/09)	4
Undefeated (30/08/08–27/09/08)	5	Without conceding (13/12/08–26/12/08)	3
Without win (28/12/08–28/03/09)	18	Scoring (23/08/08–27/09/08)	6

CARDS RECEIVED

76   7

QUICK-FIRE GOALS

From the start of a match
Ryan Lowe (v Aldershot) 0:49

By a substitute after coming on
N/A

GOALS SCORED/CONCEDED PER FIVE-MINUTE INTERVALS

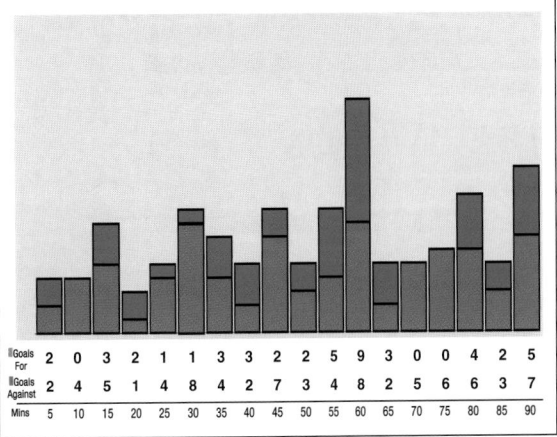

Goals For	2	0	3	2	1	1	3	3	2	2	5	9	3	0	0	4	2	5
Goals Against	2	4	5	1	4	8	4	2	7	3	4	8	2	5	6	6	3	7
Mins	5	10	15	20	25	30	35	40	45	50	55	60	65	70	75	80	85	90

CHESTERFIELD will start the 2009/10 season under a new manager as the club ruled that the end of the last campaign was time for a change.

The Spireites dismissed Lee Richardson but were boosted by the news that chairman Dave Allen was to invest £4million in the club in order to achieve their goal of promotion.

Chesterfield were among the pre-season favourites to go up to Coca-Cola League One, but just three wins in their opening 11 games put a dampener on those plans.

Surprisingly, Chesterfield's best spell of the season came following the sale of star player Jamie Ward to Sheffield United in January. The club, in mid-table at the time, lost just four times in 20 matches before their play-off hopes were ended with defeat at Accrington on the penultimate weekend of the campaign.

CLUB SUMMARY

FORMED	1866
MANAGER	TBC
GROUND	Recreation Ground
CAPACITY	8,504
NICKNAME	The Spireites
WEBSITE	www.chesterfield-fc.co.uk

The New **Football Pools** PLAYER OF THE SEASON

Jack Lester

OVERALL

P	W	D	L	F	A	GD
52	17	17	18	70	69	1

COCA-COLA FOOTBALL LEAGUE TWO

Pos	P	W	D	L	F	A	GD	Pts
10	46	16	15	15	62	57	5	63

HOME

Pos	P	W	D	L	F	A	GD	Pts
15	23	8	8	7	32	28	4	32

AWAY

Pos	P	W	D	L	F	A	GD	Pts
8	23	8	7	8	30	29	1	31

CUP PROGRESS DETAILS

Competition	Round reached	Knocked out by
FA Cup	R3	Ipswich
JP Trophy	R1	Grimsby
Carling Cup	R1	Preston

BIGGEST WIN (ALL COMPS)
28/10/08 6–1 v Exeter **FL2**

BIGGEST DEFEAT (ALL COMPS)
13/09/08 0–3 v Dag & Red **FL2**

ATTENDANCE RECORD

High	Low	Average
4,951	2,451	3,449

v Rotherham (06/09/2008)   v Macclesfield (12/12/2008)

RESULTS 2008/09

August
9th ● Barnet ....a W 1–3   **Att:** 2,237 — **Scorers:** Lester[2], Ward. **Booked:** Goodall, Page, Lester
12th ● Preston ....a L 2–0   **Att:** 5,150 — **Booked:** Niven
16th ● Bury ....h L 1–3   **Att:** 3,728 — **Scorers:** Kerry. **Booked:** Austin
23rd ● Grimsby ....a W 0–1   **Att:** 3,306 — **Scorers:** Ward. **Booked:** Goodall, Harsley, Kerry
30th ● Wycombe ....h L 0–1   **Att:** 3,175 — **Booked:** Kerry

September
3rd ● Grimsby ....h D 2–2   **Att:** 1,665 — **Scorers:** Kerry, Lester (Lost 4–1 on pens)
6th ● Rotherham ....h W 1–0   **Att:** 4,951 — **Scorers:** Goodall. **Booked:** Winter
13th ● Dag & Red ......a L 3–0   **Att:** 1,682 — **Booked:** Goodall, Niven. **Dismissed:** Kerry, Page
20th ● Rochdale ....a L 2–1   **Att:** 2,884 — **Scorers:** Ward. **Booked:** Robertson, Downes, Carson, Ward. **Dismissed:** Ward
27th ● Brentford ....h L 0–1   **Att:** 3,188 — **Booked:** Winter, Austin, Lester

October
4th ● Morecambe ......a D 2–2   **Att:** 1,734 — **Scorers:** Robertson, Ward
11th ● Chester ....h D 1–1   **Att:** 3,042 — **Scorers:** Ward. **Booked:** Goodall, Ward
18th ● Lincoln City .....a L 3–1   **Att:** 4,326 — **Scorers:** Lester. **Booked:** Harsley, Kerry, Hall
22nd ● Aldershot ....h W 5–1   **Att:** 3,079 — **Scorers:** Lester, Niven, Ward[3]. **Booked:** Page
25th ● Notts County ...h W 3–1   **Att:** 4,134 — **Scorers:** Goodall, Harsley, Ward
28th ● Exeter ....a W 1–6   **Att:** 5,093 — **Scorers:** Currie, Goodall, Lester[2], Ward, Winter

November
1st ● Bournemouth ....a D 1–1   **Att:** 4,082 — **Scorers:** Kerry. **Booked:** Winter, Goodall
8th ● Mansfield ....h W 3–1   **Att:** 6,612 — **Scorers:** Ward, Winter[2]
14th ● Shrewsbury .....h D 2–2   **Att:** 4,099 — **Scorers:** Currie, Ward. **Booked:** Lester
22nd ● Accrington S ...h D 1–1   **Att:** 3,215 — **Scorers:** Lester. **Booked:** Austin
25th ● Bradford ....a L 3–2   **Att:** 12,145 — **Scorers:** Currie, Lester. **Booked:** Goodall, Page, Ward. **Dismissed:** Goodall

December
6th ● Gillingham .....a L 2–1   **Att:** 4,622 — **Scorers:** Lester. **Booked:** Ward, Lowry, Page, Lester, Kerry, Austin
9th ● Droylsden........h D 2–2   **Att:** 5,698 — **Scorers:** Lester, Ward
12th ● Macclesfield ...h L 2–4   **Att:** 2,451 — **Scorers:** Ward[2]. **Booked:** Kerry, Winter. **Dismissed:** Goodall
16th ● Droylsden..........a A–A   **Att:** 2,261 — **Scorers:** Currie, Lester. **Booked:** Robertson (abandoned after 72 minutes due to floodlight failure)
20th ● Port Vale ....a W 0–1   **Att:** 5,011 — **Scorers:** Downes. **Booked:** Hall, Harsley, Lowry
23rd ● Droylsden* ......a L 2–1   **Att:** 2,824 — **Scorers:** Hall, Harsley. **Booked:** Lester
26th ● Luton ....h D 2–2   **Att:** 4,243 — **Scorers:** Boden, Ward
28th ● Darlington ....a D 0–0   **Att:** 3,352 — **Booked:** Robertson

January
3rd ● Ipswich ....a L 3–0   **Att:** 12,524 — **Booked:** Kerry, Boden
17th ● Chester ....a W 1–3   **Att:** 1,806 — **Scorers:** Kerry, Winter, Wilson OG.
24th ● Morecambe .....h L 1–2   **Att:** 3,283 — **Scorers:** Gritton. **Booked:** Winter, Downes
28th ● Exeter ....h W 2–1   **Att:** 2,894 — **Scorers:** Lester[2]. **Booked:** Downes, Lester
31st ● Notts County ....a W 0–1   **Att:** 4,953 — **Scorers:** Talbot. **Booked:** Hall, Gritton. **Dismissed:** Hall

February
14th ● Shrewsbury ......a L 2–1   **Att:** 4,873 — **Scorers:** Boden. **Booked:** McDonald
20th ● Bournemouth ...h W 1–0   **Att:** 3,130 — **Scorers:** Lester.
28th ● Barnet ....h D 1–1   **Att:** 3,068 — **Scorers:** Hall. **Booked:** Hall

March
3rd ● Bury ....a W 1–2   **Att:** 2,077 — **Scorers:** Downes, Lester. **Booked:** Gray, Talbot, Lester. **Dismissed:** Robertson
7th ● Wycombe ....a D 1–1   **Att:** 4,809 — **Scorers:** Lester. **Booked:** Austin, Hall, Kerry, Lester
11th ● Grimsby ....h W 2–1   **Att:** 2,999 — **Scorers:** Niven, Talbot
14th ● Dag & Red ....h D 1–1   **Att:** 3,007 — **Scorers:** Gritton. **Booked:** Austin
17th ● Brentford ....a W 0–1   **Att:** 4,541 — **Scorers:** Gritton
21st ● Rotherham ....a L 3–0   **Att:** 4,658 — **Booked:** Talbot. **Dismissed:** Talbot
25th ● Rochdale ....h W 3–0   **Att:** 3,271 — **Scorers:** Lester[2], Robertson. **Booked:** Niven
28th ● Port Vale ....h W 2–1   **Att:** 3,511 — **Scorers:** Lester[2]. **Booked:** Niven
31st ● Aldershot ....a D 1–1   **Att:** 2,482 — **Scorers:** Lester. **Booked:** Talbot, Lester

April
4th ● Macclesfield......a D 1–1   **Att:** 2,276 — **Scorers:** Gritton
7th ● Lincoln City .....h D 1–1   **Att:** 3,419 — **Scorers:** Lester
11th ● Darlington ....h D 0–0   **Att:** 3,642 — **Booked:** Robertson, Lowry
13th ● Luton ....a D 0–0   **Att:** 6,494 — **Booked:** Lowry
18th ● Gillingham ....h L 0–1   **Att:** 3,933
25th ● Accrington S ....a L 1–0   **Att:** 1,795 — **Booked:** Niven, Winter. **Dismissed:** Lester

May
2nd ● Bradford ....h L 0–2   **Att:** 3,859

*Droylsden expelled for fielding ineligible player

● Coca-Cola League 2/Play-Offs ● FA Cup ● Carling Cup ● Johnstone's Paint Trophy

LEAGUE TWO GOALKEEPER STATS

Player	Appearances	Match starts	Completed matches	Sub appearances	Subbed off	Clean sheets	Yellow cards	Red cards
Trevor Carson	18	18	18	0	0	2	1	0
Tommy Lee	28	28	28	0	0	8	0	0

LEAGUE TWO OUTFIELD PLAYER STATS

Player	Appearances	Match starts	Completed matches	Substitute appearances	Subbed off	Goals scored	Yellow cards	Red cards
Ben Algar	3	1	1	2	0	0	0	0
Lee Askham	1	0	0	1	0	0	0	0
Kevin Austin	35	27	22	8	5	0	6	0
Luke Boden	4	4	0	0	4	0	0	0
Scott Boden	11	3	2	8	1	2	0	0
Jordan Bowery	3	0	0	3	0	0	0	0
Darren Currie	27	14	7	13	7	3	0	0
Aaron Downes	42	40	37	2	3	2	3	0
Alan Goodall	28	21	11	7	8	3	6	2
Dan Gray	25	20	15	5	5	0	1	0
Martin Gritton	20	19	12	1	7	4	1	0
Daniel Hall	25	25	21	0	3	1	5	1
Paul Harsley	17	7	5	10	2	1	3	0
Lloyd Kerry	33	28	24	5	3	3	6	1
Jack Lester	37	37	30	0	6	20	8	1
Jamie Lowry	42	37	30	5	7	0	4	0
Clayton McDonald	2	1	1	1	0	0	1	0
Lewis Montrose	12	11	4	1	7	0	0	0
Derek Niven	31	21	19	10	2	2	4	0
Robert Page	16	16	15	0	0	0	4	1
Phil Picken	11	9	8	2	1	0	0	0
Gregor Robertson	38	32	28	6	3	2	3	1
Drew Talbot	17	17	10	0	6	2	3	1
Val Teixeira	5	0	0	5	0	0	0	0
Peter Till	16	14	3	2	11	0	0	0
Jamie Ward	23	23	20	0	2	14	4	1
Jared Wilson	16	15	14	1	1	0	0	0
Jamie Winter	24	18	8	6	10	2	6	0

SEASON INFORMATION

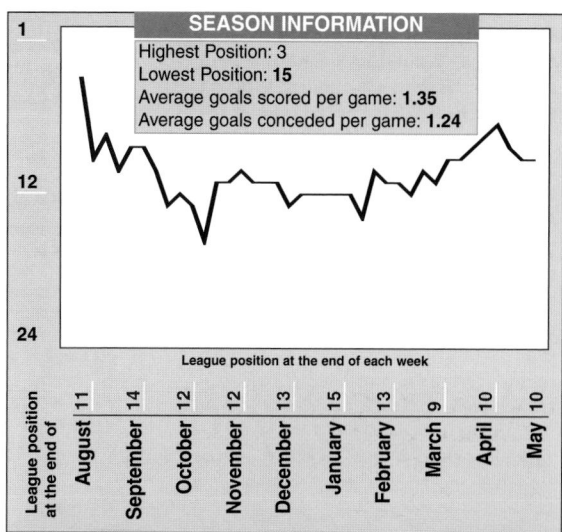

Highest Position: **3**
Lowest Position: **15**
Average goals scored per game: **1.35**
Average goals conceded per game: **1.24**

League position at the end of each week

League position at the end of: August 11, September 14, October 12, November 12, December 13, January 15, February 13, March 9, April 10, May 10

LONGEST SEQUENCES

Wins (22/10/08–28/10/08)	3	Undefeated home (28/01/09–11/04/09)	9
Losses (on two occasions)	3	Undefeated away (20/12/08–31/01/09)	4
Draws (31/03/09–13/04/09)	5	Without scoring (11/04/09–02/05/09)	5
Undefeated (on two occasions)	7	Without conceding (11/04/09–13/04/09)	2
Without win (31/03/09–02/05/09)	8	Scoring (04/10/08–26/12/08)	14

CARDS RECEIVED

69 **9**

QUICK-FIRE GOALS

From the start of a match
Aaron Downes (v Bury) 1:07

By a substitute after coming on
Paul Harsley (v Notts County) 5:49

GOALS SCORED/CONCEDED PER FIVE-MINUTE INTERVALS

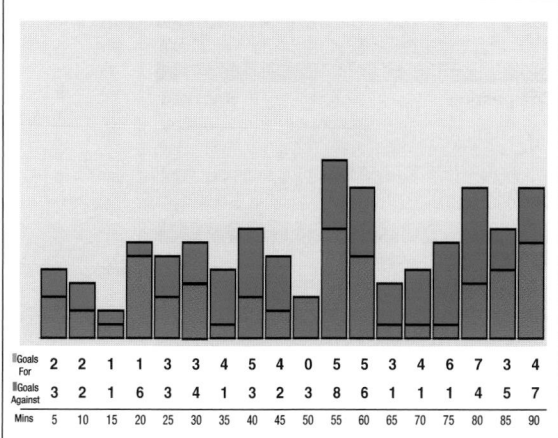

Goals For	2	2	1	1	3	3	4	5	4	0	5	5	3	4	6	7	3	4
Goals Against	3	2	1	6	3	4	1	3	2	3	8	6	1	1	1	4	5	7
Mins	5	10	15	20	25	30	35	40	45	50	55	60	65	70	75	80	85	90

THE DAGGERS were cruelly denied a play-off place by Shrewsbury, who snatched seventh spot with a 2–1 win at Victoria Road on the final day of the regular season.

The Daggers had been in and around the top six for most of the season and, despite the last-day disappointment, fans will look back with pride as their side had only just escaped relegation straight back down to the Conference during the previous campaign.

Manager John Still ensured Dagenham punched above their weight by adding some astute signings to the squad he had spent several seasons knitting together. He also enjoyed better fortune with regard to injuries.

But several of the Daggers' key performers, such as Ben Strevens and Paul Benson, have attracted interest and Still will be hoping to keep most of his squad intact for next season.

CLUB SUMMARY

FORMED	1992
MANAGER	John Still
GROUND	Victoria Road
CAPACITY	6,078
NICKNAME	The Daggers
WEBSITE	www.daggers.co.uk

The New **Football Pools** PLAYER OF THE SEASON — **Magnus Okuonghae**

OVERALL

P	W	D	L	F	A	GD
53	22	12	19	87	66	21

COCA-COLA FOOTBALL LEAGUE TWO

Pos	P	W	D	L	F	A	GD	Pts
8	46	19	11	16	77	53	24	68

HOME

Pos	P	W	D	L	F	A	GD	Pts
8	23	12	3	8	44	24	20	39

AWAY

Pos	P	W	D	L	F	A	GD	Pts
11	23	7	8	8	33	29	4	29

CUP PROGRESS DETAILS

Competition	Round reached	Knocked out by
FA Cup	R2	Leicester
JP Trophy	FLTSQ	Shrewsbury
Carling Cup	R1	Reading

BIGGEST WIN (ALL COMPS)

09/08/08 6–0 v Chester **FL2**

BIGGEST DEFEAT (ALL COMPS)

04/11/08 0–5 v Shrewsbury **FLTSQ**

ATTENDANCE RECORD

High	Low	Average
4,791	1,302	2,048

v Shrewsbury (02/05/2009) v Lincoln City (03/03/2009)

RESULTS 2008/09

August
9th	● Chester	...........h W 6–0	Att: 1,434 — **Scorers:** Benson, Green, Nwokeji, Saunders[2], Strevens. **Booked:** Gain
12th	● Reading	...........a L 1–2	Att: 2,360 — **Scorers:** Taiwo
16th	● Lincoln City	......a W 1–3	Att: 3,581 — **Scorers:** Benson, Strevens[2]. **Booked:** Saunders
23rd	● Port Vale	.........h D 1–1	Att: 1,843 — **Scorers:** Benson
30th	● Morecambe	......a W 1–2	Att: 1,571 — **Scorers:** Saunders, Taiwo

September
2nd	● Barnet	..............h W 4–2	Att: 1,412 — **Scorers:** Benson[2], Nwokeji, Southam. **Booked:** Nwokeji, Graham
6th	● Brentford	.........a L 2–1	Att: 4,519 — **Scorers:** Saunders
13th	● Chesterfield	....h W 3–0	Att: 1,682 — **Scorers:** Benson, Nwokeji, Saunders
20th	● Wycombe	.........a L 2–1	Att: 4,132 — **Scorers:** Strevens. **Booked:** Saunders, Nurse
27th	● Rotherham	.......h D 1–1	Att: 1,805 — **Scorers:** Benson

October
4th	● Rochdale	.........a W 0–2	Att: 2,566 — **Scorers:** Benson, Ritchie. **Booked:** Gain
7th	● Peterborough	....a W 0–1	Att: 2,644 — **Scorers:** Nwokeji
10th	● Barnet	..............h W 2–0	Att: 2,629 — **Scorers:** Ritchie, Strevens. **Booked:** Okuonghae
18th	● Bury	..................h L 1–3	Att: 2,364 — **Scorers:** Saunders. **Booked:** Okuonghae
21st	● Bournemouth	....a L 2–1	Att: 3,554 — **Scorers:** Nurse
25th	● Darlington	........a L 3–0	Att: 3,070 — **Booked:** Ritchie, Taiwo
28th	● Grimsby	...........h W 4–0	Att: 1,622 — **Scorers:** Arber, Benson, Strevens[2]

November
1st	● Accrington S	...h D 0–0	Att: 1,433
4th	● Shrewsbury	......a L 5–0	Att: 2,747 — **Booked:** Okuonghae
8th	● Hereford	.........a D 0–0	Att: 1,825
15th	● Luton	................a L 2–1	Att: 5,402 — **Scorers:** Okuonghae. **Booked:** Gain, Strevens, Uddin
18th	● Hereford	.........h W 2–1	Att: 1,409 — **Scorers:** Benson, Taiwo. **Booked:** Ritchie
22nd	● Notts County	....h W 6–1	Att: 1,743 — **Scorers:** Benson[3], Okuonghae, Ritchie, Strevens
25th	● Shrewsbury	......h L 2–1	Att: 4,590 — **Scorers:** Saunders. **Booked:** Uddin, Saunders, Okuonghae, Foster
29th	● Leicester	..........a L 3–2	Att: 7,791 — **Scorers:** Ritchie, Strevens. **Booked:** Foster

December
6th	● Bradford	............a D 1–1	Att: 12,145 — **Scorers:** Ritchie. **Booked:** Strevens
20th	● Macclesfield	....a W 0–4	Att: 1,909 — **Scorers:** Benson[2], Saunders, Taiwo. **Booked:** Taiwo
26th	● Gillingham	......h W 2–0	Att: 2,844 — **Scorers:** Benson, Strevens. **Booked:** Nurse
28th	● Aldershot	.........a W 1–2	Att: 3,697 — **Scorers:** Nurse, Taiwo. **Booked:** Griffiths, Gain

January
3rd	● Rotherham	.......a D 1–1	Att: 3,307 — **Scorers:** Ritchie. **Booked:** Okuonghae
17th	● Barnet	..............a D 1–1	Att: 2,366 — **Scorers:** Nwokeji. **Booked:** Arber, Strevens
20th	● Exeter	...............h L 1–2	Att: 2,053 — **Scorers:** Strevens
24th	● Rochdale	.........h W 3–2	Att: 1,808 — **Scorers:** Arber, Ritchie, Southam. **Booked:** Benson, Southam. **Dismissed:** Saunders
27th	● Grimsby	...........a D 1–1	Att: 3,431 — **Scorers:** Nurse. **Booked:** Taiwo
31st	● Darlington	........h L 0–1	Att: 1,832 — **Booked:** Okuonghae, Benson, Southam

February
7th	● Bury	..................a D 2–2	Att: 2,530 — **Scorers:** Nurse, Strevens. **Booked:** Arber, Southam, Nurse
14th	● Luton	................h W 2–1	Att: 2,310 — **Scorers:** Foster[2]. **Booked:** Southam
17th	● Wycombe	.........h L 0–1	Att: 2,242 — **Booked:** Loft
21st	● Accrington S	...a D 0–0	Att: 1,123
24th	● Bournemouth	...h L 0–1	Att: 1,602
28th	● Chester	...........a D 2–2	Att: 1,416 — **Scorers:** Ritchie, Strevens. **Booked:** Southam

March
3rd	● Lincoln City	......h L 0–3	Att: 1,302
7th	● Morecambe	......h L 0–2	Att: 1,403 — **Booked:** Strevens
10th	● Port Vale	.........a W 0–1	Att: 4,090 — **Scorers:** Guy. **Booked:** Foster, Taiwo
14th	● Chesterfield	.....a D 1–1	Att: 3,007 — **Booked:** Saunders
28th	● Macclesfield	....h W 2–1	Att: 1,347 — **Scorers:** Benson, Ritchie

April
4th	● Exeter	...............a L 2–1	Att: 5,123 — **Scorers:** Strevens. **Booked:** Taiwo
11th	● Aldershot	.........h W 3–1	Att: 1,586 — **Scorers:** Benson, Ritchie, Saunders. **Booked:** Ritchie
13th	● Gillingham	.......a L 2–1	Att: 6,945 — **Scorers:** Saunders. **Booked:** Strevens, Okuonghae, Arber, Saunders
18th	● Bradford	............h W 3–0	Att: 1,883 — **Scorers:** Benson, Saunders, Strevens.
21st	● Brentford	.........h W 3–1	Att: 3,537 — **Scorers:** Arber, Saunders, Taiwo. **Booked:** Saunders
25th	● Notts County	....a W 0–3	Att: 4,419 — **Scorers:** Ritchie[2], Saunders. **Booked:** Gain

May
2nd	● Shrewsbury	......h L 1–2	Att: 4,791 — **Scorers:** Benson. **Booked:** Taiwo

● Coca-Cola League 2/Play-Offs ● FA Cup ● Carling Cup ● Johnstone's Paint Trophy

LEAGUE TWO GOALKEEPER STATS

Player	Appearances	Match starts	Completed matches	Sub appearances	Subbed off	Clean sheets	Yellow cards	Red cards
David Button	3	3	3	0	0	2	0	0
David Hogan	1	0	0	1	0	0	0	0
Tony Roberts	43	43	41	0	2	10	0	0
Ed Thompson	1	0	0	1	0	0	0	0

LEAGUE TWO OUTFIELD PLAYER STATS

Player	Appearances	Match starts	Completed matches	Substitute appearances	Subbed off	Goals scored	Yellow cards	Red cards
Mark Arber	42	42	39	0	3	3	3	0
Paul Benson	33	31	25	2	6	17	2	0
Daniel Charge	1	0	0	1	0	0	0	0
Danny Foster	38	38	34	0	4	2	2	0
Peter Gain	31	30	30	1	0	0	5	0
Richard Graham	5	3	0	2	3	0	0	0
Dominic Green	2	2	0	0	2	1	0	0
Scott Griffiths	44	43	41	1	2	0	1	0
Jamie Guy	9	5	3	4	2	1	0	0
Shane Huke	1	0	0	1	0	0	0	0
Doug Loft	11	10	8	1	2	0	1	0
Graeme Montgomery	5	0	0	5	0	0	0	0
Jon Nurse	34	16	7	18	9	4	3	0
Mark Nwokeji	16	3	0	13	3	3	0	0
Magnus Okuonghae	45	45	43	0	2	2	6	0
Aiden Palmer	3	3	2	0	1	0	0	0
Matt Ritchie	37	36	26	1	10	11	2	0
Sam Saunders	40	40	32	0	7	14	5	1
Glen Southam	30	17	12	13	5	1	5	0
Ben Strevens	46	46	39	0	7	14	5	0
Solomon Taiwo	40	39	31	1	8	4	6	0
Tommy Tejan-Sie	1	0	0	1	0	0	0	0
Wesley Thomas	5	1	1	4	0	0	0	0
Anwar Uddin	17	10	10	7	0	0	2	0

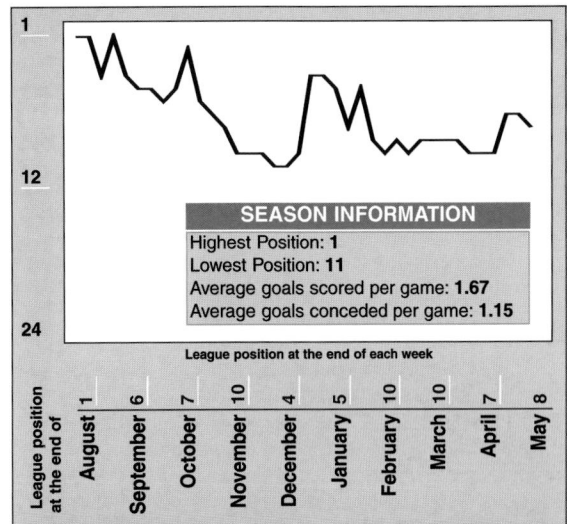

League position at the end of each week

SEASON INFORMATION
Highest Position: **1**
Lowest Position: **11**
Average goals scored per game: **1.67**
Average goals conceded per game: **1.15**

LONGEST SEQUENCES

Wins (on two occasions)	3	Undefeated home (09/08/08–10/10/08)	5
Losses (18/10/08–25/10/08)	3	Undefeated away (06/12/08–14/03/09)	11
Draws (03/01/09–17/01/09)	2	Without scoring (17/02/09–24/02/09)	3
Undefeated (06/12/08–17/01/09)	6	Without conceding (on three occasions)	2
Without win (17/02/09–07/03/09)	6	Scoring (09/08/08–21/10/08)	12

CARDS RECEIVED
48 **1**

QUICK-FIRE GOALS
From the start of a match
Ben Strevens (v Gillingham) 0:34

By a substitute after coming on
Jon Nurse (v Bournemouth) 2:58

GOALS SCORED/CONCEDED PER FIVE-MINUTE INTERVALS

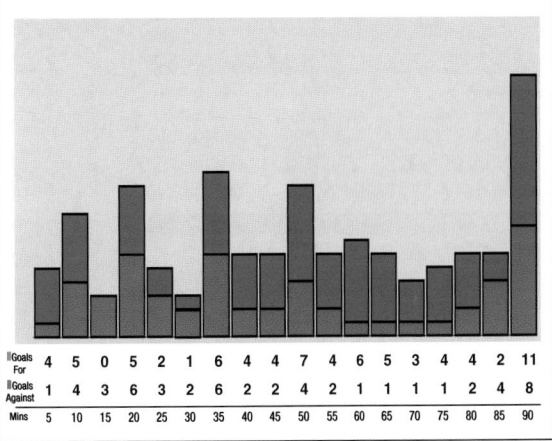

Goals For	4	5	0	5	2	1	6	4	4	7	4	6	5	3	4	4	2	11
Goals Against	1	4	3	6	3	2	6	2	2	4	2	1	1	1	1	2	4	8
Mins	5	10	15	20	25	30	35	40	45	50	55	60	65	70	75	80	85	90

HAD IT not been for a 10-point penalty for entering administration, Darlington would have reached the Coca-Cola League Two play-offs.

However, after officially entering administration in February, citing dwindling crowds at the club's 25,000-capacity stadium and the economic downturn as key factors, the club were docked crucial points.

It was a major blow for boss Dave Penney after what had been an otherwise successful season, with a nine-game unbeaten run from October to November a particular highlight. In contrast, a low point was the FA Cup first-round defeat at the hands of non-League Droylsden.

Penney quit the club for Oldham at the end of the season, with former Bolton and Bradford boss Colin Todd taking over the reins.

CLUB SUMMARY

FORMED	1883
MANAGER	Colin Todd
GROUND	Darlington Arena
CAPACITY	25,000
NICKNAME	The Quakers
WEBSITE	www.darlington-fc.net

The New **Football Pools** PLAYER OF THE SEASON — **Neil Austin**

OVERALL

P	W	D	L	F	A	GD
53	23	14	16	67	49	18

COCA-COLA FOOTBALL LEAGUE TWO

Pos	P	W	D	L	F	A	GD	Pts
12	46	20	12	14	61	44	17	62

HOME

Pos	P	W	D	L	F	A	GD	Pts
10	23	11	6	6	36	23	13	39

AWAY

Pos	P	W	D	L	F	A	GD	Pts
5	23	9	6	8	25	21	4	33

CUP PROGRESS DETAILS

Competition	Round reached	Knocked out by
FA Cup	R1	Droylsden
JP Trophy	SF	Rotherham
Carling Cup	R2	Watford

BIGGEST WIN (ALL COMPS)
30/08/08 6–0 v Macclesfield **FL2**

BIGGEST DEFEAT (ALL COMPS)
1–3 on three occasions

ATTENDANCE RECORD

High	Low	Average
3,868	2,180	2,932
v Brentford (25/04/2009)	v Wycombe (07/04/2009)	

RESULTS 2008/09

August
9th	● Exeter ....h D 1–1	Att: 3,559 — **Scorers:** Purdie
12th	● Walsall ....a W 1–2	Att: 2,702 — **Scorers:** Clarke, Kennedy
16th	● Notts County ....a D 0–0	Att: 4,352 — **Booked:** Clarke, Ravenhill
23rd	● Gillingham ......h L 1–2	Att: 2,831 — **Scorers:** Purdie. **Booked:** Ravenhill
26th	● Watford............a L 2–1	Att: 5,236 — **Scorers:** Blundell. **Booked:** G. Blundell (AET)
30th	● Macclesfield......a W 0–6	Att: 1,554 — **Scorers:** Austin, Clarke[4], Walker OG

September
6th	● Aldershot ....a L 2–1	Att: 3,460 — **Scorers:** Hulbert. **Booked:** Ravenhill
13th	● Port Vale ....h W 2–1	Att: 3,040 — **Scorers:** Burgmeier, Hatch
20th	● Accrington S ....h W 3–0	Att: 2,814 — **Scorers:** Clarke[2], White
27th	● Bournemouth ...a L 3–1	Att: 4,124 — **Scorers:** Hatch. **Booked:** Foster, Austin, Purdie, Hatch

October
4th	● Shrewsbury ...h D 1–1	Att: 2,899 — **Scorers:** White. **Booked:** Ravenhill, Kennedy, Hatch
7th	● Huddersfield......h W 1–0	Att: 1,791 — **Scorers:** White. **Booked:** Ravenhill
11th	● Luton ....a W 1–2	Att: 5,560 — **Scorers:** Blundell, Clarke. **Booked:** Ryan, Austin, Hatch
18th	● Wycombe.........a D 1–1	Att: 5,345 — **Scorers:** Kennedy. **Booked:** Burgmeier, White, Foster, Kennedy. **Dismissed:** Ryan
20th	● Bradford ....h W 2–1	Att: 3,034 — **Scorers:** Austin, Burgmeier. **Booked:** Austin, Burgmeier
25th	● Dag & Red ....h W 3–0	Att: 3,070 — **Scorers:** Hatch[2], Kennedy. **Booked:** Hatch, Ravenhill, Burgmeier
28th	● Rotherham........a W 0–1	Att: 3,322 — **Scorers:** Ravenhill

November
1st	● Grimsby ....a W 1–2	Att: 3,509 — **Scorers:** Clarke, Ravenhill. **Booked:** Clarke, White, Ravenhill
4th	● Bury ....h W 1–0	Att: 1,651 — **Scorers:** White. **Booked:** Proudlock
8th	● Droylsden.........h D 0–0	Att: 2,479
15th	● Lincoln City ...h W 2–0	Att: 3,534 — **Scorers:** Foran, Hatch. **Dismissed:** Foster
18th	● Droylsden.........a L 1–0	Att: 1,672 — **Booked:** Valentine, White, Hatch
22nd	● Brentford ....a D 1–1	Att: 4,837 — **Scorers:** Foran. **Booked:** Ravenhill, Burgmeier, Oakes, Valentine, Foran
25th	● Chester ....h L 1–2	Att: 2,416 — **Scorers:** Purdie. **Booked:** Ryan

December
13th	● Morecambe ......a L 1–0	Att: 1,873 — **Booked:** Hatch, White, Foran
16th	● Rotherham........a D 1–1	Att: 2,706 — **Booked:** Hatch, Foran (Lost 2–4 on pens)
20th	● Barnet ....h D 2–2	Att: 2,770 — **Scorers:** Hatch[2]. **Booked:** Ravenhill
26th	● Bury ....a D 2–2	Att: 3,454 — **Scorers:** Foran, Miller. **Booked:** Valentine
28th	● Chesterfield ......h D 0–0	Att: 3,352 — **Booked:** Foran

January
3rd	● Bournemouth ...h W 2–1	Att: 2,571 — **Scorers:** Abbott, Purdie. **Booked:** Hatch, Ryan, Abbott
17th	● Luton ....h W 5–1	Att: 3,319 — **Scorers:** Austin, Blundell, Hatch[2], Purdie. **Booked:** Austin
24th	● Shrewsbury ......a L 1–0	Att: 5,140 — **Booked:** Ravenhill, Foster. **Dismissed:** Ravenhill
27th	● Rotherham........h W 1–0	Att: 2,431 — **Scorers:** Carlton. **Booked:** Ryan, Hulbert, Burgmeier. **Dismissed:** Hulbert
31st	● Dag & Red........a W 0–1	Att: 1,832 — **Scorers:** Abbott. **Booked:** Valentine, Foster, Carlton, Ravenhill

February
17th	● Bradford ....a D 0–0	Att: 12,782 — **Booked:** White, Carlton
21st	● Grimsby ....h W 1–0	Att: 3,418 — **Scorers:** Main. **Booked:** White
24th	● Rochdale ....h L 1–2	Att: 2,858 — **Scorers:** Abbott. **Booked:** Hatch, Carlton. **Dismissed:** Ravenhill
28th	● Exeter ....a L 2–0	Att: 4,851 — **Booked:** Ryan, White. **Dismissed:** White

March
3rd	● Notts County ....h W 1–0	Att: 2,450 — **Scorers:** Hulbert. **Booked:** Valentine, Kennedy
7th	● Macclesfield ......h L 1–2	Att: 2,995 — **Scorers:** Poole. **Booked:** Poole, Foster
10th	● Gillingham ....a L 1–0	Att: 4,730 — **Booked:** Valentine, Poole
14th	● Port Vale ....a L 3–1	Att: 4,860 — **Scorers:** Carlton. **Booked:** Hatch, White
17th	● Lincoln City .....a W 0–1	Att: 2,835 — **Scorers:** Purdie
21st	● Aldershot ....h W 2–0	Att: 2,532 — **Scorers:** Carlton, Main
24th	● Accrington S ....a L 1–0	Att: 1,086 — **Booked:** Burgmeier, Valentine
28th	● Barnet ....a W 0–1	Att: 2,069 — **Scorers:** Abbott. **Booked:** White

April
4th	● Morecambe ......h D 0–0	Att: 2,560
7th	● Wycombe.........h L 1–2	Att: 2,180 — **Scorers:** Kennedy. **Booked:** Hatch
11th	● Chesterfield ......a D 0–0	Att: 3,642
13th	● Bury ....h D 2–2	Att: 2,927 — **Scorers:** Abbott, Kennedy. **Booked:** White, Ryan
18th	● Rochdale ....a W 0–0	Att: 3,789 — **Scorers:** Kennedy, McArdle OG. **Booked:** White, Ravenhill
25th	● Brentford ....h L 1–3	Att: 3,868 — **Scorers:** Abbott. **Booked:** Valentine, Abbott. **Dismissed:** White

May
2nd	● Chester ....a W 1–2	Att: 1,945 — **Scorers:** Abbott[2]

● Coca-Cola League 2/Play-Offs ● FA Cup ● Carling Cup ● Johnstone's Paint Trophy

LEAGUE TWO GOALKEEPER STATS

Player	Appearances	Match starts	Completed matches	Sub appearances	Subbed off	Clean sheets	Yellow cards	Red cards
Simon Brown	22	22	22	0	0	6	0	0
Dean Gerken	7	7	7	0	0	4	0	0
Przemyslaw Kazimierczak	8	7	7	1	0	4	0	0
Andy Oakes	10	10	9	0	1	4	1	0

LEAGUE TWO OUTFIELD PLAYER STATS

Player	Appearances	Match starts	Completed matches	Substitute appearances	Subbed off	Goals scored	Yellow cards	Red cards
Pawel Abbott	18	15	9	3	6	8	2	0
Neil Austin	33	29	23	4	6	3	4	0
Corey Barnes	3	2	0	1	2	0	0	0
Gregg Blundell	20	2	2	18	0	2	0	0
Franz Burgmeier	35	30	13	5	17	2	6	0
Danny Carlton	17	16	14	1	2	4	3	0
Sebastien Carole	6	3	2	3	1	0	0	0
Billy Clarke	20	18	8	2	10	8	2	0
Michael Flynn	4	4	4	0	0	0	0	0
Richie Foran	9	7	6	2	1	3	3	0
Clayton Fortune	7	3	1	4	2	0	0	0
Stephen Foster	34	34	33	0	0	0	5	1
Josh Gray	5	1	0	4	2	0	0	0
Adam Griffin	17	9	4	8	5	0	0	0
Danny Groves	1	0	0	1	0	0	0	0
Liam Hatch	26	23	13	3	10	9	9	0
Robin Hulbert	27	9	3	18	5	2	1	1
Jason Kennedy	46	44	35	2	9	5	3	0
Curtis Main	18	5	1	13	4	2	0	0
Ian Miller	21	16	16	5	0	1	0	0
David Poole	26	18	9	8	9	1	2	0
Adam Proudlock	8	3	0	5	3	0	0	0
Robert Purdie	40	39	34	1	5	5	2	0
Richard Ravenhill	38	37	26	1	9	2	11	2
Tim Ryan	24	21	16	3	4	0	6	1
Carl Tremarco	2	2	1	0	1	0	0	0
Ryan Valentine	31	30	28	1	2	0	7	0
Alan White	40	40	37	0	1	2	10	2

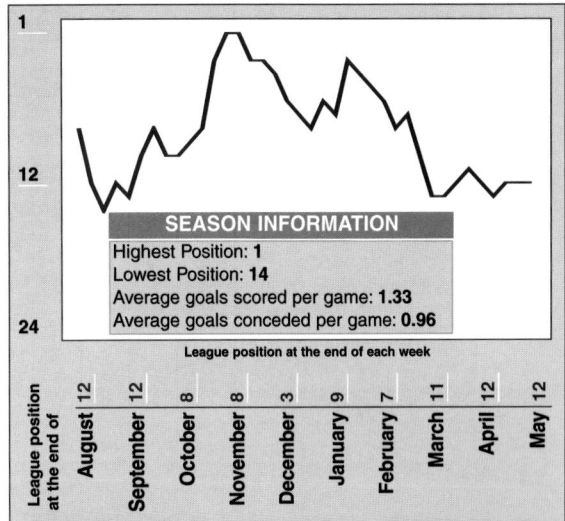

League position at the end of each week

SEASON INFORMATION
Highest Position: **1**
Lowest Position: **14**
Average goals scored per game: **1.33**
Average goals conceded per game: **0.96**

League position at the end of: August 12, September 12, October 8, November 8, December 3, January 9, February 7, March 11, April 12, May 12

LONGEST SEQUENCES

Wins (20/10/08–15/11/08)	5	Undefeated home (on two occasions)	6
Losses (07/03/09–14/03/09)	3	Undefeated away (11/10/08–22/11/08)	5
Draws (20/12/08–28/12/08)	3	Without scoring (–)	
Undefeated (04/10/08–22/11/08)	9	Without conceding (27/01/09–21/02/09)	4
Without win (22/11/08–28/12/08)	6	Scoring (23/08/08–25/11/08)	16

CARDS RECEIVED

77   7

QUICK-FIRE GOALS

From the start of a match
Jason Kennedy (v Rochdale) 3:28

By a substitute after coming on
Curtis Main (v Grimsby) 3:10

GOALS SCORED/CONCEDED PER FIVE-MINUTE INTERVALS

Goals For	3	5	2	0	3	4	2	3	3	1	4	7	3	3	5	3	3	7
Goals Against	1	2	1	1	2	5	3	4	2	0	5	1	1	2	3	2	2	7
Mins	5	10	15	20	25	30	35	40	45	50	55	60	65	70	75	80	85	90

RICHARD LOGAN'S goal in a 1–0 win at Rotherham on the final day of the season was enough to secure back-to-back promotions for Paul Tisdale's Exeter side.

The Grecians made a late run into the automatic promotion spots having spent the majority of the season in the play-off places, with a sequence of just two defeats in their last 19 matches seeing them over the line. They made the cut without scoring a hatful, with Adam Stansfield their highest scorer with just 10 goals, although midfielder Matthew Gill weighed in with nine, veteran Marcus Stewart rolled back the years with seven crucial strikes, and Craig McAllister also grabbed seven.

Promotion made up for a shock exit from the FA Cup at the hands of Curzon Ashton as the St James Park club finished the season as runners-up to Brentford.

CLUB SUMMARY

FORMED	1904
MANAGER	Paul Tisdale
GROUND	St James Park
CAPACITY	9,036
NICKNAME	The Grecians
WEBSITE	www.exetercityfc.co.uk

The New **Football Pools** PLAYER OF THE SEASON

Paul Jones

OVERALL

P	W	D	L	F	A	GD
49	22	13	14	69	58	11

COCA-COLA FOOTBALL LEAGUE TWO

Pos	P	W	D	L	F	A	GD	Pts
2	46	22	13	11	65	50	15	79

HOME

Pos	P	W	D	L	F	A	GD	Pts
4	23	13	5	5	36	25	11	44

AWAY

Pos	P	W	D	L	F	A	GD	Pts
4	23	9	8	6	29	25	4	35

CUP PROGRESS DETAILS

Competition	Round reached	Knocked out by
FA Cup	R1	Curzon Ashton
JP Trophy	R1	Shrewsbury
Carling Cup	R1	Southampton

BIGGEST WIN (ALL COMPS)
10/02/09 4–0 v Macclesfield FL2

BIGGEST DEFEAT (ALL COMPS)
28/10/08 1–6 v Chesterfield FL2

ATTENDANCE RECORD

High	Low	Average
8,544	2,839	4,939

v Morecambe (25/04/2009) v Macclesfield (10/02/2009)

RESULTS 2008/09

August
9th	● Darlington	a	D 1–1	Att: 3,559 — **Scorers:** Seaborne
12th	● Southampton	h	L 1–3	Att: 6,471 — **Scorers:** Moxey
16th	● Shrewsbury	h	L 0–1	Att: 4,916
23rd	● Bournemouth	a	W 0–1	Att: 5,350 — **Scorers:** Harley. **Booked:** Seaborne, Moxey
30th	● Luton	h	L 0–1	Att: 5,328

September
2nd	● Shrewsbury	h	L 1–2	Att: 1,530 — **Scorers:** Harley. **Booked:** Moxey
6th	● Accrington S	a	W 2–1	Att: 3,930 — **Scorers:** Gill, Watson
13th	● Bradford	a	L 4–1	Att: 12,683 — **Scorers:** Gill. **Booked:** Tully
20th	● Notts County	h	D 2–2	Att: 4,341 — **Scorers:** Gill, Taylor. **Booked:** Gill, Logan
27th	● Macclesfield	a	W 1–4	Att: 1,854 — **Scorers:** Gill, Harley, Stansfield[2]. **Booked:** Seaborne

October
4th	● Gillingham	h	W 3–0	Att: 4,819 — **Scorers:** Logan, Stansfield[2]. **Booked:** Stewart
11th	● Bury	a	W 0–1	Att: 3,220 — **Scorers:** Logan. **Booked:** Tully, Taylor
18th	● Grimsby	h	D 0–0	Att: 5,177 — **Booked:** Edwards
21st	● Port Vale	a	W 1–3	Att: 5,493 — **Scorers:** Gill, Sercombe, Stewart
25th	● Barnet	a	W 0–1	Att: 2,887 — **Scorers:** Gill. **Booked:** Logan
28th	● Chesterfield	h	L 1–6	Att: 5,093 — **Scorers:** Stansfield

November
1st	● Chester	h	W 2–0	Att: 4,448 — **Scorers:** Stansfield, Taylor
8th	● Curzon Ashton	a	L 3–2	Att: 1,259 — **Scorers:** Basham, Moxey. **Booked:** Taylor, Seaborne. **Dismissed:** Gill
15th	● Aldershot	a	L 1–0	Att: 3,784 — **Booked:** Edwards, Taylor, Moxey
22nd	● Morecambe	a	D 1–1	Att: 2,003 — **Scorers:** Panther. **Booked:** Murray, Moxey, Tully. **Dismissed:** Cozic
25th	● Rotherham	h	D 1–1	Att: 3,402 — **Scorers:** Watson

December
6th	● Lincoln City	h	W 2–1	Att: 3,916 — **Scorers:** McAllister , Moxey. **Booked:** Watson
20th	● Rochdale	h	W 4–1	Att: 4,326 — **Scorers:** Basham[2], McAllister [2]. **Booked:** Moxey
26th	● Wycombe	a	D 1–1	Att: 6,094 — **Scorers:** Panther. **Booked:** McAllister , Stewart
28th	● Brentford	h	L 0–2	Att: 6,791 — **Booked:** Harley, Murray

January
10th	● Notts County	a	L 2–1	Att: 3,832 — **Scorers:** Stewart. **Booked:** Stewart, Moxey, Murray
17th	● Bury	h	D 0–0	Att: 4,158
20th	● Dag & Red	a	W 1–2	Att: 2,053 — **Scorers:** McAllister [2]. **Booked:** Edwards
24th	● Gillingham	a	L 1–0	Att: 5,638 — **Booked:** Edwards, Stansfield, Moxey
28th	● Chesterfield	a	L 2–1	Att: 2,894 — **Scorers:** Moxey
31st	● Barnet	h	W 2–1	Att: 4,145 — **Scorers:** Gill, Saunder

February
7th	● Grimsby	a	D 2–2	Att: 3,324 — **Scorers:** Harley, Stewart. **Booked:** Edwards
10th	● Macclesfield	h	W 4–0	Att: 2,839 — **Scorers:** Logan, McAllister, Saunders, Stansfield
14th	● Aldershot	h	W 3–2	Att: 4,840 — **Scorers:** Saunders, Stewart, Harding OG. **Booked:** Gill
21st	● Chester	a	D 0–0	Att: 1,640
28th	● Darlington	h	W 2–0	Att: 4,851 — **Scorers:** Gill, McAllister . **Booked:** Archibald-Henville

March
3rd	● Shrewsbury	a	D 1–1	Att: 4,679 — **Scorers:** Stewart. **Booked:** Gill
7th	● Luton	a	W 1–2	Att: 6,460 — **Scorers:** Sercombe, Stansfield. **Booked:** Archibald-Henville
10th	● Bournemouth	h	L 1–3	Att: 4,946 — **Scorers:** Stansfield
14th	● Bradford	h	W 1–0	Att: 5,253 — **Scorers:** Moxey
21st	● Accrington S	a	L 2–1	Att: 1,169 — **Scorers:** Stansfield
28th	● Rochdale	a	D 2–2	Att: 3,364 — **Scorers:** Stewart[2]. **Booked:** Archibald-Henville
31st	● Port Vale	h	W 1–0	Att: 4,235 — **Scorers:** Prosser OG. **Booked:** Seaborne, Cozic. **Dismissed:** Seaborne

April
4th	● Dag & Red	h	W 2–1	Att: 5,123 — **Scorers:** Fleetwood[2]
11th	● Brentford	a	D 1–1	Att: 8,234 — **Scorers:** Fleetwood. **Booked:** Edwards
13th	● Wycombe	h	W 1–0	Att: 8,183 — **Scorers:** Gill. **Booked:** Fleetwood
18th	● Lincoln City	a	W 0–1	Att: 3,934 — **Scorers:** Burch OG. **Booked:** Archibald-Henville
25th	● Morecambe	h	D 2–2	Att: 8,544 — **Scorers:** Harley, Moxey. **Booked:** Cozic, Moxey

May
2nd	● Rotherham	a	W 0–1	Att: 6,184 — **Scorers:** Logan

● Coca-Cola League 2/Play-Offs ● FA Cup ● Carling Cup ● Johnstone's Paint Trophy

LEAGUE TWO GOALKEEPER STATS

Player	Appearances	Match starts	Completed matches	Sub appearances	Subbed off	Clean sheets	Yellow cards	Red cards
Paul Jones	46	46	46	0	0	15	0	0

LEAGUE TWO OUTFIELD PLAYER STATS

Player	Appearances	Match starts	Completed matches	Substitute appearances	Subbed off	Goals scored	Yellow cards	Red cards
Troy Archibald-Henville	19	19	15	0	4	0	4	0
Steve Basham	23	12	2	11	10	2	0	0
Bertrand Cozic	20	14	9	6	4	0	2	1
Rob Edwards	44	44	40	0	4	0	6	0
Stuart Fleetwood	9	7	4	2	3	3	1	0
George Friend	4	4	3	0	1	0	0	0
Matthew Gill	43	43	41	0	2	9	3	0
Ryan Harley	31	25	23	6	2	4	1	0
Richard Logan	30	18	7	12	11	4	2	0
Craig McAllister	30	8	2	22	6	7	1	0
Dean Moxey	43	41	40	2	1	4	7	0
Fred Murray	6	3	3	3	0	0	3	0
Jack Obersteller	7	3	0	4	3	0	0	0
Emmanuel Panther	22	15	12	7	3	2	0	0
Alex Russell	7	7	6	0	1	0	0	0
Neil Saunders	17	15	8	2	7	3	0	0
Daniel Seaborne	33	31	30	2	0	1	3	1
Liam Sercombe	29	16	9	13	7	2	0	0
Chris Shephard	2	0	0	2	0	0	0	0
Adam Stansfield	37	32	8	5	24	10	1	0
Marcus Stewart	36	35	24	1	11	7	3	0
Matthew Taylor	31	29	29	2	0	2	2	0
Steve Tully	36	35	32	1	3	0	3	0
Ben Watson	12	4	0	8	4	2	1	0

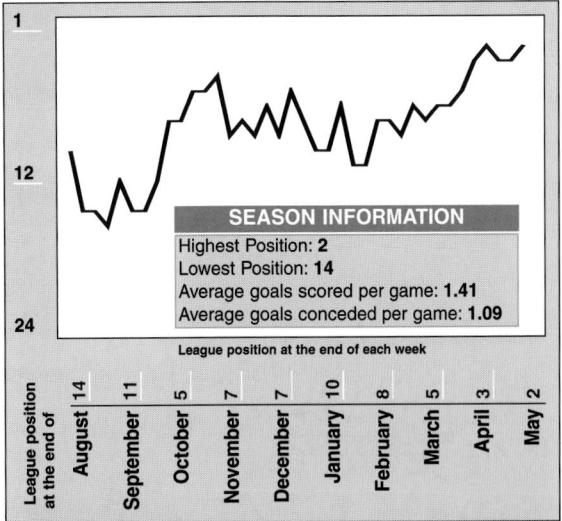

SEASON INFORMATION
Highest Position: **2**
Lowest Position: **14**
Average goals scored per game: **1.41**
Average goals conceded per game: **1.09**

League position at the end of each week

LONGEST SEQUENCES

Wins (27/09/08–11/10/08)	3	Undefeated home (17/01/09–28/02/09)	5
Losses (on two occasions)	2	Undefeated away (on two occasions)	4
Draws (22/11/08–25/11/08)	2	Without scoring (–)	
Undefeated (31/01/09–07/03/09)	8	Without conceding (04/10/08–18/10/08)	3
Without win (26/12/08–17/01/09)	4	Scoring (06/09/08–11/10/08)	6

CARDS RECEIVED

43 **2**

QUICK-FIRE GOALS

From the start of a match
Adam Stansfield (v Macclesfield) 0:46

By a substitute after coming on
Craig McAllister (v Lincoln City) 2:08

GOALS SCORED/CONCEDED PER FIVE-MINUTE INTERVALS

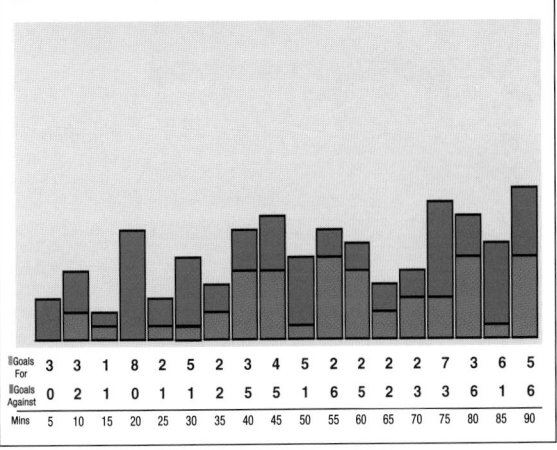

Goals For	3	3	1	8	2	5	2	3	4	5	2	2	2	7	3	6	5
Goals Against	0	2	1	0	1	1	2	5	5	1	6	5	2	3	3	6	1	6
Mins	5	10	15	20	25	30	35	40	45	50	55	60	65	70	75	80	85	90

OFFICIAL FOOTBALL YEARBOOK OF THE ENGLISH & SCOTTISH LEAGUES 2009–2010

GILLINGHAM ensured that their stay in the basement division would be for just one season by winning the Coca-Cola League Two play-off final against Shrewsbury.

It was a patchy start to the campaign for the Gills – including a 7–0 defeat against the Shrews in September – but the turning point came off the pitch following a 3–0 defeat at Exeter in October.

Andrew Crofts was replaced as captain by Barry Fuller, whose first league game with the armband saw a 5–0 win over Morecambe, and the Gills never looked back, picking up more away league wins this season (nine) than in the previous three campaigns put together.

A run of four games without a win in March and April cost them automatic promotion, but 21-goal hero Simeon Jackson pounced in the last minute at Wembley to ensure they went up.

CLUB SUMMARY

FORMED	1893
MANAGER	Mark Stimson
GROUND	Priestfield Stadium
CAPACITY	11,582
NICKNAME	The Gills
WEB	www.gillinghamfootballclub.com

The New **Football Pools** PLAYER OF THE SEASON

Simon King

OVERALL

P	W	D	L	F	A	GD
55	25	14	16	65	61	4

COCA-COLA FOOTBALL LEAGUE TWO

Pos	P	W	D	L	F	A	GD	Pts
5	46	21	12	13	58	55	3	75

HOME

Pos	P	W	D	L	F	A	GD	Pts
6	23	12	7	4	38	21	17	43

AWAY

Pos	P	W	D	L	F	A	GD	Pts
7	23	9	5	9	20	34	-14	32

CUP PROGRESS DETAILS

Competition	Round reached	Knocked out by
FA Cup	R3	Aston Villa
JP Trophy	R2	Colchester
Carling Cup	R1	Colchester

BIGGEST WIN (ALL COMPS)

11/10/08 5–0 v Morecambe FL2

BIGGEST DEFEAT (ALL COMPS)

13/09/08 0–7 v Shrewsbury FL2

ATTENDANCE RECORD

High	Low	Average
8,360	4,029	5,307
v Bury (25/04/2009)	v Rochdale (25/11/2008)	

RESULTS 2008/09

August
9th ● Bournemouth ....a D 1–1 Att: 5,377 — Scorers: Mulligan. Booked: King, McCammon
12th ● Colchester ....a L 0–1 Att: 2,566 — Booked: Fuller
16th ● Luton ....h L 0–1 Att: 5,339 — Booked: Jackson
23rd ● Darlington ....a W 1–2 Att: 2,831 — Scorers: Jackson, Richards. Booked: McCammon, Southall, Fuller
30th ● Accrington S ....h W 1–0 Att: 4,733 — Scorers: Oli

September
6th ● Grimsby ....h W 3–0 Att: 4,912 — Scorers: Daniels, Jackson, McCammon. Booked: Daniels
13th ● Shrewsbury ......a L 7–0 Att: 5,319 — Booked: Fuller, Weston, Miller, Daniels
20th ● Aldershot ....a L 2–1 Att: 4,198 — Scorers: Jackson. Booked: Bentley. Dismissed: McCammon
27th ● Port Vale ....h W 1–0 Att: 4,986 — Scorers: McCombe OG

October
4th ● Exeter ....a L 3–0 Att: 4,819 — Booked: Weston, Lewis
7th ● Colchester ....h L 0–1 Att: 1,557 — Booked: King, Bentley
11th ● Morecambe ......h W 5–0 Att: 4,316 — Scorers: Bentley, Jackson[2], McCammon, Artell OG
18th ● Bradford ....a D 2–2 Att: 12,432 — Scorers: Jackson[2]. Booked: Nutter, Fuller. Dismissed: Bentley
21st ● Notts County ....h D 2–2 Att: 4,396 — Scorers: Mulligan, Southall
25th ● Chester ....h W 2–0 Att: 4,852 — Scorers: Barcham, Mills
28th ● Lincoln City .....a L 2–0 Att: 4,396 — Booked: Mills

November
1st ● Macclesfield......a W 0–1 Att: 1,635 — Scorers: Miller. Booked: Weston, Barcham, Fuller
8th ● Bury ....a W 0–1 Att: 2,161 — Scorers: Barcham. Booked: Miller, Bentley
15th ● Rotherham ....h W 4–0 Att: 5,304 — Scorers: Cumbers, King, Miller, Richards. Booked: Miller, Fuller
22nd ● Bury ....a L 4–0 Att: 2,068 — Booked: Nutter
25th ● Rochdale ....h D 1–1 Att: 4,029 — Scorers: Jackson
29th ● Stockport ....h D 0–0 Att: 4,419 — Booked: Jarrett, Miller

December
6th ● Chesterfield .....h W 2–1 Att: 4,622 — Scorers: Jackson, Miller. Booked: Bentley, King, Weston
9th ● Stockport ....a W 1–2 Att: 3,329 — Scorers: Barcham[2]
13th ● Barnet ....a D 2–2 Att: 2,248 — Scorers: Barcham, Jackson. Booked: Nutter, Miller
20th ● Brentford ....h D 1–1 Att: 5,521 — Scorers: Jackson. Booked: Fuller, Bentley. Dismissed: Fuller
26th ● Dag & Red ....a L 2–0 Att: 2,844
28th ● Wycombe ....h D 1–1 Att: 5,979 — Scorers: Weston

January
4th ● Aston Villa ....h L 1–2 Att: 10,107 — Scorers: Jackson. Booked: King, Barcham, Bentley, Lewis
17th ● Morecambe ......a W 0–1 Att: 2,027 — Scorers: Weston. Booked: Jackson
20th ● Port Vale ....a W 1–3 Att: 4,539 — Scorers: Jackson, Miller, Oli. Booked: King
24th ● Exeter ....h W 1–0 Att: 5,638 — Scorers: Miller
27th ● Lincoln City .....h L 1–2 Att: 4,525 — Scorers: Jackson. Booked: Bentley, Miller
31st ● Chester ....a W 0–1 Att: 1,541 — Scorers: Barcham. Booked: Weston, Nutter, Miller

February
7th ● Bradford ....h L 0–2 Att: 4,866 — Booked: Miller
14th ● Rotherham ....a L 2–0 Att: 2,757 — Booked: Bentley
17th ● Aldershot ....h D 4–4 Att: 5,974 — Scorers: Barcham, McCammon, Miller, Weston.
Booked: Bentley, Mulligan, Southall
21st ● Macclesfield.....h W 3–1 Att: 4,620 — Scorers: Barcham[2], King
28th ● Bournemouth ...h W 1–0 Att: 5,353 — Scorers: Southall. Booked: Weston, McCammon

March
3rd ● Luton ....a D 0–0 Att: 5,739 — Booked: Miller, King, Nutter, Jackson
7th ● Accrington S ....a W 0–2 Att: 1,308 — Scorers: Jackson, Oli
10th ● Darlington ....h W 1–0 Att: 4,730 — Scorers: Jackson
14th ● Shrewsbury ......h D 2–2 Att: 6,023 — Scorers: Southall, Weston
17th ● Notts County ....a W 0–1 Att: 3,189 — Scorers: Jackson. Booked: Fuller
21st ● Grimsby ....a L 3–0 Att: 6,406
28th ● Brentford ....h D 1–1 Att: 7,908 — Scorers: Jackson. Booked: Jackson, McCammon

April
4th ● Barnet ....h L 0–2 Att: 6,033 — Booked: Richards
11th ● Wycombe ....a L 1–0 Att: 6,306 — Booked: King, Miller, Barcham, Jackson
13th ● Dag & Red ....h W 2–0 Att: 6,945 — Scorers: McCammon, Oli. Booked: Richards
18th ● Chesterfield .....a W 0–1 Att: 3,933 — Scorers: McCammon. Booked: Fuller
25th ● Bury ....h D 0–0 Att: 8,360 — Booked: Lewis

May
2nd ● Rochdale ....a W 0–1 Att: 3,480 — Scorers: Weston. Booked: Jarrett
7th ● Rochdale ....a D 0–0 Att: 4,450 — Booked: Nutter, Lewis
10th ● Rochdale ....h W 2–1 Att: 9,585 — Scorers: Jackson[2]
23rd ● Shrewsbury ......n W 1–0 Att: 53,706 — Scorers: Jackson. Booked: Weston

● Coca-Cola League 2/Play-Offs ● FA Cup ● Carling Cup ● Johnstone's Paint Trophy

actim

LEAGUE TWO GOALKEEPER STATS

Player	Appearances	Match starts	Completed matches	Sub appearances	Subbed off	Clean sheets	Yellow cards	Red cards
Alan Julian	4	4	4	0	0	2	0	0
Simon Royce	42	42	42	0	0	18	0	0

LEAGUE TWO OUTFIELD PLAYER STATS

Player	Appearances	Match starts	Completed matches	Substitute appearances	Subbed off	Goals scored	Yellow cards	Red cards
Andy Barcham	33	31	25	2	6	6	2	0
Mark Bentley	39	34	29	5	4	1	6	1
Tyrone Berry	5	2	1	3	1	0	0	0
Andrew Crofts	9	7	7	2	0	0	0	0
Luis Cumbers	7	0	0	7	0	1	0	0
Charlie Daniels	5	5	4	0	1	1	2	0
Barry Fuller	37	37	36	0	0	0	8	1
Simeon Jackson	41	37	26	4	11	17	5	0
Albert Jarrett	16	11	4	5	7	0	1	0
Simon King	43	43	38	0	5	2	5	0
Stuart Lewis	21	13	11	8	2	0	2	0
Mark McCammon	31	21	12	10	8	5	4	1
Adam Miller	35	32	23	3	9	6	8	0
Leigh Mills	7	6	6	1	0	1	1	0
Gary Mulligan	26	12	3	14	9	2	1	0
John Nutter	45	43	43	2	0	0	5	0
Dennis Oli	31	20	10	11	10	4	0	0
Jack Payne	2	0	0	2	0	0	0	0
Jaime Peters	3	1	0	2	1	0	0	0
Andy Pugh	1	0	0	1	0	0	0	0
Garry Richards	36	26	24	10	2	2	2	0
Nicky Southall	36	28	20	8	8	3	2	0
Rene Steer	5	3	1	2	2	0	0	0
Curtis Weston	45	43	28	2	15	5	6	0
Josh Wright	5	5	2	0	3	0	0	0

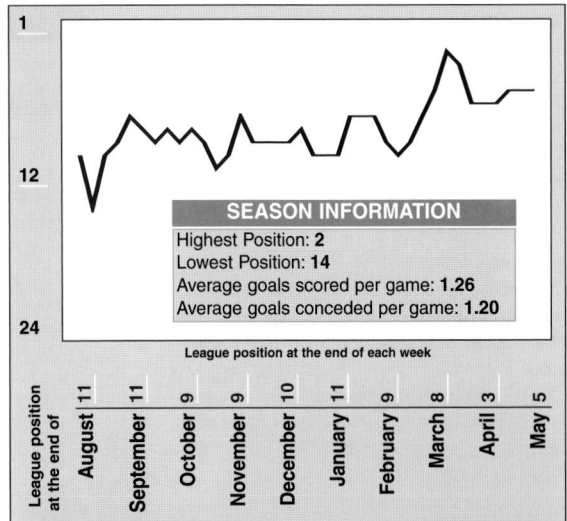

SEASON INFORMATION

Highest Position: **2**
Lowest Position: **14**
Average goals scored per game: **1.26**
Average goals conceded per game: **1.20**

League position at the end of each week

LONGEST SEQUENCES

Wins (on two occasions)	3	Undefeated home (30/08/08–24/01/09)	12
Losses (on three occasions)	2	Undefeated away (on two occasions)	3
Draws (on two occasions)	2	Without scoring (on two occasions)	2
Undefeated (17/02/09–17/03/09)	8	Without conceding (28/02/09–10/03/09)	4
Without win (on two occasions)	4	Scoring (28/12/08–31/01/09)	6

CARDS RECEIVED

60   **3**

QUICK-FIRE GOALS

From the start of a match
Simon King (v Macclesfield) 1:57

By a substitute after coming on
Luis Cumbers (v Rotherham) 3:06

GOALS SCORED/CONCEDED PER FIVE-MINUTE INTERVALS

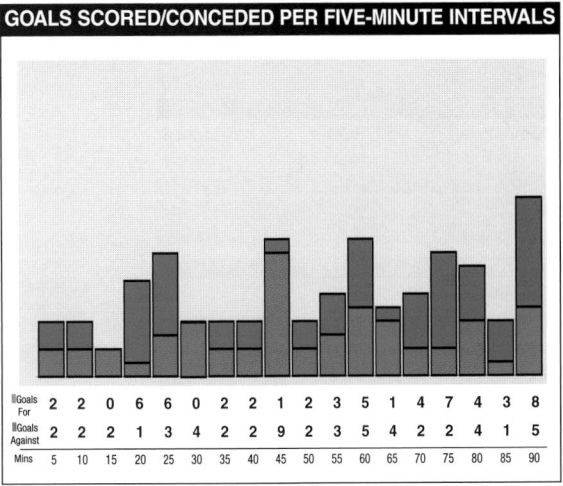

	Goals For	Goals Against
5	2	2
10	2	2
15	0	2
20	6	1
25	6	3
30	0	4
35	2	2
40	2	2
45	1	9
50	2	2
55	3	3
60	5	5
65	1	4
70	4	2
75	7	2
80	4	4
85	3	1
90	8	5

GRIMSBY left it late to secure their survival in Coca-Cola League Two after a torrid start to the season that cost manager Alan Buckley his job. The club stalwart was relieved of his post just nine games into the campaign, with Mike Newell taking the reins at Blundell Park.

The Mariners did not register a league win until a November victory at Bury – their 16th game of the season. Their fortunes did not dramatically improve until later in the year, when, boosted by a number of loan signings – in particular striker Barry Conlon and goalkeeper Wayne Henderson – they began to deliver positive results.

Conlon scored five goals in his eight games, almost single-handedly delivering safety with a week to spare, although Adam Proudlock was the Mariners' top scorer with eight goals.

CLUB SUMMARY

FORMED	1878
MANAGER	Mike Newell
GROUND	Blundell Park
CAPACITY	9,953
NICKNAME	The Mariners
WEBSITE	www.gtfc.co.uk

The New Football Pools PLAYER OF THE SEASON — Ryan Bennett

OVERALL
P	W	D	L	F	A	GD
51	10	15	26	58	79	-21

COCA-COLA FOOTBALL LEAGUE TWO
Pos	P	W	D	L	F	A	GD	Pts
22	46	9	14	23	51	69	-18	41

HOME
Pos	P	W	D	L	F	A	GD	Pts
20	23	6	7	10	31	28	3	25

AWAY
Pos	P	W	D	L	F	A	GD	Pts
24	23	3	7	13	20	41	-21	16

CUP PROGRESS DETAILS
Competition	Round reached	Knocked out by
FA Cup	R1	Morecambe
JP Trophy	R2	Scunthorpe
Carling Cup	R2	Blackburn

BIGGEST WIN (ALL COMPS)
07/03/09 5–1 v Lincoln City **FL2**

BIGGEST DEFEAT (ALL COMPS)
16/08/08 0–4 v Brentford **FL2**

ATTENDANCE RECORD
High	Low	Average
7,095	2,644	4,475

v Aldershot (28/03/2009)   v Morecambe (24/02/2009)

RESULTS 2008/09

August
9th	● Rochdale	h	D 0–0	Att: 4,213 — **Booked:** Butler, Hope
12th	● Tranmere	h	W 2–0	Att: 1,858 — **Scorers:** Hunt, Chorley OG
16th	● Brentford	a	L 4–0	Att: 4,009 — **Booked:** Heywood
23rd	● Chesterfield	h	L 0–1	Att: 3,306
27th	● Blackburn	a	L 4–1	Att: 8,379 — **Scorers:** Newey. **Booked:** Boshell, Bennett
30th	● Lincoln City	a	D 1–1	Att: 4,573 — **Scorers:** Till. **Booked:** Hegarty, Newey

September
3rd	● Chesterfield	a	D 2–2	Att: 1,665 — **Scorers:** Jarman, North. **Booked:** Heywood (Won 4–1 on pens)
6th	● Gillingham	a	L 3–0	Att: 4,912 — **Booked:** Newey
13th	● Chester	h	L 1–3	Att: 2,950 — **Scorers:** North
20th	● Morecambe	a	D 1–1	Att: 1,989 — **Scorers:** Till
27th	● Barnet	h	L 0–1	Att: 3,713 — **Booked:** Stockdale

October
4th	● Rotherham	a	L 4–1	Att: 3,889 — **Scorers:** Boshell
7th	● Scunthorpe	a	L 2–1	Att: 4,844 — **Scorers:** Hegarty. **Booked:** Hunt, Jarman
11th	● Wycombe	h	D 1–1	Att: 4,562 — **Scorers:** Hegarty
18th	● Exeter	a	D 0–0	Att: 5,177 — **Booked:** Newey, Trotter
21st	● Luton	h	D 2–2	Att: 4,021 — **Scorers:** Bennett, Bore. **Booked:** Barnes, Jarman
24th	● Bradford	h	L 1–3	Att: 4,470 — **Scorers:** Trotter
28th	● Dag & Red	a	L 4–0	Att: 1,622 — **Booked:** Heywood, Trotter

November
1st	● Darlington	h	L 1–2	Att: 3,509 — **Scorers:** Kalala. **Booked:** North, Kalala
8th	● Morecambe	a	L 2–1	Att: 1,713 — **Scorers:** Stockdale
15th	● Bury	a	W 0–2	Att: 2,549 — **Scorers:** Jarman, Trotter.
				Booked: Kalala, Proudlock. **Dismissed:** Kalala
21st	● Bournemouth	h	D 3–3	Att: 4,353 — **Scorers:** Atkinson, Bennett, Clarke
25th	● Macclesfield	a	L 1–0	Att: 1,182 — **Booked:** Trotter

December
6th	● Port Vale	a	L 2–1	Att: 5,058 — **Scorers:** Proudlock
13th	● Shrewsbury	h	W 1–0	Att: 3,283 — **Scorers:** Proudlock. **Booked:** Proudlock
20th	● Aldershot	a	D 2–2	Att: 3,605 — **Scorers:** Hegarty, Kalala.
				Booked: Proudlock, Hope, Hegarty, Stockdale
26th	● Notts County	h	L 0–1	Att: 5,432
28th	● Accrington S	a	L 3–1	Att: 1,200 — **Scorers:** Proudlock. **Booked:** Jarman

January
17th	● Wycombe	a	W 0–1	Att: 4,461 — **Scorers:** Jarman. **Booked:** Jarman
24th	● Rotherham	h	W 3–0	Att: 4,559 — **Scorers:** Proudlock, Sinclair, Widdowson
27th	● Dag & Red	h	D 1–1	Att: 3,431 — **Scorers:** Elliott.
31st	● Bradford	a	L 2–0	Att: 12,816 — **Booked:** Clarke. **Dismissed:** Atkinson

February
7th	● Exeter	h	D 2–2	Att: 3,324 — **Scorers:** Jarman². **Booked:** Forbes, Jarman
10th	● Barnet	a	D 3–3	Att: 1,554 — **Scorers:** Bennett, Elliott, Forbes. **Booked:** Sinclair, Jarman
14th	● Bury	h	L 1–2	Att: 3,673 — **Scorers:** Proudlock. **Booked:** Boshell
21st	● Darlington	a	L 1–0	Att: 3,418 — **Booked:** Widdowson, Jarman
24th	● Morecambe	h	L 2–3	Att: 2,644 — **Scorers:** Forbes². **Dismissed:** Llewellyn
28th	● Rochdale	a	L 2–0	Att: 3,076 — **Booked:** Clarke, Boshell, Henderson

March
3rd	● Brentford	h	L 0–1	Att: 3,001 — **Booked:** Akpa Akpro
7th	● Lincoln City	h	W 5–1	Att: 5,133 — **Scorers:** Akpa Akpro², Proudlock³. **Booked:** Boshell, Newey, Hegarty
11th	● Chesterfield	a	L 2–1	Att: 2,999 — **Scorers:** Bennett. **Booked:** Proudlock, Jarman
14th	● Chester	a	D 1–1	Att: 2,836 — **Scorers:** Hegarty. **Booked:** Newey, Jarman
17th	● Luton	a	L 2–1	Att: 5,830 — **Scorers:** Bennett. **Booked:** Akpa Akpro, Hegarty, Bore, Henderson
21st	● Gillingham	h	W 3–0	Att: 6,406 — **Scorers:** Akpa Akpro, Conlon, Hegarty. **Booked:** Sweeney
28th	● Aldershot	h	W 1–0	Att: 7,095 — **Scorers:** Conlon. **Booked:** Atkinson

April
4th	● Shrewsbury	a	D 1–1	Att: 5,535 — **Scorers:** Conlon. **Booked:** Llewellyn, Stockdale, Hegarty
11th	● Accrington S	h	L 4–0	Att: 6,453 — **Booked:** Widdowson, Sweeney, Forbes
13th	● Notts County	a	W 0–2	Att: 5,890 — **Scorers:** Atkinson, Boshell
18th	● Port Vale	h	W 3–0	Att: 6,511 — **Scorers:** Conlon², Jarman. **Booked:** Proudlock, Forbes
25th	● Bournemouth	a	L 2–1	Att: 9,008 — **Scorers:** Jarman.
				Booked: Boshell, Bennett, Widdowson, Jarman, Hegarty.
				Dismissed: Boshell, Widdowson

May
2nd	● Macclesfield	h	D 0–0	Att: 6,876 — **Booked:** Akpa Akpro, Atkinson, Forbes

● Coca-Cola League 2/Play-Offs ● FA Cup ● Carling Cup ● Johnstone's Paint Trophy

LEAGUE TWO GOALKEEPER STATS

Player	Appearances	Match starts	Completed matches	Sub appearances	Subbed off	Clean sheets	Yellow cards	Red cards
Phillip Barnes	32	32	32	0	0	6	1	0
Wayne Henderson	14	14	14	0	0	5	2	0

LEAGUE TWO OUTFIELD PLAYER STATS

Player	Appearances	Match starts	Completed matches	Substitute appearances	Subbed off	Goals scored	Yellow cards	Red cards
Jean-Louis Akpa Akpro	20	19	13	1	6	3	3	0
Tomi Ameobi	2	2	0	0	2	0	0	0
Robert Atkinson	31	30	29	1	0	2	2	1
Ryan Bennett	45	45	45	0	0	5	1	0
Peter Bore	27	10	8	17	2	1	1	0
Danny Boshell	24	18	13	6	4	2	4	1
Martin Butler	3	3	2	0	1	0	1	0
Jamie Clarke	32	31	28	1	3	1	2	0
Barry Conlon	8	8	6	0	2	5	0	0
Stuart Elliott	11	9	6	2	3	2	0	0
Adrian Forbes	15	8	2	7	6	3	4	0
Josh Fuller	1	0	0	1	0	0	0	0
Nick Hegarty	35	32	25	3	7	4	6	0
Simon Heslop	8	5	2	3	3	0	0	0
Matthew Heywood	18	16	15	2	1	0	2	0
Richard Hope	6	6	6	0	0	0	2	0
James Hunt	22	21	16	1	5	0	0	0
Nathan Jarman	33	25	11	8	14	6	9	0
JP Kalala	21	21	17	0	3	2	2	1
Malvin Kamara	2	1	1	1	0	0	0	0
Chris Llewellyn	28	13	4	15	8	0	1	1
Tom Newey	24	23	22	1	1	0	5	0
Grant Normington	1	0	0	1	0	0	0	0
Danny North	15	2	1	13	1	1	1	0
Adam Proudlock	28	22	11	6	11	8	5	0
Dean Sinclair	9	9	7	0	2	1	1	0
Robbie Stockdale	20	19	18	1	1	0	3	0
Peter Sweeney	8	8	7	0	1	0	2	0
Andy Taylor	6	3	1	3	2	0	0	0
Peter Till	16	15	11	1	4	2	0	0
Liam Trotter	15	15	14	0	1	2	3	0
Javan Vidal	3	2	1	1	1	0	0	0
Joe Widdowson	20	19	16	1	2	1	3	1

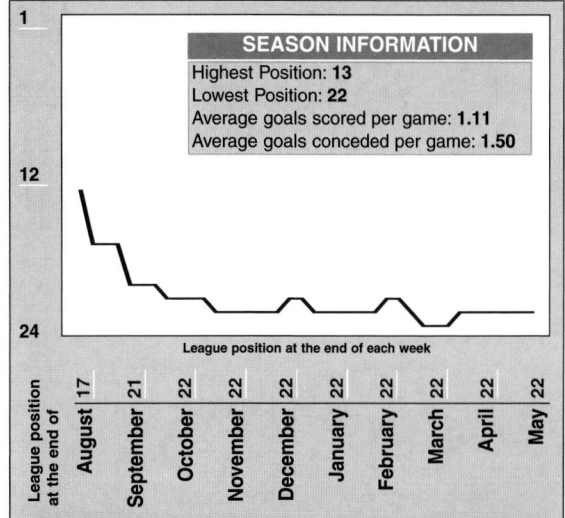

SEASON INFORMATION
Highest Position: **13**
Lowest Position: **22**
Average goals scored per game: **1.11**
Average goals conceded per game: **1.50**

League position at the end of each week

League position at the end of August 17, September 21, October 22, November 22, December 22, January 22, February 22, March 22, April 22, May 22

LONGEST SEQUENCES

Wins (on three occasions)	2	Undefeated home (on two occasions)	3
Losses (14/02/09–03/03/09)	5	Undefeated away (on two occasions)	2
Draws (11/10/08–21/10/08)	3	Without scoring (09/08/08–23/08/08)	3
Undefeated (on three occasions)	3	Without conceding (on three occasions)	2
Without win (09/08/08–01/11/08)	15	Scoring (07/03/09–04/04/09)	7

CARDS RECEIVED

66 **5**

QUICK-FIRE GOALS

From the start of a match
Peter Bore (v Luton) 0:36

By a substitute after coming on
Danny North (v Chester) 0:43

GOALS SCORED/CONCEDED PER FIVE-MINUTE INTERVALS

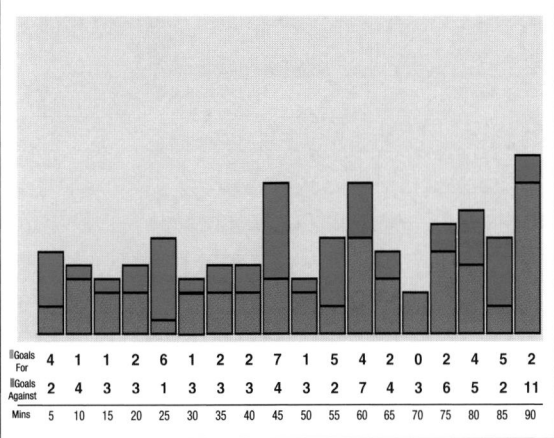

Goals For	4	1	1	2	6	1	2	2	7	1	5	4	2	0	2	4	5	2
Goals Against	2	4	3	1	3	3	3	4	3	2	7	4	3	6	5	2	11	
Mins	5	10	15	20	25	30	35	40	45	50	55	60	65	70	75	80	85	90

LINCOLN CITY

IT was a frustrating campaign for Lincoln City as the club's push for promotion never really got going, with a failure to win at Sincil Bank ultimately costing them.

Boss Peter Jackson declared it was going to be a successful season for the Imps having brought in the likes of Frank Sinclair and Stefan Oakes, but his big names failed to produce and he was forced to eat humble pie.

One success story, though, was that of Romanian striker Adrian Patulea, who was found running around the training ground carrying his wife on his back.

He was offered a deal and responded by top scoring with 11 goals, while Frenchman Dany N'Guessan produced some effervescent displays on the wing.

A late bid for the play-offs came to a halt after failing to win any of their final six games.

CLUB SUMMARY

FORMED	1884
MANAGER	Peter Jackson
GROUND	Sincil Bank
CAPACITY	10,147
NICKNAME	The Red Imps
WEBSITE	www.redimps.com

The New Football Pools PLAYER OF THE SEASON

Dany N'Guessan

OVERALL
P	W	D	L	F	A	GD
50	14	19	17	56	58	-2

COCA-COLA FOOTBALL LEAGUE TWO
Pos	P	W	D	L	F	A	GD	Pts
13	46	14	17	15	53	52	1	59

HOME
Pos	P	W	D	L	F	A	GD	Pts
17	23	6	11	6	26	22	4	29

AWAY
Pos	P	W	D	L	F	A	GD	Pts
10	23	8	6	9	27	30	-3	30

CUP PROGRESS DETAILS
Competition	Round reached	Knocked out by
FA Cup	R1	Kettering
JP Trophy	R2	Leicester
Carling Cup	R1	Derby

BIGGEST WIN (ALL COMPS)
12/12/08 5–1 v Accrington Stanley **FL2**

BIGGEST DEFEAT (ALL COMPS)
07/03/09 1–5 v Grimsby **FL2**

ATTENDANCE RECORD
High	Low	Average
6,156	2,478	3,940
v Bradford (26/12/2008)	v Macclesfield (31/03/2009)	

RESULTS 2008/09

August
9th	● Rotherham ....a L 1–0	**Att:** 4,748

9th ● Rotherham ....a L 1–0 **Att:** 4,748
12th ● Derby ....a L 3–1 **Att:** 10,091 — **Scorers:** Wright. **Booked:** John–Lewis, Oakes (AET)
16th ● Dag & Red........h L 1–3 **Att:** 3,581 — **Scorers:** John-Lewis
23rd ● Wycombe ....a L 1–0 **Att:** 4,112
30th ● Grimsby ....h D 1–1 **Att:** 4,573 — **Scorers:** Frecklington. **Booked:** N'Guessan, Sinclair, Kovacs

September
6th ● Barnet ....h W 2–0 **Att:** 3,417 — **Scorers:** N'Guessan, Patulea
13th ● Bury ....a L 3–1 **Att:** 2,663 — **Scorers:** Buchanan OG. **Booked:** Patulea
20th ● Brentford ....a D 1–1 **Att:** 4,557 — **Scorers:** Patulea. **Booked:** Beevers, Frecklington, Kovacs
23rd ● Leicester ....a D 0–0 **Att:** 8,046 — **Booked:** Beevers (Lost 1–3 on penalties)
27th ● Morecambe ......h D 1–1 **Att:** 5,003 — **Scorers:** Frecklington. **Booked:** Hone

October
4th ● Chester ....a W 0–2 **Att:** 1,962 — **Scorers:** Kovacs, Patulea. **Booked:** Kovacs, Green, A. Brown
10th ● Rochdale ....h D 1–1 **Att:** 4,510 — **Scorers:** Hone. **Booked:** John-Lewis
18th ● Chesterfield ......h W 3–1 **Att:** 4,326 — **Scorers:** Kovacs, Oakes, Patulea **Booked:** N'Guessan. **Dismissed:** Hone
21st ● Macclesfield......a W 1–2 **Att:** 1,247 — **Scorers:** Beevers, Frecklington. **Booked:** Beevers
25th ● Bournemouth ....a W 0–1 **Att:** 4,464 — **Scorers:** John-Lewis. **Booked:** Oakes, Frecklington
28th ● Gillingham ....h W 2–0 **Att:** 4,396 — **Scorers:** Frecklington, N'Guessan. **Booked:** Sinclair

November
1st ● Port Vale ....h L 0–1 **Att:** 4,793
8th ● Kettering ....a D 1–1 **Att:** 3,314 — **Scorers:** N'Guessan. **Booked:** Kovacs, Green
15th ● Darlington ....a L 2–0 **Att:** 3,534
18th ● Kettering ....h L 1–2 **Att:** 3,953 — **Scorers:** John-Lewis
22nd ● Shrewsbury ......h D 0–0 **Att:** 3,517
25th ● Aldershot ....a L 2–0 **Att:** 2,625 — **Booked:** Kovacs

December
6th ● Exeter ....a L 2–1 **Att:** 3,916 — **Scorers:** John-Lewis. **Booked:** Patulea, Hone. **Dismissed:** N'Guessan
12th ● Accrington S ....h W 5–1 **Att:** 2,625 — **Scorers:** Brown, Frecklington, Patulea², Wright. **Booked:** Patulea, Brown
20th ● Notts County ....a W 0–1 **Att:** 4,568 — **Scorers:** Patulea. **Booked:** Hone, Brown
26th ● Bradford ....h D 0–0 **Att:** 6,156 — **Booked:** Beevers, Hone
28th ● Luton ....a L 3–2 **Att:** 6,643 — **Scorers:** John-Lewis, Patulea. **Booked:** N'Guessan, Kerr

January
10th ● Brentford ....h D 2–2 **Att:** 3,932 — **Scorers:** Elding, N'Guessan. **Dismissed:** Green
17th ● Rochdale ....a D 2–2 **Att:** 2,897 — **Scorers:** N'Guessan, Kennedy OG
24th ● Chester ....h D 1–1 **Att:** 3,760 — **Scorers:** Frecklington. **Booked:** Frecklington
27th ● Gillingham ....a W 1–2 **Att:** 4,525 — **Scorers:** Horsfield, N'Guessan. **Booked:** Burch, Horsfield
31st ● Bournemouth ....h D 3–3 **Att:** 3,634 — **Scorers:** Beevers, Frecklington, N'Guessan. **Booked:** Green, Beevers, Patulea

February
10th ● Morecambe ......a D 1–1 **Att:** 1,471 — **Scorers:** Green. **Booked:** Green
20th ● Port Vale ....a W 0–1 **Att:** 5,097 — **Scorers:** N'Guessan. **Booked:** Kovacs, Oakes, Mullarkey
28th ● Rotherham ....h L 0–1 **Att:** 4,336 — **Booked:** Green, Horsfield, Kovacs

March
3rd ● Dag & Red........a W 0–3 **Att:** 1,302 — **Scorers:** Brown, Elding, Kovacs. **Booked:** Kovacs
7th ● Grimsby ....a L 5–1 **Att:** 5,133 — **Scorers:** N'Guessan. **Booked:** Oakes, Wright, Kerr, O'Connor
10th ● Wycombe ....h W 1–0 **Att:** 2,562 — **Scorers:** Elding. **Booked:** Kerr
14th ● Bury ....h D 1–1 **Att:** 3,642 — **Scorers:** Wright. **Booked:** Elding, Kerr. **Dismissed:** Elding
17th ● Darlington ....h L 0–1 **Att:** 2,835
21st ● Barnet ....a L 3–2 **Att:** 1,979 — **Scorers:** O'Connor, Patulea. **Booked:** Patulea, O'Connor
28th ● Notts County ....h D 1–1 **Att:** 4,027 — **Scorers:** Mullarkey
31st ● Macclesfield......h W 1–0 **Att:** 2,478 — **Scorers:** Patulea

April
4th ● Accrington S ....a W 0–2 **Att:** 1,139 — **Scorers:** Kerr²
7th ● Chesterfield .....a D 1–1 **Att:** 3,419 — **Scorers:** Patulea. **Booked:** Patulea
11th ● Luton ....h D 0–0 **Att:** 4,664 — **Booked:** O'Connor
13th ● Bradford ....a D 1–1 **Att:** 12,932 — **Scorers:** Hutchinson
18th ● Exeter ....h L 0–1 **Att:** 3,934
25th ● Shrewsbury ......a D 0–0 **Att:** 6,740 — **Booked:** Hutchinson, Swaibu, Kovacs

May
2nd ● Aldershot ....h L 0–2 **Att:** 3,910 — **Booked:** Kerr, Beevers

● Coca-Cola League 2/Play-Offs ● FA Cup ● Carling Cup ● Johnstone's Paint Trophy

LEAGUE TWO GOALKEEPER STATS

Player	Appearances	Match starts	Completed matches	Sub appearances	Subbed off	Clean sheets	Yellow cards	Red cards
Robert Burch	46	46	45	0	1	14	1	0
Ayden Duffy	1	0	0	1	0	1	0	0

LEAGUE TWO OUTFIELD PLAYER STATS

Player	Appearances	Match starts	Completed matches	Substitute appearances	Subbed off	Goals scored	Yellow cards	Red cards
Nathan Adams	2	0	0	2	0	0	0	0
Lee Beevers	44	43	43	1	0	2	5	0
Aaron Brown	39	33	28	6	5	2	3	0
Shane Clarke	23	13	9	10	4	0	0	0
Luca Colman-Carr	1	0	0	1	0	0	0	0
Anthony Elding	15	15	11	0	3	3	1	1
Lee Frecklington	27	25	18	2	7	7	3	0
Kevin Gall	9	6	3	3	0	0	0	0
David Graham	9	2	0	7	2	0	0	0
Paul Green	33	33	30	0	2	1	4	1
Daniel Hone	19	17	15	2	1	1	4	1
Geoff Horsfield	17	14	2	3	12	1	2	0
Andrew Hutchinson	4	3	0	1	3	1	1	0
Lenell John-Lewis	27	21	11	6	10	4	1	0
Scott Kerr	45	45	40	0	5	2	5	0
Gary King	5	2	0	3	0	0	0	0
Janos Kovacs	45	45	43	0	2	3	8	0
Kern Miller	1	0	0	1	0	0	0	0
Sam Mullarkey	18	7	5	11	2	1	1	0
Dany N'Guessan	45	43	37	2	5	8	3	1
Michael O'Connor	10	9	6	1	3	1	3	0
Stefan Oakes	28	21	13	7	8	1	3	0
Adrian Patulea	31	17	7	14	10	11	6	0
Frank Sinclair	23	21	17	2	4	0	2	0
Moses Swaibu	10	10	10	0	0	0	1	0
Ben Wright	33	15	5	18	10	2	1	0

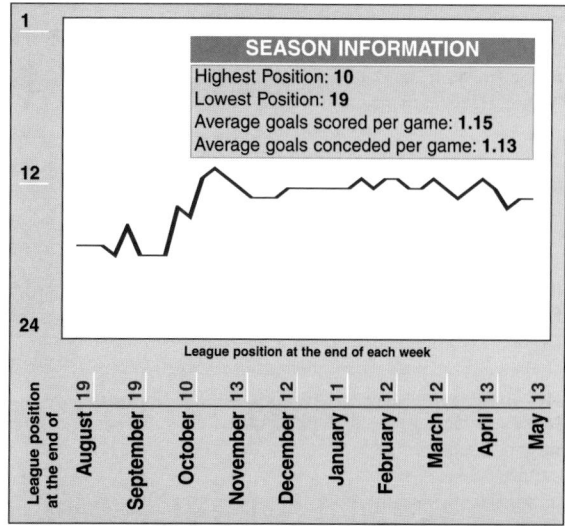

SEASON INFORMATION
Highest Position: **10**
Lowest Position: **19**
Average goals scored per game: **1.15**
Average goals conceded per game: **1.13**

League position at the end of each week

LONGEST SEQUENCES

Wins (18/10/08–28/10/08)	4	Undefeated home (on two occasions)	6
Losses (09/08/08–23/08/08)	3	Undefeated away (17/01/09–03/03/09)	5
Draws (on two occasions)	3	Without scoring (01/11/08–25/11/08)	4
Undefeated (20/09/08–28/10/08)	8	Without conceding (on three occasions)	2
Without win (07/04/09–02/05/09)	6	Scoring (30/08/08–28/10/08)	11

CARDS RECEIVED

58   **4**

QUICK-FIRE GOALS

From the start of a match
Scott Kerr (v Accrington Stanley) 3:29

By a substitute after coming on
Sam Mullarkey (v Notts County) 12:54

GOALS SCORED/CONCEDED PER FIVE-MINUTE INTERVALS

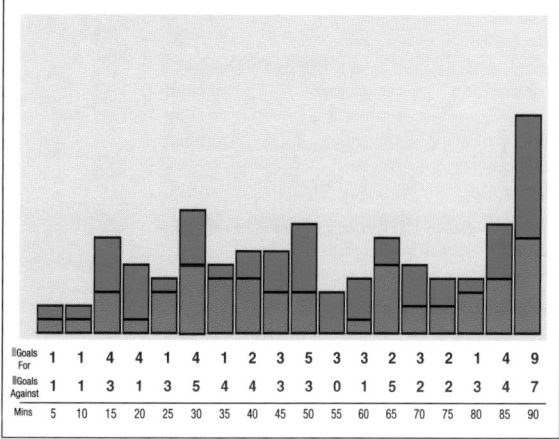

Goals For	1	1	4	1	4	1	2	3	5	3	3	2	3	2	1	4	9
Goals Against	1	1	3	1	3	5	4	4	3	3	0	1	5	2	2	3	4	7
Mins	5	10	15	20	25	30	35	40	45	50	55	60	65	70	75	80	85	90

LUTON TOWN

THE 2008/09 campaign will go down in history as the season Luton's 89-year stay in the Football League came to an end.

Due to financial irregularities overseen by the club's previous owners, Luton were docked a staggering 30 points before a ball had been kicked, leaving Mick Harford and his squad with the near-impossible task of achieving Football League survival.

Despite a noble battle, Luton eventually had their relegation confirmed after a draw with Chesterfield in April, but there was to be a richly-deserved silver lining for the Hatters.

Harford's men cemented their place in the club's history books for more positive reasons as they came from behind to beat Coca-Cola League One high-flyers Scunthorpe 3–2 after extra-time to lift the Johnstone's Paint Trophy in front of 55,378 fans at Wembley.

CLUB SUMMARY

FORMED	1885
MANAGER	Mick Harford
GROUND	Kenilworth Road
CAPACITY	10,226
NICKNAME	The Hatters
WEBSITE	www.lutontown.co.uk

Keith Keane
PLAYER OF THE SEASON

OVERALL
P	W	D	L	F	A	GD
57	17	22	18	70	78	-8

COCA-COLA FOOTBALL LEAGUE TWO
Pos	P	W	D	L	F	A	GD	Pts
24	46	13	17	16	58	65	-7	26

HOME
Pos	P	W	D	L	F	A	GD	Pts
18	23	7	8	8	34	34	0	29

AWAY
Pos	P	W	D	L	F	A	GD	Pts
12	23	6	9	8	24	31	-7	27

CUP PROGRESS DETAILS
Competition	Round reached	Knocked out by
FA Cup	R2	Southend
JP Trophy	Won	–
Carling Cup	R2	Reading

BIGGEST WIN (ALL COMPS)
13/09/08 3–1 v Aldershot **FL2**

BIGGEST DEFEAT (ALL COMPS)
26/08/08 1–5 v Reading **LC2**

ATTENDANCE RECORD
High	Low	Average
7,149	5,248	6,019
v Port Vale (09/08/2008)	v Brentford (25/11/2008)	

RESULTS 2008/09

August
9th	● Port Vale	..........h	L 1–3	Att: 7,149 — Scorers: Parkin. Booked: Gnakpa
12th	● Plymouth	..........h	W 2–0	Att: 2,682 — Scorers: Jarvis, Plummer
16th	● Gillingham	..........a	W 0–1	Att: 5,339 — Scorers: Parkin. Booked: Davis, Parkin, Gnakpa
23rd	● Notts County	..........h	D 1–1	Att: 6,085 — Scorers: Martin. Booked: Martin, Nicholls
26th	● Reading	..........a	L 5–1	Att: 7,498 — Scorers: Charles. Booked: Martin
30th	● Exeter	..........a	W 0–1	Att: 5,328 — Scorers: Parkin

September
6th	● Macclesfield	....a	L 2–1	Att: 2,349 — Scorers: Charles. Booked: Jarvis
13th	● Aldershot	..........h	W 3–1	Att: 6,462 — Scorers: Hall, Martin, Spillane. Booked: Parkin, Jarvis
20th	● Rotherham	....a	L 1–0	Att: 4,095 — Booked: Gnakpa
27th	● Chester	..........h	D 1–1	Att: 5,731 — Scorers: Hall. Booked: Spillane, Martin

October
4th	● Bradford	..........a	D 1–1	Att: 13,083 — Scorers: Spillane. Booked: Martin, Gnakpa, Keane
7th	● Brentford	..........h	D 2–2	Att: 2,029 — Scorers: Martin[2]. Booked: Gnakpa (Won 4–3 on penalties)
11th	● Darlington	..........h	L 1–2	Att: 5,560 — Scorers: Gnakpa
18th	● Accrington S	....h	L 1–2	Att: 5,492 — Scorers: Hall. Booked: Spillane
21st	● Grimsby	..........a	D 2–2	Att: 4,021 — Scorers: Craddock[2]. Booked: Spillane, Jarvis, Parkin
25th	● Bury	..........a	W 1–2	Att: 3,052 — Scorers: Craddock, Roper. Booked: T. Craddock, Howells

November
1st	● Shrewsbury	....a	L 3–0	Att: 6,188
4th	● Walsall	..........a	W 0–1	Att: 1,844 — Scorers: Jarvis. Booked: Spillane
8th	● Altrincham	..........h	D 0–0	Att: 3,200
15th	● Dag & Red	........h	W 2–1	Att: 5,402 — Scorers: Davis, McVeigh. Booked: Nicholls
18th	● Altrincham	..........a	D 0–0	Att: 2,397 — Booked: Keane, Martin. Dismissed: Davis (Won 4–2 on pens)
22nd	● Rochdale	..........a	L 2–0	Att: 2,901 — Booked: Keane, O'Connor, Roper, Martin, Logan
25th	● Brentford	..........h	L 0–1	Att: 5,248 — Booked: Spillane. Dismissed: Keane
29th	● Southend	..........a	L 3–1	Att: 4,111 — Scorers: Spillane. Booked: Roper, Andrews, Watson

December
2nd	● Bournemouth	....h	D 3–3	Att: 6,773 — Scorers: Gallen, McVeigh, Garry OG. Booked: Gnakpa
6th	● Barnet	..........h	W 3–1	Att: 5,536 — Scorers: Martin, McVeigh, Townsend OG. Booked: Howells, Roper
13th	● Wycombe	..........a	D 0–0	Att: 5,567 — Booked: Martin, McVeigh
16th	● Colchester	..........h	W 1–0	Att: 2,638 — Scorers: Gnakpa. Booked: Talbot, Howells, Martin
20th	● Morecambe	..........h	D 1–1	Att: 5,664 — Scorers: Spillane. Booked: Keane
26th	● Chesterfield	..........a	D 2–2	Att: 4,243 — Scorers: Craddock, Roper. Booked: T. Craddock
28th	● Lincoln City	......h	W 3–2	Att: 6,643 — Scorers: Martin[2], Roper. Booked: Emanuel, Spillane

January
13th	● Chester	..........a	D 2–2	Att: 1,652 — Scorers: Emanuel, Martin
17th	● Darlington	..........a	L 5–1	Att: 3,319 — Scorers: Martin. Booked: Roper
20th	● Brighton	..........a	D 0–0	Att: 6,127 — Booked: Davis, Jarvis, Gnakpa
24th	● Bradford	..........h	D 3–3	Att: 6,053 — Scorers: Hall[2], Wasiu. Booked: Roper, Spillane, Nicholls, Parkin. Dismissed: Martin
27th	● Bournemouth	....a	D 1–1	Att: 5,230 — Scorers: Hollands OG. Booked: Nicholls, Hall, Roper
31st	● Bury	..........h	L 1–2	Att: 5,545 — Scorers: Hall

February
14th	● Dag & Red	........a	L 2–1	Att: 2,310 — Scorers: Henderson. Booked: Gallen, Henderson, Roper
17th	● Brighton	..........h	D 1–1	Att: 8,711 — Scorers: Craddock. Booked: Davis (Won 4–3 on pens)
21st	● Shrewsbury	......h	W 3–1	Att: 5,661 — Scorers: Craddock, Hall, Parkin. Booked: Davis
24th	● Accrington S	....a	D 0–0	Att: 1,033 — Booked: Craddock, Hall
28th	● Port Vale	..........a	W 1–3	Att: 5,689 — Scorers: Gallen, Hall, Martin. Booked: Bower, Gnakpa

March
3rd	● Gillingham	........h	D 0–0	Att: 5,739 — Booked: Asafu–Adjaye
7th	● Exeter	..........h	L 1–2	Att: 6,460 — Scorers: Craddock. Booked: Bower
10th	● Notts County	....a	W 0–2	Att: 2,886 — Scorers: Craddock, Martin. Booked: Spillane
14th	● Aldershot	..........a	L 2–1	Att: 3,098 — Scorers: Craddock.
17th	● Grimsby	..........h	W 2–1	Att: 5,830 — Scorers: Bower, Hall. Booked: Bower, Nicholls, Craddock
21st	● Macclesfield	......h	W 1–0	Att: 5,363 — Scorers: Craddock. Booked: Emanuel
28th	● Morecambe	......a	W 1–2	Att: 2,599 — Scorers: Gallen, Martin. Booked: Pilkington, Craddock
31st	● Rotherham	......h	L 2–4	Att: 5,975 — Scorers: Hall, Martin. Booked: Martin

April
5th	● Scunthorpe	......n	W 3–2	Att: 55,378 — Scorers: Craddock, Gnakpa, Martin. Booked: Nicholls, Martin (AET)
11th	● Lincoln City	......a	D 0–0	Att: 4,664 — Booked: Livermore
13th	● Chesterfield	......h	D 0–0	Att: 6,494 — Booked: Nicholls
18th	● Barnet	..........a	D 1–1	Att: 2,808 — Scorers: Jarvis. Booked: Nicholls, Davis. Dismissed: Nicholls
21st	● Wycombe	..........h	L 0–1	Att: 6,553 — Booked: Henderson
25th	● Rochdale	..........h	D 1–1	Att: 7,025 — Scorers: Craddock. Booked: Livermore

May
2nd	● Brentford	..........a	L 2–0	Att: 10,223 — Booked: Martin

● Coca-Cola League 2/Play-Offs ● FA Cup ● Carling Cup ● Johnstone's Paint Trophy

LEAGUE TWO GOALKEEPER STATS

Player	Appearances	Match starts	Completed matches	Sub appearances	Subbed off	Clean sheets	Yellow cards	Red cards
Dean Brill	23	23	23	0	0	8	0	0
Conrad Logan	22	22	22	0	0	1	1	0
Lewis Price	1	1	1	0	0	0	0	0

LEAGUE TWO OUTFIELD PLAYER STATS

Player	Appearances	Match starts	Completed matches	Substitute appearances	Subbed off	Goals scored	Yellow cards	Red cards
Wayne Andrews	7	1	0	6	1	0	0	0
Ed Asafu-Adjaye	19	17	15	2	2	0	1	0
George Beavan	4	3	2	1	1	0	0	0
Mark Bower	16	16	14	0	2	1	3	0
Ryan Charles	10	0	0	10	0	1	0	0
Tom Craddock	27	27	22	0	5	10	5	0
Sol Davis	24	22	14	2	8	1	3	0
Lewis Emanuel	20	17	10	3	7	1	2	0
Kevin Gallen	29	26	19	3	7	3	1	0
Claude Gnakpa	27	19	14	8	5	1	6	0
Asa Hall	42	35	30	7	5	10	2	0
Ian Henderson	19	14	4	5	10	1	2	0
Jake Howells	28	14	14	14	0	0	2	0
Rossi Jarvis	35	31	15	4	16	1	3	0
Keith Keane	40	40	37	0	2	0	3	1
Josh Klein-Davies	1	0	0	1	0	0	0	0
David Livermore	8	8	6	0	2	0	2	0
Chris Martin	40	39	27	1	11	11	7	1
Paul McVeigh	13	9	8	4	1	3	1	0
Kevin Nicholls	19	16	11	3	4	0	7	1
Garreth O'Connor	3	3	0	0	3	0	1	0
Sam Parkin	23	15	14	8	1	4	4	0
Jordan Patrick	2	0	0	2	0	0	0	0
George Pilkington	18	18	15	0	3	0	1	0
Tristan Plummer	5	0	0	5	0	0	0	0
Marc Pugh	4	3	2	1	1	0	0	0
Ian Roper	19	18	17	1	1	3	6	0
Michael Spillane	39	35	32	4	3	3	7	0
Drew Talbot	7	4	0	3	4	0	0	0
Akanni-Sunday Wasiu	5	2	1	3	1	1	0	0
Kevin Watson	6	2	1	4	1	0	0	0
Harry Worley	8	6	6	2	0	0	0	0

SEASON INFORMATION

Highest Position: 24
Lowest Position: 24
Average goals scored per game: **1.26**
Average goals conceded per game: **1.41**

League position at the end of each week

League position at the end of	August 24	September 24	October 24	November 24	December 24	January 24	February 24	March 24	April 24	May 24

LONGEST SEQUENCES

Wins (17/03/09–28/03/09)	3	Undefeated home (02/12/08–24/01/09)	5
Losses (on three occasions)	2	Undefeated away (on four occasions)	3
Draws (on two occasions)	3	Without scoring (on two occasions)	2
Undefeated (02/12/08–13/01/09)	7	Without conceding (11/04/09–13/04/09)	2
Without win (11/04/09–03/05/09)	7	Scoring (20/12/08–21/02/09)	10

CARDS RECEIVED

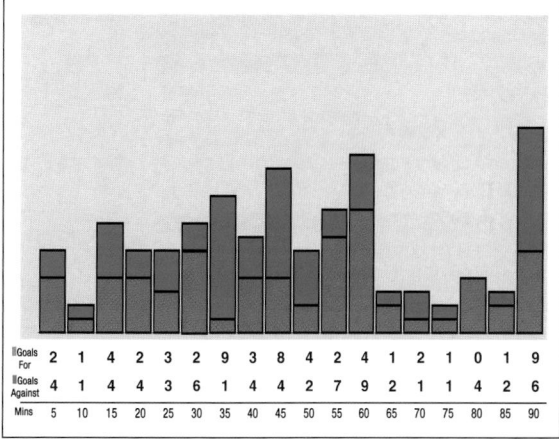

70 **3**

QUICK-FIRE GOALS

From the start of a match
Sam Parkin (v Gillingham) 2:48

By a substitute after coming on
Asa Hall (v Grimsby) 28:58

GOALS SCORED/CONCEDED PER FIVE-MINUTE INTERVALS

Goals For	2	1	4	2	3	2	9	3	8	2	4	1	2	1	0	1	9
Goals Against	4	1	4	4	3	6	1	4	4	2	7	9	2	1	1	4	2	6
Mins	5	10	15	20	25	30	35	40	45	50	55	60	65	70	75	80	85	90

MACCLESFIELD boss Keith Alexander was set to embark on a major overhaul of his squad in the summer after a disappointing campaign. The Silkmen struggled badly all season, losing 25 of their 46 Coca-Cola League Two outings and leaking plenty of goals along the way.

No other side conceded as many as the 37 that Macclesfield shipped at home and the 40 that they conceded on their travels gave them a dreadful goal difference of minus 32.

Simon Yeo retires this summer and several other players will be shown the door, but Alexander can call on a number of promising youngsters. John Rooney, the 18-year-old brother of Manchester United's Wayne, showed rich promise towards the end of the season and is expected to feature more prominently as Alexander seeks to put the focus on youth.

CLUB SUMMARY

FORMED	1874
MANAGER	Keith Alexander
GROUND	Moss Rose
CAPACITY	6,335
NICKNAME	The Silkmen
WEBSITE	www.mtfc.co.uk

The New **Football Pools** PLAYER OF THE SEASON — **Paul Morgan**

OVERALL

P	W	D	L	F	A	GD
52	16	8	28	53	86	-33

COCA-COLA FOOTBALL LEAGUE TWO

Pos	P	W	D	L	F	A	GD	Pts
20	46	13	8	25	45	77	-32	47

HOME

Pos	P	W	D	L	F	A	GD	Pts
21	23	7	4	12	23	37	-14	25

AWAY

Pos	P	W	D	L	F	A	GD	Pts
18	23	6	4	13	22	40	-18	22

CUP PROGRESS DETAILS

Competition	Round reached	Knocked out by
FA Cup	R3	Everton
JP Trophy	R1	Crewe
Carling Cup	R2	West Ham

BIGGEST WIN (ALL COMPS)
20/09/08 4–1 v Port Vale **FL2**

BIGGEST DEFEAT (ALL COMPS)
30/08/08 0–6 v Darlington **FL2**

ATTENDANCE RECORD

High	Low	Average
2,556	1,182	1,898
v Bradford (16/08/2008)	v Grimsby (25/11/2008)	

RESULTS 2008/09

August
9th	●	Shrewsbury	a	L 4–0	Att: 5,812 — **Booked:** Hessey, Walker, Yeo
12th	●	Blackpool	h	W 2–0	Att: 1,631 — **Scorers:** Brisley, Gritton. **Booked:** Brisley. **Dismissed:** Dunfield
16th	●	Bradford	h	L 0–2	Att: 2,556 — **Booked:** Tolley
23rd	●	Accrington S	a	L 2–0	Att: 1,323
27th	●	West Ham	a	L 4–1	Att: 10,055 — **Scorers:** Evans. **Booked:** Green, Reid, Yeo. **Dismissed:** Reid (AET)
30th	●	Darlington	h	L 0–6	Att: 1,554 — **Booked:** Dunfield

September
2nd	●	Crewe	a	L 3–0	Att: 2,463 — **Booked:** Gritton, Bell, Flynn. **Dismissed:** Gritton
6th	●	Luton	h	W 2–1	Att: 2,349 — **Scorers:** Morgan, Yeo
13th	●	Bournemouth	a	W 0–1	Att: 3,922 — **Scorers:** Evans. **Booked:** Flynn, Jennings, Brain. **Dismissed:** Evans
20th	●	Port Vale	h	W 1–4	Att: 6,645 — **Scorers:** Dunfield, Reid, Yeo². **Booked:** Flynn
27th	●	Exeter	h	L 1–4	Att: 1,854 — **Scorers:** Yeo

October
4th	●	Brentford	a	L 1–0	Att: 4,773 — **Booked:** Hessey, Flynn
11th	●	Aldershot	h	W 4–2	Att: 1,857 — **Scorers:** Evans, Green, Thomas². **Booked:** Bell
18th	●	Notts County	a	D 1–1	Att: 4,600 — **Scorers:** Yeo. **Booked:** Evans, Brisley, Bell. **Dismissed:** Evans
21st	●	Lincoln City	h	L 1–2	Att: 1,247 — **Scorers:** Yeo
25th	●	Rotherham	h	L 1–2	Att: 2,020 — **Scorers:** Green. **Booked:** Jennings, Bell, Dunfield. **Dismissed:** Jennings

November
1st	●	Gillingham	h	L 0–1	Att: 1,635 — **Booked:** Harvey
8th	●	Harlow	a	W 0–2	Att: 2,149 — **Scorers:** Brisley, Dunfield
15th	●	Rochdale	a	D 1–1	Att: 3,013 — **Scorers:** Brown
22nd	●	Barnet	a	W 1–3	Att: 1,579 — **Scorers:** Brown, Green, Gritton. **Booked:** Dunfield
25th	●	Grimsby	h	W 1–0	Att: 1,182 — **Scorers:** Brown
28th	●	Port Vale	a	W 1–3	Att: 4,684 — **Scorers:** Green², Gritton

December
2nd	●	Wycombe	a	L 4–0	Att: 3,770
6th	●	Bury	h	D 1–1	Att: 2,431 — **Scorers:** Gritton. **Booked:** Flynn, Gritton. **Dismissed:** Flynn
12th	●	Chesterfield	a	W 2–4	Att: 2,451 — **Scorers:** Bell, Evans, Gritton². **Booked:** Hessey, Dunfield. **Dismissed:** Green
20th	●	Dag & Red	h	L 0–4	Att: 1,909 — **Booked:** Gritton
26th	●	Morecambe	a	L 4–1	Att: 2,578 — **Scorers:** Reid. **Booked:** Evans, Brisley, Flynn
28th	●	Chester	h	W 3–1	Att: 2,219 — **Scorers:** Brown, Evans, Gritton

January
3rd	●	Everton	h	L 0–1	Att: 6,008
17th	●	Aldershot	a	D 1–1	Att: 3,018 — **Scorers:** Evans. **Booked:** Bell, Brown
24th	●	Brentford	h	W 2–0	Att: 1,942 — **Scorers:** Evans, Sinclair. **Booked:** E. Sinclair
27th	●	Wycombe	h	D 0–0	Att: 1,306 — **Booked:** Evans, Walker, Jennings
31st	●	Rotherham	a	L 2–0	Att: 2,945 — **Booked:** Elliott, Morgan, Walker

February
10th	●	Exeter	a	L 4–0	Att: 2,839 — **Booked:** Bell
14th	●	Rochdale	h	L 0–1	Att: 2,396 — **Booked:** Thomas, Brain, E. Sinclair
17th	●	Notts County	h	D 1–1	Att: 1,370 — **Scorers:** Yeo
21st	●	Gillingham	a	L 3–1	Att: 4,620 — **Scorers:** Evans. **Booked:** Bell
25th	●	Port Vale	h	L 0–2	Att: 2,267
28th	●	Shrewsbury	h	W 3–0	Att: 2,553 — **Scorers:** Brown, Evans, Cansdell-Sherriff OG. **Booked:** Hadfield, Hessey, Yeo

March
3rd	●	Bradford	a	L 1–0	Att: 11,908 — **Booked:** Flynn
7th	●	Darlington	a	W 1–2	Att: 2,995 — **Scorers:** Evans². **Booked:** Flynn, Morgan, Brown
10th	●	Accrington S	a	L 0–2	Att: 1,746 — **Booked:** Hadfield
14th	●	Bournemouth	h	L 0–2	Att: 1,589 — **Booked:** Hadfield
21st	●	Luton	a	L 1–0	Att: 5,363 — **Booked:** Sinclair, Bell, Rooney, Flynn
28th	●	Dag & Red	h	L 2–1	Att: 1,347 — **Scorers:** Rooney. **Booked:** Bell, Deen, Daniel
31st	●	Lincoln City	a	L 1–0	Att: 2,478 — **Booked:** Hadfield, Evans

April
4th	●	Chesterfield	h	D 1–1	Att: 2,276 — **Scorers:** Evans
11th	●	Chester	a	W 0–2	Att: 2,248 — **Scorers:** Evans, Rooney
13th	●	Morecambe	h	L 0–1	Att: 1,773
18th	●	Bury	a	L 3–0	Att: 3,499 — **Booked:** Tolley
25th	●	Barnet	h	W 2–1	Att: 1,619 — **Scorers:** Brown, Dennis. **Booked:** Bell

May
2nd	●	Grimsby	a	D 0–0	Att: 6,876

● Coca-Cola League 2/Play-Offs ● FA Cup ● Carling Cup ● Johnstone's Paint Trophy

LEAGUE TWO GOALKEEPER STATS

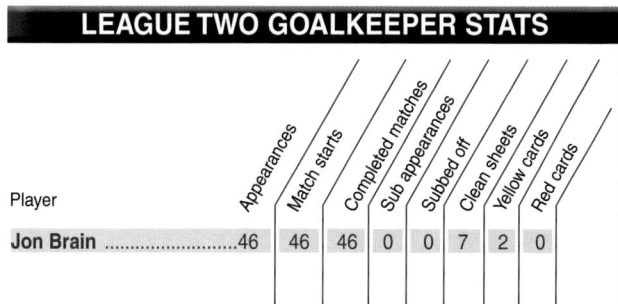

Player	Appearances	Match starts	Completed matches	Sub appearances	Subbed off	Clean sheets	Yellow cards	Red cards
Jon Brain	46	46	46	0	0	7	2	0

LEAGUE TWO OUTFIELD PLAYER STATS

Player	Appearances	Match starts	Completed matches	Substitute appearances	Subbed off	Goals scored	Yellow cards	Red cards
Rikki Bains	2	1	1	1	0	0	0	0
Lee Bell	41	37	28	4	9	1	9	0
Shaun Brisley	38	38	34	0	4	0	2	0
Nathaniel Brown	30	29	28	1	1	6	2	0
Colin Daniel	8	8	4	0	4	0	1	0
Ahmed Deen	28	19	18	9	1	0	1	0
Kristian Dennis	3	0	0	3	0	1	0	0
Terry Dunfield	20	19	18	1	1	1	4	0
Tom Elliott	6	4	1	2	3	0	1	0
Gareth Evans	40	35	22	5	11	12	4	2
Matthew Flynn	28	23	17	5	5	0	8	1
Kyle Fraser-Allen	2	0	0	2	0	0	0	0
Francis Green	24	9	5	15	3	3	0	1
Martin Gritton	21	13	8	8	5	5	2	0
Jordan Hadfield	16	14	10	2	4	0	4	0
Neil Harvey	5	0	0	5	0	0	1	0
Sean Hessey	33	29	20	4	9	0	4	0
James Jennings	18	13	5	5	7	0	3	1
Patrece Liburd	1	1	1	0	0	0	0	0
Clayton McDonald	2	2	0	0	2	0	0	0
Christian Millar	2	0	0	2	0	0	0	0
Paul Morgan	39	38	35	1	3	1	2	0
Vinny Mukendi	1	0	0	1	0	0	0	0
Izak Reid	38	30	27	8	3	2	0	0
John Rooney	14	10	7	4	3	2	1	0
Emile Sinclair	17	14	6	3	8	1	3	0
Danny Thomas	40	24	12	16	12	2	1	0
Jamie Tolley	16	14	9	2	5	0	2	0
Richard Walker	15	14	12	1	2	0	3	0
Simon Yeo	33	22	6	11	16	7	2	0

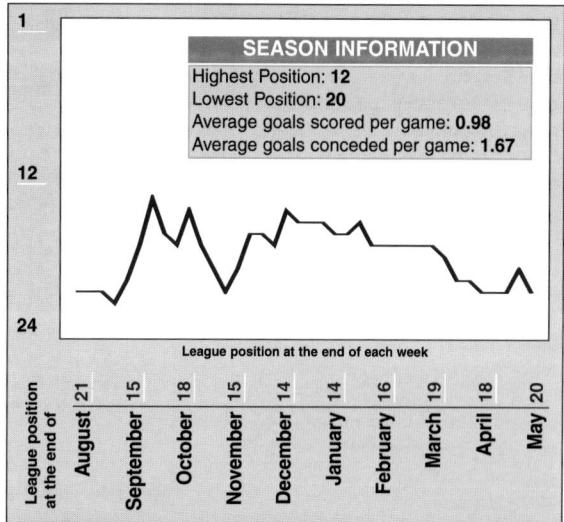

SEASON INFORMATION
Highest Position: **12**
Lowest Position: **20**
Average goals scored per game: **0.98**
Average goals conceded per game: **1.67**

League position at the end of each week

LONGEST SEQUENCES

Wins (06/09/08–20/09/08)	3	Undefeated home (28/12/08–27/01/09)	3
Losses (10/03/09–31/03/09)	5	Undefeated away (18/10/08–22/11/08)	3
Draws (–)		Without scoring (on two occasions)	4
Undefeated (28/12/08–27/01/09)	4	Without conceding (24/01/09–27/01/09)	2
Without win (27/01/09–25/02/09)	7	Scoring (on three occasions)	4

CARDS RECEIVED

62   **5**

QUICK-FIRE GOALS
From the start of a match
Gareth Evans (v Bournemouth) 1:05

By a substitute after coming on
Francis Green (v Aldershot) 9:12

GOALS SCORED/CONCEDED PER FIVE-MINUTE INTERVALS

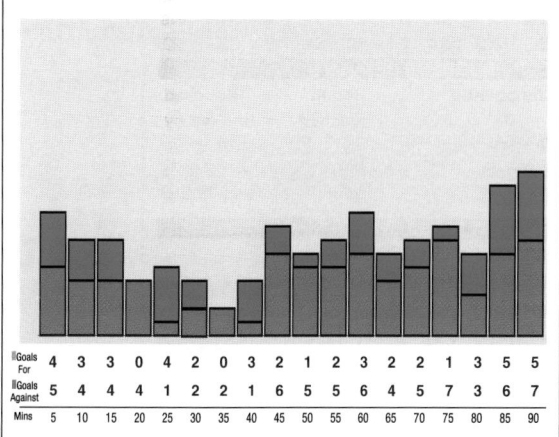

Goals For	4	3	0	0	4	2	0	3	2	1	2	3	2	2	1	3	5	5
Goals Against	5	4	4	1	2	2	1	6	5	5	6	4	5	7	3	6	7
Mins	5	10	15	20	25	30	35	40	45	50	55	60	65	70	75	80	85	90

MORECAMBE

IT WAS a season of promise at Morecambe, with boss Sammy McIlroy sowing the seeds for a potential promotion push next term.

The pre-season priority of assuring survival was easily surpassed by the Shrimps' creditable 11th-place finish, while an exceptional end-of-season run of one defeat in 17 even had the Morecambe faithful daring to dream of a late surge towards the play-offs.

Fired by the goals of Stuart Drummond and on-loan Peterborough striker Rene Howe, as well as the resolute leadership of fans' favourite and captain Jim Bentley, McIlroy's men have established themselves in the League. However, the Shrimps' progress now depends on squad-strengthening in the summer transfer market as well as the completion of an all-new stadium at Westgate in time for the club's 2010/11 campaign.

CLUB SUMMARY

FORMED	1920
MANAGER	Sammy McIlroy
GROUND	Christie Park
CAPACITY	6,400
NICKNAME	The Shrimps
WEBSITE	www.morecambefc.com

The New Football Pools PLAYER OF THE SEASON — Barry Roche

OVERALL

P	W	D	L	F	A	GD
52	16	20	16	59	67	-8

COCA-COLA FOOTBALL LEAGUE TWO

Pos	P	W	D	L	F	A	GD	Pts
11	46	15	18	13	53	56	-3	63

HOME

Pos	P	W	D	L	F	A	GD	Pts
14	23	9	9	5	29	24	5	36

AWAY

Pos	P	W	D	L	F	A	GD	Pts
13	23	6	9	8	24	32	-8	27

CUP PROGRESS DETAILS

Competition	Round reached	Knocked out by
FA Cup	R2	Cheltenham
JP Trophy	FLTNQ	Tranmere
Carling Cup	R1	Nottm Forest

BIGGEST WIN (ALL COMPS)

26/12/08 4–1 v Macclesfield **FL2**

BIGGEST DEFEAT (ALL COMPS)

11/10/08 0–5 v Gillingham **FL2**

ATTENDANCE RECORD

High	Low	Average
4,546	1,253	2,153
v Bradford (10/04/2009)	v Brentford (03/02/2009)	

RESULTS 2008/09

August
9th	● Wycombe	a	D 1–1	**Att:** 4,021 — **Scorers:** Artell
13th	● Nottm Forest	a	L 4–0	**Att:** 4,030 — **Booked:** Howe, McLachlan
16th	● Rotherham	h	L 1–3	**Att:** 2,606 — **Scorers:** Wainwright
23rd	● Bury	a	L 2–1	**Att:** 2,679 — **Scorers:** Howe. **Booked:** Blinkhorn, McStay
30th	● Dag & Red	h	L 1–2	**Att:** 1,571 — **Scorers:** O'Carroll

September
2nd	● Oldham	a	D 1–1	**Att:** 2,016 — **Scorers:** Drummond (Won 5–4 on pens)
6th	● Shrewsbury	h	W 1–0	**Att:** 2,318 — **Scorers:** Howe. **Booked:** McCann
13th	● Barnet	a	D 1–1	**Att:** 1,776 — **Scorers:** O'Carroll. **Booked:** Howe, McCann, Artell
20th	● Grimsby	h	D 1–1	**Att:** 1,989 — **Scorers:** Curtis. **Booked:** O'Carroll
27th	● Lincoln City	a	D 1–1	**Att:** 5,003 — **Scorers:** Stanley. **Booked:** McCann, Howe

October
4th	● Chesterfield	h	D 2–2	**Att:** 1,734 — **Scorers:** Drummond, Howe
7th	● Chester	a	D 1–1	**Att:** 926 — **Scorers:** Howe. **Booked:** Artell (Won 3–1 on pens)
11th	● Gillingham	a	L 5–0	**Att:** 4,316 — **Booked:** McCann
18th	● Rochdale	h	D 1–1	**Att:** 2,572 — **Scorers:** Taylor. **Booked:** Howe
21st	● Brentford	a	L 3–1	**Att:** 3,733 — **Scorers:** Drummond
25th	● Port Vale	a	L 2–1	**Att:** 5,629 — **Scorers:** Bentley. **Booked:** McStay
28th	● Accrington S	h	D 1–1	**Att:** 2,044 — **Scorers:** Stanley

November
1st	● Aldershot	h	W 2–0	**Att:** 1,897 — **Scorers:** Drummond, McGivern. **Booked:** McStay
4th	● Tranmere	a	L 1–0	**Att:** 2,110
8th	● Grimsby	h	W 2–1	**Att:** 1,713 — **Scorers:** Taylor². **Booked:** McCann
15th	● Chester	a	W 1–2	**Att:** 1,647 — **Scorers:** Howe, Stanley. **Booked:** Adams. **Dismissed:** Adams
22nd	● Exeter	h	D 1–1	**Att:** 2,003 — **Scorers:** Howe. **Booked:** Carlton, McStay
25th	● Bournemouth	a	D 0–0	**Att:** 3,068 — **Booked:** Adams
29th	● Cheltenham	h	A –A	**Att:** 1,984 — **Scorers:** Howe. **Booked:** McCann. (Abandoned due to fog after 65 mis)

December
2nd	● Cheltenham	h	L 2–3	**Att:** 1,758 — **Scorers:** Howe, McStay. **Booked:** McLachlan
6th	● Notts County	a	L 1–0	**Att:** 3,671 — **Booked:** McLachlan, McCann
13th	● Darlington	h	W 1–0	**Att:** 1,873 — **Scorers:** Howe. **Booked:** Carlton, Bentley
20th	● Luton	a	D 1–1	**Att:** 5,664 — **Scorers:** Carlton. **Booked:** Carlton
26th	● Macclesfield	h	W 4–1	**Att:** 2,578 — **Scorers:** Carlton, Drummond, Howe, McStay. **Booked:** Drummond, Carlton
28th	● Bradford	a	L 4–0	**Att:** 13,105 — **Booked:** Drummond

January
17th	● Gillingham	h	L 0–1	**Att:** 2,027 — **Booked:** Bentley
24th	● Chesterfield	a	W 1–2	**Att:** 3,283 — **Scorers:** Howe, Stanley
27th	● Accrington S	a	L 1–0	**Att:** 1,407 — **Booked:** McLachlan, Wainwright
31st	● Port Vale	h	D 1–1	**Att:** 1,823 — **Scorers:** Stanley. **Booked:** Drummond

February
3rd	● Brentford	h	W 2–0	**Att:** 1,253 — **Scorers:** Howe, Twiss. **Booked:** Bentley, Howe
10th	● Lincoln City	h	D 1–1	**Att:** 1,471 — **Scorers:** Bentley
14th	● Chester	h	W 3–1	**Att:** 1,795 — **Scorers:** Curtis², Taylor
17th	● Rochdale	a	D 1–1	**Att:** 3,347 — **Scorers:** Twiss. **Booked:** Bentley
21st	● Aldershot	a	W 0–2	**Att:** 2,872 — **Scorers:** Curtis, Drummond. **Booked:** Twiss, Wainwright, Hunter
24th	● Grimsby	a	W 2–3	**Att:** 2,644 — **Scorers:** Hunter, O'Carroll, Twiss. **Booked:** Twiss, Duffy
28th	● Wycombe	h	D 0–0	**Att:** 2,005 — **Booked:** Hunter

March
7th	● Dag & Red	a	W 0–2	**Att:** 1,403 — **Scorers:** Drummond, O'Carroll. **Booked:** Wainwright
10th	● Bury	h	D 0–0	**Att:** 2,165
14th	● Barnet	h	W 2–1	**Att:** 1,899 — **Scorers:** Artell, Curtis
21st	● Shrewsbury	a	D 0–0	**Att:** 5,426 — **Booked:** Hunter, Howe
28th	● Luton	h	L 1–2	**Att:** 2,599 — **Scorers:** Drummond

April
4th	● Darlington	a	D 0–0	**Att:** 2,560 — **Booked:** Adams, Hunter
10th	● Bradford	h	W 2–1	**Att:** 4,546 — **Scorers:** Drummond, Howe. **Booked:** Artell, Curtis, Yates, Howe
13th	● Macclesfield	a	W 0–1	**Att:** 1,773 — **Scorers:** Artell
18th	● Notts County	h	W 1–0	**Att:** 2,161 — **Scorers:** Duffy. **Booked:** Adams, Twiss
21st	● Rotherham	a	L 3–2	**Att:** 2,078 — **Scorers:** Bentley, O'Carroll. **Booked:** Howe
25th	● Exeter	a	D 2–2	**Att:** 8,544 — **Scorers:** Drummond²

May
2nd	● Bournemouth	h	L 0–4	**Att:** 2,601

● Coca-Cola League 2/Play-Offs ● FA Cup ● Carling Cup ● Johnstone's Paint Trophy

352 OFFICIAL FOOTBALL YEARBOOK OF THE ENGLISH & SCOTTISH LEAGUES 2009–2010

LEAGUE TWO GOALKEEPER STATS

Player	Appearances	Match starts	Completed matches	Sub appearances	Subbed off	Clean sheets	Yellow cards	Red cards
Barry Roche	46	46	46	0	0	13	0	0

LEAGUE TWO OUTFIELD PLAYER STATS

Player	Appearances	Match starts	Completed matches	Substitute appearances	Subbed off	Goals scored	Yellow cards	Red cards
Danny Adams	39	39	37	0	1	0	4	1
David Artell	37	35	35	2	0	3	2	0
Jim Bentley	45	45	44	0	1	3	4	0
Matthew Blinkhorn	11	5	4	6	1	0	1	0
Danny Carlton	8	8	6	0	2	2	4	0
Michael Carr	7	4	1	3	3	0	0	0
Wayne Curtis	32	23	20	9	3	5	1	0
Stuart Drummond	44	41	38	3	3	10	3	0
Mark Duffy	9	4	4	5	0	1	1	0
Rene Howe	37	35	29	2	6	10	7	0
Garry Hunter	29	23	19	6	4	1	4	0
Ryan McCann	13	11	8	2	3	0	5	0
Ryan McGivern	5	5	4	0	1	1	0	0
Fraser McLachlan	27	21	12	6	9	0	2	0
Henry McStay	20	17	15	3	2	1	4	0
Diarmuid O'Carroll	29	15	7	14	8	5	1	0
Andy Parrish	13	10	9	3	1	0	0	0
Dan Smith	2	0	0	2	0	0	0	0
Craig Stanley	24	22	20	2	2	5	0	0
Aaron Taylor	17	7	0	10	8	2	0	0
Michael Twiss	28	26	17	2	9	3	3	0
Neil Wainwright	38	32	15	6	17	1	3	0
Adam Yates	32	32	30	0	2	0	1	0

SEASON INFORMATION

Highest Position: **10**
Lowest Position: **20**
Average goals scored per game: **1.15**
Average goals conceded per game: **1.22**

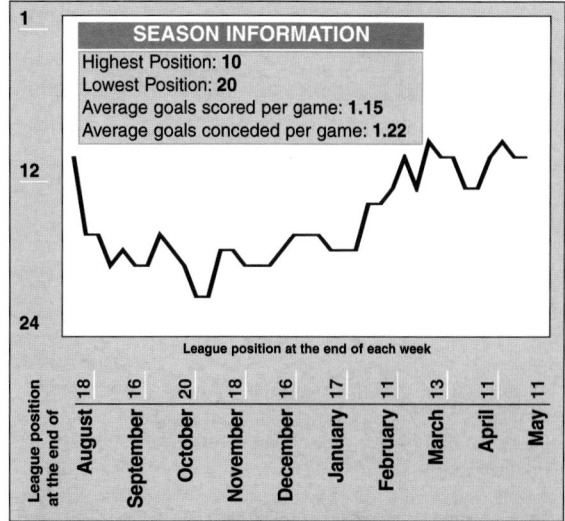

League position at the end of each week

LONGEST SEQUENCES

Wins	3		Undefeated home	9
(10/04/09–18/04/09)			(06/09/08–26/12/08)	
Losses	3		Undefeated away	7
(16/08/08–30/08/08)			(17/02/09–13/04/09)	
Draws	4		Without scoring	2
(13/09/08–04/10/08)			(on two occasions)	
Undefeated	12		Without conceding	3
(31/01/09–21/03/09)			(28/02/09–10/03/09)	
Without win	9		Scoring	9
(13/09/08–28/10/08)			(09/08/08–04/10/08)	

CARDS RECEIVED

50 **1**

QUICK-FIRE GOALS

From the start of a match
Rene Howe (v Shrewsbury) 3:09

By a substitute after coming on
Diarmuid O'Carroll (v Dag & Red) 1:21

GOALS SCORED/CONCEDED PER FIVE-MINUTE INTERVALS

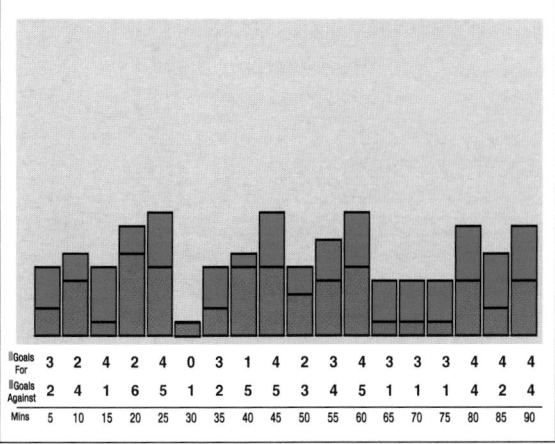

Goals For	3	2	4	2	4	0	3	1	4	2	3	4	3	3	3	4	4	4
Goals Against	2	4	1	6	5	1	2	5	5	3	4	5	1	1	1	4	2	4
Mins	5	10	15	20	25	30	35	40	45	50	55	60	65	70	75	80	85	90

IAN McPARLAND'S first full season in charge brought little improvement. After finishing fourth-bottom of the League in 2007/08, they were better by two places this season, but collected fewer points.

Elimination from the FA Cup at the hands of non-League Kettering in a second-round replay was probably the low point of the season.

Arguably the high point came in just the second game of the campaign when they knocked Coca-Cola Championship newcomers Doncaster out of the League Cup.

Perhaps the news that the club will have a training ground for the first time in their 147-year history in 2009/10 will improve their fortunes. Wholesale changes were expected over the summer with Adam Tann, Richard Butcher, Adam Nowland, Gavin Strachan and Jamie Forrester set to be released.

CLUB SUMMARY

FORMED	1862
MANAGER	Ian McParland
GROUND	Meadow Lane
CAPACITY	20,300
NICKNAME	The Magpies
WEBSITE	www.nottscountyfc.co.uk

The New **Football Pools** PLAYER OF THE SEASON — **Matthew Hamshaw**

OVERALL
P	W	D	L	F	A	GD
52	13	15	24	54	78	-24

COCA-COLA FOOTBALL LEAGUE TWO
Pos	P	W	D	L	F	A	GD	Pts
19	46	11	14	21	49	69	-20	47

HOME
Pos	P	W	D	L	F	A	GD	Pts
22	23	6	6	11	22	31	-9	24

AWAY
Pos	P	W	D	L	F	A	GD	Pts
17	23	5	8	10	27	38	-11	23

CUP PROGRESS DETAILS
Competition	Round reached	Knocked out by
FA Cup	R2	Kettering
JP Trophy	R1	Scunthorpe
Carling Cup	R2	Wigan

BIGGEST WIN (ALL COMPS)
15/11/08 4–0 v Barnet **FL2**

BIGGEST DEFEAT (ALL COMPS)
22/11/08 1–6 v Dag & Red **FL2**

ATTENDANCE RECORD
High	Low	Average
6,686	2,886	4,446

v Rotherham (28/12/2008)   v Luton (10/03/2009)

RESULTS 2008/09

August
9th	● Bradford	a	L 2–1	Att: 14,038 — Scorers: Butcher. Booked: Canham
12th	● Doncaster	h	W 1–0	Att: 3,272 — Scorers: Weston. Booked: MacKenzie (AET)
16th	● Darlington	h	D 0–0	Att: 4,352
23rd	● Luton	a	D 1–1	Att: 6,085 — Scorers: Forrester. Booked: Johnson
26th	● Wigan	a	L 4–0	Att: 4,100
30th	● Shrewsbury	h	D 2–2	Att: 4,697 — Scorers: Butcher, Edwards

September
2nd	● Scunthorpe	a	L 2–1	Att: 1,755 — Scorers: Butcher
6th	● Bournemouth	h	D 1–1	Att: 4,362 — Scorers: Forrester. Booked: Mayo, Smith, Butcher, Johnson
13th	● Accrington S	a	D 1–1	Att: 1,404 — Scorers: Canham. Booked: Smith, Mayo
20th	● Exeter	a	D 2–2	Att: 4,341 — Scorers: Canham, Johnson
27th	● Aldershot	h	W 2–1	Att: 6,033 — Scorers: Butcher, Johnson

October
4th	● Port Vale	a	W 1–2	Att: 6,247 — Scorers: Forrester, Weston. Booked: Johnson
13th	● Brentford	h	D 1–1	Att: 6,012 — Scorers: Forrester
18th	● Macclesfield	h	D 1–1	Att: 4,600 — Scorers: Facey
21st	● Gillingham	a	D 2–2	Att: 4,396 — Scorers: Butcher, Facey. Booked: Smith
25th	● Chesterfield	a	L 3–1	Att: 4,134 — Scorers: Facey. Booked: Nowland
28th	● Rochdale	h	L 1–2	Att: 3,610 — Scorers: Forrester. Booked: Smith

November
1st	● Bury	h	L 0–1	Att: 4,391
8th	● Sutton Utd	a	W 0–1	Att: 2,041 — Scorers: Butcher. Booked: Edwards, Neal
15th	● Barnet	a	W 0–4	Att: 1,934 — Scorers: Butcher, Forte[3]. Booked: Weston, Thompson
22nd	● Dag & Red	a	L 6–1	Att: 1,743 — Scorers: Forte. Booked: Thompson, Beardsley
25th	● Wycombe	h	L 0–2	Att: 2,964
30th	● Kettering	h	D 1–1	Att: 4,451 — Scorers: Canham

December
6th	● Morecambe	h	W 1–0	Att: 3,671 — Scorers: Canham. Booked: Clapham, Thompson
10th	● Kettering	a	L 2–1	Att: 3,019 — Scorers: Smith. Booked: Thompson
13th	● Chester	a	L 2–0	Att: 1,767 — Booked: Johnson, Hanson. Dismissed: Forrester
20th	● Lincoln City	h	L 0–1	Att: 4,568 — Booked: Johnson
26th	● Grimsby	a	W 0–1	Att: 5,432 — Scorers: Facey. Booked: Johnson, Hanson, Canham, Thompson
28th	● Rotherham	h	L 0–3	Att: 6,686

January
10th	● Exeter	h	W 2–1	Att: 3,832 — Scorers: Facey, Strachan
17th	● Brentford	a	D 1–1	Att: 5,465 — Scorers: Johnson, Weston, Thompson, Pilkington
20th	● Aldershot	a	D 2–2	Att: 2,491 — Scorers: Clapham, Hamshaw. Booked: Hunt, Hamshaw
24th	● Port Vale	h	W 4–2	Att: 4,447 — Scorers: Forrester[3], Weston. Booked: Hamshaw
27th	● Rochdale	a	L 3–0	Att: 2,289 — Booked: Wedderburn, Nowland
31st	● Chesterfield	h	L 0–1	Att: 4,953 — Booked: Thompson

February
14th	● Barnet	h	W 2–0	Att: 3,830 — Scorers: Clapham, Hamshaw
17th	● Macclesfield	a	D 1–1	Att: 1,370 — Scorers: Hamshaw. Booked: Picken
21st	● Bury	a	L 2–0	Att: 2,810 — Booked: Hamshaw
28th	● Bradford	h	W 3–1	Att: 5,138 — Scorers: Facey, Forte[2]. Booked: Forte, Thompson

March
3rd	● Darlington	a	L 1–0	Att: 2,450 — Booked: Tann, Edwards, Picken
7th	● Shrewsbury	a	L 3–2	Att: 5,192 — Scorers: Butcher, Forte. Booked: Clapham, Facey
10th	● Luton	h	L 0–2	Att: 2,886 — Booked: Picken
14th	● Accrington S	h	D 1–1	Att: 3,701 — Scorers: Facey
17th	● Gillingham	h	L 0–1	Att: 3,189 — Booked: Edwards
21st	● Bournemouth	a	W 0–1	Att: 5,510 — Scorers: Weston. Booked: Weston, Thompson
28th	● Lincoln City	a	D 1–1	Att: 4,027 — Scorers: Facey

April
4th	● Chester	h	L 1–2	Att: 4,025 — Scorers: Edwards
11th	● Rotherham	a	L 2–1	Att: 2,945 — Scorers: Forte. Booked: Hamshaw, Picken
13th	● Grimsby	h	L 0–2	Att: 5,890 — Booked: Thompson, Johnson
18th	● Morecambe	a	L 1–0	Att: 2,161 — Booked: Thompson
25th	● Dag & Red	h	L 0–3	Att: 4,419 — Booked: Johnson

May
2nd	● Wycombe	a	W 1–2	Att: 9,625 — Scorers: Thompson[2]

● Coca-Cola League 2/Play-Offs ● FA Cup ● Carling Cup ● Johnstone's Paint Trophy

LEAGUE TWO GOALKEEPER STATS

Player	Appearances	Match starts	Completed matches	Sub appearances	Subbed off	Clean sheets	Yellow cards	Red cards
Russell Hoult	16	16	16	0	0	2	0	0
Josh Lillis	5	5	5	0	0	1	0	0
Kevin Pilkington	25	25	25	0	0	3	1	0

LEAGUE TWO OUTFIELD PLAYER STATS

Player	Appearances	Match starts	Completed matches	Substitute appearances	Subbed off	Goals scored	Yellow cards	Red cards
Jason Beardsley	11	11	10	0	1	0	1	0
Richard Butcher	34	29	27	5	2	6	1	0
Sean Canham	23	7	3	16	4	3	2	0
Jamie Clapham	40	40	37	0	3	2	2	0
Mike Edwards	43	42	41	1	1	2	2	0
Delroy Facey	45	44	38	1	6	9	1	0
Ben Fairclough	8	2	0	6	2	0	0	0
Jamie Forrester	30	27	5	3	21	8	0	1
Jonathan Forte	18	15	14	3	1	8	1	0
Matthew Hamshaw	41	39	33	2	6	3	4	0
Mitchell Hanson	5	5	3	0	2	0	2	0
Stephen Hunt	11	8	8	3	0	0	1	0
Michael Johnson	29	29	21	0	8	2	9	0
Neil MacKenzie	1	0	0	1	0	0	0	0
Paul Mayo	12	10	9	2	1	0	2	0
Lewis Neal	4	4	4	0	0	0	0	0
Adam Nowland	20	16	6	4	10	0	2	0
Phil Picken	22	22	21	0	1	0	4	0
Matt Richards	1	0	0	1	0	0	0	0
Jay Smith	13	6	5	7	1	0	4	0
Gavin Strachan	18	13	6	5	7	1	0	0
Adam Tann	14	9	7	5	2	0	1	0
John Thompson	35	35	35	0	0	2	10	0
Nathaniel Wedderburn	9	3	1	6	2	0	1	0
Spencer Weir-Daley	10	0	0	10	0	0	0	0
Myles Weston	44	44	44	0	0	3	3	0

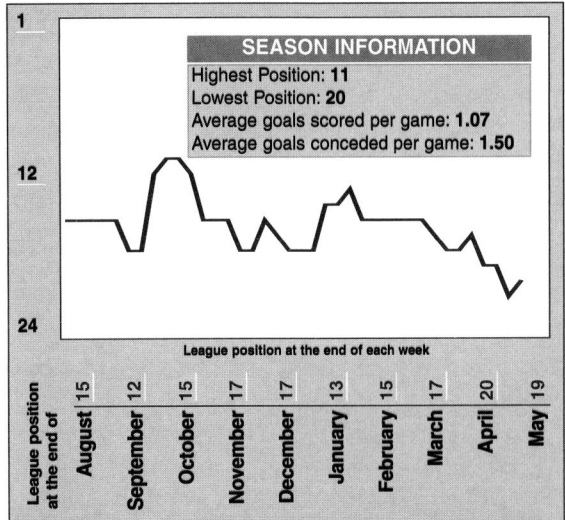

SEASON INFORMATION
Highest Position: **11**
Lowest Position: **20**
Average goals scored per game: **1.07**
Average goals conceded per game: **1.50**

League position at the end of each week

LONGEST SEQUENCES

Wins (27/09/08–04/10/08)	2	Undefeated home (16/08/08–18/10/08)	6
Losses (04/04/09–25/04/09)	5	Undefeated away (23/08/08–21/10/08)	5
Draws (16/08/08–20/09/08)	6	Without scoring (13/04/09–25/04/09)	3
Undefeated (16/08/08–21/10/08)	11	Without conceding (–)	
Without win (09/08/08–20/09/08)	7	Scoring (23/08/08–28/10/08)	12

CARDS RECEIVED

54   1

QUICK-FIRE GOALS

From the start of a match
Jamie Forrester (v Port Vale) 5:13

By a substitute after coming on
Sean Canham (v Accrington S) 11:44

GOALS SCORED/CONCEDED PER FIVE-MINUTE INTERVALS

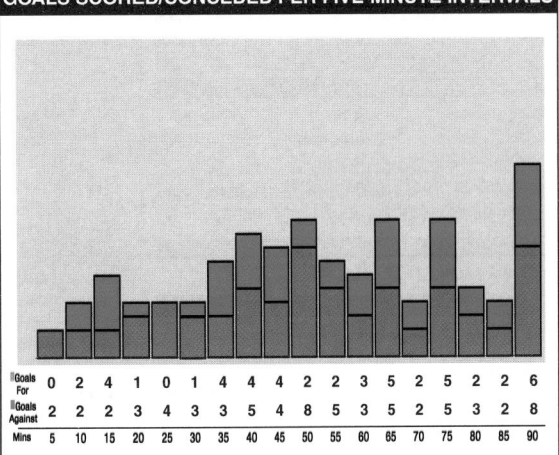

Goals For	0	2	4	1	0	1	4	4	4	2	2	3	5	2	5	2	2	6
Goals Against	2	2	2	3	4	3	3	5	4	8	5	3	5	2	5	3	2	8
Mins	5	10	15	20	25	30	35	40	45	50	55	60	65	70	75	80	85	90

PORT VALE

THE 2008/09 campaign was a season to forget for Port Vale fans.

Having been relegated in 2007/08, hopes of an immediate return to Coca-Cola League One were high, highlighted by the sale of more than 6,000 season tickets. However, it was soon clear that promotion was not a realistic ambition.

After losing six of their opening nine games, manager Lee Sinnott was sacked. Assistant Dean Glover was appointed until the end of the season, much to the anger of some Vale fans.

Glover secured what was asked of him – survival – with Vale finishing in 18th position. But a series of poor performances resulted in the club looking elsewhere for a permanent boss, with Micky Adams taking over in June.

With the possibility of new investment coming in, and Adams at the helm, optimism will again be rife when 2009/10 begins.

CLUB SUMMARY

FORMED	1876
MANAGER	Micky Adams
GROUND	Vale Park
CAPACITY	18,982
NICKNAME	The Valiants
WEBSITE	www.port-vale.co.uk

The New Football Pools PLAYER OF THE SEASON — Joe Anyon

OVERALL

P	W	D	L	F	A	GD
50	14	9	27	50	76	-26

COCA-COLA FOOTBALL LEAGUE TWO

Pos	P	W	D	L	F	A	GD	Pts
18	46	13	9	24	44	66	-22	48

HOME

Pos	P	W	D	L	F	A	GD	Pts
23	23	6	6	11	23	33	-10	24

AWAY

Pos	P	W	D	L	F	A	GD	Pts
16	23	7	3	13	21	33	-12	24

CUP PROGRESS DETAILS

Competition	Round reached	Knocked out by
FA Cup	R2	Macclesfield
JP Trophy	R1	Stockport
Carling Cup	R1	Sheffield Utd

BIGGEST WIN (ALL COMPS)

27/01/09 3–0 v Chester **FL2**

BIGGEST DEFEAT (ALL COMPS)

20/09/08 1–4 v Macclesfield **FL2**

ATTENDANCE RECORD

High	Low	Average
7,273	4,090	5,522
v Bradford (06/09/2008)	v Dag & Red (10/03/2009)	

RESULTS 2008/09

August
9th	● Luton	a W 1–3	Att: 7,149 — **Scorers:** Dodds, Richards, Taylor. **Booked:** Dodds
13th	● Sheff Utd	a L 3–1	Att: 7,694 — **Scorers:** Rodgers. **Booked:** Stockley
16th	● Accrington S	h L 0–2	Att: 6,643 — **Booked:** Taylor
23rd	● Dag & Red	a D 1–1	Att: 1,843 — **Scorers:** Richards. **Booked:** Stockley, Griffith. **Dismissed:** Stockley
30th	● Bournemouth	h W 3–1	Att: 6,048 — **Scorers:** McCombe, Richards, Richman. **Booked:** Richards

September
2nd	● Stockport	a L 1–0	Att: 2,290 — **Booked:** Perry, Prosser, McCombe, Taylor, Griffith
6th	● Bradford	h L 0–2	Att: 7,273 — **Booked:** Howland
13th	● Darlington	a L 2–1	Att: 3,040 — **Scorers:** Rodgers. **Booked:** Richman, Prosser, Collins
20th	● Macclesfield	h L 1–4	Att: 6,645 — **Scorers:** Dodds. **Booked:** Howland, Prosser
27th	● Gillingham	a L 1–0	Att: 4,986 — **Booked:** Prosser

October
4th	● Notts County	h L 1–2	Att: 6,247 — **Scorers:** Rodgers
11th	● Shrewsbury	a W 1–2	Att: 7,162 — **Scorers:** Dodds, Richards. **Booked:** Davidson, Collins, Griffith, Edwards, Howland, Anyon
19th	● Chester	a W 1–2	Att: 3,102 — **Scorers:** Richards, Richman. **Booked:** Richards
21st	● Exeter	h L 1–3	Att: 5,493 — **Scorers:** Rodgers. **Booked:** Howland
25th	● Morecambe	h W 2–1	Att: 5,629 — **Scorers:** Richards, Rodgers
28th	● Aldershot	a L 1–0	Att: 3,039

November
1st	● Lincoln City	a W 0–1	Att: 4,793 — **Scorers:** Howland. **Booked:** Richards, Prosser, Edwards
8th	● Huddersfield	a W 3–4	Att: 6,942 — **Scorers:** Dodds[2], Howland, Richards. **Booked:** McCrory, Dodds, Glover
15th	● Brentford	h L 0–3	Att: 6,058 — **Booked:** Richards. **Dismissed:** Davidson
22nd	● Wycombe	a L 4–2	Att: 4,521 — **Scorers:** Brown, Richards. **Booked:** Prosser, Edwards, Dodds
25th	● Barnet	h D 0–0	Att: 4,617 — **Booked:** Glover
28th	● Macclesfield	h L 1–3	Att: 4,684 — **Scorers:** Dodds. **Booked:** Griffith

December
6th	● Grimsby	h W 2–1	Att: 5,058 — **Scorers:** Richards, Richman
13th	● Bury	a L 3–0	Att: 2,651 — **Booked:** Richman, Glover, Stockley
20th	● Chesterfield	h L 0–1	Att: 5,011 — **Booked:** Owen, Davidson, Dodds. **Dismissed:** Richards
26th	● Rotherham	h L 0–2	Att: 4,350
28th	● Rochdale	h W 2–1	Att: 5,720 — **Scorers:** Glover, Thompson. **Booked:** Glover. **Dismissed:** Glover

January
17th	● Shrewsbury	h D 1–1	Att: 7,068 — **Scorers:** Thompson. **Booked:** McCombe, Griffith, Prosser. **Dismissed:** Perry
20th	● Gillingham	h L 1–3	Att: 4,539 — **Scorers:** Richards. **Booked:** Dodds
24th	● Notts County	a L 4–2	Att: 4,447 — **Scorers:** Dodds, Richman. **Booked:** Edwards
27th	● Chester	h W 3–0	Att: 4,448 — **Scorers:** Glover, Lawrie, Taylor. **Booked:** Howland
31st	● Morecambe	a D 1–1	Att: 1,823 — **Scorers:** Richman. **Booked:** Edwards

February
14th	● Brentford	a L 2–0	Att: 4,702 — **Booked:** Ahmed, Prosser
20th	● Lincoln City	h L 0–1	Att: 5,097 — **Booked:** Ahmed
25th	● Macclesfield	a W 0–2	Att: 2,267 — **Scorers:** Ahmed, Dodds
28th	● Luton	h L 1–3	Att: 5,689 — **Scorers:** McCombe. **Booked:** Ahmed

March
7th	● Bournemouth	a D 0–0	Att: 5,924 — **Booked:** McCombe
10th	● Dag & Red	h L 0–1	Att: 4,090 — **Booked:** Griffith
14th	● Darlington	h W 3–1	Att: 4,860 — **Scorers:** Dodds, Richards, Taylor. **Booked:** Griffith
17th	● Accrington S	a L 2–0	Att: 1,144 — **Booked:** Edwards
21st	● Bradford	a W 0–1	Att: 12,436 — **Scorers:** Howland. **Booked:** Griffith, Howland, Prosser, Edwards
28th	● Chesterfield	a L 2–1	Att: 3,511 — **Scorers:** Marshall. **Booked:** Stockley
31st	● Exeter	a L 1–0	Att: 4,235 — **Booked:** Prosser, Glover

April
4th	● Bury	h D 1–1	Att: 5,763 — **Scorers:** Lawrie. **Booked:** Marshall, McCombe
7th	● Aldershot	h D 0–0	Att: 4,140
11th	● Rochdale	a L 1–0	Att: 3,100 — **Booked:** Brammer
13th	● Rotherham	h D 0–0	Att: 4,814
18th	● Grimsby	a L 3–0	Att: 6,511
25th	● Wycombe	h D 1–1	Att: 6,047 — **Scorers:** Collins. **Booked:** Stockley, Taylor, Edwards, Collins

May
2nd	● Barnet	a W 1–2	Att: 2,305 — **Scorers:** Dodds, Glover

● Coca-Cola League 2/Play-Offs ● FA Cup ● Carling Cup ● Johnstone's Paint Trophy

LEAGUE TWO GOALKEEPER STATS

Player	Appearances	Match starts	Completed matches	Sub appearances	Subbed off	Clean sheets	Yellow cards	Red cards
Joe Anyon	36	36	35	0	1	6	1	0
Chris Martin	11	10	10	1	0	2	0	0

LEAGUE TWO OUTFIELD PLAYER STATS

Player	Appearances	Match starts	Completed matches	Substitute appearances	Subbed off	Goals scored	Yellow cards	Red cards
Adnan Ahmed	5	4	3	1	1	1	3	0
David Brammer	13	13	7	0	6	0	1	0
Scott Brown	18	18	13	0	5	1	0	0
Lee Collins	39	39	38	0	0	1	3	1
Ross Davidson	23	15	11	8	3	0	2	1
Louis Dodds	44	37	24	7	13	7	4	0
Paul Edwards	31	29	24	2	5	0	8	0
Kevin Gall	7	7	4	0	3	0	0	0
Danny Glover	23	11	6	12	4	3	4	1
Anthony Griffith	38	37	36	1	1	0	6	0
David Howland	40	35	26	5	9	2	6	0
James Lawrie	18	8	6	10	2	2	0	0
Neil MacKenzie	2	2	1	0	1	0	0	0
Anthony Malbon	1	0	0	1	0	0	0	0
Paul Marshall	13	13	13	0	0	1	1	0
John McCombe	31	30	28	1	2	2	3	0
Damien McCrory	12	10	8	2	2	0	0	0
Gareth Owen	12	12	11	0	1	0	1	0
Kyle Perry	15	9	3	6	5	0	0	1
Luke Prosser	26	24	23	2	1	0	9	0
Marc Richards	30	30	23	0	6	10	4	1
Simon Richman	37	20	8	17	12	5	2	0
Luke Rodgers	15	10	6	5	4	4	0	0
Chris Slater	6	6	6	0	0	0	0	0
Sam Stockley	22	21	19	1	1	0	4	1
Tom Taiwo	4	2	0	2	2	0	0	0
Robert Taylor	20	10	0	10	10	3	2	0
Stephen Thompson	17	5	0	12	5	2	0	0
Shane Tudor	5	3	0	2	3	0	0	0

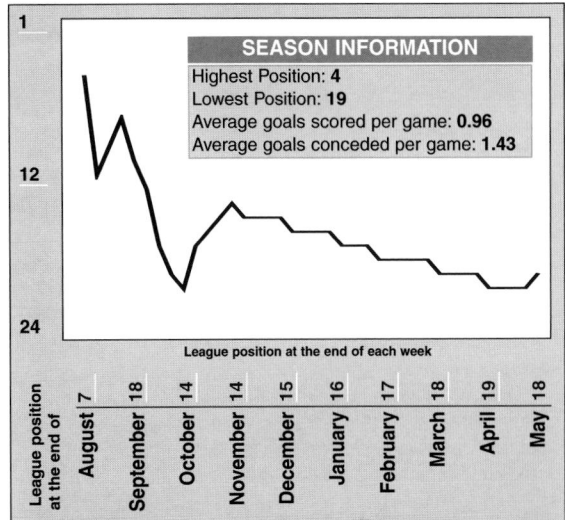

SEASON INFORMATION
Highest Position: **4**
Lowest Position: **19**
Average goals scored per game: **0.96**
Average goals conceded per game: **1.43**

League position at the end of each week

LONGEST SEQUENCES

Wins (11/10/08–19/10/08)	2	Undefeated home (14/03/09–25/04/09)	5
Losses (06/09/08–04/10/08)	5	Undefeated away (on three occasions)	2
Draws (04/04/09–07/04/09)	2	Without scoring (07/04/09–18/04/09)	4
Undefeated (on seven occasions)	2	Without conceding (–)	
Without win (28/03/09–25/04/09)	8	Scoring (28/12/08–31/01/09)	6

CARDS RECEIVED

64 **6**

QUICK-FIRE GOALS

From the start of a match
Marc Richards (v Dag & Red) 6:24

By a substitute after coming on
Louis Dodds (v Macclesfield) 2:59

GOALS SCORED/CONCEDED PER FIVE-MINUTE INTERVALS

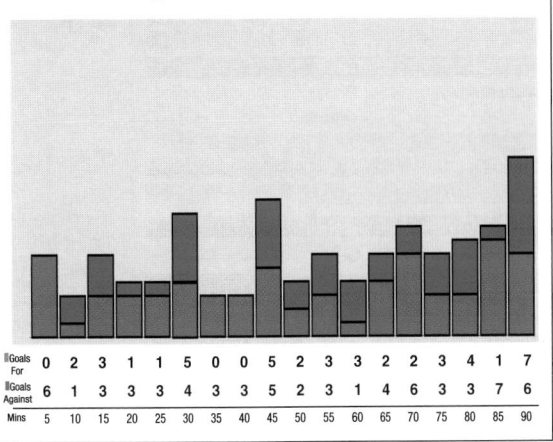

Goals For	0	2	3	1	1	5	0	0	5	2	3	3	2	2	3	4	1	7
Goals Against	6	1	3	3	4	3	3	5	2	3	1	4	6	3	3	7	6	
Mins	5	10	15	20	25	30	35	40	45	50	55	60	65	70	75	80	85	90

ROCHDALE

ROCHDALE'S valiant bid to win their first promotion since 1969 ended in depressingly familiar fashion.

The club, who have resided in the bottom tier longer than any other – since 1974 – will ply their trade there again in 2009/10.

Defeat to Gillingham denied them a second successive Coca-Cola League Two play-off final showdown at Wembley, and left boss Keith Hill searching for answers to many questions.

That Hill has fashioned a talented young side at Spotland is undeniable, but his men again fell just short when it mattered most, and he could now lose key players.

Winger Will Buckley and striker Adam Le Fondre are said to be coveted by higher-placed clubs and could start the new season elsewhere if Dale receive sizeable offers that they cannot afford to turn down.

CLUB SUMMARY

FORMED	1907
MANAGER	Keith Hill
GROUND	Spotland
CAPACITY	10,249
NICKNAME	The Dale
WEBSITE	www.rochdalefc.co.uk

The New Football Pools **PLAYER OF THE SEASON** — **Tom Kennedy**

OVERALL
P	W	D	L	F	A	GD
54	20	17	17	77	69	8

COCA-COLA FOOTBALL LEAGUE TWO
Pos	P	W	D	L	F	A	GD	Pts
6	46	19	13	14	70	59	11	70

HOME
Pos	P	W	D	L	F	A	GD	Pts
9	23	11	6	6	40	24	16	39

AWAY
Pos	P	W	D	L	F	A	GD	Pts
9	23	8	7	8	30	35	-5	31

CUP PROGRESS DETAILS
Competition	Round reached	Knocked out by
FA Cup	R2	Forest Green
JP Trophy	FLTNQ	Scunthorpe
Carling Cup	R1	Oldham

BIGGEST WIN (ALL COMPS)
21/10/08 6–1 v Chester FL2

BIGGEST DEFEAT (ALL COMPS)
04/04/09 0–4 v Bournemouth FL2

ATTENDANCE RECORD
High	Low	Average
5,500	2,162	3,222
v Bradford (10/03/2009)	v Chester (21/10/2008)	

RESULTS 2008/09

August
9th	● Grimsby	a D 0–0	Att: 4,213 — Booked: Stanton, Keltie
12th	● Oldham	h D 0–0	Att: 5,786 — (Lost 4–1 on pens)
16th	● Barnet	h W 3–1	Att: 2,442 — Scorers: Dagnall, Rundle, Shaw. Booked: Rundle
23rd	● Bradford	a L 2–0	Att: 13,154 — Booked: Ramsden, Keltie, Wiseman
30th	● Bury	h D 1–1	Att: 5,492 — Scorers: Le Fondre. Booked: Keltie

September
6th	● Wycombe	h L 0–1	Att: 2,880 — Booked: Stanton
13th	● Rotherham	a D 2–2	Att: 3,569 — Scorers: Buckley, Rhodes. Booked: Keltie. Dismissed: Thorpe
20th	● Chesterfield	h W 2–1	Att: 2,884 — Scorers: Buckley, Kennedy. Booked: McArdle
28th	● Accrington S	a W 1–3	Att: 2,417 — Scorers: Buckley, Le Fondre, Rhodes. Booked: Le Fondre, McArdle

October
4th	● Dag & Red	h L 0–2	Att: 2,566 — Booked: Keltie
7th	● Carlisle	h D 2–2	Att: 1,608 — Scorers: Dagnall, Thorpe (Won 4–3 on pens)
10th	● Lincoln City	a D 1–1	Att: 4,510 — Booked: McArdle, Thorpe
18th	● Morecambe	a D 1–1	Att: 2,572 — Scorers: Dagnall
21st	● Chester	h W 6–1	Att: 2,162 — Scorers: Buckley, Dagnall[3], Le Fondre, Thorpe
25th	● Aldershot	h W 3–1	Att: 2,750 — Scorers: Buckley, Rundle, Thompson
28th	● Notts County	a W 1–2	Att: 3,610 — Scorers: Thorpe[2]

November
1st	● Brentford	a W 1–2	Att: 4,291 — Scorers: Buckley, McArdle
4th	● Scunthorpe	a L 1–0	Att: 2,474
8th	● Barnet	a D 1–1	Att: 1,782 — Scorers: Dagnall. Booked: G. Jones, M. Jones
15th	● Macclesfield	h D 1–1	Att: 3,013 — Scorers: Rundle. Booked: Stanton
18th	● Barnet	h W 3–2	Att: 2,339 — Scorers: Le Fondre[3]. Booked: McArdle (AET)
22nd	● Luton	h W 2–0	Att: 2,901 — Scorers: Le Fondre, Thorpe. Booked: Wiseman, Stanton
25th	● Gillingham	a D 1–1	Att: 4,029 — Scorers: Le Fondre. Booked: Thompson, Keltie
29th	● Forest Green	a L 2–0	Att: 1,715

December
13th	● Bournemouth	h D 1–1	Att: 2,285 — Scorers: Le Fondre. Booked: Ramsden, Stanton
20th	● Exeter	a L 4–1	Att: 4,326 — Scorers: Keltie. Booked: McArdle. Dismissed: Wiseman
26th	● Shrewsbury	h W 2–1	Att: 4,159 — Scorers: McEvilly[2]. Booked: Keltie, Ramsden
28th	● Port Vale	a L 2–1	Att: 5,720 — Scorers: Le Fondre

January
3rd	● Accrington S	h W 3–1	Att: 3,126 — Scorers: Buckley, Higginbotham, Le Fondre. Booked: McArdle, McEvilly
17th	● Lincoln City	h D 2–2	Att: 2,897 — Scorers: Le Fondre, McEvilly
24th	● Dag & Red	a L 3–2	Att: 1,808 — Scorers: Adams, Kennedy
27th	● Notts County	h W 3–0	Att: 2,289 — Scorers: Buckley, Dagnall, Le Fondre
31st	● Aldershot	a W 2–4	Att: 3,018 — Scorers: Thompson[3], Toner. Dismissed: Stanton

February
3rd	● Chester	a W 0–2	Att: 1,357 — Scorers: McEvilly, Thompson
14th	● Macclesfield	a W 0–1	Att: 2,396 — Scorers: Kennedy. Booked: Dagnall, Stanton
17th	● Morecambe	h D 1–1	Att: 3,347 — Scorers: Buckley
21st	● Brentford	h L 1–2	Att: 3,412 — Scorers: Kennedy. Booked: McArdle
24th	● Darlington	a W 1–2	Att: 2,858 — Scorers: Le Fondre, Rundle. Booked: Thorpe, Stanton
28th	● Grimsby	h W 2–0	Att: 3,076 — Scorers: Le Fondre, Rundle. Booked: Stanton

March
3rd	● Barnet	a L 2–1	Att: 1,332 — Scorers: McEvilly. Booked: Kennedy. Dismissed: Dagnall
7th	● Bury	a L 2–1	Att: 7,589 — Scorers: Buckley. Booked: Keltie
10th	● Bradford	h W 3–0	Att: 5,500 — Scorers: Le Fondre[2], McArdle. Booked: M. Jones, McArdle, Thorpe
14th	● Rotherham	h L 1–2	Att: 3,201 — Scorers: Le Fondre. Booked: Keltie
21st	● Wycombe	a W 0–1	Att: 6,055 — Scorers: Le Fondre. Booked: Adams, Thorpe, Wiseman
25th	● Chesterfield	a L 3–0	Att: 3,271 — Booked: Le Fondre
28th	● Exeter	h D 2–2	Att: 3,364 — Scorers: Le Fondre, Thorpe. Booked: Thorpe, Stanton

April
4th	● Bournemouth	a L 4–0	Att: 5,092
11th	● Port Vale	h W 1–0	Att: 3,100 — Scorers: Buckley
13th	● Shrewsbury	a L 2–0	Att: 6,234 — Scorers: Dagnall. Booked: Thompson, Thorpe, Dagnall, Stanton
18th	● Darlington	h L 0–2	Att: 3,789 — Booked: Keltie
25th	● Luton	a D 1–1	Att: 7,025 — Scorers: Rundle. Booked: Thorpe, Dagnall

May
2nd	● Gillingham	h L 0–1	Att: 3,480 — Booked: Flitcroft
7th	● Gillingham	h D 0–0	Att: 4,450
10th	● Gillingham	a L 2–1	Att: 9,585 — Scorers: Dagnall. Booked: McArdle, Kennedy, G. Jones, Stanton

● Coca-Cola League 2/Play-Offs ● FA Cup ● Carling Cup ● Johnstone's Paint Trophy

LEAGUE TWO GOALKEEPER STATS

Player	Appearances	Match starts	Completed matches	Sub appearances	Subbed off	Clean sheets	Yellow cards	Red cards
Frank Fielding	23	23	23	0	0	8	0	0
Sam Russell	23	23	23	0	0	2	0	0

LEAGUE TWO OUTFIELD PLAYER STATS

Player	Appearances	Match starts	Completed matches	Substitute appearances	Subbed off	Goals scored	Yellow cards	Red cards
Nicky Adams	14	12	3	2	9	1	1	0
William Buckley	37	28	13	9	15	11	0	0
Chris Dagnall	39	25	8	14	16	7	3	1
David Flitcroft	1	0	0	1	0	0	1	0
Kallum Higginbotham................	7	3	1	4	2	1	0	0
Marcus Holness	7	4	4	3	0	0	0	0
Gary Jones	28	28	25	0	3	0	0	0
Mark Jones	9	7	6	2	1	0	1	0
Clark Keltie..............................	31	26	22	5	4	1	10	0
Thomas Kennedy	45	45	44	0	1	4	1	0
Kyle Lambert	1	0	0	1	0	0	0	0
Adam Le Fondre	44	28	13	16	15	17	2	0
Gary Madine	3	1	0	2	1	0	0	0
Rory McArdle	41	41	40	0	1	2	7	0
Lee McEvilly	16	4	1	12	3	5	1	0
Tom Newey	2	1	1	1	0	0	0	0
Simon Ramsden........................	28	25	23	3	2	0	3	0
Jordan Rhodes	5	5	3	0	2	2	0	0
Adam Rundle	44	32	22	12	10	7	1	0
Jon Shaw	6	5	2	1	3	1	0	0
Nathan Stanton	39	39	36	0	2	0	10	1
Joe Thompson	30	21	12	9	9	5	2	0
Lee Thorpe	28	18	10	10	7	5	7	1
Keiran Toner	37	32	26	5	6	1	0	0
Scott Wiseman	32	30	27	2	2	0	3	1

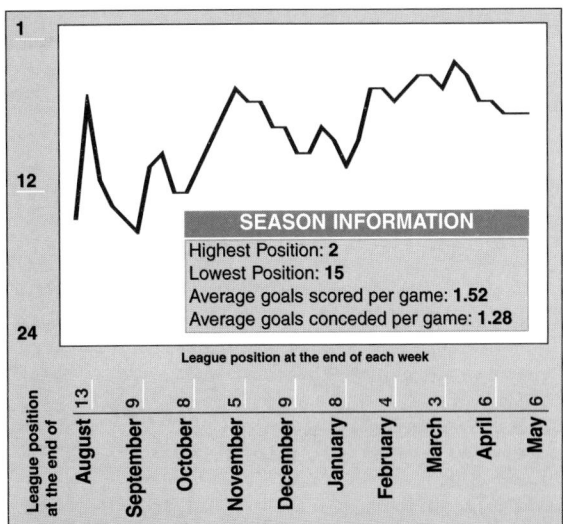

SEASON INFORMATION
Highest Position: **2**
Lowest Position: **15**
Average goals scored per game: **1.52**
Average goals conceded per game: **1.28**

League position at the end of each week

LONGEST SEQUENCES

Wins (on two occasions)	4	Undefeated home (21/10/08–17/02/09)	10
Losses (03/03/09–07/03/09)	2	Undefeated away (13/09/08–25/11/08)	7
Draws (on two occasions)	2	Without scoring (–)	
Undefeated (10/10/08–13/12/08)	10	Without conceding (03/02/09–14/02/09)	2
Without win (23/08/08–13/09/08)	4	Scoring (10/10/08–21/03/09)	29

CARDS RECEIVED

53   **4**

QUICK-FIRE GOALS

From the start of a match
Lee Thorpe (v Luton) 1:34

By a substitute after coming on
Adam Le Fondre (v Chester) 4:33

GOALS SCORED/CONCEDED PER FIVE-MINUTE INTERVALS

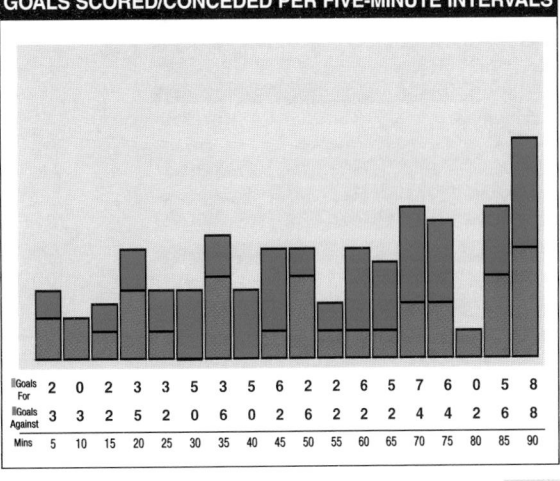

Goals For	2	0	2	3	3	5	3	5	6	2	2	6	5	7	6	0	5	8
Goals Against	3	3	2	5	2	0	6	0	2	6	2	2	2	4	4	2	6	8
Mins	5	10	15	20	25	30	35	40	45	50	55	60	65	70	75	80	85	90

ROTHERHAM must look back on 2008/09 as a major success following the financial strife and relegation that soured the previous campaign.

The Millers adapted well to life at the Don Valley Stadium, after being forced to leave Millmoor, and would have qualified for the play-offs had it not been for the 17-point deduction imposed at the start of the season because of their failure to meet League insolvency rules.

The Millers' steady progress, allied to an eye-catching run in the League Cup – they beat Sheffield Wednesday, Wolves and Southampton before losing 2–0 at Stoke – showed that, in Mark Robins, they have a young manager with a big future in the game.

The Millers' board will be hoping that, despite the club's difficulties, the 39-year-old can inspire a push for promotion in 2009/10.

CLUB SUMMARY

FORMED	1870
MANAGER	Mark Robins
GROUND	Don Valley Stadium
CAPACITY	25,000
NICKNAME	The Millers
WEBSITE	www.themillers.co.uk

The New Football Pools PLAYER OF THE SEASON — Ian Sharps

OVERALL
P	W	D	L	F	A	GD
57	24	16	17	73	61	12

COCA-COLA FOOTBALL LEAGUE TWO
Pos	P	W	D	L	F	A	GD	Pts
14	46	21	12	13	60	46	14	58

HOME
Pos	P	W	D	L	F	A	GD	Pts
12	23	11	6	6	32	21	11	39

AWAY
Pos	P	W	D	L	F	A	GD	Pts
3	23	10	6	7	28	25	3	36

CUP PROGRESS DETAILS
Competition	Round reached	Knocked out by
FA Cup	R1	Aldershot
JP Trophy	R2	Scunthorpe
Carling Cup	R4	Stoke

BIGGEST WIN (ALL COMPS)
10/03/09 5–1 v Chester FL2

BIGGEST DEFEAT (ALL COMPS)
15/11/08 0–4 v Gillingham FL2

ATTENDANCE RECORD
High	Low	Average
6,184	2,078	3,583
v Exeter (02/05/2009)	v Morecambe (21/04/2009)	

RESULTS 2008/09

August
9th	● Lincoln City	h	W 1–0	**Att:** 4,748 — **Scorers:** Reid
12th	● Sheff Wed	a	D 2–2	**Att:** 16,298 — **Scorers:** Reid, Rhodes. **Dismissed:** Joseph (Won 5–3 on pens)
16th	● Morecambe	a	W 1–3	**Att:** 2,606 — **Scorers:** Lynch[2], Taylor. **Booked:** Reid, Lynch
23rd	● Chester	h	W 3–1	**Att:** 3,462 — **Scorers:** Reid, Rhodes, Sharps. **Booked:** Yates
26th	● Wolves	h	D 0–0	**Att:** 5,404 — **Booked:** Broughton, D. Harrison (Won 4–3 on pens)
30th	● Brentford	a	D 0–0	**Att:** 4,381 — **Booked:** Reid

September
6th	● Chesterfield	a	L 1–0	**Att:** 4,951 — **Booked:** Lynch, Hudson, Fenton, Nicholas, Rhodes
13th	● Rochdale	h	D 2–2	**Att:** 3,569 — **Scorers:** Reid, McArdle OG. **Booked:** Reid
20th	● Luton	h	W 1–0	**Att:** 4,095 — **Scorers:** Rhodes
23rd	● Southampton	h	W 3–1	**Att:** 5,147 — **Scorers:** Broughton, Fenton, Harrison. **Booked:** Mills, Broughton
27th	● Dag & Red	a	D 1–1	**Att:** 1,805 — **Scorers:** Burchill

October
4th	● Grimsby	h	W 4–1	**Att:** 3,889 — **Scorers:** Barker, Cummins, Hudson, Reid
8th	● Leeds	h	W 4–2	**Att:** 4,658 — **Scorers:** Broughton, Fenton, Hudson, Sharps
11th	● Bournemouth	a	D 0–0	**Att:** 4,530
18th	● Barnet	h	L 3–4	**Att:** 3,801 — **Scorers:** Burchill, Fenton, Sharps. **Booked:** Nicholas
21st	● Bury	a	W 1–2	**Att:** 2,362 — **Scorers:** Broughton, Reid. **Booked:** Barker, Mills
25th	● Macclesfield	a	W 1–2	**Att:** 2,020 — **Scorers:** Nicholas, Tonge. **Booked:** Fenton, Sharps. **Dismissed:** Sharps
28th	● Darlington	h	L 0–1	**Att:** 3,322

November
1st	● Wycombe	h	D 0–0	**Att:** 3,471
4th	● Leicester	h	W 2–0	**Att:** 4,255 — **Scorers:** Broughton, Tonge
8th	● Aldershot	a	D 1–1	**Att:** 2,632 — **Scorers:** Cummins. **Booked:** Broughton, Barker
11th	● Stoke	a	L 2–0	**Att:** 13,731 — **Booked:** Reid
15th	● Gillingham	a	L 4–0	**Att:** 5,304 — **Booked:** Reid, Mills. **Dismissed:** Harrison
18th	● Aldershot	h	L 0–3	**Att:** 2,431
22nd	● Bradford	h	L 0–2	**Att:** 4,586
25th	● Exeter	a	D 1–1	**Att:** 3,402 — **Scorers:** Reid. **Booked:** Broughton, Joseph, Sharps

December
6th	● Shrewsbury	a	L 1–0	**Att:** 5,314 — **Booked:** Broughton. **Dismissed:** Broughton, Stockdale
16th	● Darlington	h	D 1–1	**Att:** 2,706 — **Scorers:** Fenton (Won 4–2 on pens)
20th	● Accrington S	a	W 1–3	**Att:** 1,172 — **Scorers:** Broughton, Burchill[2]. **Booked:** Hudson
26th	● Port Vale	h	W 1–0	**Att:** 4,350 — **Scorers:** Broughton. **Dismissed:** Joseph
28th	● Notts County	a	W 0–3	**Att:** 6,686 — **Scorers:** Broughton, Cummins, Reid

January
3rd	● Dag & Red	h	D 1–1	**Att:** 3,307 — **Scorers:** Sharps
17th	● Bournemouth	h	W 1–0	**Att:** 3,270 — **Scorers:** Hudson
20th	● Scunthorpe	a	L 2–0	**Att:** 6,038 — **Booked:** Hudson
24th	● Grimsby	a	L 3–0	**Att:** 4,559 — **Booked:** Nicholas, Sharps
27th	● Darlington	a	L 1–0	**Att:** 2,431 — **Booked:** J. Taylor, Hudson, Mills
31st	● Macclesfield	h	W 2–0	**Att:** 2,945 — **Scorers:** Hudson, Reid

February
14th	● Gillingham	h	W 2–0	**Att:** 2,757 — **Scorers:** Clarke, Green. **Booked:** Tonge
17th	● Scunthorpe	h	L 0–1	**Att:** 6,555
23rd	● Wycombe	a	D 0–0	**Att:** 3,739
28th	● Lincoln City	a	W 0–1	**Att:** 4,336 — **Scorers:** Cummins. **Booked:** Fenton

March
7th	● Brentford	h	D 0–0	**Att:** 3,406
10th	● Chester	a	W 1–5	**Att:** 1,235 — **Scorers:** Broughton, Cummins, Reid[3]. **Booked:** Tonge
14th	● Rochdale	a	W 1–2	**Att:** 3,201 — **Scorers:** Reid, Taylor. **Booked:** Reid
17th	● Aldershot	h	L 1–2	**Att:** 2,769 — **Scorers:** Clarke
21st	● Chesterfield	h	W 3–0	**Att:** 4,658 — **Scorers:** Mills, Reid[2]. **Booked:** Tonge, Hudson
24th	● Bury	h	D 1–1	**Att:** 2,890 — **Scorers:** Reid. **Booked:** Green
28th	● Accrington S	h	D 0–0	**Att:** 2,804 — **Booked:** Broughton, Mills
31st	● Luton	a	W 2–4	**Att:** 5,975 — **Scorers:** Broughton, Harrison, Hudson, Reid. **Booked:** Mills, Sharps, Broughton

April
4th	● Aldershot	a	W 0–1	**Att:** 2,643 — **Scorers:** Reid. **Booked:** Broughton, Sharps
7th	● Barnet	a	L 2–0	**Att:** 1,508
11th	● Notts County	h	W 2–0	**Att:** 2,945 — **Scorers:** Hudson, Reid
13th	● Port Vale	a	D 0–0	**Att:** 4,814 — **Booked:** Tonge, D. Harrison
18th	● Shrewsbury	h	L 1–2	**Att:** 3,106 — **Scorers:** Taylor. **Booked:** D. Harrison, Reid
21st	● Morecambe	h	W 3–2	**Att:** 2,078 — **Scorers:** Burchill, Taylor, Taylor. **Booked:** Mills
25th	● Bradford	a	L 3–0	**Att:** 13,242 — **Booked:** Fenton

May
2nd	● Exeter	h	L 0–1	**Att:** 6,184 — **Dismissed:** Tonge

● Coca-Cola League 2/Play-Offs ● FA Cup ● Carling Cup ● Johnstone's Paint Trophy

LEAGUE TWO GOALKEEPER STATS

Player	Appearances	Match starts	Completed matches	Sub appearances	Subbed off	Clean sheets	Yellow cards	Red cards
Steven Cann	2	0	0	2	0	1	0	0
David Stockdale	8	8	7	0	0	3	0	1
Andy Warrington	38	38	38	0	0	14	0	0

LEAGUE TWO OUTFIELD PLAYER STATS

Player	Appearances	Match starts	Completed matches	Substitute appearances	Subbed off	Goals scored	Yellow cards	Red cards
Richard Barker	13	4	0	9	4	1	1	0
Stephen Brogan	1	0	0	1	0	0	0	0
Drewe Broughton	40	33	12	7	20	6	5	1
Mark Burchill	24	10	2	14	8	5	0	0
Jamie Clarke	11	7	2	4	5	2	0	0
Michael Cummins	35	30	25	5	5	4	0	0
Nick Fenton	45	45	42	0	3	1	4	0
Omar Garcia	2	2	1	0	1	0	0	0
Jamie Green	31	29	25	2	4	1	1	0
Danny Harrison	33	27	22	6	4	1	2	1
Peter Holmes	3	2	2	1	0	0	0	0
Mark Hudson	42	35	29	7	6	5	4	0
Marc Joseph	25	13	9	12	3	0	1	1
Mark Lynch	8	7	6	1	1	2	2	0
Pablo Mills	35	34	29	1	5	1	6	0
Andrew Nicholas	19	19	17	0	2	1	3	0
Reuben Reid	41	38	24	3	14	18	6	0
Alex Rhodes	18	14	10	4	4	2	1	0
Ian Sharps	45	45	42	0	2	3	5	1
Jason Taylor	15	9	5	6	4	1	1	0
Ryan Taylor	32	16	10	16	6	4	0	0
Simon Thomas	2	2	0	0	2	0	0	0
Dale Tonge	39	39	37	0	1	1	4	1
Jamie Yates	3	0	0	3	0	0	1	0

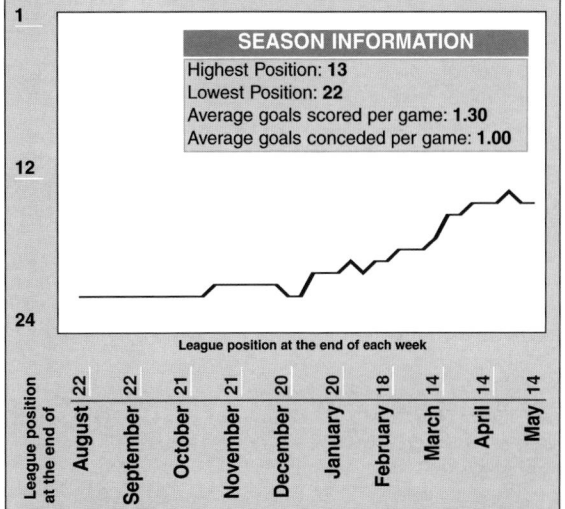

SEASON INFORMATION
Highest Position: **13**
Lowest Position: **22**
Average goals scored per game: **1.30**
Average goals conceded per game: **1.00**

League position at the end of each week

League position at the end of — August 22, September 22, October 21, November 21, December 20, January 20, February 18, March 14, April 14, May 14

LONGEST SEQUENCES

Wins (on two occasions)	3	Undefeated home (26/12/08–07/03/09)	6
Losses (on three occasions)	2	Undefeated away (23/02/09–04/04/09)	6
Draws (24/03/09–28/03/09)	2	Without scoring (28/10/08–22/11/08)	4
Undefeated (31/01/09–14/03/09)	7	Without conceding (31/01/09–07/03/09)	5
Without win (28/10/08–06/12/08)	6	Scoring (on two occasions)	5

CARDS RECEIVED

47 **6**

QUICK-FIRE GOALS

From the start of a match
Reuben Reid (v Bury) 1:16

By a substitute after coming on
Jason Taylor (v Morecambe) 2:17

GOALS SCORED/CONCEDED PER FIVE-MINUTE INTERVALS

	5	10	15	20	25	30	35	40	45	50	55	60	65	70	75	80	85	90
Goals For	4	3	6	1	1	2	0	4	4	4	3	1	2	6	2	5	5	7
Goals Against	0	1	3	2	1	2	2	2	4	2	2	3	2	2	7	4	2	5
Mins	5	10	15	20	25	30	35	40	45	50	55	60	65	70	75	80	85	90

SHREWSBURY TOWN

SHREWSBURY'S campaign ended with disappointment in the Coca-Cola League Two play-off final.

The Shrews were in the promotion shake-up all season thanks to the best home record in the fourth tier and, having won only one game away from the Prostar Stadium, they triumphed in their final two to secure seventh spot.

Two exhilarating matches followed as they scraped past Bury 4–3 on a penalty shoot-out before eventually missing out on promotion courtesy of Simeon Jackson's 90th-minute winner for Gillingham at Wembley.

Shrews also lost by a penalty shoot-out to Brighton in the area semi-final of the Johnstone's Paint Trophy, but the form of League Two golden boot winner Grant Holt, who bagged 28 in all competitions, gives plenty of cause for optimism.

CLUB SUMMARY

FORMED	1886
MANAGER	Paul Simpson
GROUND	Prostar Stadium
CAPACITY	10,000
NICKNAME	The Shrews
WEBSITE	www.shrewsburytown.com

The New Football Pools PLAYER OF THE SEASON

Grant Holt

OVERALL
P	W	D	L	F	A	GD
55	21	19	15	77	51	26

COCA-COLA FOOTBALL LEAGUE TWO
Pos	P	W	D	L	F	A	GD	Pts
7	46	17	18	11	61	44	17	69

HOME
Pos	P	W	D	L	F	A	GD	Pts
1	23	14	6	3	41	16	25	48

AWAY
Pos	P	W	D	L	F	A	GD	Pts
19	23	3	12	8	20	28	-8	21

CUP PROGRESS DETAILS
Competition	Round reached	Knocked out by
FA Cup	R1	Blyth Spartans
JP Trophy	SF	Brighton
Carling Cup	R1	Carlisle

BIGGEST WIN (ALL COMPS)
7–0 on two occasions

BIGGEST DEFEAT (ALL COMPS)
28/02/09 0–3 v Macclesfield **FL2**

ATTENDANCE RECORD
High	Low	Average
7,162	4,134	5,664
v Port Vale (11/10/2008)	v Accrington S (03/02/2009)	

RESULTS 2008/09

August
9th	Macclesfield	h	W 4–0	Att: 5,812 — Scorers: Cansdell-Sherriff, Coughlan, Hibbert, Holt
12th	Carlisle	h	L 0–1	Att: 3,337 — Booked: Holt
16th	Exeter	a	W 0–1	Att: 4,916 — Scorers: Murray. Booked: Murray, Hindmarch
23rd	Aldershot	h	W 1–0	Att: 5,422 — Scorers: Holt. Booked: Cansdell-Sherriff, Holt
30th	Notts County	a	D 2–2	Att: 4,697 — Scorers: Hibbert, Symes. Booked: Moss, McIntyre, Holt

September
2nd	Exeter	a	W 1–2	Att: 1,530 — Scorers: Davies, McIntyre
6th	Morecambe	a	L 1–0	Att: 2,318 — Booked: Cansdell-Sherriff
13th	Gillingham	h	W 7–0	Att: 5,319 — Scorers: Cansdell-Sherriff, Coughlan, Davies[2], Hibbert, Holt, Jackson. Booked: Cansdell-Sherriff, Holt
21st	Chester	a	D 1–1	Att: 2,891 — Scorers: Holt. Booked: McIntyre, Cansdell-Sherriff, Herd, Jackson
27th	Bradford	h	W 2–0	Att: 6,517 — Scorers: Davies, Walker. Booked: Jackson, Herd

October
4th	Darlington	a	D 1–1	Att: 2,899 — Scorers: Thornton. Booked: Jackson, Coughlan, Holt, Thornton, Herd
7th	Wycombe	a	W 0–7	Att: 1,730 — Scorers: Cansdell-Sherriff, Holt[5], McIntyre.
11th	Port Vale	h	L 1–2	Att: 7,162 — Scorers: Symes. Booked: Herd
18th	Bournemouth	h	W 4–1	Att: 5,738 — Scorers: Davies[2], Sigurdsson, Walker. Booked: Tierney, McIntyre
21st	Accrington S	a	L 2–1	Att: 1,249 — Scorers: Davies. Booked: Holt
25th	Brentford	a	D 1–1	Att: 5,362 — Scorers: Humphrey. Booked: Sigurdsson, Cansdell-Sherriff, Coughlan, McIntyre
28th	Barnet	h	D 2–2	Att: 5,163 — Scorers: Davies, Holt.

November
1st	Luton	h	W 3–0	Att: 6,188 — Scorers: Davies, Holt, Murray. Booked: Jackson, Tierney
4th	Dag & Red	h	W 5–0	Att: 2,747 — Scorers: Coughlan, Holt[2], Leslie, Walker. Booked: Holt
8th	Blyth Spartans	a	L 3–1	Att: 2,742 — Scorers: Holt. Booked: Murray, Herd, Hindmarch, Coughlan
14th	Chesterfield	a	D 2–2	Att: 4,099 — Scorers: Holt[2]. Booked: Walker, Jackson
22nd	Lincoln City	a	D 0–0	Att: 3,517 — Dismissed: Walker
25th	Dag & Red	h	W 2–1	Att: 4,590 — Scorers: Holt, White. Booked: Moss

December
6th	Rotherham	h	W 1–0	Att: 5,314 — Scorers: Holt. Booked: Langmead, Holt
13th	Grimsby	a	L 1–0	Att: 3,283 — Booked: Langmead, Hunt
16th	Brighton	h	D 0–0	Att: 4,052 — (Lost 5–4 on pens)
20th	Wycombe	h	L 0–1	Att: 6,160 — Booked: Holt
26th	Rochdale	a	L 2–1	Att: 4,159 — Scorers: Holt
28th	Bury	h	W 1–0	Att: 7,127 — Scorers: Holt

January
3rd	Bradford	a	D 0–0	Att: 12,877 — Booked: Murray, Holt
17th	Port Vale	a	D 1–1	Att: 7,068 — Scorers: Walker. Dismissed: Pugh
24th	Darlington	h	W 1–0	Att: 5,140 — Scorers: Walker. Booked: Coughlan, Ashton
27th	Barnet	a	D 0–0	Att: 1,568
31st	Brentford	h	L 1–3	Att: 5,674 — Scorers: Holt. Booked: Ashton

February
3rd	Accrington S	h	W 2–0	Att: 4,134 — Scorers: Coughlan, Holt. Booked: Jackson, Hibbert
7th	Bournemouth	a	L 1–0	Att: 4,187 — Booked: Jackson, Cansdell-Sherriff, Coughlan, Holt. Dismissed: Moss
14th	Chesterfield	h	W 2–1	Att: 4,873 — Scorers: Davies, Jackson. Booked: Davies
17th	Chester	h	W 1–0	Att: 6,133 — Scorers: Walker
21st	Luton	a	L 3–1	Att: 5,661 — Scorers: Davies. Booked: Humphrey
28th	Macclesfield	a	L 3–0	Att: 2,553 — Booked: Herd

March
3rd	Exeter	h	D 1–1	Att: 4,679 — Scorers: Holt. Booked: Holt, Murray
7th	Notts County	h	W 3–2	Att: 5,192 — Scorers: Ashikodi, Coughlan, Holt
10th	Aldershot	a	D 0–0	Att: 2,090 — Booked: Worrall, Moss
14th	Gillingham	a	D 2–2	Att: 6,023 — Scorers: Holt[2]. Booked: Leslie
21st	Morecambe	h	D 0–0	Att: 5,426 — Booked: Ashikodi, Moss
28th	Wycombe	a	D 1–1	Att: 4,803 — Scorers: Davies. Booked: Coughlan

April
4th	Grimsby	h	D 1–1	Att: 5,535 — Scorers: Davies. Booked: Murray
10th	Bury	a	L 2–1	Att: 4,850 — Scorers: Chadwick. Booked: Coughlan
13th	Rochdale	h	D 1–1	Att: 6,234 — Scorers: Holt. Booked: Hibbert, Leslie
18th	Rotherham	a	W 1–2	Att: 3,106 — Scorers: Chadwick, Sharps OG.
25th	Lincoln City	h	D 0–0	Att: 6,740 — Booked: Murray, Holt

May
2nd	Dag & Red	a	W 1–2	Att: 4,791 — Scorers: Holt, Humphrey. Booked: Daniels
7th	Bury	h	L 0–1	Att: 8,429 — Booked: Moss
10th	Bury	a	W 0–1	Att: 7,673 — Scorers: McIntyre. Booked: Davies. Dismissed: Leslie (Won 4–3 on pens)
23rd	Gillingham	n	L 1–0	Att: 53,706 — Booked: Coughlan, Murray, Holt

● Coca-Cola League 2/Play-Offs ● FA Cup ● Carling Cup ● Johnstone's Paint Trophy

LEAGUE TWO GOALKEEPER STATS

Player	Appearances	Match starts	Completed matches	Sub appearances	Subbed off	Clean sheets	Yellow cards	Red cards
Luke Daniels	38	38	38	0	0	14	1	0
Glyn Garner	4	4	4	0	0	1	0	0
Matthew Gilks	4	4	4	0	0	2	0	0

LEAGUE TWO OUTFIELD PLAYER STATS

Player	Appearances	Match starts	Completed matches	Substitute appearances	Subbed off	Goals scored	Yellow cards	Red cards
Moses Ashikodi	8	4	0	4	4	1	1	0
Neil Ashton	31	24	21	7	3	0	2	0
Shane Cansdell-Sherriff	31	27	18	4	9	2	6	0
Nick Chadwick	15	9	1	6	8	2	0	0
Graham Coughlan	42	42	40	0	2	4	6	0
Ben Davies	42	42	35	0	7	12	1	0
Terry Dunfield	17	15	11	2	4	0	0	0
Ben Herd	21	20	19	1	1	0	5	0
Dave Hibbert	23	9	2	14	7	3	2	0
Steven Hindmarch	3	0	0	3	0	0	1	0
Grant Holt	43	43	42	0	1	20	11	0
Chris Humphrey	37	24	11	13	13	2	1	0
David Hunt	2	0	0	2	0	0	1	0
Michael Jackson	21	21	20	0	1	2	7	0
Joss Labadie	1	1	1	0	0	0	0	0
Kelvin Langmead	33	29	29	4	0	0	2	0
Steven Leslie	27	12	8	15	3	0	2	0
Kevin McIntyre	26	25	20	1	5	0	4	0
Darren Moss	29	28	25	1	2	0	4	1
Paul Murray	32	31	9	1	22	2	5	0
Marc Pugh	7	0	0	7	0	0	0	1
Omer Riza	2	0	0	2	0	0	0	0
Gylfi Sigurdsson	5	4	3	1	1	1	1	0
Michael Symes	8	1	0	7	1	2	0	0
Sean Thornton	5	5	5	0	0	1	1	0
Marc Tierney	18	18	17	0	1	0	2	0
Richard Walker	27	16	1	11	14	5	1	1
Jamie White	9	3	1	6	2	1	0	0
David Worrall	9	7	4	2	3	0	1	0

League position at the end of each week

League position at the end of: August 2, September 3, October 6, November 4, December 5, January 6, February 5, March 7, April 8, May 7

SEASON INFORMATION
Highest Position: **1**
Lowest Position: **9**
Average goals scored per game: **1.33**
Average goals conceded per game: **0.96**

LONGEST SEQUENCES

Wins (09/08/08–23/08/08)	3	Undefeated home (03/02/09–25/04/09)	9
Losses (13/12/08–26/12/08)	3	Undefeated away (on four occasions)	3
Draws (10/03/09–04/04/09)	5	Without scoring (13/12/08–20/12/08)	2
Undefeated (on two occasions)	7	Without conceding (09/08/08–23/08/08)	3
Without win (10/03/09–13/04/09)	7	Scoring (13/09/08–14/11/08)	11

CARDS RECEIVED
68   **3**

QUICK-FIRE GOALS
From the start of a match
Paul Murray (v Luton) 3:32

By a substitute after coming on
Chris Humphrey (v Brentford) 2:34

GOALS SCORED/CONCEDED PER FIVE-MINUTE INTERVALS

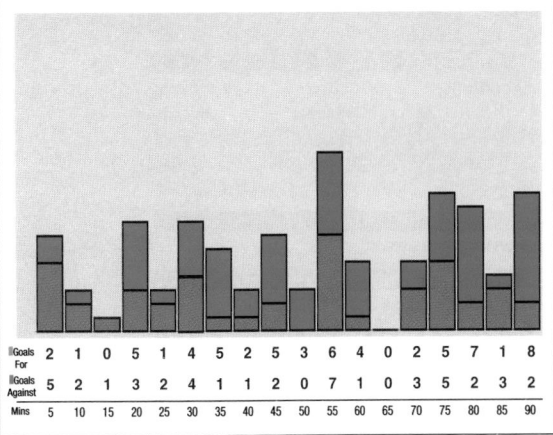

Goals For	2	1	0	5	1	4	5	2	5	3	6	4	0	2	5	7	1	8
Goals Against	5	2	1	3	2	4	1	1	2	0	7	1	0	3	5	2	3	2
Mins	5	10	15	20	25	30	35	40	45	50	55	60	65	70	75	80	85	90

PETER TAYLOR celebrated promotion at the first attempt as Wycombe returned to Coca-Cola League One after a five-season absence.

Taylor's new side started the campaign in sensational fashion as they went unbeaten in the League until early December, at which time they held a six-point lead at the top of the table. That run was based on a solid defence, but they began to wobble at the turn of the year as Brentford stole a march at the top.

Taylor reacted by signing John Akinde on loan from Bristol City and the striker's run of seven goals in 11 games pushed the Chairboys back on track for promotion.

A point on the final day at home to Notts County was all that was required but, while Taylor saw his side slump to a 2–1 defeat, they were promoted on goal difference.

CLUB SUMMARY

FORMED	1887
MANAGER	Peter Taylor
GROUND	Adams Park
CAPACITY	10,000
NICKNAME	The Chairboys
WEBSITE	www.wwfc.com

The New **Football Pools** PLAYER OF THE SEASON

Tommy Doherty

OVERALL

P	W	D	L	F	A	GD
50	21	18	11	58	47	11

COCA-COLA FOOTBALL LEAGUE TWO

Pos	P	W	D	L	F	A	GD	Pts
3	46	20	18	8	54	33	21	78

HOME

Pos	P	W	D	L	F	A	GD	Pts
7	23	11	9	3	32	16	16	42

AWAY

Pos	P	W	D	L	F	A	GD	Pts
2	23	9	9	5	22	17	5	36

CUP PROGRESS DETAILS

Competition	Round reached	Knocked out by
FA Cup	R2	Eastwood Town
JP Trophy	R2	Shrewsbury
Carling Cup	R1	Birmingham

BIGGEST WIN (ALL COMPS)
02/12/08 4–0 v Macclesfield FL2

BIGGEST DEFEAT (ALL COMPS)
07/10/08 0–7 v Shrewsbury FLTS2

ATTENDANCE RECORD

High	Low	Average
9,625	3,713	5,109
v Notts Cnty (02/05/2009)	v Chester (03/03/2009)	

RESULTS 2008/09

August
9th	● Morecambe	h	D 1–1	**Att:** 4,021 — **Scorers:** Spence. **Booked:** Doherty, Spence
13th	● Birmingham	h	L 0–4	**Att:** 2,735
16th	● Chester	a	W 0–2	**Att:** 1,419 — **Scorers:** McGleish, Mousinho. **Booked:** Doherty
23rd	● Lincoln City	h	W 1–0	**Att:** 4,112 — **Scorers:** Woodman
30th	● Chesterfield	a	W 0–1	**Att:** 3,175 — **Scorers:** Williamson. **Booked:** Williamson

September
6th	● Rochdale	a	W 0–1	**Att:** 2,880 — **Scorers:** Zebroski
13th	● Brentford	h	D 0–0	**Att:** 5,799 — **Booked:** Williamson
20th	● Dag & Red	h	W 2–1	**Att:** 4,132 — **Scorers:** Williamson[2]. **Booked:** Zebroski, Doherty, Mousinho. **Dismissed:** Church
27th	● Bury	a	D 0–0	**Att:** 3,597 — **Booked:** McGleish, Doherty, Zebroski

October
4th	● Bournemouth	h	W 3–1	**Att:** 5,005 — **Scorers:** Harrold, McGleish, Zebroski
7th	● Shrewsbury	h	L 0–7	**Att:** 1,730 — **Booked:** Zebroski, McGleish
11th	● Grimsby	a	D 1–1	**Att:** 4,562 — **Scorers:** Johnson. **Booked:** McCracken. **Dismissed:** Doherty
18th	● Darlington	h	D 1–1	**Att:** 5,345 — **Scorers:** McGleish. **Booked:** Holt, Harrold. **Dismissed:** Zebroski
21st	● Barnet	a	D 1–1	**Att:** 2,258 — **Scorers:** Zebroski
25th	● Accrington S	a	W 0–1	**Att:** 1,217 — **Scorers:** Zebroski

November
1st	● Rotherham	a	D 0–0	**Att:** 3,471
10th	● AFC Wimbledon	a	W 1–4	**Att:** 4,528 — **Scorers:** Harrold[3], Phillips
15th	● Bradford	h	W 1–0	**Att:** 5,002 — **Scorers:** Hunt
22nd	● Port Vale	h	W 4–2	**Att:** 4,521 — **Scorers:** Harrold[2], Zebroski[2]. **Booked:** Harrold
25th	● Notts County	a	W 0–2	**Att:** 2,964 — **Scorers:** Harrold, Spence. **Booked:** Balanta
29th	● Eastwood Town	a	L 2–0	**Att:** 1,955

December
2nd	● Macclesfield	h	W 4–0	**Att:** 3,770 — **Scorers:** Balanta, Johnson, Vieira[2]
6th	● Aldershot	a	L 3–2	**Att:** 3,915 — **Scorers:** Balanta, Phillips. **Booked:** Spence, McCracken, Doherty
13th	● Luton	h	D 0–0	**Att:** 5,567 — **Booked:** Phillips, Bloomfield
20th	● Shrewsbury	a	W 0–1	**Att:** 6,160 — **Scorers:** Harrold. **Booked:** Hunt, Johnson
26th	● Exeter	h	D 1–1	**Att:** 6,094 — **Scorers:** Harrold. **Booked:** Balanta, Doherty
28th	● Gillingham	h	D 1–1	**Att:** 5,979 — **Scorers:** Lewis OG. **Booked:** Antwi

January
3rd	● Bury	h	W 2–1	**Att:** 4,961 — **Scorers:** Balanta, Harrold
17th	● Grimsby	h	L 0–1	**Att:** 4,461 — **Booked:** Zebroski, Balanta
24th	● Bournemouth	a	L 3–1	**Att:** 5,946 — **Scorers:** Harrold. **Booked:** Doherty, Bloomfield, McGleish
27th	● Macclesfield	a	D 0–0	**Att:** 1,306 — **Booked:** McCracken
31st	● Accrington S	h	W 2–1	**Att:** 6,166 — **Scorers:** Harrold, Murdock OG

February
14th	● Bradford	a	L 1–0	**Att:** 12,689 — **Booked:** Johnson, Doherty. **Dismissed:** Zebroski
17th	● Dag & Red	a	W 0–1	**Att:** 2,242 — **Scorers:** Pittman
23rd	● Rotherham	h	D 0–0	**Att:** 3,739
28th	● Morecambe	a	D 0–0	**Att:** 2,005 — **Booked:** Phillips, Woodman

March
3rd	● Chester	h	W 2–0	**Att:** 3,713 — **Scorers:** Phillips, Pittman
7th	● Chesterfield	h	D 1–1	**Att:** 4,809 — **Scorers:** Pittman. **Booked:** Beavon
10th	● Lincoln City	a	L 1–0	**Att:** 2,562 — **Booked:** Harrold, Phillips
14th	● Brentford	a	D 3–3	**Att:** 10,642 — **Scorers:** Akinde[2], Mousinho. **Booked:** Harrold, Mousinho, Antwi. **Dismissed:** Doherty
21st	● Rochdale	h	L 0–1	**Att:** 6,055 — **Booked:** Antwi, Woodman
28th	● Shrewsbury	h	D 1–1	**Att:** 4,803 — **Scorers:** Holt
31st	● Barnet	h	D 1–1	**Att:** 4,066 — **Scorers:** Akinde. **Booked:** Young, Zebroski

April
7th	● Darlington	a	W 1–2	**Att:** 2,180 — **Scorers:** Akinde, Zebroski. **Booked:** Akinde, Sawyer
11th	● Gillingham	h	W 1–0	**Att:** 6,306 — **Scorers:** Akinde. **Booked:** Harrold, Woodman
13th	● Exeter	a	L 1–0	**Att:** 8,183
18th	● Aldershot	h	W 3–0	**Att:** 5,440 — **Scorers:** Akinde, Phillips, Newman OG
21st	● Luton	a	W 0–1	**Att:** 6,553 — **Scorers:** Akinde. **Booked:** Phillips, Akinde
25th	● Port Vale	a	D 1–1	**Att:** 6,047 — **Scorers:** Sawyer. **Booked:** Sawyer

May
2nd	● Notts County	h	L 1–2	**Att:** 9,625 — **Scorers:** McCracken

● Coca-Cola League 2/Play-Offs ● FA Cup ● Carling Cup ● Johnstone's Paint Trophy

LEAGUE TWO GOALKEEPER STATS

Player	Appearances	Match starts	Completed matches	Sub appearances	Subbed off	Clean sheets	Yellow cards	Red cards
Scott Shearer	29	29	29	0	0	14	0	0
Marek Stech	2	2	2	0	0	0	0	0
Jamie Young	15	15	15	0	0	7	1	0

LEAGUE TWO OUTFIELD PLAYER STATS

Player	Appearances	Match starts	Completed matches	Substitute appearances	Subbed off	Goals scored	Yellow cards	Red cards
John Akinde	11	11	4	0	7	7	2	0
Will Antwi	6	4	4	2	0	0	3	0
Nathan Ashton	11	0	0	11	0	0	0	0
Angelo Balanta	11	9	2	2	7	3	3	0
Stuart Beavon	8	2	0	6	2	0	1	0
Matt Bloomfield	20	15	6	5	9	0	2	0
Chris Casement	12	12	8	0	4	0	0	0
Simon Church	9	6	1	3	4	0	0	1
Leon Crooks	2	2	1	0	1	0	0	0
Tommy Doherty	34	34	25	0	7	0	8	2
Gavin Grant	10	9	4	1	5	0	0	0
Matt Harrold	37	28	23	9	5	9	5	0
Gary Holt	33	33	24	0	9	1	1	0
Lewis Hunt	20	20	19	0	1	1	1	0
Leon Johnson	29	29	26	0	3	2	2	0
David McCracken	39	39	36	0	3	1	2	0
Scott McGleish	15	10	5	5	5	3	2	0
Thomas Moncur	2	0	0	2	0	0	0	0
John Mousinho	34	21	17	13	4	2	2	0
Franck Moussa	9	7	4	2	3	0	0	0
Luke Oliver	8	1	1	7	0	0	0	0
Matt Phillips	37	18	5	19	13	3	4	0
Jon-Paul Pittman	17	11	4	6	7	3	0	0
Robert Rice	1	0	0	1	0	0	0	0
Lee Sawyer	9	8	3	1	5	1	2	0
Frank Sinclair	9	9	9	0	0	0	0	0
Lewwis Spence	30	21	13	9	8	2	2	0
Magno Vieira	14	2	1	12	1	2	0	0
Mike Williamson	22	22	22	0	0	3	2	0
Craig Woodman	46	46	45	0	1	1	3	0
Chris Zebroski	33	31	25	2	4	7	4	2

League position at the end of each week

League position at the end of

August	September	October	November	December	January	February	March	April	May
4	2	1	1	1	1	2	4	2	3

SEASON INFORMATION

Highest Position: **1**
Lowest Position: **12**
Average goals scored per game: **1.17**
Average goals conceded per game: **0.72**

LONGEST SEQUENCES

Wins (on two occasions)	4	Undefeated home (09/08/08–03/01/09)	12
Losses (17/01/09–24/01/09)	2	Undefeated away (09/08/08–25/11/08)	10
Draws (11/10/08–21/10/08)	3	Without scoring (23/02/09–28/02/09)	2
Undefeated (09/08/08–02/12/08)	18	Without conceding (16/08/08–13/09/08)	5
Without win (07/03/09–31/03/09)	6	Scoring (on three occasions)	5

CARDS RECEIVED

53 5

QUICK-FIRE GOALS

From the start of a match
Mike Williamson (v Chesterfield) 3:38

By a substitute after coming on
Scott McGleish (v Bournemouth) 15:07

GOALS SCORED/CONCEDED PER FIVE-MINUTE INTERVALS

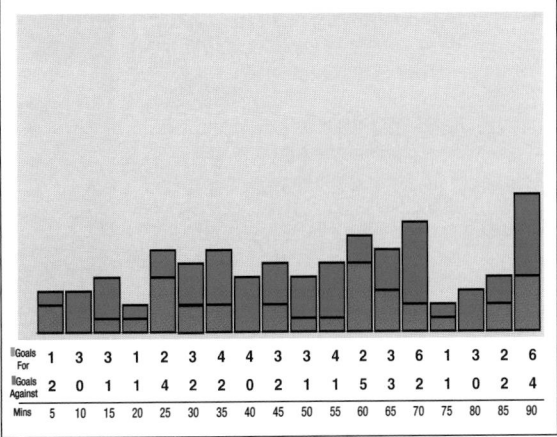

Goals For	1	3	3	1	2	3	4	4	3	3	4	2	3	6	1	3	2	6
Goals Against	2	0	1	1	4	2	2	0	2	1	1	5	3	2	1	0	2	4
Mins	5	10	15	20	25	30	35	40	45	50	55	60	65	70	75	80	85	90

THE New Football Pools has contributed £1.1billion to good causes over the years.

Supporting the community has always been at the very heart of the Football Pools. Since its humble beginnings in 1923, the Football Pools has donated more than one billion pounds to the arts, sporting and good causes, with almost £530million given to British football alone.

The funding channelled into football via the Football Grounds Improvement Trust and then via the Football Trust can be seen across Scotland in the new and rebuilt stadiums from Inverness to Livingston. A very substantial contribution – in excess of £5million – was made available to the Scottish Football Association to assist with the renovation of their national stadium at Hampden Park.

Less visible proof of the value of the Football Trust's work can also be found in the scores of new changing facilities and drainage projects for grassroots football, the provision of five-a-side playing facilities, and the funding for a variety of successful anti-racism projects.

And it's not just football that has benefited from the Pools. Other sports have also received vital help, including the Murrayfield stadium, which received major financial contributions.

The regeneration of Scottish football's national stadium, Hampden Park, above, was aided by funds from The New Football Pools via the Football Trust. Murrayfield, below, also received substantial funds

FIT FOR FOOTBALL, FIT FOR LIFE

The New Football Pools is committed to continuing its support of football in Scotland. In a major new scheme, The New Football Pools has joined forces with the Scottish Football League to launch Fit for Football, Fit for Life.

Just under £1million has been invested by The New Football Pools in this multi-channelled scheme that will tackle serious issues within the game, such as young people's heart screening, alcohol awareness training, under-17 and under-19 training, as well as the donations of a defibrillator to every football club across the Leagues.

SCOTTISH PREMIER LEAGUE

Further funding is planned by The New Football Pools to be injected into the Scottish Premier League's community projects in the 2009/10 season.

CLASSIC POOLS

PREMIER LEAGUE | THE FOOTBALL LEAGUE
OFFICIAL LICENSEE

S·P·L SPL
OFFICIAL PARTNER

The New Football Pools
www.footballpools.com

THE NEW FOOTBALL POOLS PLAYER OF THE SEASON

For the 2008/09 football season, selecting just one player to receive this accolade has been a difficult task with team and individual performances across the Leagues having been outstanding. The New Football Pools panel of football experts and pundits has produced its definitive 2008/09 'Player of the Season' for The Official Football Yearbook, having analysed player performances across all Scottish Premier League and Football League clubs. Criteria such as clean sheets, goals scored, assists and man of the match performances has combined to select those players who made the biggest impact during the exhilarating 2008/09 campaign. We'd like to congratulate each and every winner of this terrific accolade, including those pictured below. Read on to see whether your favourite player matches the verdict of our Panel....

Majid Bougherra (Rangers)

Rob Jones (Hibernian)

Calum Woods (Dunfermline)

Kevin Rutkiewicz (St Johnstone)

THE NEW FOOTBALL POOLS: A SHORT HISTORY

20s In 1923 John Moores and two friends began their venture – handing out the first 4,000 Littlewoods Football Pools coupons outside Manchester United's Old Trafford.
30s Playing the pools was by now a national pastime with millions across the UK taking part, full of hope that this would be their week. Life-changing sums of money were handed out and winning cheques reached the hands of more than 60 million people.
40s During World War II, Littlewoods turned into a parachute-making operation when John and Cecil Moores offered the Littlewoods building to the government to help the nation's combat efforts.
50s Australian matches were introduced on the pools, and pools collectors were first introduced, which later grew to a network of more than 70,000 people.
60s With icebergs floating down the River Mersey and no Saturday football, the winter of 1962/63 saw the Pools Panel born. On 26th January 1963 the panel of former players and referees provided expert opinion on 52 of the 55 postponed games that week. The Panel continues to sit every week.
70s In 1973 Spot the Ball launched as a weekly game, quickly becoming another favourite of the British public.
80s 1986 saw nurse Margaret Francis and her colleagues become the first pools millionaires, sharing £1,017,890.
90s Littlewoods Football Pools launched its first TV advertising campaign.
00s In 2007 Littlewoods, Vernons and Zetters football pools all came under the ownership of Sportech plc and re-launched as The New Football Pools in 2008. The New Football Pools became an Official Licensee of the Premier League and Football Leagues and an Official Partner of the Scottish Premier League and Scottish Football Leagues. The company also joined forces with football experts Alan Hansen, John Barnes and Tony Cascarino, who became The New Football Pools Pundits.

SEASON REVIEW

CLYDESDALE BANK PREMIER LEAGUE STATISTICS

Player of the season
Gary Caldwell (Celtic)

Manager of the season
Csaba Laszlo (Hearts)

The player with the most...

Shots on target	
Kris Boyd (Rangers)	67
Shots off target	
Kris Boyd (Rangers)	52
Shots without scoring	
Joel Thomas (Hamilton)	29
Shots per goal	
Stephen Hughes (Motherwell)	32
Assists	
Shunsuke Nakamura (Celtic)	11
Offsides	
Derek Riordan (Hibernian)	56
Fouls	
David Fernandez (Kilmarnock)	77
Fouls without a card	
John Sutton (Motherwell)	51
Free-kicks won	
Lee Miller (Aberdeen)	126
Penalties scored	
Kris Boyd (Rangers)	7
Goals scored direct from free-kicks	
Charlie Mulgrew (Aberdeen)	4
Saves made	
Graeme Smith (Motherwell)	177
Defensive clearances	
Rob Jones (Hibernian)	83
Defensive blocks	
Rob Jones (Hibernian)	21

The team with the most...

Shots on target	Rangers	283
Shots off target	Rangers	250
Shots per goal	St Mirren	9.9
Corners	Celtic	247
Fouls	Falkirk	561
Woodwork strikes	Hibernian	13
Offsides	Hibernian	138
Penalties conceded	Kilmarnock	10
Yellow cards	Kilmarnock	92
Red cards	Hearts	9

TOTALS 2008/09

Goals	
Total	548
Home	301
Away	247
Cards	
Yellow	755
Average per game	3.31
Red	54
Average per game	0.24
Attendances	
Total	3,542,527

THE 2008/09 Clydesdale Bank Premier League season was one of the most dramatic in recent memory: a title triumph, a relegation decider, a battle for European football and two managerial departures – and all in the final weekend of the season.

Walter Smith brought Rangers' long wait for the title to an end when they triumphed with a 3–0 win over Dundee United at Tannadice on the last day, ending three years of league dominance by Glasgow rivals Celtic. Goals from Kyle Lafferty, Pedro Mendes and Kris Boyd saw the Ibrox side claim the silverware in a final-day decider for the third time in seven seasons.

The championship had proved impossible to predict with the balance of power shifting between the Old Firm giants throughout the course of the campaign. At one stage, Celtic had looked odds-on favourites to clinch the top prize for a fourth successive season when they boasted a seven-point lead over Rangers at the turn of the year following a 1–0 win at Ibrox.

In the end, the Hoops surrendered meekly to Hearts in an uninspiring stalemate at Parkhead in what proved to be Gordon Strachan's last act as Celtic manager. He quit 24 hours after losing the title, but not before Jimmy Calderwood had parted company with Aberdeen after guiding the Dons to a 2–1 win over Hibernian to pip Dundee United to claim fourth place and a Europa League berth.

United had needed a point against Rangers on the final day to guarantee European football, but it was poor results at Tannadice in the latter half of the season which ultimately cost them for the second year running.

United and Aberdeen both had aspirations of finishing third, but the top prize for those outside the Old Firm went to Hearts, with new boss Csaba Laszlo surprising many and proving to be a breath of fresh air in his first season in Scottish football. As well as being a colourful character off the pitch, the coach successfully turned around the fortunes of a club who had finished the previous season in eighth place, despite several tough periods of financial uncertainty and speculation behind the scenes.

Hamilton Academical were the surprise package of the SPL, however, as they finished their first top-flight season for 19 years in a respectable ninth position and

> **Celtic boasted a seven-point lead over Rangers at the turn of the year following a win at Ibrox**

never really looked in danger of dropping straight back into the Irn-Bru First Division. Their talented mix of youth and experience adapted superbly to the demands of the SPL, as they picked up important wins – most notably in the new year as they managed six victories on the bounce in all competitions.

Instead, it was St Mirren, Falkirk and Inverness who were involved in a three-way battle for survival as the season came to a close, although Saints knew they would have to lose by at least three goals to the Accies on the final day of their campaign to lose their top-flight status.

So it was that Falkirk took on Inverness in their last game of the season, with Caley Thistle two points clear of their rivals. Michael Higdon proved to be the hero for Falkirk, grabbing the only goal of the game on a thrilling afternoon at the Caledonian Stadium, as Inverness were consigned to the Scottish Football League. Their demotion came despite the best efforts of former Rangers and England skipper Terry Butcher, who had revived the beleaguered Highlanders after taking over the hotseat in January.

Kilmarnock had also feared for their SPL status in the final weeks of the campaign for the second consecutive year. However, they will be striving for better things next term if they can retain star striker Kevin Kyle, who proved to be a revelation following his January arrival.

Hibs will be hoping to have a bigger impact in 2009/10 after finishing just inside the top six, despite having a major say in the title race with draws against both Rangers and Celtic.

Motherwell failed to live up to the highs of the previous year, having to settle for a seventh-place finish after claiming third spot 12 months earlier. However, a Europa League spot awarded by the Scottish Football Association through the Fair Play system helped to soften the blow for the Steelmen ahead of the new campaign.

FINAL CLYDESDALE BANK PREMIER LEAGUE TABLE

		HOME					AWAY						
		P	W	D	L	F	A	W	D	L	F	A	GD	Pts
1	Rangers	38	15	2	2	44	15	11	6	2	33	13	49	86
2	Celtic	38	14	4	1	48	13	10	6	3	32	20	47	82
3	Hearts	38	11	5	3	28	18	5	6	8	12	19	3	59
4	Aberdeen	38	9	5	5	22	17	5	6	8	19	23	1	53
5	Dundee Utd	38	7	8	4	25	24	6	6	7	22	26	-3	53
6	Hibernian	38	6	7	6	23	23	5	7	7	19	23	-4	47
7	Motherwell	38	7	6	6	24	27	6	3	10	22	24	-5	48
8	Kilmarnock	38	7	3	9	18	22	5	5	9	20	26	-10	44
9	Hamilton	38	7	2	10	18	20	5	3	11	12	33	-23	41
10	Falkirk	38	6	4	9	19	20	3	7	9	18	32	-15	38
11	St Mirren	38	3	8	8	14	21	6	2	11	19	31	-19	37
12	Inverness CT	38	4	5	10	18	27	6	2	11	19	31	-21	37

**COLIN NISH
(HIBERNIAN)**

**DAVID CLARKSON
(MOTHERWELL)**

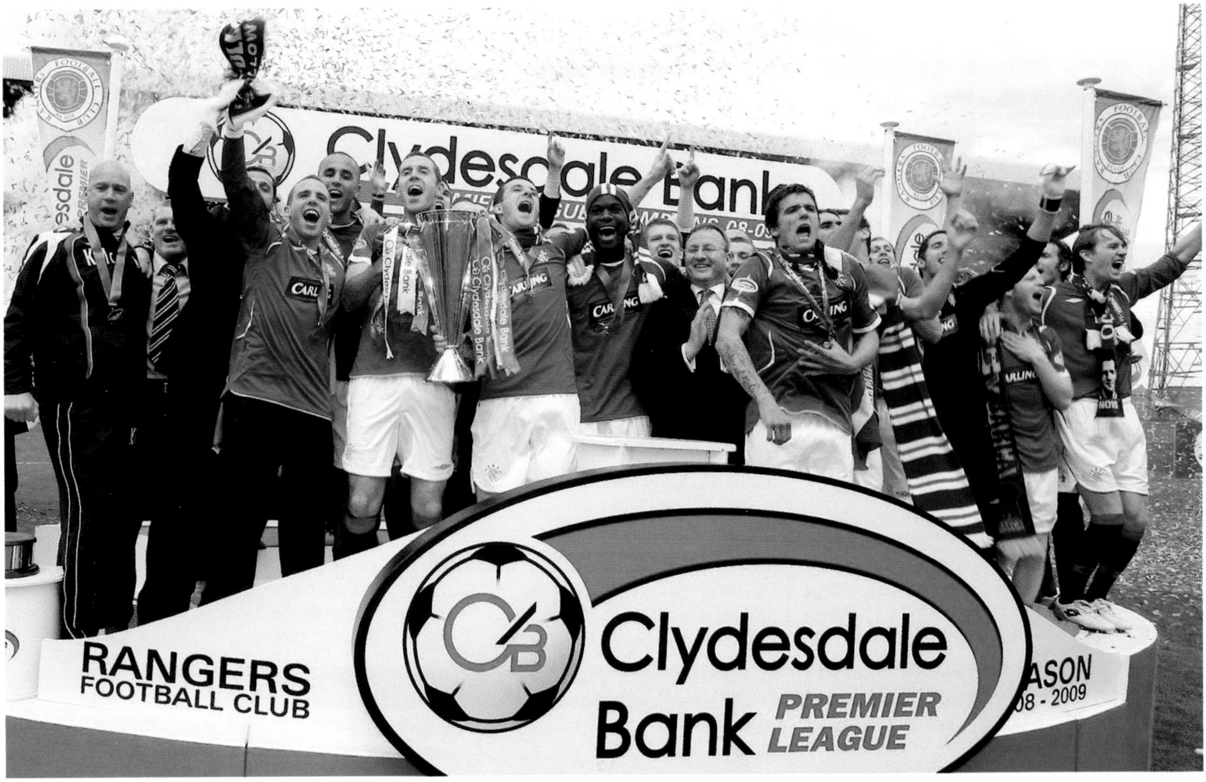

Rangers celebrate winning their first Clydesdale Bank Premier League title since 2004/05, having beaten off Celtic's challenge with victory against Dundee United on the final afternoon of the season

CLYDESDALE BANK PREMIER LEAGUE RESULTS

	Aberdeen	Celtic	Dundee Utd	Falkirk	Hamilton	Hearts	Hibernian	Inverness CT	Kilmarnock	Motherwell	Rangers	St Mirren
Aberdeen	–	4-2, 1-3	0-1, 2-2	2-1	1-2, 1-0	1-0, 0-0	1-2, 2-1	0-2, 1-0	1-0, 0-0	2-0	1-1, 0-0	2-0
Celtic	3-2, 2-0	–	2-2, 2-1	3-0, 4-0	4-0, 4-0	1-1, 0-0	4-2, 3-1	1-0	3-0	2-0	2-4, 0-0	1-0, 7-0
Dundee Utd	2-1, 1-1	1-1, 2-2	–	1-0	1-1	3-0, 0-1	2-0, 2-2	2-1, 1-1	0-2, 0-0	0-4	2-2, 0-3	2-0, 3-2
Falkirk	0-1, 1-0	0-3	0-0, 0-1	–	4-1, 1-2	2-1, 0-0	1-1	1-2, 4-0	1-1	1-0, 2-1	0-1, 0-1	1-2, 0-2
Hamilton	2-0	1-2	3-1, 0-1	1-1, 0-1	–	1-2, 2-0	0-1, 0-1	1-0	1-0, 2-1	2-0, 0-3	1-3, 0-1	1-2, 0-0
Hearts	1-1, 2-1	0-2, 1-1	0-0, 3-0	2-1	1-0	–	0-0, 0-1	1-0, 3-2	1-2, 3-1	3-2, 2-1	2-1	2-1, 1-1
Hibernian	2-2, 0-0	2-0, 0-0	2-1, 1-2	3-2, 0-0	2-0	1-1, 1-0	–	1-2	2-4	0-1, 1-1	0-3, 2-3, 1-1	2-0
Inverness CT	0-3	1-2, 0-0	1-3	1-1, 0-1	0-1, 1-1, 1-1	0-1	1-1, 2-0	–	3-1, 2-1	1-2, 1-2	0-3	1-2, 2-1
Kilmarnock	1-2	1-3, 1-2	2-0	1-2, 3-0, 1-1	1-0, 0-1	0-2	1-0, 1-1	1-2, 1-0	–	1-0, 0-0	0-4	0-1, 2-1
Motherwell	0-1, 1-1	2-4, 1-1	1-1, 2-1	3-2, 1-1	2-0, 1-0	1-0	1-4	3-2, 2-2	0-2, 1-2	–	0-0	2-1, 0-2
Rangers	2-0, 2-1	0-1, 1-0	3-3, 2-0	3-1	7-1	2-0, 2-2, 2-0	1-0	5-0, 0-1	2-1, 3-1	2-1, 3-1	–	2-1
St Mirren	0-1, 1-1	1-3	0-2	1-1, 2-2	1-0, 0-1	0-1	0-0, 1-1	2-0, 1-2	0-0, 1-1	0-0, 1-3	1-0, 1-2	–

KRIS BOYD (RANGERS)

LEADING SCORERS

Player	(Team)	Goals
Kris Boyd	(Rangers)	27
Scott McDonald	(Celtic)	16
Georgios Samaras	(Celtic)	15
David Clarkson	(Motherwell)	13
Derek Riordan	(Hibernian)	12
Steven Fletcher	(Hibernian)	11
Andy Dorman	(St Mirren)	10
Francisco Sandaza	(Dundee U)	10
John Sutton	(Motherwell)	10
Kenny Miller	(Rangers)	10
Lee Miller	(Aberdeen)	10
Colin Nish	(Hibernian)	8
Shunsuke Nakamura	(Celtic)	8
Steve Lovell	(Falkirk)	8

ON THE CLOCK CLYDESDALE BANK PREMIER LEAGUE

FROM THE START OF A MATCH

Quickest goal
Colin Nish 0:21
(Hibernian v Falkirk)

Quickest card
◼ Steven Hammell 0:40
(Motherwell v Dundee Utd)

Last-gasp goal
Kyle Lafferty 93:44
(Rangers v Dundee Utd)

BY A SUBSTITUTE

Quickest goal
Gary McDonald 1:04
(Aberdeen v Motherwell)

Quickest card
◼ Denes Rosa 0:46
(Hibernian v Falkirk)

Substitute being substituted
Laryea Kingston 5:51
(Hearts v St Mirren)

ARTUR BORUC (CELTIC)

LEADING GOALKEEPERS

Player	(Team)	Clean Sheets
Artur Boruc	(Celtic)	15
Jamie Langfield	(Aberdeen)	14
Allan McGregor	(Rangers)	12
Alan Combe	(Kilmarnock)	12
Lukasz Zaluska	(Dundee Utd)	11
Mark Howard	(St Mirren)	10
Graeme Smith	(Motherwell)	9
Tomas Cerny	(Hamilton)	8
Yves Ma-Kalambay	(Hibernian)	7
Dani Mallo	(Falkirk)	6
Janos Balogh	(Hearts)	6
Grzegorz Szamotulski	(Hibernian)	5
Marian Kello	(Hearts)	5
Neil Alexander	(Rangers)	5

REFEREE STATS

Referee	M	Yel	Red	Cards/game	Referee	M	Yel	Red	Cards/game	Referee	M	Yel	Red	Cards/game
S Dougal	5	15	3	5.6	C Murray	18	60	5	3.61	B Winter	11	34	1	3.18
S Finnie	6	24	3	4.5	C Thomson	19	65	2	3.53	D Somers	12	36	2	3.16
W Collum	17	70	5	4.41	E Smith	17	58	2	3.52	M Tumilty	11	29	0	2.63
I Brines	19	80	2	4.32	C Boyle	8	24	4	3.5	S Conroy	15	35	4	2.6
E Norris	6	22	1	3.83	S O'Reilly	7	23	1	3.42	M McCurry	10	18	5	2.3
A Muir	8	29	1	3.75	D McDonald	20	62	6	3.4	S Nicholls	1	2	0	2
C Allan	8	26	4	3.75	C Richmond	10	29	3	3.2					

DISCIPLINARY RECORDS

Player	Team	Fouls	Y	R
Sol Bamba	Hibernian	61	12	2
Ross Tokely	Inverness CT	58	12	1
Manuel Pascali	Kilmarnock	56	13	0
David Fernandez	Kilmarnock	77	11	0
Hugh Murray	St Mirren	63	11	0
Alex Neil	Hamilton	67	10	0
Ian Black	Inverness CT	72	10	0
Lee Wilkie	Dundee Utd	50	10	0
Mark Kerr	Aberdeen	30	6	2
Marius Zaliukas	Hearts	29	4	3
Andrew Considine	Aberdeen	30	7	1
Ian Murray	Hibernian	28	7	1
Madjid Bougherra	Rangers	30	7	1
Sasa Papac	Rangers	30	5	2
Lee Miller	Aberdeen	55	8	0
Maros Klimpl	Motherwell	48	8	0
David Clarkson	Motherwell	44	6	1
James McArthur	Hamilton	66	6	1
Michael Stewart	Hearts	46	6	1
Richard Offiong	Hamilton	46	6	1

SOL BAMBA (HIBERNIAN)

PLAYER WITH THE MOST...

Shots on target

Kris Boyd (Rangers)		67
Derek Riordan (Hibernian)		55
Scott McDonald (Celtic)		48
Georgios Samaras (Celtic)		38
Kenny Miller (Rangers)		34
Shunsuke Nakamura (Celtic)		34
Steven Fletcher (Hibernian)		33
Dougie Imrie (Inverness CT)		31
David Clarkson (Motherwell)		30
Pedro Mendes (Rangers)		30

Shots off target

Kris Boyd (Rangers)		52
Steven Fletcher (Hibernian)		48
Scott McDonald (Celtic)		37
Derek Riordan (Hibernian)		36
Dougie Imrie (Inverness CT)		35
Aiden McGeady (Celtic)		29
David Clarkson (Motherwell)		28
Scott Arfield (Falkirk)		27
Ian Black (Inverness CT)		27
Andy Dorman (St Mirren)		27

Shots without scoring

Joel Thomas (Hamilton)		29
Kevin McBride (Falkirk)		24
Sol Bamba (Hibernian)		23
Morgaro Gomis (Dundee Utd)		19
Kirk Broadfoot (Rangers)		18
Mark Kerr (Aberdeen)		18
Daniel Swanson (Dundee Utd)		18
Steven Hammell (Motherwell)		17
Iain Vigurs (Inverness CT)		17
Mark McLaughlin (Hamilton)		15

Assists

Shunsuke Nakamura (Celtic)		11
Kenny Miller (Rangers)		9
Paul Dixon (Dundee Utd)		8
Steven Hammell (Motherwell)		8
Charlie Mulgrew (Aberdeen)		8
Steven Davis (Rangers)		7
Dougie Imrie (Inverness CT)		7
Scott McDonald (Celtic)		7
Mehdi Taouil (Kilmarnock)		7
Sone Aluko (Aberdeen)		6

Offsides

Derek Riordan (Hibernian)		56
Scott McDonald (Celtic)		48
Kris Boyd (Rangers)		43
Kenny Miller (Rangers)		33
David Fernandez (Kilmarnock)		31
Darren Mackie (Aberdeen)		31
Steven Fletcher (Hibernian)		30
Colin Nish (Hibernian)		29
Billy Mehmet (St Mirren)		28
Michael Higdon (Falkirk)		23

Fouls commited

David Fernandez (Kilmarnock)		77
Michael Higdon (Falkirk)		74
Ian Black (Inverness CT)		72
Alex Neil (Hamilton)		67
Kris Boyd (Rangers)		66
James McArthur (Hamilton)		66
Hugh Murray (St Mirren)		63
Sol Bamba (Hibernian)		61
Simon Mensing (Hamilton)		60
Scott Arfield (Falkirk)		58

TEAM STATISTICS

Club	Played	Shots on	Shots off	Corners	Hit woodwork	Caught offside	Offside trap	Fouls	Yellow cards	Red cards	Pens awarded	Pens con
Aberdeen	38	166	183	188	10	93	55	424	59	5	4 (3)	4
Celtic	38	275	227	**247**	7	95	86	438	49	2	6 (3)	2
Dundee Utd	38	172	174	234	7	78	119	551	72	2	7 (5)	5
Falkirk	38	128	168	156	8	81	69	**561**	66	7	5 (4)	5
Hamilton	38	113	167	167	9	79	105	553	62	7	4 (3)	6
Hearts	38	174	172	195	10	71	105	491	55	**9**	4 (2)	5
Hibernian	38	174	203	137	**13**	**138**	92	502	75	4	5 (4)	4
Inverness CT	38	152	200	178	4	59	**125**	503	60	4	4 (3)	5
Kilmarnock	38	148	143	178	5	87	64	542	**92**	2	4 (3)	**10**
Motherwell	38	168	171	190	9	92	**125**	481	49	3	3 (2)	3
Rangers	38	**283**	**250**	243	11	115	61	459	65	5	9 (8)	2
St Mirren	38	156	166	196	7	82	62	412	51	4	4 (2)	8

Offside trap – number of times a side has caught the opposition offside. **Pens awarded** (scored in brackets). **Pens con** – number of penalties awarded to opposition. **Bold** – biggest total

Total league games played this season: **228** • Home wins: **96** (42%) •Away wins: **73** (32%)
•Draws: **59** (26%) • Average goals scored per match **2.4**

ABERDEEN

CLUB SUMMARY

FORMED	1903
MANAGER	TBC
GROUND	Pittodrie
CAPACITY	21,421
NICKNAME	The Dons
WEBSITE	www.afc.co.uk

The New Football Pools PLAYER OF THE SEASON — **Jamie Langfield**

OVERALL

P	W	D	L	F	A	GD
44	17	13	14	52	46	6

CLYDESDALE BANK PREMIER LEAGUE

Pos	P	W	D	L	F	A	GD	Pts
4	38	14	11	13	41	40	1	53

HOME

Pos	P	W	D	L	F	A	GD	Pts
4	19	9	5	5	22	17	5	32

AWAY

Pos	P	W	D	L	F	A	GD	Pts
6	19	5	6	8	19	23	-4	21

CUP PROGRESS DETAILS

Competition	Round reached	Knocked out by
Co-op Insurance Cup	R3	Kilmarnock
Scottish Cup	QF	Dunfermline

BIGGEST WIN (ALL COMPS)

17/02/09 5–0 v East Fife **TSC5**

BIGGEST DEFEAT (ALL COMPS)

24/09/08 2–4 v Kilmarnock **SLC3**

THE PLAYER WITH THE MOST

Shots on target
Lee Miller.................................... 30

Shots off target
Sone Aluko 26

Shots without scoring
Mark Kerr.................................... 18

Assists
Charlie Mulgrew 8

Offsides
Darren Mackie.............................. 31

Fouls
Lee Miller.................................... 55

Fouls without a card
Jamie Smith................................. 11

Free-kicks won
Lee Miller.................................. 126

Defensive clearances
Zander Diamond 28

ATTENDANCE RECORD

High	Low	Average
20,441	8,909	12,929
v Rangers (24/01/2009)	v Falkirk (13/12/2008)	

ABERDEEN sneaked into Europe on the final day of the Clydesdale Bank Premier League season, but then announced the departure of manager Jimmy Calderwood just a few hours later.

Calderwood secured the fourth top-four finish of his five-year reign by leading the Dons to a 2–1 victory over Hibernian, but it proved to be his last game in charge of the club as the former Dunfermline boss soon left his post 'by mutual consent'.

The result that hurt Calderwood most was the Homecoming Scottish Cup quarter-final defeat by his former club as the Irn-Bru First Division Pars won through on penalties following a goalless replay at Pittodrie. That shock loss came on the back of cup defeats by Queen of the South and Queen's Park in previous seasons and Aberdeen's inability to reach a Hampden final is something they will be keen to address next year.

The Dons also endured a disappointing Co-operative Insurance Cup campaign, conceding four goals inside the first 33 minutes at Kilmarnock to exit in the third round.

It was to their credit, however, that Aberdeen rallied to finish the season strongly after what had been a poor start to the campaign. The club were bottom of the SPL after eight games before a 1–0 victory at Falkirk proved pivotal, and the Dons were firmly ensconced in the top half of the table at New Year following four consecutive wins.

January saw them beat Celtic 4–2 in a Pittodrie thriller and claim a creditable draw with

Dons players celebrate beating Celtic 4–2 at Pittodrie

Rangers, but they also lost to Hamilton and Falkirk.

The Dons comfortably qualified for the top six to keep up Calderwood's record of finishing each season among the top teams, a 1–0 victory over Inverness in their first home game since the Dunfermline cup loss securing their status.

They then managed crucial draws against Dundee United and Hearts to go into the final SPL game knowing that victory could take them into the inaugural Europa League.

First-half goals from Lee Miller and Charlie Mulgrew earned them that victory over Hibs at Pittodrie as they finished the season on a high.

That result secured what should have been a night of celebration, but news quickly emerged of Calderwood's shock departure – the former boss having apparently failed to meet the club's expectations during his time in charge.

> **News quickly emerged of Calderwood's shock departure**

RESULTS 2008/09

August

9th	● Inverness CT ....h	L 0–2	**Att:** 12,659. **Ref:** M Tumilty — **Booked:** Considine, Miller
16th	● Motherwell ....a	W 0–1	**Att:** 5,872. **Ref:** S Conroy — **Scorers:** Mulgrew. **Booked:** Foster, Kerr, Young, Wright
23rd	● Rangers ....h	D 1–1	**Att:** 16,489. **Ref:** C Thomson — **Scorers:** Young. **Booked:** Mackie, Considine
27th	● Ayr ....a	W 0–1	**Att:** 3,173. **Ref:** B Winter — **Scorers:** Maguire
30th	● St Mirren............................a	W 0–1	**Att:** 4,680. **Ref:** W Collum — **Scorers:** Mackie. **Booked:** Miller, Maguire

September

13th	● Hamilton ....h	L 1–2	**Att:** 10,865. **Ref:** A Muir — **Scorers:** McDonald. **Booked:** Miller, Mulgrew
20th	● Dundee Utd ....h	L 0–1	**Att:** 11,041. **Ref:** C Murray — **Booked:** Kerr
24th	● Kilmarnock ....a	L 4–2	**Att:** 4,339. **Ref:** D McDonald — **Scorers:** McDonald, Miller. **Booked:** Mulgrew, Diamond, Aluko, Miller
27th	● Celtic................................a	L 3–2	**Att:** 58,565. **Ref:** E Smith — **Scorers:** Mulgrew[2]

October

4th	● Hibernian ....h	L 1–2	**Att:** 10,793. **Ref:** M McCurry — **Scorers:** Miller. **Booked:** Mair, Severin. **Dismissed:** Mulgrew
18th	● Falkirk ....a	W 0–1	**Att:** 5,662. **Ref:** W Collum — **Scorers:** Miller. **Booked:** Aluko
25th	● Hearts................................a	D 1–1	**Att:** 14,265. **Ref:** S Conroy — **Scorers:** Mackie. **Booked:** Considine

November

1st	● Kilmarnock ....h	W 1–0	**Att:** 10,599. **Ref:** D Somers — **Scorers:** Aluko. **Booked:** Diamond
8th	● Dundee Utd ....a	L 2–1	**Att:** 9,490. **Ref:** W Collum — **Scorers:** Mackie. **Booked:** Diamond, De Visscher
11th	● St Mirren............................h	W 2–0	**Att:** 9,452. **Ref:** B Winter — **Scorers:** Aluko, Considine. **Booked:** Kerr, Considine
15th	● Hibernian ....a	D 2–2	**Att:** 11,640. **Ref:** S O'Reilly — **Scorers:** Diamond, Mackie
22nd	● Rangers ....a	L 2–0	**Att:** 50,166. **Ref:** C Thomson — **Booked:** Diamond
29th	● Motherwell ....h	W 2–0	**Att:** 10,302. **Ref:** C Boyle — **Scorers:** McDonald, Miller. **Booked:** Miller, Maguire

December

13th	● Falkirk ....h	W 2–1	**Att:** 8,909. **Ref:** C Allan — **Scorers:** Miller[2]. **Booked:** McDonald
20th	● Inverness CT ....a	W 0–3	**Att:** 5,862. **Ref:** C Murray — **Scorers:** Mackie, McDonald, Mulgrew. **Booked:** Kerr
27th	● Hearts................................h	W 1–0	**Att:** 18,021. **Ref:** I Brines — **Scorers:** Miller. **Booked:** Mackie, Miller, Considine, Severin

January

3rd	● Hamilton ....a	L 2–0	**Att:** 4,334. **Ref:** S Finnie — **Booked:** Foster, Kerr
10th	● Alloa ....a	W 1–2	**Att:** 3,012. **Ref:** S Nicholls — **Scorers:** Aluko, Miller. **Booked:** Severin, Foster
13th	● Kilmarnock ....a	W 1–2	**Att:** 4,354. **Ref:** E Smith — **Scorers:** Miller[2]. **Booked:** Considine, Mackie, Diamond
18th	● Celtic................................h	W 4–2	**Att:** 18,100. **Ref:** D McDonald — **Scorers:** Diamond[2], Duff, McDonald. **Booked:** Kerr, Mackie
24th	● Rangers ....h	D 0–0	**Att:** 20,441. **Ref:** C Murray — **Booked:** McDonald
31st	● Falkirk ....a	L 1–0	**Att:** 5,605. **Ref:** E Norris — **Booked:** Mair

February

14th	● Hearts................................a	L 2–1	**Att:** 15,049. **Ref:** C Richmond — **Scorers:** Mackie. **Booked:** Foster
17th	● East Fife ....h	W 5–0	**Att:** 8,960. **Ref:** S Conroy — **Scorers:** Maguire[2], Vidal, Wright, McDonald OG
21st	● Dundee Utd ....h	D 2–2	**Att:** 14,673. **Ref:** W Collum — **Scorers:** Diamond, Severin. **Booked:** Diamond, Mair, Miller
28th	● Kilmarnock ....h	D 0–0	**Att:** 11,457. **Ref:** D McDonald — **Booked:** Aluko, Maguire

March

3rd	● St Mirren............................a	D 1–1	**Att:** 4,383. **Ref:** C Boyle — **Scorers:** Wright. **Booked:** Severin
7th	● Dunfermline ....a	D 1–1	**Att:** 9,696. **Ref:** C Thomson — **Scorers:** Aluko.
14th	● Hamilton ....h	W 1–0	**Att:** 10,312. **Ref:** E Norris — **Scorers:** Maguire. **Booked:** Wright, Severin
18th	● Dunfermline ....h	D 0–0	**Att:** 13,567. **Ref:** E Smith — **Booked:** Foster (Lost 2–4 on pens)
21st	● Hibernian ....a	D 0–0	**Att:** 11,754. **Ref:** M McCurry — **Dismissed:** Kerr

April

4th	● Motherwell ....a	D 1–1	**Att:** 4,686. **Ref:** C Allan — **Scorers:** Maguire. **Booked:** Mair, Considine, Miller. **Dismissed:** Considine
11th	● Inverness CT ....h	W 1–0	**Att:** 11,114. **Ref:** A Muir — **Scorers:** McDonald
18th	● Celtic................................a	L 2–0	**Att:** 58,581. **Ref:** D McDonald

May

2nd	● Celtic................................h	L 1–3	**Att:** 14,752. **Ref:** D McDonald — **Scorers:** Maguire. **Booked:** Pawlett
7th	● Dundee Utd ....a	D 1–1	**Att:** 10,407. **Ref:** C Boyle — **Scorers:** Miller. **Booked:** Miller, Foster **Dismissed:** Kerr
12th	● Hearts................................h	D 0–0	**Att:** 11,588. **Ref:** S Finnie — **Booked:** Foster, Mulgrew
16th	● Rangers ....a	L 2–1	**Att:** 50,295. **Ref:** S Dougal — **Scorers:** Paton. **Booked:** Vidal. **Dismissed:** Mulgrew
24th	● Hibernian ....h	W 2–1	**Att:** 14,083. **Ref:** D Somers — **Scorers:** Miller, Mulgrew. **Booked:** McDonald

● Clydesdale Bank Premier League ● Scottish FA Cup ● Co-op Insurance Cup ● UEFA Champions League ● UEFA Cup

ABERDEEN

CLYDESDALE BANK PREMIER LEAGUE GOALKEEPER STATS

Player	Minutes on pitch	Appearances	Match starts	Completed matches	Sub appearances	Subbed off	Saved with feet	Punched	Parried	Tipped over	Fumbled	Tipped round	Caught	Blocked	Clean sheets	Goals conceded	Minutes since conceding	Save %	Saved	Resulting in goals	Opposition miss	Yellow cards	Red cards
Bertrand Bossu 42	1	0	0	1	0	0	0	0	0	0	0	0	2	0	1	0	-	0	0	0	0	0	0
Jamie Langfield 3537	38	38	37	0	1	1	21	16	8	0	10	101	0	14	40	46	80.10	0	4	0	0	0

CLYDESDALE BANK PREMIER LEAGUE OUTFIELD PLAYER STATS

Player	Minutes on pitch	Appearances	Match starts	Completed matches	Substitute appearances	Subbed off	Goals scored	Minutes since scoring	Assists	Shots on target	Shots off target	Crosses	Defensive clearances	Defensive blocks	Fouls committed	Free-kicks won	Caught offside	Yellow cards	Red cards
Sone Aluko 2647	32	28	19	4	9	2	1973	6	21	26	35	1	0	32	58	15	2	0
Andrew Considine 1621	20	17	14	3	2	1	818	2	2	3	2	19	1	30	16	1	7	1
Jeffrey De Visscher.................526	10	6	2	4	4	0	-	0	3	6	4	0	0	7	7	2	1	0
Zander Diamond 2387	28	26	24	2	2	4	465	0	11	7	0	28	12	25	44	0	5	0
Stuart Duff 995	20	9	4	11	5	1	734	1	2	1	6	7	0	7	10	1	0	0
Richard Foster 2977	34	30	30	4	0	0	-	1	4	5	10	9	2	15	14	1	5	0
Jared Hodgkiss 501	7	6	2	1	4	0	-	1	0	2	2	1	2	6	2	0	0	0
Mark Kerr 2875	32	31	26	1	3	0	-	2	7	11	7	25	4	30	31	0	6	2
Darren Mackie 2251	29	25	16	4	9	6	336	1	15	9	7	4	0	44	27	31	4	0
Christopher Maguire 1393	31	13	3	18	10	3	234	1	14	18	3	2	1	25	31	13	3	0
Lee Mair 1897	24	21	18	3	3	0	-	0	4	5	2	14	5	23	13	0	4	0
Gary McDonald 2373	28	24	23	4	1	5	587	1	12	15	4	9	1	24	33	6	3	0
Lee Miller 3016	34	34	23	0	11	10	72	2	30	23	3	16	0	55	126	20	8	0
Charlie Mulgrew 2888	35	32	27	3	2	5	51	8	18	13	129	18	3	14	27	1	2	2
Michael Paton 71	4	0	0	4	0	1	31	0	1	0	0	0	0	0	1	1	0	0
Peter Pawlett 200	5	2	0	3	2	0	-	0	2	0	0	1	0	4	2	0	1	0
Scott Severin 3404	37	37	35	0	2	1	1186	2	10	14	19	24	11	31	43	0	4	0
Jamie Smith..............................849	12	9	5	3	4	0	-	0	3	11	4	0	0	11	14	0	0	0
Sammy Stewart 5	1	0	0	1	0	0	-	0	0	0	0	0	0	0	0	0	0	0
Javan Vidal 877	13	9	5	4	4	0	-	0	0	2	5	4	1	10	8	0	1	0
Tommy Wright 469	15	4	0	11	4	1	272	0	2	6	0	0	0	13	11	1	2	0
Derek Young 1392	22	17	6	5	11	1	1222	0	5	6	13	4	0	18	19	0	1	0

SEASON TOTALS

Goals scored	41
Goals conceded	40
Clean sheets	14
Shots on target	166
Shots off target	183
Shots per goal	8.51
Pens awarded	4
Pens scored	3
Pens conceded	4
Offsides	93
Corners	188
Crosses	255
Players used	24
Fouls committed	424
Free-kicks won	545

CARDS RECEIVED

59 **5**

SEQUENCES

Wins	4
(29/11/08–27/12/08)	
Losses	4
(13/09/08–04/10/08)	
Draws	3
(21/02/09–03/03/09)	
Undefeated	7
(21/02/09–11/04/09)	
Without win	6
(24/01/09–03/03/09)	
Undefeated home	11
(01/11/08–11/04/09)	
Undefeated away	3
(03/03/09–04/04/09)	
Without scoring	2
(24/01/09–31/01/09)	
Without conceding	2
(on two occasions)	
Scoring	8
(27/09/08–15/11/08)	
Conceding	4
(13/09/08–04/10/08)	

League position at the end of each week

League position at the end of: August 6, September 11, October 8, November 5, December 5, January 5, February 5, March 4, April 5, May 4

SEASON INFORMATION
Highest Position: 3
Lowest Position: 12
Average goals scored per game: 1.08
Average goals conceded per game: 1.05

MATCH RECORDS

Goals scored per match

		W	D	L	Pts
Failed to score	10	0	4	6	4
Scored 1 goal	18	7	5	6	26
Scored 2 goals	8	5	2	1	17
Scored 3 goals	1	1	0	0	3
Scored 4+ goals	1	1	0	0	3

Goals conceded per match

		W	D	L	Pts
Clean sheet	14	10	4	0	34
Conceded 1 goal	10	3	5	2	14
Conceded 2 goals	12	1	2	9	5
Conceded 3 goals	2	0	0	2	0
Conceded 4+ goals	0	0	0	0	0

QUICK-FIRE GOALS

From the start of a match
Charlie Mulgrew
(v Inverness CT) 5:45

By a substitute after coming on
Gary McDonald
(v Motherwell) 1:04

LAST-GASP GOALS

From the start of a match
Tommy Wright
(v St Mirren) 92:45

By a substitute after coming on
Tommy Wright
(v St Mirren) 53:49

GOAL DETAILS

How the goals were struck

SCORED		CONCEDED
16	Right foot	22
12	Left foot	8
12	Headers	10
1	Others	0

How the goals were struck

SCORED		CONCEDED
22	Open play	27
3	Cross	2
3	Corner	4
3	Penalties	4
4	Direct from free-kick	0
6	Free-kick	1
0	Own goals	2

Distance from goal

SCORED		CONCEDED
15	6yds	21
20	18yds	19
6	18+yds	0

GOALS SCORED/CONCEDED PER FIVE-MINUTE INTERVALS

Goals For	0	2	2	2	2	2	2	2	5	2	3	3	2	3	2	4	0	3
Goals Against	0	3	3	0	3	1	2	1	4	1	4	2	1	4	2	4	0	5
Mins	5	10	15	20	25	30	35	40	45	50	55	60	65	70	75	80	85	90

OFFICIAL FOOTBALL YEARBOOK OF THE ENGLISH & SCOTTISH LEAGUES 2009–2010   **375**

CELTIC

CLUB SUMMARY

FORMED	1888
MANAGER	TBC
GROUND	Celtic Park
CAPACITY	60,355
NICKNAME	The Bhoys
WEBSITE	www.celticfc.net

The New Football Pools PLAYER OF THE SEASON — Scott Brown

OVERALL

P	W	D	L	F	A	GD
51	30	13	8	97	44	53

CLYDESDALE BANK PREMIER LEAGUE

Pos	P	W	D	L	F	A	GD	Pts
2	38	24	10	4	80	33	47	82

HOME

Pos	P	W	D	L	F	A	GD	Pts
2	19	14	4	1	48	13	35	46

AWAY

Pos	P	W	D	L	F	A	GD	Pts
2	19	10	6	3	32	20	12	36

CUP PROGRESS DETAILS

Competition	Round reached	Knocked out by
Co-op Insurance Cup	Won	–
Scottish Cup	QF	St Mirren
Champions League	Group stage	–

BIGGEST WIN (ALL COMPS)

28/02/09 7–0 v St Mirren **SPL**

BIGGEST DEFEAT (ALL COMPS)

21/10/08 0–3 v Man Utd **EUROPE**

THE PLAYER WITH THE MOST

Shots on target

Scott McDonald 48

Shots off target

Scott McDonald 37

Shots without scoring

Willo Flood 13

Assists

Shunsuke Nakamura 11

Offsides

Scott McDonald 48

Fouls

Scott Brown 55

Fouls without a card

Shunsuke Nakamura 24

Free-kicks won

Scott Brown 59

Defensive clearances

Gary Caldwell 36

ATTENDANCE RECORD

High	Low	Average
59,685	55,117	57,671
v Hearts (24/05/2009)	v Inverness CT (29/11/2008)	

Scott McDonald lets fly for Celtic in the final clash of the season against Hearts

WHAT can we make of this rather erratic season for Celtic, which ended with manager Gordon Strachan stepping down 24 hours after losing the Clydesdale Bank Premier League title to Rangers?

Strachan's departure was no surprise, but it does leave the club with something of a rebuilding job to do before the start of the next campaign.

A poor performance in the UEFA Champions League saw Celtic go out at the group stages – mainly due to the fact they failed to take more than one point from two games against Danish side Aalborg. It hurt all the more because they did not even have the parachute of the UEFA Cup to fall back on.

After reaching the last 16 of the Champions League in the previous two seasons, it was a huge blow. However, Strachan's side did pick up the first silverware of the season when the Co-operative Insurance Cup was captured in March thanks to a victory over Rangers, with former youth-team

players Darren O'Dea and Aiden McGeady the scorers.

The Homecoming Scottish Cup journey had come to an end a month earlier after a 1–0 defeat at St Mirren.

In the SPL, Celtic did manage to build up an eight-point lead over Rangers in January – albeit for only 24 hours – but their poor away form cost them dearly in the end.

On the final day of the season, the Bhoys had to beat Hearts and hope Dundee United would draw or even beat Rangers at Tannadice for them to clinch the title. But a goalless draw at Celtic Park meant the Gers clinched the SPL title.

Strachan's exit was confirmed by the club soon after the climax to the campaign to mark the beginning of a new era at Celtic.

> **Strachan's departure leaves the club with a rebuilding job**

RESULTS 2008/09

August

10th	● St Mirren.................h	W 1–0	**Att:** 57,441. **Ref:** E Smith — **Scorers:** Robson. **Booked:** Vennegoor of Hesselink
17th	● Dundee Utd ....a	D 1–1	**Att:** 11,648. **Ref:** C Richmond — **Scorers:** Hartley. **Booked:** McGeady
23rd	● Falkirk.................h	W 3–0	**Att:** 56,031. **Ref:** I Brines — **Scorers:** McManus, Samaras². **Booked:** S. Brown
31st	● Rangers ....h	L 2–4	**Att:** 58,595. **Ref:** D McDonald — **Scorers:** Nakamura, Samaras. **Booked:** McManus, Samaras. **Dismissed:** Vennegoor of Hesselink

September

13th	● Motherwell ....a	W 2–4	**Att:** 8,407. **Ref:** C Thomson — **Scorers:** Maloney, McDonald, Samaras². **Booked:** McDonald, Robson, Samaras
17th	● AaB...................h	D 0–0	**Att:** 57,432. **Ref:** M Trefoloni — **Booked:** McManus, Samaras
21st	● Kilmarnock ....a	W 1–3	**Att:** 8,111. **Ref:** M McCurry — **Scorers:** Maloney, Samaras². **Booked:** McManus, Maloney. **Dismissed:** Caldwell
23rd	● Livingston ....h	W 4–0	**Att:** 23,644. **Ref:** W Collum — **Scorers:** Brown, Loovens, Samaras²
27th	● Aberdeen ....h	W 3–2	**Att:** 58,565. **Ref:** E Smith — **Scorers:** McDonald, Vennegoor of Hesselink². **Booked:** Boruc
30th	● Villarreal ....a	L 1–0	**Att:** 25,000. **Ref:** V Kassai — **Booked:** Robson, S. Brown

October

4th	● Hamilton ....h	W 4–0	**Att:** 55,881. **Ref:** S Conroy — **Scorers:** McDonald, McGeady, Nakamura, Samaras. **Booked:** Caldwell
18th	● Inverness CT ....a	W 1–2	**Att:** 7,143. **Ref:** I Brines — **Scorers:** Brown, Loovens. **Booked:** Crosas, S. Brown, McGeady
21st	● Man Utd ....a	L 3–0	**Att:** 74,655. **Ref:** F De Bleeckere — **Booked:** Hartley, Loovens
25th	● Hibernian ....h	W 4–2	**Att:** 58,337. **Ref:** C Murray — **Scorers:** Brown, Loovens, McManus, Sheridan. **Booked:** McDonald, Hartley
29th	● Kilmarnock ....a	W 1–3	**Att:** 6,319. **Ref:** C Thomson — **Scorers:** McDonald, McGeady, Nakamura. **Booked:** Nakamura, Wilson

November

2nd	● Hearts...............a	W 0–2	**Att:** 15,460. **Ref:** C Thomson — **Scorers:** Caldwell, Maloney. **Booked:** Hartley
5th	● Man Utd ....h	D 1–1	**Att:** 58,903. **Ref:** T Ovrebo — **Scorers:** McDonald
8th	● Motherwell ....h	W 2–0	**Att:** 56,504. **Ref:** D McDonald — **Scorers:** Hartley, McDonald. **Booked:** Robson
12th	● Kilmarnock ....h	W 3–0	**Att:** 55,347. **Ref:** M Tumilty — **Scorers:** Nakamura, Sheridan²
16th	● Hamilton ....a	W 1–2	**Att:** 5,550. **Ref:** S Conroy — **Scorers:** Hartley, Nakamura. **Booked:** Hartley
22nd	● St Mirren..................a	W 1–3	**Att:** 7,433. **Ref:** W Collum — **Scorers:** Nakamura, Samaras, Sheridan. **Booked:** Boruc
25th	● AaB..................a	L 2–1	**Att:** 12,647. **Ref:** K Plautz — **Scorers:** Robson.
29th	● Inverness CT ....h	W 1–0	**Att:** 55,117. **Ref:** D Somers — **Scorers:** Maloney. **Booked:** Boruc

December

7th	● Hibernian ....a	L 2–0	**Att:** 14,289. **Ref:** C Thomson — **Booked:** Caldwell
10th	● Villarreal ....h	W 2–0	**Att:** 58,104. **Ref:** C Circhetta — **Scorers:** Maloney, McGeady. **Booked:** Caldwell, McGowan
13th	● Hearts...............h	D 1–1	**Att:** 56,079. **Ref:** C Richmond — **Scorers:** McManus
21st	● Falkirk...............a	W 0–3	**Att:** 6,543. **Ref:** E Smith — **Scorers:** McDonald, Mizuno, Samaras. **Booked:** Mizuno
27th	● Rangers ....a	W 0–1	**Att:** 50,403. **Ref:** C Thomson — **Scorers:** McDonald. **Booked:** Naylor, Caldwell

January

3rd	● Dundee Utd ....h	D 2–2	**Att:** 59,558. **Ref:** S Conroy — **Scorers:** Samaras². **Booked:** McManus
10th	● Dundee...............h	W 2–1	**Att:** 23,070. **Ref:** C Murray — **Scorers:** Brown, McGeady. **Booked:** S. Brown
18th	● Aberdeen ....a	L 4–2	**Att:** 18,100. **Ref:** D McDonald — **Scorers:** Brown, McDonald. **Booked:** McGeady, S. Brown
24th	● Hibernian ....h	W 3–1	**Att:** 58,930. **Ref:** D Somers — **Scorers:** McDonald², McManus
28th	● Dundee Utd ....n	D 0–0	**Att:** 19,258. **Ref:** C Murray — **Booked:** Loovens (Won 11–10 on pens)

February

1st	● Inverness CT ....a	D 0–0	**Att:** 7,007. **Ref:** C Richmond — **Booked:** McManus, Robson
7th	● Queens Park..................h	W 2–1	**Att:** 22,223. **Ref:** W Collum — **Scorers:** Caldwell, McDonald. **Booked:** McDonald
15th	● Rangers ....h	D 0–0	**Att:** 58,766. **Ref:** C Murray — **Booked:** Vennegoor of Hesselink, Hartley, S. Brown
22nd	● Motherwell ....a	D 1–1	**Att:** 8,593. **Ref:** I Brines — **Scorers:** McDonald. **Booked:** S. Brown
28th	● St Mirren..................h	W 7–0	**Att:** 58,286. **Ref:** C Allan — **Scorers:** Brown², Crosas, Nakamura³, Potter OG. **Booked:** O'Dea

March

4th	● Kilmarnock ....a	W 1–2	**Att:** 6,712. **Ref:** C Thomson — **Scorers:** McDonald². **Booked:** McGeady, O'Dea
7th	● St Mirren..................a	L 1–0	**Att:** 5,925. **Ref:** C Richmond — **Booked:** McManus, Vennegoor of Hesselink
15th	● Rangers ....n	W 2–0	**Att:** 51,193. **Ref:** D McDonald — **Scorers:** McGeady, O'Dea. **Booked:** Hinkel, O'Dea, McGeady, Boruc (AET)
22nd	● Dundee Utd ....a	D 2–2	**Att:** 12,043. **Ref:** S Conroy — **Scorers:** McDonald, Naylor. **Booked:** McDonald

April

4th	● Hamilton ....h	W 4–0	**Att:** 58,961. **Ref:** B Winter — **Scorers:** McGeady, Samaras², Vennegoor of Hesselink
8th	● Falkirk...............h	W 4–0	**Att:** 57,669. **Ref:** W Collum — **Scorers:** Caldwell, McGeady, O'Dea, Vennegoor of Hesselink. **Booked:** S. Brown
11th	● Hearts...............a	D 1–1	**Att:** 16,514. **Ref:** C Thomson — **Scorers:** Vennegoor of Hesselink. **Booked:** McManus
18th	● Aberdeen ....h	W 2–0	**Att:** 58,581. **Ref:** D McDonald — **Scorers:** McDonald, Vennegoor of Hesselink. **Booked:** McDonald

May

2nd	● Aberdeen ....a	W 1–3	**Att:** 14,752. **Ref:** D McDonald — **Scorers:** McDonald², Considine OG. **Booked:** McDonald
9th	● Rangers ....a	L 1–0	**Att:** 50,321. **Ref:** C Thomson — **Booked:** Hartley, Caldwell, Naylor
12th	● Dundee Utd ....h	W 2–1	**Att:** 57,407. **Ref:** S Dougal — **Scorers:** Loovens, Samaras. **Booked:** Loovens, Hartley
17th	● Hibernian ....a	D 0–0	**Att:** 14,074. **Ref:** I Brines — **Booked:** S. Brown
24th	● Hearts...............h	D 0–0	**Att:** 59,685. **Ref:** C Thomson

● Clydesdale Bank Premier League ● Scottish FA Cup ● Co-op Insurance Cup ● UEFA Champions League ● UEFA Cup

CLYDESDALE BANK PREMIER LEAGUE GOALKEEPER STATS

Player	Minutes on pitch	Appearances	Match starts	Completed matches	Sub appearances	Subbed off	SAVES BREAKDOWN: Saved with feet	Punched	Parried	Tipped over	Fumbled	Tipped round	Caught	Blocked	Clean sheets	Goals conceded	Minutes since conceding	Save %	PENALTIES: Saved	Resulting in goals	Opposition miss	Yellow cards	Red cards
Artur Boruc	3185	34	34	34	0	0	3	13	17	4	0	7	69	0	15	28	222	80.69	1	1	0	3	0
Mark Brown	373	4	4	4	0	0	1	0	0	1	0	0	8	0	2	5	15	66.67	0	0	0	0	0

CLYDESDALE BANK PREMIER LEAGUE OUTFIELD PLAYER STATS

Player	Minutes on pitch	Appearances	Match starts	Completed matches	Substitute appearances	Subbed off	Goals scored	Minutes since scoring	Assists	Shots on target	Shots off target	Crosses	Defensive clearances	Defensive blocks	Fouls committed	Free-kicks won	Caught offside	Yellow cards	Red cards
Scott Brown	3287	36	36	31	0	5	5	825	5	19	26	4	8	3	55	59	2	7	0
Paul Caddis	128	5	0	0	5	0	0	-	0	0	1	2	0	0	1	0	0	0	0
Gary Caldwell	3319	36	36	33	0	2	2	726	1	11	12	2	36	6	40	35	1	4	1
Marc Crosas	1305	18	14	7	4	7	1	703	2	3	6	1	3	0	16	14	0	1	0
Massimo Donati	193	4	2	1	2	1	0	-	1	0	0	0	2	0	1	3	0	0	0
Willo Flood	170	5	2	0	3	2	0	-	0	0	1	1	1	0	1	2	0	0	0
Paul Hartley	1906	25	20	18	5	2	3	1151	0	11	9	19	5	1	30	28	0	6	0
Andreas Hinkel	2944	32	32	31	0	1	0	-	6	7	5	43	14	2	14	26	0	0	0
Ben Hutchinson	38	3	0	0	3	0	0	-	0	0	2	0	0	0	0	0	0	0	0
Chris Killen	19	1	0	0	1	0	0	-	0	0	0	0	0	0	0	0	0	0	0
Glenn Loovens	1345	17	13	13	4	0	3	259	0	5	5	1	14	2	16	6	0	1	0
Shaun Maloney	1239	21	14	7	7	7	4	306	4	21	18	12	0	0	10	25	12	1	0
Patrick McCourt	33	4	0	0	4	0	0	-	1	1	1	0	0	0	0	1	0	0	0
Scott McDonald	2931	34	33	19	1	14	16	354	7	48	37	7	2	2	38	52	48	5	0
Aiden McGeady	2166	29	21	16	8	5	3	585	4	22	29	36	0	0	18	53	3	4	0
Stephen McManus	2730	31	31	27	0	4	4	801	1	12	7	0	27	11	27	22	0	5	0
Koki Mizuno	226	10	2	1	8	1	1	117	0	1	3	5	0	0	1	5	0	1	0
Shunsuke Nakamura	2655	32	30	21	2	9	8	933	11	34	21	82	3	1	24	51	0	0	0
Lee Naylor	1773	23	19	17	4	2	1	498	1	4	2	16	5	3	18	21	0	2	0
Darren O'Dea	754	10	7	6	3	1	1	177	0	2	1	4	6	2	3	6	0	2	0
Barry Robson	1217	17	13	8	4	5	1	1154	2	3	3	16	6	1	28	28	1	3	0
Georgios Samaras	1743	31	19	4	12	15	15	130	3	38	18	3	9	1	39	22	12	2	0
Cillian Sheridan	614	12	6	3	6	3	4	128	0	11	2	1	0	0	11	7	6	0	0
Jan Vennegoor of Hesselink	1412	25	15	5	10	9	6	320	5	19	14	2	14	0	42	16	8	2	1
Mark Wilson	1370	18	15	11	3	4	0	-	1	3	4	13	4	1	4	10	2	0	0

actim

Clydesdale Bank
PREMIER LEAGUE

SEASON TOTALS

Goals scored	80
Goals conceded	33
Clean sheets	17
Shots on target	275
Shots off target	227
Shots per goal	6.28
Pens awarded	6
Pens scored	3
Pens conceded	2
Offsides	95
Corners	247
Crosses	270
Players used	27
Fouls committed	438
Free-kicks won	495

CARDS RECEIVED

49   **2**

SEQUENCES

Wins	12
(13/09/08–29/11/08)	
Losses	
(–)	
Draws	3
(01/02/09–22/02/09)	
Undefeated	12
(on two occasions)	
Without win	3
(01/02/09–22/02/09)	
Undefeated home	16
(27/09/08–24/05/09)	
Undefeated away	7
(17/08/08–22/11/08)	
Without scoring	2
(01/02/09–15/02/09)	
Without conceding	3
(02/11/08–12/11/08)	
Scoring	16
(10/08/08–29/11/08)	
Conceding	4
(31/08/08–27/09/08)	

League position at the end of each week

League position at the end of: August 4, September 2, October 1, November 1, December 1, January 1, February 2, March 1, April 1, May 2

SEASON INFORMATION
Highest Position: 1
Lowest Position: 4
Average goals scored per game: 2.11
Average goals conceded per game: 0.87

MATCH RECORDS

Goals scored per match

		W	D	L	Pts
Failed to score	6	0	4	2	4
Scored 1 goal	7	3	4	0	13
Scored 2 goals	11	7	2	2	23
Scored 3 goals	8	8	0	0	24
Scored 4+ goals	6	6	0	0	18

Goals conceded per match

		W	D	L	Pts
Clean sheet	17	13	4	0	43
Conceded 1 goal	13	8	4	1	28
Conceded 2 goals	6	3	2	1	11
Conceded 3 goals	0	0	0	0	0
Conceded 4+ goals	2	0	0	2	0

GOALS SCORED/CONCEDED PER FIVE-MINUTE INTERVALS

Goals For	4	3	2	3	6	4	3	4	5	2	5	5	4	4	4	8	7	7
Goals Against	0	0	1	1	3	0	2	3	1	2	3	5	2	2	1	4	1	2
Mins	5	10	15	20	25	30	35	40	45	50	55	60	65	70	75	80	85	90

QUICK-FIRE GOALS

From the start of a match
Jan Vennegoor of Hesselink (v Hearts) 0:26

By a substitute after coming on
Cillian Sheridan (v St Mirren) 3:00

LAST-GASP GOALS

From the start of a match
Scott McDonald (v Falkirk) 93:04

By a substitute after coming on
Jan Vennegoor of Hesselink (v Falkirk) 46:13

GOAL DETAILS

How the goals were struck

SCORED		CONCEDED
47	Right foot	16
21	Left foot	10
11	Headers	7
1	Others	0

How the goals were struck

SCORED		CONCEDED
64	Open play	24
2	Cross	0
4	Corner	2
3	Penalties	1
2	Direct from free-kick	3
3	Free-kick	3
2	Own goals	0

Distance from goal

SCORED		CONCEDED
40	6yds	16
31	18yds	12
9	18+yds	5

CLUB SUMMARY

FORMED	1909
MANAGER	Craig Levein
GROUND	Tannadice Park
CAPACITY	14,223
NICKNAME	The Terrors
WEBSITE	www.dundeeunitedfc.co.uk

The New **Football Pools** PLAYER OF THE SEASON — **Lee Wilkie**

OVERALL

P	W	D	L	F	A	GD
44	17	15	12	60	53	7

CLYDESDALE BANK PREMIER LEAGUE

Pos	P	W	D	L	F	A	GD	Pts
5	38	13	14	11	47	50	-3	53

HOME

Pos	P	W	D	L	F	A	GD	Pts
5	19	7	8	4	25	24	1	29

AWAY

Pos	P	W	D	L	F	A	GD	Pts
3	19	6	6	7	22	26	-4	24

CUP PROGRESS DETAILS

Competition	Round reached	Knocked out by
Co-op Insurance Cup	SF	Celtic
Scottish Cup	R5	Hamilton

BIGGEST WIN (ALL COMPS)

26/08/08 5–1 v Cowdenbeath **SLC2**

BIGGEST DEFEAT (ALL COMPS)

18/01/09 0–4 v Motherwell **SPL**

THE PLAYER WITH THE MOST

Shots on target
Francisco Sandaza 23

Shots off target
Jon Daly 21

Shots without scoring
Morgaro Gomis 19

Assists
Paul Dixon 8

Offsides
Francisco Sandaza 20

Fouls
Lee Wilkie 50

Fouls without a card
Paul Dixon 28

Free-kicks won
Craig Conway 90

Defensive clearances
Lee Wilkie 80

ATTENDANCE RECORD

High	Low	Average
14,077	5,926	8,654
v Rangers (24/05/2009)	v Inverness CT (14/02/2009)	

ANOTHER Clydesdale Bank Premier League season, another case of what might have been for Dundee United.

Craig Levein's men headed into the 2008/09 campaign hoping that this would be the season they established themselves as the third force in Scottish football.

Despite a poor start, losing 3–1 away from home to newly-promoted Hamilton, the Terrors quickly recovered and gradually began to demonstrate their credentials in the race to be crowned 'best of the rest' behind the Old Firm.

However, everyone associated with the Terrors was left reeling on 15th October with the news that much-loved chairman Eddie Thompson had lost his long battle with cancer.

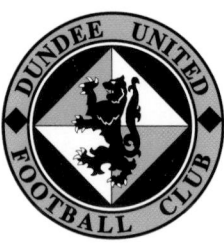

The day-to-day running of the club passed on to his son, Stephen, but focusing on matters on the pitch at such a difficult time was tough. Despite the gloom, Levein's Terrors continued to put points on the board and, by the turn of the year, they were in the coveted third spot and three points ahead of

'Levein's Terrors continued to put points on the board'

nearest rivals Hearts. But they could not maintain the momentum into 2009.

The previous year had seen United pipped to the Co-operative Insurance Cup by Rangers. This time around, Celtic stood between them and another crack at glory as the two teams battled through a tense, goalless semi-final. Another penalty shoot-out brought yet more heartache as Celtic triumphed 11–10. Loan-star Willo Flood missed the decisive spot-kick for United, just days before signing for Celtic.

Results in the League also began to suffer – a shock 4–0 defeat to Motherwell, a draw with struggling Inverness, a damaging loss to Hearts and a stalemate with Kilmarnock.

A 3–0 reverse to Hearts – who ultimately clinched third position – in the penultimate game left United's European hopes hanging by a thread and they headed into the final game against Rangers needing a point to claim a Europa League berth – or hope others slipped up.

Instead, they were unwanted guests at a title party as Rangers celebrated winning the championship – 12 months after Celtic had also triumphed at Tannadice. A 2–1 win for Aberdeen saw the Dons snatch fourth place – 12 months after pipping United to the same position by a point. Not for the first time over the course of the season, there was a horrible sense of déjà vu for the Terrors.

Francisco Sandaza celebrates one of his 10 league goals

RESULTS 2008/09

August

11th	● Hamilton ....a	L 3–1	**Att:** 4,385. **Ref:** S Dougal — **Scorers:** McLaughlin OG. **Booked:** Buaben, Grainger, Flood, Swanson
17th	● Celtic....................................h	D 1–1	**Att:** 11,648. **Ref:** C Richmond — **Scorers:** Sandaza. **Booked:** O'Donovan
23rd	● Motherwell ....a	D 1–1	**Att:** 5,149. **Ref:** D McDonald — **Scorers:** Wilkie. **Booked:** Gomis, Buaben, Sandaza, Grainger
26th	● Cowdenbeath ....a	W 1–5	**Att:** 1,435. **Ref:** E Morris — **Scorers:** Daly³, Goodwillie².
30th	● Kilmarnock ....h	L 0–2	**Att:** 6,823. **Ref:** M Tumilty — **Booked:** Sandaza

September

13th	● Hibernian ....a	L 2–1	**Att:** 13,390. **Ref:** D Somers — **Scorers:** Wilkie. **Booked:** Kovacevic, Wilkie
20th	● Aberdeen ....a	W 0–1	**Att:** 11,041. **Ref:** C Murray — **Scorers:** Sandaza. **Booked:** Wilkie, Goodwillie, S. Robertson
23rd	● Airdrie Utd ....h	W 2–0	**Att:** 3,444. **Ref:** M Tumilty — **Scorers:** Goodwillie, S. Robertson. **Booked:** Dixon
27th	● Hearts.................................h	W 3–0	**Att:** 8,004. **Ref:** D McDonald — **Scorers:** Conway, Daly, S. Robertson

October

4th	● Inverness CT ....h	W 2–1	**Att:** 6,279. **Ref:** I Brines — **Scorers:** Daly, Wilkie. **Booked:** Flood
25th	● St Mirren.............................h	W 2–0	**Att:** 11,378. **Ref:** B Winter — **Scorers:** Conway, O'Donovan. **Booked:** Flood
28th	● Dunfermline ....h	W 1–0	**Att:** 5,350. **Ref:** D McDonald — **Scorers:** S. Robertson

November

1st	● Falkirk................................a	D 0–0	**Att:** 5,608. **Ref:** I Brines — **Booked:** Gomis **Dismissed:** O'Donovan
4th	● Rangers ....a	D 3–3	**Att:** 48,686. **Ref:** C Thomson — **Scorers:** D. Robertson, Sandaza². **Booked:** Flood, Dods, Goodwillie
8th	● Aberdeen ....h	W 2–1	**Att:** 9,490. **Ref:** W Collum — **Scorers:** Feeney, Sandaza. **Booked:** Sandaza, O'Donovan, Flood
12th	● Hibernian ....h	W 2–0	**Att:** 7,490. **Ref:** E Smith — **Scorers:** Dods, Sandaza. **Booked:** Wilkie
15th	● Kilmarnock ....a	L 2–0	**Att:** 4,652. **Ref:** E Norris — **Booked:** Conway
22nd	● Hamilton ....h	D 1–1	**Att:** 6,108. **Ref:** C Allan — **Scorers:** Easton OG. **Booked:** Flood, Wilkie, S. Robertson, Sandaza
29th	● St Mirren.............................a	W 0–2	**Att:** 4,013. **Ref:** C Murray — **Scorers:** Daly²

December

6th	● Inverness CT ....a	W 1–3	**Att:** 3,560. **Ref:** B Winter — **Scorers:** Conway, Daly, D. Robertson. **Booked:** Swanson, Kovacevic
13th	● Rangers ....h	D 2–2	**Att:** 11,362. **Ref:** I Brines — **Scorers:** Feeney, Wilkie. **Booked:** Gomis
20th	● Hearts.................................h	D 0–0	**Att:** 16,442. **Ref:** W Collum — **Booked:** Daly
27th	● Falkirk................................h	W 1–0	**Att:** 7,972. **Ref:** C Boyle — **Scorers:** D. Robertson

January

3rd	● Celtic....................................a	D 2–2	**Att:** 59,558. **Ref:** S Conroy — **Scorers:** Dixon, Feeney. **Booked:** Feeney
11th	● East Stirling ....a	W 0–4	**Att:** 2,153. **Ref:** M Tumilty — **Scorers:** Buaben, Daly, Dods, Russell. **Booked:** Dods
18th	● Motherwell ....h	L 0–4	**Att:** 7,090. **Ref:** E Smith — **Booked:** Dillon, Kenneth
24th	● St Mirren.............................h	W 3–2	**Att:** 6,556. **Ref:** S O'Reilly — **Scorers:** Buaben, Feeney². **Booked:** Daly, Flood, Wilkie, Feeney
28th	● Celtic....................................n	D 0–0	**Att:** 19,258. **Ref:** C Murray — **Booked:** Buaben, Dixon (Lost 10–11 on pens)
31st	● Rangers ....a	L 2–0	**Att:** 49,918. **Ref:** I Brines — **Booked:** Grainger

February

7th	● Hamilton ....a	L 2–1	**Att:** 3,058. **Ref:** C Richmond — **Scorers:** Grainger. **Booked:** Conway, Feeney
14th	● Inverness CT ....h	D 1–1	**Att:** 5,926. **Ref:** C Thomson — **Scorers:** Wilkie. **Booked:** Sandaza
21st	● Aberdeen ....a	D 2–2	**Att:** 14,673. **Ref:** W Collum — **Scorers:** D. Robertson, Sandaza. **Booked:** Dods, D. Robertson
28th	● Hearts.................................h	L 0–1	**Att:** 8,529. **Ref:** E Smith — **Booked:** Caddis, Feeney, Kovacevic, Conway

March

3rd	● Falkirk................................a	W 0–1	**Att:** 4,385. **Ref:** D McDonald — **Scorers:** Conway. **Booked:** Dods
14th	● Motherwell ....a	L 2–1	**Att:** 4,798. **Ref:** I Brines — **Scorers:** Sandaza. **Booked:** Gomis, Wesolowski, Swanson, Wilkie
22nd	● Celtic....................................h	D 2–2	**Att:** 12,043. **Ref:** S Conroy — **Scorers:** Sandaza². **Booked:** Feeney

April

4th	● Hibernian ....h	D 2–2	**Att:** 6,623. **Ref:** E Smith — **Scorers:** Goodwillie, Kenneth. **Booked:** Wesolowski
11th	● Hamilton ....a	W 0–1	**Att:** 3,025. **Ref:** C Murray — **Scorers:** Conway. **Booked:** Wilkie, Shala
18th	● Kilmarnock ....h	D 0–0	**Att:** 6,627. **Ref:** W Collum — **Booked:** Wesolowski, Wilkie **Dismissed:** Dixon

May

2nd	● Hibernian ....a	W 1–2	**Att:** 10,591. **Ref:** S O'Reilly — **Scorers:** Feeney, Goodwillie. **Booked:** D. Robertson, Grainger
7th	● Aberdeen ....h	D 1–1	**Att:** 10,407. **Ref:** C Boyle — **Scorers:** Goodwillie. **Booked:** Buaben, Dods
12th	● Celtic....................................a	L 2–1	**Att:** 57,407. **Ref:** S Dougal — **Scorers:** D. Robertson. **Booked:** Wilkie, Conway
16th	● Hearts.................................a	L 3–0	**Att:** 15,664. **Ref:** B Winter — **Booked:** Sandaza, Kenneth, Swanson
24th	● Rangers ....h	L 0–3	**Att:** 14,077. **Ref:** D McDonald — **Booked:** Wilkie, Buaben, Sandaza

● Clydesdale Bank Premier League ● Scottish FA Cup ● Co-op Insurance Cup ● UEFA Champions League ● UEFA Cup

DUNDEE UNITED

CLYDESDALE BANK PREMIER LEAGUE GOALKEEPER STATS

Player	Minutes on pitch	Appearances	Match starts	Completed matches	Sub appearances	Subbed off	Saved with feet	Punched	Parried	Tipped over	Fumbled	Tipped round	Caught	Blocked	Clean sheets	Goals conceded	Minutes since conceding	Save %	Saved	Resulting in goals	Opposition miss	Yellow cards	Red cards
Lukasz Zaluska 3577	38	38	38	0	0	1	16	21	12	0	5	91	2	11	50	39	74.62	1	4	0	0	0

CLYDESDALE BANK PREMIER LEAGUE OUTFIELD PLAYER STATS

Player	Minutes on pitch	Appearances	Match starts	Completed matches	Substitute appearances	Subbed off	Goals scored	Minutes since scoring	Assists	Shots on target	Shots off target	Crosses	Defensive clearances	Defensive blocks	Fouls committed	Free-kicks won	Caught offside	Yellow cards	Red cards
Prince Buaben 1805	22	20	17	2	3	1	1378	0	11	13	7	13	1	26	28	1	4	0
Paul Caddis 960	11	10	7	1	3	0	-	1	5	1	15	5	3	1	11	0	1	0
Craig Conway 2699	36	28	19	8	9	5	485	4	23	16	143	1	1	36	90	7	3	0
Jon Daly 1422	23	16	10	7	6	5	716	2	14	21	3	7	0	32	14	8	2	0
Sean Dillon 1642	19	18	17	1	1	0	-	1	1	0	60	18	2	12	14	0	1	0
Paul Dixon 2653	29	28	27	1	0	1	1274	8	4	5	104	27	2	28	26	0	0	1
Darren Dods 1770	19	19	18	0	1	1	895	1	9	7	2	42	11	47	13	0	4	0
Warren Feeney 1686	23	18	8	5	10	6	79	1	10	16	13	5	1	15	24	10	4	0
Willo Flood 1731	20	20	13	0	7	0	-	4	5	7	56	5	3	18	30	2	7	0
Morgaro Gomis 3376	37	36	32	1	4	0	-	2	8	11	23	10	1	50	51	1	4	0
David Goodwillie 454	16	3	0	13	0	3	254	0	8	5	6	0	0	15	4	5	2	0
Daniel Grainger 823	9	9	8	0	1	0	-	0	2	2	17	7	1	15	11	1	4	0
Garry Kenneth 2130	25	22	22	0	3	0	645	0	4	7	8	40	9	29	22	0	2	0
Mihael Kovacevic 1540	17	17	14	0	3	0	-	0	0	4	11	9	2	26	11	0	3	0
Roy O'Donovan 588	11	7	1	4	5	1	254	0	8	5	3	2	1	15	6	8	2	1
David Robertson 1032	19	12	5	7	3	3	152	3	8	2	8	1	0	12	15	1	2	0
Scott Robertson..................2044	23	22	20	1	2	3	245	1	6	9	2	12	1	38	52	2	2	0
Francisco Sandaza 2102	31	23	6	8	17	10	484	3	23	16	14	2	1	43	26	20	7	0
Andis Shala 343	8	3	1	5	2	0	-	0	3	3	3	2	0	11	0	1	1	0
Daniel Swanson 1084	30	7	2	23	5	0	-	1	7	11	27	1	0	13	22	1	4	0
James Wesolowski 536	8	7	3	1	4	0	-	0	2	1	1	2	1	19	7	0	3	0
Lee Wilkie 3258	35	35	34	0	1	5	1017	0	11	12	1	80	14	50	33	10	10	0

actim

SEASON TOTALS

Goals scored	47
Goals conceded	50
Clean sheets	11
Shots on target	172
Shots off target	174
Shots per goal	7.36
Pens awarded	7
Pens scored	5
Pens conceded	5
Offsides	78
Corners	234
Crosses	527
Players used	23
Fouls committed	551
Free-kicks won	516

CARDS RECEIVED

72   2

SEQUENCES

Wins	4
(20/09/08–25/10/08)	
Losses	3
(12/05/09–24/05/09)	
Draws	2
(on five occasions)	
Undefeated	8
(20/09/08–12/11/08)	
Without win	5
(11/08/08–13/09/08)	
Undefeated home	8
(27/09/08–27/12/08)	
Undefeated away	4
(29/11/08–03/01/09)	
Without scoring	2
(16/05/09–24/05/09)	
Without conceding	2
(on four occasions)	
Scoring	5
(on two occasions)	
Conceding	7
(03/01/09–28/02/09)	

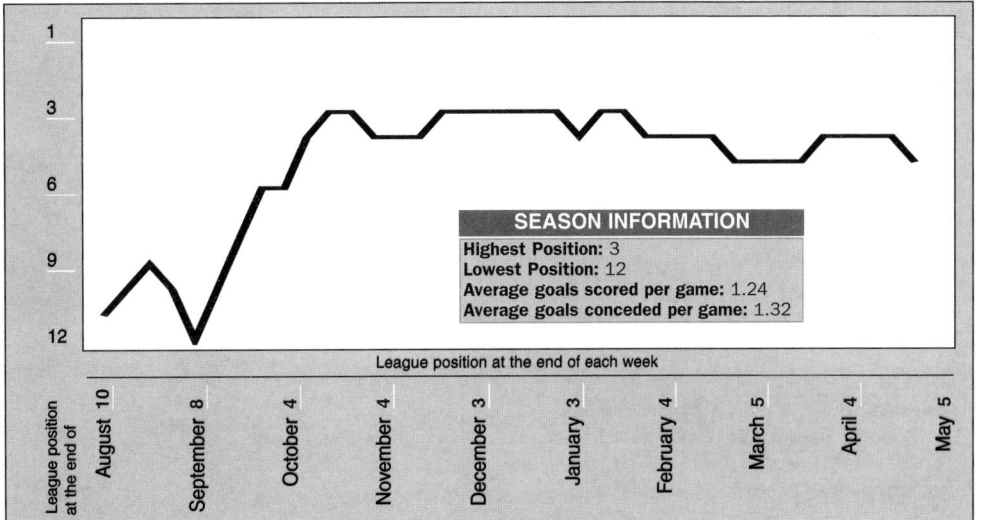

League position at the end of each week

League position at the end of: August 10, September 8, October 4, November 4, December 3, January 3, February 4, March 5, April 4, May 5

SEASON INFORMATION
Highest Position: 3
Lowest Position: 12
Average goals scored per game: 1.24
Average goals conceded per game: 1.32

MATCH RECORDS
Goals scored per match

		W	D	L	Pts
Failed to score	10	0	3	7	3
Scored 1 goal	13	4	5	4	17
Scored 2 goals	11	6	5	0	23
Scored 3 goals	4	3	1	0	10
Scored 4+ goals	0	0	0	0	0

Goals conceded per match

		W	D	L	Pts
Clean sheet	11	8	3	0	27
Conceded 1 goal	10	4	5	1	17
Conceded 2 goals	12	1	5	6	8
Conceded 3 goals	4	0	1	3	1
Conceded 4+ goals	1	0	0	1	0

GOALS SCORED/CONCEDED PER FIVE-MINUTE INTERVALS

Goals For	1	1	2	1	2	3	0	5	1	4	5	6	3	0	2	3	2	6
Goals Against	0	4	4	2	4	4	3	4	2	1	3	2	5	1	4	3	1	3
Mins	5	10	15	20	25	30	35	40	45	50	55	60	65	70	75	80	85	90

QUICK-FIRE GOALS

From the start of a match
Craig Conway
(v Hamilton) 3:28

By a substitute after coming on
Francisco Sandaza
(v Motherwell) 5:45

LAST-GASP GOALS

From the start of a match
David Goodwillie
(v Hibernian) 91:41

By a substitute after coming on
David Goodwillie
(v Hibernian) 30:05

GOAL DETAILS
How the goals were struck

SCORED		CONCEDED
28	Right foot	23
5	Left foot	15
14	Headers	11
0	Others	1

How the goals were struck

SCORED		CONCEDED
30	Open play	30
3	Cross	7
3	Corner	4
5	Penalties	4
1	Direct from free-kick	1
3	Free-kick	3
2	Own goals	1

Distance from goal

SCORED		CONCEDED
26	6yds	18
17	18yds	24
4	18+yds	8

FALKIRK

CLUB SUMMARY

FORMED	1876
MANAGER	John Hughes
GROUND	Falkirk Stadium
CAPACITY	7,190
NICKNAME	The Bairns
WEBSITE	www.falkirkfc.co.uk

The New **Football Pools** PLAYER OF THE SEASON — **Jackie McNamara**

OVERALL

P	W	D	L	F	A	GD
47	16	11	20	51	60	-9

CLYDESDALE BANK PREMIER LEAGUE

Pos	P	W	D	L	F	A	GD	Pts
10	38	9	11	18	37	52	-15	38

HOME

Pos	P	W	D	L	F	A	GD	Pts
10	19	6	4	9	19	20	-1	22

AWAY

Pos	P	W	D	L	F	A	GD	Pts
12	19	3	7	9	18	32	-14	16

CUP PROGRESS DETAILS

Competition	Round reached	Knocked out by
Co-op Insurance Cup	SF	Rangers
Scottish Cup	Final	Rangers

BIGGEST WIN (ALL COMPS)

21/03/09 4–0 v Inverness CT SPL

BIGGEST DEFEAT (ALL COMPS)

08/04/09 0–4 v Celtic SPL

THE PLAYER WITH THE MOST

Shots on target	
Scott Arfield	20
Shots off target	
Scott Arfield	27
Shots without scoring	
Kevin McBride	24
Assists	
Neil McCann	6
Offsides	
Michael Higdon	23
Fouls	
Michael Higdon	74
Fouls without a card	
Graham Barrett	6
Free-kicks won	
Michael Higdon	42
Defensive clearances	
Lee Bullen	41

ATTENDANCE RECORD

High	Low	Average
6,853	4,385	5,640
v Rangers (05/04/2009)	v Dundee Utd (03/03/2009)	

AN INCREDIBLE season for Falkirk saw them make the Homecoming Scottish Cup final – and avoid relegation on the final day of the SPL campaign.

The Bairns enjoyed a day to remember at Hampden Park in May after a brilliant run to the Cup final. While Rangers eventually came out on top 1–0, Falkirk secured European football for the first time in the club's history.

It was the climax to a season in which Falkirk had looked to be on their way out of the Clydesdale Bank Premier League. Eventually, they forced the relegation issue to the final day and came up with a crucial win when they needed it most.

The season had begun with a narrow 1–0 defeat to Rangers, but Falkirk failed to build on a decent display, spending the majority of the campaign languishing at the wrong end of the table.

Inverness had also started badly and looked favourites for the drop around the turn of the year, but their fortunes changed after Terry Butcher was installed as the club's new boss.

While Caley Thistle improved under Butcher, Falkirk struggled to pick up points in the SPL and slipped further into trouble.

By the time the two clubs met on 21st March at the Falkirk Stadium, John Hughes' men were four points adrift and had been written off in some quarters. However, instead of sealing their fate, the match ended with an emphatic 4–0 victory for the home side and gave them hope that survival

Jackie McNamara and Burton O'Brien challenge Rangers' Madjid Bougherra in the Scottish Cup final

FALKIRK

was still a real possibility. Falkirk chiefs stood by their manager, and a late resurgence saw the Bairns head into the crucial last game of the season at Inverness with their survival hopes still alive.

Michael Higdon claimed the only goal of the game – and probably the biggest of his career – at the Caledonian Stadium

as Falkirk stayed up and consigned Caley Thistle to relegation instead.

With their SPL status having been secured, Falkirk could then focus on the Cup final as they sought to continue their memorable run.

They had beaten Hearts, Inverness and Dunfermline on their way to the season finale at Hampden.

Ultimately, they were defeated by a superb goal from half-time substitute Nacho Novo as Rangers successfully defended the trophy, but it was a close game and will surely have boosted their confidence ahead of the 2009/10 campaign.

> **The Bairns enjoyed a day to remember at Hampden Park**

RESULTS 2008/09

August

9th	● Rangers ....h	L 0–1	**Att:** 6,669. **Ref:** D McDonald
16th	● Hibernian ....a	L 3–2	**Att:** 12,445. **Ref:** W Collum — **Scorers:** Higdon². **Booked:** Bullen
23rd	● Celtic............................a	L 3–0	**Att:** 56,031. **Ref:** I Brines — **Booked:** M. Stewart, Cregg
26th	● Raith ....a	W 1–3	**Att:** 2,090. **Ref:** C Thomson — **Scorers:** Higdon, M. Stewart, J. Stewart. **Booked:** Cregg
30th	● Inverness CT ....h	L 1–2	**Att:** 4,730. **Ref:** M McCurry — **Scorers:** M. Stewart

September

13th	● Hearts...........................h	W 2–1	**Att:** 5,960. **Ref:** S Conroy — **Scorers:** Arfield, McCann. **Booked:** Scobbie, Higdon, McBride
20th	● St Mirren......................a	D 1–1	**Att:** 4,134. **Ref:** E Norris — **Scorers:** Barrett. **Booked:** Barr, McBride
23rd	● Queen of South ....h	W 2–1	**Att:** 2,058. **Ref:** E Smith — **Scorers:** Lovell, McCann. **Booked:** Higdon, Aafjes, Cregg
27th	● Hamilton ....h	W 4–1	**Att:** 4,734. **Ref:** M Tumilty — **Scorers:** Arfield², Lovell, O'Brien

October

5th	● Motherwell ....a	L 3–2	**Att:** 4,509. **Ref:** S O'Reilly — **Scorers:** Barrett, Lovell. **Booked:** Scobbie, Higdon
18th	● Aberdeen ....h	L 0–1	**Att:** 5,662. **Ref:** W Collum — **Booked:** Higdon, Barr, Cregg, Holden. **Dismissed:** Bullen
25th	● Kilmarnock ....a	W 1–2	**Att:** 4,267. **Ref:** M McCurry — **Scorers:** Arfield, Lovell. **Booked:** Barr. **Dismissed:** Lovell
28th	● Inverness CT ....h	W 1–0	**Att:** 3,007. **Ref:** D Somers — **Scorers:** McCann. **Booked:** McCann

November

1st	● Dundee Utd ....h	D 0–0	**Att:** 5,608. **Ref:** I Brines — **Booked:** McNamara
8th	● Hamilton ....a	D 1–1	**Att:** 2,600. **Ref:** C Murray — **Scorers:** Higdon. **Booked:** O'Brien
12th	● Inverness CT ....a	D 1–1	**Att:** 3,111. **Ref:** C Thomson — **Scorers:** Higdon. **Booked:** McBride, Holden
15th	● Motherwell ....h	W 1–0	**Att:** 5,279. **Ref:** W Collum — **Scorers:** Higdon
22nd	● Hearts...........................a	L 2–1	**Att:** 13,009. **Ref:** E Smith — **Scorers:** Lovell. **Booked:** Riera, Mitchell
29th	● Hibernian ....h	D 1–1	**Att:** 6,260. **Ref:** A Muir — **Scorers:** Barr. **Booked:** Riera

December

6th	● St Mirren......................h	L 1–2	**Att:** 4,828. **Ref:** D McDonald — **Scorers:** Lovell. **Booked:** Higdon, Cregg. **Dismissed:** McNamara
13th	● Aberdeen ....a	L 2–1	**Att:** 8,909. **Ref:** C Allan — **Scorers:** Lovell. **Booked:** Aafjes, McBride
21st	● Celtic............................h	L 0–3	**Att:** 6,543. **Ref:** E Smith — **Booked:** Bullen, Mitchell, Finnigan
27th	● Dundee Utd ....a	L 1–0	**Att:** 7,972. **Ref:** C Boyle — **Booked:** Higdon, Barr. **Dismissed:** Barr

January

3rd	● Kilmarnock ....h	D 1–1	**Att:** 5,375. **Ref:** I Brines — **Scorers:** Lovell. **Booked:** Scobbie, McCann, Lovell, Holden
10th	● Queen of South ....h	W 4–2	**Att:** 3,423. **Ref:** C Richmond — **Scorers:** Arfield², Barrett². **Booked:** Higdon, M. Stewart
17th	● Rangers ....a	L 3–1	**Att:** 48,811. **Ref:** W Collum — **Scorers:** Lovell. **Booked:** McNamara, Bullen, Arfield. **Dismissed:** Cregg
24th	● Motherwell ....a	D 1–1	**Att:** 5,018. **Ref:** C Allan — **Scorers:** Holden. **Booked:** McBride, Holden, Mitchell
27th	● Rangers ....a	L 3–0	**Att:** 24,507. **Ref:** C Richmond — **Booked:** Pressley, Barr
31st	● Aberdeen ....a	W 1–0	**Att:** 5,605. **Ref:** E Norris — **Scorers:** Higdon. **Booked:** Holden, Pressley, Lovell

February

7th	● Hearts...........................a	W 0–1	**Att:** 14,569. **Ref:** D McDonald — **Scorers:** Lovell. **Booked:** Arfield, Riera, Finnigan, McCann, Pressley, Higdon. **Dismissed:** Arfield
14th	● St Mirren......................a	D 2–2	**Att:** 5,504. **Ref:** M Tumilty — **Scorers:** Arfield, Finnigan. **Booked:** Pressley, Finnigan, Arfield, Bullen, O'Brien
21st	● Hamilton ....h	L 1–2	**Att:** 5,307. **Ref:** C Murray — **Scorers:** Swailes OG. **Booked:** Arfield, McCann
28th	● Hibernian ....a	D 0–0	**Att:** 10,682. **Ref:** S Finnie

March

3rd	● Dundee Utd ....h	L 0–1	**Att:** 4,385. **Ref:** D McDonald — **Booked:** Barr, Pressley
7th	● Inverness CT ....a	W 0–1	**Att:** 3,024. **Ref:** S Conroy — **Scorers:** Finnigan. **Booked:** Pressley, Barr, Dani Mallo
21st	● Inverness CT ....h	W 4–0	**Att:** 5,523. **Ref:** C Murray — **Scorers:** Arfield, Finnigan², M. Stewart

April

5th	● Rangers ....h	L 0–1	**Att:** 6,853. **Ref:** I Brines — **Booked:** Cregg
8th	● Celtic............................a	L 4–0	**Att:** 57,669. **Ref:** W Collum — **Booked:** McBride, Finnigan
11th	● Kilmarnock ....a	L 3–0	**Att:** 5,835. **Ref:** C Richmond — **Booked:** Bullen, McCann
18th	● Hearts...........................h	D 0–0	**Att:** 6,156. **Ref:** E Smith — **Booked:** Higdon, Riera
26th	● Dunfermline ....n	W 2–0	**Att:** 17,124. **Ref:** D McDonald — **Scorers:** Arfield, Scobbie. **Booked:** Riera, Scobbie

May

2nd	● Motherwell ....h	W 2–1	**Att:** 4,937. **Ref:** W Collum — **Scorers:** Finnigan, Scobbie. **Booked:** Finnigan, Riera. **Dismissed:** Aafjes
9th	● Kilmarnock ....a	D 1–1	**Att:** 5,955. **Ref:** A Muir — **Scorers:** Barr. **Booked:** Pressley
13th	● Hamilton ....a	W 0–1	**Att:** 3,710. **Ref:** M McCurry — **Scorers:** Arfield. **Booked:** Scobbie, Pressley
16th	● St Mirren......................h	L 0–2	**Att:** 6,744. **Ref:** C Boyle — **Dismissed:** Pressley
23rd	● Inverness CT ....a	W 0–1	**Att:** 6,489. **Ref:** E Smith — **Scorers:** Higdon. **Booked:** Cregg
30th	● Rangers ....n	L 0–1	**Att:** 50,956. **Ref:** C Thomson — **Booked:** Barr, Finnigan, McNamara

● Clydesdale Bank Premier League ● Scottish FA Cup ● Co-op Insurance Cup ● UEFA Champions League ● UEFA Cup

FALKIRK

CLYDESDALE BANK PREMIER LEAGUE GOALKEEPER STATS

Player	Minutes on pitch	Appearances	Match starts	Completed matches	Sub appearances	Subbed off	Saved with feet	Punched	Parried	Tipped over	Fumbled	Tipped round	Caught	Blocked	Clean sheets	Goals conceded	Minutes since conceding	Save %	Saved	Resulting in goals	Opposition miss	Yellow cards	Red cards
Castro Dani Mallo 1416	15	15	15	0	0	0	14	9	1	0	3	47	0	6	17	-	81.32	0	2	0	0	0
Scott Flinders 749	8	8	8	0	0	1	5	5	0	0	0	17	0	0	7	-	80.00	0	0	0	0	0
Robert Olejnik 1404	15	15	15	0	0	1	14	11	2	0	1	54	0	0	28	-	75.00	0	3	0	0	0

CLYDESDALE BANK PREMIER LEAGUE OUTFIELD PLAYER STATS

Player	Minutes on pitch	Appearances	Match starts	Completed matches	Substitute appearances	Subbed off	Goals scored	Minutes since scoring	Assists	Shots on target	Shots off target	Crosses	Defensive clearances	Defensive blocks	Fouls committed	Free-kicks won	Caught offside	Yellow cards	Red cards
Gerard Aafjes 1026	17	10	7	7	2	0	-	2	2	4	8	12	1	14	8	0	1	1
Scott Arfield 3315	37	35	34	2	1	7	222	0	20	27	31	4	1	58	42	1	3	0
Darren Barr 3257	35	35	33	0	1	2	320	0	6	9	2	34	14	39	39	1	5	1
Graham Barrett 866	15	9	1	6	8	2	514	4	6	7	10	1	1	6	20	7	0	0
Lee Bullen..............................2800	32	29	25	3	3	0	-	0	3	6	24	41	6	31	29	1	5	1
Patrick Cregg 1461	23	16	9	7	6	0	-	0	4	2	8	3	1	48	11	0	5	1
Carl Finnigan 1029	14	10	10	4	0	4	417	0	10	3	6	6	0	32	24	10	4	0
Michael Higdon 2676	34	27	23	7	4	7	26	5	19	24	3	21	1	74	42	23	6	0
Dean Holden...........................1528	19	16	11	3	5	1	374	1	3	2	15	13	2	13	14	3	5	0
Russell Latapy..........................157	3	2	0	1	2	0	-	0	2	0	3	0	0	0	0	1	0	0
Steve Lovell 2297	28	25	18	3	6	8	831	4	17	21	0	1	2	42	29	22	2	1
Sean Lynch................................37	2	0	0	2	0	0	-	0	0	0	0	0	0	1	0	0	0	0
Kevin McBride 2316	28	25	18	3	7	0	-	1	7	17	33	8	3	44	38	1	6	0
Dermott McCaffrey 102	2	1	1	1	0	0	-	0	0	0	0	0	0	1	0	0	0	0
Neil McCann 1910	24	22	15	2	7	1	1907	6	4	3	56	1	2	27	30	5	3	0
Jackie McNamara......................2478	29	29	21	0	7	0	-	4	2	1	22	27	5	25	27	1	2	1
Chris Mitchell...........................329	9	3	2	6	1	0	-	0	1	1	6	1	0	7	1	1	3	0
Kevin Moffat..............................47	4	0	0	4	0	0	-	0	1	0	0	0	0	0	0	0	0	0
Burton O'Brien.........................2740	32	30	25	2	5	1	2479	2	6	20	38	6	2	26	38	0	2	0
Steven Pressley 1334	16	15	10	1	4	0	-	0	0	2	3	15	1	23	29	0	5	1
Arnau Riera 1087	17	14	3	3	11	0	-	0	0	2	1	5	0	20	10	0	4	0
Dayne Robertson.........................54	4	0	0	4	0	0	-	0	0	2	0	0	0	0	0	0	0	0
Thomas Scobbie 1681	20	18	17	2	1	1	414	0	5	4	19	13	2	23	26	0	4	0
John Stewart 326	4	4	1	0	3	0	-	0	3	1	0	0	1	4	4	2	0	0
Mark Stewart 636	20	5	1	15	4	2	145	0	7	10	3	0	0	5	7	2	1	0

actim · Clydesdale Bank PREMIER LEAGUE

SEASON TOTALS

Goals scored	37
Goals conceded	52
Clean sheets	8
Shots on target	128
Shots off target	168
Shots per goal	8.00
Pens awarded	5
Pens scored	4
Pens conceded	5
Offsides	81
Corners	156
Crosses	291
Players used	28
Fouls committed	561
Free-kicks won	471

CARDS RECEIVED

66   7

SEQUENCES

Wins	
(–)	
Losses	4
(on two occasions)	
Draws	3
(01/11/08–12/11/08)	
Undefeated	5
(25/10/08–15/11/08)	
Without win	9
(22/11/08–24/01/09)	
Undefeated home	3
(01/11/08–29/11/08)	
Undefeated away	3
(on three occasions)	
Without scoring	4
(05/04/09–18/04/09)	
Without conceding	
(–)	
Scoring	7
(08/11/08–13/12/08)	
Conceding	10
(09/08/08–25/10/08)	

SEASON INFORMATION

Highest Position: 7
Lowest Position: 12
Average goals scored per game: 0.97
Average goals conceded per game: 1.37

League position at the end of each week

League position at the end of:
August 12 · September 9 · October 11 · November 8 · December 10 · January 11 · February 11 · March 12 · April 12 · May 10

MATCH RECORDS

Goals scored per match

		W	D	L	Pts
Failed to score	13	0	3	10	3
Scored 1 goal	17	4	7	6	19
Scored 2 goals	6	3	1	2	10
Scored 3 goals	0	0	0	0	0
Scored 4+ goals	2	2	0	0	6

Goals conceded per match

		W	D	L	Pts
Clean sheet	8	5	3	0	18
Conceded 1 goal	16	4	7	5	19
Conceded 2 goals	7	0	1	6	1
Conceded 3 goals	6	0	0	6	0
Conceded 4+ goals	1	0	0	1	0

QUICK-FIRE GOALS

From the start of a match
Neil McCann (v Hearts) 2:12

By a substitute after coming on
Michael Higdon (v Inverness CT) 2:54

LAST-GASP GOALS

From the start of a match
Carl Finnigan (v Inverness CT) 90:18

By a substitute after coming on
Michael Higdon (v Hamilton) 3:24

GOAL DETAILS

How the goals were struck

SCORED		CONCEDED
25	Right foot	31
6	Left foot	8
6	Headers	11
0	Others	2

How the goals were struck

SCORED		CONCEDED
28	Open play	36
1	Cross	2
2	Corner	3
4	Penalties	5
0	Direct from free-kick	1
1	Free-kick	4
1	Own goals	1

Distance from goal

SCORED		CONCEDED
11	6yds	27
24	18yds	21
2	18+yds	4

GOALS SCORED/CONCEDED PER FIVE-MINUTE INTERVALS

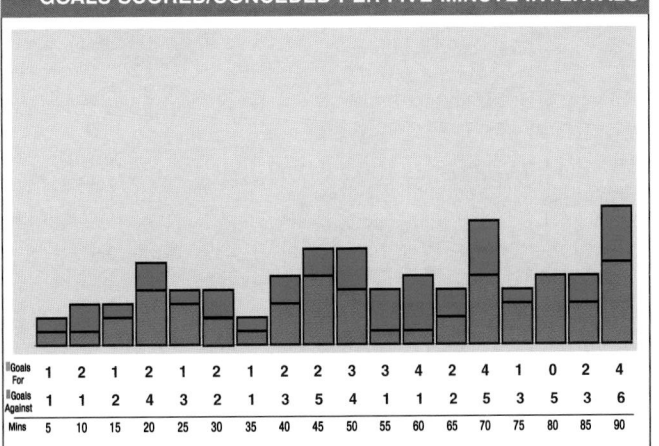

Goals For	1	2	1	2	1	2	1	2	2	3	3	4	2	4	1	0	2	4
Goals Against	1	1	2	4	3	2	1	3	5	4	1	1	2	5	3	5	3	6
Mins	5	10	15	20	25	30	35	40	45	50	55	60	65	70	75	80	85	90

HAMILTON ACADEMICAL

CLUB SUMMARY

FORMED	1874
MANAGER	Billy Reid
GROUND	New Douglas Park
CAPACITY	6,078
NICKNAME	The Accies
WEBSITE	www.acciesfc.co.uk

The New Football Pools PLAYER OF THE SEASON — James McCarthy

OVERALL

P	W	D	L	F	A	GD
44	16	5	23	39	63	-24

CLYDESDALE BANK PREMIER LEAGUE

Pos	P	W	D	L	F	A	GD	Pts
9	38	12	5	21	30	53	-23	41

HOME

Pos	P	W	D	L	F	A	GD	Pts
9	19	7	2	10	18	20	-2	23

AWAY

Pos	P	W	D	L	F	A	GD	Pts
11	19	5	3	11	12	33	-21	18

CUP PROGRESS DETAILS

Competition	Round reached	Knocked out by
Co-op Insurance Cup	QF	Rangers
Scottish Cup	QF	Rangers

BIGGEST WIN (ALL COMPS)

3–1 on two occasions

BIGGEST DEFEAT (ALL COMPS)

06/12/08 1–7 v Rangers SPL

THE PLAYER WITH THE MOST

Shots on target
Richard Offiong 17

Shots off target
Richard Offiong 22

Shots without scoring
Joel Thomas 29

Assists
Brian Easton 5

Offsides
Richard Offiong 22

Fouls
Alex Neil 67

Fouls without a card
James Gibson 10

Free-kicks won
James McCarthy 66

Defensive clearances
Mark McLaughlin............................... 24

ATTENDANCE RECORD

High	Low	Average
5,895	2,600	3,823
v Rangers (28/02/2009)	v Falkirk (08/11/2008)	

James McArthur, mobbed after scoring against Rangers, was a key man in 2008/09

IN WHAT was their first top-flight campaign for 19 years, battling Hamilton defied the odds to ensure a second successive season in the Clydesdale Bank Premier League.

Inspired by mercurial teenager James McCarthy and fellow youngster James McArthur, Accies initially took the division by storm before opposition teams worked out a way to combat their open brand of football.

It was a dream start to life in the SPL for Billy Reid's men, who won their opening two games to share top spot in the table. That was as good as it got, however, as reality soon began to bite for the newcomers.

A win at Aberdeen in September was the only bright spot in a run that ultimately extended to eight defeats in nine league matches.

They did also manage a Co-operative Insurance Cup victory at arch-rivals Motherwell in September, but a 10-match winless run in the SPL saw them propping up the table in November.

A 7–1 defeat at Rangers the following month was the low mark of the season, but it also proved to be something of a turning point. Hamilton

had beaten Kilmarnock 1–0 the previous weekend and that was the catalyst for a six-match winning streak at home.

A more cautious approach was beginning to pay dividends. Indeed, it was not just on home turf that Hamilton were proving hard to beat. Accies won all five games in January without conceding, a remarkable run that saw them sweep that month's Clydesdale Bank Premier League awards. Those results propelled them up the table, but a spate of injuries, which Reid described as the worst of his career, began to bite.

Hamilton suffered another heavy defeat at Rangers – this time in the Homecoming Scottish Cup – as they went on an eight-match winless run in all competitions. However, they had already managed to put enough points on the board before the SPL split to keep them away from the threat of relegation.

> **Accies won all five games in January without conceding**

RESULTS 2008/09

August

11th	● Dundee Utd ....h	W 3–1	**Att:** 4,385. **Ref:** S Dougal — **Scorers:** Graham, McArthur, Stevenson. **Booked:** McLaughlin, Graham
16th	● Inverness CT ....a	W 0–1	**Att:** 3,595. **Ref:** S O'Reilly — **Scorers:** Offiong. **Booked:** Neil, Cerny
23rd	● Kilmarnock ....a	L 1–0	**Att:** 5,339. **Ref:** C Allan — **Booked:** Stevenson. **Dismissed:** Graham
26th	● Clyde ....h	W 3–1	**Att:** 1,146. **Ref:** D Somers — **Scorers:** Grady, Stevenson, Thomas. **Booked:** Mensing
30th	● Hearts..................................h	L 1–2	**Att:** 4,210. **Ref:** C Thomson — **Scorers:** Lyle. **Booked:** Neil, Offiong

September

13th	● Aberdeen ....a	W 1–2	**Att:** 10,865. **Ref:** A Muir — **Scorers:** Graham, McCarthy. **Booked:** Neil, Canning, Akins
20th	● Hibernian ....h	L 0–1	**Att:** 4,058. **Ref:** D McDonald — **Booked:** Sorsa, Mensing
24th	● Motherwell a	W 1–2	**Att:** 5,586. **Ref:** I Brines — **Scorers:** Ettien, Graham. **Booked:** Corcoran, Casement, Neil, Mensing, McArthur, Ettien, McCarthy, Thomas (AET)
27th	● Falkirk ....a	L 4–1	**Att:** 4,734. **Ref:** M Tumilty — **Scorers:** Olejnik OG. **Booked:** McCarthy

October

4th	● Celtic...................................a	L 4–0	**Att:** 55,881. **Ref:** S Conroy — **Booked:** Neil
18th	● St Mirren ....h	L 1–2	**Att:** 3,397. **Ref:** D Somers — **Scorers:** Corcoran. **Booked:** Neil, Offiong
25th	● Rangers ....h	L 1–3	**Att:** 4,613. **Ref:** D McDonald — **Scorers:** Easton
28th	● Rangers ....a	L 2–0	**Att:** 32,083. **Ref:** E Smith —

November

1st	● Motherwell ....a	L 2–0	**Att:** 6,205. **Ref:** M Tumilty — **Booked:** McArthur, Cerny
8th	● Falkirk ....h	D 1–1	**Att:** 2,600. **Ref:** C Murray — **Scorers:** McCarthy. **Booked:** Offiong, McCarthy, Canning
12th	● Hearts..................................a	L 1–0	**Att:** 12,030. **Ref:** D McDonald — **Booked:** Mensing
16th	● Celtic...................................h	L 1–2	**Att:** 5,550. **Ref:** S Conroy — **Scorers:** Offiong. **Booked:** McArthur. **Dismissed:** Canning
22nd	● Dundee Utd ....a	D 1–1	**Att:** 6,108. **Ref:** C Allan — **Scorers:** Offiong. **Booked:** McCarthy, McLaughlin, Mensing. **Dismissed:** Mensing
29th	● Kilmarnock ....h	W 1–0	**Att:** 2,903. **Ref:** I Brines — **Scorers:** Offiong. **Booked:** McClenahan

December

6th	● Rangers ....a	L 7–1	**Att:** 48,282. **Ref:** C Murray — **Scorers:** McArthur. **Booked:** Mensing. **Dismissed:** Canning
13th	● Hibernian ....a	L 2–0	**Att:** 10,437. **Ref:** B Winter — **Booked:** Offiong, Thomas, Ettien
20th	● Motherwell ....h	W 2–0	**Att:** 3,527. **Ref:** I Brines — **Scorers:** McCarthy[2]. **Booked:** Neil, McCarthy
27th	● St Mirren ....a	L 1–0	**Att:** 4,794. **Ref:** M Tumilty — **Booked:** Swailes

January

3rd	● Aberdeen ....h	W 2–0	**Att:** 4,334. **Ref:** S Finnie — **Scorers:** Mensing, Offiong. **Booked:** Elebert, Offiong. **Dismissed:** Offiong
10th	● Ross County ....a	W 0–1	**Att:** 1,503. **Ref:** C Allan — **Scorers:** Swailes. **Booked:** Swailes, McArthur, Cerny, McGowan. **Dismissed:** McArthur
17th	● Inverness CT ....h	W 1–0	**Att:** 3,070. **Ref:** B Winter — **Scorers:** Mensing. **Booked:** McLaughlin
25th	● Kilmarnock ....a	W 0–1	**Att:** 5,063. **Ref:** C Thomson — **Scorers:** Offiong. **Booked:** McGowan, McCarthy, McMillan
31st	● Hearts..................................h	W 2–0	**Att:** 3,567. **Ref:** E Smith — **Scorers:** Mensing[2]. **Booked:** Offiong

February

7th	● Dundee Utd ....h	W 2–1	**Att:** 3,058. **Ref:** C Richmond — **Scorers:** Swailes[2]. **Booked:** Offiong, Easton
14th	● Motherwell ....a	L 1–0	**Att:** 5,917. **Ref:** D McDonald — **Booked:** McArthur, Easton
21st	● Falkirk ....a	W 1–2	**Att:** 5,307. **Ref:** C Murray — **Scorers:** McGowan, Mensing
28th	● Rangers ....h	L 0–1	**Att:** 5,895. **Ref:** C Thomson — **Booked:** Mensing, Neil

March

4th	● Hibernian ....h	L 0–1	**Att:** 4,046. **Ref:** S O'Reilly
8th	● Rangers ....a	L 5–1	**Att:** 27,588. **Ref:** I Brines — **Scorers:** Quinn. **Booked:** McGowan, Swailes
14th	● Aberdeen ....a	L 1–0	**Att:** 10,312. **Ref:** E Norris — **Booked:** McMillan, Neil, Canning
21st	● St Mirren ....h	D 0–0	**Att:** 3,072. **Ref:** S Finnie — **Booked:** Evans, McLaughlin. **Dismissed:** Cerny

April

4th	● Celtic...................................a	L 4–0	**Att:** 58,961. **Ref:** B Winter — **Booked:** McArthur
11th	● Dundee Utd ....h	L 0–1	**Att:** 3,025. **Ref:** C Murray — **Booked:** McArthur, Thomas
18th	● Inverness CT ....a	D 1–1	**Att:** 3,646. **Ref:** C Boyle — **Scorers:** Gibson. **Booked:** McLaughlin, Lyle

May

2nd	● Kilmarnock ....h	W 2–1	**Att:** 3,289. **Ref:** M Tumilty — **Scorers:** McCarthy[2]
10th	● Inverness CT ....a	D 1–1	**Att:** 3,623. **Ref:** C Richmond — **Scorers:** Canning. **Booked:** Canning. **Dismissed:** McArthur
13th	● Falkirk ....h	L 0–1	**Att:** 3,710. **Ref:** M McCurry — **Booked:** Taylor
16th	● Motherwell ....h	L 0–3	**Att:** 3,383. **Ref:** A Muir — **Booked:** McArthur, Neil, McLaughlin
23rd	● St Mirren ....a	W 0–1	**Att:** 6,747. **Ref:** C Murray — **Scorers:** Mensing. **Booked:** Neil, Thomas

● Clydesdale Bank Premier League ● Scottish FA Cup ● Co-op Insurance Cup ● UEFA Champions League ● UEFA Cup

CLYDESDALE BANK PREMIER LEAGUE GOALKEEPER STATS

Player	Minutes on pitch	Appearances	Match starts	Completed matches	Sub appearances	Subbed off	Saved with feet	Punched	Parried	Tipped over	Fumbled	Tipped round	Caught	Blocked	Clean sheets	Goals conceded	Minutes since conceding	Save %	Saved	Resulting in goals	Opposition miss	Yellow cards	Red cards
								SAVES BREAKDOWN										PENALTIES					
Tomas Cerny	3330	36	36	34	0	1	1	17	23	13	0	6	89	0	8	47	7	75.74	1	5	0	2	1
Sean Murdoch	258	4	2	2	2	0	0	0	0	1	0	0	8	0	2	6	103	71.43	0	0	0	0	0

CLYDESDALE BANK PREMIER LEAGUE OUTFIELD PLAYER STATS

Player	Minutes on pitch	Appearances	Match starts	Completed matches	Substitute appearances	Subbed off	Goals scored	Minutes since scoring	Assists	Shots on target	Shots off target	Crosses	Defensive clearances	Defensive blocks	Fouls committed	Free-kicks won	Caught offside	Yellow cards	Red cards
Lucas Akins	415	11	4	0	7	5	0	-	0	2	4	1	1	0	4	10	2	1	0
Derek Asamoah	132	3	1	0	2	1	0	-	0	0	1	0	0	0	1	6	1	0	0
Martin Canning	2642	30	29	26	1	1	1	313	0	4	7	1	16	6	30	13	2	4	2
Chris Casement	48	1	0	0	1	0	0	-	0	0	0	2	0	0	1	0	0	0	0
Mark Corcoran	492	13	3	1	10	2	1	260	0	1	5	3	0	0	2	10	5	0	0
Kenny Deuchar	368	9	3	0	6	3	0	-	0	5	0	1	1	6	6	4	0	0	
Brian Easton	3248	35	35	33	0	2	1	2374	5	4	5	15	21	1	27	33	1	1	0
David Elebert	1319	17	14	11	3	3	0	-	0	3	5	0	14	2	30	8	1	1	0
Stephen Ettien	187	6	0	0	6	0	0	-	0	1	1	4	0	0	4	3	0	1	0
Grant Evans	163	3	2	0	1	2	0	-	0	0	0	1	0	4	2	0	1	0	
James Gibson	859	17	7	5	10	2	1	213	0	2	1	4	3	0	10	7	0	0	0
David Graham	921	16	11	2	5	8	2	683	0	5	5	15	0	0	5	10	0	1	1
Derek Lyle	858	22	8	3	14	5	1	830	0	4	7	7	0	13	8	1	1	0	
James McArthur	3414	37	37	32	0	4	2	1917	2	12	18	9	11	2	66	65	4	6	1
James McCarthy	3278	37	33	24	4	9	6	361	2	16	19	9	6	3	52	66	13	5	0
Trent McClenahan	1881	23	20	16	3	4	0	-	1	1	1	9	2	0	26	21	0	1	0
Paul McGowan	903	14	11	4	3	7	1	549	1	3	7	7	0	0	6	26	3	1	0
Mark McLaughlin	2402	27	27	22	0	0	0	-	1	5	10	1	24	8	34	29	1	6	0
Jordan McMillan	250	4	3	2	1	1	0	-	0	0	0	0	0	0	3	9	0	2	0
Simon Mensing	3014	33	33	27	0	5	6	67	3	10	15	8	17	2	60	31	2	5	1
Stuart Mills	66	1	1	0	0	1	0	-	0	0	0	0	0	0	0	1	0	0	0
Alex Neil	3023	33	33	30	0	3	0	-	2	4	6	16	12	6	67	45	1	10	0
Richard Offiong	2047	30	24	8	6	15	6	644	2	17	22	3	17	1	46	21	22	6	1
Rocco Quinn	32	2	0	0	2	0	0	-	0	0	0	0	0	0	0	0	0	0	0
Sebastian Sorsa	157	2	2	1	0	1	0	-	0	0	0	0	0	0	2	3	0	1	0
Anthony Stevenson	546	7	7	3	0	3	1	517	0	1	1	21	1	0	2	1	1	1	0
Chris Swailes	1855	25	22	13	3	9	0	-	0	3	6	4	22	3	24	6	0	1	0
Stuart Taylor	37	2	0	0	2	0	0	-	0	1	1	0	0	0	1	0	0	1	0
Joel Thomas	1148	26	10	4	16	6	0	-	0	14	15	4	2	0	24	16	15	3	0

actim

Clydesdale Bank *PREMIER LEAGUE*

SEASON TOTALS

Goals scored	30
Goals conceded	53
Clean sheets	9
Shots on target	113
Shots off target	167
Shots per goal	9.33
Pens awarded	4
Pens scored	3
Pens conceded	6
Offsides	79
Corners	167
Crosses	143
Players used	31
Fouls committed	553
Free-kicks won	462

CARDS RECEIVED

62 **7**

SEQUENCES

Wins	4
(03/01/09–31/01/09)	
Losses	6
(20/09/08–01/11/08)	
Draws	
(–)	
Undefeated	4
(03/01/09–31/01/09)	
Without win	10
(20/09/08–22/11/08)	
Undefeated home	5
(29/11/08–31/01/09)	
Undefeated away	3
(18/04/09–23/05/09)	
Without scoring	6
(28/02/09–11/04/09)	
Without conceding	4
(03/01/09–31/01/09)	
Scoring	4
(on two occasions)	
Conceding	13
(23/08/08–22/11/08)	

SEASON INFORMATION
Highest Position: 2
Lowest Position: 12
Average goals scored per game: 0.79
Average goals conceded per game: 1.39

League position at the end of each week

(Chart: League position at the end of, with months August 7, September 7, October 12, November 11, December 12, January 8, February 8, March 8, April 10, May 9)

MATCH RECORDS

Goals scored per match

		W	D	L	Pts
Failed to score	16	0	1	15	1
Scored 1 goal	15	5	4	6	19
Scored 2 goals	6	6	0	0	18
Scored 3 goals	1	1	0	0	3
Scored 4+ goals	0	0	0	0	0

Goals conceded per match

		W	D	L	Pts
Clean sheet	9	8	1	0	25
Conceded 1 goal	18	4	4	10	16
Conceded 2 goals	5	0	0	5	0
Conceded 3 goals	2	0	0	2	0
Conceded 4+ goals	4	0	0	4	0

QUICK-FIRE GOALS

From the start of a match
James McArthur
(v Rangers) 1:50

By a substitute after coming on
Derek Lyle
(v Hearts) 18:16

LAST-GASP GOALS

From the start of a match
Brian Easton
(v Dundee Utd) 92:58

By a substitute after coming on
James McCarthy
(v Aberdeen) 26:11

GOAL DETAILS

How the goals were struck

SCORED		CONCEDED
16	Right foot	32
5	Left foot	14
7	Headers	7
2	Others	0

How the goals were struck

SCORED		CONCEDED
18	Open play	36
0	Cross	5
4	Corner	3
3	Penalties	5
1	Direct from free-kick	0
3	Free-kick	1
1	Own goals	3

Distance from goal

SCORED		CONCEDED
10	6yds	22
17	18yds	26
3	18+yds	5

GOALS SCORED/CONCEDED PER FIVE-MINUTE INTERVALS

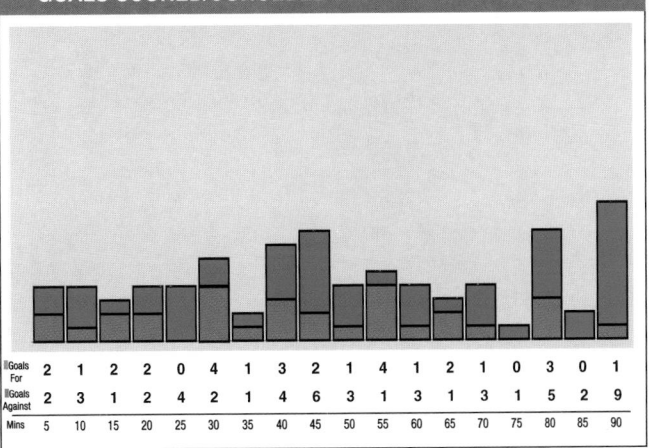

Goals For	2	1	2	2	0	4	1	3	2	1	4	1	2	1	0	3	0	1
Goals Against	2	3	1	2	4	2	1	4	6	3	1	3	1	3	1	5	2	9
Mins	5	10	15	20	25	30	35	40	45	50	55	60	65	70	75	80	85	90

HEART OF MIDLOTHIAN

CLUB SUMMARY

FORMED	1874
MANAGER	Csaba Laszlo
GROUND	Tynecastle
CAPACITY	17,402
NICKNAME	The Jam Tarts
WEBSITE	www.heartsfc.co.uk

The New Football Pools PLAYER OF THE SEASON — Lee Wallace

OVERALL

P	W	D	L	F	A	GD
41	17	12	12	42	38	4

CLYDESDALE BANK PREMIER LEAGUE

Pos	P	W	D	L	F	A	GD	Pts
3	38	16	11	11	40	37	3	59

HOME

Pos	P	W	D	L	F	A	GD	Pts
3	19	11	5	3	28	18	10	38

AWAY

Pos	P	W	D	L	F	A	GD	Pts
7	19	5	6	8	12	19	-7	21

CUP PROGRESS DETAILS

Competition	Round reached	Knocked out by
Co-op Insurance Cup	R2	Airdrie Utd
Scottish Cup	R5	Falkirk

BIGGEST WIN (ALL COMPS)

16/05/09 3–0 v Dundee Utd **SPL**

BIGGEST DEFEAT (ALL COMPS)

27/09/08 0–3 v Dundee Utd **SPL**

THE PLAYER WITH THE MOST

Shots on target
Andrew Driver 28

Shots off target
Bruno Aguiar 21

Shots without scoring
Christophe Berra 16

Assists
Andrew Driver 5

Offsides
Christian Nade 17

Fouls
Christian Nade 48

Fouls without a card
Andrew Driver 27

Free-kicks won
Christian Nade 54

Defensive clearances
Marius Zaliukas 32

ATTENDANCE RECORD

High	Low	Average
17,244	12,030	14,398

v Hibernian (03/01/2009) v Hamilton (12/11/2008)

'CSABA who?' was the response of most Hearts fans when they learned the identity of their new manager last summer. But a year on, there cannot be a football follower in Scotland who has not heard of the colourful and often eccentric Csaba Laszlo.

The Romania-born Hungarian's appointment to the role may have come as something of a surprise, but few can argue that Laszlo has produced results – immediately restoring Hearts to the position of the third force in the Clydesdale Bank Premier League.

He has rebuilt the club following their eighth-place finish the previous season, and also secured European football at the first attempt.

It was not all plain sailing for the new man in charge, though. Speculation over the club's financial position could have proved to be an unwelcome distraction for

the players, and the Jambos also had to cope with the loss of their influential captain Christophe Berra after he was sold to Wolves during the January transfer window.

It was not until November that they really got going

On the field, Hearts did not make the most auspicious of starts. Despite a decent August, it was not until November that they really got going, winning five SPL games in a row, including their memorable 2–1 victory over eventual champions Rangers.

That thrust them right into the race for Europe – even leading some people to suggest that they could separate the Old Firm. But a poor run of form in December put paid to that dream and it soon became a case of battling it out with Dundee United and Aberdeen for the title of 'best of the rest'.

Lacking a prolific goalscorer, Laszlo was forced to play to his squad's strengths, but the results were clear for all to see as he was named Manager of the Season by Scottish Football Writers and SPL sponsors, Clydesdale Bank.

The Jambos' charge was led by the likes of former Benfica star Bruno Aguiar and Michael Stewart, both of whom enjoyed an impressive campaign, while Lee Wallace and Andrew Driver also proved integral with a series of commanding displays.

At the back end of the season, Hearts crucially proved stronger than their closest rivals – rounding off the campaign with a creditable 0–0 draw at deposed champions Celtic.

That gave Laszlo and his men that coveted third spot in the table, and plenty to build on for 2009/10.

Christian Nade celebrates scoring against rivals Hibernian

RESULTS 2008/09

August

9th	● Motherwell ....h	W 3–2	**Att:** 14,219. **Ref:** I Brines — **Scorers:** Ksanavicius, Mikoliunas, Stewart. **Booked:** Ksanavicius, M. Stewart, Banks
16th	● Rangers ....a	L 2–0	**Att:** 48,191. **Ref:** S Dougal — **Booked:** Kingston, Mikoliunas **Dismissed:** Mikoliunas
23rd	● St Mirren........................h	W 2–1	**Att:** 13,357. **Ref:** C Murray — **Scorers:** Mole, Stewart. **Booked:** L Wallace, Nade
27th	● Airdrie Utd ....h	D 0–0	**Att:** 6,844. **Ref:** E Smith — **Booked:** Jonsson, M. Stewart, Ksanavicius (Lost 4–3 on pens)
30th	● Hamilton ....a	W 1–2	**Att:** 4,210. **Ref:** C Thomson — **Scorers:** Driver, Zaliukas

September

13th	● Falkirk...............................a	L 2–1	**Att:** 5,960. **Ref:** S Conroy — **Scorers:** M. Stewart. **Booked:** Mikoliunas
20th	● Inverness CT ....h	W 1–0	**Att:** 12,890. **Ref:** W Collum — **Scorers:** Mikoliunas. **Booked:** Ksanavicius, M. Stewart, Zaliukas
27th	● Dundee Utd ....a	L 3–0	**Att:** 8,004. **Ref:** D McDonald — **Booked:** M. Stewart, Jonsson, Nade

October

4th	● Kilmarnock ....h	L 1–2	**Att:** 13,189. **Ref:** C Thomson — **Scorers:** Kingston. **Booked:** Mole
19th	● Hibernian ....a	D 1–1	**Att:** 17,223. **Ref:** C Thomson — **Scorers:** Aguiar. **Booked:** Berra, Aguiar
25th	● Aberdeen ....h	D 1–1	**Att:** 14,265. **Ref:** S Conroy — **Scorers:** Wallace. **Booked:** Mikoliunas

November

2nd	● Celtic..................................h	L 0–2	**Att:** 15,460. **Ref:** C Thomson — **Dismissed:** Zaliukas
8th	● St Mirren...........................a	W 0–1	**Att:** 4,192. **Ref:** M McCurry — **Scorers:** Jonsson. **Dismissed:** M. Stewart
12th	● Hamilton ....h	W 1–0	**Att:** 12,030. **Ref:** D McDonald — **Scorers:** Nade. **Booked:** Mole
15th	● Inverness CT ....a	W 0–1	**Att:** 4,011. **Ref:** M Tumilty — **Scorers:** Aguiar. **Booked:** Zaliukas
22nd	● Falkirk...............................h	W 2–1	**Att:** 13,009. **Ref:** E Smith — **Scorers:** Aguiar, Driver. **Booked:** Wallace
29th	● Rangers ....h	W 2–1	**Att:** 15,710. **Ref:** D McDonald — **Scorers:** Kingston, Zaliukas. **Booked:** Wallace

December

13th	● Celtic..................................a	D 1–1	**Att:** 56,079. **Ref:** C Richmond — **Scorers:** Driver. **Booked:** Neilson, Kingston, Balogh
20th	● Dundee Utd ....h	D 0–0	**Att:** 16,442. **Ref:** W Collum — **Booked:** Nade, Karipidis
27th	● Aberdeen ....a	L 1–0	**Att:** 18,021. **Ref:** I Brines — **Booked:** Berra, Zaliukas, Nade **Dismissed:** Zaliukas

January

3rd	● Hibernian ....h	D 0–0	**Att:** 17,244. **Ref:** C Murray — **Booked:** Berra
7th	● Motherwell ....a	L 1–0	**Att:** 4,928. **Ref:** D Somers
11th	● Hibernian ....a	W 0–2	**Att:** 14,837. **Ref:** C Thomson — **Scorers:** Glen, Nade. **Booked:** Berra, Zaliukas
17th	● Kilmarnock ....a	W 0–2	**Att:** 5,469. **Ref:** C Richmond — **Scorers:** Aguiar, Karipidis. **Booked:** Aguiar, Jonsson, Obua
24th	● Inverness CT ....h	W 3–2	**Att:** 13,224. **Ref:** S Conroy — **Scorers:** Kingston, Obua[2]
31st	● Hamilton ....a	L 2–0	**Att:** 3,567. **Ref:** E Smith — **Booked:** Obua

February

7th	● Falkirk...............................h	L 0–1	**Att:** 14,569. **Ref:** D McDonald — **Booked:** Driver, M. Stewart
14th	● Aberdeen ....h	W 2–1	**Att:** 15,049. **Ref:** C Richmond — **Scorers:** Driver, Nade. **Booked:** Nade, M. Stewart
21st	● St Mirren...........................h	D 1–1	**Att:** 13,609. **Ref:** D Somers — **Scorers:** Jonsson. **Booked:** Nade, Palazuelos
28th	● Dundee Utd ....a	W 0–1	**Att:** 8,529. **Ref:** E Smith — **Scorers:** Stewart. **Booked:** Wallace, Neilson

March

4th	● Motherwell ....h	W 2–1	**Att:** 13,306. **Ref:** B Winter — **Scorers:** Driver, Palazuelos. **Booked:** Mrowiec
14th	● Hibernian ....a	L 1–0	**Att:** 15,091. **Ref:** C Richmond — **Booked:** M. Stewart
21st	● Rangers ....a	D 2–2	**Att:** 50,310. **Ref:** C Thomson — **Scorers:** Karipidis, Palazuelos. **Booked:** Nade, Tullberg, Aguiar

April

4th	● Kilmarnock ....h	W 3–1	**Att:** 13,659. **Ref:** D Somers — **Scorers:** Aguiar, Elliot[2]
11th	● Celtic..................................h	D 1–1	**Att:** 16,514. **Ref:** C Thomson — **Scorers:** Aguiar
18th	● Falkirk...............................a	D 0–0	**Att:** 6,156. **Ref:** E Smith — **Booked:** Palazuelos, Aguiar

May

3rd	● Rangers ....a	L 2–0	**Att:** 49,663. **Ref:** I Brines — **Booked:** M. Stewart, Neilson
7th	● Hibernian ....h	L 0–1	**Att:** 14,714. **Ref:** S Conroy — **Dismissed:** Karipidis
12th	● Aberdeen ....a	D 0–0	**Att:** 11,588. **Ref:** S Finnie — **Booked:** Zaliukas, Aguiar, Templeton, Jonsson. **Dismissed:** Zaliukas
16th	● Dundee Utd ....h	W 3–0	**Att:** 15,664. **Ref:** B Winter — **Scorers:** Aguiar, Jonsson, Wallace
24th	● Celtic..................................a	D 0–0	**Att:** 59,685. **Ref:** C Thomson — **Booked:** Mrowiec

● Clydesdale Bank Premier League ● Scottish FA Cup ● Co-op Insurance Cup ● UEFA Champions League ● UEFA Cup

CLYDESDALE BANK PREMIER LEAGUE GOALKEEPER STATS

Player	Minutes on pitch	Appearances	Match starts	Completed matches	Sub appearances	Subbed off	SAVES BREAKDOWN								Clean sheets	Goals conceded	Minutes since conceding	Save %	PENALTIES			Yellow cards	Red cards
							Saved with feet	Punched	Parried	Tipped over	Fumbled	Tipped round	Caught	Blocked					Saved	Resulting in goals	Opposition miss		
Janos Balogh 1708	19	18	17	1	0	1	8	7	1	0	0	43	0	7	12	94	82.19	1	0	1	1	1
Steve Banks 94	1	1	0	0	1	0	0	0	0	0	0	1	0	0	2	13	33.33	0	0	0	1	0
Marian Kello 1184	13	13	12	0	1	2	12	5	2	0	3	56	0	4	13	299	87.23	0	1	0	0	0
Jamie MacDonald 619	7	6	6	1	0	0	4	4	0	0	1	16	0	2	10	47	71.43	0	2	0	0	0

CLYDESDALE BANK PREMIER LEAGUE OUTFIELD PLAYER STATS

Player	Minutes on pitch	Appearances	Match starts	Completed matches	Substitute appearances	Subbed off	Goals scored	Minutes since scoring	Assists	Shots on target	Shots off target	Crosses	Defensive clearances	Defensive blocks	Fouls committed	Free-kicks won	Caught offside	Yellow cards	Red cards
Bruno Aguiar 2249	26	26	13	0	13	7	62	1	17	21	95	10	1	27	42	3	5	0
Christophe Berra 2177	23	23	23	0	0	0	-	3	5	11	2	25	7	32	34	0	3	0
Deividas Cesnauskis 322	13	2	0	11	2	0	-	0	1	2	5	0	1	6	4	1	0	0
Andrew Driver 2623	29	29	23	0	6	5	541	5	28	14	59	2	0	27	35	13	0	0
Calum Elliot 766	12	8	2	4	6	2	640	3	8	8	3	1	0	11	22	6	0	0
Gary Glen 282	8	2	0	6	2	0	-	0	2	2	0	0	0	3	5	0	0	0
Eggert Jonsson 2514	30	27	24	3	2	3	107	0	4	3	6	6	5	36	20	1	3	1
Christos Karipidis 3200	34	34	31	0	2	2	671	0	3	9	3	24	4	33	32	0	1	1
Laryea Kingston...................1230	19	15	4	4	11	3	83	1	18	14	28	0	0	30	21	5	2	0
Audrius Ksanavicius 349	9	4	0	5	4	1	310	2	1	0	4	2	0	3	9	1	2	0
Juho Makela 37	4	0	0	4	0	0	-	0	0	0	0	0	0	0	2	0	0	0
Saulius Mikoliunas 606	12	6	0	6	5	2	522	0	5	9	5	1	2	11	12	1	3	1
Jamie Mole 685	14	8	2	6	6	1	469	0	7	4	2	0	0	5	6	5	2	0
Adrian Mrowiec 543	10	6	4	2	2	0	-	0	1	1	3	2	1	8	6	3	2	0
Christian Nade 2121	36	20	4	16	16	2	574	1	18	21	4	3	1	48	54	17	7	0
Robbie Neilson....................2473	27	25	24	2	1	0	-	0	1	2	17	17	9	42	34	2	3	0
Arvydas Novikovas 42	1	0	0	1	0	0	-	0	0	0	0	0	0	1	0	1	0	0
David Obua........................2063	27	21	16	6	5	2	1438	3	12	16	13	26	4	26	22	6	2	0
Ruben Palazuelos 1835	25	18	18	7	0	2	404	0	6	6	2	15	1	16	22	0	2	0
Johnny Stewart 13	1	0	0	1	0	0	-	0	0	0	0	0	0	0	0	0	0	0
Michael Stewart 2971	34	33	25	1	7	4	1016	4	22	9	24	10	0	46	41	3	6	1
David Templeton 115	3	1	0	2	2	0	-	0	1	0	0	0	0	4	3	0	1	0
Jason Thomson.....................720	11	8	7	3	1	0	-	0	1	0	12	4	3	8	6	1	0	0
Mike Tullberg 197	7	2	0	5	2	0	-	0	1	3	0	0	0	2	1	2	1	0
Lee Wallace.......................3147	34	34	31	0	2	2	178	1	5	6	26	6	1	36	37	0	4	1
Marius Zaliukas 2544	28	28	24	0	1	2	1240	2	7	11	2	32	9	29	40	0	4	3

SEASON TOTALS

Goals scored	40
Goals conceded	37
Clean sheets	12
Shots on target	174
Shots off target	172
Shots per goal	8.65
Pens awarded	4
Pens scored	2
Pens conceded	5
Offsides	71
Corners	195
Crosses	315
Players used	30
Fouls committed	491
Free-kicks won	518

CARDS RECEIVED

55   9

SEQUENCES

Wins	5
(08/11/08–29/11/08)	
Losses	2
(on two occasions)	
Draws	2
(on three occasions)	
Undefeated	7
(08/11/08–20/12/08)	
Without win	5
(on three occasions)	
Undefeated home	11
(12/11/08–11/04/09)	
Undefeated away	4
(19/10/08–13/12/08)	
Without scoring	4
(on two occasions)	
Without conceding	3
(08/11/08–15/11/08)	
Scoring	6
(08/11/08–13/12/08)	
Conceding	5
(on three occasions)	

League position at the end of each week

League position at the end of: August 3, September 3, October 5, November 3, December 4, January 4, February 3, March 3, April 3, May 3

SEASON INFORMATION

Highest Position: 2
Lowest Position: 8
Average goals scored per game: 1.05
Average goals conceded per game: 0.97

MATCH RECORDS

Goals scored per match

		W	D	L	Pts
Failed to score	14	0	5	9	5
Scored 1 goal	12	5	5	2	20
Scored 2 goals	8	7	1	0	22
Scored 3 goals	4	4	0	0	12
Scored 4+ goals	0	0	0	0	0

Goals conceded per match

		W	D	L	Pts
Clean sheet	12	7	5	0	26
Conceded 1 goal	16	7	5	4	26
Conceded 2 goals	9	2	1	6	7
Conceded 3 goals	1	0	0	1	0
Conceded 4+ goals	0	0	0	0	0

QUICK-FIRE GOALS

From the start of a match
Christian Nade
(v Hamilton) 5:57

By a substitute after coming on
Laryea Kingston
(v Inverness CT) 3:45

LAST-GASP GOALS

From the start of a match
Ruben Palazuelos
(v Motherwell) 91:27

By a substitute after coming on
Saulius Mikoliunas
(v Motherwell) 4:44

GOAL DETAILS

How the goals were struck

SCORED		CONCEDED
21	Right foot	22
9	Left foot	6
10	Headers	9
0	Others	0

How the goals were struck

SCORED		CONCEDED
25	Open play	21
2	Cross	3
1	Corner	2
2	Penalties	3
3	Direct from free-kick	2
7	Free-kick	5
0	Own goals	1

Distance from goal

SCORED		CONCEDED
19	6yds	12
12	18yds	21
9	18+yds	4

GOALS SCORED/CONCEDED PER FIVE-MINUTE INTERVALS

Mins	5	10	15	20	25	30	35	40	45	50	55	60	65	70	75	80	85	90
Goals For	0	2	1	3	6	2	2	2	3	2	0	2	3	2	2	5	1	2
Goals Against	3	3	4	4	0	1	1	3	2	1	1	1	1	1	0	4	2	5

HIBERNIAN

CLUB SUMMARY

FORMED	1875
MANAGER	TBC
GROUND	Easter Road
CAPACITY	17,400
NICKNAME	The Hibees
WEBSITE	www.hibernianfc.co.uk

The New Football Pools PLAYER OF THE SEASON — Rob Jones

OVERALL

P	W	D	L	F	A	GD
40	11	14	15	45	52	-7

CLYDESDALE BANK PREMIER LEAGUE

Pos	P	W	D	L	F	A	GD	Pts
6	38	11	14	13	42	46	-4	47

HOME

Pos	P	W	D	L	F	A	GD	Pts
7	19	6	7	6	23	23	0	25

AWAY

Pos	P	W	D	L	F	A	GD	Pts
4	19	5	7	7	19	23	-4	22

CUP PROGRESS DETAILS

Competition	Round reached	Knocked out by
Co-op Insurance Cup	R2	Morton
Scottish Cup	R4	Hearts

BIGGEST WIN (ALL COMPS)

22/11/08 4–1 v Motherwell **SPL**

BIGGEST DEFEAT (ALL COMPS)

28/09/08 0–3 v Rangers **SPL**

THE PLAYER WITH THE MOST

Shots on target
Derek Riordan 55

Shots off target
Steven Fletcher 48

Shots without scoring
Sol Bamba.................................... 23

Assists
Colin Nish 6

Offsides
Derek Riordan 56

Fouls
Sol Bamba.................................... 61

Fouls without a card
Darren McCormack 11

Free-kicks won
Colin Nish 58

Defensive clearances
Rob Jones 83

ATTENDANCE RECORD

High	Low	Average
17,223	10,317	12,684
v Hearts (19/10/2008)	v St Mirren (17/01/2009)	

John Rankin slots home the first goal in a 2–0 win over Celtic at Easter Road

HIBERNIAN were left to reflect on a campaign of might-have-beens as they failed to mount a serious challenge for silverware and missed out on qualification for Europe.

The Easter Road side were the first Scottish club out of the traps on 6th July when they played and lost to Elfsborg over two legs in the Intertoto Cup.

The early start to the season, as well as the disappointment of seeing their European ambitions ended almost before they had begun, seemed to affect Mixu Paatelainen's side in the opening weeks of the regular season. In August, they crashed out of the Co-operative Insurance Cup in the second round to Irn-Bru First Division side Morton after extra-time.

A 2–0 Clydesdale Bank Premier League win over Celtic at Easter Road in December, their best result up until that point, offered some hope to the Hibs fans, but there was further disappointment when they lost out to arch-rivals

Hearts in the Homecoming Scottish Cup fourth round – going down 2–0 to extend their drought in a competition they have not won since 1902.

That left Hibs with only their SPL campaign to

focus upon, and after 33 games they made it in to the top six by just a single point ahead of Motherwell.

There was cause for optimism when they secured a couple of high-profile draws against both Old Firm clubs – results that would help play a defining role in the SPL title race.

A derby win against Hearts at Tynecastle also gave former Finland striker Paatelainen something to draw cheer from.

The enigmatic Derek Riordan proved to be the hero that day as he scored the winner to give the visiting fans local bragging rights to carry them through the summer, despite Hearts' third-place finish in the SPL table.

However, there was surprise all round when, just days after the end of the campaign, Paatelainen decided to resign.

Whoever replaces him will be expected to build for next term, and they could face a tough close season with captain Rob Jones linked with a return to England.

Striker Steven Fletcher could also be the subject of a bidding war from clubs on both sides of the border after another impressive campaign.

> **Paatelainen decided to resign at the end of the season**

RESULTS 2008/09

July
6th	● IF Elfsborg ....h	L 0–2	**Att:** 7,809. **Ref:** A Toussaint	
12th	● IF Elfsborg ....a	L 2–0	**Att:** 3,523. **Ref:** M Strahonja	

August
9th	● Kilmarnock ....a	L 1–0	**Att:** 6,168. **Ref:** C Murray — **Booked:** Hogg, Chisholm
16th	● Falkirk ....h	W 3–2	**Att:** 12,445. **Ref:** W Collum — **Scorers:** Hanlon, Nish². **Booked:** Keenan, van Zanten
23rd	● Inverness CT ....a	D 1–1	**Att:** 4,022. **Ref:** E Smith — **Scorers:** Nish
26th	● Morton ....h	L 3–4	**Att:** 6,329. **Ref:** I Brines — **Scorers:** Keenan, Pinau, Shiels. **Booked:** Stevenson, Hogg (AET)
30th	● Motherwell ....h	L 0–1	**Att:** 11,285. **Ref:** S Dougal —

September
13th	● Dundee Utd ....h	W 2–1	**Att:** 13,390. **Ref:** D Somers — **Scorers:** Fletcher². **Booked:** Bamba, Murray **Dismissed:** Bamba
20th	● Hamilton ....a	W 0–1	**Att:** 4,058. **Ref:** D McDonald — **Scorers:** Riordan. **Booked:** Rankin, van Zanten
28th	● Rangers ....h	L 0–3	**Att:** 15,292. **Ref:** C Murray — **Booked:** Jones

October
4th	● Aberdeen ....a	W 1–2	**Att:** 10,793. **Ref:** M McCurry — **Scorers:** Riordan². **Booked:** Nish
19th	● Hearts.................................h	D 1–1	**Att:** 17,223. **Ref:** C Thomson — **Scorers:** Fletcher. **Booked:** Jones, Thicot, Murray
25th	● Celtic..................................a	L 4–2	**Att:** 58,337. **Ref:** C Murray — **Scorers:** Fletcher, Nish. **Booked:** Riordan, Bamba, Shiels

November
1st	● St Mirren ....a	D 0–0	**Att:** 4,588. **Ref:** S Finnie — **Booked:** Bamba
8th	● Inverness CT ....h	L 1–2	**Att:** 11,688. **Ref:** C Boyle — **Scorers:** Riordan. **Booked:** Fletcher, Murray
12th	● Dundee Utd ....a	L 2–0	**Att:** 7,490. **Ref:** E Smith — **Booked:** Bamba
15th	● Aberdeen ....h	D 2–2	**Att:** 11,640. **Ref:** S O'Reilly — **Scorers:** Fletcher, Jones. **Booked:** Jones
22nd	● Motherwell ....a	W 1–4	**Att:** 4,957. **Ref:** C Richmond — **Scorers:** Fletcher, Rankin, Riordan, Shiels. **Booked:** Jones, Hogg, Bamba
29th	● Falkirk ....a	D 1–1	**Att:** 6,260. **Ref:** A Muir — **Scorers:** Nish. **Booked:** Nish

December
7th	● Celtic..................................h	W 2–0	**Att:** 14,289. **Ref:** C Thomson — **Scorers:** Nish, Rankin. **Booked:** Ma-Kalambay
13th	● Hamilton ....h	W 2–0	**Att:** 10,437. **Ref:** B Winter — **Scorers:** Jones, Riordan. **Booked:** van Zanten
20th	● Rangers ....a	L 1–0	**Att:** 49,538. **Ref:** S Conroy — **Booked:** van Zanten
27th	● Kilmarnock ....h	L 2–4	**Att:** 12,117. **Ref:** E Norris — **Scorers:** Shiels². **Booked:** van Zanten, Nish, Thicot, Fletcher

January
3rd	● Hearts.................................a	D 0–0	**Att:** 17,244. **Ref:** C Murray — **Booked:** Stevenson, Riordan, Murray
11th	● Hearts.................................h	L 0–2	**Att:** 14,837. **Ref:** C Thomson — **Booked:** Stevenson, Riordan, Rankin. **Dismissed:** Fletcher
17th	● St Mirren ....h	W 2–0	**Att:** 10,317. **Ref:** I Brines — **Scorers:** Jones, Riordan. **Booked:** Bamba, Johansson
24th	● Celtic..................................a	L 3–1	**Att:** 58,930. **Ref:** D Somers — **Scorers:** Jones. **Booked:** Bamba, Johansson
31st	● Motherwell ....h	D 1–1	**Att:** 10,903. **Ref:** M McCurry — **Scorers:** Riordan. **Booked:** Stevenson

February
14th	● Kilmarnock ....a	D 1–1	**Att:** 4,649. **Ref:** C Boyle — **Scorers:** Riordan. **Booked:** Chisholm
21st	● Inverness CT ....a	L 2–0	**Att:** 4,116. **Ref:** A Muir — **Booked:** Bamba, Nish, Keenan
28th	● Falkirk ....h	D 0–0	**Att:** 10,682. **Ref:** S Finnie — **Booked:** Johansson, Bamba, Rosa

March
4th	● Hamilton ....a	W 0–1	**Att:** 4,046. **Ref:** S O'Reilly — **Scorers:** Fletcher. **Booked:** Rosa, Stevenson, Rankin, Nish
14th	● Hearts.................................h	W 1–0	**Att:** 15,091. **Ref:** C Richmond — **Scorers:** Fletcher. **Dismissed:** Bamba
21st	● Aberdeen ....h	D 0–0	**Att:** 11,754. **Ref:** M McCurry — **Booked:** Murray, Jones

April
4th	● Dundee Utd ....a	D 2–2	**Att:** 6,623. **Ref:** E Smith — **Scorers:** Nish². **Booked:** Hogg, Fletcher
13th	● St Mirren ....a	D 1–1	**Att:** 5,151. **Ref:** I Brines — **Scorers:** Fletcher. **Booked:** Bamba, Jones, Nish, Chisholm
19th	● Rangers ....h	L 2–3	**Att:** 14,014. **Ref:** S Conroy — **Scorers:** Fletcher, Rankin. **Booked:** Stevenson, Jones

May
2nd	● Dundee Utd ....h	L 1–2	**Att:** 10,591. **Ref:** S O'Reilly — **Scorers:** Fletcher. **Booked:** Rankin. **Dismissed:** Hogg
7th	● Hearts.................................a	W 0–1	**Att:** 14,714. **Ref:** S Conroy — **Scorers:** Riordan. **Booked:** Stevenson, Rankin, van Zanten
13th	● Rangers ....h	D 1–1	**Att:** 13,765. **Ref:** E Smith — **Scorers:** Riordan. **Booked:** Bamba, Fletcher
17th	● Celtic..................................h	D 0–0	**Att:** 14,074. **Ref:** I Brines — **Booked:** Murray, Rankin, Ma-Kalambay, Bamba, Riordan
24th	● Aberdeen ....a	L 2–1	**Att:** 14,083. **Ref:** D Somers — **Scorers:** Riordan. **Booked:** Murray, Thicot, Chisholm. **Dismissed:** Murray

● Clydesdale Bank Premier League ● Scottish FA Cup ● Co-op Insurance Cup ● UEFA Champions League ● UEFA Cup ● UEFA Intertoto Cup

HIBERNIAN

CLYDESDALE BANK PREMIER LEAGUE GOALKEEPER STATS

Player	Minutes on pitch	Appearances	Match starts	Completed matches	Sub appearances	Subbed off	Saved with feet	Punched	Parried	Tipped over	Fumbled	Tipped round	Caught	Blocked	Clean sheets	Goals conceded	Minutes since conceding	Save %	Saved	Resulting in goals	Opposition miss	Yellow cards	Red cards
							SAVES BREAKDOWN												PENALTIES				
Yves Ma-Kalambay	1916	21	21	20	0	1	1	17	16	0	0	9	68	2	7	24	51	82.96	1	1	0	2	0
Andrew McNeil	517	6	5	5	1	0	0	3	0	1	0	1	17	2	0	9	40	68.75	0	0	0	0	0
Grzegorz Szamotulski	1138	12	12	12	0	0	0	11	5	2	0	8	38	0	5	13	21	83.12	1	1	0	0	0

CLYDESDALE BANK PREMIER LEAGUE OUTFIELD PLAYER STATS

Player	Minutes on pitch	Appearances	Match starts	Completed matches	Substitute appearances	Subbed off	Goals scored	Minutes since scoring	Assists	Shots on target	Shots off target	Crosses	Defensive clearances	Defensive blocks	Fouls committed	Free-kicks won	Caught offside	Yellow cards	Red cards
Sol Bamba	2620	29	29	23	0	4	0	-	0	8	15	1	31	5	61	41	1	12	2
Ross Campbell	15	2	0	0	2	0	0	-	0	0	1	0	0	0	0	1	0	0	0
Martin Canning	95	1	1	1	0	0	0	313	0	0	0	0	0	0	1	1	0	0	0
Ross Chisholm	993	19	10	6	9	4	0	-	2	2	0		4	0	17	14	0	4	0
Steven Fletcher	2956	34	34	26	0	8	11	408	2	33	48	11	7	1	51	57	30	4	0
Paul Hanlon	555	7	6	5	1	1	1	410	1	1	1	3	10	3	6	2	0	0	0
Chris Hogg	2900	31	31	29	0	1	0	-	0	0		7	43	8	32	27	0	3	1
Jonatan Johansson	536	9	5	3	4	2	0	-	1	4	1	2	1	0	14	2	8	3	0
Rob Jones	2875	32	32	29	0	3	4	1142	2	8	7	0	83	21	43	26	1	7	0
Joe Keenan	831	15	9	2	6	7	0	-	0	2	5	4	2	0	9	13	0	0	0
Darren McCormack	576	8	7	4	1	3	0	-	0	0	0	1	4	0	11	2	0	0	0
Filipe Morais	62	2	0	0	2	0	0	207	0	0	1	0	0	0	2	1	0	0	0
Ian Murray	2246	28	23	21	5	1	0	-	2	1	5	6	26	7	28	31	3	7	1
Colin Nish	2308	31	27	18	4	9	8	225	6	20	25	14	18	1	42	58	29	6	0
Alan O'Brien	1350	24	14	5	10	9	0	-	1	1	8	15	0	1	9	7	1	0	0
Steve Pinau	216	8	0	0	8	0	0	-	0	0	3	1	0	0	3	6	0	0	0
John Rankin	2788	33	30	27	3	3	3	477	3	24	15	25	15	3	44	45	3	5	0
Derek Riordan	2755	32	28	22	4	6	12	46	6	55	36	39	1	0	15	20	56	3	0
Denes Rosa	923	12	10	7	2	3	0	-	0	1	6	2	5	0	7	8	3	2	0
Dean Shiels	1455	19	16	9	3	7	3	82	0	8	13	14	2		17	25	1	1	0
Lewis Stevenson	2408	29	26	25	3	1	0	-	1	1	3	7	16	2	33	27	0	5	0
Steven Thicot	1396	20	15	8	5	7	0	-	0	2	2	2	10	1	20	6	0	3	0
Fabian Yantorno	207	7	1	1	6	0	0	-	0	2	0	1	5	0	4	4	1	0	0
Merouane Zemmama	30	1	0	0	1	0	0	-	0	0	0	1	0	0	0	0	0	0	0
David van Zanten	2494	29	26	23	3	3	0	-	0	1	0	13	14	5	33	22	0	6	0

SEASON TOTALS

Goals scored	42
Goals conceded	46
Clean sheets	12
Shots on target	174
Shots off target	203
Shots per goal	8.98
Pens awarded	5
Pens scored	4
Pens conceded	4
Offsides	138
Corners	137
Crosses	170
Players used	28
Fouls committed	502
Free-kicks won	452

CARDS RECEIVED

75 **4**

SEQUENCES

Wins	2
(on three occasions)	
Losses	2
(on three occasions)	
Draws	3
(21/03/09–13/04/09)	
Undefeated	6
(28/02/09–13/04/09)	
Without win	6
(19/10/08–15/11/08)	
Undefeated home	5
(17/01/09–21/03/09)	
Undefeated away	4
(04/03/09–07/05/09)	
Without scoring	2
(21/02/09–28/02/09)	
Without conceding	4
(28/02/09–21/03/09)	
Scoring	6
(04/04/09–13/05/09)	
Conceding	5
(on two occasions)	

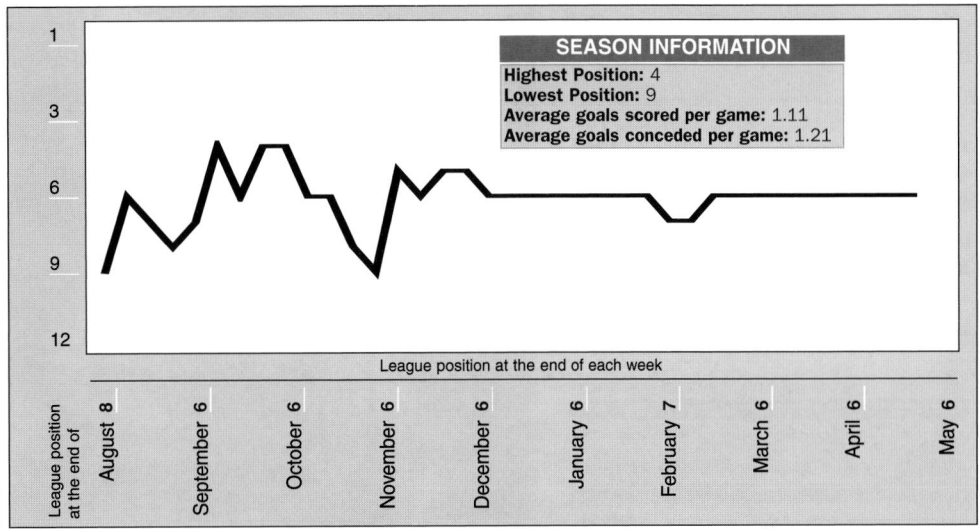

League position at the end of each week

League position at the end of — August 8 · September 6 · October 6 · November 6 · December 6 · January 6 · February 7 · March 6 · April 6 · May 6

SEASON INFORMATION
Highest Position: 4
Lowest Position: 9
Average goals scored per game: 1.11
Average goals conceded per game: 1.21

MATCH RECORDS

Goals scored per match

		W	D	L	Pts
Failed to score	11	0	5	6	5
Scored 1 goal	15	4	7	4	19
Scored 2 goals	10	5	2	3	17
Scored 3 goals	1	1	0	0	3
Scored 4+ goals	1	1	0	0	3

Goals conceded per match

		W	D	L	Pts
Clean sheet	12	7	5	0	26
Conceded 1 goal	13	3	7	3	16
Conceded 2 goals	8	1	2	5	5
Conceded 3 goals	3	0	0	3	0
Conceded 4+ goals	2	0	0	2	0

GOALS SCORED/CONCEDED PER FIVE-MINUTE INTERVALS

Goals For	2	4	2	1	2	0	2	4	6	4	1	0	3	1	0	3	3	4	
Goals Against	3	1	3	0	1	4	2	3	5	2	5	1	2	1	2	8	1	2	
Mins	5	10	15	20	25	30	35	40	45	50	55	60	65	70	75	80	85	90	

QUICK-FIRE GOALS

From the start of a match
Colin Nish
(v Falkirk) 0:21

By a substitute after coming on
Derek Riordan
(v Hamilton) 0:57

LAST-GASP GOALS

From the start of a match
Steven Fletcher
(v Aberdeen) 93:08

By a substitute after coming on
Derek Riordan
(v Hamilton) 21:32

GOAL DETAILS

How the goals were struck

SCORED		CONCEDED
18	Right foot	24
13	Left foot	11
11	Headers	10
0	Others	1

How the goals were struck

SCORED		CONCEDED
31	Open play	32
1	Cross	1
4	Corner	3
4	Penalties	2
0	Direct from free-kick	3
2	Free-kick	5
0	Own goals	0

Distance from goal

SCORED		CONCEDED
15	6yds	20
19	18yds	17
8	18+yds	9

INVERNESS CALEDONIAN THISTLE

CLUB SUMMARY

FORMED	1994
MANAGER	Terry Butcher
GROUND	Caledonian Stadium
CAPACITY	7,753
NICKNAME	Caley Thistle
WEBSITE	www.ictfc.co.uk

The New **Football Pools** PLAYER OF THE SEASON — Ross Tokely

OVERALL

P	W	D	L	F	A	GD
44	13	8	23	46	63	-17

CLYDESDALE BANK PREMIER LEAGUE

Pos	P	W	D	L	F	A	GD	Pts
12	38	10	7	21	37	58	-21	37

HOME

Pos	P	W	D	L	F	A	GD	Pts
12	19	4	5	10	18	27	-9	17

AWAY

Pos	P	W	D	L	F	A	GD	Pts
10	19	6	2	11	19	31	-12	20

CUP PROGRESS DETAILS

Competition	Round reached	Knocked out by
Co-op Insurance Cup	QF	Falkirk
Scottish Cup	QF	Falkirk

BIGGEST WIN (ALL COMPS)

10/01/09 3–0 v Partick **TSC4**

BIGGEST DEFEAT (ALL COMPS)

01/11/08 0–5 v Rangers **SPL**

THE PLAYER WITH THE MOST

Shots on target
Dougie Imrie 31

Shots off target
Dougie Imrie 35

Shots without scoring
Iain Vigurs 17

Assists
Dougie Imrie 7

Offsides
Andrew Barrowman 15

Fouls
Ian Black 72

Fouls without a card
Brian Kerr 19

Free-kicks won
Dougie Imrie 82

Defensive clearances
Ross Tokely 56

ATTENDANCE RECORD

High	Low	Average
7,143	3,110	4,457
v Celtic (18/10/2008)	v Motherwell (25/10/2008)	

Richie Foran scored three goals after joining from Darlington in January

THERE cannot be many teams who have won at Ibrox and been relegated in the same season, but that is exactly what happened to Inverness.

The Highlanders appeared doomed when they slipped five points adrift at the foot of the Clydesdale Bank Premier League in January.

But the appointment of Terry Butcher as manager proved to be a turning point. In little over a month, the former Rangers captain had hauled Caley Thistle off the bottom of the table and clear of danger.

However, one win in the last seven games of the season saw them sucked back into the dogfight and they ultimately failed to hold their nerve when it mattered, losing their final-weekend relegation decider against Falkirk to go down by two goals. That ended their five-year

stay in the SPL, the first time they had been relegated since the club's formation in 1994.

Before Butcher's arrival,

they had won only one of 11 SPL games in front of their own fans. Their reasonable away form had been keeping them afloat but, once that dried up, an eight-match barren run ensued, ultimately costing

Craig Brewster his job. Butcher made an instant impact, leading the club to an encouraging goalless draw against Celtic in his first match in charge in February.

After a decent run of results, the shock 1–0 win at leaders Rangers on 4th March, in which Ian Black scored the winner from the penalty spot, saw Inverness haul themselves off the foot of the table for the first time in 2009.

However, Butcher had been unable to address a lack of goals within the squad and they began to struggle. Following the split, they crucially lost their final two league games and with them their SPL status.

> **The appointment of Butcher proved to be a turning point**

RESULTS 2008/09

August

9th	● Aberdeen ....a	W 0–2	**Att:** 12,659. **Ref:** M Tumilty — **Scorers:** Barrowman, McBain. **Booked:** Tokely
16th	● Hamilton ....h	L 0–1	**Att:** 3,595. **Ref:** S O'Reilly — **Booked:** Duff
23rd	● Hibernian ....h	D 1–1	**Att:** 4,022. **Ref:** E Smith — **Scorers:** Cowie. **Booked:** Tokely, Black, Hastings
27th	● Arbroath a	D 2–2	**Att:** 596. **Ref:** A Muir — **Scorers:** Vigurs, Wood. **Booked:** Djebi-Zadi, Barrowman, Esson, McGuire, Imrie. **Dismissed:** Barrowman. (Won 4-2 on pens)
30th	● Falkirk ....a	W 1–2	**Att:** 4,730. **Ref:** M McCurry — **Scorers:** Cowie, Imrie. **Booked:** McBain

September

13th	● St Mirren ....h	L 1–2	**Att:** 3,501. **Ref:** I Brines — **Scorers:** Rooney. **Booked:** Tokely
20th	● Hearts ....a	L 1–0	**Att:** 12,890. **Ref:** W Collum — **Booked:** Tokely, Wood
23rd	● Morton ....a	W 1–2	**Att:** 2,023. **Ref:** M McCurry — **Scorers:** Hastings, Imrie. **Booked:** Tokely, Wood (AET)
27th	● Kilmarnock ....h	W 3–1	**Att:** 3,426. **Ref:** B Winter — **Scorers:** Barrowman, Black, McGuire. **Booked:** Vigurs

October

4th	● Dundee Utd ....a	L 2–1	**Att:** 6,279. **Ref:** I Brines — **Scorers:** Wilkie OG. **Booked:** B Wilson, Munro
18th	● Celtic..........................h	L 1–2	**Att:** 7,143. **Ref:** I Brines — **Scorers:** Wood. **Booked:** Black, Imrie, Tokely
25th	● Motherwell ....h	L 1–2	**Att:** 3,110. **Ref:** E Norris — **Scorers:** Rooney
28th	● Falkirk ....a	L 1–0	**Att:** 3,007. **Ref:** 10120 — **Booked:** Hastings, Munro

November

1st	● Rangers ....a	L 5–0	**Att:** 49,255. **Ref:** C Allan — **Booked:** Tokely
8th	● Hibernian ....a	W 1–2	**Att:** 11,688. **Ref:** C Boyle — **Scorers:** Black, Cowie. **Booked:** Vigurs, Black
12th	● Falkirk ....h	D 1–1	**Att:** 3,111. **Ref:** C Thomson — **Scorers:** Rooney. **Booked:** Vigurs
15th	● Hearts ....h	L 0–1	**Att:** 4,011. **Ref:** M Tumilty
22nd	● Kilmarnock ....a	W 1–2	**Att:** 4,328. **Ref:** S Finnie — **Scorers:** Imrie, Wood. **Booked:** Black, Wood, Tokely
29th	● Celtic..........................a	L 1–0	**Att:** 55,117. **Ref:** D Somers

December

6th	● Dundee Utd ....h	L 1–3	**Att:** 3,560. **Ref:** B Winter — **Scorers:** Rooney. **Booked:** Proctor
13th	● St Mirren..........................a	L 2–0	**Att:** 3,364. **Ref:** S Conroy — **Booked:** Barrowman
20th	● Aberdeen ....h	L 0–3	**Att:** 5,862. **Ref:** C Murray — **Booked:** Duncan, Hastings, Tokely
27th	● Motherwell ....a	L 3–2	**Att:** 4,521. **Ref:** C Richmond — **Scorers:** Rooney, Tokely. **Booked:** Munro, Tokely, Proctor

January

4th	● Rangers ....h	L 0–3	**Att:** 7,056. **Ref:** D McDonald — **Booked:** Proctor
10th	● Partick..........................h	W 3–0	**Att:** 1,803. **Ref:** E Smith — **Scorers:** Morais², Vigurs
17th	● Hamilton ....a	L 1–0	**Att:** 3,070. **Ref:** B Winter — **Booked:** Barrowman, Vigurs, Imrie, Wood
24th	● Hearts..........................a	L 3–2	**Att:** 13,224. **Ref:** S Conroy — **Scorers:** Imrie, Mihadjuks. **Booked:** Tokely, McBain, Imrie, Wood. **Dismissed:** McBain

February

1st	● Celtic..........................h	D 0–0	**Att:** 7,007. **Ref:** C Richmond — **Booked:** Black, Rooney
7th	● Kilmarnock ....h	W 2–0	**Att:** 2,578. **Ref:** I Brines — **Scorers:** Mihadjuks, Rooney. **Booked:** Mihadjuks, Proctor
14th	● Dundee Utd ....a	D 1–1	**Att:** 5,926. **Ref:** C Thomson — **Scorers:** Odhiambo. **Booked:** Foran, McBain. **Dismissed:** Duncan
21st	● Hibernian ....h	W 2–0	**Att:** 4,116. **Ref:** A Muir — **Scorers:** Foran, Proctor. **Booked:** Foran
28th	● Motherwell ....h	L 1–2	**Att:** 3,611. **Ref:** M McCurry — **Scorers:** Munro

March

4th	● Rangers ....a	W 0–1	**Att:** 48,129. **Ref:** C Murray — **Scorers:** Black. **Booked:** Black
7th	● Falkirk ....h	L 0–1	**Att:** 3,024. **Ref:** S Conroy — **Booked:** Duncan. **Dismissed:** Djebi-Zadi
14th	● Kilmarnock ....h	W 2–1	**Att:** 4,005. **Ref:** M Tumilty — **Scorers:** Black, Foran
21st	● Falkirk ....a	L 4–0	**Att:** 5,523. **Ref:** C Murray — **Booked:** Foran **Dismissed:** Esson

April

4th	● St Mirren ....h	W 2–1	**Att:** 3,794. **Ref:** W Collum — **Scorers:** Morais². **Booked:** Barrowman
11th	● Aberdeen ....a	L 1–0	**Att:** 11,114. **Ref:** A Muir — **Booked:** Tokely
18th	● Hamilton ....h	D 1–1	**Att:** 3,646. **Ref:** C Boyle — **Scorers:** Kerr. **Booked:** Black, Duncan, Foran

May

2nd	● St Mirren..........................a	W 1–2	**Att:** 4,171. **Ref:** S Conroy — **Scorers:** Munro, Tokely. **Booked:** Black
10th	● Hamilton ....h	D 1–1	**Att:** 3,623. **Ref:** C Richmond — **Scorers:** Foran
13th	● Motherwell ....a	D 2–2	**Att:** 2,818. **Ref:** D McDonald — **Scorers:** Imrie, Morais. **Booked:** Foran, Munro
16th	● Kilmarnock ....h	L 1–0	**Att:** 6,096. **Ref:** W Collum — **Booked:** Proctor, Foran, Black, Tokely
23rd	● Falkirk ....h	L 0–1	**Att:** 6,489. **Ref:** E Smith — **Booked:** Black, Djebi-Zadi. **Dismissed:** Tokely

● Clydesdale Bank Premier League ● Scottish FA Cup ● Co-op Insurance Cup ● UEFA Champions League ● UEFA Cup

INVERNESS CALEDONIAN THISTLE

CLYDESDALE BANK PREMIER LEAGUE GOALKEEPER STATS

Player	Minutes on pitch	Appearances	Match starts	Completed matches	Sub appearances	Subbed off	Saved with feet	Punched	Parried	Tipped over	Fumbled	Tipped round	Caught	Blocked	Clean sheets	Goals conceded	Minutes since conceding	Save %	Saved	Resulting in goals	Opposition miss	Yellow cards	Red cards
							SAVES BREAKDOWN												PENALTIES				
Ryan Esson 1969	21	21	20	0	0	2	12	10	4	0	2	51	0	3	31	79	74.11	0	1	3	0	1
Michael Fraser 1605	18	17	17	1	0	0	2	8	4	0	1	33	0	1	27	26	62.34	0	2	0	0	0

CLYDESDALE BANK PREMIER LEAGUE OUTFIELD PLAYER STATS

Player	Minutes on pitch	Appearances	Match starts	Completed matches	Substitute appearances	Subbed off	Goals scored	Minutes since scoring	Assists	Shots on target	Shots off target	Crosses	Defensive clearances	Defensive blocks	Fouls committed	Free-kicks won	Caught offside	Yellow cards	Red cards
Andrew Barrowman 1378	30	14	3	16	11	2	922	1	6	9	1	3	0	42	18	15	3	0
Ian Black 2842	34	34	20	0	14	4	878	1	15	27	45	12	4	72	61	2	10	0
Don Cowie 1913	22	21	18	1	3	3	953	4	15	19	36	7	1	5	18	4	0	0
Lionel Djebi-Zadi 1451	16	15	15	1	0	0	-	2	3	4	16	5	10	23	0	1	0	
Jamie Duff 746	12	7	6	5	1	0	-	1	0	0	0	8	2	9	2	0	1	0
Russell Duncan 2144	27	24	17	3	6	0	-	0	4	6	10	3	28	23	0	2	1	
Richie Foran 1340	15	15	9	0	6	3	327	0	8	15	2	15	0	35	17	6	6	0
Thierry Gathuessi 17	1	1	0	0	0	0	-	0	0	0	0	0	0	0	0	0	0	0
Richard Hastings 2091	25	22	22	3	0	0	-	0	1	3	14	9	3	15	19	0	2	0
Dougie Imrie 3047	38	33	22	5	11	4	222	7	31	35	36	3	1	57	82	12	3	0
Brian Kerr 943	10	10	10	0	0	1	477	2	5	2	3	4	0	19	6	0	0	0
Rory McAllister 44	3	0	0	3	0	0	-	0	0	1	0	0	0	1	0	0	0	0
Roy McBain 1880	27	21	9	6	11	1	1790	1	5	7	8	5	0	19	12	1	3	1
Phil McGuire 914	11	10	9	1	1	1	330	0	5	4	0	7	1	11	4	0	0	0
Pavels Mihadjuks 1124	12	12	11	0	1	1	970	0	3	1	0	14	1	8	12	0	0	0
Filipe Morais 779	12	9	2	3	7	3	207	1	15	10	4	0	0	5	13	2	0	0
Grant Munro 3201	34	34	34	0	0	2	458	0	3	5	4	32	9	29	30	1	3	0
Eric Odhiambo 263	8	3	0	5	3	1	239	0	2	2	0	0	0	1	0	2	0	0
David Proctor 2399	26	25	24	1	1	1	1089	0	1	2	5	10	4	21	21	1	4	0
Adam Rooney 1348	30	10	4	20	4	6	465	2	14	15	2	0	0	19	21	11	1	0
Zander Sutherland 29	3	0	0	3	0	0	-	0	0	0	0	0	0	0	0	0	0	0
Ross Tokely 3325	36	36	34	0	1	2	326	2	5	14	28	56	6	58	37	1	12	1
Iain Vigurs 1077	17	12	4	5	8	0	-	1	4	13	10	5	0	17	13	0	4	0
Barry Wilson 266	12	1	0	11	1	0	-	0	0	2	8	4	0	2	3	0	1	0
Garry Wood 1033	18	11	4	7	7	2	409	1	7	5	2	2	1	18	31	1	4	0

actim∄

SEASON TOTALS

Goals scored	37
Goals conceded	58
Clean sheets	4
Shots on target	152
Shots off target	200
Shots per goal	9.51
Pens awarded	4
Pens scored	3
Pens conceded	5
Offsides	59
Corners	178
Crosses	222
Players used	27
Fouls committed	503
Free-kicks won	471

CARDS RECEIVED

60 **4**

SEQUENCES

Wins	2
(04/03/09–14/03/09)	
Losses	8
(29/11/08–24/01/09)	
Draws	2
(on two occasions)	
Undefeated	4
(18/04/09–13/05/09)	
Without win	10
(29/11/08–14/02/09)	
Undefeated home	4
(14/03/09–10/05/09)	
Undefeated away	2
(on four occasions)	
Without scoring	2
(on two occasions)	
Without conceding	
(–)	
Scoring	5
(14/02/09–14/03/09)	
Conceding	22
(16/08/08–24/01/09)	

SEASON INFORMATION

Highest Position: 2
Lowest Position: 12
Average goals scored per game: 0.97
Average goals conceded per game: 1.53

League position at the end of each week

League position at the end of: August 5, September 4, October 10, November 9, December 11, January 12, February 12, March 11, April 11, May 12

MATCH RECORDS

Goals scored per match

		W	D	L	Pts
Failed to score	14	0	1	13	1
Scored 1 goal	12	1	5	6	8
Scored 2 goals	11	8	1	2	25
Scored 3 goals	1	1	0	0	3
Scored 4+ goals	0	0	0	0	0

Goals conceded per match

		W	D	L	Pts
Clean sheet	4	3	1	0	10
Conceded 1 goal	20	7	5	8	26
Conceded 2 goals	7	0	1	6	1
Conceded 3 goals	5	0	0	5	0
Conceded 4+ goals	2	0	0	2	0

QUICK-FIRE GOALS

From the start of a match
Grant Munro (v St Mirren) 11:14

By a substitute after coming on
Dougie Imrie (v Falkirk) 2:12

LAST-GASP GOALS

From the start of a match
Ian Black (v Rangers) 92:26

By a substitute after coming on
Adam Rooney (v Motherwell) 46:05

GOAL DETAILS

How the goals were struck

SCORED		CONCEDED
17	Right foot	34
11	Left foot	8
9	Headers	16
0	Others	0

How the goals were struck

SCORED		CONCEDED
22	Open play	42
1	Cross	3
5	Corner	3
3	Penalties	3
2	Direct from free-kick	2
3	Free-kick	5
1	Own goals	0

Distance from goal

SCORED		CONCEDED
15	6yds	23
19	18yds	28
3	18+yds	7

GOALS SCORED/CONCEDED PER FIVE-MINUTE INTERVALS

Goals For	0	0	3	2	3	2	0	4	3	4	0	2	1	2	1	1	3	6
Goals Against	1	5	1	4	1	4	0	5	3	4	3	2	6	3	1	7	4	4
Mins	5	10	15	20	25	30	35	40	45	50	55	60	65	70	75	80	85	90

KILMARNOCK

CLUB SUMMARY

FORMED	1869
MANAGER	Jim Jefferies
GROUND	Rugby Park
CAPACITY	18,128
NICKNAME	Killie
WEBSITE	www.kilmarnockfc.co.uk

The New Football Pools PLAYER OF THE SEASON — Craig Bryson

OVERALL

P	W	D	L	F	A	GD
44	15	9	20	50	58	-8

CLYDESDALE BANK PREMIER LEAGUE

Pos	P	W	D	L	F	A	GD	Pts
8	38	12	8	18	38	48	-10	44

HOME

Pos	P	W	D	L	F	A	GD	Pts
8	19	7	3	9	18	22	-4	24

AWAY

Pos	P	W	D	L	F	A	GD	Pts
8	19	5	5	9	20	26	-6	20

CUP PROGRESS DETAILS

Competition	Round reached	Knocked out by
Co-op Insurance Cup	QF	Celtic
Scottish Cup	R5	Inverness CT

BIGGEST WIN (ALL COMPS)
11/04/09 3–0 v Falkirk **SPL**

BIGGEST DEFEAT (ALL COMPS)
09/11/08 0–4 v Rangers **SPL**

THE PLAYER WITH THE MOST

Shots on target		
Kevin Kyle		21
Shots off target		
Kevin Kyle		16
Shots without scoring		
David Lilley		3
Assists		
Mehdi Taouil		7
Offsides		
David Fernandez		31
Fouls		
David Fernandez		77
Fouls without a card		
Conor Sammon		15
Free-kicks won		
Mehdi Taouil		92
Defensive clearances		
Frazer Wright		55

ATTENDANCE RECORD

High	Low	Average
10,153	4,267	5,727
v Rangers (09/11/2008)	v Falkirk (25/10/2008)	

KILMARNOCK retained their Clydesdale Bank Premier League status with a game to spare, and all credit must go to manager Jim Jefferies and his staff.

They proved once again that they are as good as anyone in the business at working miracles on a shoestring budget, as Killie made light of their financial concerns away from the pitch to win their battle for survival on it.

Things did not look good in March, when the Rugby Park club slipped to within five points of the SPL's bottom side, Falkirk. But Jefferies ensured his squad remained focused on the job in hand throughout the remainder of the campaign.

The road to SPL safety was not an easy one and was fuelled more by perspiration than inspiration.

Veteran goalkeeper Alan Combe was a mainstay for the club over the course of

the season, behind a hard-working defence and popular midfielder Manuel Pascali. And when flair players such as David Fernandez and Mehdi Taouil were fit, they offered

Alan Combe was a mainstay over the course of the season

Killie something more than just hard work.

A real standout player was midfielder Craig Bryson, who has been tipped by many to go on to great things. The former Clyde player has grown in confidence and assurance since moving to Rugby Park in 2007 and, while he has signed a new contract recently, that is unlikely to ward off potential suitors.

There is no doubt, though, that former Hearts and Bradford boss Jefferies ultimately had his most recent signing, Kevin Kyle, to thank for ensuring the club's survival.

The big striker arrived on a free transfer and scored on his debut against St Mirren at the end of January. He was then sent off in the following game against Inverness in the Homecoming Scottish Cup, but seven goals in a six-match spell were worth their weight in gold.

Kyle's overall impact following his arrival at the club was such that there has even been talk of him earning an international recall from Scotland manager George Burley.

Such publicity is likely to make it difficult for Jefferies to hang on to the former Sunderland player, but there is a feeling that, even if he does stay to see out the last year of his contract, next season could still prove to be another battle for the Ayrshire club.

Kevin Kyle made a huge impression for Killie

RESULTS 2008/09

August

9th	● Hibernian ....h	W 1–0	**Att:** 6,168. **Ref:** C Murray — **Scorers:** Hamill. **Booked:** Pascali
16th	● St Mirren............a	D 0–0	**Att:** 4,176. **Ref:** D Somers — **Booked:** Fowler, Pascali
23rd	● Hamilton ....h	W 1–0	**Att:** 5,339. **Ref:** C Allan — **Scorers:** Pascali. **Booked:** Ford, Fernandez, Hay
27th	● Brechin ....a	W 0–2	**Att:** 803. **Ref:** S Conroy — **Scorers:** Bryson, Wright
30th	● Dundee Utd ....a	W 0–2	**Att:** 6,823. **Ref:** M Tumilty — **Scorers:** Invincibile, Skelton. **Booked:** Taouil, Pascali, Hay

September

13th	● Rangers ....a	L 2–1	**Att:** 50,019. **Ref:** C Murray — **Scorers:** Wright. **Booked:** Skelton, Pascali
21st	● Celtic.................h	L 1–3	**Att:** 8,111. **Ref:** M McCurry — **Scorers:** Taouil. **Booked:** Fernandez
24th	● Aberdeen ....h	W 4–2	**Att:** 4,339. **Ref:** D McDonald — **Scorers:** Fernandez, Sammon², Taouil. **Booked:** Lilley, Hamill
27th	● Inverness CT ......a	L 3–1	**Att:** 3,426. **Ref:** B Winter — **Scorers:** Sammon. **Booked:** Combe, Fowler, Wright, Hamill, Fernandez. **Dismissed:** Fowler

October

4th	● Hearts................a	W 1–2	**Att:** 13,189. **Ref:** C Thomson — **Scorers:** Bryson, Taouil. **Booked:** Taouil, Ford, Fernandez, Pascali, Wright, Lilley
18th	● Motherwell ....h	W 1–0	**Att:** 5,113. **Ref:** A Muir — **Scorers:** Bryson. **Booked:** Invincibile, Wright, Bryson
25th	● Falkirk...............h	L 1–2	**Att:** 4,267. **Ref:** M McCurry — **Scorers:** Simmonds. **Booked:** Fernandez
29th	● Celtic.................h	L 1–3	**Att:** 6,319. **Ref:** C Thomson — **Scorers:** Invincibile. **Booked:** Fowler, Pascali, Lilley, Skelton

November

1st	● Aberdeen ....a	L 1–0	**Att:** 10,599. **Ref:** D Somers — **Booked:** Fowler, Murray, Lilley, Gibson
9th	● Rangers ....h	L 0–4	**Att:** 10,153. **Ref:** E Smith — **Booked:** Bryson
12th	● Celtic.................a	L 3–0	**Att:** 55,347. **Ref:** M Tumilty — **Booked:** Skelton, Pascali
15th	● Dundee Utd ....h	W 2–0	**Att:** 4,652. **Ref:** E Norris — **Scorers:** Fernandez, Hamill. **Booked:** Taouil, Fowler, Hamill
22nd	● Inverness CT ......h	L 1–2	**Att:** 4,328. **Ref:** S Finnie — **Scorers:** Gibson. **Booked:** Hay, Wright, Fernandez, Hamill
29th	● Hamilton ....a	L 1–0	**Att:** 2,903. **Ref:** I Brines — **Booked:** Wright, Taouil, Bryson

December

15th	● Motherwell ....a	W 0–2	**Att:** 3,339. **Ref:** M Tumilty — **Scorers:** Pascali, Russell. **Booked:** Murray
20th	● St Mirren............h	L 0–1	**Att:** 5,183. **Ref:** S O'Reilly — **Booked:** Fernandez, Murray, Pascali
27th	● Hibernian ....a	W 2–4	**Att:** 12,117. **Ref:** E Norris — **Scorers:** Hay, Invincibile², Russell. **Booked:** Skelton. **Dismissed:** Combe

January

3rd	● Falkirk...............a	D 1–1	**Att:** 5,375. **Ref:** I Brines — **Scorers:** Fernandez. **Booked:** Skelton, Russell, Fowler, Gibson
10th	● Ayr ....a	D 2–2	**Att:** 9,280. **Ref:** S Conroy — **Scorers:** Bryson, Pascali. **Booked:** Wright
13th	● Aberdeen ....h	L 1–2	**Att:** 4,354. **Ref:** E Smith — **Scorers:** Russell. **Booked:** Pascali, Gibson, Taouil, Fernandez
17th	● Hearts................h	L 0–2	**Att:** 5,469. **Ref:** C Richmond — **Booked:** Bryson
22nd	● Ayr ....h	W 3–1	**Att:** 11,563. **Ref:** S Conroy — **Scorers:** Ford², Taouil. **Booked:** Gibson. **Dismissed:** Fernandez
25th	● Hamilton ....h	L 0–1	**Att:** 5,063. **Ref:** C Thomson — **Booked:** Wright, Pascali
31st	● St Mirren............a	D 1–1	**Att:** 7,542. **Ref:** W Collum — **Scorers:** Kyle. **Booked:** Taouil, Combe, Bryson, Fernandez

February

7th	● Inverness CT ......a	L 2–0	**Att:** 2,578. **Ref:** I Brines — **Dismissed:** Kyle
14th	● Hibernian ....h	D 1–1	**Att:** 4,649. **Ref:** C Boyle — **Scorers:** Hamill. **Booked:** Hay, Pascali, Murray
21st	● Rangers ....a	L 3–1	**Att:** 50,301. **Ref:** B Winter — **Scorers:** Hamill. **Booked:** Skelton, Combe
28th	● Aberdeen ....a	D 0–0	**Att:** 11,457. **Ref:** D McDonald — **Booked:** Bryson, Pascali

March

4th	● Celtic.................h	L 1–2	**Att:** 6,712. **Ref:** C Thomson — **Scorers:** Invincibile. **Booked:** Hamill, Ford
14th	● Inverness CT ......a	L 2–1	**Att:** 4,005. **Ref:** M Tumilty — **Scorers:** Ford. **Booked:** Bryson, Clancy
21st	● Motherwell ....h	D 0–0	**Att:** 5,434. **Ref:** D McDonald — **Booked:** Lilley, Hamill, Fernandez

April

4th	● Hearts................a	L 3–1	**Att:** 13,659. **Ref:** D Somers — **Scorers:** Invincibile. **Booked:** Taouil, Pascali, Kyle
11th	● Falkirk...............h	W 3–0	**Att:** 5,835. **Ref:** C Richmond — **Scorers:** Kyle³. **Booked:** Kyle
18th	● Dundee Utd ....a	D 0–0	**Att:** 6,627. **Ref:** W Collum — **Booked:** Gibson

May

2nd	● Hamilton ....a	L 2–1	**Att:** 3,289. **Ref:** M Tumilty — **Scorers:** Hamill. **Booked:** Clancy
9th	● Falkirk...............h	D 1–1	**Att:** 5,955. **Ref:** A Muir — **Scorers:** Kyle. **Booked:** Lilley, Kyle
13th	● St Mirren............h	W 2–1	**Att:** 5,927. **Ref:** C Allan — **Scorers:** Kyle². **Booked:** Clancy
16th	● Inverness CT ......h	W 1–0	**Att:** 6,096. **Ref:** W Collum — **Scorers:** Kyle. **Booked:** Hay, Gibson, Fernandez, Pascali
23rd	● Motherwell ....a	W 1–2	**Att:** 4,186. **Ref:** S Nicholls — **Scorers:** Invincibile, Taouil. **Booked:** Lilley

● Clydesdale Bank Premier League ● Scottish FA Cup ● Co-op Insurance Cup ● UEFA Champions League ● UEFA Cup

KILMARNOCK

CLYDESDALE BANK PREMIER LEAGUE GOALKEEPER STATS

Player	Minutes on pitch	Appearances	Match starts	Completed matches	Sub appearances	Subbed off	Saved with feet	Punched	Parried	Tipped over	Fumbled	Tipped round	Caught	Blocked	Clean sheets	Goals conceded	Minutes since conceding	Save %	Saved	Resulting in goals	Opposition miss	Yellow cards	Red cards
Cameron Bell	93	1	1	1	0	0	0	0	0	0	0	0	1	0	0	1	12	66.67	0	0	0	0	0
Alan Combe	3101	34	34	32	0	1	3	16	15	3	0	8	100	0	12	40	98	78.92	2	4	2	3	1
Damien Rascle	388	5	3	3	2	0	0	2	1	0	0	2	15	0	1	7	35	71.43	0	2	0	0	0

CLYDESDALE BANK PREMIER LEAGUE OUTFIELD PLAYER STATS

Player	Minutes on pitch	Appearances	Match starts	Completed matches	Substitute appearances	Subbed off	Goals scored	Minutes since scoring	Assists	Shots on target	Shots off target	Crosses	Defensive clearances	Defensive blocks	Fouls committed	Free-kicks won	Caught offside	Yellow cards	Red cards
Scott Anson	14	1	0	0	1	0	0	-	0	0	0	0	0	0	0	0	0	0	0
Craig Bryson	2920	33	31	26	2	5	2	2100	0	15	8	11	11	4	31	50	4	7	0
Tim Clancy	1124	13	12	11	1	1	0	-	0	0	0	7	12	3	14	11	0	3	0
Martyn Corrigan	92	1	1	1	0	0	0	-	0	0	0	0	0	0	0	0	0	0	0
David Cox	29	2	0	0	2	0	0	-	0	0	0	0	0	0	0	0	0	0	0
David Fernandez	2568	32	28	16	4	12	2	961	3	10	9	36	2	1	77	64	31	11	0
Iain Flannigan	220	7	1	1	6	0	0	-	0	1	2	4	0	0	1	0	0	0	0
Simon Ford	2267	27	27	20	0	7	1	674	0	4	3	1	25	6	21	11	3	3	0
James Fowler	2284	26	23	19	3	3	0	-	2	1	1	6	14	3	14	22	0	5	1
William Gibson	1247	21	10	8	11	2	1	978	6	4	10	26	7	0	23	30	2	5	0
Jamie Hamill	2592	33	28	23	5	5	5	378	0	14	13	52	11	5	35	18	7	5	0
Garry Hay	2736	30	30	26	0	4	1	1668	6	5	6	95	18	6	15	33	0	5	0
Danny Invincibile	1907	25	21	16	4	5	6	66	1	16	10	25	8	2	36	22	3	1	0
Kevin Kyle	1030	11	11	10	0	1	8	14	0	21	16	3	12	0	30	27	14	3	0
David Lilley	1763	20	20	18	0	2	0	-	0	1	2	1	19	10	32	8	0	5	0
Grant Murray	812	11	10	8	1	2	0	-	0	2	0	0	3	2	13	1	0	4	0
Ryan O'Leary	90	3	1	0	2	1	0	-	0	0	1	0	0	0	1	1	0	0	0
Manuel Pascali	2815	32	31	27	1	4	2	1356	1	9	16	1	24	1	56	34	2	13	0
Allan Russell	640	11	8	0	3	8	3	206	0	10	6	1	2	1	18	9	10	1	0
Conor Sammon	1041	19	10	4	9	6	1	683	0	5	7	2	5	1	15	18	3	0	0
Donovan Simmonds	611	19	4	2	15	2	1	502	1	6	11	3	0	0	8	9	6	0	0
Gavin Skelton	1888	27	20	15	7	5	1	1841	1	5	6	7	4	4	34	28	0	5	0
Mehdi Taouil	2701	34	30	20	4	10	3	2		13	12	44	2	1	29	92	2	7	0
Frazer Wright	2394	27	23	22	4	1	1	2032	0	6	4	0	55	17	37	19	0	6	0

SEASON TOTALS

Goals scored	38
Goals conceded	48
Clean sheets	12
Shots on target	148
Shots off target	143
Shots per goal	7.66
Pens awarded	4
Pens scored	3
Pens conceded	10
Offsides	87
Corners	178
Crosses	325
Players used	27
Fouls committed	542
Free-kicks won	519

CARDS RECEIVED

92 **2**

SEQUENCES

Wins	3
(13/05/09–23/05/09)	
Losses	4
(25/10/08–12/11/08)	
Draws	2
(31/01/09–14/02/09)	
Undefeated	4
(on two occasions)	
Without win	12
(03/01/09–04/04/09)	
Undefeated home	5
(21/03/09–16/05/09)	
Undefeated away	4
(15/12/08–31/01/09)	
Without scoring	3
(01/11/08–12/11/08)	
Without conceding	4
(09/08/08–30/08/08)	
Scoring	8
(23/08/08–25/10/08)	
Conceding	9
(20/12/08–21/02/09)	

SEASON INFORMATION

Highest Position: 2
Lowest Position: 10
Average goals scored per game: 1.00
Average goals conceded per game: 1.26

League position at the end of each week

League position at the end of: August 2, September 5, October 3, November 7, December 7, January 9, February 9, March 9, April 8, May 8

MATCH RECORDS

Goals scored per match

		W	D	L	Pts
Failed to score	11	0	4	7	4
Scored 1 goal	19	4	4	11	16
Scored 2 goals	6	6	0	0	18
Scored 3 goals	1	1	0	0	3
Scored 4+ goals	1	1	0	0	3

Goals conceded per match

		W	D	L	Pts
Clean sheet	12	8	4	0	28
Conceded 1 goal	11	3	4	4	13
Conceded 2 goals	9	1	0	8	3
Conceded 3 goals	5	0	0	5	0
Conceded 4+ goals	1	0	0	1	0

QUICK-FIRE GOALS

From the start of a match
Conor Sammon
(v Inverness CT) 3:43

By a substitute after coming on
Jamie Hamill
(v Hibernian) 5:24

LAST-GASP GOALS

From the start of a match
Donovan Simmonds
(v Falkirk) 91:56

By a substitute after coming on
William Gibson
(v Inverness CT) 26:07

GOAL DETAILS

How the goals were struck

SCORED		CONCEDED
16	Right foot	25
9	Left foot	14
13	Headers	9
0	Others	0

How the goals were struck

SCORED		CONCEDED
24	Open play	28
4	Cross	4
5	Corner	6
3	Penalties	6
1	Direct from free-kick	1
1	Free-kick	3
0	Own goals	0

Distance from goal

SCORED		CONCEDED
17	6yds	22
17	18yds	21
4	18+yds	5

GOALS SCORED/CONCEDED PER FIVE-MINUTE INTERVALS

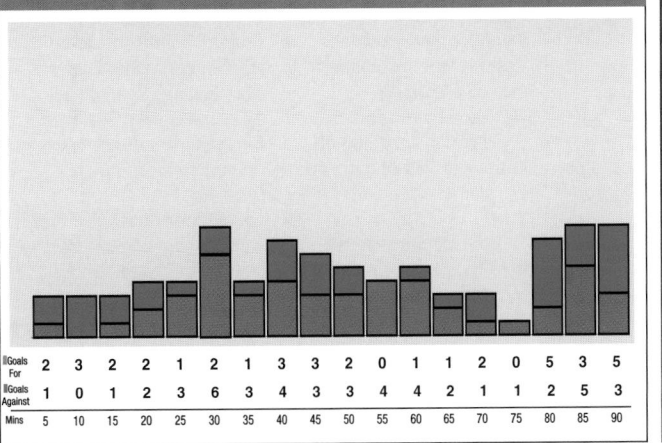

Goals For	2	3	2	2	1	2	1	3	3	2	0	1	1	2	0	5	3	5
Goals Against	1	0	1	2	3	6	3	4	3	3	4	4	2	1	1	2	5	3
Mins	5	10	15	20	25	30	35	40	45	50	55	60	65	70	75	80	85	90

CLUB SUMMARY

FORMED	1886
MANAGER	Mark McGhee
GROUND	Fir Park Stadium
CAPACITY	13,677
NICKNAME	The Steelmen
WEBSITE	www.motherwellfc.co.uk

PLAYER OF THE SEASON — Stephen Craigan

OVERALL

P	W	D	L	F	A	GD
44	14	10	20	51	58	-7

CLYDESDALE BANK PREMIER LEAGUE

Pos	P	W	D	L	F	A	GD	Pts
7	38	13	9	16	46	51	-5	48

HOME

Pos	P	W	D	L	F	A	GD	Pts
6	19	7	6	6	24	27	-3	27

AWAY

Pos	P	W	D	L	F	A	GD	Pts
5	19	6	3	10	22	24	-2	21

CUP PROGRESS DETAILS

Competition	Round reached	Knocked out by
Co-op Insurance Cup	R2	Hamilton
Scottish Cup	R5	St Mirren
UEFA Cup	R1	AS Nancy

BIGGEST WIN (ALL COMPS)

18/01/09 4–0 v Dundee Utd **SPL**

BIGGEST DEFEAT (ALL COMPS)

22/11/08 1–4 v Hibernian **SPL**

THE PLAYER WITH THE MOST

Shots on target
David Clarkson 30

Shots off target
David Clarkson 28

Shots without scoring
Steven Hammell 17

Assists
Steven Hammell 8

Offsides
Chris Porter... 27

Fouls
Keith Lasley.. 56

Fouls without a card
John Sutton 51

Free-kicks won
David Clarkson 75

Defensive clearances
Mark Reynolds 29

ATTENDANCE RECORD

High	Low	Average
9,600	2,818	5,522
v Rangers (12/11/2008)	v Inverness CT (13/05/2009)	

MOTHERWELL never quite lived up to the raised expectations set by Mark McGhee's first season in charge – but they still qualified for Europe for the second successive year.

The Steelmen – who finished third in the Clydesdale Bank Premier League in 2007/08 – just missed out on the top six, but their position in the Fair Play League handed them a place in the UEFA Europa League qualifiers.

That earned Motherwell the status of being the last Scottish club to play in the UEFA Cup and the first to appear in the new Europa League tournament.

Their UEFA Cup campaign proved something of an anti-climax as they lost 3–0 on aggregate to French club AS Nancy. A Graeme Smith penalty save kept the tie alive after a difficult away leg, but two early goals from set-pieces gave the Ligue 1 side a comfortable evening at Fir Park.

Motherwell made a decent start to the SPL season without hitting the heights of the previous year as they adapted to life without Ross McCormack, who was pivotal to their attacking play before leaving for Cardiff. But they were knocked out of the Co-operative Insurance Cup by arch-rivals Hamilton following striker Chris Porter's sending off in the first half of a thrilling 2–1 defeat after extra-time.

Their league season then took a downward turn following injury to skipper Stephen Craigan and the loss of Scotland striker David Clarkson to injury and suspension. Five straight defeats left them

Steven Hammell in UEFA Cup action against AS Nancy

joint bottom of the table on Christmas Day.

However, the return of Craigan, Clarkson and on-loan Slovakian midfielder Maros Klimpl sparked a 12-game unbeaten run that put Motherwell firmly on course for a top-six spot. After selling top scorer Porter to Derby, that eluded them as St Mirren beat them 2–0 to consign

McGhee's men to the bottom six. But feelings of disappointment soon lifted slightly as UEFA confirmed Scotland had gained an extra European place after finishing in the top three of their Fair Play rankings. With Motherwell in pole position to take advantage under the Scottish Football Association's ratings system, fans watched the post-split fixtures with more concern about yellow cards than goals.

And, with seventh place comfortably secured, they got their best 'result' of the season three days after it actually ended when their European qualification was confirmed.

> **Fans had more concern about yellow cards than scoring goals**

RESULTS 2008/09

August

9th	● Hearts.................a	L 3–2	**Att:** 14,219. **Ref:** I Brines — **Scorers:** Clarkson². **Booked:** Malcolm, Lasley
16th	● Aberdeen ....h	L 0–1	**Att:** 5,872. **Ref:** S Conroy
23rd	● Dundee Utd ....h	D 1–1	**Att:** 5,149. **Ref:** D McDonald — **Scorers:** Sutton. **Booked:** Clarkson, Reynolds
30th	● Hibernian ....a	W 0–1	**Att:** 11,285. **Ref:** S Dougal — **Scorers:** Sutton

September

13th	● Celtic.................h	L 2–4	**Att:** 8,407. **Ref:** C Thomson — **Scorers:** Clarkson, Sutton. **Booked:** Lasley, Craigan, Reynolds
18th	● AS Nancy ....a	L 1–0	**Att:** 16,094. **Ref:** V Hrinak — **Booked:** Lasley
21st	● Rangers ....a	L 2–1	**Att:** 49,448. **Ref:** E Smith — **Scorers:** Clarkson. **Booked:** Quinn, Craigan
24th	● Hamilton ....h	L 1–2	**Att:** 5,586. **Ref:** I Brines — **Scorers:** Murphy. **Booked:** Hammell, Reynolds. **Dismissed:** Porter (AET)
27th	● St Mirren ....h	W 2–1	**Att:** 4,786. **Ref:** S Conroy — **Scorers:** Malcolm, Sutton. **Booked:** Fitzpatrick

October

2nd	● AS Nancy ....h	L 0–2	**Att:** 11,318. **Ref:** E Berntsen
5th	● Falkirk................h	W 3–2	**Att:** 4,509. **Ref:** S O'Reilly — **Scorers:** Murphy, Porter, Sutton
18th	● Kilmarnock ....a	L 1–0	**Att:** 5,113. **Ref:** A Muir — **Booked:** Clarkson, G. Smith, Hammell
25th	● Inverness CT ....a	W 1–2	**Att:** 3,110. **Ref:** E Norris — **Scorers:** Malcolm, Porter. **Booked:** Malcolm

November

1st	● Hamilton ....h	W 2–0	**Att:** 6,205. **Ref:** M Tumilty — **Scorers:** Porter². **Booked:** Malcolm, Lasley, Hammell
8th	● Celtic.................a	L 2–0	**Att:** 56,504. **Ref:** D McDonald — **Booked:** Reynolds. **Dismissed:** Clarkson
12th	● Rangers ....h	D 0–0	**Att:** 9,600. **Ref:** S Conroy
15th	● Falkirk................a	L 1–0	**Att:** 5,279. **Ref:** W Collum
22nd	● Hibernian ....h	L 1–4	**Att:** 4,957. **Ref:** C Richmond — **Scorers:** Malcolm. **Booked:** Malcolm, Lasley
29th	● Aberdeen ....a	L 2–0	**Att:** 10,302. **Ref:** C Boyle — **Booked:** G. Smith, Malcolm, Reynolds

December

15th	● Kilmarnock ....h	L 0–2	**Att:** 3,339. **Ref:** M Tumilty
20th	● Hamilton ....a	L 2–0	**Att:** 3,527. **Ref:** I Brines — **Booked:** Klimpl, McGarry, Quinn
27th	● Inverness CT ....h	W 3–2	**Att:** 4,521. **Ref:** C Richmond — **Scorers:** Porter³

January

3rd	● St Mirren ....a	D 0–0	**Att:** 10,189. **Ref:** A Muir — **Booked:** Lasley
7th	● Hearts.................h	W 1–0	**Att:** 4,928. **Ref:** D Somers — **Scorers:** Porter. **Booked:** Craigan
18th	● Dundee Utd ....a	W 0–4	**Att:** 7,090. **Ref:** E Smith — **Scorers:** Clarkson, Fitzpatrick, Klimpl, Porter. **Booked:** Hammell
24th	● Falkirk................h	D 1–1	**Att:** 5,018. **Ref:** C Allan — **Scorers:** Clarkson. **Booked:** Klimpl
31st	● Hibernian ....a	D 1–1	**Att:** 10,903. **Ref:** M McCurry — **Scorers:** Clarkson

February

2nd	● Inverurie Loco Works ....a	W 0–3	**Att:** 2,500. **Ref:** W Collum — **Scorers:** Clarkson, Sutton². **Booked:** Klimpl, Lasley
7th	● St Mirren ....h	D 1–1	**Att:** 5,695. **Ref:** C Thomson — **Scorers:** Hughes
14th	● Hamilton ....h	W 1–0	**Att:** 5,917. **Ref:** D McDonald — **Scorers:** Clarkson. **Booked:** Quinn
19th	● St Mirren ....a	L 1–0	**Att:** 4,555. **Ref:** C Thomson — **Booked:** Craigan
22nd	● Celtic.................h	D 1–1	**Att:** 8,593. **Ref:** I Brines — **Scorers:** Quinn. **Booked:** Klimpl, Hughes
28th	● Inverness CT ....a	W 1–2	**Att:** 3,611. **Ref:** M McCurry — **Scorers:** Sheridan, Sutton. **Booked:** Klimpl

March

4th	● Hearts.................a	L 2–1	**Att:** 13,306. **Ref:** B Winter — **Scorers:** Hughes. **Booked:** Klimpl
14th	● Dundee Utd ....h	W 2–1	**Att:** 4,798. **Ref:** I Brines — **Scorers:** Clarkson, Sutton. **Booked:** Klimpl, Clarkson
21st	● Kilmarnock ....a	D 0–0	**Att:** 5,434. **Ref:** D McDonald — **Booked:** Reynolds, Klimpl

April

4th	● Aberdeen ....h	D 1–1	**Att:** 4,686. **Ref:** C Allan — **Scorers:** O'Brien
11th	● Rangers ....a	L 3–1	**Att:** 50,080. **Ref:** D Somers — **Scorers:** Sutton. **Booked:** G. Smith, Clarkson
18th	● St Mirren ....h	L 0–2	**Att:** 6,626. **Ref:** M McCurry

May

2nd	● Falkirk................a	L 2–1	**Att:** 4,937. **Ref:** W Collum — **Scorers:** Clarkson. **Booked:** Hammell, Lasley, Reynolds, McLean
9th	● St Mirren ....a	W 1–3	**Att:** 4,002. **Ref:** B Winter — **Scorers:** Clarkson², Murphy. **Booked:** Clarkson
13th	● Inverness CT ....h	D 2–2	**Att:** 2,818. **Ref:** D McDonald — **Scorers:** McLean, Sutton.
16th	● Hamilton ....a	W 0–3	**Att:** 3,383. **Ref:** A Muir — **Scorers:** Clarkson, Sheridan, Sutton. **Booked:** Clarkson, Klimpl
23rd	● Kilmarnock ....h	L 1–2	**Att:** 4,186. **Ref:** S Nicholls — **Scorers:** McLean. **Booked:** Quinn

● Clydesdale Bank Premier League ● Scottish FA Cup ● Co-op Insurance Cup ● UEFA Champions League ● UEFA Cup

MOTHERWELL

CLYDESDALE BANK PREMIER LEAGUE GOALKEEPER STATS

Player	Minutes on pitch	Appearances	Match starts	Completed matches	Sub appearances	Subbed off	Saved with feet	Punched	Parried	Tipped over	Fumbled	Tipped round	Caught	Blocked	Clean sheets	Goals conceded	Minutes since conceding	Save %	Saved	Resulting in goals	Opposition miss	Yellow cards	Red cards
Artur Krysiak 93	1	1	1	0	0	0	0	0	0	0	0	0	1	0	0	2	2	33.33	0	0	0	0	0
Graeme Smith 3469	37	37	37	0	0	2	28	27	2	0	5	107	1	9	49	131	78.32	1	2	0	3	0

Columns: SAVES BREAKDOWN spans (Saved with feet, Punched, Parried, Tipped over, Fumbled, Tipped round, Caught, Blocked). PENALTIES spans (Saved, Resulting in goals, Opposition miss).

CLYDESDALE BANK PREMIER LEAGUE OUTFIELD PLAYER STATS

Player	Minutes on pitch	Appearances	Match starts	Completed matches	Substitute appearances	Subbed off	Goals scored	Minutes since scoring	Assists	Shots on target	Shots off target	Crosses	Defensive clearances	Defensive blocks	Fouls committed	Free-kicks won	Caught offside	Yellow cards	Red cards
David Clarkson...............2643	33	30	17	3	12	13	150	3	30	28	9	3	0	44	75	21	6	1
Stephen Craigan 2032	22	22	20	0	2	0	-	0	2	1	3	19	3	21	26	0	3	0
Marc Fitzpatrick..............1405	23	14	11	9	3	1	431	1	2	8	2	4	0	11	13	2	1	0
Steven Hammell 3431	37	37	36	0	1	0	-	0	8	8	9	50	12	0	26	36	0	4	0
Stephen Hughes 3238	35	35	33	0	2	1	953	4	18	14	16	25	4	37	32	4	1	0
Shaun Hutchinson.............95	1	1	1	0	0	0	-	0	0	0	0	1	0	1	0	0	0	0
Maros Klimpl....................1843	21	20	16	1	4	1	1249	0	7	8	1	2	1	48	36	0	8	0
Keith Lasley 2182	28	24	20	4	4	0	-	3	3	4	8	3	1	56	25	0	6	0
Bob Malcolm 1027	13	11	8	2	3	3	248	1	6	2	4	6	1	26	9	0	5	0
Steve McGarry 1355	23	16	4	7	12	0	-	1	5	4	10	1	0	16	19	0	1	0
Robert McHugh 25	2	0	0	2	0	0	-	0	0	0	0	0	0	2	0	0	0	0
Brian McLean 1085	12	12	10	0	2	2	12	1	4	8	1	8	2	11	10	0	1	0
Jamie Murphy...................1185	30	11	1	19	10	2	224	0	8	3	14	0	0	3	16	8	0	0
Jim O'Brien......................1926	29	19	13	10	6	1	637	3	9	14	35	1	1	26	37	3	0	0
Chris Porter.....................1949	22	21	17	1	4	9	100	2	23	20	2	5	0	33	43	27	0	0
Paul Quinn 3021	33	33	30	0	1	1	848	3	6	7	9	10	6	16	28	5	4	2
Mark Reynolds..................3374	36	36	36	0	0	0	-	0	1	2	3	29	8	42	24	0	6	0
Steven Saunders...............219	3	2	2	1	0	0	-	0	1	1	0	0	0	3	3	0	0	0
Cillian Sheridan................842	13	9	5	4	4	2	128	2	7	14	2	0	0	4	9	6	0	0
Paul Slane 7	1	0	0	1	0	0	-	0	0	0	0	0	0	1	0	0	0	0
Darren Smith 392	16	1	0	15	2	0	-	0	1	0	3	0	0	3	4	0	0	0
John Sutton 2216	28	26	17	2	9	10	69	1	27	24	2	4	0	51	27	16	0	0

SEASON TOTALS

Goals scored	46
Goals conceded	51
Clean sheets	9
Shots on target	168
Shots off target	171
Shots per goal	7.37
Pens awarded	3
Pens scored	2
Pens conceded	3
Offsides	92
Corners	190
Crosses	175
Players used	24
Fouls committed	481
Free-kicks won	480

CARDS RECEIVED

49 **3**

SEQUENCES

Wins	2
(on three occasions)	
Losses	5
(15/11/08–20/12/08)	
Draws	2
(on two occasions)	
Undefeated	9
(27/12/08–28/02/09)	
Without win	7
(08/11/08–20/12/08)	
Undefeated home	7
(27/12/08–04/04/09)	
Undefeated away	4
(03/01/09–28/02/09)	
Without scoring	3
(on two occasions)	
Without conceding	3
(03/01/09–18/01/09)	
Scoring	9
(07/01/09-14/03/09)	
Conceding	6
(on three occasions)	

SEASON INFORMATION

Highest Position: 3
Lowest Position: 12
Average goals scored per game: 1.21
Average goals conceded per game: 1.34

League position at the end of each week

League position at the end of

August 9 | September 10 | October 7 | November 10 | December 9 | January 7 | February 6 | March 7 | April 7 | May 7

MATCH RECORDS

Goals scored per match

		W	D	L	Pts
Failed to score	11	0	3	8	3
Scored 1 goal	14	3	5	6	14
Scored 2 goals	8	5	1	2	16
Scored 3 goals	4	4	0	0	12
Scored 4+ goals	1	1	0	0	3

Goals conceded per match

		W	D	L	Pts
Clean sheet	9	6	3	0	21
Conceded 1 goal	13	5	5	3	20
Conceded 2 goals	12	2	1	9	7
Conceded 3 goals	2	0	0	2	0
Conceded 4+ goals	2	0	0	2	0

GOALS SCORED/CONCEDED PER FIVE-MINUTE INTERVALS

Goals For	0	2	2	1	3	4	4	3	3	1	3	3	2	3	1	6	3	2
Goals Against	2	5	0	0	3	2	1	5	4	4	2	4	3	3	2	3	1	7
Mins	5	10	15	20	25	30	35	40	45	50	55	60	65	70	75	80	85	90

QUICK-FIRE GOALS

From the start of a match
Chris Porter
(v Inverness CT) 7:46

By a substitute after coming on
David Clarkson
(v Dundee Utd) 5:36

LAST-GASP GOALS

From the start of a match
David Clarkson
(v Rangers) 86:53

By a substitute after coming on
John Sutton
(v Inverness CT) 13:04

GOAL DETAILS

How the goals were struck

SCORED		CONCEDED
25	Right foot	30
9	Left foot	14
12	Headers	7
0	Others	0

How the goals were struck

SCORED		CONCEDED
33	Open play	44
4	Cross	0
3	Corner	4
2	Penalties	2
2	Direct from free-kick	1
2	Free-kick	0
0	Own goals	0

Distance from goal

SCORED		CONCEDED
16	6yds	20
24	18yds	23
6	18+yds	8

RANGERS

CLUB SUMMARY

FORMED	1873
MANAGER	Walter Smith
GROUND	Ibrox Stadium
CAPACITY	51,076
NICKNAME	The Gers
WEBSITE	www.rangers.co.uk

The New **Football Pools** PLAYER OF THE SEASON — **Majid Bougherra**

OVERALL

P	W	D	L	F	A	GD
49	34	9	6	100	34	66

CLYDESDALE BANK PREMIER LEAGUE

Pos	P	W	D	L	F	A	GD	Pts
1	38	26	8	4	77	28	49	86

HOME

Pos	P	W	D	L	F	A	GD	Pts
1	19	15	2	2	44	15	29	47

AWAY

Pos	P	W	D	L	F	A	GD	Pts
1	19	11	6	2	33	13	20	39

CUP PROGRESS DETAILS

Competition	Round reached	Knocked out by
Co-op Insurance Cup	Final	Celtic
Scottish Cup	Won	–
Champions League	Qualifying R2	FBK Kaunas

BIGGEST WIN (ALL COMPS)

06/12/08 7–1 v Hamilton **SPL**

BIGGEST DEFEAT (ALL COMPS)

15/03/09 0–2 v Celtic **SLCF**

THE PLAYER WITH THE MOST

Shots on target	
Kris Boyd	67
Shots off target	
Kris Boyd	52
Shots without scoring	
Kirk Broadfoot	18
Assists	
Kenny Miller	9
Offsides	
Kris Boyd	43
Fouls	
Kris Boyd	66
Fouls without a card	
Nacho Novo	14
Free-kicks won	
Kris Boyd	56
Defensive clearances	
David Weir	60

ATTENDANCE RECORD

High	Low	Average
50,403	48,129	49,534
v Celtic (27/12/2008)	v Inverness CT (04/03/2009)	

IT SEEMS that Rangers no longer do straightforward title wins.

For the third time in seven seasons the Ibrox side triumphed on the final day of the campaign, as fingernails were once again bitten to the quick. Alex McLeish had been a past master of the dramatic climax, presiding over a 6–1 win against Dunfermline at Ibrox in 2003, and repeating the feat two years later with a win over Hibernian.

This time around, Walter Smith secured the Clydesdale Bank Premier League title thanks to a 3–0 win against Dundee United at Tannadice, as Celtic's draw against Hearts at Celtic Park handed Rangers a winning margin of four points.

Less than a week later, the double was secured courtesy of a 1–0 win over Falkirk in the Homecoming Scottish Cup final.

Six months earlier, such a haul of both those domestic trophies had seemed to be highly unlikely.

Rangers had recovered sufficiently from their disappointing UEFA Champions League qualifying-stage exit at the hands of Lithuanian minnows FBK Kaunas to record a superb 4–2 victory over Celtic in the first Old Firm derby of the season. But inconsistency saw them drop points against St Mirren, Dundee United and Motherwell, and the title was slipping from their grasp as 2008 came to a close.

By the time Scott McDonald's goal earned Celtic a 1–0 win at Ibrox on 27th December, Rangers were seven points adrift and had been all but written off. Even Smith has since admitted he feared there was no way back as his side headed into 2009 desperately hoping to rebuild their challenge.

However, if one thing was certain in this incredible campaign, it was to expect the unexpected. The first turning point came in the final Old Firm derby when a Steven Davis strike sealed the points and propelled Rangers two points clear at the summit.

Then, just four days later, came another defining moment. Smith's men appeared to have blown their chances after being held to a 1–1 draw at Hibernian, but Mixu Paatelainen's side were to have another major say in the destination of the title when they also earned a draw against Celtic at Easter Road in the penultimate game to force the title race to the wire.

Once again, Rangers saved the best for last and, this time, there was no need for the helicopter carrying the SPL trophy to change direction – as it had in 2005 – as goals from Kyle Lafferty, Pedro Mendes and the prolific Kris Boyd gave Rangers the decisive win they needed and sparked jubilant celebrations.

Top scorer Kris Boyd and Lee McCulloch hold the Scottish Cup trophy

RESULTS 2008/09

July
30th	● FBK Kaunas ....h	D 0–0	**Att:** 34,847. **Ref:** K Blom — **Booked:** McCulloch

August
5th	● FBK Kaunas ....a	L 2–1	**Att:** 5,500. **Ref:** S Johannesson — **Scorers:** Thomson. **Booked:** McCulloch, Thomson
9th	● Falkirk ....a	W 0–1	**Att:** 6,669. **Ref:** D McDonald — **Scorers:** Velicka. **Booked:** Dailly, Whittaker, Lafferty
16th	● Hearts............................h	W 2–0	**Att:** 48,191. **Ref:** S Dougal — **Scorers:** Boyd, Lafferty. **Booked:** Thomson
23rd	● Aberdeen ....a	D 1–1	**Att:** 16,489. **Ref:** C Thomson — **Scorers:** Weir
31st	● Celtic..............................a	W 2–4	**Att:** 58,595. **Ref:** D McDonald — **Scorers:** Cousin, Mendes, Miller[2]
			Booked: Thomson, Cousin, Adam, McGregor, Broadfoot **Dismissed:** Cousin

September
13th	● Kilmarnock ....h	W 2–1	**Att:** 50,019. **Ref:** C Murray — **Scorers:** Boyd[2]. **Booked:** Boyd, Papac, Mendes. **Dismissed:** Papac
21st	● Motherwell ....h	W 2–1	**Att:** 49,448. **Ref:** E Smith — **Scorers:** Davis, Novo. **Booked:** Weir, Boyd
24th	● Partick...........................a	W 1–2	**Att:** 6,497. **Ref:** S Conroy — **Scorers:** Boyd, Mendes. **Booked:** Thomson (AET)
28th	● Hibernian ....a	W 0–3	**Att:** 15,292. **Ref:** C Murray — **Scorers:** Bougherra, Miller[2]. **Booked:** Broadfoot, Darcheville

October
5th	● St Mirren.......................a	L 1–0	**Att:** 7,520. **Ref:** W Collum — **Booked:** Mendes, Lafferty
25th	● Hamilton ....a	W 1–3	**Att:** 4,613. **Ref:** D McDonald — **Scorers:** Boyd[2], Novo
28th	● Hamilton ....h	W 2–0	**Att:** 32,083. **Ref:** E Smith — **Scorers:** Boyd, Lafferty

November
1st	● Inverness CT ....h	W 5–0	**Att:** 49,255. **Ref:** C Allan — **Scorers:** Boyd[3], Miller, Novo
4th	● Dundee Utd ....h	D 3–3	**Att:** 48,686. **Ref:** C Thomson — **Scorers:** Davis, Papac, Thomson. **Booked:** Papac
9th	● Kilmarnock ....a	W 0–4	**Att:** 10,153. **Ref:** E Smith — **Scorers:** Boyd, Miller, Weir, Whittaker. **Booked:** Papac, Broadfoot
12th	● Motherwell ....a	D 0–0	**Att:** 9,600. **Ref:** S Conroy — **Booked:** Bougherra
15th	● St Mirren.......................h	W 2–1	**Att:** 49,321. **Ref:** D Somers — **Scorers:** Boyd, Davis. **Booked:** Mendes, Miller
22nd	● Aberdeen ....h	W 2–0	**Att:** 50,166. **Ref:** C Thomson — **Scorers:** Boyd, Darcheville. **Booked:** Broadfoot
29th	● Hearts............................a	L 2–1	**Att:** 15,710. **Ref:** D McDonald — **Scorers:** Karipidis OG. **Booked:** Bougherra, Boyd, Whittaker, Lafferty

December
6th	● Hamilton ....h	W 7–1	**Att:** 48,282. **Ref:** C Murray — **Scorers:** Boyd[3], Davis, Lafferty, Miller, Novo. **Booked:** Bougherra
13th	● Dundee Utd ....a	D 2–2	**Att:** 11,362. **Ref:** I Brines — **Scorers:** Boyd, Lafferty. **Booked:** Ferguson, Weir, Whittaker
20th	● Hibernian ....h	W 1–0	**Att:** 49,538. **Ref:** S Conroy — **Scorers:** Boyd
27th	● Celtic..............................h	L 0–1	**Att:** 50,403. **Ref:** C Thomson — **Booked:** Adam

January
4th	● Inverness CT ....a	W 0–3	**Att:** 7,056. **Ref:** D McDonald — **Scorers:** Boyd[2], Mendes
13th	● St Johnstone ....a	W 0–2	**Att:** 7,746. **Ref:** D McDonald — **Scorers:** Novo, McCaffrey OG. **Booked:** Bougherra, Mendes
17th	● Falkirk ....h	W 3–1	**Att:** 48,811. **Ref:** W Collum — **Scorers:** Boyd, Davis. **Booked:** Miller. **Dismissed:** Papac
24th	● Aberdeen ....a	D 0–0	**Att:** 20,441. **Ref:** C Murray — **Booked:** McCulloch
27th	● Falkirk ....h	W 3–0	**Att:** 24,507. **Ref:** C Richmond — **Scorers:** Boyd, Novo[2]
31st	● Dundee Utd ....h	W 2–0	**Att:** 49,918. **Ref:** I Brines — **Scorers:** Fleck, Lafferty. **Booked:** Fleck

February
15th	● Celtic..............................a	D 0–0	**Att:** 58,766. **Ref:** C Murray — **Booked:** Weir, Naismith, Ferguson, McCulloch, Mendes
18th	● Forfar ....h	W 0–4	**Att:** 248336. **Ref:** — **Scorers:** Miller[2], Niguez, Papac. **Booked:** Papac, Niguez
21st	● Kilmarnock ....h	W 3–1	**Att:** 50,301. **Ref:** B Winter — **Scorers:** Boyd, Miller[2]. **Booked:** Boyd
28th	● Hamilton ....a	W 0–1	**Att:** 5,895. **Ref:** C Thomson — **Scorers:** Ferguson. **Booked:** Ferguson, Davis

March
4th	● Inverness CT ....h	L 0–1	**Att:** 48,129. **Ref:** C Murray — **Booked:** Bougherra **Dismissed:** Weir
8th	● Hamilton ....h	W 5–1	**Att:** 27,588. **Ref:** I Brines — **Scorers:** Davis, Lafferty[2], Niguez, Whittaker. **Booked:** Papac
15th	● Celtic..............................a	L 2–0	**Att:** 51,193. **Ref:** D McDonald — **Booked:** Novo, Weir, McCulloch. **Dismissed:** Broadfoot (AET)
21st	● Hearts............................h	D 2–2	**Att:** 50,310. **Ref:** C Thomson — **Scorers:** Ferguson, Lafferty. **Booked:** Mendes

April
5th	● Falkirk ....a	W 0–1	**Att:** 6,853. **Ref:** I Brines — **Scorers:** Boyd. **Booked:** McCulloch, Whittaker, Boyd, Bougherra
8th	● St Mirren.......................a	W 1–2	**Att:** 6,231. **Ref:** E Smith — **Scorers:** Boyd, Edu. **Booked:** Bougherra, Boyd
11th	● Motherwell ....h	W 3–1	**Att:** 50,080. **Ref:** D Somers — **Scorers:** Boyd[2], Velicka. **Booked:** Dailly
19th	● Hibernian ....a	W 2–3	**Att:** 14,014. **Ref:** S Conroy — **Scorers:** Edu, Velicka, Whittaker
25th	● St Mirren.......................n	W 3–0	**Att:** 32,431. **Ref:** C Murray — **Scorers:** Boyd, Miller, Velicka. **Booked:** Dailly

May
3rd	● Hearts............................h	W 2–0	**Att:** 49,663. **Ref:** I Brines — **Scorers:** Boyd, Velicka. **Booked:** Smith
9th	● Celtic..............................h	W 1–0	**Att:** 50,321. **Ref:** C Thomson — **Scorers:** Davis. **Booked:** Smith, Miller, Lafferty
13th	● Hibernian ....a	D 1–1	**Att:** 13,765. **Ref:** E Smith — **Scorers:** Novo. **Booked:** Bougherra, Mendes, Lafferty
16th	● Aberdeen ....h	W 2–1	**Att:** 50,295. **Ref:** S Dougal — **Scorers:** Miller, Foster OG. **Booked:** Lafferty, Papac. **Dismissed:** Bougherra
24th	● Dundee Utd ....a	W 0–3	**Att:** 14,077. **Ref:** D McDonald — **Scorers:** Boyd, Lafferty, Mendes. **Booked:** Weir, Papac
30th	● Falkirk ....h	W 1–0	**Att:** 50,956 .**Ref:** C Thomson — **Scorers:** Novo. **Booked:** Dailly, Novo, Whittaker

● Clydesdale Bank Premier League ● Scottish FA Cup ● Co-op Insurance Cup ● UEFA Champions League ● UEFA Cup

CLYDESDALE BANK PREMIER LEAGUE GOALKEEPER STATS

Player	Minutes on pitch	Appearances	Match starts	Completed matches	Sub appearances	Subbed off	SAVES BREAKDOWN								Clean sheets	Goals conceded	Minutes since conceding	Save %	PENALTIES			Yellow cards	Red cards
							Saved with feet	Punched	Parried	Tipped over	Fumbled	Tipped round	Caught	Blocked					Saved	Resulting in goals	Opposition miss		
Neil Alexander 1043	11	11	11	0	0	0	1	4	2	0	1	33	0	5	7	-	85.42	0	0	0	0	0
Allan McGregor 2520	27	27	27	0	0	1	8	18	4	0	3	51	1	12	21	-	80.19	1	1	0	1	0

CLYDESDALE BANK PREMIER LEAGUE OUTFIELD PLAYER STATS

Player	Minutes on pitch	Appearances	Match starts	Completed matches	Substitute appearances	Subbed off	Goals scored	Minutes since scoring	Assists	Shots on target	Shots off target	Crosses	Defensive clearances	Defensive blocks	Fouls committed	Free-kicks won	Caught offside	Yellow cards	Red cards
Charlie Adam.........................583	9	7	2	2	5	0	-	2	4	10	22	4	1	11	10	0	2	0
DaMarcus Beasley 443	10	6	0	4	6	0	-	1	4	3	12	1	0	2	17	1	0	0
Madjid Bougherra 2849	31	31	30	0	0	1	2215	2	3	16	14	30	2	30	39	0	7	1
Kris Boyd 2957	35	33	20	2	13	27	14	5	67	52	7	15	0	66	56	43	6	0
Kirk Broadfoot 2519	27	27	27	0	0	0	-	3	10	8	70	21	10	21	32	4	4	0
Chris Burke 68	2	0	0	2	0	0	-	1	0	1	5	0	0	0	2	0	0	0
Daniel Cousin 78	2	1	0	1	0	1	38	0	1	2	0	0	0	6	3	1	1	1
Christian Dailly 744	9	7	7	2	0	0	-	0	1	1	15	5	0	9	4	0	2	0
Jean Claude Darcheville...........346	8	4	0	4	4	1	97	0	3	5	7	0	0	2	8	3	1	0
Steven Davis.........................3189	34	34	34	0	0	6	341	7	20	20	100	7	4	25	15	7	1	0
Maurice Edu 1003	12	11	9	1	2	2	494	0	3	5	5	4	1	11	21	0	0	0
Barry Ferguson 1714	22	17	17	5	0	2	97	1	12	14	4	4	1	26	23	0	3	0
John Fleck............................538	8	7	2	1	5	1	291	0	5	4	28	0	1	3	9	2	1	0
Kyle Lafferty 1197	25	11	4	14	7	6	77	3	27	6	13	8	0	31	13	4	6	0
Rory Loy 35	1	0	0	1	0	0	-	0	0	0	0	0	0	0	0	0	0	0
Lee McCulloch........................874	12	10	7	2	3	0	-	0	3	3	0	17	5	20	14	0	3	0
Pedro Mendes 3205	35	35	32	0	3	3	45	5	30	24	43	14	5	46	32	1	6	0
Kenny Miller 2267	30	25	13	5	12	10	97	9	34	25	28	3	1	18	30	33	3	0
Steven Naismith 220	7	1	1	6	0	0	-	0	0	1	0	0	0	6	5	1	1	0
Aaron Niguez 48	3	0	0	3	0	0	-	1	1	0	6	0	0	1	1	0	0	0
Nacho Novo 1120	29	7	2	22	5	5	70	6	20	21	17	1	2	14	15	12	0	0
Sasa Papac..........................2596	29	29	23	0	4	1	1725	1	9	9	53	11	7	30	22	1	5	2
Steven Smith 360	5	5	1	0	4	0	-	1	1	0	9	1	0	7	4	0	2	0
Kevin Thomson 934	11	11	7	0	4	1	84	4	6	4	20	2	1	15	15	0	2	0
Andrius Velicka 400	8	6	0	2	6	4	53	0	5	3	0	1	0	11	1	2	0	0
David Weir 3372	36	36	35	0	2	2	2388	0	4	7	7	60	13	30	36	0	4	1
Steven Whittaker 1832	24	19	18	5	1	2	566	3	10	6	46	16	3	18	19	0	4	0

SEASON TOTALS

Goals scored	77
Goals conceded	28
Clean sheets	17
Shots on target	283
Shots off target	250
Shots per goal	6.92
Pens awarded	9
Pens scored	8
Pens conceded	2
Offsides	115
Corners	243
Crosses	531
Players used	29
Fouls committed	459
Free-kicks won	463

CARDS RECEIVED

65 **5**

SEQUENCES

Wins	6
(05/04/09–09/05/09)	
Losses	
(–)	
Draws	
(–)	
Undefeated	10
(21/03/09–24/05/09)	
Without win	2
(04/03/09–21/03/09)	
Undefeated home	9
(16/08/08–20/12/08)	
Undefeated away	10
(13/12/08–24/05/09)	
Without scoring	
(–)	
Without conceding	3
(24/01/09–15/02/09)	
Scoring	7
(09/08/08–28/09/08)	
Conceding	4
(23/08/08–21/09/08)	

SEASON INFORMATION
Highest Position: 1
Lowest Position: 5
Average goals scored per game: 2.03
Average goals conceded per game: 0.74

League position at the end of each week

League position at the end of: August 1, September 1, October 2, November 2, December 2, January 2, February 1, March 2, April 2, May 1

MATCH RECORDS

Goals scored per match

		W	D	L	Pts
Failed to score	6	0	3	3	3
Scored 1 goal	8	5	2	1	17
Scored 2 goals	11	9	2	0	29
Scored 3 goals	9	8	1	0	25
Scored 4+ goals	2	2	0	0	6

Goals conceded per match

		W	D	L	Pts
Clean sheet	17	14	3	0	45
Conceded 1 goal	15	10	2	3	32
Conceded 2 goals	5	2	2	1	8
Conceded 3 goals	1	0	1	0	1
Conceded 4+ goals	0	0	0	0	0

GOALS SCORED/CONCEDED PER FIVE-MINUTE INTERVALS

Goals For	3	6	5	2	1	4	4	5	6	3	6	2	6	3	2	8	1	10
Goals Against	1	1	1	3	1	2	1	2	2	1	1	3	1	1	0	2	2	3
Mins	5	10	15	20	25	30	35	40	45	50	55	60	65	70	75	80	85	90

QUICK-FIRE GOALS

From the start of a match
Steven Whittaker
(v Hibernian) 1:41

By a substitute after coming on
Kyle Lafferty
(v Hamilton) 3:49

LAST-GASP GOALS

From the start of a match
Kyle Lafferty
(v Dundee Utd) 93:44

By a substitute after coming on
Nacho Novo
(v Hibernian) 34:02

GOAL DETAILS

How the goals were struck

SCORED		CONCEDED
49	Right foot	13
18	Left foot	10
10	Headers	5
0	Others	0

How the goals were struck

SCORED		CONCEDED
46	Open play	17
11	Cross	5
7	Corner	1
8	Penalties	1
0	Direct from free-kick	1
3	Free-kick	3
2	Own goals	0

Distance from goal

SCORED		CONCEDED
34	6yds	12
33	18yds	11
10	18+yds	5

ST MIRREN

CLUB SUMMARY

FORMED	1877
MANAGER	Gus MacPherson
GROUND	St Mirren Park
CAPACITY	8,029
NICKNAME	The Buddies
WEBSITE	www.saintmirren.net

The New Football Pools
PLAYER OF THE SEASON

Jack Ross

OVERALL

P	W	D	L	F	A	GD
45	13	11	21	46	59	-13

CLYDESDALE BANK PREMIER LEAGUE

Pos	P	W	D	L	F	A	GD	Pts
11	38	9	10	19	33	52	-19	37

HOME

Pos	P	W	D	L	F	A	GD	Pts
11	19	3	8	8	14	21	-7	17

AWAY

Pos	P	W	D	L	F	A	GD	Pts
9	19	6	2	11	19	31	-12	20

CUP PROGRESS DETAILS

Competition	Round reached	Knocked out by
Co-op Insurance Cup	R3	Dunfermline
Scottish Cup	SF	Rangers

BIGGEST WIN (ALL COMPS)

26/08/08 7–0 v Dumbarton **SLC2**

BIGGEST DEFEAT (ALL COMPS)

28/02/09 0–7 v Celtic **SPL**

THE PLAYER WITH THE MOST

Shots on target	
Andy Dorman	25
Shots off target	
Andy Dorman	27
Shots without scoring	
Scott Cuthbert	11
Assists	
Andy Dorman	4
Offsides	
Billy Mehmet	28
Fouls	
Hugh Murray	63
Fouls without a card	
Steven Robb	6
Free-kicks won	
Hugh Murray	60
Defensive clearances	
John Potter	44

ATTENDANCE RECORD

High	Low	Average
10,189	3,364	5,411

v Motherwell (03/01/2009) v Inverness CT (13/12/2008)

ST MIRREN showed signs of improvement during their third season back in the top flight – yet still only survived on goal difference.

Victories over both Old Firm teams in the Clydesdale Bank Premier League and Homecoming Scottish Cup showed their potential, but their SPL status was still only preserved on the final day.

Their play was pleasing on the eye, but an inability to convert chances meant a season of struggle. Strikers Billy Mehmet, Craig Dargo, Jim Hamilton and Dennis Wyness only scored 15 league goals between them, and the Buddies did not win an SPL game at their new stadium following their move in January.

Andy Dorman's 12 goals ultimately proved crucial as St Mirren endured a difficult end to a season that promised more on occasions. Their best SPL victory came in October when a superb Stephen McGinn strike earned them a 1–0 win over Rangers at Love Street.

The Paisley side had an inconsistent winter, taking one point out of 18 in a difficult run of fixtures in November before Gus MacPherson claimed the Manager of the Month award for December after four successive wins.

Saints said farewell to

"Dorman got into his stride after a slow start to the campaign"

Love Street – their home for 114 years – with a goalless draw against Motherwell before moving to nearby Greenhill Road. But a league win at the new St Mirren Park eluded them, despite memorable cup triumphs at home to Motherwell and Celtic.

Those victories set up a Scottish Cup semi-final – the club's first appearance in the last four since their 1987 triumph – but, after conceding in the first minute, they were beaten 3–0 by Rangers.

Dorman claimed the Clydesdale Bank Player of the Month award in both February and April as he got into his stride after a slow start to the campaign following a pre-season injury. The midfielder netted eight goals in 12 games to make St Mirren's position look comfortable before the split.

A 2–0 win over Motherwell left the Buddies six points ahead of bottom club Falkirk with five games left, but three consecutive defeats plunged them to the bottom of the table before their trip to play the Bairns in the penultimate fixture.

Defeat could have relegated Saints, but goals from Mehmet and Dorman earned them a 2–0 win thanks to one of their best displays of the season.

However, St Mirren still endured a nervous finale as a 1–0 home defeat by Hamilton left them sweating before avoiding the drop by two goals.

Billy Mehmet celebrates scoring in a 1–0 win over Celtic

RESULTS 2008/09

August
10th	● Celtic........................a	L 1–0	**Att:** 57,441. **Ref:** E Smith — **Dismissed:** Haining
16th	● Kilmarnock ....h	D 0–0	**Att:** 4,176. **Ref:** D Somers — **Booked:** Mehmet
23rd	● Hearts.......................a	L 2–1	**Att:** 13,357. **Ref:** C Murray — **Scorers:** Mehmet. **Booked:** Tonet, Hamilton, Ross. **Dismissed:** Tonet
26th	● Dumbarton ....h	W 7–0	**Att:** 1,747. **Ref:** S O'Reilly — **Scorers:** Dargo, Dorman, Mason, Mehmet³, Robb
30th	● Aberdeen ....h	L 0–1	**Att:** 4,680. **Ref:** W Collum — **Booked:** Ross, Dargo, Dorman

September
13th	● Inverness CT ....a	W 1–2	**Att:** 3,501. **Ref:** I Brines — **Scorers:** Brady, Mehmet. **Booked:** Howard
20th	● Falkirk ....h	D 1–1	**Att:** 4,134. **Ref:** E Norris — **Scorers:** Mehmet. **Booked:** Dargo
23rd	● Dunfermline ....a	L 2–0	**Att:** 2,319. **Ref:** C Murray — **Booked:** Miranda, Haining
27th	● Motherwell ....a	L 2–1	**Att:** 4,786. **Ref:** S Conroy — **Scorers:** Mehmet. **Booked:** Mehmet, Potter, McAusland. **Dismissed:** Miranda

October
5th	● Rangers ....h	W 1–0	**Att:** 7,520. **Ref:** W Collum — **Scorers:** McGinn. **Booked:** McGinn, Brady
18th	● Hamilton ....a	W 1–2	**Att:** 3,397. **Ref:** D Somers — **Scorers:** Mehmet, Miranda. **Booked:** Potter
25th	● Dundee Utd ....a	L 2–0	**Att:** 11,378. **Ref:** B Winter — **Booked:** Mehmet, Wyness

November
1st	● Hibernian ....h	D 0–0	**Att:** 4,588. **Ref:** S Finnie — **Booked:** Murray
8th	● Hearts.......................h	L 0–1	**Att:** 4,192. **Ref:** M McCurry
11th	● Aberdeen ....a	L 2–0	**Att:** 9,452. **Ref:** B Winter — **Booked:** Howard, Hamilton
15th	● Rangers ....a	L 2–1	**Att:** 49,321. **Ref:** D Somers — **Scorers:** Miranda. **Booked:** Murray
22nd	● Celtic.......................h	L 1–3	**Att:** 7,433. **Ref:** W Collum — **Scorers:** Hamilton. **Booked:** Potter, Murray
29th	● Dundee Utd ....h	L 0–2	**Att:** 4,013. **Ref:** C Murray — **Booked:** Hamilton

December
6th	● Falkirk ....a	W 1–2	**Att:** 4,828. **Ref:** D McDonald — **Scorers:** Hamilton, Wyness. **Booked:** Murray
13th	● Inverness CT ....h	W 2–0	**Att:** 3,364. **Ref:** S Conroy — **Scorers:** Brady, Dorman
20th	● Kilmarnock ....a	W 0–1	**Att:** 5,183. **Ref:** S O'Reilly — **Scorers:** Dorman. **Booked:** Murray
27th	● Hamilton ....h	W 1–0	**Att:** 4,794. **Ref:** M Tumilty — **Scorers:** Dargo. **Booked:** Ross, Miranda

January
3rd	● Motherwell ....h	D 0–0	**Att:** 10,189. **Ref:** A Muir — **Booked:** Murray, Brighton
13th	● Brechin ....a	W 1–3	**Att:** 1,026. **Ref:** S Finnie — **Scorers:** Hamilton², Wyness
17th	● Hibernian ....a	L 2–0	**Att:** 10,317. **Ref:** I Brines — **Booked:** Miranda
24th	● Dundee Utd ....a	L 3–2	**Att:** 6,556. **Ref:** S O'Reilly — **Scorers:** Mehmet, Ross. **Booked:** Dargo, Miranda
31st	● Kilmarnock ....h	D 1–1	**Att:** 7,542. **Ref:** W Collum — **Scorers:** Wyness. **Booked:** Wyness

February
7th	● Motherwell ....a	D 1–1	**Att:** 5,695. **Ref:** C Thomson — **Scorers:** Dorman. **Booked:** Mehmet, Hamilton
14th	● Falkirk ....h	D 2–2	**Att:** 5,504. **Ref:** M Tumilty — **Scorers:** Dorman². **Booked:** Ross
19th	● Motherwell ....h	W 1–0	**Att:** 4,555. **Ref:** C Thomson — **Scorers:** Mehmet. **Booked:** Cuthbert, Barron, Murray
21st	● Hearts.......................a	D 1–1	**Att:** 13,609. **Ref:** D Somers — **Scorers:** Dorman. **Booked:** Murray, Hamilton, Cuthbert, Dorman
28th	● Celtic.......................a	L 7–0	**Att:** 58,286. **Ref:** C Allan — **Booked:** Thomson, Murray. **Dismissed:** Ross

March
3rd	● Aberdeen ....h	D 1–1	**Att:** 4,383. **Ref:** C Boyle — **Scorers:** Dargo
7th	● Celtic.......................h	W 1–0	**Att:** 5,925. **Ref:** C Richmond — **Scorers:** Mehmet. **Booked:** Dorman, Thomson
21st	● Hamilton ....a	D 0–0	**Att:** 3,072. **Ref:** S Finnie — **Booked:** Thomson

April
4th	● Inverness CT ....a	L 2–1	**Att:** 3,794. **Ref:** W Collum — **Scorers:** Dorman. **Booked:** Mehmet, Potter
8th	● Rangers ....h	L 1–2	**Att:** 6,231. **Ref:** E Smith — **Scorers:** Dorman. **Booked:** Camara, Ross
13th	● Hibernian ....h	D 1–1	**Att:** 5,151. **Ref:** I Brines — **Scorers:** Dorman
18th	● Motherwell ....a	W 0–2	**Att:** 6,626. **Ref:** M McCurry — **Scorers:** Dorman, Thomson. **Booked:** Murray, Haining
25th	● Rangers ....n	L 3–0	**Att:** 32,431. **Ref:** C Murray

May
2nd	● Inverness CT ....h	L 1–2	**Att:** 4,171. **Ref:** S Conroy — **Scorers:** Hamilton
9th	● Motherwell ....h	L 1–3	**Att:** 4,002. **Ref:** B Winter — **Scorers:** O'Donnell
13th	● Kilmarnock ....a	L 2–1	**Att:** 5,927. **Ref:** C Allan — **Scorers:** Wyness. **Booked:** Mason, Murray
16th	● Falkirk ....h	W 0–2	**Att:** 6,744. **Ref:** C Boyle — **Scorers:** Dorman, Mehmet
23rd	● Hamilton ....h	L 0–1	**Att:** 6,747. **Ref:** C Murray — **Booked:** Murray

● Clydesdale Bank Premier League ● Scottish FA Cup ● Co-op Insurance Cup ● UEFA Champions League ● UEFA Cup

ST MIRREN

CLYDESDALE BANK PREMIER LEAGUE GOALKEEPER STATS

Player	Minutes on pitch	Appearances	Match starts	Completed matches	Sub appearances	Subbed off	SAVES BREAKDOWN								Clean sheets	Goals conceded	Minutes since conceding	Save %	PENALTIES			Yellow cards	Red cards
							Saved with feet	Punched	Parried	Tipped over	Fumbled	Tipped round	Caught	Blocked					Saved	Resulting in goals	Opposition miss		
Mark Howard	3194	34	34	34	0	0	3	14	17	7	0	8	120	2	10	41	67	80.48	1	5	0	2	0
Chris Smith	378	4	4	4	0	0	1	2	2	0	0	3	15	0	0	11	1	67.65	1	1	0	0	0

CLYDESDALE BANK PREMIER LEAGUE OUTFIELD PLAYER STATS

Player	Minutes on pitch	Appearances	Match starts	Completed matches	Substitute appearances	Subbed off	Goals scored	Minutes since scoring	Assists	Shots on target	Shots off target	Crosses	Defensive clearances	Defensive blocks	Fouls committed	Free-kicks won	Caught offside	Yellow cards	Red cards
David Barron	585	9	5	5	4	0	0	-	0	2	2	18	9	1	3	6	0	0	0
Garry Brady	2730	34	31	16	3	15	2	1357	0	9	19	29	5	5	8	25	1	1	0
Tom Brighton	107	5	1	0	4	1	0	-	0	0	0	0	0	0	1	2	0	1	0
Sean Burns	43	2	0	0	2	0	0	-	0	0	0	0	0	0	1	0	0	0	0
Mohammed Camara	873	10	10	8	0	2	0	-	0	2	2	8	3	0	5	5	0	1	0
Scott Cuthbert	2659	29	28	27	1	1	0	-	0	4	7	3	26	8	18	24	0	1	0
Craig Dargo	1354	27	12	7	15	5	2	507	3	14	5	7	0	0	21	28	22	3	0
Andy Dorman	2934	36	32	24	4	8	10	108	4	25	27	59	5	4	24	38	7	2	0
Will Haining	1571	19	17	14	2	2	0	-	0	2	5	3	25	8	10	18	0	1	1
James Hamilton	1267	24	13	4	11	9	3	1	2	12	14	3	12	0	27	33	6	4	0
Gary Mason	1759	23	20	14	3	6	0	-	0	6	2	0	5	3	36	22	0	1	0
Marc McAusland	132	5	0	0	5	0	0	-	0	0	1	0	0	0	2	0	0	1	0
Stephen McGinn	1790	28	17	11	11	6	1	1606	2	12	9	13	4	0	19	41	1	1	0
Billy Mehmet	2596	34	28	19	6	9	7	147	3	24	17	8	6	0	51	47	28	4	0
Franco Miranda	2021	22	22	19	0	2	2	841	0	11	11	62	13	5	24	35	0	3	1
Hugh Murray	2564	30	28	23	2	5	0	-	3	4	4	23	16	2	63	60	5	11	0
Stephen O'Donnell	306	8	3	1	5	2	1	49	0	2	2	4	0	0	5	4	1	0	0
John Potter	3241	35	35	32	0	3	0	-	0	1	8	3	44	12	26	34	0	4	0
Steven Robb	891	16	11	5	5	6	0	-	2	4	19	1	1	6	10	2	0	0
Jack Ross	3224	36	36	32	0	3	0	1179	2	4	6	61	29	8	37	40	3	5	1
Steven Thomson	1179	14	12	12	2	0	1	390	1	6	3	1	2	2	15	12	0	2	0
Tonet Gilareo	126	3	2	0	1	1	0	-	0	0	1	2	1	0	3	2	0	1	1
Dennis Wyness	1534	31	17	3	14	14	3	8	1	14	17	5	1	0	7	32	7	2	0

SEASON TOTALS

Goals scored	33
Goals conceded	52
Clean sheets	10
Shots on target	156
Shots off target	166
Shots per goal	9.76
Pens awarded	4
Pens scored	2
Pens conceded	8
Offsides	82
Corners	196
Crosses	332
Players used	25
Fouls committed	412
Free-kicks won	525

CARDS RECEIVED

51 **4**

SEQUENCES

Wins	4
(06/12/08–27/12/08)	
Losses	5
(08/11/08–29/11/08)	
Draws	3
(31/01/09–21/02/09)	
Undefeated	5
(06/12/08–03/01/09)	
Without win	12
(03/01/09–13/04/09)	
Undefeated home	6
(13/12/08–03/03/09)	
Undefeated away	2
(06/12/08–20/12/08)	
Without scoring	4
(25/10/08–11/11/08)	
Without conceding	4
(13/12/08–03/01/09)	
Scoring	8
(04/04/09–16/05/09)	
Conceding	7
(17/01/09–03/03/09)	

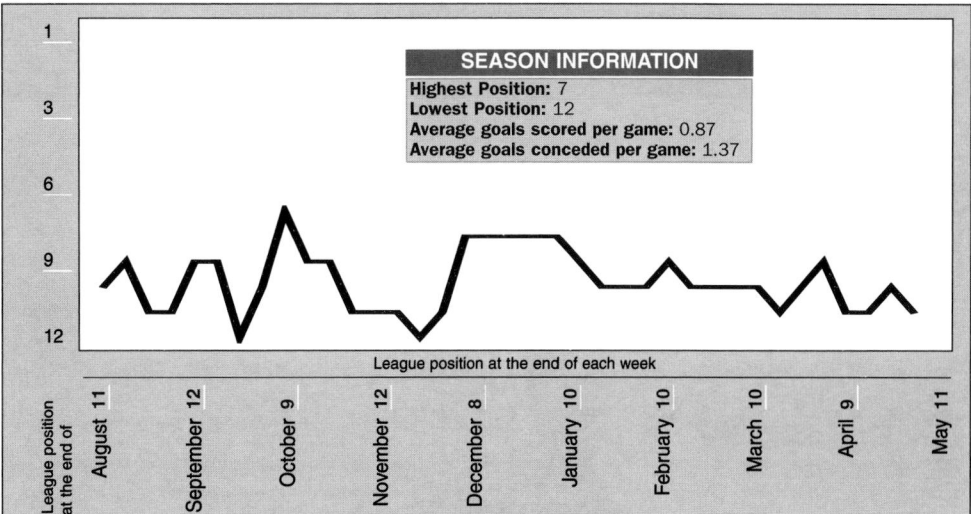

SEASON INFORMATION
Highest Position: 7
Lowest Position: 12
Average goals scored per game: 0.87
Average goals conceded per game: 1.37

League position at the end of each week

League position at the end of

August 11 | September 12 | October 9 | November 12 | December 8 | January 10 | February 10 | March 10 | April 9 | May 11

MATCH RECORDS

Goals scored per match

		W	D	L	Pts
Failed to score	13	0	4	9	4
Scored 1 goal	17	3	5	9	14
Scored 2 goals	8	6	1	1	19
Scored 3 goals	0	0	0	0	0
Scored 4+ goals	0	0	0	0	0

Goals conceded per match

		W	D	L	Pts
Clean sheet	10	6	4	0	22
Conceded 1 goal	12	3	5	4	14
Conceded 2 goals	12	0	1	11	1
Conceded 3 goals	3	0	0	3	0
Conceded 4+ goals	1	0	0	1	0

GOALS SCORED/CONCEDED PER FIVE-MINUTE INTERVALS

Goals For	0	1	0	4	0	2	0	2	2	2	0	1	1	2	4	6	2	4
Goals Against	1	1	3	3	1	3	3	2	4	4	2	2	4	2	2	5	5	5
Mins	5	10	15	20	25	30	35	40	45	50	55	60	65	70	75	80	85	90

QUICK-FIRE GOALS

From the start of a match
Andy Dorman
(v Inverness CT) 6:10

By a substitute after coming on
Dennis Wyness
(v Kilmarnock) 4:06

LAST-GASP GOALS

From the start of a match
Andy Dorman (v Hearts)
90:12

By a substitute after coming on
Craig Dargo (v Hamilton)
9:41

GOAL DETAILS

How the goals were struck

SCORED		CONCEDED
24	Right foot	30
7	Left foot	7
2	Headers	15
0	Others	0

How the goals were struck

SCORED		CONCEDED
29	Open play	35
0	Cross	0
0	Corner	6
2	Penalties	6
0	Direct from free-kick	1
2	Free-kick	3
0	Own goals	1

Distance from goal

SCORED		CONCEDED
16	6yds	21
15	18yds	25
2	18+yds	6

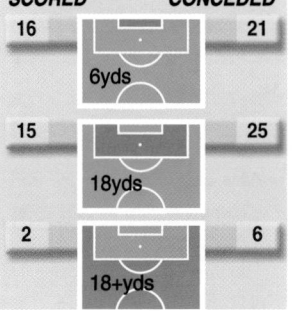

THIS WILL be remembered as the season in which St Johnstone exorcised the demons of 2006/07 and ended their seven-year exile from the elite of Scottish football.

The Saints were famously pipped to promotion by a last-gasp Gretna goal two years ago and suffered something of a hangover in 2007/08. But there was no stopping them this time around as Derek McInnes' men won the Irn-Bru First Division by a massive 10 points.

At the other end, Clyde finished bottom of the table but it was their finances which proved of most concern, with the club forced to ask their manager to step down while planning to terminate the contracts of most of their players.

Airdrie finished second-bottom and lost their play-off final to Second Division runners-up Ayr. Indeed, Division Two provided arguably the most thrilling title scrap in Scotland, with Ayr and Raith taking the race almost to the wire. The two teams were neck and neck for months but in the end it was Raith who clinched promotion with a game to spare. Brechin had to make do with third and Peterhead fourth, with both comfortably beaten in the play-offs.

It was a season to forget for rock-bottom Stranraer, who managed just three wins and conceded 90 goals.

Queen's Park finished ninth to set up a play-off semi-final with Third Division Stenhousemuir, but they were unable to overturn a 2–1 first-leg defeat. Indeed, despite only just sneaking into the play-offs, Stenhousemuir ended up promoted after a play-off final penalty shoot-out against Cowdenbeath. That piled on the misery for the Blue Brazil, who had blown a 10-point lead to finish runners-up to Dumbarton.

East Stirling also made the play-offs, while Elgin finished in bottom place in the Scottish Football League.

St Johnstone's Kevin Moon

PLAY-OFF RESULTS

FIRST DIVISION SEMI-FINAL FIRST LEG
Brechin...................0 Ayr 2
Peterhead................0 Airdrie 2

FIRST DIVISION SEMI-FINAL SECOND LEG
Ayr ....3 Brechin 2
Ayr win 5–2 on aggregate
Airdrie ....2 Peterhead 1
Airdrie win 4–1 on aggregate

FIRST DIVISION FINAL FIRST LEG
Ayr ....2 Airdrie 2

FIRST DIVISION FINAL SECOND LEG
Airdrie ....0 Ayr 1
Ayr win 3–2 on aggregate

SECOND DIVISION SEMI-FINAL FIRST LEG
East Stirling.............1 Cowdenbeath..........2
Stenhousemuir ....2 Queen's Park 1

SECOND DIVISION SEMI-FINAL SECOND LEG
Cowdenbeath ....1 East Stirling 1
Cowdenbeath win 3–2 on aggregate
Queen's Park ....0 Stenhousemuir........0
Stenhousemuir win 2–1 on aggregate

SECOND DIVISION FINAL FIRST LEG
Cowdenbeath...........0 Stenhousemuir........0

SECOND DIVISION FINAL SECOND LEG
Stenhousemuir ....0 Cowdenbeath..........0
0–0 on aggregate.
Stenhousemuir win 5–4 on penalties

IRN-BRU FIRST DIVISION RESULTS

	Airdrie	Clyde	Dundee	Dunfermline	Livingston	Morton	Partick	Qn of the South	Ross County	St Johnstone
Airdrie	–	0-2, 1-0	0-0, 1-0	1-3, 1-1	0-0, 4-4	5-0, 1-0	0-1, 0-1	2-0, 2-0	0-2, 1-0	1-1, 0-4
Clyde	1-0, 3-0	–	1-0, 2-0	0-2, 1-4	2-1, 0-1	1-1, 2-4	1-1, 2-4	0-2, 1-1	2-2, 2-0	2-2, 1-3
Dundee	1-1, 0-1	1-0, 2-1	–	0-0, 1-0	0-3, 4-1	1-0, 0-0	0-0, 4-0	2-0, 2-3	1-2, 2-0	1-1, 0-1
Dunfermline	0-0, 1-1	4-4, 1-1	0-1, 1-1	–	1-2, 1-0	0-1, 2-1	1-0, 0-1	2-1, 0-2	3-1, 1-2	1-2, 1-3
Livingston	1-2, 1-1	2-1, 1-1	1-2, 0-1	2-3, 4-2	–	1-0, 0-2	3-1, 2-4	2-0, 2-2	2-0, 4-2	0-1, 1-0
Morton	2-0, 0-0	1-0, 2-0	2-0, 2-0	1-1, 2-1	1-2, 2-2	–	2-0, 0-1	0-0, 2-2	2-1, 0-2	2-2, 0-0
Partick	2-1, 0-1	2-0, 0-1	0-0, 1-1	1-0, 2-3	2-1, 1-0	2-1, 1-0	–	2-0, 0-2	0-1, 0-2	4-0, 0-0
Qn of the South	0-0, 4-0	0-2, 7-1	3-1, 0-1	1-2, 0-3	6-1, 3-3	1-4, 1-1	2-0, 2-2	–	1-0, 1-2	2-2, 3-3
Ross County	2-0, 0-0	3-0, 0-0	1-2, 1-1	2-1, 1-3	1-4, 2-2	3-0, 1-1	1-0, 0-2	0-2, 1-0	–	1-2, 2-2
St Johnstone	3-1, 3-0	2-3, 1-0	2-0, 0-0	0-3, 0-0	2-0, 1-0	1-0, 3-1	3-0, 1-1	0-0, 2-3	2-1, 0-0	–

FINAL IRN-BRU FIRST DIVISION TABLE

			HOME				AWAY						
		P	W	D	L	F	A	W	D	L	F	A	GD	Pts
1	ST JOHNSTONE	36	10	5	3	26	13	7	9	2	29	22	20	65
2	Partick	36	9	3	6	20	14	7	4	7	19	24	1	55
3	Dunfermline	36	5	5	8	20	24	9	4	5	32	20	8	51
4	Dundee	36	8	5	5	22	14	5	6	7	11	18	1	50
5	Queen of the South	36	6	6	6	37	28	6	5	7	20	22	7	47
6	Morton	36	8	7	3	23	14	4	4	10	17	26	0	47
7	Livingston	36	8	3	7	29	25	5	5	8	27	33	-2	47
8	Ross County	36	6	6	6	22	22	7	2	9	20	24	4	47
9	Airdrie	36	7	5	6	20	19	3	7	8	9	24	-14	42
10	Clyde	36	6	5	7	24	28	4	4	10	17	30	-17	39

LEADING SCORERS

Player	(Team)	Goals
Stephen Dobbie ......(Queen of South)		24
Leigh Griffiths..........(Livingston)		18
Andy Kirk ....(Dunfermline)		15
M Antoine-Curier ....(Dundee)		14
Steven Milne ....(St Johnstone)		14
Patrick Clarke ....(Clyde)		11
Sean Higgins ....(Ross County)		10
Simon Lynch............(Airdrie)		10
Steven Craig ....(Ross County)		10

AWARDS

Irn-Bru Phenomenal Player of the Season
Gary Harkins (Partick)
Irn-Bru Phenomenal Manager of the Season
Derek McInnes (St Johnstone)

IRN-BRU SECOND DIVISION RESULTS

	Alloa	Arbroath	Ayr	Brechin	East Fife	Peterhead	Queen's Park	Raith	Stirling	Stranraer
Alloa	–	2–1, 2–0	0–2, 3–2	2–1, 3–2	0–3, 0–1	1–0, 1–2	1–3, 0–0	1–1, 0–0	4–3, 2–3	5–1, 2–2
Arbroath	4–1, 1–0	–	0–3, 1–3	1–2, 0–0	0–1, 0–2	4–0, 2–2	1–1, 3–0	0–2, 0–2	1–2, 1–2	1–0, 2–0
Ayr	3–0, 1–1	2–1, 2–1	–	1–1, 4–2	4–2, 2–0	2–0, 0–0	2–1, 1–1	0–0, 2–2	1–1, 3–1	3–2, 5–0
Brechin	3–1, 1–0	3–1, 0–1	0–1, 1–0	–	2–1, 2–1	2–2, 1–1	2–1, 2–0	2–0, 0–4	2–1, 1–2	1–0, 2–1
East Fife	1–0, 0–2	3–2, 0–0	3–0, 0–1	0–0, 2–1	–	0–2, 0–3	1–2, 4–2	0–2, 0–1	0–1, 0–3	1–2, 4–0
Peterhead	1–0, 2–2	1–1, 1–0	3–0, 2–3	5–1, 0–1	0–1, 2–0	–	4–1, 1–1	1–2, 2–1	1–1, 1–1	4–0, 1–0
Queen's Park	1–0, 1–2	1–2, 0–1	0–3, 0–3	1–1, 0–0	0–0, 3–1	0–1, 2–1	–	1–2, 0–1	1–1, 3–1	2–2, 1–1
Raith	4–1, 3–1	2–1, 0–0	3–2, 0–1	2–2, 2–0	1–1, 1–0	3–0, 3–3	2–0, 1–0	–	1–1, 1–1	2–1, 2–1
Stirling	3–2, 0–0	0–2, 1–1	2–2, 2–0	1–2, 2–3	1–1, 2–0	0–0, 2–1	0–3, 4–0	2–1, 0–1	–	3–2, 1–2
Stranraer	2–2, 1–3	2–2, 1–5	1–3, 1–4	1–2, 0–3	0–4, 0–1	0–3, 0–1	0–0, 2–2	0–2, 0–3	1–0, 2–8	–

FINAL IRN-BRU SECOND DIVISION TABLE

		HOME					AWAY						
		P	W	D	L	F	A	W	D	L	F	A	GD	Pts
1	RAITH	36	11	6	1	33	16	11	4	3	27	11	33	76
2	AYR	36	11	7	0	38	16	11	1	6	33	22	33	74
3	Brechin	36	12	2	4	27	18	6	6	6	24	27	6	62
4	Peterhead	36	9	5	4	32	16	6	6	6	22	23	15	56
5	Stirling	36	7	5	6	26	23	7	6	5	33	26	10	53
6	East Fife	36	6	2	10	19	24	7	3	8	20	20	-5	44
7	Arbroath	36	6	3	9	22	23	5	5	8	22	23	-2	41
8	Alloa	36	8	4	6	29	27	3	4	11	18	32	-12	41
9	Queen's Park	36	4	6	8	17	23	3	6	9	18	31	-19	33
10	Stranraer	36	1	4	13	14	48	2	3	13	17	42	-59	16

LEADING SCORERS

Player	(Team)	Goals
Kevin Smith ....(Raith)		18
Bryan Prunty ....(Ayr)		15
David McKenna ......(Stirling)		13
Paul McManus ....(East Fife)		12
Martin Grehan ....(Stirling)		11
Ryan Stevenson ......(Ayr)		10
David Gormley ....(Ayr)		9
Graeme Sharp..........(Peterhead)		9

AWARDS

Irn-Bru Phenomenal Player of the Season
Bryan Prunty (Ayr)

Irn-Bru Phenomenal Manager of the Season
John McGlynn (Raith)

IRN-BRU THIRD DIVISION RESULTS

	Albion	Annan	Berwick	Cowdenbeath	Dumbarton	East Stirling	Elgin	Forfar	Montrose	Stenhousemuir
Albion	–	0–1, 2–1	2–0, 2–1	3–1, 0–0	1–3, 1–1	0–2, 0–2	2–1, 0–3	1–3, 2–0	0–1, 0–1	1–2, 1–2
Annan	2–4, 1–1	–	1–2, 1–1	0–1, 3–1	2–1, 1–3	2–1, 4–0	5–0, 6–0	1–3, 1–0	1–2, 2–1	1–1, 1–1
Berwick	0–3, 1–1	3–0, 1–1	–	2–3, 1–0	1–2, 1–2	2–1, 1–2	1–1, 2–1	2–2, 0–2	3–2, 0–1	3–2, 0–3
Cowdenbeath	2–1, 2–1	1–4, 1–0	2–1, 2–0	–	2–0, 0–0	0–0, 2–0	4–1, 1–1	0–0, 2–2	2–1, 2–1	1–2, 1–0
Dumbarton	1–1, 1–0	4–1, 0–2	5–2, 2–0	2–1, 1–1	–	1–1, 1–0	2–0, 6–0	3–0, 4–0	1–1, 1–1	1–2, 1–0
East Stirling	1–0, 0–1	2–1, 1–1	1–0, 0–4	1–4, 0–2	5–2, 3–1	–	5–2, 1–0	0–3, 3–2	5–0, 2–1	0–2, 0–3
Elgin	1–6, 1–0	1–2, 0–1	0–2, 2–0	0–2, 1–1	1–1, 0–2	0–4, 0–2	–	0–1, 1–4	1–2, 1–0	4–2, 2–0
Forfar	0–0, 4–0	2–1, 2–1	2–1, 5–4	0–1, 1–1	2–2, 0–2	2–3, 0–2	0–1, 1–1	–	0–1, 0–3	1–0, 4–4
Montrose	1–2, 1–0	1–1, 0–3	1–1, 1–1	0–1, 2–1	1–2, 1–0	3–0, 0–2	1–0, 3–1	1–0, 1–3	–	0–3, 5–3
Stenhousemuir	1–0, 2–0	0–0, 1–0	2–0, 1–2	1–0, 1–0	1–1, 0–2	1–1, 1–4	3–0, 4–2	1–1, 0–1	2–2, 1–3	–

FINAL IRN-BRU THIRD DIVISION TABLE

		HOME					AWAY						
		P	W	D	L	F	A	W	D	L	F	A	GD	Pts
1	DUMBARTON	36	11	5	2	38	13	8	5	5	27	23	29	67
2	Cowdenbeath	36	11	5	2	27	15	7	4	7	21	19	14	63
3	East Stirlingshire	36	10	1	7	30	29	9	3	6	27	21	7	61
4	STENHOUSEMUIR	36	8	5	5	23	19	8	3	7	32	27	9	56
5	Montrose	36	8	3	7	23	24	8	3	7	24	24	-1	54
6	Forfar Athletic	36	6	5	7	26	28	8	4	6	27	23	2	51
7	Annan Athletic	36	8	4	6	35	23	6	4	8	21	22	11	50
8	Albion Rovers	36	6	2	10	18	25	5	4	9	21	22	-8	39
9	Berwick Rangers	36	6	4	8	24	29	4	3	11	22	32	-15	37
10	Elgin City	36	5	2	11	16	32	2	3	13	15	47	-48	26

LEADING SCORERS

Player	(Team)	Goals
Mike Jack ....(Annan)		15
Scott Dalziel............(Stenhousemuir)		15
Andrew Rodgers ......(East Stirling)		14
Brian Graham ....(East Stirling)		14
Darren Gribben ....(Berwick)		14
Ross Clark ....(Dumbarton)		14
Ross Campbell ....(Forfar)		13

AWARDS

Irn-Bru Phenomenal Player of the Season
Bobby Barr (Albion)

Irn-Bru Phenomenal Manager of the Season
Jim Chapman (Dumbarton)

AIRDRIE UNITED

AIRDRIE were relegated from the Irn-Bru Second Division, but had the consolation of an ALBA Challenge Cup triumph.

They made a decent start to the season – keeping five consecutive clean sheets in August – and knocked Hearts out of the Co-operative Insurance Cup. But the Challenge Cup was the highlight of their campaign and a penalty shoot-out victory following a 2–2 draw with Ross County earned them the trophy.

The competitive nature of the First Division meant they ended up second bottom despite amassing 42 points, a total that would have seen them safe in the other two SFL divisions.

Too many draws – a dozen – and only nine away goals cost them dear and they lost their play-off final against Ayr 3–2 on aggregate despite being two goals up at half-time in the first leg at Somerset Park.

CLUB SUMMARY

FORMED	2002
MANAGER	Kenny Black
GROUND	Excelsior Stadium
CAPACITY	10,171
NICKNAME	The Diamonds
WEBSITE	www.airdrieunitedfc.com

The New Football Pools PLAYER OF THE SEASON

Stephen Robertson

OVERALL
P	W	D	L	F	A	GD
48	18	14	16	50	55	-5

IRN-BRU FIRST DIVISION
Pos	P	W	D	L	F	A	GD	Pts
9	36	10	12	14	29	43	-14	42

HOME
Pos	P	W	D	L	F	A	GD	Pts
6	18	7	5	6	20	19	1	26

AWAY
Pos	P	W	D	L	F	A	GD	Pts
10	18	3	7	8	9	24	-15	16

CUP PROGRESS DETAILS
Competition	Round reached	Knocked out by
Co-op Insurance Cup	R3	Dundee Utd
Scottish Cup	R5	Dunfermline
Challenge Cup	Won	–

BIGGEST WIN (ALL COMPS)
30/08/08 5–0 v Morton **SC1**

BIGGEST DEFEAT (ALL COMPS)
0–4 on two occasions

ATTENDANCE RECORD
High	Low	Average
2,165	633	1,356
v Partick (09/08/2008)	v St Johnstone (11/05/2009)	

RESULTS 2008/09

July
26th ● Dumbarton........h W 3–2 **Att:** 808 — **Scorers:** Cardle, Di Giacomo, Noble. **Booked:** McDonald, Smyth

August
2nd ● Queen of South a D 0–0 **Att:** 2,914 — **Booked:** Nixon
5th ● Ross County ....a W 2–3 **Att:** 869 — **Scorers:** Di Giacomo², Noble (AET)
9th ● Partick ....h L 0–1 **Att:** 2,165
13th ● East Fife...........a W 0–2 **Att:** 606 — **Scorers:** Lynch, Smith
16th ● Dundee ....h D 0–0 **Att:** 1,787 — **Booked:** Di Giacomo, McKenna
23rd ● Dunfermline .....a D 0–0 **Att:** 3,407 — **Booked:** Lynch, Di Giacomo, B. Donnelly
27th ● Hearts ....a D 0–0 **Att:** 6,844 — **Booked:** Cardle, McDonald, McKenna. **Dismissed:** McDonald (Won 4–3 on pens)
30th ● Morton ....h W 5–0 **Att:** 1,793 — **Scorers:** Di Giacomo, Lynch, McLaughlin², Nixon

September
7th ● Cowdenbeath....a W 1–2 **Att:** 640 — **Scorers:** Di Giacomo². **Booked:** Smyth
13th ● Livingston.........a W 1–2 **Att:** 1,710 — **Scorers:** Lynch, McLaughlin
20th ● Clyde ....h L 0–2 **Att:** 1,489 — **Booked:** Nixon, Smyth
23rd ● Dundee Utd ......a L 2–0 **Att:** 3,444
27th ● Ross County .....a L 2–0 **Att:** 2,259

October
4th ● St Johnstone ...a L 3–1 **Att:** 2,259 — **Scorers:** Nixon. **Booked:** McDougall, Nixon
12th ● Partick ....a W 0–1 **Att:** 2,761 — **Scorers:** Di Giacomo
18th ● Queen of South h W 2–0 **Att:** 1,524 — **Scorers:** Cardle, Lynch

November
1st ● Dundee ....a D 1–1 **Att:** 3,456 — **Scorers:** Lynch. **Booked:** McDonald, D. Smith, Nixon
4th ● Dunfermline .....h L 1–3 **Att:** 1,099 — **Scorers:** Di Giacomo. **Booked:** Smyth
8th ● Livingston.........h D 0–0 **Att:** 1,201 — **Booked:** Smyth
16th ● Ross County .....n D 2–2 **Att:** 4,091 — **Scorers:** McKenna, Dowie OG. **Booked:** Smyth, Cardle, McDonald (Won 3–2 on pens)
22nd ● Ross County .....h L 0–2 **Att:** 939 — **Booked:** McDonald
25th ● Morton ....a L 2–0 **Att:** 1,685 — **Booked:** Hazley, Di Giacomo, Cardle
29th ● Cove Rangers ..h W 3–0 **Att:** 821 — **Scorers:** Cardle, Lynch²

December
13th ● Partick ....a L 2–1 **Att:** 2,296 — **Scorers:** Lynch. **Booked:** Cardle, B. Donnelly
16th ● Clyde ....a L 1–0 **Att:** 836 — **Booked:** Cardle
20th ● St Johnstone ....h D 1–1 **Att:** 1,175 — **Scorers:** Mcguire. **Booked:** McLachlan, Nixon
27th ● Morton ....h W 1–0 **Att:** 1,663 — **Scorers:** Lynch. **Booked:** Di Giacomo

January
3rd ● Livingston.........a D 1–1 **Att:** 1,462 — **Scorers:** Lynch. **Booked:** McDonald, McKenna
10th ● Spartans ....h W 2–1 **Att:** 1,460 — **Scorers:** Di Giacomo, Lynch
17th ● Dunfermline .....a D 1–1 **Att:** 2,913 — **Scorers:** Lynch. **Booked:** Cardle
24th ● Dundee ....h W 1–0 **Att:** 1,278 — **Scorers:** Di Giacomo
31st ● Partick ....h L 0–1 **Att:** 1,988 — **Booked:** McLachlan

February
14th ● Queen of South a L 4–0 **Att:** 2,443 — **Booked:** McLachlan, Robertson. **Dismissed:** McDonald
17th ● Dunfermline .....a L 1–2 **Att:** 1,772 — **Scorers:** McLaughlin. **Booked:** McKenna, Robertson, Smyth, Lynch, McLachlan
22nd ● Clyde ....h W 1–0 **Att:** 1,189 — **Scorers:** Di Giacomo. **Booked:** Hazley
28th ● Ross County .....a D 0–0 **Att:** 2,290

March
7th ● Livingston.........h D 4–4 **Att:** 1,100 — **Scorers:** Baird², Di Giacomo, Smyth. **Booked:** Hazley. **Dismissed:** Cardle
10th ● Morton ....a D 0–0 **Att:** 1,865 — **Booked:** B. Donnelly
14th ● Queen of South h W 2–0 **Att:** 1,320 — **Scorers:** McLaughlin, Smyth. **Booked:** D. Smith
21st ● St Johnstone ....a L 3–0 **Att:** 2,561

April
4th ● Dunfermline .....h D 1–1 **Att:** 1,136 — **Scorers:** Smith. **Booked:** McDonald, Baird
11th ● Dundee ....a W 0–1 **Att:** 2,870 — **Scorers:** Lynch. **Booked:** B. Donnelly, Smyth, McKenna
18th ● Clyde ....a L 3–0 **Att:** 1,613 — **Booked:** McLachlan, D. Smith
25th ● Ross County .....h W 1–0 **Att:** 927 — **Scorers:** McKenna. **Booked:** McKenna

May
2nd ● Partick ....a W 0–1 **Att:** 3,255 — **Scorers:** Lynch. **Booked:** McKenna, McLaughlin
11th ● St Johnstone ...h L 0–4 **Att:** 633
14th ● Peterhead ....a W 0–2 **Att:** 1,364 — **Scorers:** Baird, McLaughlin. **Booked:** Di Giacomo
17th ● Peterhead ....h W 1–0 **Att:** 1,008 — **Scorers:** Baird, Smyth. **Booked:** McLachlan, Smyth, McKenna
20th ● Ayr ....a D 2–2 **Att:** 3,378 — **Scorers:** Baird, Di Giacomo. **Booked:** Lovering, B. Donnelly
24th ● Ayr ....h L 0–1 **Att:** 3,303 — **Booked:** McKenna, D. Smith, Smyth

● Irn-Bru First Division ● Scottish FA Cup ● Scottish League Cup ● Scottish Challenge Cup

FIRST DIVISION GOALKEEPER STATS

Player	Appearances	Match starts	Completed matches	Sub appearances	Subbed off	Clean sheets	Yellow cards	Red cards
Lee Hollis	3	3	3	0	0	1	0	0
Stephen Robertson	33	33	33	0	0	14	1	0

FIRST DIVISION OUTFIELD PLAYER STATS

Player	Appearances	Match starts	Completed matches	Substitute appearances	Subbed off	Goals scored	Yellow cards	Red cards
Jamie Bain	1	1	1	0	0	0	0	0
John Baird	13	9	6	4	3	2	1	0
Michael Brown	11	2	2	9	0	0	0	0
Joe Cardle	24	21	14	3	6	1	4	1
Paul Di Giacomo	33	30	17	3	13	5	4	0
Keiran Donnaghy	1	0	0	1	0	0	0	0
Bobby Donnelly	31	31	29	0	2	0	4	0
Ryan Donnelly	1	0	0	1	0	0	0	0
Liam Floan	1	1	1	0	0	0	0	0
Matthew Hazley	19	17	13	2	4	0	3	0
Fraser Keast	1	1	0	0	1	0	0	0
Paul Lovering	11	10	6	1	3	0	0	1
Simon Lynch	33	24	8	9	16	10	1	0
Patrick McCabe	1	1	1	0	0	0	0	0
Stefan McCluskey	1	0	0	1	0	0	0	0
Kevin McDonald	32	27	18	5	8	0	4	1
Steven McDougall	30	20	8	10	12	0	1	0
Stephen McKenna	35	35	35	0	0	1	5	0
William McLachlan	18	18	18	0	0	0	4	0
Scott McLaughlin	34	28	28	6	0	4	1	0
Stephen Mcguire	11	3	0	8	3	1	0	0
David Nixon	32	28	22	4	6	2	5	0
Stuart Noble	16	3	1	13	2	1	0	0
Darren Smith	22	15	4	7	11	1	3	0
Liam Smith	1	1	1	0	0	0	0	0
Marc Smyth	32	32	31	0	1	2	4	0
David Taylor	1	1	1	0	0	0	0	0
Kevin Watt	6	1	0	5	1	0	0	0

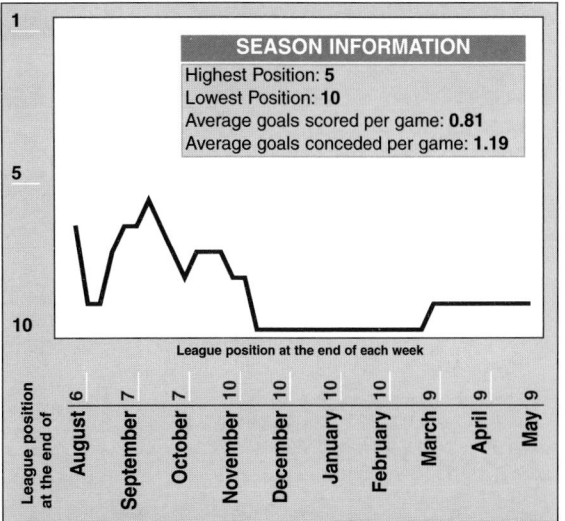

SEASON INFORMATION
Highest Position: 5
Lowest Position: 10
Average goals scored per game: 0.81
Average goals conceded per game: 1.19

League position at the end of each week

LONGEST SEQUENCES

Wins (on two occasions)	2	Undefeated home (22/02/09–25/04/09)	5
Losses (22/11/08–16/12/08)	4	Undefeated away (02/08/08–13/09/08)	3
Draws (28/02/09–10/03/09)	3	Without scoring (02/08/08–23/08/08)	4
Undefeated (on two occasions)	5	Without conceding (16/08/08–30/08/08)	3
Without win (01/11/08–20/12/08)	8	Scoring (20/12/08–24/01/09)	5

CARDS RECEIVED

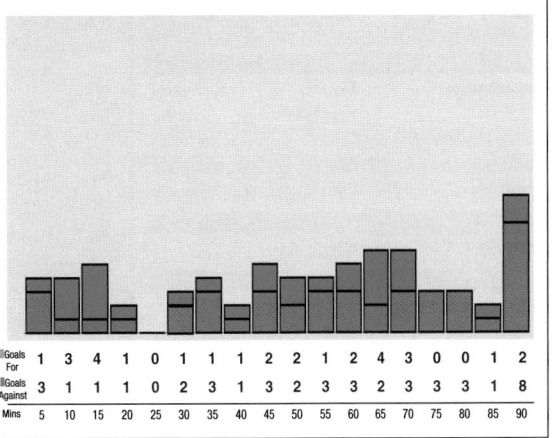

45   3

QUICK-FIRE GOALS
From the start of a match
Paul Di Giacomo (v Clyde) 5:00

By a substitute after coming on
Stephen Mcguire (v St Johnstone) 4:00

GOALS SCORED/CONCEDED PER FIVE-MINUTE INTERVALS

Goals For	1	3	4	1	0	1	1	1	2	2	1	2	4	3	0	0	1	2
Goals Against	3	1	1	1	0	2	3	1	3	2	3	3	2	3	3	3	1	8
Mins	5	10	15	20	25	30	35	40	45	50	55	60	65	70	75	80	85	90

CLYDE

CLYDE are set for Irn-Bru Second Division football next term after a disappointing campaign which ended with the heartache of relegation.

Former Rangers hardman John Brown failed to steer his side away from the relegation zone, as an inconsistent start saw the Cumbernauld men slip to ninth place after 10 games.

An encouraging run in November and December saw them pick up 11 points out of a possible 15, leaving the side sitting pretty in fifth place on Christmas Day.

However, results went awry as the season's end drew closer with an embarrassing 7–1 defeat against Queen of the South a low point.

On-loan Rangers players Alan Lowing and Paul Emslie could not help Clyde stay up, although Pat Clarke impressed with a healthy total of 14 goals for the season.

CLUB SUMMARY

FORMED	1877
MANAGER	John Brown
GROUND	Broadwood Stadium
CAPACITY	8,006
NICKNAME	The Bully Wee
WEBSITE	www.clydefc.co.uk

Billy Gibson

OVERALL
P	W	D	L	F	A	GD
43	14	9	20	52	65	-13

IRN-BRU FIRST DIVISION
Pos	P	W	D	L	F	A	GD	Pts
10	36	10	9	17	41	58	-17	39

HOME
Pos	P	W	D	L	F	A	GD	Pts
9	18	6	5	7	24	28	-4	23

AWAY
Pos	P	W	D	L	F	A	GD	Pts
9	18	4	4	10	17	30	-13	16

CUP PROGRESS DETAILS
Competition	Round reached	Knocked out by
Co-op Insurance Cup	R2	Hamilton
Scottish Cup	R4	Dunfermline
Challenge Cup	QF	Ross County

BIGGEST WIN (ALL COMPS)
05/08/08 4–1 v Queens Park **SLC1**

BIGGEST DEFEAT (ALL COMPS)
25/04/09 1–7 v Queen of the South **SC1**

ATTENDANCE RECORD
High	Low	Average
2,114	776	1,236
v Partick (13/09/2008)	v Ross County (24/01/2009)	

RESULTS 2008/09

July
26th ● Annan Athletic ..h W 2–0 **Att:** 688 — **Scorers:** Trouten[2]. **Booked:** Gemmill, Clarke

August
5th ● Queens Park ....h W 4–1 **Att:** 690 — **Scorers:** Gibson, Roddy MacLennan, McSwegan[2]. **Booked:** Kettlewell
9th ● Dundee ....a L 1–0 **Att:** 4,042
12th ● Alloa................a W 0–2 **Att:** 414 — **Scorers:** Clarke, Gibson. **Booked:** Ruari MacLennan, Clarke
16th ● Ross County ...h D 2–2 **Att:** 973 — **Scorers:** Clarke, MacLennan. **Booked:** Ohnesorge, Clarke
23rd ● Livingston........a L 2–1 **Att:** 1,068 — **Scorers:** Clarke. **Booked:** Ruari MacLennan, Higgins
26th ● Hamilton..........a L 3–1 **Att:** 1,146 — **Scorers:** Clarke. **Booked:** Ohnesorge, Cherrie. **Dismissed:** Ohnesorge
27th ● Morton ....h D 1–1 **Att:** 1,638 — **Scorers:** Brown. **Booked:** McGregor, Higgins
30th ● St Johnstone ...a W 2–3 **Att:** 2,412 — **Scorers:** Gemmill, McKay, Waddell. **Booked:** Brown

September
7th ● Ross County ...h L 0–1 **Att:** 756 — **Booked:** McGregor, Emslie
13th ● Partick ....h D 1–1 **Att:** 2,114 — **Scorers:** Clarke. **Booked:** Ohnesorge
20th ● Airdrie Utd ....a W 0–2 **Att:** 1,489 — **Scorers:** Ruari MacLennan, Waddell. **Booked:** Gemmill, Ohnesorge, McGregor, Kettlewell, Clarke, Gibson
27th ● Queen of South h L 0–2 **Att:** 1,095 — **Booked:** McSwegan, McKay, Emslie

October
4th ● Dunfermline ....h L 0–2 **Att:** 1,273 — **Booked:** Clarke, Waddell, Emslie, McSwegan
18th ● Morton ....a L 1–0 **Att:** 2,062 — **Booked:** Ruari MacLennan, Gemmill, Wilson, Waddell, McSwegan, Trouten
25th ● Livingston..........h W 2–1 **Att:** 820 — **Scorers:** McSwegan, Trouten. **Booked:** Wilson, Emslie, Higgins, Trouten

November
1st ● Ross County ....a L 3–0 **Att:** 2,205 — **Booked:** Waddell
8th ● Partick ....a L 2–0 **Att:** 3,003 — **Booked:** Brown, McLaren, Higgins
15th ● St Johnstone ...h D 2–2 **Att:** 1,417 — **Scorers:** Clarke[2]. **Booked:** McLaren, Higgins, Hutton, Kettlewell
22nd ● Queen of South a W 0–2 **Att:** 2,324 — **Booked:** Emslie, Lowing
29th ● Montrose ....h W 2–0 **Att:** 677 — **Scorers:** Clarke, McKay. **Booked:** Emslie

December
13th ● Dundee ....h W 1–0 **Att:** 1,179 — **Scorers:** McLaren. **Booked:** Lithgow, Gemmill, Brown. **Dismissed:** Gemmill
16th ● Airdrie Utd ....h W 1–0 **Att:** 836 — **Scorers:** Trouten. **Booked:** McLaren, McKay, Higgins. **Dismissed:** Ruari MacLennan
27th ● St Johnstone ...a L 1–0 **Att:** 3,291 — **Booked:** Hutton, Higgins, Waddell. **Dismissed:** McSwegan

January
3rd ● Partick ....h L 2–4 **Att:** 2,031 — **Scorers:** Clarke[2]. **Booked:** Lithgow, Gibson
10th ● Dunfermline .....a L 2–0 **Att:** 2,871 — **Booked:** Kettlewell, McLaren
17th ● Livingston........a D 1–1 **Att:** 1,481 — **Scorers:** McLaren. **Booked:** McLaren, Clarke, Wilson
20th ● Dunfermline .....a D 4–4 **Att:** 3,489 — **Scorers:** Clarke[2], Higgins, Trouten.
24th ● Ross County ....h W 2–0 **Att:** 776 — **Scorers:** McLaren, Waddell. **Booked:** Kettlewell, Tade, Gemmill, McKay, Waddell
31st ● Dundee ....a L 2–1 **Att:** 3,217 — **Scorers:** McLaren. **Booked:** Waddell, McLaren, Wilson

February
22nd ● Airdrie Utd ....a L 1–0 **Att:** 1,189 — **Booked:** Trouten, Ruari MacLennan, McLaren

March
3rd ● Morton ....h L 2–4 **Att:** 1,165 — **Scorers:** Gemmill, Ruari MacLennan. **Booked:** Gibson. **Dismissed:** Gibson
7th ● Partick ....a W 0–1 **Att:** 3,378 — **Scorers:** Maxwell OG. **Booked:** Lithgow, Ruari MacLennan, Tade
10th ● St Johnstone ...h L 1–3 **Att:** 1,159 — **Scorers:** Lithgow. **Booked:** Trouten
14th ● Morton ....a L 2–0 **Att:** 2,168 — **Booked:** Hutton. **Dismissed:** Hutton
21st ● Dunfermline .....h L 1–4 **Att:** 1,109 — **Scorers:** Ruari MacLennan. **Booked:** Trouten

April
4th ● Livingston..........h L 0–1 **Att:** 957 — **Booked:** Higgins, Gibson, Wilson, Kettlewell, Hutton, Ruari MacLennan
11th ● Ross County ....a D 0–0 **Att:** 2,078 — **Booked:** Wilson
18th ● Airdrie Utd ....h W 3–0 **Att:** 1,613 — **Scorers:** Ruari MacLennan[2], Waddell. **Booked:** Waddell, McKay, Ruari MacLennan
25th ● Queen of South a L 7–1 **Att:** 2,601 — **Scorers:** McLaren. **Booked:** Higgins

May
2nd ● Dundee ....h W 2–0 **Att:** 944 — **Scorers:** McLaren, Shinnie OG. **Booked:** Ruari MacLennan
9th ● Dunfermline .....a D 1–1 **Att:** 2,418 — **Scorers:** Higgins. **Booked:** Wilson, Lithgow, Brown

● Irn-Bru First Division ● Scottish FA Cup ● Scottish League Cup ● Scottish Challenge Cup

FIRST DIVISION GOALKEEPER STATS

Player	Appearances	Match starts	Completed matches	Sub appearances	Subbed off	Clean sheets	Yellow cards	Red cards
Peter Cherrie	5	5	5	0	0	1	0	0
David Hutton	31	31	30	0	0	8	4	1

FIRST DIVISION OUTFIELD PLAYER STATS

Player	Appearances	Match starts	Completed matches	Substitute appearances	Subbed off	Goals scored	Yellow cards	Red cards
Mark Brown	26	24	19	2	5	1	4	0
Patrick Clarke	29	28	22	1	5	11	4	1
Paul Emslie	9	9	9	0	0	0	4	0
Scott Gemmill	30	23	11	7	11	2	5	1
Billy Gibson	30	30	28	0	1	0	4	1
Chris Higgins	32	30	28	2	2	2	9	0
Stuart Kettlewell	26	26	16	0	10	0	4	0
Alan Lithgow	22	22	21	0	1	1	4	0
Alan Lowing	17	17	14	0	3	0	1	0
Ruari MacLennan	29	16	13	13	2	6	7	1
Roddy MacLennan	3	1	0	2	1	1	0	0
Marc McCusker	1	0	0	1	0	0	0	0
David McGowan	1	0	0	1	0	0	0	0
Neil McGregor	7	7	6	0	1	0	2	0
David McKay	30	14	7	16	7	1	4	0
William McLaren	24	24	15	0	8	6	6	1
Gary McSwegan	16	2	0	14	2	1	3	1
Jordan Murch	1	0	0	1	0	0	0	0
Craig O'Reilly	3	0	0	3	0	0	0	0
Michael Ohnesorge	10	10	6	0	4	0	3	0
Connor Stevenson	2	0	0	2	0	0	0	0
Anthony Stevenson	9	9	5	0	4	0	0	0
Gregory Tade	13	11	7	2	4	0	2	0
Alan Trouten	27	15	12	12	3	4	5	0
Richard Waddell	28	24	18	4	6	4	7	0
Marvyn Wilson	19	14	8	5	6	0	7	0
Robert Winters	5	4	1	1	3	0	0	0

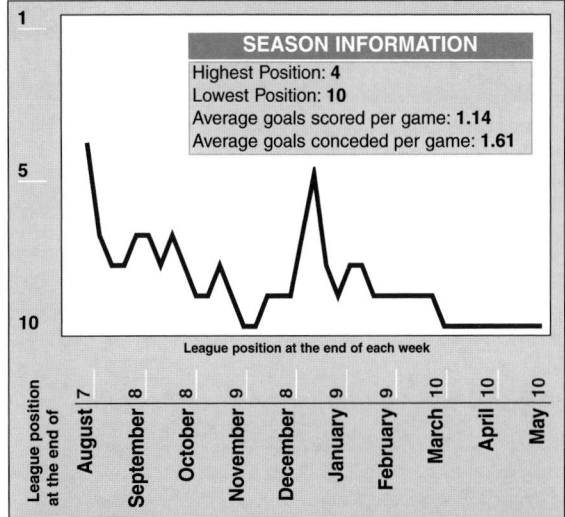

SEASON INFORMATION
Highest Position: **4**
Lowest Position: **10**
Average goals scored per game: **1.14**
Average goals conceded per game: **1.61**

League position at the end of each week

LONGEST SEQUENCES

Wins (22/11/08–16/12/08)	3	Undefeated home (25/10/08–16/12/08)	4
Losses (10/03/09–04/04/09)	4	Undefeated away (on two occasions)	2
Draws (–)		Without scoring (27/09/08–18/10/08)	3
Undefeated (15/11/08–20/12/08)	5	Without conceding (22/11/08–16/12/08)	3
Without win (10/03/09–11/04/09)	5	Scoring (on two occasions)	5

CARDS RECEIVED

89 **7**

QUICK-FIRE GOALS

From the start of a match
Alan Trouten (v Dunfermline) 1:00

By a substitute after coming on
Ruari MacLennan (v Airdrie Utd) 10:00

GOALS SCORED/CONCEDED PER FIVE-MINUTE INTERVALS

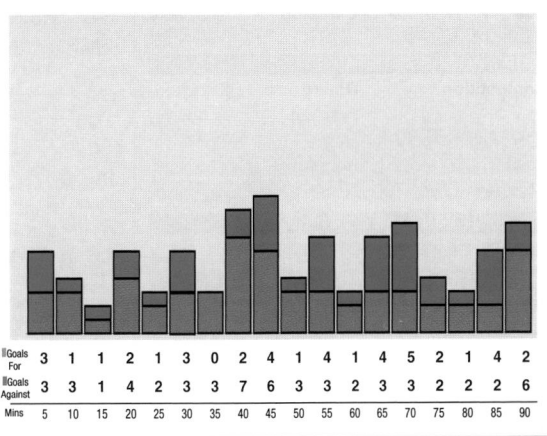

Goals For	3	1	1	2	1	3	0	2	4	1	4	1	4	5	2	1	4	2
Goals Against	3	3	1	4	2	3	3	7	6	3	3	2	3	3	2	2	2	6
Mins	5	10	15	20	25	30	35	40	45	50	55	60	65	70	75	80	85	90

DUNDEE

THE 2007/08 season saw the return of a familiar face at Dundee, with Jocky Scott coming back to Dens Park as manager for a third time following the sacking of Alex Rae.

Rae left the club in October, as the Dees sought to recover from a disappointing eight-match run without a win.

It was Mickael Antoine-Curier that finally ended the drought, scoring in the 1–0 away victory against Dunfermline. Antoine-Curier proved to be crucial for the Dens Park side, the prolific Guadeloupe forward returning the faith shown in him after he was signed permanently following a loan spell in the final months of the 2007/08 season.

As the season drew to a close, results varied but, with only one defeat in March, a degree of stability returned to the Dark Blues' results and they secured a fourth-place finish.

CLUB SUMMARY

FORMED	1893
MANAGER	Jocky Scott
GROUND	Dens Park
CAPACITY	11,800
NICKNAME	Dark Blues
WEBSITE	www.dundeefc.co.uk

The New Football Pools
PLAYER OF THE SEASON

Rab Douglas

OVERALL
P	W	D	L	F	A	GD
39	13	11	15	36	38	-2

IRN-BRU FIRST DIVISION
Pos	P	W	D	L	F	A	GD	Pts
4	36	13	11	12	33	32	1	50

HOME
Pos	P	W	D	L	F	A	GD	Pts
4	18	8	5	5	22	14	8	29

AWAY
Pos	P	W	D	L	F	A	GD	Pts
6	18	5	6	7	11	18	-7	21

CUP PROGRESS DETAILS
Competition	Round reached	Knocked out by
Co-op Insurance Cup	R2	Partick
Scottish Cup	R4	Celtic
Challenge Cup	R1	Alloa

BIGGEST WIN (ALL COMPS)
09/05/09 4–0 v Partick SC1

BIGGEST DEFEAT (ALL COMPS)
20/09/08 0–3 v Livingston SC1

ATTENDANCE RECORD
High	Low	Average
6,537	2,831	3,955

v St Johnstone (29/11/2008) v Partick (09/05/2009)

RESULTS 2008/09

July
26th	● Alloa...............a L 2–1	Att: 793 — **Scorers:** Antoine-Curier

August
2nd	● Ross County ....a W 1–2	Att: 3,444 — **Scorers:** Antoine-Curier, Paton. **Booked:** McHale, Cowan, Malone
9th	● Clyde ....h W 1–0	Att: 4,042 — **Scorers:** Antoine-Curier
16th	● Airdrie Utd ....a D 0–0	Att: 1,787 — **Booked:** Antoine-Curier, Paton, Douglas
23rd	● Morton ....h W 1–0	Att: 4,032 — **Scorers:** Paton. **Booked:** McMenamin
26th	● Partick ....h L 1–2	Att: 2,507 — **Scorers:** McHale. **Booked:** MacKenzie
30th	● Queen of South a L 3–1	Att: 3,339 — **Scorers:** Posniak. **Booked:** Gilhaney

September
13th	● Dunfermline .....h D 0–0	Att: 4,259 — **Booked:** McHale
20th	● Livingston.........h L 0–3	Att: 3,631 — **Booked:** McKeown, Davidson, Cameron
27th	● St Johnstone ....a L 2–0	Att: 4,307 — **Booked:** Cowan

October
4th	● Partick ....a D 0–0	Att: 2,556
18th	● Ross County ....h L 1–2	Att: 3,228 — **Scorers:** Antoine-Curier. **Booked:** Dodds
25th	● Morton ....a L 2–0	Att: 1,769 — **Booked:** McKeown

November
1st	● Airdrie Utd ....h D 1–1	Att: 3,456 — **Scorers:** Antoine-Curier. **Booked:** Deasley, Malone, Williams
8th	● Dunfermline .....a W 0–1	Att: 3,798 — **Scorers:** Antoine-Curier. **Booked:** Paton
15th	● Queen of South h W 2–0	Att: 3,630 — **Scorers:** Deasley, Paton
29th	● St Johnstone ...h D 1–1	Att: 6,537 — **Scorers:** Antoine-Curier

December
13th	● Clyde ....a L 1–0	Att: 1,179 — **Booked:** Shinnie. **Dismissed:** Young
20th	● Partick ....h D 0–0	Att: 3,569 — **Booked:** Williams, Malone
27th	● Queen of South a W 0–1	Att: 2,616 — **Scorers:** McMenamin. **Booked:** Cowan, McKeown

January
3rd	● Dunfermline .....h W 1–0	Att: 5,033 — **Scorers:** Paton
10th	● Celtic ....a L 2–1	Att: 23,070 — **Scorers:** McMenamin
17th	● Morton ....h D 0–0	Att: 3,738 — **Booked:** McHale, Shinnie
24th	● Airdrie Utd ....a L 1–0	Att: 1,278 — **Booked:** Shinnie, McKeown, Paton
31st	● Clyde ....h W 2–1	Att: 3,217 — **Scorers:** Antoine-Curier, McMenamin

February
7th	● Livingston.........a W 1–2	Att: 1,531 — **Scorers:** Antoine-Curier, Efrem.
		Booked: McKeown, McHale, Malone
21st	● Livingston.........h W 4–1	Att: 3,679 — **Scorers:** Antoine-Curier[2], Efrem, Shinnie
28th	● St Johnstone ....a D 0–0	Att: 7,238 — **Booked:** McMenamin, MacKenzie

March
10th	● Queen of South h L 2–3	Att: 3,757 — **Scorers:** Antoine-Curier[2]
14th	● Ross County ....h W 2–0	Att: 3,381 — **Scorers:** Antoine-Curier, McMenamin
22nd	● Partick ....a D 1–1	Att: 3,303 — **Scorers:** McMenamin. **Booked:** Efrem, McHale
28th	● Ross County ....a D 1–1	Att: 2,296 — **Scorers:** Antoine-Curier.
		Booked: McHale, MacKenzie, McMenamin. **Dismissed:** McHale, MacKenzie
31st	● Dunfermline .....a D 1–1	Att: 2,565 — **Scorers:** Malone

April
4th	● Morton ....a L 2–0	Att: 2,133 — **Booked:** McHale, Paton
11th	● Airdrie Utd ....h L 0–1	Att: 2,870 — **Booked:** Paton, MacKenzie
18th	● Livingston.........a W 0–1	Att: 1,988 — **Scorers:** Young. **Booked:** McMenamin, MacKenzie.
		Dismissed: MacKenzie
25th	● St Johnstone ....h L 0–1	Att: 6,305 — **Booked:** Young, Malone. **Dismissed:** Antoine-Curier

May
2nd	● Clyde ....a L 2–0	Att: 944 — **Booked:** Benedictus
9th	● Partick ....h W 4–0	Att: 2,831 — **Scorers:** McMenamin[3], Young

● Irn-Bru First Division ● Scottish FA Cup ● Scottish League Cup ● Scottish Challenge Cup

actim

SCOTTISH FOOTBALL LEAGUE

FIRST DIVISION GOALKEEPER STATS

Player	Appearances	Match starts	Completed matches	Sub appearances	Subbed off	Clean sheets	Yellow cards	Red cards
Rab Douglas	36	36	35	0	1	15	1	0
Ludovic Roy	1	0	0	1	0	1	0	0

FIRST DIVISION OUTFIELD PLAYER STATS

Player	Appearances	Match starts	Completed matches	Substitute appearances	Subbed off	Goals scored	Yellow cards	Red cards
Mickael Antoine-Curier	32	29	25	3	3	14	1	1
Kyle Benedictus	11	10	9	1	1	0	1	0
Colin Cameron	9	7	7	2	0	0	1	0
David Cowan	18	15	14	3	1	0	3	0
Frederic Daquin	19	16	8	3	8	0	0	0
Robert Davidson	12	6	5	6	1	0	1	0
Bryan Deasley	13	9	5	4	4	1	1	0
Rhian Dodds	4	4	4	0	0	0	1	0
Georgios Efrem	8	8	7	0	1	2	1	0
Craig Forsyth	1	0	0	1	0	0	0	0
Mark Gilhaney	19	13	7	6	6	0	1	0
James Lauchlan	16	15	12	1	3	0	0	0
Gary MacKenzie	19	17	14	2	1	0	4	2
Eddie Malone	35	35	34	0	1	1	5	0
Paul McHale	23	21	17	2	3	0	7	1
Craig McKeown	21	19	19	2	0	0	5	0
Colin McMenamin	29	24	20	5	4	7	4	0
Eddie Mearns	3	1	1	2	0	0	0	0
David O'Brien	24	18	13	6	5	0	0	0
Eric Paton	31	31	29	0	2	4	5	0
Christopher Posniak	26	23	17	3	6	1	0	0
Andrew Shinnie	20	19	16	1	3	1	3	0
Darren Williams	19	16	10	3	6	0	2	0
Darren Young	7	4	3	3	0	2	1	1

SEASON INFORMATION

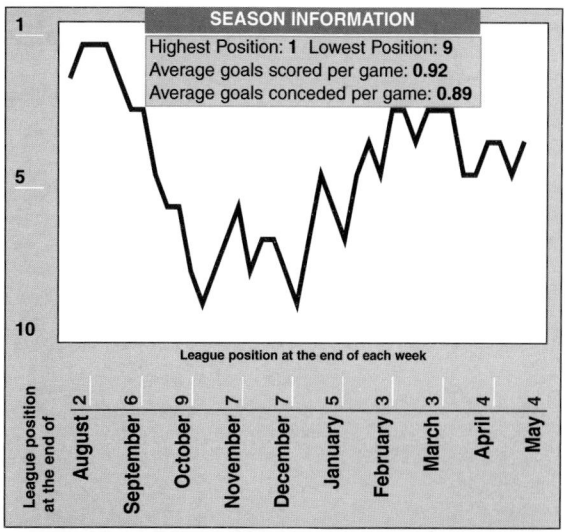

Highest Position: **1** Lowest Position: **9**
Average goals scored per game: **0.92**
Average goals conceded per game: **0.89**

League position at the end of each week

| League position at the end of | August 2 | September 6 | October 9 | November 7 | December 7 | January 5 | February 3 | March 3 | April 4 | May 4 |

LONGEST SEQUENCES

Wins (31/01/09–21/02/09)	3	Undefeated home (01/11/08–21/02/09)	8
Losses (on four occasions)	2	Undefeated away (07/02/09–31/03/09)	5
Draws (22/03/09–31/03/09)	3	Without scoring (13/09/08–04/10/08)	4
Undefeated (on five occasions)	4	Without conceding (20/12/08–17/01/09)	4
Without win (30/08/08–01/11/08)	8	Scoring (10/03/09–31/03/09)	5

CARDS RECEIVED

48   5

QUICK-FIRE GOALS

From the start of a match
Mickael Antoine-Curier (v Livingston) 1:00

By a substitute after coming on
Mickael Antoine-Curier (v Ross County) 12:00

GOALS SCORED/CONCEDED PER FIVE-MINUTE INTERVALS

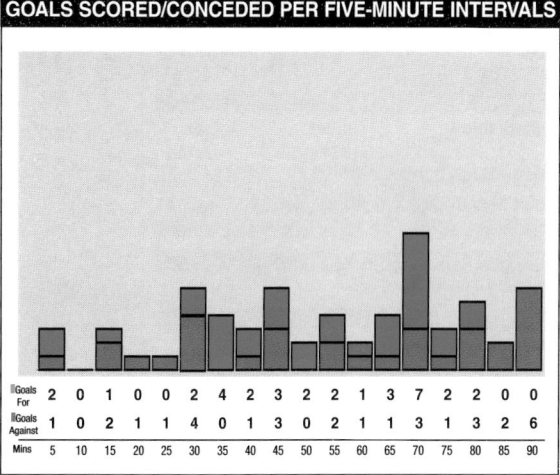

Goals For	2	0	1	0	0	2	4	2	3	2	2	1	3	7	2	2	0	0
Goals Against	1	0	2	1	1	4	0	1	3	0	2	1	1	3	1	3	2	6
Mins	5	10	15	20	25	30	35	40	45	50	55	60	65	70	75	80	85	90

DUNFERMLINE ATHLETIC

IT IS now two years since Dunfermline's relegation from the top flight and they must wait for at least another 12 months to return.

It was an indifferent start to the 2008/09 season for Jim McIntyre's side, who lost to Partick on the opening day and were also beaten by Livingston before the end of August.

The Pars struggled to instill any sense of consistency in the League, with their run to the Homecoming Scottish Cup semi-finals perhaps proving a distraction.

Their away form was vital, as they recorded a greater number of wins outside East End Park than at home, leaving fans wondering how to rouse their team to victory.

Ex-Hearts and Northern Ireland striker Andy Kirk proved to be a standout performer after his move from Yeovil.

CLUB SUMMARY

FORMED	1885
MANAGER	Jim McIntyre
GROUND	East End Park
CAPACITY	11,780
NICKNAME	The Pars
WEBSITE	www.dafc.co.uk

The New Football Pools PLAYER OF THE SEASON — Calum Woods

OVERALL
P	W	D	L	F	A	GD
47	20	11	16	65	51	14

IRN-BRU FIRST DIVISION
Pos	P	W	D	L	F	A	GD	Pts
3	36	14	9	13	52	44	8	51

HOME
Pos	P	W	D	L	F	A	GD	Pts
10	18	5	5	8	20	24	-4	20

AWAY
Pos	P	W	D	L	F	A	GD	Pts
1	18	9	4	5	32	20	12	31

CUP PROGRESS DETAILS
Competition	Round reached	Knocked out by
Co-op Insurance Cup	QF	Dundee Utd
Scottish Cup	SF	Falkirk
Challenge Cup	R2	Queen of South

BIGGEST WIN (ALL COMPS)
21/03/09 4–1 v Clyde **SC1**

BIGGEST DEFEAT (ALL COMPS)
10/03/09 2–4 v Livingston **SC1**

ATTENDANCE RECORD
High	Low	Average
4,998	1,438	3,255

v St Johnstone (01/11/2008) v Morton (05/05/2009)

RESULTS 2008/09

July
26th ● Stirling ....h W 3–0 — **Att:** 1,327 — **Scorers:** Burke, Phinn, Williamson

August
2nd ● Partick ....a L 1–0 — **Att:** 3,092 — **Booked:** Bayne, Glass
5th ● Peterhead ....a W 0–2 — **Att:** 1,291 — **Scorers:** Kirk, Phinn. **Booked:** Wilson
9th ● Queen of South h W 2–1 — **Att:** 2,995 — **Scorers:** Kirk². **Booked:** Wilson, Williamson
16th ● St Johnstone ....a W 0–3 — **Att:** 3,697 — **Scorers:** Bayne, Phinn, Williamson. **Booked:** Wilson
20th ● Queen of South h L 0–2 — **Att:** 1,371
23rd ● Airdrie Utd ....h D 0–0 — **Att:** 3,407 — **Booked:** Phinn, Shields, Wilson. **Dismissed:** Phinn
26th ● Alloa................h W 1–0 — **Att:** 1,326 — **Scorers:** Kirk. **Booked:** Wilson, Woods, Bayne, Bell
30th ● Livingston.........h L 1–2 — **Att:** 3,700 — **Scorers:** Kirk. **Booked:** Bayne, McCann, Wilson

September
13th ● Dundee ....a D 0–0 — **Att:** 4,259 — **Booked:** Wilson, Bayne, Gallacher. **Dismissed:** Woods
20th ● Ross County ......h W 3–1 — **Att:** 2,894 — **Scorers:** Bell, Phinn, Thomson
23rd ● St Mirren ....h W 2–0 — **Att:** 2,319 — **Scorers:** Bayne, Wiles. **Booked:** Bayne
27th ● Morton ....a D 1–1 — **Att:** 2,156 — **Booked:** Glass, Woods

October
4th ● Clyde ....a W 0–2 — **Att:** 1,273 — **Scorers:** Harper, Kirk. **Booked:** McCann, Harper
18th ● Partick ....h W 1–0 — **Att:** 3,534 — **Scorers:** Kirk
28th ● Dundee Utd ......a L 1–0 — **Att:** 5,350 — **Booked:** Gallacher

November
1st ● St Johnstone ....h L 1–2 — **Att:** 4,998 — **Scorers:** Wilson. **Booked:** Glass
4th ● Airdrie Utd ....a W 1–3 — **Att:** 1,099 — **Scorers:** Glass, Phinn, Woods. **Booked:** Phinn, Kirk
8th ● Dundee ....h L 0–1 — **Att:** 3,798 — **Booked:** Wilson
15th ● Livingston.........a W 2–3 — **Att:** 1,929 — **Scorers:** Bayne, Kirk². **Booked:** Wilson
22nd ● Morton ....h L 0–1 — **Att:** 4,400

December
13th ● Queen of South a W 1–2 — **Att:** 2,312 — **Scorers:** Bayne, Phinn. **Booked:** Shields
20th ● Clyde ....h D 4–4 — **Att:** 3,489 — **Scorers:** Glass, Kirk², Phinn. **Booked:** Bayne
30th ● Livingston.........h W 1–0 — **Att:** 3,140 — **Scorers:** Shields. **Booked:** Ross, Wilson, Bell, Bayne

January
3rd ● Dundee ....a L 1–0 — **Att:** 5,033 — **Booked:** Bell
10th ● Clyde ....h W 2–0 — **Att:** 2,871 — **Scorers:** Bayne, Phinn. **Booked:** Shields, Woods, Bell
17th ● Airdrie Utd ....h D 1–1 — **Att:** 2,913 — **Scorers:** Loy. **Booked:** Phinn
31st ● Queen of South h L 0–2 — **Att:** 2,847 — **Booked:** Bayne

February
14th ● Partick ....a W 2–3 — **Att:** 2,957 — **Scorers:** Bell, Kirk, Loy. **Booked:** D. Graham, Wilson, Holmes, Mole
17th ● Airdrie Utd ....a W 1–2 — **Att:** 1,772 — **Scorers:** Bayne, Holmes. **Booked:** S. Thomson, McCann
21st ● Ross County ......h L 1–2 — **Att:** 3,325 — **Scorers:** Bayne. **Booked:** Woods
28th ● Morton ....a L 2–1 — **Att:** 2,092 — **Scorers:** Kirk

March
7th ● Aberdeen ....h D 1–1 — **Att:** 9,696 — **Scorers:** Phinn. **Booked:** Glass
10th ● Livingston.........a L 4–2 — **Att:** 1,288 — **Scorers:** Bell, D. Graham
14th ● Partick ....h L 0–1 — **Att:** 2,934
18th ● Aberdeen ....a D 0–0 — **Att:** 13,567 — (Won 4–2 on penalties)
21st ● Clyde ....a W 1–4 — **Att:** 1,109 — **Scorers:** Burke, Phinn², Woods. **Booked:** Bayne
24th ● Ross County .....a L 2–1 — **Att:** 1,782 — **Scorers:** Bayne. **Booked:** Wilson, D. Graham
31st ● Dundee ....h D 1–1 — **Att:** 2,565 — **Scorers:** Woods. **Booked:** Burke, Glass

April
4th ● Airdrie Utd ....a D 1–1 — **Att:** 1,136 — **Scorers:** Ross. **Booked:** Glass
7th ● St Johnstone ....a D 0–0 — **Att:** 3,199 — **Booked:** Bell
11th ● St Johnstone ....h L 1–3 — **Att:** 3,791 — **Scorers:** Kirk. **Booked:** McCann, Kirk, Bayne. **Dismissed:** Wilson
18th ● Ross County ......h W 2–1 — **Att:** 2,413 — **Scorers:** Bayne, Kirk, Woods
26th ● Falkirk ....n L 2–0 — **Att:** 17,124 — **Booked:** Woods

May
2nd ● Queen of South a W 0–3 — **Att:** 2,750 — **Scorers:** Kirk, Phinn, Woods
5th ● Morton ....h W 2–1 — **Att:** 1,438 — **Scorers:** Kirk, Loy
9th ● Clyde ....h D 1–1 — **Att:** 2,418 — **Scorers:** D. Graham. **Booked:** Muirhead

● Irn-Bru First Division ● Scottish FA Cup ● Scottish League Cup ● Scottish Challenge Cup

FIRST DIVISION GOALKEEPER STATS

Player	Appearances	Match starts	Completed matches	Sub appearances	Subbed off	Clean sheets	Yellow cards	Red cards
Paul Gallacher	36	36	36	0	0	8	1	0

FIRST DIVISION OUTFIELD PLAYER STATS

Player	Appearances	Match starts	Completed matches	Substitute appearances	Subbed off	Goals scored	Yellow cards	Red cards
Craig Bald	1	1	1	0	0	0	0	0
Sol Bamba	1	1	1	0	0	0	0	0
Graham Bayne	31	31	27	0	4	6	8	0
Steven Bell	24	19	13	5	6	3	3	0
Alex Burke	32	29	18	3	11	1	1	0
Ross Campbell	1	0	0	1	0	0	0	0
Stephen Glass	26	26	22	0	4	2	5	0
Lee Graham	1	1	1	0	0	0	0	0
David Graham	14	13	6	1	7	2	2	0
Kevin Harper	14	12	3	2	9	1	1	0
Graeme Holmes	7	4	3	3	1	0	1	0
Andy Kirk	32	27	18	5	9	15	2	0
Rory Loy	18	6	3	12	3	3	0	0
Austin McCann	32	30	26	2	4	0	3	0
Jim McIntyre	2	0	0	2	0	0	0	0
Jamie Mole	9	3	1	6	2	0	1	0
Scott Muirhead	19	8	6	11	2	0	1	0
Nick Phinn	35	33	25	2	7	8	3	1
Greg Ross	15	9	5	6	4	1	1	0
Greg Shields	28	27	26	1	1	1	2	0
Scott Thomson	27	21	16	6	5	1	0	0
Simon Wiles	9	2	0	7	3	1	0	0
Iain Williamson	9	2	0	7	2	1	1	0
Paul Willis	3	0	0	3	0	0	0	0
Scott Wilson	29	29	24	0	4	1	10	1
Calum Woods	30	25	20	5	4	5	2	1

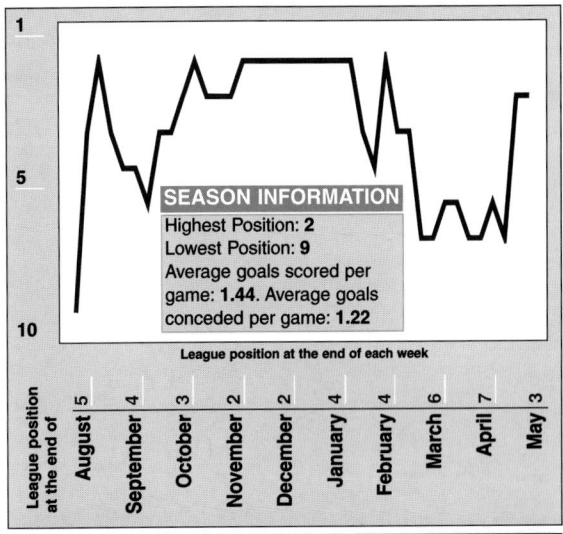

SEASON INFORMATION

Highest Position: **2**
Lowest Position: **9**
Average goals scored per game: **1.44**. Average goals conceded per game: **1.22**

League position at the end of each week

LONGEST SEQUENCES

Wins (18/04/09–05/05/09)	3	Undefeated home (20/12/08–17/01/09)	3
Losses (21/02/09–14/03/09)	4	Undefeated away (16/08/08–13/12/08)	7
Draws (31/03/09–07/04/09)	3	Without scoring (–)	
Undefeated (13/09/08–18/10/08)	5	Without conceding (16/08/08–23/08/08)	2
Without win (24/03/09–11/04/09)	5	Scoring (20/09/08–04/11/08)	6

CARDS RECEIVED

48   **3**

QUICK-FIRE GOALS

From the start of a match
Calum Woods (v Airdrie Utd) 4:00

By a substitute after coming on
Greg Ross (v Airdrie Utd) 11:00

GOALS SCORED/CONCEDED PER FIVE-MINUTE INTERVALS

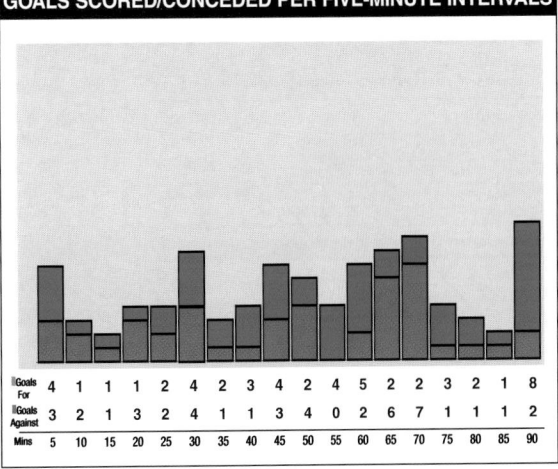

Goals For	4	1	1	1	2	4	2	3	4	2	4	5	2	2	3	2	1	8
Goals Against	3	2	1	3	2	4	1	1	3	4	0	2	6	7	1	1	1	2
Mins	5	10	15	20	25	30	35	40	45	50	55	60	65	70	75	80	85	90

LIVINGSTON suffered highly-publicised off-the-field problems in a tough season in the Irn-Bru First Division.

With Paul Hegarty in charge, they enjoyed an impressive start to the campaign but, ultimately, failed to capitalise on their early-season form, finishing in seventh position.

The Almondvale side picked up six wins in their first eight games, thrusting them into first place. However, Hegarty was then suspended – pending further investigation – and old favourite Davie Hay stepped in as a temporary manager at the end of April.

One highlight was the form of 18-year-old Leigh Griffiths, who scored 19 goals. He was rewarded with a place in the Scotland B squad, scoring on his first appearance, and could well make a futher impact on the national team in years to come.

CLUB SUMMARY

FORMED	1943
MANAGER	David Hay (interim)
GROUND	Almondvale Stadium
CAPACITY	10,016
NICKNAME	The Livi Lions
WEBSITE	www.livingstonfc.co.uk

The New **Football Pools** PLAYER OF THE SEASON — **Lee Griffiths**

OVERALL

P	W	D	L	F	A	GD
43	17	8	18	66	68	-2

IRN-BRU FIRST DIVISION

Pos	P	W	D	L	F	A	GD	Pts
7	36	13	8	15	56	58	-2	47

HOME

Pos	P	W	D	L	F	A	GD	Pts
5	18	8	3	7	29	25	4	27

AWAY

Pos	P	W	D	L	F	A	GD	Pts
7	18	5	5	8	27	33	-6	20

CUP PROGRESS DETAILS

Competition	Round reached	Knocked out by
Co-op Insurance Cup	R3	Celtic
Scottish Cup	R3	East Stirling
Challenge Cup	QF	Partick

BIGGEST WIN (ALL COMPS)
26/07/08 4–0 v Stranraer **SLCC1SW**

BIGGEST DEFEAT (ALL COMPS)
04/10/08 1–6 v Queen of South **SC1**

ATTENDANCE RECORD

High	Low	Average
2,876	1,068	1,728
v Partick (28/02/2009)	v Clyde (23/08/2008)	

RESULTS 2008/09

July
26th ● Stranraer ....h W 4–0　Att: 642 — Scorers: Griffiths², Hamill, McParland. **Booked:** McPake

August
2nd ● St Johnstone ....a L 2–0　Att: 2,692 — **Booked:** Talbot
6th ● East Stirling ......a W 1–2　Att: 491 — Scorers: Fox, Smith. **Booked:** Griffiths (AET)
9th ● Ross County ......h W 2–0　Att: 1,725 — Scorers: Griffiths, Talbot
12th ● Forfar ....h W 1–0　Att: 656 — Scorers: Griffiths. **Booked:** Fox
16th ● Morton ....a W 1–2　Att: 2,305 — Scorers: Davidson, Griffiths. **Booked:** Fox, McPake
23rd ● Clyde ....h W 2–1　Att: 1,068 — Scorers: Griffiths, McParland. **Booked:** Innes
26th ● St Johnstone ....h W 2–1　Att: 979 — Scorers: Cuenca, Griffiths. **Booked:** Fox, Miller, Quinn (AET)
30th ● Dunfermline ......a W 1–2　Att: 3,700 — Scorers: Griffiths²

September
7th ● Partick ....h L 0–2　Att: 1,339
13th ● Airdrie Utd ....h L 1–2　Att: 1,710 — **Scorers:** Elliot
20th ● Dundee ....a W 0–3　Att: 3,631 — Scorers: Elliot², Innes. **Booked:** Giarrizzo
23rd ● Celtic ....a L 4–0　Att: 23,644
27th ● Partick ....h W 3–1　Att: 2,150 — Scorers: Davidson, Elliot²

October
4th ● Queen of South a L 6–1　Att: 3,266 — Scorers: MacKay. **Dismissed:** Elliot
18th ● St Johnstone ....h L 0–1　Att: 2,169 — **Booked:** Talbot
25th ● Clyde ....a L 2–1　Att: 820 — **Scorers:** Elliot. **Booked:** Hamill, Fox, McPake, Davidson

November
1st ● Morton ....h W 1–0　Att: 1,727 — Scorers: Elliot. **Booked:** Elliot
8th ● Airdrie Utd ....a D 0–0　Att: 1,201 — **Booked:** Elliot, Davidson
15th ● Dunfermline ......h L 2–3　Att: 1,929 — Scorers: Elliot, McPake. **Booked:** Fox, Talbot
22nd ● Partick ....a L 2–1　Att: 2,416 — Scorers: MacKay. **Booked:** Elliot, Fox, MacKay
29th ● East Stirling ......a L 2–1　Att: 563 — Scorers: Fox. **Booked:** MacKay, McPake, Ke. Jacobs

December
13th ● Ross County ......a W 1–4　Att: 2,180 — Scorers: Davidson, Elliot, Griffiths, Quinn. **Booked:** Innes, Quinn
20th ● Queen of South h W 2–0　Att: 1,492 — Scorers: Elliot, McPake
30th ● Dunfermline ......a L 1–0　Att: 3,140 — **Booked:** Griffiths, Elliot, McPake

January
3rd ● Airdrie Utd ....h D 1–1　Att: 1,462 — Scorers: Elliot. **Booked:** McPake
17th ● Clyde ....h D 1–1　Att: 1,481 — Scorers: Winters. **Booked:** Innes
24th ● Morton ....a D 2–2　Att: 2,307 — Scorers: Griffiths, Smith OG
31st ● Ross County ......h W 4–2　Att: 1,374 — Scorers: Davidson, Griffiths, MacKay, One

February
7th ● Dundee ....h L 1–2　Att: 1,531 — Scorers: McParland
　　Booked: Griffiths, MacDonald, MacKay, Innes. **Dismissed:** Griffiths
14th ● St Johnstone ....a L 1–0　Att: 2,752 — **Booked:** MacDonald, Innes
21st ● Dundee ....a L 4–1　Att: 3,679 — Scorers: De Vita. **Booked:** Hamill, Innes
28th ● Partick ....h L 2–4　Att: 2,876 — Scorers: Griffiths²

March
7th ● Airdrie Utd ....a D 4–4　Att: 1,100 — Scorers: Griffiths², One². **Booked:** Miller
10th ● Dunfermline ......h W 4–2　Att: 1,288 — Scorers: Davidson², Griffiths, McParland
14th ● St Johnstone ....h W 1–0　Att: 1,882 — Scorers: Griffiths. **Booked:** Davidson, One
21st ● Queen of South a D 3–3　Att: 2,487 — Scorers: Griffiths², Winters. **Booked:** Halliday, Davidson, Griffiths

April
4th ● Clyde ....a W 0–1　Att: 957 — Scorers: Hamill. **Booked:** Winters
11th ● Morton ....h L 0–2　Att: 1,594
18th ● Dundee ....h L 0–1　Att: 1,988 — **Booked:** One, Griffin
25th ● Partick ....a L 1–0　Att: 2,803 — **Booked:** Fox, Hamill

May
2nd ● Ross County ......a D 2–2　Att: 2,567 — Scorers: Griffiths, Halliday. **Booked:** Malone, MacDonald
9th ● Queen of South h D 2–2　Att: 1,652 — Scorers: Griffiths, Winters. **Booked:** Miller

● Irn-Bru First Division ● Scottish FA Cup ● Scottish League Cup ● Scottish Challenge Cup

FIRST DIVISION GOALKEEPER STATS

Player	Appearances	Match starts	Completed matches	Sub appearances	Subbed off	Clean sheets	Yellow cards	Red cards
Pierre Martini	13	12	12	1	0	3	0	0
Roddy McKenzie	24	24	23	0	1	5	0	0

FIRST DIVISION OUTFIELD PLAYER STATS

Player	Appearances	Match starts	Completed matches	Substitute appearances	Subbed off	Goals scored	Yellow cards	Red cards
Phill Cave	3	2	1	1	1	0	0	0
Jean-Jose Cuenca	8	2	1	6	1	0	0	0
Murray Davidson	29	29	23	0	6	6	4	0
Raffaele De Vita	7	2	0	5	2	1	0	0
Calum Elliot	13	13	12	0	0	11	4	1
Liam Fox	20	18	15	2	3	0	5	0
Fernando Giarrizzo	4	2	1	2	1	0	1	0
Danny Griffin	17	17	17	0	0	0	1	0
Leigh Griffiths	27	25	21	2	3	18	3	1
Andrew Halliday	13	7	1	6	6	1	1	0
Joe Hamill	33	32	30	1	2	1	3	0
Chris Innes	30	30	28	0	2	1	6	0
Keaghan Jacobs	14	2	1	12	1	0	0	0
Kyle Jacobs	1	0	0	1	0	0	0	0
Devon Jacobs	1	0	0	1	0	0	0	0
Cameron MacDonald	17	12	10	5	2	0	3	0
David MacKay	26	26	24	0	2	3	2	0
Chris Malone	8	8	6	0	2	0	1	0
David McKay	2	2	1	0	1	0	0	0
James McPake	18	18	18	0	0	2	4	0
Anthony McParland	36	36	22	0	14	3	0	0
Gary Miller	23	13	4	10	9	0	2	0
Armand One	15	12	8	3	4	3	2	0
Rocco Quinn	15	14	13	1	1	1	1	0
David Sinclair	1	0	0	1	0	0	0	0
Gordon Smith	4	1	1	3	0	1	0	0
Jason Talbot	28	24	20	4	4	1	3	0
Millan Thomas	1	1	1	0	0	0	0	0
Mark Torrance	4	2	1	2	1	0	0	0
David Winters	14	10	6	4	4	3	1	0

SEASON INFORMATION

Highest Position: **1**
Lowest Position: **10**
Average goals scored per game: **1.56**
Average goals conceded per game: **1.61**

League position at the end of each week

League position at the end of: August 1 · September 1 · October 4 · November 5 · December 3 · January 3 · February 5 · March 4 · April 6 · May 7

LONGEST SEQUENCES

Wins (09/08/08–30/08/08)	4	Undefeated home (20/12/08–31/01/09)	4
Losses (07/02/09–28/02/09)	4	Undefeated away (on two occasions)	3
Draws (03/01/09–24/01/09)	3	Without scoring (11/04/09–25/04/09)	3
Undefeated (07/03/09–04/04/09)	5	Without conceding (01/11/08–08/11/08)	2
Without win (on two occasions)	5	Scoring (09/08/08–04/10/08)	8

CARDS RECEIVED

47   2

QUICK-FIRE GOALS

From the start of a match
James McPake (v Dunfermline) 5:00

By a substitute after coming on
David Winters (v Queen of South) 3:00

GOALS SCORED/CONCEDED PER FIVE-MINUTE INTERVALS

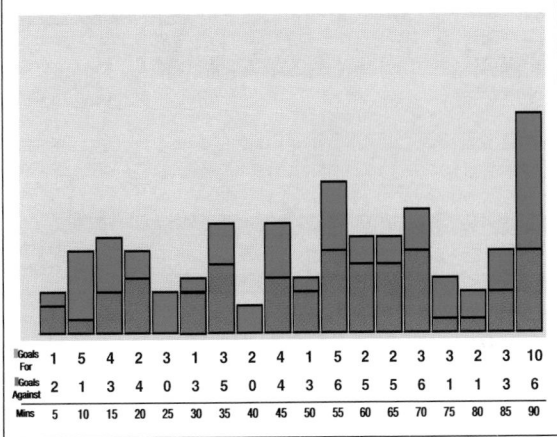

Goals For	1	5	4	2	3	1	3	2	4	1	5	2	2	3	3	2	3	10
Goals Against	2	1	3	4	0	3	5	0	4	3	6	5	5	6	1	1	3	6
Mins	5	10	15	20	25	30	35	40	45	50	55	60	65	70	75	80	85	90

GREENOCK MORTON endured a horrific start to the season, but managed to salvage their campaign to finish in sixth spot.

Manager Davie Irons came into the 2008/09 season on a high having saved Morton from relegation during the previous season, but his side made an awful start to the new campaign.

It took the 'Ton some 10 games to register a victory, which came in the shape of a 1–0 win over eventual basement club Clyde. This proved to be a catalyst for the rest of the season, with wins over Dundee and Dunfermline among those to follow soon after.

March and April saw the Greenock side notch up a seven-game unbeaten run, consolidating their respectable league position and banishing the memories of a campaign that had begun so worryingly with four draws and five defeats.

CLUB SUMMARY

FORMED	1874
MANAGER	Davie Irons
GROUND	Cappielow Park
CAPACITY	11,612
NICKNAME	The 'Ton
WEBSITE	www.gmfc.net

The New **Football Pools** PLAYER OF THE SEASON

Stewart Greacen

OVERALL

P	W	D	L	F	A	GD
43	16	11	16	58	54	4

IRN-BRU FIRST DIVISION

Pos	P	W	D	L	F	A	GD	Pts
6	36	12	11	13	40	40	0	47

HOME

Pos	P	W	D	L	F	A	GD	Pts
2	18	8	7	3	23	14	9	31

AWAY

Pos	P	W	D	L	F	A	GD	Pts
8	18	4	4	10	17	26	-9	16

CUP PROGRESS DETAILS

Competition	Round reached	Knocked out by
Co-op Insurance Cup	R3	Inverness CT
Scottish Cup	R3	Peterhead
Challenge Cup	SF	Ross County

BIGGEST WIN (ALL COMPS)

05/08/08 6–3 v Stranraer **SLC1**

BIGGEST DEFEAT (ALL COMPS)

30/08/08 0–5 v Airdrie Utd **SC1**

ATTENDANCE RECORD

High	Low	Average
3,323	1,685	2,279
v Partick (18/04/2009)	v Airdrie Utd (25/11/2008)	

RESULTS 2008/09

August

2nd	● Clyde	a	D 1–1	**Att:** 1,638 — **Scorers:** Newby.
				Booked: Walker, Wake, Paartalu, McAlister, McGuffie. **Dismissed:** Wake
5th	● Stranraer	a	W 3–6	**Att:** 317 — **Scorers:** McGuffie, Paartalu, Russell[2], Wake[2].
				Booked: Wake, Shimmon, Masterton, Walker
9th	● St Johnstone	h	D 2–2	**Att:** 2,820 — **Scorers:** McGuffie, Paartalu. **Booked:** Russell
13th	● East Stirling	a	W 0–3	**Att:** 698 — **Scorers:** Masterton, McGuffie[2]. **Booked:** Russell, Wake, Masterton
16th	● Livingston	h	L 1–2	**Att:** 2,305 — **Scorers:** Wake. **Booked:** Masterton
23rd	● Dundee	a	L 1–0	**Att:** 4,032
26th	● Hibernian	a	W 3–4	**Att:** 6,329 — **Scorers:** Harding, Masterton, Russell[2].
				Booked: Paartalu, McManus (AET)
30th	● Airdrie Utd	h	L 5–0	**Att:** 1,793 — **Booked:** Shimmon, McAlister. **Dismissed:** McManus

September

7th	● Queen of South	a	W 0–2	**Att:** 2,991 — **Scorers:** McGuffie, Wake. **Booked:** McGuffie
13th	● Queen of South	h	D 0–0	**Att:** 2,235 — **Booked:** Walker
20th	● Partick	a	L 2–1	**Att:** 3,368 — **Scorers:** Russell. **Booked:** Walker, Weatherson
23rd	● Inverness CT	h	L 1–2	**Att:** 2,023 — **Scorers:** McAlister. **Booked:** Paartalu (AET)
27th	● Dunfermline	h	D 1–1	**Att:** 2,156 — **Scorers:** Wake. **Booked:** Paartalu

October

4th	● Ross County	a	L 3–0	**Att:** 2,361 — **Booked:** Shimmon
12th	● Ross County	a	L 4–1	**Att:** 1,334 — **Scorers:** Weatherson.
				Booked: Cuthbert, Smith. **Dismissed:** McManus
18th	● Clyde	h	W 1–0	**Att:** 2,062 — **Scorers:** Grady. **Booked:** Finlayson, Greacen, Masterton
25th	● Dundee	h	W 2–0	**Att:** 1,769 — **Scorers:** McGuffie, Weatherson

November

1st	● Livingston	a	L 1–0	**Att:** 1,727 — **Booked:** Finlayson, Jenkins
8th	● Queen of South	a	W 1–4	**Att:** 2,944 — **Scorers:** Greacen, Jenkins, Weatherson[2].
				Booked: McAlister, Wake, McManus
22nd	● Dunfermline	a	W 0–1	**Att:** 4,400 — **Scorers:** Paartalu. **Booked:** Weatherson
25th	● Airdrie Utd	h	W 2–0	**Att:** 1,685 — **Scorers:** Jenkins, Wake. **Booked:** Shimmon, Smith, Wake
29th	● Peterhead	a	L 2–1	**Att:** 817 — **Scorers:** Masterton. **Booked:** Greacen. **Dismissed:** Weatherson

December

13th	● St Johnstone	a	L 1–0	**Att:** 2,699 — **Booked:** Finlayson
20th	● Ross County	h	W 2–1	**Att:** 1,779 — **Scorers:** Masterton, Wake. **Booked:** McAlister, Shimmon
27th	● Airdrie Utd	a	L 1–0	**Att:** 1,663 — **Booked:** Masterton. **Dismissed:** Cuthbert
30th	● Partick	h	W 2–0	**Att:** 2,812 — **Scorers:** Masterton, Weatherson. **Booked:** Masterton

January

3rd	● Queen of South	h	D 2–2	**Att:** 2,742 — **Scorers:** Weatherson[2]. **Booked:** Finlayson, Jenkins
17th	● Dundee	a	D 0–0	**Att:** 3,738 — **Booked:** McManus
24th	● Livingston	h	D 2–2	**Att:** 2,307 — **Scorers:** McGuffie, Wake. **Booked:** Smith
31st	● St Johnstone	h	D 0–0	**Att:** 2,810 — **Booked:** McGuffie, Smith

February

21st	● Partick	a	L 1–0	**Att:** 3,348 — **Booked:** Finlayson
28th	● Dunfermline	h	W 2–1	**Att:** 2,092 — **Scorers:** Greacen, Weatherson

March

3rd	● Clyde	a	W 2–4	**Att:** 1,165 — **Scorers:** Paartalu, Russell, Wake[2]. **Booked:** Jenkins, Weatherson
7th	● Queen of South	a	D 1–1	**Att:** 2,643 — **Scorers:** Grady. **Booked:** Weatherson, McManus
10th	● Airdrie Utd	h	D 0–0	**Att:** 1,865 — **Booked:** Greacen
14th	● Clyde	h	W 2–0	**Att:** 2,168 — **Scorers:** Jenkins, Masterton. **Booked:** Paartalu
21st	● Ross County	a	D 1–1	**Att:** 2,236 — **Scorers:** Russell

April

4th	● Dundee	h	W 2–0	**Att:** 2,133 — **Scorers:** Weatherson[2].
11th	● Livingston	a	W 0–2	**Att:** 1,594 — **Scorers:** Wake[2]. **Booked:** McAlister, Masterton
18th	● Partick	h	L 0–1	**Att:** 3,323 — **Booked:** Walker

May

2nd	● St Johnstone	a	L 3–1	**Att:** 6,453 — **Scorers:** McGuffie. **Booked:** Greacen, Wake
5th	● Dunfermline	a	L 2–1	**Att:** 1,438 — **Scorers:** Monti
9th	● Ross County	h	L 0–2	**Att:** 1,956

● Irn-Bru First Division ● Scottish FA Cup ● Scottish League Cup ● Scottish Challenge Cup

FIRST DIVISION GOALKEEPER STATS

Player	Appearances	Match starts	Completed matches	Sub appearances	Subbed off	Clean sheets	Yellow cards	Red cards
Kevin Cuthbert	34	34	31	0	2	13	0	1
Colin Stewart	4	2	2	2	0	3	0	0

FIRST DIVISION OUTFIELD PLAYER STATS

Player	Appearances	Match starts	Completed matches	Substitute appearances	Subbed off	Goals scored	Yellow cards	Red cards
Kevin Finlayson	32	27	23	5	4	0	5	0
James Grady	22	16	3	6	13	2	0	0
Stewart Greacen	28	28	27	0	1	2	3	0
Ryan Harding	8	7	7	1	0	1	0	0
Allan Jenkins	29	20	17	9	3	3	3	0
David MacGregor	8	8	8	0	0	0	0	0
Steven Masterton	28	21	17	7	4	3	5	0
James McAlister	35	35	33	0	2	0	5	0
David McGregor	2	2	2	0	0	0	0	0
Ryan McGuffie	32	31	18	1	13	4	2	0
Allan McManus	19	18	17	1	0	0	3	1
Carrol Monti	4	3	3	1	0	1	0	0
Jon Newby	4	3	1	1	2	0	0	0
Erik Paartalu	27	19	10	8	9	3	3	0
Alan Reid	2	2	1	1	0	0	0	0
Ian Russell	25	11	9	14	2	3	1	0
Dominic Shimmon	21	21	19	0	2	0	4	0
Chris Smith	20	18	15	2	3	0	3	0
Brian Wake	32	18	12	14	5	9	4	1
Alex Walker	24	23	21	1	2	0	4	0
Peter Weatherson	34	31	20	3	11	9	4	0

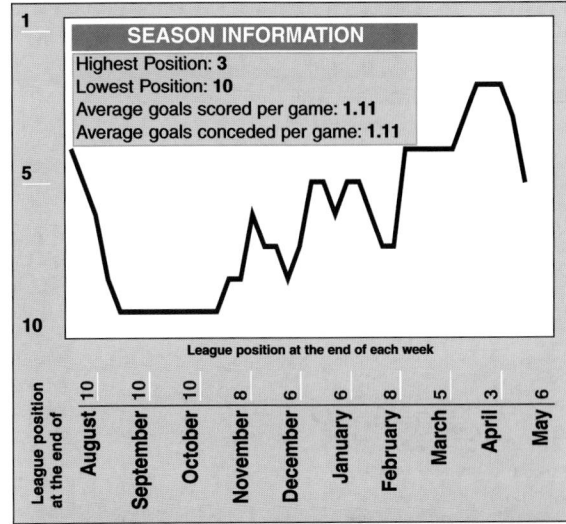

SEASON INFORMATION
Highest Position: **3**
Lowest Position: **10**
Average goals scored per game: **1.11**
Average goals conceded per game: **1.11**

League position at the end of each week

LONGEST SEQUENCES

Wins (08/11/08–25/11/08)	3	Undefeated home (13/09/08–04/04/09)	14
Losses (18/04/09–09/05/09)	4	Undefeated away (03/03/09–11/04/09)	4
Draws (03/01/09–31/01/09)	4	Without scoring (23/08/08–13/09/08)	3
Undefeated (28/02/09–11/04/09)	8	Without conceding (on four occasions)	2
Without win (02/08/08–04/10/08)	9	Scoring (14/03/09–11/04/09)	4

CARDS RECEIVED

49   **3**

QUICK-FIRE GOALS

From the start of a match
Ryan McGuffie (v St Johnstone) 5:00

By a substitute after coming on
Ian Russell (v Clyde) 4:00

GOALS SCORED/CONCEDED PER FIVE-MINUTE INTERVALS

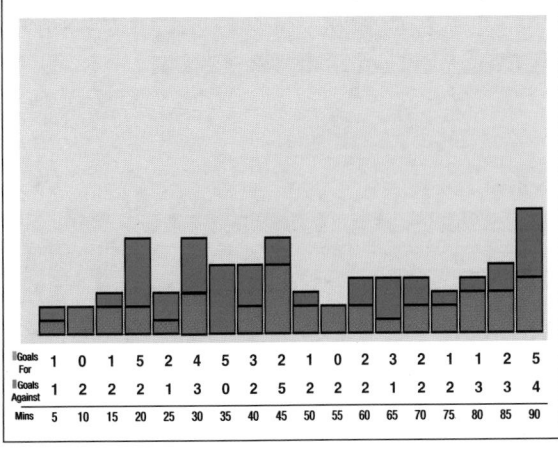

Goals For	1	0	1	5	2	4	5	3	2	1	0	2	3	2	1	1	2	5
Goals Against	1	2	2	2	1	3	0	2	5	2	2	2	1	2	2	3	3	4
Mins	5	10	15	20	25	30	35	40	45	50	55	60	65	70	75	80	85	90

PARTICK THISTLE

PARTICK ended the season as runners-up in the Irn-Bru First Division, with Ian McCall's team making up for their disappointing sixth-place finish of 2007/08.

Thistle's early-season form was indifferent, with the jewel in the crown – a 4–0 hammering of eventual champions St Johnstone – lying amongst disappointing defeats to Queen of the South and Livingston.

By mid-November, Partick were lingering in fifth place, but a steady stream of victories and draws in the remainder of the season lifted them up the table. They stayed in second place for the majority of 2009, heading a chasing group including Dunfermline and Dundee.

Former Blackburn youth Gary Harkins was outstanding for the Jags, netting nine goals, while Simon Donnelly and Ian Maxwell gave the team some valuable experience.

CLUB SUMMARY

FORMED	1876
MANAGER	Ian McCall
GROUND	Firhill Stadium
CAPACITY	10,887
NICKNAME	The Jags
WEBSITE	www.ptfc.co.uk

 **Gary Harkins**

The New **Football Pools**
PLAYER OF THE SEASON

OVERALL

P	W	D	L	F	A	GD
45	22	7	16	57	53	4

IRN-BRU FIRST DIVISION

Pos	P	W	D	L	F	A	GD	Pts
2	36	16	7	13	39	38	1	55

HOME

Pos	P	W	D	L	F	A	GD	Pts
3	18	9	3	6	20	14	6	30

AWAY

Pos	P	W	D	L	F	A	GD	Pts
3	18	7	4	7	19	24	-5	25

CUP PROGRESS DETAILS

Competition	Round reached	Knocked out by
Co-op Insurance Cup	R3	Rangers
Scottish Cup	R4	Inverness CT
Challenge Cup	SF	Airdrie Utd

BIGGEST WIN (ALL COMPS)
23/08/08 4–0 v St Johnstone **SC1**

BIGGEST DEFEAT (ALL COMPS)
09/05/09 0–4 v Dundee **SC1**

ATTENDANCE RECORD

High	Low	Average
3,378	2,296	2,956
v Clyde (07/03/2009)	v Airdrie Utd (13/12/2008)	

RESULTS 2008/09

July
26th ● Queens Park ....h W 2–1 Att: 1,386 — Scorers: Gray, Roberts. Booked: Rowson

August
2nd ● Dunfermline ......h W 1–0 Att: 3,092 — Scorers: McKeown. Booked: Maxwell
5th ● Forfar ....h W 4–3 Att: 1,195 — Scorers: Chaplain, Gray², McKeown (AET)
9th ● Airdrie Utd ....a W 0–1 Att: 2,165 — Scorers: Gray
12th ● Peterhead ....h W 4–2 Att: 1,133 — Scorers: Donnelly, Harkins, McKeown². Booked: Kinniburgh
17th ● Queen of South a L 2–0 Att: 3,272 — Booked: Twaddle, Paton, Chaplain, Maxwell
23rd ● St Johnstone ....h W 4–0 Att: 2,863 — Scorers: Harkins, Maxwell, Paton, Robertson
26th ● Dundee ....a W 1–2 Att: 2,507 — Scorers: Harkins, Maxwell.
30th ● Ross County ......h L 0–1 Att: 2,945 — Dismissed: Robertson

September
7th ● Livingston..........a W 0–2 Att: 1,339 — Scorers: Turner, Twaddle. Booked: Harkins
13th ● Clyde ....a D 1–1 Att: 2,114 — Scorers: Chaplain. Booked: Turner
20th ● Morton ....h W 2–1 Att: 3,368 — Scorers: Harkins, Maxwell. Booked: Rowson
24th ● Rangers ....h L 1–2 Att: 6,497 — Scorers: McKeown.
    Booked: Storey (AET)
27th ● Livingston..........a L 3–1 Att: 2,150 — Scorers: Maxwell

October
4th ● Dundee ....h D 0–0 Att: 2,556
12th ● Airdrie Utd ....h L 0–1 Att: 2,761 — Booked: Rowson, McKinlay
18th ● Dunfermline ......a L 1–0 Att: 3,534
25th ● St Johnstone ....a L 3–0 Att: 2,772 — Booked: Tuffey, Harkins, McKinlay. Dismissed: Storey

November
1st ● Queen of South h W 2–0 Att: 2,971 — Scorers: Harkins, McKinlay. Booked: Harkins, Kinniburgh
8th ● Clyde ....h W 2–0 Att: 3,003 — Scorers: Buchanan, McKeown. Booked: McKeown
22nd ● Livingston..........h W 2–1 Att: 2,416 — Scorers: Buchanan, McKeown
25th ● Ross County .....a L 1–0 Att: 1,625 — Booked: Rowson
29th ● Stirling ....a W 2–3 Att: 1,472 — Scorers: Buchanan, Chaplain, Harkins. Booked: Roberts, Tuffey

December
13th ● Airdrie Utd ....h W 2–1 Att: 2,296 — Scorers: Harkins, McLaughlin OG
20th ● Dundee ....a D 0–0 Att: 3,569 — Booked: Kinniburgh
27th ● Ross County .....h L 0–2 Att: 2,465 — Booked: Twaddle, Archibald. Dismissed: Twaddle
30th ● Morton ....a L 2–0 Att: 2,812 — Booked: Kinniburgh

January
3rd ● Clyde ....a W 2–4 Att: 2,031 — Scorers: Buchanan, Donnelly, Harkins, Paton.
    Booked: Archibald, Chaplain, Roberts
10th ● Inverness CT ....a L 3–0 Att: 1,803
17th ● St Johnstone ....h D 0–0 Att: 3,353 — Booked: Paton, Kinniburgh
24th ● Queen of South a D 2–2 Att: 2,811 — Scorers: Chaplain, Doolan. Booked: Paton, Paton, Harkins, Akins
31st ● Airdrie Utd ....a W 0–1 Att: 1,988 — Scorers: Buchanan. Booked: Paton, McKeown, McKinlay

February
14th ● Dunfermline ......h L 2–3 Att: 2,957 — Scorers: Buchanan, Doolan. Dismissed: Maxwell
21st ● Morton ....h W 1–0 Att: 3,348 — Scorers: Doolan. Booked: Paton
28th ● Livingston..........a W 2–4 Att: 2,876 — Scorers: Harkins², Paton, Rowson. Booked: Twaddle

March
7th ● Clyde ....h L 0–1 Att: 3,378
10th ● Ross County .....a W 0–2 Att: 2,017 — Scorers: Doolan². Booked: McKinlay
14th ● Dunfermline ......a W 0–1 Att: 2,934 — Scorers: Harkins
22nd ● Dundee ....h D 1–1 Att: 3,303 — Scorers: McKinlay. Booked: Kinniburgh, Akins

April
4th ● St Johnstone ....a D 1–1 Att: 4,909 — Scorers: Harkins. Booked: Archibald
11th ● Queen of South h L 0–2 Att: 2,830 — Booked: McKinlay, Harkins
18th ● Morton ....a W 0–1 Att: 3,323 — Scorers: Akins
25th ● Livingston..........h W 1–0 Att: 2,803 — Scorers: Buchanan. Booked: Archibald, Buchanan

May
2nd ● Airdrie Utd ....h L 0–1 Att: 3,255 — Booked: Donnelly, Robertson, Storey
9th ● Dundee ....a L 4–0 Att: 2,831 — Booked: Storey, Harkins

● Irn-Bru First Division ● Scottish FA Cup ● Scottish League Cup ● Scottish Challenge Cup

FIRST DIVISION GOALKEEPER STATS

Player	Appearances	Match starts	Completed matches	Sub appearances	Subbed off	Clean sheets	Yellow cards	Red cards
Jonny Tuffey	36	36	36	0	0	14	1	0

FIRST DIVISION OUTFIELD PLAYER STATS

Player	Appearances	Match starts	Completed matches	Substitute appearances	Subbed off	Goals scored	Yellow cards	Red cards
Lucas Akins	9	6	1	3	5	1	2	0
Alan Archibald	20	19	19	1	0	0	4	0
Liam Buchanan	19	17	5	2	12	6	1	0
Scott Chaplain	29	13	6	16	7	2	2	0
Simon Donnelly	31	19	6	12	13	1	1	0
Kris Doolan	16	15	7	1	8	5	0	0
Damon Gray	10	5	2	5	3	1	0	0
Gary Harkins	34	34	27	0	7	9	5	0
William Kinniburgh	18	14	12	4	2	0	5	0
Steven Lennon	9	5	2	4	3	0	0	0
Richard Little	1	0	0	1	0	0	0	0
Ian Maxwell	24	21	19	3	1	3	2	1
Stephen McKeown	25	18	10	7	8	3	2	0
Kevin McKinlay	29	12	9	17	3	2	4	0
Ryan McStay	3	1	0	2	1	0	0	0
Paul Paton	35	32	29	3	3	3	6	0
Mark Roberts	15	6	2	9	4	0	1	0
John Robertson	28	28	26	0	1	1	1	1
David Rowson	35	35	30	0	5	1	2	0
Simon Storey	32	31	26	1	4	0	2	1
Chris Turner	2	1	0	1	1	0	1	0
Marc Twaddle	30	28	24	2	3	0	3	1

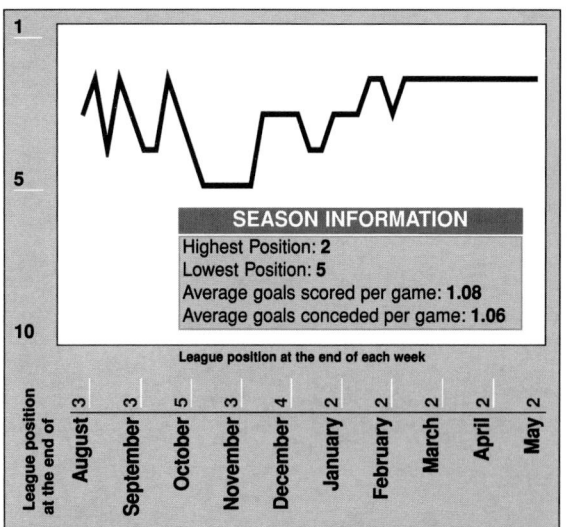

SEASON INFORMATION
Highest Position: **2**
Lowest Position: **5**
Average goals scored per game: **1.08**
Average goals conceded per game: **1.06**

League position at the end of each week

LONGEST SEQUENCES

Wins (01/11/08–22/11/08)	3	Undefeated home (20/09/08–13/12/08)	6
Losses (on two occasions)	2	Undefeated away (03/01/09–18/04/09)	8
Draws (on two occasions)	2	Without scoring (on two occasions)	3
Undefeated (on two occasions)	4	Without conceding (on four occasions)	2
Without win (27/09/08–25/10/08)	4	Scoring (24/01/09–28/02/09)	5

CARDS RECEIVED

45 4

QUICK-FIRE GOALS

From the start of a match
John Robertson (v St Johnstone) 6:00

By a substitute after coming on
Stephen McKeown (v Dunfermline) 8:00

GOALS SCORED/CONCEDED PER FIVE-MINUTE INTERVALS

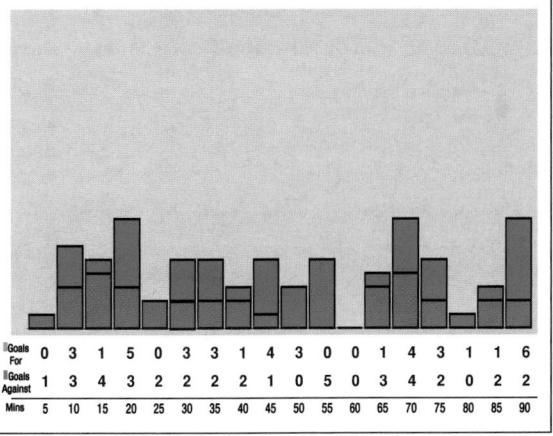

Goals For	0	3	1	5	0	3	3	1	4	3	0	0	1	4	3	1	1	6
Goals Against	1	3	4	3	2	2	2	2	1	0	5	0	3	4	2	0	2	2
Mins	5	10	15	20	25	30	35	40	45	50	55	60	65	70	75	80	85	90

QUEEN OF THE SOUTH

ASIDE from their short stint in the UEFA Cup, Queen of the South's season will be remembered for the scoring exploits of the impressive Stephen Dobbie.

The ex-Hibernian forward will leave the Doonhamers in the summer after agreeing a free transfer to Swansea, but can go with his head held high after finishing the season as the Irn-Bru First Division's top scorer with 24 goals.

The men from Palmerston Park went on a seven-game unbeaten run at the start of the campaign, topping the table after 10 matches. However, despite their free scoring – with a 6–1 mauling of Livingston and a 7–1 victory over Clyde – results were mixed from that point on.

While there is no shame in a fifth-place finish, the season was a reality check after they reached the Homecoming Scottish Cup final in 2007/08.

CLUB SUMMARY

FORMED	1919
MANAGER	Gordon Chisholm
GROUND	Palmerston Park
CAPACITY	6,412
NICKNAME	The Doonhammers
WEBSITE	www.qosfc.co.uk

The New
Football Pools
PLAYER OF THE SEASON

Stephen Dobbie

OVERALL
P	W	D	L	F	A	GD
43	14	11	18	69	63	6

IRN-BRU FIRST DIVISION
Pos	P	W	D	L	F	A	GD	Pts
5	36	12	11	13	57	50	7	47

HOME
Pos	P	W	D	L	F	A	GD	Pts
7	18	6	6	6	37	28	9	24

AWAY
Pos	P	W	D	L	F	A	GD	Pts
4	18	6	5	7	20	22	-2	23

CUP PROGRESS DETAILS
Competition	Round reached	Knocked out by
Co-op Insurance Cup	R3	Falkirk
Scottish Cup	R4	Falkirk
Challenge Cup	QF	Morton
UEFA Cup	Qual2	FC Nordsjaelland

BIGGEST WIN (ALL COMPS)
25/04/09 7–1 v Clyde **SC1**

BIGGEST DEFEAT (ALL COMPS)
08/11/08 1–4 v Morton **SC1**

ATTENDANCE RECORD
High	Low	Average
3,339	2,029	2,720
v Dundee (30/08/2008)	v Ross Cnty (04/04/2009)	

RESULTS 2008/09

July
26th ● Berwick ....a W 1-5 — **Att:** 655 — **Scorers:** Barr, Kean[2], O'Connor[2]. **Booked:** Barr

August
2nd ● Airdrie Utd ....h D 0–0 — **Att:** 2,914 — **Dismissed:** Thomson
9th ● Dunfermline .....h L 2–1 — **Att:** 2,995 — **Scorers:** Kean. **Booked:** Barr, Arbuckle. **Dismissed:** Aitken
14th ● FC Nordsjaelland h L 1–2 — **Att:** 4,406 — **Scorers:** O'Connor. **Booked:** Reid, O'Connor
17th ● Partick ....h W 2–0 — **Att:** 3,272 — **Scorers:** Dobbie, Tosh. **Booked:** Barr
20th ● Dunfermline .....a W 0–2 — **Att:** 1,371 — **Scorers:** Kean, O'Connor. **Booked:** Thomson
26th ● FC Nordsjaelland a L 2–1 — **Att:** 3,452 — **Scorers:** Harris. **Booked:** Adams
30th ● Dundee ....h W 3–1 — **Att:** 3,339 — **Scorers:** Barr, Dobbie[2]. **Booked:** Parratt

September
3rd ● Ross County ....h W 1–0 — **Att:** 2,525 — **Scorers:** Weatherston. **Booked:** Barr
7th ● Morton ....h L 0–2 — **Att:** 2,991 — **Booked:** Robertson, McQuilken
13th ● Morton ....a D 0–0 — **Att:** 2,235 — **Booked:** Sives, Bell, Tosh, Barr, McGowan. **Dismissed:** Tosh
20th ● St Johnstone ...h D 2–2 — **Att:** 2,831 — **Scorers:** Dobbie, Thomson. **Booked:** Sives
23rd ● Falkirk ....h L 2–1 — **Att:** 2,058 — **Scorers:** Kean. **Booked:** Barr, Thomson
27th ● Clyde ....a W 0–2 — **Att:** 1,095 — **Scorers:** Arbuckle, Dobbie

October
4th ● Livingston...........h W 6–1 — **Att:** 3,266 — **Scorers:** Burns, Dobbie[2], McQuilken, Weatherston[2]
18th ● Airdrie Utd ......a L 2–0 — **Att:** 1,524 — **Booked:** Tosh
25th ● Ross County ....a W 0–2 — **Att:** 2,232 — **Scorers:** Dobbie, McGowan. **Booked:** Simmons, McQuilken

November
1st ● Partick ....a L 2–0 — **Att:** 2,971 — **Booked:** Sives, Thomson, Barr. **Dismissed:** Thomson
8th ● Morton ....h L 1–4 — **Att:** 2,944 — **Scorers:** O'Connor. **Booked:** Aitken, McQuilken, Tosh
15th ● Dundee ....a L 2–0 — **Att:** 3,630 — **Booked:** MacFarlane
22nd ● Clyde ....h L 0–2 — **Att:** 2,324

December
6th ● St Johnstone ...a D 0–0 — **Att:** 3,068 — **Booked:** Burns, Aitken, Thomson
13th ● Dunfermline .....h L 1–2 — **Att:** 2,312 — **Scorers:** McQuilken. **Booked:** Simmons
20th ● Livingston...........a L 2–0 — **Att:** 1,492 — **Booked:** Barr, Kinniburgh, Reid. **Dismissed:** Barr
27th ● Dundee ....h L 0–1 — **Att:** 2,616 — **Booked:** Reid

January
3rd ● Morton ....a D 2–2 — **Att:** 2,742 — **Scorers:** Arbuckle, Wilson. **Booked:** McQuilken, Harris, MacFarlane
10th ● Falkirk ....a L 4–2 — **Att:** 3,423 — **Scorers:** Harris, Wilson. **Booked:** Barr, Wilson, Harris
17th ● Ross County ....a L 1–0 — **Att:** 2,323 — **Booked:** Tosh, MacFarlane
24th ● Partick ....h D 2–2 — **Att:** 2,811 — **Scorers:** Dobbie, Tosh.
      Booked: Wilson, Wilson, Lancaster, Lancaster
31st ● Dunfermline .....a W 0–2 — **Att:** 2,847 — **Scorers:** Burns, Dobbie.
      Booked: MacFarlane, Harris, Barr, Lancaster

February
14th ● Airdrie Utd ....h W 4–0 — **Att:** 2,443 — **Scorers:** Dobbie[2], Harris, Weatherston. **Booked:** O'Connor
21st ● St Johnstone ...h D 3–3 — **Att:** 2,857 — **Scorers:** Burns, Dobbie, Wilson. **Booked:** Barr, McQuilken
28th ● Clyde ....a D 1–1 — **Att:** 1,151 — **Scorers:** Tosh. **Booked:** Burns

March
7th ● Morton ....h D 1–1 — **Att:** 2,643 — **Scorers:** Lancaster. **Booked:** Robertson, Lancaster
10th ● Dundee ....a W 2–3 — **Att:** 3,757 — **Scorers:** Dobbie, Lancaster, Wilson
14th ● Airdrie Utd ....a L 2–0 — **Att:** 1,320 — **Booked:** Tosh, Harris
21st ● Livingston...........h D 3–3 — **Att:** 2,487 — **Scorers:** Dobbie[2], Wilson

April
4th ● Ross County ....h L 1–2 — **Att:** 2,029 — **Scorers:** Dobbie. **Booked:** Tosh
11th ● Partick ....a W 0–2 — **Att:** 2,830 — **Scorers:** Dobbie, Tosh. **Booked:** Burns
19th ● St Johnstone ....a W 2–3 — **Att:** 3,294 — **Scorers:** Dobbie[2], Kean
25th ● Clyde ....h W 7–1 — **Att:** 2,601 — **Scorers:** Dobbie[4], Harris, Kean, Tosh. **Booked:** Scally, Tosh

May
2nd ● Dunfermline .....h L 0–3 — **Att:** 2,750 — **Booked:** Lancaster, Wilson. **Dismissed:** Thomson
9th ● Livingston...........a D 2–2 — **Att:** 1,652 — **Scorers:** McLaughlan, Tosh

● Irn-Bru First Division ● UEFA Cup ● Scottish FA Cup ● Scottish League Cup ● Scottish Challenge Cup

actim

FIRST DIVISION GOALKEEPER STATS

Player	Appearances	Match starts	Completed matches	Sub appearances	Subbed off	Clean sheets	Yellow cards	Red cards
Cameron Bell	15	15	15	0	0	6	1	0
Bryn Halliwell	4	4	4	0	0	1	0	0
Lee Robinson	17	17	17	0	0	3	0	0

FIRST DIVISION OUTFIELD PLAYER STATS

Player	Appearances	Match starts	Completed matches	Substitute appearances	Subbed off	Goals scored	Yellow cards	Red cards
Jamie Adams	3	2	1	1	1	0	0	0
Andrew Aitken	13	9	7	4	1	0	2	1
Gary Arbuckle	8	5	2	3	3	2	1	0
Craig Barr	24	22	19	2	2	1	8	1
Paul Burns	29	28	25	1	3	3	3	0
Stephen Dobbie	33	30	20	3	10	24	0	0
Robert Harris	21	21	15	0	6	2	3	0
Stewart Kean	31	19	14	12	5	3	0	0
Stephen Kinniburgh	2	2	0	0	2	0	1	0
Martyn Lancaster	15	15	13	0	2	2	5	0
Neil MacFarlane	33	26	20	7	6	0	4	0
Ryan McCann	12	8	7	4	1	0	0	0
Michael McGowan	13	8	5	5	3	1	1	0
Gerry McLaughlan	1	1	1	0	0	1	0	0
Jamie McQuilken	34	24	18	10	6	2	4	0
Sean O'Connor	28	22	11	6	11	1	1	0
Tom Parratt	9	9	7	0	2	0	1	0
Craig Reid	15	12	10	3	2	0	2	0
Scott Robertson	10	5	2	5	3	0	1	0
Lee Robinson	17	17	17	0	0	0	0	0
Neil Scally	11	10	9	1	4	0	1	0
Stephen Simmons	10	6	3	4	3	0	2	0
Craig Sives	10	10	10	0	0	0	3	0
Jim Thomson	24	22	16	2	3	1	2	3
Steven Tosh	29	26	18	3	7	6	7	1
David Weatherston	20	4	1	16	3	4	0	0
Barry Wilson	16	14	6	2	8	4	3	0

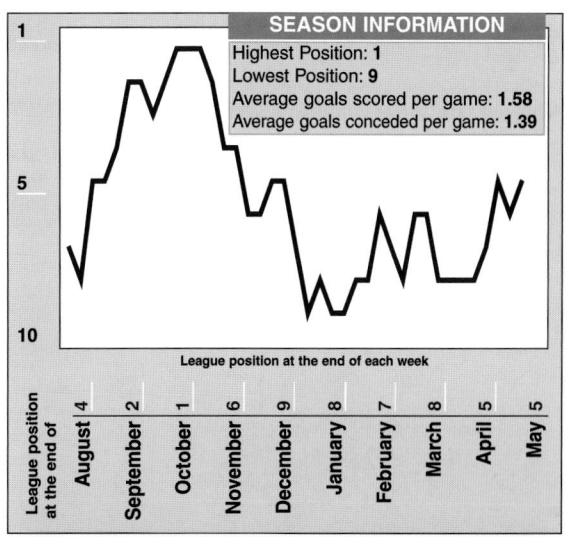

SEASON INFORMATION

Highest Position: **1**
Lowest Position: **9**
Average goals scored per game: **1.58**
Average goals conceded per game: **1.39**

League position at the end of each week

League position at the end of

August 4 — September 2 — October 1 — November 6 — December 9 — January 8 — February 7 — March 8 — April 5 — May 5

LONGEST SEQUENCES

Wins (on three occasions)	3	Undefeated home (02/08/08-04/10/08)	6
Losses (01/11/08-22/11/08)	4	Undefeated away (31/01/09-10/03/09)	3
Draws (21/02/09-07/03/09)	3	Without scoring (15/11/08-06/12/08)	3
Undefeated (on two occasions)	7	Without conceding (on two occasions)	2
Without win (01/11/08-24/01/09)	11	Scoring (24/01/09-10/03/09)	7

CARDS RECEIVED

56   **6**

QUICK-FIRE GOALS

From the start of a match
Stephen Dobbie (v Livingston) 3:00

By a substitute after coming on
Steven Tosh (v Partick) 1:00

GOALS SCORED/CONCEDED PER FIVE-MINUTE INTERVALS

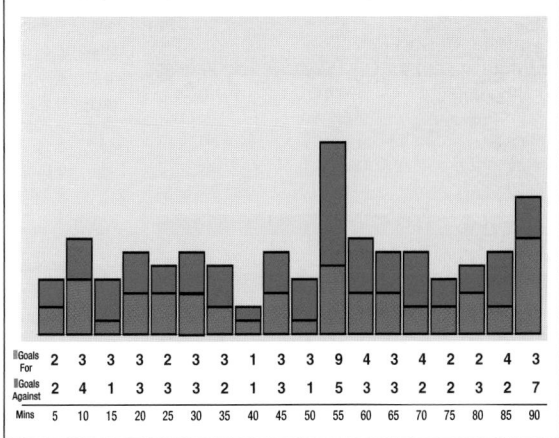

Goals For	2	3	3	2	2	3	3	1	3	3	9	4	3	4	2	2	4	3
Goals Against	2	4	1	3	3	3	2	1	3	1	5	3	3	2	2	3	2	7
Mins	5	10	15	20	25	30	35	40	45	50	55	60	65	70	75	80	85	90

ROSS COUNTY

ROSS COUNTY retained their Irn-Bru First Division status on the final day of the season with an impressive 2–0 win over Greenock Morton at Cappielow. Goals from Craig Brittain and Sean Higgins ensured the Highland club left Airdrie facing a relegation play-off.

County endured a fraught and often controversial season after having won promotion from the Second Division in 2007/08, but manager Derek Adams – a former player at the club – can look to several positives.

Record books will show that County finished the campaign with 47 points, the same as Queen of the South, Morton and Livingston. The Dingwall club also reached the Challenge Cup final, only to lose to Airdrie after extra-time and penalties, while their reserves reached the final of the SFL Reserve Cup.

CLUB SUMMARY

FORMED	1929
MANAGER	Derek Adams
GROUND	Victoria Park
CAPACITY	6,310
NICKNAME	The Staggies
WEB	www.rosscountyfootballclub.co.uk

The New Football Pools PLAYER OF THE SEASON — **Mark McCulloch**

OVERALL

P	W	D	L	F	A	GD
45	18	10	17	59	58	1

IRN-BRU FIRST DIVISION

Pos	P	W	D	L	F	A	GD	Pts
8	36	13	8	15	42	46	-4	47

HOME

Pos	P	W	D	L	F	A	GD	Pts
8	18	6	6	6	22	22	0	24

AWAY

Pos	P	W	D	L	F	A	GD	Pts
5	18	7	2	9	20	24	-4	23

CUP PROGRESS DETAILS

Competition	Round reached	Knocked out by
Co-op Insurance Cup	R1	Airdrie Utd
Scottish Cup	R4	Hamilton
Challenge Cup	Final	Airdrie Utd

BIGGEST WIN (ALL COMPS)

12/10/08 4–1 v Morton **SLCCSF**

BIGGEST DEFEAT (ALL COMPS)

13/12/08 1–4 v Livingston **SC1**

ATTENDANCE RECORD

High	Low	Average
3,444	1,625	2,279
v Dundee (02/08/2008)	v Partick (25/11/2008)	

RESULTS 2008/09

July
26th ● St Johnstone ....h W 2–1 **Att:** 1,308 — **Scorers:** Higgins, Winters. **Booked:** Lawson, Higgins, Hart

August
2nd ● Dundee ....h L 1–2 **Att:** 3,444 — **Scorers:** Daal. **Booked:** Brittain
5th ● Airdrie Utd ......h L 2–3 **Att:** 869 — **Scorers:** Daal, Hart. **Booked:** Lawson. (AET)
9th ● Livingston.........a L 2–0 **Att:** 1,725 — **Booked:** Higgins, Bullock, Watt, Hart, Dowie, Lawson, Scott. **Dismissed:** Craig, Higgins
12th ● Raith ....a W 1–2 **Att:** 1,080 — **Scorers:** Keddie². **Booked:** Strachan
16th ● Clyde ....a D 2–2 **Att:** 973 — **Scorers:** Craig, Morrison. **Booked:** A. Keddie
30th ● Partick ....a W 0–1 **Att:** 2,945 — **Scorers:** Craig. **Booked:** M. McCulloch, Brittain

September
3rd ● Queen of South a L 1–0 **Att:** 2,525 — **Booked:** Craig, Keddie, Daal
7th ● Clyde ....h W 0–1 **Att:** 756 — **Scorers:** Craig
13th ● St Johnstone ....h L 1–2 **Att:** 2,474 — **Scorers:** Brittain. **Booked:** Hart, Higgins, Dowie
20th ● Dunfermline .....a L 3–1 **Att:** 2,894 — **Scorers:** Craig. **Booked:** Hart, Scott. **Dismissed:** Hart
27th ● Airdrie Utd ......h W 2–0 **Att:** 2,259 — **Scorers:** Craig, Smyth OG. **Booked:** Daal, Boyd

October
4th ● Morton ....h W 3–0 **Att:** 2,361 — **Scorers:** Craig, Hart, Higgins. **Booked:** McCulloch
12th ● Morton ....h W 4–1 **Att:** 1,334 — **Scorers:** Craig, Daal², Dowie
18th ● Dundee ....a W 1–2 **Att:** 3,228 — **Scorers:** Craig, Dowie. **Booked:** Brittain, Boyd
25th ● Queen of South h L 0–2 **Att:** 2,232

November
1st ● Clyde ....h W 3–0 **Att:** 2,205 — **Scorers:** Gardyne, Hart, Higgins. **Booked:** Keddie, Hart
8th ● St Johnstone ....a L 2–1 **Att:** 2,714 — **Scorers:** McCulloch. **Booked:** Keddie
16th ● Airdrie Utd ......n D 2–2 **Att:** 4,091 — **Scorers:** Higgins, Nixon OG. **Booked:** Keddie, Boyd, Higgins (Lost 2–3 on pens)
22nd ● Airdrie Utd ......a W 0–2 **Att:** 939 — **Scorers:** Brittain, Higgins. **Booked:** Boyd, Daal, Scott
25th ● Partick ....h W 1–0 **Att:** 1,625 — **Booked:** Daal. **Booked:** Strachan, Brittain, McCulloch, Daal
29th ● Dumbarton .....h D 2–2 **Att:** 1,200 — **Scorers:** Higgins². **Booked:** Watt, Bullock, Dowie. **Dismissed:** Daal

December
13th ● Livingston.........h L 1–4 **Att:** 2,180 — **Scorers:** McCulloch. **Booked:** Strachan
15th ● Dumbarton .....a W 1–2 **Att:** 557 — **Scorers:** Brittain, Hart. **Booked:** McCulloch
20th ● Morton ....a L 2–1 **Att:** 1,779 — **Scorers:** Morrison. **Booked:** Craig, Bullock, Keddie, Watt
27th ● Partick ....a W 0–2 **Att:** 2,465 — **Scorers:** Higgins²

January
10th ● Hamilton..........h L 0–1 **Att:** 1,503 — **Booked:** Watt, Brittain, Higgins, Stewart
17th ● Queen of South h W 1–0 **Att:** 2,323 — **Scorers:** Daal. **Booked:** Boyd
24th ● Clyde ....a L 2–0 **Att:** 776 — **Booked:** Higgins
31st ● Livingston.........a L 4–2 **Att:** 1,374 — **Scorers:** Hart, Higgins. **Booked:** Higgins

February
7th ● St Johnstone ....h D 2–2 **Att:** 2,240 — **Scorers:** Craig, McCulloch. **Booked:** Daal. **Dismissed:** Boyd
21st ● Dunfermline .....a W 1–2 **Att:** 3,325 — **Scorers:** Brewster, Higgins
28th ● Airdrie Utd ......h D 0–0 **Att:** 2,290

March
7th ● St Johnstone ....a D 0–0 **Att:** 2,727 — **Booked:** Higgins, Lawson, Craig, Corrigan
10th ● Partick ....h L 0–2 **Att:** 2,017 — **Booked:** Watt, Corrigan
14th ● Dundee ....a L 2–0 **Att:** 3,381
21st ● Morton ....h D 1–1 **Att:** 2,236 — **Scorers:** Keddie
24th ● Dunfermline .....h W 2–1 **Att:** 1,782 — **Scorers:** Brewster, Brittain. **Booked:** Watt, Boyd, Brittain
28th ● Dundee ....h D 1–1 **Att:** 2,296 — **Scorers:** Higgins. **Booked:** Craig, Hart, Keddie

April
4th ● Queen of South a W 1–2 **Att:** 2,029 — **Scorers:** Brewster, Higgins. **Booked:** Keddie, Boyd, Brewster
11th ● Clyde ....h D 0–0 **Att:** 2,078 — **Booked:** McCulloch. **Dismissed:** Brittain
18th ● Dunfermline .....h L 1–3 **Att:** 2,413 — **Scorers:** Craig
25th ● Airdrie Utd ......a L 1–0 **Att:** 927 — **Booked:** Golabek, Watt

May
2nd ● Livingston.........h D 2–2 **Att:** 2,567 — **Scorers:** Craig². **Booked:** Watt. **Dismissed:** Keddie
9th ● Morton ....a W 0–2 **Att:** 1,956 — **Scorers:** Brittain, Higgins. **Booked:** Higgins

● Irn-Bru First Division ● Scottish FA Cup ● Scottish League Cup ● Scottish Challenge Cup

actim

FIRST DIVISION GOALKEEPER STATS

Player	Appearances	Match starts	Completed matches	Sub appearances	Subbed off	Clean sheets	Yellow cards	Red cards
Tony Bullock	16	16	16	0	0	6	2	0
Joe Malin	8	7	7	1	0	2	0	0
Derek Soutar	13	13	12	0	1	6	0	0

FIRST DIVISION OUTFIELD PLAYER STATS

Player	Appearances	Match starts	Completed matches	Substitute appearances	Subbed off	Goals scored	Yellow cards	Red cards
Scott Boyd	28	28	27	0	0	0	6	1
Craig Brewster	10	10	3	0	7	3	1	0
Richard Brittain	30	30	25	0	4	4	5	1
Martyn Corrigan	10	10	9	0	1	0	2	0
Steven Craig	31	26	16	5	9	10	4	1
Dyron Daal	28	16	6	12	10	3	5	0
Andrew Dowie	29	28	26	1	2	1	2	0
Michael Gardyne	27	9	4	18	5	1	0	0
Stuart Golabek	15	14	14	1	0	0	1	0
Richard Hart	33	24	15	9	8	3	5	1
Sean Higgins	31	23	8	8	14	10	6	1
Alex Keddie	29	25	22	4	2	1	7	1
Paul Lawson	20	18	8	2	10	0	2	0
Mark McCulloch	35	35	35	0	0	3	4	0
Scott Morrison	15	7	5	8	2	2	0	0
Martin Scott	25	16	7	9	9	0	3	0
Dene Shields	1	0	0	1	0	0	0	0
John Stewart	9	3	1	6	2	0	0	0
Adam Strachan	24	12	7	12	5	0	2	0
Steven Watt	24	23	17	1	6	0	6	0
David Winters	6	3	0	3	3	0	0	0

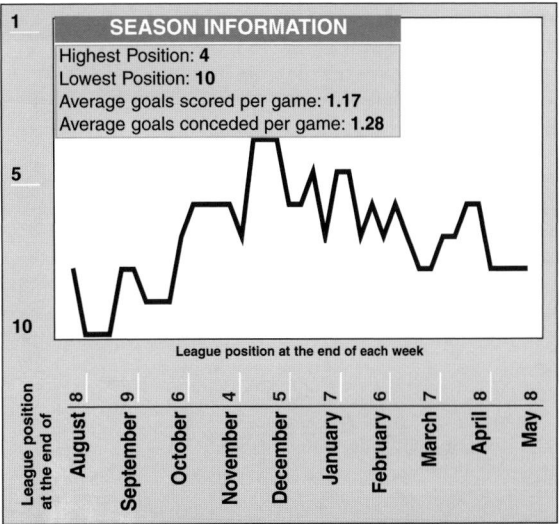

SEASON INFORMATION

Highest Position: **4**
Lowest Position: **10**
Average goals scored per game: **1.17**
Average goals conceded per game: **1.28**

League position at the end of each week

League position at the end of: August 8, September 9, October 6, November 4, December 5, January 7, February 6, March 7, April 8, May 8

LONGEST SEQUENCES

Wins (27/09/08–18/10/08)	3	Undefeated home (21/03/09–11/04/09)	4
Losses (03/09/08–20/09/08)	3	Undefeated away (on two occasions)	2
Draws (28/02/09–07/03/09)	2	Without scoring (28/02/09–14/03/09)	4
Undefeated (21/03/09–11/04/09)	5	Without conceding (on four occasions)	2
Without win (28/02/09–21/03/09)	5	Scoring (01/11/08–17/01/09)	8

CARDS RECEIVED

63 **6**

QUICK-FIRE GOALS

From the start of a match
Sean Higgins (v Queen of South) 5:00

By a substitute after coming on
Sean Higgins (v Morton) 12:00

GOALS SCORED/CONCEDED PER FIVE-MINUTE INTERVALS

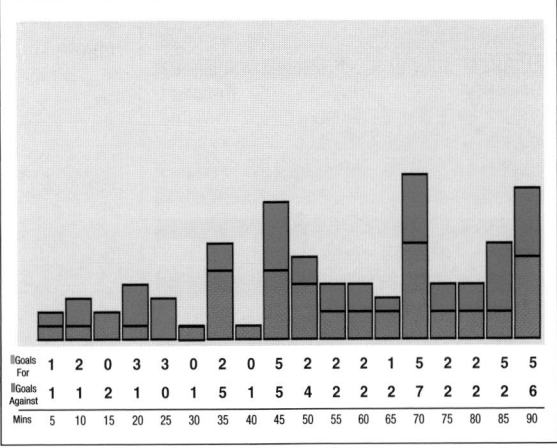

Goals For	1	2	0	3	3	0	2	0	5	2	2	2	1	5	2	2	5	5
Goals Against	1	1	2	1	0	1	5	1	5	4	2	2	7	2	2	2	2	6
Mins	5	10	15	20	25	30	35	40	45	50	55	60	65	70	75	80	85	90

ST JOHNSTONE

ST JOHNSTONE wrapped up the Irn-Bru First Division title with a game to spare, ending their seven-year exile from the elite of the Scottish game.

Derek McInnes' men shook off a poor start to the season to lead the table from the start of November, breaking a 125-year club record by going 22 games unbeaten in the League.

However, a large number of draws in that sequence meant that they were never able to pull clear of their rivals, while a run of just two wins in six games in March and April allowed Partick to stay in touch at the top. Fortunately for the Saints, they did eventually rediscover their form, while Partick ran out of steam.

Steven Milne's goals proved crucial in the league run-in, the former Dundee striker maintaining his fine record since joining the club from Plymouth in 2005.

CLUB SUMMARY

FORMED	1884
MANAGER	Derek McInnes
GROUND	McDiarmid Park
CAPACITY	10,673
NICKNAME	The Saints
WEBSITE	www.stjohnstone.co.uk

The New Football Pools PLAYER OF THE SEASON

Kevin Rutkiewicz

OVERALL

P	W	D	L	F	A	GD
40	18	14	8	62	42	20

IRN-BRU FIRST DIVISION

Pos	P	W	D	L	F	A	GD	Pts
1	36	17	14	5	55	35	20	65

HOME

Pos	P	W	D	L	F	A	GD	Pts
1	18	10	5	3	26	13	13	35

AWAY

Pos	P	W	D	L	F	A	GD	Pts
2	18	7	9	2	29	22	7	30

CUP PROGRESS DETAILS

Competition	Round reached	Knocked out by
Co-op Insurance Cup	R2	Livingston
Scottish Cup	R4	Rangers
Challenge Cup	R1	Ross County

BIGGEST WIN (ALL COMPS)

05/08/08 5–1 v Stenhousemuir **SLC1**

BIGGEST DEFEAT (ALL COMPS)

23/08/08 0–4 v Partick **SC1**

ATTENDANCE RECORD

High	Low	Average
7,238	2,259	3,502
v Dundee (28/02/2009)	v Airdrie Utd (04/10/2008)	

RESULTS 2008/09

July
26th	● Ross County	....a	L 2–1	**Att:** 1,308 — **Scorers:** Samuel. **Booked:** Craig, McCaffrey

August
2nd	● Livingston	..........h	W 2–0	**Att:** 2,692 — **Scorers:** MacDonald, Sheerin. **Booked:** Millar. **Dismissed:** Craig
5th	● Stenhousemuir	..a	W 1–5	**Att:** 613 — **Scorers:** Hardie, Holmes[2], Milne, Sheerin
9th	● Morton	..........a	D 2–2	**Att:** 2,820 — **Scorers:** Milne, Swankie. **Booked:** Hardie
16th	● Dunfermline	......h	L 0–3	**Att:** 3,697
23rd	● Partick	..........a	L 4–0	**Att:** 2,863 — **Booked:** MacDonald, McCaffrey, Millar, Hardie
26th	● Livingston	..........a	L 2–1	**Att:** 979 — **Scorers:** Craig. **Booked:** Jackson, Craig, Anderson (AET)
30th	● Clyde	................h	L 2–3	**Att:** 2,412 — **Scorers:** Holmes, McCaffrey. **Booked:** McCaffrey, Craig

September
13th	● Ross County	....a	W 1–2	**Att:** 2,474 — **Scorers:** Samuel[2]. **Booked:** McCaffrey, Irvine, Anderson
20th	● Queen of South	a	D 2–2	**Att:** 2,831 — **Scorers:** Holmes, Thomson OG. **Booked:** Rutkiewicz, Hardie
27th	● Dundee	...........h	W 2–0	**Att:** 4,307 — **Scorers:** Milne, Sheerin.
				Booked: Rutkiewicz, Samuel, Millar, Swankie, McCaffrey

October
4th	● Airdrie Utd	........h	W 3–1	**Att:** 2,259 — **Scorers:** Milne[2], Swankie. **Booked:** McKoy
18th	● Livingston	..........a	W 0–1	**Att:** 2,169 — **Scorers:** Milne. **Booked:** Rutkiewicz, Hardie
25th	● Partick	..............h	W 3–0	**Att:** 2,772 — **Scorers:** Craig, McCaffrey, Milne.
				Booked: Hardie, Holmes, Rutkiewicz

November
1st	● Dunfermline	......a	W 1–2	**Att:** 4,998 — **Scorers:** Craig, Hardie. **Booked:** McCaffrey, Irvine
8th	● Ross County	....h	W 2–1	**Att:** 2,714 — **Scorers:** Hardie, Samuel. **Booked:** Hardie
15th	● Clyde	................a	D 2–2	**Att:** 1,417 — **Scorers:** Craig, Rutkiewicz. **Booked:** Craig, Hardie, Anderson
29th	● Dundee	...........a	D 1–1	**Att:** 6,537 — **Scorers:** Milne. **Booked:** Millar, Moon

December
6th	● Queen of South	h	D 0–0	**Att:** 3,068 — **Booked:** Morris
13th	● Morton	..............h	W 1–0	**Att:** 2,699 — **Scorers:** Rutkiewicz. **Booked:** McCaffrey
20th	● Airdrie Utd	........h	D 1–1	**Att:** 1,175 — **Scorers:** Craig
27th	● Clyde	................h	W 1–0	**Att:** 3,291 — **Scorers:** Milne

January
13th	● Rangers	...........h	L 0–2	**Att:** 7,746 — **Booked:** Millar, Rutkiewicz
17th	● Partick	..............a	D 0–0	**Att:** 3,353 — **Booked:** Sheerin, Craig, Irvine, McCaffrey
31st	● Morton	..............a	D 0–0	**Att:** 2,810

February
7th	● Ross County	....a	D 2–2	**Att:** 2,240 — **Scorers:** Holmes, McCaffrey. **Booked:** Gartland, Millar, Holmes
14th	● Livingston	..........h	W 1–0	**Att:** 2,752 — **Scorers:** Samuel
21st	● Queen of South	a	D 3–3	**Att:** 2,857 — **Scorers:** Holmes, Millar, Rutkiewicz. **Booked:** Sheerin
28th	● Dundee	...........h	D 0–0	**Att:** 7,238

March
7th	● Ross County	....h	D 0–0	**Att:** 2,727
10th	● Clyde	................a	W 1–3	**Att:** 1,159 — **Scorers:** Milne[2], Swankie. **Booked:** Moon, Millar
14th	● Livingston	..........a	L 1–0	**Att:** 1,882 — **Booked:** Rutkiewicz
21st	● Airdrie Utd	........h	W 3–0	**Att:** 2,561 — **Scorers:** Samuel[2], Sheerin

April
4th	● Partick	..............h	D 1–1	**Att:** 4,909 — **Scorers:** Milne
7th	● Dunfermline	......h	D 0–0	**Att:** 3,199
11th	● Dunfermline	......a	W 1–3	**Att:** 3,791 — **Scorers:** Craig, Hardie, Irvine. **Booked:** Gartland, Hardie
19th	● Queen of South	h	L 2–3	**Att:** 3,294 — **Scorers:** Holmes, Millar. **Booked:** Hardie
25th	● Dundee	...........a	W 0–1	**Att:** 6,305 — **Scorers:** Milne. **Booked:** Hardie, Irvine, Barrett

May
2nd	● Morton	..............h	W 3–1	**Att:** 6,453 — **Scorers:** Hardie, Milne[2]. **Booked:** McCaffrey
11th	● Airdrie Utd	........a	W 0–4	**Att:** 633 — **Scorers:** Anderson, Barrett, May, Swankie

● Irn-Bru First Division ● Scottish FA Cup ● Scottish League Cup ● Scottish Challenge Cup

FIRST DIVISION GOALKEEPER STATS

Player	Appearances	Match starts	Completed matches	Sub appearances	Subbed off	Clean sheets	Yellow cards	Red cards
Alan Main	32	32	32	0	0	14	0	0
Euan McLean	4	4	4	0	0	2	0	0

FIRST DIVISION OUTFIELD PLAYER STATS

Player	Appearances	Match starts	Completed matches	Substitute appearances	Subbed off	Goals scored	Yellow cards	Red cards
Steven Anderson	15	11	9	4	2	1	2	0
Graham Barrett	9	4	1	5	3	1	1	0
Richie Byrne	5	5	3	0	2	0	0	0
Liam Craig	34	31	27	3	3	5	3	1
Steven Doris	2	1	1	1	0	0	0	0
Graham Gartland	7	7	5	0	2	0	2	0
Paul Hanlon	2	2	2	0	0	0	0	0
Martin Hardie	24	20	10	4	10	4	10	0
Derek Holmes	35	22	12	13	10	5	2	0
Gary Irvine	35	34	34	1	0	1	4	0
Andrew Jackson	10	5	0	5	5	0	0	0
Kevin James	4	4	4	0	0	0	0	0
Jonathon Lindisay	1	1	1	0	0	0	0	0
Peter MacDonald	12	2	0	10	2	1	1	0
Steve May	1	0	0	1	0	1	0	0
Stuart McCaffrey	26	25	24	1	1	3	8	0
Nicholas McKoy	5	2	0	3	2	0	1	0
Chris Millar	34	30	25	4	5	2	6	0
Steven Milne	32	26	16	6	10	14	0	0
Kevin Moon	22	12	8	10	4	0	2	0
Alan Morgan	4	2	0	2	2	0	0	0
Jody Morris	14	10	8	4	2	0	1	0
Stephen Reynolds	1	1	0	0	1	0	0	0
Kevin Rutkiewicz	34	34	33	0	1	3	5	0
Collin Samuel	28	20	9	8	11	6	1	0
Paul Sheerin	34	29	22	5	7	3	2	0
Daniel Smith	3	3	3	0	0	0	0	0
Gavin Swankie	27	17	1	10	16	4	1	0
David Weatherston	1	0	0	1	0	0	0	0

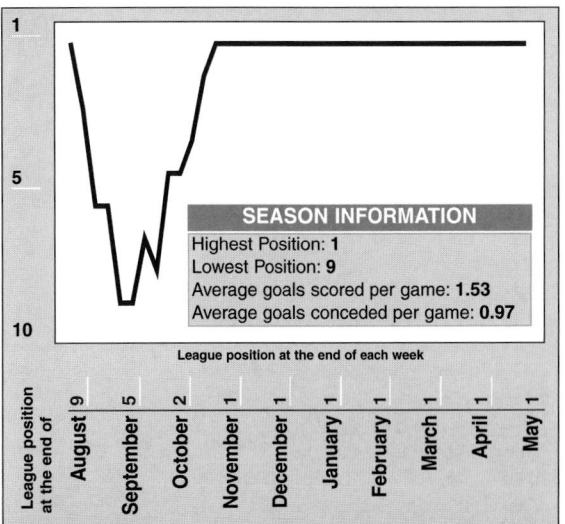

League position at the end of each week

SEASON INFORMATION
Highest Position: **1**
Lowest Position: **9**
Average goals scored per game: **1.53**
Average goals conceded per game: **0.97**

LONGEST SEQUENCES

Wins (27/09/08–08/11/08)	6	Undefeated home (27/09/08–07/04/09)	13
Losses (16/08/08–30/08/08)	3	Undefeated away (13/09/08–10/03/09)	12
Draws (on three occasions)	3	Without scoring (on three occasions)	2
Undefeated (13/09/08–10/03/09)	22	Without conceding (27/12/08–31/01/09)	3
Without win (09/08/08–30/08/08)	4	Scoring (30/08/08–29/11/08)	11

CARDS RECEIVED

52 **1**

QUICK-FIRE GOALS

From the start of a match
Steven Milne (v Dundee) 2:00

By a substitute after coming on
Collin Samuel (v Ross County) 2:00

GOALS SCORED/CONCEDED PER FIVE-MINUTE INTERVALS

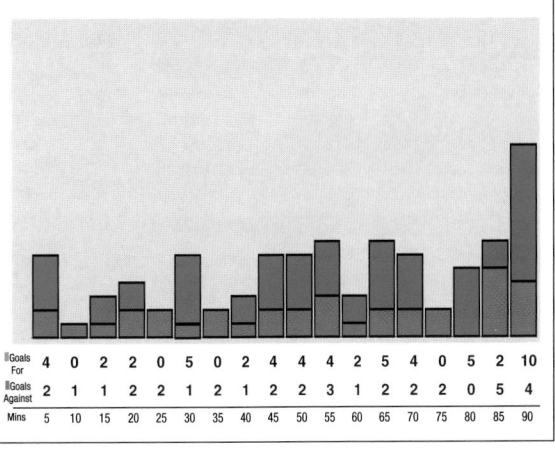

Goals For	4	0	2	0	5	0	2	4	4	4	2	5	4	0	5	2	10
Goals Against	2	1	1	2	2	1	2	1	2	2	3	1	2	2	2	0	5	4
Mins	5	10	15	20	25	30	35	40	45	50	55	60	65	70	75	80	85	90

ALLOA took a step backwards in the Irn-Bru Second Division after the previous season's fourth-place finish, having to make do with eighth this time round.

Allan Maitland's team suffered a poor start, recording only two wins and a draw in their first 10 games which left them mingling with fellow-strugglers Arbroath at the bottom of the table.

Results improved somewhat, but remained unspectacular and, by the end of February, the Wasps had eked their way up the table to eighth place.

Alloa held onto that position, with Stranraer unable to avoid relegation and Queen's Park slipping down to ninth place. Brown 'Bomber' Ferguson had another superb year for the Wasps collecting not only the Player of the Year award, but also the Young Supporters' Club trophy.

CLUB SUMMARY

FORMED	1878
MANAGER	Allan Maitland
GROUND	Recreation Park
CAPACITY	3,100
NICKNAME	The Wasps
WEBSITE	www.alloaathletic.co.uk

The New Football Pools PLAYER OF THE SEASON — **Brown Ferguson**

OVERALL

P	W	D	L	F	A	GD
43	14	9	20	54	66	-12

IRN-BRU SECOND DIVISION

Pos	P	W	D	L	F	A	GD	Pts
8	36	11	8	17	47	59	-12	41

HOME

Pos	P	W	D	L	F	A	GD	Pts
5	18	8	4	6	29	27	2	28

AWAY

Pos	P	W	D	L	F	A	GD	Pts
9	18	3	4	11	18	32	-14	13

CUP PROGRESS DETAILS

Competition	Round reached	Knocked out by
Co-op Insurance Cup	R2	Dunfermline
Scottish Cup	R4	Aberdeen
Challenge Cup	R2	Clyde

BIGGEST WIN (ALL COMPS)
30/08/08 5–1 v Stranraer SC2

BIGGEST DEFEAT (ALL COMPS)
1–4 on two occasions

ATTENDANCE RECORD

High	Low	Average
1,057	331	637
v Stirling (07/03/2009)	v Peterhead (25/10/2008)	

RESULTS 2008/09

July
26th ● Dundee ....h W 2–1 **Att:** 793 — **Scorers:** Stevenson, Townsley. **Booked:** P. Scullion, McClune

August
2nd ● Arbroath...........a L 4–1 **Att:** 611 — **Scorers:** A. Ferguson. **Booked:** Grant, P. Scullion, Townsley
5th ● Elgin................h W 2–0 **Att:** 269 — **Scorers:** Kelly, Scott. **Booked:** Stevenson, P. Scullion
9th ● Ayr ....h L 0–2 **Att:** 569 — **Booked:** Campbell, Brown, MacAulay
12th ● Clyde ....h L 0–2 **Att:** 414 — **Booked:** McKeown, Hill
16th ● Raith ....h D 1–1 **Att:** 899 — **Scorers:** Brown. **Booked:** Brown, McKeown, Grant
23rd ● Peterhead ....a L 1–0 **Att:** 500 — **Booked:** Grant
26th ● Dunfermline .....a L 1–0 **Att:** 1,326 — **Booked:** P. Scullion, Buist , Campbell, Hill
30th ● Stranraer ....h W 5–1 **Att:** 408 — **Scorers:** Brown, Buist , MacAulay², Scott. **Booked:** A. Ferguson, Townsley

September
13th ● Stirling ....a L 3–2 **Att:** 907 — **Scorers:** A. Ferguson, Wilson. **Booked:** Hill, McClune, Campbell
20th ● East Fife...........h L 0–3 **Att:** 776 — **Booked:** Buist , B. Ferguson
27th ● Queen's Park ....a L 1–0 **Att:** 518 — **Booked:** McKeown, Stevenson

October
4th ● Brechin............a L 3–1 **Att:** 412 — **Scorers:** Townsley. **Booked:** Hill, Grant, Townsley
18th ● Arbroath...........h W 2–1 **Att:** 508 — **Scorers:** Forrest, MacAulay. **Booked:** A. Ferguson, Townsley, Grant, Campbell
25th ● Peterhead ......h W 1–0 **Att:** 331 — **Scorers:** Grant. **Booked:** Grant, Scott, Townsley

November
1st ● Raith ....a L 4–1 **Att:** 1,669 — **Scorers:** Scott. **Booked:** Grant, Townsley, Campbell
8th ● Stirling ....h W 4–3 **Att:** 1,001 — **Scorers:** B. Ferguson, Forrest, MacAulay, Stevenson. **Booked:** Forrest
15th ● Stranraer ....a D 2–2 **Att:** 186 — **Scorers:** Hill, Scott. **Booked:** Stevenson, McKeown
22nd ● Queen's Park ...h L 1–3 **Att:** 557 — **Scorers:** MacAulay. **Dismissed:** Jellema
29th ● Raith ....a D 0–0 **Att:** 1,493 — **Booked:** J. Scullion, B. Ferguson

December
6th ● East Fife...........a L 1–0 **Att:** 653 — **Booked:** Hill, Scott
9th ● Raith ....h W 2–1 **Att:** 860 — **Scorers:** B. Ferguson². **Booked:** Forrest
13th ● Ayr ....a L 3–0 **Att:** 1,077 — **Booked:** Buist . **Dismissed:** Buist
20th ● Brechin...........h W 2–1 **Att:** 405 — **Scorers:** A. Ferguson, Stevenson. **Booked:** Townsley, Wilson, J. Scullion
27th ● Stranraer ....h D 2–2 **Att:** 463 — **Scorers:** B. Ferguson, Scott. **Booked:** Campbell, Scott, B. Ferguson

January
10th ● Aberdeen ....h L 1–2 **Att:** 3,012 — **Scorers:** Scott. **Booked:** Campbell, Buist, Townsley, McClune
17th ● Peterhead ....a D 2–2 **Att:** 601 — **Scorers:** Scott, Wilson. **Booked:** Hill
24th ● Raith ....h D 0–0 **Att:** 953
31st ● Arbroath...........a L 1–0 **Att:** 478 — **Booked:** Hill

February
7th ● Ayr ....h W 3–2 **Att:** 752 — **Scorers:** Carrigan², Grant. **Booked:** Grant, Campbell, Hill
14th ● Queen's Park ....a W 1–2 **Att:** 606 — **Scorers:** Noble, Spence. **Booked:** Townsley, Grant
21st ● East Fife...........h L 0–1 **Att:** 695 — **Booked:** Grant, Scott
28th ● Stranraer ....a W 1–3 **Att:** 291 — **Scorers:** Campbell, B. Ferguson, Noble. **Booked:** Campbell, Scott, Grant, J. Scullion

March
3rd ● Stirling ....a D 0–0 **Att:** 768 — **Booked:** Noble, Noble
7th ● Stirling ....h L 2–3 **Att:** 1,057 — **Scorers:** Noble, Scullion. **Booked:** B. Ferguson, Grant, Hill
14th ● Arbroath...........h W 2–0 **Att:** 505 — **Scorers:** Campbell, McClune. **Booked:** Scott
21st ● Brechin............a L 1–0 **Att:** 421 — **Booked:** Buist

April
4th ● Peterhead ....h L 1–2 **Att:** 479 — **Scorers:** Wilson. **Booked:** Wilson
11th ● Raith ....a L 3–1 **Att:** 1,770 — **Scorers:** B. Ferguson. **Booked:** Campbell, Wilson, Buist
18th ● East Fife...........a W 0–2 **Att:** 623 — **Scorers:** Noble, Scott
25th ● Queen's Park ....h D 0–0 **Att:** 704 — **Booked:** Grant, Hill

May
2nd ● Ayr ....a D 1–1 **Att:** 2,195 — **Scorers:** Spence
9th ● Brechin...........h W 3–2 **Att:** 401 — **Scorers:** Scott, Spence²

● Irn-Bru Second Division ● Scottish FA Cup ● Scottish League Cup ● Scottish Challenge Cup

SECOND DIVISION GOALKEEPER STATS

Player	Appearances	Match starts	Completed matches	Sub appearances	Subbed off	Clean sheets	Yellow cards	Red cards
Raymond Jellema 35	35	34	0	0	6	0	1	
Michael White 1	1	1	0	0	0	0	0	

SECOND DIVISION OUTFIELD PLAYER STATS

Player	Appearances	Match starts	Completed matches	Substitute appearances	Subbed off	Goals scored	Yellow cards	Red cards
Steven Barker 4	0	0	4	0	0	0	0
Graeme Brown 11	8	2	3	6	2	2	0
Scot Buist 27	27	23	0	3	1	4	1
Iain Campbell 30	30	24	0	6	2	8	0
Brian Carrigan 9	6	2	3	4	2	0	0
Gary Carroll 6	4	1	2	3	0	0	0
Andrew Ferguson 11	8	4	3	4	3	2	0
Brown Ferguson 31	30	25	1	5	4	3	0
Mark Ferguson 2	1	0	1	1	0	0	0
Fraser Forrest 10	9	9	1	0	2	1	0
John Grant 28	24	22	4	2	2	13	0
Jamie Hay 4	1	0	3	1	0	0	0
Dougie Hill 32	30	26	2	4	1	8	0
Francis Kelly 6	0	0	6	1	1	0	0
Hugh Kerr 2	0	0	2	0	0	0	0
Kyle MacAulay 30	21	14	9	7	5	1	0
Marc McCafferty 4	4	4	0	0	0	0	0
David McClune 26	23	23	3	0	1	1	0
Steven McKeown 13	9	6	4	3	0	3	0
Stuart Noble 14	14	11	0	3	4	2	0
Martin O'Neill..............................1	0	0	1	0	0	0	0
Andrew Scott 30	24	12	6	12	7	6	0
James Scullion.........................12	10	5	2	5	0	2	0
Pat Scullion 18	11	7	7	4	1	1	0
Greig Spence 18	6	3	12	3	4	0	0
Jamie Stevenson 16	13	12	3	1	2	2	0
Chris Townsley 31	31	30	0	1	1	8	0
Douglas Wilson 21	16	8	5	8	3	3	0

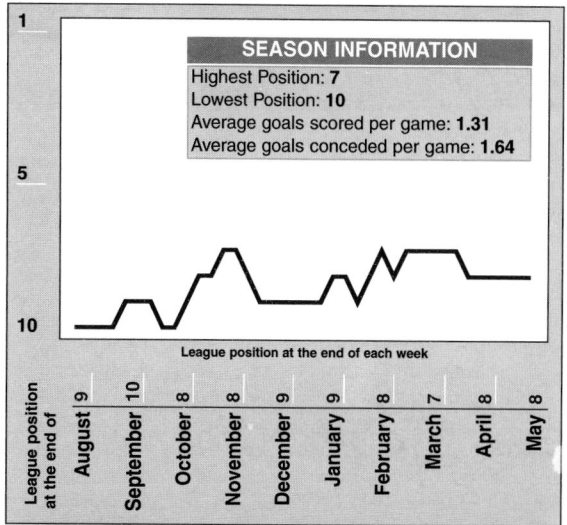

SEASON INFORMATION
Highest Position: **7**
Lowest Position: **10**
Average goals scored per game: **1.31**
Average goals conceded per game: **1.64**

League position at the end of each week

League position at the end of: August 9, September 10, October 8, November 8, December 9, January 9, February 8, March 7, April 8, May 8

LONGEST SEQUENCES

Wins (on two occasions)	2	Undefeated home (20/12/08–07/02/09)	4
Losses (13/09/08–04/10/08)	4	Undefeated away (14/02/09–03/03/09)	3
Draws (27/12/08–24/01/09)	3	Without scoring (on three occasions)	2
Undefeated (on two occasions)	4	Without conceding (18/04/09–25/04/09)	2
Without win (on four occasions)	4	Scoring (04/10/08–22/11/08)	7

CARDS RECEIVED

70 **2**

QUICK-FIRE GOALS

From the start of a match
Brown Ferguson (v Stranraer) 2:00

By a substitute after coming on
Fraser Forrest (v Arbroath) 55:00

GOALS SCORED/CONCEDED PER FIVE-MINUTE INTERVALS

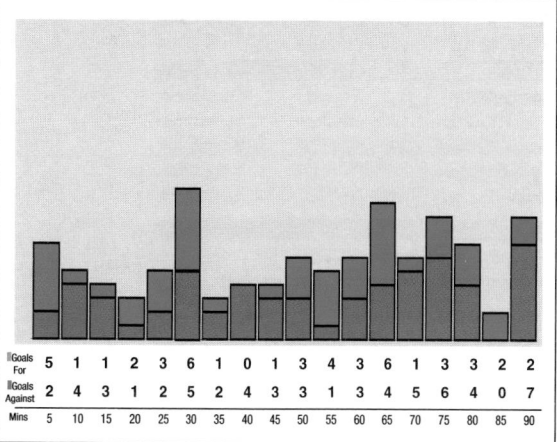

Goals For	5	1	1	2	3	6	1	0	1	3	4	3	6	1	3	3	2	2
Goals Against	2	4	3	1	2	5	2	4	3	3	1	3	4	5	6	4	0	7
Mins	5	10	15	20	25	30	35	40	45	50	55	60	65	70	75	80	85	90

ARBROATH

JOHN McGLASHAN led Arbroath into the Irn-Bru Second Division through the play-offs in 2007/08, and secured safety in 2008/09 with a seventh-place finish.

But it was a real topsy-turvy campaign for the club. After thrashing Alloa 4–1 on the opening day of the season, they embarked on a 12-match run without a victory and were left rooted to the foot of the table.

They reversed that horrible streak with a four-match winning run and, despite losing the four subsequent games, results steadied towards the end of the season, lifting McGlashan and his men out of trouble.

The experience of central defender Robbie Raeside helped to inspire the rest of the team from the back as he continued to prove himself a crucial cog for the team following his move from Peterhead in 2006.

CLUB SUMMARY

FORMED	1878
MANAGER	John McGlashan
GROUND	Gayfield Park
CAPACITY	4,415
NICKNAME	The Red Lichties
WEBSITE	www.arbroathfc.co.uk

The New **Football Pools** PLAYER OF THE SEASON

Robbie Raeside

OVERALL
P	W	D	L	F	A	GD
40	12	9	19	50	54	-4

IRN-BRU SECOND DIVISION
Pos	P	W	D	L	F	A	GD	Pts
7	36	11	8	17	44	46	-2	41

HOME
Pos	P	W	D	L	F	A	GD	Pts
7	18	6	3	9	22	23	-1	21

AWAY
Pos	P	W	D	L	F	A	GD	Pts
7	18	5	5	8	22	23	-1	20

CUP PROGRESS DETAILS
Competition	Round reached	Knocked out by
Co-op Insurance Cup	R2	Inverness CT
Scottish Cup	R3	East Fife
Challenge Cup	R1	Forfar

BIGGEST WIN (ALL COMPS)
14/02/09 5–1 v Stranraer **SC2**

BIGGEST DEFEAT (ALL COMPS)
01/11/08 0–3 v Ayr **SC2**

ATTENDANCE RECORD
High	Low	Average
921	411	638
v Raith (21/03/2009)	v Stranraer (22/11/2008)	

RESULTS 2008/09

July
26th	● Forfar	h	L 1–2	Att: 543 — Scorers: Scott. **Booked:** Scott, Black, McMullan

August
2nd	● Alloa	h	W 4–1	Att: 611 — Scorers: Rattray, Reilly, Scott, Sellars. **Booked:** Rattray, Gates
6th	● Stirling	h	W 3–2	Att: 448 — Scorers: Bishop, McMullan, Wright
9th	● Peterhead	a	D 1–1	Att: 631 — Scorers: Masson. **Booked:** Lunan, Black
16th	● Ayr	a	L 2–1	Att: 1,296 — **Scorers:** McMullan. **Booked:** Rennie, Fraser
23rd	● East Fife	h	L 0–1	Att: 766 — **Booked:** Fraser, McMullan, Weir
27th	● Inverness CT	h	D 2–2	Att: 596 — Scorers: Sellars, Tosh. **Booked:** Raeside, McMullan, Gates. (Lost 4–2 on pens)
30th	● Stirling	h	L 1–2	Att: 631 — Scorers: Gates. **Booked:** Fraser, Lunan, Sellars

September
13th	● Brechin	a	L 3–1	Att: 615 — Scorers: Gates. **Booked:** McMullan, Bishop, Raeside. **Dismissed:** Tosh
20th	● Queen's Park	h	D 1–1	Att: 523 — Scorers: Sellars. **Booked:** Rattray, McMullan
27th	● Stranraer	a	D 2–2	Att: 124 — Scorers: Sellars[2]. **Booked:** Bishop, McMullan, Lunan, Sellars, Weir, Tosh, Gates

October
4th	● Raith	h	L 0–2	Att: 855 — **Booked:** Raeside, Weir
18th	● Alloa	a	L 2–1	Att: 508 — Scorers: McGowan. **Booked:** Fraser
25th	● East Fife	a	L 3–2	Att: 677 — Scorers: McGowan, Weir. **Booked:** Lunan, Raeside

November
1st	● Ayr	h	L 0–3	Att: 535 — **Booked:** Weir, Sellars, Lunan, Gates. **Dismissed:** Sellars
8th	● Brechin	h	L 1–2	Att: 702 — Scorers: Scott. **Booked:** Raeside
15th	● Stirling	a	W 0–2	Att: 509 — Scorers: Scott, Sellars
22nd	● Stranraer	a	W 1–0	Att: 411 — Scorers: Scott
29th	● East Fife	a	L 2–0	Att: 729 — **Booked:** Sellars, Scott

December
6th	● Queen's Park	a	W 1–2	Att: 637 — Scorers: Scott, Little OG. **Booked:** Sellars
13th	● Peterhead	h	W 4–0	Att: 451 — Scorers: Dorris, Scott, Weir[2]. **Booked:** McMullan
20th	● Raith	a	L 2–1	Att: 1,477 — Scorers: Dorris. **Booked:** Bishop, Black
27th	● Stirling	h	L 1–2	Att: 635 — Scorers: Gibb OG. **Booked:** Tosh, Masson, McMullan

January
17th	● East Fife	h	L 0–2	Att: 731 — **Booked:** McCulloch, Lunan
25th	● Ayr	a	L 2–1	Att: 1,245 — Scorers: Weir. **Booked:** Raeside, Lunan
31st	● Alloa	h	W 1–0	Att: 478 — Scorers: Weir. **Booked:** Weir

February
14th	● Stranraer	a	W 1–5	Att: 280 — Scorers: McGowan, McMullan, Raeside. **Booked:** Lunan
21st	● Queen's Park	h	W 3–0	Att: 568 — Scorers: Dobbins, Raeside, Sellars. **Booked:** Raeside, Sellars, Ross, McGowan, Scott
28th	● Stirling	a	D 1–1	Att: 578 — Scorers: Raeside. **Booked:** Rattray. **Dismissed:** Sellars

March
7th	● Brechin	h	D 0–0	Att: 749 — **Booked:** Weir
10th	● Peterhead	a	L 1–0	Att: 466 — **Booked:** Sellars, McCulloch
14th	● Alloa	a	L 2–0	Att: 505 — **Booked:** Weir
21st	● Raith	h	L 0–2	Att: 921 — **Booked:** Rattray
28th	● Brechin	a	W 0–1	Att: 560 — Scorers: Forsyth. **Booked:** Scott

April
4th	● East Fife	a	D 0–0	Att: 629 — **Booked:** Sellars
11th	● Ayr	h	L 1–3	Att: 821 — Scorers: Bishop. **Booked:** Raeside, Hill, Gibson, Weir
18th	● Queen's Park	a	W 0–1	Att: 722 — Scorers: Ross. **Booked:** Raeside, Bishop, Ross, Lunan
25th	● Stranraer	h	W 2–0	Att: 506 — Scorers: Forsyth, Ross. **Booked:** Gibson

May
2nd	● Peterhead	h	D 2–2	Att: 599 — Scorers: Rennie, Ross
9th	● Raith	a	D 0–0	Att: 4,426

● Irn-Bru Second Division ● Scottish FA Cup ● Scottish League Cup ● Scottish Challenge Cup

SECOND DIVISION GOALKEEPER STATS

Player	Appearances	Match starts	Completed matches	Sub appearances	Subbed off	Clean sheets	Yellow cards	Red cards
Darren Hill	35	35	35	0	0	11	1	0
Scott Morrison	1	1	1	0	0	0	0	0

SECOND DIVISION OUTFIELD PLAYER STATS

Player	Appearances	Match starts	Completed matches	Substitute appearances	Subbed off	Goals scored	Yellow cards	Red cards
Jamie Bishop	25	24	22	1	2	1	4	0
Roddy Black	22	18	15	4	3	0	2	0
Colin Cameron	3	3	1	0	2	0	0	0
Alan Campbell	8	8	7	0	1	0	0	0
Joe Dingwall		0	0	0	0	0	0	0
Ian Dobbins	15	15	15	0	0	1	0	0
Steven Dorris	6	6	3	0	3	2	0	0
Craig Forsyth	26	26	24	0	2	2	0	0
John Fraser	12	10	4	2	6	0	4	0
Scott Gates	23	12	7	11	5	2	3	0
Keith Gibson	8	8	7	0	1	0	2	0
Paul Lunan	25	25	21	0	4	0	9	0
Terry Masson	12	1	1	11	0	1	1	0
Marc McCulloch	11	11	10	0	1	0	2	0
David McGowan	14	10	7	4	3	3	1	0
Kevin McMullan	31	26	18	5	8	2	6	0
Robbie Raeside	31	31	28	0	3	3	8	0
Alan Rattray	15	15	11	0	3	1	4	1
Andy Reilly	8	1	0	7	1	1	0	0
Steven Rennie	34	30	28	4	2	1	1	0
Robbie Ross	13	7	2	6	5	3	2	0
Bryan Scott	21	16	5	5	11	6	2	0
Barry Sellars	31	31	25	0	4	6	7	2
Sean Simpson	4	1	0	3	1	0	0	0
Nicky Smith	4	1	0	3	1	0	0	0
Paul Tosh	12	3	0	9	2	0	2	1
Paul Watson	7	4	3	3	1	0	0	0
Steven Weir	24	15	2	9	13	5	8	0
Kenny Wright	3	0	0	3	0	0	0	0

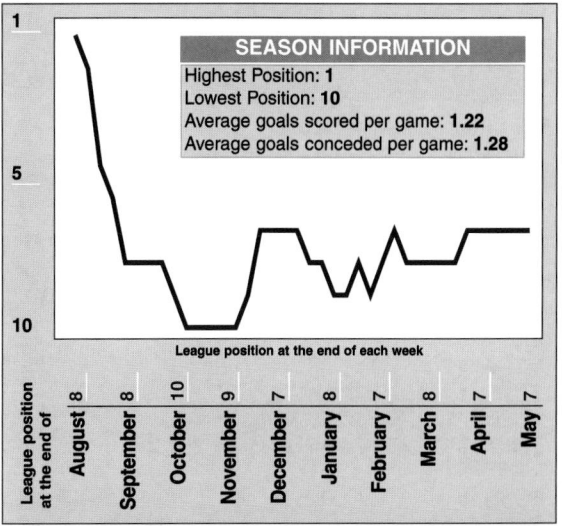

SEASON INFORMATION

Highest Position: **1**
Lowest Position: **10**
Average goals scored per game: **1.22**
Average goals conceded per game: **1.28**

League position at the end of each week

LONGEST SEQUENCES

Wins (15/11/08–13/12/08)	4	Undefeated home (31/01/09–07/03/09)	3
Losses (04/10/08–08/11/08)	5	Undefeated away (on four occasions)	2
Draws (on two occasions)	2	Without scoring (07/03/09–21/03/09)	4
Undefeated (31/01/09–07/03/09)	5	Without conceding (on three occasions)	2
Without win (09/08/08–08/11/08)	12	Scoring (08/11/08–27/12/08)	7

CARDS RECEIVED

69   **4**

QUICK-FIRE GOALS

From the start of a match
Bryan Scott (v Queens Park) 3:00

By a substitute after coming on
Andy Reilly (v Alloa) 14:00

GOALS SCORED/CONCEDED PER FIVE-MINUTE INTERVALS

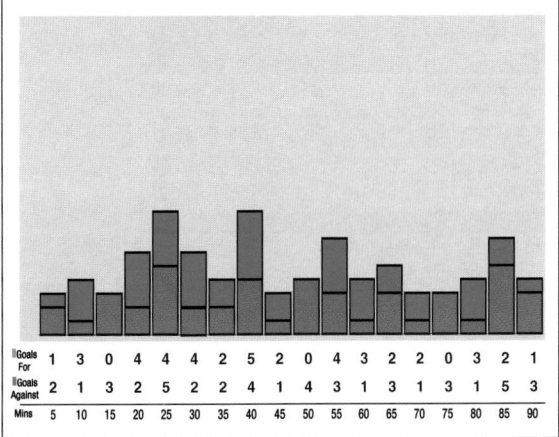

Goals For	1	3	0	4	4	4	2	5	2	0	4	3	2	2	0	3	2	1	
Goals Against	2	1	3	2	5	2	2	4	1	4	3	1	3	1	3	1	5	3	
Mins	5	10	15	20	25	30	35	40	45	50	55	60	65	70	75	80	85	90	

AYR UNITED

WHEN Ayr United forced a Homecoming Scottish Cup replay with Kilmarnock in January with Alex Williams' last-minute goal, the roar that followed shook the foundations of Somerset Park.

What manager Brian Reid was anxious to avoid, though, was all the excitement being misplaced. He feared it bringing the house down on their promotion hopes.

Reid always insisted it was the Irn-Bru Second Division that mattered most and he made sure his players understood that. The replay with Killie was lost and so was the battle for automatic promotion by just two points.

That meant a play-off with Airdrie, and Ryan Stevenson's goal in the away leg was enough to secure a 3–2 aggregate win and promotion. Now Reid's side must prosper despite being the only part-time club in the First Division.

CLUB SUMMARY

FORMED	1910
MANAGER	Brian Reid
GROUND	Somerset Park
CAPACITY	10,185
NICKNAME	The Honest Men
WEBSITE	www.ayrunitedfc.co.uk

 The New **Football Pools** PLAYER OF THE SEASON — **Bryan Prunty**

OVERALL
P	W	D	L	F	A	GD
47	27	11	9	89	53	36

IRN-BRU SECOND DIVISION
Pos	P	W	D	L	F	A	GD	Pts
2	36	22	8	6	71	38	33	74

HOME
Pos	P	W	D	L	F	A	GD	Pts
1	18	11	7	0	38	16	22	40

AWAY
Pos	P	W	D	L	F	A	GD	Pts
2	18	11	1	6	33	22	11	34

CUP PROGRESS DETAILS
Competition	Round reached	Knocked out by
Co-op Insurance Cup	R2	Aberdeen
Scottish Cup	R4	Kilmarnock
Challenge Cup	R1	East Stirling

BIGGEST WIN (ALL COMPS)
07/03/09 5–0 v Stranraer **SC2**

BIGGEST DEFEAT (ALL COMPS)
27/09/08 0–3 v East Fife **SC2**

ATTENDANCE RECORD
High	Low	Average
2,363	1,057	1,477
v Raith (31/01/2009)	v Stirling (25/10/2008)	

RESULTS 2008/09

July
27th	● East Stirling ......a	L 2–1	Att: 729 — **Scorers:** Williams

August
2nd	● Raith ....h	D 0–0	Att: 1,373 — **Booked:** Keenan, Easton
6th	● Berwick ....h	W 2–1	Att: 716 — **Scorers:** Aitken, Williams
9th	● Alloa.................a	W 0–2	Att: 569 — **Scorers:** Prunty, Williams. **Booked:** Dempsie
16th	● Arbroath ....h	W 2–1	Att: 1,296 — **Scorers:** Prunty, Stevenson. **Booked:** Williams, Keenan, Stevenson, Prunty, Dempsie
23rd	● Stirling ....a	D 2–2	Att: 877 — **Scorers:** Prunty². **Booked:** Keenan, Stevenson
27th	● Aberdeen ....a	L 0–1	Att: 3,173 — **Booked:** Dempsie
30th	● Queen's Park ....h	W 2–1	Att: 1,427 — **Scorers:** Prunty²

September
13th	● Stranraer ....a	W 1–3	Att: 768 — **Scorers:** Aitken, Borris, Prunty. **Booked:** Keenan
21st	● Brechin.............h	D 1–1	Att: 1,494 — **Scorers:** Stevenson
27th	● East Fife...........a	L 3–0	Att: 1,010 — **Booked:** Walker, Campbell. **Dismissed:** Aitken

October
4th	● Peterhead ....h	W 2–0	Att: 1,100 — **Scorers:** Stevenson, Williams. **Booked:** Borris, Keenan
18th	● Raith ....a	L 3–2	Att: 1,746 — **Scorers:** Gormley, Walker
25th	● Stirling ....h	D 1–1	Att: 1,057 — **Scorers:** Aitken. **Booked:** Stevenson. **Dismissed:** Stevenson

November
1st	● Arbroath...........a	W 0–3	Att: 535 — **Scorers:** Campbell, Easton, Prunty
8th	● Stranraer ....h	W 3–2	Att: 1,358 — **Scorers:** Easton, Gormley, Prunty. **Booked:** Dempsie, Stevenson, McGowan
15th	● Queen's Park ....a	W 0–3	Att: 1,009 — **Scorers:** Prunty³. **Booked:** Dempsie, Borris
22nd	● East Fife...........h	W 4–2	Att: 1,254 — **Scorers:** Easton, Gormley, Keenan, Stevenson. **Booked:** Borris, McGowan. **Dismissed:** McGowan

December
13th	● Alloa.................h	W 3–0	Att: 1,077 — **Scorers:** Agnew, Williams². **Booked:** Easton, Walker
17th	● Lochee Utd ......a	D 1–1	Att: 1,223 — **Scorers:** Williams
20th	● Peterhead ....a	L 3–0	Att: 556
23rd	● Lochee Utd ......h	W 3–1	Att: 2,049 — **Scorers:** Gormley, McGowan, Prunty. **Booked:** Walker
30th	● Brechin.............a	W 0–1	Att: 548 — **Scorers:** Prunty. **Booked:** Keenan, Williams, Walker

January
10th	● Kilmarnock ....h	D 2–2	Att: 9,280 — **Scorers:** Keenan, Williams. **Booked:** Keenan, Stevenson, Prunty, Easton
17th	● Stirling ....a	L 2–0	Att: 779 — **Booked:** Prunty
22nd	● Kilmarnock ....a	L 3–1	Att: 11,563 — **Scorers:** Prunty. **Booked:** Keenan, Williams, Stevenson
25th	● Arbroath ....h	W 2–0	Att: 1,245 — **Scorers:** Stevenson, Williams. **Booked:** Gormley
31st	● Raith ....h	D 2–2	Att: 2,363 — **Scorers:** Agnew, Stevenson. **Booked:** Williams, Keenan

February
7th	● Alloa.................a	L 3–2	Att: 752 — **Scorers:** Gormley²
21st	● Brechin.............h	W 4–2	Att: 1,402 — **Scorers:** Aitken, Roberts², Stevenson. **Booked:** Aitken, Keenan
28th	● Queen's Park ....a	W 0–3	Att: 1,139 — **Scorers:** Connolly, Roberts, Stevenson. **Booked:** Borris

March
4th	● Queen's Park ....h	D 1–1	Att: 1,360 — **Scorers:** Borris. **Booked:** Campbell, Walker
7th	● Stranraer ....h	W 5–0	Att: 1,570 — **Scorers:** Aitken, McGowan, Prunty, Stevenson, Williams. **Booked:** Dempsie
14th	● Raith ....a	W 0–1	Att: 1,294 — **Scorers:** Gormley. **Booked:** James, Dempsie
18th	● East Fife...........a	W 0–1	Att: 832 — **Scorers:** Prunty. **Booked:** Aitken, James
21st	● Peterhead ....h	D 0–0	Att: 1,601
28th	● Stranraer ....a	W 1–4	Att: 891 — **Scorers:** Borris, Connolly, Easton, Nicoll OG

April
4th	● Stirling ....h	W 3–1	Att: 1,573 — **Scorers:** Gormley², Williams. **Booked:** Dempsie, Connolly
11th	● Arbroath ....a	W 1–3	Att: 821 — **Scorers:** Aitken, Stevenson². **Booked:** Gormley
18th	● Brechin.............h	L 1–0	Att: 712 — **Booked:** Roberts, Keenan
25th	● East Fife...........h	W 2–0	Att: 1,849 — **Scorers:** Connolly, Roberts

May
2nd	● Alloa.................h	D 1–1	Att: 2,195 — **Scorers:** Roberts. **Booked:** Prunty, Stevenson
9th	● Peterhead ....a	W 2–3	Att: 602 — **Scorers:** Agnew, Connolly, Gormley
13th	● Brechin.............a	W 0–2	Att: 902 — **Scorers:** Aitken². **Booked:** Prunty
16th	● Brechin.............h	W 3–2	Att: 1,974 — **Scorers:** Aitken, Connolly, Prunty. **Booked:** Grindlay
20th	● Airdrie Utd ....h	D 2–2	Att: 3,378 — **Scorers:** Roberts². **Booked:** McGowan, Walker. **Dismissed:** McGowan
24th	● Airdrie Utd ....a	W 0–1	Att: 3,303 — **Scorers:** Stevenson. **Booked:** Keenan, Prunty, Gormley

● Irn-Bru Second Division ● Scottish FA Cup ● Scottish League Cup ● Scottish Challenge Cup

SECOND DIVISION GOALKEEPER STATS

Player	Appearances	Match starts	Completed matches	Sub appearances	Subbed off	Clean sheets	Yellow cards	Red cards
Stephen Grindlay	36	36	36	0	0	13	0	0

SECOND DIVISION OUTFIELD PLAYER STATS

Player	Appearances	Match starts	Completed matches	Substitute appearances	Subbed off	Goals scored	Yellow cards	Red cards
Scott Agnew	17	7	5	10	2	3	0	0
Chris Aitken	29	27	22	2	4	5	2	1
Ryan Borris	28	25	19	3	6	3	4	0
Martin Campbell	28	28	21	0	7	1	2	0
Kenneth Connolly	18	13	9	5	4	4	1	0
Allan Dempsie	32	31	26	1	5	0	7	0
William Easton	29	25	16	4	9	4	2	0
Iain Fisher	1	0	0	1	0	0	0	0
David Gillies	1	0	0	1	0	0	0	0
David Gormley	36	17	11	19	6	9	2	0
Murray Henderson	2	1	1	1	0	0	0	0
Kevin James	5	5	5	0	0	0	2	0
Dean Keenan	34	33	31	1	2	1	9	0
Neil McGowan	27	24	19	3	4	1	2	1
Bryan Prunty	31	29	15	2	14	15	3	0
Mark Roberts	14	12	6	2	6	5	1	0
Ryan Stevenson	34	32	29	2	2	10	5	1
Scott Walker	34	33	32	1	1	1	4	0
Paul Weaver	5	1	0	4	1	0	0	0
Alex Williams	33	16	5	17	11	7	3	0
Alastair Woodburn	6	1	1	5	0	0	0	0

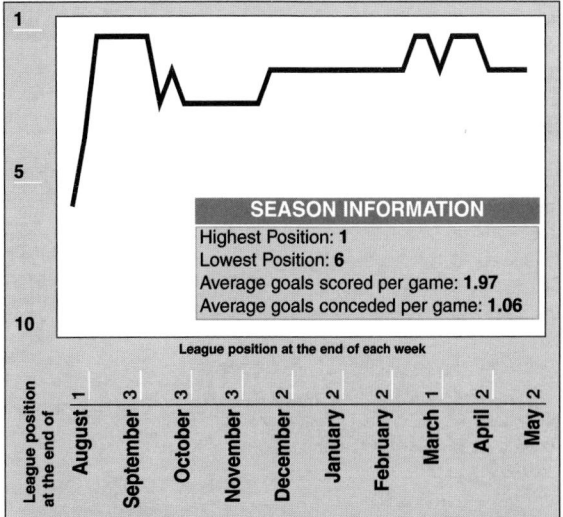

League position at the end of each week

League position at the end of

| | August 1 | September 3 | October 3 | November 3 | December 2 | January 2 | February 2 | March 1 | April 2 | May 2 |

SEASON INFORMATION
Highest Position: **1**
Lowest Position: **6**
Average goals scored per game: **1.97**
Average goals conceded per game: **1.06**

LONGEST SEQUENCES

Wins	5		Undefeated home	18
(01/11/08–13/12/08)			(02/08/08–02/05/09)	
Losses			Undefeated away	5
(–)			(28/02/09–11/04/09)	
Draws			Without scoring	
(–)			(–)	
Undefeated	10		Without conceding	4
(21/02/09–11/04/09)			(07/03/09–21/03/09)	
Without win	2		Scoring	9
(on three occasions)			(25/01/09–18/03/09)	

CARDS RECEIVED

49 **3**

QUICK-FIRE GOALS
From the start of a match
Bryan Prunty (v Queens Park) 2:00

By a substitute after coming on
David Gormley (v Raith) -4:00

GOALS SCORED/CONCEDED PER FIVE-MINUTE INTERVALS

Goals For	3	4	5	2	5	5	2	4	5	5	4	3	4	1	4	4	7	4
Goals Against	0	2	3	2	0	3	4	2	0	3	2	1	3	2	4	2	1	4
Mins	5	10	15	20	25	30	35	40	45	50	55	60	65	70	75	80	85	90

BRECHIN CITY will spend another year in the Irn-Bru Second Division after suffering their second play-off defeat in three years.

Former Dundee and Hibernian boss Jim Duffy arrived in January to replace Michael O'Neill, who left to take charge of Shamrock Rovers.

Duffy did enough to lead City to third place in the table, but they lost both legs of their play-off semi-final with runners-up Ayr United.

It was still an improvement on the previous season's sixth-place finish, but extended the club's exile from the First Division to three years and counting.

Brechin were right in touch at the top of the table until the turn of the year. Then, as well as losing their manager, they saw star striker Gary Twigg follow O'Neill to Ireland. Twigg had netted 13 goals in all competitions before his departure and proved a huge loss.

CLUB SUMMARY

FORMED	1906
MANAGER	Jim Duffy
GROUND	Glebe Park
CAPACITY	3,960
NICKNAME	The Hedgemen
WEBSITE	www.brechincity.com

The New **Football Pools** PLAYER OF THE SEASON

Neil Janczyk

OVERALL
P	W	D	L	F	A	GD
43	20	8	15	60	56	4

IRN-BRU SECOND DIVISION
Pos	P	W	D	L	F	A	GD	Pts
3	36	18	8	10	51	45	6	62

HOME
Pos	P	W	D	L	F	A	GD	Pts
3	18	12	2	4	27	18	9	38

AWAY
Pos	P	W	D	L	F	A	GD	Pts
6	18	6	6	6	24	27	-3	24

CUP PROGRESS DETAILS
Competition	Round reached	Knocked out by
Co-op Insurance Cup	R2	Kilmarnock
Scottish Cup	R4	St Mirren
Challenge Cup	R1	East Fife

BIGGEST WIN (ALL COMPS)
06/08/08 0-3 v East Fife **SLC1**

BIGGEST DEFEAT (ALL COMPS)
01/11/08 5-1 v Peterhead **SC2**

ATTENDANCE RECORD
High	Low	Average
780	315	552
v Raith (24/03/2009)	v Stranraer (10/03/2009)	

RESULTS 2008/09

July
26th ● East Fife.........h L 0–1 Att: 446 — Booked: Janczyk. Dismissed: Nimmo

August
2nd ● Stirling ....h W 2–1 Att: 535 — Scorers: D. Smith, Twigg. Booked: C. Nelson, White
6th ● East Fife.........a W 0–3 Att: 523 — Scorers: Twigg, Ward, White. Booked: White, Dyer
9th ● Stranraer ....a W 1–2 Att: 245 — Scorers: Diack[2]
16th ● Peterhead ....h D 2–2 Att: 524 — Scorers: Nimmo[2]. Booked: White, Murie, Ward
23rd ● Queen's Park ....a D 1–1 Att: 613 — Scorers: Twigg. Booked: Murie
27th ● Kilmarnock.......h L 0–2 Att: 803 — Booked: Nimmo
30th ● East Fife.........a D 0–0 Att: 726

September
13th ● Arbroath ....h W 3–1 Att: 615 — Scorers: Byers, C. Smith[2]. Booked: Janczyk, Murie, Byers
21st ● Ayr ....a D 1–1 Att: 1,494 — Scorers: Twigg. Booked: Dyer, Nimmo, Seeley
27th ● Raith ....h W 2–0 Att: 769 — Scorers: Paton, White. Booked: Janczyk

October
4th ● Alloa................h W 3–1 Att: 412 — Scorers: King[2], Twigg
18th ● Stirling ....a W 1–2 Att: 577 — Scorers: Byers, Twigg
25th ● Queen's Park ....h W 2–1 Att: 483 — Scorers: Byers, D. Smith. Booked: Janczyk, Baird

November
1st ● Peterhead ....a L 5–1 Att: 573 — Scorers: D. Smith
8th ● Arbroath ....a W 1–2 Att: 702 — Scorers: Twigg[2]. Booked: Baird
15th ● East Fife.........h W 2–1 Att: 691 — Scorers: Byers, Diack. Booked: Murie, King, Nimmo
22nd ● Raith ....a D 2–2 Att: 2,229 — Scorers: Diack, Twigg. Booked: Murie

December
8th ● Edinburgh City ..a W 0–3 Att: 1,026 — Scorers: Diack[3]. Booked: A. Nelson
20th ● Alloa................a L 2–1 Att: 405 — Scorers: Twigg. Booked: Baird
27th ● East Fife.........a L 2–1 Att: 857 — Scorers: Dyer. Booked: White
30th ● Ayr ....h L 0–1 Att: 548 — Booked: Janczyk

January
13th ● St Mirren ....h L 1–3 Att: 1,026 — Scorers: Janczyk
17th ● Queen's Park ....a D 0–0 Att: 466
24th ● Peterhead ....h D 1–1 Att: 517 — Scorers: Twigg
31st ● Stirling ....h L 1–2 Att: 565 — Scorers: Walker

February
7th ● Stranraer ....a W 0–3 Att: 223 — Scorers: Byers, Twigg[2]. Booked: King
21st ● Ayr ....a L 4–2 Att: 1,402 — Scorers: Byers, McAllister. Booked: Dyer
28th ● East Fife.........h W 2–1 Att: 596 — Scorers: Byers, Janczyk. Booked: Ward, D. Smith, King

March
7th ● Arbroath ....a D 0–0 Att: 749
10th ● Stranraer ....h W 1–0 Att: 315 — Scorers: McAllister. Booked: McAllister
14th ● Stirling ....a W 2–3 Att: 529 — Scorers: Ettien[2], McAllister
21st ● Alloa................h W 1–0 Att: 421 — Scorers: McAllister. Booked: McAllister
24th ● Raith ....h L 0–4 Att: 780 — Booked: McAllister
28th ● Arbroath ....h L 0–1 Att: 560 — Booked: Harvey, Dyer. Dismissed: Harvey

April
4th ● Queen's Park ....h W 2–0 Att: 467 — Scorers: King[2]
11th ● Peterhead ....a W 0–1 Att: 739 — Scorers: D. Smith. Booked: Walker
18th ● Ayr ....h W 1–0 Att: 712 — Scorers: McAllister. Booked: McAllister
25th ● Raith ....a L 2–0 Att: 2,529 — Booked: Murie, Dyer

May
2nd ● Stranraer ....h W 2–1 Att: 418 — Scorers: Ettien, Nimmo
9th ● Alloa................a L 3–2 Att: 401 — Scorers: Ettien, Townsley OG
13th ● Ayr ....h L 0–2 Att: 902 — Booked: Ettien, McAllister
16th ● Ayr ....a L 3–2 Att: 1974 — Scorers: McAllister[2]. Booked: Byers, Canning, D. Smith, Fusco

● Irn-Bru Second Division ● Scottish FA Cup ● Scottish League Cup ● Scottish Challenge Cup

SECOND DIVISION GOALKEEPER STATS

Player	Appearances	Match starts	Completed matches	Sub appearances	Subbed off	Clean sheets	Yellow cards	Red cards
Craig Nelson	36	36	36	0	0	10	1	0

SECOND DIVISION OUTFIELD PLAYER STATS

Player	Appearances	Match starts	Completed matches	Substitute appearances	Subbed off	Goals scored	Yellow cards	Red cards
John Baird	9	5	5	4	0	0	3	0
Kevin Byers	30	27	20	3	7	7	1	0
Stevie Canning	12	5	2	7	3	0	0	0
Iain Diack	12	8	4	4	4	4	0	0
William Dyer	35	35	35	0	0	1	4	0
Steven Ettien	14	8	7	6	1	4	0	0
Gary Fusco	19	15	11	4	4	0	0	0
Ross Harvey	3	0	0	3	0	0	1	1
Neil Janczyk	31	30	21	1	9	1	4	0
Charlie King	35	26	15	9	11	4	3	0
Rory McAllister	15	13	7	2	6	5	4	0
David Murie	18	12	8	6	4	0	6	0
Adam Nelson	7	1	0	6	1	0	0	0
Ian Nimmo	33	27	15	6	12	3	2	0
Michael Paton	8	7	6	1	1	1	0	0
Jonathon Seeley	18	17	17	1	0	0	1	0
Barry Smith	14	14	13	0	1	0	0	0
Calum Smith	5	0	0	5	0	2	0	0
Darren Smith	26	21	13	5	8	4	1	0
Gary Twigg	23	23	19	0	4	12	0	0
Richard Walker	34	28	27	6	1	1	1	0
John Ward	21	20	17	1	3	0	2	0
David White	18	18	17	0	1	1	3	0

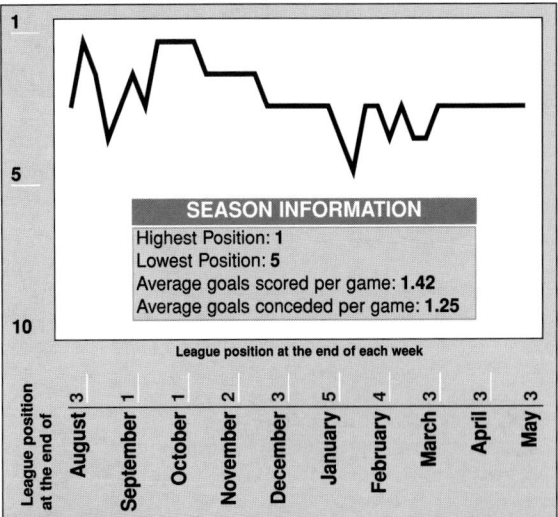

League position at the end of each week

SEASON INFORMATION

Highest Position: **1**
Lowest Position: **5**
Average goals scored per game: **1.42**
Average goals conceded per game: **1.25**

LONGEST SEQUENCES

Wins (27/09/08–25/10/08)	4	Undefeated home (02/08/08–15/11/08)	7
Losses (20/12/08–30/12/08)	3	Undefeated away (02/08/08–18/10/08)	6
Draws (16/08/08–30/08/08)	3	Without scoring (on two occasions)	2
Undefeated (02/08/08–25/10/08)	11	Without conceding (04/04/09–18/04/09)	3
Without win (22/11/08–31/01/09)	7	Scoring (13/09/08–27/12/08)	12

CARDS RECEIVED

37   **1**

QUICK-FIRE GOALS

From the start of a match
Steven Ettien (v Stranraer) 2:00

By a substitute after coming on
Iain Diack (v Raith) 3:00

GOALS SCORED/CONCEDED PER FIVE-MINUTE INTERVALS

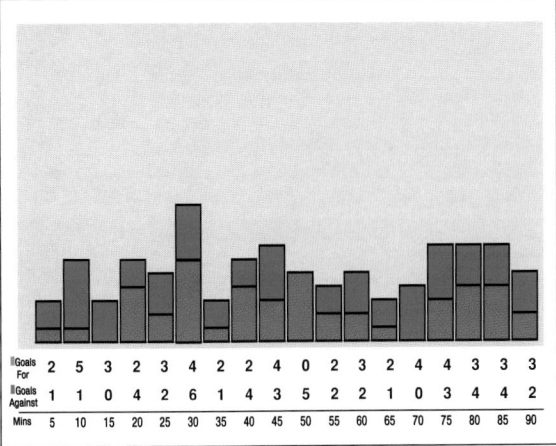

Goals For	2	5	3	2	3	4	2	2	4	0	2	3	2	4	4	3	3	3
Goals Against	1	1	0	4	2	6	1	4	3	5	2	2	1	0	3	4	4	2
Mins	5	10	15	20	25	30	35	40	45	50	55	60	65	70	75	80	85	90

EAST FIFE

IRN-BRU Division Two newcomers East Fife secured sixth place after their comfortable promotion of the previous season. The Fifers experienced a managerial change towards the end of the campaign, but managed a respectable finish.

It took Dave Baikie's side four games to taste victory and subsequent results were mixed, with any positive results soon offset by defeats and draws.

Despite Paul McManus' regular goals, a run of just one win in eight games led to Baikie's departure on 14th April, with veteran striker Stevie Crawford taking over the reins on a caretaker basis. The 35-year-old former Scotland star tasted defeat in three of his four games in charge before the end of the season, but was nevertheless given the manager's job on a permanent basis.

CLUB SUMMARY

FORMED	1903
MANAGER	Stevie Crawford
GROUND	Bayview Stadium
CAPACITY	1,992
NICKNAME	The Fifers
WEBSITE	www.eastfife.org

The New **Football Pools**
PLAYER OF THE SEASON

Bobby Linn

OVERALL

P	W	D	L	F	A	GD
42	16	5	21	43	54	-11

IRN-BRU SECOND DIVISION

Pos	P	W	D	L	F	A	GD	Pts
6	36	13	5	18	39	44	-5	44

HOME

Pos	P	W	D	L	F	A	GD	Pts
8	18	6	2	10	19	24	-5	20

AWAY

Pos	P	W	D	L	F	A	GD	Pts
4	18	7	3	8	20	20	0	24

CUP PROGRESS DETAILS

Competition	Round reached	Knocked out by
Co-op Insurance Cup	R1	Brechin
Scottish Cup	R5	Aberdeen
Challenge Cup	R2	Airdrie Utd

BIGGEST WIN (ALL COMPS)
4–0 on two occasions

BIGGEST DEFEAT (ALL COMPS)
17/02/09 0–5 v Aberdeen TSC5

ATTENDANCE RECORD

High	Low	Average
1,980	533	864
v Raith (08/11/2008)	v Stranraer (21/03/2009)	

RESULTS 2008/09

July
26th ● Brechin............a W 0–1 **Att:** 446 — **Scorers:** Templeman. **Booked:** Smart, Templeman

August
2nd ● Peterhead ....h L 0–2 **Att:** 888
6th ● Brechin............h L 0–3 **Att:** 523 — **Booked:** Smart, Stewart, McCulloch
9th ● Stirling ....a D 1–1 **Att:** 686 — **Scorers:** Cameron. **Booked:** McManus
13th ● Airdrie Utd ......h L 0–2 **Att:** 606
16th ● Queen's Park ...h L 1–2 **Att:** 789 — **Scorers:** Templeman
23rd ● Arbroath ....a W 0–1 **Att:** 766 — **Scorers:** Fotheringham. **Booked:** Linn, McDonald
30th ● Brechin............h D 0–0 **Att:** 726 — **Booked:** Linn

September
13th ● Raith ....a D 1–1 **Att:** 3,637 — **Scorers:** Fotheringham.
Booked: Fotheringham, McCulloch, McManus, Linn
20th ● Alloa................a W 0–3 **Att:** 776 — **Scorers:** McManus[3]. **Booked:** Fagan, Linn, McCulloch, Fotheringham
27th ● Ayr ....h W 3–0 **Att:** 1,010 — **Scorers:** McManus[2], Young.
Booked: Shields, Young, Templeman. **Dismissed:** Fagan

October
4th ● Stranraer ....h L 1–2 **Att:** 730 — **Scorers:** Templeman. **Booked:** Cameron, Templeman
18th ● Peterhead ....a W 0–1 **Att:** 680 — **Scorers:** McManus
25th ● Arbroath ....h W 3–2 **Att:** 677 — **Scorers:** Cameron, McManus, Tweed.
Dismissed: Fotheringham, Fagan

November
1st ● Queen's Park ....a D 0–0 **Att:** 752
8th ● Raith ....h L 0–2 **Att:** 1,980 — **Booked:** Fotheringham, Shields
15th ● Brechin............a L 2–1 **Att:** 691 — **Scorers:** McDonald. **Booked:** Cameron
22nd ● Ayr ....a L 4–2 **Att:** 1,254 — **Scorers:** Fotheringham, Linn.
Booked: Campbell, Cameron, Crawford
29th ● Arbroath ....h W 2–0 **Att:** 729 — **Scorers:** Crawford, O'Reilly. **Booked:** Fotheringham

December
6th ● Alloa................h W 1–0 **Att:** 653 — **Scorers:** McManus. **Booked:** Fotheringham, Fagan
13th ● Stirling ....h L 0–1 **Att:** 593 — **Booked:** Smart
20th ● Stranraer ....a W 0–4 **Att:** 172 — **Scorers:** Crawford, McDonald, McManus, Nugent.
Booked: Fagan, Tweed
27th ● Brechin............h W 2–1 **Att:** 857 — **Scorers:** Linn, McManus. **Booked:** Linn

January
3rd ● Raith ....a L 1–0 **Att:** 4,812 — **Booked:** Smart, Tweed
10th ● Stenhousemuir..a W 0–1 **Att:** 784 — **Scorers:** Linn. **Booked:** Young
17th ● Arbroath ....a W 0–2 **Att:** 731 — **Scorers:** Linn[2]
24th ● Queen's Park ....h W 4–2 **Att:** 785 — **Scorers:** Crawford[2], McDonald, Templeman
31st ● Peterhead ....h L 0–3 **Att:** 698

February
17th ● Aberdeen ....a L 5–0 **Att:** 8,960 — **Booked:** Templeman. **Dismissed:** McCulloch
21st ● Alloa................a W 0–1 **Att:** 695 — **Scorers:** McDonald
28th ● Brechin............a L 2–1 **Att:** 596 — **Scorers:** McManus. **Booked:** McManus, Cameron

March
7th ● Raith ....h L 0–1 **Att:** 1,980 — **Booked:** McDonald, Fagan
14th ● Peterhead ....a L 2–0 **Att:** 556 — **Booked:** Fagan
18th ● Ayr ....h L 0–1 **Att:** 832 — **Booked:** Stewart, Fagan
21st ● Stranraer ....h W 4–0 **Att:** 533 — **Scorers:** Linn[2], Makel, Templeman
28th ● Stirling ....a L 2–0 **Att:** 636 — **Booked:** Templeman, Fotheringham

April
4th ● Arbroath ....h D 0–0 **Att:** 629
11th ● Queen's Park ....a L 3–1 **Att:** 601 — **Scorers:** McManus. **Booked:** Fagan, Young, Smart
18th ● Alloa................h L 0–2 **Att:** 623 — **Booked:** Cameron
25th ● Ayr ....a L 2–0 **Att:** 1,849 — **Booked:** Linn, Fagan. **Dismissed:** Linn

May
2nd ● Stirling ....h L 0–3 **Att:** 569 — **Booked:** Fagan, Nugent
9th ● Stranraer ....a W 0–1 **Att:** 249 — **Scorers:** Kane OG. **Booked:** Smart, Cargill

● Irn-Bru Second Division ● Scottish FA Cup ● Scottish League Cup ● Scottish Challenge Cup

SECOND DIVISION GOALKEEPER STATS

Player	Appearances	Match starts	Completed matches	Sub appearances	Subbed off	Clean sheets	Yellow cards	Red cards
Michael Brown	13	13	13	0	0	4	0	0
Willie McCulloch	23	23	23	0	0	9	2	0

SECOND DIVISION OUTFIELD PLAYER STATS

Player	Appearances	Match starts	Completed matches	Substitute appearances	Subbed off	Goals scored	Yellow cards	Red cards
Ryan Blackadder	1	0	0	1	0	0	0	0
Douglas Cameron	36	36	33	0	3	2	5	0
Robert Campbell	10	5	1	5	4	0	1	0
Stuart Cargill	4	0	0	4	0	0	1	0
Stevie Crawford	27	22	14	5	8	3	1	0
Shaun Fagan	23	18	12	5	4	0	9	2
Kevin Fotheringham	24	23	17	1	5	3	5	1
Kevin Gordon	2	0	0	2	0	0	0	0
Bobby Linn	34	32	22	2	9	6	6	1
Lee Makel	8	7	5	1	2	1	0	0
Greig McDonald	24	23	19	1	4	5	2	0
Paul McManus	33	30	19	3	11	12	3	0
Johnny McRae	1	0	0	1	0	0	0	0
David Muir	19	14	13	5	1	0	0	0
Paul Nugent	21	19	15	2	4	0	1	0
Craig O'Reilly	11	0	0	11	0	0	0	0
Jordyn Sheerin	4	1	0	3	1	0	0	0
John Sheran	1	0	0	1	0	0	0	0
Dene Shields	9	7	5	2	2	0	2	0
Jonathan Smart	28	28	23	0	5	0	4	0
Goran Stanik	13	11	8	2	3	0	0	0
Paul Stewart	30	21	19	9	2	0	1	0
Chris Templeman	33	25	13	8	12	4	3	0
Darren Thomson	1	0	0	1	0	0	0	0
Steven Tweed	16	16	14	0	2	1	2	0
Paul Walker	1	0	0	1	0	0	0	0
Lloyd Young	32	22	18	10	4	1	2	0

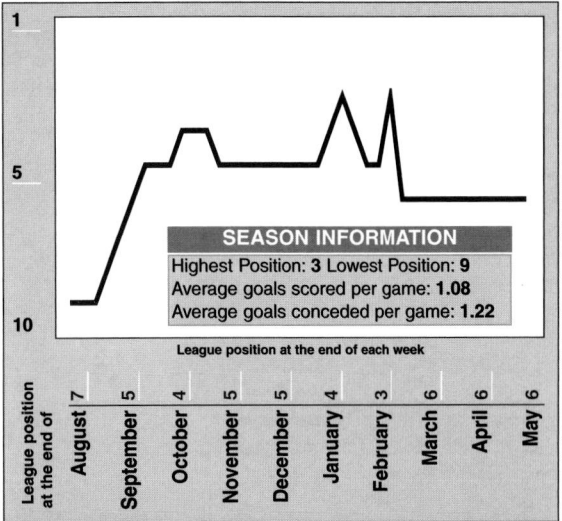

League position at the end of each week

SEASON INFORMATION
Highest Position: **3** Lowest Position: **9**
Average goals scored per game: **1.08**
Average goals conceded per game: **1.22**

LONGEST SEQUENCES

Wins (on four occasions)	2	Undefeated home (on two occasions)	2
Losses (on two occasions)	4	Undefeated away (09/08/08–01/11/08)	6
Draws (30/08/08–13/09/08)	2	Without scoring (on two occasions)	3
Undefeated (23/08/08–27/09/08)	5	Without conceding (on two occasions)	2
Without win (28/03/09–02/05/09)	6	Scoring (13/09/08–25/10/08)	6

CARDS RECEIVED

50 **4**

QUICK-FIRE GOALS

From the start of a match
Paul McManus (v Queen's Park) 1:00

By a substitute after coming on
Paul McManus (v Alloa) 9:00

GOALS SCORED/CONCEDED PER FIVE-MINUTE INTERVALS

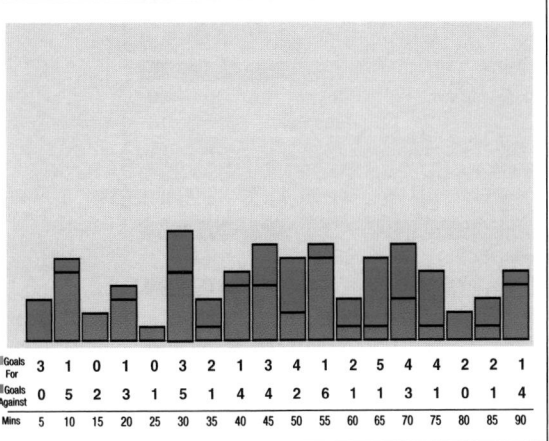

Goals For	3	1	0	1	0	3	2	1	3	4	1	2	5	4	4	2	2	1
Goals Against	0	5	2	3	1	5	1	4	4	2	6	1	1	3	1	0	1	4
Mins	5	10	15	20	25	30	35	40	45	50	55	60	65	70	75	80	85	90

PETERHEAD will face another season in the Irn-Bru Second Division after a 4–1 aggregate defeat in their play-off semi-final clash against Airdrie United.

The Blue Toon gave themselves a mountain to climb when they lost the first leg 2–0 at their Balmoor Stadium home. Despite giving themselves a lifeline in the return game in Lanarkshire, when Stuart McKay's header reduced the deficit, United came back with second-half goals from Marc Smyth and John Baird to mean Airdrie will remain in the First Division for at least another year.

Neale Cooper's men pushed their full-time counterparts all the way and will have taken plenty of confidence from their efforts. However, the Highland club will have to re-group before they launch another promotion bid in 2009/10.

CLUB SUMMARY

FORMED	1890
MANAGER	Neale Cooper
GROUND	Balmoor Stadium
CAPACITY	4,000
NICKNAME	The Blue Toon
WEBSITE	www.peterheadfc.org

The New **Football Pools** PLAYER OF THE SEASON — Callum MacDonald

OVERALL

P	W	D	L	F	A	GD
44	17	12	15	67	53	14

IRN-BRU SECOND DIVISION

Pos	P	W	D	L	F	A	GD	Pts
4	36	15	11	10	54	39	15	56

HOME

Pos	P	W	D	L	F	A	GD	Pts
4	18	9	5	4	32	16	16	32

AWAY

Pos	P	W	D	L	F	A	GD	Pts
5	18	6	6	6	22	23	-1	24

CUP PROGRESS DETAILS

Competition	Round reached	Knocked out by
Co-op Insurance Cup	R1	Dunfermline
Scottish Cup	R4	Queens Park
Challenge Cup	R2	Partick

BIGGEST WIN (ALL COMPS)
26/07/08 6–0 v Montrose **SLCC1NE**

BIGGEST DEFEAT (ALL COMPS)
13/12/08 0–4 v Arbroath **SC2**

ATTENDANCE RECORD

High	Low	Average
855	400	615
v Stirling (25/04/2009)	v Stirling (22/11/2008)	

RESULTS 2008/09

July
26th ⚫ Montrose ....h W 6–0 **Att:** 514 — **Scorers:** Bavidge[2], Gunn[3], Cumming OG

August
2nd ⚫ East Fife............a W 0–2 **Att:** 888 — **Scorers:** Gunn, Sharp. **Booked:** McVitie
5th ⚫ Dunfermline ......h L 0–2 **Att:** 1,291 — **Booked:** Anderson
9th ⚫ Arbroath............h D 1–1 **Att:** 631 — **Scorers:** McKay. **Booked:** Mann, Mann, McKay, McVitie
12th ⚫ Partick ....a L 4–2 **Att:** 1,133 — **Scorers:** Gunn, Kozminski. **Booked:** Skinner, Kozminski
16th ⚫ Brechin............a D 2–2 **Att:** 524 — **Scorers:** Bavidge, Gunn. **Booked:** Sharp, MacDonald, McKay, Gunn
23rd ⚫ Alloa.................h W 1–0 **Att:** 500 — **Scorers:** Anderson. **Booked:** MacDonald
30th ⚫ Raith ....h L 1–2 **Att:** 837 — **Scorers:** Anderson

September
13th ⚫ Queens Park ....a W 0–1 **Att:** 578 — **Scorers:** Anderson
20th ⚫ Stranraer ....h W 4–0 **Att:** 488 — **Scorers:** Gunn, MacDonald, Ross[2]. **Booked:** McKay
27th ⚫ Stirling ....a D 0–0 **Att:** 527

October
4th ⚫ Ayr ....a L 2–0 **Att:** 1,100 — **Booked:** Skinner, Bavidge, McKay, Anderson
18th ⚫ East Fife............h L 0–1 **Att:** 680
25th ⚫ Alloa.................a L 1–0 **Att:** 331 — **Booked:** Gunn

November
1st ⚫ Brechin............h W 5–1 **Att:** 573 — **Scorers:** Bavidge[2], Cowie, Ross, Sharp
8th ⚫ Queens Park ....h W 4–1 **Att:** 564 — **Scorers:** Bavidge[3], Sharp. **Booked:** McVitie
15th ⚫ Raith ....a L 3–0 **Att:** 1,597 — **Dismissed:** McVitie
22nd ⚫ Stirling ....h D 1–1 **Att:** 400 — **Scorers:** Sharp
29th ⚫ Morton ....h W 2–1 **Att:** 817 — **Scorers:** Bavidge, Ross. **Booked:** Sharp, Skinner

December
13th ⚫ Arbroath............a L 4–0 **Att:** 451 — **Booked:** Sharp, Kozminski
20th ⚫ Ayr ....h W 3–0 **Att:** 556 — **Scorers:** Bavidge, Gunn, Sharp. **Booked:** Donald
27th ⚫ Raith ....h W 2–1 **Att:** 796 — **Scorers:** Ross[2]. **Booked:** Anderson

January
3rd ⚫ Queens Park ....a L 2–1 **Att:** 617 — **Scorers:** McKay. **Booked:** Anderson
10th ⚫ Queens Park ....h D 2–2 **Att:** 842 — **Scorers:** Anderson, Bavidge. **Booked:** McKay
17th ⚫ Alloa.................h D 2–2 **Att:** 601 — **Scorers:** McKay, Ross
20th ⚫ Queens Park ....a L 1–0 **Att:** 782
24th ⚫ Brechin.............a D 1–1 **Att:** 517 — **Scorers:** Bavidge
31st ⚫ East Fife............a W 0–3 **Att:** 698 — **Scorers:** McKay[2], Sharp

February
21st ⚫ Stranraer ....h W 1–0 **Att:** 531 — **Scorers:** Bavidge. **Booked:** Anderson, Sharp
28th ⚫ Raith ....a D 3–3 **Att:** 1,564 — **Scorers:** MacDonald[2], McKay. **Booked:** McVitie, Mann

March
4th ⚫ Stranraer ....a W 0–3 **Att:** 131 — **Scorers:** McVitie, Moore[2]
7th ⚫ Queens Park ....h D 1–1 **Att:** 695 — **Scorers:** Anderson
10th ⚫ Arbroath............h W 1–0 **Att:** 466 — **Scorers:** Anderson. **Booked:** Jarvie, Gunn
14th ⚫ East Fife............h W 2–0 **Att:** 556 — **Scorers:** MacDonald, Sharp
17th ⚫ Stirling ....a L 2–1 **Att:** 404 — **Scorers:** MacDonald
21st ⚫ Ayr ....a D 0–0 **Att:** 1,601 — **Booked:** McKay. **Dismissed:** Sharp, McKay

April
4th ⚫ Alloa.................a W 1–2 **Att:** 479 — **Scorers:** Kozminski, MacDonald. **Booked:** Gunn, Moore, Anderson
11th ⚫ Brechin.............h L 0–1 **Att:** 739
18th ⚫ Stranraer ....a W 0–1 **Att:** 221 — **Scorers:** Mann
25th ⚫ Stirling ....h D 1–1 **Att:** 855 — **Scorers:** Mann

May
2nd ⚫ Arbroath............a D 2–2 **Att:** 599 — **Scorers:** Anderson[2]. **Booked:** Anderson, MacDonald
9th ⚫ Ayr ....h L 2–3 **Att:** 602 — **Scorers:** Sharp[2]
14th ⚫ Airdrie Utd ....h L 0–2 **Att:** 1,364
17th ⚫ Airdrie Utd ....a L 2–1 **Att:** 1,008 — **Scorers:** McKay. **Booked:** Mann

⚫ Irn-Bru Second Division ⚫ Scottish FA Cup ⚫ Scottish League Cup ⚫ Scottish Challenge Cup

SECOND DIVISION GOALKEEPER STATS

Player	Appearances	Match starts	Completed matches	Sub appearances	Subbed off	Clean sheets	Yellow cards	Red cards
Paul Jarvie	11	11	10	0	1	4	1	0
Michal Kula	26	25	25	1	0	8	0	0

SECOND DIVISION OUTFIELD PLAYER STATS

Player	Appearances	Match starts	Completed matches	Substitute appearances	Subbed off	Goals scored	Yellow cards	Red cards
Stuart Anderson	36	35	31	1	4	7	6	0
Andrew Bagshaw	6	4	0	2	4	0	0	0
Martin Bavidge	33	32	25	1	7	9	1	0
Dean Cowie	7	2	1	5	1	1	0	0
Lewis Davidson	1	0	0	1	0	0	0	0
David Donald	36	36	35	0	1	0	1	0
Ryan Duncan	2	0	0	2	0	0	0	0
Sean Fleming	7	5	3	2	2	0	0	0
Craig Gunn	36	26	15	10	11	4	4	0
Konrad Kozminski	17	1	1	16	0	1	1	0
Callum MacDonald	34	34	34	0	0	6	3	0
Robert Mann	21	17	15	4	2	2	3	0
Stuart McKay	35	32	22	3	9	6	5	1
Neil McVitie	24	24	18	0	5	1	4	1
Daniel Moore	33	32	28	1	4	2	1	0
David Ross	30	16	10	14	6	6	0	0
Graeme Sharp	30	29	21	1	7	9	3	1
Martin Skinner	14	13	12	1	1	0	1	0
Stuart Smith	22	22	22	0	0	0	0	0

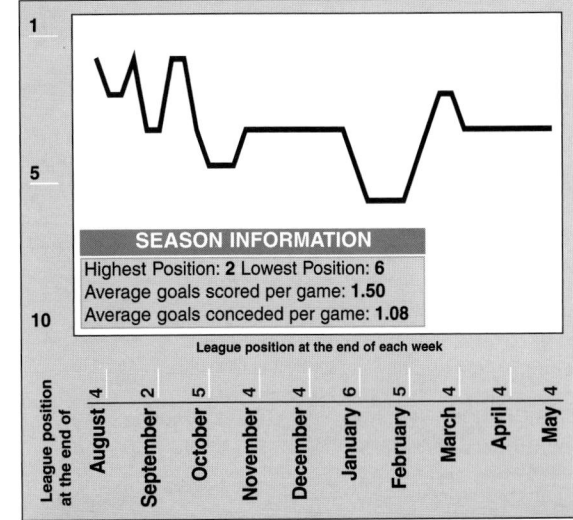

SEASON INFORMATION
Highest Position: **2** Lowest Position: **6**
Average goals scored per game: **1.50**
Average goals conceded per game: **1.08**

League position at the end of each week

LONGEST SEQUENCES

Wins	2	Undefeated home	10
(on five occasions)		(01/11/08–14/03/09)	
Losses	3	Undefeated away	4
(04/10/08–25/10/08)		(on three occasions)	
Draws	2	Without scoring	4
(on three occasions)		(27/09/08–25/10/08)	
Undefeated	9	Without conceding	3
(17/01/09–14/03/09)		(13/09/08–27/09/08)	
Without win	4	Scoring	13
(27/09/08–25/10/08)		(20/12/08–17/03/09)	

CARDS RECEIVED

34 **3**

QUICK-FIRE GOALS

From the start of a match
Stuart Anderson (v Alloa) 6:00

By a substitute after coming on
Dean Cowie (v Brechin) 3:00

GOALS SCORED/CONCEDED PER FIVE-MINUTE INTERVALS

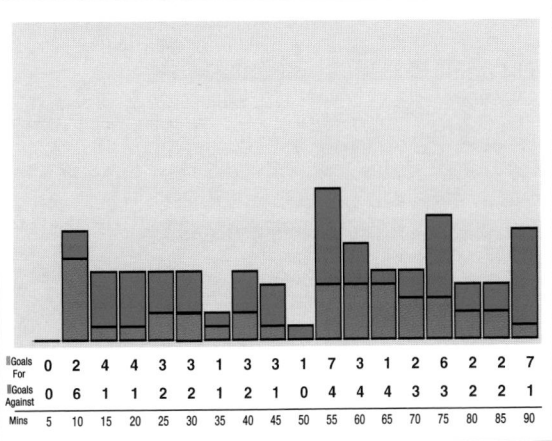

Goals For	0	2	4	4	3	3	1	3	3	1	7	3	1	2	6	2	2	7
Goals Against	0	6	1	1	2	2	1	2	1	0	4	4	4	3	3	2	2	1
Mins	5	10	15	20	25	30	35	40	45	50	55	60	65	70	75	80	85	90

QUEEN'S PARK

QUEEN'S PARK had the consolation of the memory of a Celtic Park adventure to take from a disappointing season that saw them drop down to the Irn-Bru Third Division.

The Spiders drew more games than any other team in the division, 12, to finish in second-bottom place as an inability to take their chances cost them dear. They also failed to beat fellow strugglers Stranraer and Arbroath, undermining victories at East Fife and Stirling. Their demotion came after defeat to Stenhousemuir in the play-offs.

The highlight of the campaign was Adam Coakley's strike at Celtic Park, the final goal of a 2–1 fifth-round Homecoming Scottish Cup defeat. Coakley was later sent off, after initially being booked for his celebrations, which all but ended Queen's Park's hopes of pressing for an equaliser against the Glasgow giants.

CLUB SUMMARY

FORMED	1867
MANAGER	Gardner Speirs
GROUND	Hampden Park
CAPACITY	52,5000
NICKNAME	The Spiders
WEBSITE	www.queensparkfc.co.uk

The New Football Pools PLAYER OF THE SEASON

Barry Douglas

OVERALL

P	W	D	L	F	A	GD
44	9	14	21	44	67	-23

IRN-BRU SECOND DIVISION

Pos	P	W	D	L	F	A	GD	Pts
9	36	7	12	17	35	54	-19	33

HOME

Pos	P	W	D	L	F	A	GD	Pts
9	18	4	6	8	17	23	-6	18

AWAY

Pos	P	W	D	L	F	A	GD	Pts
8	18	3	6	9	18	31	-13	15

CUP PROGRESS DETAILS

Competition	Round reached	Knocked out by
Co-op Insurance Cup	R1	Clyde
Scottish Cup	R5	Celtic
Challenge Cup	R1	Partick

BIGGEST WIN (ALL COMPS)
20/12/08 3–0 v Stirling SC2

BIGGEST DEFEAT (ALL COMPS)
11/05/09 0–4 v Stirling SC2

ATTENDANCE RECORD

High	Low	Average
1,763	466	730
v Raith (02/05/2009)	v Brechin (17/01/2009)	

RESULTS 2008/09

July
26th ● Partick ....a L 2–1 **Att:** 1,386 — **Scorers:** Henry. **Dismissed:** Sinclair

August
2nd ● Stranraer ....h D 2–2 **Att:** 611 — **Scorers:** Cairney, Dunn. **Booked:** Harkins
5th ● Clyde ....a L 4–1 **Att:** 690 — **Scorers:** Harkins. **Booked:** Harkins, Brough, Neill
9th ● Raith ....a L 2–0 **Att:** 1,507 — **Booked:** Douglas, Sinclair. **Dismissed:** Cairney
16th ● East Fife..........a W 1–2 **Att:** 789 — **Scorers:** Coakley, Dunlop
23rd ● Brechin.............h D 1–1 **Att:** 613 — **Scorers:** Douglas. **Booked:** Sinclair
30th ● Ayr ....a L 2–1 **Att:** 1,427 — **Scorers:** Quinn. **Booked:** Quinn, Brough

September
13th ● Peterhead ....h L 0–1 **Att:** 578
20th ● Arbroath ....a D 1–1 **Att:** 523 — **Scorers:** Brough. **Booked:** Douglas
27th ● Alloa ....h W 1–0 **Att:** 518 — **Scorers:** Harkins. **Booked:** Little, Brough, Neill

October
4th ● Stirling ....h D 1–1 **Att:** 713 — **Scorers:** Watt. **Booked:** Little
18th ● Stranraer ....a D 0–0 **Att:** 284 — **Booked:** Cairney, Ronald, Coakley. **Dismissed:** Ronald
25th ● Brechin.............a L 2–1 **Att:** 483 — **Scorers:** Watt. **Booked:** Little, Quinn

November
1st ● East Fife..........h D 0–0 **Att:** 752
8th ● Peterhead ....a L 4–1 **Att:** 564 — **Scorers:** Coakley
15th ● Ayr ....h L 0–3 **Att:** 1,009 — **Booked:** McGrady, Little
22nd ● Alloa................a W 1–3 **Att:** 557 — **Scorers:** Cairney, Harkins, Watt. **Booked:** Agostini, Coakley
29th ● Albion..............a W 1–2 **Att:** 619 — **Scorers:** Cairney, Watt. **Booked:** Holms, Holms, Brough, Little

December
6th ● Arbroath ....h L 1–2 **Att:** 637 — **Scorers:** Cairney
13th ● Raith ....h L 1–2 **Att:** 735 — **Scorers:** Nicholas. **Booked:** Cairney, Nicholas
20th ● Stirling ....a W 0–3 **Att:** 525 — **Scorers:** Brough, Coakley, Holms

January
3rd ● Peterhead ....h W 2–1 **Att:** 617 — **Scorers:** Cairney, Watt. **Booked:** Brough, Sinclair
10th ● Peterhead ....a D 2–2 **Att:** 842 — **Scorers:** Brough, Cairney. **Booked:** Watt, Sinclair, Brough
17th ● Brechin.............h D 0–0 **Att:** 466
20th ● Peterhead ....h W 1–0 **Att:** 782 — **Scorers:** Holms
24th ● East Fife..........a L 4–2 **Att:** 785 — **Scorers:** Cairney, Watt. **Booked:** Quinn
31st ● Stranraer ....h D 1–1 **Att:** 474 — **Scorers:** Douglas

February
7th ● Celtic ....a L 2–1 **Att:** 22,223 — **Scorers:** Coakley.
Booked: Ure, Coakley, Quinn, Brough. **Dismissed:** Coakley
14th ● Alloa................h L 1–2 **Att:** 606 — **Scorers:** Harkins.
Booked: Douglas, Watt, Quinn. **Dismissed:** Douglas
21st ● Arbroath ....a L 3–0 **Att:** 568 — **Booked:** Harkins, Neill, Sinclair, Watt
28th ● Ayr ....h L 0–3 **Att:** 1,139 — **Booked:** Sinclair

March
4th ● Ayr ....a D 1–1 **Att:** 1,360 — **Scorers:** Odenewo. **Booked:** Brough, Holms. **Dismissed:** Brough
7th ● Peterhead ....a D 1–1 **Att:** 695 — **Scorers:** Watt. **Booked:** Sinclair
14th ● Stranraer ....a D 2–2 **Att:** 338 — **Scorers:** Barry, Cairney. **Booked:** Reilly, Neill
17th ● Raith ....a L 1–0 **Att:** 1,294 — **Booked:** Reilly
21st ● Stirling ....h W 3–1 **Att:** 594 — **Scorers:** Cairney, Harkins, Odenewo

April
4th ● Brechin.............a L 2–0 **Att:** 467
11th ● East Fife..........h W 3–1 **Att:** 601 — **Scorers:** Cairney, Harkins, Holms. **Booked:** Odenewo, Brough
18th ● Arbroath ....h L 0–1 **Att:** 722 — **Booked:** Sinclair
25th ● Alloa................a D 0–0 **Att:** 704 — **Booked:** Sinclair

May
2nd ● Raith ....h L 0–1 **Att:** 1,763 — **Booked:** Watt. **Dismissed:** McGinn
11th ● Stirling ....a L 4–0 **Att:** 284
14th ● Stenhousemuir..a L 1–2 **Att:** 617 — **Scorers:** Harkins
17th ● Stenhousemuir..h D 0–0 **Att:** 854 — **Booked:** Reilly

● Irn-Bru Second Division ● Scottish FA Cup ● Scottish League Cup ● Scottish Challenge Cup

SECOND DIVISION GOALKEEPER STATS

Player	Appearances	Match starts	Completed matches	Sub appearances	Subbed off	Clean sheets	Yellow cards	Red cards
Alex Cowie	13	13	13	0	0	1	0	0
David Crawford	23	23	23	0	0	5	0	0

SECOND DIVISION OUTFIELD PLAYER STATS

Player	Appearances	Match starts	Completed matches	Substitute appearances	Subbed off	Goals scored	Yellow cards	Red cards
Damiano Agostini	16	14	13	2	1	0	1	0
Steven Baillie	1	0	0	1	0	0	0	0
Douglas Barry	1	1	1	0	0	1	0	0
Andrew Boslem	7	3	3	4	0	0	0	0
James Brough	33	32	30	1	1	2	5	1
Paul Cairney	33	33	30	0	2	8	2	1
Giuseppe Capuano	1	0	0	1	0	0	0	0
Adam Coakley	21	12	4	9	8	3	2	0
Barry Douglas	30	30	29	0	0	2	3	1
Ross Dunlop	27	17	13	10	4	1	0	0
Robert Dunn	7	2	0	5	2	1	0	0
Paul Harkins	30	27	19	3	8	5	2	0
Jack Henry	4	3	0	1	3	0	0	0
Ryan Holms	31	25	14	6	11	2	1	0
Richard Little	11	11	11	0	0	0	4	0
Paul McGinn	1	0	0	1	0	0	0	1
Stuart McGrady	10	5	1	5	4	0	1	0
Anthony McGrogan	7	0	0	7	0	0	0	0
David Murray	13	5	2	8	3	0	0	0
John Neill	20	20	15	0	5	0	3	0
Steven Nicholas	17	16	5	1	11	1	1	0
Steven Odenewo	10	10	3	0	7	2	1	0
Anthony Quinn	23	22	19	1	3	1	4	0
Steven Reilly	7	6	5	1	1	0	2	0
Paul Ronald	11	4	2	7	1	0	1	1
Richard Sinclair	17	17	12	0	5	0	8	0
Martin Ure	24	24	22	0	2	0	0	0
David Waters	5	5	5	0	0	0	0	0
Ian Watt	29	16	11	13	5	6	3	0

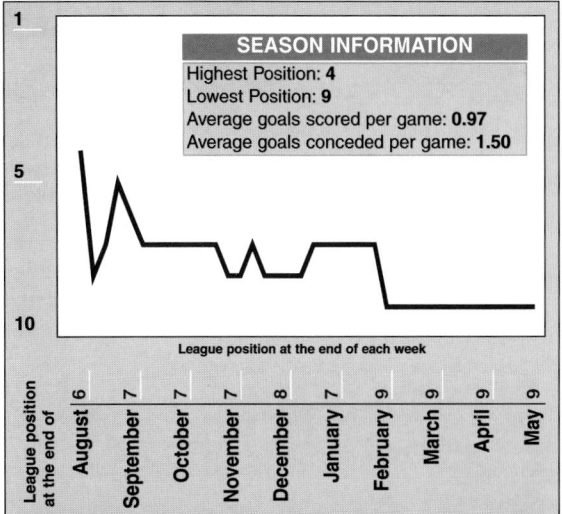

SEASON INFORMATION

Highest Position: **4**
Lowest Position: **9**
Average goals scored per game: **0.97**
Average goals conceded per game: **1.50**

League position at the end of each week

LONGEST SEQUENCES

Wins (20/12/08–03/01/09)	2	Undefeated home (on two occasions)	3
Losses (14/02/09–28/02/09)	3	Undefeated away (04/03/09–14/03/09)	3
Draws (04/03/09–14/03/09)	3	Without scoring (18/04/09–11/05/09)	4
Undefeated (20/09/08–18/10/08)	4	Without conceding (–)	
Without win (17/01/09–17/03/09)	10	Scoring (22/11/08–03/01/09)	5

CARDS RECEIVED

QUICK-FIRE GOALS

From the start of a match
Adam Coakley (v Peterhead) 8:00

By a substitute after coming on
Robert Dunn (v Stranraer) 4:00

GOALS SCORED/CONCEDED PER FIVE-MINUTE INTERVALS

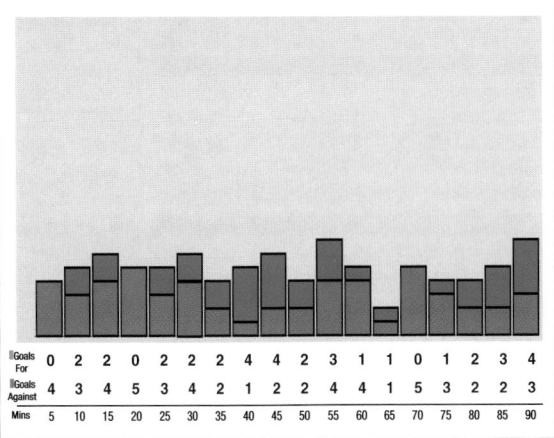

Goals For	0	2	2	0	2	2	2	4	4	2	3	1	1	0	1	2	3	4
Goals Against	4	3	4	5	3	4	2	1	2	2	4	4	1	5	3	2	2	3
Mins	5	10	15	20	25	30	35	40	45	50	55	60	65	70	75	80	85	90

RAITH ROVERS

DESPITE a period of financial uncertainty, Raith ended the season back in the Irn-Bru First Division after comfortably securing promotion.

The Kirkcaldy side were sniffing about the top of the table from the season's start, and managed to assume pole position in November.

John McGlynn's men refused to relinquish their grasp on first place and enjoyed a consistent lead over their rivals. Goals were flowing too, with 10 scored and none conceded in a four-game period in the spring.

Kevin Smith blasted in 18 goals and ended the season as the division's top scorer, whilst Graham Weir also chipped in with a healthy nine goals. And, with the return of fans' favourite Marvin Andrews from injury, Rovers will believe they can make a positive impact upon the First Division in 2009/10.

CLUB SUMMARY

FORMED	1883
MANAGER	John McGlynn
GROUND	Stark's Park
CAPACITY	10,104
NICKNAME	The Rovers
WEBSITE	www.raithrovers.com

The New Football Pools PLAYER OF THE SEASON — **Graham Weir**

OVERALL

P	W	D	L	F	A	GD
41	22	12	7	63	34	29

IRN-BRU SECOND DIVISION

Pos	P	W	D	L	F	A	GD	Pts
1	36	22	10	4	60	27	33	76

HOME

Pos	P	W	D	L	F	A	GD	Pts
2	18	11	6	1	33	16	17	39

AWAY

Pos	P	W	D	L	F	A	GD	Pts
1	18	11	4	3	27	11	16	37

CUP PROGRESS DETAILS

Competition	Round reached	Knocked out by
Co-op Insurance Cup	R2	Falkirk
Scottish Cup	R3	Alloa
Challenge Cup	R2	Ross County

BIGGEST WIN (ALL COMPS)
24/03/09 4–0 v Brechin SC2

BIGGEST DEFEAT (ALL COMPS)
26/08/08 1–3 v Falkirk SLC2

ATTENDANCE RECORD

High	Low	Average
4,812	1,294	2,106
v East Fife (03/01/2009)	v Queen's Park (17/03/2009)	

RESULTS 2008/09

August
2nd	● Ayr	a	D 0–0	Att: 1,373 — Booked: Ellis, Smith
5th	● Albion	a	D 0–0	Att: 415 — Booked: Davidson. Dismissed: Davidson (Won 4–3 on pens).
9th	● Queen's Park	h	W 2–0	Att: 1,507 — Scorers: Smith, Walker. Booked: Cook, Smith. Dismissed: Cook
12th	● Ross County	h	L 1–2	Att: 1,080 — Scorers: Weir. Booked: Wardlaw
16th	● Alloa	a	D 1–1	Att: 899 — Scorers: Smith. Booked: Wilson, Weir, Smith
23rd	● Stranraer	h	W 2–1	Att: 1,483 — Scorers: Campbell, Smith. Booked: Ellis
26th	● Falkirk	h	L 1–3	Att: 2,090 — Scorers: Campbell. Booked: C. Silvestro, McGurn
30th	● Peterhead	a	W 1–2	Att: 837 — Scorers: Smith, Wardlaw

September
13th	● East Fife	h	D 1–1	Att: 3,637 — Scorers: Ellis
20th	● Stirling	h	D 1–1	Att: 1,648 — Scorers: Smith. Booked: Davidson, Campbell
27th	● Brechin	a	L 2–0	Att: 769 — Booked: Campbell

October
4th	● Arbroath	a	W 0–2	Att: 855 — Scorers: Ferry, Walker. Booked: Wilson
18th	● Ayr	h	W 3–2	Att: 1,746 — Scorers: Smith, Wales, Weir. Booked: Weir, Walker, Ellis
25th	● Stranraer	a	W 0–2	Att: 253 — Scorers: Smith, Wales. Booked: Smith, Campbell

November
1st	● Alloa	h	W 4–1	Att: 1,669 — Scorers: Ferry, Smith², Wales. Booked: Weir
8th	● East Fife	a	W 0–2	Att: 1,980 — Scorers: Sloan, Smith
15th	● Peterhead	h	W 3–0	Att: 1,597 — Scorers: Wales², Weir. Booked: Wales
22nd	● Brechin	h	D 2–2	Att: 2,229 — Scorers: Wales, Wardlaw. Booked: Wales, Wilson
29th	● Alloa	h	D 0–0	Att: 1,493

December
9th	● Alloa	a	L 2–1	Att: 860 — Scorers: Wales. Booked: Walker, Sloan
13th	● Queen's Park	a	W 1–2	Att: 735 — Scorers: Smith². Booked: Wilson, Sloan, Davidson
20th	● Arbroath	h	W 2–1	Att: 1,477 — Scorers: Davidson, Ferry. Booked: Davidson, Wales
27th	● Peterhead	h	L 2–1	Att: 796 — Scorers: Wales. Booked: Davidson

January
3rd	● East Fife	h	W 1–0	Att: 4,812 — Scorers: Ferry. Booked: Campbell, Wales
10th	● Stirling	a	L 2–1	Att: 906 — Scorers: Sloan. Booked: Lumsden, Ellis
17th	● Stranraer	h	W 2–1	Att: 1,455 — Scorers: Weir, Wilson. Booked: Wilson
24th	● Alloa	a	D 0–0	Att: 953
31st	● Ayr	a	D 2–2	Att: 2,363 — Scorers: Campbell, Ferry. Booked: Simmons, Smith

February
21st	● Stirling	h	D 1–1	Att: 1,770 — Scorers: Smith. Booked: Davidson
28th	● Peterhead	h	D 3–3	Att: 1,564 — Scorers: Campbell, Smith, Weir. Booked: Simmons

March
7th	● East Fife	a	W 0–1	Att: 1,980 — Scorers: Weir. Booked: Wilson, Weir, Simmons, Wales, Walker
14th	● Ayr	h	L 0–1	Att: 1,294
17th	● Queen's Park	h	W 1–0	Att: 1,294 — Scorers: Weir
21st	● Arbroath	a	W 0–2	Att: 921 — Scorers: Campbell, Sloan. Booked: Wales, Campbell, Sloan, Hislop. Dismissed: Davidson
24th	● Brechin	a	W 0–4	Att: 780 — Scorers: Campbell, Smith², Wales

April
4th	● Stranraer	a	W 0–3	Att: 367 — Scorers: Hislop, Sloan, Williamson
11th	● Alloa	h	W 3–1	Att: 1,770 — Scorers: Smith², Weir. Booked: Andrews, Simmons. Dismissed: Simmons
18th	● Stirling	a	W 0–1	Att: 1,125 — Scorers: Hislop. Booked: Hislop
25th	● Brechin	h	W 2–0	Att: 2,529 — Scorers: Sloan, Weir. Booked: Campbell, Wilson, Davidson, Weir

May
2nd	● Queen's Park	a	W 0–1	Att: 1,763 — Scorers: Weir. Booked: Simmons, Wardlaw
9th	● Arbroath	h	D 0–0	Att: 4,426

● Irn-Bru Second Division ● Scottish FA Cup ● Scottish League Cup ● Scottish Challenge Cup

actim

SECOND DIVISION GOALKEEPER STATS

Player	Appearances	Match starts	Completed matches	Sub appearances	Subbed off	Clean sheets	Yellow cards	Red cards
David McGurn	30	30	29	0	1	15	0	0
Gary O'Connor	7	6	6	1	0	2	0	0

SECOND DIVISION OUTFIELD PLAYER STATS

Player	Appearances	Match starts	Completed matches	Substitute appearances	Subbed off	Goals scored	Yellow cards	Red cards
Marvin Andrews	10	10	9	0	1	0	1	0
David Armstrong	1	0	0	1	0	0	0	0
Lee Bryce	12	0	0	12	0	0	0	0
Mark Campbell	31	31	25	0	6	5	6	0
Andrew Cook	18	13	12	5	0	0	1	1
Iain Davidson	33	33	32	0	0	1	6	1
Joe Dunbar	3	0	0	3	0	0	0	0
Laurie Ellis	28	28	24	0	4	1	4	0
Mark Ferry	35	27	23	8	4	5	0	0
Thomas Graham	2	0	0	2	0	0	0	0
Juan Guerrero	1	0	0	1	1	0	0	0
Steven Hislop	11	3	0	8	3	2	2	0
Todd Lumsden	11	10	9	1	1	0	1	0
Chris Silvestro	11	8	3	3	5	0	0	0
Stephen Simmons	12	12	10	0	1	0	5	1
Robert Sloan	33	31	27	2	4	5	2	0
Kevin Smith	28	25	9	3	16	18	5	0
Gary Wales	23	20	14	3	6	8	6	0
Allan Walker	32	24	20	8	4	2	2	0
Gareth Wardlaw	20	4	1	16	3	2	1	0
Graham Weir	36	34	17	2	17	9	5	0
Ian Williamson	12	9	3	3	6	1	0	0
Craig Wilson	36	36	36	0	0	1	7	0

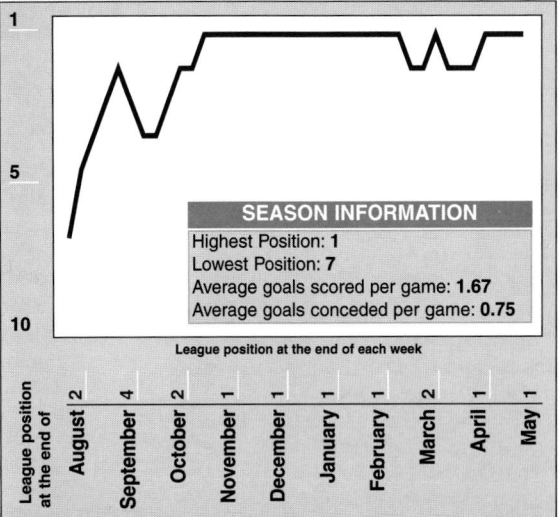

League position at the end of each week

SEASON INFORMATION

Highest Position: **1**
Lowest Position: **7**
Average goals scored per game: **1.67**
Average goals conceded per game: **0.75**

LONGEST SEQUENCES

Wins (17/03/09–02/05/09)	8	Undefeated home (02/08/08–28/02/09)	14
Losses (–)		Undefeated away (04/10/08–13/12/08)	4
Draws (24/01/09–28/02/09)	4	Without scoring (–)	
Undefeated (on two occasions)	9	Without conceding (17/03/09–04/04/09)	4
Without win (24/01/09–28/02/09)	4	Scoring (04/10/08–17/01/09)	13

CARDS RECEIVED

55   3

QUICK-FIRE GOALS

From the start of a match
Graham Weir (v Stranraer) 1:00

By a substitute after coming on
Mark Ferry (v East Fife) 1:00

GOALS SCORED/CONCEDED PER FIVE-MINUTE INTERVALS

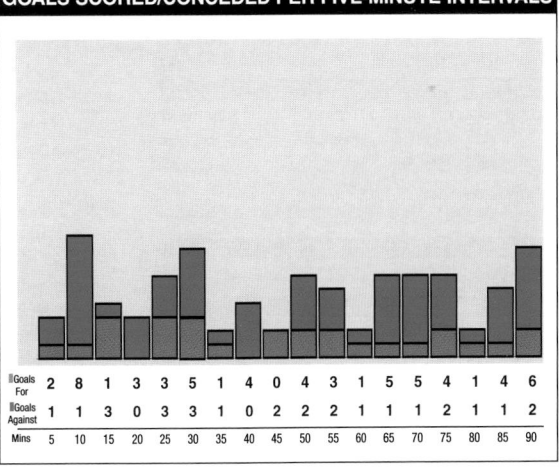

Goals For	2	8	1	3	3	5	1	4	0	4	3	1	5	5	4	1	4	6
Goals Against	1	1	3	0	3	3	1	0	2	2	2	1	1	1	2	1	1	2
Mins	5	10	15	20	25	30	35	40	45	50	55	60	65	70	75	80	85	90

STIRLING ALBION

AFTER the previous season's relegation, Stirling found themselves marooned in the middle of the Irn-Bru Second Division table, finishing in fifth place.

It was a patchy start to the campaign, with only two wins from the first 11 games. Results picked up at the turn of the year, with Allan Moore's men enjoying a nine-match unbeaten run from January to March, including an 8–2 mauling of Stranraer and a 2–1 victory over eventual champions Raith.

Former St Mirren striker David McKenna helped to strengthen Stirling's position with an impressive goal haul and former Motherwell player Martin Grehan similarly found his shooting boots. Their contributions helped to maintain a respectable standing but, after having dropped down from the First Division, more was expected of the club's season.

CLUB SUMMARY

FORMED	1945
MANAGER	Allan Moore
GROUND	Forthbank Stadium
CAPACITY	3,808
NICKNAME	The Binos
WEBSITE	www.stirlingalbionfc.co.uk

The New Football Pools PLAYER OF THE SEASON — Andy Graham

OVERALL
P	W	D	L	F	A	GD
39	14	11	14	63	58	5

IRN-BRU SECOND DIVISION
Pos	P	W	D	L	F	A	GD	Pts
5	36	14	11	11	59	49	10	53

HOME
Pos	P	W	D	L	F	A	GD	Pts
6	18	7	5	6	26	23	3	26

AWAY
Pos	P	W	D	L	F	A	GD	Pts
3	18	7	6	5	33	26	7	27

CUP PROGRESS DETAILS
Competition	Round reached	Knocked out by
Co-op Insurance Cup	R1	Arbroath
Scottish Cup	R3	Partick
Challenge Cup	R1	Dunfermline

BIGGEST WIN (ALL COMPS)
24/01/09 8–2 v Stranraer **SC2**

BIGGEST DEFEAT (ALL COMPS)
0–3 on two occasions

ATTENDANCE RECORD
High	Low	Average
1,125	284	642
v Raith (18/04/2009)	v Queen's Park (11/05/2009)	

RESULTS 2008/09

July
26th ● Dunfermline ......a L 3–0 **Att:** 1,327 — **Booked:** Lowing

August
2nd ● Brechin.............a L 2–1 **Att:** 535 — **Scorers:** White OG. **Booked:** Devine
6th ● Arbroath ....a L 3–2 **Att:** 448 — **Scorers:** Graham, Harty. **Booked:** O'Neil, Lowing
9th ● East Fife...........h D 1–1 **Att:** 686 — **Scorers:** O'Neil. **Booked:** Grehan, Harty, O'Neill
16th ● Stranraer ....a L 1–0 **Att:** 233 — **Booked:** Lawrie, Graham
23rd ● Ayr ....h D 2–2 **Att:** 877 — **Scorers:** Harty, Taggart. **Booked:** Lowing, Corr
30th ● Arbroath ....a W 1–2 **Att:** 631 — **Scorers:** McKenna, O'Neill. **Booked:** Harty, Lowing. **Dismissed:** Docherty

September
13th ● Alloa.................h W 3–2 **Att:** 907 — **Scorers:** Corr, Graham, Harty
20th ● Raith ....a D 1–1 **Att:** 1,648 — **Scorers:** Taggart. **Booked:** O'Neill, Lowing
27th ● Peterhead ....h D 0–0 **Att:** 527

October
4th ● Queen's Park ....a D 1–1 **Att:** 713 — **Scorers:** Harty. **Booked:** Molloy, Docherty
18th ● Brechin.............h L 1–2 **Att:** 577 — **Scorers:** Grehan. **Booked:** Forsyth
25th ● Ayr ....a D 1–1 **Att:** 1,057 — **Scorers:** O'Neill. **Booked:** O'Neill, Graham, Forsyth, Molloy

November
1st ● Stranraer ....h W 3–2 **Att:** 489 — **Scorers:** Grehan, Molloy[2]. **Booked:** Corr, Taggart
8th ● Alloa.................a L 4–3 **Att:** 1,001 — **Scorers:** Grehan, Murphy, Hill OG. **Booked:** Harty, Graham, Devine
15th ● Arbroath ....h L 0–2 **Att:** 509 — **Booked:** Gibb, Grehan
22nd ● Peterhead ....a D 1–1 **Att:** 400 — **Scorers:** O'Neill. **Booked:** Gibb, Graham
29th ● Partick ....h L 2–3 **Att:** 1,472 — **Scorers:** Molloy, Murphy. **Booked:** Lowing, Gibb, Murphy, Grehan

December
13th ● East Fife...........a W 0–1 **Att:** 593 — **Scorers:** Fotheringham OG. **Booked:** Docherty, Murphy, O'Neill
20th ● Queen's Park ....h L 0–3 **Att:** 525 — **Booked:** Gibb
27th ● Arbroath ....a W 1–2 **Att:** 635 — **Scorers:** McKenna[2]. **Booked:** Hamilton, Boyle

January
10th ● Raith ....h W 2–1 **Att:** 906 — **Scorers:** McKenna, O'Neill. **Booked:** Gibb, Murphy, Roycroft
17th ● Ayr ....h W 2–0 **Att:** 779 — **Scorers:** Grehan, McCord. **Booked:** Gibb, Grehan. **Dismissed:** Forsyth
24th ● Stranraer ....a W 2–8 **Att:** 191 — **Scorers:** Gibb, Grehan[2], Hamilton[3], McKenna, McKinstry OG. **Booked:** O'Neill
31st ● Brechin.............a W 1–2 **Att:** 565 — **Scorers:** Graham, Grehan. **Booked:** O'Neil

February
21st ● Raith ....h D 1–1 **Att:** 1,770 — **Scorers:** McKenna. **Booked:** Murphy
28th ● Arbroath ....h D 1–1 **Att:** 578 — **Scorers:** Docherty. **Booked:** Gibb, Graham. **Dismissed:** McCord

March
3rd ● Alloa.................h D 0–0 **Att:** 768 — **Booked:** Grehan
7th ● Alloa.................a W 2–3 **Att:** 1,057 — **Scorers:** Grehan, McKenna[2]. **Booked:** Forsyth, McKenna, Roycroft
14th ● Brechin.............h L 2–3 **Att:** 529 — **Scorers:** O'Neill, Roycroft
17th ● Peterhead ....h W 2–1 **Att:** 404 — **Scorers:** Grehan, McKenna. **Booked:** Lawrie
21st ● Queen's Park ....a L 3–1 **Att:** 594 — **Scorers:** Docherty. **Booked:** Christie, Murphy, Devine
28th ● East Fife...........h W 2–0 **Att:** 636 — **Scorers:** McKenna[2]. **Booked:** Grehan

April
4th ● Ayr ....a L 3–1 **Att:** 1,573 — **Scorers:** Grehan. **Booked:** Mullen, Roycroft, Lowing, Forsyth. **Dismissed:** Roycroft
11th ● Stranraer ....h L 1–2 **Att:** 459 — **Scorers:** McKenna.
18th ● Raith ....h L 0–1 **Att:** 1,125 — **Booked:** O'Neill, Grehan
25th ● Peterhead ....a D 1–1 **Att:** 855 — **Scorers:** Murphy. **Booked:** O'Neill

May
2nd ● East Fife...........a W 0–3 **Att:** 569 — **Scorers:** McKenna, Mullen[2]. **Booked:** Lawrie
11th ● Queen's Park ....h W 4–0 **Att:** 284 — **Scorers:** Docherty, Grehan, Hamilton, Mullen.

● Irn-Bru Second Division ● Scottish FA Cup ● Scottish League Cup ● Scottish Challenge Cup

actim

SECOND DIVISION GOALKEEPER STATS

Player	Appearances	Match starts	Completed matches	Sub appearances	Subbed off	Clean sheets	Yellow cards	Red cards
Scott Christie	19	19	18	0	1	3	1	0
Myles Hogarth	18	17	17	1	0	3	0	0

SECOND DIVISION OUTFIELD PLAYER STATS

Player	Appearances	Match starts	Completed matches	Substitute appearances	Subbed off	Goals scored	Yellow cards	Red cards
Jonathan Boyle	11	2	1	9	1	0	1	0
Liam Corr	24	12	4	12	8	1	2	0
Stewart Devine	22	19	14	3	5	0	3	0
Mark Docherty	29	22	13	7	8	3	2	1
Robert Dunn	5	0	0	5	0	0	0	0
Shaun Fagan	1	0	0	1	0	0	0	0
Kenneth Feaks	3	2	2	1	0	0	0	0
Ross Forsyth	27	26	24	1	1	0	4	1
Scott Gibb	20	20	19	0	1	1	6	0
Andy Graham	26	25	23	1	2	2	5	0
Martin Grehan	33	30	18	3	12	11	6	0
Chris Hamilton	20	12	2	8	10	4	1	0
Ian Harty	13	12	7	1	5	3	3	0
Andrew Lawrie	26	25	25	1	0	0	3	0
David Lowing	21	20	15	1	5	0	4	0
Ryan McCord	7	3	2	4	0	1	0	1
David McKenna	34	26	15	8	11	13	1	0
Craig Molloy	11	11	9	0	2	2	2	0
Michael Mullen	12	5	2	7	3	3	1	0
Paul Murphy	32	26	24	6	2	2	4	0
John O'Neill	31	30	25	1	5	6	8	0
Sean Roycroft	20	20	15	0	4	1	3	1
Nathan Taggart	13	11	6	2	5	2	1	0
Steven Waddell	8	0	0	8	0	0	0	0

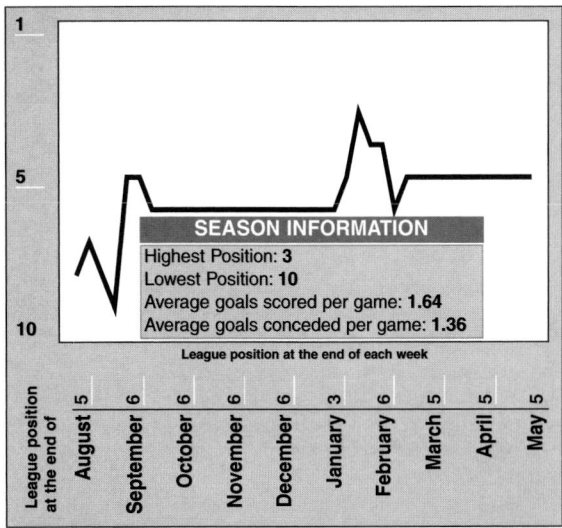

SEASON INFORMATION
Highest Position: **3**
Lowest Position: **10**
Average goals scored per game: **1.64**
Average goals conceded per game: **1.36**

League position at the end of each week

LONGEST SEQUENCES

Wins (27/12/08–31/01/09)	5	Undefeated home (09/08/08–27/09/08)	4
Losses (04/04/09–18/04/09)	3	Undefeated away (22/11/08–07/03/09)	7
Draws (on two occasions)	3	Without scoring (–)	
Undefeated (27/12/08–07/03/09)	9	Without conceding (–)	
Without win (20/09/08–25/10/08)	5	Scoring (on two occasions)	7

CARDS RECEIVED

61   4

QUICK-FIRE GOALS

From the start of a match
David McKenna (v Raith) 2:00

By a substitute after coming on
Ryan McCord (v Ayr) 4:00

GOALS SCORED/CONCEDED PER FIVE-MINUTE INTERVALS

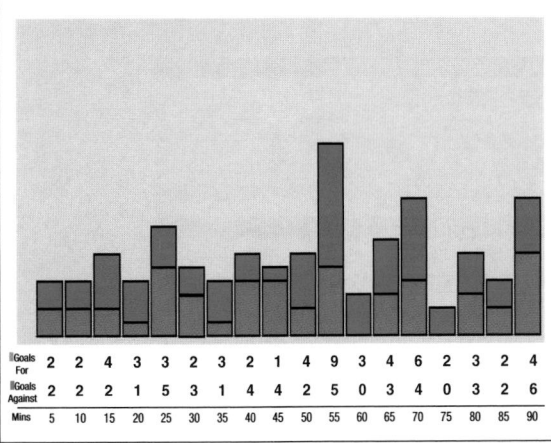

	5	10	15	20	25	30	35	40	45	50	55	60	65	70	75	80	85	90
Goals For	2	2	4	3	3	2	3	2	1	4	9	3	4	6	2	3	2	4
Goals Against	2	2	2	1	5	3	1	4	4	2	5	0	3	4	0	3	2	6

RELEGATED Stranraer finished off a disappointing season in the Irn-Bru Second Division with a 1–0 defeat to East Fife, a result which summed up their campaign.

It was the club's 26th league defeat of the season, with only three victories recorded. Despite being the Blues Supporters' Player of the Year, John Kane scored an own goal against East Fife, symbolising what was an awful campaign for the Stair Park club.

In January, cash-strapped Stranraer parted company with manager Derek Ferguson following an 8–2 home defeat by Stirling. Local boy Keith Knox, a former captain of the club, was made caretaker manager and his position was confirmed as permanent a month later. However, there was to be no fairytale rescue and relegation was confirmed on 4th April following a 3–0 defeat to Raith.

CLUB SUMMARY

FORMED	1870
MANAGER	Keith Knox
GROUND	Stair Park
CAPACITY	5,600
NICKNAME	The Blues
WEBSITE	www.stranraerfc.org

The New **Football Pools** PLAYER OF THE SEASON — **Stuart McColm**

OVERALL
P	W	D	L	F	A	GD
39	3	7	29	34	102	-68

IRN-BRU SECOND DIVISION
Pos	P	W	D	L	F	A	GD	Pts
10	36	3	7	26	31	90	-59	16

HOME
Pos	P	W	D	L	F	A	GD	Pts
10	18	1	4	13	14	48	-34	7

AWAY
Pos	P	W	D	L	F	A	GD	Pts
10	18	2	3	13	17	42	-25	9

CUP PROGRESS DETAILS
Competition	Round reached	Knocked out by
Co-op Insurance Cup	R1	Morton
Scottish Cup	R3	Forfar
Challenge Cup	R1	Livingston

BIGGEST WIN (ALL COMPS)
2–1 on two occasions

BIGGEST DEFEAT (ALL COMPS)
24/01/09 2–8 v Stirling **SC2**

ATTENDANCE RECORD
High	Low	Average
891	124	303
v Ayr (28/03/2009)	v Arbroath (27/09/2008)	

RESULTS 2008/09

July
26th ● Livingston..........a L 4–0 **Att:** 642 — **Booked:** Dobbins, Black, Frizzel, McBride. **Dismissed:** Nicoll

August
2nd ● Queen's Park....a D 2–2 **Att:** 611 — **Scorers:** McBride, Tade. **Booked:** D. Mitchell. **Dismissed:** White
5th ● Morton ....h L 3–6 **Att:** 317 — **Scorers:** Frizzel, Gibson, McColm. **Booked:** Kane, Creaney
9th ● Brechin.............h L 1–2 **Att:** 245 — **Scorers:** Frizzel
16th ● Stirling ....h W 1–0 **Att:** 233 — **Scorers:** Tade. **Booked:** Dobbins
23rd ● Raith ....a L 2–1 **Att:** 1,483 — **Scorers:** Tade. **Booked:** Creaney, McBride
30th ● Alloa.................a L 5–1 **Att:** 408 — **Scorers:** Tade. **Booked:** Frizzel. **Dismissed:** Nicol

September
13th ● Ayr ....h L 1–3 **Att:** 768 — **Scorers:** McConalogue. **Booked:** Tade, Kane, Dobbins, Creaney. **Dismissed:** Tade
20th ● Peterhead ....a L 4–0 **Att:** 488 — **Booked:** McBride, Frizzel, Creaney, Gibson
27th ● Arbroath ....h D 2–2 **Att:** 124 — **Scorers:** Mitchell². **Booked:** D. Mitchell, Nicoll, Gibson. **Dismissed:** D. Mitchell

October
4th ● East Fife...........a W 1–2 **Att:** 730 — **Scorers:** McConalogue, Nicoll. **Booked:** Tade, Nicoll. **Dismissed:** Tade
18th ● Queen's Park....h D 0–0 **Att:** 284 — **Booked:** Nicoll
25th ● Raith ....h L 0–2 **Att:** 253

November
1st ● Stirling ....a L 3–2 **Att:** 489 — **Scorers:** Dobbins, Tade. **Booked:** Nicoll
8th ● Ayr ....a L 3–2 **Att:** 1,358 — **Scorers:** Tade, White. **Booked:** McKinstry, Gibson, Nicoll
15th ● Alloa.................h D 2–2 **Att:** 186 — **Scorers:** Kane, Tade
22nd ● Arbroath ....a L 1–0 **Att:** 411 — **Booked:** Dobbins, Tade

December
15th ● Forfar ....a L 2–0 **Att:** 305 — **Booked:** Nicoll, Dobbins, McKinstry, Gibson. **Dismissed:** Dobbins, McKinstry
20th ● East Fife...........h L 0–4 **Att:** 172 — **Booked:** Nicoll, Gibson
27th ● Alloa.................a D 2–2 **Att:** 463 — **Scorers:** McConalogue, Mullen. **Booked:** McKinstry, Mullen, D. Mitchell, Dobbins, McBride

January
17th ● Raith ....a L 2–1 **Att:** 1,455 — **Scorers:** Mullen. **Booked:** Nicoll, G. Mitchell
24th ● Stirling ....h L 2–8 **Att:** 191 — **Scorers:** McConalogue, Mullen
31st ● Queen's Park....a D 1–1 **Att:** 474 — **Scorers:** Frizzel. **Booked:** McConalogue

February
7th ● Brechin.............h L 0–3 **Att:** 223
14th ● Arbroath ....h L 1–5 **Att:** 280 — **Scorers:** McConalogue. **Booked:** Black, Kane, McGrath, McBride, Frizzel. **Dismissed:** McBride
21st ● Peterhead ....a L 1–0 **Att:** 531 — **Booked:** Creaney
28th ● Alloa.................h L 1–3 **Att:** 291 — **Scorers:** McBride. **Booked:** D. Mitchell, Moore

March
4th ● Peterhead ....h L 0–3 **Att:** 131
7th ● Ayr ....a L 5–0 **Att:** 1,570 — **Booked:** Moore, D. Mitchell, Creaney
10th ● Brechin.............a L 1–0 **Att:** 315 — **Booked:** D. Mitchell
14th ● Queen's Park....h D 2–2 **Att:** 338 — **Scorers:** Mitchell²
21st ● East Fife...........a L 4–0 **Att:** 533
28th ● Ayr ....h L 1–4 **Att:** 891 — **Booked:** McBride, Nicoll

April
4th ● Raith ....h L 0–3 **Att:** 367
11th ● Stirling ....a W 1–2 **Att:** 459 — **Scorers:** McColm, Moore. **Booked:** Nicoll
18th ● Peterhead ....h L 0–1 **Att:** 221
25th ● Arbroath ....a L 2–0 **Att:** 506 — **Booked:** McKinstry, Moore

May
2nd ● Brechin.............a L 2–1 **Att:** 418 — **Scorers:** Mitchell
9th ● East Fife...........h L 0–1 **Att:** 249 — **Booked:** Gibson, Noble

● Irn-Bru Second Division ● Scottish FA Cup ● Scottish League Cup ● Scottish Challenge Cup

SECOND DIVISION GOALKEEPER STATS

Player	Appearances	Match starts	Completed matches	Sub appearances	Subbed off	Clean sheets	Yellow cards	Red cards
Scott Black	26	26	25	0	1	2	1	0
Fraser Cantley	2	1	1	1	0	0	0	0
Duncan Crosthwaite	9	9	9	0	0	0	0	0

SECOND DIVISION OUTFIELD PLAYER STATS

Player	Appearances	Match starts	Completed matches	Substitute appearances	Subbed off	Goals scored	Yellow cards	Red cards
Stephen Aitken	10	9	5	1	4	0	0	0
Craig Bradley	7	0	0	7	0	0	0	0
Marc Campbell	1	0	0	1	0	0	0	0
Steven Connolly	3	1	0	2	1	0	0	0
Roddy Cooksley	4	0	0	4	0	0	0	0
David Craig	3	3	3	0	0	0	0	0
James Creaney	20	13	12	7	1	0	5	0
Ian Dobbins	16	16	15	0	1	1	4	0
Craig Frizzel	32	26	11	6	15	2	3	0
Andrew Gibson	28	26	20	2	6	0	5	0
Darren Hogan	1	0	0	1	0	0	0	0
Richard Jones	4	3	1	1	2	0	0	0
John Kane	36	36	35	0	1	1	2	0
John Kiltie	1	0	0	1	0	0	0	0
Martin McBride	25	23	16	2	6	2	5	1
Stuart McColm	21	11	6	10	5	1	0	0
Stephen McConalogue	34	28	13	6	15	6	1	0
Philip McGrath	7	5	2	2	3	0	1	0
Steven McGregor	1	1	1	0	0	0	0	0
James McKinstry	29	26	22	3	4	0	3	0
Ian Miller	1	0	0	1	0	0	0	0
Glen Mitchell	1	1	1	0	0	0	1	0
Danny Mitchell	32	26	25	6	0	5	6	1
Michael Moore	8	6	4	2	2	1	3	0
Michael Mullen	18	11	5	7	6	3	1	0
Alan Murdoch	4	0	0	4	0	0	0	0
Jordan Mutch	2	1	0	1	1	0	0	0
Steven Nicol	1	1	0	0	0	0	0	1
Kevin Nicoll	21	20	15	1	4	1	9	1
Steven Noble	31	27	22	4	5	0	1	0
Robert Paisley	4	1	0	3	1	0	0	0
Jay Ritchie	1	0	0	1	0	0	0	0
Gregory Tade	16	16	14	0	0	7	3	2

SEASON INFORMATION

Highest Position: **5**
Lowest Position: **10**
Average goals scored per game: **0.86**
Average goals conceded per game: **2.50**

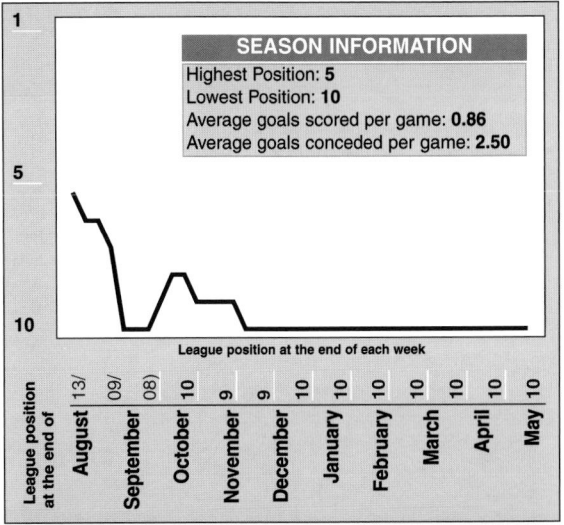

League position at the end of each week

LONGEST SEQUENCES

Wins		Undefeated home	2
(–)		(27/09/08–18/10/08)	
Losses	7	Undefeated away	
(07/02/09–10/03/09)		(–)	
Draws		Without scoring	3
(–)		(04/03/09–10/03/09)	
Undefeated	3	Without conceding	
(27/09/08–18/10/08)		(–)	
Without win	22	Scoring	6
(18/10/08–04/04/09)		(02/08/08–13/09/08)	

CARDS RECEIVED

54 **7**

QUICK-FIRE GOALS

From the start of a match
Michael Mullen (v Alloa) 4:00

By a substitute after coming on
Alex White (v Ayr) 11:00

GOALS SCORED/CONCEDED PER FIVE-MINUTE INTERVALS

Goals For	1	0	2	4	2	2	2	4	1	3	1	0	0	2	1	2	0	4
Goals Against	8	3	0	7	5	3	3	4	4	3	9	5	10	3	5	5	9	4
Mins	5	10	15	20	25	30	35	40	45	50	55	60	65	70	75	80	85	90

ALBION ROVERS

ALBION endured a difficult season in which they could not lift themselves from the lower reaches of the Irn-Bru Third Division.

Paul Martin's side enjoyed a fairly successful opening to the campaign, notching up numerous wins, but their form slipped as 2008/09 drew to a close and their league position suffered as a result.

Rovers' good start saw them thump Elgin 6–1, while they also put three goals past high-flying Cowdenbeath. After a strong new year period, which included six wins from eight, the Cliftonhill side saw their form dip. By late April they were languishing near the foot of the table, and they stayed in that position until the end of the season.

Albion tried to galvanise their squad with loan signings from top-flight clubs, but they could only manage an eighth-place finish.

CLUB SUMMARY

FORMED	1882
MANAGER	Paul Martin
GROUND	Cliftonhill
CAPACITY	2,496
NICKNAME	The Wee Rovers
WEBSITE	www.albionrovers.co.uk

The New **Football Pools** PLAYER OF THE SEASON — **Michael McGowan**

OVERALL
P	W	D	L	F	A	GD
41	13	7	21	45	53	-8

IRN-BRU THIRD DIVISION
Pos	P	W	D	L	F	A	GD	Pts
8	36	11	6	19	39	47	-8	39

HOME
Pos	P	W	D	L	F	A	GD	Pts
9	18	6	2	10	18	25	-7	20

AWAY
Pos	P	W	D	L	F	A	GD	Pts
8	18	5	4	9	21	22	-1	19

CUP PROGRESS DETAILS
Competition	Round reached	Knocked out by
Co-op Insurance Cup	R1	Raith
Scottish Cup	R3	Queens Park
Challenge Cup	R2	Cowdenbeath

BIGGEST WIN (ALL COMPS)
20/09/08 6–1 v Elgin SC3

BIGGEST DEFEAT (ALL COMPS)
14/03/09 0–4 v Forfar SC3

ATTENDANCE RECORD
High	Low	Average
452	237	312

v Cowdenbeath (11/04/2009) v Elgin (03/03/2009)

RESULTS 2008/09

July
26th	● Stenhousemuir..a W 0–1	Att: 210 — Scorers: Donnelly. Booked: Barr

August
2nd	● Forfar ....h L 1–3	Att: 298 — Scorers: Barr. Booked: McGowan
5th	● Raith ....h D 0–0	Att: 415 — Booked: Donnelly, Reid (Lost 3–4 on pens)
9th	● East Stirling ......a L 1–0	Att: 348 — Booked: Donnelly, Ferry
12th	● Cowdenbeath....a L 3–2	Att: 204 — Scorers: Barr, Martin
16th	● Cowdenbeath....a L 2–1	Att: 288 — Scorers: P. Walker. Booked: P. Walker, Reid
23rd	● Berwick ....h W 2–0	Att: 253 — Scorers: P. Walker²
30th	● Annan Athletic ..a W 2–4	Att: 937 — Scorers: Barr, Pollock, P. Walker²

September
13th	● Dumbarton........h L 1–3	Att: 327 — Scorers: P. Walker. Booked: McGowan, Adam
20th	● Elgin................a W 1–6	Att: 407 — Scorers: Barr³, Watt³. Booked: Benton, Harris
27th	● Stenhousemuir..h L 1–2	Att: 279 — Scorers: Adam

October
4th	● Montrose ....h L 0–1	Att: 237 — Booked: Benton, Donnelly
18th	● Forfar ....a D 0–0	Att: 426 — Booked: McGowan
25th	● Berwick ....a W 1–2	Att: 259 — Scorers: Harris. Booked: R. Walker

November
1st	● Cowdenbeath....h W 3–1	Att: 259 — Scorers: Barr, Benton, Harris
8th	● Berwick ....a W 0–3	Att: 288 — Scorers: Barr, Harris². Booked: McGowan, Canning
15th	● Annan Athletic ..h L 0–1	Att: 310 — Booked: Canning
22nd	● Dumbarton.......a D 1–1	Att: 647 — Scorers: Donnelly. Booked: Donnelly, Barr
29th	● Queens Park ....h L 1–2	Att: 619 — Scorers: Barr. Booked: Barr, Barr, Donnelly

December
13th	● Stenhousemuir..a L 1–0	Att: 508 — Booked: McCusker, Benton
20th	● Montrose ....a W 1–2	Att: 321 — Scorers: Andreoni, Barr. Booked: Reid, McGowan, Barr, Andreoni

January
17th	● Berwick ....h W 2–1	Att: 264 — Scorers: Harty, McCusker. Booked: McGowan
24th	● Cowdenbeath....a L 2–1	Att: 409 — Scorers: Harty. Booked: Benton, Donnelly
31st	● Forfar ....h W 2–0	Att: 289 — Scorers: Barr, Harty

February
7th	● East Stirling ......a W 0–1	Att: 435 — Scorers: Barr. Booked: Benton, McKeown
21st	● Elgin................a L 1–0	Att: 357 — Booked: Benton
28th	● Annan Athletic ..h W 2–1	Att: 427 — Scorers: Donnelly, McKeown. Booked: R. Walker, Donnelly

March
3rd	● Elgin................h W 2–1	Att: 237 — Scorers: Crozier, Harty
7th	● Dumbarton........a L 1–0	Att: 692 — Booked: Reid, Barr, Donnelly. Dismissed: Barr
10th	● East Stirling ......h L 0–2	Att: 420
14th	● Forfar ....a L 4–0	Att: 390
17th	● Dumbarton........h D 1–1	Att: 346 — Scorers: Barr
21st	● Montrose ....h L 0–1	Att: 263 — Booked: Donnelly
25th	● Annan Athletic ..a D 1–1	Att: 864 — Scorers: Adam. Booked: Reid, R. Walker
31st	● Stenhousemuir..h L 1–2	Att: 335 — Scorers: Donnelly. Booked: Ferry, McGowan, Benton, Donnelly

April
4th	● Berwick ....a D 1–1	Att: 323 — Scorers: Harty. Booked: Benton, Ewings
11th	● Cowdenbeath....h D 0–0	Att: 452
18th	● Elgin................h L 0–3	Att: 275 — Booked: Crozier
25th	● Stenhousemuir..a L 2–0	Att: 428

May
2nd	● East Stirling ......h L 0–2	Att: 346 — Dismissed: Benton
9th	● Montrose ....a L 1–0	Att: 324 — Booked: Ewings, Fleming. Dismissed: Ewings

● Irn-Bru Third Division ● Scottish FA Cup ● Scottish League Cup ● Scottish Challenge Cup

THIRD DIVISION GOALKEEPER STATS

Player	Appearances	Match starts	Completed matches	Sub appearances	Subbed off	Clean sheets	Yellow cards	Red cards
Jamie Ewings	19	19	18	0	0	3	2	1
Chris McCluskey	7	7	7	0	0	1	0	0
David Scott	11	10	10	1	0	2	0	0

THIRD DIVISION OUTFIELD PLAYER STATS

Player	Appearances	Match starts	Completed matches	Substitute appearances	Subbed off	Goals scored	Yellow cards	Red cards
Callan Adam	19	18	12	1	6	2	1	0
Marco Andreoni	16	8	3	8	5	1	1	0
Mark Archdeacon	10	3	1	7	2	0	0	0
Robert Barr	32	31	29	1	1	11	3	1
Alan Benton	20	20	18	0	1	1	8	1
Stevie Canning	7	7	5	0	2	0	2	0
Mark Casey	2	2	1	0	1	0	0	0
Tommy Coyne	1	0	0	1	0	0	0	0
Brendan Crozier	20	8	2	12	6	1	1	0
Ciaran Donnelly	31	31	27	0	4	3	8	0
Graham Eaglesham	6	1	0	5	1	0	0	0
Danny Ferry	25	17	11	8	6	0	2	0
Sean Fleming	17	16	15	1	1	0	1	0
Ross Harris	21	17	10	4	7	3	1	0
Ian Harty	15	15	9	0	6	5	0	0
Chris Hughes	4	3	3	1	0	0	0	0
Todd Lumsden	9	9	8	0	1	0	0	0
William Martin	3	2	0	1	2	0	0	0
Marc McCusker	3	3	2	0	1	1	1	0
Martin McGoldrick	9	6	5	3	1	0	0	0
Michael McGowan	33	33	30	0	3	0	7	0
Gary McKenna	3	0	0	3	0	0	0	0
Steven McKeown	17	17	16	0	1	1	1	0
Marc Pollock	33	19	10	14	9	1	0	0
Alan Reid	32	32	28	0	4	0	4	0
Brian Smith	3	2	0	1	2	0	0	0
Patrick Walker	6	5	3	1	2	6	1	0
Robert Walker	27	24	24	3	0	0	2	0
Kevin Watt	4	3	2	1	1	3	0	0
Robert Wright	4	2	1	2	1	0	0	0

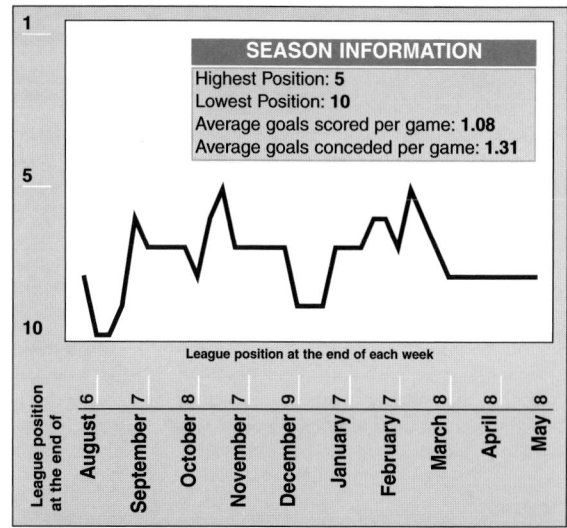

SEASON INFORMATION
Highest Position: **5**
Lowest Position: **10**
Average goals scored per game: **1.08**
Average goals conceded per game: **1.31**

League position at the end of each week

LONGEST SEQUENCES

Wins (on five occasions)	2	Undefeated home (17/01/09–03/03/09)	4
Losses (02/08/08–16/08/08)	3	Undefeated away (30/08/08–22/11/08)	5
Draws (04/04/09–11/04/09)	2	Without scoring (11/04/09–09/05/09)	5
Undefeated (18/10/08–08/11/08)	3	Without conceding (31/01/09–07/02/09)	2
Without win (07/03/09–09/05/09)	13	Scoring (16/08/08–27/09/08)	6

CARDS RECEIVED

47   **3**

QUICK-FIRE GOALS

From the start of a match
Brendan Crozier (v Elgin) 3:00

By a substitute after coming on
Marc Pollock (v Annan Athletic) 22:00

GOALS SCORED/CONCEDED PER FIVE-MINUTE INTERVALS

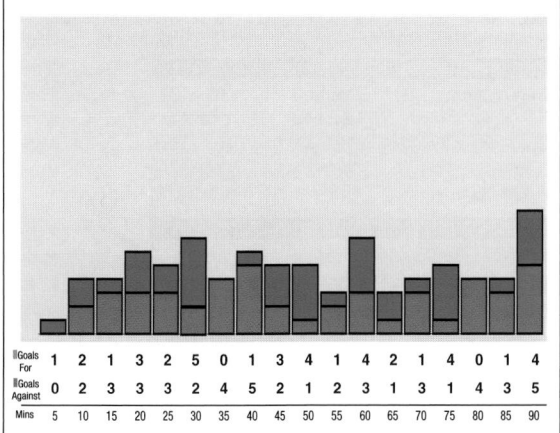

Goals For	1	2	1	3	2	5	0	1	3	4	1	4	2	1	4	0	1	4	
Goals Against	0	2	3	3	3	2	4	5	2	1	2	3	1	3	1	4	3	5	
Mins	5	10	15	20	25	30	35	40	45	50	55	60	65	70	75	80	85	90	

ANNAN made the most of Gretna's demise by making a competent start to their life in the Irn-Bru Scottish Football League.

The Black and Golds – who successfully applied to join the League after Gretna were dissolved – achieved a creditable seventh-place finish in their debut season.

Harry Cairney's side made a perfect start to the campaign with a 4–1 away win at Cowdenbeath but, soon after, went on a six-game losing streak which left the club languishing near the bottom of the table.

However, their form picked up, and by mid-March they were five points off a promotion place, sitting in fifth position.

One of Annan's standout players was Mike Jack, the ex-Carlisle striker chipping in with a valuable 15 goals and finishing as the division's top scorer.

CLUB SUMMARY

FORMED	1942
MANAGER	Harry Cairney
GROUND	Galabank Stadium
CAPACITY	3,500
NICKNAME	The Black and Golds
WEBSITE	www.annanathleticfc.com

The New **Football Pools** PLAYER OF THE SEASON — Craig Summersgill

OVERALL

P	W	D	L	F	A	GD
39	14	9	16	58	50	8

IRN-BRU THIRD DIVISION

Pos	P	W	D	L	F	A	GD	Pts
7	36	14	8	14	56	45	11	50

HOME

Pos	P	W	D	L	F	A	GD	Pts
5	18	8	4	6	35	23	12	28

AWAY

Pos	P	W	D	L	F	A	GD	Pts
7	18	6	4	8	21	22	-1	22

CUP PROGRESS DETAILS

Competition	Round reached	Knocked out by
Co-op Insurance Cup	R1	Dumbarton
Scottish Cup	R2	Spartans
Challenge Cup	R1	Clyde

BIGGEST WIN (ALL COMPS)

07/03/09 6–0 v Elgin SC3

BIGGEST DEFEAT (ALL COMPS)

04/10/08 1–4 v Dumbarton SC3

ATTENDANCE RECORD

High	Low	Average
1,343	422	734

v Dumbarton (09/05/2009)   v Elgin (22/11/2008)

RESULTS 2008/09

July

26th	● Clyde	a	L 2–0	**Att:** 688 — **Booked:** Hill

August

2nd	● Cowdenbeath	a	W 1–4	**Att:** 595 — **Scorers:** Archibald, Jack², Johnstone. **Booked:** Townsley
5th	● Dumbarton		D 1–1	**Att:** 459 — **Scorers:** Jack.
				Booked: Archibald, Inglis, Sloan, Johnstone. (Lost 4–5 on pens)
9th	● Stenhousemuir	h	D 1–1	**Att:** 1,132 — **Scorers:** Jack. **Booked:** Grainger, Jack
16th	● East Stirling	h	W 2–1	**Att:** 968 — **Scorers:** Jack, Sloan
23rd	● Montrose	a	D 1–1	**Att:** 425 — **Scorers:** Bell. **Booked:** Jardine, Johnstone
30th	● Albion	h	L 2–4	**Att:** 937 — **Scorers:** Neilson, Townsley

September

13th	● Elgin	a	W 1–2	**Att:** 468 — **Scorers:** Jack². **Booked:** Inglis, Summersgill, Jack.
				Dismissed: Grainger
20th	● Forfar	h	L 1–3	**Att:** 690 — **Scorers:** Dunbar. **Booked:** Jardine, Hill
27th	● Berwick	a	L 3–0	**Att:** 502 — **Booked:** Townsley. **Dismissed:** Brown

October

4th	● Dumbarton	a	L 4–1	**Att:** 636 — **Scorers:** Inglis
18th	● Cowdenbeath	h	L 0–1	**Att:** 698 — **Booked:** Townsley, Jack. **Dismissed:** Neilson, Jack

November

1st	● Spartans	h	L 1–2	**Att:** 652 — **Scorers:** Neilson
8th	● Montrose	h	L 1–2	**Att:** 505 — **Scorers:** Hoolickin. **Booked:** Townsley
12th	● East Stirling	a	L 2–1	**Att:** 343 — **Scorers:** Hoolickin
15th	● Albion	a	W 0–1	**Att:** 310 — **Scorers:** Jack. **Booked:** Hoolickin
22nd	● Elgin	h	W 5–0	**Att:** 422 — **Scorers:** Bell, Jack², Johnstone, Neilson

December

13th	● Berwick	h	L 1–2	**Att:** 423 — **Scorers:** Neilson. **Booked:** Neilson. **Dismissed:** Archibald
20th	● Dumbarton	h	W 2–1	**Att:** 647 — **Scorers:** Neilson². **Booked:** Hoolickin
27th	● Stenhousemuir	a	D 0–0	**Att:** 524

January

17th	● Montrose	a	W 0–3	**Att:** 329 — **Scorers:** Anson, Bell, McLeod OG. **Booked:** Anson, Hoolickin
24th	● East Stirling	h	W 4–0	**Att:** 714 — **Scorers:** Anson, Bell, Jack²
31st	● Cowdenbeath	a	L 1–0	**Att:** 326 — **Booked:** Gilfillan, Neilson, Townsley

February

7th	● Stenhousemuir	h	D 1–1	**Att:** 805 — **Scorers:** McBeth
21st	● Forfar	h	W 1–0	**Att:** 542 — **Scorers:** Bell. **Booked:** Hoolickin, Townsley
24th	● Berwick	a	D 1–1	**Att:** 306 — **Scorers:** Hoolickin. **Booked:** Townsley, Bell
28th	● Albion	a	L 2–1	**Att:** 427 — **Scorers:** Jack. **Booked:** Watson, Campbell

March

3rd	● Forfar	a	L 2–1	**Att:** 366 — **Scorers:** Adamson. **Booked:** Hoolickin. **Dismissed:** McBeth
7th	● Elgin	h	W 6–0	**Att:** 487 — **Scorers:** Bell², Dunbar², Jack, Storey. **Booked:** Hoolickin, Neilson
14th	● Cowdenbeath	h	W 3–1	**Att:** 629 — **Scorers:** Dunbar, Sloan, Storey. **Booked:** Neilson
21st	● Dumbarton	a	W 0–2	**Att:** 724 — **Scorers:** Jack, Neilson. **Booked:** Watson, Muirhead
25th	● Albion	h	D 1–1	**Att:** 864 — **Scorers:** Bell
28th	● Elgin	a	W 0–1	**Att:** 321 — **Scorers:** Storey. **Booked:** Hoolickin, Watson

April

4th	● Montrose	h	W 2–1	**Att:** 617 — **Scorers:** Dunbar, Jack. **Booked:** Neilson, Watson
11th	● East Stirling	a	D 1–1	**Att:** 508 — **Scorers:** Storey. **Booked:** Inglis, Storey
18th	● Forfar	a	L 2–1	**Att:** 463 — **Scorers:** Storey. **Booked:** Townsley, Adamson, Summersgill, McBeth
25th	● Berwick	h	D 1–1	**Att:** 786 — **Scorers:** Storey. **Booked:** McBeth

May

2nd	● Stenhousemuir	a	L 1–0	**Att:** 581 — **Booked:** Neilson
9th	● Dumbarton	h	L 1–3	**Att:** 1,343 — **Scorers:** Watson

● Irn-Bru Third Division ● Scottish FA Cup ● Scottish League Cup ● Scottish Challenge Cup

THIRD DIVISION GOALKEEPER STATS

Player	Appearances	Match starts	Completed matches	Sub appearances	Subbed off	Clean sheets	Yellow cards	Red cards
Dougie Calder 3	2	2	1	0	0	0	0
Craig Summersgill............34	34	34	0	0	9	2	0

THIRD DIVISION OUTFIELD PLAYER STATS

Player	Appearances	Match starts	Completed matches	Substitute appearances	Subbed off	Goals scored	Yellow cards	Red cards
Ryan Adamson.............................28	10	5	18	5	1	1	0
Scott Anson.................................3	3	3	0	0	2	1	0
Steven Archibald 11	7	2	4	4	1	0	1
James Batey 1	0	0	1	0	0	0	0
Graeme Bell 29	26	10	3	16	8	1	0
Gary Brown.................................13	13	11	0	1	0	0	1
Hugh Cameron 4	2	0	2	2	0	0	0
Robert Campbell 11	7	3	4	4	0	1	0
Liam Cuseck 3	2	0	1	2	0	0	0
Jamie Dunbar 28	24	15	4	9	5	0	0
Bryan Gilfillan 6	6	4	0	2	0	1	0
Ian Grainger...............................4	3	0	1	2	0	1	1
Stuart Hill...................................7	7	4	0	3	0	1	0
Lee Hoolickin 26	26	20	0	6	3	7	0
Alan Inglis..................................20	18	17	2	1	1	2	0
Mike Jack 33	33	31	0	1	15	3	1
Chris Jardine 17	14	12	3	2	0	2	0
Darren Johnstone 16	12	7	4	5	2	1	0
Adam Kassim 1	0	0	1	0	0	0	0
John McBeth 16	15	13	1	1	1	2	1
Aaron Muirhead 11	9	8	2	1	0	1	0
Kevin Neilson 32	32	30	0	1	6	6	1
Grant Parker 1	0	0	1	0	0	0	0
Steven Sloan 34	34	33	0	1	2	0	0
Phil Storey 18	7	6	11	1	6	1	0
Derek Townsley 27	27	26	0	1	1	8	0
Lewis Walker 5	0	0	5	0	0	0	0
Peter Watson 25	23	23	2	0	1	4	0

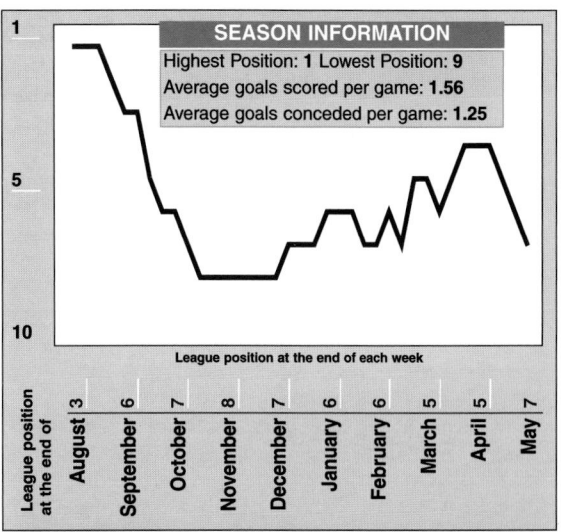

SEASON INFORMATION
Highest Position: **1** Lowest Position: **9**
Average goals scored per game: **1.56**
Average goals conceded per game: **1.25**

League position at the end of each week

League position at the end of — August 3, September 6, October 7, November 8, December 7, January 6, February 6, March 5, April 5, May 7

LONGEST SEQUENCES

Wins (07/03/09–21/03/09)	3	Undefeated home (20/12/08–25/04/09)	9
Losses (20/09/08–12/11/08)	6	Undefeated away (on three occasions)	3
Draws (–)		Without scoring (–)	
Undefeated (07/03/09–11/04/09)	7	Without conceding (27/12/08–24/01/09)	3
Without win (20/09/08–12/11/08)	6	Scoring (07/02/09–25/04/09)	14

CARDS RECEIVED

46   6

QUICK-FIRE GOALS

From the start of a match
Graham Bell (v Elgin) 4:00

By a substitute after coming on
Jamie Dunbar (v Elgin) 0:00

GOALS SCORED/CONCEDED PER FIVE-MINUTE INTERVALS

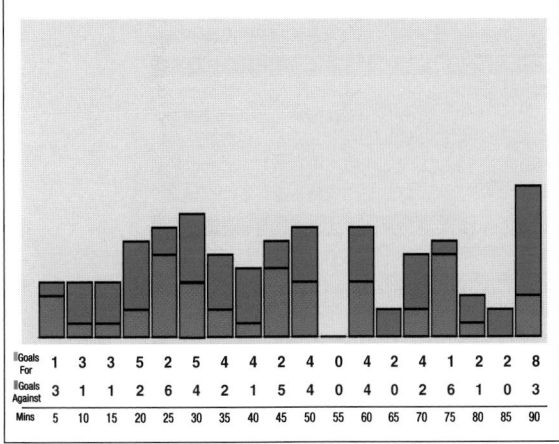

Goals For	1	3	3	5	2	5	4	4	2	4	0	4	2	4	1	2	2	8
Goals Against	3	1	1	2	6	4	2	1	5	4	0	4	0	2	6	1	0	3
Mins	5	10	15	20	25	30	35	40	45	50	55	60	65	70	75	80	85	90

BERWICK had little to shout about as they ended the season second from the bottom of the Irn-Bru Third Division table.

After being relegated from the Second Division the previous season, Jimmy Crease's side struggled to make an impact upon the fourth tier and, if not for the poor form of Elgin, might have been at risk of finishing bottom once again. They recorded just two wins in their first 14 games, although they still managed to engineer breathing space between themselves and Elgin.

Their fans had a December to remember with four wins in a row, but they then reverted to type, despite picking up valuable wins against Stenhousemuir and Cowdenbeath.

Striker Darren Gribben was crucial, belying his team's poor form by finishing the season as one of the division's top scorers.

CLUB SUMMARY

FORMED	1881
MANAGER	Jimmy Crease
GROUND	Shielfield Park
CAPACITY	4,131
NICKNAME	The Borderers
WEBSITE	www.berwickrangers.net

 **Jamie Ewart**

PLAYER OF THE SEASON

OVERALL

P	W	D	L	F	A	GD
39	10	7	22	49	70	-21

IRN-BRU THIRD DIVISION

Pos	P	W	D	L	F	A	GD	Pts
9	36	10	7	19	46	61	-15	37

HOME

Pos	P	W	D	L	F	A	GD	Pts
8	18	6	4	8	24	29	-5	22

AWAY

Pos	P	W	D	L	F	A	GD	Pts
9	18	4	3	11	22	32	-10	15

CUP PROGRESS DETAILS

Competition	Round reached	Knocked out by
Co-op Insurance Cup	R1	Ayr
Scottish Cup	R2	Albion
Challenge Cup	R1	Queen of the South

BIGGEST WIN (ALL COMPS)

14/03/09 0-4 v East Stirling **SC3**

BIGGEST DEFEAT (ALL COMPS)

26/07/08 1-5 v Queen of South **SLCC1SW**

ATTENDANCE RECORD

High	Low	Average
570	288	414

v East Stirling (02/08/2008) v Albion (08/11/2008)

RESULTS 2008/09

July
26th	● Queen of South h	L 1–5	**Att:** 655 — **Scorers:** Little

August
2nd	● East Stirling ......h	W 2–1	**Att:** 570 — **Scorers:** Dillon, Gribben. **Booked:** Gribben
6th	● Ayr ....a	L 2–1	**Att:** 716 — **Scorers:** Greenhill. **Booked:** Gribben
9th	● Montrose ....a	D 1–1	**Att:** 344 — **Scorers:** Howat. **Booked:** Ewart
16th	● Dumbarton........h	L 1–2	**Att:** 516 — **Scorers:** Gribben. **Booked:** Ewart
23rd	● Albion...............a	L 2–0	**Att:** 253
30th	● Forfar ....h	D 2–2	**Att:** 390 — **Scorers:** Gribben². **Booked:** Ewart, Bonar

September
13th	● Cowdenbeath....a	L 2–1	**Att:** 385 — **Scorers:** Ewart. **Booked:** Lennox
20th	● Stenhousemuir..a	L 2–0	**Att:** 446 — **Booked:** Bonar
27th	● Annan Athletic ..h	W 3–0	**Att:** 502 — **Scorers:** Dillon², Ewart. **Booked:** McLaren, Lennox, G. Greenhill

October
4th	● Elgin.................h	D 1–1	**Att:** 367 — **Scorers:** Lister. **Booked:** G. Greenhill
18th	● East Stirling ......a	L 1–0	**Att:** 397 — **Booked:** Dillon, Ewart
25th	● Albion...............h	L 1–2	**Att:** 259 — **Scorers:** Gribben. **Booked:** Dillon

November
1st	● Dumbarton........a	L 5–2	**Att:** 679 — **Scorers:** Cr. Anderson, Ewart.
			Booked: McMahon , D. Greenhill, McMenamin. **Dismissed:** G. Greenhill
8th	● Albion...............h	L 0–3	**Att:** 288 — **Booked:** McLaren, McMenamin, Horn
15th	● Forfar ....a	L 2–1	**Att:** 362 — **Scorers:** Ewart. **Booked:** Robertson
22nd	● Cowdenbeath....h	L 2–3	**Att:** 389 — **Scorers:** Gribben². **Booked:** Horn

December
6th	● Stenhousemuir..h	W 3–2	**Att:** 367 — **Scorers:** McLaren, McMenamin, Thom OG.
			Booked: D. Greenhill, Guy, Dillon
13th	● Annan Athletic ..a	W 1–2	**Att:** 423 — **Scorers:** Horn, McMenamin. **Booked:** Fraser
20th	● Elgin.................a	W 0–2	**Att:** 304 — **Scorers:** Gribben². **Booked:** Dillon
27th	● Montrose ....h	W 3–2	**Att:** 510 — **Scorers:** Callaghan, Gribben, McMenamin.
			Booked: G. Greenhill, Lunn. **Dismissed:** Little

January
13th	● Cowdenbeath....a	L 2–0	**Att:** 282 — **Booked:** Gribben, Callaghan. **Dismissed:** Callaghan
17th	● Albion...............a	L 2–1	**Att:** 264 — **Scorers:** Andreoni OG. **Booked:** Guy
24th	● Dumbarton........h	L 1–2	**Att:** 425 — **Scorers:** Callaghan.
			Booked: Horn, Bonar, Callaghan, Ewart, Forrest. **Dismissed:** Forrest

February
7th	● Montrose ....a	D 1–1	**Att:** 318 — **Scorers:** Guy. **Booked:** Bonar, Callaghan. **Dismissed:** Mearns
21st	● Stenhousemuir..a	W 1–2	**Att:** 439 — **Scorers:** Callaghan, McLaren. **Booked:** Ewart
24th	● Annan Athletic ..h	D 1–1	**Att:** 306 — **Scorers:** Forrest. **Booked:** Dillon, Callaghan
28th	● Forfar ....a	L 5–4	**Att:** 382 — **Scorers:** McLaren³, Tod OG. **Booked:** McLaren

March
7th	● Cowdenbeath....h	W 1–0	**Att:** 523 — **Scorers:** Bonar. **Booked:** Callaghan
14th	● East Stirling ......a	W 0–4	**Att:** 441 — **Scorers:** Gribben³, McLaren. **Booked:** Mearns
17th	● Forfar ....h	L 0–2	**Att:** 382
21st	● Elgin.................h	W 2–1	**Att:** 348 — **Scorers:** Callaghan, McLaren. **Booked:** Gribben
28th	● East Stirling ......h	L 1–2	**Att:** 431 — **Scorers:** Gribben. **Booked:** Horn, Gribben, Ewart, D. Greenhill

April
4th	● Albion...............h	D 1–1	**Att:** 323 — **Scorers:** McLaren. **Booked:** Gribben, Ewart
11th	● Dumbarton........a	L 2–0	**Att:** 770 — **Booked:** Ewart, Callaghan, Little. **Dismissed:** Dillon
18th	● Stenhousemuir..h	L 0–3	**Att:** 390
25th	● Annan Athletic ..a	D 1–1	**Att:** 786 — **Scorers:** Gribben. **Booked:** D. Greenhill, Lennox, Gribben, Callaghan

May
2nd	● Montrose ....h	L 0–1	**Att:** 418 — **Booked:** Callaghan
9th	● Elgin.................a	L 2–0	**Att:** 429 — **Booked:** Ewart, D. Greenhill. **Dismissed:** Ewart

● Irn-Bru Third Division ● Scottish FA Cup ● Scottish League Cup ● Scottish Challenge Cup

THIRD DIVISION GOALKEEPER STATS

Player	Appearances	Match starts	Completed matches	Sub appearances	Subbed off	Clean sheets	Yellow cards	Red cards
Jamie Barclay	13	13	13	0	0	2	0	0
Mark Lunn	2	2	2	0	0	0	1	0
Ryan McGurk	21	21	21	0	0	2	0	0

THIRD DIVISION OUTFIELD PLAYER STATS

Player	Appearances	Match starts	Completed matches	Substitute appearances	Subbed off	Goals scored	Yellow cards	Red cards
Chris Anderson	19	2	1	17	1	0	0	0
Craig Anderson	7	5	2	2	3	1	0	0
Steven Bonar	27	24	16	3	8	1	4	0
Stuart Callaghan	31	28	24	3	3	4	8	1
John Dillon	28	28	26	0	1	3	4	1
Jamie Ewart	35	35	32	0	2	4	10	1
Fraser Forrest	12	10	9	2	0	1	1	1
Stuart Fraser	7	5	2	2	3	0	1	0
David Grant	7	0	0	7	0	0	0	0
Gary Greenhill	9	8	0	1	7	0	3	1
David Greenhill	33	23	15	10	8	0	5	0
Darren Gribben	34	31	22	3	9	14	6	0
Graham Guy	21	20	15	1	5	1	2	0
Steven Hampshire	7	6	4	1	2	0	0	0
Robert Horn	27	24	23	3	1	1	4	0
Andrew Howat	3	1	0	2	1	1	0	0
Steven Kiczynski	3	3	3	0	0	0	0	0
Tommy Lennox	16	13	8	3	5	0	3	0
Jim Lister	9	9	6	0	3	1	0	0
Ian Little	17	6	3	11	2	0	1	1
Fraser McLaren	34	34	31	0	3	8	3	0
Andrew McLean	3	2	1	0	0	0	0	0
Peter McMahon	16	13	9	3	4	0	1	0
Christopher McMenamin	24	22	15	2	7	3	2	0
Eddie Mearns	9	5	2	4	3	0	1	0
Dayne Robertson	2	2	2	0	0	0	1	0

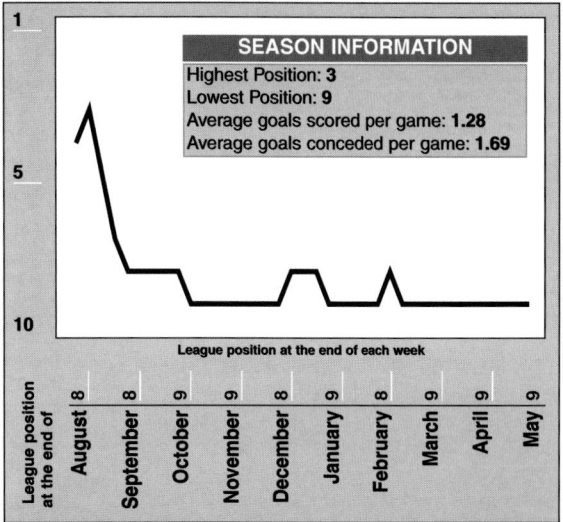

SEASON INFORMATION
Highest Position: **3**
Lowest Position: **9**
Average goals scored per game: **1.28**
Average goals conceded per game: **1.69**

League position at the end of each week

League position at the end of: August 8, September 8, October 9, November 9, December 8, January 9, February 8, March 9, April 9, May 9

LONGEST SEQUENCES

Wins (06/12/08–27/12/08)	4	Undefeated home (30/08/08–04/10/08)	3
Losses (18/10/08–22/11/08)	5	Undefeated away (on three occasions)	2
Draws (–)		Without scoring (on two occasions)	2
Undefeated (06/12/08–27/12/08)	4	Without conceding (07/03/09–14/03/09)	2
Without win (28/03/09–09/05/09)	7	Scoring (17/01/09–14/03/09)	8

CARDS RECEIVED

61   7

QUICK-FIRE GOALS

From the start of a match
Darren Gribben (v Cowdenbeath) 11:00

By a substitute after coming on
Andrew Howat (v Montrose) 5:00

GOALS SCORED/CONCEDED PER FIVE-MINUTE INTERVALS

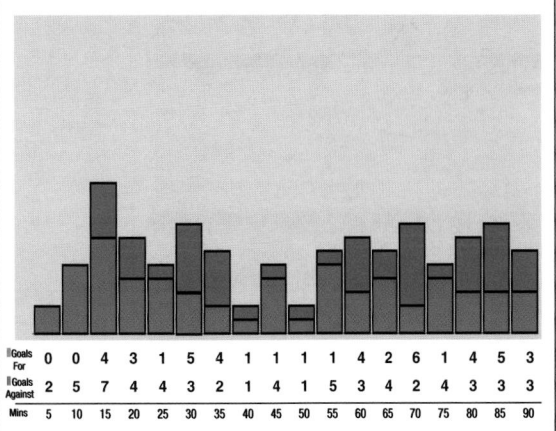

Goals For	0	0	4	3	1	5	4	1	1	1	1	4	2	6	1	4	5	3
Goals Against	2	5	7	4	4	3	2	1	4	1	5	3	4	2	4	3	3	3
Mins	5	10	15	20	25	30	35	40	45	50	55	60	65	70	75	80	85	90

COWDENBEATH finished eight points ahead of Stenhousemuir in the Irn-Bru Third Division, but it was not enough to be playing Second Division football ahead of them next season.

Jay Stein became the reluctant villain with a penalty shoot-out miss in the play-off final second leg at Ochilview that meant Stenhousemuir were the team promoted.

After finishing second behind Dumbarton in the Third Division, Cowdenbeath had overcome East Stirling 3–2 on aggregate in the semi-final through a late John Dempster goal.

Cowdenbeath had led Dumbarton for much of the season only to collapse in the closing months. Known affectionately as the Blue Brazil, Danny Lennon's young team simply drew too many matches in the run-in, but will still consider the campaign a success.

CLUB SUMMARY

FORMED	1881
MANAGER	Danny Lennon
GROUND	Central Park
CAPACITY	4,370
NICKNAME	The Blue Brazil
WEBSITE	www.cowdenbeathfc.com

The New Football Pools PLAYER OF THE SEASON

John Gemmell

OVERALL

P	W	D	L	F	A	GD
46	22	12	12	61	47	14

IRN-BRU THIRD DIVISION

Pos	P	W	D	L	F	A	GD	Pts
2	36	18	9	9	48	34	14	63

HOME

Pos	P	W	D	L	F	A	GD	Pts
2	18	11	5	2	27	15	12	38

AWAY

Pos	P	W	D	L	F	A	GD	Pts
6	18	7	4	7	21	19	2	25

CUP PROGRESS DETAILS

Competition	Round reached	Knocked out by
Co-op Insurance Cup	R2	Dundee Utd
Scottish Cup	R2	Elgin
Challenge Cup	QF	Airdrie Utd

BIGGEST WIN (ALL COMPS)

08/11/08 4–1 v Elgin **SC3**

BIGGEST DEFEAT (ALL COMPS)

26/08/08 1–5 v Dundee Utd **SLC2**

ATTENDANCE RECORD

High	Low	Average
1,181	193	415

v Dumbarton (18/04/2009)   v Elgin (08/11/2008)

RESULTS 2008/09

July
26th ● Elgin.................a W 0–2   **Att:** 379 — **Scorers:** McGregor, McQuade. **Booked:** Fairbairn

August
2nd ● Annan Athletic ..h L 1–4   **Att:** 595 — **Scorers:** McQuade
5th ● Montrose ....a W 0–2   **Att:** 352 — **Scorers:** Fairbairn, McGregor.
Booked: Ramsay, McGregor, Shields, Gemmell
9th ● Forfar ....a W 0–1   **Att:** 412 — **Scorers:** Ramsay
12th ● Albion................h W 3–2   **Att:** 204 — **Scorers:** Fairbairn, Gemmell, McQuade
16th ● Albion................h W 2–1   **Att:** 288 — **Scorers:** Fairbairn, Gemmell. **Booked:** Adamson, Hodge
23rd ● Elgin.................a W 0–2   **Att:** 537 — **Scorers:** Gemmell, McGregor. **Booked:** McGregor
26th ● Dundee Utd ......h L 1–5   **Att:** 1,435 — **Scorers:** Dempster. **Booked:** Gemmell, Fleming, Dempster
30th ● Stenhousemuir..a L 1–0   **Att:** 456 — **Booked:** Adamson, Gemmell, Fleming

September
7th ● Airdrie Utd ......h L 1–2   **Att:** 640 — **Scorers:** Fairbairn. **Dismissed:** Baxter
13th ● Berwick ....h W 2–1   **Att:** 385 — **Scorers:** Fairbairn, Gemmell
20th ● Dumbarton.......a L 2–1   **Att:** 826 — **Scorers:** McQuade. **Booked:** Ross, Fleming
27th ● Montrose ....h W 2–1   **Att:** 296 — **Scorers:** Gemmell, McQuade. **Booked:** Stein

October
4th ● East Stirling ......h D 0–0   **Att:** 331 — **Booked:** Gemmell
18th ● Annan Athletic ..a W 0–1   **Att:** 698 — **Scorers:** McQuade. **Booked:** McGregor, Shields
25th ● Elgin.................h L 1–2   **Att:** 328 — **Scorers:** McQuade. **Booked:** Gallacher, Tomana

November
1st ● Albion................a L 3–1   **Att:** 259 — **Scorers:** Armstrong. **Booked:** Adamson
8th ● Elgin.................h W 4–1   **Att:** 193 — **Scorers:** Armstrong[2], McQuade[2].
15th ● Stenhousemuir..h L 1–2   **Att:** 406 — **Scorers:** McQuade.
Booked: Baxter, Shields, Fleming, McQuade. **Dismissed:** Shields
22nd ● Berwick ....a W 2–3   **Att:** 389 — **Scorers:** Armstrong, Dempster, McQuade

December
13th ● Montrose ....a W 0–1   **Att:** 334 — **Scorers:** Dempster. **Booked:** McGregor, Shields
20th ● East Stirling ......a W 1–4   **Att:** 457 — **Scorers:** Adamson, Fairbairn[2], McQuade. **Booked:** Armstrong

January
10th ● Dumbarton.......h W 2–0   **Att:** 416 — **Scorers:** Adamson, McQuade
13th ● Berwick ....h W 2–0   **Att:** 282 — **Scorers:** Dempster, Tomana. **Booked:** MacKay
17th ● Elgin.................a D 1–1   **Att:** 382 — **Scorers:** Brown
24th ● Albion................h W 2–1   **Att:** 409 — **Scorers:** Gemmell[2]. **Booked:** McGregor
31st ● Annan Athletic ..h W 1–0   **Att:** 326 — **Scorers:** Gemmell. **Booked:** Fleming

February
21st ● Dumbarton.......a D 1–1   **Att:** 846 — **Scorers:** Dempster. **Booked:** Shields
28th ● Stenhousemuir..h W 1–0   **Att:** 459 — **Scorers:** Dempster

March
3rd ● Stenhousemuir..a L 1–0   **Att:** 368 — **Booked:** Armstrong, Gemmell, Shields, Fleming
7th ● Berwick ....a L 1–0   **Att:** 523
10th ● Forfar ....h D 0–0   **Att:** 317 — **Booked:** Ramsay. **Dismissed:** Fairbairn
14th ● Annan Athletic ..a L 3–1   **Att:** 629 — **Scorers:** MacKay. **Booked:** Gemmell, Ramsay
17th ● Montrose ....h W 2–1   **Att:** 303 — **Scorers:** Gemmell[2]
21st ● East Stirling ......h W 2–0   **Att:** 430 — **Scorers:** Armstrong, Fairbairn
31st ● Forfar ....a D 1–1   **Att:** 621 — **Scorers:** Gemmell

April
4th ● Elgin.................h D 1–1   **Att:** 331 — **Scorers:** Gemmell
11th ● Albion................a D 0–0   **Att:** 452 — **Booked:** Gemmell
18th ● Dumbarton.......h D 0–0   **Att:** 1,181 — **Booked:** Shields, Dempster, Armstrong. **Dismissed:** Shields
25th ● Montrose ....a L 2–1   **Att:** 403 — **Scorers:** Gemmell

May
2nd ● Forfar ....h D 2–2   **Att:** 527 — **Scorers:** Stein[2]. **Booked:** Shields
9th ● East Stirling ......a W 0–2   **Att:** 434 — **Scorers:** Ferguson[2]
13th ● East Stirling ......a W 1–2   **Att:** 605 — **Scorers:** Gemmell, Stein
16th ● East Stirling ......h D 1–1   **Att:** 633 — **Scorers:** Dempster. **Booked:** Shields
20th ● Stenhousemuir..h D 0–0   **Att:** 775 — **Booked:** Gemmell. **Dismissed:** McGregor
23rd ● Stenhousemuir..a D 0–0   **Att:** 1,530 — **Booked:** Robertson, Armstrong (Lost 5–4 on pens)

● Irn-Bru Third Division ● Scottish FA Cup ● Scottish League Cup ● Scottish Challenge Cup

IRN BRU
SCOTTISH FOOTBALL LEAGUE

THIRD DIVISION GOALKEEPER STATS

Player	Appearances	Match starts	Completed matches	Sub appearances	Subbed off	Clean sheets	Yellow cards	Red cards
Scott Gallacher 7	7	7	0	0	2	0	0
David Hay 29	29	29	0	0	12	0	0

THIRD DIVISION OUTFIELD PLAYER STATS

Player	Appearances	Match starts	Completed matches	Substitute appearances	Subbed off	Goals scored	Yellow cards	Red cards
Kenny Adamson.....................25	21	20	4	1	2	3	0
John Armstrong.....................31	31	31	0	0	5	3	0
Mark Baxter 26	24	20	2	4	0	1	0
Graeme Brown 17	8	1	9	7	1	0	0
Gary Cennerazzo 1	1	1	0	0	0	0	0
John Dempster......................26	17	12	9	5	5	1	0
Dene Droudge 4	3	2	1	1	0	0	0
Brian Fairbairn 28	20	9	8	10	5	0	1
John Ferguson 2	1	1	1	0	2	0	0
Derek Fleming 24	19	18	5	1	0	5	0
Mark Forbes 1	0	0	1	0	0	0	0
John Gemmell 31	25	14	6	11	12	5	0
Sandy Hodge 12	12	9	0	3	0	1	0
Daniel Lennon 1	0	0	1	0	0	0	0
Scott Linton 9	5	4	4	1	0	0	0
Daniel MacKay 19	19	13	0	6	1	1	0
Joe Mbu 19	18	16	1	2	0	0	0
Darren McGregor 34	34	34	0	0	1	4	0
Daniel McKay..........................3	2	2	1	0	0	0	0
Paul McQuade 23	20	14	3	6	10	1	0
John O'Neil 1	0	0	1	0	0	0	0
Mark Ramsay 32	26	17	6	9	1	2	0
Jamie Reid 1	1	1	0	0	0	0	0
Jon Robertson 9	3	1	6	2	0	0	0
Greg Ross 4	2	1	2	1	0	1	0
Jay Shields 22	20	11	2	7	0	7	2
Jay Stein 19	10	7	9	3	2	1	0
Marek Tomana 27	18	5	9	13	1	0	0
Derek Wallace 1	0	0	1	0	0	0	0
Callum Young 1	0	0	1	0	0	0	0

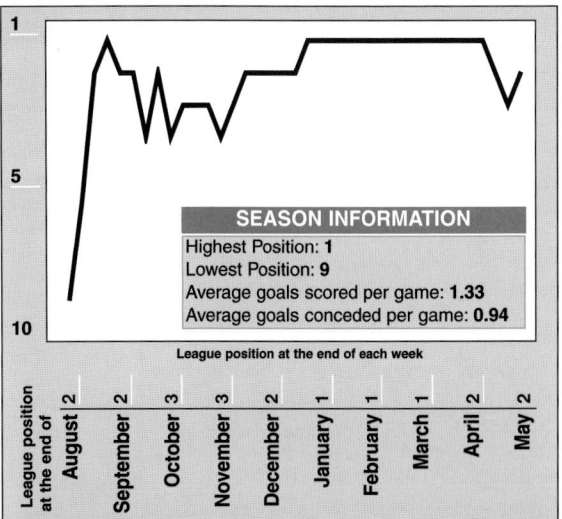

League position at the end of each week

| League position at the end of | August 2 | September 2 | October 3 | November 3 | December 2 | January 1 | February 1 | March 1 | April 2 | May 2 |

SEASON INFORMATION
Highest Position: **1**
Lowest Position: **9**
Average goals scored per game: **1.33**
Average goals conceded per game: **0.94**

LONGEST SEQUENCES

Wins	5	Undefeated home	11
(22/11/08–13/01/09)		(10/01/09–02/05/09)	
Losses	2	Undefeated away	5
(03/03/09–07/03/09)		(22/11/08–21/02/09)	
Draws	4	Without scoring	3
(31/03/09–18/04/09)		(03/03/09–10/03/09)	
Undefeated	10	Without conceding	2
(22/11/08–28/02/09)		(on three occasions)	
Without win	6	Scoring	14
(31/03/09–02/05/09)		(18/10/08–28/02/09)	

CARDS RECEIVED

36 **3**

QUICK-FIRE GOALS

From the start of a match
John Gemmell (v Berwick) 2:00

By a substitute after coming on
Marek Tomana (v Berwick) 3:00

GOALS SCORED/CONCEDED PER FIVE-MINUTE INTERVALS

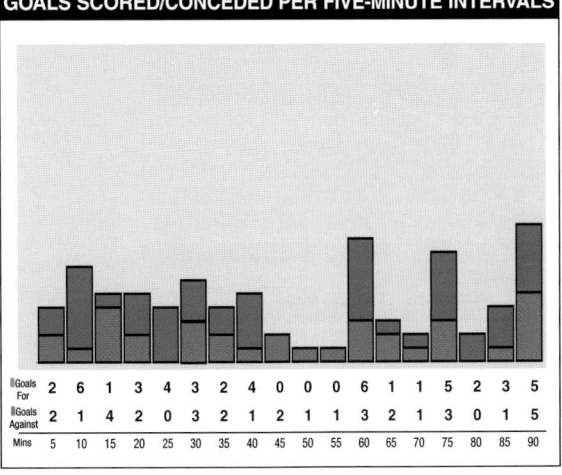

	Goals For																		
Goals For	2	6	1	3	4	3	2	4	0	0	0	6	1	1	5	2	3	5
Goals Against	2	1	4	2	0	3	2	1	2	1	1	3	2	1	3	0	1	5
Mins	5	10	15	20	25	30	35	40	45	50	55	60	65	70	75	80	85	90

DUMBARTON ended a 17-year wait for a trophy when they clinched the Irn-Bru Third Division title with a 3–1 win against Annan on the final day of the season.

The achievement was all the more laudable given that manager Jim Chapman recruited a total of 16 new players to the Strathclyde Homes Stadium at the start of the season before bolstering his squad again in January.

The new-look side took time to gel and Cowdenbeath looked like they would stroll to the title in March when they went 10 points clear of the Sons at the top of the table.

However, Chapman's side continued fighting and slowly began to cut the lead and, even though they conceded for the first time in eight games at Annan, goals from top scorer Ross Clark, Denis McLaughlin and Derek Carcary sparked wild celebrations.

CLUB SUMMARY

FORMED	1872
MANAGER	Jim Chapman
GROUND	Strathclyde Homes Stadium
CAPACITY	2,025
NICKNAME	The Sons
WEB	www.dumbartonfootballclub.com

The New Football Pools PLAYER OF THE SEASON   **Ross Clark**

OVERALL

P	W	D	L	F	A	GD
42	20	12	10	72	51	21

IRN-BRU THIRD DIVISION

Pos	P	W	D	L	F	A	GD	Pts
1	36	19	10	7	65	36	29	67

HOME

Pos	P	W	D	L	F	A	GD	Pts
1	18	11	5	2	38	13	25	38

AWAY

Pos	P	W	D	L	F	A	GD	Pts
2	18	8	5	5	27	23	4	29

CUP PROGRESS DETAILS

Competition	Round reached	Knocked out by
Co-op Insurance Cup	R2	St Mirren
Scottish Cup	R3	Ross County
Challenge Cup	R1	Airdrie Utd

BIGGEST WIN (ALL COMPS)

02/05/09 6–0 v Elgin **SC3**

BIGGEST DEFEAT (ALL COMPS)

26/08/08 0–7 v St Mirren **SLC2**

ATTENDANCE RECORD

High	Low	Average
1,396	462	716
v Elgin (02/05/2009)	v East Stirling (03/03/2009)	

RESULTS 2008/09

July
26th ● Airdrie Utd ....a L 3–2   **Att:** 808 — **Scorers:** Carcary, Clark. **Booked:** Keegan, Canning, Gray

August
2nd ● Montrose ....h D 1–1   **Att:** 602 — **Scorers:** Clark. **Booked:** Clark, Brittain
5th ● Annan Athletic ..h D 1–1   **Att:** 459 — **Scorers:** Logan. **Booked:** Gordon, Geggan, Logan.
    Dismissed: Geggan (Won 5–4 on pens)
9th ● Elgin.................a D 1–1   **Att:** 462 — **Scorers:** Logan. **Booked:** Murray, Logan
16th ● Berwick ....a W 1–2   **Att:** 516 — **Scorers:** Lennon[2]. **Booked:** O'Byrne
23rd ● Stenhousemuir..h L 1–2   **Att:** 676 — **Scorers:** Keegan. **Booked:** Gordon, Logan
26th ● St Mirren ....a L 7–0   **Att:** 1,747
30th ● East Stirling ......h D 1–1   **Att:** 587 — **Scorers:** Murray

September
13th ● Albion................a W 1–3   **Att:** 327 — **Scorers:** Clark, Gordon, McLeod. **Booked:** O'Byrne
20th ● Cowdenbeath....h W 2–1   **Att:** 826 — **Scorers:** Carcary, Gordon.
    Booked: O'Byrne, Canning, Wilson, Murray, M. Moore
27th ● Forfar ....a D 2–2   **Att:** 473 — **Scorers:** McLeod, Tulloch OG

October
4th ● Annan Athletic ..h W 4–1   **Att:** 636 — **Scorers:** Clark, Keegan, Watson OG, Watson OG. **Booked:** O'Byrne
18th ● Montrose ....a W 1–2   **Att:** 570 — **Scorers:** Clark, McLeod
25th ● Fraserburgh ......a W 0–1   **Att:** 517 — **Scorers:** Chisholm. **Booked:** Clark, Wilson, Lennon

November
1st ● Berwick ....h W 5–2   **Att:** 679 — **Scorers:** Clark[2], Cusack, McLeod, Murray
8th ● Stenhousemuir..a D 1–1   **Att:** 724 — **Scorers:** Murray. **Dismissed:** Wilson
15th ● East Stirling ......a L 5–2   **Att:** 516 — **Scorers:** Carcary, Gordon. **Booked:** Geggan, O'Byrne
22nd ● Albion...............h D 1–1   **Att:** 647 — **Scorers:** Clark. **Booked:** Canning, Murray, M. Moore, Geggan
29th ● Ross County .....a D 2–2   **Att:** 1,200 — **Scorers:** Carcary[2]

December
13th ● Forfar ....h W 3–0   **Att:** 569 — **Scorers:** Chisholm, Keegan, McLeod
15th ● Ross County .....h L 1–2   **Att:** 557 — **Scorers:** Gordon. **Booked:** Murray, Gordon, Canning
20th ● Annan Athletic ..a L 2–1   **Att:** 647 — **Scorers:** Clark. **Booked:** Chisholm

January
10th ● Cowdenbeath....a L 2–0   **Att:** 416 —**Booked:** Dunlop, Canning. **Dismissed:** Dunlop
17th ● Stenhousemuir..h W 1–0   **Att:** 737 — **Scorers:** Chisholm. **Booked:** Geggan
24th ● Berwick ....a W 1–2   **Att:** 425 — **Scorers:** Carcary, McLeod.
31st ● Montrose ....h D 1–1   **Att:** 652 — **Scorers:** Carcary

February
21st ● Cowdenbeath....h D 1–1   **Att:** 846 — **Scorers:** Boyle. **Booked:** Forbes, Lennon, Canning
28th ● East Stirling ......a L 3–1   **Att:** 526 — **Scorers:** Clark. **Booked:** Clark, Canning, Geggan, D. McLaughlin

March
3rd ● East Stirling ......h W 2–0   **Att:** 462 — **Scorers:** Craig, McLaughlin. **Booked:** D. McLaughlin
7th ● Albion...............h W 1–0   **Att:** 692 — **Scorers:** Boyle
10th ● Elgin.................h W 2–0   **Att:** 474 — **Scorers:** Carcary, McLaughlin
14th ● Montrose ....a L 1–0   **Att:** 347 —**Booked:** Dunlop, Forbes
17th ● Albion...............a D 1–1   **Att:** 346 — **Scorers:** Clark. **Booked:** Forbes
21st ● Annan Athletic ..h L 0–2   **Att:** 724 —**Booked:** Gordon
31st ● Elgin.................a W 0–2   **Att:** 276 — **Scorers:** McLaughlin, Edwards OG. **Booked:** McStay

April
4th ● Stenhousemuir..a W 0–2   **Att:** 588 — **Scorers:** Clark, Gordon
7th ● Forfar ....a W 0–2   **Att:** 513 — **Scorers:** Clark[2]. **Booked:** Murray, Lennon, D. McLaughlin
11th ● Berwick ....h W 2–0   **Att:** 770 — **Scorers:** Boyle, Forbes. **Booked:** Carcary, D. McLaughlin
18th ● Cowdenbeath....a D 0–0   **Att:** 1,181 —**Booked:** Lennon, Gordon
25th ● Forfar ....h W 4–0   **Att:** 917 — **Scorers:** Brannan, Carcary, McLaughlin, Smith OG. **Booked:** Forbes

May
2nd ● Elgin.................h W 6–0   **Att:** 1,396 — **Scorers:** Carcary[4], McLaughlin, Murray
9th ● Annan Athletic ..a W 1–3   **Att:** 1,343 — **Scorers:** Carcary, Clark, McLaughlin. **Booked:** Dunlop

● Irn-Bru Third Division ● Scottish FA Cup ● Scottish League Cup ● Scottish Challenge Cup

THIRD DIVISION GOALKEEPER STATS

Player	Appearances	Match starts	Completed matches	Sub appearances	Subbed off	Clean sheets	Yellow cards	Red cards
David McEwan	22	22	21	0	1	7	0	0
Mark McGeown	15	14	14	1	0	5	0	0

THIRD DIVISION OUTFIELD PLAYER STATS

Player	Appearances	Match starts	Completed matches	Substitute appearances	Subbed off	Goals scored	Yellow cards	Red cards
Patrick Boyle	17	17	17	0	0	3	0	0
Kieran Brannan	6	0	0	6	0	1	0	0
Craig Brittain	3	3	3	0	0	0	1	0
Mark Canning	20	10	5	10	5	0	5	0
Derek Carcary	33	25	12	8	13	11	2	0
Iain Chisholm	27	15	14	12	1	2	1	0
Ross Clark	31	30	20	1	10	14	2	0
Paul Craig	3	3	3	0	0	1	0	0
Liam Cusack	9	1	0	8	1	1	0	0
Michael Dunlop	21	21	20	0	0	0	3	1
Ross Forbes	18	15	10	3	5	1	4	0
Andrew Geggan	25	23	21	2	2	0	4	0
Ben Gordon	36	36	33	0	3	4	3	0
Alan Gourlay	3	0	0	3	0	0	0	0
David Gray	7	2	0	5	2	0	0	0
Paul Keegan	21	12	2	9	10	3	0	0
Gordon Lennon	34	32	31	2	1	2	3	0
Raymond Logan	6	4	3	2	1	1	2	0
Kieran McAnespie	4	2	1	2	1	0	0	0
Richard McKillen	2	2	2	0	0	0	0	0
Denis McLaughlin	16	16	9	0	7	6	4	0
Paul McLeod	24	19	10	5	9	6	0	0
Martin McNiff	1	0	0	1	0	0	0	0
Ryan McStay	12	11	8	1	3	0	1	0
Michael Moore	6	0	0	6	0	0	2	0
Stevie Murray	35	34	22	1	12	4	4	0
Michael O'Byrne	13	13	13	0	0	0	5	0
Fergus Tiernan	4	2	1	2	1	0	0	0
Steven Weir	1	1	0	0	1	0	0	0
Gary Wilson	8	8	7	0	0	0	1	1

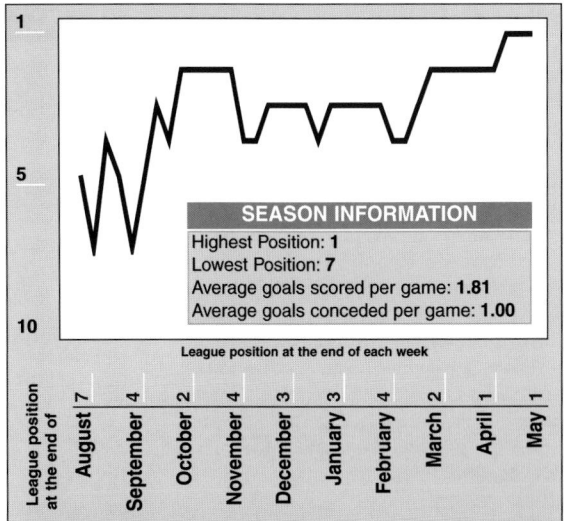

League position at the end of each week

League position at the end of	August	September	October	November	December	January	February	March	April	May
	7	4	2	4	3	3	4	2	1	1

SEASON INFORMATION
Highest Position: **1**
Lowest Position: **7**
Average goals scored per game: **1.81**
Average goals conceded per game: **1.00**

LONGEST SEQUENCES

Wins (31/03/09–11/04/09)	4	Undefeated home (30/08/08–10/03/09)	12
Losses (20/12/08–10/01/09)	2	Undefeated away (02/08/08–08/11/08)	7
Draws (on two occasions)	2	Without scoring (–)	
Undefeated (on two occasions)	8	Without conceding (31/03/09–02/05/09)	7
Without win (on three occasions)	3	Scoring (02/08/08–20/12/08)	16

CARDS RECEIVED

47 **2**

QUICK-FIRE GOALS

From the start of a match
Derek Carcary (v Montrose) 5:00

By a substitute after coming on
Paul Keegan (v Forfar) 5:00

GOALS SCORED/CONCEDED PER FIVE-MINUTE INTERVALS

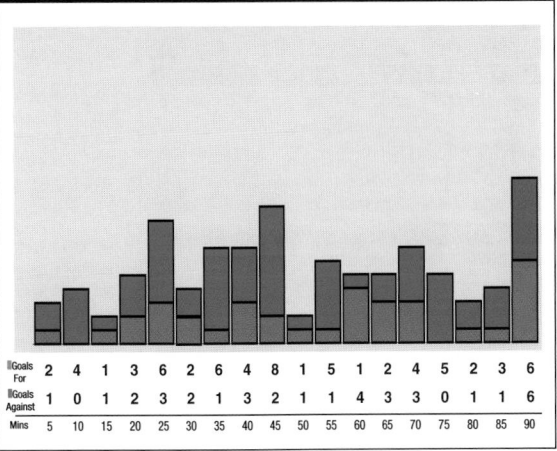

Goals For	2	4	1	3	6	2	6	4	8	1	5	1	2	4	5	2	3	6
Goals Against	1	0	1	2	3	2	1	3	2	1	1	4	3	3	0	1	1	6
Mins	5	10	15	20	25	30	35	40	45	50	55	60	65	70	75	80	85	90

EAST STIRLINGSHIRE

THE Jim McInally revolution continued apace at East Stirlingshire this season, but what looked set to be a dream campaign in the Irn-Bru Third Division, ultimately ended in disappointment.

The club's 3–2 play-off semi-final defeat to Cowdenbeath was all too much for McInally, who aimed an angry outburst at the Blue Brazil bench towards the end of the second leg, for which he later apologised. That incident soured what had otherwise been a superb campaign for a club who only avoided finishing bottom of the League by a point in 2007/08.

Forced to play their home matches on the artificial surface at Stenhousemuir's Ochilview ground as their own Firs Park was deemed unsuitable, the Shire managed to take the title race down to the final day of the season, but a defeat meant settling for a play-off place.

CLUB SUMMARY

FORMED	1881
MANAGER	Jim McInally
GROUND	Ochilview Park
CAPACITY	3,776
NICKNAME	The Shire
WEBSITE	www.eaststirlingfc.co.uk

The New Football Pools PLAYER OF THE SEASON — **Andy Rodgers**

OVERALL
	P	W	D	L	F	A	GD
	44	22	5	17	68	66	2

IRN-BRU THIRD DIVISION
Pos	P	W	D	L	F	A	GD	Pts
3	36	19	4	13	57	50	7	61

HOME
Pos	P	W	D	L	F	A	GD	Pts
3	18	10	1	7	30	29	1	31

AWAY
Pos	P	W	D	L	F	A	GD	Pts
1	18	9	3	6	27	21	6	30

CUP PROGRESS DETAILS
Competition	Round reached	Knocked out by
Co-op Insurance Cup	R1	Livingston
Scottish Cup	R4	Dundee Utd
Challenge Cup	R2	Morton

BIGGEST WIN (ALL COMPS)
06/12/08 5–0 v Montrose SC3

BIGGEST DEFEAT (ALL COMPS)
0–4 on three occasions

ATTENDANCE RECORD
High	Low	Average
812	343	450

v Stenhousemuir (03/01/2009) v Annan Athletic (12/11/2008)

RESULTS 2008/09

July
27th ● Ayr ....h W 2–1 **Att:** 729 — **Scorers:** Richardson, Rodgers. **Booked:** Cramb, Dunn, Nicholls

August
2nd ● Berwick ....a L 2–1 **Att:** 570 — **Scorers:** Rodgers. **Booked:** Rodgers, Ure, Cramb, Gibson. **Dismissed:** Cramb
6th ● Livingston..........h L 1–2 **Att:** 491 — **Scorers:** Graham. **Booked:** Moffat, Graham. (AET)
9th ● Albion...............h W 1–0 **Att:** 348 — **Scorers:** Forrest. **Booked:** Moffat, Gibson, McKenzie
13th ● Morton ....h L 0–3 **Att:** 698 — **Booked:** Hay, Forrest
16th ● Annan Athletic ..a L 2–1 **Att:** 968 — **Scorers:** Cramb. **Booked:** Gibson
23rd ● Forfar ....h L 0–3 **Att:** 394 — **Booked:** Ure, Tully
30th ● Dumbarton........a D 1–1 **Att:** 587 — **Scorers:** McKenzie. **Booked:** Richardson, Bolochoweckyj, Rodgers, Hay, Forrest, McKenzie. **Dismissed:** Tully

September
13th ● Stenhousemuir..h L 0–2 **Att:** 511 — **Booked:** Ure
20th ● Montrose ....a L 3–0 **Att:** 363 — **Booked:** Kelly, Graham. **Dismissed:** Graham
27th ● Elgin.................h W 5–2 **Att:** 352 — **Scorers:** Cramb, Donaldson, Richardson, Rodgers, Kaczan OG. **Booked:** Richardson

October
4th ● Cowdenbeath....a D 0–0 **Att:** 331 — **Booked:** Forrest, Richardson, Tully
18th ● Berwick ....h W 1–0 **Att:** 397 — **Scorers:** Bolochoweckyj. **Booked:** Ure, Tully, Cramb. **Dismissed:** Ure
26th ● Preston Ath ......h W 4–2 **Att:** 382 — **Scorers:** Anderson, Cramb, Graham, Rodgers. **Booked:** Barclay, Graham

November
8th ● Forfar ....a W 2–3 **Att:** 427 — **Scorers:** Bolochoweckyj, Cramb, Rodgers. **Booked:** Forrest, Richardson
12th ● Annan Athletic ..h W 2–1 **Att:** 343 — **Scorers:** Cramb, Graham. **Booked:** Richardson, Cramb
15th ● Dumbarton........h W 5–2 **Att:** 516 — **Scorers:** Donaldson, Dunn, Graham[2], Rodgers. **Booked:** Rodgers, Forrest, Bolochoweckyj
22nd ● Stenhousemuir..a D 1–1 **Att:** 737 — **Scorers:** Graham. **Booked:** Bolochoweckyj, Graham, Tully, Forrest, Hay. **Dismissed:** Hay
29th ● Livingston.........h W 2–1 **Att:** 563 — **Scorers:** Forrest, Graham. **Booked:** Bolochoweckyj, Tully

December
6th ● Montrose ....h W 5–0 **Att:** 427 — **Scorers:** Bolochoweckyj, Cramb[2], Graham[2]. **Booked:** Ure
13th ● Elgin.................a W 0–4 **Att:** 366 — **Scorers:** Graham, Rodgers[3].
20th ● Cowdenbeath....h L 1–4 **Att:** 457 — **Scorers:** Forrest. **Booked:** Forrest

January
3rd ● Stenhousemuir..h L 0–3 **Att:** 812 — **Booked:** Richardson, Hay
11th ● Dundee Utd ......h L 0–4 **Att:** 2,153
17th ● Forfar ....h W 3–2 **Att:** 405 — **Scorers:** Cramb, Dunn, Rodgers. **Booked:** Graham, Ure
24th ● Annan Athletic ..a L 4–0 **Att:** 714 — **Booked:** Kelly

February
7th ● Albion...............h L 0–1 **Att:** 435 — **Booked:** Tully
14th ● Elgin.................h W 1–0 **Att:** 389 — **Scorers:** Rodgers. **Booked:** Bolochoweckyj
21st ● Montrose ....a W 0–2 **Att:** 400 — **Scorers:** Cramb, Stevenson. **Booked:** Hay, Rodgers, Graham
28th ● Dumbarton........h W 3–1 **Att:** 526 — **Scorers:** Cramb, Rodgers, Stevenson. **Booked:** Stevenson, Weaver, Tully, Rodgers

March
3rd ● Dumbarton........a L 2–0 **Att:** 462 — **Booked:** Bolochoweckyj, Cramb. **Dismissed:** Cramb
7th ● Stenhousemuir..a W 1–4 **Att:** 805 — **Scorers:** Donaldson, Graham[2], Stevenson. **Booked:** Kelly, Graham, Bolochoweckyj
10th ● Albion...............a W 0–2 **Att:** 420 — **Scorers:** Graham, Hay. **Booked:** Richardson
14th ● Berwick ....h L 0–4 **Att:** 441 — **Booked:** Forrest, Ure, Peat, Tully. **Dismissed:** Forrest
21st ● Cowdenbeath....a L 2–0 **Att:** 430 — **Booked:** Dunn
28th ● Berwick ....a W 1–2 **Att:** 431 — **Scorers:** Rodgers[2]. **Booked:** Bolochoweckyj, Forrest, Stevenson

April
4th ● Forfar ....a W 0–2 **Att:** 491 — **Scorers:** Bolochoweckyj, McKenzie. **Booked:** Ure, King
11th ● Annan Athletic ..h D 1–1 **Att:** 508 — **Scorers:** Graham. **Booked:** Graham, Stevenson, Ure, Bolochoweckyj, Weaver
18th ● Montrose ....h W 2–1 **Att:** 401 — **Scorers:** Graham[2]. **Booked:** Graham
25th ● Elgin.................a W 0–2 **Att:** 381 — **Scorers:** Graham[2]. **Booked:** Rodgers, Bolochoweckyj

May
2nd ● Albion...............a W 0–2 **Att:** 346 — **Scorers:** Rodgers, Stevenson.
9th ● Cowdenbeath....h L 0–2 **Att:** 434 — **Booked:** Kelly, Forrest, Dunn
13th ● Cowdenbeath....h L 1–2 **Att:** 605 — **Scorers:** Rodgers. **Booked:** Bolochoweckyj
16th ● Cowdenbeath....a D 1–1 **Att:** 633 — **Scorers:** Graham. **Booked:** Stevenson

● Irn-Bru Third Division ● Scottish FA Cup ● Scottish League Cup ● Scottish Challenge Cup

THIRD DIVISION GOALKEEPER STATS

Player	Appearances	Match starts	Completed matches	Sub appearances	Subbed off	Clean sheets	Yellow cards	Red cards
Jamie Barclay	11	11	11	0	0	2	0	0
Barry John Corr	2	0	0	0	0	0	0	0
John Hillcoat	3	3	3	0	0	1	0	0
Greg Mitchell	2	2	2	0	0	0	0	0
Jamie Newman	1	0	0	1	0	1	0	0
Mark Peat	16	16	15	0	1	7	1	0
Mark Peters	2	2	0	0	0	0	0	0

THIRD DIVISION OUTFIELD PLAYER STATS

Player	Appearances	Match starts	Completed matches	Substitute appearances	Subbed off	Goals scored	Yellow cards	Red cards
Sean Anderson	26	16	7	10	9	1	0	0
Michael Bolochoweckyj	33	33	30	0	3	4	9	0
Colin Cramb	21	15	4	6	9	9	4	2
Craig Donaldson	30	26	19	4	7	3	0	0
David Dunn	33	18	7	15	11	2	2	0
Jason Elliot	1	0	0	1	0	0	0	0
Eddie Forrest	26	25	22	1	2	2	9	1
James Gibson	3	2	2	1	0	0	3	0
Brian Graham	33	29	17	4	11	14	7	1
Paul Hay	32	31	23	1	7	1	4	1
Gary Kelly	25	14	10	11	4	0	4	0
David King	7	7	7	0	0	0	1	0
Balsa Krivokapic	2	1	0	1	1	0	0	0
Marc McKenzie	34	1	1	33	0	2	2	0
Gordon Moffat	1	0	0	1	0	0	1	0
David Nicholls	4	4	1	0	3	0	0	0
Gary O'Hara	1	1	1	0	0	0	0	0
John O'Neill	2	1	0	1	1	0	0	0
Stephen Oates	2	2	1	0	1	0	0	0
Steven Page	1	0	0	1	0	0	0	0
Dean Richardson	25	19	10	6	9	1	7	0
Andy Rodgers	30	28	18	2	10	14	6	0
Jamie Stevenson	13	13	4	0	9	4	3	0
David Thornton	2	1	1	1	0	0	0	0
Craig Tully	27	27	24	0	2	0	7	1
Derek Ure	32	31	28	1	2	0	9	1
Paul Weaver	15	15	14	0	1	0	2	0

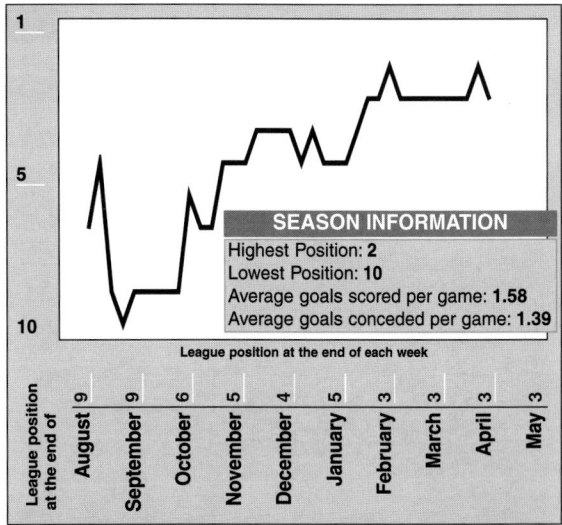

League position at the end of each week

SEASON INFORMATION

Highest Position: **2**
Lowest Position: **10**
Average goals scored per game: **1.58**
Average goals conceded per game: **1.39**

LONGEST SEQUENCES

Wins	4	Undefeated home	5
(18/10/08–15/11/08)		(27/09/08–06/12/08)	
Losses	2	Undefeated away	4
(on five occasions)		(04/10/08–13/12/08)	
Draws		Without scoring	2
(–)		(on three occasions)	
Undefeated	9	Without conceding	2
(27/09/08–13/12/08)		(on four occasions)	
Without win	5	Scoring	8
(16/08/08–20/09/08)		(18/10/08–20/12/08)	

CARDS RECEIVED

81   7

QUICK-FIRE GOALS

From the start of a match
Colin Cramb (v Annan Athletic) 1:00

By a substitute after coming on
David Dunn (v Dumbarton) 2:00

GOALS SCORED/CONCEDED PER FIVE-MINUTE INTERVALS

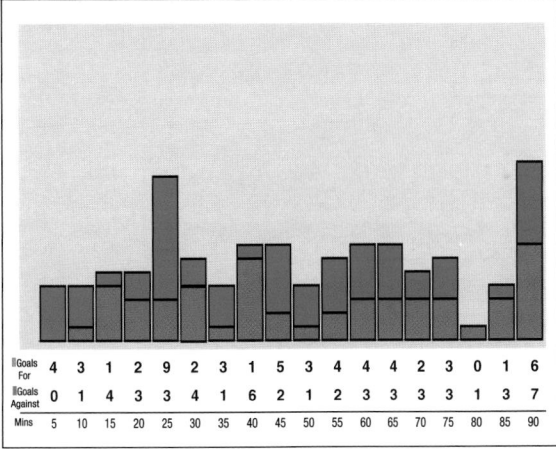

Goals For	4	3	1	2	9	2	3	1	5	3	4	4	4	2	3	0	1	6
Goals Against	0	1	4	3	3	4	1	6	2	1	2	3	3	3	3	1	3	7
Mins	5	10	15	20	25	30	35	40	45	50	55	60	65	70	75	80	85	90

ELGIN CITY

ELGIN endured a torrid time in the Irn-Bru Third Division and seemed destined to finish bottom of the table from almost the first kick of the 2008/09 season.

There was a managerial change too, with former Clachnacuddin boss Robbie Williamson parting ways with the club in December after a run of poor results and being replaced by Ross County assistant Ross Jack.

Season low points included a 6–1 home thrashing by Albion – in which they had three men sent off – and 6–0 defeats to both Annan and Dumbarton.

Elgin could take some solace from a 3–0 revenge victory at Albion, but wins were hard to come by. Darren Shallicker chipped in with a healthy, if modest, goal tally but could not help to alter City's position as the League's least-prolific team.

CLUB SUMMARY

FORMED	1893
MANAGER	Ross Jack
GROUND	Borough Briggs
CAPACITY	3,927
NICKNAME	The Black and Whites
WEBSITE	www.elgincity.com

The New **Football Pools** PLAYER OF THE SEASON — Paul Kaczan

OVERALL

P	W	D	L	F	A	GD
41	9	5	27	36	87	-51

IRN-BRU THIRD DIVISION

Pos	P	W	D	L	F	A	GD	Pts
10	36	7	5	24	31	79	-48	26

HOME

Pos	P	W	D	L	F	A	GD	Pts
10	18	5	2	11	16	32	-16	17

AWAY

Pos	P	W	D	L	F	A	GD	Pts
10	18	2	3	13	15	47	-32	9

CUP PROGRESS DETAILS

Competition	Round reached	Knocked out by
Challenge Cup	R1	Cowdenbeath
Co-op Insurance Cup	R1	Alloa
Scottish Cup	R3	Spartans

BIGGEST WIN (ALL COMPS)
18/04/09 3–0 v Albion SC3

BIGGEST DEFEAT (ALL COMPS)
0–6 on two occasions

ATTENDANCE RECORD

High	Low	Average
537	276	392

v Cowdenbeath (23/08/2008) v Dumbarton (31/03/2009)

RESULTS 2008/09

July
26th	● Cowdenbeath....h	L 0–2	Att: 379 — Booked: Campbell, Gilbert

August
2nd	● Stenhousemuir..a	L 3–0	Att: 320 — Dismissed: Gilbert
5th	● Alloa................a	L 2–0	Att: 269 — Booked: A. MacDonald, Shallicker
9th	● Dumbarton.......h	D 1–1	Att: 462 — Scorers: MacKay. Booked: Crooks, Lindsay
16th	● Forfar ....a	W 0–1	Att: 377 — Scorers: MacKay. Booked: O'Donoghue. Dismissed: O'Donoghue
23rd	● Cowdenbeath....h	L 0–2	Att: 537 — Booked: Hind, Shallicker. Dismissed: MacKay
30th	● Montrose ....a	L 1–0	Att: 294

September
13th	● Annan Athletic ..h	L 1–2	Att: 468 — Scorers: Shallicker. Booked: Nicolson
20th	● Albion...............h	L 1–6	Att: 407 — Scorers: Shallicker. Booked: Gilbert, Nicolson, Campbell, Shallicker. Dismissed: Niven, Campbell, Gilbert
27th	● East Stirling ......a	L 5–2	Att: 352 — Scorers: Kerr, Wright. Booked: Nicolson, Hind

October
4th	● Berwick ....a	D 1–1	Att: 367 — Scorers: Shallicker. Booked: Wright. Dismissed: Wright
18th	● Stenhousemuir..h	W 4–2	Att: 359 — Scorers: Campbell, Kaczan, Kerr, Shallicker. Booked: McNulty, Nicolson
25th	● Cowdenbeath....a	W 1–2	Att: 328 — Scorers: Kaczan, Wright. Booked: McNulty

November
1st	● Forfar ....h	L 0–1	Att: 491 — Booked: Gilbert, Nicolson, Kaczan
8th	● Cowdenbeath....h	L 4–1	Att: 193 — Scorers: Shallicker
15th	● Montrose ....h	L 1–2	Att: 376 — Scorers: O'Donoghue. Booked: Niven, Keogh, Nicolson
22nd	● Annan Athletic ..a	L 5–0	Att: 422 — Booked: Nicolson, MacKay

December
6th	● Spartans ....h	W 2–1	Att: 519 — Scorers: Nicolson, Wright. Dismissed: Wright
13th	● East Stirling ......h	L 0–4	Att: 366 — Booked: Malin, Campbell
15th	● Spartans ....h	L 1–2	Att: 551 — Scorers: MacKay. Booked: Hind, Nicolson, MacKay, Niven, Gilbert. Dismissed: Nicolson
20th	● Berwick ....h	L 0–2	Att: 304

January
10th	● Montrose ....a	L 3–1	Att: 296 — Scorers: Wright. Booked: Niven
17th	● Cowdenbeath....h	D 1–1	Att: 382 — Scorers: Wright. Booked: McKenzie
31st	● Stenhousemuir..a	L 4–2	Att: 311 — Scorers: Wright[2]. Booked: Kaczan, McNulty, Campbell. Dismissed: Campbell

February
14th	● East Stirling ......a	L 1–0	Att: 389
21st	● Albion...............h	W 1–0	Att: 357 — Scorers: MacKay. Booked: Gillespie
28th	● Montrose ....h	W 1–0	Att: 364 — Scorers: Crooks. Booked: Nicolson

March
3rd	● Albion...............a	L 2–1	Att: 237 — Scorers: Crooks. Booked: Jack
7th	● Annan Athletic ..a	L 6–0	Att: 487 — Booked: O'Donoghue. Dismissed: McNulty
10th	● Dumbarton.......a	L 2–0	Att: 474 — Booked: Niven, Kaczan
14th	● Stenhousemuir..h	W 2–0	Att: 318 — Scorers: Campbell, MacKay
21st	● Berwick ....a	L 2–1	Att: 348 — Scorers: Wright
24th	● Forfar ....a	D 1–1	Att: 578 — Scorers: Brown OG. Booked: Kaczan, Nicolson
28th	● Annan Athletic ..h	L 0–1	Att: 321 — Booked: Nicolson, D. Craig
31st	● Dumbarton.......h	L 0–2	Att: 276 — Booked: D. Craig, Kaczan, Nicolson

April
4th	● Cowdenbeath....a	D 1–1	Att: 331 — Scorers: Shallicker. Booked: Edwards
11th	● Forfar ....h	L 1–4	Att: 452 — Scorers: Shallicker. Booked: Shallicker, Kaczan, MacKay
18th	● Albion...............a	W 0–3	Att: 275 — Scorers: Campbell[2], Nicolson. Booked: Campbell
25th	● East Stirling ......a	L 0–2	Att: 381 — Booked: O'Donoghue

May
2nd	● Dumbarton.......a	L 6–0	Att: 1,396
9th	● Berwick ....h	W 2–0	Att: 429 — Scorers: MacDonald, Nicolson. Booked: Niven

● Irn-Bru Third Division ● Scottish FA Cup ● Scottish League Cup ● Scottish Challenge Cup

actim

THIRD DIVISION GOALKEEPER STATS

Player	Appearances	Match starts	Completed matches	Sub appearances	Subbed off	Clean sheets	Yellow cards	Red cards
Joe Malin	2	2	2	0	0	0	1	0
Andy McNulty	19	19	16	0	2	5	2	1
Ally Ridgers	18	15	15	3	0	1	0	0

THIRD DIVISION OUTFIELD PLAYER STATS

Player	Appearances	Match starts	Completed matches	Substitute appearances	Subbed off	Goals scored	Yellow cards	Red cards
David Allan	8	1	0	7	1	0	0	0
Liam Archibald	1	0	0	1	0	0	0	0
Brian Cameron	14	4	1	10	3	0	0	0
Craig Campbell	29	29	25	0	2	4	4	2
Colin Charlesworth	1	0	0	1	0	0	0	0
David Craig	26	16	12	10	3	0	2	1
Jason Crooks	33	26	16	7	10	2	1	0
Steven Edwards	7	5	4	2	1	0	1	0
Kenny Gilbert	9	9	6	0	1	0	2	2
Dale Gillespie	17	16	13	1	3	0	1	0
David Hind	13	10	5	3	5	0	2	0
Alexander Jack	11	6	2	5	4	0	1	0
Paul Kaczan	28	27	24	1	3	1	6	0
Liam Keogh	5	5	1	0	4	0	1	0
Guy Kerr	14	13	11	1	2	2	0	0
Allan Lindsay	3	2	2	1	0	0	1	0
Tony Low	6	2	1	4	1	0	0	0
Ally MacDonald	31	31	24	0	7	1	0	0
Steven MacKay	26	23	19	3	3	4	2	1
Stephen McKenzie	9	2	1	7	1	0	1	0
Duncan McPhee	4	2	2	2	0	0	0	0
Graham Munro	7	7	5	0	2	0	0	0
Mark Nicolson	33	33	33	0	0	2	11	0
David Niven	19	17	14	2	2	0	4	1
David Nixon	1	1	1	0	0	0	0	0
Ross O'Donoghue	33	33	31	0	1	1	3	1
Derek Ramsay	3	0	0	3	1	0	0	0
Darren Shallicker	29	22	14	7	8	7	3	0
Daniel Smith	1	0	0	1	0	0	0	0
Gary Tweedie	1	0	0	1	0	0	0	0
Kenny Wright	23	20	7	3	12	6	1	1

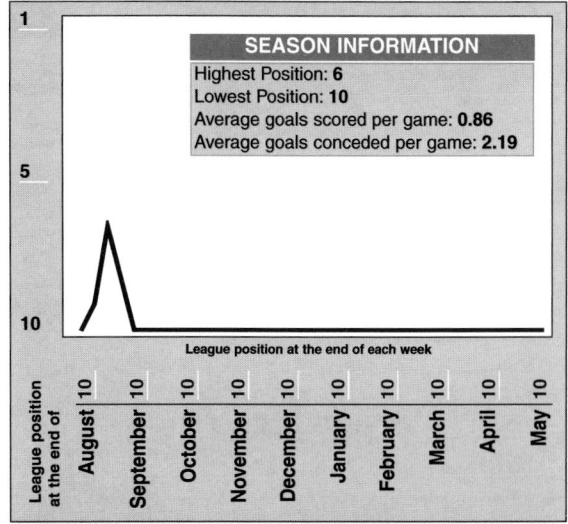

SEASON INFORMATION
Highest Position: **6**
Lowest Position: **10**
Average goals scored per game: **0.86**
Average goals conceded per game: **2.19**

League position at the end of each week

LONGEST SEQUENCES

Wins	2	Undefeated home	4
(21/02/09–28/02/09)		(17/01/09–14/03/09)	
Losses	7	Undefeated away	3
(01/11/08–10/01/09)		(on two occasions)	
Draws		Without scoring	3
(–)		(22/11/08–20/12/08)	
Undefeated	2	Without conceding	2
(on three occasions)		(21/02/09–28/02/09)	
Without win	10	Scoring	5
(01/11/08–14/02/09)		(13/09/08–18/10/08)	

CARDS RECEIVED

50 10

QUICK-FIRE GOALS

From the start of a match
Kenny Wright (v Montrose) 6:00

By a substitute after coming on
Darren Shallicker (v Annan Athletic) 7:00

GOALS SCORED/CONCEDED PER FIVE-MINUTE INTERVALS

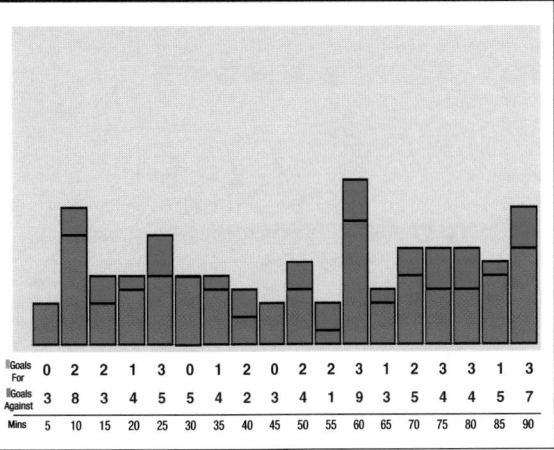

Goals For	0	2	2	1	3	0	1	2	0	2	2	3	1	2	3	3	1	3
Goals Against	3	8	3	4	5	5	4	2	3	4	1	9	3	5	4	4	5	7
Mins	5	10	15	20	25	30	35	40	45	50	55	60	65	70	75	80	85	90

FORFAR ATHLETIC

DICK CAMPBELL rescued Forfar from the doldrums, improving on their rock-bottom finish of the previous season.

The ex-Partick manager took the helm before the start of the campaign and gave the Loons a boost as they attempted to forget their disappointing 2007/08.

Forfar's form was unpredictable, with the team finding it difficult to maintain any sort of rhythm. They went on a five-game unbeaten run in the autumn, propelling them to fourth in the League, but struggled after the turn of the year.

Their season was summed up by a 5–4 victory against Berwick, an exciting game that highlighted Forfar's defensive frailties.

Former Dunfermline veteran defender Andy Tod signed for free, after a successful loan spell at Station Park, and helped to ensure a respectable sixth-place finish.

CLUB SUMMARY

FORMED	1885
MANAGER	Dick Campbell
GROUND	Station Park
CAPACITY	5,177
NICKNAME	The Loons
WEBSITE	www.forfarathletic.co.uk

The New Football Pools **PLAYER OF THE SEASON** — Ross Campbell

OVERALL
P	W	D	L	F	A	GD
43	18	9	16	69	63	6

IRN-BRU THIRD DIVISION
Pos	P	W	D	L	F	A	GD	Pts
6	36	14	9	13	53	51	2	51

HOME
Pos	P	W	D	L	F	A	GD	Pts
7	18	6	5	7	26	28	-2	23

AWAY
Pos	P	W	D	L	F	A	GD	Pts
3	18	8	4	6	27	23	4	28

CUP PROGRESS DETAILS
Competition	Round reached	Knocked out by
Co-op Insurance Cup	R1	Partick
Scottish Cup	R5	Rangers
Challenge Cup	R2	Livingston

BIGGEST WIN (ALL COMPS)
13/01/09 6–1 v Forres Mechanics **TSC4**

BIGGEST DEFEAT (ALL COMPS)
0–4 on two occasions

ATTENDANCE RECORD
High	Low	Average
621	362	460
v Montrose (28/03/2009)	v Berwick (15/11/2008)	

RESULTS 2008/09

July
26th ● Arbroath ....a W 1–2 **Att:** 543 — **Scorers:** Kilgannon, McLeish. **Booked:** Lilley, Winter, Dunn

August
2nd ● Albion................a W 1–3 **Att:** 298 — **Scorers:** Manson, McLeish, Winter.
Booked: Tulloch, Brady, E. Smith, Fotheringham
5th ● Partick ....a L 4–3 **Att:** 1,195 — **Scorers:** Fotheringham, Lilley, E. Smith.
Booked: Tulloch, Winter (AET)
9th ● Cowdenbeath.....h L 0–1 **Att:** 412 — **Booked:** Campbell, Tulloch
12th ● Livingston.........a L 1–0 **Att:** 656 — **Booked:** Fotheringham, Campbell
16th ● Elgin................h L 0–1 **Att:** 377 — **Booked:** Winter, Kilgannon. **Dismissed:** Ferguson
23rd ● East Stirling ......a W 0–3 **Att:** 394 — **Scorers:** Lilley, Russell². **Booked:** Dunn, Duell
30th ● Berwick ....a D 2–2 **Att:** 390 — **Scorers:** McLeish, Gibson. **Booked:** Winter, Dunn, Brady

September
13th ● Montrose ....h L 0–1 **Att:** 518 — **Booked:** Tulloch, Winter
20th ● Annan Athletic ..a W 1–3 **Att:** 690 — **Scorers:** Fotheringham, Gibson, Russell.
Booked: Lilley, McLeish, E. Smith
27th ● Dumbarton........h D 2–2 **Att:** 473 — **Scorers:** Gibson, Russell.
Booked: E. Smith, Tulloch, Winter, Lilley, Campbell, Brady

October
4th ● Stenhousemuir ..a D 1–1 **Att:** 429 — **Scorers:** Kilgannon. **Booked:** McLeish, Brady
18th ● Albion................h D 0–0 **Att:** 426 — **Booked:** McLeish
25th ● Brora ....a W 1–3 **Att:** 200 — **Scorers:** Campbell, Dunn, Gordon. **Booked:** Lilley, McNally

November
1st ● Elgin................a W 0–1 **Att:** 491 — **Scorers:** Campbell. **Booked:** Winter, Brown
8th ● East Stirling ......h L 2–3 **Att:** 427 — **Scorers:** Campbell, Gibson. **Booked:** Brown, Russell
15th ● Berwick ....h W 2–1 **Att:** 362 — **Scorers:** Lilley, McLeish. **Booked:** Winter, Dunn, Donachie
22nd ● Montrose ....a L 1–0 **Att:** 465 — **Booked:** Lilley, Campbell, Brady, Tulloch, Donachie

December
13th ● Dumbarton........a L 3–0 **Att:** 569 — **Booked:** Lilley, McNally, Ferguson
15th ● Stranraer ....h W 2–0 **Att:** 305 — **Scorers:** Gibson, Kilgannon. **Booked:** E. Smith, Winter
20th ● Stenhousemuir..h W 1–0 **Att:** 468 — **Scorers:** Kilgannon. **Booked:** Winter, Lilley

January
13th ● Forres Mechs....h W 6–1 **Att:** 775 — **Scorers:** Campbell, Gibson, Gordon², Tulloch, Milne OG
17th ● East Stirling ......a L 3–2 **Att:** 405 — **Scorers:** Fotheringham, Tulloch. **Booked:** Lilley
31st ● Albion................a L 2–0 **Att:** 289 — **Booked:** Fotheringham

February
18th ● Rangers ....h L 0–4 **Att:** 4,718 — **Booked:** Tulloch, Brady, McGuigan. **Dismissed:** E. Smith
21st ● Annan Athletic ..a L 1–0 **Att:** 542 — **Booked:** C. Smith, McNally
28th ● Berwick ....h W 5–4 **Att:** 382 — **Scorers:** Campbell, Gibson, Gordon, Russell, Tulloch

March
3rd ● Annan Athletic ..h W 2–1 **Att:** 366 — **Scorers:** Campbell²
7th ● Montrose ....a W 1–3 **Att:** 530 — **Scorers:** Campbell², McNally.
Booked: Fotheringham, Winter, Donachie
10th ● Cowdenbeath....a D 0–0 **Att:** 317 — **Booked:** Derden
14th ● Albion................h W 4–0 **Att:** 390 — **Scorers:** Brady, Divine, Fotheringham, Gordon
17th ● Berwick ....a W 0–2 **Att:** 382 — **Scorers:** Campbell, Russell
21st ● Stenhousemuir..a W 0–1 **Att:** 399 — **Scorers:** Gibson. **Booked:** Campbell, Tulloch, Fotheringham
24th ● Elgin................h D 1–1 **Att:** 578 — **Scorers:** Campbell. **Booked:** Campbell
28th ● Montrose ....h L 0–3 **Att:** 621 — **Booked:** Divine, Brady. **Dismissed:** McNally
31st ● Cowdenbeath....h D 1–1 **Att:** 621 — **Scorers:** Campbell. **Booked:** Brady

April
4th ● East Stirling ......h L 0–2 **Att:** 491 — **Booked:** Winter, Lilley
7th ● Dumbarton........h L 0–2 **Att:** 513 — **Booked:** Tod, Lilley
11th ● Elgin................a W 1–4 **Att:** 452 — **Scorers:** Campbell, Russell, Tulloch, Kaczan OG. **Booked:** Tod
18th ● Annan Athletic ..h W 2–1 **Att:** 463 — **Scorers:** Campbell, Fotheringham. **Booked:** Campbell, Tulloch, Lilley
25th ● Dumbarton........a L 4–0 **Att:** 917 — **Booked:** Winter

May
2nd ● Cowdenbeath....a D 2–2 **Att:** 527 — **Scorers:** Gordon, Russell. **Booked:** Winter, G. Gibson, Fotheringham
9th ● Stenhousemuir..h D 4–4 **Att:** 392 — **Scorers:** Campbell, Gibson, Gordon². **Booked:** Donachie

● Irn-Bru Third Division ● Scottish FA Cup ● Scottish League Cup ● Scottish Challenge Cup

THIRD DIVISION GOALKEEPER STATS

Player	Appearances	Match starts	Completed matches	Sub appearances	Subbed off	Clean sheets	Yellow cards	Red cards
Ally Brown	32	32	32	0	0	8	2	0
John Gibson	4	4	4	0	0	0	0	0

THIRD DIVISION OUTFIELD PLAYER STATS

Player	Appearances	Match starts	Completed matches	Substitute appearances	Subbed off	Goals scored	Yellow cards	Red cards
Darren Brady	30	30	27	0	3	1	7	0
Stewart Cairns	12	12	12	0	0	0	0	0
Ross Campbell	31	24	12	7	12	13	6	0
Stuart Derden	1	1	0	0	1	0	1	0
Alistair Divine	15	14	9	1	5	1	1	0
Barry Donachie	12	6	4	6	2	0	4	0
Bryan Duell	3	0	0	3	0	0	1	0
David Dunn	11	10	9	1	1	0	3	0
Stuart Ferguson	4	4	2	0	1	0	1	1
Martyn Fotheringham	32	22	12	10	10	4	5	0
Graham Gibson	29	27	20	2	7	6	1	0
Kevin Gordon	29	24	11	5	13	5	0	0
Pat Keogh	2	2	2	0	0	0	0	0
Sean Kilgannon	16	7	3	9	3	2	1	1
Derek Lilley	26	23	11	3	12	2	9	0
Stephen Manson	4	0	0	4	0	1	0	0
Kevin McLeish	18	11	8	7	3	3	3	0
Stephen McNally	27	20	15	7	4	1	2	1
Johnny Russell	26	25	16	1	9	8	1	0
Sean Simpson	8	3	1	5	2	0	0	0
Alan Simpson	2	0	0	2	0	0	0	0
Callum Smith	16	3	2	13	1	0	1	0
Elliot Smith	18	14	10	4	4	0	3	0
Andy Tod	23	23	20	0	3	0	2	0
Steven Tosh	2	2	2	0	0	0	1	0
Stephen Tulloch	33	33	33	0	0	3	7	0
Craig Winter	33	21	13	12	8	1	11	0

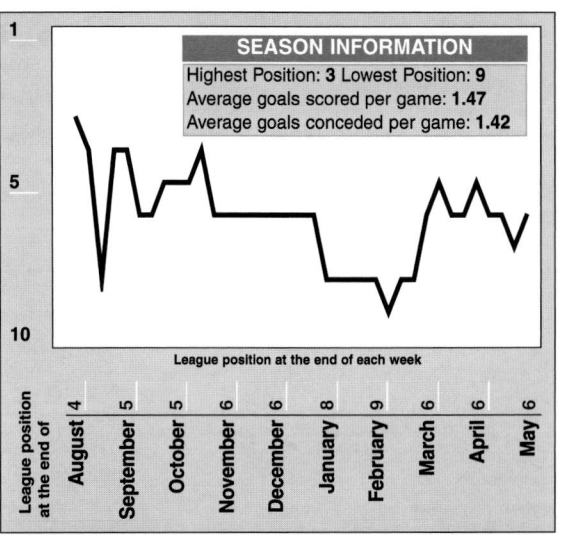

SEASON INFORMATION
Highest Position: 3 Lowest Position: 9
Average goals scored per game: 1.47
Average goals conceded per game: 1.42

League position at the end of each week

LONGEST SEQUENCES

Wins (on two occasions)	3	Undefeated home (15/11/08–24/03/09)	6
Losses (17/01/09–21/02/09)	3	Undefeated away (02/08/08–01/11/08)	6
Draws (27/09/08–18/10/08)	3	Without scoring (on four occasions)	2
Undefeated (28/02/09–24/03/09)	8	Without conceding (10/03/09–21/03/09)	4
Without win (24/03/09–07/04/09)	5	Scoring (14/03/09–24/03/09)	4

CARDS RECEIVED

73   3

QUICK-FIRE GOALS
From the start of a match
Kevin Gordon (v Cowdenbeath) 3:00

By a substitute after coming on
Stephen Manson (v Albion) 6:00

GOALS SCORED/CONCEDED PER FIVE-MINUTE INTERVALS
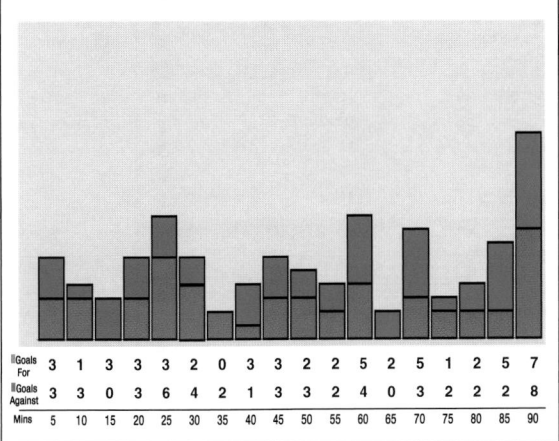

Goals For	3	1	3	3	2	0	3	3	2	2	5	2	5	1	2	5	7
Goals Against	3	3	0	3	6	4	2	1	3	3	2	4	0	3	2	2	8
Mins	5	10	15	20	25	30	35	40	45	50	55	60	65	70	75	80	85	90

MONTROSE

MONTROSE missed out on a play-off spot by a single place, but it was a decent season for Steven Tweed's side.

The Links Park men's first four games all ended in draws, with the team struggling to overcome their opponents. However, they started to pick up victories, which lifted them up the table, and they found themselves in second spot at the end of November.

After the turn of the year, their form hit peaks and troughs. Wins came against the likes of the resurgent Dumbarton and Cowdenbeath, but they also suffered a number of defeats, including a run of three to Forfar and East Stirling and lowly Elgin.

Ex-Aberdeen defender Jamie Buchan gave the Gable Endies some much-needed experience at the back as the side improved on the previous season's eighth-place finish.

CLUB SUMMARY

FORMED	1879
MANAGER	Steven Tweed
GROUND	Links Park
CAPACITY	3,292
NICKNAME	The Gable Endies
WEBSITE	www.montrosefc.co.uk

The New Football Pools PLAYER OF THE SEASON — Hugh Davidson

OVERALL
P	W	D	L	F	A	GD
40	17	6	17	49	58	-9

IRN-BRU THIRD DIVISION
Pos	P	W	D	L	F	A	GD	Pts
5	36	16	6	14	47	48	-1	54

HOME
Pos	P	W	D	L	F	A	GD	Pts
6	18	8	3	7	23	24	-1	27

AWAY
Pos	P	W	D	L	F	A	GD	Pts
5	18	8	3	7	24	24	0	27

CUP PROGRESS DETAILS
Competition	Round reached	Knocked out by
Co-op Insurance Cup	R1	Cowdenbeath
Scottish Cup	R3	Clyde
Challenge Cup	R1	Peterhead

BIGGEST WIN (ALL COMPS)
3–0 on two occasions

BIGGEST DEFEAT (ALL COMPS)
26/07/08 0–6 v Peterhead **SLCC1NE**

ATTENDANCE RECORD
High	Low	Average
570	294	379
v Dumbarton (18/10/2008)	v Elgin (30/08/2008)	

RESULTS 2008/09

July
26th	● Peterhead	a	L 6–0	**Att:** 514 — **Booked:** Cumming, Worrell

August
2nd	● Dumbarton	a	D 1–1	**Att:** 602 — **Scorers:** Stewart. **Booked:** Hegarty, Thomson, Stein. **Dismissed:** Stein
5th	● Cowdenbeath	h	L 0–2	**Att:** 352 — **Booked:** Davidson, Thomson, Stein, McLeod
9th	● Berwick	h	D 1–1	**Att:** 344 — **Scorers:** McLeod
16th	● Stenhousemuir	a	D 2–2	**Att:** 413 — **Scorers:** Baird, Bradley. **Booked:** Black, Anson, Baird
23rd	● Annan Athletic	h	D 1–1	**Att:** 425 — **Scorers:** Anson. **Dismissed:** Davidson
30th	● Elgin	h	W 1–0	**Att:** 294 — **Scorers:** Buchan

September
13th	● Forfar	a	W 0–1	**Att:** 518 — **Scorers:** Anson. **Dismissed:** McLeod
20th	● East Stirling	h	W 3–0	**Att:** 363 — **Scorers:** Anson, Bradley, Buchan. **Booked:** Anson, Stewart, Baird, Bradley
27th	● Cowdenbeath	a	L 2–1	**Att:** 296 — **Scorers:** Baird. **Dismissed:** McLeod

October
4th	● Albion	a	W 0–1	**Att:** 237 — **Scorers:** Bradley
18th	● Dumbarton	h	L 1–2	**Att:** 570 — **Scorers:** Black. **Booked:** Thomson, Bradley
25th	● Huntly	h	W 2–0	**Att:** 523 — **Scorers:** Davidson, Smith. **Booked:** Bradley

November
1st	● Stenhousemuir	h	L 0–3	**Att:** 419 — **Booked:** Bradley, Black
8th	● Annan Athletic	a	W 1–2	**Att:** 505 — **Scorers:** Bradley[2]. **Booked:** McLeod, McLaughlan
15th	● Elgin	a	W 1–2	**Att:** 376 — **Scorers:** Hunter[2]. **Booked:** Hegarty, Smith
22nd	● Forfar	h	W 1–0	**Att:** 465 — **Scorers:** Davidson. **Booked:** Hegarty
29th	● Clyde	a	L 2–0	**Att:** 677 — **Booked:** Hegarty, Davidson

December
6th	● East Stirling	a	L 5–0	**Att:** 427 — **Booked:** Black, Gibson
13th	● Cowdenbeath	h	L 0–1	**Att:** 334 — **Booked:** McLaughlan, Hegarty. **Dismissed:** Hunter
20th	● Albion	h	L 1–2	**Att:** 321 — **Scorers:** Smith. **Booked:** Davidson, McLeod. **Dismissed:** Bradley
27th	● Berwick	a	L 3–2	**Att:** 510 — **Scorers:** Black, Davidson. **Booked:** McLeod, McLaughlan

January
10th	● Elgin	h	W 3–1	**Att:** 296 — **Scorers:** Gibson, Hegarty, Hunter. **Booked:** Crighton, Gibson
17th	● Annan Athletic	h	L 0–3	**Att:** 329 — **Booked:** Gibson
24th	● Stenhousemuir	a	W 1–3	**Att:** 447 — **Scorers:** Hunter[2], Ovenstone OG
31st	● Dumbarton	a	D 1–1	**Att:** 652 — **Scorers:** Hunter

February
7th	● Berwick	h	D 1–1	**Att:** 318 — **Scorers:** Gibson, Hegarty. **Booked:** Pope, Cox. **Dismissed:** Cox
21st	● East Stirling	h	L 0–2	**Att:** 400 — **Booked:** Hegarty
28th	● Elgin	a	L 1–0	**Att:** 364

March
7th	● Forfar	h	L 1–3	**Att:** 530 — **Scorers:** Cox. **Booked:** Bullock
14th	● Dumbarton	h	W 1–0	**Att:** 347 — **Booked:** Pope
17th	● Cowdenbeath	a	L 2–1	**Att:** 303 — **Scorers:** McKenzie. **Booked:** Hegarty, Crighton
21st	● Albion	a	W 0–1	**Att:** 263 — **Scorers:** Nicol. **Booked:** O'Reilly, McKenzie
28th	● Forfar	a	W 0–3	**Att:** 621 — **Scorers:** Cox, Davidson, Stewart. **Booked:** Cox, Tweed, Milligan

April
4th	● Annan Athletic	a	L 2–1	**Att:** 617 — **Scorers:** O'Reilly. **Booked:** Milligan, Bullock
11th	● Stenhousemuir	h	W 5–3	**Att:** 338 — **Scorers:** Hunter[2], O'Reilly[2], Tweed
18th	● East Stirling	a	L 2–1	**Att:** 401 — **Scorers:** Hunter. **Booked:** Bradley, Davidson
25th	● Cowdenbeath	h	W 2–1	**Att:** 403 — **Scorers:** Hegarty, Tweed. **Booked:** Tweed

May
2nd	● Berwick	a	W 0–1	**Att:** 418 — **Scorers:** Bradley
9th	● Albion	h	W 1–0	**Att:** 324 — **Scorers:** Pope

● Irn-Bru Third Division ● Scottish FA Cup ● Scottish League Cup ● Scottish Challenge Cup

actim

THIRD DIVISION GOALKEEPER STATS

Player	Appearances	Match starts	Completed matches	Sub appearances	Subbed off	Clean sheets	Yellow cards	Red cards
Tony Bullock	16	16	16	0	0	5	2	0
Greg Kelly	16	16	16	0	0	4	0	0
Mark Peat	3	3	3	0	0	0	0	0
Fraser Stark	1	1	0	0	0	1	0	0

THIRD DIVISION OUTFIELD PLAYER STATS

Player	Appearances	Match starts	Completed matches	Substitute appearances	Subbed off	Goals scored	Yellow cards	Red cards
Kieran Adams	1	0	0	1	0	0	0	0
Scott Anson	10	9	6	1	3	3	2	0
John Baird	8	8	4	0	4	2	2	0
Stephen Black	32	30	20	2	10	2	3	0
Kevin Bradley	32	23	16	9	6	6	4	1
Jamie Buchan	28	28	25	0	3	2	0	0
David Cox	11	10	8	1	1	2	2	1
David Craig	3	3	2	0	1	0	0	0
Sean Crighton	18	18	18	0	0	0	2	0
Stuart Cumming	2	1	1	1	0	0	0	0
Hugh Davidson	30	30	28	0	1	3	2	1
Steven Doris	5	5	3	0	2	0	0	0
Ross Gardiner	1	0	0	1	1	0	0	0
Keith Gibson	20	18	16	2	2	2	3	0
Mik Gray	1	0	0	1	0	0	0	0
David Hannah	1	1	1	0	0	0	0	0
Chris Hegarty	28	24	17	4	7	2	6	0
Rod Hunter	25	18	9	7	8	9	0	1
Jordan Leyden	1	0	0	1	0	0	0	0
John Maitland	9	3	1	6	2	0	0	0
Ryan McCay	2	2	0	0	2	0	0	0
Jamie McKenzie	5	5	3	0	2	1	1	0
Gerry McLaughlan	13	12	12	1	0	0	3	0
Chris McLeod	14	13	10	1	1	1	3	2
Fraser Milligan	9	8	2	1	6	0	2	0
Daryl Nicol	16	2	1	14	1	1	0	0
Craig O'Reilly	8	8	5	0	3	3	1	0
Gordon Pope	16	16	16	0	0	1	2	0
Mark Russell	2	0	0	2	0	0	0	0
Aaron Sinclair	1	1	1	0	0	0	0	0
Callum Smith	10	7	4	3	3	1	1	0
Jay Stein	3	1	0	2	0	0	1	1
Paul Stewart	31	14	6	17	8	2	1	0
Stephen Thomson	11	11	8	0	3	0	2	0
Steven Tweed	16	15	14	1	1	2	2	0
Josh Winton	1	0	0	1	0	0	0	0
David Worrell	13	12	12	1	0	0	1	0
Kyle Wright	1	0	0	1	0	0	0	0

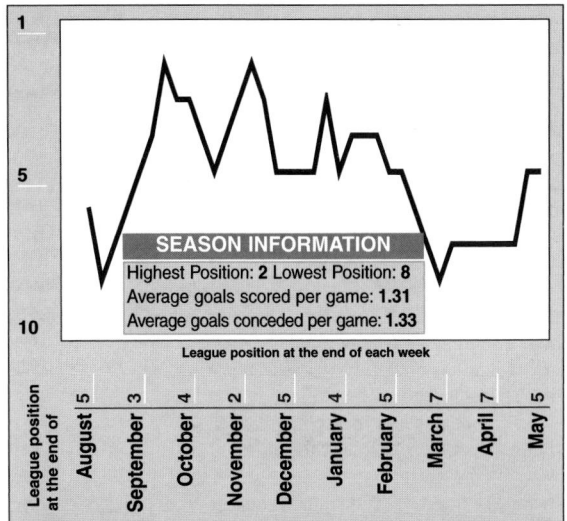

SEASON INFORMATION

Highest Position: **2** Lowest Position: **8**
Average goals scored per game: **1.31**
Average goals conceded per game: **1.33**

League position at the end of each week

LONGEST SEQUENCES

Wins	3	Undefeated home	5	
(on two occasions)		(02/08/08–20/09/08)		
Losses	4	Undefeated away	3	
(06/12/08–27/12/08)		(on two occasions)		
Draws	4	Without scoring	2	
(02/08/08–23/08/08)		(on two occasions)		
Undefeated	7	Without conceding	3	
(02/08/08–20/09/08)		(30/08/08–20/09/08)		
Without win	5	Scoring	10	
(31/01/09–07/03/09)		(02/08/08–18/10/08)		

CARDS RECEIVED

47 **7**

QUICK-FIRE GOALS

From the start of a match
Hugh Davidson (v Forfar) 2:00

By a substitute after coming on
Rod Hunter (v East Stirling) 6:00

GOALS SCORED/CONCEDED PER FIVE-MINUTE INTERVALS

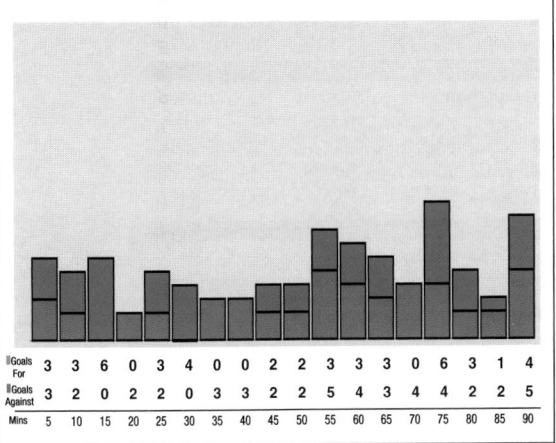

Goals For	3	3	6	0	3	4	0	0	2	2	3	3	3	0	6	3	1	4	
Goals Against	3	2	0	2	2	0	3	3	2	2	5	4	3	4	4	2	2	5	
Mins	5	10	15	20	25	30	35	40	45	50	55	60	65	70	75	80	85	90	

STENHOUSEMUIR will play Irn-Bru Second Division football for the first time since 2004 after a dramatic penalty shoot-out win over Cowdenbeath at Ochilview.

A long, arduous season came to an end in the most exciting of circumstances as John Coughlin's side survived a tense play-off final second-leg against the Blue Brazil, who had finished seven points ahead of them in the Third Division.

With the tie poised at 0–0 from the first leg, neither side did enough to break the deadlock after 120 minutes at Ochilview. The penalty shoot-out saw Cowdenbeath's Jay Stein miss the visitors' third penalty after the Warriors had scored their opening three.

Andy Brand was left with the crucial spot-kick, and he made no mistake to seal his side's promotion for the first time in five years.

CLUB SUMMARY

FORMED	1884
MANAGER	John Coughlin
GROUND	Ochilview Park
CAPACITY	3,776
NICKNAME	The Warriors
WEBSITE	www.stenhousemuirfc.com

The New Football Pools PLAYER OF THE SEASON — Kevin Motion

OVERALL
P	W	D	L	F	A	GD
43	18	10	15	66	53	13

IRN-BRU THIRD DIVISION
Pos	P	W	D	L	F	A	GD	Pts
4	36	16	8	12	55	46	9	56

HOME
Pos	P	W	D	L	F	A	GD	Pts
4	18	8	5	5	23	19	4	29

AWAY
Pos	P	W	D	L	F	A	GD	Pts
4	18	8	3	7	32	27	5	27

CUP PROGRESS DETAILS
Competition	Round reached	Knocked out by
Co-op Insurance Cup	R1	St Johnstone
Scottish Cup	R4	East Fife
Challenge Cup	R1	Albion

BIGGEST WIN (ALL COMPS)
5–0 on two occasions

BIGGEST DEFEAT (ALL COMPS)
05/08/08 1–5 v St Johnstone SLC1

ATTENDANCE RECORD
High	Low	Average
805	311	496

v East Stirling (07/03/2009) v Elgin (31/01/2009)

RESULTS 2008/09

July
26th	● Albion	h	L 0–1	Att: 210

August
2nd	● Elgin	h	W 3–0	Att: 320 — Scorers: Brand[2], Hampshire
5th	● St Johnstone	h	L 1–5	Att: 613 — Scorers: Love
9th	● Annan Athletic	a	D 1–1	Att: 1,132 — Scorers: Brand. Booked: Tyrrell. Dismissed: Tyrrell
16th	● Montrose	h	D 2–2	Att: 413 — Scorers: Dalziel[2]. Booked: C. McGroarty, Thomson
23rd	● Dumbarton	a	W 1–2	Att: 676 — Scorers: Motion, Shirra. Booked: C. McGroarty, S. Ferguson
30th	● Cowdenbeath	h	W 1–0	Att: 456 — Scorers: Motion. Booked: Lyle, Brand, S. Ferguson

September
13th	● East Stirling	a	W 0–2	Att: 511 — Scorers: Motion[2]. Booked: Lyle, Dalziel, Motion
20th	● Berwick	h	W 2–0	Att: 446 — Scorers: Dalziel, Ovenstone. Booked: McGroarty

October
4th	● Forfar	h	D 1–1	Att: 429 — Scorers: Dalziel. Booked: Motion, Dalziel, S. Ferguson
18th	● Elgin	a	L 4–2	Att: 359 — Scorers: Brand, Motion. Booked: S. Ferguson, Motion
25th	● Threave Rovers	h	W 5–0	Att: 247 — Scorers: Motion, Shirra[2], Thom, Thomson

November
1st	● Montrose	a	W 0–3	Att: 419 — Scorers: Dalziel, Motion, Shirra. Booked: Ovenstone
8th	● Dumbarton	h	D 1–1	Att: 724 — Scorers: Brand. Booked: Lyle, Ovenstone. Dismissed: Motion
15th	● Cowdenbeath	a	W 1–2	Att: 406 — Scorers: Dalziel, Thom. Booked: S. Ferguson. Dismissed: Lyle
22nd	● East Stirling	h	D 1–1	Att: 737 — Scorers: Dalziel
29th	● Clachnacuddin	a	W 0–5	Att: 350 — Scorers: Dalziel[3], Desmond, Hampshire. Booked: McEwan

December
6th	● Berwick	a	L 3–2	Att: 367 — Scorers: Hampshire, Love. Booked: Thom
13th	● Albion	h	W 1–0	Att: 508 — Scorers: Thomson. Dismissed: S. Ferguson
20th	● Forfar	a	L 1–0	Att: 468 — Booked: Tyrrell. Dismissed: Shirra
27th	● Annan Athletic	h	D 0–0	Att: 524

January
3rd	● East Stirling	a	W 0–3	Att: 812 — Scorers: Dalziel[2], Motion. Booked: Dalziel, Lyle
10th	● East Fife	h	L 0–1	Att: 784 — Booked: S. Ferguson, Thom, Motion
17th	● Dumbarton	a	L 1–0	Att: 737 — Booked: Smith
24th	● Montrose	h	L 1–3	Att: 447 — Scorers: Motion. Booked: Motion, McGroarty
31st	● Elgin	h	W 4–2	Att: 311 — Scorers: Dalziel, Love, McLeod, Smith. Booked: Dalziel

February
7th	● Annan Athletic	a	D 1–1	Att: 805 — Scorers: McLeod. Booked: Dalziel, Thomson
28th	● Cowdenbeath	a	L 1–0	Att: 459 — Booked: Molloy

March
3rd	● Cowdenbeath	h	W 1–0	Att: 368 — Scorers: Dalziel. Booked: Lyle, Motion
7th	● East Stirling	h	L 1–4	Att: 805 — Scorers: Motion. Booked: Lyle, Motion
14th	● Elgin	a	L 2–0	Att: 318
21st	● Forfar	h	L 0–1	Att: 399 — Booked: Smith
31st	● Albion	a	W 1–2	Att: 335 — Scorers: Motion, Ovenstone. Booked: Thomson, Molloy

April
4th	● Dumbarton	h	L 0–2	Att: 588
11th	● Montrose	a	L 5–3	Att: 338 — Scorers: Love[2], Ovenstone. Booked: Molloy
18th	● Berwick	a	W 0–3	Att: 390 — Scorers: Dalziel, Diack, Thom. Booked: Love
25th	● Albion	h	W 2–0	Att: 428 — Scorers: Diack, Motion. Booked: Diack, Lyle

May
2nd	● Annan Athletic	h	W 1–0	Att: 581 — Scorers: Smith. Booked: Brazil
9th	● Forfar	a	D 4–4	Att: 392 — Scorers: Dalziel[2], Stirling, Thomson
14th	● Queen's Park	h	W 2–1	Att: 617 — Scorers: Dalziel, Love. Booked: Diack, Lyle
17th	● Queen's Park	a	D 0–0	Att: 854 — Booked: McLeod
20th	● Cowdenbeath	a	D 0–0	Att: 775 — Booked: McLeod, Molloy. Dismissed: McLeod
23rd	● Cowdenbeath	h	D 0–0	Att: 1530 — Booked: Molloy, Lyle, Diack (Won 5–4 on pens)

● Irn-Bru Third Division ● Scottish FA Cup ● Scottish League Cup ● Scottish Challenge Cup

actim

THIRD DIVISION GOALKEEPER STATS

Player	Appearances	Match starts	Completed matches	Sub appearances	Subbed off	Clean sheets	Yellow cards	Red cards
Scott Bennett	24	24	24	0	0	8	0	0
Craig Rankin	1	1	0	0	0	0	0	0
Keiron Renton	11	11	11	0	0	4	0	0

THIRD DIVISION OUTFIELD PLAYER STATS

Player	Appearances	Match starts	Completed matches	Substitute appearances	Subbed off	Goals scored	Yellow cards	Red cards
Andrew Brand	30	25	16	5	9	5	1	0
Alan Brazil	10	8	2	2	6	0	1	0
Steven Connolly	3	1	1	2	0	0	0	0
Scott Dalziel	35	28	20	7	8	15	5	0
Steven Desmond	7	2	0	5	2	1	0	0
Ian Diack	14	13	5	1	8	2	1	0
Andrew Ferguson	3	2	2	1	0	0	0	0
Steven Ferguson	17	16	13	1	2	0	6	1
Graham Gibson	2	0	0	2	0	0	0	0
Steven Hampshire	14	8	2	6	6	2	0	0
Robert Love	23	12	1	11	11	4	1	0
William Lyle	28	28	27	0	0	0	7	1
Craig McEwan	6	3	2	3	1	0	0	0
Christopher McGroarty	24	24	22	0	2	0	3	0
Chris McGroarty	6	6	5	0	1	0	2	0
Chris McLeod	11	11	11	0	0	2	1	0
Scott McManus	1	0	0	1	0	0	0	0
Craig Molloy	13	12	9	1	3	0	3	0
Alan Morgan	7	4	1	3	3	0	0	0
Kevin Motion	32	28	25	4	2	12	6	1
John Ovenstone	31	31	31	0	0	3	2	0
Alan Reid	6	6	6	0	0	0	0	0
Andrew Shirra	23	11	6	12	4	2	2	1
Jordan Smith	25	24	22	1	2	2	3	0
Andrew Stirling	4	1	1	3	0	1	0	0
Gary Thom	16	15	14	1	1	2	1	0
Iain Thomson	29	26	20	3	6	2	3	0
Paul Tyrrell	17	13	10	4	2	0	2	1

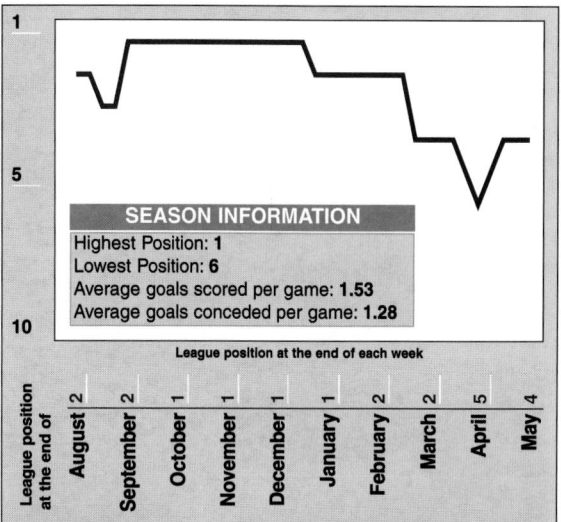

League position at the end of each week

SEASON INFORMATION
Highest Position: **1**
Lowest Position: **6**
Average goals scored per game: **1.53**
Average goals conceded per game: **1.28**

LONGEST SEQUENCES

Wins	5	Undefeated home	9	
(23/08/08–27/09/08)		(02/08/08–27/12/08)		
Losses	3	Undefeated away	5	
(07/03/09–21/03/09)		(02/08/08–27/09/08)		
Draws	2	Without scoring	2	
(09/08/08–16/08/08)		(on two occasions)		
Undefeated	9	Without conceding	3	
(02/08/08–04/10/08)		(on two occasions)		
Without win	3	Scoring	16	
(on two occasions)		(02/08/08–13/12/08)		

CARDS RECEIVED

50 **5**

QUICK-FIRE GOALS

From the start of a match
Jordan Smith (v Elgin) 1:00

By a substitute after coming on
Scott Dalziel (v Berwick) 2:00

GOALS SCORED/CONCEDED PER FIVE-MINUTE INTERVALS

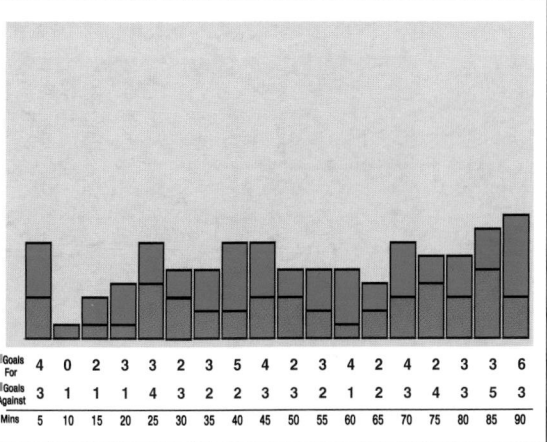

Goals For	4	0	2	3	3	2	3	5	4	2	3	4	2	4	2	3	3	6
Goals Against	3	1	1	1	4	3	2	2	3	3	2	1	2	3	4	3	5	3
Mins	5	10	15	20	25	30	35	40	45	50	55	60	65	70	75	80	85	90

Manchester United's Champions League dreams are undone by goals from Lionel Messi, above, and Samuel Eto'o, below, in the competition's final in Rome

LIONEL MESSI hung in the air for what seemed like an age.

Then the cross from Xavi Hernandez came in and Messi's looping header evaded the grasp of Manchester United goalkeeper Edwin van der Sar and the UEFA Champions League trophy was on its way to Barcelona. To a team with a football game based on possession and penetration. To a team full of radiant stars such as Andres Iniesta, Thierry Henry, Xavi and Messi. To Josep Guardiola, a manager in his rookie year who incredibly also won La Liga and Copa del Rey to land a treble unprecedented in Spanish football.

It was a deserved 2–0 victory for Barcelona in Rome's Stadio Olimpico, striker Samuel Eto'o having slotted the first goal to leave United manager Sir Alex Ferguson lamenting his side's 'shoddy' defending. It was a particularly hard defeat to take as United were bidding to become the first club to successfully defend the trophy in its current format and were hoping to commemorate what would have been former United manager Sir Matt Busby's 100th birthday the day before with a historic win.

The truth, however, was that Barcelona were the better, more technically gifted and more imaginative team and United's big guns, Cristiano Ronaldo and Wayne Rooney, failed to make telling contributions. 'It was very disappointing,' said Ferguson. 'But credit to Barcelona. They are a fantastic football team.'

And Guardiola is some rookie manager, having already won the Champions League in its inaugural year back in 1992 as a player with Barcelona. After the match Guardiola insisted Messi had eclipsed Ronaldo as the best player in the world, adding: 'I am very happy, very excited. We have done something magnificent. We attacked, we defended and we won. We are the best team in the world. We wanted to say we played and were not cowards and the players have done a great job.'

He was right. It was a masterful final performance by the Spaniards but, in truth, it had been a tournament dominated once more by the big squads of English teams, illustrating the power of the Barclays Premier League. All four sides – Manchester United, Chelsea, Arsenal and Liverpool – eased through the group stages before revealing their might in the last 16.

CLOCKWISE FROM ABOVE: Arsenal's William Gallas in action against Roma; Portsmouth line up against AC Milan; Manchester City's Richard Dunne faces SV Hamburg; Frank Lampard scores in Chelsea's dramatic 4–4 draw with Liverpool at Stamford Bridge

United saw off Jose Mourinho's Inter Milan, Arsenal defeated Roma and Chelsea eased past Juventus in a clean sweep over Italian opposition.

The tie of the round, however, saw Liverpool beat Real Madrid 1–0 in the Bernabeu and complete a spectacular rout with a 4–0 victory at Anfield. If ever a result sent out a message to football's elite it was that one. Liverpool looked good enough to reach their third final in five seasons. They probably would have done, too, if Chelsea had not thrown off their natural caution and unexpectedly attacked them at Anfield to come away with a 3–1 first-leg lead in the quarter-finals. Even then the tie was in doubt when Liverpool raced into a 2–0 lead to even up the aggregate score, before a Frank Lampard-inspired Chelsea hit back in a 4–4 match which will live long in Champions League memory.

By contrast, the semi-finals were a disappointment as Chelsea retreated to their defensive default against Barcelona who won the tie with their only second-leg

shot on goal, Iniesta's injury-time strike. United, meanwhile, proved how far Arsenal still have to travel if Arsène Wenger is ever to get his hands on the trophy, with a crushing 3–1 win at the Emirates Stadium for a 4–1 aggregate scoreline.

But if England's clubs dominated the Champions League, it was a different story in the final UEFA Cup – the tournament is revamped as the Europa League next season – in which Ukraine's Shakhtar Donetsk won their first European title by beating German side Werder Bremen 2–1 in the final after extra-time. The winner came from Brazilian midfielder Jadson, whose 15-yard shot slipped through the grasp of Werder goalkeeper Tim Wiese in the 97th minute.

Shakhtar had dispatched Tottenham in the first knockout round with a 2–0 victory in Ukraine and a creditable draw at White Hart Lane.

Everton were beaten in the first round after going down to Standard Liège, while 2008 FA Cup winners Portsmouth went out at the group stage after losing 3–2 to

German team Wolfsburg, having earlier drawn at home against AC Milan.

Aston Villa, meanwhile, showed their priorities lay with the Barclays Premier League by sending a skeleton side to Russia for their tie with CSKA Moscow. Villa had drawn the first leg 1–1 with a goal from John Carew cancelling out an early strike from Brazilian Vagner Love, but Martin O'Neill's youngsters went down 2–0 in Moscow.

O'Neill later hosted a dinner to explain his reasons for his selection to the fans who went to Russia, saying: 'I accept that it was different to what are my normal positive values, and that's my disappointment. I'm disappointed with myself for even having to think about it.'

Manchester City went the furthest of the English contingent, going out in the quarter-finals after beating SV Hamburg 2–1 at home but losing 4–3 on aggregate.

A disappointing end then for both blue and red in Manchester. But a season, ultimately, which belonged to a fabulous Barcelona side.

GROUP A

16/09/2008

Chelsea (2) 4 Bordeaux (0) 0
Lampard 14, Cole 30 — Att: 39,635
Malouda 82, Anelka 90

Roma (1) 1 CFR Cluj-Napoca (1) 2
Panucci 17 — Culio 27, 49
Att: 25,000

01/10/2008

Bordeaux (1) 1 Roma (0) 3
Gourcuff 18 — Vucinic 64
Att: 27,000 — Julio Baptista 71, 83

CFR Cluj-Napoca (0) 0 Chelsea (0) 0
Att: 22,000

22/10/2008

Bordeaux (0) 1 CFR Cluj-Napoca (0) 0
Cadu 54 og — Att: 24,000

Chelsea (1) 1 Roma (0) 0
Terry 78 — Att: 41,002

04/11/2008

CFR Cluj-Napoca (1) 1 Bordeaux (2) 2
Dani 10 — Gourcuff 6
Att: 20,500 — Wendell 38

Roma (1) 3 Chelsea (0) 1
Panucci 34 — Terry 75
Vucinic 48, 58 — Att: 38,425

26/11/2008

Bordeaux (0) 1 Chelsea (0) 1
Diarra 83 — Anelka 60
Att: 34,307

CFR Cluj-Napoca (1) 1 Roma (2) 3
Kone 30 — Brighi 11, 64
Att: 20,000 — Totti 23

09/12/2008

Chelsea (1) 2 CFR Cluj-Napoca (0) 1
Kalou 40 — Kone 55
Drogba 71 — Att: 41,060

Roma (0) 2 Bordeaux (0) 0
Brighi 61, Totti 79 — Att: 20,000

	P	W	D	L	F	A	Gd	Pts
Roma	6	4	0	2	12	6	6	12
Chelsea	6	3	2	1	9	5	4	11
Bordeaux	6	2	1	3	5	11	-6	7
CFR Cluj-Napoca	6	1	1	4	5	9	-4	4

GROUP B

16/09/2008

Panathinaikos (0) 0 Inter Milan (1) 2

Werder Bremen (0) 0 A Famagusta (0) 0

01/10/2008

A Famagusta (2) 3 Panathinaikos (1) 1

Inter Milan (1) 1 Werder Bremen (0) 1

22/10/2008

Inter Milan (1) 1 A Famagusta (0) 0

Panathinaikos (1) 2 Werder Bremen (1) 2

04/11/2008

A Famagusta (2) 3 Inter Milan (2) 3

Werder Bremen (0) 0 Panathinaikos (0) 0

26/11/2008

A Famagusta (0) 2 Werder Bremen (0) 2

Inter Milan (0) 0 Panathinaikos (0) 2

09/12/2008

Panathinaikos (0) 1 A Famagusta (0) 0

Werder Bremen (0) 2 Inter Milan (0) 1

	P	W	D	L	F	A	Gd	Pts
Panathnks	6	3	1	2	8	7	1	10
Inter Milan	6	2	2	2	8	7	1	8
W Bremen	6	1	4	1	7	9	-2	7
A Famagusta	6	1	3	2	8	8	0	6

GROUP C

16/09/2008

Barcelona (1) 3 Sporting (0) 1

Basle (0) 1 Shakhtar Donetsk (2) 2

01/10/2008

Shakhtar Donetsk (1) 1 Barcelona (0) 2

Sporting (0) 2 Basle (0) 1

22/10/2008

Basle (0) 0 Barcelona (3) 5

Shakhtar Donetsk (0) 0 Sporting (0) 1

04/11/2008

Barcelona (0) 1 Basle (0) 1

Sporting (0) 1 Shakhtar Donetsk (0) 0

26/11/2008

Shakhtar Donetsk (1) 5 Basle (0) 0

Sporting (0) 2 Barcelona (2) 5

09/12/2008

Barcelona (0) 2 Shakhtar Donetsk (1) 3

Basle (0) 0 Sporting (1) 1

	P	W	D	L	F	A	Gd	Pts
Barcelona	6	4	1	1	18	8	10	13
Sporting	6	4	0	2	8	8	0	12
Sh Donetsk	6	3	0	3	11	7	4	9
Basle	6	0	1	5	2	16	-14	1

GROUP D

16/09/2008

Marseille (1) 1 Liverpool (2) 2
Cana 23 — Gerrard 26, 32 pen
Att: 45,000

PSV (0) 0 Atletico Madrid (2) 3
Att: 28,000 — Aguero 9, 36, Maniche 54

01/10/2008

Atletico Madrid (2) 2 Marseille (1) 1
Aguero 4 — Niang 16
Raul Garcia 22 — Att: 43,290

Liverpool (2) 3 PSV (0) 1
Kuyt 5 — Koevermans 78
Keane 34, Gerrard 76 — Att: 41,097

22/10/2008

Atletico Madrid (0) 1 Liverpool (1) 1
Simao 83 — Keane 14
Att: 44,500

PSV (0) 2 Marseille (0) 0
Koevermans 71, 85 — Att: 30,000

04/11/2008

Liverpool (0) 1 Atletico Madrid (1) 1
Gerrard 90 pen — Maxi 37
Att: 42,010

Marseille (1) 3 PSV (0) 0
Kone 30, Niang 63, 71 — Att: 40,000

26/11/2008

Atletico Madrid (2) 2 PSV (0) 1
Simao 14 — Koevermans 47
Maxi 28 — Att: 44,500

Liverpool (1) 1 Marseille (0) 0
Gerrard 23 — Att: 40,024

09/12/2008

Marseille (0) 0 Atletico Madrid (0) 0
Att: 52,000

PSV (1) 1 Liverpool (1) 3
Lazovic 36 — Babel 45
Att: 35,000 — Riera 69, Ngog 77

	P	W	D	L	F	A	Gd	Pts
Liverpool	6	4	2	0	11	5	6	14
Atletico Madrid	6	3	3	0	9	4	5	12
Marseille	6	1	1	4	5	7	-2	4
PSV	6	1	0	5	5	14	-9	3

GROUP E

17/09/2008

Celtic (0) 0 AaB (0) 0
Att: 57,432

Manchester Utd (0) 0 Villarreal (0) 0
Att: 74,944

30/09/2008

AaB (0) 0 Manchester Utd (1) 3
Att: 10,346 — Rooney 22
Berbatov 55, 79

Villarreal (0) 1 Celtic (0) 0
Senna 67 — Att: 25,000

21/10/2008

Manchester Utd (1) 3 Celtic (0) 0
Berbatov 30, 51, Rooney 76 — Att: 74,655

Villarreal (2) 6 AaB (2) 3
Rossi 28, Capdevila 33 — Saganowski 20
Llorente 67, 70, 84, Pires 79 — Enevoldsen 36
Att: 22,000 — Johansson 77

05/11/2008

AaB (0) 2 Villarreal (1) 2
Curth 54 — Rossi 41, Franco 77
Due 81 — Att: 9,500

Celtic (1) 1 Manchester Utd (0) 1
McDonald 13 — Giggs 84
Att: 58,903

25/11/2008

AaB (0) 2 Celtic (0) 1
Caca 73 — Robson 53
Caldwell 87 og — Att: 12,647

Villarreal (0) 0 Manchester Utd (0) 0
Att: 26,000

10/12/2008

Celtic (2) 2 Villarreal (0) 0
Maloney 14, McGeady 45 — Att: 58,104

Manchester Utd (1) 2 AaB (2) 2
Tevez 3, Rooney 52 — Jakobsen 32
Att: 74,382 — Curth 45

	P	W	D	L	F	A	Gd	Pts
Manchester Utd	6	2	4	0	9	3	6	10
Villarreal	6	2	3	1	9	7	2	9
AaB	6	1	3	2	9	14	-5	6
Celtic	6	1	2	3	4	7	-3	5

GROUP F

17/09/2008

Lyon (0) 2 Fiorentina (2) 2

Steaua Bucuresti (0) 0 Bayern Munich (1) 1

30/09/2008

Bayern Munich (0) 1 Lyon (1) 1

Fiorentina (0) 0 Steaua Bucuresti (0) 0

21/10/2008

Bayern Munich (2) 3 Fiorentina (0) 0

Steaua Bucuresti (3) 3 Lyon (2) 5

05/11/2008

Fiorentina (1) 1 Bayern Munich (1) 1

Lyon (1) 2 Steaua Bucuresti (0) 0

25/11/2008

Bayern Munich (0) 3 Steaua Bucuresti (0) 0

Fiorentina (1) 1 Lyon (2) 2

10/12/2008

Lyon (0) 2 Bayern Munich (3) 3

Steaua Bucuresti (0) 0 Fiorentina (0) 1

	P	W	D	L	F	A	Gd	Pts
B Munich	6	4	2	0	12	4	8	14
Lyon	6	3	2	1	14	10	4	11
Fiorentina	6	1	3	2	5	8	-3	6
Steaua Bucuresti	6	0	1	5	3	12	-9	1

GROUP G

17/09/2008

Dynamo Kiev (0) ....1 Arsenal (0) 1
Bangoura 64 pen | Gallas 88
Att: 20,000

FC Porto (2) ....3 Fenerbahce (1) 1
Lopez 11 | Guiza 30
Gonzalez 14, Lino 90 | Att: 43,000

30/09/2008

Arsenal (2) ....4 FC Porto (0) 0
Van Persie 31, 48 | Att: 59,623
Adebayor 40, 71 pen

Fenerbahce (0) ....0 Dynamo Kiev (0) 0
Att: 40,000

21/10/2008

FC Porto (0) ....0 Dynamo Kiev (1) 1
Att: 37,000 | Aliev 27

Fenerbahce (1) ....2 Arsenal (3) 5
Silvestre 19 og | Adebayor 10, Walcott 11
Guiza 78 | Diaby 21, Song 49
Att: 49,521 | Ramsey 90

05/11/2008

Arsenal (0) ....0 Fenerbahce (0) 0
Att: 60,003

Dynamo Kiev (1) ....1 FC Porto (0) 2
Milevskiy 21 | Rolando 69
Att: 16,000 | Gonzalez 90

25/11/2008

Arsenal (0) ....1 Dynamo Kiev (0) 0
Bendtner 87 | Att: 59,374

Fenerbahce (0) ....0 FC Porto (2) 2
Kazim-Richards 64 | Lopez 18, 28
Att: 35,000

10/12/2008

Dynamo Kiev (1) ....1 Fenerbahce (0) 0
Eremenko 20 | Att: 1,500

FC Porto (1) ....2 Arsenal (0) 0
Bruno Alves 39, Lopez 54 | Att: 37,602

	P	W	D	L	F	A	Gd	Pts
FC Porto	6	4	0	2	9	8	1	12
Arsenal	6	3	2	1	11	5	6	11
Dynamo Kiev	6	2	2	2	4	4	0	8
Fenerbahce	6	0	2	4	4	11	-7	2

GROUP H

17/09/2008

Juventus (0) ....1 Zenit St Petersburg (0)0

Real Madrid (1) ....2 BATE (0) 0

30/09/2008

BATE (2) ....2 Juventus (2) 2

Zenit St Petersburg (1)1 Real Madrid (2) 2

21/10/2008

Juventus (1) ....2 Real Madrid (0) 1

Zenit St Petersburg (0)1 BATE (0) 1

05/11/2008

BATE (0) ....0 Zenit St Petersburg (1)2

Real Madrid (0) ....0 Juventus (1) 2

25/11/2008

BATE (0) ....0 Real Madrid (1) 1

Zenit St Petersburg (0)0 Juventus (0) 0

10/12/2008

Juventus (0) ....0 BATE (0) 0

Real Madrid (1) ....3 Zenit St Petersburg (0)0

	P	W	D	L	F	A	Gd	Pts
Juventus	6	3	3	0	7	3	4	12
Real Madrid	6	4	0	2	9	5	4	12
Z St Petersburg	6	1	2	3	4	7	-3	5
BATE	6	0	3	3	3	8	-5	3

FIRST KNOCKOUT ROUND FIRST LEG

24/02/2009

Arsenal (1) ....1 Roma (0) 0
Van Persie 37 pen | Att: 60,003

Atletico Madrid (2) .....2 FC Porto (1) 2
Maxi 4, Forlan 45 | Lopez 22, 72; Att: 54,000

Inter Milan (0) ....0 Manchester Utd (0) 0
Att: 84,000

Lyon (1) ....1 Barcelona (0) 1
Juninho 7 | Henry 67; Att: 40,000

25/02/2009

Chelsea (1) ....1 Juventus (0) 0
Drogba 13 | Att: 38,079

Real Madrid (0) ....0 Liverpool (0) 1
Att: 85,000 | Benayoun 82

Sporting (0) ....0 Bayern Munich (0) 5
Att: 35,163 | Ribery 41, 63 pen
| Klose 57, Toni 84, 90

Villarreal (0) ....1 Panathinaikos (0) 1
Rossi 67 pen | Karagounis 59; Att: 25,500

FIRST KNOCKOUT ROUND SECOND LEG

10/03/2009

Bayern Munich (4) ....7 Sporting (1) 1
Podolski 8, 34, Polga 39 og | Joao Moutinho 42
Schweinsteiger 43 | Att: 66,000
Van Bommel 74, Klose 82 pen
Muller 90
Bayern win 12–1 on aggregate

Juventus (1) ....2 Chelsea (1) 2
Iaquinta 19 | Essien 45, Drogba 83
Del Piero 74 pen | Att: 28,500
Chelsea win 3–2 on aggregate

Liverpool (2) ....4 Real Madrid (0) 0
Torres 16, Gerrard 28 pen, 47 | Att: 42,550
Dossena 88
Liverpool win 5–0 on aggregate

Panathinaikos (0) ....1 Villarreal (0) 2
Mantzios 55 | Ibagaza 49
Att: 63,150 | Llorente 70
Villarreal win 3–2 on aggregate

11/03/2009

Barcelona (4) ....5 Lyon (1) 2
Henry 25, 27, Messi 40 | Makoun 44, Juninho 48
Eto 43, Keita 90 | Att: 93,062
Barcelona win 6–3 on aggregate

FC Porto (0) ....0 Atletico Madrid (0) 0
Att: 49,500
3–3 on aggregate. Atletico win on away goals

Manchester Utd (1) ....2 Inter Milan (0) 0
Vidic 4, Ronaldo 49 | Att: 74,769
Manchester Utd win 2–0 on aggregate

Roma (1) ....1 Arsenal (0) 0
Juan 10 | Att: 81,000
1–1 on aggregate. Arsenal win 7–6 on penalties.

QUARTER-FINAL FIRST LEG

07/04/2009

Manchester Utd (1) ....2 FC Porto (1) 2
Rooney 15 | Rodriguez 4, Gonzalez 89
Tevez 85 | Att: 74,517

Villarreal (1) ....1 Arsenal (1) 1
Senna 10 | Adebayor 66; Att: 25,000

08/04/2009

Barcelona (4) ....4 Bayern Munich (0) 0
Messi 9, 38 | Att: 97,000
Eto'o 12, Henry 43

Liverpool (1) ....1 Chelsea (1) 3
Torres 6 | Ivanovic 39, 62
Att: 42,543 | Drogba 67

QUARTER-FINAL SECOND LEG

14/04/2009

Bayern Munich (0) ....1 Barcelona (0) 1
Ribery 47 | Keita 73; Att: 65,000
Barcelona win 5–1 on aggregate

Chelsea (0) ....4 Liverpool (2) 4
Drogba 52, Alex 57 | Aurelio 19, Alonso 28 pen
Lampard 76, 89 | Lucas 81, Kuyt 82
Att: 38,286
Chelsea win 7–5 on aggregate

15/04/2009

Arsenal (1) ....3 Villarreal (0) 0
Walcott 10, Adebayor 60 | Att: 58,233
Van Persie 69 pen
Arsenal win 4–1 on aggregate

FC Porto (0) ....0 Manchester Utd (1) 1
Att: 50,000 | Ronaldo 6
Manchester Utd win 3–2 on aggregate

SEMI-FINAL FIRST LEG

28/04/2009

Barcelona (0) ....0 Chelsea (0) 0
Att: 95,000
Barcelona: Valdes, Dani Alves, Marquez (Puyol 52), Pique, Abidal, Xavi, Toure Yaya, Iniesta, Messi, Eto'o (Bojan 82), Henry (Hleb 87). Subs (not used): Jorquera, Gudjohnsen, Keita, Sylvinho. Booked: Puyol, Toure Yaya.
Chelsea: Cech, Ivanovic, Alex, Terry, Bosingwa, Mikel, Ballack (Anelka 90), Essien, Lampard (Belletti 71), Malouda, Drogba. Subs (not used): Hilario, Di Santo, Kalou, Mancienne, Stoch. Booked: Alex, Ballack.
Referee: Wolfgang Stark (Germany).

29/04/2009

Manchester Utd (1) ....1 Arsenal (0) 0
O'Shea 18 | Att: 74,733
Manchester Utd: Van der Sar, O'Shea, Ferdinand (Evans 78), Vidic, Evra, Fletcher, Carrick, Anderson (Giggs 66), Ronaldo, Tevez (Berbatov 66), Rooney. Subs (not used): Foster, Park, Scholes, Rafael. Booked: Tevez.
Arsenal: Almunia, Sagna, Toure, Silvestre, Gibbs, Song, Diaby, Walcott (Bendtner 70), Fabregas, Nasri, Adebayor (Eduardo 78). Subs (not used): Fabianski, Denilson, Ramsey, Djourou, Eboue.
Referee: Claus Bo Larsen (Denmark).

SEMI-FINAL SECOND LEG

05/05/2009

Arsenal (0) ....1 Manchester Utd (2) 3
Van Persie 76 pen | Park 8
Att: 59,867 | Ronaldo 11, 61
Manchester Utd win 4–1 on aggregate
Arsenal: Almunia, Sagna, Toure, Djourou, Gibbs (Eboue 45), Walcott (Bendtner 63), Fabregas, Song, Nasri, Van Persie (Vela 79), Adebayor. Subs (not used): Fabianski, Silvestre, Diaby, Denilson. Booked: Adebayor, Eboue, Nasri.
Manchester Utd: Van der Sar, O'Shea, Ferdinand, Vidic, Evra (Rafael 65), Fletcher, Carrick, Anderson (Giggs 63), Park, Ronaldo, Rooney (Berbatov 66). Subs (not used): Kuszczak, Evans, Scholes, Tevez. Dismissed: Fletcher.
Referee: Roberto Rosetti (Italy).

06/05/2009

Chelsea (1) ....1 Barcelona (0) 1
Essien 9 | Iniesta 90; Att: 37,857
1–1 on aggregate. Barcelona win on away goals
Chelsea: Cech, Bosingwa, Alex, Terry, Cole, Lampard, Essien, Ballack, Anelka, Drogba (Belletti 72), Malouda. Subs (not used): Hilario, Ivanovic, Di Santo, Mikel, Kalou, Mancienne. Booked: Alex, Ballack, Essien.
Barcelona: Valdes, Dani Alves, Toure Yaya, Pique, Abidal, Busquets (Bojan 85), Xavi, Keita, Messi, Eto'o (Sylvinho 46), Iniesta (Gudjohnsen 90). Subs (not used): Pinto, Caceres, Hleb, Pedrito. Booked: Dani Alves, Eto'o. Dismissed: Abidal.
Referee: Tom Ovrebo (Norway).

FINAL

27/05/2009

Barcelona (1) ....2 Manchester Utd (0) 0
Eto'o 10, Messi 70 | Att 72,700
Barcelona: Valdes, Puyol, Toure Yaya, Pique, Sylvinho, Xavi, Busquets, Iniesta (Pedrito 90), Messi, Eto'o, Henry (Keita 72). Subs (not used): Pinto, Caceres, Muniesa, Gudjohnsen, Bojan. Booked: Pique.
Manchester Utd: Van der Sar, O'Shea, Ferdinand, Vidic, Evra, Anderson (Tevez 46), Carrick, Giggs (Scholes 75), Park (Berbatov 66), Ronaldo, Rooney. Subs (not used): Kuszczak, Rafael, Evans, Nani. Booked: Ronaldo, Scholes, Vidic.
Referee: Massimo Busacca (Switzerland).

GROUP A

23/10/2008
FC Twente (1) 1	Racing Santander (0)....0	
Schalke 04 (2) 3	PSG (0) 1	

6/11/2008
Manchester City (1) ..3	FC Twente (1) 2
Racing Santander (0)..1	Schalke 04 (0) 1

27/11/2008
PSG (2) 2	Racing Santander (1)...2
Schalke 04 (0) 0	Manchester City (1)....2

3/12/2008
FC Twente (1) 2	Schalke 04 (0) 1
Manchester City (0) ..0	PSG (0) 0

18/12/2008
PSG (2) 4	FC Twente (0) 0
Racing Santander (2)..3	Manchester City (0)....1

	P	W	D	L	F	A	Gd	Pts
Manchester City	4	2	1	1	6	5	1	7
FC Twente	4	2	0	2	5	8	-3	6
PSG	4	1	2	1	7	5	2	5
Racing Santander	4	1	2	1	6	5	1	5
Schalke 04	4	1	1	2	5	6	-1	4

GROUP B

23/10/2008
Galatasaray (1) 1	Olympiacos (0) 0
Hertha Berlin (0) 1	Benfica (0) 1

6/11/2008
Benfica (0) 0	Galatasaray (0) 2
FC Met Kharkiv (0)....0	Hertha Berlin (0) 0

27/11/2008
Galatasaray (0) 0	FC Met Kharkiv (0)....1
Olympiacos (4) 5	Benfica (1) 1

3/12/2008
FC Met Kharkiv (0)....1	Olympiacos (0) 0
Hertha Berlin (0) 0	Galatasaray (0) 1

18/12/2008
Benfica (0) 0	FC Met Kharkiv (0)....1
Olympiacos (0) 4	Hertha Berlin (0) 0

	P	W	D	L	F	A	Gd	Pts
FC Met Kharkiv	4	3	1	0	3	0	3	10
Galatasaray	4	3	0	1	4	1	3	9
Olympiacos	4	2	0	2	9	3	6	6
Hertha Berlin	4	0	2	2	1	6	-5	2
Benfica	4	0	1	3	2	9	-7	1

GROUP C

23/10/2008
Partizan Belgrade (1)..1	Sampdoria (1) 2
Sevilla (2) 2	VfB Stuttgart (0) 0

6/11/2008
Standard Liège (1).....1	Sevilla (0) 0
VfB Stuttgart (0) 2	Partizan Belgrade (0)...0

27/11/2008
Partizan Belgrade (0)..0	Standard Liège (1).....1
Sampdoria (1) 1	VfB Stuttgart (1) 1

3/12/2008
Sevilla (1) 3	Partizan Belgrade (0)...0
Standard Liège (3)....3	Sampdoria (0) 0

18/12/2008
Sampdoria (0) 1	Sevilla (0) 0
VfB Stuttgart (1) 3	Standard Liège (0).....0

	P	W	D	L	F	A	Gd	Pts
Standard Liège	4	3	0	1	5	3	2	9
VfB Stuttgart	4	2	1	1	6	3	3	7
Sampdoria	4	2	1	1	4	5	-1	7
Sevilla	4	2	0	2	5	2	3	6
Partizan Belgrade	4	0	0	4	1	8	-7	0

GROUP D

23/10/2008
Dinamo Zagreb (1) ...3	NEC (1) 2
Udinese (1) 1	Tottenham (0) 0

6/11/2008
Spartak Moscow (1) ..1	Udinese (0) 0
Tottenham (2) 4	Dinamo Zagreb (0) 0

27/11/2008
Dinamo Zagreb (0) 0	Spartak Moscow (0) 1
NEC (0) 0	Tottenham (1) 1

3/12/2008
Spartak Moscow (1) ..1	NEC (0) 2
Udinese (1) 2	Dinamo Zagreb (0) 1

18/12/2008
NEC (0) 2	Udinese (0) 0
Tottenham (0) 2	Spartak Moscow (2)....2

	P	W	D	L	F	A	Gd	Pts
Udinese	4	3	0	1	6	4	2	9
Tottenham	4	2	1	1	7	4	3	7
NEC	4	2	0	2	6	5	1	6
Sp Moscow	4	1	1	2	5	6	-1	4
Dinamo Zagreb	4	1	0	3	4	9	-5	3

GROUP E

23/10/2008
Braga (1) 3	Portsmouth (0) 0
Heerenveen (0) 1	AC Milan (2) 3

6/11/2008
AC Milan (0) 1	Braga (0) 0
Wolfsburg (2) 5	Heerenveen (1) 1

27/11/2008
Braga (1) 2	Wolfsburg (1) 3
Portsmouth (0) 2	AC Milan (0) 2

4/12/2008
Heerenveen (1) 1	Braga (1) 2
Wolfsburg (2) 3	Portsmouth (2) 2

17/12/2008
AC Milan (1) 2	Wolfsburg (0) 2
Portsmouth (2) 3	Heerenveen (0) 0

	P	W	D	L	F	A	Gd	Pts
Wolfsburg	4	3	1	0	13	7	6	10
AC Milan	4	2	2	0	8	5	3	8
Braga	4	2	0	2	7	5	2	6
Portsmouth	4	1	1	2	7	8	-1	4
Heerenveen	4	0	0	4	3	13	-10	0

GROUP F

23/10/2008
Aston Villa (2) 2	Ajax (1) 1
MSK Zilina (0) 1	Hamburg (2) 2

6/11/2008
Ajax (1) 1	MSK Zilina (0) 0
Slavia Prague (0)........0	Aston Villa (1) 1

27/11/2008
Hamburg (0) 0	Ajax (0) 0
MSK Zilina (0) 0	Slavia Prague (0) 0

4/12/2008
Aston Villa (1) 1	MSK Zilina (2) 2
Slavia Prague (0)........0	Hamburg (1) 2

17/12/2008
Ajax (1) 2	Slavia Prague (2) 2
Hamburg (2) 3	Aston Villa (0) 1

	P	W	D	L	F	A	Gd	Pts
Hamburg	4	3	0	1	7	3	4	9
Ajax	4	2	1	1	5	4	1	7
Aston Villa	4	2	0	2	5	6	-1	6
MSK Zilina	4	1	1	2	3	4	-1	4
Slavia Prague	4	0	2	2	2	5	-3	2

GROUP G

23/10/2008
FC Copenhagen (0) 1	St Etienne (2) 3
Rosenborg (0) 0	Club Brugge (0) 0

6/11/2008
St Etienne (0) 3	Rosenborg (0) 0
Valencia (0) 1	FC Copenhagen (0) 1

27/11/2008
Club Brugge (0) 1	St Etienne (1) 1
Rosenborg (0) 0	Valencia (1) 4

4/12/2008
FC Copenhagen (0) 1	Rosenborg (1) 0
Valencia (0) 1	Club Brugge (1) 1

17/12/2008
Club Brugge (0) 0	FC Copenhagen (1) 1
St Etienne (2) 2	Valencia (1) 2

	P	W	D	L	F	A	Gd	Pts
St Etienne	4	2	2	0	9	4	5	8
Valencia	4	1	3	0	8	4	4	6
FC Copenhagen	4	1	2	1	4	5	-1	5
Club Brugge	4	0	3	1	2	3	-1	3
Rosenborg	4	0	2	2	1	8	-7	2

GROUP H

23/10/2008
AS Nancy (0) 3	Feyenoord (0) 0
CSKA Moscow (2) 3	Deportivo La Coruna (0).0

6/11/2008
Feyenoord (1) 1	CSKA Moscow (2) 3
Lech Poznan (2) 2	AS Nancy (1) 2

27/11/2008
CSKA Moscow (2) 2	Lech Poznan (0) 1
Deportivo La Coruna (1)3	Feyenoord (0) 0

4/12/2008
AS Nancy (1) 3	CSKA Moscow (2) 4
Lech Poznan (1) 1	Deportivo La Coruna (1).1

17/12/2008
Deportivo La Coruna (0)1	AS Nancy (0) 0
Feyenoord (0) 0	Lech Poznan (1) 1

	P	W	D	L	F	A	Gd	Pts
CSKA Moscow	4	4	0	0	12	5	7	12
Deportivo	4	2	1	1	5	4	1	7
Lech Poznan	4	1	2	1	5	5	0	5
AS Nancy	4	1	1	2	8	7	1	4
Feyenoord	4	0	0	4	1	10	-9	0

ROUND OF 32 FIRST LEG

18/02/2009

AaB (0) 3	Deportivo La Coruna (0).0	
Aston Villa (0) 1	CSKA Moscow (1) 1	
Bordeaux (0) 0	Galatasaray (0)............0	
Braga (2) 3	Standard Liège (0).......0	
Dynamo Kiev (0) 1	Valencia (1)...............1	
NEC (0) 0	Hamburg (2)...............3	
Olympiacos (0) 1	St Etienne (2)............3	
PSG (0) 2	Wolfsburg (0)............0	
Sampdoria (0) 0	FC Met Kharkiv (1).....1	
Werder Bremen (0) ...1	AC Milan (1)..............1	
Zenit St Petersburg (2)2	VfB Stuttgart (1)........1	

19/02/2009

FC Copenhagen (0) 2	Manchester City (1)....2
Fiorentina (0)............0	Ajax (0).....................1
Lech Poznan (0).........0	Udinese (0)................2
Marseille (0) 0	FC Twente (1) 1
Shakhtar Donetsk (0)..2	Tottenham (0)............0

ROUND OF 32 SECOND LEG

26/02/2009

AC Milan (2) ......2 Werder Bremen (0) 2
3–3 on aggregate. Werder Bremen win on away goals

Ajax (0)................1 Fiorentina (0)...........1
Ajax win 2–1 on aggregate

CSKA Moscow (1) ..2 Aston Villa (0) 0
CSKA Moscow win 3–1 on aggregate

Deportivo La Coruna (1) 1 AaB (3) 3
AaB win 6–1 on aggregate

FC Met Kharkiv (2)..2 Sampdoria (0)............0
FC Metalist Kharkiv win 3–0 on aggregate

FC Twente (1) ....0 Marseille (0)..............0
1–1 on aggregate. Marseille win 7–6 on penalties

Galatasaray (2) ......4 Bordeaux (1) 3
Galatasaray win 4–3 on aggregate

Hamburg (1) ....2 NEC (0) 0
Hamburg win 4–0 on aggregate

Manchester City (2) ..2 FC Copenhagen (0)....1
Manchester City win 4–2 on aggregate

St Etienne (1) ....2 Olympiacos (0) 0
St Etienne win 5–2 on aggregate

Standard Liège (0) ..1 Braga (0).................0
Braga win 4–1 on aggregate

Tottenham (0) ....1 Shakhtar Donetsk (0) ..1
Shakhtar Donetsk win 3–1 on aggregate

Udinese (0) ....2 Lech Poznan (1).........0
Udinese win 4–3 on aggregate

Valencia (1) ....1 Dynamo Kiev (1) 2
3–3 on aggregate. Dynamo Kiev win on away goals

VfB Stuttgart (0) ....1 Zenit St Petersburg (1)2
Zenit St Petersburg win 4–2 on aggregate

Wolfsburg (0) ....1 PSG (1) 3
PSG win 5–1 on aggregate

FOURTH ROUND FIRST LEG

12/03/2009

CSKA Moscow (0) ......1 Shakhtar Donetsk (0) ..0
Vagner Love 50 pen   Att: 19,700

Dynamo Kiev (0) ....1 FC Met Kharkiv (0)......0
Vukojevic 54   Att: 17,800

Hamburg (0) ....1 Galatasaray (1)...........1
Jansen 50   Akman 33
Att: 50,000

Manchester City (2) ..2 AaB (0) 0
Caicedo 8   Att: 24,502
Wright-Phillips 30

Marseille (2) ....2 Ajax (1).....................1
Cheyrou 19   Suarez 36 pen
Niang 33   Att: 27,829

PSG (0) ....0 Braga (0)...................0
Att: 35,000

Udinese (0) ....2 Zenit St Petersburg (0)0
Quagliarella 85   Att: 17,000
Di Natale 88 pen

Werder Bremen (1) ....1 St Etienne (0).............0
Naldo 20   Att: 30,116

FOURTH ROUND SECOND LEG

18/03/2009

Ajax (1)...................2 Marseille (1)...............2
Enoh 33   Niang 35
Sulejmani 74   Mears 110
Att: 47,650
AET: Score after 90 mins 2–1
Marseille win 4–3 on aggregate

St Etienne (0) ....2 Werder Bremen (2) 2
Benalouane 64   Prodl 6
Grax 90   Pizarro 27
Att: 33,522
Werder Bremen win 3–2 on aggregate

19/03/2009

AaB (0) ....2 Manchester City (0)....0
Shelton 85   Att: 10,734
Jakobsen 90 pen
AET: Score after 90 mins 2–0
2–2 on aggregate.
Manchester City win 4–3 on penalties

Braga (0) ....0 PSG (0) 1
Att: 16,371   Hoarau 81
PSG win 1–0 on aggregate

FC Metalist Kharkiv (1)3 Dynamo Kiev (0) 2
Slyusar 29   Sablic 68
Coelho 56   Berezovchuk 79 og
Acevedo 70   Att: 26,000
3–3 on aggregate.
Dynamo Kiev win on away goals

Galatasaray (1) ....2 Hamburg (0)...............3
Kewell 42 pen   Guerrero 57, 60
Baros 49   Olic 90
Att: 23,500
Hamburg win 4–3 on aggregate

Shakhtar Donetsk (0) 2 CSKA Moscow (0) 0
Fernandinho 54 pen   Att: 25,000
Luiz Adriano 70
Shakhtar Donetsk win 2–1 on aggregate

Zenit St Petersburg (1)1 Udinese (0) 0
Tymoschuk 34   Att: 19,500
Udinese win 2–1 on aggregate

QUARTER-FINAL FIRST LEG

09/04/2009

Hamburg (1) ....3 Manchester City (1)....1
Mathijsen 9   Ireland 1
Trochowski 64 pen   Att: 50,500
Guerrero 79

PSG (0) ....0 Dynamo Kiev (0) 0
Att: 41,000

Shakhtar Donetsk (1) 2 Marseille (0)...............0
Hubschman 39   Att: 25,500
Jadson 65

Werder Bremen (1) ....3 Udinese (0) 1
Diego 34, 67   Quagliarella 87
Hugo Almeida 69   Att: 32,548

QUARTER-FINAL SECOND LEG

16/04/2009

Dynamo Kiev (2) ....3 PSG (0) 0
Bangoura 4   Att: 16,900
Landreau 15 og
Vukojevic 61
Dynamo Kiev win 3–0 on aggregate

Manchester City (1) ..2 Hamburg (1)...............1
Elano 17 pen   Guerrero 12
Caicedo 50   Att: 47,009
Hamburg win 4–3 on aggregate

Marseille (1) ....1 Shakhtar Donetsk (1) ..2
Ben Arfa 43   Fernandinho 29
Att: 50,000   Luiz Adriano 90
Shakhtar Donetsk win 4–1 on aggregate

Udinese (3) ....3 Werder Bremen (1) 3
Inler 15   Diego 29, 59
Quagliarella 31, 38   Pizarro 74
Att: 30,000
Werder Bremen win 6–4 on aggregate

SEMI-FINAL FIRST LEG

30/04/2009

Dynamo Kiev (1) ....1 Shakhtar Donetsk (0) ..1
Chigrinsky 22 og   Fernandinho 68
Att: 17,000
Dynamo Kiev: Bogush, Betao, Sablic, Yussuf, El Kaddouri, Vukojevic, Correa (Cernat 82), Ninkovic, Aliev, Bangoura (Ghioane 46), Milevskiy. Subs (not used): Shovkovskiy, Nesmachniy, Kravchenko, Gusev, Zozulya. Booked: Correa, Vukojevic
Shakhtar Donetsk: Pyatov, Srna, Kucher, Chigrinsky, Rat, Hubschman, Duljaj, Ilsinho (Willian 56), Fernandinho, Jadson (Lewandowski 76), Luiz Adriano (Gladkyy 46). Subs (not used): Khudzamov, Ischenko, Gai, Moreno. Booked: Kucher
Referee: Konrad Plautz (Austria)

Werder Bremen (0) ....0 Hamburg (1)...............1
Att: 37,500   Trochowski 28
Werder Bremen: Wiese, Fritz (Prodl 85), Mertesacker, Naldo, Boenisch, Tziolis, Frings, Diego, Ozil, Pizarro, Hugo Almeida (Rosenberg 61). Subs (not used): Mielitz, Tosic, Baumann, Vranjes, Harnik. Booked: Tziolis
Hamburg: Rost, Demel, Gravgaard, Mathijsen, Aogo (Benjamin 79), Jarolim, Da Silva (Boateng 75), Pitroipa, Guerrero, Trochowski, Olic (Torun 90). Subs (not used): Hesl, Choupo-Moting, Ndjeng, Rincon. Booked: Aogo, Da Silva, Guerrero
Referee: Howard Webb (England)

SEMI-FINAL SECOND LEG

07/05/2009

Hamburg (1) ....2 Werder Bremen (1) 3
Olic 12, 87   Diego 29
Att: 51,200   Pizarro 66
                                      Baumann 83
3–3 on aggregate
Werder Bremen win on away goals
Hamburg: Rost, Demel (Boateng 63), Gravgaard, Mathijsen, Jansen (Aogo 77), Pitroipa, Jarolim, Da Silva (Benjamin 72), Trochowski, Petric, Olic. Subs (not used): Hesl, Atouba, Torun, Rincon. Booked: Boateng, Da Silva, Jarolim
Werder Bremen: Wiese, Fritz, Mertesacker (Prodl 54), Naldo, Boenisch, Frings, Baumann, Ozil, Pizarro (Niemeyer 89), Diego, Rosenberg (Hugo Almeida 62). Subs (not used): Mielitz, Tosic, Tziolis, Harnik. Booked: Diego, Hugo Almeida, Naldo
Referee: Frank De Bleeckere (Belgium)

Shakhtar Donetsk (1) 2 Dynamo Kiev (0).........1
Jadson 17   Bangoura 47
Ilsinho 88   Att: 24,000
Shakhtar Donetsk win 3–2 on aggregate
Shakhtar Donetsk: Pyatov, Srna, Ischenko, Chigrinsky, Rat, Ilsinho (Lewandowski 90), Hubschman, Gai (Willian 70), Fernandinho, Jadson, Luiz Adriano (Gladkyy 70). Subs (not used): Khudzamov, Duljaj, Seleznyov, Chyzhov. Booked: Gladkyy, Hubschman
Dynamo Kiev: Bogush, Betao, Sablic, Yussuf, El Kaddouri, Eremenko (Correa 75), Vukojevic, Ninkovic, Bangoura, Aliev, Milevskiy. Subs (not used): Shovkovskiy, Ghioane, Kravchenko, Nesmachniy, Zozulya, Yarmolenko. Booked: Aliev, Bangoura, El Kaddouri, Vukojevic
Referee: Olegario Benquerenca (Portugal)

FINAL

20/05/2009

Shakhtar Donetsk (1)..2 Werder Bremen (1) 1
Luiz Adriano 25   Naldo 35
Jadson 97
Att: 53,100
AET: Score after 90 mins 1–1
Shakhtar Donetsk: Pyatov, Srna, Kucher, Chigrinsky, Rat, Lewandowski, Fernandinho, Ilsinho (Gai 99), Jadson (Duljaj 112), Willian , Luiz Adriano (Gladkyy 89). Subs (not used): Khudzamov, Ischenko, Chyzhov, Moreno. Booked: Ilsinho, Lewandowski, Srna
Werder Bremen: Wiese, Fritz (Pasanen 94), Prodl, Naldo, Boenisch, Niemeyer (Tziolis 103), Frings, Baumann, Ozil, Pizarro, Rosenberg (Hunt 78). Subs (not used): Vander, Tosic, Vranjes, Harnik. Booked: Boenisch, Frings, Fritz, Tziolis
Referee: Luis Medina Cantalejo (Spain)

QUICK SEARCH

Trace the progress of all the clubs from the first round of the competition

BARCLAYS PREMIER LEAGUE

	Reached 2008/09
Arsenal	Semi-final
Aston Villa	Round 5
Blackburn	Round 5
Bolton	Round 3
Chelsea	Final
Everton	Final
Fulham	Quarter-final
Hull	Quarter-final
Liverpool	Round 4
Manchester City	Round 3
Manchester Utd	Semi-final
Middlesbrough	Quarter-final
Newcastle	Round 3
Portsmouth	Round 4
Stoke	Round 3
Sunderland	Round 4
Tottenham	Round 4
West Brom	Round 4
West Ham	Round 5
Wigan	Round 3

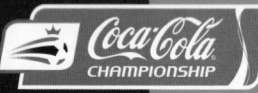

Coca-Cola CHAMPIONSHIP

Barnsley	Round 3
Birmingham	Round 3
Blackpool	Round 3
Bristol City	Round 3
Burnley	Round 5
Cardiff	Round 4
Charlton	Round 4
Coventry	Quarter-final
Crystal Palace	Round 4
Derby	Round 5
Doncaster	Round 4
Ipswich	Round 4
Norwich	Round 3
Nottm Forest	Round 4
Plymouth	Round 3
Preston	Round 3
QPR	Round 3
Reading	Round 3
Sheff Utd	Round 5
Sheff Wed	Round 3
Southampton	Round 3
Swansea	Round 5
Watford	Round 5
Wolverhampton	Round 4

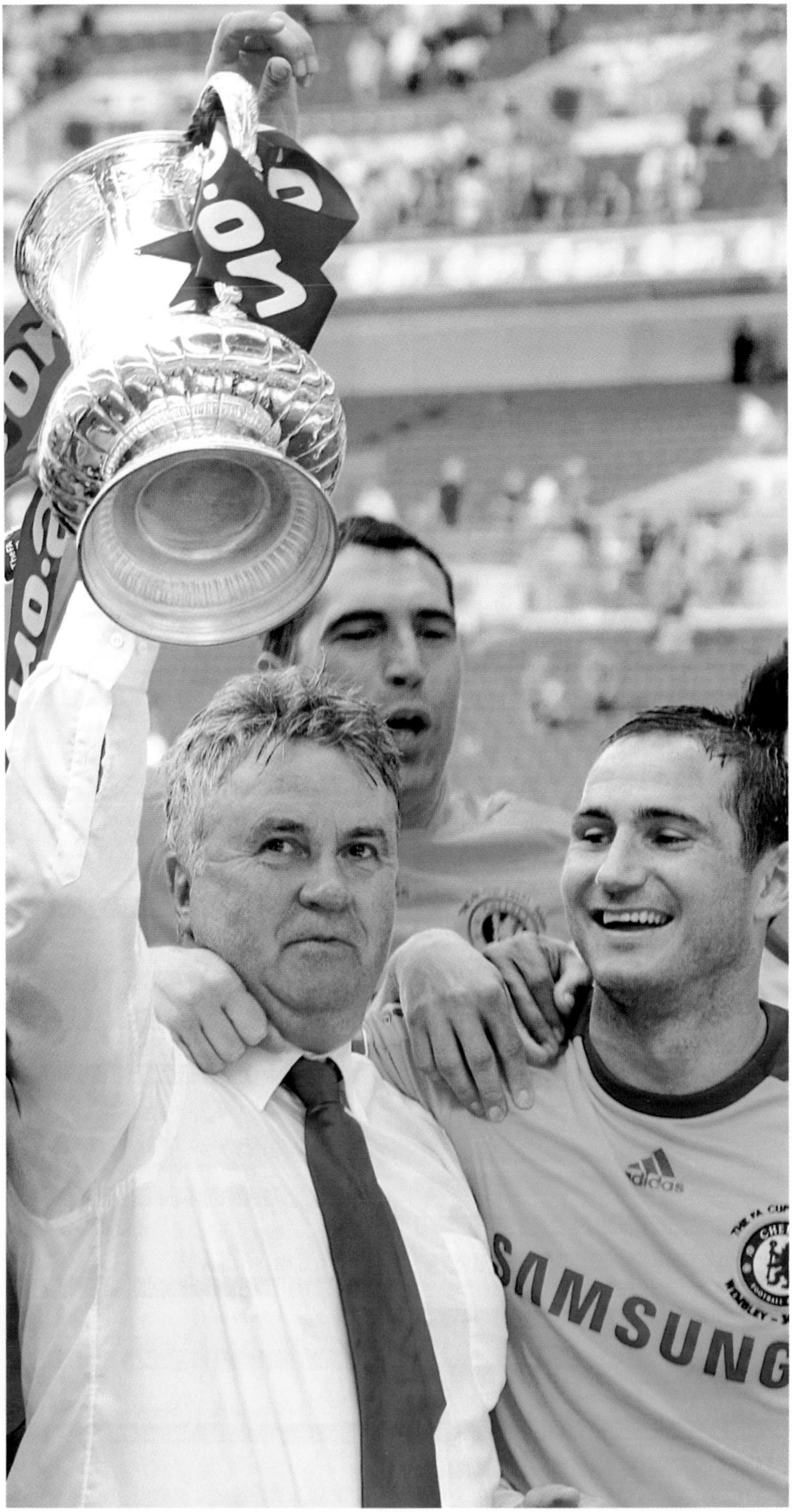

GUUS HIDDINK was only in England for three-and-a-half months, but he left to resume coaching duties with Russia as a winner after masterminding Chelsea's victory over Everton on a sunny May day at Wembley.

Hiddink has coached all over the world. Yet, as a Dutchman brought up on a diet of English football, the FA Cup has a special place in his heart.

And he certainly has a special place in Chelsea's hearts after helping them to win the trophy for the second time in three years at the new Wembley. Chelsea deserved it too, just as defender Ashley Cole deserved his man-of-the-match award for becoming the first player since the 19th century to win five winner's medals in the world's oldest domestic cup competition.

Not that it came without a fright against the Toffees, who went in front thanks to the fastest goal in FA Cup final history courtesy of Louis Saha, who took just 25 seconds to find the net.

However, Didier Drogba equalised before half-time and Chelsea were well on top by the time Frank Lampard drilled home from 20 yards 18 minutes from time.

It left Chelsea as the only ones standing from a starting field that totalled 762 teams last August, the competition providing its usual thrills and spills along the way.

Given the entire semi-final line-up came from the Barclays Premier League's top five – with the only absentee, Liverpool, who lost to Everton at the fourth-round stage – many would argue the tournament lacked sparkle compared to 12 months earlier, when three of the last four did not even play in the top flight. On closer inspection, the argument could be easily dismissed.

Chelsea survived a massive scare in the third round, which played a major part in their manager being dumped, while Manchester City's expensively-assembled team suffered a humiliating home defeat to Nottingham Forest.

Fifteen years ago, few would have expected the names of Leeds and Wimbledon to go into the hat along with Dorchester, Fleetwood and Brackley at the

Continued on page 495

CLOCKWISE FROM FAR LEFT: Guus Hiddink lifts the FA Cup trophy with Frank Lampard; Didier Drogba heads Chelsea's equaliser in the final; Louis Saha celebrates with his Everton teammates after scoring the fastest goal in FA Cup final history

FA CUP

QUICK SEARCH

Trace the progress of all the clubs from the first round of the competition

Coca-Cola LEAGUE 1

Reached 2008/09

Club	Reached
Brighton	Round 1
Bristol Rovers	Round 1
Carlisle	Round 2
Cheltenham	Round 3
Colchester	Round 1
Crewe	Round 3
Hartlepool	Round 4
Hereford	Round 1
Huddersfield	Round 1
Leeds	Round 2
Leicester	Round 3
Leyton Orient	Round 3
Millwall	Round 4
MK Dons	Round 1
Northampton	Round 1
Oldham	Round 1
Peterborough	Round 3
Scunthorpe	Round 3
Southend	Round 3
Stockport	Round 2
Swindon	Round 2
Tranmere	Round 2
Walsall	Round 1
Yeovil	Round 1

Coca-Cola LEAGUE 2

Club	Reached
Accrington Stanley	Round 1
Aldershot	Round 2
Barnet	Round 1
Bournemouth	Round 2
Bradford	Round 2
Brentford	Round 2
Bury	Round 1
Chester	Round 1
Chesterfield	Round 3
Dag & Red	Round 2
Darlington	Round 1
Exeter	Round 1
Gillingham	Round 3
Grimsby	Round 1
Lincoln City	Round 1
Luton	Round 2
Macclesfield	Round 3
Morecambe	Round 2
Notts County	Round 2
Rochdale	Round 2
Port Vale	Round 2
Rotherham	Round 2
Shrewsbury	Round 1
Wycombe	Round 2

FIRST ROUND

07/11/2008

Leeds (1) ....1 Northampton (1) 1
Robinson 37 pen   McGleish 9
Att: 9,531

08/11/2008

AFC Telford (0) ....2 Southend (1) 2
Adams 70, 83   Laurent 34
Att: 3,631   Christophe 90

Accrington Stanley (0) 0 Tranmere (0) 0
Att: 2,126

Aldershot (0) ....1 Rotherham (0) 1
Grant 90 pen   Cummins 54
Att: 2,632

Alfreton Town (1) ......4 Bury Town (2) 2
McIntosh 4   Johnson 23
Fortune-West 61   Reed 34
Law 65 pen, Clayton 90   Att: 1,060

Barnet (0) ....1 Rochdale (0) 1
Yakubu 67   Dagnall 49
Att: 1,782

Blyth Spartans (2) ......3 Shrewsbury (0) 0
Reay 1, 29   Holt 68
Leeson 53   Att: 2,742

Bournemouth (0) ....1 Bristol Rovers (0) 0
Pearce 76   Att: 3,935

Brighton (2) ....3 Hartlepool (0) 3
McLeod 19   Hawkins 53 og
Cox 38   Brown 55, Monkhouse 69
Fraser 78   Att: 2,545

Bury (0) ....0 Gillingham (0) 1
Att: 2,161   Barcham 71

Carlisle (0) ....1 Grays Athletic (0) 1
Madine 84   Stuart 52
Att: 3,921

Cheltenham (2) ....2 Oldham (0) 2
Murray 5   Taylor 49, Whitaker 76
Owusu 45 pen   Att: 2,585

Chester (0) ....0 Millwall (0) 3
Att: 1,932   Grabban 76
   Harris 79, Grimes 90

Chesterfield (1) ....3 Mansfield (0) 1
Winter 32, 58   Arnold 78
Ward 51   Att: 6,612

Colchester (0) ....0 Leyton Orient (0) 1
Att: 4,600   Demetriou 80

Crewe (1) ....1 Ebbsfleet United (0) 0
Donaldson 34   Att: 2,593

Curzon Ashton (1)........3 Exeter (0) 2
Worsley 26   Basham 84, Moxey 90
Ogoo 56, Norton 79   Att: 1,259

Darlington (0) ....0 Droylsden (0) 0
Att: 2,479

Eastbourne Boro (0) ....0 Barrow (0) 0
Att: 1,216

Eastwood Town (0) ......2 Brackley (1) 1
Cooke 54   Winters 20
Meikle 65   Att: 960

Harlow (0) ....0 Macclesfield (0) 2
Att: 2,149   Brisley 65, Dunfield 86

Hereford (0) ....0 Dag & Red (0) 0
Att: 1,825

Histon (0) ....1 Swindon (0) 0
Wright 66   Att: 1,541

Huddersfield (1) ....3 Port Vale (1) 4
Collins 45, Craney 51   Dodds 27, 85
Williams 65   Howland 79, Richards 90
Att: 6,942

Kettering (0) ....1 Lincoln City (0)...........1
Geohaghan 85   N'Guessan 86
Att: 3,314

Kidderminster (1) ....1 Cambridge Utd (0) 0
Richards 17 pen   Att: 1,717

Leicester (1)...........3 Stevenage (0) 0
Dyer 37   Att: 7,586
Fryatt 52, King 69

Leiston (0) ....0 Fleetwood Town (0) 0
Att: 1,250

Luton (0) ....0 Altrincham (0) 0
Att: 3,200

MK Dons (1).................1 Bradford (1) 2
Johnson 43   Daley 2
Att: 5,542   Lee 82

Morecambe (1)...........2 Grimsby (0)...........1
Taylor 45, 77   Stockdale 88; Att: 1,713

Oxford Utd (0) ....0 Dorchester (0) 0
Att: 3,196

Sutton Utd (0) ....0 Notts County (0)...........1
Att: 2,041   Butcher 75

Torquay (1)...........2 Evesham (0)...........0
Sills 28, 75   Att: 2,275

Walsall (1)...........1 Scunthorpe (1)...........3
Ricketts 25   Hooper 42, 58
Att: 2,318   Hurst 90

Yeovil (0) ....1 Stockport (1)...........1
Skiverton 60   Davies 44; Att: 3,582

09/11/2008

AFC Hornchurch (0) ....0 Peterborough (0) 1
Att: 3,000   Mackail-Smith 90

Havant and W (0) ....1 Brentford (1) 3
Simpemba 73   Williams 42
Att: 1,631   MacDonald 66, Elder 83

Team Bath (0) ....0 Forest Green (0) 1
Att: 906   Mohamed 75

10/11/2008

AFC Wimbledon (0)....1 Wycombe (2) 4
Hatton 56   Harrold 9, 36, 74
Att: 4,528   Phillips 62

REPLAYS

13/11/2008

Tranmere (0) ....1 Accrington Stanley (0) 0
Shuker 69   Att: 2,560

17/11/2008

Northampton (1)...........2 Leeds (4) 5
Crowe 44, 90   Beckford 13, 45, 55
Att: 3,960   Howson 28, Parker 41

18/11/2008

Altrincham (0) ....0 Luton (0) 0
Att: 2,397
AET: Score after 90 mins 0–0
Luton win 4–2 on penalties

Dag & Red (2) ....2 Hereford (1) 1
Benson 17, Taiwo 33   Taylor 34; Att: 1,409

Dorchester (1) ....1 Oxford Utd (0) 3
Mudge 22   Constable 78
Att: 1,474   Trainer 110, Odubade 120
AET: Score after 90 mins 1–1

Droylsden (1) ....1 Darlington (0)...........0
Tipton 26   Att: 1,672

Fleetwood Town (1) ....2 Leiston (0) 0
Bell 48, Warlow 79   Att: 2,010

Grays Athletic (A)........A Carlisle (A)...........A
Sloma 19
Abandoned after 20min due to floodlight failure

Hartlepool (0) ....2 Brighton (1) 1
Porter 67 pen, Liddle 70   Forster 28; Att: 3,288

Lincoln City (0)...........1 Kettering (0) 2
John-Lewis 54   Westcarr 68
Att: 3,953   Christie 90

Oldham (0) ....0 Cheltenham (1)...........1
Att: 2,552   Montrose 22

Rochdale (0)...........3 Barnet (2) 2
Le Fondre 56, 73, 105   O'Flynn 10
Att: 2,339   Adomah 19
AET: Score after 90 mins 2–2

Rotherham (0) ....0 Aldershot (1) 3
Att: 2,431   Hudson 15, 81, Morgan 55

Southend (0) ....2 AFC Telford (0)...........0
Francis 74, Walker 79   Att: 4,415

Stockport (3) ....5 Yeovil (0) 0
Dicker 6, Rose 16, McNeil 42   Att: 3,260
Pilkington 48, Vincent 90

Barrow (1) ....4 Eastbourne Borough (0)0
Brodie 45, Brown 47   Att: 2,131
Henney 57, Logan 76

29/11/2008

Grays Athletic (0) ....0 Carlisle (1)...........2
Att: 1,217   Graham 27, Kavanagh 52

SECOND ROUND

28/11/2008

Barrow (1) ....2 Brentford (0) 1
Brown 39 pen   MacDonald 50
Henney 71   Att: 3,120

Port Vale (0).............1 Macclesfield (1) 3
Dodds 71   Green 9, 73
Att: 4,684   Gritton 90

29/11/2008

Bournemouth (0) ....0 Blyth Spartans (0) 0
Att: 4,165

Bradford (0) ....1 Leyton Orient (1) 2
Boulding 58   Demetriou 14
Att: 5,065   Granville 65

Chesterfield (0) ....A Droylsden (1) ....A
Lamb 35
Abandoned due to fog at half-time

Eastwood Town (1) ......2 Wycombe (0) 0
Meikle 34   Att: 1,955
Knox 90

Fleetwood Town (1) ......2 Hartlepool (1).............3
Bell 14   Mackay 17, 47
Warlow 66   Porter 56
Att: 3,280

Forest Green (1) ....2 Rochdale (0)..............0
Smith 27, Low 56   Att: 1,715

Gillingham (0)..............0 Stockport (0) 0
Att: 4,419

Kidderminster (1) ....2 Curzon Ashton (0)........0
Moore 38   Att: 2,070
Creighton 65

Leicester (2)................3 Dag & Red (2) 2
Fryatt 11, 30 pen, 55   Ritchie 9
Att: 7,791   Strevens 25

Millwall (1) ....3 Aldershot (0)..............0
Alexander 30, 77, Grimes 88   Att: 6,159

Morecambe (1)...........A Cheltenham (0) ....A
Howe 15 pen   Hayles 54
Att: 1,984
Abandoned due to fog after 65 minutes

Peterborough (0) ....0 Tranmere (0) 0
Att: 5,980

Scunthorpe (1) ....4 Alfreton Town (0) 0
May 30   Att: 4,249
Hooper 62, 83, Togwell 90

Southend (1) ....3 Luton (0) 1
Stanislas 34, 84   Spillane 80
Walker 90   Att: 4,111

Torquay (1)................2 Oxford Utd (0) 0
Benyon 41, 83   Att: 2,647

30/11/2008

Histon (1)..................1 Leeds (0) 0
Langston 39   Att: 4,500

Notts County (1)..........1 Kettering (1) 1
Canham 34   Solkhon 18
Att: 4,451

02/12/2008

Morecambe (2)............2 Cheltenham (2)...........3
McStay 5   Vincent 23, 54
Howe 27 pen   Finnigan 36 pen
Att: 1,758

03/12/2008

Carlisle (0) ....0 Crewe (2) 2
Att: 2,755   Miller 3, 12

09/12/2008

Chesterfield (1) ....2 Droylsden (0) 2
Ward 31   Brown 50, Halford 82
Lester 79   Att: 5,698

REPLAYS

09/12/2008

Stockport (1) ....1 Gillingham (2).............2
Gleeson 17   Barcham 25, 34
Att: 3,329

Tranmere (0) ....1 Peterborough (0) 2
Kay 47   Mclean 90
Att: 3,139   Mackail-Smith 114
AET: Score after 90 mins 1–1

10/12/2008

Kettering (0) ....2 Notts County (1)..........1
Solkhon 53   Smith 43
Seddon 54   Att: 3,019

16/12/2008

Blyth Spartans (0) ......1 Bournemouth (0) 0
Dalton 90   Att: 4,040

Droylsden (0) ....A Chesterfield (1) ....A
Att: 2,261   Lester 25, Currie 53
Abandoned after 72 minutes due to floodlight failure

23/12/2008

Droylsden (1) ....2 Chesterfield (1) 1
Newton 31, 55 pen   Lester 35; Att: 2,824

THIRD ROUND

02/01/2009

Tottenham (0)..............3 Wigan (0) 1
Pavlyuchenko 52 pen, 90   Camara 88
Modric 76   Att: 34,040

03/01/2009

Arsenal (0) ....3 Plymouth (0) 1
Van Persie 47, 85   Duguid 53
Bendtner 50   Att: 59,424

Cardiff (0) ....2 Reading (0) 0
McCormack 57, Ledley 83   Att: 12,448

Charlton (1) ....1 Norwich (0) 1
Shelvey 20   Lupoli 71
Att: 12,615

Chelsea (1) ....1 Southend (1) 1
Kalou 31   Clarke 90
Att: 41,090

Coventry (0) ....2 Kidderminster (0) 0
McKenzie 52, Best 82   Att: 13,652

Forest Green (2) ....3 Derby (2) 4
Smith 14   Hulse 40
Lawless 20   Albrechtsen 45
Stonehouse 72   Green 76
Att: 4,836   Davies 87 pen

Hartlepool (0)..............2 Stoke (0) 0
Nelson 49, Foley 76   Att: 5,367

Hull (0)......................0 Newcastle (0).............0
Att: 20,557

Kettering (1) ....2 Eastwood Town (0) 1
Westcarr 24   Robinson 60
Seddon 58   Att: 5,090

Leicester (0)...............0 Crystal Palace (0)........0
Att: 15,976

Macclesfield (0) ....0 Everton (1) 1
Att: 6,008   Osman 43

Manchester City (0) ....0 Nottm Forest (2) 3
Att: 31,869   Tyson 38
    Earnshaw 42, Garner 75

Middlesbrough (1) ......2 Barrow (0) 1
Alves 23, 62   Walker 80
Att: 25,132

Millwall (2).................2 Crewe (1) 2
Laird 40   Lawrence 12, Shelley 58
Frampton 45   Att: 5,754

Portsmouth (0)............0 Bristol City (0) 0
Att: 14,446

Preston (0)..................0 Liverpool (1) 2
Att: 23,046   Riera 25
    Torres 90

QPR (0) ....0 Burnley (0) 0
Att: 8,896

Sheffield Wed (1) ....1 Fulham (1) 2
Spurr 21   Johnson 12, 88
Att: 18,377

Sunderland (0) ....2 Bolton (0)..................1
Jones 57   Smolarek 79
Cisse 67   Att: 20,685

Torquay (1) ....1 Blackpool (0) 0
Green 32   Att: 3,654

Watford (0)..................1 Scunthorpe (0) 0
Rasiak 67   Att: 8,690

West Brom (0) ....1 Peterborough (0) 1
Olsson 64   Mackail-Smith 87
Att: 18,659

West Ham (2) ....3 Barnsley (0) 0
Ilunga 10   Att: 28,869
Noble 39 pen
Cole 68

Ipswich (0) ....3 Chesterfield (0) 0
Walters 50 pen   Att: 12,524
Counago 53
Stead 88

04/01/2009

Gillingham (0)..............1 Aston Villa (1) 2
Jackson 57   Milner 13, 79 pen
Att: 10,107

Southampton (0)..........0 Manchester Utd (1) 3
Att: 31,901   Welbeck 20
    Nani 48 pen
    Gibson 81

05/01/2009

Blyth Spartans (0) ......0 Blackburn (0) 1
Att: 3,445   Villanueva 58

13/01/2009

Birmingham (0)...........0 Wolverhampton (1) 2
Att: 22,232   Keogh 38
    Vokes 51

Cheltenham (0)............0 Doncaster (0) 0
Att: 4,417

Histon (0)..................1 Swansea (2) 2
Simpson 84   Pintado 22
Att: 2,821   Bauza 38

Leyton Orient (1) ....1 Sheffield Utd (0) 4
Melligan 38 pen   Halford 59, 78
Att: 4,527   Sharp 62
    Naughton 69

REPLAYS

13/01/2009

Bristol City (0) ....0 Portsmouth (1) 2
Att: 14,302   Crouch 38
    Kranjcar 88

Burnley (0) ....2 QPR (0) 1
Thompson 60   Di Carmine 54
Rodriguez 120   Att: 3,760
AET: Score after 90 mins 1–1

Crewe (1)...................2 Millwall (1).................3
Murphy 7   Barron 8
Miller 58   Harris 54
Att: 3,060   Whitbread 86

Norwich (0) ....0 Charlton (1) 1
Att: 13,997   Ambrose 6

Peterborough (0) ....0 West Brom (2) 2
Att: 10,735   Simpson 18
    Robinson 37

14/01/2009

Newcastle (0)...............0 Hull (0)......................1
Att: 31,380   Cousin 81

Crystal Palace (1)........2 Leicester (0)...............1
Ifill 38   Gradel 90
Scannell 55   Att: 6,023

Southend (1) ....1 Chelsea (1) 4
Barrett 16   Ballack 45
Att: 11,314   Kalou 60
    Anelka 78, Lampard 90

20/01/2009

Doncaster (2)..............3 Cheltenham (0)...........0
Stock 26, 58   Att: 5,345
Hird 36

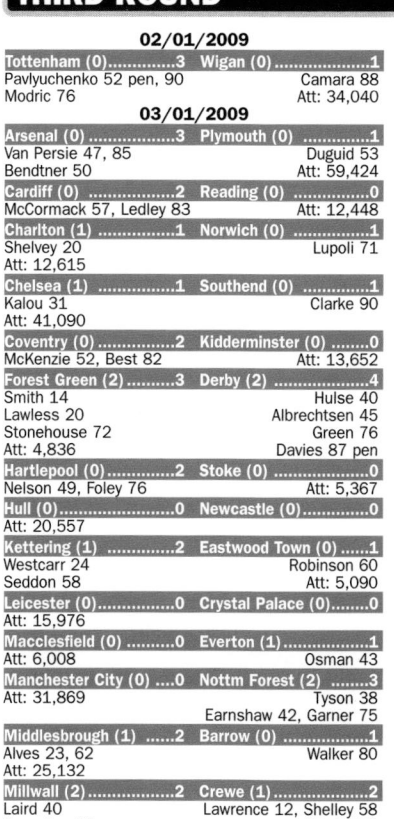

FA CUP

FOURTH ROUND

23/01/2009

Derby (1) ....1 Nottm Forest (0) 1
Hulse 36 — Earnshaw 64; Att: 32,035
Derby: Bywater, Connolly, Addison, Albrechtsen, Stewart, Barazite (Villa 89), Green, Savage, Teale (Commons 72), Hulse, Barnes (Varney 64). Subs (not used): Carroll, Nyatanga, Hanson, Beardsley. Booked: Connolly.
Nottm Forest: Smith, Chambers, Wilson, Breckin, Lynch (McCleary 46), Anderson (Davies 78), Perch, McGugan, Cohen, Tyson, Earnshaw (Garner 90). Subs (not used): Darlow, Byrne, Thornhill, Heath. Booked: Cohen, McCleary.
Referee: Howard Webb (S Yorkshire).

24/01/2009

Chelsea (1) ....3 Ipswich (1)...................1
Ballack 16, 59 — Bruce 34
Lampard 85 — Att: 41,137
Chelsea: Cech, Bosingwa, Carvalho (Ivanovic 70), Alex, Cole, Belletti, Ballack (Deco 79), Lampard, Malouda (Drogba 58), Kalou, Anelka. Subs (not used): Cudicini, Ferreira, Mancienne, Stoch.
Ipswich: R Wright, D Wright, McAuley, Bruce, Garvan, Miller (Quinn 81), Counago, Norris, Balkestein, Haynes (Lisbie 60), Walters (Stead 71). Subs (not used): Supple, Bowditch, Shumulikoski, Thatcher. Booked: Bruce, Garvan, Norris.
Referee: Alan Wiley (Staffordshire).

Doncaster (0) ....0 Aston Villa (0) 0
Att: 13,517
Doncaster: Sullivan, O'Connor, Mills, Hird, Roberts, Woods, Stock, Wellens, Coppinger (Price 76), Guy (Heffernan 76), Spicer (Lockwood 90). Subs (not used): Taylor, Van Nieuwstadt, Wilson, Byfield.
Aston Villa: Friedel, Davies, Cuellar, Knight, Reo-Coker (Gardner 70), Sidwell, Petrov, Barry, Shorey, Milner, Agbonlahor. Subs (not used): Harewood, Delfouneso, Salifou, Guzan, Osbourne, Clark.
Referee: Mark Halsey (Lancashire)

Hartlepool (0).............0 West Ham (2).............2
Att: 6,849 — Behrami 44, Noble 45 pen
Hartlepool: Lee-Barrett, Sweeney, Nelson, Clark, Humphreys, Monkhouse, Jones (Foley 85), Liddle, Robson, Mackay (Henderson 56), Porter. Subs (not used): Budtz, McCunnie, Collins, Power, Rowell.
West Ham: Green, Faubert, Collins, Tomkins, Ilunga, Behrami, Parker, Noble, Collison (Boa Morte 64), Cole (Sears 78), Di Michele (Mullins 75). Subs (not used): Stech, Neill, Spector, Tristan. Booked: Cole, Collins, Ilunga.
Referee: Lee Mason (Lancashire).

Hull (1).......................2 Millwall (0).................0
Turner 15, Ashbee 84 — Att: 18,639
Hull: Warner, Ricketts, Turner, Zayatte, Dawson, Garcia, Ashbee, Marney, Halmosi (Featherstone 66), Cousin, Manucho (Folan 75). Subs (not used): Duke, Doyle, Geovanni, France, Mendy. Booked: Folan.
Millwall: Forde, Dunne, Robinson, Craig, Frampton, Grabban (Hackett 77), Laird, Abdou, Martin (Grimes 77), Harris, McLeod (Alexander 74). Subs (not used): Pidgeley, Kandol, O'Connor, Fuseini. Booked: Dunne, Grimes, Harris, Martin.
Referee: Stuart Attwell (Warwickshire).

Kettering (1) ....2 Fulham (1) 4
Westcarr 36, 83 pen — Davies 12, Murphy 77
Att: 5,406 — Johnson 88, Zamora 89
Kettering: Harper, Eaden, Geohaghan, Dempster, Jaszczun (Potter 71), Bennett, Boucaud, Solkhon, Graham (Marna 89), Westcarr, Seddon (Beardsley 73). Subs (not used): Wrack, Galbraith. Booked: Dempster, Graham, Westcarr.
Fulham: Schwarzer, Stoor, Hangeland, Hughes, Konchesky, Davies, Andreasen, Etuhu (Murphy 69), Gera (Zamora 69), Johnson, Dempsey. Subs (not used): Zuberbuhler, Pantsil, Nevland, Kallio, Baird. Booked: Hangeland.
Referee: Mike Riley (Yorkshire).

Manchester Utd (2) ....2 Tottenham (1).............1
Scholes 35 — Pavlyuchenko 5
Berbatov 36 — Att: 75,014
Manchester Utd: Foster, O'Shea, Neville, Vidic, Rafael (Eckersley 53), Welbeck (Fletcher 86), Carrick, Scholes, Ronaldo (Tosic 72), Berbatov, Tevez. Subs (not used): Kuszczak, Giggs, Possebon, Chester. Booked: Tevez, Vidic.
Tottenham: Alnwick, Gunter, Corluka, Dawson, Assou-Ekotto, Bentley (Defoe 72), Huddlestone, Zokora, Bale (Taarabt 67), Modric (Giovani 46), Pavlyuchenko. Subs (not used): Gomes, Gilberto, Rocha, Dervite.
Referee: Peter Walton (Northamptonshire).

Portsmouth (0)...........0 Swansea (2)..................2
Att: 17,357 — Dyer 26, Scotland 45 pen
Portsmouth: James, Cranie, Campbell, Distin, Belhadj, Nugent (Kanu 46), Hughes (Kaboul 84), Davis, Traore (Hreidarsson 46), Pennant, Crouch. Subs (not used): Begovic, Pamarot, Utaka, Mvuemba. Booked: Belhadj, Distin.
Swansea: Konstantopoulos, Rangel, Williams, Monk, Tate, Britton, Pratley, Allen (Pintado 61), Gomez, Scotland, Dyer (Gower 79). Subs (not used): De Vries, Orlandi, Tudur-Jones, Bauza, Serran. Booked: Britton, Pratley, Rangel, Tate.
Referee: Andre Marriner (W Midlands).

Sheffield Utd (1).........2 Charlton (0) 1
Webber 26, Hendrie 62 — Dickson 69; Att: 15,957
Sheffield Utd: Bennett, Jihai (Howard 83), Morgan, Kilgallon, Naysmith, Halford, Naughton, Montgomery, Webber (Hendrie 56), Sharp, Henderson. Subs (not used): Haber, Cotterill, Carney, Walker.
Charlton: Elliot, Moutaouakil, Fortune, Hudson, Youga, Shelvey (Dickson 58), Bailey, Ambrose, Holland (Racon 78), Sam, Burton (Gray 59). Subs (not used): Randolph, Wagstaff, Basey, Clark. Booked: Dickson.
Referee: Tony Bates (Staffordshire).

Sunderland (0) ....0 Blackburn (0) 0
Att: 22,634
Sunderland: Fulop, Chimbonda, Ferdinand, Collins, Bardsley (McCartney 65), Edwards, Leadbitter, Malbranque, Reid, Healy (Jones 67), Chopra. Subs (not used): Colgan, Cisse, Diouf, Murphy, Yorke.
Blackburn: Robinson, Simpson, Samba, Nelsen, Warnock (Givet 73), Olsson (Haworth 56), Mokoena, Grella, Pedersen, Santa Cruz (Villanueva 67), McCarthy. Subs (not used): Bunn, Emerton, Khizanishvili, Andrews. Booked: Mokoena, Olsson, Samba.
Referee: Lee Probert (Wiltshire).

Torquay (0).................0 Coventry (0) 1
Att: 6,018 — Ward 8703
Torquay: Bevan, Mansell, Hodges, Woods, Nicholson, Carlisle (Stevens 90), Wroe, Hargreaves, DSane (Carayol 90), Sills, Green (Benyon 80). Subs (not used): Poke, Robertson, Thompson, Adams. Booked: Mansell.
Coventry: Westwood, Gunnarsson (Ward 45), Hall, Turner, Fox, Mifsud, Doyle, Beuzelin (Thornton 64), McKenzie, Eastwood, Morrison. Subs (not used): Marshall, Dann, Walker, Fraser, Wynter. Booked: Gunnarsson.
Referee: Kevin Friend (Leicestershire).

Watford (2)..................4 Crystal Palace (0).......3
DeMerit 17, Cork 27 — Hill 48, Ifill 83, 90
Hoskins 67, Rasiak 70 — Att: 10,006
Watford: Loach, Hoyte (Kiernan 90), DeMerit, Mariappa, Doyley, Cork, McAnuff, Harley, Jenkins, Rasiak (O'Toole 77), Hoskins (Bridcutt 86). Subs (not used): Searle, Sadler, Eustace, Bangura.
Crystal Palace: Speroni, Clyne (Butterfield 76), Lawrence, Fonte, Hill, Derry (Fletcher 75), Danns, Ifill, Oster, Lee (Kuqi 78), Moses. Subs (not used): Carle, Flahavan, Scannell, Hills. Booked: Danns, Fonte, Lee.
Referee: Michael Oliver (Northumberland).

West Brom (2) ....2 Burnley (1) 2
Koren 31, Kim 45 — Alexander 25 pen
Att: 18,294 — Paterson 89
West Brom: Carson, Hoefkens, Pele, Donk (Zuiverloon 72), Robinson, Kim, Greening (Borja Valero 40), Filipe Teixeira (Brunt 71), Koren, Simpson, Bednar. Subs (not used): Kiely, Cech, Dorrans, Fortuné.
Burnley: Jensen, Duff (Thompson 66), Carlisle, Caldwell, Kalvenes (Rodriguez 86), Elliott, Alexander, McCann, Eagles (Gudjonsson 60), Blake, Paterson. Subs (not used): Penny, McDonald, Mahon, MacDonald.
Referee: Mike Dean (Wirral).

Wolverhampton (0) ......1 Middlesbrough (1) 2
Vokes 63 — Alves 44
Att: 18,013 — Emnes 83
Wolverhampton: Hennessey, Edwards, Shackell, Collins, Hill, Jarvis (Ebanks-Blake 81), Henry, Jones, Reid (Kightly 65), Iwelumo (Keogh 52), Vokes. Subs (not used): Craddock, Friend, Ikeme, Foley. Booked: Jones.
Middlesbrough: Jones, Bates, Wheater, Riggott, Taylor (McMahon 7), O'Neil, Sanli, Shawky (Hoyte 46), Johnson, Downing, Alves (Emnes 70). Subs (not used): Porritt, Bennett, Turnbull, Craddock. Booked: O'Neil.
Referee: Rob Styles (Hampshire).

25/01/2009

Cardiff (0) ....0 Arsenal (0) 0
Att: 20,079
Cardiff: Enckelman, McNaughton, Gyepes, R Johnson, Kennedy, Rae, Parry, Ledley, Burke (Capaldi 79), Bothroyd (E Johnson 90), McCormack. Subs (not used): Heaton, Purse, McPhail, Comminges, Blake.
Arsenal: Fabianski, Sagna, Toure, Djourou, Gibbs, Nasri, Ramsey (Diaby 59), Song Billong, Eboue (Adebayor 66), Van Persie, Bendtner (Wilshere 87). Subs (not used): Almunia, Gallas, Vela, Denilson. Booked: Eboue, Van Persie.
Referee: Martin Atkinson (W Yorkshire).

Liverpool (0) ....1 Everton (1)..................1
Gerrard 54 — Lescott 27; Att: 43,524
Liverpool: Reina, Arbeloa, Skrtel, Carragher, Dossena, Kuyt, Alonso, Mascherano, Babel (Riera 75), Gerrard, Torres. Subs (not used): Cavalieri, Hyypia, Aurelio, Benayoun, Lucas, Ngog. Booked: Alonso, Carragher.
Everton: Howard, Hibbert, Jagielka, Lescott, Baines, Anichebe (Gosling 71), Castillo (Rodwell 76), Neville, Osman, Pienaar, Cahill. Subs (not used): Nash, Yobo, Van der Meyde, Jacobsen, Jutkiewicz. Booked: Cahill, Pienaar.
Referee: Steve Bennett (Kent).

REPLAYS

03/02/2009

Burnley (1) ....3 West Brom (0) 1
Elliott 45 — Zuiverloon 60
Thompson 52, 88 — Att: 6,635
Burnley: Jensen, Alexander, Duff, Caldwell, Kalvenes, McDonald (Gudjonsson 80), Elliott, McCann, Blake, Paterson (Rodriguez 90), Thompson (MacDonald 90). Subs (not used): Penny, Carlisle, Akinbiyi, Mahon. Booked: Caldwell.
West Brom: Carson, Zuiverloon, Donk, Pele, Cech, Kim, Dorrans, Simpson (Brunt 36), Filipe Teixeira (Hoefkens 57), Fortuné, Bednar. Subs (not used): Kiely, Robinson, Koren, Martis, Morrison.
Referee: Mike Jones (Cheshire).

04/02/2009

Aston Villa (2) ....3 Doncaster (1) 1
Sidwell 15, Carew 19 — Price 45
Delfouneso 61 — Att: 24,203
Aston Villa: Guzan, L Young, Davies, Cuellar, Shorey, Gardner, Salifou, Sidwell, A Young (Osbourne 78), Delfouneso, Carew. Subs (not used): Friedel, Barry, Milner, Agbonlahor, Knight, Lowry. Booked: Sidwell.
Doncaster: Sullivan, O'Connor, Mills, Hird, Chambers, Coppinger (Byfield 76), Wellens, Woods, Stock, Spicer (Guy 75), Price (Heffernan 75). Subs (not used): Roberts, Van Nieuwstadt, Taylor, Lockwood. Booked: Hird.
Referee: Lee Mason (Lancashire).

Blackburn (1) ....2 Sunderland (1) 1
Mokoena 37, McCarthy 118 — Healy 7; Att: 10,112
AET: Score after 90 mins 1–1
Blackburn: Robinson, Simpson, Khizanishvili, Nelsen (Ooijer 87), Givet, Villanueva, Mokoena, Dunn (Kerimoglu 61), Treacy, Santa Cruz (McCarthy 72), Roberts. Subs (not used): Bunn, Pedersen, Olsson, Doran. Booked: Mokoena, Simpson, Treacy.
Sunderland: Gordon, Kay (Bardsley 56), Ferdinand, Collins, McCartney (Luscombe 106), Edwards, Leadbitter, Reid, Malbranque (Yorke 76), Healy, Murphy. Subs (not used): Colgan, Whitehead, Richardson, Colback. Booked: Kay, Leadbitter.
Referee: Phil Dowd (Staffordshire).

Everton (0)..................1 Liverpool (0) 0
Gosling 118 — Att: 37,918
AET: Score after 90 mins 0–0
Everton: Howard, Hibbert, Jagielka, Lescott, Baines, Osman, Fellaini (Gosling 52), Neville (Van der Meyde 106), Arteta, Pienaar (Rodwell 60), Cahill. Subs (not used): Nash, Yobo, Castillo, Jacobsen. Booked: Arteta, Cahill, Hibbert, Neville, Pienaar.
Liverpool: Reina, Dossena, Carragher, Skrtel, Arbeloa, Kuyt, Alonso, Gerrard (Benayoun 16), Lucas, Riera (Mascherano 80), Torres (Babel 101). Subs (not used): Cavalieri, Hyypia, Agger, El Zhar. Booked: Alonso, Lucas. Dismissed: Lucas.
Referee: Alan Wiley (Staffordshire).

Nottm Forest (2) ....2 Derby (1) 3
Cohen 2, Tyson 14 pen — Hulse 27, Green 60
Att: 29,001 — Commons 74
Nottm Forest: Smith, Chambers, Morgan, Breckin, Wilson, McCleary (Heath 81), Perch (Byrne 70), McGugan, Thornhill, Cohen, Tyson (Newbold 85). Subs (not used): Darlow, Bencherif, Reid, Whitehurst. Booked: McGugan.
Derby: Bywater, Connolly, Albrechtsen, McEveley, Nyatanga, Barazite, Green, Savage, Teale, Commons, Hulse (Ellington 81). Subs (not used): Carroll, Stewart, Villa, Sterjovski, Todd, Pearson. Booked: Bywater, Nyatanga.
Referee: Chris Foy (Merseyside).

16/02/2009

Arsenal (2) ....4 Cardiff (0) 0
Eduardo 20, 60 pen — Att: 57,237
Bendtner 34, Van Persie 89
Arsenal: Fabianski, Sagna, Toure, Gallas, Gibbs, Nasri (Ramsey 67), Denilson, Song, Vela (Bischoff 74), Eduardo (Van Persie 67), Bendtner. Subs (not used): Almunia, Wilshere, Clichy. Booked: Bendtner, Gallas.
Cardiff: Heaton, McNaughton, Purse (Blake 68), R Johnson, Kennedy, Burke, Rae (Scimeca 74), Ledley, Parry (Whittingham 68), Bothroyd, McCormack. Subs (not used): Sak, Capaldi, E Johnson, Comminges.
Referee: Mark Halsey (Lancashire).

Southend's Peter Clarke beats the Chelsea defence in their titanic third-round clash. Although Chelsea eventually triumphed after a replay, the tie effectively cost Blues boss Luiz Felipe Scolari his job

FIFTH ROUND

14/02/2009

Blackburn (1) ....2 Coventry (0) 2
Santa Cruz 2   Gunnarsson 61, Doyle 76
Samba 90   Att: 15,053
Blackburn: Robinson, Simpson, Samba, Khizanishvili, Givet, Villanueva, Dunn (Treacy 71), Tugay (Andrews 65), Warnock, Santa Cruz, Roberts (McCarthy 78). Subs (not used): Bunn, Nelsen, Grella, Doran. Booked: Khizanishvili, Samba.
Coventry: Marshall, Osbourne, McPake (Dann 46), Ward, Fox, Henderson, Beuzelin (Best 53), Gunnarsson, Doyle, Eastwood, Morrison. Subs (not used): Hall, Dann, Simpson, Thornton, Cain. Booked: Best, Beuzelin, Eastwood.
Referee: Steve Tanner (Somerset).

Sheffield Utd (1) ....1 Hull (1).......................1
Halford 7   Zayatte 34
Att: 22,283
Sheffield Utd: Kenny, Jihai (Naughton 60), Morgan (Webber 31), Kilgallon, Naysmith, Cotterill, Montgomery, Quinn, Hendrie (Howard 73), Halford, Sharp. Subs (not used): Bennett, Walker.
Hull: Myhill, Ricketts, Turner, Gardner, Dawson, Mendy (France 88), Marney, Zayatte, Garcia (Manucho 79), Geovanni (Barmby 73), Folan. Subs (not used): Warner, Doyle, Halmosi, Featherstone. Booked: Garcia, Mendy, Turner.
Referee: Andre Marriner (W Midlands).

Swansea (0) ....1 Fulham (1) 1
Scotland 52   Monk 44 og
Att: 16,573
Swansea: De Vries, Rangel, Williams, Monk, Tate, Britton, Gomez, Allen (Bauza 81), Gower (Orlandi 71), Dyer, Scotland. Subs (not used): Cornell, Tudur-Jones, Bessone, Serran, Butler. Booked: Williams.
Fulham: Schwarzer, Stoor, Hangeland, Hughes, Konchesky, Nevland (Zamora 75), Gera, Murphy, Davies, Dacourt (Dempsey 60), Johnson (Gray 85). Subs (not used): Zuberbuhler, Pantsil, Milsom, Kallio. Booked: Dacourt.
Referee: Howard Webb (S Yorkshire).

Watford (0)..................1 Chelsea (0) 3
Priskin 69   Anelka 75, 77, 90
Att: 16,851
Watford: Loach, Hoyte, Mariappa, DeMerit, Doyley, Smith, Jenkins, Williamson (Cowie 67), McAnuff, Rasiak (Priskin 66), Hoskins (O'Toole 76). Subs (not used): Lee, Sadler, Harley, Parkes. Booked: O'Toole.
Chelsea: Cech, Mancienne, Alex, Ivanovic, Cole, Lampard, Ballack (Belletti 83), Mikel (Stoch 73), Kalou, Anelka, Drogba. Subs (not used): Hilario, Di Santo, Quaresma, Ferreira, Deco. Booked: Cole.
Referee: Mike Dean (Wirral).

West Ham (0) ....1 Middlesbrough (1) 1
Ilunga 83   Downing 22
Att: 33,658

West Ham: Green, Neill, Collins, Upson, Ilunga, Collison, Parker, Noble (Nsereko 74), Boa Morte (Sears 49), Di Michele, Cole (Tristan 33). Subs (not used): Lastuvka, Lopez, Kovac, Spector. Booked: Di Michele, Noble.
Middlesbrough: Jones, Hoyte, Huth, Wheater, Pogatetz, Johnson, O'Neil, Digard, Arca (Walker 77), Downing, Alves (Sanli 74). Subs (not used): Turnbull, Emnes, Bates, McMahon, Bennett. Booked: O'Neil.
Referee: Peter Walton (Northamptonshire).

15/02/2009

Derby (0) ....1 Manchester Utd (2) 4
Addison 56   Nani 29
Att: 32,103   Gibson 44
                                            Ronaldo 48
                                            Welbeck 81
Derby: Bywater, Connolly, Addison, Albrechtsen, Stewart, Barazite (Sterjovski 63), Green, Savage (Pearson 82), Teale, Commons, Hulse (Porter 68). Subs (not used): Carroll, Nyatanga, Davies, Todd. Booked: Connolly.
Manchester Utd: Foster, Rafael, Ferdinand, Evans, Evra (O'Shea 55), Park (Welbeck 55), Fletcher, Gibson, Nani, Giggs, Ronaldo (Possebon 72). Subs (not used): Kuszczak, Vidic, Scholes, Tevez.
Referee: Alan Wiley (Staffordshire).

Everton (2)..................3 Aston Villa (1) 1
Rodwell 4   Milner 8 pen
Arteta 24 pen
Cahill 76
Att: 32,979
Everton: Howard, Hibbert, Jagielka, Lescott, Baines, Gosling, Neville, Arteta (Castillo 90), Rodwell, Cahill, Anichebe (Yobo 88). Subs (not used): Nash, Van der Meyde, Jacobsen, Baxter, Wallace. Booked: Cahill, Hibbert, Rodwell.
Aston Villa: Friedel, Gardner, Knight, Davies, L Young, Milner, Sidwell (Delfouneso 83), Petrov, A Young, Agbonlahor, Carew. Subs (not used): Guzan, Harewood, Salifou, Shorey, Albrighton, Lowry. Booked: Milner, Petrov, Sidwell.
Referee: Martin Atkinson (W Yorkshire).

08/03/2009

Arsenal (1) ....3 Burnley (0) 0
Vela 25   Att: 57,454
Eduardo 51
Eboue 84
Arsenal: Fabianski, Sagna, Djourou, Gallas, Gibbs, Eduardo (Walcott 71), Song, Diaby (Ramsey 71), Vela (Van Persie 60), Eboue, Arshavin. Subs (not used): Almunia, Clichy, Bendtner, Bischoff.
Burnley: Jensen, Alexander, Caldwell, Carlisle, Kalvenes, McDonald (MacDonald 75), McCann, Gudjonsson (Thompson 58), Eagles (Elliott 53), Paterson, Blake. Subs (not used): Penny, Mahon, Rodriguez, Jordan. Booked: McDonald.
Referee: Chris Foy (Merseyside).

REPLAYS

24/02/2009

Coventry (0) ....1 Blackburn (0) 0
Best 59   Att: 22,793
Coventry: Westwood, Wright, Ward, Turner, Fox, Henderson, Gunnarsson, Doyle, Eastwood (Simpson 87), Best, Morrison. Subs (not used): Marshall, Hall, Beuzelin, Osbourne, Thornton, Cain. Booked: Gunnarsson, Ward, Westwood.
Blackburn: Brown, Simpson, Samba, Khizanishvili (Givet 81), Olsson, Villanueva (Santa Cruz 68), Mokoena, Tugay, Treacy (Warnock 68), McCarthy, Roberts. Subs (not used): Robinson, Nelsen, Pedersen, Doran. Booked: Brown.
Referee: Mike Riley (Yorkshire).

Fulham (0) ....2 Swansea (0) 1
Dempsey 77   Scotland 47
Zamora 81   Att: 12,316
Fulham: Schwarzer, Pantsil, Hughes, Hangeland, Konchesky, Davies, Dacourt (Murphy 59), Etuhu, Dempsey (Kamara 90), Nevland (Gera 60), Zamora. Subs (not used): Zuberbuhler, Milsom, Kallio, Baird. Booked: Etuhu.
Swansea: De Vries, Rangel, Williams (Bessone 90), Serran, Tate, Gower (Tudur-Jones 55), Britton, Gomez, Dyer, Scotland, Bauza (Butler 72). Subs (not used): Cornell, O'Leary, Orlandi, Collins. Booked: Bauza.
Referee: Mark Halsey (Lancashire).

25/02/2009

Middlesbrough (2) ......2 West Ham (0) 0
Downing 5   Att: 15,602
Sanli 20
Middlesbrough: Jones, Hoyte, Wheater, Huth, Pogatetz, O'Neil, Bates, Arca (Walker 88), Downing, Sanli (Johnson 81), Aliadière (Emnes 67). Subs (not used): Turnbull, Taylor, Alves, McMahon. Booked: O'Neil.
West Ham: Green, Neill, Tomkins, Upson, Ilunga, Behrami, Parker, Noble (Collison 56), Kovac (Tristan 69), Cole, Sears (Di Michele 57). Subs (not used): Lastuvka, Lopez, Nsereko, Spector. Booked: Behrami.
Referee: Steve Bennett (Kent).

26/02/2009

Hull (1)........................2 Sheffield Utd (1) 1
Naughton 24 og   Sharp 32
Halmosi 56   Att: 17,239
Hull: Myhill, Doyle, Turner, Zayatte, Ricketts, Mendy, France, Marney, Halmosi, Barmby (Garcia 73), Folan (Manucho 65). Subs (not used): Warner, Geovanni, Cousin, Featherstone, Gardner. Booked: Marney.
Sheffield Utd: Kenny, Naughton, Morgan, Walker, Naysmith (Jihai 88), Cotterill, Howard, S Quinn, Hendrie (Tahar 90), Halford, Sharp. Subs (not used): Bennett, K Quinn, Starosta. Booked: Naughton, Sharp.
Referee: Peter Walton (Northamptonshire).

2008/2009 STATISTICS

Total goals scored	416
Total penalties scored	27
Total red cards	19
Total yellow cards	422
Number of penalty shoot-outs	2

THE TEAM WITH THE MOST...

Shots on target	
Chelsea 63	
Shots off target	
Chelsea 59	
Shots per goal	
Bournemouth 43	
Corners	
Chelsea 69	
Fouls	
Everton 103	
Offsides	
Kettering 27	
Woodwork strikes	
Doncaster 5	
Penalties conceded	
Cheltenham 3	
Yellow cards	
Hull, Everton 15	
Red cards	
Bournemouth 2	

LEADING GOALSCORERS

Player	Team	Goals
C Westcarr	(Kettering)	4
R van Persie	(Arsenal)	4
N Anelka	(Chelsea)	4
G Hooper	(Scunthorpe)	4
M Fryatt	(Leicester)	4
P Ifill	(Crystal P)	3
Eduardo	(Arsenal)	3
R Pavlyuchenko	(Tottenham)	3
C Mackail-Smith	(Peterborough)	3
M Ballack	(Chelsea)	3
J Milner	(Aston Villa)	3
L Dodds	(Port Vale)	3
F Lampard	(Chelsea)	3
G Halford	(Sheff Utd)	3
A Barcham	(Gillingham)	3
D Drogba	(Chelsea)	3
J Beckford	(Leeds)	3
S Miller	(Crewe)	3

Tim Howard leads the celebrations after his Everton side saw off Manchester United in the semi-finals at Wembley following a dramatic penalty shoot-out

QUARTER-FINALS

07/03/2009

Coventry (0) .... 0 **Chelsea (1)** 2
Att: 31,407 — Drogba 15, Alex 72
Coventry: Westwood, Wright, Dann, Turner, Hall, Henderson, Gunnarsson, Doyle (Beuzelin 59), Eastwood, Best, Morrison. Subs (not used): Marshall, Ward, Osbourne, McPake, Simpson, Thornton. Booked: Beuzelin.
Chelsea: Cech, Bosingwa, Terry, Alex, Cole, Lampard, Mikel (Essien 65), Ballack, Malouda, Drogba (Di Santo 80), Kalou (Quaresma 46). Subs (not used): Hilario, Carvalho, Belletti, Mancienne.
Referee: Steve Bennett (Kent).

Fulham (0) .... 0 **Manchester Utd (2)** 4
Att: 24,662 — Tevez 20, 35, Rooney 50, Park 81
Fulham: Schwarzer, Pantsil, Hangeland, Hughes, Konchesky, Davies, Etuhu, Murphy (Dacourt 57), Dempsey, Zamora (Gera 67), Johnson (Kamara 60). Subs (not used): Zuberbuhler, Nevland, Stoor, Kallio. Booked: Dacourt, Pantsil.
Manchester Utd: Van der Sar, O'Shea (Eckersley 52), Ferdinand (Evans 46), Vidic, Evra, Fletcher, Carrick, Anderson, Park, Rooney (Welbeck 64), Tevez. Subs (not used): Foster, Berbatov, Giggs, Scholes.
Referee: Mike Dean (Wirral).

08/03/2009

Everton (0) .... 2 **Middlesbrough (1)** 1
Fellaini 50, Saha 56 — Wheater 44; Att: 37,856
Everton: Howard, Neville, Yobo, Jagielka, Lescott, Pienaar (Gosling 89), Rodwell (Saha 46), Osman, Baines, Fellaini, Cahill. Subs (not used): Nash, Van der Meyde, Castillo, Jacobsen, Wallace.
Middlesbrough: Jones, Hoyte, Huth, Wheater, Pogatetz, O'Neil, Arca, Bates (Johnson 72), Downing, Sanli, Aliadière (Emnes 68). Subs (not used): Turnbull, Taylor, McMahon, Franks, Walker.
Referee: Mark Halsey (Lancashire).

17/03/2009

Arsenal (0) .... 2 **Hull (1)** 1
Van Persie 74, Gallas 84 — Barmby 13; Att: 55,641
Arsenal: Fabianski, Sagna, Gallas, Djourou, Gibbs, Walcott (Eboue 82), Song (Bendtner 64), Diaby, Vela (Nasri 64), Van Persie, Arshavin. Subs (not used): Mannone, Toure, Denilson, Silvestre. Booked: Gallas, Nasri.
Hull: Myhill, Ricketts, Gardner, Zayatte, Dawson, Ashbee (Hughes 46), Barmby (France 76), Geovanni, Fagan, Manucho, Halmosi (Mendy 67). Subs (not used): Duke, Garcia, Folan, Featherstone. Booked: Dawson, France, Halmosi, Manucho, Myhill.
Referee: Mike Riley (Yorkshire).

SEMI-FINALS

18/04/2009

Arsenal (1) .... 1 **Chelsea (1)** 2
Walcott 18 — Malouda 33, Drogba 84
Att: 88,103
Arsenal: Fabianski, Eboue, Toure, Silvestre, Gibbs, Walcott, Fabregas, Diaby, Denilson (Nasri 86), Van Persie (Arshavin 75), Adebayor (Bendtner 83). Subs (not used): Mannone, Vela, Ramsey, Song. Booked: Denilson, Toure.
Chelsea: Cech, Ivanovic, Alex, Terry, Cole, Ballack, Lampard, Essien, Malouda, Anelka (Kalou 82), Drogba. Subs (not used): Hilario, Carvalho, Di Santo, Mikel, Belletti, Mancienne. Booked: Ballack, Drogba, Ivanovic.
Referee: Martin Atkinson (W Yorkshire).

19/04/2009

Manchester Utd (0) .... 0 **Everton (0)** 0
Att: 88,141
AET: Score after 90 mins 0–0
Everton win 4–2 on penalties
Manchester Utd: Foster, Rafael, Ferdinand, Vidic, Fabio (Evra 63), Welbeck, Gibson, Anderson, Park (Scholes 67), Tevez, Macheda (Berbatov 91). Subs (not used): Kuszczak, Neville, Nani, Evans. Booked: Rafael, Scholes, Tevez.
Everton: Howard, Hibbert, Jagielka, Lescott, Baines, Osman, Neville, Fellaini (Vaughan 102), Pienaar, Cahill, Saha (Rodwell 70). Subs (not used): Nash, Yobo, Castillo, Jacobsen, Gosling. Booked: Cahill, Fellaini.
Referee: Mike Riley (Yorkshire).

FINAL

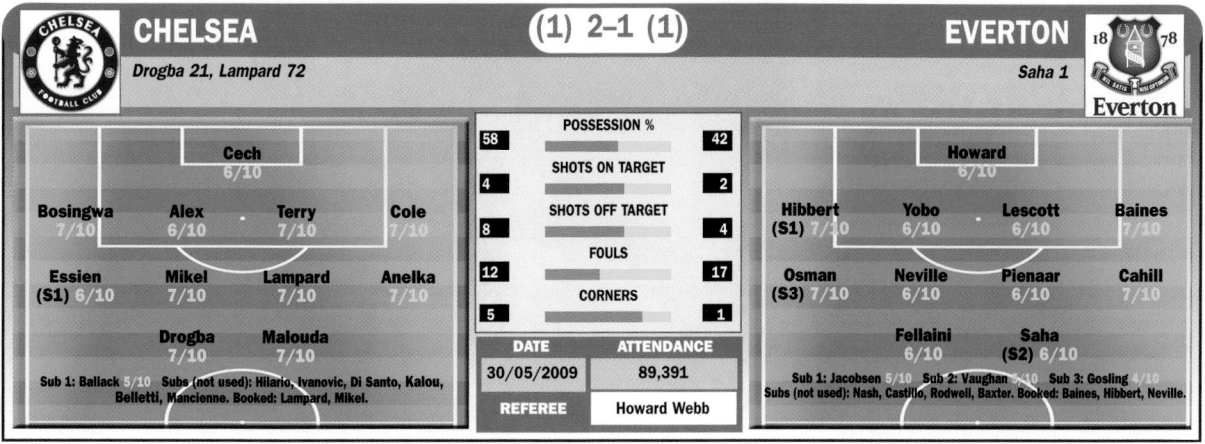

CHELSEA (1) 2–1 (1) **EVERTON**

Drogba 21, Lampard 72 — Saha 1

CHELSEA
Cech 6/10
Bosingwa 7/10 — Alex 6/10 — Terry 7/10 — Cole 7/10
Essien (S1) 6/10 — Mikel 7/10 — Lampard 7/10 — Anelka 7/10
Drogba 7/10 — Malouda 7/10

Sub 1: Ballack 5/10 Subs (not used): Hilario, Ivanovic, Di Santo, Kalou, Belletti, Mancienne. Booked: Lampard, Mikel.

EVERTON
Howard 6/10
Hibbert (S1) 7/10 — Yobo 6/10 — Lescott 6/10 — Baines 7/10
Osman (S3) 7/10 — Neville 6/10 — Pienaar 6/10 — Cahill 7/10
Fellaini 6/10 — Saha (S2) 6/10

Sub 1: Jacobsen 6/10 Sub 2: Vaughan 5/10 Sub 3: Gosling 4/10
Subs (not used): Nash, Castillo, Rodwell, Baxter. Booked: Baines, Hibbert, Neville.

	POSSESSION %	
58		42
	SHOTS ON TARGET	
4		2
	SHOTS OFF TARGET	
8		4
	FOULS	
12		17
	CORNERS	
5		1

DATE	ATTENDANCE
30/05/2009	89,391

REFEREE	
	Howard Webb

Continued from page 489

start of the FA Cup proper. For Leeds, winners in 1972 and UEFA Champions League semi-finalists as recently as 2001, it was a reminder of how far their fortunes have plummeted.

However, at AFC Wimbledon the complete opposite is true. Their existence may have been due to controversy and misery, but only smiles surround the club now. An appearance at this stage of the competition for the first time since they were formed may have been brief as they were beaten 4–1 at Kingsmeadow by Wycombe, but those famous blue and yellow shirts that triumphed over Liverpool in 1988 are on an upward trend. They will be back.

Leeds survived that round, but not the next. Don't tell the people of dear old Histon that this year's FA Cup was shock-free, a 1–0 win at Bridge Road taking the Conference outfit through to join the high and mighty, along with seven other non-League outfits. It should have been eight others, given that Droylsden defeated Chesterfield at Butchers Arms. Their joy lasted just eight days before they were kicked out by an FA disciplinary committee after being found to have fielded an ineligible player.

There was honour in third-round defeat for Barrow and Blyth, who went down narrowly to Middlesbrough and Blackburn respectively. Of those outside the top four

tiers, the top prize went to Torquay as they eliminated Blackpool.

The big stories were at Stamford Bridge and Eastlands. Chelsea, starting to falter badly under manager Luiz Felipe Scolari, failed to account for Southend at the first attempt. The Blues made amends in the replay at Roots Hall, but owner Roman Abramovich was not impressed and the Brazilian's reign came to an end soon afterwards.

Manchester City's even richer owners kept their nerve after Mark Hughes' side were hammered by Nottingham Forest. There were 10 full internationals in the Blues side booed off after a 3–0 home defeat that set up a mouthwatering fourth-round tie for the east midlands outfit.

With the cinematic version of The Damned United getting close to release, the Clough family name was being spoken about again. Nigel's appointment as Derby manager to replace Billy Davies, who had been installed at Forest, just created more of a talking point. That the two east midlands rivals, who bear the Clough connection like a badge of honour, should be paired together in the last 32 was a fantastic

coincidence. Clough and Derby came through after a City Ground replay.

On the same night, Liverpool's dreams came crashing down as teenager Dan Gosling struck for Everton in extra-time at Goodison Park. Everton then added Aston Villa to their list of scalps in round five and Middlesbrough at the quarter-final stage.

When semi-final weekend dawned, three of the big four were represented. Chelsea's power was too much for an Arsenal side that started well but eventually faded, with Didier Drogba brilliantly breaking clear to score the winner.

Twenty-four hours later, a very inexperienced Manchester United side had the better of a goalless 120 minutes against Everton, but then got stuck as the Toffees won in a penalty shoot-out to reach their first FA Cup final for 14 years.

The fact that Chelsea eventually triumphed was a fitting end to Hiddink's brief spell in charge, although it was tough on Everton's Dave Moyes (left). Hiddink had been brought in to steady the club and was able to sign off with some silverware to appease fans whose club were second best in both the Barclays Premier League and Champions League.

QUICK SEARCH

Trace the progress of all the clubs from the first round of the competition Reached 2008/09

BARCLAYS PREMIER LEAGUE

Arsenal	Quarter-final
Aston Villa	Round 3
Blackburn	Quarter-final
Bolton	Round 2
Chelsea	Round 4
Everton	Round 3
Fulham	Round 3
Hull	Round 2
Liverpool	Round 4
Manchester City	Round 2
Manchester Utd	Final
Middlesbrough	Round 3
Newcastle	Round 3
Portsmouth	Round 3
Stoke	Quarter-final
Sunderland	Round 4
Tottenham	Final
West Brom	Round 2
West Ham	Round 3
Wigan	Round 4

Coca-Cola CHAMPIONSHIP

Barnsley	Round 1
Birmingham	Round 2
Blackpool	Round 1
Bristol City	Round 2
Burnley	Semi-final
Cardiff	Round 3
Charlton	Round 1
Coventry	Round 2
Crystal Palace	Round 2
Derby	Semi-final
Doncaster	Round 1
Ipswich	Round 3
Norwich	Round 1
Nottm Forest	Round 2
Plymouth	Round 1
Preston	Round 2
QPR	Round 4
Reading	Round 3
Sheff Utd	Round 3
Sheff Wed	Round 1
Southampton	Round 3
Swansea	Round 4
Watford	Quarter-final
Wolverhampton	Round 2

Ben Foster holds the Carling Cup trophy, above, after becoming Manchester United's hero in the Wembley final. The goalkeeper saved from Jamie O'Hara, below, in the penalty shoot-out to seal United's win

IF EVER a football match demonstrated the attention to detail that goes into winning sport's top prizes it was the 2009 Carling Cup final.

With Manchester United and Tottenham deadlocked at 0–0 after extra-time, players swigged from water bottles, physios massaged tired limbs and the managers, Sir Alex Ferguson and Harry Redknapp, busied themselves with informing the officials who would take the penalty kicks.

Yet, unseen and unremarked, away on the touchline near the United dugout, the final was effectively being won in a two-man huddle which dragged football firmly into the age of new technology. Ben Foster, playing instead of United's regular goalkeeper Edwin van der Sar, was studying some video footage on an iPod supplied by goalkeeping coach Eric Steele. It featured the penalty-taking technique of Tottenham's players.

When Jamie O'Hara stepped up to take Tottenham's first spot-kick, Foster knew exactly which way and height to dive. O'Hara's shot, as the iPod footage indicated it might, went low to Foster's left and the goalkeeper flung himself full length to palm the ball away.

'It is a new innovation for us,' Foster explained. 'Eric brought it when he came to the club. We have done a lot of research into the way each player is going to put their penalty. I have never seen anything like it, it is a fantastic tool.'

United, of course, still had to slot home their own spot-kicks, but they did so with consummate composure – Ryan Giggs, Carlos Tevez, Cristiano Ronaldo and Anderson all scoring convincingly while Tottenham's David Bentley contrived to miss the target altogether.

Predictably, after such a cruel and dramatic finale, the tears flowed for Bentley and O'Hara. For United, however, the celebrations began: the champagne flowed, Ferguson wrapped his arms around yet another major trophy in his glittering career and Foster was dubbed the 'iPod hero'.

FROM ABOVE: Carlos Vela impressed in Arsenal's thrashing of Sheffield United, while Manchester United's Carlos Tevez and Blackburn's Benni McCarthy leave the field after United's 5–3 win in the quarter-finals

That is how the 2009 final will be remembered by the 88,217 fans inside Wembley stadium and the millions who tuned in on television. It has to be said that much of the football that went before was forgettable, perhaps because Spurs were missing the cup-tied Robbie Keane and Jermain Defoe while United were without Wayne Rooney, due to a virus, and Ferguson had stuck with youngsters such as Danny Welbeck, Darron Gibson and Jonny Evans who had given such commendable service throughout the competition.

There were some memorable moments: Foster's second-half save from the impressive Aaron Lennon and Ronaldo's dribble and shot that came back off the post two minutes into stoppage time in normal time were the two prime examples. Foster also made one fine stop with his legs from Darren Bent in extra-time.

There was controversy too, mainly in the decision by referee Chris Foy to book Ronaldo for diving in the penalty area when television replays appeared to confirm he had been fouled by Tottenham defender Ledley King.

In the main, however, it was a final that never quite lived up to the attacking traditions of two clubs with such an exciting heritage in cup football. The same

 It was a final that never quite lived up to the attacking traditions of two clubs with such an exciting heritage

QUICK SEARCH

Trace the progress of all the clubs from the first round of the competition

Coca-Cola LEAGUE 1	Reached 2008/09
Brighton	Round 3
Bristol Rovers	Round 1
Carlisle	Round 2
Cheltenham	Round 2
Colchester	Round 2
Crewe	Round 3
Hartlepool	Round 3
Hereford	Round 1
Huddersfield	Round 2
Leeds	Round 4
Leicester	Round 2
Leyton Orient	Round 1
Millwall	Round 1
MK Dons	Round 2
Northampton	Round 3
Oldham	Round 2
Peterborough	Round 1
Scunthorpe	Round 1
Southend	Round 1
Stockport	Round 1
Swindon	Round 1
Tranmere	Round 1
Walsall	Round 1
Yeovil	Round 2

Coca-Cola LEAGUE 2	
Accrington Stanley	Round 1
Aldershot	Round 1
Barnet	Round 1
Bournemouth	Round 1
Bradford	Round 1
Brentford	Round 1
Bury	Round 1
Chester	Round 1
Chesterfield	Round 1
Dag & Red	Round 1
Darlington	Round 2
Exeter	Round 1
Gillingham	Round 1
Grimsby	Round 2
Lincoln City	Round 1
Luton	Round 2
Macclesfield	Round 2
Morecambe	Round 1
Notts County	Round 2
Port Vale	Round 1
Rochdale	Round 1
Rotherham	Round 4
Shrewsbury	Round 1
Wycombe	Round 1

FROM TOP: Burnley's Kevin McDonald scores in the defeat of Arsenal; the Clarets celebrate beating Chelsea (above); Michael Ball's missed penalty saw Manchester City lose to Brighton; Kris Commons gives Derby a semi-final lead against Manchester United

FROM ABOVE: Tottenham's Aaron Lennon beats Darron Gibson at Wembley, while David Bentley attempts to find a way past Patrice Evra

could not be said of the rest of the competition, which marked the 49th season of the Football League Cup. Football's enduring fixture congestion means that these days the competition, especially in the early rounds, has become a stage for the top clubs to blood some of their future stars while providing an opportunity for the game's smaller teams to demonstrate the talent and desire outside the elite Barclays Premier League.

At the Emirates Stadium in September, Arsène Wenger fielded virtually a youth team against Sheffield United and watched on as his youngsters won 6–0. The scoreline featured a hat-trick from Mexican Carlos Vela and a goal from a 16-year-old English midfielder Jack Wilshere, of whom we will no doubt hear plenty in the future. If ever there was an advertisement for the Carling Cup's ability to capture the imagination, it came that night.

There were other memorable nights too, not least at Stamford Bridge as Burnley, having already disposed of Fulham, knocked out Chelsea 5–4 on penalties in a match that contained a wonderful solo goal from Didier Drogba, an equaliser from Ade

"Clough watched on from the stands as Commons scored"

Akinbiyi and a decisive missed penalty from John Obi Mikel. Chelsea's boss at the time, Luiz Felipe Scolari, fielded an experimental team, but it still included Drogba, Deco and Florent Malouda with Frank Lampard and John Terry on the bench.

Burnley's adventure continued as they knocked out Arsenal 2–0 before finally losing to Tottenham in the semi-final, but only after threatening the comeback of the season following a 4–1 defeat in the first leg at White Hart Lane. They led 3–0 in the return leg and looked to be going through until Roman Pavlyuchenko and Jermain Defoe scored inside the last three minutes of extra-time to deny the Clarets a famous final appearance.

Other commendable performances saw wins for Hartlepool and Northampton in the second round against West Brom and Bolton respectively, and for the romantic, how about Brighton's victory against Manchester City, the richest club in the world according to some, 5–3 on penalties?

In the third round, Watford's 1–0 win against West Ham and QPR's 1–0 defeat of Aston Villa at Villa Park continued the rout of the Barclays Premier League sides. Then, of course, there was Derby, who beat Stoke in the quarter-finals and provided the competition's joint leading scorer in Nathan Ellington. The Rams then beat Manchester United 1–0 in the first leg of their semi-final just hours after new manager Nigel Clough had been unveiled to the press. Clough watched from the stands as Kris Commons scored with a ferocious shot, yet they could not repeat the feat at Old Trafford as United turned on the style to win 4–2.

That brings us back to the final, which Ferguson described as a 'bonus' amid a hectic quest for football's major trophies at home and in Europe.

'We would have lost without Ben,' said Ferguson afterwards. 'He made some terrific saves.' And so the 'iPod hero' went down in history, while the Carling Cup took its place in the Old Trafford trophy cabinet.

2008/09 STATISTICS

Total goals scored	290
Total penalties scored	16
Total red cards	15
Total yellow cards	205
Number of penalty shoot-outs	8

THE TEAM WITH THE MOST...

Shots on target	Manchester Utd 59
Shots off target	Manchester Utd 54
Shots per goal	West Brom 21
Corners	Manchester Utd 48
Fouls	Burnley, Derby 91
Offsides	Burnley 26
Woodwork strikes	Derby 5
Penalties conceded	Hull, Barnsley, Stoke 2
Yellow cards	Derby 14
Red cards	Macclesfield 2

LEADING GOALSCORERS

Player	Team	Goals
N Ellington	(Derby)	6
R Pavlyuchenko	(Tottenham)	6
C Tevez	(Man Utd)	6
M Paterson	(Burnley)	5
J Beckford	(Leeds)	4
E Villa	(Derby)	4
J Henry	(Reading)	4
C Alberto Vela	(Arsenal)	4
L Nani	(Man Utd)	3
E Jorge Ledesma	(QPR)	3
M Derbyshire	(Blackburn)	3
H Camara	(Wigan)	3
J Porter	(Hartlepool)	3
R Earnshaw	(Nottm Forest)	3
B McCarthy	(Blackburn)	2
C Iwelumo	(Wolves)	2
C Ronaldo	(Man Utd)	2
J Rodriguez	(Burnley)	2

FIRST ROUND

12/08/08

Bournemouth (1) ....1 Cardiff (2) 2
Kuffour 28 — Parry 7, 12
Att: 3,399

Brighton (4) ....4 Barnet (0) 0
Virgo 2, 35 — Att: 2,571
Forster 28
Richards 43

Bristol City (0) ....2 Peterborough (1) 1
Carey 53 — Boyd 17
Brooker 85 — Att: 5,684

Bury (0) ....0 Burnley (1) 2
Att: 4,276 — Paterson 40, 90

Charlton (0) ....0 Yeovil (1) 1
Att: 6,239 — Warne 28

Chester (1) ....2 Leeds (5) 5
Lowe 15, 75 pen — Beckford 3, 25, 35
Att: 3,644 — Snodgrass 10
— Robinson 31

Crewe (2) ....2 Barnsley (0) 0
O'Connor 14 pen — Att: 2,492
Elding 36 pen

Crystal Palace (1)........2 Hereford (1) 1
Carle 45 — Ashikodi 41
Oster 49 — Att: 3,094

Dag & Red (0) ....1 Reading (1) 2
Taiwo 68 — Henry 26
Att: 2,360 — Hunt 89

Derby (0) ....3 Lincoln City (0)...........1
Ellington 83, 100, 105 — Wright 48
Att: 10,091
AET: Score after 90 mins 1–1

Exeter (0) ....1 Southampton (1).........3
Moxey 85 — Holmes 29
Att: 6,471 — McGoldrick 77, 90 pen

Gillingham (0)..............0 Colchester (1) 1
Att: 2,566 — Heath 11

Grimsby (1) ....2 Tranmere (0) 0
Hunt 20 — Att: 1,858
Chorley 54 og

Hartlepool (0).............3 Scunthorpe (0) 0
Porter 51 — Att: 2,076
Foley 58
Brown 76

Huddersfield (0) ....4 Bradford (0) 0
Worthington 48 — Att: 8,932
Roberts 62, 80, Williams 75

Ipswich (3) ....4 Leyton Orient (0) 1
Haynes 20, 44 — Boyd 49
Miller 22 — Att: 1,477
Lee 48

Leicester (1) ....1 Stockport (0) 0
Howard 36 — Att: 7,386

Luton (1) ....2 Plymouth (0) 0
Jarvis 15 — Att: 2,682
Plummer 77

Macclesfield (1) ....2 Blackpool (0) 0
Brisley 25 — Att: 1,631
Gritton 59

Millwall (0) ....0 Northampton (1)..........1
Att: 3,525 — Crowe 16

MK Dons (1) ....1 Norwich (0) 0
Baldock 34 — Att: 6,261

Notts County (0) ....1 Doncaster (0) 0
Weston 106 — Att: 3,272
AET: Score after 90 mins 0–0

Preston (1) ....2 Chesterfield (0) 0
Mellor 37, 90 — Att: 5,150

Rochdale (0) ....0 Oldham (0) 0
Att: 5,786
AET: Score after 90 mins 0-0
Oldham win 4–1 on penalties

Sheffield Wed (1) ....2 Rotherham (1) 2
Esajas 14, 117 — Rhodes 15
Att: 16,298 — Reid 119
AET: Score after 90 mins 1–1
Rotherham win 5–3 on penalties

Shrewsbury (0) ....0 Carlisle (1) 1
Att: 3,337 — Murphy 41

Southend (0) ....0 Cheltenham (0)...........1
Att: 2,998 — Gill 115
AET: Score after 90 mins 0–0

Swansea (1) ....2 Brentford (0) 0
MacDonald 31, 69 — Att: 5,366

Swindon (2) ....2 QPR (1) 3
Cox 34 — Balanta 32
Paynter 41 — Blackstock 46
Att: 7,230 — Delaney 54

Walsall (1) ....1 Darlington (1) 2
Ricketts 11 — Kennedy 31
Att: 2,702 — Clarke 67

Watford (0) ....1 Bristol Rovers (0) 0
Hoskins 88 — Att: 5,574

Wolverhampton (0) .....3 Accrington Stanley (1) 2
Iwelumo 73, 102 — Mullin 40
Davies 106 — Craney 104
Att: 9,424
AET: Score after 90 mins 1–1

13/08/08

Coventry (1) ....3 Aldershot (1) 1
Morrison 31 — Morgan 37
Simpson 58, 65 — Att: 9,293

Nottm Forest (1) ....4 Morecambe (0)...........0
Cohen 14 — Att: 4,030
Earnshaw 62, 89
Newbold 81

Sheffield Utd (1) ....3 Port Vale (0) 1
Hendrie 41 — Rodgers 53
Quinn 71 — Att: 7,694
Webber 90 pen

Wycombe (0) ....0 Birmingham (1)...........4
Att: 2,735 — Nafti 14
— Larsson 64
— Jerome 73
— Owusu-Abeyie 86

SECOND ROUND

26/08/08

Bolton (0)..................1 Northampton (2).........2
Nolan 82 — Akinfenwa 22 pen, 28
Att: 7,136
Bolton: Jaaskelainen, Steinsson, Cahill, Shittu, Samuel (Nolan 64), McCann (O'Brien 39), Muamba, O'Brien, Riga (Davies 64), Helguson, Gardner. **Subs not used:** Al Habsi, Hunt, Dzemaili, Fojut. **Dismissed:** Cahill
Northampton: Bunn, Little, Hughes, Doig, Crowe, Gilligan (Dolman 71), Jackman, Osman, Coke (Taylor 90), Holt, Akinfenwa (Henderson 75). **Subs not used:** Dunn, Davis, Dyer, Guttridge.
Referee: Graham Laws (Tyne & Wear).

Burnley (1) ....3 Oldham (0) 0
McCann 12
Paterson 63,79 — Att: 5,528
Burnley: Jensen, Alexander, Duff (Blake 58), Caldwell, Carlisle, Kalvenes, Elliott, McDonald (Gudjonsson 57), McCann (Mahon 80), Eagles, Paterson. **Subs not used:** Penny, Akinbiyi, Jordan, Anderson. **Booked:** Elliott
Oldham: Fleming, Eardley, Stam, Hazell, Lomax, Taylor, Allott, Maher (Lee 67), Whitaker, O'Grady (Hughes 67), Smalley (Alessandra 68). **Subs not used:** Crossley, Kalala, Stephens, Liddell. **Booked:** Hazell
Referee: Andy Penn (W Midlands).

SECOND ROUND

Cardiff (1) ....2 Milton Keynes Dons (0)1
McCormack 45 (pen) O'Hanlon 75
Whittingham 58 Att: 6,334
Cardiff: Heaton, Blake (Parry 20), Johnson, Purse, Capaldi (Comminges 10), Whittingham, McPhail, Scimeca (Morris 45), Ledley, Johnson, McCormack. **Subs not used:** Enckelman, Bothroyd, Dennehy, Thompson.
Milton Keynes Dons: Gueret, Stirling (O'Hanlon 65), Diallo, Lewington (King 65), Cummings, Johnson, Mitchell, Navarro, Chicksen, Baldock, Dobson. **Subs not used:** Abbey, Wright, Regan, Leven, Belson. **Booked:** Stirling
Referee: Rob Shoebridge (Derbyshire).

Cheltenham (0)...........2 Stoke (0) 3
Vincent 57, Russell 90 Whelan 51, Cresswell 54
Att: 3,600 Parkin 78
Cheltenham: Higgs, J Gill, Townsend, Duff (Gallinagh 61), Wright, Armstrong, Lindegaard, B Gill (Caines 79), Russell, Vincent (Ledgister 88), Connor. **Subs not used:** Brown, Ridley, Watkins, Emery. **Booked:** Armstrong
Stoke: Simonsen, Wilkinson (Shotton 90), Buxton, Shawcross, Dickinson (Phillips 79), Cresswell, Diao (Matteo 75), Whelan, Pugh, Parkin, Pericard. **Subs not used:** De Laet, Phillips, Wedderburn. **Booked:** Pericard
Referee: Darren Deadman (Cambridgeshire).

Coventry (1)..............2 Newcastle (2)............3
Morrison 45, Dann 90 Dann 21 (og), Milner 38
Att: 19,249 Owen 97
AET: Score after 90 mins 2–2
Coventry: Marshall, Hall, Ward, Dann, Fox, Beuzelin (Doyle 63), Mifsud, Gunnarsson, Tabb (Simpson 88), McKenzie (Gray 74), Morrison. **Subs not used:** Ireland, Turner, Thornton, Clarke. **Booked:** Hall, Fox
Newcastle: Given, Beye, Coloccini, Bassong, Jose Enrique, Milner, Geremi (Owen 75), Butt, Guthrie, N'Zogbia, Gutierrez. **Subs not used:** Harper, Taylor, Edgar, Tozer, Donaldson, Ranger.
Referee: Tony Bates (Staffordshire).

Crewe (1)...................2 Bristol City (0) 1
Elding 24, Moore 76 Wilson 79; Att: 3,227
Crewe: Collis, Woodards, O'Donnell, Baudet, Bailey, Moore, O'Connor, Rix (Schumacher 86), Grant (Donaldson 87), Pope, Elding (Carrington 78). **Subs not used:** Legzdins, Miller, McManus, Westwood.
Bristol City: Weale, Orr, Fontaine, Carey, McAllister (Webster 21), Wilson, Skuse (Trundle 78), Johnson, McIndoe, Maynard, Adebola (Brooker 59). **Subs not used:** Basso, Noble, Sproule, Williams.
Referee: Andy Hall (W Midlands).

Hartlepool (0).............3 West Brom (0) 1
Porter 61 Koren 87
Foley 102, Barker 105 Att: 3,387
AET: Score after 90 mins 1–1
Hartlepool: Lee-Barrett, Sweeney, Nelson, Collins, Humphreys, Jones, McCunnie, Liddle, Monkhouse (Robson 57), Brown (Foley 85), Porter (Barker 85). **Subs not used:** Budtz, Power, Mackay, Rowell.
West Brom: Kiely, Hoefkens, Barnett, Meite, Cech, Koren (Pele 94), Greening, Borja Valero, Brunt (MacDonald 46), Bednar (Beattie 64), Moore. **Subs not used:** Dorrans, Carson, Slusarski, Martis. **Booked:** Bednar, MacDonald
Referee: Mark Haywood (W Yorkshire).

Ipswich (1)................2 Colchester (0) 1
Counago 28, Lisbie 56 Gillespie 87; Att: 17,084
Ipswich: Wright, Casement, McAuley, Naylor, Thatcher, Walters, Campo (Miller 76), Trotter, Quinn, Counago, Lisbie (Haynes 73). **Subs not used:** Supple, Lee, Balkestein, Smith, Rhodes. **Booked:** Quinn, Casement
Colchester: Gerken, Reid, Coyne, Heath, Ifil, Yeates, Jackson, Hammond (Izzet 73), Wordsworth (Perkins 62), Vernon, Platt (Gillespie 62). **Subs not used:** Cousins, Baldwin, Wasiu, Elito. **Booked:** Coyne
Referee: Richard Beeby (Northamptonshire).

Leeds (2) ....4 Crystal Palace (0).......0
Douglas 11, Beckford 32
Becchio 52, Showunmi 76 Att: 10,765
Leeds: Lucas, Richardson, Michalik, Telfer, White (Johnson 73), Hughes, Douglas, Delph, Kilkenny, Beckford (Howson 78), Becchio (Showunmi 57). **Subs not used:** Martin, Marques, Robinson, Snodgrass.
Crystal Palace: Flahavan, Ertl, Lawrence, McCarthy, Hill, Soares, Watson (Fletcher 88), Carle (Hills 63), Djilali, Andrew, Moses (Ifill 66). **Subs not used:** Speroni, Thomas, Oster, Griffit.
Referee: Kevin Friend (Leicestershire).

Middlesbrough (3) ......5 Yeovil (1) 1
Mido 11 Tomlin 45
Digard 23, Aliadière 32
Emnes 47, Johnson 66 Att: 15,651
Middlesbrough: Turnbull, Hoyte, Riggott, Pogatetz (Williams 74), Grounds, Aliadière (O'Neil 60), Digard, Shawky (Walker 60), Johnson, Emnes, Mido. **Subs not used:** Steele, Downing, Sanli, Alves.
Yeovil: Wagenaar, Jones, Skiverton, Forbes, Peltier (Alcock 83), Murtagh, Roberts, Way (Bircham 63), Dayton, Tomlin, Warne (McCollin 62). **Subs not used:** Irish, Owusu, Brown, Smith. **Booked:** Bircham
Referee: Scott Mathieson (Cheshire).

Preston (0).................0 Derby (1) 1
Att: 8,037 Green 40
Preston: Lonergan, Hart, Jones, St. Ledger, Hill, Sedgwick (Whaley 68), McKenna, Carter (Chaplow 82), Wallace, Mellor, Hawley. **Subs not used:** Neal, Mawene, Jarrett, Nicholson, Ormerod.
Derby: Carroll, Connolly, Leacock, Albrechtsen, Stewart, Kazmierczak (Mears 77), Addison, Green, Commons, Hulse (Davies 77), Villa. **Subs not used:** Bywater, McEveley, Sterjovski, Pearson, Pereplotkins. **Booked:** Leacock, Addison, Villa
Referee: Jon Moss (W Yorkshire).

QPR (0) ....4 Carlisle (0) 0
Stewart 48, Ledesma 56, 63, 85 Att: 8,021
QPR: Cerny, Ramage, Stewart, Connolly, Delaney (Gorkss 68), Ledesma, Rowlands, Mahon (Bolder 68), Cook, Di Carmine (Balanta 70), Parejo. **Subs not used:** Camp, Alberti, Ephraim, Ainsworth. **Booked:** Delaney
Carlisle: Williams, Raven, Livesey, Murphy, Horwood, Taylor, Bridge-Wilkinson, Thirlwell, Hackney (Smith 72), Bridges (Smith 74), Madine. **Subs not used:** Howarth, Graham, Carlton, Keogh, Campion.
Referee: Keith Hill (Hertfordshire).

Reading (2) ....5 Luton (0) 1
N.Hunt 11, S.Hunt 15, Pearce 54 Charles 80
Karacan 55, Henry 76 Att: 7,498
Reading: Federici, Kelly, Pearce, Duberry (Ingimarsson 21), Golbourne, Henry, Karacan, Harper (Sigurdsson 59), N.Hunt, S.Hunt, Long (Mooney 59). **Subs not used:** Andersen, Kebe, Convey, Rosenior. **Booked:** N.Hunt
Luton: Logan, Gnakpa, Keane, Pilkington, Davis (Jarvis 46), Plummer, Nicholls, Watson, Emanuel, Parkin (Charles 64), Martin (Hall 82). **Subs not used:** Brill, Roper, Asafu-Adjaye, Spillane. **Booked:** Martin
Referee: Dean Whitestone (Northamptonshire).

Rotherham (0) ....0 Wolves (0) 0
Att: 5,404
AET: Score after 90 mins 0–0
Rotherham win 4–3 on penalties
Rotherham: Warrington, Lynch, Sharps, Fenton, Nicholas, Cummins (Mills 116), Harrison, Hudson, Rhodes (Burchill 115), Broughton (Taylor 106), Reid. **Subs not used:** Cann, Tonge, Yates, Green. **Booked:** Harrison, Broughton
Wolves: Ikeme, Foley, Collins, Stearman, Gray (Elliott 79), Kightly, Edwards (Jones 100), Henry, Ward, Ward, Keogh (Iwelumo 46). **Subs not used:** Davies, Jones, Potter, Hennessey.
Referee: Neil Swarbrick (Lancashire).

Southampton (1)..........2 Birmingham (0)...........0
Holmes 17, Lallana 86 Att: 11,331
Southampton: Bialkowski, James, Thomas, Cork, Surman, Gillett (Mills 60), Lallana, Wotton, Schneiderlin (John 56), Holmes, McGoldrick. **Subs not used:** Forecast, Dyer, Lancashire, White, Wright-Phillips.
Birmingham: Doyle, Parnaby, Ridgewell, Kelly, Murphy, Agustien, Carsley, O'Connor (Phillips 46), Owusu-Abeyie, Bent, McSheffrey (Mutch 46). **Subs not used:** Taylor, Taylor, Jaidi, Queudrue, Aydilek. **Booked:** Mutch, Ridgewell
Referee: Grant Hegley (Hertfordshire).

Swansea (0)................2 Hull (1)......................1
Pintado 63, Gomez 105 pen Windass 11; Att: 8,622
AET: Score after 90 mins 1–1
Swansea: De Vries, Painter, Monk, Collins (Rangel 55), Serran, Orlandi, Gomez, Tudur Jones, MacDonald, Allen (Pintado 54), Bauza (Brandy 81). **Subs not used:** O'Leary, Tate, Gower, Lawrence. **Booked:** Bauza
Hull: Duke, Brown, Mendy, Doyle, Cooper (Turner 91), Barmby (Featherstone 72), Hughes, France, Halmosi, Folan, Windass (King 62). **Subs not used:** Atkinson, Garcia, Welsh, Warner. **Booked:** Halmosi, Brown, Mendy
Referee: Mike Russell (Hertfordshire).

Watford (1).................2 Darlington (0).............1
Francis 37, O'Toole 116 Blundell 90; Att: 5,236
AET: Score after 90 mins 1–1
Watford: Loach, Doyley, Bromby, Mariappa, Sadler, Ainsworth, Francis (Bangura 75), Jenkins, Young, Hoskins (O'Toole 62), Priskin (Henderson 75). **Subs not used:** Poom, Gibson, Avinel, Parkes.**Booked:** Ainsworth, O'Toole
Darlington: Brown, Austin, Foster, Miller, Valentine (Purdie 62), Kennedy, Ravenhill, Burgmeier (Poole 71), Hulbert (Griffin 71), Blundell, Clarke. **Subs not used:** Kazimierczak, Smith, Main, White. **Booked:** Blundell
Referee: Fred Graham (Essex).

Wigan (1)...................4 Notts County (0).........0
Camara 32, 62, Zaki 60, Kupisz 90 Att: 4,100
Wigan: Nash, Montrose, Bramble, Boyce, Figueroa, De Ridder, Valencia (Kupisz 63), Brown, Kilbane (Bouaouzan 70), Camara, Heskey (Zaki 46). **Subs not used:** Pollitt, Palacios, Cattermole, Cywka.
Notts County: Hoult, Beardsley, Edwards, Tann, Mayo, Fairclough, MacKenzie (Hamshaw 62), Butcher, Smith, Weir-Daley (Weston 57), Facey (Canham 74). **Subs not used:** Pilkington, Johnson, Forrester.
Referee: Colin Webster (Tyne & Wear).

27/08/08

Blackburn (3) ....4 Grimsby (1) 1
Villanueva 18 Newey 7
Derbyshire 32, 55, Emerton 39 Att: 8,379
Blackburn: Brown, Simpson, Khizanishvili, Nelsen (Judge 67), Treacy, Emerton (Gallagher 70), Mokoena, Tugay, Pedersen (Marshall 76), Derbyshire, Villanueva. **Subs not used:** Robinson, Santa Cruz, Kane, Hodge. **Booked:** Simpson
Grimsby: Barnes, Bennett, Newey, Heywood, Hegarty, Clarke, Boshell, Hunt, Heslop, Till (Taylor 66), Jarman (Butler 66). **Subs not used:** Montgomery, Llewellyn, Bore, North. **Booked:** Boshell, Bennett
Referee: Michael Oliver (Northumberland).

Fulham (1) ....3 Leicester (0)...............2
Gera 31 Dickov 46, King 48
Bullard 83, Murphy 90 Att: 7,584
Fulham: Schwarzer, Stoor, Hangeland, Hughes, Kallio, Davies, Bullard, Murphy, Gera, Zamora, Seol (Nevland 59). **Subs not used:** Zuberbuhler, Pantsil, Teymourian, Dempsey, Andreasen, Baird.
Leicester: Martin, Gilbert, Morrison, Tunchev, Powell, Dickov (Campbell 87), Wesolowski, King, Dyer, Fryatt (Gradel 46), Howard. **Subs not used:** Henderson, Kishishev, Adams, Hobbs, King.
Referee: Paul Taylor (Hertfordshire).

Huddersfield (1) ....1 Sheffield Utd (0)..........2
Flynn 34; Att: 9,552 Henderson 82, Naughton 83
Huddersfield: Glennon, Holdsworth, Lucketti, Clarke, Williams (Kamara 88), Roberts, Flynn, Worthington (Jevons 85), Cadamarteri, Beckett (Goodwin 77), Parker. **Subs not used:** Skarz, Collins, Unsworth, Smithies.
Sheffield Utd: Bennett, Geary (Sharp 80), Morgan, Kilgallon, Jihai, Carney (Naughton 69), Tonge, Spring, Cotterill, Henderson, Stead (Webber 46). **Subs not used:** Kenny, Montgomery, Robertson, Ehiogu. **Booked:** Jihai, Henderson
Referee: Nigel Miller (Durham).

Nottm Forest (0) ....1 Sunderland (0) 2
Earnshaw 60; Att: 9,198 Bardsley 86, Healy 93
AET: Score after 90 mins 1–1
Nottm Forest: Smith, Chambers, Morgan, Breckin, Bennett, Perch, Moussi (Sinclair 108), Thornhill (Cole 95), McCleary (Tyson 79), Earnshaw, Cohen. **Subs not used:** Roberts, Moloney, Heath, Reid. **Booked:** Cohen, Bennett
Sunderland: Gordon, Chimbonda, Nosworthy, Collins, Bardsley, Malbranque (Miller 19), Whitehead (Leadbitter 57), Reid, Murphy (Healy 62), Diouf, Cisse. **Subs not used:** Ward, Edwards, Higginbotham, Stokes. **Booked:** Chimbonda, Healy
Referee: Iain Williamson (Berkshire).

West Ham (0).............4 Macclesfield (1) 1
Bowyer 74, Cole 100 Evans 5
Hines 105, Reid 117 Att: 10,055
AET: Score after 90 mins 1–1
West Ham: Green, Behrami (Hines 27), Davenport, Upson, McCartney (Reid 55), Faubert, Mullins, Bowyer, Boa Morte, Sears (Cole 58), Ashton. **Subs not used:** Lastuvka, Parker, Widdowson, Spence. **Booked:** Boa Morte
Macclesfield: Brain, Brisley, Hessey, Walker, Reid, Tolley, Bell, Thomas (Yeo 63), Deen, Evans (Rooney 104), Green (Hadfield 81). **Subs not used:** Towns, Gritton, Jennings, Flynn. **Booked:** Green, Yeo, Reid. **Dismissed:** Reid
Referee: Clive Penton (Sussex).

24/09/08

Brighton (0) ....2 Manchester City (0) 2
Murray 89 Fernandes 64, Ireland 108
Anyinsah 95 Att: 8,729
AET: Score after 90 mins 1–1
Brighton win 5–3 on penalties
Brighton: Kuipers, Whing (Cook 85), El-Abd, Thomson, Richards, Livermore, Murray, Loft (Anyinsah 68), Fraser (Cox 74), Virgo, Elphick. **Subs not used:** Sullivan, Hart, Robinson, Wills. **Booked:** El-Abd, Livermore
Man City: Schmeichel, Zabaleta, Dunne, Ben-Haim, Ball, Kompany, Ireland, Johnson (Elano 102), Fernandes, Sturridge (Evans 60), Jo (Caicedo 91). **Subs not used:** Hart, Garrido, Hamann, Logan.
Referee: Andy D'Urso (Essex).

THIRD ROUND

23/09/08

Arsenal (3) ....6 Sheffield Utd (0).........0
Bendtner 31, 42
Vela 44, 50, 87, Wilshere 57 Att: 56,632
Arsenal: Fabianski, Hoyte, Djourou, Song (Lansbury 70), Gibbs, Randall, Ramsey, Merida (Coquelin 71), Wilshere, Bendtner (Simpson 71), Vela. **Subs not used:** Mannone, Emmanuel-Thomas, Ogogo, Frimpong.
Sheffield Utd: Kenny, Halford, Morgan, Kilgallon, Naysmith, Cotterill (Naughton 46), Speed (Hendrie 73), Quinn, Montgomery, Beattie (Robertson 76), Webber. **Subs not used:** Bennett, Sharp, Geary, Ehiogu. **Booked:** Halford
Referee: Phil Dowd (Staffordshire).

Burnley (0) ....1 Fulham (0) 0
Rodriguez 88 Att: 7,119
Burnley: Jensen, Anderson (Duff 12), Carlisle, Caldwell, Jordan, Alexander, Elliott, Gudjonsson, McCann, Paterson (Rodriguez 85), Blake (Eagles 75). **Subs not used:** Penny, Kalvenes, Mahon, Van der Schaaf.
Fulham: Zuberbuhler, Baird, Stoor, Andreasen, Konchesky, Teymourian, Seol (Milsom 90), Gera (Pantsil 73), Dempsey, Kallio, Johnson (Nevland 72). **Subs not used:** Stockdale, Leijer, Brown. **Booked:** Kallio
Referee: M Jones (Mansfield).

Leeds (1) ....3 Hartlepool (2).............2
Snodgrass 14 Monkhouse 2, Porter 33
Showunmi 58, Robinson 90 Att: 14,599
Leeds: Ankergren, Hughes, Michalik, Huntington, Parker, Prutton (Delph 83), Kilkenny, Howson, Robinson, Snodgrass (Beckford 35), Showunmi (Becchio 70). **Subs not used:** Lucas, Webb, White, Elliott.
Hartlepool: Lee-Barrett, McCunnie, Collins, Nelson, Humphreys, Sweeney (Barker 68), Liddle, Jones, Monkhouse (Robson 90), Porter, Brown (Mackay 90). **Subs not used:** Budtz, Clark, Power, Rowell. **Booked:** Collins
Referee: Andy Penn (W Midlands).

Liverpool (1)...............2 Crewe (1)...................1
Agger 15, Lucas 58 O'Connor 25; Att: 28,591
Liverpool: Cavalieri, Degen (Carragher 73), Hyypia, Agger, Insua, Pennant, Lucas, Plessis, El Zhar (Keane 87), Babel, Ngog (Torres 66). **Subs not used:** Gulacsi, Dossena, Alonso, Skrtel.
Crewe: Collis, Woodards, Baudet, O'Donnell, Jones, Moore, Bailey, O'Connor, Carrington (Grant 81), Zola (Miller 78), Pope (Elding 87). **Subs not used:** Tomlinson, Abbey, Rix, Schumacher.
Referee: Michael Oliver (Northumberland).

Manchester Utd (1) ....3 Middlesbrough (0) 1
Ronaldo 25 Johnson 56
Giggs 79, Nani 90 Att: 53,729
Manchester Utd: Amos, Rafael, Vidic, Brown, O'Shea, Nani, Possebon (Gibson 72), Anderson, Giggs (Manucho 84), Welbeck, Ronaldo (Tevez 61). **Subs not used:** Zieler, Cleverley, Gray, Eckersley.
Middlesbrough: Jones, Hoyte, Wheater, Pogatetz, Taylor, Downing, Digard (Riggott 72), O'Neil, Shawky (Johnson 46), Aliadière, Alves (Emnes 85). **Subs not used:** Turnbull, Arca, Walker, Craddock. **Booked:** Johnson.
Dismissed: Pogatetz
Referee: Andre Marriner (W Midlands).

Rotherham (1) ....3 Southampton (0).........1
Fenton 20 John 61
Harrison 56, Broughton 69 Att: 5,147
Rotherham: Warrington, Tonge, Nicholas, Sharps, Fenton, Harrison, Mills, Cummins, Rhodes, Reid, Broughton. **Subs not used:** Cann, Hudson, Burchill, Garcia, Green, Yates, Joseph. **Booked:** Mills, Broughton
Southampton: Bialkowski, Svensson, Perry (Pekhart 77), Cork, Mills (John 55), James, Surman, Wotton, Wright-Phillips (Dyer 63), Lallana, McGoldrick. **Subs not used:** Forecast, Paterson, Hatch, Thomson.**Booked:** Svensson
Referee: Rob Shoebridge (Derbyshire).

Stoke (1) ....2 Reading (1) 2
Pericard 9, Sidibe 50 Henry 45 pen, 75; Att: 9,141
AET: Score after 90 mins 2–2
Stoke win 4–3 on penalties
Stoke: Simonsen, Wilkinson, Shawcross, Higginbotham (Cort 101), Dickinson, Lawrence, Buxton, Whelan, Cresswell (Fuller 78), Sidibe (Phillips 63), Pericard. **Subs not used:** Sorensen, De Laet, Davies, Wedderburn. **Booked:** Whelan
Reading: Federici, Kelly, Bikey, Ingimarsson, Golbourne, Henry, Gunnarsson (Sigurdsson 95), Cisse (Pearce 98), Convey (Mooney 106), Long, Lita. **Subs not used:** Andersen, Sodje, Bozanic, Spence. **Booked:** Bikey, Cisse, Henry
Referee: Lee Probert (Wiltshire).

Sunderland (0) ....2 Northampton (1).........2
Stokes 86, 90; Att: 21,082 Larkin 20, Guttridge 81
Sunderland win 4–3 on penalties
Sunderland: Fulop, Bardsley, Nosworthy, Ferdinand, Collins, Edwards (Richardson 46), Leadbitter (Stokes 78), Whitehead, Reid, Healy (Chopra 46), Murphy. **Subs not used:** Colgan, Miller, Yorke, Chimbonda. **Booked:** Murphy
Northampton: Fielding, Crowe, Little, Hughes, Holt (Jackman 99), Davis, Coke (Gilligan 67), Larkin (Akinfenwa 98), Osman, Guttridge, Constantine. **Subs not used:** Dunn, Henderson, Dolman, Dyer. **Booked:** Davis
Referee: Tony Bates (Staffordshire).

Swansea (0)...............1 Cardiff (0) 0
Gomez 57 Att: 17,411
Swansea: De Vries, Williams, Monk, Bessone, Rangel, Bodde, Britton, Gower (Pintado 66), Gomez, Butler, Scotland (Brandy 85). **Subs not used:** Tate, Orlandi, Tudur Jones, Serran, Krysiak. **Booked:** Gomez
Cardiff: Enckelman, McNaughton, Purse, Johnson, Comminges, Ledley (Whittingham 64), McPhail, Rae, Parry, Bothroyd, Johnson (McCormack 46). **Subs not used:** Heaton, Kennedy, Blake, Morris, Dennehy.
Booked: Whittingham, McCormack, Comminges, Ledley, McPhail. **Dismissed:** McPhail
Referee: Alan Wiley (Staffordshire).

Watford (0).................1 West Ham (0).............0
Mullins 70 (og) Att: 12,914
Watford: Loach, Mariappa, Parkes, Bromby, DeMerit, Williamson (Bennett 71), Ainsworth, Bangura, Jenkins, Smith (Harley 70), Hoskins (Young 80). **Subs not used:** Lee, Eustace, Avinel, Oshodi. **Booked:** Jenkins
West Ham: Lastuvka, Neill, Lopez, Upson, Etherington, Boa Morte (Parker 62), Noble, Mullins, Faubert, Di Michele (Reid 71), Sears. **Subs not used:** Green, Ilunga, Behrami, Collison, Stanislas.
Referee: Peter Walton (Northamptonshire).

24/09/08

Aston Villa (0) ....0 QPR (0) 1
Att: 21,541 Stewart 58
Aston Villa: Guzan, Gardner, Cuellar, Knight, Shorey, Osbourne (Routledge 67), Petrov, Barry, Young, Harewood (Agbonlahor 67), Carew. **Subs not used:** Friedel, Delfouneso, Davies, Salifou, Reo-Coker. **Booked:** Cuellar, Gardner
QPR: Cerny, Connolly, Hall, Stewart, Delaney, Mahon, Rowlands, Parejo, Ledesma (Balanta 90), Buzsaky (Leigertwood 81), Agyemang (Di Carmine 66). **Subs not used:** Camp, Blackstock, Gorkss, Ephraim. **Booked:** Delaney
Referee: Lee Mason (Lancashire).

Blackburn (1) ....1 Everton (0)..................0
Olsson 10 Att: 14,366
Blackburn: Robinson (Brown 12), Simpson, Ooijer, Khizanishvili, Olsson, Villanueva (Santa Cruz 72), Tugay, Warnock, Treacy (Pedersen 75), Derbyshire, Fowler. **Subs not used:** Samba, Nelsen, Kane, Roberts. **Booked:** Warnock, Villanueva
Everton: Howard, Neville, Yobo, Jagielka, Lescott, Rodwell, Castillo (Cahill 46), Fellaini (Yakubu 46), Vaughan (Baxter 83), Saha, Osman. **Subs not used:** Turner, Hibbert, Baines, Nuno Valente. **Booked:** Neville, Vaughan
Referee: Martin Atkinson (W Yorkshire).

Ipswich (0) ....1 Wigan (0) 4
Walters 61 Cattermole 52, Kapo 64
Att: 13,803 Scharner 70, Camara 90
Ipswich: Wright, Volz, Bruce, McAuley, Thatcher (Balkestein 46), Norris, Campo, Miller, Quinn (Haynes 72), Walters, Lisbie (Bowditch 82). **Subs not used:** Supple, Garvan, Peters, Shumulikoski. **Booked:** Volz
Wigan: Kirkland, Cattermole, Boyce, Bramble, Kilbane, Valencia, Scharner, Palacios (De Ridder 71), Kapo, Heskey (Camara 75), Zaki (Koumas 82). **Subs not used:** Pollitt, Taylor, Kupisz, Figueroa. **Booked:** Scharner
Referee: Mike Dean (Wirral).

Newcastle (0).............1 Tottenham (0).............2
Owen 90 Pavlyuchenko 62
Att: 20,577 O'Hara 66
Newcastle: Given, Geremi, Taylor, Coloccini, Bassong, Cacapa (Edgar 72), Butt, N'Zogbia, Owen, Duff (Xisco 72), Martins. **Subs not used:** Harper, Ameobi, Tozer, Doninger, Donaldson. **Booked:** Butt
Tottenham: Gomes, Corluka, King, Woodgate, Assou-Ekotto, Lennon (Campbell 62), Jenas, Zokora, O'Hara, Bale (Giovani 53), Pavlyuchenko (Modric 75). **Subs not used:** Cesar, Bentley, Bent, Gilberto. **Booked:** Giovani, Zokora, O'Hara, Corluka
Referee: Chris Foy (Merseyside).

Portsmouth (0)...........0 Chelsea (2) 4
Att: 15,339 Lampard 36 pen, 49
Malouda 45, Kalou 64
Portsmouth: James, Johnson, Pamarot, Distin, Hreidarsson, Utaka, Mvuemba, Kaboul, Hughes (Wilson 80), Belhadj (Traore 69), Crouch (Kanu 69). **Subs not used:** Ashdown, Defoe, Traore, Little. **Booked:** Johnson, Hughes, Hreidarsson
Chelsea: Cech, Ivanovic, Terry, Alex, Bridge, Belletti, Ballack (Ferreira 69), Lampard (Sinclair 74), Kalou, Malouda, Drogba (Di Santo 79). **Subs not used:** Cudicini, Mikel, Mancienne, Stoch. **Booked:** Ballack
Referee: Steve Bennett (Kent).

04/11/08

Brighton (1) ....1 Derby (2) 4
Elphick 36 Villa 28, 73, 87
Att: 6,625 Ellington 34
Brighton: Sullivan, Whing, Elphick, Richards, Hawkins (El-Abd 77), Anyinsah, Cox (McLeod 69), Thomson, Thornton, Fleetwood, Murray (Livermore 78). **Subs not used:** Kuipers, Loft, Robinson, Fraser.
Derby: Carroll, Connolly, Addison, Nyatanga, Leacock (Zadkovich 58), Stewart, Kazmierczak (Teale 66), Green, Commons, Ellington, Villa (Hanson 89). **Subs not used:** Bywater, Hulse, Sterjovski, Pereplotkins.
Booked: Nyatanga, Addison
Referee: Kevin Friend (Leicestershire).

FOURTH ROUND

11/11/08

Arsenal (1).................3 Wigan (0)...................0
Simpson 42, 66, Vela 70 Att: 59,665
Arsenal: Fabianski, Hoyte, Song, Djourou, Gibbs, Wilshere (Bischoff 76), Randall, Ramsey, Merida, Simpson (Lansbury 76), Vela (Fonte 84). **Subs not used:** Mannone, Coquelin, Ogogo, Frimpong. **Booked:** Ramsey
Wigan: Kirkland, Cattermole (Brown 67), Boyce, Bramble, Melchiot, Valencia, Koumas (Camara 58), Palacios, De Ridder, Figueroa, Zaki. **Subs not used:** Kingson, Taylor, Scharner, Kilbane, Cywka.
Referee: Steve Tanner (Somerset).

Derby (2) ....2 Leeds (1) 1
Villa 6, Ellington 18 Becchio 40; Att: 18,540
Derby: Carroll, Connolly, Davis, Nyatanga, Stewart, Teale (Zadkovich 46), Green, Kazmierczak, Commons, Ellington (Sterjovski 81), Villa (Hulse 70). **Subs not used:** Bywater, McEveley, Hanson, Pereplotkins. **Booked:** Davis
Leeds: Ankergren, Richardson, Telfer, Michalik, Parker (White 75), Snodgrass, Kilkenny (Howson 80), Douglas, Robinson (Beckford 64), Delph, Becchio. **Subs not used:** Lucas, Prutton, Showunmi, Hughes.
Referee: Graham Laws (Tyne & Wear).

Manchester Utd (0) ....1 QPR (0) 0
Tevez 76 (pen) Att: 62,539
Manchester Utd: Kuszczak, Rafael, Neville (Vidic 89), Evans, O'Shea, Gibson, Possebon (Welbeck 72), Anderson, Nani, Tevez, Park. **Subs not used:** Foster, Carrick, Manucho, Cleverley, Gray.
QPR: Cerny, Ramage, Hall, Stewart, Connolly, Buzsaky (Agyemang 33), Rowlands, Mahon, Cook (Di Carmine 78), Parejo (Ledesma 46), Blackstock. **Subs not used:** Cole, Delaney, Gorkss, Ephraim.
Referee: Phil Dowd (Staffordshire).

Stoke (1) ....2 Rotherham (0) 0
Whelan 21, Pugh 59 Att: 13,731
Stoke: Simonsen, Wilkinson, Cort, Shawcross, Dickinson, Pugh, Whelan, Olofinjana (Faye 58), Cresswell, Kitson, Pericard (Fuller 73). **Subs not used:** Sorensen, Delap, Phillips, Sonko, Wedderburn.
Rotherham: Warrington, Mills, Sharps, Fenton, Nicholas, Rhodes, Harrison (Taylor 70), Cummins, Tonge, Broughton (Yates 88), Reid. **Subs not used:** Annerson, Hudson, Joseph, Green, Garcia. **Booked:** Reid
Referee: Mark Halsey (Lancashire).

Swansea (0) ....0 Watford (1).................1
Att: 9,549 Williamson 21
Swansea: Konstantopoulos, Tate, Monk, O'Halloran, Serran, MacDonald, Bodde, Tudur Jones (Gomez 57), Brandy (Scotland 85), Bauza (Gower 57), Pintado. **Subs not used:** Krysiak, O'Leary, Pratley, Collins. **Booked:** Pintado, Tudur Jones
Watford: Lee, Doyley, DeMerit, Bromby, Harley, McAnuff (Hoskins 80), Williamson (O'Toole 87), Mariappa, Smith, Jenkins, Priskin (Rasiak 75). **Subs not used:** Tyler, Sadler, Eustace, Robinson.
Booked: Williamson, Mariappa, Priskin, Bromby
Referee: Andy D'Urso (Essex).

FOURTH ROUND

12/11/08

Chelsea (1) ....1 Burnley (0) 1
Drogba 27   Akinbiyi 69; Att: 41,369
AET: Score after 90 mins 1–1. Burnley win 5–4 on pens.
Chelsea: Cudicini, Ivanovic, Alex, Belletti (Lampard 25), Bridge, Ferreira, Deco (Mikel 46), Mineiro, Malouda, Drogba (Di Santo 68), Kalou. **Subs not used:** Hilario, Sinclair, Terry, Woods.
Burnley: Jensen, Alexander, Duff, Caldwell, Jordan, Eagles, Gudjonsson (McDonald 97), McCann, Elliott, Blake (Mahon 76), Paterson (Akinbiyi 60). **Subs not used:** Penny, Rodriguez, Kay, MacDonald. **Booked:** Akinbiyi, Eagles, Caldwell. **Dismissed:** Caldwell
Referee: Keith Stroud (Hampshire).

Sunderland (0) ....1 Blackburn (0) 2
Jones 71   Santa Cruz 65
Att: 18,555   Bardsley 70 (og)
Sunderland: Fulop, Bardsley, Nosworthy, Ferdinand, Collins, Henderson (Leadbitter 80), Whitehead, Richardson, Malbranque (Reid 71) Cisse, Jones (Murphy 80). **Subs not used:** Colgan, Tainio, Diouf, Kay. **Booked:** Leadbitter
Blackburn: Robinson, Simpson, Khizanishvili, Samba, Olsson, Tugay, Derbyshire, Mokoena, Treacy (Warnock 67), Fowler (Villanueva 78) Haworth (Santa Cruz 62). **Subs not used:** Brown, Ooijer, Nelsen, Judge. **Booked:** Mokoena, Treacy
Referee: Rob Styles (Hampshire).

Tottenham (3)............4 Liverpool (0) 2
Pavlyuchenko 38, 52   Plessis 49, Hyypia 63
Campbell 42, 45   Att: 33,242
Tottenham: Gomes (Cesar 74), Hutton, Dawson, Corluka, Bale, Lennon, Zokora, Huddlestone, O'Hara, Pavlyuchenko (Boateng 90), Campbell (Bent 90). **Subs not used:** Campbell, Pavlyuchenko.
Liverpool: Cavalieri, Dossena, Hyypia, Agger, Degen (Darby 84), Babel, Lucas, Ngog, Plessis (Alonso 66), Torres (Insua 56), El Zhar. **Subs not used:** Gulacsi, Riera, Benayoun, Carragher. **Booked:** Babel, Lucas, Plessis, Torres
Referee: Mike Riley (Yorkshire).

QUARTER-FINALS

02/12/08

Burnley (1) ....2 Arsenal (0) 0
McDonald 6, 57   Att: 19,045
Burnley: Jensen, Duff, Carlisle, Caldwell, Jordan, Alexander, Blake (Elliott 77), McDonald (Gudjonsson 61), McCann, Eagles, Paterson (Akinbiyi 74). **Subs not used:** Penny, Mahon, Rodriguez, MacDonald.
Arsenal: Fabianski, Hoyte, Silvestre, Ramsey, Gibbs, Rodgers (Lansbury 46), Randall (Bischoff 72), Merida, Wilshere (Simpson 63), Bendtner, Vela. **Subs not used:** Mannone, Coquelin, Steer, Fringpong, Merida, Randall
Referee: Andre Marriner (W Midlands).

Stoke (0) ....0 Derby (0) 1
Att: 22,034   Ellington 90 pen
Stoke: Simonsen, Griffin, Cort, Sonko, Higginbotham, Delap, Olofinjana (Pugh 81), Whelan, Cresswell, Sidibe, Fuller. **Subs not used:** Sorensen, Pericard, Faye, Davies, Faye, Dickinson.

Derby: Carroll, Connolly, Powell, Tomkins, Stewart, Kazmierczak, Green (Teale 90), Addison, Commons, Hulse (Villa 86), Ellington. **Subs not used:** Bywater, Sterjovski, Nyatanga, Zadkovich, Camara. **Booked:** Addison, Powell
Referee: Rob Styles (Hampshire).

03/12/08

Manchester Utd (2) ....5 Blackburn (0) 3
Tevez 36, 51 pen   McCarthy 48, 90
54, 90   Derbyshire 8
Nani 40
Att: 53,997
Manchester Utd: Foster, Rafael, Neville, Evans, O'Shea (Evra 66), Nani, Gibson, Possebon (Scholes 66), Anderson, Giggs (Manucho 71), Tevez. **Subs not used:** Kuszczak, Park, Vidic, Welbeck.

Blackburn: Robinson, Olsson, Nelsen, Ooijer, Warnock, Treacy, Tugay (Pedersen 70), Mokoena, Emerton (McCarthy 46), Derbyshire, Santa Cruz (Fowler 76). **Subs not used:** Brown, Villanueva, Judge, Roberts. **Booked:** Nelsen
Referee: Alan Wiley (Staffordshire).

Watford (1)..................1 Tottenham (1) 2
Priskin 13   Pavlyuchenko 45 (pen)
Att: 16,501   Bent 76
Watford: Loach, Mariappa, DeMerit (Doyley 58), Bromby, Jenkins (O'Toole 78), Harley, Williamson, McAnuff (Hoskins 83), Bridcutt, Smith, Priskin. **Subs not used:** Lee, Robinson, Bangura, Henderson. **Booked:** McAnuff, Priskin
Tottenham: Gomes, Corluka, Dawson, Woodgate, Assou-Ekotto, Zokora, Lennon, Jenas, O'Hara, Pavlyuchenko, Campbell (Bent 65). **Subs not used:** Cesar, Bale, Bentley, Huddlestone, Gunter, Boateng. **Booked:** Assou-Ekotto
Referee: Phil Dowd (Staffordshire).

SEMI-FINALS

FIRST LEG
06/01/09

Tottenham (0) ....4 Burnley (1) 1
Dawson 47, O'Hara 52   Paterson 15
Pavlyuchenko 65, Duff 68 (og)   Att: 31,377
Tottenham: Gomes, Corluka, Dawson, Woodgate, Bale, Lennon, Modric, Zokora, Bentley (O'Hara 46), Pavlyuchenko, Campbell. **Subs not used:** Alnwick, Gunter, Giovani, Taarabt, Boateng, Rocha.
Burnley: Jensen, Alexander, Duff, Carlisle, Jordan, Gudjonsson (McDonald 30), Eagles, Paterson (Akinbiyi 86), Elliott, Blake (Rodriguez 75), McCann. **Subs not used:** Penny, Kalvenes, Mahon, MacDonald. **Booked:** Duff, Jordan
Referee: Martin Atkinson (W Yorkshire).

07/01/09

Derby (1) ....1 Manchester Utd (0) 0
Commons 30   Att: 30,194

Derby: Carroll, Connolly, Todd (Savage 87), Nyatanga, Camara, Sterjovski (Teale 58), Green, Addison, Commons, Hulse, Davies (Barazite 81). **Subs not used:** Bywater, Dickinson, Powell, Hines. **Booked:** Connolly, Teale
Manchester Utd: Kuszczak, Rafael, Vidic, Evans, O'Shea, Anderson (Carrick 74), Scholes (Rooney 63), Gibson, Nani, Tevez, Welbeck (Rooney 63). **Subs not used:** Amos, Giggs, Fletcher, Possebon. **Booked:** Rafael
Referee: Phil Dowd (Staffordshire).

SECOND LEG
20/01/09

Manchester Utd (3) ....4 Derby (0) 2
Nani 16, O'Shea 22   Barnes 80 pen, 90
Tevez 34, Ronaldo 89 (pen)   Att: 73,374
Manchester Utd: Foster, Rafael (Fletcher 42), Neville (Chester 67), Evans, O'Shea, Nani, Gibson, Anderson, Giggs (Ronaldo 58), Welbeck, Tevez. **Subs not used:** Kuszczak, Tosic, Scholes, Possebon. **Booked:** Fletcher, Rafael

Derby: Carroll, Connolly, Albrechtsen, Todd (Barazite 62), Stewart, Teale, Addison, Green, Davies (Savage 46), Commons (Barnes 68), Hulse. **Subs not used:** Bywater, Villa, Nyatanga, Hines. **Booked:** Green, Addison, Carroll
Referee: Mike Dean (Wirral).

21/01/09

Burnley (1) ....3 Tottenham (0) 2
Blake 34, McCann 73   Pavlyuchenko 118
Rodriguez 88   Defoe 120; Att: 19,533
AET: Score after 90 mins 3–0
Burnley: Jensen, Alexander, Duff, Carlisle, Jordan (Kalvenes 39), Elliott, Eagles, Gudjonsson (Rodriguez 81), McCann, Blake, Paterson (Akinbiyi 100). **Subs not used:** Penny, McDonald, Mahon, MacDonald.**Booked:** Duff, McCann
Tottenham: Alnwick, Gunter (Taarabt 95), Woodgate, Dawson, Assou-Ekotto, Bentley, Zokora, Huddlestone, O'Hara (Bale 62), Modric (Pavlyuchenko 65), Defoe. **Subs not used:** Cesar, Giovani, Campbell, Rocha. **Booked:** Bentley
Referee: Mark Halsey (Lancashire).

FINAL

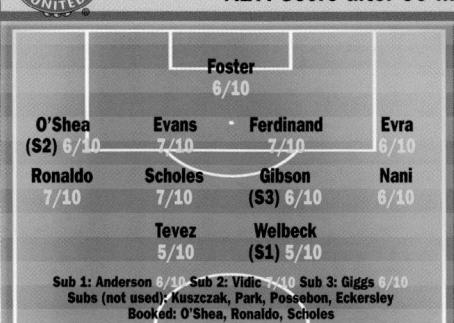
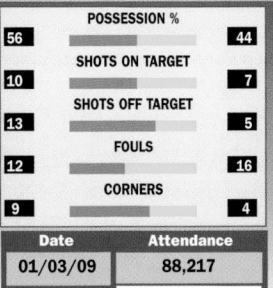

Manchester Utd (0) 0-0 (0) Tottenham H

AET: Score after 90 mins 0–0. Manchester United win 4–1 on penalties

POSSESSION %		
56		44
SHOTS ON TARGET		
10		7
SHOTS OFF TARGET		
13		5
FOULS		
12		16
CORNERS		
9		4

Manchester Utd:
Foster 6/10
O'Shea (S2) 6/10, Evans 7/10, Ferdinand 7/10, Evra 6/10
Ronaldo 7/10, Scholes 7/10, Gibson (S3) 6/10, Nani 6/10
Tevez 5/10, Welbeck (S1) 5/10
Sub 1: Anderson 6/10 Sub 2: Vidic 7/10 Sub 3: Giggs 6/10
Subs (not used): Kuszczak, Park, Possebon, Eckersley
Booked: O'Shea, Ronaldo, Scholes

Tottenham:
Gomes 7/10
Corluka 6/10, Dawson 8/10, King 7/10, Assou-Ekotto 6/10
Lennon (S3) 8/10, Jenas (S2) 6/10, Zokora 6/10, Modric 8/10
Bent 5/10, Pavlyuchenko (S1) 5/10
Sub 1: O'Hara 7/10 Sub 2: Bale 6/10 Sub 3: Bentley 6/10
Subs (not used): Alnwick, Huddlestone, Gunter, Taarabt

Date	Attendance
01/03/09	88,217
Referee	**Chris Foy**

2008/09 STATISTICS

Total goals scored	120
Total penalties scored	9
Total red cards	4
Total yellow cards	114
Number of penalty shoot-outs	12

THE TEAM WITH THE MOST...

Shots on target	
Scunthorpe 59	
Shots off target	
Scunthorpe 57	
Shots per goal	
Bury 18	
Corners	
Scunthorpe 66	
Fouls	
Luton 88	
Offsides	
Colchester, Brighton 24	
Woodwork strikes	
Scunthorpe 4	
Penalties conceded	
Swindon 2	
Yellow cards	
Luton 11	
Red cards	
Huddersfield, Brighton, Macclesfield, Milton Keynes Dons 1	

LEADING GOALSCORERS

Player	Team	Goals
G Holt	(Shrewsbury)	7
P Hayes	(Scunthorpe)	3
T Craddock	(Luton)	2
L Sawyer	(Southend)	2
S Cox	(Swindon)	2
D Broughton	(Rotherham)	2
C Gnakpa	(Luton)	2
A White	(Darlington)	2
R Jarvis	(Leyton Orient)	2
P Benson	(Dag & Red)	2
A Birchall	(Barnet)	2
G Hooper	(Scunthorpe)	2
C Martin	(Luton)	2
G Poole	(Brentford)	2
M Nwokeji	(Dag & Red)	2

Luton's players lift the Johnstone's Paint Trophy after beating Scunthorpe

UNDERDOGS Luton claimed the Johnstone's Paint Trophy after a thrilling Wembley final win over Scunthorpe.

The Hatters, the lowest-ranked team in the competition, dug deep to complete what their manager Mick Harford called 'a fairytale' for the Bedfordshire club.

Luton were bottom of the Football League and on the brink of relegation, but they brought an incredible 40,000 fans for the showpiece. The hoards of orange-clad supporters were later in dreamland when Claude Gnakpa struck in extra-time to secure a 3–2 victory over their Coca-Cola League One opponents.

Harford is no stranger to Wembley, having lifted the League Cup with Luton as a player back in 1988, but he claimed leading the Hatters to a dramatic victory eclipsed even that historic day.

'It's definitely up there with my finest achievements and it might even be the greatest,' he said. 'It's a fantastic achievement for the club and for the town.'

Luton's prospects did not look so bright when Gary Hooper fired Scunthorpe into a 14th-minute lead. However, the Coca-Cola League Two outfit hit back through classy strikes from Chris Martin and Tom Craddock to lead 2–1 until Grant McCann forced extra-time with a 25-yard curler.

It was Gnakpa who settled a match with a strike worthy of any cup final, and wrote himself into Luton folklore, when he raced onto Keith Keane's long-range pass and lifted the ball over advancing goalkeeper Joe Murphy to clinch the game and the trophy.

Luton's first steps on the road to Wembley were no less dramatic. Having received a bye in round one, they were 2–0 down against Brentford at Kenilworth Road before battling back to draw 2–2 and going on to win on penalties.

Scunthorpe were seconds from going out at the first hurdle themselves, and needed two stoppage-time goals from Paul Hayes to get past Notts County.

Holders MK Dons exited in round two, going out to Bournemouth, while Scunthorpe beat 2008 runners-up Grimsby.

Leeds were shocked by Rotherham, but the performance of the early rounds came from Shrewsbury striker Grant Holt, who scored five goals in a 7–0 rout of Wycombe.

A last-minute Rossi Jarvis goal sent Luton into the Southern Area semi-finals at the expense of Walsall, while Scunthorpe edged past Rochdale in the Northern Section courtesy of David Mirfin's strike, while Rotherham added Leicester to their list of scalps.

Gnakpa scored to see off Colchester and Scunthorpe left it late as a 93rd-minute free-kick from Hayes sent them through against Tranmere. The Iron ended Rotherham's dreams in the Northern Area final with a comfortable 3–0 aggregate win, while Luton needed a penalty shoot-out to see off Brighton.

The Hatters' amazing journey was complete when captain Kevin Nicholls held aloft the trophy at Wembley.

NORTHERN SECTION

FIRST ROUND

02/09/08

Crewe (3) ....3 Macclesfield (0) 0
Schumacher 5   Att: 2,463
Jones 27
O'Donnell 42

Hartlepool (0) ....0 Leicester (0).............3
Att: 2,807   Howard 52
                                    Adams 66
                                    Fryatt 87

Leeds (2) ....2 Bradford (0)............1
Robinson 8 pen   Conlon 71
Becchio 42   Att: 20,128

Oldham (0) ....1 Morecambe (0)..........1
Whitaker 56   Drummond 65
Att: 2,016
Morecambe win 5–4 on penalties

Scunthorpe (0) ....2 Notts County (1)..........1
Hayes 90, 90   Butcher 9
Att: 1,755

Stockport (1) ....1 Port Vale (0).............0
McSweeney 4   Att: 2,290

Tranmere (0) ....1 Accrington Stanley (0).0
Sonko 49   Att: 2,410

03/09/08

Chesterfield (1) ....2 Grimsby (1)............2
Lester 18   Jarman 32
Kerry 52   North 78
Att: 1,665
Grimsby win 4–1 on penalties

SECOND ROUND

23/09/08

Leicester (0)..............0 Lincoln City (0)..........0
Att: 8,046
Leicester win 3–1 on penalties

06/10/08

Tranmere (0) ....1 Crewe (0)..............0
Shuker 86   Att: 2,626

07/10/08

Bury (0) ....1 Stockport (0) 0
Bishop 77   Att: 2,384

Chester (0)............1 Morecambe (1)..........1
Ellison 82   Howe 42
Att: 926
Morecambe win 3–1 on penalties

Darlington (1) ....1 Huddersfield (0).........0
White 45   Att: 1,791

Rochdale (2).............2 Carlisle (1) 2
Thorpe 10   Bridges 4
Dagnall 16   Madine 71
Att: 1,608
Rochdale win 4–3 on penalties

Scunthorpe (2) ....2 Grimsby (0)............1
Togwell 38   Hegarty 48
Morris 42   Att: 4,844

08/10/08

Rotherham (2) ....4 Leeds (1)............2
Sharps 17   Howson 31
Hudson 44   Showunmi 56
Broughton 48, Fenton 53   Att: 4,658

QUARTER-FINALS

04/11/08

Darlington...........1 Bury 0
White 53
                                    Att: 1,651

Rotherham ....2 Leicester 0
Broughton 45
Tonge 58   Att 4,255

Scunthorpe ....1 Rochdale............0
Mirfin 90   Att 2,474

Tranmere ....1 Morecambe............0
Shotton 45   Att 2,110

SEMI-FINALS

16/12/08

Rotherham (0) ....1 Darlington (1)............1
Fenton 74   Foster 35
Att: 2,706
Rotherham win 4–2 on penalties

Scunthorpe (1) ....2 Tranmere (0)............1
May 26   Moore 53
Hayes 90   Att: 2,669

AREA FINAL FIRST LEG

20/01/09

Scunthorpe (0) ....2 Rotherham (0)............0
Woolford 60   Att: 6,038
Pearce 67

AREA FINAL SECOND LEG

17/02/09

Rotherham (0) ....0 Scunthorpe (0)............1
Att: 6,555   Hooper 74

SOUTHERN SECTION

FIRST ROUND

02/09/08

Aldershot (1) ....2 Swindon (1)...............2
Elvins 45   Cox 32
Davies 48 pen   Ifil 83
Att: 1,814
Swindon win 7–6 on penalties

Bournemouth (1) ....3 Bristol Rovers (0) 0
Goulding 38   Att: 2,220
Igoe 67
Hollands 76

Brentford (2) ....2 Yeovil (1)...............2
Poole 28 pen   Bircham 39
O'Connor 37   Tomlin 77 pen
Att: 1,339
Brentford win 4–2 on penalties

Dag & Red (3) ....4 Barnet (2) 2
Benson 4, 34   Birchall 6, 18
Nwokeji 28   Att: 1,412
Southam 75 pen

Exeter (1)...............1 Shrewsbury (1)...........2
Harley 22   McIntyre 9
Att: 1,530   Davies 90

Millwall (0)............0 Colchester (1)............1
Att: 2,456   Perkins 8

Northampton (0)..........0 Brighton (0).............1
Att: 2,047   McLeod 68

Southend (2) ....2 Leyton Orient (2)..........4
Sawyer 13, 34   Jarvis 20
Att: 3,499   Chambers 25
                                    Melligan 48
                                    Boyd 86 pen

SECOND ROUND

07/10/08

Brighton (2) ....2 Leyton Orient (1) 2
Virgo 5 pen   Jarvis 21
Anyinsah 14   Boyd 72 pen
Att: 2,157
Brighton win 5–4 on penalties

Cheltenham (1)...........1 Walsall (0)...............2
Low 4   Ibehre 61
Att: 1,741   Ricketts 74

Gillingham (0)..............0 Colchester (0)............1
Att: 1,557   Yeates 60

Hereford (1) ....1 Swindon (1)...............2
Done 30   Cox 45
Att: 1,458   Peacock 84

Luton (1) ....2 Brentford (2)...........2
Hall 39   Poole 18
Martin 55   Williams 37
Att: 2,029
Luton win 4–3 on penalties

Milton Keynes Dons (0)0 Bournemouth (0) 1
Att: 4,329   Anderton 77

Peterborough (0) ....0 Dag & Red (0) 1
Att: 2,644   Nwokeji 65

Wycombe (0) ....0 Shrewsbury (3) 7
Att: 1,730   Holt 12, 27, 80, 81, 86
                                    McIntyre 39
                                    Cansdell-Sherriff 74

QUARTER-FINALS

04/11/08

Bournemth ....0 Colchester............1
                                    Williams 17
                                    Att 2,275

Shrewsbry ....5 Dagenham............0
Holt 13, 45
Leslie 22
Walker 69
Coughlan 81   Att 2,747

Walsall ....0 Luton............1
                                    Jarvis 90
                                    Att 1,844

12/11/08

Brighton ....2 Swindon............0
Forster 24 pen
Livermore 75   Att 2,234

SEMI-FINALS

16/12/08

Luton (1) ....1 Colchester (0) 0
Gnakpa 29   Att: 2,638

Shrewsbury (0) ....0 Brighton (0)............0
Att: 4,052
Brighton win 5–4 on penalties

AREA FINAL FIRST LEG

20/01/09

Brighton (0) ....0 Luton (0)...............0
Att: 6,127

AREA FINAL SECOND LEG

17/02/09

Luton (1) ....1 Brighton (1)...........1
Craddock 2   Forster 20
Att: 8,711
Luton win 4–3 on penalties

FINAL

05/04/09

Luton (1) ....3 Scunthorpe (1) 2
Martin 32   Hooper 14
Craddock 70   McCann 88
Gnakpa 95   Att: 55,378
AET: Score after 90 mins 2–2
Luton: Brill, Asafu-Adjaye, Pilkington, Spillane, Emanuel, Keane, Nicholls, Hall, Jarvis (Parkin 117), Martin, Craddock (Gnakpa 85). **Subs not used:** Button, Davis, Roper. **Booked:** Martin, Nicholls.
Scunthorpe: Murphy, Byrne, Pearce (Wright 85), Mirfin, Williams, Sparrow (Woolford 77), Lansbury, McCann, Hurst (Togwell 63), Hooper, Hayes. **Subs not used:** Lillis, May. **Booked:** Wright.
Referee: Phil Crossley (Kent).

QUICK SEARCH

Trace how far each club progressed in the 2008/09 Scottish Cup

Team	Reached 2008/09
SCOTTISH PREMIER LEAGUE	
Aberdeen	Quarter-final
Celtic	Quarter-final
Dundee Utd	Round 5
Falkirk	Final
Hamilton	Quarter-final
Hearts	Round 5
Hibernian	Round 4
Inverness	Quarter-final
Kilmarnock	Round 5
Motherwell	Round 5
Rangers	Final
St Mirren	Semi-final
FIRST DIVISION	
Airdrie	Round 5
Clyde	Round 4
Dundee	Round 4
Dunfermline	Semi-final
Livingston	Round 3
Morton	Round 3
Partick	Round 4
Queen of the South	Round 4
Ross County	Round 4
St Johnstone	Round 4
SECOND DIVISION	
Alloa	Round 4
Arbroath	Round 3
Ayr	Round 4
Brechin	Round 4
East Fife	Round 5
Peterhead	Round 4
Queen's Park	Round 5
Raith	Round 3
Stirling	Round 3
Stranraer	Round 3
THIRD DIVISION	
Albion	Round 3
Annan	Round 2
Berwick	Round 2
Cowdenbeath	Round 2
Dumbarton	Round 3
East Stirling	Round 4
Elgin	Round 3
Forfar	Round 5
Montrose	Round 3
Stenhousemuir	Round 4

Rangers celebrate after their 1–0 Scottish Cup final win over Falkirk

RANGERS ensured there were no shocks in the Homecoming Scottish Cup final as they successfully defended the trophy to see their name engraved on it for the 33rd time.

This season's showpiece at Hampden Park proved a perfect way to sign off the campaign for both sides, with Rangers and Falkirk arriving at the national stadium following very different success stories in the Clydesdale Bank Premier League.

The Bairns started the celebrations on the final weekend of the league campaign when a dramatic win at Inverness allowed them to retain their SPL status after they had looked doomed going into the run-in.

Twenty-four hours later, the champagne corks were popping again when Rangers claimed the title for the first time in four years, finishing four points ahead of Celtic.

The final was yet another day to remember for the Ibrox faithful. Rangers had beaten Queen of the South 12 months earlier, and their display against a battling Falkirk side ensured they kept the trophy. A superb strike from half-time substitute Nacho Novo – less than 30 seconds after coming on to the pitch – separated the sides and completed a domestic double for Walter Smith's men.

Considering Rangers' impressive record in finals over recent years, the outcome was not surprising, but Falkirk could count themselves unfortunate not to have claimed the silverware for the first time since 1957.

The earlier rounds had plenty of drama,

with junior side Lochee United earning a third-round replay against Irn-Bru Second Division outfit Ayr. The Somerset Park side managed to progress at the second attempt and went on to force a dramatic replay of their own after holding Ayrshire rivals Kilmarnock to a 2–2 draw in the fourth round, before eventually crashing out at Rugby Park.

The Old Firm entered the tournament with Celtic easing past Dundee, and Rangers overcoming eventual First Division champions St Johnstone.

Motherwell also booked their place in the fifth round with victory over Highlanders Inverurie Locos at the fifth attempt, after weather conditions had played havoc with the fixture.

Hamilton secured the result of the fifth round when they sent Dundee United crashing out, but it was the quarter-finals that threw up the major shocks. SPL strugglers St Mirren hit the headlines by disposing of Celtic, before First Division Dunfermline triumphed over Aberdeen in a dramatic penalty shoot-out after a goalless replay at Pittodrie.

Falkirk's run in the competition continued with victory over Inverness, as Rangers cruised past Hamilton 5–1.

St Mirren and Dunfermline were the teams who fell at the penultimate hurdle, as Falkirk and Rangers progressed to a meeting at Hampden. And, despite their defeat, the Bairns had the consolation of securing European football for the first time in the club's history.

FIRST ROUND

27/09/2008

Banks O'Dee (5) ....10 Fort William (0) 0
Carstairs 24, 35
Reid 30, 38
Taylor 44, 72, 86 pen
Whyte 69 pen
Brownhill 70
Phillips 89

Clachnacuddin (2) ......4 Burntisland S (R) 0
Macmillan 19 og
Lawrie 29
Ross 64
Morrison 77

Dalbeattie Star (0) .....5 Lossiemouth (1)...........1
Milligan 68, 86, 89, 90   Lasley 27
Sloan 81

Edinburgh City (1) ......2 Nairn County (0) 0
Ross 25
Bruce 53

Edinburgh Univ (1) ......1 Civil Service Stroll's (0)2
Dick 10   Burgess 64
                                            Dickson 82

Fraserburgh (4)............6 Hawick Royal A (1) 3
Stephen 7, 45   Smith 35
Clark 17 og   Hamilton 51
West 27   Knox 78
Main 77
Johnstone 80

Glasgow Univ (0) ....0 Vale Of Leithen (0).......1
                                            Shortreed 82

Golspie Sutherland (0) 0 Threave Rovers (1) 3
                                            Cook 28, 59
                                            Beattie 89

Huntly (1) ....1 Girvan (0) 0
Soane 10

Inverurie Loco Works (4)5 Deveronvale (0) 2
Simpson 21   McKenzie 58 pen, 79
McLean 33
Smith 36
Gauld 39
Coull 47

Lochee Utd (RS) ....3 Bathgate Thistle (RS) ...1
Hagen 64   P Harvey 23
Robertson 80
Cargill 82

Newton Stewart (0) ....1 Brora (1) 1
Sutherland 89 pen   Cameron 12

Pollok (1) ....1 Spartans (1) 1
Dingwall 15   Walker 29 pen

Preston Ath (2) ....3 Gala Fairydean (1) 1
Miller 2   Gibson 24
Manson 31, 56

Rothes (1) ....1 Buckie Thistle (0) 3
Shortreed 45   Charlesworth 58
                                            Low 71
                                            Shewan 89

Selkirk (0) ....1 Coldstream (0) 1
Stephen 90 pen   Bolton 85

St Cuthbert Wndrs (0) 0 Wick Academy (1) 3
                                            Weir 23, 48, 89

Wigtown & Bladnoch (1) 2 Forres Mechanics (1)...2
McClymont 43   Sharp 11
White 57   Allan 86 pen

FIRST-ROUND REPLAYS

04/10/2008

Brora (1) ....2 Newton Stewart (0) 1
Inglis 24   McColm 48
MacKay-Steven 95
AET: Score after 90 mins 1–1

Coldstream (0) ....2 Selkirk (0) 2
Travis 86, Ingles 89   Waldie 50, Pritchard 60
AET: Score after 90 mins 2–2
Selkirk win 3–2 on penalties

Forres Mechanics (1) ..2 Wigtn & Bladnoch (0) ..0
Sharp 21, Hendry 75

Spartans (RS) ....1 Pollok (RS) 0
Walker 86

SECOND ROUND

25/10/2008

Berwick (1) ....1 Albion (1) 2
Gribben 32   Coyne 35, Harris 71

Brora (0) ....1 Forfar (1) 3
MacKay 69 pen   Gordon 17
                                            Dunn 52
                                            Campbell 76

Clachnacuddin (1) ......1 Crichton (0)..................0
Ross 20

Cove Rangers (0) ....1 Whitehill Welfare (0)....0
Stephen 59

Cowdenbeath (0) ....1 Elgin (1) 2
McQuade 50   Kaczan 27
                                            Wright 71

Dalbeattie Star (2) .....6 Selkirk (0) 0
Milligan 19, 69, 79
Redpath 31
Kerr 65
Harkness 89

Edinburgh City (0) ......0 Wick Academy (0) 0

Forres Mechanics (1) ..1 Keith (0)......................1
Collins 40   Lennox 69

Fraserburgh (0)............0 Dumbarton (0) 1
                                            Chisholm 54

Inverurie Loco Works (2)5 Banks O'Dee (0) 1
Forbes 2 og   Taylor 77
Smith 23
Ross 46
Milne 81, 83

Lochee Utd (1) ....3 Buckie Thistle (0) 0
Robertson 32, 55
Middleton 75

Montrose (1) ....2 Huntly (0) 0
Davidson 13
Smith 67

Stenhousemuir (1) ......5 Threave Rovers (0) 0
Thom 32
Motion 53
Shirra 67, 90
Thomson 73

26/10/2008

East Stirling (1) ....4 Preston Ath (1) 2
Rodgers 25 pen   Miller 14
Graham 72   McAuley 48 pen
Cramb 84
Anderson 90

01/11/2008

Annan (1) ....1 Spartans (0) 2
Neilson 10   Malin 48
                                            Archibald 50

Civil Service Stroll's (0) 0 Vale Of Leithen (0).......1
                                            Summerville 77

SECOND-ROUND REPLAY

01/11/2008

Keith (0) ....1 Forres Mechanics (0)...1
Wood 65   Penwright 66
AET: Score after 90 mins 1–1
Forres Mechanics win 3–0 on penalties

Wick Academy (1) ......1 Edinburgh City (1) 4
Weir 45   Ross 19, 51, 57
                                            Hall 90

THIRD ROUND

29/11/2008

Airdrie (3) ....3 Cove Rangers (0).........0
Cardle 20
Lynch 38, 41
Att: 821

Albion (0) ....1 Queen's Park (1) 2
Barr 63   Watt 11
Att: 619   Cairney 52 pen

Clachnacuddin (0) ......0 Stenhousemuir (2) 5
Att: 350   Dalziel 13, 28, 78
                                            Desmond 53
                                            Hampshire 90

Clyde (1) ....2 Montrose (0) 0
McKay 38
Clarke 87 pen
Att: 677

East Fife (0) ....2 Arbroath (0) 0
Crawford 70
O'Reilly 90
Att: 729

East Stirling (1) ....2 Livingston (1) 1
Forrest 9   Fox 39
Graham 55
Att: 563

Peterhead (0) ....2 Morton (1) 1
Ross 74   Masterton 24
Bavidge 90
Att: 817

Raith (0) ....0 Alloa (0) 0
Att: 1,493

Ross County (1) ....2 Dumbarton (0) 2
Higgins 23, 57   Carcary 80, 83
Att: 1,200

Stirling (0) ....2 Partick (2) 3
Molloy 55   Chaplain 28
Murphy 89   Harkins 33 pen
Att: 1,472   Buchanan 83

06/12/2008

Elgin (0) ....2 Spartans (0) 1
Wright 52   Henretty 83
Nicolson 63   Att: 519

Forres Mechanics (1) ..2 Dalbeattie Star (0)......2
Sharp 30   Steele 85
Collins 77   Sloan 89 pen
Att: 378

08/12/2008

Edinburgh City (0) ......0 Brechin (3) 3
Att: 600   Diack 5, 16, 43 pen

13/12/2008

Inverurie Loco Works (2)4 Vale Of Leithen (0).......0
Tan 1   Att: 608
Milne 22
Smith 55, 62

15/12/2008

Forfar (0) ....2 Stranraer (0)................0
Gibson 83
Kilgannon 90
Att: 305

Elgin (1) ....1 Spartans (1) 2
MacKay 5 pen   Kader 36
Att: 551   Malin 72

17/12/2008

Lochee Utd (0) ....1 Ayr (0) 1
Hagan 86   Williams 60
Att: 1,223

SCOTTISH CUP

THIRD-ROUND REPLAYS

09/12/2008

Alloa (0) ....2 Raith (0) 1
Ferguson 79, 81   Wales 57
Att: 860

15/12/2008

Dumbarton (0) ....1 Ross County (2) 2
Gordon 46   Brittain 24 pen
Att: 557   Hart 37

Dalbeattie Star (1) ......2 Forres Mechanics (0)...4
MacBeth 22   Allan 66 pen
Redpath 94   Green 92
Att: 378   Whyte 101, 112
AET: Score after 90 mins 1–1

23/12/2008

Ayr (1) ....3 Lochee Utd (0) 1
McGowan 36   Blackwood 76
Gormley 53
Prunty 58
Att: 2,049

FOURTH ROUND

10/01/2009

Airdrie (2)...................2 Spartans (0) 1
Di Giacomo 26   Malin 54
Lynch 43
Att: 1,460

Alloa (1) ....1 Aberdeen (1) 2
Scott 42 pen   Miller 9
Att: 3,012   Aluko 57

Ayr (1) ....2 Kilmarnock (1)............2
Keenan 15   Pascali 9
Williams 90   Bryson 54
Att: 9,280

Celtic (2) ....2 Dundee (1) 1
Brown 37   McMenamin 14
McGeady 44
Att: 23,070

Dunfermline (1)...........2 Clyde (0) 0
Phinn 20   Att: 2,871
Bayne 66

Falkirk (1) ....4 Queen of South (1) 2
Arfield 37 pen, 48   Wilson 41
Barrett 68, 81   Harris 48
Att: 3,423

Inverness (1) ....3 Partick (0) 0
Morais 28, 56
Vigurs 46
Att: 1,803

Peterhead (1) ....2 Queen's Park (2) 2
Bavidge 17   Brough 35
Anderson 73   Cairney 43
Att: 842

Ross County (0) ....0 Hamilton (1) 1
Att: 1,503   Swailes 22

Stenhousemuir (0) ......0 East Fife (0) 1
Att: 784   Linn 84

11/01/2009

East Stirling (0) ....0 Dundee Utd (3).........4
Att: 2,153   Buaben 15
                                 Dods 40
                                 Daly 43
                              Russell 55 pen

Hibernian (0) ....0 Hearts (1) 2
Att: 14,837   Nade 38
                                 Glen 90

13/01/2009

Brechin (0) ....1 St Mirren (1) 3
Janczyk 46   Hamilton 25 pen, 70
Att: 1,026   Wyness 56

Forfar (5) ....6 Forres Mechanics (1)...1
Gibson 2   Green 23
Milne 4 og
Tulloch 24
Campbell 31
Gordon 43, 54
Att: 775

St Johnstone (0) ....0 Rangers (1) 2
Att: 7,746   McCaffrey 43 og
                                 Novo 79

02/02/2009

Inverurie Loco Works (0)0 Motherwell (1)...........3
Att: 2,500   Sutton 2, 69
                               Clarkson 57

FOURTH-ROUND REPLAYS

20/01/2009

Queen's Park (0) ....1 Peterhead (0) 0
Holms 51
Att: 782

22/01/2009

Kilmarnock (0) ....3 Ayr (1) 1
Ford 50, 80   Prunty 10
Taouil 76
Att: 11,563

FIFTH ROUND

07/02/2009

Celtic (2) ....2 Queen's Park (0) 1
Caldwell 19   Coakley 66
McDonald 45   Att: 22,223

Hamilton (0) ....2 Dundee Utd (1) 1
Swailes 47, 55   Grainger 35
Att: 3,058

Hearts (0) ....0 Falkirk (0) 1
Att: 14,569   Lovell 59

Inverness (1) ....2 Kilmarnock (0)............0
Mihadjuks 36
Rooney 90   Att: 2,578

Motherwell (0) ....1 St Mirren (1) 2
Hughes 65   Dorman 12
Att: 5,695

17/02/2009

Aberdeen (3) ....5 East Fife (0) 0
Wright 11   Att: 8,960
Vidal 16
McDonald 29 og
Maguire 82, 84

Airdrie (1)...................1 Dunfermline (1)..........2
McLaughlin 14 pen   Holmes 2
Att: 1,772   Bayne 73

18/02/2009

Forfar (0) ....0 Rangers (1) 4
Att: 4,718   Papac 8
                              Miller 54, 90
                               Niguez 84

FIFTH-ROUND REPLAY

19/02/2009

St Mirren (0) ....1 Motherwell (0)............0
Mehmet 85   Att: 4,555

QUARTER-FINALS

07/03/2009

Dunfermline (0)............1 Aberdeen (0) 1
Phinn 82   Aluko 61
Att: 9,696

Inverness (0) ....0 Falkirk (1) 1
Att: 3,024   Finnigan 31 pen

St Mirren (0) ....1 Celtic (0)....................0
Mehmet 55 pen
Att: 5,925

08/03/2009

Rangers (3) ....5 Hamilton (1) 1
Whittaker 15   Quinn 26
Lafferty 35, 81
Niguez 45 pen
Davis 53
Att: 27,588

QUARTER-FINAL REPLAY

18/03/2009

Aberdeen (0) ....0 Dunfermline (0)...........0
Att: 13,567
AET: Score after 90 mins 0–0
Dunfermline win 4–2 on penalties

SEMI-FINALS

25/04/2009

Rangers (1) ....3 St Mirren (0) 0
Velicka 2
Boyd 66
Miller 70
Att: 32,431
Rangers: Alexander, Dailly, Bougherra, Weir, Whittaker, Davis, Mendes (Novo 41), Edu, Smith, Boyd (Little 81), Velicka (Miller 60). Subs (not used): McGregor, Wilson. Booked: Dailly
St Mirren: Howard, Ross, Haining, Cuthbert, Camara, Dorman, Thomson (Burns 89), Murray, McGinn (Brady 67), Mehmet, Wyness (Hamilton 67). Subs (not used): Mathers, Potter
Referee: C Murray

26/04/2009

Falkirk (0) ....2 Dunfermline (0)..........0
Scobbie 54
Arfield 89 pen
Att: 17,124
Falkirk: Dani Mallo, McNamara, Scobbie, Aafjes, Barr, Arfield, McCann (Cregg 90), Riera (McBride 87), O'Brien, Finnigan (Stewart 71), Higdon. Subs (not used): Olejnik, Bullen. Booked: Riera, Scobbie
Dunfermline: Gallacher, Woods, Wilson, Thomson (Ross 56), McCann, Phinn, Bell (Kirk 63), Glass, Bayne, Mole (Loy 71), Burke. Subs (not used): Paterson, Muirhead. Booked: Woods
Referee: D McDonald

FINAL

Rangers (0) ....1 Falkirk (0) 0
Novo 46
Att: 50,956
Rangers: Alexander, Whittaker, Bougherra, Weir, Papac, Davis, Ferguson, McCulloch, Lafferty (Dailly 88), Boyd (Novo 46), Miller (Naismith 85). Subs (not used): McGregor, Wilson. Booked: Dailly, Novo, Whittaker
Falkirk: Dani Mallo, McNamara, Barr, Aafjes, Scobbie, Arfield, Cregg (Finnigan 74), McBride (Higdon 74), O'Brien, McCann (Stewart 74), Lovell. Subs (not used): Olejnik, Pressley. Booked: Barr, Finnigan, McNamara
Referee: C Thomson

AIRDRIE UNITED emulated the success of their predecessors when they brought the ALBA Challenge Cup back to Lanarkshire following an exciting penalty shoot-out triumph over Ross County in the final. The conquest was the club's second trophy win since they formed in 2002 out of the ashes of Airdrieonians, who won the Challenge Cup themselves back in 1995, 2000 and 2001.

The final at McDiarmid Park, which was screened live by Gaelic channel BBC ALBA, lived up to supporters' expectations, with Airdrie midfielder Stephen McKenna forcing extra-time with a well-struck 80th-minute equaliser after Alex Keddie's header had been deflected past his own goalkeeper by the unfortunate David Nixon. Another own goal, from Andy Dowie, then put Airdrie ahead for the first time but Sean Higgins headed home for Ross County with seven minutes of the extra period remaining to force penalties.

The penalty shoot-out was a tense affair, with four spot-kicks missed before Marc Smyth sealed a 3–2 victory for the Diamonds.

Airdrie had reached the final against the odds after Paul Di Giacomo's early goal had seen them overcome fellow Irn-Bru First Division outfit Partick Thistle in the semi-final. The Diamonds had secured comfortable wins at East Coast sides East Fife and Cowdenbeath in the previous rounds, but their run had almost come to a premature end in the first round. Irn-Bru Third Division side Dumbarton led 2–0 at half-time at the Excelsior Stadium, but goals from Stuart Noble, Joe Cardle and Di Giacomo ensured a stirring comeback to propel Airdrie on their way in what proved to be a memorable cup campaign.

The first round also saw Annan Athletic play their first competitive game as a Scottish Football League club following their admission on the back of the dramatic demise of neighbours Gretna. There was no fairytale for the newcomers, however, as an Alan Trouten double earned Clyde a comfortable 2–0 victory at Broadwood Stadium. The Bully Wee eventually exited the competition themselves at the hands of Ross County in the quarter-finals.

Airdrie's players celebrate their ALBA Challenge Cup triumph at McDiarmid Park

FIRST ROUND NORTH-EAST

26/07/08

Alloa (0) ....2 Dundee (0) 1
Townsley 59 — Antoine-Curier 88
Stevenson 83 — Att: 793

Arbroath (1) ....1 Forfar (0) 2
Scott 44 — Kilgannon 62 pen
Att: 563 — McLeish 71 pen

Brechin (0) ....0 East Fife (0) 1
Att: — Templeman 69

Dunfermline (1) ....3 Stirling (0) 0
Burke 4 — Att: 1,340
Phinn 61, Williamson 74

Elgin (0) ....0 Cowdenbeath (1) 2
Att: 379 — McGregor 13, McQuade 80

Peterhead (2) ....6 Montrose (0) 0
Bavidge 24, 78 — Att: 503
Cumming 45 og
Gunn 52, 58, 68 pen

Ross County (0) ....2 St Johnstone (0) 1
Winters 53 — Samuel 84
Higgins 65 — Att: 2,365

FIRST ROUND SOUTH-WEST

26/07/08

Airdrie (0) ....3 Dumbarton (2) 2
Noble 53 — Clark 25
Cardle 58 — Carcary 43
Di Giacomo 75 — Att: 808

Berwick (0) ....1 Queen of the South (2) 5
Little 47 — O'Connor 12, 58
Att: 655 — Kean 31, 65, Barr 80

Clyde (0) ....2 Annan (0) 0
Trouten 61 pen, 74 — Att: 700

Livingston (1) ....4 Stranraer (0) 0
Griffiths 33, 72
Hamill 67, McParland 70

Partick (2) ....2 Queen's Park (1) 1
Roberts 9, Gray 9 — Henry 17; Att: 1,382

Stenhousemuir (0) ......0 Albion (1) 1
Att: 323 — Donnelly 87 pen

27/07/08

East Stirling (0) ....2 Ayr (1) 1
Richardson 86 — Williams 15
Rodgers 89 — Att: 761

SECOND ROUND

12/08/08

Alloa (0) ....0 Clyde (0) 2
Att: 414 — Clarke 58, Gibson 76

Cowdenbeath (1) ....3 Albion (1) 2
McQuade 8 — Barr 30, Martin 75
Gemmell 54, Fairbairn 89 — Att: 204

Livingston (0) ....1 Forfar (0) 0
Griffiths 51 — Att: 800

Partick (0) ....4 Peterhead (1) 2
Donnelly 52 — Gunn 23
McKeown 92, 115 — Kozminski 103
Harkins 112 — Att: 1,133
AET: Score after 90 mins 1–1

Raith (0) ....1 Ross County (0) 2
Weir 74 — Keddie 52, 54
Att: 1,080

13/08/08

East Fife (0) ....0 Airdrie (1) 2
Att: 606 — Lynch 10, Smith 84

East Stirling (0) ....0 Morton (2) 3
Att: 753 — Masterton 22
McGuffie 32, 53

20/08/08

Dunfermline (0) ....0 Queen of the South (1) 2
Att: 1,373 — Kean 3, O'Connor 75

QUARTER-FINALS

07/09/08

Clyde (0) ....0 Ross County (1) 1
Att: 756 — Craig 25

Cowdenbeath (0) ....1 Airdrie (0) 2
Fairbairn 79 — Di Giacomo 53, 75
Att: 643

Livingston (0) ....0 Partick (0) 2
Att: 1,340 — Turner 75
Twaddle 78

Queen of the South (0) 0 Morton (0) 2
Att: 2,991 — Wake 48, McGuffie 77

SEMI-FINALS

12/10/08

Partick (0) ....0 Airdrie (1) 1
Att: 2,761 — Di Giacomo 4

Ross County (2) ....4 Morton (0) 1
Craig 6 — Weatherson 77
Daal 42, 62, Dowie 84 — Att: 1,396

FINAL

16/11/08

Airdrie (0) ....2 Ross County (0) 2
McKenna 80 — Nixon 59 og, Higgins 113
Dowie 103 og — Att: 4,091
AET: Score after 90 mins 1–1
Airdrie won 3–2 on penalties

The co-operative insurance cup

QUICK SEARCH

Trace how far each club progressed in the 2008/09 Co-operative Insurance Cup

Team	Round reached
SCOTTISH PREMIER LEAGUE	
Aberdeen	Round 3
Celtic	Final
Dundee Utd	Semi-final
Falkirk	Semi-final
Hamilton	Quarter-final
Hearts	Round 2
Hibernian	Round 2
Inverness	Quarter-final
Kilmarnock	Quarter-final
Motherwell	Round 3
Rangers	Final
St Mirren	Round 3
FIRST DIVISION	
Airdrie	Round 3
Clyde	Round 2
Dundee	Round 2
Dunfermline	Quarter-final
Livingston	Round 3
Morton	Round 3
Partick	Round 3
Queen of the South	Round 3
Ross County	Round 1
St Johnstone	Round 2
SECOND DIVISION	
Alloa	Round 2
Arbroath	Round 2
Ayr	Round 2
Brechin	Round 2
East Fife	Round 1
Peterhead	Round 1
Queen's Park	Round 1
Raith	Round 2
Stirling	Round 1
Stranraer	Round 1
THIRD DIVISION	
Albion	Round 1
Annan	Round 1
Berwick	Round 1
Cowdenbeath	Round 2
Dumbarton	Round 2
East Stirling	Round 1
Elgin	Round 1
Forfar	Round 1
Montrose	Round 1
Stenhousemuir	Round 1

Winners 2009

Triumphant Celtic hold aloft the Co-operative Insurance Cup trophy

CELTIC'S Co-operative Insurance Cup triumph over Rangers at Hampden did more than just end the Parkhead club's 20-year wait for a cup-final victory over their Glasgow neighbours.

Extra-time goals courtesy of Darren O'Dea and Aiden McGeady – the first a header, the second from the penalty spot – indicated that Gordon Strachan's men were ready to seize the initiative from their rivals in the race for major honours.

It was Strachan's sixth trophy in three and a half years and it left his Rangers counterpart Walter Smith having to fend off difficult questions about his side's tactical approach.

Yet, at kick-off time at the national stadium, the team from Govan had looked arguably the better bet. Celtic led the Light Blues at the top of the Clydesdale Bank Premier League by three points but had just crashed out of the Homecoming Scottish Cup at the hands of St Mirren – a week after having thrashed the Paisley side 7–0 in the League. Strachan had finally lost patience with strikers Jan Vennegoor of Hesselink and Georgios Samaras, leaving McGeady to partner Scott McDonald in attack. Rangers, though, were weakened by the loss of their best defender Madjid Bougherra, who failed a late fitness test.

Both teams started with only one striker – McDonald for Celtic and Kenny Miller for Rangers – which did not bode well for those hoping for a classic. It therefore came as little surprise that the game went to extra-time – at one point in the match there were eight centre-halves on the pitch. However, it took little more than a minute of the added period for the breakthrough to arrive as O'Dea headed Shunsuke Nakamura's free-kick past Allan McGregor for his first goal in two years.

In the second half of extra-time, the Hoops' superior fitness told and, after Kirk Broadfoot conceded a penalty and earned a red card for his trip on McGeady, the Celtic midfielder sealed the win as he sent McGregor the wrong way from the spot.

Celtic's journey to Hampden had taken them past Livingston, Kilmarnock and then Dundee United in the semi-final, which was decided by a dramatic penalty shoot-out that ended 11–10 to the Hoops.

Rangers needed extra-time to get past Irn-Bru First Division Partick Thistle 2–1, before victories over Hamilton and Falkirk.

The first round produced few shocks but, in the second round, Hibernian crashed out to First Division Morton after extra-time while Hearts lost to Airdrie United on penalties and Inverness needed spot-kicks to get past Arbroath.

In the third round, Hamilton beat Lanarkshire rivals Motherwell 2–1 to set up their meeting with Rangers while Killie's impressive 4–2 win over Aberdeen earned them a place against Celtic.

Falkirk beat Inverness in the quarter-finals and Dundee United reached the last four with a narrow 1–0 home win over Dunfermline, but it was the Old Firm who dug deep to steal all the headlines.

FIRST ROUND

05/08/2008

Albion (0) ....0 Raith (0) 0
Att: 415
AET: Score after 90 mins 0–0.
Raith Rovers win 4–3 on penalties

Alloa (0) ....2 Elgin (0) 0
Scott 71, Kelly 78   Att: 269

Clyde (1) ....4 Queen's Park (1) 1
R MacLennan 15   Harkins 82
Gibson 63
McSwegan 86, 88   Att: 690

Dumbarton (0) ....1 Annan (0) 1
Logan 115   Jack 103 (pen)
Att: 462
AET: Score after 90 mins 0–0
Dumbarton win 5–4 on penalties

Montrose (0) ....0 Cowdenbeath (1) 2
Att: 382   McGregor 6, Fairbairn 81

Partick (1) ....4 Forfar (1) 3
McKeown 39   Fotheringham 13
Gray 70, 97   Lilley 65
Chaplain 112   Smith 103
Att: 1,192
AET: Score after 90 mins 2–2

Peterhead (0) ....0 Dunfermline (0) 2
Att: 1,291   Phinn 46, Kirk 50

Ross County (1) ....2 Airdrie (1) 3
Daal 43   Di Giacomo 23, 112
Hart 76   Noble 86
Att: 869
AET: Score after 90 mins 2–2

Stenhousemuir (1) ....1 St Johnstone (1) 5
Love 12   Sheerin 23 (pen)
                                            Milne 78
Att: 687   Holmes 79, 83, Hardie 88

Stranraer (1) ....3 Morton (5) 6
Frizzel 37   McGuffie 5, Wake 12, 85
McColm 72, Gibson 84   Russell 23, 32
Att: 317   Paartalu 40

06/08/2008

Arbroath (0) ....3 Stirling (1) 2
McMullan 48   Graham 5
Wright 64   Harty 63
Bishop 80   Att: 448

Ayr (2) ....2 Berwick (1) 1
Aitken 40   Greenhill 12
Williams 45   Att: 523

East Fife (0) ....0 Brechin (1) 3
                                            Twigg 44
                                            White 65
Att: 523   Ward 74

East Stirling (0) ....1 Livingston (0) 2
Graham 90   Fox 80
Att: 360   Smith 113
AET: Score after 90 mins 1–1

SECOND ROUND

26/08/2008

Cowdenbeath (0) ....1 Dundee Utd (2) 5
Dempster 74   Daly 30, 47, 80
Att: 1,423   Goodwillie 41, 60

Dundee (0) ....1 Partick Thistle (0) 1
McHale 80   Maxwell 78
Att: 2,507   Harkins 87 (pen)

Dunfermline (1)...........1 Alloa Ath (0) 0
Kirk 8   Att: 1,326

Hamilton Acad (1) .....3 Clyde (1) 1
Grady 17   Clarke 19
Thomas 81
Stevenson 90 (pen)   Att: 1,146

Hibernian (0) ....3 Morton (1) 4
Keenan 80   Russell 29, 115 (pen)
Shiels 85   Masterston 66
Pinao 91   Harding 118
Att: 6,329
AET: Score after 90 mins 2–2

Livingston (0) ....2 St Johnstone (0) 1
Griffiths 58   Craig 46
Cuenca 95   Att: 979
AET: Score after 90 mins 1–1

Raith (0) ....1 Falkirk (2) 3
Campbell 74   Higdon 16
                                    J Stewart 35 (pen)
Att: 2,090   M Stewart 84

St Mirren (3) ....7 Dumbarton (0) 0
Robb 18
Mehmet 33, 50, 52
Dorman 39
Dargo 75, Mason 77   Att: 1,747

27/08/2008

Arbroath (1) ....2 Inverness (1) 2
Tosh 21   Vigurs 18
Sellars 87 (pen)   Wood 64
Att: 596
AET: Score after 90 mins 2–2
Inverness win 4–2 on penalties

Ayr (0) ....0 Aberdeen (1) 1
Att: 2,979   Maguire 40

Brechin (0) ....0 Kilmarnock (0) 2
Att: 802   Wright 58, Bryson 65

Hearts (0) ....0 Airdrie (0) 0
Att: 6,844
AET: Score after 90 mins 0–0
Airdrie win 4–3 on penalties

THIRD ROUND

23/09/2008

Celtic (1) ....4 Livingston (0) 0
Loovens 24
Samaras 64, 85 (pen)
S Brown 81   Att: 23,569

Dundee Utd (2) ....2 Airdrie (0) 0
Goodwillie 33
S Robertson 42   Att: 3,444

Dunfermline (0) ....2 St Mirren (0) 0
Bayne 69, Wiles 74   Att: 2,186

Falkirk (1) ....2 Queen of Sth (0) 1
McCann 29   Kean 58
Lovell 73   Att: 2,058

Morton (1) ....1 Inverness (0) 2
McAlister 34   R Hastings 79
Att: 2,023   Imrie 111
AET: Score after 90 mins 1–1

24/09/2008

Kilmarnock (4) ....4 Aberdeen (2) 2
Sammon 2, 33   McDonald 6
Fernandez 12   Miller 26 (pen)
Taouil 17 (pen)   Att: 4,339

Motherwell (0) ....1 Hamilton (0) 1
Murphy 66   Graham 53
Att: 5,590   Ettien 95
AET: Score after 90 mins 1–1

Partick (1) ....1 Rangers (1) 2
McKeown 33   Boyd 25
Att: 6,497   Mendes 116
AET: Score after 90 mins 1–1

QUARTER-FINALS

28/10/2008

Dundee Utd (1) ....1 Dunfermline (0) 0
S Robertson 16   Att: 5,350
Dundee Utd: Zaluska, Dillon, Wilkie, Dods, Dixon, Flood,
Scott Robertson, Gomis, Conway, O'Donovan, Sandaza
(Feeney 68). **Subs not used:** McGovern, David Robertson,
Swanson, Kenneth.

Dunfermline Ath: Gallacher, Woods, Shields, Wilson,
McCann, Harper (Bell 88), Phinn, Burke (Wiles 82), Glass,
Bayne, Kirk (Williamson 82). **Subs not used:** Reidford,
Thomson. **Booked:** Gallacher.
Referee: D McDonald.

Falkirk (1) ....1 Inverness (0) 0
McCann 36   Att: 3,007
Falkirk: Flinders, McNamara, Aafjes, Barr, Holden,
McBride, Arfield, O'Brien, McCann (Cregg 90), Barrett
(Latapy 62), Higdon. **Subs not used:** Olejnik, Bullen,
Riera. **Booked:** McCann.
Inverness CT: Esson, Tokely, Duff, Munro, Hastings, Imrie
(Vigurs 80), Duncan, Cowie, McBain (Wilson 63), Rooney,
Wood (Barrowman 63). **Subs not used:** Fraser, Proctor.
Booked: Hastings, Munro.

Rangers (1) ....2 Hamilton (0) 0
Boyd 25, Lafferty 50   Att: 32,083
Rangers: McGregor, Broadfoot, Bougherra, Weir, Papac,
Davis, Mendes, Edu, Lafferty, Darcheville (Novo 73),
Boyd. **Subs not used:** Alexander, Ferguson, Smith,
Whittaker.
Hamilton Acad: Cerny, McClenahan, Swailes (Corcoran
75), Elebert, Easton, Graham, McArthur, Neil, McCarthy
(Ettien 69), Gibson, Akins (Offiong 59). **Subs not used:**
Murdoch, Casement.
Referee: E Smith.

29/10/2008

Kilmarnock (0) ....1 Celtic (2) 3
Invincibile 68   McDonald 11
Att: 6,319   Nakamura 45, McGeady 71
Kilmarnock: Combe, Murray, Hamill, Lilley, Wright
(Skelton 33), Bryson, Fowler, Pascali, Fernandez,
Invincibile (Sammon 84), Taouil (Simmonds 84). **Subs not
used:** Rascle, Gibson. **Booked:** Fowler, Lilley, Pascali,
Skelton.
Celtic: Boruc, Hinkel, Wilson, O'Dea, Caldwell, S Brown,
Donati, Nakamura (Hartley 46), McGeady, McDonald
(Sheridan 76), Maloney. **Subs not used:** M Brown, Robson,
McCourt. **Booked:** Nakamura, Wilson.
Referee: C Thomson.

SEMI-FINALS

27/01/2009

Rangers (2) ....3 Falkirk (0) 0
Novo 8, 40, Boyd 88   Att: 24,507
Rangers: McGregor, Broadfoot, Bougherra, Weir, Papac,
Davis, Mendes, Ferguson (McCulloch 86), Naismith (Fleck
77), Boyd, Novo. **Subs not used:** Whittaker, Miller,
Alexander.
Falkirk: Dani Mallo, McNamara, Bullen (Higdon 60), Barr,
Pressley, Scobbie, Arfield, McBride, Cregg (Stewart 70),
McCann, Lovell. **Subs not used:** O'Brien, Holden, Olejnik.
Booked: Barr, Pressley.
Referee: C Richmond.

28/01/2009

Celtic (0) ....0 Dundee Utd (0) 0
Att: 19,258
AET: Score after 90 mins 0–0
Celtic win 11–10 on penalties
Celtic: Boruc, Hinkel, Caldwell, Loovens, Naylor,
Nakamura, S Brown, Crosas, McGeady (Robson 75),
McDonald, Vennegoor of Hesselink (Samaras 73). **Subs
not used:** M Brown, Hartley, O'Dea. **Booked:** Loovens.
Dundee Utd: Zaluska, Dixon, Wilkie, Kenneth, Kovacevic,
Flood, Gomis, Buaben (Robertson 90), Conway, Feeney,
Sandaza (Daly 86). **Subs not used:** McGovern, Dillon,
Swanson. **Booked:** Buaben, Dixon.
Referee: C Murray.

FINAL

15/03/2009

Celtic ....2 Rangers......................0
O'Dea 91, McGeady 120 (pen)   Att: 51,193
AET: Score after 90 mins 0–0
Celtic: Boruc, Hinkel, Loovens, McManus, O'Dea (Wilson
105), Caldwell, Nakamura, S Brown, Hartley (G Samaras
72 (Vennegoor of Hesselink 120)), McGeady, McDonald.
Subs not used: M Brown, Crosas. **Booked:** Boruc, Hinkel,
McGeady, O'Dea.
Rangers: McGregor, Whittaker, Weir, Broadfoot, Papac,
Davis, McCulloch (Dailly 82), Ferguson, Mendes, Miller
(Novo 58), Lafferty (Boyd 76). **Subs not used:** Alexander,
Edu. **Booked:** McCulloch, Novo, Weir. **Dismissed:**
Broadfoot.
Referee: D McDonald.